BIOGRAPHICAL DICTIONARY OF
MODERN
WORLD LEADERS
1992 TO THE PRESENT

JOHN C. FREDRIKSEN

Facts On File, Inc.

Biographical Dictionary of Modern World Leaders: 1992 to the Present

Facts On File, Inc.
132 West 31st Street
New York NY 10001

Library of Congress Cataloging-in-Publication Data
 Biographical dictionary of modern world leaders : 1992 to the present / [compiled] by John C. Fredriksen.
     p. cm.
 Includes bibliographical references and index.
 ISBN 0-8160-4723-5
 1. Statesmen—Biography—Dictionaries. 2. Heads of state—Biography—Dictionaries. 3. Biography—20th century—Dictionaries. 4. Biography—21st century—Dictionaries. I. Fredriksen, John C.
 D412.B55 2003
 909.82'9'0922—dc21   [B]2002192849

Facts On File books are available at special discounts when purchased in bulk quantities for businesses, associations, institutions or sales promotions. Please call our Special Sales Department in New York at (212) 967-8800 or (800) 322-8755.

You can find Facts On File on the World Wide Web at http://www.factsonfile.com

Text design by Joan M. Toro
Cover design by Cathy Rincon

Printed in the United States of America

VB FOF 10 9 8 7 6 5 4 3 2 1

This book is printed on acid-free paper.

CONTENTS

LIST OF ENTRIES

v

INTRODUCTION

Since the end of the cold war, the global community has undergone profound geopolitical changes. The breakup of the Soviet Union alone resulted in a bevy of new national entities stretching from eastern Europe to Asia. This, in turn, stimulated ideological readjustment among the Western democracies to compensate for a seemingly more hospitable clime. The Arabic and Muslim worlds, meanwhile, have also experienced a surge in Islamic fundamentalism, marked by a concomitant rise in global terrorism. The apocalyptic events of September 11, 2001, have put the United States on notice that, despite its unique status as the only surviving superpower, perfidy knows no boundaries. So, unlike the relatively stable state of world affairs occasioned by the cold war, new nations have arrived in a world that is patently unpredictable and, therefore, highly dangerous. Under such unsettling circumstances, the need for understanding mind-sets and political systems around the world has never been greater. The book you hold is a concerted effort to address all these issues by proffering capsule biographies of the leaders in charge. Collectively, they delineate the path of global political developments over the past 10 years. This knowledge may also provide insight towards possible trends in the decade that follows.

The approach to writing these 400 essays was relatively conventional; they range from 700 to 1,500 words, depending on the relative significance of each subject. Here I touch upon such diverse considerations as ethnic background, religion, education level, party affiliation, and performance in office. Wherever possible, I also cite a direct quotation to liven up an otherwise dour recital of facts and give greater perspective to the individual in question. In designing this reference book, I also decided to cast as wide a net as possible to afford complete world coverage. Thus, all 190 of the world's countries, ranging from newly constituted Afghanistan to newly independent East Timor and quasi-independent Kosovo, are represented. However, the chronological limitations are absolute and restricted to heads of state who were either in power as of 1992, or have risen to power since then through election or other means. A handful of prominent contemporary figures such as Jörg Haider and Ian Paisley are also included.

There are other biographical dictionaries extant, and of varying quality and merit. However, as a trained reference librarian and researcher, I notice a disturbing trend in terms of bibliographic citations. Lately, many authors seem content to simply cite newspaper essays or news magazine articles pertaining to given subjects. I find this practice self-defeating from a reference standpoint, seeing how, in most circumstances, these sources can only be accessed on microfilm. Most students, particularly at the undergraduate level, usually lack the discipline and resolve to retrieve such materials and, hence, their research efforts are discouraged. To counter this, I chose to cite only those books and scholarly journals most likely to remain in hard copy for years to come. This makes them readily available, either by accessing them on the shelf or through interlibrary loan. Also, great care has been taken to cull only the latest and most comprehensive works available. I relied almost exclusively on such useful sites as the Library of Congress and WorldCat to gather requisite materials, which include not only published data like books and articles but also unpublished works such as master's theses and dissertations. Thus readers are exposed to the fullest possible range of political and biographical research. Autobiographical matter or writings were my strongest criteria for inclusion, but I occasionally cite national or political studies for greater context. All told, I hold this approach to confer more utility to youthful users than chasing slender and hard-to-find newspaper citations on microfilm.

Another distinctive feature of this book was the methodology underlying its compilation. As librarians and researchers, we live in an automated information age whereby the newest and most recent information on a given person or circumstance is but a few clicks away. Therefore, I crafted every essay based largely on news postings available through such on-line wonders as CNN.com and BBC.com to keep events as absolutely current as possible. On-line databases such as Infotrac and EBSCO were also regularly combed for the latest-breaking developments, worldwide.

Biographical Dictionary of Modern World Leaders will go far in promoting research and awareness of world politics, along with the varied individuals and systems it is made up of. No effort was spared in terms of providing comprehensive coverage or recency of citations so, as a reference tool, it remains in a class by itself. I would like to thank my editor, Owen Lancer, for suggesting this project to me. It proved an arduous undertaking, but also a valuable learning experience—for which I remain highly gratified.

—John C. Fredriksen

A

Abacha, Sani (1943–1998) *president of Nigeria*

Sani Abacha was born in Kano, Kano state, Nigeria, on September 20, 1943, a member of the influential Hausa-Fulani-speaking peoples of northern Nigeria. This group wields an inordinate degree of national influence because it traditionally dominates the upper echelons of the military. From 1957 to 1962 Abacha was a student at the local primary and secondary schools, and in 1962 he joined the army. A promising soldier, he was allowed to pass through the Nigerian Military Training College at Kaduna, 1962–63, before being commissioned a second lieutenant. Abacha then received additional training in the United States and also attended several prestigious military schools in the United Kingdom. He thereafter climbed steadily through the ranks, rising to brigadier general by 1980. Throughout this period, Nigeria, which had won its independence from Great Britain in 1960, had been subject to a series of military coups that usually deposed—then restored—civilian rulers. Now part of the military elite, Abacha proved himself a willing accomplice in several of these disturbances, and struck up close relationships with several senior military figures.

In December 1983 Abacha figured prominently in a coup that toppled the regime of Shehu Shagari, which ended the Second Republic and ushered General Muhammed Buhari into power. Two years later he helped orchestrate a second coup which deposed Buhari and elevated General IBRAHIM BABANGIDA to supremacy. While in power, Babangida always promised to restore Nigeria's democracy and in 1993 he allowed the nation's first free elections in nearly two decades. However, when a member of the opposition party apparently won the contest, Babangida quickly annulled the results and resumed control. This act prompted much civil and political unrest against the military regime, and he eventually resigned from office and appointed a civilian, Ernest Shonekan, to succeed him. Abacha was then installed as defense secretary, but on November 17, 1993, Abacha, having moved steadily closer to the centers of national power, staged a bloodless coup of his own, ousted Shonekan, and declared himself president.

For the most part, Nigerians willingly accepted new military regimes for the stability and reform they represented. However, Abacha's intentions and methods were entirely different. Like his predecessors, he paid the usual lip service to restoring democracy—but then severely clamped down on the entire political process. By degrees, he dissolved all of Nigeria's political institutions, including the national assembly, local government, and the constitution. Moreover, he banned all political parties and replaced sitting civilian governors with military officers. The Abacha regime proved both

1

brutal and intolerant of enemies, either real or perceived, and it arrested, tortured, or executed dissidents by the score. Among them were OLUSEGUN OBASANJO, a former president, MOSHOOD ABIOLA, winner of the annulled 1993 elections, and world renowned writer-environmentalist Ken Saro-Wiwa. Both Abiola and Wiwa died while in prison. Abacha's paranoia even extended to members of his own ruling circle, for in December 1997 he arrested Oladipo Diya, his own second-in-command.

While in power, the Abacha regime did little else than systematically plunder Nigeria of revenues accruing from the sale of oil. During his five-year tenure in office national poverty rates skyrocketed from 21 percent to nearly 80 percent, while the ruling clique amassed fantastic fortunes. All the while, Abacha buttressed his rule with large-scale police forces, undercover agents, and a determination to wield them ruthlessly. However, by 1998 international pressure was brought to bear upon Nigeria and, to forestall the possibility of economic sanctions, Abacha scheduled elections for August of that year. However, the dictator did not live to see the results of his handiwork for on June 8, 1998, Abacha died suddenly of a heart attack in Abuja, Nigeria. When elections were finally held the former president Obasanjo was returned to office and has since restored democratic rule to the country.

Since Abacha's death and the restoration of democracy, the Nigerian government has been pressing the Abacha family for an estimated $3 billion looted from the national treasury and deposited in foreign banks. In April 2002 the government of Switzerland agreed to return $535 million from accounts there alone. However, the political settlement caused consternation at home for, as part of the deal, criminal proceedings were dropped against members of Abacha's family, who also kept an estimated $100 million acquired before the general took power. The entire episode also proved an embarrassment to Switzerland, which had previously enacted laws intended to prevent such laundered funds from reaching its financial institutions.

Further Reading

Fayemi, Kayode. *Nigeria: Crisis of Manhood.* London: Parliamentary Human Rights Group, 1996.
Igwara, Obi. "Ethnicity, Nationalism, and Nation-Building in Nigeria." Unpublished Ph.D. dissertation, University of London, 1973.
Ihonvbere, Julius O. "Are Things Falling Apart? The Military Crisis of Democratization in Nigeria." *Journal of Modern African Studies* 34 (June 1996): 193–226.
Njoku, Raphael C. "Deconstructing Abacha: Demilitarization and Democratic Consolidation in Nigeria after the Abacha Era." *Government and Opposition* 36, no. 1 (2001): 71–97.
Onadipe, A. "Nigeria: The World's Newest Pariah State." *Contemporary Review* 268 (February 1996): 69–74.

Abdullah II (1962–) *king of Jordan*
Abdullah ibn al-Hussein was born in Amman, Jordan, on January 30, 1962, the youngest son of King HUSSEIN I and his second wife, a British subject. At the age of four he was enrolled at St Edmund's School in Surrey, England, and he subsequently passed through the Deerfield Academy, Massachusetts. Abdullah, in view of this Western-style education, is fluent in English and speaks it better than Arabic. In 1980, the young prince attended the Royal Military Academy at Sandhurst, England, and three years later studied international affairs at prestigious Oxford University. He then returned home in 1984 to commence a long and distinguished career in the Jordanian military. Beginning as a platoon commander in the 40th Armored Brigade, Abdullah advanced steadily through the ranks through ability, rising to the rank of major general within the nation's special forces. He also found the time to attend the School of Foreign Service and Georgetown University in Washington, D.C., before the mantle of leadership was suddenly and unexpectedly thrust upon him.

Prior to 1999, Abdullah was never a serious contender for the Jordanian throne. This was accorded to his older half-brother Hassan, the formal crown prince. However, King Hussein's dissatisfaction with Hassan's penchant for palace intrigue led him to choose the 39-year-old Abdullah to succeed him. Consequently, following the king's death on February 7, 1999, he ascended to the throne as Abdullah II, and declared his loyalty to the country before a joint session of the Jordanian parliament. Mindful of his father's moderate legacy, he then declared in a televised address that "Today you are my brothers and sisters and you are dear to me. We will preserve the course that Hussein set." Given Abdullah's Western-style outlook and half-European heritage, it was not known if his tenure would incite resentment among Jordan's increasingly restless population. Criticism proved muted, possibly because his wife, the reigning Queen RANIA, is a native-born Palestinian. They have three children.

King Abdullah II presently holds the unenviable position of running a small but strategic country that borders four potentially hostile neighbors: Israel to the west, Syria to the north, Iraq to the east, and Saudi Arabia to the south. Hence, like his father, Abdullah's foreign policy is calculated to follow a fine balancing act between national priorities and popular passions. This feat is made all the more perilous by the fact that fully half of Jordan's population consists of Palestinians, many of whom support the violent creation of their own state. Abdullah's determination to remain on good terms with Israel remains a flash point with many Palestinians, especially given the climate of hostility over the fate of the West Bank and continuing Israeli occupation. It is perhaps a good indication of the youthful monarch's character that he remains committed his father's policy of peace with the Jewish state. To underscore his determination, on April 23, 2000, two months after being sworn in, Abdullah conducted his first state visit to Israel to confer with his counterpart, EHUD BARAK. The result was continuation of a previous agreement of Israel to supply Jordan with freshwater, an essential commodity for his desert kingdom.

Abdullah faces even greater challenges with the country's economy, which remains in deep recession. With a national debt of $7 billion and an unemployment rate of 15–20 percent, he actively promotes a free-market economy at home and encourages investment from abroad. The king takes inspiration from the success of Singapore and is determined to structure the Jordanian economy around new information technology to break the poverty and despair gripping the majority of his people. Such widespread dislocation, in turn, has fueled the rise of Islamic fundamentalism and mounting calls from militant clergymen for increasing terrorism against Israel and its chief sponsor, the United States. Furthermore, the September 11, 2001, destruction of the World Trade Center only reaffirmed Abdullah's determination, in his own words, "to fight evil," however unpopular at home. Three weeks after the attack, he met with President GEORGE W. BUSH in Washington and pledged Jordan's wholehearted cooperation in the fight against international terrorism. Consequently, Bush pronounced him a "strong friend of America" and signed a free trade agreement with Jordan, only the fourth country to enjoy such

King Abdullah II and Queen Rania *(Jordan Information Bureau)*

a privilege. Abdullah is also committed to freedom of the press and increasing democratization of Jordan, but at a slower, more controlled pace than would be accepted in the West. "Democracy is a learning experience," the young king insists. "Down the line you will see a shift of responsibility as institutions mature." Initially dismissed as a novice and a political lightweight, Abdullah is forcefully stepping into the strategic niche carved out by his father. He will undoubtedly function as a voice for peace and moderation throughout this very volatile region.

Further Reading

Fischbach, Michael R. *State, Society, and Land in Jordan.* Boston: Brill, 2000.

Jarman, Robert L. *Palestine and Jordan.* Slough, England: Archives Editions, 2001.

Joffe, E. G. H. *Jordan in Transition.* New York: Palgrave, 2001.

Milton-Edwards, Beverly, and Peter Hinchcliffe. *Jordan: A Hashemite Legacy.* London: Routledge, 2001.

Ryan, Curtis R. *Jordan in Transition: From Hussein to Ab-dullah.* Boulder, Colo.: Lynne Rienner Publishers, 2002.

Rubin, Barry, ed. *Revolutionaries and Reformers: Contemporary Islamist Movements in the Middle East.* Albany: State University of New York Press, 2003.

Tamini, Azzam. *Islam and Democracy: Jordan and the Muslim Brotherhood.* Tokyo: Islamic Area Studies Project, 2000.

Abiola, Moshood (1937–1998) *president of Nigeria*

Moshood Kashimawa Abiola was born on August 24, 1937, in Abeokuta, Ogun state, Nigeria, the son of a Muslim family from the Yoruba tribal grouping. None of the family's previous 22 children had survived past infancy, so his middle name means "Let us see if he will survive." Abiola endured a hardscrabble existence and was allegedly so poor that he had to sell firewood to pay for his school books. Nonetheless, he attended a nearby Baptist missionary school, proved bright academically, and subsequently won a scholarship to the University of Glasgow, Scotland. There Abiola studied public accounting and earned his master's degree by 1965. After returning home he was employed by the Lagos University Teaching Hospital and by a large pharmaceutical firm, but his big break occurred in 1968 when he joined the African division of ITT, a telecommunications concern. He flourished as company chairman, amassing a fortune and expanding his commercial empire to include oil exports, shipping, and publishing. By 1974 he had become one of the world's richest men, and he became celebrated for lavish philanthropic spending. Among his beneficiaries were the education system, political groups, and his own soccer team. Abiola also gained a degree of international notoriety in 1992 when he castigated Western powers for enslaving black Africans and demanded that reparations be paid. And, as the nation's leading business figure, it was inevitable that Abiola would, by necessity, establish cordial relations with the military establishment, which had run the nation since the late 1960s. Accordingly, Abiola became closely associated with General IBRAHIM BABANGIDA, who administered Nigeria for eight years after promising free elections.

Abiola's political aspirations dated back at least as far as 1979, when he joined the National Party of Nigeria (NPN). However, when he ran as a presidential candidate in 1982 he was bested by Shehu Shagari for the party's nomination, and he resigned from the party altogether. Babangida, meanwhile, established a June 1993 deadline for new elections, but he reserved the right to choose the two parties that would be allowed to run, as well as their candidates. He selected Bashir Tofa, a northerner and a Muslim, to stand as the government-sponsored candidate of the National Republican Convention (NRC), while Abiola headed the new Social Democratic Party ticket. As such he was the first southern Nigerian to run for national office. This proved quite symbolic, as the nation suffered from political tensions between the Muslim North and the Christian South. Abiola, himself a Muslim, garnered considerable support from the Christian community, and when elections were held on June 15, 1993, he won an unexpected victory with 58.4 percent of votes cast. This outcome angered Babangida, and on June 17, 1993, the general unilaterally annulled the election. The population found this incredulous, especially the Southerners, who rioted for several days. Abiola himself traveled abroad to Europe and the United States, decrying the stolen election and demanding implementation of international sanctions. Nonetheless, Babangida ignored rising protests and substituted a new man, Ernest Shonekan, as Nigeria's legitimate president. Nigeria's return to democracy had been thwarted once again.

Shonekan's presidency lasted only a few months for, on November 17, 1993, he was ousted by a new strongman, General SANI ABACHA. Abiola, previously on good terms with Abacha, interpreted this as an opportunity to reclaim the mandate stolen by Babangida. In June 1994 he campaigned through Nigeria, demanding that the presidency was rightfully his. Abacha, unfortunately, responded with an arrest warrant, and Abiola was detained and charged with treason. He was then held in close confinement in a small cell, without visitors or medical personnel allowed to see him. Abiola languished in jail for four years while rumors of mistreatment, beatings, and torture abounded. On June 4, 1996, Kudirat Abiola, one of his four wives and an outspoken critic of the government, was apparently assassinated. Yet the sudden death of Abacha on June 9, 1998, heightened public expectations of Abiola's release as a new leader, General Abdulsalem Abubakar, began to free political prisoners. International pressure then mounted on Nigeria for Abiola's release, and United Nations Secretary-General Kofi Annan paid him a visit, along with several leading American politicians. All this good will came to naught on July 7, 1998, when Abiola died of an apparent heart attack in the presence of foreign dignitaries. Public resentment over his death, seemingly brought on by government misconduct, exploded onto the streets and rioting continued for several days. But the wheels of justice continued rolling—if slowly. In February 2002 the family of Abiola and other detainees sued General Abubakar in U.S. courts for his wrongful death and millions of dollars in damages. The case is still pending but the former tycoon remains a symbol of Nigeria's determination to achieve true democracy.

Further Reading

Aborisade, Oladimeji, and Robert J. Mundt. *Politics in Nigeria.* New York: Longman, 2002.

Edozie, Rtia K. *People Power and Democracy: The Popular Movement against Military Despotism in Nigeria, 1989–1999.* Trenton, N.J.: Africa World Press, 2002.

Mimiko, Nahzeem O. "Between Yugoslavia and Czechoslovakia: The Abacha Coup, the National Conference, and Prospects for Peace and Democracy in Nigeria." *Social Justice* 22 (Fall 1995): 129–143.

Momoh, Abukar, and Said Adejumobi. *The National Question in Nigeria: Comparative Perspectives.* Burlington, Vt.: Ashgate, 2002.

Olukotun, Ayo. "Traditional Protest Media and Anti-Military Struggle in Nigeria, 1988–1999." *African Affairs* 101 (April 2002): 193–202.

Adamkus, Valdas (1926–) *president of Lithuania*

Born in Kaunas, Lithuania, on November 3, 1926, Valdas Adamkus was the son of dedicated civil servants. His father was head of the Lithuanian Air Force School while his mother worked for the Ministry of Communications. In 1940 Soviet forces under Josef Stalin invaded and occupied Lithuania in anticipation of World War II. Adamkus joined an underground resistance movement and published a clandestine newspaper called *Jaunime, budek!* (Youth Be on Guard!) until the invaders were driven back by the German army in 1941. By July 1944 the fortunes of war had reversed, and the Red Army was once again at the gates of Kaunas. Adamkus then joined the Homeland Defense Team, fought in the Battle of Seda, and was forced to live in Germany when his country again suffered Soviet occupation. During the postwar period, he returned to school and received an advanced degree from the Faculty of Natural Science at Munich University. Adamkus then worked for the YMCA settling displaced refugees, and he also found time to win two medals at the Olympic Games of the Enslaved Nations in 1948.

In 1949 Adamkus and his family relocated to the United States and settled in Chicago, Illinois, the site of a large and politically active Lithuanian community. In between bouts as an autoworker and engineering draftsman, Adamkus attended the Illinois Institute of Technology, where he received a civil engineering degree in 1960. He was also active in numerous Lithuanian social organizations that protested the continuing occupation of that country by Soviet forces. "I knew the day would come when my country would be free," he subsequently reflected. In 1970 Adamkus gained employment with the U.S. Environmental Protection Agency, rising to the rank of deputy administrator of the Great Lakes region.

Valdas Adamkus *(Embassy of the Republic of Lithuania)*

Two years later, his dream of returning home was realized when he visited Lithuania to assist environmental institutions there. In this capacity he served as an important conduit for information and technology for hard-pressed Lithuanian ecologists, who were ill-equipped to combat rampant environmental damage caused by the Soviet Union. He also befriended many Lithuanian political dissidents, making a name for himself as a champion of political liberty. In light of his tireless work protecting the environment, Adamkus also received a gold medal from the U.S. Environmental Protection Agency and a letter of thanks from President BILL CLINTON. He then retired from the civil service with little ceremony in June 1997.

Following the collapse of the Soviet Union in 1991, Adamkus returned to Lithuania repeatedly and dabbled in national politics. In 1993 he headed the presidential campaign of Stasys Lozoraitis and subsequently worked at uniting a diverse bloc of conservative forces. His efforts paid handsome dividends in 1997 when Adamkus was nominated for president of Lithuania, to which office he gained election on January 4, 1998. This was achieved only after four candidates failed to secure a clear majority, and then Adamkus squeaked through in a runoff by winning 50.4 percent of the vote. The former refugee and environmental engineer took his oath of office on February 26, 1998, and, consistent with Lithuanian law, resigned his American citizenship.

Once in office, 71-year-old Adamkus began addressing the needs of his tiny nation of 3.8 million people, which rests upon the margins of northwestern Russia. Steeped in the American tradition of ethnic tolerance, he strongly argued for the civil rights of Russians and Poles still in residence and, consequently, in contrast to Estonia and Latvia, Lithuania enjoys good relations with both countries. He then moved energetically to address unemployment, economic reform, and public safety. Adamkus also strongly insisted on preserving and protecting the environment of his homeland, which suffered badly at the hands of Soviet occupiers. Mindful of the past, he eagerly solicits Lithuania's full membership in the North Atlantic Treaty Organization (NATO) and the European Union (EU) as an added measure of protection. "For us, the enlargement of NATO is not just another technical foreign policy issue," he declared. "It is an opportunity to come home and a chance to regain our place in the Western Community of nations whose values and spirit we have always shared." Never-

theless, Adamkus is eager to court good relations with his giant neighbor and on December 19, 2001, he cordially welcomed Russian president VLADIMIR PUTIN to the capital of Vilnius. Despite Russia's edginess over the presence of NATO on its western border, Adamkus also advocates Russian membership in that organization to ensure peace and stability throughout Europe.

Further Reading

Donskis, Leonidas. *Identity and Freedom: Mapping Nationalism and Social Criticism in Twentieth-Century Lithuania.* New York: Routledge, 2002.

Krickus, Richard J. *Showdown: The Lithuanian Rebellion and the Breakup of the Soviet Union.* London: Brassey's, 1997.

Lane, A. T. *Lithuania: Stepping Westward.* London: Routledge, 2001.

Steen, Anton. *Between Past and Future: Elites, Democracy, and the State in Post-Communist Countries: A Comparison of Estonia, Latvia, and Lithuania.* Brookfield, Vt.: Ashgate, 1997.

Adams, Gerry (1948–) *Northern Ireland politician*

Gerry Adams was born on October 6, 1948, in Belfast, Northern Ireland, the son of a laborer. He belonged to a staunchly Roman Catholic family with a long tradition of fighting with the outlawed Irish Republican Army (IRA) against the British army and Protestant extremists. Adams worked as a barkeeper for many years until 1964, when street riots against the British—followed by a severe police crackdown—induced him to join Sinn Féin ("By Ourselves" in Gaelic), the political wing of the IRA. Like its more violent counterpart, membership of which Adams always denied, Sinn Féin was dedicated to the eventual unification of the six largely Protestant counties with the overwhelmingly Catholic Republic of Ireland to the south. Inspired by the ongoing Civil Rights movement in the United States, Adams became an active organizer of peace marches, protests, and sit-ins on behalf of better treatment for Catholics. However, by 1972 the onset of sectarian warfare between the IRA, the British-controlled constabulary, and militant Protestant loyalists resulted in suspension of the Northern Ireland constitution. On two occasions, Adams was summarily arrested and detained without being charged, although he partook in secret negotiations to end the violence. His repeated incarcerations also made him a folk hero and, following his release in 1977, he was elected vice president of Sinn Féin. A year later he became its president and the most vocal proponent of political resistance to Protestant domination.

Britain restored home rule to Northern Ireland by 1982 and the following year Adams was elected to parliament from West Belfast. However, he refused to be seated in London as this required taking an oath of loyalty to the Queen. He continued as a pro-Irish activist, and in 1984 was nearly killed in an assassination attempt. However, he kept his lines of communication to the British government open and maintained a continuing dialogue whenever possible. By December 1993, and thanks to heroic efforts by British prime minister TONY BLAIR and Irish prime minister ALBERT REYNOLDS, the Downing Street Declaration emerged as an initial step toward peace in Northern Ireland. This enabled Catholics to enjoy a measure of self-rule and representation, so the IRA declared a cease-fire in August 1994. At best, only an uneasy truce prevailed. Adams bore a full measure in the secret proceedings, but afterward he refused to denounce IRA violence as long as Catholics suffered at the hands of Protestant Unionists. Violence resumed in February 1996, at which point former U.S. senator George Mitchell arrived to orchestrate the first face-to-face negotiations between the warring factions. Adams was again closely engaged, but communication proved difficult as ranking Protestants like DAVID TRIMBLE refused to deal with him in person. Negotiations dragged on fruitlessly until Prime Minister Blair, in a fit of exasperation, declared that April 9, 1998, would end the process—whether it succeeded or not. Intense deliberations followed and were only concluded several hours after the deadline. But the ensuing Good Friday Agreement was a historic first for the beleaguered region, granting Northern Ireland self-rule without changing its political status. Furthermore, the Irish constitution was altered to renounce the republic's claim upon the territory, and joint institutions were founded for mutual interest. The agreement was subsequently ratified by voters in the republic and Northern Ireland in May 1998 and elections were held for the new Northern Ireland Assembly. Adams ran for office and won, as did 18 other members of Sinn Féin. And, although he was not nominated for the Nobel Peace Prize as Trimble and Catholic leader David Hume were, he is acknowledged as having played a decisive, behind-the-scenes role.

Despite this most promising start, the peace process has since floundered over the issue of IRA disarmament. Protestant Unionists demand this as a precondition to a multiparty cabinet but Adams, though acknowledging the obligation to disarm, does not link the two processes together. The impasse has all but killed the Good Friday Agreement and violence has flared anew between armed bands of Catholics and Protestants. Blair has since threatened to reintroduce British troops and crack down upon IRA operatives to curtail their use of terror. In July 2002 Adams pronounced the British declaration "a surreal sideshow," and he further noted that Catholics "will find it crazy that the prime minister is zeroing in on republicans when they are the victims of a loyalist campaign." Many Protestant leaders also demand Sinn Féin's ejection from the coalition government. Moreover, Unionists have refused to disarm until the IRA does likewise, and extremists like IAN PAISLEY call for wholesale rejection of the entire peace process. Adams and Sinn Féin, meanwhile, continue walking the tight rope of restraining sectarian violence while advancing their ultimate goal of Irish reunification. It remains a dangerous game.

Further Reading

Adams, Gerry. *Before the Dawn: An Autobiography.* Dingle: Brandon, 2001.

Coogan, Tim Pat. *The IRA.* New York: St. Martin's Press, 2002.

MacGinty, Roger. *Guns and Government: The Management of the Northern Ireland Peace Process.* New York: Palgrave, 2002.

Nic Creath, Mairead. *Culture and Identity Politics in Northern Ireland.* New York: Palgrave, 2003.

O'Brien, Brendan. *The Long War: The IRA and Sinn Féin, 1985 to Today.* Syracuse, N.Y.: Syracuse University Press, 1999.

Sharrock, David. *Man of War, Man of Peace? The Unauthorized Biography of Gerry Adams.* London: Pan, 1998.

Afwerki, Isaias (1946–) *president of Eritrea*

Isaias Afwerki was born in Asmara, the capital of Eritrea, on February 2, 1946. Eritrea at that time was a British-controlled UN mandate, but in 1962 Emperor Haile Selassie forcibly annexed it to neighboring Ethiopia. After graduating from the Prince Mekonnen

Secondary School in his home town, Afwerki ventured to Ethiopia and studied engineering at the University of Addis Ababa. Like many Eritreans, he resented the forced takeover of his country. In 1966 he dropped out of school to join the Eritrean Liberation Front (ELF) and fought as a guerrilla. He rose rapidly through the ranks of the ELF, becoming a deputy divisional commander by 1967. However, dissatisfaction with ELF leadership prompted that movement to fracture by 1970, and Afwerki became as a rising star within a new movement, the Eritrean Popular Liberation Front (EPLF). And, unlike many senior political figures, Afwerki did not base himself in Europe for political exposure, but rather remained at home to fight. Consequently, he gained a reputation as an inspirational leader and was sent to China to receive advanced military training. Combat was internecine and relentless with Ethiopian forces, and the rebels were further stymied by frequent pitched battles between ELF and EPLF factions. Nonetheless, in May 1991, Ethiopia withdrew from the disputed region and Eritrea finally regained its independence. In April 1993, a referendum was held on the question of Eritrean sovereignty, and it received overwhelming support. Afwerki, the new country's most visible and popular wartime leader, was ushered in as its first president by the National Assembly on May 24 of that year.

Immediately, Afwerki was confronted with the task of reconstructing a nation ravaged by 30 years of war. Eritrea, on the strategic Horn of Africa, was previously a food exporter of considerable wealth. However, the damage wrought proved so extensive that, for the first time in its history, the region became dependent upon outside food sources to survive. Discomfiture has also been compounded by periodic droughts that have devastated agriculture. Fortunately, Afwerki, despite his Marxist background, proved himself remarkably pragmatic and not given to dogmatic responses. He worked swiftly to stamp out corruption and embarked on pursuing a mixed economy that features government control, but also elements of free market, foreign investment, and joint ventures. Moreover, this Christian president extended his hand in friendship to the sizable Muslim community and appointed several Muslims as ministers. Presently, Afwerki's biggest challenge is the resettlement of an estimated 750,000 war refugees and securing the wherewithal to feed them. Given the growing but underdeveloped economy, Eritrea will undoubtedly be depend upon foreign aid and technical assistance for several decades to come.

When he first swept to power in 1993, Afwerki pledged himself to the growth of democracy, but with the caveat that it should be accompanied by stability. In a country almost completely lacking infrastructure and continually threatened by famine, this proved a very tall order. Events were further complicated by border fighting with neighboring Sudan in 1994, which continued sporadically up through 1998. Elections were initially promised for May of that year, but these were then suspended because of deteriorating relations with Ethiopia's new leader, MELES ZENAWI. Fighting flared up along the border that month, with Eritrean forces giving up considerable ground before the invaders. Hostilities were finally concluded by June 2000, but at the cost of nearly 100,000 dead and half a million new refugees. Peace and secure border arrangements have finally been secured with Ethiopia and Sudan. The Eritrean people, moreover, seem solidly behind Afwerki, which can only facilitate endeavors to lead his nation on a path to economic self-sufficiency.

Further Reading

Fessehatzion, Tekic. *Eritrea and Ethiopia: From Conflict to Cooperation to Conflict.* Lawrenceville, N.J.: Red Sea Press, 1999.

Gilkes, Patrick, and Martin Plant. *War in the Horn: The Conflict between Eritrea and Ethiopia.* London: Royal Institute for International Affairs, 1999.

Jacquin-Berdal, Dominique. *Nationalism and Ethnicity in the Horn of Africa: A Critique of the Ethnic Interpretation.* Lewiston, N.Y.: Edwin Mellen Press, 2003.

Negash, Tekeste. *Brothers at War: Making Sense of the Eritrea-Ethiopia War.* Oxford: James Currey, 2000.

Pool, David. *From Guerrillas to Government: The Eritrean People's Liberation Front.* Athens, Ohio: Ohio University Press, 2001.

Ahern, Bertie (1951–) *prime minister of Ireland*

Bartholomew (Bertie) Patrick Ahern was born in Dublin, Ireland, on September 12, 1951, to parents of working-class backgrounds. His father, a farmer, had previously fought with the Irish Republican Army against Britain in the 1920s, and he was a strong supporter of the Fianna Fáil party. This enthusiasm for politics carried over to his son for, having trained as an accountant at the Rathmines College of Commerce and University College, Dublin, Ahern commenced organizing hospital workers. A charismatic figure with a common touch, he became a frequent sight in the working-class districts north of Dublin, and residents there elected him to the lower house of the Irish Parliament (the Dail) in 1977. Ahern proved himself an astute party player, and up through the 1980s he filled a number of posts within both Fianna Fáil and the national government. By 1983 he had risen to party vice president, a position he occupied for 10 years. However, Ahern's political stock vastly improved in 1986 when he gained appointment as lord mayor of Dublin, which greatly increased his national visibility. He then capitalized on his rising popularity by successively serving as minister of labor and minister of finance, 1989–91, in the Charles Haughey administration.

It was while functioning as finance minister that Ahern made a positive and dramatic impact upon Ireland's economic well-being. The country, strapped by four decades of semi-socialist policies, was in debt and on the brink of economic collapse. But Ahern moved swiftly to jettison outmoded practices by cutting personal and corporate taxes, trimming governmental expenditures, and campaigning vigorously for foreign investment. Within months, nearly 500 American and European corporations had settled in Ireland to take advantage of an available, well-educated workforce. Ahern also established policies to keep the country competitive by investing in infrastructure, high technology, and pharmaceuticals. Through this bold expedient, Ireland was slowly transformed from a traditional agrarian exporter to an industrial and technological powerhouse. The net result of this "Irish Economic Miracle" was a growth rate and level of prosperity surpassing all other countries in the European Union (EU).

In 1994, a scandal forced Taoiseach (Prime Minister) ALBERT REYNOLDS from office, and Ahern was a natural selection to fill the void. However, some interparty coalition squabbling between Fianna Fáil and the Labour Party resulted in the election of JOHN BRUTON, from the opposition Fine Gael, to succeed him. Ahern lost, but he assumed the mantle of president of his party. By 1997 the country was beset by rising crime, inflation, and a new government scandal, so Bruton called for a general election. By dint of hard campaigning, Fianna Fáil won 77 seats in the Dail, which, once combined those of the

Bertie Ahern *(Department of Foreign Affairs, Dublin)*

allied Progressive Democrats, ousted Bruton as prime minister on an 85 to 78 vote. When Ahern finally became taoiseach on June 26, 1997, he was also the youngest politician ever to lead the country.

Ahern's primary concern as prime minister was to achieve peace in Northern Ireland, which was rocked by religious violence and remained a Protestant-dominated region controlled by Great Britain. His efforts paid off on April 10, 1998, when Ahern and British prime minister TONY BLAIR signed the so-called Good Friday Agreement, whereby both leaders agreed to establish a new form of government for Northern Ireland. As part of the deal, the militant Irish Republican Army would be required to disarm, something they had previously been loath to do. "We have seized the initiative from the men of violence," he trumpeted, "let's not relinquish it, now or ever." Sporadic fighting continues in Northern Ireland to this day, but the two sides have never been closer to resolving this ongoing, bloody struggle between Roman Catholics and Protestants.

Ahern was also active in keeping Ireland in the forefront of continental affairs by attempting to alter Ireland's traditional neutrality in aligning its policies closely with the European Union (EU). In 2001 European leaders hammered out the Nice Treaty, which aimed to integrate the Irish economy and currency into the fold. Ahern campaigned strongly for Irish passage of the agreement in a public referendum held on June 15, 2001, but he was singularly rebuffed. The resolution, attacked by a unique coalition of the Green Party, neutralists, and Ahern's political opponents, went down to defeat by a margin of 54 to 46 percent. It was a particularly stinging defeat for Ahern, who enjoyed the support of his government, the main opposition parties, and employer and trade unions. Defeat also entails that a new treaty must now be hammered out in a fashion more palatable to Irish tastes and voted on again. However, Ahern remains cautiously optimistic and waxes confident that Ireland will align itself with fellow EU members when the next opportunity arises. His hand was greatly strengthened by elections held in May 2002, whereby Fianna Fáil captured 70 seats in parliament. On June 6, 2002, Ahern was resounding reelected by a parliamentary vote of 93 to 68. His hand considerably strengthened, the taoisech then recommitted himself to reaching a peace agreement in Northern Ireland. "Building a lasting and a just peace on this island is my great political goal," he declared, "the priority that I have and will continue to put above all else."

Further Reading

"Ahern, Bertie." *Current Biography* (July 1998): 7–10.
Collins, Neil, and Terry Cradden. *Irish Politics Today.* New York: Manchester University Press, 2001.
Hanifin, Will. *De Little Book of Bertie.* Dublin: Merlin, 2001.
Kavanagh, Ray. *Spring, Summer & Fall: The Rise and Fall of the Labour Party, 1986–99.* Dublin: Blackwater Press, 2001.
Taylor, George, ed. *Issues in Irish Public Policy.* Portland, Oreg.: Irish Academic Press, 2002.
Whelan, Ken. *Bertie Ahern: Taoiseach and Peacemaker.* Edinburgh: Mainstream Pub. Co., 1998.

Aidid, Mohammad Farah (c. 1930–1996)

president of Somalia

Mohammad Farah Aidid was born in Italian Somaliland around 1930, a member of Habar Gedir subclan of the larger Hawiye clan, the country's largest grouping. His family was poor and he worked many years as a laborer before joining the Italian gendarmes in 1950. Aidid proved himself a competent soldier and underwent advanced training in Europe at the NATO infantry school. When Somalia acquired its independence in July 1960, Aidid's unit hoisted the national flag for the first time. He remained in the army throughout the 1960s and subsequently attended various military schools in the Soviet Union. However, in 1969 the Somali government was overthrown by General Mohammad Siad Barre, who imprisoned Aidid for six years. He was then released, promoted to brigadier general, and sent south to fight in the Ogaden war against Soviet-backed Ethiopia. Aidid performed well, and after 1980 Siad Barre determined to rid himself of a potential competitor by appointing him ambassador to India. Aidid remained in New Delhi until 1989, when he returned home to help found a resistance movement, the United Somali Congress (USC). This group was dedicated to the overthrow of Siad Barre, a ruthless dictator, and the USC also appointed Aidid its chairman. He waged a successful campaign against his opponent's forces and evicted them from the capital of Mogadishu by January 1991. Aidid then hounded Siad Barre out of the country until he took refuge in Kenya. Unfortunately, in his absence, factions with the USC appointed Mohammad Ali Mahdi, a member of the competing Agbal subclan, to serve as interim president of Somalia. This move angered Aidid, for he had not been consulted and it was his men who had done all the fighting, and, as head of the Hebr Gadir clan, he felt the presidency rightfully belonged to him. Aidid, commanding the biggest armies in Somalia, then declared himself president. He proceeded to back that claim with force.

Ali Mahdi enjoyed little influence outside of Mogadishu, but he controlled part of the national capital and his faction was strongly entrenched. Commencing in 1992, large-scale urban warfare broke out between competing gangs, which basically flattened the city. Worse, as violence and anarchy fanned out into the countryside, farmers were unable to either plant or harvest their crops and widespread famine ensued. Both sides eagerly employed food as a weapon but Aidid, by virtue of his vast holdings, enjoyed greater success. The chaos soon garnered international attention, and the images of starving children prompted President George H. W. Bush to deploy troops on a humanitarian mission in December 1991. Ironically, one of the U.S. Marines dispatched was Hussein Aidid, the president's son, who was also an American citizen. They were followed by thousands of United Nations peacekeeping forces and, for a while, it appeared that stability might be restored to Somalia's fractured polity.

Aidid did not interfere with the UN's humanitarian efforts until they began concerted efforts to disarm competing factions. He ordered his men to fight back and in June 1993 they ambushed and killed 24 Pakistani peacekeepers and wounded 59. He was then branded a war criminal by UN authorities, and a new U.S. president, BILL CLINTON, decided to up the ante by capturing him. "The UN and the U.S. are trying to impose colonial rule on us," he declared, "God will destroy Washington as surely as they have destroyed Mogadishu." Several attempts to snare the elusive warlord failed, and on October 3, 1999, Somali militiamen downed several American helicopters in Aidid-controlled territory. A tremendous firefight erupted during rescue attempts and a further 18 U.S. servicemen and 500 to 1,000 Somalis died in action. The defeat so rattled the United States that it summarily withdrew its forces, and the UN followed suite in 1994. The war in Somalia, waged between rag-tag bands of heavily-armed thugs for mere parcels of land, continued without interruption.

Aidid's defeat of the Americans rendered him a national hero and enhanced his political status. In March 1994 the United States managed to bring all the warring factions to a peace conference in Nairobi, Kenya, where Aidid convinced several breakaway republics that they were best served by remaining within a united Somalia. Unfortunately, fighting flared anew and in one skirmish Aidid was severely wounded. He died from complications on August 1, 1996, the most notorious—and successful—warlord of the Somali civil war. He was succeeded by his son Hussein, who still commands the largest and best-trained paramilitary forces in the capital. For this and similar reasons, a peaceful solution to ongoing factional violence remains elusive.

Further Reading

Ahmed, Ali Jimale. *The Invention of Somalia.* Lawrenceville, N.J.: Red Sea Press, 1995.

Bowden, Mark. *Black Hawk Down: A Story of Modern War.* New York: Atlantic Monthly Press, 1999.

Clarke, Walter, and Jeffrey Herbst. *Learning from Somalia: The Lessons of Armed Humanitarian Intervention.* Boulder, Colo.: Westview Press, 1997.

Jacquin-Berdal, Dominique. *Nationalism and Ethnicity in the Horn of Africa: A Critique of the Ethnic Interpretation.* Lewiston, N.Y.: Edwin Mellen Press, 2003.

Knigge, Timothy M. *Operation Casablanca: Nine Hours in Hell.* Chapel Hill, N.C.: Professional Press, 1995.

Samatar, Ahmed I., ed. *The Somali Challenge: From Catastrophe to Renewal?* Boulder, Colo.: Lynne Rienner Publishers, 1994.

Akayev, Askar (1944–) *president of Kyrgyzstan*
Askar Akayevich Akayev was born in the village of Kyzyl-Bairak, Kyrgyzstan, on November 10, 1944, into an ethnic Kyrgz family. At that time his country was a republic within the Soviet Union. An accomplished student, he was educated at the Leningrad (now St. Petersburg) Institute of Precision Mechanics and Optics, where he obtained a doctorate in optical physics. He returned home to teach at the Funze Polytechnic Institute, where he excelled as a scientist and was appointed departmental chair. Akayev's accomplishments led to his admission into the Communist Party and advancement as head of the Central Committee's Department of Scientific and Educational Institutions. By 1989 he was also functioning as president of the Kyrgyz Academy of Sciences.

Commencing in 1991 Soviet chairman Mikhail Gorbachev began experimenting with liberal reforms in an attempt to stimulate the moribund Soviet economy and to make society less repressive. However, the hard-line Communist leader of Kyrgyzstan, Absamat Masaliev, strongly opposed such change, which induced Akayev, a dedicated reformer, to challenge him in the legislature. In a surprise vote, Akayev trounced Masaliev handily and became the republic's new president. Like Gorbachev, he championed broad liberalization in economic and political affairs, which greatly endeared him to the populace. Moreover, once the tottering Soviet Union collapsed after August 1991, Kyrgyzstan declared its independence and held free elections to determine the new president. Not surprisingly, the popular Akayev won by a resounding 95 percent of the vote, and he reaffirmed his commitment to a pluralistic political system and a free-market economy. The transition to independence and freedom was so smooth and peaceful that it has since been hailed as the "Silk Revolution." Consequently, Kyrgystan enjoys the only free press in Central Asia and a modestly expanding national economy.

The new country suddenly faced problems never experienced under communism. With Soviet controls lifted from religious activities, Kyrgyzstan experienced a surge of of Muslim fundamentalism in the form of terrorism. Religious extremists and Arab fighters began routinely slipping through the porous border with Uzbekistan, taking hostages, and fomenting an uprising against the government. Akayev, though nominally Muslim himself, was completely against religious extremism, and he took vigorous measures to disarm and arrest all provocateurs. He also had to confront the problem of mass Russian immigration from Kyrgyzstan, as members of this ethnic group held key positions in government and industry. He accomplished this by granting the Russian language equal status with the native tongue in regions where Russians constitute the majority. This apparently deterred many would-be emigrants from leaving, and thus Kyrgyzstan maintains this valuable pool of skilled foreign labor.

In 1993 Akayev encouraged passage of a new state constitution, which established a democratic presidential system, separation of powers, and guarantees of human rights. Despite traversing an oftentimes bumpy road, Akayev maintained his high standing among voters, and in December 1995 they returned him to office with 72 percent of the vote. In July 1998, a Constitutional Court decision allowed him to run for office a third time in the year 2000. That May he won another convincing victory, garnering 74.5 percent of the vote against three other candidates. The former scientist was inaugurated for a third time on December 9, 2000, and he continued along his proven path of political liberalization and economic growth. His stance against militant Islam also acquired greater urgency after the September 11, 2001, destruction of the World Trade Center in New York, and he subsequently pledged use of several airfields to U.S. forces operating against Afghanistan. He also permitted South Korean and Australian troops to be deployed in Kyrgyzstan in conjunction with the war against terrorism. To the extent that Kyrgyzstan, a tiny landlocked nation, needs peaceful neighbors and good relations with its giant neighbors Russia and China to survive, Akayev has placed special emphasis on demilitarizing both borders, and he encourages the expansion of trade. He has similarly cultivated closer ties to nearby Muslim states to control the expansion of religious fanaticism. The culmination of Akayev's progressive reforms was Kyrgyzstan's admission to the World Trade Organization in 1998.

Further Reading

Anderson, John. *Kyrgyzstan: Central Asia's Island of Democracy?* Amsterdam: Harwood Academic Publishers, 1999.

Eshingkanov, Melis. *A. Akayev: The First President of Independent Kyrgyzstan.* Bishbek: Asaaba, 1995.

Handrahan, Lori. *Gendering Ethnicity: Implications for Democracy Assistance.* New York: Routledge, 2002.

Hyman, Anthony. *Power and Politics in Central Asia's New Republics.* London: Research Institute for the Study of Conflict and Terrorism, 1994.

Kumar, Narendra. *President Akayev of Kyrgyzstan: A Political Biography.* New Delhi: Har-Annand, 1998.

Meyer, Karl E. *The Dust of Empire: The Race for Mastery in the Asian Heartland.* New York: Public Affairs, 2003.

Alemán, Arnoldo (1946–) *president of Nicaragua*

Arnoldo Alemán Lacayo was born in Managua, Nicaragua, on January 23, 1946, the son of an education minister. He studied law at the Universidad Autónoma

Askar Akayev *(Embassy of Kyrgyzstan)*

de León in 1961 and maintained a legal practice up through 1979. That year Alemán became politically active on behalf of the Somoza dictatorship and in opposition to the mounting Sandinista revolution. Over the next decade he established politically conservative credentials by forging links with the Cuban exile community in Miami, and he served as the vice president of the National Farmers Union and president of the Nicaraguan Coffee Growers Union. In 1990 Alemán took advantage of mounting dissatisfaction with the Marxist regime of Daniel Ortega by defeating the Sandinista candidate for mayor of Managua. He also lent his political support to VIOLETA CHAMORRO of the umbrella UNO party when she decisively defeated Ortega in the 1991 presidential elections. Over the next five years Alemán continued consolidating his political base through the country, using as his platform the very conservative Liberal Party. Through this expedient he outmaneuvered Minister of State Antonio Lacayo, Chamorro's son-in-law, to become the presidential candidate. This move was viewed as essential to prevent Ortega and the Sandinistas from returning to power. On October 20, 1996, he did exactly that, winning 51 percent of the vote amidst charges of irregularities. Ortega, after several days of stalling, finally conceded defeat. This event seemed to confirm the extinction of the Sandinistas as a viable national party.

Like Chamorro, Alemán continued the trend of rolling back Sandinista policies of centralized economic planning and encouraging a free-market economy. This was a daunting task for any Nicaraguan leader, for the country is the hemisphere's second-poorest after Haiti. In 2000, after a decade of reform, the country was still saddled with huge debts and unemployment rates approaching 70 percent, while around 40 percent of the population subsists on a daily income of $1. For this reason, Alemán has courted technocrats, the business and religious communities, and conservative politicians committed to promoting free trade, especially with the country's largest trading partner and benefactor, the United States. Initially, he was thwarted by Ortega and the Sandinistas, who orchestrated a transportation strike in 1998 that all but paralyzed the country. Alemán was also stung by allegations of corruption, and by the charge that his presidential plane had been stolen from the United States and was being employed to smuggle cocaine from Colombia. Alemán denied the charges and the issue was dropped, but lingering suspicions remained.

Arnoldo Alemán *(Embassy of Nicaragua)*

On the international front, Alemán weathered a military crisis when, in March 2000, the Honduran navy accosted several Nicaraguan fishing vessels on the grounds of having violating Honduran territorial waters. The Nicaraguan government made official protests and solicited the support of neighboring Costa Rica, but as yet control of the Gulf of Fonseca remains disputed. Another unresolved issue in Nicaraguan politics is that of returning the land appropriated by the Sandinistas and given to their supporters. This process continues on a graduated basis, but amid much protest from adherents of the former Marxist regime. But the biggest crisis facing Alemán was the familiar charge of corruption. In August 1998 the state comptroller, Agustín Jarquín, formally accused him of increasing his personal wealth by 900 percent while he held public office. The president responded by having him arrested on similar charges, tried, and jailed, but pressure from the international community forced his release. Alemán then forced through a restructuring of the comptroller's office with a view to restraining its inquiries, but the new head, Luis Angel Montenegro, has accused Alemán of building an expensive helicopter pad on his property at public expense. Newspapers have also asserted that Alemán acquired an expensive American-built helicopter for his personal use, but registered it to a nonexistent company to avoid paying taxes.

Alemán weathered all these charges and remained in office until November 4, 2000, when Vice President Enrique Bolanos defeated Daniel Ortega for a third time to succeed him. It remained to be seen if the former Nicaraguan president would confront these irregularities, and their concomitant penalties, in a court of law. On December 12, 2002, the Nicaraguan National Assembly stripped him of his congressional immunity, and he was placed under house arrest. The attorney general has charged Alemán with misappropriation of up to $100 million in public funds. If tried and convicted, he faces a maximum of 30 years in prison. Appearing in court the following day, Alemán waxed defiant, insisting that his immunity "has not been removed from me, so no judge or tribunal in the republic can have jurisdiction to prosecute me."

Further Reading

Brown, Timothy C. *When the AK-47s Fall Silent: Revolutionaries, Guerrillas, and the Dangers of Peace.* Stanford, Calif.: Hoover Institute Press, 2000.

Dye, David R., Jack Spence, and George Vickers. *Patchwork Democracy: Nicaraguan Politics Ten Years after the Fall.* Cambridge, Mass.: Hemisphere Initiatives, 2000.

Kodrich, Ken. *Tradition and Change in the Nicaraguan Press: Newspapers and Journalists in a New Democratic Era.* Lanham, Md.: University Press of America, 2001.

Paige, Jeffrey M. *Coffee and Power: Revolution and the Rise of Democracy in Central America.* Cambridge, Mass.: Harvard University Press, 1998.

Alia, Ramiz (1925–) *president of Albania*

Ramiz Alia was born in Shkodër, Albania, on October 18, 1925, the son of poor Muslim parents. His family subsequently relocated to the capital of Tirana, and he was educated at the city gymnasium. Following the Italian occupation of Albania in April 1939, Alia enrolled in the fascist-oriented Lictor Youth Group, but later dropped out to join the Communist Youth Organization. In this capacity he entered guerrilla forces under Enver Hoxha, a hard-line Stalinist, and distinguished himself in combat in World War II. By war's end he had risen to the rank of lieutenant colonel and had also

struck up cordial relations with Hoxha, who emerged as Albania's leader. In the immediate postwar period, Hoxha steered Albania on a decidedly pro-Soviet course and Alia was sent to study in Moscow. He obtained his advanced degree in political science by 1954, and he returned home to serve as minister of education and culture. Like his mentor, Hoxha, Alia was a doctrinaire Stalinist by inclination, and he rose steadily through the ranks of the Albanian Party of Labor (ALP, or Communist). He supported Hoxha's break with the Soviet Union and Yugoslavia over ideological issues after 1956, and he moved to embrace the stridently ideological Red China of Mao Zedong. Following the death of Mao in 1976, Hoxha and Alia broke off relations with China, thereby increasing Albania's diplomatic isolation. Alia remained a doctrinaire Marxist-Leninist up to the time of Hoxha's own demise in 1985, and he managed to engineer his appointment as the party's first secretary and heir apparent. He accomplished this by outmaneuvering another longtime Hoxha ally, Prime Minister Mehmet Shehu, whose supporters were also purged.

Though in undisputed control of the political apparatus, Alia could do little to improve the failing socialist system he had inherited. By 1985 the collectivized agricultural system was breaking down and proved unable to feed the nation. Hunger and mounting economic shortcomings led to increasing social unrest, even in this tightly controlled, one-party state. In 1988 Alia felt he had little recourse but to distance himself from his communist indoctrination and to begin experimenting with varying degrees of decentralization. He also sought to gradually break Albania's traditional isolation by making diplomatic overtures to both the Soviet Union and the United States. However, the Albanian political and economic infrastructure proved so tottering that conditions only worsened. By January 1990 Alia felt he had no choice but to implement a 25-point reform program intended to liberalize the economy in line with more capitalist practices, encourage private enterprise and foreign investment, and enhance long-suppressed civil liberties. These changes were largely welcomed by the populace, but the 1989 execution of Romanian dictator Nicolae Ceauşescu served as a catalyst for greater change. Bowing to the inevitable, in 1991, Alia authorized a new constitution that, for the first time in Albanian history, allowed for multiparty elections.

Surprisingly, in March 1991 the communist-inspired Albanian Party of Labor won the first round of elections by defeating four, divided opposition parties. Alia himself had lost his seat in Tiranë, but the following month the parliament reappointed him president. This, however, forced him to relinquish his post as party first secretary and other positions held in the Politburo and central committee. But Alia was unwilling to approve of additional reforms to assist the sagging economy and, in elections held that June, the Communists were finally defeated by a four-party coalition. Alia at that point seemed resigned to the inevitable and, after a multiparty coalition won an outright majority in parliament in March 1992, he resigned from office the following April in favor of SALI BERISHA of the Democratic Party. He became reviled as the second and last communist ruler of Albania, but he did manage to steer his nation toward democracy and political pluralism.

The legacy of Albanian political oppression engendered considerable resentment among the polity, and in September 1992 Alia was arrested and charged with abuse of power during his five-year reign. He was put on trial in April 1994, found guilty, and sentenced to nine years in prison. However, he only served a year before being released for humanitarian reasons. However, in 1996, Alia was arrested again and charged with crimes against humanity while in power. During his trial, a riot erupted and Alia escaped to Sweden with his family. He remained there for several years before the charges were dropped against him, and in 1998 Alia returned to the former Stalinist stronghold, now basking in the light of freedom and democracy. The former leader remains an unpopular figure at home, but he has made his mark on history for overseeing a peaceful transition from totalitarianism to freedom.

Further Reading

Artisien, P. "Albania at the Crossroads." *Journal of Communist Studies* 3 (September 1987): 231–49.

Biberaj, Elez. *Albania in Transition: The Rocky Road to Democracy.* Boulder, Colo.: Westview Press, 1998.

Kadare, Ismail. *Albanian Spring: The Anatomy of Tyranny.* London: Saqi Books, 1994.

Murati, Teuta. "The Emergence of the Albanian Nation: The Effect of Nationalism on Politics and Society." Unpublished master's thesis, East Stroudsburg University, 2000.

Vickers, Miranda, and James Pettifer. *Albania: From Anarchy to a Balkan Tragedy.* London: Hurst, 1999.

Aliyev, Heydar (1923–   ) *president of Azerbaijan*

Heydar Aliyev was born in the Nakhichevan Autonomous Republic of Azerbaijan, then part of the Soviet Union, on May 10, 1923, to working-class parents. Intelligent and aspiring, he joined the All Union People's Commissariat of Internal Affairs (NKVD, the dreaded secret police) in 1941 and was allowed to join the Communist Party four years later. Over the next 20 years he filled a number of state security positions throughout Russia and Azerbaijan, taking time off only to obtain a degree in history from Azerbaijan State University in 1957. After 1964 he formed a close working relationship with Soviet premier Leonid Brezhnev, who continually advanced his political career. Aliyev's fortunes crested in 1982 when he became a full member of the Politburo, the Soviet Union's governing body. In 1985 Aliyev supported the rise of reformist Mikhail Gorbachev as general secretary of the Communist Party, although two years later he was stripped of his party posts over charges of corruption. For the next six years Aliyev lived in relative obscurity in Moscow and Azerbaijan until 1991, the year the Soviet Union collapsed.

Azerbaijan quickly declared its independence from Moscow and installed Abulfaz Elchibey as its first democratically elected president in June 1992. However, the economy soured and, worse, fighting broke out between Azerbaijan and Armenia over the disputed Nagorno-Karabakh region. Azerbaijan subsequently lost 20 percent of its territory and faced an influx of over 1 million refugees. Aliyev, judging the moment right, then overthrew the ineffective Elchibey to popular acclaim. Azerbaijanis clearly desired a firmer hand at the tiller, and this is exactly what they received. After a sham election held on October 3, 1993, Aliyev, the former secret policeman, quickly reverted to a style of governance that was both autocratic and authoritarian. The population overlooked these tendencies initially, as the need for order and security became pressing. Aliyev reached an accord with Armenia in 1993 and, although territorial disputes remain, the cease-fire has held. He also easily crushed a police-supported coup against him in 1994, and he further clamped down with a mass arrest of perceived political opponents. Again moving swiftly and decisively to consolidate his control, Aliyev drafted a new constitution that was officially ratified by 90 percent of voters in a nationwide referendum. It proclaimed, among other things, freedom of religion in this Muslim-dominated state, a national language (Azeri), and allowances for token opposition in the form of small parties. He also pledged to develop a viable market economy and stamp out corruption, which had become a staple of political life. These changes are largely cosmetic, however, and he continues to run Azerbaijan like a personal fiefdom. But Aliyev's goal has always been the pursuit of stability in the quest for national survival, and to the extent that he has succeeded, his fellow countrymen concur.

One reason for Aliyev's apparent success is oil. Azerbaijan is one of the world's richest petroleum-producing regions and he has unhesitatingly offered it to the outside world. He cleverly—if cynically—deduced that criticism of his heavy-handed regime would be muted once oil and natural gas starting flowing through European and American pipelines. Consequently, the influx of revenues have shored up Azerbaijan's shaky economy and raised otherwise marginal standards of living. Moreover, in July 1997, Aliyev became the first Azerbaijan head of state to visit the United States, where he was cordially received by President BILL CLINTON, and he signed several lucrative treaties. However, this seeming subservience to the West has generated resentment in Russia and Iran, who also have vested interests in and around the Caspian Sea. Iran, in particular, has a sizable Azeri population within its boundaries, and its treatment of them remains a point of contention with the nationalistic Aliyev. Russia has also applied pressure on Azerbaijan to insure that its oil flows in pipes through Russia, and not Turkey, as the United States desires. Nonetheless, throughout 2000, the 78-year-old leader mounted state visits to both nations to smooth out differences and enhance trade. Russian president VLADIMIR PUTIN, himself a former KGB agent, was quite conciliatory in negotiating with Aliyev, praising him for his treatment of ethnic Russians residing in Azerbaijan. Putin also received assurances that Azerbaijan was not aiding separatist rebels in the breakaway republic of Chechnya.

Though ailing in recent years, Aliyev has indicated that he has no intention of relinquishing power. In fact, he hopes to perpetuate his legacy by grooming his son to succeed him. "No one was born a democrat in this country, including myself," he declared. "Maybe if we establish conditions of democracy, my grandson will have democracy." However, many Azerbaijanis fear that his political heirs will lack the sheer will and dynamism of Heydar Aliyev, and that the country might slip back into the chaotic state that occasioned his rise.

Further Reading

Atabaki, Touraj. *Azerbaijan: Ethnicity and the Struggle for Power in Iran.* New York; I. B. Tauris, 2000.

Croissant, Cynthia. *Azerbaijan, Oil, and Geopolitics.* Commack, N.Y.: Nova Science Publishers, 1998.

Dragadze, Tamara. *Azerbaijan.* London: Melisende, 2000.

Shaffer, Branda. *Borders and Brethren: Iran and the Challenge of Azerbaijan Identity.* Cambridge, Mass.: MIT Press, 2002.

Thomas, Paul. *Azerbaijan: The Next Big Oil Play.* London: Financial Times Energy Pubs., 1998.

Amarjargal, Rinchinnyamiin (1961–)
prime minister of Mongolia

Rinchinnyamiin Amarjargal was born in Ulaanbaatar, Mongolia, on February 27, 1961. His country was then a republic aligned with the Soviet Union and he was educated in state-sponsored schools at home and in Moscow. In 1982 Amarjargal received a degree in finance from the Plekhanov Economics Institute before securing work at the Central Council of Mongolian Trade Unions. In 1990 Amarjargal was selected to lecture at the Mongolian Technical University, where he became an early advocate of free-market economics. This came at a time when the Soviet Union collapsed and splintered in August 1991, whereupon Mongolia declared its independence. However, Amarjargal continued on as head of the college until 1996, when he earned an advanced degree in economics from the University of Bradford, England. Despite his preoccupation with teaching, he became active in politics and joined the Mongolian National Democratic Party (MNDP) in 1992. Four years later he tested the political waters by gaining election to the Great Khural (parliament) as the party's leading economic reformer.

Amarjargal took readily to politics with an aptitude that belied his relative youth. From April to December 1998 he functioned as minister of external relations within the government and was spoken of as a possible contender for prime minister. This move was quashed by opponents that year, but another opportunity arose in July 1999 when the government of Prime Minister Janlavyn Narantsatsralt became ensnared in a scandal involving the privatization of copper mines. He resigned after only seven months in office and the Democratic Alliance, to which the MNDP belonged, nominated

Amarjargal to succeed him. After some internal wrangling, the Great Khural elected him to the post of prime minister in July 1999. That November he also assumed the mantle of chairman of the MNDP.

Once in office, Amarjargal focused upon his trademark specialty, the formation and development of a free-market economy. Another priority was the privatization of inefficient state-run industries, which comprised 80 percent of the country's economy. "I firmly believe that liberalism throughout every segment of society is the engine of prosperity for Mongolia," he declared. Unfortunately, Mongolia's break with the Soviet Union meant a loss of subsidies to keep the economy afloat, and there was a corresponding increase in social dislocation and hardship. Amarjargal therefore directed several campaigns to address issues such as homelessness, hunger, and crime, which only deflected his attention from other priorities. To regain funding in the form of foreign aid, Amarjargal took the unprecedented step of visiting both China and South Korea in the quest for investment. He was also diplomatic in his dealing with the new Russian Federation, and careful not to display favoritism toward China, for Mongolian security and survival depends on peaceful relations with both its giant neighbors.

The decisive point in Amarjargal's tenure as prime minister occurred during the winter of 1999–2000 when the entire country was hit by a "zud," the Mongolian term for a severe storm. Snow and intense cold wiped out millions of heads of cattle, which are essential to the survival of this largely pastoral nation. Intense suffering resulted, particularly among nomadic herdsmen residing in remote locations. Amarjargal mobilized scanty government resources to help alleviate the disaster, but the magnitude proved overwhelming. "No doubt, it will be very painful, demanding a lot of human resources," he told a BBC reporter, "But I don't expect this will force my fellow countrymen, even those from the territories under trouble, to leave their country en masse." Unfortunately, Amarjargal underestimated the suffering of his people and their impatience to receive timely assistance. When new elections were held on July 2, 2000, both he and his entire cabinet were swept from office. His replacement as prime minister, Nambaryn Enkhbayar, pledged to forgo economic reforms in favor of placing increased emphasis on social welfare and poverty reduction.

Further Reading
Akaha, Tsuneo. *Politics and Economics in Northeast Asia: Nationalism and Regionalism in Contention.* New York: St. Martin's Press, 1999.

Badarch, Dendiviia, and Raymond A. Zilinskas. *Mongolia Today: Science, Culture, Environment, and Development.* Richmond, Va.: Curzon, 2001.

Bulag, Uradyn E. *The Mongols at China's Edge: History and the Politics of National Unity.* Lanham, Md.: Rowman and Littlefield, 2002.

Namjin, Tumurin. *The Economy of Mongolia: From Traditional Times to the Present.* Bloomington, Ind.: Mongolia Society, 2000.

Kotkin, Stephen. *Mongolia in the Twentieth Century: Landlocked Cosmopolitan.* Armonk, N.Y.: M. E. Sharpe, 1999.

Amato, Giuliano (1938–) *prime minister of Italy*

Giuliano Amato was born on May 13, 1938, in Turin, Italy, and he majored in law at the Normale University in Pisa. In 1962 he pursued an advanced degree in law from Columbia University in New York City before returning home to teach at the prestigious University of Rome. He is the author of several highly regarded books on constitutional and international law and speaks fluent English. Amato joined the Socialist Party in 1958, becoming a lifelong adherent. He first gained election to parliament in 1983 and struck up a close working relationship with Socialist Bettino Craxi. From 1983 to 1987, Amato was chosen to serve as cabinet chief, and from 1987 to 1989 he functioned as treasury minister. Part of his success lay in Craxi's determination to rid the Socialist Party of its Marxist inheritance and all the ideological baggage that alienated most middle-class voters. Amato, a political realist, heartily concurred, and the two embarked on the twin goals of both party and national reform. He then gained renown as a Socialist willing to break with failed policies of the past, and he initiated cuts in government spending and a reduction in overall bureaucracy. These efforts were also undertaken to enhance Italy's chances of joining the European Monetary Union in 1999. In the course of gaining greater public exposure, Amato received high marks for intelligence, wit, and personal honesty from the Italian people. As a degree of affection, they nicknamed the diminutive politician "Topolino"—the Italian version of Mickey Mouse.

Although Amato basked in popularity during his days in office, Craxi was indicted as one of Italy's most corrupt politicians and was forced from office in 1992. The Socialist Party consequently fell into immediate disarray, and many questioned Amato's integrity over his silence during a long and fruitful association with the disgraced prime minister. However, he was cleared of any wrongdoing and apologized publicly for not doing more to stop party corruption. Craxi, then a fugitive from justice in Tunisia, allegedly never forgave Amato for his remarks, but the public did. In 1992 he was asked to serve as prime minister, and he remained in office for a tempestuous 10 months. Italy was then in the grip of a sagging economy, a resurgent Mafia in political life, and public disgust over rampant corruption. On April 22, 1993, Amato subsequently resigned after another scandal involving his cabinet, but he again emerged with his personal reputation unscathed. He then resumed teaching for several years before returning to politics as reform minister in the government of MASSIMO D'ALEMA in 1998, and as his treasury minister, 1999–2000. On April 21, 2000, Amato was himself appointed prime minister under some of the most unusual circumstances in Italian political history.

Since the collapse of the Socialist Party, Amato basically served as a freelance opportunist, bereft of party alignment. For this reason, he came to power under the aegis of a crazy-quilt center-left coalition of no less than 12 disparate parties. He had no allegiance to any of them, nor they to him, other than that they collectively wielded a slim majority in parliament—and he was the only candidate they backed. Consequently, this proved an unholy alliance among the Green Party, Socialists, Catholics, Communists, and other malcontents who, more often than not, were at cross purposes with each other. However, the smooth-talking, urbane Amato was perhaps the only politician in Italy who could keep such discordant allies from splitting apart.

Amato's control of events was tenuous, and he was singularly unable to pass major legislation, including a long-overdue reform of the Italian electoral system. He also toyed with the necessity of updating the outdated pension system: Italy, with one of the lowest birth rates in Europe, can no longer support its rapidly aging population. Unfortunately, the Italian polity is one of Europe's most volatile, and it quickly tired of Amato's

inability to promote change. He called for elections on May 13, 2001, in an effort to thwart conservative media magnate SILVIO BERLUSCONI from taking power. The result was a debacle for Amato's coalition as the Conservatives won a clear majority of seats in both houses of parliament. Accordingly, Amato tendered his resignation on June 8, 2001, having unsuccessfully served as the 58th Italian prime minister since 1945.

Further Reading

Agnew, John A. *Place and Politics in Modern Italy.* Chicago: University of Chicago Press, 2002.

Bedani, Gino, and B. A. Haddock. *The Politics of Italian National Identity: A Multidisciplinary Perspective.* Cardiff: University of Wales Press, 2000.

Bufacci, Vittorio, and Simon Burgess. *Italy since 1989: Events and Interpretations.* Basingstoke, England: Palgrave, 2001.

Gilbert, Mark, and Gianfranco Pasquino. *Italian Politics: The Faltering Transition.* New York: Berghahn Books, 2000.

Ginsburg, Paul. *Italy and Its Discontents.* London: Allen Lane, 2001.

Andreotti, Giulio (1919–) *prime minister of Italy*

Giulio Andreotti was born in Rome on January 14, 1919, the son of a schoolteacher. He obtained a law degree from the University of Rome in 1940 and thereafter became closely associated with Catholic student associations. Toward the end of the World War II he joined forces with Alcide De Gaspari to help found a new political party, the Christian Democrats (DC), and in 1946 he was part of a political convention tasked with drafting a new constitution. His relationship with De Gaspari held him in good stead afterward and, despite his youth, he was always at the center of DC politics. He also held an appointment as undersecretary of the presidency of ministers until De Gaspari's death in 1954. Andreotti was first elected to the Constituent Assembly from his district in Rome in 1947 and remained in office, one way or another, up through 1992. Furthermore, he served as prime minister no less than seven times—in 1972, 1976, 1978, 1979, 1989–91, and 1991–92. He was also defense minister eight times and foreign minister five times in various governments. Andreotti has since become renowned as the quintessential postwar Italian politician, a figure of both impressive longevity and legendary bargaining abilities.

Andreotti's most important national service occurred during the late 1970s, when the nation was wracked by left-wing inspired terrorism and the ascent of the Italian Communist Party (PCI). For many months, the conservative-minded Christian Democrats feared that they might actually be supplanted as Italy's largest party by the Communists, with detrimental effects upon relations with the United States and NATO. However, Andreotti diffused the crisis with a typical admixture of pragmatism and guile. Rather than face a political showdown with the surging Communists, during his 1978 tenure as prime minister he invited them to serve as part of his administration in a government of national unity. This was done with the understanding that it was a first step toward a formal alliance between the two feuding parties, whereby Communists would be appointed to ministerial posts. However, Andreotti carefully crafted a minority cabinet that excluded any Communist members, while at the same time cementing their support in the assembly. It was an unholy alliance between two staunch adversaries, but the arrangement is witness to Andreotti's ability to strike a bargain. In this manner the Christian Democrats retained power with Communist support, and they never made but token efforts to secure a formal political alliance. Consequently, the PCI lost the confidence of its own voters, and they supported the party with dwindling numbers over the years. As Andreotti, a literary wit, dryly remarked, "power corrodes those who do not have it."

Andreotti's style of leadership was firmly in the Western camp, and he established close relationships with a number of American presidents. He also demonstrated, despite his working relationship with Communists, that Italy was a reliable NATO ally in its dealings with the Soviet Union. Ever a popular politician, he was also tapped to serve as foreign minister in the Socialist administration of Bettino Craxi during the 1980s. However, following the collapse of European communism in the late 1990s, Andreotti weathered the most controversial storm in his lengthy career. After his last tenure as prime minister in 1992, the Italian senate voted to remove his immunity from prosecution stemming from charges of complicity with the Mafia. Apparently, Andreotti was viewed as having close political ties to Toto Riina, a leading Sicilian mob boss. Worse, rumors began circulating that in 1979 Andreotti ordered the murder of Mino Pecorelli, a Roman journalist, to prevent investigations into his financial dealings. At length the weight of scandal began impacting the political fortunes of the DC, and in 1993 they suffered their worse political showing ever.

Though forced to resign from office and politics, Andreotti strenuously maintained his innocence. He insisted that, because he had conducted one of the biggest anticrime sweeps in Italian history, the numerous criminal kingpins indicted were simply tarring him to get even. He went on trial in September 1995 for corruption and murder in what was billed as the most sensational trial of Italian political history. After six years of testimony from witnesses, intense deliberations, and cross-examinations, a three-judge panel finally acquitted the former prime minister of any underworld connections. Earlier, he had also been cleared of complicity in the death of Pecorelli. "Obviously, I'm delighted," Andreotti proclaimed. "It wasn't so great to have to wait so many years. I consider the case closed now." The former prime minister still continues to enjoy his reputation as one of his nation's most legendary senior statesmen. His reputation as "Mr. Italy" also remains intact. In July 2000 state prosecutors called for his retrial but, in light of Andreotti's age and ill health, no further actions have been taken.

Further Reading

Andreotti, Giulio. *The U.S.A. Up Close: From the Atlantic Pact to Bush.* New York: New York University Press, 1992.

"Foreign Policy in the Italian Democracy." *Political Science Quarterly* 109 (Summer 1999): 529–38.

Gilbert, Mark. *The Italian Revolution: The End of Politics, Italian Style?* Boulder, Colo.: Westview Press, 1995.

Orlando, Leoluca. *Fighting the Mafia and Renewing Sicilian Culture.* San Francisco: Encounter Books, 2001.

Robb, Peter. *Midnight in Sicily: On Art, Food, History, Travel, and the Cosa Nostra.* Boston: Faber and Faber, 1998.

Annan, Kofi (1938–) *secretary-general of the United Nations*

Kofi Atta Annan was born on April 8, 1938, in Kumasi, Gold Coast (now Ghana), the son of a Fante tribal chief. After receiving an economics degree from Macalester

College, Minnesota, in 1961, he conducted advanced studies at the Institut Universitaire des Hautes Etudes Internationales in Geneva, Switzerland. By 1971 Annan had joined the United Nations as part of the World Health Organization. He then pursued a master's degree in management from the Massachusetts Institute of Technology. In 1980 he advanced to serve as deputy director of administration of the office of the UN High Commissioner for Refugees, winning plaudits for efficiency and personal diplomacy. He then spent a decade in planning, budgeting, and finance, all of which he fulfilled with consummate skill and honesty. By 1993 Annan's reputation was such that he became undersecretary general for peacekeeping operations by Secretary-General BOUTROS BOUTROS-GHALI, a high-visibility posting. In the wake of the cold war, ethnic fighting was rife in such diverse regions as Somalia, the Balkans, and Rwanda. Boutros-Ghali strove mightily to have UN forces deployed as peacekeepers but the results, owing to a lack of money and troops, were far from uniform. In Rwanda and Bosnia-Herzegovina, where peacekeeping forces failed to halt the slaughter of unarmed civilians, the UN was criticized for burgeoning bureaucracy and incompetence. Annan, however, continued distinguishing himself in difficult ventures abroad, including negotiating the safe removal of 500,000 Asian workers from Kuwait in 1990 and arranging the arrival of 50,000 peacekeepers to Balkan states. In light of UN disasters elsewhere, Annan's genteel persona belied a steely resolve that the organization badly needed. His star was on the ascent.

Dissatisfaction with UN operations crested in 1996 when the United States, paying an annual $2 billion in dues, opposed a second term for Boutros-Ghali. However, the African bloc, which remained entitled to nominate a candidate from their region, selected Annan as his replacement that December. His credentials as a modest, objective, and determined bureaucrat had been well established in two decades of work for the United Nations, and he gained easy approval by the General Assembly. Annan thus became the seventh secretary-general and the first black African from south of the Sahara. He was also the first leader to rise entirely through the organization's bureaucracy. "There is no lack of ideas or debate," he addressed the session. "Our task now is to find common ground, to shape together the changes that will move this organization forward."

Kofi Annan *(United Nations)*

From the onset, Annan faced formidable if not impossible tasks of providing humanitarian assistance to the world's poor, intervening to stop wars, and providing troops to maintain the peace. He set about his work dutifully, while trying to achieve the paradoxical goals of streamlining bureaucracy and reducing costs. Boutros-Ghali's failure to implement change resulted in U.S. suspension of annual dues to the UN but Annan, with deliberation and tact, convinced the United States to resume funding. Throughout 1998 he was busily employed in the Middle East, restraining violence between the United States and Iraq and between Israel and the Palestinians. The following year he proved instrumental in hammering out an agreement allowing UN troops to patrol Serbia's strife-torn province of Kosovo. By 2000, UN operations had been active in East Timor, Sierra Leone, and the Democratic Republic of the Congo, all of which suffered from sectarian violence. And, in contrast to his predecessor, the smooth-talking Ghanaian enjoyed uniform success and international popularity. His efforts culminated in June 2001 when the UN unanimously approved a second five-year term as secretary-general. That October Annan received the Nobel Peace Prize.

Despite Annan's best efforts, the world continues to be a very dangerous place, especially following the 2001 destruction of New York's World Trade Center. "If today, after the horror of 11 September, we can see better and we see further, we will realize that humanity is indivisible," he declared. "New threats make no distinction between races, nations, or regions." Annan unflinchingly endorsed the U.S. war against international terrorists in Afghanistan, while simultaneously working to increase humanitarian assistance to beleaguered civilians. But his chores, while onerous, are not without their rewards. On May 7, 2002, Annan accompanied XANANA GUSMÃO to Dili, capital of East Timor, to commemorate celebrations marking the independence of that land from Indonesia. It also joined the UN, becoming its 190th member. "As Secretary-General, I am proud of the part the United Nations has played in that struggle, and especially in its last phase," he affirmed, "I pledge that this will mark not an end, but a new beginning." The affable Annan will remain secretary-general until 2006, at which point his mandate concludes.

Further Reading

Emmerij, Levis. *Ahead of the Curve? UN Ideas and Global Challenges*. Bloomington, Ind.: Indiana University Press, 2001.

Gareau, Frederick H. *The United Nations and Other Institutions: A Critical Analysis*. Chicago: Burnham, 2001.

Kille, Kent J. "Leadership and Influence in the United Nations: A Comparative Analysis of the Secretaries General." Unpublished Ph.D. dissertation, Ohio State University, 2001.

Loescher, Gil. *The UNCHR and World Politics: A Perilous Path*. New York: Oxford University Press, 2001.

Ryan, Stephen. *The United Nations and International Politics*. New York: St. Martin's Press, 2000.

Antall, Jozsef (1932–1993) *prime minister of Hungary*

Jozsef Antall, Jr., was born in Hungary on April 8, 1932, the son of a government interior minister, Jozsef Antall, Sr., who was also a member of the conservative Independent Smallholders Party. During World War II Hungary was occupied by Nazi forces, yet the elder Antall distinguished himself by saving the lives of thousands of Jews and East European refugees. Antall witnessed his father being arrested for his humanity, and the experience indelibly impressed him. Thereafter he became personally committed to liberal political traditions and joined the Smallholders Party youth organization. Unfortunately, the end of World War II witnessed the Soviet occupation of Hungary, and, by 1948, the Soviet Union had installed a communist puppet regime. Antall, meanwhile, attended Eitvos University in Budapest, where he eventually obtained a doctorate in history. Thereafter he sought work as a historian with the National Archives and also taught at the Eitvos secondary school. When Hungarian dissatisfaction with communism erupted in a major uprising in 1956, Antall actively participated in antigovernment demonstrations and was jailed. The revolt was subsequently crushed by Russian tanks and, following a brief imprisonment, he was forbidden to teach or publish until 1963.

Antall eventually became attracted to medical history, which did not entail an ideological slant, and so for many years he served as director of the Semmelweis Museum for the History of Medicine. By 1972 he had risen to director and was allowed to travel outside of the country. During these forays Antall became closely acquainted with the Christian Democratic parties of Austria and Hungary, and he wished to impart their religion-based principles to the Hungarian polity. His quest was abetted by the slow disintegration of the Soviet bloc in the late 1980s, whereby entrenched economic failures stimulated massive public clamoring for change. In 1988 Antall became a co-founder and chairman of a new movement, the Hungarian Freedom Forum (MDF), which called for Western-style multiparty democracy and liberalized economics. Following the withdrawal of Soviet forces from Eastern Europe in 1989, the Hungarian Communist Party had little recourse but to accede to demands for greater political freedom, and the nation's first multiparty elections were scheduled for the spring of 1990. In two rounds of elections the MDF gathered the most seats and, in concert with two other center-right parties, Antall became Hungary's first democratically elected prime minister in 40 years. "I always have had an interest in politics," he declared, "but only in a democracy with parliament and freedom." However, success was only achieved by making the head of the opposition Alliance of Free Democrats, Árpád Göncz, president of Hungary. Once installed, the two leaders skirmished frequently.

Antall did not have long to savor his victory, for the nation was in desperate economic straits, needing drastic reform. Still, to mitigate the social shock of liberalization, the prime minister insisted on a slower, more gradual pace of privatization. This approach surprised many conservatives within the MDF, but Antall determined to avoid the social dislocation caused by radical reform plans, such as those adopted by Poland. However, the government nevertheless clearly reoriented itself toward Western Europe, both politically and economically, so foreign investors were also invited in. Antall then oversaw the drafting of a new constitution that enshrined the principles of freedom and democracy after four decades of brutal Soviet oppression. During a 1991 trip to the Soviet Union, whose days were also numbered, Antall also advocated dissolving the Warsaw Pact, an outdated military alliance bent upon preserving communist rule in Eastern Europe.

As a student of Hungarian history, Antall was acutely aware that two-thirds of his nation's land had been stripped away thanks to the Trianon Treaty, signed in the wake of World War I. He also knew that large numbers of Hungarians were forced to reside in neighboring Romania, where they suffered discrimination. Therefore, in many speeches to the national assembly, he dropped veiled hints about an emergence of a "greater Hungary," which to many suggested that force might be used to regain traditional lands. Antall never publicly advocated such a position, but it was a long-suppressed notion, and popular among nationalists. By 1993 Antall had become Eastern Europe's longest-serving prime minister and Hungary was well on its way to becoming an economic powerhouse in its own right. However, he did not live long enough to witness the fruits of his labors. On December 12, 1993, Antall died of cancer and was succeeded by Peter Boross, the interior minister. He is fondly remembered as the bookish historian who helped his country make the difficult transition from tyranny to freedom and a market economy. His MDF party did not fare as well in public opinion, and, in the 1994 elections, they were removed from power by former Communists, now posing as reform Socialists.

Further Reading

Anderson, Ruth M., and J. M. Anderson. *Barbed Wire for Sale: The Hungarian Transition to Democracy,* *1988–1991.* Graham, Wash.: Poetic License, 1999.

Masat, Melissa. "The Social Agenda of the New Hungarian Government: The Reconstruction of A Post-Communist Society." *Journal of Social, Political, and Economic Studies* 15 (Winter 1990): 423–35.

Renwick, John. "Combining Rational Choice and Political Culture: The Case of Institutional Choice in Hungary, 1989–1990." Unpublished M. Phil., Oxford University, 2000.

Schatz, Sara. "The Consideration of an Imagined National Identity in Post-Communist Hungary: The Jozsef Antall Cabinet." *Canadian Review of Studies in Nationalism* 25, nos. 1, 2 (1998): 63–68.

Schmidt, Maria, and Laszlo G. Toth. *From Totalitarianism to Democratic Hungary: Evolution and Transformation, 1990–2000.* Highlands, N.J.: Atlantic Research and Publications, 2000.

Anthony, Kenny (1951–   ) *prime minister of St. Lucia*

Kenny Anthony was born on St. Lucia, a small Caribbean Island, on January 8, 1951. He received his education at the Vieux Fort Senior Secondary School before attending the St. Lucia's Teacher's School. Anthony subsequently received a degree in law at the University of the West Indies and a doctorate in law at the University of Birmingham, England. After several years of teaching and tutoring at the University of the West Indies, Anthony gained appointment as department head of the Caribbean Justice Improvement Department Project in 1993, and he also served as a consultant with the United Nations Development Program. In 1996 he first tested the political waters of St. Lucia by winning election as a leader within the St. Lucia Labour Party (SLP), which was established shortly after the island's independence in 1946. But since 1964, the island had been ruled by the conservative United Worker's Party (UWP). In May 1997, the urbane, articulate Anthony was nominated to run for prime minister against the sitting UWP candidate, Vaughn Lewis. Lewis, a stiff, colorless technocrat, was unprepared for Anthony's brand of populist politics. The election held in May 1996 proved a resounding triumph for the Labour Party, which carried 60 percent of votes cast and now held 16 to 17 seats in the national assembly. This victory elevated Anthony to prime minister and also ended for the SLP an 18-year spell as the minority opposition. "I solemnly pledge that we will effectively and fearlessly attack all those problems which today remain unsolved," he declared. "We promise you a better, richer, and more satisfied St. Lucia."

Once in office, Anthony followed through on several of his campaign pledges. These included fiscal reform with tighter accountability, a reduction in government portfolios to reduce expenditures, and appointment of new leaders to head the state corporations. His greatest challenge, however, was the sagging economy which, like many islands in the Caribbean, is contingent upon tourism. To combat unemployment, which had risen to 29 percent in 1996, he expanded public sector jobs and implemented high-tech training and education. These endeavors helped to reduce the jobless rate by 10 points by 1999, which would pay political dividends in the upcoming election. Anthony was also mindful of the importance of agriculture to the island economy, particularly the export of bananas, its principal cash crop. For this reason the government has proved willing to help absorb the mounting debts of the St. Lucia Banana Growers Association, and it has modified the tax code to encourage cultivation of nontraditional crops. Anthony has also been active on the international scene. He made several high-visibility trips to Japan and Cuba seeking foreign investment, and he established diplomatic relations with the People's Republic of China. He also sought to deepen cultural and economic ties with neighboring Guadeloupe and Martinique, islands that share St. Lucia's heritage, which is partly French.

Unlike his predecessors, Anthony has also maintained a squeaky-clean image by not courting Libyan money and scrupulously steering clear of embarrassing off-shore banking scandals. The inhabitants of St. Lucia gladly welcomed the changes wrought by the prime minister and his Labour Party. When elections were held again on December 3, 2001, the SLP again carried the day with 14 seats. The youngish, well-educated Anthony is thus slated to lead his island until elections in 2005.

Further Reading

Francois, Martinus. *Reforming Government: Connecting Social Justice to Economic Vision.* Castries, St. Lucia: Freedom Publications, 1999.

Molloy, Linda. *Saint Lucia Past: A Pictorial History.* Swanage, England: Linda Molloy, 1996.

Theodore, Percita M. *The Politics of Constituency Development: Challenge and Perspectives.* Ottawa: Tamari Books, 1998.

Arafat, Yasser (1929–) *president of the Palestinian Authority*

Mohammed Abdel-Raouf Arafat was born in Cairo, Egypt, on August 24, 1929, the son of a successful merchant who was also Palestinian by birth. At some point in his life he adopted the nickname Yasser ("Easy"). Following the death of his mother in 1933, Arafat resided with an uncle in the Palestinian city of Jerusalem, then ruled as a British protectorate. It was here that he first became exposed to Jewish immigrants arriving in the Holy Land, Zionists intent upon reclaiming the biblical state of Israel from the Arabs. Arafat subsequently returned to Egypt to study engineering at the University of Fuad I (now Cairo University), but when war was erupted between Arabs and Jews in 1948 he quickly lent his support to the Egyptian military. However, the Jewish settlers were completely successful, and the new state of Israel added additional Arab lands, displacing nearly 1 million Palestinians. The experience of defeat only hardened Arafat's stance toward the Jews and, like many contemporaries, he became a strident Palestinian nationalist. He swore to destroy Israel.

Throughout the 1950s, Arafat's growing militancy coalesced around the creation of Fatah, a Palestinian guerrilla group dedicated to the creation of a Palestinian state. After 1964 this faction became part of a larger umbrella association, the Palestine Liberation Organization (PLO). Arafat, who despite his short stature, was a charismatic, forceful leader, emerged as the head of the PLO, and by 1965 he was directing guerrilla raids and terrorism against Israel. In 1967 Israeli forces were brilliantly successful in the Six-Day War, and they conquered the Golan Heights from Syria, and, from Jordan, the West Bank of the Jordan River and the holy city of East Jerusalem, sacred to Jews and Muslims alike. Arafat was forced to relocate operations to Jordan, with some success, although his growing military strength induced King Hussein to evict the Palestinians after a brief war in 1971. Thereafter the PLO staged its attacks from neighboring Lebanon with the tacit support of President

HAFEZ AL-ASSAD of Syria. It also became stigmatized for the brutal murder of Israeli athletes at the 1972 Munich Olympics, which brought world condemnation. Thereafter, Arafat sought to soften and moderate his image, and, in 1974, he addressed the United Nations in New York, which voted the PLO observer status and declared that the Palestinian people merited rights to self-determination. Arafat also began hinting at his willingness to negotiate with the Israelis to reach a political settlement over a Palestinian homeland.

However, little progress was made toward founding a Palestinian state, and the homeless refugees, poverty-stricken and lacking hope, turned to increasingly desperate measures. By 1982 a renewed spate of bloody guerrilla attacks against Israel brought a sharp military response, and the PLO was forcibly evicted from Lebanon. Arafat survived the onslaught, however, and he reestablished his headquarters in Tunisia. A few years later he also miraculously survived a plane crash. Meanwhile, in 1988 the PLO leadership declared an independent Palestinian state on the West Bank and Gaza Strip, although hinting at recognizing Israel's right to exist. Arafat took the process a step further at the United Nations by formally renouncing terrorism and supporting the right for all contenders to live in peace, including the Jews. Secret negotiations between both sides continued and in 1990 the PLO formally recognized Israel's right to exist. Progress on future bargaining received a setback during the Iraqi invasion of Kuwait that same year, which Arafat supported. This stance cost him the support of the moderate Arab Gulf states and the loss of considerable financial support. It was not until three years later that talks culminated in a formal agreement, the Oslo peace accords, signed by Arafat and Israeli prime minister YITZHAK RABIN. By the terms of this settlement, Israel agreed to withdraw its military forces from the Gaza Strip and part of the West Bank, with the exception of Jewish settlements already extant. The Palestinians were also allowed to create their own homeland government, the Palestinian Authority, to govern the newly freed territories. The breakthrough and the prospects for peace were lauded worldwide, and, in 1994, Arafat, Rabin, and SHIMON PERES all shared the Nobel Peace Prize. On January 20, 1996, the first elections were held for the 88-seat Palestinian Council, and Arafat won 83 percent of the popular vote to serve as its president. Expectations for a Palestinian state were at an all-time high.

Despite this glimmering start, the prospects for genuine peace and accommodation remain bleak. The notion of peaceful coexistence did not sit well among more radical elements of the PLO, notably Hamas, and guerrilla attacks continued. Arafat condemned the killing but was in turn condemned for his inability or unwillingness to stop such actions. Worse, after Rabin was assassinated by a Jewish fanatic in November 1995, a period of conservative Likud governments began in Israel under BINYAMIN NETANYAHU and ARIEL SHARON, who steadfastly refuse to surrender occupied lands in the West Bank. Israeli intransigence, in turn, led to new rounds of deadly guerrilla attacks and a sustained popular uprising, the *intifada*. Again, Arafat condemned the violence on both sides but could not stem the course of events. In turn, he was loudly criticized by Israelis and Palestinians alike for corruption and an increasingly autocratic demeanor. Events crested in the spring of 2002 when a wave of suicidal bombings killed scores of Israelis and prompted Prime Minister Sharon to invade the West Bank with military forces. For 34 days Arafat was surrounded in his Ramallah headquarters and virtually held hostage, while the Israelis extracted a stiff toll upon the settlement of Jenin, home of many suicide extremists. The attackers finally withdrew in late May, but Arafat defiantly postponed reforming the Palestinian Authority and refused to hold new elections until the Israelis completely withdrew from Arab territory. This caused considerable unrest among the Palestinians themselves, who had grown restive under Arafat's seemingly ineffectual leadership, and he promised new elections by 2003 whether the Israelis withdrew or not. The need for reform received additional impetus when the Israeli government declared that elections were a precondition for further peace talks. Meanwhile, a bloody impasse has been reached in which suicide attacks and military retaliation continue unabated. Hamas, in particular, has sworn to continue such tactics, even in defiance of the Palestinian Authority. It is unknown if Arafat can fully rein in the terror machine he is partly responsible for creating, or if he has finally painted himself into the corner of political irrelevance. His historical legacy as the father of a Palestinian homeland, even at this late juncture, remains problematic at best.

Further Reading

Aburish, Said K. *Arafat: From Defender to Dictator.* New York: Bloomsbury, 1999.

Brown, Nathan J. *Palestinian Politics After the Oslo Accords: Resuming Arab Palestine.* Berkeley: University of California Press, 2003.

Gowers, Andrew, and Tony Walker. *Arafat: The Biography.* London: Virgin, 1994.

Hart, Alan. *Arafat: A Political Biography.* London: Sidgwick and Jackson, 1994.

Minton, Tony S. *Yasir Arafat in His Own Words: Prospects for a Mideast Peace.* Virginia Beach, Va.: Regent University, 1994.

Nehme, Michel G. *Fear and Anxiety in the Arab World.* Gainesville: University Press of Florida, 2003.

Wallach, Janet, and John Wallach. *Arafat: In the Eyes of the Beholder.* Secaucus, N.J.: Carol Publishing Group, 1997.

Aristide, Jean-Bertrand (1953–) *president of Haiti*

Jean-Bertrand Aristide was born in Douyon, Haiti, on July 15, 1953, into a poor working-class family. His father died during his childhood, and his mother relocated the family to the capital of Port-au-Prince. There Aristide was educated at numerous Catholic schools run by the Society of St. Francis de Sales and he subsequently attended the University of Haiti. He emerged as an excellent student, fluent in several languages, and was sent to Israel and the University of Montreal to further his religious studies. Quite independently, and personally cognizant of Haiti's grinding poverty and political oppression, he also inculcated the tenets of "liberation theology," the notion that clergymen ought to become directly involved in the struggle for social justice. Aristide was finally ordained a priest and member of the Salesian Order in 1982 and received his first assignment to preach and serve the poor community of the slum of St-Jean Bosco.

From his pulpit, Aristide became a vocal opponent of the brutal regime of Jean-Claude "Baby Doc" Duvalier, and his radical rhetoric accorded him great popularity among poor parishioners. His verbal attacks drew the ire of the Duvalier regime and on January 31, 1986, Aristide survived the first of three assassination attempts. Undeterred, the young clergyman continue assailing the regime and agitating for mass political activity to oust it. He was partly successful, for in February 1986 "Baby Doc" fled the country for France while a military government under General Henri Namphy seized control. This did little to mitigate Aristide's strident attacks upon the extremes of poverty and privilege in Haiti, and at length the military branded him a "radical firebrand." After two more failed assassination attempts, in which several parishioners were killed, a representative from the Vatican instructed Aristide to tone down his criticism. When he refused, Aristide was dropped from the Salesian order, although not defrocked. Thereafter, he confined his activities to helping the poor of Port-au-Prince and serving the needs of street children. But he had also acquired a legendary reputation among Haiti's desperately poor.

By 1989, international pressure on Haiti convinced the military to hold free and open democratic elections. In an unexpected move at the last moment, Aristide decided to toss his hat into the political arena and run for president. Little was expected to result from his campaign, but to everybody's surprise, he won the presidency with an overwhelming 67 percent of the vote, mostly from the poor. Furthermore, his rise seemed to confirm the return of democracy to Haiti. But despite his popular impulses, Aristide could do very

Jean-Bertrand Aristide *(Embassy of Haiti)*

little to affect the course of poverty in his country, for his Lavalas (Landslide) Party failed to secure a majority in parliament. Furthermore, his radical rhetoric only alarmed the commercial and landowning elites of Haiti, and he alienated the military by promising a violent crackdown against secret Duvallierists still in the country. Events crested on September 30, 1991, when military forces under General RAOUL CÉDRAS overthrew Aristide, forcing him to flee to Venezuela. He eventually made his way to the United States, previously one of the objects of his rhetorical wrath, and he continued railing against the poverty and injustice of his homeland. These charges, President BILL CLINTON realized, might engender a wave of illegal immigrants landing by the boatload in Florida. To circumvent this potential situation, which might prove politically embarrassing, Clinton and the United Nations brought increasing diplomatic and economic pressure to bear upon the Cédras regime. Negotiations were successful, and in September 1993 the United States deployed 27,000 troops in "Operation Restore Democracy," whereby Cédras departed for Panama and Aristide was restored to office. He finished the remaining 27 months of his single, nonrenewable term, without further incident, then resigned following the election of his hand-picked successor, RENÉ PRÉVAL.

Apparently, Aristide and Préval experienced a falling out while the latter was still in office. The former president then used his influence to stymie Préval's attempts to pass a budget through the legislature, which lasted for several years. The sitting president's decision to rule by decree thereafter also did little to enhance either his popularity or his international standing. Riding the tide of political unrest, Aristide then announced his candidacy for the next presidential campaign, and on November 26, 2000, he was swept back into power with 91.7 percent of votes cast. Detractors immediately claimed wholesale fraud prior to the vote and largely boycotted the process. Nonetheless, Aristide was both exultant and magnanimous, inviting several opposition leaders to serve in his administration. He continues in office, very popular with the poor and sworn to alleviate appalling poverty, rampant drug-trafficking, and rising crime that render Haiti the poorest nation in the Western Hemisphere. However, genuine results have yet to materialize, and realistic solutions undoubtedly lie beyond the realm of populist rhetoric. In June 2001 opposition leaders rejected Aristide's offer to hold new elections to end the ongoing political crisis. They thus far refuse to recognize the legitimacy of his victory, which, in turn, does little to strengthen Haiti's fledgling democratic process.

Further Reading

Aristide, Jean-Bernard. *Dignity.* Charlottesville, Va.: University Press of Virginia, 1996.

———. *Aristide: A Biography.* Maryknoll, N.Y.: Orbis Books, 1993.

Chin, Pat. *Haiti: The People Rise.* New York: World View Forum, 1993.

Clements, Christopher I. "Returning Aristide: The Contradictions of U.S. Foreign Policy in Haiti." *Race and Class* 39, no. 2 (1997): 21–36.

Griffiths, Leslie. *The Aristide Factor.* Oxford: Lion, 2000.

Arthur, Owen (1949–   ) *prime minister of Barbados*

Owen Arthur was born on the Caribbean island of Barbados on October 17, 1949. He received his primary education at the All Saints Boys School before obtaining a bachelor's degree in economics at the University of the West Indies, Jamaica. Having acquired a reputation as a highly competent technocrat, he remained in Jamaica several years working for the Planning Agency, as director of economics at the Jamaican Bauxite Institute, and on the board of directors of the Jamaican Scientific Research Council. Arthur returned to Barbados armed with an impressive resumé and quickly found work as chief analyst in the ministry of finance and planning, and he also served as a lecturer at the University of the West Indies Cave Hill campus, Barbados. At this point he decided to enter politics by joining the Barbados Labour Party (BLP) in 1983, and the following year he was elected to the island parliament. However, the party suffered badly in 1986 and 1994 at the hands of the Democratic Labour Party (DLP), and Arthur was elevated to head of his party and opposition leader in parliament. His smooth style of campaigning and populist appeal reversed Labor's fortunes on September 6, 1994, when they won an impressive 26 seats in parliament while the DLP held on to only two. Consistent with his philosophy of inclusion, he stated: "No country can ever truly develop unless it finds the means of engrossing everyone in the task of nation building, whatever their class, creed, color, or political persuasion."

Despite his socialist background, Arthur, a trained economist, has approached economic affairs with considerable restraint. Nonetheless, his first priority was to break the recession gripping the island's economy by promoting tourism, encouraging more diversified agriculture for export, and engendering greater employment through construction and the service sector. Consequently, the jobless rate dwindled from a high of 23 percent in 1992 to 15.9 percent in 1997. Arthur was also determined to carry through on his policy of inclusion. High on his list of priorities was the creation of a computer-based information system that would afford equal access to Barbadians of any race or class. Furthermore, the prime minister is pledged to enhance free, universal education by spending $100 million on updating schools and the University of the West Indies campus. The government also embarked on a strategy to develop human resources through extensive job training, and it aspires to enact minimum wage legislation to insure a satisfactory standard of living. This can be achieved only when every citizen has access to proper training from adequate schools.

Arthur is also committed to creation of a single Caribbean economy, which would ease competition between Barbados and other small islands. To this end he works assiduously to cultivate closer economic ties with the United States, Canada, the United Kingdom, and the Commonwealth, and he is seeking preferential trading arrangements with the European Union and other free trade organizations. He hopes that by 2005 Barbados will be transformed into the most competitive country in the Caribbean. He also aspires to transform his tiny nation into a republic. The inhabitants of Barbados appreciate Arthur's political vision and the positive impact it has exuded thus far. During elections held in January 1999, the Barbados Labour Party won 26 seats while opposition forces were able to maintain only two. Under Arthur's continuing tutelage, Barbados will undoubtedly be a leading force in the future Caribbean economy.

Further Reading

Beckles, Hilary. *A History of Barbados: From Amerindian Settlement to Nation State.* Cambridge: Cambridge University Press, 1990.

Foster, Cecil. *Island Wings: A Memoir.* Toronto: Harper-Collins, 1994.

Howe, Glenford D., and Don D. Marshall. *The Empowering Impulse: The Nationalist Tradition of Barbados.* Barbados: Canoe Press, 2001.

Sandiford, L. Erksine. *Politics and Society in Barbados and the Caribbean: An Introduction.* Barbados: Cassia Pub., 2000.

Assad, Bashar al- (1965–) *president of Syria*

Bashar al-Assad was born in Damascus, Syria, on September 11, 1965, a son of one of the Middle East's most intractable dictators, HAFEZ AL-ASSAD. He received his primary education at the al-Houria Institute before attending Damascus University to study ophthalmology. After graduating in 1988 al-Assad joined the Syrian military as an eye doctor, and, four years, later he ventured to England for additional medical training. There he favorably impressed many contemporaries with his good humor and easy-going demeanor. However, in February 1994 he was summoned home following the death of his brother Basil in a car crash. This loss was completely unanticipated, for Bashar was never really intended as a potential successor. Unlike his iron-fisted father, the younger Assad displayed a relaxed and friendly personality. Fluent in French and English, he is very open to Western technology and helped introduce the first Internet service to Syria, over the objections of state security forces. Once home, Assad resumed his military career commanding an armored division, and he distinguished himself by removing old and incompetent officers from positions of authority. By 1999 he had advanced in rank to colonel, although he remained a bachelor and highly interested in computers and programming. However, when Hafez al-Assad died on June 10, 2000, he was immediately selected to succeed him by the People's Assembly, which altered the national constitution by lowering the minimum age from 40 to 34 years of age. On July 10, 2000, Bashar al-Assad was formally sworn in as president of the Syrian Republic.

No one in this previously authoritarian state knew what to expect from this easy-going eye doctor, although it was popularly anticipated he would eventually move against the political and military old guard that allowed him to rule. However, Assad has yet to directly challenge his power base and appears to promote change and reform through osmosis. For example, his ascension was marked by a general relaxation of press censorship and greater freedom of speech. When new newspapers and hundreds of previously suppressed discussion groups emerged overnight, he did nothing to interfere. This may have grated upon traditionalists in the ruling Baath Party, but Assad, a man whose Western education has tempered his political beliefs, was determined to place Syria on the path of modernization. As a further indication of this, he made the eradication of traditional political corruption a centerpiece of his administration. "No one would be above the law," he insisted. The young leader has also staffed his new cabinet with members who are not part of the Baath Party, indicating that expertise in a given field is far more important than political credentials. And, unlike his megalomanic father, he studiously avoided promoting a cult of personality for himself, for his portrait is rarely displayed outside of state functions.

Regardless of his domestic reforms, the younger Assad seems outwardly intent upon pursuing the hardline foreign policies of his father. He remains "officially" hostile to Israel and refuses any peace settlement that does not return lands seized in the 1967 Arab-Israeli War. For Syria this entails acquisition of the strategic Golan Heights overlooking the Sea of Galilee. Assad reiterated this anti-Israeli stance during an audience with Pope JOHN PAUL II, and he was widely condemned by the Vatican and the U.S. government for it. However, it is not known to what extent Assad actually endorses such extreme views: it is more likely he is parroting his father's line to placate traditionalists at home. In fact, Assad has been far more accommodating toward his neighbors Jordan, Iraq, and Turkey than was his father, and in many instances he has opened rail and commercial air routes that have been closed for 20 years.

Since coming to power, Assad's emphasis on openness and press freedom has slowed somewhat, possibly as a concession to the entrenched establishment. Political prisoners continued to be freed and moves toward a free-market economy continue, but nothing has been done to promote greater democracy or modify the one-party state that has controlled Syrian politics for four decades. It is also unclear if Assad will adopt more pragmatic attitudes toward peace in the Middle East, or continue his father's uncompromising line against the Jewish state. In the interest of his own political survival, this well-intentioned neophyte will most likely place expedience ahead of idealism and pursue economic and political liberalization at a slower pace.

Further Reading

George, Alan. *Syria: Neither Grand nor Freedom.* New York: Zed Books, 2003.

Ghadbian, Najib. "The New Assad: Dynamics of Continuity and Change in Syria." *Middle East Journal* 55 (Autumn 2000): 624–42.

Moaddel, Mansoor. *Jordanian Exceptionalism: A Comparative Analysis of State-Religion Relationships in Egypt, Iran, Jordan, and Syria.* New York: Palgrave, 2002.

Rabil, Robert G. *Embattled Neighbors: Israel, Syria, Lebanon.* Boulder, Colo.: Lynne Reinner Publishers, 2003.

Quilliam, Neill. *Syria and the New World Order.* Reading, England: Ithaca Press, 1999.

Ziser, Etal. *Assad's Legacy: Syria in Transition.* New York: New York University Press, 2001.

Assad, Hafez al- (1930–2000) *president of Syria*

Hafez al-Assad was born in Qardaha, Syria, on October 6, 1930, the son of a farmer. He was also a member of the minority Alawite sect of the Shiite branch of Islam, which distinguishes him from the resident, majority Sunni Islamic community. Assad proved adept as a pupil and was allowed to attend the Homs Military Academy in 1952. Three years later he also graduated from the air academy as a pilot and went to the Soviet Union for further military training. Assad arrived in Cairo, Egypt, in 1959 as a squadron leader, and at a time when the governments of that country and Syria were temporarily joined to form the United Arab Republic. Assad, a staunch pan-Arabist, opposed Syria's break from the UAR in 1961, and he was immediately demoted to a civilian post by pro-secessionist superiors. Undeterred, he then joined the clandestine Military Committee of the ruling Baath (Socialist) Party and helped engineer the March 8, 1963, coup that ousted the government. Assad subsequently supported a second coup that removed the Baath moderates from power, and the radicals now in charge promoted him to minister of defense and air force chief. However, during the ill-fated Six-Day War with Israel in 1967, the Syrian air force was severely pummeled, and Assad assumed responsibility for the disaster. Syria also lost the strategic Golan Heights, the return of which subsequently became a lynchpin of national foreign policy. But Assad's candor and overall competence as a military leader elevated his standing among fellow nationalists, and on

November 13, 1970, he toppled the civilian faction of the Baath Party from power. He then installed himself as president of the Republic of Syria, a fact confirmed in 1971 when he was elected to fill the first of four seven-year terms.

Syria is a relatively small country with a weak, socialist economy, but Assad proved himself to be a master diplomat and power broker. Unable to wage war against Israel alone, he solidified his nationalist credentials by joining Egypt's Anwar Sadat during the bloody Yom Kippur War of October 1973. Syrian forces were again defeated, but Assad emerged with his pan-Arab reputation enhanced. And, at the urging of U.S. secretary of state Henry Kissinger, he also consented to resumption of diplomatic relations with the United States, which had been severed in 1967. Realizing he could not confront the Israelis alone, Assad next turned to secure allies from among the violent, unpredictable factions fighting for supremacy in the Middle East.

Assad had earlier struck up a working relationship with Palestinian leader YASSER ARAFAT, and he supported the latter's efforts to destabilize the kingdom of Jordan in 1970. However, Arafat refused to submit to Syrian control, and Assad did nothing to prevent Jordanian forces from driving the Palestine Liberation Organization (PLO) into neighboring Lebanon. This move only complicated an already explosive situation, and Assad masterfully played the PLO off against Maronite Christians, the Shiite majority, and new, Islamic fundamentalist militant groups like Hezbollah. Their infighting gave Syria a pretext for intervening directly in the civil war, and eventually Assad wielded control over the northern half of the country. From here, and with his tactic support, Hezbollah guerrillas launched repeated attacks against Israel settlements. In 1982 the Israelis invaded and managed to drive the PLO to Tunisia, but the occupation quickly became a military quagmire. As usual, Assad kept the guerrillas fed and supplied, and he also allowed religious and material support from revolutionary Iran to arrive. At length the Israelis were forced to withdrew from Lebanon while Syria reexerted its control over the entire country. It was a masterful play from a position of weakness, and the de facto Syrian "protectorate" over Lebanon remains intact to this day.

Nor was Assad hesitant to fight fellow Arabs when it suited his purpose. He engaged in a long and bloody row with neighboring Iraqi dictator SADDAM HUSSEIN, and throughout the Iran-Iraq War of the 1980s he assisted the Iranians against his fellow Arabs. In 1990, Assad also confounded his critics by lending 20,000 troops in the Gulf War to drive Hussein from Kuwait. This brought him praise and aid from both the moderate Arabic Gulf states, along with friendly overtures from the United States and Great Britain. However, it did nothing to resolve the issue of the Golan Heights, and in the 1990s a succession of right-wing Israeli governments flatly refused to return the land for peace. Assad, in turn, snubbed any peace overtures or negotiated settlement pending unfettered return of all Syrian territories. The impasse only fueled Assad's desire to fight a proxy war through use of Hezbollah and other militant groups, and they struck repeatedly at Israel's northern border. The contest was never settled during his lifetime and it remains a hotly disputed issue.

Assad may have converted Syria into a regional power of note, but this was done by clamping down severely on dissent. In fact, his authoritarian regime enjoyed a terrible human rights record. At one point, during a rebellion by the Sunni-based Muslim Brotherhood, Assad's troops reputedly killed 20,000 rebels without mercy. Other dissidents have been routine arrested, tortured or executed. Syria was also branded by the United States and Great Britain as one of five countries that openly sponsor terrorist organizations. But Assad's willingness to act as Israel's most implacable adversary enhanced his standing in the Arab world and generated widespread sympathy for his cause. Through such carefully Machiavellian means, Assad fully lived up to his name, which means "Lion" in Arabic. He displayed singular determination to keep the Arab agenda in the world's headlines, sometimes at great cost to Israel but at relatively little cost to himself. More often than not he succeeded. This fearsome and capable political survivor succumbed suddenly to a heart attack on January 10, 2000. He was immediately succeeded by his youngest son BASHIR AL-ASSAD, upon whom hopes for a peaceful resolution with Israel rest.

Further Reading

Dam, Nikolas van. *The Struggle for Power in Syria: Politics and Society under Assad and the Ba'th Party.* New York: I. B. Tauris, 1996.

Kedar, Mordecal. *Assad in Search of Legitimacy: Messages and Rhetoric in the Syrian Press, 1970–2000.* Portland, Oreg.: Sussex Academic Press, 2002.

Moubayed, Sami M. *Damascus between Democracy and Dictatorship.* Lanham, Md.: University Press of America, 2000.

Patterson, Charles. *Hafiz Al-Assad of Syria.* Lincoln, Nebr.: iUniverse.com, 1991.

Talhami, Ghada H. *Syria and the Palestinians: The Clash of Nationalisms.* Gainesville: University Press of Florida, 2001.

Aung San Suu Kyi (1945–) *Burmese politician*

Aung San Suu Kyi was born in Rangoon, Burma, on June 19, 1945. Her father, General Aung San, was a leading figure in the Burmese fight for independence from Great Britain. However, he was assassinated in 1947 before his dream could be realized. Suu Kyi was then raised by her mother, a career diplomat, who was posted as ambassador to India. She subsequently attended Oxford University and obtained her master's degree in political science in 1967. Suu Kyi then circulated among academic circles, worked for the United Nations in New York, and lectured at the University of Kyoto, Japan. In 1972 she also married Michael V. Aris, a respected authority on Central Asia, and continued living and studying abroad until April 1988. That year her mother suffered a stroke, and Suu Kyi returned to Burma to assist her. Unexpectedly, this slender unassuming woman was suddenly thrust into the role of an international dissident.

Suu Kyi's decision to visit Burma proved a watershed in her life. That nation, now called Myanmar, had been ruled by General Ne Win for more than two decades. He installed a socialist-oriented military regime that stifled political opposition and drove the country into poverty. This left Burma's population in desperation, and for the first time massed public demonstrations against the regime arose. Suu Kyi was quickly drawn into the protest movement, and she began making public appearances, denouncing the military. Moreover, she called for the establishment of human rights and political pluralism, something that the government was unwilling to concede. Suu Kyi soon gained recognition as a dissident leader of note, and that year she founded the National League for Democracy (NLD). However, once Ne Win stepped down from power he was replaced by a collective leadership, the State Law and Order Council (SLORC), which had no intention of surrendering power. Elections were promised by the government, but in July 1989 Suu Kyi was arrested and placed under house arrest. Nonetheless, when elections transpired in 1990, they were overwhelmingly won by the NLD, which garnered 80 percent of the vote. The military, whose rule was now directly threatened, simply annulled the results amid talk of a new constitution. This act triggered widespread protests and led to the death of several hundred demonstrators, but the SLORC remained firmly in control. Suu Kyi's efforts at peacefully spreading democracy did not go unnoticed, fortunately, and in 1991 she received the Nobel Peace Prize.

Suu Kyi remained under house arrest until 1995, becoming one of the world's most celebrated dissidents. She was only freed after Western powers applied economic sanctions for her release. All the while the SLORC held talks with various political opposition groups, giving the impression that progress was being made toward a new constitution. Suu Kyi immediately resumed her role as head of the NLD, and she railed against government attempts at legitimizing their dictatorship. She also recommended her impassioned prodemocracy speeches, calling for peaceful resistance to the regime, and denouncing political oppression in Myanmar. "The struggle for democracy and human rights in Burma is a struggle for life and dignity," she affirmed. "It is a struggle that encompasses our political, social, and economic aspirations." Her message resonated with thousands of people who gathered to hear her, and by January 1997 Prime Minister Than Shwe felt sufficiently threatened to restrain her under "unofficial" house arrest. Suu Kyi was then routinely harassed whenever she tried to travel, and, while trying to depart Rangoon, she was forced to spend a week in her car. Throughout all her ordeals, the frail Burmese dissident adamantly insists that the military respect the will of the people—and abide by the 1990 elections. The junta vindictively countered by restricting all public access to her, and in March 1999 her husband died of cancer after they refused him an entrance visa.

The impasse over Burma's budding democratic movement continued for many years, but a corner was turned on May 6, 2002, when Suu Kyi was finally released from house arrest. This apparently occurred after 18 months of negotiations between the dissident and the government, along with a pressing need to have economic sanctions lifted. She then immediately drove to various parts of the country, flaunting her newfound freedom, and was greeted by adoring throngs as she drove by. "Nothing is permanent, so if you are faced with defeat just keep working toward the goal," she declared to supporters at a rally in Moulmein. "With the support and strength of the people, the NLD will be able to achieve its goal toward democracy faster." Aung San Suu Kyi remains a potent symbol of Burma's quest for political freedom through nonviolent struggle. Her fate and that of her country remain closely intertwined.

Further Reading

Ang, Chin Geok. *Aung San Suu Kyi: Towards a New Freedom*. London: Prentice Hall, 1998.

Aung San Suu Ki. *The Voice of Hope*. New York: Seven Stories Press, 1997.

Ling, Bettina. *Aung San Suu Kyi: Standing Up for Democracy in Burma*. New York: Feminist Press at the City University of New York, 1999.

Steinberg, David I. *Burma: The State of Myanmar*. Washington, D.C.: Georgetown University Press, 2001.

Victor, Barbara. *The Lady: Aung San Suu Kyi, Nobel Laureate and Burma's Prisoner*. Boston: Farber and Farber, 1998.

Aylwin, Patricio (1918–) *president of Chile*

Patricio Aylwin Azocar was born in Viña del Mar, Chile, on November 26, 1918, the son of a prominent lawyer and president of the Supreme Court. Like his father, Aylwin decided to pursue a legal career, and in 1943 he graduated from the University of Chile law school. Aylwin was a conservative, and by 1946 he was writing and speaking on behalf of the Falange Nacional, a Christian-oriented group seeking social change without the violence espoused by the Communists. At length these conservative interests coalesced into a new association, the Christian Democratic Party, in the 1950s, of which Aylwin was repeatedly elected president. His political career commenced in 1965 when he was elected to the Senate. At that time Chile was governed by Eduardo Frei Montalva, the country's first Christian Democratic president, who remained in office until 1970. However, national fortunes took a dramatic turn that year when Salvador Allende Gossens, an avowed Socialist, was elected president with a slim plurality of votes. His rise proved a dramatic turning point in Chile's political history.

Once in power, Allende initiated sweeping programs of economic nationalization that destabilized the entire country. Aylwin, now a leading opposition figure, met repeatedly with the president in a failed attempt to mitigate the excesses of his policies. Social discontent resulted in a wave of strikes against the administration, and in 1973 Allende declared martial law to preserve order. At this juncture the military intervened on September 11, 1973, to save the country. They overthrew Allende, killing him in the process, and installed a military regime under General Augusto Pinochet Ugarte. Aylwin, like many Christian Democrats, initially supported both the coup and the military, for they promised to quickly restore order and democracy. However, Pinochet evinced no inclination to relinquish power and, in fact, initiated a brutally repressive administration lasting 17 years. As before, Aylwin emerged as a leading opposition figure and a champion of democratic rights. In 1987 he skillfully managed to have Pinochet consider a national plebiscite over his continuance in power and the general, anticipating an easy victory, agreed. Surprisingly, on October 5, 1988, Chilean voters rejected government by military rule by a wide margin, and the general gracefully consented to free multiparty elections the following year. The ensuing contest was not even close. On December 14, 1989, Aylwin won a resounding victory with 55 percent of the vote, becoming Chile's first democratically elected leader in nearly two decades. He accomplished this by presiding over a broad-based coalition of 17 disparate parties, all united in their hatred for Pinochet. Aylwin was formally sworn into office in March 1990.

The Christian Democrats were clearly not revolutionaries, but they were determined to address long-standing human rights abuses committed in Chile. Once empowered, Aylwin quickly released thousands of political prisoners and initiated official investigations into the disappearance of thousands more. His most notable success was in obtaining guilty verdicts against two of Pinochet's henchmen, Generals Manuel Contreras and Pedro Espinoza, for the assassination of Chilean foreign minister Orlando Letelier in Washington, D.C. However, the Christian Democrats enjoyed less success in confronting Pinochet himself, and he remained the titular head of the military while many officers continued enjoying political amnesty. He continued to loom in the background of Chilean national politics for many years thereafter.

Equally pressing to the Aylwin administration was the issue of poverty and social injustice. The Christian Democrats were committed to obviating poverty through economic growth, and the government quickly enacted a wide-ranging stimulus package. Within three years, the national economy rebounded to a 7.5 percent annual growth rate, which lifted 1.3 million Chileans out of poverty. Aylwin also orchestrated a 40 percent increase in social spending to further assist the needy, while the minimum wage was increased by 36 percent. All told, his single term in office was a startling success and a tribute to long-held political convictions. In 1992 he became the first Chilean leader to visit Washington, D.C., in 30 years and he was hailed by President George H. W. Bush as proof of democracy's resiliency. "We are not asking for help," Aylwin declared to his audience, "but for help and understanding." A temporary constitutional provision limited Aylwin's tenure in office to four years, although his successor, EDUARDO FREI, son of the former president, succeeded him with a six-year term on March 1, 1994. Aylwin's rise to power, and his peaceful transfer out of it, signaled the successful return of true democracy to Chile.

Further Reading

Fuentes, Claudio A. "After Pinochet: Civilian Policies towards the Military in the 1990s Chilean Democracy." *Journal of Interamerican Studies and World Affairs* 42 (Fall 2000): 111–142.

Londregan, John B. *Legislative and Institutional Ideology in Chile.* Cambridge: Cambridge University Press, 2000.

Loveman, Brian. "?Mission complida? Civil-military Relations and the Chilean Political Transition." *Journal of Interamerican Studies and World Affairs* 33 (Fall 1991): 35–40.

Oppenheim, L. H. *Politics in Chile: Democracy, Authoritarianism, and the Search for Development.* Boulder, Colo.: Westview Press, 1993.

Rabkin, Rhoda. "The Aylwin Government and Tutelary Democracy: A Concept in Search of a Case?" *Journal of Interamerican Studies and World Affairs* 34 (Winter 1992–1993): 199–94.

Azali, Assoumani (ca. 1959–   ) *president of Comoros*

Assoumani Azali was born on Great Comoro Island around 1959, although little is known about him. He received military training in France and Morocco and had risen to the rank of chief of staff by 1998. The Comoros are a group of three small islands off the coast of Mozambique: Great Comoro, the largest, followed by Anjouan and Mohéli, the smallest. The population is part African and part Muslim in terms of culture and religion, and they were ruled as a French colony since 1843. The islands obtained political independence in 1975 and that July received their first appointed president, Ahmed Abdallah. However, Abdallah was overthrown the following month by Ali Soilih, who recruited a force of white mercenaries under the notorious French soldier of fortune, Bob Denard. In 1978 Soilih was himself toppled by Denard, who subsequently ran the Comoros as his personal fiefdom for the next 11 years. In 1984 Abdallah reemerged as president, although Denard really directed affairs until 1989. That year Abdallah was assassinated by Denard, who continued ruling the three islands more or less on his own until new elections were held in March 1996. The winner was Mohamed Taki Abdulkarim, who also presided over the nation's first peaceful transition of power. However, a declining economy and social strife among the three islands, fiercely independent from each other, led to violence and disorder. Worse, Taki died of a heart attack in November 1998, and his successor, Tadjiddine Ben Massonde, failed to restore stability when the islands of Anjouan and Mohéli threatened to secede from Great Comoro. It was at this juncture, on April 30, 1998, that Colonel Azali stepped in and overthrew Massonde in a bloodless coup. "I have seized power," he declared, "to save the Comoros from falling into chaos and anarchy." His was the fifth successful putsch since the islands gained their independence in 1975.

Once ensconced in power, Azali was formally sworn in as president on May 5, 1999. He thereupon assumed the portfolios of premier and defense minister, summarily dissolved all elected institutions, and suspended the constitution. Moreover, the blunt-talking chief of staff announced that he would form a 12-person executive body, the Committee of State, that would conduct national affairs. Azali pledged himself to reinstate democratic institutions once a new constitution was drawn up and agreed upon by all three islands, but he remains firmly in control of the archipelago. He has since subscribed to an accord put forth by the Organization of African Unity (OAU), which encouraged more independence for the islands, but also an end to secession. It has not been agreed to by the island rebels, and, hence, Azali's dominance remains unchallenged. However, his coup was strongly denounced by the OAU, France, and South Africa, which responded with an economic boycott. Nor is the military regime recognized by any government, with a corresponding decline in foreign aid. This is unfortunate, as the Comoros is one of the poorest nations on earth, and its living standards have deteriorated even more since the upheaval. Matters were further complicated when soldiers under Captain Abderamane Abdallah, the former president's son, failed to overthrow Azali in March 2000. An OAU-brokered agreement was thereupon cemented that granted the islands greater autonomy, but soldiers on the island of Anjouan attempted a coup against their own leader, Colonel Said Abeid in August 2001. Azali remains in power for the foreseeable future.

Further Reading

Alphers, Edward A. "A Complex Relationship: Mozambique and the Comoro Islands in the 19th and 20th Centuries." *Cahiers d'études Africaines* 41, no. 161 (2000): 73–93.

Ostheimer, John M., ed. *The Politics of the Western Indian Ocean Islands*. New York: Praeger, 1975.

Ottenheimer, Martin, and Harriet Otterheimer. *Historical Dictionary of the Comoros Islands*. Metuchen, N.J.: Scarecrow Press, 1994.

Weinberg, Samantha. *Last of the Pirates: The Search for Bob Denard*. New York: Pantheon Books, 1994.

Aznar, José María (1953–   ) *prime minister of Spain*

José María Aznar López was born in Madrid, Spain, on February 25, 1953, the scion of a politically conservative household. Both his father and grandfather were closely associated with the right-wing fascist regime of dictator Francisco Franco, who ruled Spain with an iron fist from 1939 to 1975. Aznar was educated at the University of Madrid, where he studied law, and shortly after he entered politics. After a brief tenure as inspector in Madrid, he joined a conservative party, the Popular Alliance (PA). Spain at that time was firmly under the control of the Socialist Party of Felipe González since 1983, but that party was then experiencing a decline in popularity. Aznar, meanwhile, first came to national prominence by winning election to parliament in 1982, which also occasioned his rise within the ranks of the

PA. He was foremost among party leaders who urged a clean break with the past, and he denounced the extreme right-wing policies of Franco. His message resonated with the new generation of conservatives, who in 1989 appointed Aznar head of the party, now renamed the Popular Party (PP). Still, the bulk of Spanish voters did not trust the right wing, despite mounting disenchantment with Socialist policies and a lackluster economy. In 1989 and 1993, the PP under Aznar's direction tried and failed to topple the entrenched leftists. However, as the popularity of the Socialists tumbled in the wake of numerous scandals, Aznar made ethics a vociferous campaign issue. The tactic worked, for in the elections of March 3, 1993, the Socialists took a pounding at the polls, losing 156 seats to the Popular Party. They were still 20 seats short of a complete majority in the Congress of Deputies, but González nonetheless resigned. Aznar was subsequently sworn in as prime minister. His rise marked a historic occasion, signaling only the second time in 60 years that political power passed from one party to the other in Spain.

True to his conservative credentials, Aznar embarked on a scheme to trim government expenditures, cut taxes, and reform the bloated welfare state erected by the Socialists. In this he was helped by Jordi Puljol of the Catalan Convergence and Union (CiU) Party, who provide the margin of seats necessary to control the government. He undertook these austerity measures for the sole purpose of preparing for Spain's entry into the common European currency. Moreover, these deficit-reduction policies also served to spur the economy and reduce the 25 percent unemployment rate to 15 percent by 2000. Meanwhile, the Socialist party was unable to mount meaningful opposition to Aznar's reform and, worse, suffered from continuing revelations about corruption. Consequently, during the elections held in March 2000, the Conservative Popular Alliance captured 183 seats in the Congress of Deputies, enough to formulate an outright majority. Aznar, buoyed by his successes, has since continued on his avowed course of fiscal restraint, privatization of state-owned assets, and economic reform. And, by distancing himself from the excesses of the Franco regime, he has relegitimized conservative politics in the eyes of many Spaniards.

One conspicuous failure of the Aznar administration, and those before it, was the question of Basque separatism. Militants in this non-Spanish region of northern Spain are seeking an independent state and have resorted to violence to achieve it. During Aznar's tenure they renounced a cease-fire and commenced a campaign of kidnaping, murder, and bombing. The prime minister, however, refused to negotiate with the terrorists, and he stepped up the police campaign against them. But by September 1998, the ETA rebels announced a new cease-fire, and the government reciprocated by transferring all Basque prisoners from the Balearic and Canary Islands back to the mainland. The overarching issue of Basque independence re-mains unresolved for, in Aznar's words, "Spain is one nation."

Troubles of a different sort arose in October 1988, when Spanish judge Baltasar Garzón requested British authorities to extradite aged Chilean dictator Augusto Pinochet to Spain, where he was wanted for murdering Spanish citizens. There was much fury on the right for Aznar's eventual decision to allow the process to continue, but ultimately Pinochet was released from England for humanitarian reasons. However, more international trouble looms, as the Spanish judiciary has declared its intentions to investigate human-rights abuses in Central and South America. Through it all, Aznar's political fortunes seemed tied more to the booming Spanish economy than to foreign affairs. With his policies in place, a majority in the government, and much popularity at home, he is poised to guide Spain's restoration as a credible European power.

Further Reading

Anderson, Wayne. *The ETA: Spain's Basque Terrorists.* New York: Rosen Group, 2003.

Gibbons, John. *Spanish Politics Today.* Manchester, England: University of Manchester Press, 1999.

Granell, Francisco. "Europe's Evolving Identity: Spain's Role." *Mediterranean Politics* 5 (Summer 2000): 64–75.

Jones, Benjamin. "Aznar Stuns Socialists: Popular Party Victory Marks a Turning Point in Spanish Politics." *Europe,* no. 396 (2000): 22–25.

Mangen, Stephen P. *Spanish Society after Franco: Regime Transition and the Welfare State.* New York: Palgrave, 2001.

Romero Salvado, Francisco J. *Twentieth-Century Spain: Politics and Society, 1989–1998.* Basingstoke, England: Palgrave, 1999.

B

Babangida, Ibrahim (1941–   ) *president of Nigeria*

Ibrahim Gbadamosi Babangida was born in the northern city of Minna, Niger State, Nigeria, on August 17, 1941. Like many young Nigerian men of Muslim origin, he sought to pursue a traditional military career, and after graduating from the government college at Bida, he attended the Nigerian Military Training College in Kaduna. An excellent student, Babangida was allowed to broaden his educational experience by studying abroad at the Indian Military Academy in 1964, the Royal Armoured Centre in Great Britain, and the U.S. Army Armor School. Once commissioned a lieutenant, he bore a conspicuous role in the Nigerian civil war, 1967–70, and emerged a national hero. Babangida then rose steadily through the ranks and, as a lieutenant colonel, helped thwart a military coup against the government in 1976. Good performance and a reputation for political reliability resulted in additional advancements, and by 1983 Babangida was functioning as army chief of staff in the civilian administration of Shehu Shagari. This placed him at the very center of national power.

Ever since gaining independence in 1960, Nigeria had been wracked by successive military coups and revolts. One reason for this instability was the apparent corruption of many civilian leaders, including Shegari, whom Babangida helped oust in 1983. This move helped install a military leader, General Muhammadu Buhari, to power. However, Babangida, as chief of staff, clashed repeatedly with Buhari and his minions, principally over economic policy. Nigeria's oil-based economy was in a tailspin owing to declining world prices, yet the generals did little or nothing to obviate the mounting social toll this engendered. A tense impasse between the two men lasted until August 27, 1985, when Babangida moved decisively against Buhari, bloodlessly disposing of him while the latter celebrated a Muslim festival in his distant hometown. Moreover, once in control, he appeared on national media to assure the populace of his intention to liberalize the economy, lift press restrictions, and enforce human rights. He also promised to return to democratic pluralism in a few months and symbolically relinquished his title as general in favor of president.

Babangida's most pressing obstacle to national harmony was the economy, which required major structural reforms. These were insisted upon by the International Monetary Fund (IMF) as a precondition for securing additional loans. Babangida, however, cleverly put these changes up before the public in a referendum, where they were soundly rejected. Having demonstrated that he could stand up to the West, the general next introduced his own brand of austerity measures to curb inflation and rising national debt. The result was increasing deprivation suffered by an already poor populace, and

35

the ensuing unrest led students and labor unions to wage mass protests. Babangida countered by closing all universities and dissolving the National Labor Council's executive committee. It began to appear to most Nigerians that his regime was only slightly less repressive than its predecessor. Discontent also mounted among various cliques within the officer corps and Babangida ruthlessly crushed two coup attempts against him.

However, the general's greatest failure was his inability to restore Nigerian democracy as promised. Initially, he held open the possibility for multiparty opposition to be reestablished, then he promptly backtracked. He then determined that only two parties, designated by himself, would be allowed to function, provided that they fulfilled exceedingly high criteria. As a sop to the creation of a more open system, Babangida also forbade previous officeholders from running for the presidency. Delay, however, was heaped upon delay, and it was not until 1993 that the first civilian elections transpired—only after Babangida had personally picked the opposing candidates himself! The unexpected winner was Moshood Abiola, a noted businessman, and he was suddenly viewed as undesirable. Babangida then annulled the election and unilaterally installed another handpicked successor, Ernest Shonekan, to succeed him. The result was widespread strikes and civil unrest across Nigeria, and on November 17, 1993, Babangida was himself overthrown by his chief of staff, General SANI ABACHA.

For many years, Babangida has lived quietly in self-imposed exile, and over the years he has steadfastly refused to appear before a human rights panel investigating charges against him. In November 2001 a Nigerian appeals court ruled that the panel lacks the ability to summon former rulers of the country. However, in April 2002, Babangida emerged from obscurity to confer with several former military associates at Langtang, Plateau State. At that time the general refused to confirm or deny if he intended to support the present ruler, OLUSEGUN OBASANJO, in the 2003 presidential election, or to run against him as a candidate. "I will only exercise my right to vote like any other Nigerian," he insisted.

Further Reading

Adeoye, Oladimeiji. *The Morning of a Coup: The Dictatorship of Nigeria; Ibrahim B. Babangida.* Chicago: Spectrum Press, 1995.

Diamond, Larry, Anthony Kirk-Greene, and Oyeleye Oyedivan. *Transition without End: Nigerian Politics and Civil Society under Babangida.* Boulder, Colo.: Lynne Rienner Publishers, 1997.

Mabry, Marcus. "Africa's Ailing Giant: Chaos Reigns in Nigeria." *Foreign Affairs* 79, no. 5 (2000): 123–27.

Nzeribe, Francis A. *Nigeria: Seven Years after Sheshushagari.* London: Kilimanjaro Publications, 1990.

Ojo, Emmanuel O. "The Military and Democratic Transition in Nigeria: An In-depth Analysis of General Babangida's Transition Program (1985–1993)." *Journal of Political and Military Sociology* 20, no. 1 (2000): 1–26.

Balaguer, Joaquín (1907–2002) *president of the Dominican Republic*

Joaquín Balaguer Ricardo was born in Villa Bisono, the Dominican Republic, on September 1, 1907, into a well-to-do middle-class family. He excelled as a student and published a volume on poetry at the age of 16. Balaguer chose to pursue a legal career, and he received advanced degrees from the University of Santo Domingo in 1929 and the University of Paris in 1932. In addition to being a man of letters, Balaguer was also a talented linguist, becoming fluent in Spanish, French, and English. He served as a public servant until 1930, when the noted dictator Rafael Trujillo came to power in a coup. Balaguer promptly allied himself with the new regime, and he was rewarded with several ambassadorial and ministerial posts over the next three decades. In 1957 Balaguer was appointed vice president of the Dominican Republic and three years later he succeeded Trujillo as president. Following Trujillo's assassination in 1961, Balaguer proved instrumental in having sanctions imposed by the Organization of American States lifted, although he himself entered self-imposed exile in New York City. This move came after he himself was ousted by air force chief Rodriguez Echeverria in January 1962.

Over the next three years, the Dominican Republic was ruled by Balaguer's main rival, Juan Bosch, until his overthrow in 1965, and the nation was plunged into chaos and civil war. Balaguer, meanwhile, had been busy organizing a new entity, the Reformist Party (PR) in exile, and in 1966 he returned home with the aid of U.S. troops to run for president. He won a resounding victory over Bosch with 57 percent of votes cast, initiating a 12-year period of uninterrupted success. Once in charge,

Balaguer took immediate steps to boost the economy, aided in large part by a massive influx of American aid and a rise in sugar prices. Consequently, the national economy grew at a rate of 10 percent a year, and Balaguer initiated several grand building programs to restore the capital of Santo Domingo. Staunchly conservative, he remained friendly and cooperative with the United States and maintained an anticommunist foreign policy. However, he also proved despotic in outlook and during this period hundreds of political opponents were either arrested by the police or killed by paramilitary forces loyal to his administration. However, by 1978, the bottom dropped out of the national economy, and Balaguer, seeking a fourth consecutive term, was defeated by Antonio Guzmán of the Dominican Revolutionary Party (DRP). Noticeably, he voluntarily stepped down despite an ardent wish by military officials that he remain in power. The DRP managed to remain in control of the country until 1982 when the aged Balaguer decided to return to politics.

Balaguer's initial attempt to regain the presidency was unsuccessful, but economic fumbling by the DRP left the country in dire straits, and in 1986 Balaguer won his fourth term in office. This time he was associated with a new organization, the Reformist Social Christian Party, which had been resurrected from his earlier Reformist Party. Again, a leading hallmark of his administration remained large-scale public construction works, especially an expensive, ornate lighthouse dedicated to Christopher Columbus on the 500th anniversary of his landing on Hispaniola. But, as an indication of his enduring popularity, in 1990 he was reelected again at the age of 90, despite vocal allegations of fraud. He was victorious again in 1994, although the results this time proved so marred by fraudulence that international pressure forced him to conclude his administration in 1996. By that time Balaguer was in poor health and nearly blind from cataracts. The 1996 election was also characterized by its acute racial tone. The PRD candidate, José Francisco Peña Gómez, was of African descent, and Balaguer openly campaigned against what he deemed the "Haitianization" of the Dominican Republic. Consequently, Lionel Fernandez, his hand-picked successor, won the presidency.

Once out of office, Balaguer became the object of several notorious lawsuits, alleging his complicity in the murder of several opposition journalists between 1975 and 1994 and his connivance in the misappropriation of $700 million in public funds. However, the charges were never proven, and the elder statesman lost little of his popularity. In April 2000 he declared his candidacy for the next round of presidential elections, which, had he succeeded, would have left him in office until the age of 99! Fortunately, Balaguer received only 24 percent of the vote and he has since retired to private life. For four decades, he was the most influential politician of the Dominican Republic since the dictator Trujillo. Beyond politics, Balaguer also gained repute as the author of a number of books on Dominican law, literature, and history. He died in July 2002.

Further Reading

Chester, Eric T. *Rag-tags, Riff-raff, and Commies: The U.S. Intervention in the Dominican Republic, 1965–1966.* New York: Monthly Review Press, 2001.

Espinal, Rosario. "Classes, Power, and Political Change in the Dominican Republic." Unpublished Ph.D. dissertation, University of Washington, 1985.

Gutierrez, Carlos M. *The Dominican Republic: Rebellion and Repression.* New York: Monthly Review Press, 1996.

Hartlyn, Jonathan. *The Struggle for Democratic Politics in the Dominican Republic.* Chapel Hill: University of North Carolina Press, 1998.

Kryzanek, Michael J. "Political Party Opposition in Latin America: The PRD, Joaquín Balaguer, and the Politics of the Dominican Republic, 1966–1973." Unpublished Ph.D. dissertation, University of Massachusetts, 1975.

Balkenende, Jan (1956–) *prime minister of the Netherlands*

Jan Peter Balkenende was born on May 7, 1956 in Kapelle, Zeeland, the Netherlands, the son of a grain trader. In 1992 he received his doctorate in philosophy from the Free University of Amsterdam, and he subsequently taught philosophy courses there. Between 1982 and 1984 he also served as a legal affairs policy officer with the Netherlands Universities Council. Balkenende concurrently developed a conservative bent in politics and eventually joined the Christian Democrats (CDA), a party that had formed part of every Dutch government since 1917. However, in August 1994 the Labor Party under WIM KOK swept the CDA from power and formed a coalition without them for the first time. The party subsequently lost two more elections over the next eight years and seemed on the verge of becoming marginalized altogether. Party elders then looked for younger, more attractive candidates to lead them out of the political wilderness. At first glance, Balkenende seemed an unlikely candidate to head the CDA, being a philosophy professor with minimal political experience who had been seated in parliament only since 1998. In fact, with his owlish glasses and moppish head of hair, he bore a striking resemblance to the fictional children's hero Harry Potter. Balkenende was publicly derided by opponents as such, but, once becoming CDA chairman in October 2001, he demonstrated a political wizardry all his own.

By the spring of 2002 Wim Kok announced his resignation as head of a successful Labor coalition government. His administration had run affairs much as it liked over the past eight years and the Netherlands prospered under his tutelage, but to placate extreme left-wing allies, Kok allowed certain radical legislation to be passed. These includes measures to legalize soft drugs and gay marriages and facilitate increased immigration in the form of both migrants and refugees. The Netherlands is probably one of the most permissive, tolerant societies in Europe but Labor, long accustomed to power, had grown smug and deaf to rising discontent. The major issue was crime, which, according to public perception, could be traced to the recent influx of Muslim immigrants. This group also appeared to many people as disproportionally represented on welfare rolls. However, as elections approached, the ruling center-left coalition ignored public clamoring and focused upon more traditional issues such as worker's rights. Nobody could have anticipated what would happen next.

In February 2002 a new party, the Pim Fortuyn List (LPF), suddenly exploded on the scene. It was headed by charismatic Pim Fortuyn, a gay record executive and millionaire who had assumed the mantle of anti-immigrant leadership. In sum, he found his niche broadcasting what everyone else was only thinking. Fortuyn was denounced as a right-wing extremist for demanding an end to immigration, expulsion of welfare cases, and mandatory assimilation by newcomers, but his xenophobic populism resonated with voters at large. Had he lived, Fortuyn might have amassed as much as a third of the popular vote. However, on May 6, 2002, he was assassinated by an animal-rights activist, which shocked the Dutch public and brought inordinate sympathy to his

cause. Balkenende was well positioned to benefit from such a backlash, for Fortuyn's positions on immigration neatly mirrored his own. Moreover, he strongly opposed legalized drugs and euthanasia, which Labor had not only supported but also signed into law. "Citizens want a different kind of politics," he insisted. At the election held on May 16, 2002, more than 80 percent of voters turned out and their verdict was unmistakable. Kok's Labor Party was swept from office while the Christian Democrats returned with 43 seats in the 150-seat parliament—making them the biggest single voting bloc. Intense negotiations followed with the LPF, which finished a strong second, and the Liberal Party (VVD) to form a viable coalition. On July 22, 2002, Balkenende, a 46-year-old philosophy professor, was sworn in as the first CDA prime minister in eight years. Considering his amateur standing as a politician, "Harry Potter" had indeed worked a miracle.

True to his pledge, Balkenende determined to sponsor legislation ending free access to soft drugs. He also sought to tighten immigration policies by making assimilation into Dutch culture and language mandatory. Furthermore, prospective migrants were now required to post a large deposit before bringing a spouse into the Netherlands, which would only be refunded once the newcomer passed assimilation courses. The government also intends to hire more police officers and commence a thorough crackdown on crime. Balkenende's victory seems to have capped a trend in Western Europe toward conservative anti-immigration sentiment, which has seen similar successes in Portugal, Norway, Denmark, Italy, and France. He also seems to have slipped easily into the role as head of state: In July 2002 Balkenende appeared in Beijing, China, to meet with Prime Minister ZHU RONGJI. The Chinese premier warmly toasted his guest, and he wished him well in his leadership post.

Further Reading

Andeweg, R. B. *Governance and Politics of the Netherlands.* New York: Palgrave, 2002.

Hendriks, Frank, and Thomas A. J. Toomen. *Polder Politics: The Re-invention of Consensus of Democracy in the Netherlands.* Burlington, Vt.: Ashgate, 2001.

Mudde, Cas. *The Ideology of the Extreme Right.* New York: Manchester University Press, 2000.

Phalet, Karen, and Antal Orkeny. *Ethnic Minorities and Inter-ethnic Realities in Context: A Dutch-Hungarian Comparison.* Burlington, Vt.: Ashgate, 2001.

Rochon, Thomas R. *The Netherlands: Negotiating Sovereignty in an Independent World.* Boulder, Colo.: Westview Press, 1999.

Timmermans, Arco. *High Politics in the Law Countries: Functions and Effects of Coalition Agreements in Belgium and the Netherlands.* Burlington, Vt.: Ashgate, 2003.

Balladur, Edouard (1929–   ) *prime minister of France*

Edouard Balladur was born in Smyrna (Izmir) Turkey, on May 2, 1929, the son of successful French merchants. His family resettled in Marseilles in 1934 and Balladur was raised in a strictly Catholic, highly conservative setting. He excelled in school and gained admittance to the prestigious Institut d'Etudes Politiques, receiving his law degree in 1950. After completing military service in North Africa, Balladur next attended the Ecole Nationale d'Administration, the training ground for future civil servants. He was sidelined by recurring bouts of tuberculosis while studying, but Balladur finally graduated in 1957 and found work in the French radio and television organization. It was while working at this post that he came to the attention of Prime Minister Georges Pompidou, who appointed him as a policy adviser on social and industrial relations in 1962. Over the next decade, the two men struck up an affable and constructive relationship, and Balladur's political star began its ascent.

As an adviser, Balladur convinced Pompidou to enact increasingly conservative social and economic policies that were friendly to business. After the public tumult of May 1968, he backtracked somewhat and advocated raising salaries, shortening the work week, and adopting a minimum wage. The following year Pompidou succeeded Charles de Gaulle as president of France, and Balladur followed him into his cabinet as secretary-general. Over the next five years Balladur introduced new policies that not only shored up the working class but also stimulated economic growth. However, following Pompidou's death in 1974, Balladur declined a position within the administration of Valéry Giscard d'Estaing and withdrew from politics altogether. For the next several years he successfully headed several large corporations, and he also struck up a working relationship with a new conservative force in French politics, JACQUES CHIRAC. Balladur, sensing that the French polity was shifting left, warned Chirac not to run for the presidency in 1981, but Chirac disregarded his advice and was totally defeated by FRANÇOIS MITTERRAND's Socialists. The leftists engaged in a spate of nationalization of key sectors of the economy and by 1986 had nearly ruined it. At that point Balladur reentered politics by winning a seat in parliament, at a time when right-wing forces obtained a majority. Socialist Mitterrand, wishing to put the best face possible on the reality of a stinging reverse, asked conservative Balladur to serve as prime minister of France through an arrangement known as "cohabitation."

As prime minister, Balladur continued his established practice of initiating conservative economic policies at the expense of the Socialists' agenda. These included liberalizing the stock market and privatizing state assets, and considerable economic growth ensued. However, the Socialists were the immediate beneficiaries of such good results, and in 1988 Mitterrand again defeated Chirac in the race for president. Balladur stepped down as prime minister and returned as an opposition leader in parliament. The Socialists, however, enjoying a complete majority in that body, again embarked on reckless big-spending social programs that increased unemployment until it reached 10 percent of the workforce. The tide turned strongly against them in the elections of March 1993, when conservatives under Chirac won an absolute majority, and once again Mitterrand approached Balladur to serve as prime minister. France was then embroiled in one of its worse economic recessions ever. He wasted no time in addressing the spiraling national debt, and he introduced a severe austerity budget, new taxes, and additional privatization schemes to fuel economic growth. This strong dose of medicine brought the economy back from the brink, and by 1995 Balladur was easily the most popular politician in France. By now it seemed inevitable that he would finally seek the presidency in the 1995 elections.

Balladur's impending election hopes were dashed by several factors. Foremost among these was rivalry with his erstwhile ally, Jacques Chirac, who also coveted the highest office. Both men posited themselves as the best candidate to represent conservative interests, and their infighting only boosted the Socialist candidate, LIONEL JOSPIN, in the polls. But the decisive factor was the whiff of scandal. Previously, Balladur projected himself as a dull, scrupulously honest candidate, devoted to his job and beyond reproach. However, once it was revealed in 1995 that his office was responsible for illegally wiretapping phones of political opponents, his fortunes began to wane. In the first round of elections he came in third behind Chirac and Jospin, and he was compelled to drop out of the race. Since then, Balladur resigned as prime minister and returned to the National Assembly, where he continues to serve as an effective spokesman for the conservative Rally for the Republic Party (RTF) and as an ally of Chirac when it suits him. In April 1998 the former prime minister also testified before a parliamentary committee about French inactivity in Rwanda during the massacres there in the 1990s, and he stated that he considered recent criticism of that role as "biased and hateful" toward France.

Further Reading

Bell, David S. *French Politics Today.* Manchester, England: University of Manchester Press, 2002.

Forbes, Jill, and Nick Hewett. *Contemporary France: Essays and Texts on Politics, Economics, and Society.* New York: Longman, 2001.

Guyomarch, Alain. *Developments in French Politics 2.* New York: Palgrave, 2001.

Levy, Jonah D. "Partisan Politics and Welfare Adjustment: The Case of France." *Journal of European Public Policy* 8 (April 2001): 265–85.

Raymond, Gino. *Structures of Power in Modern France.* New York: St. Martin's Press, 2000.

Banda, Hastings (1906?–1997) *president of Malawi*

Ngwazi Kamazu Banda was born in Kasungu, Nyasaland, on May 14, 1906 (although other records suggest 1898), to an impoverished family of the Chewa tribe. His homeland was then a British colonial protectorate. Banda was educated at a missionary school run by the Church of Scotland, where he adopted the Christian name Hastings. He was intent upon furthering his education and reputedly walked over 1,000 miles with his uncle to the mines of Dundee, Natal. There he worked as a clerk while attending night school. A few years later, missionaries made it possible for him to visit the United States and attend Wilberforce University, Ohio, in 1925. Intent upon a medical career, he graduated three years later before attending Meharry Medical College in Nashville, Tennessee, in 1937. Banda then ventured to Scotland the following year for additional training, and throughout World War II he maintained a successful practice in London and Liverpool. In this capacity he became acquainted with Jomo Kenyatta, Kwame Nkrumah, and many other future African independence leaders. Banda himself was aware of the racist state of affairs in his homeland, but he declined to become politically active. Instead, he corresponded with the nationalist Nyasaland African Congress (NAC) and provided financial contributions.

Banda finally adopted political activism in the wake of Britain's decision to combine Nyasaland and Rhodesia into the ill-fated Central African Federation. In 1953 he relocated to the Gold Coast (Ghana) at the invitation of Nkrumah, where he practiced medicine until 1958. That year Banda returned to his homeland for the first time in 30 years and began agitating for political independence from Britain. Being a medical doctor who had practiced many years among Europeans made him something of a homegrown celebrity, and Banda's fiery oratory landed him a prison sentence in March 1959. He was released a year later to become head of the newly formed Malawi Congress Party (MCP), which was pressing Great Britain for complete independence. This became a reality in 1964, and the short, smartly dressed Banda became the nation's first prime minister. Later, when Malawi became a republic within the British Commonwealth, he was elected to the presidency on July 6, 1966.

Once in office, Banda quickly established himself as a despotic leader. As the unquestioned head of a one-party state, the conservative-minded leader had to quell a left-wing mutiny within the MCP ranks when younger, leftist leaders contested his policies. Many were either jailed or died under mysterious circumstances. However, his popularity among Malawi inhabitants remained undiminished, and during a 1967 coup attempt, many residents assisted police in rounding up conspirators. Banda's influence over the day-to-day life of average citizens was far-reaching. Finding that many Western standards in clothing and fashion were offensive, he personally banned long hair and bell-bottomed jeans from men, while censors busily covered the arms and legs of women in magazine ads. Banda himself was very fond of conservative-style Western clothing, and he was always impeccably dressed in a jacket, tie, and homburg hat. Furthermore, he could not converse in his own native tongue after so long an absence from home, and many Malawians began viewing him as little different from the Europeans whom they had displaced. As if to confirm this fact, in 1971 Banda had the constitution altered to have him retitled "president for life."

For all his autocratic methods, Banda was a firm believer in the market economy, and he did much to liberalize trade and privatize government industries. Under his leadership, Malawi adhered closely to guidelines established by the International Monetary Fund (IMF), achieved a high credit rating and, with it, considerable financial assistance. Hence, in contrast to many neighboring states, Malawi enjoyed a degree of affluence not usually associated with Central Africa. The president was also a pragmatist in terms of his foreign policy. Staunchly anticommunist, he readily established close economic links to the apartheid regime in South Africa, but he also opened up diplomatic channels to the socialist-oriented administration of Angola. For 30 years Banda ran Malawi like a personal fiefdom, quashing dissent mercilessly, but willing to undertake new steps to enhance living standards for average citizens. However, the bulk of these remained poor while Banda and his cronies amassed private fortunes. It was not until 1993, after he suffered a stroke, that political conditions changed. The nation was by then under increasing international pressure to allow multiparty elections. When these transpired in 1994, Banda was defeated by BAKILI MULUZI of the United Democratic Front (UDF) and withdrew from public life. Arrested for human rights abuses, he was declared senile and unfit for trial, and he spent his remaining days in quiet retirement. Banda died in a Johannesburg hospital on November 25, 1997, one of the longest-serving African heads of state from his generation of independence leaders.

Further Reading

Baker, C. A. *Revolt of the Ministers: The Malawi Cabinet Crisis, 1964–1965.* New York: I. B. Tauris, 2001.

Forster, Peter. "Law and Society under a Democratic Dictatorship: Dr. Banda and Malawi." *Journal of Asian and African Studies* 36 (August 2001): 275–294.

Lwanda, John L. *Kamuzu Banda of Malawi: A Study in Promise and Paralysis.* Glasgow: Dudu Nsomba Publications, 1993.

Mwalilino, Walusako A. *The Making and Dethronement of the Ngonde Kings in Malawi: A Study in the Conflict between the Presidency and the Monarchy, 1964–1973.* Silver Spring, Md.: Institute of Nyakyusa-Ngonde Studies, 1998.

Muyebe, Stanislaus C., and Alexander Muyebe. *The Religious Factor within the Body of Political Symbolism in Malawi, 1964–1994: A Bibliographic Essay.* Parkland, Fla.: Universal Publishers, 1999.

Bandaranaike, Sirimavo (1916–2000)

prime minister of Sri Lanka

Sirimavo Ratwatte was born on April 17, 1916, at Ratnapura, Ceylon, then a British Crown colony. She belonged to an illustrious family of Sinhalese aristocrats, and her father had served in the island senate. Though a practicing Buddhist, Ratwatte was educated at a Roman Catholic convent and she worked for several years among poor communities. In 1940 she accepted an arranged marriage with Soloman W. R. D. Bandaranaike, an older politician, and she settled into the traditional role of housewife and mother. By 1951 Ceylon had been granted independence within the British Commonwealth and her husband founded the Sri Lankan Freedom Party (SLFP), a socialist organization. However, when he was assassinated by a Buddhist fanatic in 1959, Bandaranaike was encouraged to take up the party's banner. She did so with considerable guile, delivering tear-filled speeches and winning sympathy as the "weeping widow." The outpouring of emotion catapulted her into office in July 1960 as the world's first female prime minister. Like her husband, Bandaranaike was a cultural nationalist, and she deliberately invoked policies favoring the Sinhalese language. This, however, was done arbitrarily and at the expense of the Tamil minority, which constitutes 20 percent of Ceylon's population. When further steps were enacted giving preferential treatment to Sinhalese natives in hiring and college admissions, Tamil resentment exploded into violence. Bandaranaike proved equally unrelenting and responded with force. By 1964 her army had failed to squelch the rebellion, but the economy sank under the imposition of hard-line socialist policies. Bandaranaike was then forced into a coalition with Trotskyite factions, suffered a vote of 'no confidence' in March 1965, and was forced to resign.

Bandaranaike stayed on as opposition leader until May 1970, when the SLFP regained power and she resumed the premiership. Previously, she had melded together the United Front, an alliance between her party and numerous left-wing organizations, to enhance the coalition. The Tamils were still waging their guerrilla warfare, but the government suddenly faced a bigger military threat from an armed, left-wing insurgency, the People's Liberation Front. Fortunately the revolt was crushed, with much bloodshed, by 1972. Bandaranaike then determined to change Ceylon's status from a parliamentary government within the British Commonwealth to an independent republic. A new constitution was adopted calling for a president to share power with the prime minister. Significantly, it also bequeathed a new name to the nation, Sri Lanka, or "resplendent island" in Sinhalese. She then furthered her progressive agenda by nationalizing the business sector and instituting massive land reform. Bandaranaike also demonstrated her commitment to the nonaligned movement by expelling the American-sponsored Peace Corps and closing down the Israeli embassy. But, her personal popularity notwithstanding, Bandaranaike was unable to improve the economy. Her second term in office was plagued by low productivity, high unemployment, and grinding poverty. New elections held in July 1977 removed her from office a second time, and in October 1980 a presidential commission found her guilty of abusing power. She was consequently expelled from parliament and forbidden to run in upcoming elections. Bandaranaike regained her rights in 1988 and, as a measure of her amazing political resilience, she finished second in presidential elections held that year.

By 1993 Bandaranaike's daughter, Prime Minister CHANDRIKA KUMARATUNGA, had displaced her as head of the SLFP. The following year, continuing the island's tradition of strong female leadership, Kumaratunga was elected president of Sri Lanka and she appointed her aged mother as prime minister. By now this was more of a ceremonial position, but it constituted the only time in history whereby one female head of state peacefully succeeded another through elections. It also represents the sole instance whereby a nation's two highest offices were occupied by mother and daughter. Curiously, the new executive spent much effort overturning her mother's outdated socialist policies in favor of privatization and neoliberal economics. But Kumaratunga enjoyed little success in taming the Tamil Tigers and their protracted terrorism continued. Bandaranaike held office until August 10, 2000, when she concluded four decades of public service by stepping down for health reasons. She died three months later in Gampha, Sri Lanka, mourned by the Sinhalese majority to which she devoted her life. However, the Tamil War, which her strident policies fo-

mented, continues, with a current death toll estimated at 80,000.

Further Reading

Goonevatne, Yasmine. *Relative Merits: A Personal Memoir of the Bandaranaike Family of Sri Lanka.* New York: St. Martin's Press, 1986.

Lakshman, W. D. *Sri Lanka's Development since Independence.* Huntington, N.Y.: Nova Science Publishers, 2000.

Sabaratnam, Lakshmanan. *Ethnic Attachments in Sri Lanka: Social Change and Cultural Continuity.* New York: Palgrave, 2001.

Sivarajah, Ambalavanar. *Politics of Tamil Nationalism in Sri Lanka.* Denver, Colo.: iAcademic Books, 2000.

Werake, Mahinda, and P. V. J. Jayasekera. *Security Dilemmas of a Small State.* Denver, Colo.: iAcademic Books, 2000.

Banzer, Hugo (1926–2002) *president of Bolivia*
Hugo Banzer was born in Concepción, Bolivia, on May 10, 1926, into a family of pure Spanish ancestry. This set him apart from the bulk of his fellow citizens, 80 percent of whom are Indians. After receiving his education, Banzer attended the Bolivian Military College and graduated a cavalry lieutenant. He completed several years of routine assignments before passing through the U.S. Army School in Panama, and he subsequently received additional training at the Armored Cavalry School, Fort Hood, Texas. Banzer proved himself to be an excellent officer, and he acquired additional prestige by serving as the Bolivian military attaché in Washington, D.C. He returned home in 1969 to serve as director of the military academy. The short, nondescript Banzer also became known as "El Petiso" owing to his short stature.

Bolivia, one of the poorest nations in South America, is also one of the most unstable. Since its independence from Spain in 1825, it has weathered an average of one military coup attempt every other year. In 1970 General Juan José Torres, a strident leftist, deposed the sitting president and took over. He then embarked on a policy of nationalizing foreign companies and properties, and he invited droves of Soviet and Cuban advisers into the country. Banzer, strongly anticommunist by persuasion, attempted a failed coup against Torres and fled to exile in Argentina. However, reforms initiated by the Torres regime threw the country into social and economic chaos, which only further alienated the conservative military establishment. Banzer, meanwhile, made several clandestine visits back to Bolivia to rally political and military forces against Torres. He was captured on one occasion and this led to a successful, if bloody, military coup against the government on August 22, 1971. Banzer was then installed as head of the government.

In practice, Banzer wielded an iron fist over Bolivia to restore order, stability, and root out leftist adversaries. This entailed the arrest of 15,000 dissidents, while a similar number sought refuge in neighboring countries. He also reversed the trend toward nationalization and expelled Soviet and Cuban diplomats en masse. This had the effect of winning support from the United States and other conservative governments in the region, and the flow of badly needed foreign aid resumed. Despite the crackdown and his authoritarian style, within four years Banzer had succeeded in checking inflation, fostering economic growth and ushering in a period—at least by Bolivian standards—of prolonged political stability. He also initiated education and welfare reforms aimed at assisting poor Indians, Bolivia's majority population. By July 1978 he stepped aside in favor of free elections, although his chosen candidate, General Juan Pereda, was declared the winner. When these results were nullified by an electoral commission, Pereda led a successful coup against Banzer in 1979, who voluntarily stepped down to avoid violence.

Eager to resume his political career, Banzer founded the National Democratic Alliance (AND) in 1980 and ran five successive times for the presidency. The former dictator finally triumphed in 1997 at the age of 71. "I have fought and will fight for Bolivia," he crowed. "I will lead a political force that will consolidate the democratization process initiated in my previous government." In office Banzer has proven himself both a populist and a nationalist, which appeals to a wide spectrum of Bolivian voters. And despite his conservative instincts, he was careful to implement social welfare reforms to shore up sagging standards of living. Banzer proved himself unique among recent Bolivian politicians by championing economic growth, but not at the expense of working-class citizens. Hence the privatization of state industries proceeded apace to placate the international financial community, but it went hand in hand with programs for mitigating the displacement that such reforms produce. It was a difficult

balancing act but Banzer, a highly disciplined figure, conducted himself with both boldness and restraint. Consequently, Bolivia has enjoyed one of the most sustained periods of growth and stability in its history.

Banzer garnered considerable popularity among a wide spectrum of voters, but on August 6, 2000, he resigned as president after being diagnosed with cancer. His successor, Vice President José Quiroga served the remainder of his term in office, which expired in 2002. Meanwhile, Banzer's past came back to haunt him. In 2000 a court in Argentina formally requested his extradition to stand charges for alleged involvement in "Plan Condor," a scheme to eliminate leftists and labor opponents during the 1970s. Banzer died on May 5, 2002 before he could be prosecuted for these charges.

Further Reading

"Bolivian President Banzer Steps Down, Vice President Quiroga Sworn in." *Facts On File* 61, no. 3166 (2000): 612–614.

Crabtree, John, and Laurence Whitehead. *Towards Democratic Viability: The Bolivian Experience.* Basingstoke, England: Palgrave, 2001.

Urioste, Miguel. *Bolivia: Reform and Resistance in the Countryside, 1982–2000.* London: University of London Press, 2001.

Van Colt, Donna L. *The Friendly Liquidation of the Past: The Politics of Diversity in Latin America.* Pittsburgh, Pa.: University of Pittsburgh Press, 2000.

Barak, Ehud (1942–) *prime minister of Israel*
Ehud Barak (born Brog) was born at Kibbutz Mishmar Hasharon, British-controlled Palestine, on February 12, 1943, the son of eastern European Jewish immigrants. As a youth, he gained a reputation for unruliness and belligerence, whose only interests were classical piano and picking locks. The state of Israel won its independence in 1948, and 11 years later Brog changed his last name to Barak (Hebrew for "lightning"). The short, restless young man then joined the Israeli Defense Force (IDF) as part of the elite *sayeret matkal* ("border reconnaissance") units. He quickly established himself as a leading exponent of clandestine special forces missions, including the assassination of several ranking Palestinian terrorists. Barak rose quickly through the ranks, becoming a unit commander, head of military intelligence, and

army chief of staff by 1991. He also found time to obtain a bachelor's degree in mathematics from Hebrew University and a master's degree in systems analysis from Stanford University. Prior to retiring from the army in 1994 as Israel's youngest lieutenant general and most decorated solider, Barak helped orchestrate critical negotiations with Syria and Jordan over the return of Arab lands seized in the 1967 Six-Day War. These talks have since remained at an impasse, but they did succeed in establishing Barak as a "hawkish dove," tough on defense issues but realistic enough to compromise on the issue of territory.

In July 1995 Barak entered politics by joining the Labor Party under Prime Minister YITZHAK RABIN, another conspicuous veteran, who appointed him minister of the interior. Four months later Rabin was assassinated by an Israeli extremist, and he was succeeded by the more dovish SHIMON PERES. However, in 1996 a jittery Israeli polity turned Labor out of office in favor of BINYAMIN NETANYAHU of the right-leaning Likud Party. Barak's star was nonetheless on the ascent and by 1997 he was voted head of the Labor Party. He used his pulpit to roundly criticize Netanyahu, a former military subordinate, for strident inflexibility in dealing with the Palestinian issue. Moreover, increasing U.S. pressure forced Likud to sign the Wye Memorandum, which stipulated increasing Palestinian control over the West Bank region. This, in turn, undermined the stability of Likud, which depended upon extreme religious parties to govern as a majority. The government was also being buffeted politically by a lackluster economy. In 1999 it was clear that his coalition was no longer viable, and Prime Minister Netanyahu called for national elections. Barak was chosen as the candidate of a new association, the One Israel Party, and he soundly trounced the incumbent on May 17, 1999.

Barak served as prime minister of a country in one of the most violent, unpredictable, and dangerous regions in the world. The Middle East has been a cauldron churning with resentment against the Jewish state of Israel, and many Palestinians, either dispossessed of property and living in Jordan or residing in Israel as citizens, are increasingly motivated by terrorism. Barak, given his military background, unflinchingly ordered retaliation for each attack, but retribution undermines the prospect of negotiations with neighboring countries like Jordan, Syria, and Lebanon. The latter, an object of Israeli occupation since the 1980s, was formally abandoned by

Barak after the loss of 900 Israeli soldiers. This was done in an attempt to placate Syria, which is also demanding immediate return of the strategic Golan Heights, lost in 1967. Barak also walked a fine line in dealing with YASSER ARAFAT, chairman of the Palestine Liberation Organization (PLO) and nominal head of the Palestinian Authority, which governs Arab-controlled sections of the West Bank. In 2002, Muslim extremist groups such as Hamas unleashed a series of suicide bombings within Israel proper and even managed to assassinate the minister of tourism. Barak brooked no delays in launching retaliatory strikes against Arafat, whom he held responsible, while also holding out a chance for further negotiations. However, he was roundly criticized by Arabs and left-wing parties for allowing resumption of Israeli settlements in the occupied West Bank.

The current Arab-Israeli struggle is internecine and with apparently no end in sight. Barak had a reputation as a hard-eyed pragmatist who was willing to concede land for peace, but the Jewish state has been reluctant to proceed, given no assurance that the Palestinian Authority is in actual control of its people. It is hoped that with the accession of newer, younger Arab leaders, such as ABDULLAH II of Jordan and BASHAR AL-ASSAD of Syria, the stalled peace talks can recommence. But the violence shows little sign of abatement and seems to be forever extending its grasp into the body politic. As late as November 2001, Barak was forced to testify before a judicial commission investigating the violent deaths of 13 Israeli Arabs by the army. "The overall responsibility is that of the government," he explained. "The government needs to set policy and take responsibility." It was hoped that Barak's carrot-and-stick approach to negotiating could have ushered in a period of general peace or, at the very least, stop the escalating spiral of violence threatening Israel's survival and, with it, Middle Eastern stability. In any event, on February 6, 2002, he lost the general election to hard-liner ARIEL SHARON, who promised to take an ever harder stance against Arab extremism.

Further Reading

Chapman, Colin. *Whose Promised Land? The Continuing Crisis over Israel and Palestine.* Oxford: Lion, 2002.

Diskin, Abraham. *The Last Days in Israel: Understanding the New Israeli Democracy.* Portland, Oreg.: Frank Cass, 2003.

Hazony, Yoram. *The Jewish State: The Struggle for Israel's Soul.* New York: Basic Books, 2001.

Jones, Clive, and Emma C. Murphy. *Israel: Challenges to Identity, Democracy, and the State.* New York: Routledge, 2002.

Rabil, Robert G. *Embattled Neighbors: Syria, Israel, Lebanon.* Boulder, Colo.: Lynne Rienner Publishers, 2003.

Shakak, Israel. *Jewish History, Jewish Religion: The Weight of Three Thousand Years.* London: Pluto, 2000.

Bashir, Omar Hassan Ahmed al- (1944–)

president of Sudan

Omar Hassan Ahmen Al-Bashir was born in Sudan in 1944. A career military officer, he received his initial training in the Soviet Union before returning to the Sudanese military as a paratrooper. In this capacity, he fought with Egyptian forces against Israel during the 1973 Yom Kippur War, and he was highly decorated. Bashir then rotated back to Sudan, where he rose to the position of brigadier general of airborne forces. He spent several years in the southern part of the country fighting a long-standing struggle against Christian and animist forces who stridently resist the advance of Islam in their region. At length, an Islamic movement arose in the north which vocally agitated for the imposition of the *sharia,* or Islamic law, on the entire country. Bashir was apparently in sympathy with this aspiration for, when Prime Minister Sadiq al-Mahdi tried to restrain the growth of Islam, he was overthrown in a bloodless coup on June 30, 1989. Upon assuming the reins of power, Colonel Bashir declared to his countrymen: "As soon as we feel that the Sudanese people are capable of making good decisions free from sectarian considerations and party politics, we will relinquish power."

Once in charge, Bashir took immediate steps to consolidate his position. He dissolved the parliament, abolished the constitution, and declared a national state of emergency. He also simultaneously promoted himself to brigadier general, prime minister, and commander in chief. Thus situated, Bashir embarked on a personal, quixotic, and—for Sudan—disastrous course to transform that impoverished nation into a model Islamic state. In concert with a 15-man Command Council of National Salvation, he ordered the *sharia* officially adopted as a state-sponsored creed. This only stiffened the resolve of Christian forces in the south to resist. Bashir also struck up a cordial alliance with the National Islamic Front of Hassan al-Turabi, who more or less

functioned as the government's spiritual adviser. The net result of their efforts was a litany of human rights violations, political repression, and a return of the slave trade. The government began a concerted effort to kidnap Christian children, forcibly convert them to Islam, and have them combat their former cohorts. However, Christian forces under Colonel John Garang have resisted gamely and fought superior forces of the Sudanese government to a standoff. In return, Bashir resorted to a complete economic blockade of the south, aided by periodic drought, to starve the opposition out. Since 1980 it is estimated that at least 2 million people have died and another 4 million have been displaced by these efforts. The Bashir regime, however, was roundly condemned by the international community for not allowing humanitarian relief flights to enter the afflicted regions.

Bashir originally inherited a weak economy burdened by large foreign debt, and his continual warfare has only made a bad situation worse. He has since embarked on a program to promote economic growth and cultivate outside investors, but the attempt has enjoyed little success. This is primarily because of Bashir's radical pan-Islamic foreign policy. He supported the Iraqi invasion of Kuwait, has visited Iran and Iraq for weapons and credit, and allowed terrorist cells under Osama bin Laden to flourish on his soil. In August 1998 this sparked an angry response from the United States, which bombed a so-called pharmaceutical factory in Sudan in response to terrorist attacks. The country remains on the U.S. list of countries that sponsor terrorism, and, in the wake of the September 11, 2001, destruction of the World Trade Center in New York City, President GEORGE W. BUSH may yet schedule retaliatory attacks upon terrorist training facilities. On December 29, 2001, Bashir won reelection as president with 86 percent of the vote, but the voting was boycotted by all the opposition parties.

Given the grave economic and military situation in which he finds himself, Bashir is apparently moderating his stance on several fronts. To begin with, in December 1999 he had a falling out with al-Turabi and ordered his arrest. Next, he announced that henceforth his foreign policy would be officially "indifferent" to the Jewish state of Israel, which further distances himself from more radical regimes. Finally, he has made several attempts to negotiate a cease-fire agreement to the two-decade old Sudanese civil war that consumes most government revenues. Negotiations are continuing to this date in Eritrea, although it remains to be seen if Bashir will consent to a separation of church and state. Undoubtedly, his erratic and unpredictable leadership style, coupled with unworkable religious notions of government, have rendered Bashir one of the most ineffective leaders in Sudanese history.

Further Reading

Jendia, Catherine. *The Sudanese Civil Conflict, 1969–1985.* New York: Peter Lang, 2001.

Jok, Jok Madut. *War and Slavery in Sudan.* Philadelphia: University of Pennsylvania Press, 2000.

O'Ballance, Edgar. *Sudan, Civil War, and Terrorism, 1956–99.* New York: Macmillan Press, 2000.

Peterson, Scott. *Me against My Brother: At War in Somalia, Sudan, and Rwanda.* New York: Routledge, 2001.

Salam, A. H. Abdel., and Alexander De Waal. *The Phoenix State: Civil Society and the Future of Sudan.* Lawrenceville, N.J.: Red Sea, 2001.

Warburg, Gabriel. *Sudan: Islam, Secularism, and Politics since the Mahdiyya.* Madison: University of Wisconsin Press, 2002.

Batlle Ibáñez, Jorge Luis (1927–   )

president of Uruguay

Jorge Luis Batlle Ibáñez was born in Uruguay on October 25, 1927, into an illustrious political family. His great uncle, José Batlle y Ordóñez, was a former two-term president (1903–07, 1911–15) who helped lift the nation out of poverty by establishing the comprehensive welfare system still in operation. The younger Batlle began working as a radio journalist before joining the moderately conservative Colorado Party in 1945. Their traditional opposition was the National, or Blanco, Party. In 1956 Batlle attended the University of Montevideo, received a degree in law, and resumed his career in journalism. He then tested the political waters by being elected to the Chamber of Deputies in 1958. Spurred on by success, Batlle next ran unsuccessfully for president in 1966 and 1971. However, from 1973–84, Uruguay was ruled by an oppressive military junta, which closed Batlle's newspapers and frequently arrested him for questioning. The country then returned to civilian rule and Batlle began seeking political office. He was elected sen-

ator in November 1984, and, wishing to capitalize upon his famous name, he again ran unsuccessfully for president in 1989 and 1994.

In 1999, Batlle was once more nominated as his party's candidate for the presidency. However, the traditional rivalry between the Colorado Party and the National Party was complicated by the sudden rise and surprising strength of the Broad Front, a coalition of various center-left groupings under Tabaré Vázquez. The two established parties were somewhat stunned by the preliminary election results of October 31, 1999, when Vázquez garnered 39 percent of the vote. The 72-year-old Batlle won only 31 percent by comparison. Because neither side could claim a majority, a run-off election was scheduled for November. Both the Colorados and Nationals feared a leftist takeover, for Vázquez vowed to slow down or stop the trend toward liberalizing (privatizing) state assets. To prevent this from happening, Batlle then cut a deal with the National Party for their support. He also campaigned against Vázquez's intention to institute an income tax for the first time in Uruguayan history. By siphoning off National Party support, Batlle went on to defeat the Broad Front candidate, while also securing slim majorities in the upper and lower houses. He was sworn in on March 1, 2000, and, in return, five National Party ministers were granted portfolios within his cabinet.

Batlle inherited a reasonably sound economy, but future prospects were grim. Uruguay's major trading partners, Brazil and Argentina, were both in economic disarray, and it was only a matter of time before the reverberations were felt at home. Therefore, the president moved quickly to update antiquated ways of doing business, capped governmental spending, and made the country's products more competitive for export. He also began promoting computers and the Internet, and he pledged to help all of Uruguay's students become computer literate. "Only those societies with open economies and with a high level of technology have acceptable levels of unemployment," he declared, "Uruguay can and should transform itself into one of these nations." Batlle also reiterated his support for Mercosur, a trade pact among Uruguay, Brazil, Argentina, and Paraguay. In a recent meeting with heads of states from those nations, he pushed for the expansion of free trade by the admittance of Chile and Bolivia to the pact.

Batlle also summoned the courage to confront Uruguay's recent past. During the period of military rule between 1973 and 1984, the country was wracked by civil unrest abetted by an armed left-wing guerrilla movement, the Tupamaros. The generals responded with a crackdown on freedom, with thousands of people arrested, tortured, and, in some instances, murdered. Batlle cordially met with the families of 159 unresolved disappearances to seek closure—a formal amnesty prevents the prosecution of offending officers. Batlle thereupon announced formation of a commission, culled from the government, the opposition, the church, and families of missing persons, to investigate the fate of each. Moreover, he dismissed a ranking general who suggested that armed conflict with leftists is inevitable and ought to be resumed. Batlle enjoys considerable political popularity and is confident that the economy will rebound by 2002. Furthermore, he earnestly hopes that the movement for free trade initiated by Mercosur will expand its reach to encompass markets from Argentina in the south to the farthest reaches of North America.

Further Reading

Davis, William C. *Warnings from the South: Democracy versus Dictatorship in Uruguay, Argentina, and Chile.* Westport, Conn.: Praeger, 1995.

Gillespie, Charles. *Negotiating Democracy: Politicians and Generals in Uruguay.* New York: Cambridge University Press, 1991.

Panizza, F. "Late Institutionalization and Early Modernization: The Emergence of Uruguay's Liberal Democratic Order." *Journal of Latin American Studies* 29 (October 1997): 667–691.

Stubbs, Richard. *Political Economy and the Changing Global Order.* New York: Oxford University Press, 2000.

Uggla, Fredrik. *Disillusioned in Democracy: Labor and State in Post-transitional Chile and Uruguay.* Uppsala, Sweden: Uppsala University, 2000.

Bédié, Henri-Konan (1934–) *president of Côte d'Ivoire*

Henri-Konan Bédié was born in Dadiekro, Ivory Coast, on May 15, 1934, a member of the Baoule ethnic group. At that time his country was administered as a French colonial possession. Bédié completed his secondary education before training as a teacher, but he subsequently opted for a legal career instead. He ventured to France and attended law school in Poitiers, graduating there in 1958. That year he also befriended FÉLIX HOUPHOUËT-BOIGNY, the future president of the Côte d'Ivoire, and the two struck up cordial relations. Bédié then returned home to work as a civil servant, and was later sent to Washington, D.C., to train as a diplomat. Once the Ivory Coast gained its independence in 1960 as the Côte d'Ivoire, Bédié served as his country's first ambassador to the United States at the age of 27. Like all government officials, he was part of his nation's only official organization, the Democratic Party of Côte d'Ivoire (PDCI). He remained on station for six years before coming home in 1966 to serve in Houphouët-Boigny's cabinet as minister of economy and finances. These were boom times for Côte d'Ivoire, and for the next 11 years the nation experienced great prosperity. However, rumors began circulating that Bédié had profited considerably at the public's expense, so in 1977 President Houphouët-Boigny removed him, along with eight other ministers. However, Bédié subsequently found work with the World Bank in Washington, D.C., where he made many useful contacts among the international business community. By 1980 conditions were ripe for his return to Côte d'Ivoire, and he won a seat in the National Assembly. Soon after he demonstrated his mastery of parliamentary politics by gaining appointment as president of the assembly, where he remained for 13 years. In 1990, when multiparty democracy was finally authorized, Bédié astutely added provisions to the constitution stipulating that the president of the National Assembly would assume the presidency in the event of the incumbent's death or resignation.

When Houphouët-Boigny died suddenly on December 7, 1993, Bédié went on national television and announced his succession to the presidency. However, he did this before the Supreme Court voted on the assumption of power and while the prime minister, Alassane Ouattara, also maneuvered to secure the highest office. Fortunately, two days later the court voted in favor of Bédié and Ouattara conceded the contest. Côte d'Ivoire, in addition to being one of West Africa's wealthiest nations, was thus far unique for never having endured political coups of any kind. Bédié moved swiftly to consolidate his power within the government and it appeared that a peaceful transfer of power—the nation's first—had been effected.

Once in office, Bédié continued the economic policies of his predecessor and, given the success Côte d'Ivoire enjoyed in that field, suggested nicknaming his country the "Elephant of Africa." Unfortunately, the eve of the 1995 elections proved violent, and the president overreacted by ordering the police and army into the streets to suppress all protesters. This did little to enhance his national image or popularity. But Bédié further strengthened his political dominance by having the National Assembly pass strict residency laws stipulating that presidential candidates must have two parents who are citizens of Côte d'Ivoire. His leading rival, Ouattara, was thus rendered ineligible. In light of these none-too-subtle machinations, the opposition largely boycotted the elections of 1995, which Bédié won resoundingly—if unopposed. Three years later, to further consolidate his grip, Bédié had the assembly pass a law extending his term in office from five to seven years and also allowing him to postpone future elections if political instability threatened. Finally, the president authorized additional changes to the constitution by creating an upper chamber, or senate, to function alongside the National Assembly. Not surprisingly, Bédié reserved to himself the right to appoint one-third of its members.

The course of Côte d'Ivoire governance seemed irrevocably destined for dictatorship until December 25, 1999, when Bédié was overthrown by General Robert Guei. The former president escaped by airplane to Togo and thence to France. Citizens of Côte d'Ivoire welcomed the change and celebrated with a frenzied three-day looting spree in the capital of Abidjan. Guei cited his reason for overthrowing Bédié as increasing corruption, unpaid salaries for troops and civil servants, and all-around "bad governance." In 2000 Guei himself was forced out of office after losing an election to Laurent Gbagbo, annulling the results, and stepping down in the face of national protests. Bédié, meanwhile, remained in France until October 2001, when a reconciliation panel invited both Bédié and Guei back to Côte d'Ivoire. His arrival was greeted by thousands of former PDCI supporters and he unapologetically declared his intention "to take up new battles."

Further Reading

Bassett, Thomas J. *The Peasant Cotton Rebellion in West Africa: Côte d'Ivoire, 1880–1995.* Cambridge: Cambridge University Press, 2001.
"Côte d'Ivoire." *The Courier,* no. 133 (May–June 1992): 5–25.
Mendt, Robert J. *Historical Dictionary of Côte d'Ivoire.* Lanham, Md.: Scarecrow Press, 1995.
N'Diaye, Boubacar. "A Comparative Analysis of Civilian Control Strategies: Botswana, Ivory Coast, and Kenya." Unpublished Ph.D. dissertation, Northern Illinois University, 1998.
Nnedu, Uguchukwe. "The Impact of African Institutions and Economic Policy Traditions on Economic Growth: The Colonial and Post-colonial Experience in Nigeria and Côte d'Ivoire." Unpublished master's thesis, Auburn University, 2001.

Ben Ali, Zine el Abidine (1936–)
president of Tunisia

Zine El Abidine Ben Ali was born in the coastal town of Hammam Sousse, Tunisia, on September 3, 1936. Having received his primary education, like many youths his age he became caught up in revolutionary activities against French forces occupying his country. After independence was won in 1956, Ben Ali was allowed to visit France to attend the prestigious military academy at St.-Cyr and the artillery school at Châlons-sur-Marne. Adept in military matters, he subsequently took courses at Fort Bliss, Texas, and Fort Holabird, Maryland, in the United States. Ben Ali returned home in 1958 and, though a young man, was appointed director of military security, under President Habib Bourguiba, and as part of the Destourian Socialist Party. His main responsibility was controlling and directing state security forces and suppressing political dissent. This he accomplished skillfully and ruthlessly until 1974 when, following a disagreement with Bourguiba, he found himself reassigned as military attaché to Morocco. Ben Ali remained in disfavor six years later when he was appointed ambassador to Poland. However, mounting civil unrest in Tunisia culminated in bread riots throughout 1983–84, and he was summoned home as head of national security. With his usual promptness and efficiency, Ben Ali restored order and won favor with President Bourguiba, who successively appointed him minister of the interior, prime minister, and party general secretary.

Public dissatisfaction with the aged Bourguiba induced Ben Ali to mount a bloodless coup against the tottering incumbent on November 7, 1987. Once installed, he energetically moved to confront two rising specters stalking Tunisia's internal security. The first and most ominous was the rise of an Islamic fundamentalist party, Ennahdha, which sought to overthrow the secular government in favor of a theocracy. Sensing a real threat, Ben Ali vigorously crushed its adherents, jailing thousands and outlawing any political activity with a religious slant. This, in turn, led to riots, police brutality, and a general abuse of human rights, but also insured the government's survival. This rigid stance won him plaudits from Western governments, who overlooked Ben Ali's abuses in favor of the stability he brought the country.

The second problem confronting Tunisia was the economy. Ben Ali, who boasts an electrical engineering background, paid careful attention to economic growth, private investment, and expanded industry. His success here may be gauged by the fact that Tunisia has received more World Bank loans than any other African or Arab country in recent history. Ben Ali also encouraged fellow Tunisians to work abroad in Europe and the Persian Gulf states, thereby relieving the stress of unemployment at home. His emphasis on advanced technology, computers, active petroleum exploration and exportation, coupled with responsible fiscal discipline, has given Tunisia the most prosperous and stable government in the Arab world. The overall sense of satisfaction has also largely muted domestic criticism against him, which in any case is only vocal among religious factions. And, while seeking close economic ties to Western Europe, Ben Ali demonstrated his independence by supporting SADDAM HUSSEIN's invasion of Kuwait in 1991 and, earlier, supporting the Palestine Liberation Organization by allowing its headquarters to be based in Tunisia. He was also one of the first Arab countries to restore diplomatic relations with Egypt following that country's peace treaty with Israel. Tunisian troops, meanwhile, have been dispatched abroad to Somalia and Bosnia under the aegis of the United Nations, which further enhanced his country's international standing.

When Ben Ali first came to power in 1987, he vowed to expand democratization and political pluralism. However, he has continually reneged on the issue of political reform and, in fact, has contrived a system that virtually guarantees his monopoly on power. The government remains intolerant of any contrary group or individual views, secular or religious, which it sees as a threat to its continuation. Moreover, Ben Ali promoted the façade of democracy and popular will in 1989 and 1994 by running unopposed and emerged with an un-

Zine el Abidine Ben Ali *(Embassy of Tunisia)*

surprising 99 percent of the vote. In 1999 he allowed representatives from two minor parties to oppose him, and both he and his party, renamed the Democratic Constitutional Rally, won decisively. He has since allowed other, minor parties to flourish. Provided they parrot his antireligious views, they are granted state subsidies and time on television. But Tunisia remains, for all intents and purposes, a one-party state.

Ben Ali proved himself a master at juggling national priorities, especially in his ability to determine when and to what degree to crack down on the opposition. Unlike many contemporaries in the Arab world, he has successfully weathered the challenge of Islamic extremism and remains firmly ensconced in power. This far-sighted, highly disciplined pragmatist is likely to lead Tunisia into the 21st century for some time to come.

Further Reading

Borowiec, Andrew. *Modern Tunisia: A Democratic Apprenticeship.* Westport, Conn.: Praeger, 1998.

Chaabane, Sadok. *Ben Ali on the Road to Pluralism in Tunisia.* Washington, D.C.: American Educational Trust, 1997.

Geyer, Georgie A. "Tunisia: A Country That Works." *Washington Quarterly* 21 (Autumn 1998): 93–107.

Murphy, Emma. *Economic and Political Change in Tunisia: From Bourguiba to Ben Ali.* New York: St. Martin's Press, 1999.

Sorkin, Jerry. "The Tunisian Model." *Middle East Quarterly* 8 (Fall 2001): 25–30.

Beregovoy, Pierre (1925–1993) *prime minister of France*

Pierre Eugène Beregovoy was born in Deville-les-Rouen, France, on December 23, 1925, the son of working-class parents. His family was poor, so in 1941 he quit school to help support the family as a textile worker and railroad ticket agent. During World War II he fought the German occupation as part of the underground resistance, and he acquired a taste for left-wing politics. After the war he joined Gaz de France, the national gas company, where he remained for 31 years. Beregovoy was self-educated and displayed an endless appetite for learning. Having risen to the rank of company executive, he attended the Labor Institute of the University of Strasbourg and obtained his diploma in scientific management. Politically, Beregovoy became closely associated with the Socialist Party throughout its ongoing evolution. In 1958 he helped found the Autonomous Socialist Party before merging three years later with a new group, the Unified Socialist Party. Like many other moderates in his group, Beregovoy felt that the only way socialism could prevail in France would be under the aegis of a noncommunist left wing. He subsequently joined the newly reorganized Socialist Party in 1969, and he served many years as its national secretary for social affairs. It was while acting in this capacity that he befriended FRANÇOIS MITTERRAND, becoming one of his most trusted advisers. His political fortunes greatly accelerated in 1981 following the election of Mitterrand as France's first socialist executive. The self-taught Beregovoy found himself successively appointed secretary-general of the presidential staff and minister of social affairs in June 1982.

As a cabinet minister, Beregovoy displayed a consistent mixture of personal loyalty to Mitterrand together with an unswerving, moderate approach to governmental policies. This placed him at odds with more ideological members of his party, but Beregovoy determined not to squander an opportunity for building French socialism by kowtowing to extremists. As minister, he fully embraced a decidedly conservative approach to economics, including higher social security taxes, co-payments by beneficiaries when possible, and cost-cutting measures to balance the budget. In 1983 he also enjoyed his first election success by becoming mayor of Nevers, a post that he held for a decade. In July 1984 Mitterrand rewarded his friend with a cabinet post as minister of finance. As such he became the only member of Mitterrand's inner circle to possess a bona fide working-class background. Probably for this reason, and his own life experience, Beregovoy was much more beholden to practicality than ideology. He was therefore determined to win the confidence of the business community by enacting sound economic policies such as reductions in government spending and pursuit of a tight monetary policy to buoy up the franc. Over the objection of party stalwarts, he also overhauled the stock exchange to make it more competitive, initiated a futures exchange, and launched banking deregulation.

In 1986 the Socialists were rebuffed at the polls and Beregovoy left the cabinet, but he gained election to parliament from Nevers, and he also served as the party's national secretary. In this capacity he helped engineer Mitterrand's surprising comeback victory of 1988, and he was reinstated as his finance minister. Beregovoy fully expected to be made prime minister of France, second in command after the president but, strangely, this did not materialize. Nonetheless, he was one of the few senior Socialist leaders to enjoy public popularity in a period of mounting skepticism. Despite his best efforts, the French economy began sliding precipitously and Mitterrand's administration was also increasingly criticized for a series of scandals. In April 1992 Beregovoy was finally tapped to replace the unpopular EDITH CRESSON as prime minister. It was widely anticipated that this appointment would revitalize the sagging fortunes of the Socialists and he pledged to "lance the abscess of corruption." However, rising unemployment continued to dog the administration and, worse, Beregovoy found himself enmeshed in a scandal involving his acceptance of an interest-free loan. Despite earnest denials of wrongdoing, the public apparently refused to believe him and in March and April 1993, the Socialists took a pounding at the polls. Consequently, Beregovoy resigned as prime minister and was replaced by the conservative EDOUARD BALLADUR under a "cohabitation" agreement with Mitterrand.

Beregovoy was clearly distraught by his recent defeat and alarmed by the allegations of political impropriety against him. His friend and mentor, Mitterrand, was sympathetic but offered no public support for the disgraced minister. Deeply depressed, and rather than face continuing hounding by investigation, Beregovoy committed suicide at Nevers on May 1, 1993. His passing has since been compared to the fate of Roger Salengro, a French politician who was falsely accused of collaborating with the enemy during World War I before taking his own life in 1936. His death also prompted President Mitterrand to speak up on behalf of his old friend, declaring that nothing "could justify throwing a man's honor and ultimately his life to the dogs."

Further Reading

Bell, David S. *French Politics Today.* Manchester, England: Manchester University Press, 2002.

Cook, Linda J., and Mitchell R. Crenstein. *Left Parties and Social Policy in Post-communist Europe.* Boulder, Colo.: Westview Press, 1999.

Elgie, Robert. *The Changing French Political System.* Ilford, England: Frank Cass, 1999.

Gildea, Robert. *France since 1945.* Oxford: Oxford University Press, 2002.

Guyomarch, A. "The 1993 Parliamentary Elections in France." *Parliamentary Affairs* 46 (October 1993): 605–626.

Berisha, Sali (1944–) *president of Albania*

Sali Berisha was born in the Tropoja district of northern Albania on July 1, 1944, the son of a peasant Muslim family. At that time his country was on the verge of becoming a hard-line Stalinist state run by Communist dictator Enver Hoxha—one of the most quixotic in Europe. Berisha was educated locally before attending the University of Tiranë, from which he graduated with honors in 1967. Intent upon a medical career, Berisha next studied cardiology at the Tiranë General Hospital. By 1978 he had established himself as a leading researcher in his field and subsequently served as a medical

lecturer at the university. His reputation as an intellectual notwithstanding, he was also allowed to join the Albanian Party of Labor (ALP–Communist) in 1971, despite its ingrained distrust toward such professionals. As Berisha's medical reputation continued to grow, he received numerous awards and invitations to study abroad, including a UNESCO fellowship. He also joined the Copenhagen-based European Committee for Research in the Medical Sciences. Berisha continued working in his field, and with little fanfare until 1989, the year when the removal of Soviet troops from Eastern Europe signaled the coming collapse of communism.

In time, Berisha became an outspoken proponent of political reform and liberalization in Albania. The government, then under President Ramiz Alia, began a series of tepid reforms but the public responded with mounting impatience. Foremost among malcontents was Berisha, who, at a convention of intellectuals, directly challenged Alia to open the country up. To underscore his determination to break with the past, Berisha resigned from the Communist Party and helped found a new opposition group, the Democratic Party (DP). By December 1990, public impatience with the Alia regime spilled over onto the streets. Demonstrations and riots erupted. Sensing the inevitable, the government finally authorized Albania's first multiparty elections in four decades, whereupon Berisha was formally appointed president of the DP in February 1991. During the first round of elections held the following March, the ALP defeated the reformers and Alia was able to remain in power, although in a coalition with the DP. However, as the country began sliding into economic chaos, new elections were scheduled for March 1992. At that time, the DP was swept to power by capturing 62 percent of the popular vote and 92 of 140 seats in the National Assembly. Alia promptly resigned in consequence and on April 8, 1992, the legislature elected Berisha president. He was the first Albanian head of state who was not a Communist in 40 years. For a country with Albania's repressive past, an important political crossroads had been reached.

Berisha had little time for celebrations as, thanks to the communist tradition of state controls and centralized planning, Albania was on the verge of collapse. Immediately he responded with a scheme of economic liberalization and privatization. This produced the usual period of social dislocation and hardships, but within two years the national economy rebounded at a brisk 8 percent growth rate a year. Berisha was also committed to ending

Albania's long tradition of political and diplomatic isolation. He therefore took deliberate steps to strengthen economic and political ties with Western Europe and the United States, all the while seeking additional economic investment. By 1994 Berisha had met or exceeded most of his political objectives; the economy was in better shape than when he had inherited it, and Albania was securely ensconced among the community of nations. These successes rendered him the most popular and influential politician of his day.

Things began to go awry for Berisha commencing in 1995. That year he endorsed vindictive legislation designed to exclude former Communists from running in the 1996 elections, an act that, to many, smacked of the very authoritarianism he had campaigned against. Worse, the country became wracked by a large-scale and fraudulent pyramid investment scheme that cost Albanian citizens upwards of $2 billion. This represented the life savings of most citizens, and they responded with violence and rioting. Unrest continued into 1997 as voters became convinced that Berisha had personally profited from the scam, a fact underscored by legislative elections held in June of that year, when the Democratic Party was trounced and the Socialist (renamed Communist) Party took control. Berisha felt he had no recourse but to resign, which he did on June 29, 1997. "Though I have been elected from a fairer and more honest parliament than this present one," he maintained, "I declare my irrevocable resignation to return to the post of a deputy for the Democratic Party." Socialist Party secretary-general Rexhep Mejdani succeeded him to the presidency. Since his resignation, Berisha continues to enjoy considerable popularity in the ranks of the DP, to which he has been elected president twice, but his national ambitions have been stymied. In July 2001 he accused Socialist president Ilir Meta of rigging a runoff vote in the general election.

Further Reading

Biberaj, Elez. *Albania in Transition: The Rocky Road to Democracy.* Boulder, Colo.: Westview Press, 1998.

Kaser, Michael C. *Albania's Muscular Socialism.* London: Contemporary Review Co., 1983.

Destani, Bejtullah. *The Albanian Question.* London: Albanian Community Centre "Faik Konica," 1996.

Tarifa, Fatos. "Albania's Exit From Communism in the East European Context." Unpublished Ph.D. dissertation, University of North Carolina, 1998.

Vickers, Miranda, and James Pettifer. *Albania: From Anarchy to a Balkan Tragedy.* London: Hurst, 1999.

Berlusconi, Silvio (1936–) *prime minister of Italy*

Silvio Berlusconi was born in Milan on September 29, 1936, the son of a banker. As a young man, he exuded entrepreneurial spirit by writing essays for fellow students in high school and charging them in proportion to the grades they received. Having attended the University of Milan for a law degree, Berlusconi characteristically dove headfirst into the business world by establishing Edilnord, a construction company, in 1962. He was widely successful and in 1974 directed his attention to the media market by creating his own television station. By cleverly acquiring smaller, independent stations to compete with the three state-owned channels, Berlusconi quickly established a media empire for himself, becoming one of Italy's richest tycoons in the process. He further established himself in the popular press industry by acquiring no less than 30 magazines and newspapers as well as a leading publishing house. He also bought his own soccer team. By now, the handsome, dynamic Berlusconi was popularly viewed as an icon of success. At a time when Italian politics was becoming hopelessly mired in corruption and scandal, he became widely touted as a candidate for the next prime minister of Italy. His rising popularity and ability to accomplish difficult goals led the Italian media to dub him "Il Cavaliere" (the Knight).

Berlusconi had, in fact, political aspirations, but he was dissatisfied with the existing political atmosphere. He was no friend of the many leftist parties extant. However, the logical choice, the Christian Democrats, were losing popularity owing to repeated corruption charges. Displaying the boldness that characterized his business leadership, Berlusconi decided to found and finance his own party, Forza Italia (Go Italy!) in 1994. It was a decidedly pro-business, free-market, free-enterprise organization and represented a clean break with past political traditions. Berlusconi then announced his campaign for prime minister, stating: "I have decided to enter the fray of public affairs because I do not want to live in an unfree country governed by immature forces and men tied to past political and economic failure." With a net worth estimated at $10 billion, Berlusconi utilized his media assets to enact a slick, very American-style political campaign. The Italian polity had never before witnessed such style and confidence and, anxious for change, voted for the new party in droves on March 28, 1994. It was a feat that forever altered the Italian political landscape.

The four-month-old Forza Italia Party enjoyed a clear majority in the Chamber of Deputies, so Berlusconi was sworn into office on May 11, 1994. A revolution of some kind seemed in the offing, as the new leader promised to transform the Italian economy and political scene. However, Berlusconi's plans were derailed within months when Umberto Bossi of the Northern League, disenchanted with growing allegations of scandal against Berlusconi, pulled out of the coalition. Magistrates also began questioning him about his business practices, which were vast and seemingly byzantine. Rather than face a vote of no confidence in parliament, Berlusconi resigned his premiership after only seven months in office.

Within months power shifted back to the left-wing Socialists under MASSIMO D'ALEMA and GIULIANO AMATO. The latter came to office only in April 2000 in the wake of another party scandal, and the public was appreciably angry. Berlusconi judged the moment right and announced his candidacy for a second time. This was despite a 1997 conviction investment fraud and a 1998 conviction for bribing tax officials. On the latter he was sentenced to two years' imprisonment, which was never served, and in October 1998 Berlusconi was able to rally over 1 million supporters in Rome against the Socialists. Amato, in contrast, was beholden to a shaky coalition of 12 bickering leftist parties. On May 14, 2001, the irrepressible entrepreneur decisively defeated the Socialists, taking 168 seats in the upper chamber and 330 in the lower. This assured Forza Italia clear majorities and on June 10, 2001, Berlusconi was sworn in a second time.

The most pressing issue facing the Berlusconi administration is its hostility to the introduction of a new, standard currency, the euro. This resistance, coming after carefully negotiated agreements had been signed by prior administrations, threatened the entire deal. Nonetheless, Berlusconi posits himself as a "Europe-First" politician, provided that Italy has greater say in monetary matters. He also hosted the G-8 meeting at Genoa in July 2001, which witnessed the death of a young protester by police. Berlusconi was roundly criticized for police behavior, and then compounded his difficulties in Berlin that fall by declaring his belief in the superiority of Western civilization over Islam. This caused a strident protest from Islamic countries, and he apologized for the remark. However, the government's contentious resistance to the euro convinced Foreign Minister Renato Ruggerio to resign from the cabinet in January 2002. Berlusconi has since assumed the twin posts of prime minister and foreign minister for at least six months. Freewheeling and unflappable as ever, he purportedly declared, "I like the job." It remains to be seen if Berlusconi, this politician who melds business acumen, personal ambition, and political naivete, can succeed.

Further Reading

Bogart, Leo. *Media Moguls & Megalomania: Berlusconi, Murdoch and Turner.* London: Writers and Scholars International, 1994.

Bufacchi, Vittorio. *Italy since 1989: Events and Interpretations.* New York: St. Martin's Press, 1998.

Gold, Thomas W. *The Legal World and Contemporary Politics in Italy* New York: Palgrave, 2003.

Katz, Richard, and Piero Ignazi. *Italian Politics: The Year of the Tycoon.* Boulder, Colo.: Westview Press, 1996.

McCarthy, Patrick. *The Crisis of the Italian State: From the Origins of the Cold War to the Fall of Berlusconi.* New York: St. Martin's Press, 1997.

Russo, Pipo. "Berlusconi and Other Matters: The Era of 'Football Politics.'" *Journal of Modern Italian Studies.* 5, no. 3 (2000): 348–370.

Bhutto, Benazir (1953–) *prime minister of Pakistan*

Benazir Bhutto was born on June 21, 1953, in Karachi, Pakistan, the daughter of a noted political activist. Her father, Zulfikar Ali Bhutto, was founder of the Pakistan People's Party in the late 1940s, and then became a noted member of the left-wing opposition. He became prime minister of Pakistan in 1971. The product of an affluent upbringing, Bhutto was raised by an English governess before attending Harvard's Radcliffe College in 1969. She graduated cum laude with a bachelor's degree in comparative politics in 1973 before receiving similar honors from Oxford University in 1977. She returned home that same year intent upon entering the civil service, but the military under General Mohammad Zia ul-Haq overthrew the government and imprisoned her father on charges of corruption and treason. Two years later he was hung in consequence, and Bhutto became the sworn enemy of

Zia's regime. Both she and her mother endured intermittent prison sentences before being exiled to London in January 1984. Thereafter Bhutto worked assiduously to enhance the Pakistan People's Party from afar, and she stridently attacked the government for gross violations of civil and human rights. When martial law was finally lifted, she returned home in January 1986 to an adoring crowd of thousands. It being politically inexpedient to remain a single woman in a conservative Muslim nation, she accepted a traditional arranged marriage to businessman Asif Ali Zardari in December 1987. Bhutto also remained an outspoken adversary of Zia until August 1988, when he died in a plane crash. Immediately thereafter she declared her candidacy for the prime ministership. That November the Pakistan People's Party won a slim majority in parliament, and Bhutto gained appointment as the first female prime minister of an Islamic country in the 20th century.

As a woman and as a leftist, Bhutto was forced to tread carefully through the internecine labyrinth of Pakistani politics. To most Muslim fundamentalists, her success was an affront to Islam, and her positions in favor of repealing traditional laws deemed degrading to women proved another source of friction. Worse, her party was committed to a platform of providing greater aid to the poverty-stricken throngs of Pakistan, as well as other tenets of social justice. But, unlike her father, who was given to nationalizing key sectors of the economy, Bhutto believed in the free market and privatization to stimulate economic growth. Some gains had been made along political, social, and economic fronts when suddenly, on August 6, 1990, President Ghulam Ishaq Khah—backed by the military—dismissed Bhutto's government. Officially, she was charged with corruption, nepotism, and abuse of power (which may in fact have been aimed at her husband) and the following October the Pakistan People's Party suffered a humiliating defeat at the polls. Her strident conservative adversary, Mohammed NAWAZ SHARIF, became the new prime minister.

Bhutto spent the next three years attempting to rehabilitate her reputation and political fortunes. Sharif proved unable to resolve Pakistan's long-standing economic woes and, himself tainted by corruption, his administration was likewise dismissed. Bhutto again tossed her hat into the political arena, and in October 1993 she won a small majority in parliament to become prime minister again. Her second tenure in office proved as tumultuous as the first. Pakistan remained saddled by a sluggish economy and fundamentalist unease over being led by a woman. Worse, Bhutto experienced a falling-out with her brother, who went on to found a rival political movement before he was gunned down by police. The prime minister claimed to have no role in his death, but the nation erupted with widespread street protests and calls for her resignation. Amid increasing chaos, President Farooq Leghari dismissed Bhutto from office for a second time on November 5, 1996. Her husband was also arrested for taking bribes and pocketing government money. In February 1997 Sharif again won a landslide victory over the Pakistan People's Party, which was reduced to a mere 19 seats in parliament. In April 1999 a court convicted Bhutto and her husband on corruption charges, although the pair escaped and took up residence in London rather than face trial.

Bhutto remains in self-imposed exile to this day. On June 10, 2001, a judge sentenced her in absentia to three years in jail for failing to appear in court to face corruption charges. Nonetheless, she continues to watch events on the subcontinent closely and, like many outside observers, was horrified by the prospect of a possible nuclear war between India and Pakistan over the contested region of Kashmir. In November 2001 she ventured to New Delhi to confer with Indian prime minister ATAL BEHARI VAJPAYEE and opposition leader Sonia Gandhi. "We owe it to our children to build a world free of the threat of nuclear annihilation," she said, "Too much is at stake here; I want to play a role." However, she remains less than welcome in her own nation, and presiding leader General PERVEZ MUSHARRAF declared that neither Bhutto nor her rival Sharif will have a place in any future Pakistani government.

Further Reading

Akhund, Iqbal. *Trial and Error: The Advent and Eclipse of Benazir Bhutto.* Oxford: Oxford University Press, 2000.

Bhutto, Benazir. *Daughter of the East.* London: Arrow Books, 1988.

Hughes, Libby. *Benazir Bhutto: From Prison to Prime Minister.* Lincoln, Nebr.: iUniverse.com, 2000.

Lamb, Christina. *Waiting for Allah: Pakistan's Struggle for Democracy.* London: Penguin, 1992.

Shaqaf, Saeed. *Civil-Military Relations in Pakistan from Zulfikar to Benazir Bhutto.* Boulder, Colo.: Westview Press, 1997.

Bildt, Carl (1949–) *prime minister of Sweden*

Carl Bildt was born in Halmstad, Sweden, on July 15, 1949, into an aristocratic household. As a youth he visited Washington, D.C., on a school trip and was deeply impressed by the Lincoln Memorial. Thereafter he became indelibly pro-American in his personal and political outlook. Bildt attended the University of Stockholm in 1968 and that year he also joined the Moderate (Conservative) Party. After graduating in 1973, Bildt served on the staff of the Moderate Party chairman, and the following year he won election to the Stockholm county council at the age of 25. In 1976 the Social Democratic Party suffered a political loss and a conservative coalition took control of the country. Bildt thereupon became an adviser to the minister of economic affairs. In 1979 he also won a seat in the Riksdag, or national legislature, as a Moderate member. For the next three years Bildt fulfilled a number of minor bureaucratic positions until the Social Democrats returned to power in 1982, and he served as a member of the defense committee. Bildt was outspoken in his denunciation of the Soviet Union after one of its submarines ran aground in Swedish waters, and in 1983 he personally ventured to Washington, D.C., to brief members of the U.S. Navy over his committee findings. This led the leftish prime minister Olaf Palme to strongly question Bildt's patriotism and dedication to Swedish neutrality, but it also boosted his national exposure. In June 1986 Bildt's political fortunes accelerated when he was tapped to serve as head of the Moderate Party. His mission was nothing less than to topple the long-serving Social Democrats from power.

The elections of 1991 were in many respects a turning point in Sweden's modern political history. That nation had been renowned for its cradle-to-grave socialism, which gave its citizens low-cost health care, free education, and other benefits. However, this was achieved by raising tax rates to 60 percent, the highest in the industrialized world. But at the start of the decade Sweden's economy was suffering a downturn, with inflation and unemployment both on the rise. Incumbent prime minister INGVAR CARLSSON began some moderate tampering with the so-called Swedish model to make it more competitive, but Bildt felt the time was right for a radical overhaul. He advocated deep cuts in taxes and social services, along with a much smaller role for government in the lives of average citizens. Bildt also vowed to bring the powerful Swedish labor unions into line, along with privatizing inefficient state-run businesses. As the econ-

omy continued its downward spiral, many Swedish voters felt that it was, in fact, time for a change. Despite ominous warnings from the Social Democrats, they were turned out of office in their worst showing in nearly 70 years. The four-power conservative coalition under Bildt won 171 seats, and he was installed as prime minister on September 17, 1991. He was also the youngest person to ever hold that office.

Once in power, Bildt initiated sweeping changes in the Swedish national economy, including welfare cuts, tax cuts, and the sale of national industries. He proclaimed the end to the vaunted "Swedish model," stating that "the age of collectivism is now at an end." He also sought closer integration of Sweden with Western Europe. He aimed to achieve this even at the expense of the country's cherished principles of neutrality, and he was determined to join the European Union. In 1995 Sweden finally accomplished that goal, which put the country on the center stage in European affairs. Bildt, unfortunately, was not on hand to celebrate the festivities. His enthusiasm for dismantling the welfare state alarmed many voters, and, in September 1994, they voted the Social Democrats back into power under Carlsson. But a corner had been turned, nonetheless. Hereafter, neither the welfare state nor rigid neutrality has held overarching sway over Swedish political culture, and both have been continually pared with each successive administration.

Bildt has maintained an abiding interest in international affairs, no doubt buoyed by his fluency in English, French, and German. He is a member of the International Institute for Strategic Studies in London, and in 1992 he became chair of the International Democrat Union. In 1995 he was also tapped to serve as United Nations and EU representative in Bosnia during its war with Serbia, in which he roundly condemned the actions of SLOBODAN MILOŠEVIĆ. He continues as a UN member of the Balkans peacekeeping force, and in January 2001 he called for a new and more permanent peace settlement for the Albanian-dominated province of Kosovo. Bildt strongly maintains that unless the international community constructs more durable political structures for the entire region, no lasting peace or stability will ensue.

Further Reading

Bildt, Carl. *Peace Journey: The Struggle for Peace in Bosnia and the War in Bosnia-Herzegovina.* London: Weidenfeld and Nicolson, 1998.

Einhorn, Eric S. *Modern Welfare States: Scandinavian Politics and Policy in the Global Age.* Westport, Conn.: Praeger, 2003.

Fulcher, James. "The Social Democratic Model in Sweden: Termination or Restoration?" *Political Quarterly* 65 (April–June, 1994): 203–214.

Johnsson, Mats. "The House That Carl Bildt." *Scandinavian Review* 97 (Spring–Summer 1997): 10–15.

Malmberg, Mikael af. *Neutrality and State-Building in Sweden.* New York: Palgrave, 2001.

Ruin, Olaf. "Managing Coalition Governments: The Swedish Experience." *Parliamentary Affairs* 53 (October 2000): 710–720.

Bird, Lester (1938–) *prime minister of Antigua and Barbuda*

Lester Bryant Bird was born on Antigua on February 21, 1938, the son of VERE BIRD. His father gained local renown by becoming that island's first and longest-serving prime minister in 1981. The younger Bird was educated at the Antigua Grammar School and subsequently attended the University of Michigan to earn a law degree. While present he also distinguished himself in field and track, winning a bronze medal at the Pan American games. In 1969 Bird was admitted to the bar at Gray's Inn, England, where he practiced several years. In 1971 he returned to Antigua, where his father was prime minister and head of the Antiguan Labour Party (ALP). That year Bird was nominated as a senator in the upper house, where he served as opposition leader for several years. In 1976 his political fortunes increased when he gained election to the parliament. A spate of government positions, including deputy prime minister and minister of foreign affairs, followed as his father groomed him for succession. After being reelected in 1989, Bird held the office of External Affairs, Planning, and Trade. In 1994 Vere Bird stepped down as nominal leader of the ALP and his son succeeded him. Nevertheless, his father cast a very big shadow over subsequent elections that year, which saw Lester Bird elected prime minister by a large and popular margin.

In office, Bird perpetuated the Labour policies that had made his father so popular. These included particular attention to tourism and trade, which form a large segment of the island's income. So aggressively did Bird pursue foreign investors that many opposition leaders accused him of putting the island up for sale. He countered by stating that "investors bring jobs and development that have made Antigua one of the most prosperous Caribbean nations." However, the island was especially hard hit by hurricanes in 1995, with a corresponding decline in gross national product. Bird, fortunately, had attracted sufficient foreign investment to bail the economy out, and within a year it was back at previous levels, with a modest 5 percent unemployment rate. Since then he has been able to absorb refugees from the volcano-ridden island of Montserrat into the expanding jobs market.

Overall contentment with Bird's first administration may be gauged by the March 9, 1999, elections, where he was handily returned to power with 12 of 17 seats in the House of Representatives. Since then he has worked at improving tax collection procedures rather than impose new levies. "Our goal is not to take money away from the people's pockets, but to put more money in them," he said. The combination of modest tax rates, overseas investment, and efficient governance have rendered Antigua and neighboring Barbuda among the strongest economies in the region. As a sop to the politics of inclusion, Bird also regularly invites businessmen in to discuss public policy and discuss new strategies. In said manner, the prime minister feels the people will have greater say over the direction of their country.

Unfortunately, there are a few distinct dark clouds on Antigua's horizon. Part of this is family history. Earlier, Lester's younger brother, Vere, Jr., had been accused of fraudulent behavior as minister of public works. This was compounded by his arrest for drug possession and arms smuggling. In 1990 Vere, Jr. had been declared "unfit for public office," but Lester nonetheless appointed him minister of agriculture, lands and fisheries. In truth, happy little Antigua remains one of the world's biggest centers of offshore money laundering, squarely connected to the Colombian cocaine trade. In February 1997 the government closed down several Russian and Ukrainian "offshore" banks on suspicion of criminal activity. Still, both the United States and Great Britain have advised its own banks to closely scrutinize all dealings with their Antiguan opposites. The government has since become the first Caribbean nation to sign a treaty with the United States over issues of extradition and mutual legal assistance.

Further Reading

Coram, Robert. *Caribbean Time Bomb: The United States' Complicity in the Corruption of Antigua.* New York: Morrow, 1993.

Dyde, Brian. *A History of Antigua: The Unsuspected Isle.* London: Macmillan Caribbean, 2000.

Sanders, Ron, and Alan Aflak. *Antigua and Barbuda: A Little Bit of Paradise.* London: Hansib, 1994.

Bird, Vere (1909–1999) *prime minister of Antigua and Barbuda*

Vere Cornwall Bird was born on December 9, 1909, in St. Johns, Antigua and Barbuda, into an impoverished working-class family. He had acquired only a primary education by the time he joined the Salvation Army as a teenager. Bird then trained on Grenada and acquired the rudiments of organizing and public speaking that guided him throughout his later life. He also returned home angered by the discriminatory racial policies encountered throughout the English-speaking Caribbean, and in January 1939 he found the Antigua Trades and Labour Union (ATLU). Bird was elected president in 1943, and he held that post for the next 24 years. Though poorly educated, he was charismatic and, at seven feet tall, an unmistakably island personality. He gained election to the island's Legislative Council in 1945 and the following year also joined the Executive Council. In these capacities Bird emerged as the island's most important labor spokesman, and he pushed hard for ending poverty among the sugarcane workers. Antigua and Barbuda was then a British colony, but in 1951 constitutional amendments were introduced granting universal suffrage. Bird capitalized on this by forming a political wing of the ATLU, the Antigua Labour Party (ALP), and he was again elected to the Executive Council. Here he criticized the white "plantocracy" monopolizing the sugar trade and demanded better wages and working conditions for their mostly black workers. By 1956 a ministerial system had also been adopted, and Bird became minister of trade and production.

In 1960 the pace of movement toward self-governance and independence quickened. Bird served as chief minister and minister of planning, and elections that year brought all 10 seats on the Legislative Council under ALP control. Bird next pushed for associated statehood from Great Britain, which was achieved in 1967, and he became the island's first premier. Under this arrangement, Antigua and Barbuda conducted their own internal affairs while Britain restricted itself to defense and foreign policy matters. That year Bird also stepped down as head of the ATLU and led the ALP as

a separate political organization. A rival organization, the Progressive Labour Movement (PLM) also took root and Bird experienced a reversal of fortunes in 1971 when the ALP was badly defeated in local elections. He remained out of power until 1976 but nevertheless bounced back, and he participated in intense negotiations with Great Britain for independence. This transpired on November 1, 1981, and Bird, in recognition of his status as the "father of the country," became the first prime minister.

Once empowered, Bird continued the economic policies that served the islands so well. He was determined to break their dependence upon the wildly fluctuating sugar market, and he went to great lengths diversifying the economy. His first priority was building up a profitable tourist trade, which remains the island's greatest single source of revenue. Bird was also strongly committed to preserving and strengthening the free-market atmosphere, and he advocated privatization and an influx of foreign investment. Bird was also one of the original architects of the Caribbean Free Trade Association, which in 1973 was renamed the Caribbean Common Market (CARICOM). And, mindful of his limited education, he initiated the founding of several secondary schools, and education remains free to the public. Through Bird's economic foresight, Antigua and Barbuda have sustained growth rates of 7 percent annually, one of the highest in the region. They also enjoy one of the Caribbean's best standards of living.

Bird remained the country's most popular politician, and he was reelected prime minister in 1984 and 1989. However, his attempts to establish a family dynasty proved more controversial. Both of his sons, Vere, Jr., and LESTER BIRD, were implicated in various corruption schemes, but their father refused to dismiss them from high office. A crisis was reached in April 1990 when Vere, Jr., was convicted of selling arms to the Colombian drug cartels and was banned for life from holding public office. Bird's endless search for foreign investment also led to the rise of numerous "offshore" banks that the U.S. government has accused of routinely laundering drug money. Despite this criticism, the prime minister remained indelibly pro-American and conservative in outlook, and in 1983 he supported President Ronald Reagan's invasion of Grenada by supplying troops. By March 1994, "Papa Bird" was declining physically and he stepped aside in favor of his son, Lester. Vere Bird died on June 28, 1999, at the age of 89, a beloved national figure. His public funeral was attended by thousands of mourners, vying with each other to bid farewell to the father of their nation. At the time of his passing, Bird was also the longest-serving head of state in the English-speaking eastern Caribbean.

Further Reading

Coram, Robert. *Caribbean Time Bomb: The United States' Complicity in the Corruption of Antigua.* New York: Morrow, 1993.

Midgett, Douglas. *Eastern Caribbean Elections, 1950–1982.* Iowa City: University of Iowa Press, 1983.

O'Marde, Dorbreve. *A Decade of Development: Antigua and Barbuda Celebrate Its 10th Anniversary of Independence, 1981–1991.* St. John's, Antigua: I. Archibald and Associates, 1992.

Payne, Douglas W. *The 1994 Antigua and Barbuda Elections.* Washington, D.C.: CSIS America's Program, 1994.

Sanders, Ronald. *Antigua and Barbuda, 1966–1981: Transition, Trial, Triumph.* St. John's, Antigua: Archives Committee, 1984.

Biya, Paul (1933–) *president of Cameroon*

Paul Biya was born in the southern Cameroon village of Mvomeka'a on February 13, 1933, a member of the Boulou minority tribe residing there. At the age of seven he was enrolled at a Catholic mission at Ndem, where he excelled academically. Though originally trained for the priesthood, Biya elected to attend the Lycée General Leclerc in France, and he subsequently took advanced degrees in law and political science from the University of Paris in 1960. He then studied at the Institute of Overseas Studies before returning to Cameroon in 1962. There he was invited to join the government under President Ahmadou Ahidjo, the country's first president. Cameroon, then and now, remains a country split along a north/south axis. The product of British and French colonialism, the two sections were joined together in 1961, with Christians dominating the south and Muslims predominant in the north. Cameroonians are further divided along linguistic lines, with English competing with French for political favor. Biya nonetheless held a succession of increasingly significant posts in the government, rising to prime minister in 1975. This made him the legal successor to the ailing Ahidjo. On November 6, 1982, Ahidjo stepped down for health reasons and Biya gained appointment as Cameroon's second president. He was distinguished from his immediate predecessor by being urbane, versed in Greek and Latin, and a devotee of classical music.

It is not know what arrangement the two men worked out beforehand, for Ahidjo retained his post as head of the Cameroon National Union (CNU), the country's only legal party. If through this expedient he intended to manipulate the scholarly, worldly Biya as his puppet, the scheme backfired completely. The new leader displayed an unpardonable degree of independence from his former mentor, and in 1983 and 1984, Ahidjo, now exiled to France, was implicated in two failed coup attempts against the president. Biya countered by abolishing the old CNU in favor of a new organization, the Cameroon People's Democratic Movement (CDPM), which he tightly controlled. At first, Biya's tenure was welcomed by his constituents, who reelected him by a large margin on January 14, 1984. However, having firmly ensconced himself in power, his regime quickly became an exercise in self-enrichment.

In truth, Biya has ruled Cameroon with an iron fist for 14 years. He has cracked down on all political opposition and only grudgingly allowed the presence of other political parties. His reign also closely corresponds with a decline in Cameroon's overall economic health. Commencing in 1984, when oil prices sank markedly, a strong recession hit the country. The prices of essential exports like cocoa, cotton, coffee, and palm oil also dropped precipitously and resulted in nine consecutive years of economic contraction. Part of the problem was the large and thoroughly corrupt Cameroonian government, overstuffed with Biya's cronies, who skimmed 30 percent of business profits for their own use. Biya himself is estimated to be worth at least $75 million, and he owns, in additional to two Boeing 747 jumbo jets for his personal use, several large estates in France and Switzerland.

Naturally, the people of Cameroon grew restive under such blatant corruption, and they commenced agitating for political pluralism and change. Biya allowed the first multiparty elections in 1990, but he also skillfully manipulated the mass media, which he by and large controls, to his own ends. Consequently, in 1997 he was reelected for a second seven-year term with little difficulty, owing to the fact that all opposition parties boycotted the process. Furthermore, protests and street demonstrations were brutally repressed by force, giving Cameroon one of the worst human rights records in Africa. A major sticking point in Cameroon politics is the schism between English- and French-speaking sections of the country. Biya, as a Francophone, does everything in his power to curry favor with the French-speaking parts of the country through patronage. Such favoritism promoted secessionist movements in predominately English-speaking parts of the nation, which were suppressed by force. Moreover, linguistic resentment crystallized in the presidential campaign of John Fru Ndi, an English speaker from the north, to run against him twice in national elections. He subsequently organized boycotts when Biya refused to have the process certified by an independent electoral commission. However, to lessen charges of favoritism toward adherents of French, Biya arranged for Cameroon to join the British Commonwealth. Meanwhile he continues to masterfully subvert the democratic process in Cameroon for his personal gain and to the detriment of his people.

Further Reading

Chiabi, Emmanuel. *The Making of Modern Cameroon.* Lanham, Md.: University Press of America, 1997.

Gwellem, Jerome F. *Paul Biya: Hero of the New Deal.* Limbe, Cameroon: Gwellem Publications, 1984.

Takougang, Joseph, and Milton Krieger. *African State and Society in the 1990s: Cameroon's Political Crusade.* Boulder, Colo.: Westview Press, 1998.

Walker, S. Tjip. "Both Pretense and Promise: The Political Economy of Privatization in Africa." Unpublished Ph.D. dissertation, Indiana University, 1998.

Bizimungu, Pasteur (1951–) *president of Rwanda*

Pasteur Bizimungu was born in Bushiri, Rwanda, in 1951, a member of the Hutu tribe. This is one of two major tribal divisions in Rwanda, the other being the minority Tutsi. In large measure, ethnic polarization between these two competing groups, along with occasional outbreaks of violence, has been the defining characteristic of Rwandan political life. Bizimungu was more fortunate than many of his impoverished brethren by attending the National University of Rwanda in 1973, and he subsequently received his master's degree in France. He then returned home to function as a civil servant, and in 1990 he became a manager for the state-run utility, Electro-Gas. It was while working in this capacity that Bizimungu grew conscious of the need to change the corrupt, Hutu-dominated regime of General

JUVÉNAL HABYARIMANA, who came to power in 1973. As astute businessman, Bizimungu pressed Habyarimana for sweeping changes at Electro-Gas, including raising rates, reducing the payroll, and cutting off debtors, but the general refused. This convinced him of the need for sweeping political reform, despite the fact that fellow Hutu tribesmen were the chief beneficiaries of Habyarimana's rule. By 1990 angry Tutsis and disillusioned Hutus were pressing for multiparty democratic elections and they formed a dissenting group in exile, the Rwandan Patriotic Front (RPF). In 1990 Bizimungu denounced Habyarimana's nepotism and ethnic discrimination, and he helped convince RPF leaders that his grip on power was tenuous. That same year the RPF began the first of a long series of protracted guerrilla attacks against government forces in an attempt to bring about badly needed reforms.

On April 6, 1994, an unforeseen catalyst unleashed a human tragedy of unthinkable proportions. That month General Habyarimana and CYPRIEN NTARIYAMIRA, the president of neighboring Burundi (both Hutus) died in a plane crash. Their deaths were blamed upon the Tutsi-dominated RPF, and Hutu military and paramilitary forces went on a blood-spilling rampage. For three months they murdered thousands of Tutsis and moderate Hutus while the world looked on but did nothing. The death toll reached nearly 1 million before the RPF under General PAUL KAGAME managed to defeat government forces and subdue the countryside. Renegade Hutu, meanwhile, fled the country and sought refuge in the neighboring region of Congo. Peace was finally restored on June 15, 1994, and the killing subsided. The RPF was determined not to repeat past mistakes and installed a new government with an admixture of Hutus and Tutsis. Bizimungu, given his ethnic background and long association with the rebels, was then appointed president of Rwanda while Kagame, a Tutsi, became vice president and minister of defense. It was hoped such multiethnic, power-sharing arrangements would be a symbolic gesture of reconciliation, and encourage a more peaceful future.

Bizimungu inherited a nation on the brink of collapse. Nearly 10 percent of its population had been brutally murdered while a quarter more were refugees scattered about Central Africa. "Our nation is in pieces," he declared. "We must teach new values to the population, based on respect for universal rights." Moreover, the fighting devastated what little infrastructure existed beforehand. The civil service, running water, electricity, and telecommunications all had to be restored quickly if Rwanda were to be running as a nation again. The country also faced a potentially destabilizing situation in the form of thousands of armed Hutu militiamen still residing in Congo, and who made occasional guerrilla attacks upon RPF forces at the behest of President LAURENT KABILA. Bizimungu, for his part, appealed to the international community for help, and, in December 1997, U.S. secretary of state Madeleine Albright arrived, pledging several million dollars in aid. President BILL CLINTON also toured Rwanda in March 1998, signifying Rwanda's return to the fold of civilized nations. However, Bizimugu proved less successful addressing the issues of corruption and privilege. He skirmished continually with Vice President Paul Kagame and other senior leaders of the RPF until March 23, 2000, when he resigned in disgust over "the impunity of a powerful Tutsi clique, and unfair reprisals and corruption witch hunts against prominent Hutus." Kagame then advanced to succeed him. The following June Bizimungu helped form a new political opposition at home, the Party for Democracy and Renewal, which was outlawed by the ruling regime. In April 2002 Bizimungu was arrested at his home on what authorities claim is illegal political activity. If convicted of such charges, he faces up to 10 years' imprisonment.

Further Reading

Adelman, Howard, and Astri Suhrke. *The Path of Genocide: The Rwanda Crisis from Uganda to Zaire.* New Brunswick, N.J.: Transaction Publishers, 2000.

Des Forges, Alison. *"Leave None to Tell the Story;" Genocide in Rwanda.* New York: Human Rights Watch, 1999.

Khan, Shaharyar M. *The Shallow Graves of Rwanda.* New York: I. B. Tauris, 2000.

Kuperman, Alan J. *The Limits of Humanitarian Intervention: Genocide in Rwanda.* Washington, D.C.: Brookings Institute Press, 2001.

Mamdani, Mahmood. *When Victims Become Killers: Colonialism, Nativism, and the Genocide in Rwanda.* Princeton, N.J.: Princeton University Press, 2001.

Blair, Tony (1953–) *prime minister of Great Britain*

Anthony Charles Lynton Blair was born in Edinburgh, Scotland, on May 6, 1953. His father, a barrister (lawyer) was a political activist within the Tory (Conservative) Party, and indelibly impressed upon his son the important of public service. Blair was subsequently educated at Durham Choristers before attending the elite Fetters College in Edinburgh. His fine academic performance landed him at St. John's College, Oxford, where he pursued a law degree. When not studying, Blair also devoted inordinate amounts of time playing in a rock band, the Ugly Rumors. He was then admitted to the bar in London, where he met his wife, Cherie Booth, a fellow barrister, and the two married in 1980. He also became a committed Christian and joined the Labour Party out of a profound desire to help the disadvantaged. In 1982 Blair was defeated in his first election bid, but the following year he gained a seat in the House of Commons. His youth, intellect, and boyish good looks soon made him a party favorite and he commenced a stellar rise through the ranks.

At this time the Labour Party was in the doldrums politically for, throughout the late 1970s and into the 1980s, they had been badly drubbed by Tories under Margaret Thatcher and her successor, John Major. On July 21, 1994, Blair replaced John Smith as the youngest-ever head of the party. Being by nature an astute political observer, he divined that his party was completely off-message for the electorate of the times. Moreover, the centerpiece of his leadership campaign revolved around radically redefining both Labour and its approach to government. Taking on established interests like unions, Blair began arguing for a decidedly centrist approach to politics, a stance much closer to the average British voter. This entailed jettisoning some of Labour's most cherish ideological assumptions about the welfare state. Foremost among these was the controversial Clause Four in the party constitution, which mandated a communist-style "collective ownership of the means of production." Planks calling for full employment, welfare perks, and unilateral nuclear disarmament were also similarly discarded. Henceforth, Blair's "New Labour" stood for free markets, privatization, low taxes, and responsible spending. And, having carefully studied and analyzed U.S. president BILL CLINTON's 1992 win by co-opting Republican Party issues, Blair promised to be both "tough on crime and tough on the causes of crime." Considering the ideological obstacles in his path, Blair's remake of the Labour Party was one of the most impressive feats in modern British political history. Moreover, the country was ready for a change.

Tony Blair *(Foreign and Commonwealth Office)*

The ensuing election of 1997 was a resounding victory for the Labour Party, which had been in opposition for nearly two decades. Their candidates captured a record 165 seats in the House of Commons, which placed them in a firm majority. The well-heeled Conservatives, complacent after years of power, were also tainted by scandals and simply unable to fathom the nature of their opposition. In essence, Blair assured voters that Labour would be fiscally stringent and, in fact, would maintain the Tory monetary and spending policies already in place. This meant no new taxes, no increase in government programs, and utmost respect for values such as initiative and individual responsibility. Blair's strict emphasis on fiscal discipline, coupled with a willingness to break with tradition, resulted in his election as Britain's youngest prime minister of the 20th century on May 1, 1997.

Once in office, Blair wrought no new changes, but he did alter the direction of government services in providing greater access to education and opportunity for health care for those less fortunate. "Power without principle is barren," he affirmed, "but principle without power is futile. This is a party of government, and I will lead it as a party of government." But the emphasis now was on degree, not scope. He also followed through on a pledge to allow creation of parliaments in Scotland and Wales with limited taxing ability and a sense of regional sovereignty. In a major shift, the British government now took an activist role in promoting peace talks between Catholic and Protestant factions in Northern Ireland. Consequently, in December 1998, both Blair and his Irish counterpart, BERTIE AHERN, signed an accord that promoted a joint Catholic-Protestant governing arrangement in the six counties. The militant Irish Republican Army, however, refused to agree to disarm, although further negotiations in March 2000 prompted them to permit open inspections of their arms dumps. Finally, Blair as a politician is infinitely more receptive, but not totally committed, to the notion of integrating Britain's economy and currency with its fellow European Union members. To this end he introduced the country's first minimum wage law and a host of employees' rights legislation to bring England up to par with other nations of Europe.

Blair was also determined to maintain the "great" in Great Britain, at least on the international scene. Following the September 11, 2001, destruction of the World Trade Center in New York City, in which scores of British nationals died, he quickly and strongly announced complete support for an all-out war against international terrorism. In concert with U.S. president GEORGE W. BUSH, Blair committed air and special forces assets for the war in Afghanistan. With the Taliban regime toppled, he also pledged a sizable British contingent to be deployed for peacekeeping purposes. This stance has resurrected England's visibility as a viable military power and reaffirmed its more traditional role as America's most trusted strategic partner. Since the attack, he has constantly shuttled abroad seeking broad coalition support for Bush's war on terror, while at the same time placating Arab allies by calling for creation of a Palestinian state. It was a bravura performance seldom equaled by British leaders of the past 50 years. His high-powered approach to leadership was also widely applauded in Europe, and imitated by GERHARD SCHROEDER of Germany and WIM KOK of the Netherlands. Having proven his credentials as a strong, decisive leader in times of adversity, and buoyed by the twin benefits of a sound economy and national popularity, Blair easily remained in office following elections in 2001.

In the fall of 2002 Blair incurred considerable controversy in Labour circles for his unabashed support of President George Bush's bellicosity towards Iraqi dictator SADDAM HUSSEIN. As war became more imminent, Robin Cook, Blair's foreign secretary, resigned in protest on March 17, 2003. Nonetheless, and in spite of polls indicating 64 percent of public opinion opposed to war, British forces were in the forefront of Operation Iraqi Freedom when it commenced three days later. "In refusing to give up his weapons of mass destruction, Saddam gave us no choice," Blair stated, "now that the war had begun, it will be seen through to the end."

Further Reading

Abse, Leo. *Tony Blair: The Man behind the Smile*. London: Robson, 2001.

Blair, Tony. *New Britain: My Vision of a Young Country*. London: Fourth Estate, 1996.

Rentoul, John. *Tony Blair: Prime Minister*. London: Warner, 2001.

Seyd, Patrick, and Paul Whitely. *New Labour's Grassroots: The Transformation of the Labour Party Membership*. New York: Palgrave, 2002.

Bolger, Jim (1935–) *prime minister of New Zealand*

James Brendan Bolger was born on May 31, 1935, in Taranaki, New Zealand, into a staunchly Roman Catholic family of Irish immigrants. He attended school until 15 before quitting to work on the family farm. He married and set up his own farm in 1963, becoming wealthy by breeding sheep and cattle. Given his naturally conservative outlook, Bolger joined the National Party, and in 1972 he successfully stood for a seat in parliament. The National Party took power in 1975, and Prime Minister Robert Muldoon appointed him to parliamentary undersecretary to various government ministries. Three years later Bolger joined the cabinet as minister of labor, in which he applied his conservative philosophy with a vengeance. His most lasting mark was in abolishing compulsory trade unionism, a hallmark of New Zealand labor law since the 1930s. However, the National Party was turned out of office by 1984, and he became deputy leader in opposition. The party then began looking for more effective leadership, and in 1986 Bolger was nominated party chairman. He served there until October 17, 1990, when voter discontent placed the National Party back in power. Bolger was sworn in as prime minister the following day, becoming New Zealand's first Catholic head of state in half a century.

Prior to 1990, New Zealand boasted one of the world's most extensive—and costly—welfare states. Bolger was pledged to a conservative platform promising deep cuts across the board in health, education, housing, and defense. In April 1991 he followed through with additional reductions in social security along with cutbacks in unemployment and sickness benefits. That July Bolger shepherded through the Employment Contract Act, which negated the ability of unions to negotiate wages and conditions and led to widespread strikes and protests. Bolger, however, continued with various and painful cost-cutting measures aimed at improving New Zealand's competitiveness. Various politicians and ministers, alarmed at the prospects of their own political survival, changed parties or resigned from the cabinet. At one point Bolger sacked Winston Peters, minister of Maori affairs, because of his continual criticism. Undaunted, Peters subsequently founded his own New Zealand First Party. By December 1991, Bolger's poll ratings were at 5.5 percent, the lowest ever recorded for a sitting prime minister. However, he remained stalwart in the face of public discontent throughout the 1993 elections. Surprisingly, the National Party retained power, although their majority in the House of Representatives was reduced to a single seat.

Another unusual outcome of the 1993 elections was adoption of a German-style proportional representation system, which guaranteed seats for small parties such as Peters's New Zealand First Party. After winning the 1996 elections, Bolger was forced to ally himself with Peters's New Zealand First and small Christian Democratic parties to stay in power. This was the first coalition arrangement for New Zealand since 1935 and it placed additional strains upon the National Party to seize an outright majority. Happily, despite the rancor that Bolger's austerity measures incurred, the national economy rebounded, growing at annual rates of 4 percent while unemployment dropped to 6 percent. Emboldened by success, Bolger expanded privatization efforts by offering more state-owned utilities to the marketplace. His administration further distinguished itself from Labour predecessors by seeking improved relations with the United States, a traditional ally. That alliance had been strained since 1985 when New Zealand withheld docking rights from warships if they carried nuclear weapons, something U.S. naval vessels neither confirmed nor denied. Bolger allowed the popular ban to remain, although he established better relations with President BILL CLINTON and high-level military contacts resumed. Bolger proved equally accommodating toward the conservative Australian government of JOHN HOWARD, and the two leaders struck up an amicable rapport.

Unfortunately, many conservatives were unhappy about the National Party's marriage to New Zealand First and, with poll numbers sinking, they resolved to right the matter. In November 1997 transport minister JENNY SHIPLEY waited until Bolger was out of the country for two weeks before circulating among fellow conservatives, collecting signatures of support. When Bolger returned, Shipley presented him with her list, promising a fight for the party leadership if he did not stand down. Sensing defeat, Bolger resigned from office on December 8, 1997, while Shipley went on to become the nation's first female prime minister. After many years in retirement Bolger was appointed ambassador to the United States by Prime Minister HELEN CLARK of the Labour Party. He occupies this post at present.

Further Reading

Bolger, Jim. *Bolger: A View from the Top: My Seven Years as Prime Minister.* New York: Viking, 1998.

Boston, Jonathan. *From Campaign to Coalition: New Zealand's First Grand Election under Proportional Representation.* Palmerston North, N.Z.: Dunmore Press, 1997.

Dawe, Rufus. *From Hope to Glory: The New Zealand Economic Miracle, 1992–1995.* Wellington, N.Z.: Fighting Cock Press, 1996.

Miller, Raymond. *New Zealand: Government and Politics.* New York: Oxford University Press, 2001.

Vowles, J. "New Zealand." *European Journal of Political Research* 24 (December 1993): 505–513.

Bolkiah, Muda Hassanal (1946–)
sultan of Brunei

Muda Hassanal Bolkiah was born on July 15, 1946, in Bandar Seri Begawan, capital of the Sultanate of Brunei. This tiny Islamic state has existed since the 13th century and has been ruled continuously under the same family. After 1844 it functioned as a protectorate of Great Britain, which lasted until the late 20th century when independence was finally achieved. It has since

been officially renamed Brunei Darussalam, or Brunei, Abode of Peace. Bolkiah was educated through private tutors at home before attending private schools in Kuala Lumpur, Malaysia. He then returned home and was made crown prince in 1961, at the age of 15, to succeed his father, Sultan Muda Omar Ali Sifudden. At this time, Brunei was being pressured by Great Britain to become more democratic and to allow political activity. The sultan did so only reluctantly and for good reason. In 1962 the Brunei People's Party was formed, which captured control of the new legislature and began agitating for the fall of the sultanate. An armed insurrection then commenced, which was only put down with the aid of British troops. A state of emergency was declared, forbidding all political activity, which is still enforced today. Meanwhile, Bolkiah was allowed to visit Britain where he enrolled at the elite military academy at Sandhurst. His studies were interrupted in 1966, however, when his father abdicated the throne. Bolkiah was then enthroned as the 29th sultan of Brunei on August 1, 1967, amid much national celebration.

Brunei is a unique country and Bolkiah a unique leader. His nation, though small, is extremely wealthy owing to the great oil and natural gas resources it commands. Consequently, the sultan enjoys an estimated personal worth in excess of $40 billion and, on a scale commensurate with his title as the world's third-richest man, has two wives, countless cars, horses, airplanes, and a 1,788-room mansion—the largest ever built. Despite his vast wealth and political power, he remains personable and on friendly terms with the inhabitants of his nation-state. The great wealth accumulated from oil has spilled over to the benefit the general populace, for they enjoy one of the highest standards of living in the world. The per capita income averages over $20,000, and includes free access to health care, free education, no income taxes, and interest-free loans for consumers. This emphasis on material wealth and physical well-being has canceled out the public cry for greater political participation. Presently, there is none in the offing.

Like his father, Bolkiah has resisted all attempts at democratization, which would spell the end of his family's reign. In fact, he adheres to a closely prescribed Islamic governance of the country that discourages social change and enforces the status quo. However, he is intolerant of religious fundamentalism and will not allow militant, religious activity to flourish. His only flirtation with democracy occurred in 1985, when he allowed creation of the Brunei National Democratic Party. This body no sooner came into being than it, too, agitated for the abolition of the sultanate, and it was dissolved in 1988. The only other source of potential social unrest is the sizable ethnic Chinese population, which are predominately merchants. These are not counted as citizens, however, and they receive none of the opulent benefits accorded native Malays. Individuals who make trouble and who are not citizens find themselves usually deported back to Taiwan or Hong Kong, and thus are dispensed with peacefully.

For all its wealth, Brunei is a tiny, almost defenseless strip of territory. Since achieving its independence from Great Britain on January 1, 1984, it has depended on a small garrison of British troops to maintain security. Bolkiah has also extended his hand to neighboring countries such as Singapore, Indonesia, and Malaysia, and he has signed mutual defense alliances with them as well as cooperative economic agreements. These states, in return, have formally renounced any territorial ambitions at Brunei's expense. The sultan is also aware that Brunei's oil resources are likely to be exhausted within the next two decades, well within his lifetime. Therefore, he has embarked on a national course of diversification toward high technology and computers, thus converting Brunei into a center for banking, trade, and finance. His family has also endured greater public scrutiny after it was revealed that Jefri Bolkiah, the sultan's younger brother, had embezzled several million dollars of public money in pursuit of an outlandish lifestyle. Thus Brunei, for better or worse, continues to be ruled by Bolkiah and his immediate family, who hold all key government positions. This last of the world's absolute monarchs continues enjoying the respect and affection of his subjects, but the sultan performs a precarious balancing act between the need for innovation and the urge to preserve tradition.

Further Reading

Bartholomew, James. *The Richest Man in the World.* London: Viking, 1989.

"Bolkiah, Sir Muda Hassanal." *Current Biography Yearbook* (1989): 54–58.

Bolkiah, Mohammed. *Time and the River: Brunei Darussalam, 1947–2000: A Memoir.* Begawan: Brunei Press, 2000.

Chalfont, Arthur. *By God's Will: A Portrait of the Sultan of Brunei.* New York: Weidenfeld and Nicolson, 1989.

Gunn, Geofrey C. *Language, Power, and Ideology in Brunei Darussalam.* Athens: Ohio University Center for International Studies, 1997.

Bondevik, Kjell (1947–) *prime minister of Norway*

Kjell Magne Bondevik was born on September 3, 1947, in Molde, Norway. He matured in a rural area, inculcating the deeply held conservative values of the Norwegian countryside. Accordingly, Bondevik attended the Free Faculty of Theology at the University of Oslo, and in 1979 he became an ordained Lutheran minister. He also became interested in politics and, while still in school, served as chairman of the Norwegian Young Christian Democrats (KrF). Bondevik proved adept at politics and in 1973 he gained election to the Storting (parliament) at the age of 26. He rose rapidly through the party infrastructure, becoming vice chairman in 1975 and finally chairman by 1983. Three years later he served as deputy prime minister in a coalition government with Kare Willoch. However, at this time Norwegian politics were dominated by the Labor Party's prime minister, GRO HARLEM BRUNDTLAND, one of the most successful figures in Norway's history. For conservatives it spelled a decade in the wilderness as they vied among varying small parties to form an alternative government. Their opportunity arose when Brundtland unexpectedly stepped down in October 1996 and appointed JAGLAND THORBJOERN her successor. The national economy boomed under his stewardship, especially from the sale of oil and natural gas. However, many Norwegians felt that affluence and government spending were undermining traditional family values, a sentiment playing directly into conservative hands. Moreover, Thorbjoern declared his intention to resign if Labor did not do better than 39.6 percent in the 1997 elections. When, as expected, Labor voting totals declined slightly, he surrendered his office without ceremony. Bondevik, now viewed as one of the nations' most promising leaders, was then invited to form a government. He did so skillfully, grafting a viable minority coalition among the Christian Democrats, Liberals, and Center Party. On October 17, 1997, he was sworn in as the first conservative prime minister in over a decade. "Just a short time ago, many people did not believe we would ever succeed in making a governmental declaration," Bondevik stated, "now we are sitting here larger than life."

Norway is one of the world's wealthiest nations and, as the third-largest oil exporter after Russia and Saudi Arabia, can afford to sustain one of Europe's most generous welfare states. Given the sound economy at home, Bondevik's primary concern was events abroad. Many Scandinavian countries were in a heated rush to join the European Union (EU) for all the economic benefits it offered member states. However, Bondevik steadfastly opposed EU membership owing to the threat it posed to numerous fishing villages and small farms dotting the Norwegian political landscape. However, Norway is a member of the European Economic Area, which allows greater access to EU markets without subjecting the country to strict EU regulations. This arrangement suits the independent-minded Norwegian polity. The government also emphasized a more conservative, family-oriented agenda, including increased pensions for the elderly, better education, and a foreign policy predicated upon human rights. Bondevik was not shy about utilizing social benefits to his own advantage, and in 1998 he took over three weeks' sick leave to mitigate a well-publicized bout with depression. And, despite his conservative leanings, Bondevik evinced concerned over ecological issues. In March 2000 he argued against constructing several gas-fired power plants because of the pollution they spewed into the air. When the measure passed over his protests, he resigned from office and was replaced by Labor's chairman, JENS STOLTENBERG.

Bondevik served as head of the opposition for several months until new elections occurred on October 16, 2001. Labor, beset by criticism over high taxes and an indifferent civil service, suffered their biggest defeat in nearly a century, dropping from 65 to 43 seats in the 165-seat Storting. Bondevik was exultant and readily drew up another minority coalition as the new prime minister. "We have a good political platform," he said. "We are going to work from a long-term perspective, but as a minority government we will always have to be ready to leave." He then pledged to cut deeply into existing tax rates—among the highest in Europe—place greater emphasis on privatization, and pave the way for increased competition in the public sector. Moreover, Bondevik is determined to elevate Norway's presence on the international scene. In January 2002 he visited Shanghai, China, to sign several measures for enhancing trade. The following month Norwegian representatives arrived in Sri Lanka, where they have played a crucial role arbitrating the bloody rebellion there by Tamil Tigers. "There

can be no misunderstanding about our reasons for being involved," the priestly prime minister declared. "We only want to bring peace to the people of Sri Lanka." But Bondevik, mindful that his political strength is based in the countryside and along the coasts, remains committed to keeping Norway out of the EU for the time being. He continually advises his Liberal Party and Center Party allies that their political survival depends on it.

Further Reading

Baldershim, Harold, and Jean Pascal Daloz, eds. *Political Leadership in a Global Age: The Experience of Norway & France.* Burlington, Vt.: Ashgate, 2003.

Christensen, Tom, and Guy Peters. *Structure, Culture, and Governance: A Comparison of Norway and the United States.* Lanham, Md.: Rowman and Littlefield, 1999.

Einhorn, Eric S. *Modern Welfare States: Scandinavian Politics & Policy in the Global Age.* Westport, Conn.: Praeger, 2003.

Heidar, Knut. *Norway: Center and Periphery.* Boulder, Colo.: Westview Press, 2000.

Matthews, Donald R., and Henry Valens. *Parliamentary Representation: The Case of the Norwegian Storting.* Columbus: Ohio State University Press, 1999.

Rommetveldt, Hilmar. *The Rise of Parliament: Studies in Norwegian Parliamentary Government.* Portland, Oreg.: Frank Cass, 2003.

Shaffer, William R. *Politics, Parties, and Parliaments: Political Change in Norway.* Columbus: Ohio State University Press, 1998.

Bongo, Omar (1935–) *president of Gabon*

Albert Bernard Bongo was born in Lewal, Haut-Ogoodué province, Gabon, on December 30, 1935. At that time his country, located on the Atlantic coast of West Africa, was a French colony. Bongo received his primary education at Brazzaville in neighboring Congo, and he was conscripted into the French air force as a lieutenant in 1958. He mustered out two years later and found work with the Ministry of Foreign Affairs in 1962. This brought him to the attention of Leon Mba, the first elected president of Gabon, who subsequently appointed him to positions of authority in ministries dealing with tourism and national defense. Bongo favorably impressed Mba, who made him vice president in 1966, and he began grooming him for the succession.

He was formally elected to this office in March 1967 and, after Mba died of illness on November 28, 1967, Bongo became the second president of Gabon. His uninterrupted reign of nearly 40 years establishes him as one of the longest-serving heads of state in recent times.

Prior to Bongo's ascension, Gabon had been established as one-party state after achieving independence from France in 1960. However, intent on securing better control of his charge, the new president formally dissolved the existing party and replaced it with a new organization, the Gabonese Democratic Party (PDG) in 1968. This facilitated domination of the national polity but, in Bongo's view, also reduced the squabbling and tension between the 40 distinct language and ethnic groups comprising Gabon. Unlike most African nations, Gabon enjoys an abundance of natural resources, especially uranium and oil. Bongo, well versed in the intricacies of the free-market economy, allowed capitalism to flourish through free enterprise and foreign investment. The result was one of the continent's highest per capita incomes, a relatively high standard of living, and, by African standards, an unusually peaceful regime. "Give me a sound economy," Bongo declared, "and I will give you stable politics." However, this was achieved by maintaining a strictly authoritarian state, which discouraged political pluralism and crushed dissent outright. Bongo's control of state media, his great personal revenues, and his entrenched system of patronage have rendered him nearly immune from effective opposition. Not surprisingly, in 1973, 1979, 1986, and 1993, he was "reelected" to office despite claims of widespread voter fraud. In 1973, he also converted to Islam and adopted the name Omar.

In the 1980s, the falling price of oil rocked the erstwhile thriving Gabon economy, and created a great deal of political unrest. Bongo responded to force, as usual, but spurred on by his two largest trading partners, France and the United States, he finally acquiesced to the inevitability of a multiparty system. Naturally, his control of national resources was directed at keeping the fractured opposition parties thoroughly divided, and in 1993 and 1998 the PDG easily retained power. His ability to keep the economy growing apparently muted most domestic unrest for strikes and protests, while common, were localized and never widespread. Furthermore, he is acutely aware that oil reserves, the mainstay of his economy, are running out. He is therefore very active in promoting and directing economic diversifica-tion to wean Gabon from its dependence on oil and timber exports. The privatization of state-run agencies such as energy and water are also expected to increase revenues and, because Bongo owns controlling interests in both, he is expected to prosper and maintain his opulent lifestyle.

With such a relatively stable and prosperous country to back him, Bongo emerged as a conspicuous player on the international scene. He forged close economic ties to France and allowed that country to help develop Gabon's petroleum and mining industries. He was also firmly in the Western camp throughout the cold war, which brought him a favorable response—and financial aid—from the United States. Bongo also exerted influence as an arbiter during the internecine fighting in and around Central Africa. He has hosted numerous multinational conferences with a view to promoting regional peace and stability, particularly between the Republic of Congo and the Democratic Republic of the Congo. This is essential to Gabon as the Congo River is a major commercial artery and sensitive to military interdiction. "Those who obstruct the river traffic are looking for war," he warned the regime of LAURENT KABILA in October 2000. Bongo has consequently earned high praise from the Organization of African Unity, and he enjoys a measure of international respect and visibility not usually accorded despots ruling developing nations. Given the relative tranquillity of Gabon, his surprising suppression of tribalism and regionalism within its borders, and his tight control of its political machinery, Bongo seems destined to remain the head of his country for some time to come.

Further Reading

Barnes, James. *Gabon: Beyond the Colonial Legacy.* Boulder, Colo.: Westview Press, 1992.

Decalo, Samuel. *The Stable Minority: Civilian Rule in Africa, 1960–1990.* Gainesville, Fla.: FAP Books, 1998.

Ngolet, François. "Ideological Manipulation and Political Longevity—The Power of Omar Bongo since 1967." *African Studies Review* 43 (September 2000): 55–73.

Reed, Michael C., and James F. Barnes, eds. *Culture, Ecology, & Politics in Gabon's Rainforest.* Lewiston, N.Y.: E. Mellen Press, 2003.

Yates, Douglas A. *The Rentier State in Gabon.* Boston: African Studies Center, Boston University, 1995.

Borja Cevallos, Rodrigo (1935–) *president of Ecuador*

Rodrigo Borja Cevallos was born on June 19, 1935, in Quito, Ecuador, the descendant of Spanish aristocrats. After completing his secondary education, he attended Ecuador's Central University, majoring in law. He graduated in 1960 with honors and his dissertation reputedly became a standard text throughout Latin America. Borja then completed a stint of postgraduate work in Costa Rica, all the while developing an abiding interest in politics. This first manifested in his college days when he joined the Radical Liberal Party (PLR), one of Ecuador's two traditional political organizations. He then gained election to the national congress in 1962 and was widely regarded as one of the most promising young politicians in the country. However, the military seized power in 1963, and Borja left Ecuador to work at the United Nations in New York. When democracy resurfaced three years later he returned home and joined the law school faculty of the Central University. The big change in Borja's political destiny occurred in 1968, when the PLR candidate was defeated by José María Velasco. To achieve greater national unity, a power-sharing agreement was reached between the conservatives and liberals, which outraged more leftist members like Borja. He then summarily broke all ties with the PLR and founded a new organization—the Izquierda Democrática (ID or Democratic Left) to counter what he perceived as a sellout. In 1970 Borja returned to congress as one of the first ID members before the military again took power.

This latest coup kept Borja from taking office, and he traveled the length and breadth of Ecuador seeking to establish the ID as Ecuador's first grassroots political party. By the time the military finally stepped aside in 1978, he had collected sufficient signatures to allow the ID to run in the upcoming national election. That year Borja finished a distant fourth, but his party had commenced its climb toward legitimacy in Ecuadorian politics. Borja was subsequently reelected and served as a national spokesman for the new "center-left" politics. In 1984 he again ran for the presidency, only to lose to the better-financed conservative, León Febres Cordero. Borja then spent four years touring the country and shoring up the strength of the ID, particularly in the coastal regions. In 1988 Borja again ran for president against Abdala Bucaram, a flamboyant populist, and he defeated him with 47 percent of votes cast.

Borja was formally sworn in as president of Ecuador in August 1988, amid great rejoicing by his left-wing compatriots.

Borja's festivities were short-lived, for the Ecuadorian economy was in deep recession. The problem was further compounded by high inflation, an escalating national debt, and declining oil prices. Though sworn to end poverty and fight injustice, the lack of revenue and the sputtering economy he inherited left the government cash-strapped and, hence, no new social programs could be initiated. Worse, from a leftist standpoint, Borja had little recourse but to enact distinctly neoliberal measures to restart the economy. These included a strict austerity budget, cutbacks in state programs, and close adherence to International Monetary Fund (IMF) guidelines for continuance of foreign aid. Results throughout his tenure were mixed at best. However, Borja had decidedly greater success in establishing the tenor of his administration. Intent upon a national and nonpartisan government, he negotiated with a wide spectrum of political interests, including Communists and Christian Democrats, and he endeavored to bring them into the fold. This was the first time in Ecuadorian history that the politics of inclusion had been practiced on so wide a scale. Once consensus had been achieved he concentrated on another hallmark policy of his administration: social justice and popular welfare, ideological lynchpins of the ID Party.

For all his good intentions, Borja's austerity measures did little to revive the moribund economy and the hardship it engendered. Consequently, in the 1990 congressional elections, the ID lost its majority in congress and with it Borja's ability to formulate policy. He enjoyed better success abroad and struck cordial relationships with progressive leaders like CARLOS ANDRÉS PÉREZ of Venezuela and Alán García of Peru. In 1992 Borja honored the constitutional ban against second presidential terms, and he was replaced by Sixto Alfonso Durán Ballen. And, while he failed in his objectives, Borja's administration was the first to make more than token efforts to mitigate the suffering of Ecuador's poor and dispossessed. He continued for many years thereafter as a spokesman for the ID Party at home and abroad. In September 2000 Borja visited the People's Republic of China at the behest of that country's ruling Central Committee, and he hoped that closer relations between the two nations would develop.

Further Reading

Conaghan, Catharine M. "Ecuador Swings towards Social Democracy." *Current History* 88 (March 1989): 137–41, 154.

Isaacs, Anita. *Military Rule and Transition in Ecuador, 1972–1992.* Pittsburgh, Pa.: University of Pittsburgh Press, 1993.

Pallares, Amalia. *From Peasant Struggles to Indian Resistance: The Ecuadorian Andes in the Late Twentieth Century.* Norman, Okla.: University of Oklahoma Press, 2002.

Roos, Wilma. *Ecuador in Focus: People, Politics, and Culture.* New York: Interlink Books, 2000.

Selverston, Melina. *The 1990 Indigenous Uprising in Ecuador: Politicized Ethnicity as Social Movement.* New York: Columbia University Press, 1993.

Bouteflika, Abdelaziz (1937–) *president of Algeria*

Abdelaziz Bouteflika was born in the border town of Oujda, Morocco, on March 2, 1937, and raised in Algeria. Like many youths of his generation, he took up arms against France in 1956 during the Algerian War for Independence. In the course of fierce fighting Bouteflika distinguished himself in several actions, and he rose to captain within the National Liberation Front (FLN). Fighting ceased in 1962 when French troops evacuated the country, and Bouteflika emerged as a national hero. Accordingly, President Ahmed Ben Bella, Algeria's first president, appointed him minister of youth, sports, and tourism. Within a year the intelligent, articulate young official gained appointment as foreign minister, and he remained in office after a 1965 coup installed Colonel Houari Boumedienne as president. For many years thereafter, Bouteflika became an official spokesman for Algeria's left-leaning nationalism. He touted the nationalization of foreign assets in his country and, furthermore, expressed open sympathy for newly emerging developing countries attempting to do the same. His international reputation crested in 1974 when he chaired the United Nations special session on the new global economy. As usual, Bouteflika stridently promoted Third World interests at the expense of the established order. He was especially vocal on the issue of a Palestinian homeland and the return of Arab land captured by Israel in 1967. Under his aegis, Algeria also became highly touted as an international mediator, and he offered its services to arbitrate running disputes among poorer nations.

Despite his high visibility in the ranks of developing country diplomats, a cloud began forming over Bouteflika's reputation over the issue of corruption. He was dismissed from office in 1980 and the following year was accused of embezzling $12 million while foreign minister. Bouteflika fled Algeria for Switzerland, where he lived in posh political exile. Ever eager to be associated with international diplomacy, he also lent his credentials and expertise to several Persian Gulf nations as a well-paid political consultant. The intervening 19 years proved difficult ones for his native homeland, however. Throughout the 1980s, plunging oil prices threw the Algerian economy into chaos, and the resulting recession led to mass unemployment, civil unrest, and the rise of militant Islamic movements. One group, the Islamic Salvation Front (FIS), viewed the FLN-dominated Algerian government as hopelessly corrupt and agitated for creation of an Islamic state. Their message, rooted in the concept of *sharia,* or Islamic law, resonated with the populace, many of whom experienced genuine social distress. Accordingly, in the democratic elections held in December 1991, the FIS captured 188 seats out of 430 while the ruling FLN majority was pared back to a mere 15. This rising tide of fundamentalism greatly alarmed the Algerian military, unfortunately. In January 1992 they canceled upcoming elections—which FIS would have inevitably won—disposed of President Benjedid, and imposed rule through a High State Council. They also outlawed the FIS and began a campaign of repression that jailed thousands of its supporters. In turn, the disgruntled militants responded with a vicious, nationwide guerrilla war. It continued unabated and consumed the lives of 200,000 Algerians before new elections were scheduled in February 1999.

Bouteflika was summoned from Switzerland by the military because military leaders felt he was the only civilian candidate they could support. In the ensuing election, however, all six other candidates boycotted the vote only two days before it was held to protest fraudulence. Consequently, Bouteflika ran unopposed on April 15, 1999, garnering 74 percent of the vote. He has since been considered by many Algerians as a pawn of the military. Since coming to power, though, he has spared no effort to negotiate with more reasonable elements of the Islamic movement. These have agreed to support a general cease-fire, although a more strident faction, the Islamic Armed Group (GIA) continues staging attacks. To further placate the opposition, Bouteflika promulgated a "civil concord" or general amnesty, which released large numbers of religious prisoners and reduced the sentences of others. He also pledged to attack corruption in government, modernize the economy, and improve social services. In the wake of the September 11, 2001, destruction of the World Trade Center in New York City, Bouteflika has conferred with U.S. president GEORGE W. BUSH on the issue of international terrorism, and he has pledged to help fight it. "Terrorism is one and indivisible," he declared. "If we are going to combat terrorism, we must do it together, uniformly, with the same vigor, the same convictions, and the same financial means." But, in light of small but continuing guerrilla attacks at home, Bouteflika has yet to bring about the lasting peace so desperately sought by his countrymen. His fate, and that of his nation, depend on it.

Further Reading

Graffenried, Michael von. *Inside Algeria.* New York: Aperture, 1998.

Kiser, John W. *The Monks of Tibhirine: Faith, Love, and Terror in Algeria.* New York: St. Martin's Press, 2002.

Laremont, Ricardo R. *Islam and the Politics of Resistence in Algeria, 1783–1992.* Trenton, N.J.: African World Press, 2000.

Martinez, Luis. *The Algerian Civil War, 1990–1998.* London: C. Hurst, 1999.

Roberts, Hugh. *Commanding Disorder: Military Power and Informal Politics in Algeria.* London: I. B. Tauris, 2002.

Rubin, Barry, ed. *Revolutionaries and Reformers: Contemporary Islamist Movements in the Middle East.* Albany: State University of New York Press, 2003.

Boutros-Ghali, Boutros (1922–)
secretary-general of the United Nations

Boutros Boutros-Ghali was born on November 14, 1922, in Cairo, Egypt, the son of a government minister. He belonged to a noted Coptic Christian family and was extremely well educated. In 1946 he received a degree in law from Cairo University before pursing advanced studies at the Sorbonne, Paris, obtaining a doctorate there in 1949. Thereafter, Boutros-Ghali served as a professor of international law at Cairo University, 1949–77, while also holding a Fulbright scholarship at Columbia University and receiving similar honors at the Hague University of International Law and the University of Paris. He soon became recognized as an authority on international law, a brilliant analyst, and fluent in French, English, and Arabic. However, his career in academe concluded in October 1977 when President Anwar Sadat tapped him to serve as Egypt's minister of state. Apparently, his immediate predecessor resigned over peace efforts directed at the state of Israel. Boutros-Ghali subsequently accompanied Sadat on his famous visit to Jerusalem to initiate peace talks, and he was a key player in negotiating the 1978 Camp David accords. This established formal diplomatic relations between Egypt and Israel, in exchange for Israel's returning the Sinai Peninsula to Egypt. In 1990 he also helped negotiate the release of South African dissident Nelson Mandela from prison. Now a world-recognized diplomat, Boutros-Ghali represented Egyptian interests at the United Nations on several occasions, and he demonstrated his expertise on development issues affecting the Third World. In May 1991 President HOSNI MUBARAK appointed him deputy prime minister, a post traditionally reserved for Muslims, further heightening his international visibility.

After 1991 the sitting secretary-general of the United Nations, Javier Pérez de Cuéllar, declined to seek a third term. The African bloc of nations, feeling it was time to field a candidate to represent their interests, approached Boutros-Ghali to succeed him. Delighted, he became the first candidate to actively campaign for the post. On January 1, 1992, Boutros-Ghali became the sixth UN secretary-general, the first to originate from Africa, and also the first of Arab extraction. The cold war having ended in 1991, expectations were high for a new sense of internationalism, with the UN finally able to address development issues in depth. Boutros-Ghali brought with him, among other attributes, nearly 50 years of experience in diplomacy and international law and, more important, his vision as an activist secretary-general. Above all, he wished the agency to become directly involved in world affairs as its leading peacemaker and peacekeeper. These efforts would anticipate the mass influx of humanitarian aid to distressed regions of the globe.

Boutros-Ghali assumed office at a difficult period in the UN's history. As cold war boundaries began breaking down, ethnic fighting commenced in regions as diverse as Somalia, Rwanda, and Bosnia-Herzegovina. The secretary-general helped orchestrate large-scale peace-keeping missions with the United States, the sole remaining superpower and the UN's biggest financial contributor, playing a prominent role. However, President BILL CLINTON felt increasing pressure from the Republican-controlled Congress for the UN to streamline its bureaucracy and cut waste and fraud. Boutros-Ghali complied in large measure, but he never satiated critics in the United States. Congress then stopped paying its annual dues, amounting to $2 billion per year. This retrenchment occurred as the UN expanded its peacekeeping efforts across the globe to such remote regions as Cambodia and East Timor. The lack of funding and close cooperation compromised its effectiveness. In certain instances, such as the NATO–backed bombing campaign against Serbians in Bosnia, Boutros-Ghali also opposed armed intervention in favor of lower-profile solutions. This further angered American critics, who by 1996 opposed his candidacy for a second term. Originally, Boutros-Ghali had pledged himself to a single term in office, but he later changed his mind. However, U.S. representative Madeleine Albright declared that unless Boutros-Ghali stepped down, no more funding could be expected. Moreover, the United States would veto his nomination in the Security Council. The secretary-general denounced his critics as vindictive and narrow-minded but he compiled, becoming the only secretary-general restricted to a single term. However, he had the satisfaction of seeing a fellow African, KOFI ANNAN, succeed him.

After departing the United Nations, Boutros-Ghali resumed his academic career at Cairo University, and he was also elected to the Egyptian parliament in 1997. Despite his much-publicized row with the United States, or perhaps because of it, he has lost none of his popularity among the developing nations. In May 2002, Boutros-Ghali appeared at Nanjing University, China, to receive an honorary doctorate. He remains a major architect in the UN's newfound attempts to bring greater harmony to a discordant world, intervening where possible to curtail human suffering.

Further Reading

Boutros-Ghali, Boutros. *Unvanquished: A U.S.–U.N. Saga.* New York: Random House, 1999.
———. *Egypt's Road to Jerusalem: A Diplomat's Story of the Struggle for Peace.* New York: Random House, 1997.
Burgess, Stephen F. *The United Nations under Boutros Boutros-Ghali, 1992–1997.* Lanham, Md.: Scarecrow Press, 2001.
Meisler, Stanley. "Dateline U.N.: A New Hammerskjold?" *Foreign Policy* 98 (1995): 180–97.
Morikawa, Yukiko. "Electing the Sixth Secretary-General of the United Nations." Unpublished master's thesis, University of Oregon, 1992.

Brundtland, Gro Harlem (1939–) *prime minister of Norway*

Gro Harlem was born in Oslo, Norway, on April 20, 1939, the daughter of a Labor Party government minister. She was raised in an atmosphere of competitive equality with her brothers and encouraged to perform tasks traditionally assigned to boys her age. In 1960 she married conservative journalist Arne Olay Brundtland, and the couple raised four children. Intent upon a medical career, however, Brundtland obtained her degree from the University of Oslo in 1963, and two years later earned an advanced degree from Harvard University. She began her public career with the Board of Health in Oslo, but Labor Party connections resulted in an appointment as minister of environment in 1974. By 1979 Brundtland had expanded her political credentials by gaining election to the Norwegian Storting (parliament), where she served on committees dealing with finance, foreign policy, and constitutional matters. Early on, Brundtland established herself as a force to be reckoned with within the Labor Party by dint of her keen intellect and steely resolve. She was also a vocal advocate of equal rights for women, and in 1981 she rose to become head of the Labor Party. In this capacity she served a brief term as Norway's first woman prime minister in 1981 following the resignation of Odvar Nordli. Brundtland at that time was also Norway's youngest head of state, but the political novelty of her ascension ended seven months later when she was relegated to the post of leader of the opposition. However, the glass ceiling had finally been broken in Norwegian politics—thereafter, increasing numbers of women began serving in government.

While out of office, in 1983 Brundtland had been approached by the United Nations to chair the World Commission on Environment and Development. Four years later she authored the famous report *Our Common Future,* also known as the "Brundtland Report," which called for careful industrial development and greater respect for the earth's fragile environment. It was widely hailed for its political vision and scientific relevance, and, in 1992, it served as the blueprint document for the UN Conference on Environment and Development at Rio de Janeiro, Brazil. Success on the international stage only heightened Brundtland's popularity at home, and in 1986, following the collapse of a conservative coalition, she began her second term as prime minister. But her regular duties did little to temper her enthusiasm for environmentalism, and she also served as chairman of the World Commission of Environment from 1984 to 1987. Three years later Labor was upended again by the conservatives and Brundtland left office, still among Norway's most visible and popular figures. Fortunes shifted again the following year, and in 1990 she assumed the highest office for a third time. In 1993 Brundtland was reelected to an unprecedented fourth term in office, making her one of the most influential politicians in recent Norwegian history. Ever independent-minded, however, she had her hopes pinned on other challenges, and so, in October 1992, she stepped down as party head in favor of her protégé, THORBJOERN JAGLAND.

As a spokesperson for women's rights, Brundtland was never shy about avoiding confrontation or controversy. During the 1994 UN Population Conference in Cairo, Egypt, she raised the ire of many Muslim and Catholic participants by demanding the decriminalization of abortion. She also appointed a record number of women to serve in her cabinet, nine out of 19. In 1996 Brundtland again surprised political pundits by announcing her resignation from office a year before elections were due. She was succeeded by Jagland and left behind a legacy of solid accomplishments. The most significant of these was an invigorated Social Democratic Party at a time when conservatism was sweeping most of Europe. Curiously, Brundtland's biggest setback involved her failure to convince Norwegian voters to join the European Union (EU) in 1994—a referendum was soundly rejected. But in July 1998, she fulfilled a lifelong dream by being appointed head of the World Health Organization (WHO), a post in which she could act out her commitment to improving public health on a global scale. In this office she marshaled all her formidable personal qualities in a struggle against tobacco, malaria, and—above all—the worldwide scourge of AIDS.

Brundtland considers herself a leader in the struggle against AIDS, which afflicts 40 million people worldwide and infects an estimated 17,000 daily. Despite this alarming toll, money and lack of access to drugs continually hamper attempts to control the epidemic, especially in developing nations. Her cost-effective solution—widespread introduction of condoms—could effectively curtail and contain infection rates to acceptable levels, provided an intense educational awareness program accompanies the effort. "The world is now ready to turn back the epidemic, learning from those who have blazed a trail, scaling up the best practice and confronting AIDS systematically," she insists. Brundtland is scheduled to remain as head of WHO until 2003. By the end of her tenure many anticipate that she will completely overhaul existing practices, rendering it, in her accepted fashion, a far more efficient organization than the one she inherited.

Further Reading

Breton, Mary Joy. *Women Pioneers for the Environment.* Boston: Northeastern University, 1998.

Brundtland, Gro Harlem. *Madam Prime Minister: A Life in Power and Politics.* New York: Farrar, Strauss, and Giroux, 2002.

Fukuyama, F. "Women and the Evolution of World Politics." *Foreign Affairs* 77 (September–October 1998): 24–40.

Graf, William. "From Brandt to Brundtland and Beyond: Hegemonic-Ideological Aspects of the North-South Dialogue in the 1990s." *History of European Ideas* 15 (nos. 1–3, 1992): 399–406.

Madeley, J. "Norway's 1993 Election: The Road to Europe Blocked?" *West European Politics* 17 (April 1994): 197–203.

Bruton, John (1947–) *prime minister of Ireland*

John Gerard Bruton was born on May 18, 1947, in Dublin, to wealthy, farming landowners. He was well-educated locally, and he attended the University College, Dublin, where he obtained a bachelor's degree in law. Around this time he joined Fine Gael, one of the two traditional Irish parties, and in 1969 he gained election to the Dail, or parliament. Bruton, aged but 22 years, was then the youngest member seated. He demonstrated a flair for public service over time, and in 1973 Bruton became parliamentary secretary to the minister of education. Four years later power shifted to the rival Fianna

Fáil Party, and he served as the opposition shadow minister on agriculture. In 1981 Bruton again demonstrated his public policy expertise by authoring Fine Gael's policy statement for overhauling parliament's committee system. The party then bounced back to power through the aegis of Garret Fitzgerald in June 1981, and Bruton found himself appointed minister of finance, his first cabinet posting. In this capacity he called for an increase in the European Union's value added tax (VAT) to balance the budget, but public outcry against the measure brought Fianna Fáil back into power that year. However, within months Fine Gael's fortunes had risen again, and Bruton became minister for industry and energy. In 1986 he resumed his post as finance minister and decided to devalue the Irish currency to revive the economy. His overall good performance propelled him up the party hierarchy, and in 1987 he assumed the mantle of deputy leader. In contrast to his frequently more flamboyant opponents, Bruton, known derisively as "the Brute," was blunt, direct, and decidedly uncharismatic. However, this did not prevent him from becoming head of Fine Gael in 1990. In the spring of 1994 he strengthened his grip on party affairs by surviving a vote of no confidence, and he continued on as Fine Gael's spokesman.

Bruton's political fortunes took a major upturn in 1994 when the administration of ALBERT REYNOLDS was rocked by the revelation that its appointee to the presidency of the High Court turned out to be an attorney who had mishandled a child molestation case. The public uproar caused the Labour Party leader Dick Spring to leave the government coalition, and the administration collapsed. Bruton, however, was waiting in the wings for such an event and, through deft negotiations with Labour and the Democratic Left Party, he formed a new coalition government on December 15, 1994. Bruton thus became the youngest-ever *taoiseach* (prime minister) of Ireland. "We have joined forces now to confront and manage the changes that are reshaping our political culture," he proclaimed. "To this end, we have committed ourselves to a government of renewal."

Once in office, Bruton established a blueprint for reducing the nation's high unemployment rate, reforming the tax codes, and decreasing levies on the working poor. However, his greatest legacy was continuance of the Reynolds's policy of promoting dialogue between and among Great Britain and warring elements in Northern Ireland. Bruton, a devout Catholic, considered the Irish Republican Army (IRA) as terrorists and was loath to deal with them personally. However, in the interest of peace, he established a working rapport with the head of the IRA's political wing, Sinn Féin's GERRY ADAMS, and british prime minister JOHN MAJOR. In the course of these negotiations, he roundly denounced the IRA for its unwillingness to surrender its arms. Given the complexities and emotional forces driving the question of Northern Ireland's possible unification with the Republic of Ireland, a resolution did not materialize during Bruton's tenure in office. But his efforts were roundly praised, and in 1995 U.S. president BILL CLINTON publicly lauded the prime minister as a peacemaker. Fortunately, he enjoyed better success in narrowly passing a referendum lifting the ban on divorce in Ireland in November 1995. Earlier that year he enjoyed another controversial success by passing legislation that finally legalized abortion.

Bruton continued serving competently as prime minister until the national elections of June 1997, when he narrowly lost to BERTIE AHERN of Fianna Fail. The latter managed to assemble a small coalition majority and Fine Gael passed to the opposition. Bruton managed to remain at the head of his party for several years until February 2001, when he finally succumbed to a 39-33 vote of no confidence. Apparently, the party suffered low ratings in national opinion polls, no doubt brought on by a succession of scandals involving bribery, nepotism, and incompetence. This ended his 11-year tenure as leader of Fine Gael after failing for four years to lead them back into power. "I fully accept this democratic decision," he declared, "I am completely certain that Fine Gael will be in power after the next general election." Party members agreed, and place their faith and hopes in finding new leaders.

Further Reading

Gallagher, Michael. *Days of Blue Loyalty: The Politics of Membership of the Fine Gael Party.* Dublin: PSAI Press, 2002.

Guttman, Robert J. "Interview with John Bruton, Prime Minister of Ireland." *Europe* 358 (July–August, 1996): 14–17.

Kissane, Bill. *Explaining Irish Democracy.* Dublin: University College of Dublin, 2002.

Mulholland, Marc. *The Longest War: Northern Ireland's Troubled History.* Oxford: Oxford University Press, 2002.

O'Malley, Desmond, and Tom Gavin. *Redefining Southern Nationalism: A Political Perspective.* Dublin: University College of Dublin, 2001.

Bush, George W. (1946–) *president of the United States*

George Walker Bush was born on July 6, 1946, in New Haven, Connecticut, the son of future president George Herbert Walker Bush. His father relocated to West Texas to pursue a career in the oil industry, and the younger Bush was initially educated at public schools and then at the elite Philips Academy in Andover, Massachusetts. He then followed the family tradition by attending Yale University in 1964, which both his father and grandfather had attended. Bush obtained a bachelor's degree in history and the reputation of a gregarious partygoer of modest intellectual means. In 1968 he joined the Texas National Guard, in which he trained as a pilot and flew F-102 jet fighters for four years. Having fulfilled his military obligations, Bush next attended prestigious Harvard University, and he received an M.B.A. in 1975. He then returned to Texas to start his own oil company, and he enjoyed mixed success. He also tested the political waters by running for the U.S. House or Representatives as a Republican in 1978, but he lost to a Democrat. After another long stint in the oil business, and a successful one, he became owner of the Texas Rangers baseball team, which he successfully managed. He also campaigned actively during the senior Bush's 1988 run for the White House. Success here only whetted his appetite for more political activity.

In 1994 Bush ran for governor against a popular incumbent, Democrat Ann Richards. Throughout their campaign, she lampooned him as a political lightweight and the child of privilege, but Bush determined to remain on message. Despite Richard's acerbic taunting, he continually hammered away at the themes of decentralizing the poorly performing Texas school system, reforming the state juvenile justice system, and reducing the welfare rolls. Bush's political message, while clearly Republican in tone, was not stridently conservative, and it appealed to many voters outside his core constituency. And, while Richards maintained her shrillness, Bush appeared jovial and convivial, increasing his public appeal. On election day, this son of a president became only the second Republican governor of Texas since Reconstruction, winning with 53 percent of the vote, attracting the votes of many women, Hispanics, and younger people.

Once in office, Bush strengthened his political credentials by demonstrating his ability to work with Democrats. He wooed the Democratic-controlled legislature with compromise and common sense, to the extent that nearly all of his campaign promises were fulfilled. Foremost of these was a pledge to cut taxes, which were reduced by $3 billion. The Texas economy soared in response and in 1998, Bush won reelection by a record 69 percent of the popular vote, including record numbers of blacks, Hispanics, and women who voted for him. The stage was now set for a rendezvous with destiny.

In 1999 Bush announced his intention to run for the presidency of the United States as the Republican standard-bearer. He had no trouble raising a record $37

George Bush *(Getty Images)*

million initially, and it looked as though he would simply coast to the party's nomination, until he ran afoul of Senator John McCain of Arizona. The tough-talking McCain, a decorated Vietnam war hero, scored heavily against Bush by portraying him as too inexperienced for the White House, especially in the realm of foreign affairs. The message resonated among some party members. During the New Hampshire primary, Bush lost to McCain by 20 percentage points. But, never losing a step in a well-oiled campaign, Bush quickly retooled his image to stress personal charm and to reemphasize familiar themes of tax cuts, school reform, and increased military spending. He took the process of image makeover a step further when, taking a leaf from incumbent President BILL CLINTON, he co-opted several distinctly Democratic themes into his own platform, including Social Security reform and better Medicare coverage for the elderly. Thus was born the notion of "compassionate conservatism," which quickly became Bush's campaign mantra. McCain was unable to adjust to such fancy political footwork and in the end he was overwhelmed in the "Super Tuesday" primaries of March 2000. In view of the heated nature of their contest, it took several months before the two were formerly reconciled, although McCain agreed on principle to work on Bush's behalf in the general election.

Bush next faced off with the Democratic nominee, sitting vice president ALBERT GORE, JR. Gore enjoyed the advantages of incumbency and a relatively robust economy, but he was tainted by the numerous scandals that had rocked the Clinton administration for eight years. In three televised debates with Bush, he came across to many as a wooden and devoid of original ideas. Not surprisingly, Bush gained and held a slight lead over Gore up through election day. On November 7, 2000, he did exactly that, but only after one of the biggest election-day imbroglios in American history. Bush and Gore split the electoral college evenly, save for the essential state of Florida (Gore, however, did accrue roughly half a million more votes in the national count). Earlier that evening, the networks awarded Florida and its crucial 25 electoral votes to Gore. They then retracted their prediction and gave it—along with the election—to Bush. Subsequent counting revealed Bush's margin of victory to be a mere 327 votes out of 6 million cast, so an automated recount was in order. This he won without controversy. An angry Gore then convinced the Florida State Supreme Court, staffed entirely by Democrats, to order a manual recount of four Democratic-leaning counties, which appeared to be undercounted. This was granted and took more time than the five days allotted by the court. Katherine Harris, the Republican secretary of state, refused an extension and ordered the results certified as a Bush win. Suspicions were also increased by the fact that Bush's brother, Florida governor Jeb Bush, was in charge of the state's political apparatus. Gore again appealed to the Democratic-controlled court for another manual recount, which was again granted over objections from the Bush campaign. The latter then appealed to the U.S. Supreme Court for redress. On a five-to-four vote, the Court sided with Bush and stopped the recount on December 12, 2000. Sensing the futility of further appeals (to which he was legally entitled) Gore formally and graciously conceded the contest. Almost by default Bush became the first son of a president to win the executive's chair since John Quincy Adams in 1824. He is also the first president since 1876 to win the White House while losing the national popular vote.

Bush was formally inaugurated on January 20, 2001, as the nation's 47th president. "Together, we are changing the tone in our nation's capital," he said. "And this spirit of respect and cooperation is vital—because in the end, we will be judged not only by what we say or how we say it, but by what we are able to accomplish." However, given the closeness and controversial nature of Bush's victory, political pundits anticipated that any mandate for change was virtually nil. He was also expected to encounter resistance to passage of the most controversial of his campaign pledges, a massive tax cut, since the Republicans maintained but a razor-thin control over both houses of Congress. Bush surprised the establishment that May when the centerpiece of his legislative agenda passed. However, celebrations were cut short when Vermont senator Jim Jeffords left the Republican Party to become an Independent, thereby throwing control of the Senate over to the Democrats. Bush nevertheless prided himself in his ability to work cordially with the opposition and get the job done. Consequently, in the fall of 2001 Congress easily passed his sweeping educational reform bill, fulfilling another campaign pledge. Bush also scored another political triumph by securing fast-track authority to negotiate trade agreements. The new president also weathered his first international crisis that April when a Chinese jet accidentally rammed an American reconnaissance aircraft flying along the China coast. The damaged plane was forced to land on Chinese soil and the 24-man crew was interned. This was an egregious act of aggression but Bush, realizing the value of China as a trading partner, calmly issued a statement that he was "very sorry" for the affair, and both the crew and plane were eventually released.

Sadly and most unexpectedly, the defining moment of Bush's presidency occurred not overseas, but on American soil. On September 11, 2001, two hijacked airliners flown by suicidal Arab terrorists struck and destroyed the World Trade Center buildings in New York City. Millions of viewers recoiled in horror over the televised images of the twin towers collapsing in ruin. Meanwhile, another hijacked craft hit the Pentagon, while a fourth crashed in Pennsylvania when passengers overwhelmed the terrorists. The ensuing destruction was so vast that it appeared surreal, and loss of life amounted to over 3,000 deaths. However, Bush quickly identified known Arab terrorist Osama bin Laden as the architect of the attack and ordered the U.S. military into action. He also cobbled together an international coalition of disparate nations to wage war on terrorist cells, wherever they reside. When the militant Islamic regime of Afghanistan, the Taliban, refused to hand over bin Laden, American carrier-based and strategic aircraft commenced a concerted bombing campaign that drove them from power within weeks. Special forces teams have also been committed to a ground search for the fugitive bin Laden, in concert with air and land assets committed by Great Britain's prime minister TONY BLAIR. With the Taliban gone and a pro-Western government under HAMID KARZAI about to take power, Bush's steely resolve eliminated a major haven for bin Laden's international terrorist network.

Bush currently enjoys a national popularity rating of 80 percent and reservations as to his ability to handle a foreign crisis have all but evaporated. However, with the economy entering a period of recession, he continues to push hard for a stimulus package over Democratic obstructionism. On November 5, 2002, he did exactly that, winning three additional seats in the House. More important, the Republicans upset the Democrats by taking two additional seats in the Senate for a total of 51, thereby securing control for Bush. Such gains also represent a historic reversal of political fortunes, for parties in power have traditionally lost seats in mid-term elections.

Having consolidated his control over Congress, Bush forced his attention back toward Iraq and SADDAM HUSSEIN. He continued a military buildup in the region, over the strident objections of China, France, Germany, and Russia, and on March 17, 2003, he issued a strongly worded ultimatum to the dictator. "All the decades of deceit and cruelty have now reached an end," Bush solemnly declared on television, "Saddam Hussein and his sons must leave Iraq within 48 hours." When the deadline had passed without compliance, Bush, along with a coalition of countries that included Great Britain and Australia, commenced Operation Iraqi Freedom. After three weeks of fighting Hussein's troops, American tanks rumbled into Baghdad and effectively took control of Iraq.

Further Reading

Bruni, Frank. *Ambling into History: The Unlikely Odyssey of George W. Bush.* New York: HarperCollins, 2002.

Bush, George W. *A Charge to Keep: My Journey to the White House.* New York: Perennial, 2001.

Ide, Arthur F. *George W. Bush: Portrait of a Compassionate Conservative.* Las Colinas, Tex.: Monument Press, 2000.

Kellner, Douglas. *9/11 and the Terror War: The Dangers of the Bush Legacy.* Lanham, Md.: Rowman & Littlefield, 2003.

Minutaglio, Bill. *First Son: George W. Bush and the Bush Family Dynasty.* New York: Times Books, 1999.

Sabato, Larry. *Overtime! The Election 2000 Thriller.* New York: Longman, 2002.

Williams, Mary E., ed. *The Terrorist Attack on America.* San Diego, Calif.: Green Haven Press, 2003.

Buthelezi, Gatsha Mangosuthu (1928–)
chief of Zulu tribe

Gatsha Mangosuthu Buthelezi was born in Mahlabatini, South Africa, on August 27, 1928, the son of a Zulu chieftain. As such he received a better than average education by Zulu standards, including attendance at Fort Hare University. However, while there he engaged in political agitations against white minority rule in South Africa and temporarily joined the radical African National Congress (ANC). This was a socialist-oriented organization dedicated to the violent overthrow of the white regime. As such Buthelezi was expelled from college in 1951, but two years later he served as an interpreter with the Bantu Department of Durban. In 1957 he was also installed as the chief of the Buthelezi tribe in the Mahlabatini district. During the 1950s the white-ruled South African minority government adopted a formal policy of apartheid, or racial separation. To achieve this they divided the nation into 10 bantustans, or "homelands," in which blacks could live and govern their own affairs but were allowed no influence over national affairs. Buthelezi strongly opposed the system initially but, displaying a degree of realism and pragmatism missing in many contemporaries, he eventually decided to cooperate with the whites. This brought charges of complicity with the apartheid regime from other African leaders, but it did give the Zulu king greater leverage in dealings with them.

Patience and cooperation eventually paid dividends. In 1976 Buthelezi became chief minister of the KwaZulu homeland, which also served as his political power base. In fact the Zulu tribe, descended from a nation of famous warriors, held neighboring tribes in contempt and only reluctantly dealt with them as equals. Once the ANC commenced guerrilla activities against the South African government and began growing in numbers and popularity, Buthelezi felt pressured to found a political movement of his own. Thus emerged the Inkatha Freedom Party, which, although its origins are traced to a cultural movement of the 1920s, was in fact a miniature paramilitary group organized around ethnic lines. It soon numbered an estimated 200,000 members and became the dominant political force of the KwaZulu homeland. Buthelezi did not hesitate to unleash party members against the ANC whenever the latter threatened his authority, which, in turn, brought charges that he was fostering tribalism at the expense of black liberation. After 1985, fighting between the two black factions intensified as the end of the apartheid regime approached, and an estimated 18,000 people lost their lives. Nonetheless, backed by his army of fighters, Buthelezi was determined to be a major player in any post-apartheid settlement and he proffered Inkatha as a political counterweight to the more radical ANC.

By the time ANC leader NELSON MANDELA was released from prison in February 1990, there was a growing sense that Buthelezi was preparing to use violence to advance his own political ends. Despite their mutual antipathy against white rule, the Zulu leader refused to cooperate fully with the ANC. Furthermore, in 1991 it was revealed that throughout the 1980s Inkatha had actually been subsidized by the white government, which made the chief minister seem duplicitous. But Buthelezi, a conservative-minded individual with little regard for the ANC's left-wing policies, remained unapologetic. In fact he initially refused to participate in the first-ever free elections of April 1994 unless KwaZulu were guaranteed a degree of autonomy. Furthermore, Buthelezi insisted that he himself be included in whatever government arrangement the ANC planned to adopt. After the elections Mandela was formally elected president of the new, racially inclusive South Africa, and the bantustan system was formally disbanded. But, in an effort to maintain the façade of national unity, Mandela appointed Buthelezi minister of home affairs.

Since the end of apartheid, Buthelezi's cooperation with the government has been based largely upon perpetuation of his own self-interest. His lack of cooperation in the post-apartheid era confounds many black leaders, who view him as either a traitor or an opportunist, but the presence of Inkatha allows the Zulu chief to bargain from a position of strength. In October 1998 a report issued by the government-sponsored Truth and Reconciliation Commission concluded that Buthelezi was in fact responsible for many atrocities committed against ANC members, although he denied any culpability. In June 1999 President THABO MBEKI tendered the office of deputy vice president to the Zulu chief, but he declined to accept. Then, in April 2002, Buthelezi warned the government that an impending immigration bill, revised with a command economy quota system, would threaten the traditional power base of local leaders. "I am talking about a very serious thing for our country," he warned the ANC. Given his determination to maintain a visible profile in South African politics, Buthelezi remains a controversial figure, loved by some, hated others, but never underestimated by political opponents.

Further Reading

Berkeley, Bill. "The 'New' South Africa: Violence Works." *World Policy Journal* 13, no. 4 (1996–1997): 73–80.

Hamilton, Carolyn. *Terrific Majesty: The Powers of Shaka Zulu and the Limits of Historical Invention.* Cambridge, Mass.: Harvard University Press, 1998.

Mare, Gerhard, and Georgiana Hamilton. *An Appetite for Power: Buthelezi, Inkatha, and South Africa.* Bloomington: Indiana University Press, 1987.

Mzala. *Gatsha Buthelezi: Chief with a Double Agenda.* Atlantic Highlands, N.J.: Zed Books, 1988.

Temkin, Ben. *Buthelezi: A Biography.* Portland, Oreg.: Frank Cass, 2002.

Buyoya, Pierre (1949–   ) *president of Burundi*

Pierre Buyoya was born in Rutovu, Bururi province, Burundi, on November 24, 1949, into the minority Tutsi tribe. This small, landlocked country is the scene of some of the longest-lived and most horrific ethnic disputes on record. Burundi is shared by two major ethnic groups, the majority Hutu and the minority Tutsi, who have lived within close proximity of each other for centuries. However, an undercurrent of hostility between the two groups has long existed as the Tutsi have traditionally dominated civil and military affairs at the expense of the Hutu. The onset of Belgian colonial control in 1916 only served to exacerbate tensions, and outbreaks of violence became alarmingly frequent. Like many of his background, Buyoya was educated at home and sent to study military science abroad, in this instance the Royal Military Academy in Brussels. He returned to assume a succession of important command positions, although Buyoya was little known, even within his own country, before a coup against sitting president Jean-Baptiste Bagaza. At that time Bagaza had embarked on a crackdown against internal dissent, including attacks upon the Catholic Church, which made him highly unpopular in this highly Christianized nation. On September 3, 1987, a group of military officers bloodlessly overthrew Bagaza, then traveling abroad, and deposed him. They then appointed the trusted but little-known Buyoya to serve as interim president of Burundi.

Once empowered, Buyoya displayed a surprising degree of moderation in his policies. He tried to placate the more numerous Hutu by bringing several into his government for the first time. He also pledged a return to democracy and initiated numerous political reforms. By June 1993, Burundi was ready for its first multiparty national elections, in which Tutsi Buyoya, with 32 percent of the vote, was soundly defeated by Melchior Ndadye, a Hutu. Surprisingly, the military leader peacefully surrendered power and urged his followers to support the new administration. Unfortunately, ethnic divisions ran strong, and the following October Ndadye was killed in a coup attempt. His successor, CYPRIEN NTARYAMIRA, restored order quickly, but he was also killed in a mysterious plane crash months later. A third candidate, Sylvestre Ntibantunganya, then rallied the country, but the rapid series of changes triggered a prolonged period of bloody civil war. By 1995 an estimated 200,000 Burundians, Hutu and Tutsi alike, were slaughtered by roving gangs of ethnic militias and the president declared to the world that genocide was being committed against the Hutu of Burundi. When it became clear that Ntibantunganya could not restore order, he was overthrown by Buyoya in July 1996.

Back in office, Buyoya took the unprecedented step of appointing the nation's first Hutu prime minister, and he filled other cabinet posts with members of the same tribe. However, these measures were accomplished only after suspending the constitution, banning all political parties, and dissolving the national assembly. "We have to bring back democracy," he affirmed, "but how long it will take, we don't know; it could be 12 months, 18 months, or more." By November, the assembly had been restored and the ban lifted. Buyoya also declared a three-year transitional period in which he hoped to restore order and promulgate a new constitution. Meanwhile, warring factions in the countryside continued fighting and killing civilians on both sides. Many in the Hutu fold blame Buyoya's army for the violence, for he never appointed any high-ranking Hutu within its ranks. Buyoya, however, accuses rebels outside governmental control for continuing disturbances. An estimated 10,000 people were massacred within three months of the coup, which did little to enhance Buyoya's reputation at home or abroad. In fact, the heads of neighboring countries were so upset by his overthrow of a democratically elected government that they imposed an economic boycott against Burundi. The boycott remained in place until 1999, which only added to the suffering of Burundi's population.

In November 2001, Buyoya was sworn in to head a three-year power-sharing agreement that, it was hoped, would end the eight-year-old civil war. However, the Hutu rebels refused to lay down their arms until further agreement could be reached. Accordingly, Buyoya's representatives were dispatched to Pretoria, South Africa, to negotiate with former president Ntibantunganya for an end to the fighting. The peace deal was brokered by none other than NELSON MANDELA, and it hinges upon a release of political prisoners, restoration of the 1992 constitution, and creation of a national army with adequate Hutu representation.

Further Reading
"Buyoya: Bogeyman of Burundi." *New African,* no. 345 (2000): 10–14.

Evans, Glynne. *Responding to Crises in the African Great Lakes.* New York: Oxford University Press for the International Institute for Strategic Studies, 1997.

Jennings, Christian. *Across the River: Rwanda, Burundi, and the Heart of Darkness.* London: Phoenix, 2000.

Mwakikagile, Geoffrey. *Civil Wars in Rwanda and Burundi: Conflict Resolution in Africa.* Huntington, N.Y.: Nova Science Publishers, 2001.

Nyankanzi, Edward L. *Genocide: Rwanda and Burundi.* Rochester, Vt.: Schenkman Books, 1998.

Schrrer, Christian P. *Genocide and Crisis in Central Africa: Conflict Roots, Mass Violence, and Regional War.* Westport, Conn.: Praeger, 2002.

C

Caldera, Rafael (1916–) *president of Venezuela*
Rafael Caldera Rodríguez was born on January 24, 1916, in San Felipe, Venezuela, the son of a physician. An exceptional student, he attended the Central University and obtained his doctorate in political science. For many years thereafter he taught at the university while also becoming active in numerous Catholic civic organizations. In 1936 Caldera commenced his political career by being elected to the Chamber of Deputies but, by 1946, he was sufficiently disillusioned by establishment politics to help found the Christian Democratic Party (COPEI). In this manner, he and his adherents hoped to find a "third way" between the tyranny of Marxism and the excesses of capitalism to address Venezuela's social grievances. To underscore his belief in change, Caldera ran for the presidency in 1947 and lost to the newly founded, leftist Democratic Action Party (AD). A long interval of military rule then followed, and in 1958 Caldera was imprisoned and exiled for political agitation. He came home the following year and ran again for the presidency in 1958 and 1963, losing twice by increasingly smaller margins. Caldera then presided over the Chamber of Deputies as head of the opposition. In December 1968 he ran a fourth time for the presidency and acquired 29 percent of the vote in a multiparty election. He was sworn in on March 11, 1969, marking the first time in Venezuelan history that power transferred peacefully from one party to another.

While president, Caldera lacked a working majority in the legislature, so he had little recourse but to continue the economic and fiscal policies of his AD predecessor. Happily, Venezuela was experiencing a boom thanks to growth in the oil export industry. He embarked on only modest and gradual social reforms, all the while encouraging the growth of democracy through sponsorship of weekly television talks and press conferences. Caldera also took dramatic steps to nationalize the oil industry, which did little to endear him to the United States, but the additional revenue was channeled into helping the poor and middle classes. Furthermore, faced with a long-standing Marxist guerrilla movement, Caldera proved himself ideologically flexible enough to negotiate with them directly. To underscore his good-faith effort, he relaxed relations with Fidel Castro's Cuba, which enhanced his image with domestic leftists. By the time his first term in office ended in 1974, Venezuela was at peace and enjoyed a prosperous economy. Caldera was forbidden by the national constitution to run again for 10 years, so he left office to pursue scholarly pursuits. Several of his books were published worldwide.

After a 20-year hiatus from politics, Caldera resurfaced in 1992 as a serious presidential candidate. Now in his 78th year, he had grown disillusioned by the complacency of the Christian Democrats, and finally he broke ranks with them. Venezuela was then struggling with a deep economic crisis, one which engulfed the presidency of CARLOS ANDRÉS PÉREZ of the AD. Pérez left office after being impeached by the Senate and elections were held in December 1993. Caldera now ran as the candidate of the National Convergence Party, a crazy-quilt assemblage of 17 parties spanning the political spectrum. Opposition leaders openly derided it as the "cockroach coalition." Nonetheless, he managed to scrape together a 30 percent plurality from the crowded field of candidates and was declared the winner. This victory also represented the first time in Venezuelan history that the two mainstream parties had been defeated.

Voters initially felt reassured by Caldera's victory, as he was the nation's elder statesman and a respected figure. However, Venezuela's woes read like a litany of grievances. The country's overdependence on oil production was underscored when world prices toppled, leaving the government short of cash. Consequently, the national debt zoomed, interest rates skyrocketed, and cuts had to be made in social spending. But try as he may, Caldera's attempts at fiscal reform and budgetary austerity wielded little impact. By 1997 inflation had risen to 31 percent, the worst in Latin America, and the currency had to be devalued 40 percent. This distress only exacerbated the suffering of poor Venezuelans, the vast majority in a country in which only 10 percent of the population control nearly half the nation's wealth. Even more inexplicable, Venezuela is the second-largest oil exporter in the world after Saudi Arabia and yet billions of dollars could not be accounted for. Caldera proved singularly unable to formulate a coherent economic strategy, hamstrung as he was by the lack of a working majority in Congress. To forestall further social unrest, he agreed to end his tenure in office a year early and call for early elections.

Caldera's political misfortunes crested in December 1998, when the contest was won by HUGO CHÁVEZ, a former soldier and coup leader, who promised dramatic reforms. The ensuing contest split the nation along class lines, pitting rich and middle class against the poor, and threatened to spill onto the streets. But Caldera was adamant that law and the will of the people prevail. "The government and armed forces have promised to respect the electoral results. That respect will be sacrosanct," he lectured. "At the same time we de-

mand that the results be accepted in peace." Caldera has lived in quiet retirement since leaving office.

Further Reading

Buxton, Julia. *The Failure of Political Reform in Venezuela.* Burlington, Vt.: Ashgate, 2001.

Canache, Damarys. *Venezuela: Public Opinion and Protest in a Fragile Democracy.* Coral Gables, Fla.: North-South Center Press at the University of Miami, 2002.

Crisp, Brian F. *Democratic Institutional Design: The Powers and Incentives of Venezuelan Politicians and Interest Groups.* Stanford, Calif.: Stanford University Press, 2000.

Goodman, Louis W. *Lesson of the Venezuelan Experience.* Baltimore: Johns Hopkins University Press, 1995.

Perry, William, and Norman A. Bailey. *Venezuela, 1994: Challenges for the Caldera Administration.* Washington, D.C.: Center for Strategic and International Studies, 1994.

Calderón, Rafael (1949–) *president of Costa Rica*

Rafael Angel Calderón Fournier was born in Diriamba, Nicaragua, on March 14, 1949, the son of Rafael Calderón Guardia, former president of Costa Rica (1940–44). At that time the senior Calderón had lost a civil war to opposition forces and was living in exile. Rafael Calderón was initially educated in Mexico City, but he returned home with his family to complete his education. In 1977 he graduated from the University of Costa Rica with a law degree and, like his father before him, became deeply wedded to the notion of public service. Furthermore, his father was a beloved figure in Costa Rican politics, and his name carried considerable political weight, which transferred to his son. Calderón was elected to the national legislature in 1974, where he remained four years. By 1978 he managed to convince his followers to help form the Unidad (Unity) Coalition that elected Rodrigo Carazo Odio president. Consequently, Calderón was rewarded with the post of foreign minister from 1978 to 1982, and he also served as the head of the social security system.

Costa Rican politics now revolves around two traditional parties: the left-leaning National Liberation Party (PLN), and the more conservative Social Christian Unity Party (PUSC) formed by Calderón in 1982.

There is usually very little to choose between the two, save for varying degrees of free enterprise and the role of government control in the economy. In 1982 Calderón ran for the presidency against PLN candidate Luis Alberto Monge and lost. Four years later he ran again against Oscar Arias Sánchez and lost again. It was not until 1990 that Calderón ran a third time and finally triumphed by beating PLN candidate Manuel Castillo, 52 percent to 48 percent. His victory was due to two main factors: By constantly evoking the memory of his father and the good work for the poor that he accomplished, Calderón secured more votes from impoverished individuals than he might have done otherwise. Second, after 20 years of uncontested PLN rule, many Costa Rican voters felt the need for change before entrenched success led to outright corruption. Calderón was also greatly assisted by his own moderate campaign platform, which called for greater privatization of the economy, while still upholding the elaborate welfare state for which Costa Rica was renowned. And, at the age of 40, Calderón was, next to his father, the youngest politician ever elected president.

Once in office Calderón could do very little to set the national agenda, as the Costa Rican executive office is weak by design. He also had to contend with 130 autonomous institutions that are self-regulating and beyond presidential control. Nonetheless, Calderón had pledged to tinker with the economy while maintaining high benefit levels for the poor and middle class. In practice this was found to be increasingly impractical because of a global recession, which greatly impacted the Costa Rican economy. Declining revenues had to be accompanied by a corresponding cut in social services, which did little to enhance his political popularity. Furthermore, the International Monetary Fund (IMF) demanded imposition of strict austerity measures to shore up the country's credit rating. Over the next three years, the PLN had a field day hammering away at Calderón's economic measures, created by necessity but extracting an increasing social toll. In view of mounting political unrest, Calderón was forced to create a labor council in 1991 to investigate both labor and social issues. His austerity package, while unpopular, did managed to roll back inflation from 25 percent to 9 percent by 1994, his last year in office. But, despite his best efforts, the Costa Rican economy continued its downward spiral: growth fell from 7.7 percent in 1992 to 5.4 percent the following year and only 4.3 percent in 1994. Such lack-

luster performance naturally boded ill for the fortunes of the PUSC in upcoming national elections.

Calderón was constitutionally forbidden from serving a second term in high office, so he stepped aside. On May 8, 1994, PLN candidate María Figuerres Olsen reclaimed the presidency for her party, while Calderón continued on as head of the PUSC. In November 1997 he created a minor stir when, angered by a television show that used puppets to mock him—and other politicians—he attempted to have a patent taken out on his face and name to prevent such satire. At that time the journalistic community feared that a legal decision on Calderón's behalf would prove detrimental to the future of Costa Rican political coverage. The resolution of this issue remains unknown.

Further Reading
Booth, John A. *Costa Rica: Quest for Democracy.* Boulder, Colo.: Westview Press, 1998.

Hytrek, Gary J. "The Politics of Social Development in Costa Rica and the Dominican Republic: Social Agents, the State, and the International Political Economy." Unpublished Ph.D. dissertation, University of California, Los Angeles, 1996.

Lehovco, Fabrice E., and Ivan Molina. *Stuffing the Ballot: Fraud, Elections Reform, and Democratization in Costa Rica.* Cambridge: Cambridge University Press, 2001.

Martinez, Louis U. *Costa Rica's Leadership Role in Economic Integration.* Virginia Beach, Va.: Regent University, 1997.

Wilson, Bruce M. *Costa Rica: Politics, Economics, and Democracy.* Boulder, Colo.: Lynne Rienner Publishers, 1998.

Callejas, Rafael (1943–) *president of Honduras*

Rafael Leonardo Callejas Romero was born in Tegucigalpa, Honduras, on November 14, 1943, the son of well-to-do landowners. He attended several American-sponsored schools nearby and subsequently received his bachelor's and master's degrees at Mississippi State University in 1967. Afterward he enrolled at the Social Studies Institute in the Netherlands to study agricultural development. Once back in Honduras, Callejas was employed by the Higher Council for Economic Planning, where he remained until 1971. Success here proved a springboard to other positions, and over the next decade he held positions at the Office of Agricultural Planning, the Department of Natural Resources, and various other commercial and governmental agencies. Callejas's American-style background made him a fervent supporter of free-market economics, and in 1980 he joined the conservative National Party as its treasurer. The following year the Honduran military finally agreed to support free elections, and the fast-rising Callejas was tapped as his party's presidential nominee. He lost to Roberto Suazo Córdova of the rival Liberal Party and spent the next four years enhancing his conservative credentials by heading the National Renovation Movement faction within the National Party. This group leaned heavily toward U.S. president Ronald Reagan's Caribbean Basin Initiative, again with a view toward advancing free-market agendas. In 1985 Callejas waged a bitter campaign for the presidency, only to lose by a slight margin to Liberal Party candidate José Azcona Hoyo. The loss greatly angered the conservatives, who won an actual higher percentage of votes, but they acquiesced to a power-sharing agreement giving them five cabinet posts and five seats on the Supreme Court. This was a serious attempt at bipartisan reconciliation in a seriously polarized country, but it ultimately failed to address a sinking economy, rising crime, and ongoing friction with Sandinista-led Nicaragua.

The Liberal Party's inability to rectify many of Honduras's problems existed well into the 1989 election. Here, Callejas ran against CARLOS FLORES and defeated him by a clear margin of 51 percent to 43 percent. This victory ushered in a new era of conservative politics, for the National Party had campaigned on a pledge to liberalize the economy, fight crime, and demilitarize the region. Thus, he became only the third civilian ruler since the military takeover of 1980. And, when Callejas was sworn into office on January 27, 1993, it marked the first peaceful transfer of party from one party to another since 1932.

Once in office and enjoying a majority in Congress, Callejas pushed forward with badly needed reforms of the economic sector. Accordingly, governmental expenditures were reduced, the *lempira* (currency) devalued, and taxes and tariffs lowered. Government-held industries were also subject to wholesale privatization and put on the auction block. Wishing to maintain close economic ties with the United States, in 1993 Callejas sponsored an intellectual property law to curb widespread pirating of television and media products. In recognition of his free-trade and democratic stances, Callejas was hailed abroad for his efforts, and in 1989 he served as vice president of the International Democratic Association. He was also sternly anticommunist in his foreign policy outlook, and he harshly condemned the Nicaraguan Sandinistas for their oppression at home and acts of subversion in neighboring countries. However, following the Sandinista defeat at the polls in February 1990, Callejas worked to demilitarize Honduras by disbanding numerous contra (freedom fighter) camps along the Nicaraguan border. The government also disassociated itself from the National Investigation Directorate (DNI) of the Honduran military, which was known for human rights abuses. All told, the National Party fulfilled most of its campaign pledges to the letter, and posited itself as a legitimate alternative to the traditional, government-oriented policies of the Liberals.

Unfortunately, Honduras was beset by a global economic recession that mitigated expected gains. Despite his best efforts, Callejas, like the Liberals before him, failed to stimulate national growth for any sustained period. In fact, many of his policies gained him the ire of the unions, who claimed that his free-market reforms had actually lowered the living standards of many Hondurans. Compounding his political problems was a growing shortage of staple foodstuffs, which, in turn, led to increasing social instability. In sum, the highly touted structural adjustment policies of the National Party failed to improve the plight of average Hondurans. Callejas was forbidden by the constitution to serve more than a single four-year term, but it was perhaps just as well. In the national elections of 1993, the Liberal Party was swept back into power under the aegis of Carlos Roberto Reina. In November 1997 elections Carlos Flores of the Liberal Party was elected president. Since that time Callejas has functioned as a senior spokesman for the National Party.

Further Reading

Hammond, Tony. "The Role of Honduran Armed Forces in the Transition to Democracy." Unpublished master's thesis, University of Florida, 1991.

Karl, Terry L. *Central America in the Twentieth-first Century: The Prospects for a Democratic Region.* Notre Dame, Ind.: University of Notre Dame Press, 1994.

Kelly, Joseph H. "The Strategy of Low-Intensity Conflict and Civic Actions in Honduras." Unpublished master's thesis, University of New Mexico, 1990.

Schulz, Donald E. *The United States, Honduras, and the Crisis in Central America.* Boulder, Colo.: Westview Press, 1994.

Waddell, Rick. *In War's Shadow: Waging Peace in Central America.* New York: Ivy Books, 1997.

Campbell, Kim (1947–) *prime minister of Canada*

Avril Phaedra ("Kim") Campbell was born in Port Alberni, British Columbia, Canada, on March 10, 1947, into a working-class family. Her parents divorced while she was a child, and the experience affected her profoundly. She became her high school valedictorian in 1964 and subsequently studied political science at the University of British Columbia. Campbell graduated with honors, and from 1975 to 1978 she served as a university lecturer. She also briefly pursued an advanced degree at the University of London School of Economics on a government fellowship. By 1981 Campbell decided to abandon academics in favor of law, and she found work with the prestigious firm of Ladner Downs. That same year she became politically active by gaining election to the Vancouver School Board, and she acquired a reputation as an outspoken, contentious individual. Campbell soon came to the attention of the Social Credit Party, and in 1985 William Bennett, the premier (governor) of British Columbia, appointed her to his cabinet. A year later, Campbell banked on her rising popularity to run for the head of the party, but she was badly defeated. However, in October 1986 she gained election to the provincial legislature as a Social Credit Party member, but she gradually grew dissatisfied with the leadership of Premier William Vander Zalm. She was a vocal proponent of abortion and, despite her otherwise conservative credentials, Campbell no longer felt at home in her party. Campbell then left the Social Credit Party, feeling strongly impelled to move onto the national scene. In 1988 she advanced her personal agenda by winning a seat in the House of Commons as a member of the Progressive Conservative Party.

Campbell was not the first woman to serve in parliament but, by dint of rapier wit and articulate speech, she quickly gained national exposure. These attributes

undoubtedly inspired Prime Minister BRIAN MULRONEY to appoint her to his cabinet as the first woman minister of state and Indian affairs in 1989. The following year she again made headlines by becoming Canada's first woman minister of justice and attorney general. Here she proved instrumental in forcing through a tough gun-control bill, while also enhancing the legal status of women involved in rape cases. However, by this time the Progressive Conservatives had been in power for nine consecutive years and were appearing politically spent. Mulroney's popularity was plunging nationally so, in an attempt to regain favor, he appointed Campbell the nation's first woman minister of defense on January 1993. Her tenure there proved brief and uneventful but she claimed that "It's a matter of some pride and satisfaction for me that I happened to be the one that had the opportunity to at least put a dent in that particular glass ceiling." Clearly, bigger things were looming on the horizon.

In February 1993 Mulroney resigned as party head and prime minister and the scramble was on to succeed him. Campbell, by virtue of her gender and relatively novel status, was clearly favored to win, but she endured several runoff votes with Jean Charest of Quebec to do so. However, the Conservatives felt they needed a major facelift to stave off defeat in the upcoming fall elections, and so on June 25, 1993, Campbell was sworn in as Canada's first woman prime minister. As hoped, the decision was favorably received by most Canadians, and she initially rode a wave of popularity. Young, photogenic, and eloquent, the forceful Campbell made her appearance on the world's stage in representing Canada at the annual G7 economic conference in Tokyo, Japan. Here she stood shoulder-to-shoulder with such global luminaries as President BILL CLINTON and made a favorable impression.

Within weeks of coming to power, however, the reservoir of public good will toward Campbell rapidly dissipated in the wake of the poor state of Canada's economy. Unemployment hovered at 10 percent while many Canadians waxed resentful over Mulroney's passage of the Free Trade Agreement with the United States, which, it was feared, would cost many more jobs. Worse, while on the campaign trail, Campbell made several well-publicized gaffes that enhanced her status as a political neophyte. Unable to distance herself from the unpopular Mulroney, she led her party into one of the biggest disasters in Canadian political history. The Progressive

Conservatives, with the exception of two seats, were annihilated by the Liberal Party under JEAN CHRÉTIEN. She then resigned from office in December 1993, having completed Canada's third-shortest tenure as prime minister. The experience of defeat so embittered Campbell that she withdrew from politics altogether. Jean Charest eventually succeeded her as party head.

For several years thereafter, Campbell served as a lecturer at Harvard's John F. Kennedy School of Government in Irvine, California. In September 1996, Prime Minister Chrétien magnanimously appointed her the Canadian consul general in Los Angeles, where she serves to the present day. Her tenure as prime minister may have been brief, but Campbell's status stands for having blazed a new trail for Canadian women in national politics.

Further Reading

Bueckert, Dennis. *Kim Campbell: Above the Shoulders.* Hull, Quebec: Voyageur Publications, 1993.

Campbell, Kim. *Time and Chance: The Political Memoirs of Canada's First Woman Prime Minister.* Toronto: Seal Books, McClelland-Bantam, 1997.

———. *Sayings of Kim Campbell.* Montreal: Robert Davies Publishers, 1993.

Dobbin, Murray. *The Politics of Kim Campbell: From School Trustee to Prime Minister.* Toronto: J. Lorimer, 1993.

Fife, Robert. *Kim Campbell: The Making of a Politician.* Toronto: HarperCollins Publishers, 1993.

Cardoso, Fernando (1931–) *president of Brazil*

Fernando Henrique Cardoso was born at Rio de Janeiro, Brazil, on June 18, 1931, into a prominent military family. Intellectually inclined, however, he declined an army career in favor of pursuing academics. Having received degrees from both the University of São Paulo and the University of Paris, he accepted a teaching position at the former in 1964. That year, a military coup toppled the democratically elected presidency of João Goulart and ushered in an age of political repression. Cardoso, as an outspoken leftist intellectual, became the frequent target of harassment and threats. Rather than risk imprisonment, torture, and possibly death, he fled to Chile and took up teaching. Four years later he returned, anticipating resumption of his academic career, but he was quickly arrested and banned from the campus. Cardoso then flaunted authorities by establishing the Brazilian Analysis and Planning Center, which became a prominent left-wing think tank. When it was bombed by right-wing extremists in the 1970s, he fled again and taught sociology as a visiting lecturer at prestigious universities, including Yale, Berkeley, Stanford, and Oxford. He also became celebrated in academe for the publication of several books that delineated Brazilian dependency upon foreign investment in Marxist terms.

At length the military junta relaxed the atmosphere of repression in Brazil, and Cardoso returned home again to enter politics. Defeated in his run for the Brazilian Senate in 1978, he gained election the following year and also served as vice president of the Brazilian Democratic Movement Party (PMDB). He subsequently failed to become mayor of São Paulo in 1986, but, two years later, he was reelected to the upper house. As a senator, he proved instrumental in orchestrating creation of a new organization, the Brazilian Social Democratic Party. Cardoso by now had also become one of the best-known politicians in Brazil, and among the most respected. To many he combined formidable intellect, unquestioned honesty, and genuine concern for the nation's innumerable poor. His fellow leftists certainly expected much of him.

Cardoso's career reached a turning point following the impeachment of President FERNANDO COLLOR DE MELLO for corruption in 1992. His successor, ITAMAR FRANCO, invited him aboard as his foreign minister. Brazil at that time was wracked by crippling inflation rates that approached 50 percent a month. Having lost three successive finance ministers, Itamar then appointed Cardoso, his fourth in eight months. The bookish professor was not well versed in economics, but he nonetheless fostered relief by drawing up a new currency for the country, the real, and pegging it to the U.S. dollar to contain inflation. This strategy, the so-called Real Plan, was enacted in July 1994 and worked marvelously. Within only three months inflation had dropped to only 1 percent, and the ensuing public acclaim induced Cardoso to seek the presidency of Brazil. On October 8, 1994, he defeated a major left-wing candidate, Luis Ignacio de Silva, with 52 percent of the vote. This was the largest majority won by any presidential candidate in Brazil since 1945.

Over the next four years, this former leftist icon eschewed a radical plan to promote liberalization of the economy, greater foreign investment, and respect for free enterprise. Brazil's economy responded resoundingly, and

Fernando Cardoso *(Embassy of Brazil)*

nomic fortunes. Nearby Argentina's sagging fortunes had a dragging effect upon the Brazilian economy, as did the concurrent Asian currency crisis. Cardoso countered with greater emphasis on job creation. He sold off inefficient state-owned agencies to raise capital. The latter move greatly upset his former leftist allies in Congress, who regarded centralized control of the economy as an article of faith. The government was also forced to spend billions of dollars per month to prevent the real from being drastically devalued, an act that sparked hyperinflation. Despite his best efforts, the Brazilian economy remained sluggish and Cardoso was forced to ration energy sources, his most unpopular austerity measure to that date. Cardoso's term ended on January 1, 2003, when he was replaced by the winner of the October 2002 election, LUIZ INÁCIO LULA DA SILVA of the Worker's Party.

Further Reading

Ames, Barry. *The Deadlock of Democracy in Brazil.* Ann Arbor: University of Michigan Press, 2001.

Black, Carina A. "Fernando Henrique Cardoso: Intellectual Evolution from Exile to Presidency." Unpublished Ph.D. dissertation, University of Nevada, 1997.

Goertzel, Ted G. *Fernando Henrique Cardoso: Reinventing Democracy in Brazil.* Boulder, Colo.: Lynne Rienner Publishers, 1999.

Kingstone, Peter R., and Timothy J. Power. *Democratic Brazil: Action, Institutions, and Processes.* Pittsburgh, Pa.: University of Pittsburgh Press, 2000.

Power, Timothy J. "Blairism, Brazilian Style? Cardoso and the 'Third Way' in Brazil." *Political Science Quarterly* 116 (Winter 2001–2002): 611–636.

Samuels, David. *Ambassadors of the State: Federalism, Ambition, and Congressional Politics in Brazil.* New York: Cambridge University Press, 2002.

growth placed that nation in the forefront among developing countries. Nor did Cardoso forsake Brazil's vast disparities in income and the deep social gulf between rich and poor, and he undertook deliberate measures to increase vocational training and improve access to affordable education and housing. By 1998 Brazil seemed to have cemented its role as a major world player for the first time in its history. That same year a grateful electorate returned Cardoso to office for a second term by wide margins. As an indication of his soaring popularity, the state constitution was amended to allow presidents to serve consecutive terms. Cardoso was sworn in a second time in January 1999, becoming the first Brazilian executive of his generation to complete a full term in office.

Unfortunately for Brazil, and South America in general, the entire region was rocked by declining eco-

Carlsson, Ingvar (1934–) *prime minister of Sweden*

Ingvar Gosta Carlsson was born on November 9, 1934, in Borås, Sweden, the son of a textile worker. He was educated locally and briefly worked the mills before attending the University of Lund to obtain a degree in social science. He graduated in 1958 and became a secretary in the office of Prime Minister Tage Erlander of the Social Democratic Party. The Social Democrats are

Sweden's largest party and they more or less have monopolized national politics since 1932. Erlander himself was a politician of note and an architect of Sweden's famous "cradle to grave" welfare state that has offered the broadest social services—paid for by the highest taxes—in the world. Carlsson functioned well and in 1960 he took a sabbatical to study economics at Northwestern University, Illinois. He then returned home to enter party affairs, becoming head of the Social Democratic Youth League. In 1964 he became the youngest politician ever elected to the Riksdag (parliament) and three years later he advanced to undersecretary of state. In 1969 Erlander retired and was replaced by Olof Palme, a flamboyant, outspoken liberal, while Carlsson occupied his post as minister of education and cultural affairs. This made him, at 34, the youngest cabinet minister in Swedish history. In 1976 the Social Democrats were voted out of power, and Carlsson continued on as a member of the opposition. He also helped orchestrate the 1982 campaign that returned Palme to power, and Carlsson assumed the post of deputy prime minister. In contrast to his fiery superior, Carlsson had cemented his reputation as a calm, seemingly dull technocrat, more given to conciliation than confrontation. When Palme was assassinated on February 28, 1986, Sweden's first political killing in two centuries, the unobtrusive Carlsson was unanimously endorsed by his party to become prime minister.

By the time the new leader took power, the Swedish economy was floundering and he faced some difficult decisions, namely, how to impose austerity measures while maintaining high-benefit welfare policies. He also maintained established Social Democratic policies of strict neutrality and nuclear disarmament. This last point was underscored when several Soviet submarines intruded into Swedish waters and Carlsson, like Palme before him, strongly criticized the superpowers for their arms buildup. But he also championed Sweden's admission to the European Union (EU), which transpired in 1995, as the end of the cold war deflated anxiety over loss of traditional neutrality. The Social Democrats managed to hang on to power in the elections of September 1988, although by reduced margins, and Carlsson tried balancing fiscal responsibility with welfare politics. He introduced stark austerity measures to shore up the economy, which were defeated in parliament, and he resigned from office on February 15, 1990. He resumed power two weeks later after a watered-down version of his plan

finally passed. However, the economy continued sinking, and, in September 1991, the Social Democrats experienced their worse defeated since 1928, winning just 38 percent of the popular vote. Carlsson resigned a second time in favor of CARL BILDT of the Moderate Party.

For the next three years Carlsson served as head of the opposition until the 1996 elections returned Labor to power. He then established three new goals for the Social Democrats: to improve the economy with increased revenues and cuts in government spending, to strengthen the welfare system with regard to children and the elderly, and to adopt ecologically sound approaches to economic and industrial growth. Carlsson also sought to elevate Sweden's profile on the international scene by increasing aid to developing countries and by providing soldiers to serve as UN peacekeepers. One of his proudest moments came in November 1994 when the public referendum on EU membership passed by 52.2 percent, and Sweden formally joined the following year. The Social Democrats continued to enjoy high ratings at home, but, in October 1995, Carlsson suddenly announced his retirement from politics after a successful nine years as prime minister. After some internal party wrangling in March 1996, he was replaced by GORAN PERSSON.

Since retiring, Carlsson has been extremely active in the field of global policy. In 1997 he became a member of the advisory board of the United Nations Staff College, along with serving as chairman of the Foundation for Strategic Research. He concurrently serves as chairman of the Olof Palme International Center to promote peace-related issues. In May 1999 Secretary-General KOFI ANNAN appointed him to head an independent inquiry to investigate allegations concerning the United Nations's inactivity during the 1994 genocide in Rwanda.

Further Reading

Arter, David. "A Tale of Two Carlssons: The Swedish General Election of 1988." *Parliamentary Affairs* 42, no. 1 (1989): 84–101.

Aspalter, Christian. *Importance of Christian and Social Democratic Movements in Welfare Politics.* Huntington, N.Y.: Nova Science Publishers, 2001.

Aylott, N. "Back to the Future: The 1994 Swedish Election." *Party Politics* 1, no. 3 (1995): 419–429.

Miles, Lee. *Sweden and the European Union Evaluated.* New York: Continuum, 2000.

Ruin, Olaf. "Three Swedish Prime Ministers: Tage Erlander, Olaf Palme, and Ingvar Carlsson." *West European Politics* 14, no. 3 (1991): 58–82.

Castro, Fidel (1926–) *president of Cuba*

Fidel Castro Ruz was born on his family's sugar plantation in Birán, Cuba, on August 13, 1926. As a youth he attended Jesuit schools at Santiago de Cuba prior to attending the University of Havana in 1945. A highly intelligent, charismatic figure with a flair for showmanship, Castro was elected president of the University Students' Federation and became embroiled in revolutionary activities. In 1947 he joined a force intending to overthrow dictator Rafael Trujillo in the Dominican Republic and the following year Castro participated in violent student rebellions throughout Colombia. After receiving his law degree in 1950, he opened a practice in Havana, and he made a name for himself by defending the poor. By 1952 Castro felt that dramatic change in Cuba was imperative to alleviate social inequity, so he joined the Partido Ortodoxo as a candidate for parliament. Unfortunately, General Fulgencio Batista overthrew the presidency of Carlos Prío Socarrás and canceled all further political activity. His dictatorship proved brutal, and Castro reacted by raising a small force of revolutionaries who attacked a military barracks on July 26, 1953. They were nearly wiped out and the surviving rebels, including Castro, were arrested and sentenced to stiff prison sentences. Most were subsequently released under a general amnesty in 1955. Castro then relocated to Mexico to regroup, where he met and allied himself with Ernesto "Che" Guevara, an Argentine expatriate. On December 2, 1955, Castro and 82 men of his "26th of July" movement returned to Cuba, where they were again badly defeated in combat. He and a handful of survivors then fled to the shelter of the Sierra Maestra Mountains, where they regrouped and recruited new members. By 1958 the Cuban populace had grown tired of Batista's excesses, and Castro's rebels launched a series of successful operations against him. The hated regime was finally toppled on January 1, 1959, and the ragtag insurgents triumphantly marched into Havana. As revolutionary leader, Castro now became nominal head of the country.

The United States warily watched Castro's success, but Washington did establish formal diplomatic relations with the revolutionary regime. However, Castro, who up to this point had not espoused any clear ideological leanings, began to drift into the Soviet orbit. When he started nationalizing American holdings and signed a comprehensive trade deal with the Soviet Union, the United States broke off diplomatic relations. Worse, on April 11, 1961, a force of 1,300 Cuban exiles, armed and trained by the Central Intelligence Agency, landed at the Bay of Pigs. Castro rallied his forces and personally led the counterattack against the rebels, who surrendered, much to the embarrassment of President John F. Kennedy. By October 1962, Kennedy also uncovered the presence of Russian nuclear missiles, which were being secretly deployed on Cuban soil, and he ordered a naval blockade of the island. The world flirted dangerously with nuclear war for several days before the Soviets agreed to withdraw their weapons, while the Americans pledged not to invade Cuba. Castro then formally committed himself to establishing Cuba as a client state of the Soviet Union, and he initiated a doctrinaire Marxist-Leninist political and economic regime. The United States countered by imposing a strict economic embargo, which is enforced to the present day.

For 40 years Castro has ruled Cuba as both a virtual dictator and as something of a Third World celebrity. His regime posted impressive gains in terms of promoting literacy and health care, among the finest in Latin America, but his centrally planned economic schemes, based on export of sugar and nickel, proved disastrous. The Cuban economy performed precariously and inefficiently, even when aided by large subsidies from the Soviet Union and its allies. Hence, for most Cubans, acute shortages of nearly every possible commodity are the mainstay of everyday existence. Moreover, the Castro regime is utterly intolerant of dissent and frequently jails its internal critics for long periods without trial. The twin evils of economic deprivation and political repression resulted in a steady stream of refugees from the country, usually to the United States. Castro has been forced to relax his ideological grasp on the economy and he has loosened state control to allow some minor free trade and foreign investment. The economy, however, simply muddles along and Cuba remains one of the poorest nations of the Western Hemisphere.

Despite Castro's mishandling of economic affairs and his severe repression at home, he enjoys folk-hero status in the developing world for both defiance of America and longevity in power. For many years after the revolution, Castro sought to export revolution to other counties, particularly Latin America, which failed dismally. He has since renounced promotion of violence, but throughout the 1970s and 1980s, Cuban troops were deployed abroad to prop up tottering Marxist regimes in Africa and Nicaragua. In the fall of 1983, U.S. president Ronald Reagan forcibly captured and evicted a large Cuban garrison from the Caribbean island of Grenada, a major setback. Nor were the Cubans able to squelch the American-backed guerrillas, or contras, who opposed the Nicaraguan regime by force. The collapse of the Soviet Union in 1991, and the ensuing loss of subsidies, also contributed to the overall economic morass. However, with respect to successive American administrations, eager for his departure, the aging Castro still manages to "beard the lion in his den." In 2000 a major political flap occurred over the issue of Elián González, a six-year-old Cuban refugee whose mother drowned while escaping to Florida. Elían's father, still in Cuba, demanded the return of his son, which was refused by the Cuban exile community in Miami. Castro, meanwhile, made great political hay by orchestrating mass demonstrations in Havana, demanding the child's return. It took an armed raid by the U.S. Justice Department to repatriate the child from his American relatives and reunite him with his father. However, this move utterly outraged the Cuban-American community. Consequently, they sought to punish the Democratic administration of President BILL CLINTON by voting against his party's successor, Vice President ALBERT GORE, during the 2000 presidential election. In Florida this translated into an additional 50,000 votes for the Republican challenger, GEORGE W. BUSH, and may have proved a decisive factor in his electoral victory there.

After four decades in power, Castro carries on as an increasingly minor player on the world scene. His unwillingness to part with the rhetoric or dogma of revolutionary communism and his refusal to allow free elections at a time when democracy and freedom flourishes worldwide render him an anachronistic relic from the past. Admired in some quarters, thoroughly despised in others, he remains in office with his power unchallenged. Castro's legacy is largely one befitting a quixotic, revolutionary dictator—full of symbolism, long on charisma, and decidedly short on lasting accomplishments.

Further Reading

Azicri, Max. *Cuba Today and Tomorrow: Reinventing Socialism.* Gainesville: University of Florida Press, 2001.

Baudach, Ann Louise. *Cuba Confidential: Love and Hate in the Two Havanas.* New York: Random House, 2002.

Castro, Fidel. *On Imperialist Globalism.* New York: Zed Books, 2002.

Geyer, Georgie A. *Guerrilla Prince: The Untold Story of Fidel Castro.* Kansas City, Mo.: Andrews McNeel Pub., 2001.

Lopez, Juan J. *Democratizing Cuba: Lessons Learned from Eastern Europe and U.S. Foreign Policy.* Baltimore: Johns Hopkins University Press, 2002.

Trento, Angelo. *Castro and Cuba: From Revolution to the Present.* New York: Interlink Books, 2000.

Wright, Thomas L. *Latin America in the Age of the Cuban Revolution.* Westport, Conn.: Praeger, 2001.

Cavaco Silva, Anibal (1939–) *prime minister of Portugal*

Anibal Antonio Cavaco Silva was born in Boliqueime, Portugal, on July 15, 1939, the son of a gas station attendant. He overcame a hardscrabble existence and graduated from the Technical University of Lisbon in 1964. After several years as a finance researcher, Cavaco Silva obtained his Ph.D. from the University of York, England, in 1973 and returned home to commence a distinguished academic career. For the next six years he taught economics at the New University of Lisbon and in 1974 he joined the newly formed Portuguese Social Democratic Party (PSD), which touts a moderately conservative ideology. Since the restoration of Portuguese democracy in 1974, national politics had been dominated by the Socialist Party, which revised the national constitution to enshrine certain aspects of state control over the economy. Six years of a government-led command economy left Portugal broke and among Europe's poorest countries, and, in 1980, Cavaco Silva decided to enter politics. In January of that year he gained appointment as minister of finance in the administration of PSD prime minister Francisco Sa Carneiro. In this capacity he began an earnest rollback of Socialist nationalization policies, but he was always stymied by constitutional provisions ensuring state control. Discouraged, in January 1981, Cavaco Silva retired from politics to resume teaching and serve as an adviser to the Bank of Portugal. He remained so disposed until 1985, when a major shakeup of PSD leadership occurred.

Cavaco Silva had grown dissatisfied with the timid pace of liberalization by the PSD and he mounted a challenge for control of the party leadership. Young, urbane, and charismatic, he accomplished exactly that while also advocating breaking all ties to the Socialist Party in their coalition government. When this rupture happened, early elections were called and in 1985 Cavaco Silva became prime minister with a minority PSD government. As the nation's political leader, he enacted sweeping changes to modernize Portugal's inefficient economy by privatizing government-run industries, and he emerged as a strong advocate of Portugal's entry into the European Union (EU), which occurred on January 1, 1986. Such neoliberal policies rattled the Socialist and Communist majority in the National Assembly, and in 1987 they brought down Cavaco Silva's government with a vote of no confidence. Undeterred, the young prime minister called for new elections based upon his administration's achievements, and the PSD easily won more than 50 percent of the vote. This victory constituted the first time since 1974 that a Portuguese government was able to fulfill its four-year mandate without opposition interference.

Politically strengthened by the new vote, Cavaco Silva redoubled his efforts to liberalize the moribund national economy. He accomplished this by increasing the pace of privatization and through the wholesale reform of labor, housing, and fiscal laws. And, enjoying a majority in the National Assembly, he finally succeeded in revising the national constitution in dropping the last vestiges of Socialist-inspired economic controls. Portugal's economy posted impressive gains, and, in 1991, the voters responded by returning the PSD to power with over 50 percent of votes cast. This was a political feat rarely accomplished in post–World War II Europe, but it guaranteed that Cavaco Silva could continue with his modernizing trends. He also took deliberate steps to fully integrate the national economy with that of the EU, and he adopted the narrowly prescribed measures to reduce inflation, decrease public sector debt, and maintain a steady currency necessary to join the European Monetary Union.

By 1995 Cavaco Silva had been prime minister of Portugal for a decade. Unfortunately, that year witnessed a worsening economic climate brought on by a global recession, which complicated relations between the PSD prime minister and his Socialist president, MARIO SOARES. In January 1995 Cavaco Silva decided to with-draw from politics altogether, and he resigned as party head in favor of Fernando Nogueira. PSD fortunes were further dashed that October, when the Socialists garnered a majority vote in the National Assembly. Cavaco Silva then sought to reverse the tide by running for the presidency, but he lost to Socialist candidate Jorge Sampaio. Afterward, he returned to academe as a professor of economics and consultant to the Bank of Portugal. His political career was not entirely successful, but Cavaco Silva made history by engineering the policies that liberalized Portugal's economy and helped consolidate the nation's peaceful transition to democracy. He resurfaced briefly in December 1999 at Macao, China, where he signed a joint declaration with the Chinese government over the future of that 450-year-old Portuguese colony. This agreement guarantees continuation of Macao's capitalist economy and political system for the next 50 years under the aegis of the Macao Special Administrative Region (SAR). "I welcome it and pin great hope on it," Cavaco Silva announced.

Further Reading

Corkill, David. "Portugal Votes for Change and Stability: The Election of 1995." *West European Politics* 19 (April 1996): 403–410.

Gallagher, T. "Goodbye to Revolution: The Portuguese Election of July 1987." *West European Politics* 11 (January 1988): 139–145.

Grayson, G. W. "A Revitalized Portugal." *Current History* 89 (November 1990): 373–376, 390–391.

Storeloff, A. "Between Corporation and Class Struggle: The Portuguese Labour Movement and the Cavaco Silva Governments." *West European Politics* 15 (October 1992): 118–150.

Syrett, Stephen. *Contemporary Portugal: Dimensions of Economic and Political Change*. Brookfield, Vt.: Ashgate, 2002.

Cédras, Raoul (1949–   ) *Haitian military leader*
Raoul Cédras was born in Haiti July 9, 1949. His father had previously served as mayor of the town of Jérémie, and he was a close political supporter of dictator Jean-Claude "Baby Doc" Duvalier. After his father's death in 1971, the younger Cédras was allowed to attend the Haitian military academy. He proved himself a competent, nonpolitical professional soldier after graduating, and by 1990 he had reached the rank of brigadier general.

In this capacity Cédras functioned as security chief to JEAN-BERTRAND ARISTIDE during Haiti's first-ever democratic elections. Aristide was apparently impressed by his performance and military demeanor, for, after being sworn in, he promoted Cédras to army commander in chief in July 1992. Haiti, then the Western Hemisphere's poorest country, was also one of the most politically oppressed. For many years army troops were dispatched to support a variety of dictators, but the regime of "Baby Doc" Duvalier relied on its own paramilitary forces, the dreaded Tonton Macoutes ("Boogeymen"). These were ruthless brigands who killed and terrorized known political opponents on a lark. They even eclipsed the military in terms of brutality. But with the return of democracy in 1991, organized thugs disappeared only to be replaced by roving gangs of equally unlawful Aristide supporters. Political killings and unrest were on the rise again. For a man of Cédras's background and orientation, this became an intolerable situation.

Aristide had made his reputation as a firebrand politician and champion of the poor. His promises to redistribute land, double the minimum wage, and freeze the price on goods frightened the elite business community, who felt their lavish lifestyle threatened. Aristide also alienated large segments of the military establishment by arbitrarily sacking several top officers. For Cédras, the most threatening development occurred when Aristide invited Swiss police officials to Haiti, apparently intent on forming his own security forces independent of the army. The turning point was reached in September 1991, when the president, having delivered a fiery speech at the United Nations in New York, subsequently addressed a throng of followers at a rally. There he seemingly approved the practice of "necklacing," a method of killing political opponents by fitting them with burning tires around their necks. On September 3, 1991, a group of soldiers suddenly mutinied and called for the overthrow of Aristide. The exact role Cédras played in the uprising has never been established, but within hours the president had been detained while the general took to the airwaves. He declared: "Today the armed forces find themselves obligated to assume the heavy responsibility to keep the ship of state afloat." Aristide meanwhile was quickly flown to Venezuela for his own safety, and from there he made his way to the United States. Haiti had endured its latest coup.

Aristide may have been a dictatorial rabble-rouser in his own right, but his removal by force was widely condemned by the United Nations and the Organization of American States. President George H. W. Bush summarily imposed economic sanctions, pending the restoration of the president. Cédras, however, felt no inclination to comply. Shrugging off sanctions and threats of American force, he declared: "Democracy is a process of evolution, education. It is not something you can impose." However, by July 1993 sanctions had severely crippled the Haitian economy and unemployment had skyrocketed to 80 percent. Under these circumstances, the general felt more disposed to negotiate, and on July 3, 1993, he signed an agreement allowing Aristide's restoration in exchange for political amnesty. When the October deadline passed, Cédras insisted upon further negotiations for the president's return. He also tightened the screws upon his fellow citizens by allowing troops to rough up supporters at pro-Aristide rallies while also ejecting international human rights observers from the country. A new U.S. president, BILL CLINTON, anxious to head off a new wave of Haitian refugees arriving in Florida, again threatened to use military force to restore Aristide. Sensing that the game was finally up, Cédras once more entered into negotiations involving a last-ditch diplomatic effort headed by former president Jimmy Carter, former chief of staff Colin Powell, and Georgia senator Sam Nunn. On September 18, the four men signed an agreement just hours before American troops began landing in Haiti to restore order. As part of the deal, Cédras was allowed to fly to Panama with his family and keep his personal wealth.

The former military leader has since remained in Panama unmolested, but, in February 1998, a Haitian judge applied for his extradition to face charges in the murder of 10 Aristide supporters. The Panamanian government, citing the lack of an extradition treaty between the two countries, refused to comply. Still the wheels of justice continue rolling. In November 2000, a Haitian judge pronounced life sentences on more than 30 exiled senior army officers for crimes of murder, including one against Cédras. The general, meanwhile, continually ignores all summons and lives a life of luxury in Panama. He is allegedly writing his memoirs.

Further Reading

Avril, Prosper. *From Glory to Disgrace: The Haitian Army, 1804–1994.* Parkland, Fla.: Universal Publishers, 1999.

Fatton, Robert. *Haiti's Predatory Republic: The Unending Transition to Democracy.* Boulder, Colo.: Lynne Rienner Publishers, 2002.

Laguerre, Michel S. *The Military and Society in Haiti.* Knoxville: University of Tennessee Press, 1993.

Maguire, Robert. "Haiti: State of Terror in Mufti." *Caribbean Affairs* 7 no. 4 (1994): 78–86.

Morley, Morris, and Chris McGillion. "'Disobedient' Generals and the Politics of Redemocratization: The Clinton Administration and Haiti." *Political Science Quarterly* 112 (Fall 1997): 363–385.

Chamorro, Violeta Barrios de (1929–   )
president of Nicaragua

Violeta Barrios was born in Rivas, Nicaragua, on October 18, 1929, the daughter of a wealthy rancher. She was educated at a Roman Catholic girl's school in San Antonio, Texas, and also attended Blackstone College, Virginia, until the death of her father in 1948. Barrios then returned home to help manage the ranch before meeting Pedro Joaquín Chamorro Cardenal, publisher of the opposition newspaper *La Prensa.* They fell in love and married. Nicaragua at that time was controlled by the family of Anastasio Somoza, who monopolized the economy and brutally crushed any opposition. However, he singularly failed to silence *La Prensa,* and Pedro Chamorro endured several bouts of imprisonment and exile for criticizing the regime. Both he and his family returned to Nicaragua under an amnesty in 1960 and he resumed his journalistic war against the Somoza family. By now control of the country had passed to Somoza's eldest son, Anastasio Somoza Debayle, who proved even more ruthless than his father. On January 10, 1978, Pedro Chamorro was assassinated while his wife was out of the country. If through this grisly expedient Somoza had hoped to intimidate *La Prensa* into submission, he was sadly mistaken. Violeta Chamorro boldly assumed the mantle of leadership as editor and continued her fight against tyranny. She was joined by guerrillas of the communist-inspired Sandinista movement under Daniel Ortega. In July 1979, opponents finally disposed of the hatred regime. In recognition of her contributions to the final victory, Chamorro was invited to join a five-member civilian executive junta now running the country.

Within a year the real intentions of the Sandinista regime had become painfully apparent to Chamorro. Intent on imposing a communist-style dictatorship, Sandinista leaders cut ties with the United States and established close relations with the Soviet Union and its sole Latin American ally, Fidel Castro's Cuba. This alarmed the editor of *La Prensa,* for she was dedicated to the growth of democracy. She quit the ruling circle in 1980. Worse, discontent over Sandinista oppression fueled a growing counterinsurgency by anticommunist rebel forces (contras) funded in part by the United States. Chamorro also weighed in heavily in criticizing the government, proving so strident a critic that the Sandinistas repeatedly shut *La Prensa* down. Each time, however, international outcry forced the Ortega regime to allow the paper to resume publishing. Chamorro, having endured the same abuse previously at the hands of Somoza, was not about to be silenced by the Sandinistas—despite the fact that two of her children worked for the government. Two others sided with the contras.

The combined pressure of diplomacy and guerrilla warfare forced Ortega to accept free elections slated for February 1990. Chamorro, by virtue of her international stature, was then chosen as the candidate of UNO, a coalition of 17 disparate parties. In this capacity she railed against the Sandinistas for betraying democratic principles, ruining the economy through excessive military spending, and attempting to conquer neighboring countries, such as El Salvador, through subversion. The majority of Nicaraguans agreed, for on February 25, 1990, UNO was swept into power by taking 55 percent of the vote and also securing a majority—51 out of 92—of the seats in the National Assembly. Chamorro's victory represented the complete repudiation of communist oppression and marked an end to Soviet influence in Central America. Moreover, by dint of steely resolve, she made history by becoming Nicaragua's first woman president and also the first female head of state in the Western Hemisphere.

Once in office, Chamorro wasted no time in reversing Sandinista policies. Aid to guerrillas in El Salvador promptly ceased, the contras were integrated into the Nicaraguan army, and the size of military expenditures curtailed. She also advocated a return to promoting private property, a free-market economy, and complete freedom of the press. Chamorro's first years in office, however, were marked by an economic downturn caused in large measure by such drastic institutional restructuring. The Sandinistas, still led by Ortega and clearly the single-biggest party in the congress, did their utmost to obstruct legislation and thwart change. Nonetheless, by

1996 the economy had turned around significantly and posted annual growth rates of 5 percent. The 65-year-old grandmother then retired from politics rather than seek another term. In October 1996 Ortega was again defeated by ARNOLDO ALEMÁN of UNO, thereby confirming the demise of Sandinista designs upon Nicaragua.

Despite her advancing age, Chamorro's national popularity persists and may be measured by the fact that in March 2001 she declined repeated invitations to run for the presidency again. "My time as president is over," she declared. "Thank you so much, but I don't believe that my work is now as a candidate for president." Despite this reticence, her legacy as the silver-haired matron who first defied and then slew the Sandinista dragon is secure. Democracy seldom possessed a more unlikely heroine.

Further Reading

Chamorro, Violeta, Guido Fernandez, and Sonia Cruz de Baltodano. *Dreams of the Heart: The Autobiography of President Violeta Barrios de Chamorro of Nicaragua.* New York: Simon and Schuster, 1996.

Close, David. *Nicaragua: The Chamorro Years.* Boulder, Colo.: Lynne Rienner Publishers, 1999.

Martinez, Mario. "Property as an Instrument of Power in Nicaragua." *University of Miami Law Review* 53 (July 1999): 907–912.

Payne, Douglas W. *How the Sandinistas Lost Nicaragua's Second Revolution.* New York: Freedom House, 1990.

Prevost, Gary. "The Nicaraguan Revolution—Six Years after the Sandinista Electoral Defeat." *Third World Quarterly* 17, no. 2 (1996): 307–327.

Charles, Mary Eugenia (1919–) *prime minister of Dominica*

Mary Eugenia Charles was born in Pointe Michel, Dominica, on May 15, 1919, into an affluent and highly conservative business family. Significantly, she was the granddaughter of former slaves while her father lived to the age of 107 years. After receiving a Catholic education in neighboring Grenada, Charles attended the University of Toronto and acquired her law degree in 1947. She subsequently completed her legal studies at the Inner Temple, London, and she was called to the bar in 1949. Charles returned home that year to become the first female attorney on Dominica. From this point onward the island was experiencing the dramatic change from a British colony to an independent nation.

Granted self-rule in 1968, it was administered by chief minister Edward LeBlanc of the United Workers Party (UWP), who authored the Seditious and Undesirable Publication Act to muzzle critics. Such censorship stirred Charles into action, and that year she helped found the Dominica Freedom Party (DFP) to thwart growing leftist influence. Defeated in her run for the House of Assembly in 1970, Charles managed to become an appointed member two years later, and, in 1975, she was finally elected. A stirring, forceful personality, Charles emerged as the opposition leader against the tyrannical practices of LeBlanc's successor, Patrick Roland Jack. Once Dominica had achieved independence in 1978, Jack's government passed legislation outlawing strikes and limiting freedom of the press. This spurred the Dominica Labour Party to quit the ruling coalition and call for new elections. On June 21, 1979, the opposition DFP candidates were swept into power in a landslide. Charles, as nominal party head, became prime minister as well as minister of finance and foreign affairs. She was also the first woman prime minister to head a Caribbean nation.

Charles inherited a politically unstable polity and, in 1981, she weathered two attempted coups to restore Jack to power. Nonetheless, she remained committed to a conservative course and was determined to reverse many of the left-wing policies of her predecessors. This included greater emphasis on free enterprise, privatization of government-owned industries, and unrestricted foreign investment. "We should give the people not luxury but a little comfort—a job, the means to build a house, assistance for agricultural pursuits," she said. "We will never be rich, but I think we can be a self-reliant nation with a little thrift and development." Charles was also unswerving loyalty to Western democracies in her foreign policy, and she cultivated extremely close ties with U.S. president Ronald Reagan of the United States. She also felt that the island's military establishment was too heavily involved in drug smuggling to be of much use, so she ordered it disbanded. Dominica had become the Caribbean's bastion of conservatism.

The defining moment of Charles's career occurred in October 1983 when Prime Minister Maurice Bishop of Grenada was overthrown and brutally murdered in a communist-inspired coup. Previously, Charles had been elected chairman of the newly created Organization of Eastern Caribbean States to which Dominica and Grenada belong. In this capacity she made the first appeals to President Reagan for military intervention in Grenada to restore order and punish Bishop's murderers. On October 25, 1983, American forces stormed ashore, and during a news conference televised around the world, Charles stood by Reagan's side throughout the broadcast. Once the island was secure, she also contributed police forces to help maintain order. All told, this display of her verve earned Charles the appellation "Iron Lady of the Caribbean." Consequently, in 1991 she was knighted as a dame of the British Empire. Dominica's inhabitants also appreciated her tough, no-nonsense approach to leadership, for in 1985 and 1990 the voters returned her to power.

For 15 years Charles served as Dominica's prime minister, longer than any other incumbent. In this capacity she supported many U.S.–sponsored programs and instruments, including the Caribbean Basin Initiative and the Eastern Caribbean Regional Defense Force. In 1989, she vocally supported President George H. W. Bush's invasion of Panama to oust drug lord General Manuel Noriega from power—the only Caribbean leader to do so. But she also raised American eyebrows with her decision to open up trade with communist Cuba. "I have always said that I'll do business with the Devil if it will buy products and put money in the hands of my people," she insisted. In 1990 the DFP again proved victorious, but just barely, and the following year Charles relinquished the title of party head while still remaining prime minister. After doing much to improve the island's infrastructure, including building schools, hospitals, and tourist facilities, she resigned from office in 1995. Her hand-picked successor, foreign affairs minister Brian Alleyne, was defeated that year by the UWNP candidate Edison James.

Further Reading

Baker, Patrick L. *Centering the Periphery: Chaos, Order, and the Ethnohistory of Dominica.* Kingston, Jamaica: University of the West Indies, 1994.

Higbie, Janet. *Eugenia: The Caribbean's Iron Lady.* London: Macmillan, 1993.

Honychurch, Lennox. *The Dominica Story: A History of the Island.* London: Macmillan, 1995.

Myers, Robert A., comp. *Dominica.* Santa Barbara, Calif.: ABC-Clio, 1987.

Trouillot, Michel-Rolph. *Peasants and Capital: Dominica in the World Economy.* Baltimore: Johns Hopkins University Press, 1988.

Chaudhry, Mahendra (1942–) *prime minister of Fiji*

Mahendra Pal Chaudhry was born in Tuvua, Ba province, Fiji, on September 2, 1942, the grandson of indentured servants from India. His homeland is a collection of 322 diverse islands that became part of the British Empire in 1874. As such, the British imported several thousand Indians to work the sugar cane fields as laborers. This fact never sat easily with the indigenous Fijian population who, since gaining independence from Britain in 1970, have contrived political means to keep non-natives from holding high office. In fact, while Indians comprise the majority of Fiji's population, they are officially accorded second-class status with fewer rights and privileges. Ethnic friction continues unabated and has resulted in several military coups against the sitting government.

Chaudhry completed his primary and secondary education at schools constructed for Indian students before working at the Emperor Gold Mines in 1960. From there he rose to become branch secretary of the Fiji Public Service Association in 1968, and he commenced a long and productive association with labor and farming organizations. Chaudhry served as assistant secretary of the Fiji Trades Union Congress in 1975, rising to national secretary between 1988 and 1992. He performed much useful work promoting the export of sugar, Fiji's main cash crop. Chaudhry also helped found the National Farmers Union in 1978 and the Fiji Labor Party in 1985. In this capacity he gained election to parliament in 1987 before being tapped to serve as minister of finance and economic planning in the coalition government of Timoci Bavadra. However, native resentment against Indians in such high office culminated in a successful coup by Lieutenant Colonel Sitiveni Rabuka on May 14, 1987. Chaudhry was held hostage for six days before being released. After nearly a decade of internal wrangling and international pressure, Fiji finally adopted a new constitution designed to avoid purely ethnic politics. Furthermore, it recognizes the Great Council of Chiefs as a legitimate body for determining policies that pertain to the native Fijian population. It was under this system that, on May 20, 1999, the long-serving Chaudhry became Fiji's first prime minister of Indian descent. The Labour Party also shared in his impressive success, winning 54 out of 71 seats outright, while Colonel Rabuka's SVT Party captured only eight.

Chaudhry strove mightily to avoid ethnic friction with the majority Fijian natives, but his ensuing land policies for sugar cane growers placed them on an inevitable collision course with the government. Virtually all of the growers are of Indian or mixed heritage and they seek to lease land owned by native Fijians for the longest possible terms. Chaudhry's insistence that the growers receive assistance in grants and loans struck many Fijians as overt favoritism toward the Indian community. Moreover, many senior tribal chiefs, angered by Chaudhry's victory in the first place, refused to renew their land leases to Indians. The growing crisis erupted on May 19, 2000, nearly a year to the day after Chaudhry took office. A group of disgruntled businessmen under George Speight stormed the parliament building in Suva and held the prime minister and several senior officials hostage for 56 days. During this interval, Speight negotiated a settlement with the Fijian military. Henceforth, the constitution would be amended to prevent non-native Fijians from holding higher office. Furthermore, the new president and prime minister would be chosen by the Great Council of Chiefs. Chaudhry, once released, denounced the pact and tried rallying international support to help him regain his office. In December 2000 he was formally rebuffed by the governments of New Zealand and Australia, who nonetheless demanded a return to the 1997 constitution. Fiji, meanwhile, is currently ruled by former bank president Laisenia Qarase, who was elected head of an interim authority by the Great Council of Chiefs. The politics of ethnicity continue to dominate Fiji's political landscape.

Further Reading

Alley, Roderic. "The Coup Crisis in Fiji." *Australian Journal of Political Science* 35 (November 2000): 515–20.

Fraenkel, Jon. "The Clash of Dynasties and Rise of Demagogues: Fiji's Tauri Vakaukauwa of May 2000." *Journal of Pacific History* 35 (December 2000): 295–308.

Kelly, John D. *Represented Communities: Fiji and World Decolonization.* Chicago: University of Chicago Press, 2001.

Lal, Brij V. *Broken Waves: A History of the Fiji Islands in the Twentieth Century.* Honolulu: University of Hawaii Press, 1992.

———. "Chiefs and Thieves and Other People Besides: The Making of George Speight's Coup," *Journal of Pacific History* 35 (December 2000): 281–293.

———, and Michael Pretes. *Coup: Reflections on the Political Crisis in Fiji.* Canberra: Australian National University, 2001.

Robertson, R. T. *The Indigenous Question: Fiji and the 2000 Coup.* New York: Zed Books, 2001.

Chávez, Hugo (1954–   ) *president of Venezuela*
Hugo Chávez Frías was born in Sabaneta, Venezuela, on July 28, 1954, the son of two elementary schoolteachers. He endured a life of grinding poverty—his house had a grass roof and dirt floors—but he nonetheless distinguished himself academically. Chávez subsequently attended the prestigious Venezuelan Military Academy, the only higher education his family could afford for him, and he emerged as a lieutenant of the elite parachute forces in 1975. Political stability in Venezuela at that time was slowly being undermined by a poor economy and rampant political corruption. Chávez sought to fight the latter by clandestinely founding the Bolivarian Revolutionary Movement among like-minded soldiers. On February 4, 1992, he led 1,000 of his paratroopers in a failed coup attempt against President CARLOS ANDRÉS PÉREZ, whom the soldiers regarded as hopelessly corrupt. After severe fighting, the disenchanted officer surrendered and was placed in jail. However, the following year Pérez was brought before the Supreme Court and forced to resign from office. His replacement, RAFAEL CALDERA, subsequently released Chávez from prison under a general amnesty. Previously, while imprisoned, Chávez committed himself to studying great literature, everything from the Bible (he remains a committed Catholic) to Karl Marx. He thereafter embarked on a personal crusade to stamp out corruption, help the poor, and shore up the sagging national economy.

Once released, Chávez made a much publicized visit to Cuba's Fidel Castro, a personal hero, in 1994. He shortly afterward returned home to found the Polo Patriótico (Patriotic Pole) Party to unite diverse factions in a struggle against the established order. Chávez, a fiery and charismatic speaker, then unveiled his campaign for the presidency. During the campaign he unabashedly invoked Marxist rhetoric about helping disadvantaged citizens, and he reiterated charges of corruption and mismanagement against the government. His message was enthusiastically received among Venezuela's poor, the majority of the population, who were suffering disproportionately in this period of economic hardship. They began publicly and affectionately referring to this former paratrooper as El Comandante. On December 6, 1998, Chávez decisively defeated Henrique Salas Romer, a Yale-educated economist, by 56.5 percent to 39.5 percent of the vote, becoming the nation's youngest elected president. He also retained his personal commitment toward national reform and social justice with a vengeance.

Once in power, Chávez quickly drew up a public referendum to reform the constitution. He advocated discarding the bicameral legislature in favor of a single assembly to reduce corruption, enhancing the powers of the presidency, restricting civilian control over the military, extending a president's tenure from five to six years, and allowing the president to run for consecutive terms. The previous law, established in the late 1950s, allowed presidents to return to office only after 10 years had elapsed. Finally, in a nod toward Venezuela's revolutionary past and indebtedness to liberator Simón Bolívar, his measure called for renaming the country the Bolivarian Republic of Venezuela. In December 1999, the public approved of Chávez's reforms by 71 percent. The victory was achieved over the objections and warnings of the political establishment, who feared establishment of a dictatorship.

As president, Chávez's main objectives have been fighting poverty, reforming the fiscal system, and restructuring Venezuela's massive foreign debt. Inflation, running between 25 percent and 45 percent per month in 1998, also required immediate attention. He therefore cut back production of oil, the country's leading export, which doubled its price and brought much-needed revenues to the state coffers. He also embarked on an aggressive public works project to tackle unemployment. The dramatic reforms made significant gains in improving Venezuela's economic climate, but his task was greatly complicated by torrential floods that killed an estimated 30,000 people and left 10 times that number homeless. Nevertheless, the turn toward populism rendered Chávez a popular figure among the nation's poor—the majority of voters. On July 30, 2000, he defeated opposition candidate Francisco Arias Cárdenas with 59 percent of the vote. That November he also further enhanced his presidential powers by securing the assembly's consent to presidential rule by decree, without legislative debate, over a wide range of issues.

However well-intentioned, Chávez remains saddled with a poorly performing economy that threatens to undermine his reforms. Opposition forces, including the nation's powerful labor unions, have staged several crippling strikes to protest his increasingly authoritarian rule. *El Comandante* countered with tough talk of possible military intervention. With his popularity ratings down to the low 30 percent range, it remains to be seen if Chávez will finish his term in office in 2007 or be replaced by other means. His tenure in office took a violent—and quixotic—turn on April 11, 2002, when he ordered National Guardsmen and civilian gunmen to stop a 150,000-strong protest march from reaching the presidential palace. At least 13 people were killed and 100 wounded, and the following day the military intervened and forced Chávez to resign from office. He was then briefly replaced by his vice president, Pedro Carmona. Two days of massive counterdemonstrations then erupted during which an additional 25 protestors were killed. The generals apparently entertained second thoughts on the subject, and on April 14 the beleaguered president was released and restored to power. The

Hugo Chávez *(Embassy of Venezuela)*

experience apparently sobered Chávez, who declined seeking revenge. "I do not come with hate or rancor in my heart," he confessed, "but we must make decisions and adjust things."

Further Reading

Canache, Damarys, and Michael R. Kulisheck. *Reinventing Legitimacy: Democracy and Political Change in Venezuela.* Westport, Conn.: Greenwood Press, 1998.

Gott, Richard. *In the Shadow of the Liberator: The Impact of Hugo Chávez on Venezuela and Latin America.* London: Verso, 2001.

Kelly de Escobar, Janet. *The United States and Venezuela: Rethinking a Relationship.* New York: Routledge, 2002.

McCoy, Jennifer. "Demystifying Venezuela's Hugo Chávez." *Current History* 99 (February 2000): 66–671.

Rada Herrera, Virginia H. "President Hugo Chávez's Image in Venezuela Megaelections." Unpublished master's thesis, University of Florida, 2001.

Chen Shui-bian (1950–) *president of Taiwan*

Chen Shui-bian was born in Tainan province, Taiwan, sometime in 1950. Underweight as an infant, his mother did not register his birth for nearly a year out of concern that he would not live. Chen then eked out a hardscrabble existence from his mud-hut residence. Reputedly, his family was so poor that he walked two miles to school everyday barefoot, and frequently without lunch. Nonetheless, the young man excelled academically and in 1970 he was admitted to the prestigious National Taiwan University. Chen graduated with honors four years later, studied law, and worked as a successful corporate lawyer commencing in 1976. Within four years he was one of the most successful attorneys on Taiwan. He then cemented his financial fortunes by marrying the daughter of a wealthy doctor.

Taiwan, an island off the coast of China, had been run as an independent country ever since remnants of Jiang Jieshi's (Chiang Kai-shek) Kuomingtang (KMT or Nationalist Party) fled from the mainland to escape a Communist victory there in 1949. The island appeared to be run democratically on the surface, but it was in reality ruled as a one-party state. In 1980 Chen volunteered to defend two dissident leaders for publishing

Chen Shui-bian *(Taipei Economic and Cultural Office, Boston)*

what the government considered seditious articles. He lost the case and the defendants went to jail, but the experience convinced him of the need for political reform and greater democracy. In 1981 he became politically active by winning a seat on the Taipei city council as an anti-KMT candidate. To silence his outspoken criticism, in 1985 the government tried Chen for accusing a prominent KMT university professor of plagiarism, and he received a one-year jail sentence. His wife, Wu Shujen, was then elected to the National Assembly in his place, but she was then nearly killed when deliberately run over by a truck. This adversity only deepened Chen's commitment to reform.

Mounting dissatisfaction over KMT political dominance—and the corruption it engendered—resulted in the founding of the Democratic Progressive Party (DPP) in 1986, which the handsome, articulate Chen joined. From 1987 to 1989 he served as a member on the party's Central Standing Committee and in 1994 he won election as major of Taipei. Chen distinguished himself in office by improving traffic congestion, eliminating crime and prostitution, and creating city parks. However, when a resurgent KMT defeated him for office in 1998 he set his eyes on becoming the island's leader.

In 1999 Chen became the DPP party's candidate for president. Significantly, his vice presidential running mate, Annette Lu, was one of the defendants from the 1980 sedition trial. His KMT opponent, Lien Chan, had been previously tarred with corruption and publicly feuded with James Soong, a KMT official who broke from the party and ran as an independent. Chen ran an unconventional campaign and, to reinforce his image as an outsider, he frequently showed up at political rallies dressed up as James Bond or Superman. He emerged the victor in a three-way race, gathering a majority 39 percent of the vote, to Chan's 23 percent and Soong's 37 percent. It was a stunning upset and a historic turning point in the history of Taiwan. For the first time in 50 years, the all-powerful KMT had been turned out of office by another party. Moreover, former prisoner Annette Lu became the island's first-ever female vice president.

Chen won on a platform that promulgated stamping out corruption, promoting a better economic climate, and—above all—declaring Taiwanese independence from Communist-controlled mainland China. This stance greatly angered authorities in Beijing, who considered the island a breakaway province and threatened war if Taiwan ceded. Chen has since moderated his pledge, explaining: "We do advocate the right to self-determination, but that is not the same as advocating Taiwanese independence." In reality, he faces a more difficult task contending with domestic opponents. The KMT, while defeated, still controls most of the island's political infrastructure, and it settled upon a scorched-earth policy to thwart the DDP at every turn. Consequently, needed reforms advanced only at a snail's pace and Chen was forced to back down on his pledge to cancel a fourth nuclear power plant under construction. His unpopularity with the People's Republic has also affected relations abroad. In November 2001 Chen received the Prize for Freedom from Liberal International, a European human rights group. He was to accept his award in Belgium, but Beijing applied diplomatic pressure on Brussels and Chen was denied a passport. France, with billions of dollars tied up in Chinese trade, also refused Chen the right to visit. At length, his wife, Shu-chen,

still bound in a wheelchair since being hit by a truck, received the prize on his behalf in Strasbourg. Given the political intransigence of the KMT opposition to enact economic reforms, the Taiwanese economy, once a powerhouse of Asia, started slipping into a deep recession. However, the island's voters apparently know where to place the blame. In elections held in December 2001, Chen's DDP actually increased its numbers in the national legislature. Buoyed by his success, Chen wasted no time in tweaking the noses of mainland authorities. In August 2002, against a backdrop of increasing communist Chinese warnings about independence and war, Chen blithely exclaimed "Our Taiwan is not someone else's local government. Our Taiwan is not someone else's province."

Further Reading

Chao, Linda. *Some Implications of the Turnover of Political Power in Taiwan.* Stanford, Calif.: Hoover Institute, 2002.

Chen Shuibian. *The Son of Taiwan: The Life of Chen Shuibian and His Dreams for Taiwan.* Upland, Calif.: Taiwan Pub. Co., 2000.

Chow, Peter C. Y. *Taiwan's Modernization in Global Perspective.* Westport, Conn.: Praeger, 2002.

Corcuff, Stephanie. *Memories of the Future: National Identity and the Search for a New Taiwan.* Armonk, N.Y.: M. E. Sharpe, 2002.

Hickey, Dennis. "Cross-Strait Relations in the Aftermath of the Election of Chen Shui-bian." *Asian Affairs* 28 (Winter 2002): 201–216.

Rigger, Shelley. *Taiwan's Democratic Progressive Party: From Opposition to Power.* Boulder, Colo.: Lynne Rienner Publishers, 2001.

Roy, Denny. *Taiwan: A Political History.* Ithaca, N.Y.: Cornell University Press, 2003.

Sheng, Lijun. *China's Dilemma: The Taiwan Issue.* New York: I. B. Taurus, 2001.

Cheney, Dick (1941–) *vice president of the United States*

Richard Bruce Cheney was born in Lincoln, Nebraska, on January 30, 1941, the son of a Department of Agriculture worker. He was raised in Casper, Wyoming, and graduated from high school there in 1959. Cheney performed well enough to gain admittance to Yale University on a full scholarship, but he dropped out two semesters later. After working odd jobs for two years, he attended the University of Wyoming and obtained his bachelor's degree in political science in 1965. After receiving his masters the following year, Cheney undertook several internships with the state legislature until 1968, when he joined the staff of Republican congressman William A. Steiger of Wisconsin. Exposure to life at the center of power whetted Cheney's appetite for public service, and he began a lengthy climb up through the national political establishment. Cheney was soon tapped to serve with Donald Rumsfeld, director of the Office of Economic Opportunity, and he subsequently accompanied him to the Cost of Living Council, 1969–72. Following the resignation of President Richard Nixon in 1974, Cheney joined the staff of his successor, Gerald Ford, as deputy assistant. When Rumsfeld gained appointment as the new secretary of defense, the 34-year-old Cheney became the youngest-ever White House chief of staff. He served well in this capacity until January 1977, when Ford was defeated and replaced by President Jimmy Carter.

Cheney returned to public life, and in January 1979 he was elected as a Republican to Wyoming's sole congressional seat. He served until March 1989, being reelected five times by increasingly wide margins. Cheney solidified his reputation as a staunch but pragmatic conservative, devoid of ostentation and decidedly low-key. He also became renowned for his ability to work with Democrats across the aisle on a number of contentious issues. However, Cheney became point man for many of Ronald Reagan's conservative issues, especially the Strategic Defense Initiative (SDI, or "Star Wars"), aid to anticommunist contras in Nicaragua, and assistance to freedom fighters in Soviet-occupied Afghanistan. After the election of President George H. W. Bush in January 1989, Cheney was elected as the new secretary of defense, a position of vital national significance. Within months he became responsible for managing the November 1989 invasion of Panama, which overthrew the dictator/drug lord Manuel Noriega. However, his most severe test occurred following Iraqi dictator SADDAM HUSSEIN's invasion of Kuwait in August 1990.

The Iraqi invasion caught the United States unprepared, but Cheney quickly instituted a strategy for driving Iraqi forces out. Over the next few months he masterfully orchestrated a massive buildup of American forces in the Gulf of Arabia, and he personally convinced many reluctant heads of state there to allow U.S. forces to use their territory. His personal brand of diplomacy also proved instrumental in forming a wide-ranging coalition to oppose Hussein, which included France, England, Syria, and Egypt. When fighting commenced on February 23, 1993, the heretofore formidable Iraqi army was routed with a loss of 50,000 men in only three days of combat. Victory proved decisive, and also established Cheney as one of the most effective and far-sighted defense secretaries of the 20th century. Consequently, President Bush awarded him the Presidential Medal of Freedom, the nation's highest award for civilian service to the nation. After the victory, Cheney next turned his attention to reducing military expenditures, closing unneeded bases, and other means of fiscal retrenchment. He also played visible roles in helping formulate the START I and START II nuclear weapon reduction treaties with the Soviet Union, reduction of conventional forces in Europe, and the Chemical Weapons Convention. Each represented a triumph for Cheney and his intense personal diplomacy but, as always, he shrugged off media attention, exemplifying his usual modest persona. Following the election of President BILL CLINTON in January 1993, he resumed his business affairs as chairman of the Halliburton Corporation, a Texas-based oil corporation.

As the 2000 presidential election approached, Cheney's name was frequently mentioned as a possible Republican party standard-bearer. However, he declined the opportunity to run, citing the need for fresh new blood to invigorate the party. Texas governor GEORGE W. BUSH, the former president's son, then won the party's nomination, a feat which filled some party members with trepidation. In truth, the governor was regarded in many circles as too young and inexperienced for the nation's highest office. Hence, Cheney, a consummate politician with extensive public service, became his vice presidential candidate. Throughout the ensuing campaign, he campaigned actively and enjoyed a highly televised and sometimes uproarious debate with his Democratic opposite, Senator Joseph Lieberman of Connecticut. The two adversaries have since become personal friends. The election proved close and was only settled by the U.S. Supreme Court in December 2000, but the following month Cheney capped his political ambitions by becoming vice president of the United States. In the minds of many political pundits, he was the real power behind the throne—a solid intellectual counterweight to the president's amiable but neophyte status.

As always, Cheney performed in his quietly dignified manner, although in January 2001 he was briefly
sidelined by recurring bouts of heart disease. His performance as vice president also drew closer scrutiny in the
wake of the September 11, 2001, destruction of the
World Trade Center in New York. With President Bush
away in Florida, Cheney was in charge of running the
country for many hours. Thereafter, he remained sequestered in secret hiding places for his own security once
Bush returned to the White House. Cheney was then at
the center of military planning against Afghanistan,
which toppled the Taliban regime by December 2001.
The vice president has also warned any nations harboring
terrorists that they face "the full wrath of the United
States." Attention has since shifted to his old adversary
Iraq, which for many years resisted implementation of
United Nations weapons inspectors. Therefore, in the
spring of 2002, President Bush dispatched him on a tour
of Europe and the Middle East to drum up support for a
possible attack upon Saddam Hussein. Sadly, many Arab
leaders, caught up in popular passions generated by renewed fighting between Israelis and Palestinians, proved
either unwilling or unable to extend their support. It appears that Cheney's brand of personal diplomacy may
have reached the limits of its effectiveness. Nonetheless,
he continues on as one of the most effective and influential vice presidents in American history.

Further Reading
Ceaser, James W., and Andrew E. Busch. *The Perfect Tie:
The True Story of the 2000 Presidential Election.* Lanham, Md.: Rowman and Littlefield, 2001.
Diller, Daniel C. *The Presidents, First Ladies, and Vice Pres-
idents: White House Biographies, 1789–2001.* Wash-
ington, D.C.: CQ Press, 2001.
Pomper, Gerald, ed. *The Election of 2000: Reports and In-
terpretations.* Chatham, N.J.: Chatham House, 2001.
Purcell, L. Edward. *Vice Presidents: A Biographical Dictio-
nary.* New York: Checkmark Books, 2001.
Schumacher, Mary. *Keeping the Cold War Cold: Dick Cheney at the Department of Defense.* Cambridge, Mass.:
President and Fellows of Harvard College, 1990.

Chernomyrdin, Viktor (1938–) *prime
minister of Russia*

Viktor Stephanovich Chernomyrdin was born in
Cherny Ostrog, Orenburg region of the Soviet Union,
on April 9, 1938, the son of a truck driver. After working in the oil industry for several years, Chernomyrdin
attended the Kuybishev Polytechnical Institute, graduated in 1966, and subsequently received a master's degree in technical sciences from the All-Union
Polytechnical School six years later. Chernomyrdin then
resumed his position with the state-owned energy concern, while also advancing up the ranks of the Communist Party hierarchy. By 1989, he was entrusted to
run Gazprom, then the world's largest oil and natural
gas supplier. A colorless if efficient technocrat, Chernomyrdin performed well enough to chair the company
board from 1989 to 1992. By that time, the Communist government had collapsed and the Soviet Union
voted itself out of existence. BORIS YELTSIN was then
president of the new Commonwealth of Independent
States, and, in 1992, he appointed Chernomyrdin
deputy prime minister under acting prime minister
Yegor Gaidar.

Chernomyrdin came to power while Russia was experiencing severe economic distress, all occasioned by
the dramatic restructuring necessary to restore a market
economy. Gaidar was a vocal proponent of increased liberalization and drastic reform to jump-start the faltering
economy, but he was strenuously opposed by Chernomyrdin. "I am for reform," he insisted, "but not
through the impoverishment of the people." Accordingly, in December 1992, Yeltsin fired Gaidar and appointed Chernomyrdin prime minister in his place. But,
while he was considerably more cautious than his predecessor, the Russian economic quagmire was so profound
that the new leader had little choice but to implement
Gaidar's drastic policies. This was also done to fulfill
strict terms established by the International Monetary
Fund (IMF) for the continuance of foreign aid. "Russia
has only one path to tread," he assured Western leaders,
"that of reform—and it will not depart from it." The
long-suffering Russian people consequently endured several more months of stagnation, unemployment, and declining standards of living, but by June 1994 inflation
had dropped from 25 percent to 8 percent. Nonetheless, the former Communist Party made impressive gains
during elections, and Chernomyrdin had to survive a
vote of no confidence in October 1994. Yeltsin by that
time was fighting for his political life and was facing
possible impeachment. Chernomyrdin, by comparison,
gained national recognition and popularity by successfully negotiating the end to a hostage situation in

rebellious Chechnya. To many, he was seen as Yeltsin's logical successor.

In May 1995, Chernomyrdin seemed to be taking the first steps toward the presidency when he founded a new centrist party, Our Home Is Russia. Elections that year were again dominated by the Communists, but Chernomyrdin's party came in second place, suggesting that he had established a political power base upon which to build. In November 1995 the prime minister was required to lead the country after Yeltsin suffered a serious heart attack and was hospitalized. Again, Chernomyrdin's tenure at the top was competent, if uneventful, and reminiscent of a typical Soviet-era party boss. However, he declined to run against the ailing Yeltsin during the 1996 presidential elections, and he was reappointed prime minister over objections from the Communist-dominated Duma, or lower house. For the next two years Chernomyrdin continued implementing his market-oriented reforms, though Russia remained plagued by poor economic performance. The country was further staggered by the 1998 Asian currency crisis and conditions worsened. Seeking to shore up his own political base, Yeltsin then suddenly fired his entire cabinet on March 23, 1998. Chernomyrdin then found himself replaced by SERGEI KIRIYENKO as prime minister.

Kiriyenko tried unsuccessfully to adopt new and more drastic economic measures, including devaluating the ruble, but on August 23, 1998, Yeltsin dismissed him as well. Again he turned to the gray but capable Chernomyrdin as prime minister, only this time the Communist-dominated Duma twice refused to confirm his appointment. Rather than risk a third vote, which might have triggered a constitutional crisis, Yeltsin withdrew the nomination. After two weeks in office, the position of prime minister was filled by a compromise candidate, YEVGENY PRIMAKOV, the present foreign minister. Chernomyrdin, meanwhile, announced his long-awaited decision to run for the presidency in the 2000 elections. In the elections, he was soundly defeated by VLADIMIR PUTIN, who subsequently appointed him ambassador to Ukraine. In this capacity, he proved able to work amiably with the former Communists dominating that country and pledged continuing cooperation despite forthcoming national elections in 2002. "Russia will cooperate with the Ukrainian parliament no matter what composition it may have," he declared. "That must be understood clearly."

Further Reading

Brown, Archie. *Contemporary Russian Politics*. New York: Oxford University Press, 2001.

Hahn, Gordon M. *Russia's Revolution from Above, 1985–2000: Reform, Transition, and Revolution in the Fall of the Soviet Communist Regime*. New Brunswick, N.J.: Transaction Publishers, 2002.

Lo, Bobo. Russian *Foreign Policy in the Post-Soviet Era: Reality, Illusion, and Mythmaking*. New York: Palgrave, 2002.

Medvedev, Roy, and Michael Vale. "A Long-Term Construction Project for Russia." *Russian Politics and Law* 37 (July–August, 1999): 5–49.

Sherr, James. *Victor Chernomyrdin's Appointment to Ukraine*. Camberley, England: Conflict Studies Research Centre, Royal Military Academy, Sandhurst, 2001.

Simes, Dimitri. "Russia's Crisis and America's Complicity." *National Interest* 54 (Winter 1998–99): 12–22.

Chiluba, Frederick (1943–) *president of Zambia*

Frederick Jacob Titus Chiluba was born in Kitwe, Zambia, on April 30, 1942, the son of a copper miner. His country, which gained its independence in 1964, was the former British protectorate of Northern Rhodesia. Chiluba's family, desperately poor, lacked sufficient funding to allow him to complete school, so he migrated to neighboring Tanzania to work on a plantation. Once back home, he became interested in labor issues as a young man, and he served as a shop steward with the National Union of Building, Electrical, and General Workers. Attentive in his duties, Chiluba rose to union president by 1971 and subsequently served as president of the 3,000,000-strong Zambian Congress of Trade Unions. In this capacity Chiluba became a strident critic of President Kenneth A. Kaunda, the founder of modern Zambia, and in 1981 he was briefly jailed and charged with destabilizing the government. Once released, he and thousands of other Zambians agitated for multiparty elections, which were deemed illegal under the Kaunda regime's permanent state of emergency. However, the sitting president's popularity was being undermined by a tottering economy, itself the product of acute central planning and rampant corruption. Chiluba, vocal and articulate despite a diminutive five-foot stature, further enhanced his national standing by becoming head of the Movement for Multi-Party Democracy (MMD) in 1990. He then announced his determination to run for the presidency on a platform of democracy, a liberalized economy, and intolerance for corruption. On October 31, 1991, he engineered a sweeping 76 percent to 24 percent victory over Kaunda, who did everything in his power to derail the opposition. The MMD Party shared in his success, capturing 125 National Assembly seats out of 150. The results were widely hailed, and it was anticipated that Zambia could serve as an example for multiparty democracy for the rest of Africa.

Once in power, Chiluba initially enjoyed great support from the Zambian people, but popular approval began to wane as the economy worsened. In March 1993, he ordered a state of emergency and arrested 14 opposition leaders without charges. The order was then rescinded following protests from Western donor nations, but the affair tarnished his reputation as a democrat. More seriously, new accusations of corruption among Chiluba's various ministers surfaced, although the president himself was never tarred. However, his reputation was badly stained by the upcoming 1996 elections. Kaunda, sensing widespread dissatisfaction with Chiluba, announced his intention to recapture the presidency. Chiluba countered by amending the constitution so as to bar him from running. The MDD-controlled national assembly quickly passed new laws mandating that only citizens whose parents were native Zambians could aspire to high office. Kaunda, whose family originated from neighboring Malawi, was shut out. Consequently, Chiluba was reelected with a predictable 70 percent of the vote, even though the opposition boycotted the entire process. International observers also complained of widespread vote buying and gross irregularities in registration. These abuses triggered some vocal protests and threats from many Western aid sources; however, the International Money Fund and the World Bank continued doing business with Zambia.

Despite Chiluba's oftentimes shady politics, his handling of Zambian economic affairs brought him high marks from abroad. He was tasked with dismantling inefficient, state-owned and operated industries, which comprised 80 percent of the national economy. Chiluba therefore initiated a policy of privatization of industry, particularly of the copper mines, and currency deregulation. Consequently, inflation fell rapidly from 200

Frederick Chiluba *(Embassy of the Republic of Zambia)*

percent to 55 percent in a few years, although unemployment remained high at 22 percent. Progress, however, came not without cost. Not only did the price of maize, a staple commodity, rise fivefold, but labor leaders also feared that privatization would lead to loss of jobs and reduced social services for those still employed. In October 1997, Chiluba survived an unsuccessful coup attempt, which did little to modify his political or economic beliefs. His cronies in government also proved intractable. In 2001 a movement circulated in the MMD-controlled national assembly to amend the constitution and allow Chiluba to run for a third term. However, street protests erupted and a petition to impeach the president, signed by one-third of the assembly members, convinced the president to step down. In December 2001, Chiluba was officially succeeded by his handpicked successor, Levy Mwanawasa, who won by a scant 28.7 percent of votes cast. Chiluba's political legacy appears mixed, but may prove ultimately successful.

Further Reading

Burnell, Peter. "The Party System and Party Politics in Zambia: Constitutions Past, Present, and Future." *African Affairs* 100 (April 2001): 239–263.

"Chiluba, the Single Man." *New African,* no. 402 (2001): 40–44.

Chiluba, Frederick. *Building a Political Culture: Underpinning Democracy.* Lusaka, Zambia: Senter Pub., 2001.

Kilpatrick, Andrew L. "An Analysis of Chiluba's Imagery in His Speeches on Economic and Political Change in Zambia." Unpublished master's thesis, Baylor University, 1992.

Mphaisha, Chisepo J. J. "The State of Democratization in Zambia." *Commonwealth and Comparative Politics* 38 (November 2000): 131–146.

Weinstein, Jerry. "Africa's Scramble for Africa: Lessons of a Continental War." *Peace Research Abstracts* 38, no. 5 (2001): 603–751.

Chirac, Jacques (1932–) *president of France*

Jacques Jean Chirac was born in Paris on November 29, 1932, and he graduated from the elite, Lycée Louis-le-Grand in 1950. He continued his education by attending the Institut d'Etudes Politiques, which groomed students for careers in political office and diplomacy. Chirac subsequently spent a summer studying at Harvard University in the United States before being drafted in the army, where he saw active service during the ongoing war in Algeria. Highly decorated, he next enrolled at theEcole Nationale d'Administration (another government service school) and graduated in 1958. After a series of minor bureaucratic positions, Chirac joined the administration of Prime Minister Georges Pompidou in 1962. He fulfilled numerous cabinet-level positions, and he also served as deputy to the National Assembly for Corrèze. In 1967 a grateful Pompidou elevated him to the post of undersecretary of state. Chirac, notorious for conservative views and a forceful personality, subsequently became known as the "Bulldozer" in political circles. In 1974, after Pompidou died in office, Chirac hitched his fortunes to that of another conservative, Valéry Giscard d'Estaing, who became president in 1967. He was made prime minister in return, but a long-standing row over ideological differences led to Chirac's resignation in April 1976.

Chirac had been a lifelong adherent to the conservative Gaullist Party, and in December 1976 he reorganized it and renamed it the Rassemblement pour la République (Rally for the Republic or RPR). This party seeks to reaffirm France's role as a world leader in economic, cultural, and military spheres. The following year Chirac solidified his political base by becoming the first mayor of Paris since 1871. He also maintained his running feud with Giscard, ran against him in the general election of 1981, and both men lost to the Socialist candidate, FRANÇOIS MITTERRAND. Chirac continued serving effectively as Paris mayor until 1986, when the RPR won ascendancy in the National Assembly, and Mitterrand appointed him prime minister. It proved an awkward arrangement—"Cohabitation" of the president and prime minister holding stridently opposing viewpoints—but Chirac lost to Mitterrand again in 1988 and withdrew from high office. Reinstalled as mayor of Paris, he nonetheless remained a moving force in national politics whose support proved instrumental in passage of the Maastricht Treaty of 1992. The treaty paved the way for France's adoption of a unified European currency. Three years later, on May 7, 1995, Chirac won the French presidency by defeating Socialist LIONEL JOSPIN by 52 percent to 47 percent. His rise also occasioned a near-complete sweep of national seats by conservatives, who now controlled 80 percent of the National Assembly and 67 percent of the Senate.

France in the 1990s was an economic powerhouse, although it suffered from relatively high unemployment and burgeoning budget deficits. To spur job creation, Chirac embarked on a program to cut taxes and increase privatization of state-owned companies. He also sought to slash $55 million from the budget, including cutbacks in France's generous national health care system and national transportation network. The result was an explosion of strikes and the largest mass demonstrations in recent history. The economy continued growing strongly, but unemployment remained high, despite innumerable campaign promises, and Chirac's popularity plummeted. In May 1997 new elections returned control of Parliament to the Socialists, which compromised Chirac's ability to enact his conservative agenda.

In the field of foreign affairs, Chirac has enjoyed greater success. France has closely aligned itself with Germany, an old adversary, and the two nations work closely to promote the EU and a common European currency. He then reintegrated France back into the NATO chain of command, from which France had been withdrawn by Charles de Gaulle in 1967. Chirac has also established a close relationship with President VLADIMIR PUTIN of Russia, and he urged the 19-member NATO alliance to allow Russia to serve as a "special" 20th member. France is also second only to the United States in terms of aid to Africa, and it provides its former colonies with a wide range of humanitarian aide. Consistent with his Gaullist nationalism, Chirac strongly desired that France keep a high profile in the work of international peacekeeping, and he supplied the largest ground contingent to UN forces patrolling Bosnia-Herzegovina in 1997. However, France stirred up a hornet's nest in 1995 when it resumed nuclear testing in the Pacific. Chirac subsequently shifted his stance to working toward a global ban on nuclear tests. Worse, the hard-charging prime minister has been wracked by allegations of corruption while mayor of Paris, and he was on the defensive while heading into the May 2002 presidential elections. This entailed a rematch with the popular Socialist Jospin with the fate of the RPR apparently hang-ing in the balance. However, on May 5, 2002, Jospin was knocked out of the election by finishing a close third behind JEAN-MARIE LE PEN of the far-right National Front. Chirac registered first, but with only 20 percent of the vote, the lowest ever recorded for an incumbent president. Jospin subsequently endorsed his erstwhile implacable adversary to deny Le Pen the presidency, and Chirac took to the offensive against the far right. "The response is not extremism," he told supporters. "The leaders of the far right betrayed the French people by allying with the forces of evil and the enemies of our homeland. History has definitely disqualified them from speaking on behalf of France." Many French voters agreed and, on June 16, 2002, Chirac was resoundingly reelected by 82 percent of votes cast. The RPR also picked up a clear majority in parliament, with 392 seats to 173 for the Socialists, confirming France's conservative realignment. Such a concentration of power in the hands of a single party has not been seen since the heyday of Charles de Gaulle in the late 1960s. Chirac is now at absolute liberty to pursue his avowed goals of law and order and a 30 percent tax cut on personal and corporate incomes. In a larger sense, his victory also caps a European trend that witnessed similar conservative gains in Italy, Denmark, the Netherlands, and Portugal.

Further Reading

Buldersheim, Harold, and Jean Pascal Daloz, eds. *Political Leadership in a Global Age: The Experience of France & Norway.* Burlington, Ut.: Ashgate, 2003.
Drake, David. *Intellectuals and Politics in Post-war France.* New York: Palgrave, 2002.
Hanley, David. *Party, Society, Government: Republican Democracy in France.* Oxford: Berghahn, 2001.
Knapp, Andrew, and Vincent Wright. *The Government and Politics of France.* New York: Routledge, 2001.
Keeler, John T. S., and Martin Schain. *Chirac's Challenge: Liberalization, Europeanization, and Malaise in France.* New York: St. Martin's Press, 1996.
Tuppen, John W. *Chirac's France, 1986–88: Contemporary Issues in French Society.* New York: St. Martin's Press, 1991.

Jacques Chirac *(Embassy of France)*

Chissanó, Joaquim (1939–) *president of Mozambique*

Joaquim Alberto Chissanó was born in Malehice, Chibuto district, Mozambique, on October 22, 1939, the son of a Methodist minister. At that time his country was part of the Portuguese Empire, and most Africans were treated contemptuously, like second-class citizens. However, Chissanó was fortunate in acquiring access to primary and secondary education, being one of the few African children allowed to attend school. He subsequently ventured to Portugal on a scholarship to study medicine in 1960, but he dropped out and moved to Paris. There Chissanó became politically involved with revolutionary activities against Portugal, and in 1962 he helped found the Mozambican Liberation Front (FRELIMO). In this capacity he trained as a guerrilla fighter in Algeria, and he struck up cordial relations with Dr. Eduardo Mondlane, president of FRELIMO. The war for independence lasted from 1964–74, during which period Chissanó served as a member of the party central committee, secretary of military security, and a highly visible diplomat. The latter function became his forte, as Chissanó was intelligent, articulate, and fluent in English, Portuguese, French, and Swahili. When Mozambique won its independence in September 1974, he gained appointment as the nation's first foreign minister under President Samora Machel. Behind Mondlane and Sachel, he was the third most important member of FRELIMO.

In executing the duties of his office, Chissanó gained a reputation for competence, eloquence, and pragmatism. His government steered a closely honed Marxist-Leninist line diplomatically, and he helped forge Mozambican links to the Soviet Union and the People's Republic of China. However, he also went to great lengths to demonstrate to Western powers and investors that his nation maintained its independence from the Communist bloc, and he pushed for a nonaligned agenda in international forums. A more pressing concern was the 16-year old civil war between FRELIMO and the Mozambican National Resistance Movement (RENAMO). The civil war was supported by South Africa, which sought to destabilize the regime. In 1986 the flamboyant President Machel was killed in a plane crash and the party central committee unhesitatingly appointed the urbane and soft-spoken Chissanó his successor on November 6, 1986.

Chissanó's first priority in office was cessation of regional hostilities. Earlier, this entailed signing the Nkomati Accord with the hated South African regime in 1983, whereby both countries forbade their territory to be used as guerrilla staging areas. Next, Chissanó

opened negotiations with RENAMO officials, which finally ended the internecine struggle in 1992. An estimated 100,000 civilians died in the violence, which also wreaked havoc on large areas of the country. Two years earlier, in an attempt to shore up the tottering, centrally planned economy, Chissanó formally ditched any pretense of adhering further to Marxist-Leninist doctrines. Thereafter, he placed Mozambique on a path to privatization of state industries, a free-market economy, and multiparty democracy. "Each country must have a serious development program rooted in its own reality," he reasoned, "and promote social justice through development." In response, Western powers such as the United States and Great Britain, which had heretofore considered Mozambique to be a Soviet satellite, reestablished diplomatic and trade relations. Chissanó also labored to have the country enrolled in working agreements with the World Bank and the International Monetary Fund. The results have brought internal peace and capitalism, which have led to a significant growth in Mozambican economic strength, although the country continues to be one of the world's poorest nations.

For all his achievements in international diplomacy, Chissanó was less successful at cultivating viable, multiparty democracy. After major negotiations with RENAMO, presidential elections were held for the first time in October 1993 and Chissanó won with 53 percent of the vote. The opposition claimed widespread voter fraud, but further violence had been averted. Chissanó was then reelected to a second term with 52.3 percent of the vote in December 1999, again to a chorus of complaints from the opposition. However, Chissanó has since declared that he will not stand for reelection, despite the urging of several FRELIMO officials. His successor is expected to be nominated by the party congress in June 2004.

Further Reading

Alden, Chris. *Mozambique and the Construction of the New African State: From Negotiations to Nation Building.* Basingstoke, England: Palgrave, 2001.

Chan, Stephen, and Moises Venancio. *War and Peace in Mozambique.* New York: Macmillan Press, 1998.

Hall, Margaret. *Confronting Leviathan: Mozambique since Independence.* London: C. Hurst, 1997.

Schafer, Jessica. "Soldiers at Peace: The Post-war Politics of Demobilized Soldiers in Mozambique, 1975–1996."

Unpublished Ph.D. dissertation, Oxford University, 1999.

Sheldon, Kathleen E. *Pounders of Grain: A History of Women, Work, and Politics in Mozambique.* Portsmouth, N.H.: Heinemann, 2002.

Chrétien, Jean (1934–   ) *prime minister of Canada*

Joseph Jacques Jean Chrétien was born in Shawinigan, Quebec, on January 11, 1934, one of 19 children. As a youth he contracted infantile paralysis, which left him deaf in one ear and with the left side of his face partially deformed. Chrétien nonetheless surmounted these disabilities, entered the law school at Laval University, and was admitted to the bar in 1958. After practicing law for several years he joined the Liberal Party and was elected to the House of Commons in 1963. As a native speaker of French, one of Canada's two official languages, he realized the importance of learning English to enhance his political aspirations. While doing so, he came to the attention of Prime Minister Lester B. Pearson, who appointed him parliamentary secretary in 1965. Two years later he became the youngest finance minister in Canadian history. This act initiated Chrétien's rise to political power and over the next 15 years he held a successive series of ministerial posts, including national revenue, Indian affairs, commerce, and justice. He also became a close political ally and protégé of the legendary prime minister Pierre Trudeau for nearly a decade. Sensing his time had come, in June 1984 Chrétien challenged John Turner for leadership of the Liberal Party and lost. When the Progressive Conservatives under BRIAN MULRONEY were subsequently swept into power by a large majority, Chrétien resigned from politics and resumed his legal practice. However, as the economy weakened, popular support for the Progressive Conservatives waned, and Chrétien was reelected to parliament in 1986. In June 1990 he also became leader of the Liberal Party following Turner's resignation. On November 4, 1993, the Liberal Party handily routed the Progressive Conservatives under KIM CAMPBELL, winning 178 house seats. With this solid majority, Chrétien was elected Canada's 20th prime minister.

Immediately upon taking office, Chrétien set about restoring the Canadian economy, which was saddled by enormous debts, high unemployment, and runaway inflation. He imposed a strict regimen of fiscal austerity measures which curbed inflation and closed the budget deficit, but proved less successful at curbing unemployment. Consequently, when Chrétien called for new elections in June 1997, the Liberal Party lost several seats, although it still retained power. He has since refocused his spending priorities to those of job creation and social benefits. Popular reception to Chrétien's overall policies may be gauged by the fact that in early 2000, he defeated an attempt by Finance Minister Paul Martin to challenge him for the Liberal Party leadership. More impressively, on November 27, 2000, the Liberals reasserted their control of parliament by winning 172 of 301 seats available. His political future seems secure for the time being.

Unquestionably, the biggest and most vexing political problem facing Chrétien—and all Canadians—was Quebec. This is the only predominantly French-speaking province in Canada (the other nine are overwhelmingly English speaking), with long-standing political and cultural grievances against the majority. In truth, there remains a deep-seated cultural fissure. Over the past two decades a vocal political movement (Bloc Quebecois) arose, which agitates for the secession of Quebec from

Jean Chrétien *(Embassy of Canada)*

Canada and national independence. Tensions crested in 1980 and 1995 when provincial referendums were held over Quebec's continuing relationship within the Canadian federation. Both attempts were defeated largely because Chrétien, a Quebec native whose first language is French, campaigned arduously against them. "I will try to bring us together by appealing not to what divides us, but what unites us," he declared. Moreover, he recognizes the wish of the French minority to be recognized as a distinct culture within Canada, and he has granted numerous political concessions. This, in turn, infuriated residents in several western provinces, who deemed such actions preferential treatment. Chrétien—together with all future Canadian prime ministers—faces a delicate balancing act on the future of Canada's national integrity.

Canadians also live in the shadow of the United States and are apprehensive about being swallowed up by it culturally and economically. Chrétien has therefore adopted the traditional Liberal "distance" from his giant neighbor to the south, so as not to appear subservient. Despite that stance, in 1993 he campaigned in favor of expanding free trade with both the United States and Mexico under the North American Free Trade Agreement (NAFTA). The September 11, 2001, attack upon the World Trade Center has refocused Canadian attention to its undefended border with the United States, and many Canadians have begun questioning the validity of their own open-ended immigration policies. In the wake of the attack, Chrétien has, by default, signed on to closer scrutiny of foreign nationals in Canada and tighter border restrictions, and he pledges to support the ongoing international war against terrorism. Many of these policies go against the very grain of Liberal Party tradition, but Chrétien is placed in the awkward position of deciding between the role of either a good neighbor or a good Canadian. It remains to be seen how well he can finesse these conflicting national agendas while safeguarding Canadian national interests.

Further Reading

Baer, Douglas E. *Political Sociology: Canadian Perspectives.* Don Mills, Ontario: Oxford University Press Canada, 2002.

Bickerton, James, and Bob Rae. *Reflections on Canadian Politics.* Antigonish, Nova Scotia: St. Xavier University Press, 2001.

Chrétien, Jean. *Straight from the Heart.* Toronto: Key Porter Books, 1994.

Cross, William. *Political Parties, Representation, and Electoral Democracy in Canada.* New York: Oxford University Press, 2002.

Laycock, David H. *The New Right and Democracy in Canada: Understanding Reform and the Canadian Alliance.* New York: Oxford University Press, 2002.

McBride, Stephen K., and John Shields. *Dismantling a Nation: The Transition to Corporate Rule in Canada.* Halifax, Nova Scotia: Fernwood Pub., 1997.

Martin, Lawrence. *Chrétien.* Toronto: Lester Pub., 1995.

Pal, Leslie A., and R. Kent Weaver, eds. *The Government Taketh Away: The Politics of Pain in the United States and Canada.* Washington, D.C.: Georgetown University Press, 2003.

Chuan Leekpai (1938–) *prime minister of Thailand*

Chuan Leekpai was born in Muang district, Trang province, Thailand, on July 28, 1938, a son of Chinese immigrants. "I am an ordinary man who came from a rather poor family," he has recalled, "During my younger days I had to collect rubber from trees before going to school." After completing his primary and secondary education, Chuan studied art at the prestigious Silpakorn Pre-University, and he subsequently received a law degree from Thammasat University in 1962. He then maintained a legal practice until 1969, when he won a seat in parliament as a member of the Democratic Party. Aged but 33 years, Chuan became one of the youngest members in national government. He also quickly attained a reputation for honesty in voicing concern over the lot of poor people. Not surprisingly, he won the trust of his constituents and successfully defended his seat over the next 11 elections. Chuan also became a highly visible figure in several administrations, serving, by turns, as deputy minister of justice and minister of justice, commerce, agriculture and cooperatives, education, and public health. Chuan acquitted himself as a capable technocrat of unimpeachable integrity. He subsequently also rose within the ranks of the Democratic Party, becoming party leader in 1990.

As a political entity, Thailand has a long and established tradition of military intervention in government, with a history of 18 coups since 1932. A military junta assumed power in 1991 and installed General Suchinda

Kraprayoon as prime minister. When this act triggered an outpouring of public anger rare for Thailand, the general resigned and scheduled national elections for September 1992. The voters then elected 185 prodemocracy candidates to the House of Representatives and Chuan, who cobbled together a working coalition majority of 202 seats, gained appointment as prime minister on September 23, 1992. This proved a pivotal event, for, unlike most Thai heads of state, Chuan was unique in possessing neither an aristocratic nor a military background. Furthermore, his record of nearly three decades of public service without a single allegation of corruption set him apart from the majority of Thai politicians.

Chuan managed to retain the reins of power for nearly three years before a land reform scandal within his cabinet forced him to call for new elections in 1995. The Democratic Party was then unceremoniously turned out of power in July 1995, after enjoying one of the longest continuous tenures in recent Thai history. The quiet, unassuming Chuan then took up the mantle as opposition leader until he could form a new coalition on November 9, 1997. His presence was certainly reassuring as the Thai economy, in consequence of reckless borrowing and shady investments by the private sector, was on the verge of collapse. Furthermore, in order to retire $80 billion of national debt, the International Monetary Fund (IMF) insisted upon severe austerity measures to shore up the Thai economy and check inflation. Chuan moved quickly and closed down 56 out of 58 national banks, an unprecedented but necessary step. He also allowed the national currency (the baht) to float alongside the stronger U.S. dollar. This led to sharp price increases overall, but consumer complaints dwindled as the inflationary rate declined. Chuan's vigorous belt-tightening satisfied IMF officials and, consequently, the government received a $17 billion bailout to further stimulate the economy. By the summer of 1999, this stiff dose of medicine was paying dividends, and the Thai economy posted an impressive gain of 3 percent growth for the year. As of January 2001, the country was officially declared out of recession.

Chuan was highly engaged in the realm of regional diplomacy. He actively cultivated good relations with the nine member nations of the Association of Southeast Asian Nations (ASEAN), and he pushed strongly for a free-trade zone by 2010. Chuan also distinguished himself as a vocal advocate for human rights, and he campaigned actively for the release of Myanmar's opposition leader, AUNG SAN SUU KYI. Thailand next made a concerted effort to resolve long-standing border disputes with Cambodia, and in January 2002, Chuan signed an extradition agreement for the return of any members of the murderous Khmer Rouge organization hiding on Thai soil. The unassuming prime minister certainly accomplished more for Thailand in less time than has any other recent national leader. Yet, Thai voters remained fickle. In January 2001 the Democratic Party was turned out of office by the Thai Rak Thai Party. Chuan has since stepped down in favor of Thaksin Shinawatra, who promised widescale debt relief to farmers and grants of 1 million bahts to each of Thailand's 70,000 villages.

Further Reading

Englehart, Neil A. *Culture and Power in Traditional Siamese Government.* Ithaca, N.Y.: Cornell University Press, 2001.

Keyes, Charles F., and Shigeharu Tanabe. *Cultural Crisis and Social Memory: Politics of the Past in the Thai World.* Honolulu: University of Hawaii Press, 2002.

Kobkua Suwannathat-Pian. *Kings, Country, and Constitution: Thailand's Political Development, 1932–2000.* Richmond, Va.: Curzon, 2001.

Pasuk Phongpaichit, and Christopher J. Baker. *Thailand: Economy and Politics.* New York: Oxford University Press, 1997.

Tanabe, Shigeharu, and Charles F. Reyes. *Cultural Crisis and Social Memory: Modernity and Identity in Thailand and Laos.* Honolulu: University of Hawaii Press, 2002.

Yoshihara, Kunio. *The Nation and Economic Growth: Korea and Thailand.* Kyoto: Kyoto University Press, 1999.

Ciampi, Carlo (1920–) *president of Italy*

Carlo Azeglio Ciampi was born on December 9, 1920, in Livorno, Italy, and he studied Italian literature at the University of Pisa. Following a stint at military service in World War II, he returned to the same university to receive a law degree in 1946. That same year Ciampi began working as a clerk at the Bank of Italy, where he spent most of his professional career. By 1979 he gained appointment as the bank's governor, which he held for another 14 years. In this capacity Ciampi helped prepare Italy for entrance into the European Monetary Union. Through the years Ciampi espoused no interest in politics, and he registered no affiliation with any party or interest group. However, by 1990, Italy was wracked by a series of scandals that greatly embarrassed the political establishment. Numerous high-profile figures were either indicted for corruption or fell under suspicion, and none of the current leaders could grasp the reins of power for more than a few months. Once incumbent GIULIANO AMATO tendered his resignation, President OSCAR SCALFARO unexpectedly turned to Ciampi to serve as prime minister. At this time the former banker enjoyed impeccable credentials for honesty and efficiency. Accordingly, he was sworn into office on April 29, 1993, and he took remedial steps to ease corruption. Ciampi also pursued an aggressive economic agenda including expanded privatization, reduced deficits, and establishment of a tripartite negotiation arrangement among government, labor, and management for promoting greater harmony. Elections held in May 1994 led to his replacement by SILVIO BERLUSCONI, but two years later Ciampi was appointed treasury minister by a new prime minister, ROMANO PRODI. Ironically, when the left-leaning premier MASSIMO D'ALEMA succeeded Prodi in 1998, he not only retained the conservative-minded Ciampi but also expanded his authority to include the budget ministry. This was the first time in Italian history that two distinct departments had been merged under one individual, and Ciampi became known as the "superminister" for juggling such responsibilities. His performance was little short of miraculous, and he succeeded in transforming the usually chaotic Italian economy into a smoothly humming machine ready for its role within the European Union.

In May 1999, President Scalfaro announced his resignation and the hunt was on for a successor. He again chose Ciampi based upon his 50 years of service as an outstanding civil servant. He was an unlikely candidate, never having run for public office, but his reputation transcended party lines. Surprisingly, Ciampi was overwhelmingly approved in parliament by a two-third vote on the first ballot—an unprecedented show of unity in this otherwise factious political system. The role of the president is largely ceremonial, although it carries the important responsibilities of appointing the prime minister, signing legislation into law, and calling for elections. Ciampi, as usual, kept his head above the

political fray and in May 2001 he allowed Berlusconi, his former adversary, to form a government. The president also remains an outspoken champion of European unification as a guarantee of peace and prosperity. Ciampi considers it a moral imperative for a wealthy, unified Europe to assist the Balkans in their nationalist difficulties and help lead them toward peace and prosperity. "We must broaden our concept of Europe," he lectured. "Europe's political space must eventually coincide with its geographical border." In May 2002 Italy itself became embroiled in a political crisis when several thousand Kurdish refugees disembarked from boats and sought asylum. This event underscored the growing problem of illegal immigration and right-wing extremists called for their expulsion. But Ciampi predictably took the moral route. "This wave of immigration born out of poverty certainly causes problems, but it appears indispensable to fill the void in the workforce left by a society which lives happily and longer than before, but in which few children are born," he reasoned. "In emergencies, the humanitarian spirit must prevail above all else."

As president, Ciampi has also pressed for reforming the Italian political system, which is fractured, frayed, and has been marked by 59 governments since 1945. He therefore urges greater emphasis on devolution, namely, delegating power and authority away from the center and back to the regions. Such changes might produce more stable bipolar parliaments, which would be less dominated by numerous small parties that frequently tip the balance of power. He even wants the office of the president, traditionally chosen by legislators, opened up to direct popular vote. Ciampi will continue in office until 2006. He remains one of the few Italian politicians who enjoy both immense popularity at home and a high reputation abroad.

Further Reading

Bufacchi, Vittorio, and Simon Burgess. *Italy since 1989: Events and Interpretations.* Basingstoke, England: Palgrave, 2001.

Cananea, Giacinto D. "Reforming the State: The Policy of Administrative Reform in Italy under the Ciampi Government." *West European Politics* 19 (April 1996): 321–39.

Gilbert, Mark, and Gianfranco Pasquino. *Italian Politics: The Faltering Transition.* New York: Berghahn Books, 2000.

Pasquino, S. "No Longer a Party State? Institutions, Power, and the Problems of Italian Reform." *West European Politics* 20 (January 1997): 34–53.

Tambini, Damian. *Nationalism in Italian Politics, 1980–2000: The Stories of the Northern League, 1980–2000.* New York: Routledge, 2001.

Ciller, Tansu (1944–) *prime minister of Turkey*

Tansu Ciller was born in Istanbul, Turkey, on October 23, 1944, into a comfortably middle-class family. Her father was a political liberal and newspaper editor, and he made an indelible impression on her with his forward-looking policies. Ciller was educated in Istanbul at the American Girls' School and then Robert College, from which she acquired a bachelor's degree in 1967. Fluent in both English and German, she next embarked on graduate study in the United States, and by 1978 she had earned advanced degrees in economics from both the University of New Hampshire and the University of Connecticut. Ciller subsequently taught economics at Franklin and Marshall College, Pennsylvania, before returning home for similar work at Bosphorus University. By the 1980s she had become politically active by joining the center-right True Path Party (TPP) of SÜLEYMAN DEMIREL as an economic consultant. In this capacity she acquired a wide following based upon her youth, attractive looks, and apparent ability. By drawing up the TPP's economic policy, which was very accommodating toward the business community, Ciller helped engineer the party's rise to power in October 1991. As usual in Turkish politics, this was accomplished in concert with the Social Democratic Populist Party (SHP). That year she also won a seat in parliament, and Demirel rewarded her with appointment as minister of state.

Ciller continued functioning as a well-regarded economist until April 1993, following the sudden death of President TURGUT ÖZAL. This vacancy prompted Demirel to run for the presidency and resign as head of the TPP. New party elections were then held and Ciller won a surprising victory over several more senior candidates. Thus, by dint of her reputation at home and abroad, as well as the perceived need for fresh new faces, Ciller became both party head and prime minister of Turkey. This was a political first for that strongly Muslim country, despite its long-established tradition of secularism. Having won a vote of confidence from both the TPP and SHP, Ciller was formally inaugurated on June 13, 1995. It was anticipated her ascension would enhance Turkey's image abroad as a thoroughly modern state, one that was comfortable with women leaders.

Ciller assumed power at a difficult time in Turkey's history. The country suffered from high inflation, a shrinking economy, and a violent Kurdish-led guerrilla war. Ciller had presented a governmental platform predicated upon addressing all these problems, as well as one that advanced the cause of human rights in Turkey, but she proved unable to control her parliamentary coalition to any useful extent. Consequently, the nation remained unstable and Ciller appeared increasingly ineffective. Worse, in 1995 both she and her husband were accused of amassing a fortune through corruption. Ciller strenuously denied these accusations, but suspicions mounted when the extent of her personal holdings—$60 million in American real estate and investments—was revealed. Her dilemma was further complicated in June 1996 by the rise of the Welfare Party, part of a rising tide of Islamic fundamentalism throughout the region, which threaten to upend traditional secularism.

Ciller's problems multiplied in September 1995 after the Republican People's Party withdrew from her coalition. Forced to call new elections, she watched in dismay as the Welfare Party won 150 seats, making it the largest bloc in parliament. Still intent upon stopping Muslim fundamentalism, Ciller then engineered an alliance with the Motherland Party headed by Mesut Yilmaz, a bitter rival. A bargain was struck whereby Yilmaz would serve as prime minister for two years. However, the agreement unraveled once parliament voted to investigate Ciller's holdings, and she was forced to find new allies. Curiously, the only willing partner was NECMETTIN ERBAKAN's Welfare Party, and an unholy alliance was formed. As before, Ciller agreed to temporarily cede the prime minister's office to Erbakan for two years, while she served as foreign minister. However, elections held in June 1997 crippled the TPP's numbers in parliament, and Ciller resigned to serve as head of the opposition.

Since leaving high office, Cıller has retained a degree of popularity within her party, and, in November 1999, she was reelected party head over Koksal Toptan, the former education minister. However, she has proved unable to revive the fortunes of the TPP, which remains the minority opposition. But Ciller, true to form, remains outspoken on controversial issues. The government of Prime Minister Bulent Evecit is committed to abolishing the death penalty in Turkey, despite calls that it be applied to captured Kurdish terrorist Abdullah Ocalan. Ciller is personally opposed to such punishment, but, in February 2002, she suggested a compromise course. "First of all, the government should do what is necessary about Ocalan's death," she stated, "then we lift the death penalty." Such talk has done little to endear her to more conservative elements in the Turkish polity, which roundly calls for Ocalan's execution and supports retention of the ultimate punishment.

Further Reading

Arat, Yesim. "A Woman Prime Minister in Turkey: Did It Matter?" *Women and Politics* 19, no. 4 (1998): 1–22.

Brown, John M. "Tansu Ciller and the Question of Turkish Identity." *World Policy Journal* 11 (Fall 1994): 55–61.

Heper, Metin, and Oncu Ayse. *Turkey and the West: Changing Political Culture and Identities.* New York: I. B. Tauris, 1993.

Heper, Metin, and Sabri Sayari, eds. *Political Leaders and Democracy in Turkey.* Lanham, Md.: Lexington Books, 2002.

Meyer, James H. "Politics as Usual: Ciller, Refah, and Swurluk: Turkey's Troubled Democracy." *East European Quarterly* 32, no. 4 (1998): 489–502.

Clark, Helen (1950–) *prime minister of New Zealand*

Helen Elizabeth Clark was born in Hamilton, New Zealand, on February 26, 1950, one of four sisters. Her family were ranchers and distinctly conservative in political outlook. Having been educated at the Epsom Girls School, Clark next attended the University of Auckland to study political science. She obtained her master's degree in 1974 and spent the next seven years lecturing at the university. Throughout this period, student unrest centered around the Vietnam War, nuclear disarmament, and environmental issues. Clark actively espoused sympathy for many of these causes, and in 1971 she cast her lot with the leftist Labour Party. Shen then filled a series of important party offices before she ran for office, unsuccessfully, in 1979. However, Clark persevered and in 1981 she gained election to New Zealand's unicameral legislature, the House of Representatives. She held this position for 19 years, becoming the longest-serving woman member of parliament, and was popularly known as the "Mother of the House."

True to her Labour leanings, Clark was active in nuclear disarmament matters and in 1986 she received the Peace Prize from the Danish Peace Foundation. The following year she was invited to join the administration of John Lange, who appointed her minister of conservation, 1987–89. A brief stint as minister of housing ensued before Clark next served as minister of health, 1989–90. In this capacity she championed landmark tobacco-control legislation to restrict exposure to secondhand smoke and eliminate tobacco sponsorship of sporting events. Soon after, Lange appointed her the first woman deputy prime minister in New Zealand history, a post she held until Labour was turned out of office in 1990. Three years later Clark became the first woman to head Labour as the opposition leader. When declining economic fortunes returned Labour to power on November 27, 1999, Clark became New Zealand's second woman prime minister by defeating the incumbent, JENNY SHIPLEY. This feat seemed to proffer recognition of her nearly 30 years of service to the Labour Party.

Clark's ascension marked a dramatic turning point in modern New Zealand politics. For the previous 16 years, both Labour and Conservative governments strove to discard decades-old Socialist policies, such as control of the economy and enlargement of the welfare state. Henceforth, Clark moved swiftly to reinstate and reassert traditional government roles in everyday New Zealand life. This entailed policies in support of full employment, higher wages, equality for women, and more equitable distribution of income. Furthermore, she is particularly committed to combating long-standing discrimination against the native Maori population, the islands' original inhabitants. Foremost among these efforts is an attempt at closing social and economic gaps between citizens of European and native ancestry. Many Maori have since been elected to the parliament for the first time in New Zealand history. Clark, a lifelong devotee of opera and the arts, also advocates an expanded role for government in funding, promoting, and preserving culture and national heritage. And, in addition to fostering larger social benefits, she is determined to strike a careful balance between economic and environmental concerns. She maintains a cordial alliance with members of the radical Green Party in parliament. To this end Clark has also made it official government policy to criticize Japan for its continuing practice of whaling for "scientific" purposes. New Zealand is formally and vocally committed to creating a southern seas whale sanctuary where hunting is forbidden.

Despite her traditional Labour perspectives, Clark is no radical. Like TONY BLAIR and BILL CLINTON, she seeks a "Third Way" between liberal and conservative extremes, and she posits fiscal restraint along with social care as a policy priority. "A strong economy produces the wealth to fund our social objectives, to employ our people, to house them, and to give them the means to live in dignity," she lectured. "A strong economy must enable us to do those things, or else it has failed in its central purpose." She hopes that this mixing of market-based policies with selective government control will bring about a better economic picture—and the means to sustain social change.

In the realm of foreign policy, Clark has also markedly distinguished herself from her predecessors. She remains an outspoken advocate of nuclear disarmament and insists on creation of nuclear-free zones in the South Pacific. Clark has also questioned the utility of excessive military defense spending, and, in 2001, she decided to sell off New Zealand's only squadron of aging A-4 Skyhawk jet airplanes. Several of the navy's larger warships will also be retired and not replaced, so for the foreseeable future New Zealand will depend more heavily upon its small army for defense. This act triggered criticism from Australia's John Howard that Clark was abrogating a long-standing mutual defense pact (ANZAC) between the two nations.

Further Reading

Alves, Dora. *The Maori and the Crown: An Indigenous People's Struggle for Self-Determination.* Westport, Conn.: Greenwood Press, 1999.

Edwards, Brian. *Helen: Portrait of a Prime Minister.* Auckland: Exisle Publishing, 2001.

Fenton, Damien. "Has New Zealand Let Down the ANZAC Tradition?" *New Zealand International Review* 26 (July 2001): 19–29.

Levine, Stephen L., and Margaret Clark. *The New Zealand Politics Source Book.* Palmerston North, New Zealand: Dunmore Press, 1999.

Miller, Raymond. *New Zealand: Government and Politics.* New York: Oxford University Press, 2001.

Rudd, Chris, and B. Roper. *The Political Economy of New Zealand.* Auckland: Oxford University Press, 1997.

Clerides, Glafcos (1919–) *president of Cyprus*

Glafcos Clerides was born at Nicosia, Cyprus, on April 24, 1919, the son of a lawyer. Cyprus, the Mediterranean's third-largest island, was then a British Crown colony. Clerides was educated at the Pancyprian Gymnasium and subsequently joined the Royal Air Force during World War II. He was shot down in 1942 and remained in captivity for several months until effecting an escape. Clerides then studied law at King's College in London, from which he graduated in 1948. He returned home and established a legal practice between 1951 and 1960. During talks with Great Britain in 1959 over the issue of independence, Clerides also served as a leading negotiator.

Cyprus gained its independence in August 1960 under a specially balanced constitution. This was promulgated to reflect the competing interests of the island's two major communities, the Greek and Turkish Cypriots. Henceforth, the island was to elect a Greek president, a Turkish vice president, while also allowing disproportionate Turkish representation at every level of government. It was hoped that through such measures peace and stability could thrive between the island's inhabitants, who had a long history of internecine strife. However, the Turkish Cypriots withdrew from the government in 1963 over the issue of constitutional amendments, while the mainland governments of Greece and Turkey perpetually interfered in the island's affairs. When the military junta ruling Greece deposed the elected president of Cyprus, Turkey invaded the island on July 20, 1974. They then secured the northern third of the island, displacing large numbers of Greeks and seizing their property. This act, widely condemned by the United Nations, keeps the island separated along ethnic lines to this day. It was against this discordant backdrop that Clerides decided to enter politics.

In 1969 Clerides founded the Unified Party, a conservative organization. He followed this in 1976 by establishing another center-right group, the Democratic Rally, which has since functioned as the largest party in the House of Representatives. Clerides himself ran for the island's presidency in 1983 and 1985, being narrowly defeated on both occasions. He finally succeeded to the office on February 14, 1993, at the age of 74. However, running the island had grown increasingly complicated, as the Turkish Republic of Northern Cyprus had been established in 1983. This ethnic enclave is not diplomatically recognized by any nation but Turkey.

Both sides then began girding for what seemed like an inevitable confrontation.

Unlike many small island nations, Cyprus has become a prosperous showcase of free markets and an expansive private sector. To cement this success, in 1990 it applied for full membership into the European Union (EU). Turkey, however, strongly protested the move, asserting that the Greek section of the island was in no position to speak for the Turkish side. Events were further skewed in January 1997 when Clerides announced his decision to purchase and deploy advanced, Russian-made S-300 antiaircraft missiles on Cyprus. This weapon, which could threaten any aircraft on the Turkish side, drew a sharp response from the Turks. They threatened the use of military force to curtail their deployment, even in the event of war with Greece. The following year Clerides was reelected by a 50.8 percent margin and, after intense pressure from the EU, the United Nations and the United States, he rescinded his decision to acquire missiles. The entire episode only served to underscore the deep-seated mistrust and tension between the two communities.

Clerides has since declared that the only solution to the Cyprus problem rests with the principles of the UN charter and the European Convention on Human Rights. A settlement would entail creation of a bicommunal and bizonal federation, withdrawal of Turkish troops, and resolution of issues involving the movement and settlement of displaced residents and the return of confiscated property. Despite Turkish objections, he also remains committed to integrating the island into the EU to improve both the economy and living standards for all Cypriots. The Turkish leader, RAUF DENKTASH, had previously rejected all attempts at a UN–sponsored solution. Behind-the-scene negotiations between the two factions and UN representatives have since come to naught. However, a major breakthrough occurred on December 5, 2001, when the 83-year-old Clerides became the first Greek Cypriot to visit the occupied north in 27 years. Both he and Denktash, longtime friends before the invasion, enjoyed dinner together and publicly pledged to resolve their differences peacefully. Their long-standing amicability has since spilled over into their respective communities, so a far-reaching settlement may be at hand.

Further Reading

Borowiec, Andrew. *Cyprus: A Troubled Island.* Westport, Conn.: Praeger, 2000.

Glafcos Clerides *(Embassy of Cyprus)*

Dodd, C. H. *Storm Clouds over Cyprus: A Briefing.* Huntington, England: Eothen, 2001.

Clerides, Glafcos. *Cyprus: My Deposition.* 4 vols. Nicosia, Cyprus: Alithia, 1989–1992.

Staurinides, Zenon. *The Cyprus Conflict: National Identity and Statehood.* Lefkosa, Cyprus: CYREP, 1999.

Stefanidis, Ioannis D. *Isle of Discord: Nationalism, Imperialism, and the Making of the Cyprus Problem.* New York: New York University Press, 1999.

Clinton, Bill (1946–) *president of the United States*

William Jefferson Blythe Clinton was born on August 19, 1946, in Hope, Arkansas, just prior to losing his father to a car accident. His mother subsequently married Roger Clinton, who legally adopted him. Now known as Bill Clinton, he proved himself an exceptional student and was selected for a field trip to Washington, D.C., at which he met President John F. Kennedy. This encounter inspired Clinton to a life of public service, and, in 1964, he gained admittance to Georgetown University. Clinton graduated with honors four years later and won a Rhodes Scholarship to study at Oxford University. He returned home in 1970 and enrolled at Yale University Law School, where he met and eventually married Hillary Rodham. Clinton graduated in 1973 and came home to teach law at the University of Arkansas, Fayetteville.

Clinton, a lifelong Democrat, commenced his political career in 1974 when he unsuccessfully challenged a popular Republican incumbent for a congressional seat. Two years later he managed the Arkansas campaign of presidential contender Jimmy Carter, and he also managed to gain election as state attorney general. Clinton gained considerable popularity as an outspoken proponent of consumer rights, and in 1978 he was elected to the governor's mansion. At that time Clinton became the nation's youngest state executive. However, he spent the next two years arbitrarily raising taxes and confronting vested interests statewide, and in 1980 he was unceremoniously voted out of office. Thoroughly chastised, Clinton took the lessons to heart and thereafter he chose moderation and conciliation over confrontation. He successfully wielded his new image in 1982, and he was reelected governor by a wide margin. His political success at home may be gauged by the fact that he was continually returned to office by wide margins over the next 10 years. His ability to embrace contentious issues and emerge unscathed earned him the unflattering but appropriate moniker "Slick Willie." And throughout his tenure in Little Rock, Clinton enjoyed considerable success upgrading the state educational system, even at the expense of such traditional Democratic allies as teacher's unions. He also sought to gain national exposure by serving as chair of the National Governor's Association. More important, Clinton, long disillusioned by a string of defeated Democratic presidential candidates, determined to bring his party to the political center. As part of the Democratic Leadership Council, he worked assiduously to wean his party from its tendency toward ill-advised liberal policies, and he advanced more palatable, mainstream stances on crime, defense, and the economy.

By August 1991 Clinton felt emboldened by his striking success in Arkansas to run for the presidency. Youthful, telegenic, and politically gifted, he was the odds-on favorite to win the Democratic nomination, but a series of personal scandals that surfaced involving draft-dodging during the Vietnam War and marital infidelity nearly derailed his campaign. However, Clinton displayed amazing resilience in confronting these damaging allegations and went on to secure his party's nomination. In November 1992 he defeated Republican incumbent George H. W. Bush and independent challenger H. Ross Perot. Many voters remained unsettled by the "character issue," however, so Clinton's margin of victory was a plurality of 43 percent. Even so he had become the first Democrat to occupy the White House in over a decade and, given his youth, commitment, and capability, much was expected of him.

Once empowered, Clinton appeared initially overwhelmed by the responsibilities of command. His administration commenced a shaky start with the rejection of several high-ranking nominees, and he was also unable to fulfill several important campaign pledges. A fiscal moderate, he had campaigned on a platform to lower taxes, but, in a politically courageous move, he decided instead to raise them in an effort to bring down the massive national debt accrued by his Republic predecessors. This ploy paid great dividends for the economy in the months ahead, but it gained him the public's immediate ire. Furthermore, the move tarred him as simply another "tax-and-spend" Democrat. The president's attempts at overhauling the national health care system also backfired politically when it was entrusted to Hillary Clinton, a divisive political figure who served as a lightning rod for Republican criticism. At length, the reform attempts failed, and in November 1994 the Democrats entered the congressional elections appearing disjointed and fumbling. Consequently, the Republicans scored impressive gains, recapturing the control of both houses of Congress for the first time since 1954. It was one of the darkest moments in Clinton's presidency and many pundits were predicting the end of his administration. But, as events proved, he would again live up to his reputation as the "Comeback Kid."

Hereafter, Clinton's policies became more conservative, and he consciously and successfully co-opted many Republican issues, such as law and order and a line-item veto. Republican attempts at budgetary confrontation made them appear too extreme by comparison, and also contributed to Clinton's rising approval ratings. Buoyed by an improving economy, he was well placed to run for a second term in 1996. Wishing to deny his opponent, Senator Robert Dole, a viable campaign issue, Clinton unhesitatingly endorsed a Republican-inspired welfare reform bill that gutted social welfare programs dating back to Franklin D. Roosevelt's administration. Liberals groaned about being thrown overboard, but Clinton's political instinct for survival was hard at work. His determination to embrace centrist policies succeeded, and that November he was resoundingly reelected. Clinton again made history as the first Democrat to serve two consecutive terms since Franklin Roosevelt. But, as before, he had to settle for a plurality of 49 percent, while the Republicans retained complete control of Congress.

Clinton's second term in office proved more stormy and tempestuous than his first, and tested his talents for political survival to their utmost. He was determined to engage U.S. forces abroad in the interests of world peace, and successfully returned JEAN-BERTRAND ARISTIDE back to power in Haiti, committed troops to peacekeeping in Somalia, and initiated an air campaign against SLOBODAN MILOŠEVIĆ in Kosovo. However, success abroad was perpetually undercut by congressional investigations about allegedly shady land dealings in Arkansas, known collectively as "Whitewater," and charges of sexual harassment by Paula Jones, a former Arkansas state employee. In the spring of 1998, the tempo of legal action against Clinton greatly accelerated following revelations of his affair with Monica Lewinski, an intern half his age. After months of repeatedly denying any wrongdoing, Clinton was forced by Special Prosecutor Ken Starr to admit he had committed perjury about the Lewinski matter, apparently under oath. Such transgressions inspired the Republican-controlled Congress to initiate impeachment proceedings against him. Through a highly charged, highly divisive process, in December 1998 the president was formally impeached by the House of Representatives for perjury and obstruction of justice. From a strictly legal standpoint, either charge can be construed as felonious and grounds for removal from office and Clinton became only the second president so accused, after Andrew Johnson. However, in February 2000, a closely divided Senate acquitted him on all counts. Clinton, the political survivor, had triumphed again but at great cost to his party. In the fall of 2000, public dismay over ethical lapses detrimentally effected the candidacy of incumbent vice president ALBERT GORE, who lost to neophyte GEORGE W. BUSH despite a sound economy and record prosperity. In January 2001, on virtually his last day in office, Clinton agreed to a plea bargain arrangement whereby he formally admitted lying under oath in exchange for suspension of legal action against him. Consequently, he was fined $10,000 by the state of Arkansas and willingly suspended practicing law for five years.

Though he was out of office and far from the center of national politics, controversy continued stalking the former president. He was seriously criticized for the pardoning of Marc Rich, a millionaire fugitive wanted for tax evasion and living in Switzerland. "People are free to say that they disagreed with this or that part of the decisions I made, but there wasn't a shred of evidence that it had been done for any improper motive," he insisted. The former president has since attempted to maintain high public visibility by renting out an office in the Harlem section of New York City, where he continues as a popular public speaker. Convivial to a fault and eager to bask in the limelight, Clinton also proffered his talents as a raconteur to several television networks and offered to serve as a talk show host for $50 million a year. On a more serious note, in March 2002 President Bush dispatched him to lead the American delegation at independence celebrations held in East Timor, where he proved instrumental in securing UN peacekeeping forces. Clinton, despite all the controversy engendered by his behavior, still enjoys a degree of popularity with the American public. But the consensus of political analysts suggests that his many peccadillos deeply injured his historical reputation.

Further Reading

Brasch, Walter M. *Joy of Sax: America during the Bill Clinton Era.* Deerfield Branch, Fla.: Lighthouse Press, 2001.

Denton, Robert E., and Rachel L. Holloway, eds. *Images, Scandal, and Communications Strategies of the Clinton Presidency.* Westport, Conn.: Praeger, 2003.

Halberstam, David. *War in a Time of Peace: Bush, Clinton, and the Generals.* Waterville, Maine: Thorndike Press, 2001.

Hayden, Joseph. *Covering Clinton: The President and the Press in the 1990s.* Westport, Conn.: Praeger, 2002.

Hendrickson, Ryan C. *The Clinton Years: The Constitution, Congress, and War Powers.* Nashville, Tenn.: Vanderbilt University, 2002.

Klein, Joe. *The Natural: The Misunderstood Presidency of Bill Clinton.* Waterville, Maine: Thorndike Press, 2002.

Morris, Irvin L. *Money and the Clinton Impeachment.* Boulder, Colo.: Westview Press, 2001.

Waddan, Alex. *Clinton's Legacy: A New Democrat in Governance.* New York: Palgrave, 2002.

Collor de Mello, Fernando (1949–   )

president of Brazil

Fernando Collor de Mello was born on August 12, 1949, in Rio de Janeiro, Brazil, the son of an affluent businessman who was governor of Alagoas state. He attended the Federal University in Alagoas, obtaining a degree in economics. Collor began working for his family business empire and quickly gained celebrity status as a media mogul. He entered politics in 1979 by flaunting his flamboyant playboy reputation, and he gained election as mayor of Maceio, capital of Alagoas. By 1982 the long-serving military regime finally decided to allow democratic elections, so Collor ran for a seat in the Chamber of Deputies. He won, becoming the youngest congressman to hold office. In this capacity he gained a national reputation as a hard-line, no-nonsense political and economic reformer, intent upon spending more money in neglected regions like his home state. This stance endeared him to voters at home. In 1986 Collor ran for governor of Alagoas and won easily. Again, he championed statewide fiscal reforms and garnered a degree of notoriety for prosecuting well-paid and unproductive bureaucrats, derisively known as "Mahararjahs." Success only enhanced his political standing and, given his screen presence, boyish good looks, and fluency in five languages, Collor became touted as a possible presidential candidate in 1990.

Collor commenced his quest for the presidency in 1989 as part of the small but conservative National Reconstruction Party. He ran on a platform entitled "the New Brazil," predicated upon dramatic economic reform, privatization of state-owned industries, responsible fiscal policies, and increased protection for the environment. He was also unabashedly pro-American in outlook, in stark contrast to several leftist opponents. And, as head of a huge television empire, he orchestrated the first media blitz in Brazilian political history. In November 1990, Collor won more votes than any other candidate, but he was short of a majority, so a runoff was inevitable. The following December he beat leftist candidate Luis da Silva with a slender electoral majority of 53 percent. Surprisingly, despite his reputation as the product of privilege and monied interests, support for Collor cut across traditional class lines. He thus became the first freely elected Brazilian president since the military takeover of 1964, and the youngest executive ever to hold office. Collor, mindful of his international image, spent the next several months visiting the United States and several Latin American countries before taking the oath of office.

Collor's ascension represented a marked shift away from Brazil's traditional emphasis on developing nations. The new president was firmly in the American camp and he intended to tie Brazil's fortunes to Western democracies and the industrialized world. To achieve this, however, he first had to address the nation's soaring inflation rate, which had reached 80 percent a month. Collor quickly enacted stiff austerity measures, including the abandonment of wage and price indexing, freezes on wage increases, and a crackdown on tax evaders. Brazil's much-vaunted and controversial nuclear weapons program was also scuttled in the interest of cost-cutting. He then authorized a reduction in the bloated federal payroll and commenced renegotiating the country's $100 billion foreign debt. In less dramatic fashion, Collor also addressed various social problems, including establishing viable reservations for Brazil's native population and urging creditor nations to financially assist the preservation of Amazon rain forests.

Despite his best efforts, Collor's reform package did not produce the anticipated windfall, and his popularity ratings plunged. Worse, in the fall of 1992 he was stung by allegations of having amassed large fortunes at state expense. Collor strongly professed his innocence, but, in September 1992, he was impeached by the Chamber of Deputies. Stripped of power, he waited impotently in office while the congress debated removing him from office. The turning point in his fortunes occurred in December 1992, when a court formally indicted him on corruption charges. Collor, rather than face the ultimate humiliation, resigned from office on December 29, 1992. Vice President ITAMAR FRANCO succeeded him. The former executive was then proscribed from holding office for a period of eight years. However, in 1998, a court acquitted him of all counts of illegal enrichment. Eager to return to the political fray, in August 2000 Collor announced his candidacy for mayor of São Paulo, Brazil's largest city, but a judge canceled his efforts until the eight-year ban on politics expired that December. Since that time he has been waiting in the wings, eager and apparently determined to rehabilitate his political reputation and fortunes.

Further Reading

Bertozzi, Carlos A. "Collor de Mello: A Brazilian Neopopulist Leader?" Unpublished master's thesis, Ohio University, 2001.

Perez-Linan, Anibal S. "Crisis without Breakdown: Presidential Impeachment in Latin America." Unpublished Ph.D. dissertation, University of Notre Dame, 2001.

Rosenn, Keith S., and Richard Downes. *Corruption and Political Reform in Brazil: The Impact of Collor's Impeachment.* Coral Gables, Fla.: North-South Center Press, 1999.

Valencia, Marcio M. "The Politics of Giving in Brazil: The Rise and Demise of Collor." *Latin American Perspectives* 29 (January 2002): 115–188.

Weyland, Kurt. "The Rise and Fall of President Collor and Its Impact on Brazilian Democracy." *Journal of Interamerican Studies and World Affairs* 35 (Spring 1993): 1–38.

Compaore, Blaise (1950–) *president of Burkina Faso*

Blaise Compaore was born in Ziniare, Burkina Faso, in 1950, while his country was a French possession known as Upper Volta. The country achieved independence in 1960, but it had been under military rule of one form or another until 1980. Compaore came from a distinguished military family, and he attended an infantry school in Montpellier, France, and an officer's school at Yaoundé, Cameroon. Adept as a soldier, Compaore then trained as a paratrooper in Morocco, where he encountered and befriended Captain Thomas Sankara. The two formed a fast relationship and, when Sankara took charge of the paracommando school at home, Compaore served as his deputy. He subsequently also served as garrison commander when Sankara was transferred.

In 1983 Compaore led troops in an uprising that toppled Colonel Saye Zerbo and installed Sankara as head of state. The latter instituted a radical left-wing regime through the formation of the National Council for the Revolution, with Compaore holding down the posts of minister of state and minister of justice. Henceforth, political activity in Burkina Faso became contingent upon grassroots organizations known as Committees for the Defense of the Revolution (CDRs), which were also heavily armed. However, the radical nature of Sankara's reforms and his own unstable behavior drove a wedge between the two men. Fearing that he might be removed from office and murdered, Compaore staged a bloody coup on October 15, 1987, that saw Sankara and several other leading figures killed. The following day, despite international condemnation, he declared himself president of Burkina Faso. Compaore also publicly declared he had nothing to do with the death of Sankara, although public skepticism remained strong.

Immediately upon taking office, Compaore embarked on an official policy of "rectification" to roll back the revolutionary excesses of Sankara. This entailed creation of a new political party, the Popular Front, which was an umbrella organization of several differing groups. Moreover, the CDRs were disarmed, disbanded, and replaced by revolutionary committees drawn from factories, offices, and villages. He also dropped some unpopular taxes and raised the salaries of the bureaucracy to meld their support to his regime. However, the Compaore proved merciless toward the opposition and stifled political dissent through arrests and torture. In 1988 several military units attempted a coup against Compaore; this was also ruthlessly suppressed with the wholesale execution of rebel leaders.

By 1991 Compaore's grip on power seemed secure. He then announced the end to all Marxist-Leninist policies in place and promulgated a new constitution that granted multiparty democracy. In December 1991 he was resoundingly elected as president, although all opposition parties boycotted the process. Compaore then accelerated his economic reforms, promoting free markets, privatization, and membership in the World Bank and the International Monetary Fund (IMF). In 1996 the president orchestrated creation of the Congress for Democracy and Progress Party (CDP), and the following year the national assembly amended the constitution to allow Compaore to run for a second seven-year term. On November 15, 1998, he received 87.53 percent of ballots cast although, once again, he ran unopposed. Despite claims of widespread voter fraud, Compaore thus became the first president of Burkina Faso to fulfill his term in office and be reelected.

The citizens of Burkina Faso accepted the legitimacy of the Compaore regime with little comment until December 1998, when it became known that Nobert Zongo, a respected journalist investigating Compaore's brother, had been murdered. The countryside suddenly became rocked by mass protests and political violence. Given the magnitude of this backlash, Compaore established an independent commission to investigate the murder. He also constituted a council of tribal elders to redress problems of crime and punishment. This body recommended a government of national unity to placate the countryside, which had been seething with resentment against Compaore since the death of Sankara. The independent commission has since recommended the arrest of the president's brother and six guards for the murder of Zongo and others. To date no arrests have been made.

Compaore has enjoyed a higher profile and greater success on the international scene where he strove to function as a mediator and peacekeeper for regional disputes. However, the United States has downgraded its diplomatic presence to protest Burkina Faso's close ties with Libya, and its clandestine support for CHARLES TAYLOR's rebel group in Liberia. The country enjoys a good working relationship with many of its feuding neighbors and bilateral trade agreements with other nations in the developing world.

Further Reading

Battersby, Simon. "Burkina Faso." *African Affairs* 95, no. 381 (1996): 599–604.

Englebert, Pierre. *Burkina Faso: Unsteady Statehood in West Africa.* Boulder, Colo.: Westview Press, 1996.

Guion, Jean R. *Blaise Compaore: Realism and Integrity: Portrait of the Man behind Rectification in Burkina Faso.* Paris: Berger-Leuvault International, 1991.

Huasch, Ernst. "Burkina Faso in the Winds of Liberalization." *Review of African Political Economy* 28 (1998): 625–641.

Constantinescu, Emil (1939–) *president of Romania*

Emil Constantinescu was born in Tighina, Moldavia (now Bessarabia), on November 19, 1939. Romania was then ruled by a pro-Nazi fascist regime, but this was overthrown by Soviet troops in 1945. A new government controlled by the Communist Party then came to power. During this time Constantinescu was educated in law at the University of Bucharest in 1960 and five years later he joined the Communist Party. Such a move virtually insured his rapid rise through the government's ranks,

but, like many intellectuals behind the Iron Curtain, he was attempting to change the party from within. However, mounting disillusionment forced Constantinescu to abandon law and politics altogether. He thereupon returned to school, studied geology, and received his doctorate in 1979. Constantinescu subsequently became a committed academician, teaching geology until 1990 when he gained appointment as the university's rector. Prior to this point he expressed little interest in public affairs.

For many years, communist Romania was run with an iron fist under Nicolae Ceauşescu, who was violently overthrown in December 1989. Soon after, Constantinescu became actively involved in politics by joining the National Salvation Front. However, he felt not enough was being done to break with Romania's communist past. In the spring of 1990, when new president ION ILIESCU spoke at the University of Bucharest, he employed nearby miners to violently suppress student protests. This act prompted Constantinescu to found a new political organization, the National Convention of Romania (NCR), in November 1991. After much political squabbling and infighting, he became the party's candidate to oppose Iliescu in the 1992 presidential elections. Constantinescu, a political neophyte, campaigned badly on ideological issues and his desire to punish surviving Communists for their excesses. Moreover, his seemingly friendly invitation to allow the former King Michael back into the country allowed the opposition to tar him as a monarchist. But the election ultimately turned on the economy, which had been in tatters since the revolution of 1989. Consequently, on October 11, 1992, Constantinescu was decisively defeated in a runoff election by Iliescu, 61 percent to 38 percent. It proved a humbling experience for the former geology professor, but he had gained national recognition and a reputation for personal integrity. As events demonstrated, these became traits that the Romanian government needed to survive.

After his crushing defeat, Constantinescu remained as president of the NCR and girded himself for a rematch with Iliescu. The Romanian economy performed miserably over the next four years, and was further exacerbated by the government's refusal to accelerate badly needed reform. Romania was also swept by a seemingly endless wave of corruption that sapped the vitality of the nation. Constantinescu was by now better versed in the nuances of national politics, and, in 1996, he again

challenged Iliescu for the presidency. This time he focused his message on economic reforms and pledged to
fight corruption wherever it occurred. His opponent, in
contrast, invoked his usual scare tactic that the NCR was
prepared to grant unnecessary concessions to Romania's
Hungarian minority, and that Constantinescu secretly
intended to restore King Michael to the throne. But the
voters wanted change and on November 17, 1996, Constantinescu was swept to victory on a second ballot, winning with 51.4 percent of the vote. His accession marked
the first time that Romania enjoyed a peaceful transition of power since 1937.

Once installed, Constantinescu embarked on a path
of economic reform, embracing free markets, privatization of state-owned industries, and foreign investment.
To reduce age-old ethnic strife with the country's sizable
Hungarian minority, he also granted several government
posts to the Hungarian Democratic Federation, a staunch
political ally. He also abandoned his earlier campaign to
punish former Communists, but he did remove them
from numerous state and cultural institutions. Furthermore, Constantinescu has been pushing hard for Romania's entry into both the European Union (EU) and the
North Atlantic Treaty Organization (NATO) to further
distance his country form its Soviet past. But, more than
anything else, Constantinescu ordered a crack-down on
widespread corruption. However, after four years, the
president was dissatisfied by the slow rate of economic
growth (especially compared to other newly freed countries in Eastern Europe) and his inability to end graft. In
July 2000 he announced his intention not to seek a second term in office. "The problems Romania and Roma-
nians have are the effects of disrespect for the law,"
Constantinescu declared. "If we will go on disregarding
the law, and if theft, murder, and illegal enrichment at the
expense of others continue, deception and lies will pro-
liferate." On November 26, 2000, former president Iliescu was swept back into power by defeating Corneliu
Vadim Tudor with 66 percent of the vote.

Further Reading

Boia, Lucian. *Romania: Borderland of Europe.* London
Reaktion, 2001.
Light, Duncan, and David Phinnemore, eds. *Post-Com-
munist Romania: Coming to Terms with Transition.*
New York: Palgrove, 2001.
Neastase, Adrian. *Battle for the Future.* Boulder, Colo.:
East European Monographs, 2001.

Roper, Steven D. *Romania: The Unfinished Revolution.*
Amsterdam: Harwood Academic, 2000.
Tismayeanu, Vladimir. "Electoral Revolutions." *Society* 35
(November–December 1997): 61–66.

Conté, Lansana (1934–   ) *president of Guinea*

Lansana Conté was born at Dubreka, Guinea, in 1934,
and pursued a military career while quite young. After
training at schools in Senegal and Côte d'Ivoire, he
joined the French army in 1955 and then transferred to
the newly independent Guinean military in 1958. In
1961 he was active in forwarding supplies and support
to liberation forces under Amilcar Cabral in neighboring
Guinea-Bissau. Conté rose to colonel by 1975 and subsequently became chief of the army general staff. Guinea
was then ruled by Ahmad Sékou Touré, who had led the
country since independence. His regime was both authoritarian and dominated by left-wing socialist doctrines, including a centrally planned and controlled
economy. However, when Sékou Touré died during
heart surgery in March 1984, Conté took control during
a bloodless coup. He was assisted by the Military Committee for National Recovery (CMRN), which unilaterally decided to undo most of Sékou Touré's political
legacy.

Once in power, Conté suspended the constitution,
banned all political activity, and prepared to scale back
state control of the economy. Henceforth, Guinea followed a path toward free markets, privatization of state-
run industries, and foreign investment. Moreover, Conté
freed over 1,000 political prisoners and pushed for closer
ties to Western countries, most notably France. This decidedly antirevolutionary direction engendered some
discontent among some senior members of Sékou
Touré's military leadership. In July 1985 they staged an
unsuccessful coup against Conté, but this was thwarted
by loyalist troops. The government then responded with
exacting reprisals not only against the mutineers but also
against the Malinké tribal group to which they belonged.
This gave most Guineans an impression that Conté was
both ruthless and vindictive.

Conté may have been autocratic in tone, but his
grasp of economics proved exceptionally sound. By
closely adhering to austerity measures imposed by the
World Bank and International Monetary Fund (IMF),
Guinea's economy started rebounding after years of decline under Sékou Touré. "It is you—the farmers, crafts-

men and industrial workers who make up the riches of this nation," he declared. "It is the role of Guinean men and women to build or develop their business." Moreover, government policy redirected national wealth into rebuilding the country's infrastructure, especially transportation and communication. The nation also owns two-thirds of the world's known bauxite reserves, and several consortia based in the United States have been invited to develop it. One additional asset of this sustained growth was political stability, and in 1990 Conté deemed it prudent to enhance Guinea's image abroad by legalizing multiparty elections. That year a new constitution was adopted by public referendum and Conté ran for the top office. However, because the government owns all access to state-run media, opponents charged that he enjoyed unfair advantages in any election process. They also complained about irregularities in compiling the electoral lists and in issuing voting cards. Consequently, all opposition parties boycotted the election held on December 19, 1993, and Conté ran unopposed, garnering 51 percent of the vote. On December 14, 1998, Conté was also reelected in an uncontested bid for a second term—the maximum allowed under the constitution.

Conté's regime has thus far been characterized by the adoption of Western-style economic practices and reintegration of Guinea into the world economy. However, domestically the country has been rocked by violence stemming from election fraud and favoritism of groups like the Susa at the expense of the Malinké. Worse, in September 2000 fighting broke out in the forest regions of southeastern Guinea. It appears that elements within the Revolutionary United Front, stationed on the fringes of Liberia and Sierra Leone, are working with Guinean dissidents to overthrow the government. Fighting continues to rage in that region, but Conté has responded with both military force and a political ploy. In December 2001 he sponsored a constitutional amendment that would expand presidential terms from five to seven years and allow him to run for a third term. A referendum was held on November 11, 2001, and published results by the state-controlled media indicate an astonishing 98 percent approval rating. Opposition parties have again cried foul and boycotted the general elections slated for December 27, 2001. This tactic, in turn, has forced the government to postpone the elections, in the words of one governmental official, "for further consultation between political parties and the

department charged with organizing elections." Conté's continuing tenure in office thus remains problematic.

Further Reading

Camara, Mohamed S. "From Military Politicization to Militarization of Power in Guinea-Conakry." *Journal of Political and Military Sociology* 28, no. 2 (2000): 311–326.

Fegley, Randall. *Equatorial Guinea: An African Tragedy.* New York: P. Lang, 1989.

Liniger-Goumaz, Max. *Historical Dictionary of Equatorial Guinea.* Lanham, Md.: Scarecrow Press, 2000.

Topouzis, Daphne. "Conte." *Africa Report* 34 (November–December, 1989): 38–42.

Cresson, Edith (1934–   ) *prime minister of France*

Edith Cresson (née Campion) was born on January 27, 1934, in Boulogne-Billancourt, the daughter of a tax inspector. She received a Ph.D. in demography from the noted Hautes Etudes Commerciales of Paris, and first evinced interest in politics by joining the left-wing Convention of Republican Institutions in 1965. There she met and assisted FRANÇOIS MITTERRAND in his failed attempt to achieve the presidency that year. Mitterrand was nonetheless impressed by the highly intelligent, highly outspoken Cresson, and they formed an abiding political friendship. In 1971 she transferred her alliance to the newly formed Socialist Party and four years later ran for parliament against a conservative incumbent in the district of Châtellerault. She lost, but her feisty campaign style gained her a reputation as "the Fighter." In 1977 Cresson enjoyed better success in becoming the mayor of Thure, and two years later she solidified her credentials by gaining a seat in the European Parliament. In 1981 Mitterrand became the first Socialist president in a generation and Cresson also won a seat in the National Assembly. He then appointed Cresson France's first woman minister of agriculture. Belligerent and defiant, she antagonized the conservative-minded farming community, but she also enacted policies that raised their income by 10 percent. In 1983 she participated in municipal elections and finally won the mayorship of Châtellerault. That year she also served as the first woman minister of foreign trade and tourism, and the following year served as minister of industrial restructuring. In this capacity she displayed considerable pragmatism, despite her socialist leanings, and she adopted neoliberal positions such as tax breaks for businesses.

In 1986, when the Socialists lost the next round of legislative elections, Cresson resigned from office and worked for private industry. Two years later she was voted back into office as a deputy from Vienne, and concurrently she held the post of minister of European affairs under Prime Minister Michel Rocard. Rocard, a right-wing Socialist, did not work well with Cresson, who criticized him for failing to completely mobilize French industry. Cresson was also outspoken in her complaints about Japan and its protectionist policies. "Japan is an adversary who does not respect the rules of the game and whose overwhelming desire is to conquer the world," she blithely maintained. After continued infighting, she resigned from office again to resume work in industry, until May 15, 1991, when Mitterrand, in a surprise move, appointed her to replace Rocard, making her France's first woman prime minister. This was a calculated risk on Mitterrand's part, for the Socialists fared badly in recent elections, and he hoped that the blunt-speaking Cresson might revive the party's flagging image. "To get the country moving it is necessary to let off some bombs," Cresson said, "I shall commence the bombardment." It was a prophetic pronouncement.

Given her strident, mercurial disposition, Cresson's tenure in office was destined to be a controversial one. Intent on breaking the glass ceiling for others, she quickly named five women to her cabinet, more than any other incumbent. Cresson also moved quickly to counter what she perceived as France's industrial weakness by merging the ministries of economics and industry into a single superministry. However, her tactless demeanor outraged the male-dominated inner circles of power, and Cresson was always quick to blame political resistance to her policies on sexism. "There are three places where women have always been excluded: the military, religion, and politics," she insisted, "I would say that today, it is still in politics where they have the least access." However, the Socialist Party, rather than constructively address France's economic woes, took to infighting and fell into disarray. Cresson's popularity fell in consequence, and soon she sustained the lowest-ever popularity rating of any prime minister. Mitterrand nonetheless stuck by her until the Socialists were routed in the April 1992 regional elections. Many in the party considered this debacle a referendum on their controversial prime minister, and Cresson, not wishing to hurt Mitterrand further, resigned

on April 2, 1992. She was replaced by finance minister PIERRE BEREGOVOY.

Cresson continued on as Mitterrand's personal favorite, and, in 1994, she received the portfolio as head of the Department of Research and Education within the Commission of the European Union. Her tenure there was also contentious and occasioned numerous charges of favoritism and corruption. For example, she appointed a friend who was a dentist to serve as a high-ranking scientific adviser to coordinate AIDS research, and, although on the payroll, he never produced any work. Once word of such irregularities was leaked to the press, Cresson threatened to sue for defamation, and the ensuing public uproar forced the entire commission to resign in March 1999. To the end the former prime minister remains defiant and unapologetic, traits she inherited from her mentor Mitterrand. However, in February 2000, the European Commission lifted Cresson's immunity from prosecution and proffered charges of corruption against her. The case remains pending.

Further Reading

Benoit, Bertrand. *Social-Nationalism: An Anatomy of French Euroscepticism.* Brookfield, Vt.: Ashgate, 1997.

Friend, Julius W. *The Long Presidency: France in the Mitterrand Years, 1981–1995.* Boulder, Colo.: Westview Press, 1998.

Lilla, Mark. "Mme Gaffe: Edith Cresson's Big Mouth." *The New Republic* 205 (August 12, 1991): 10–13.

Morray, J. P. *Grand Disillusion: François Mitterrand and the French Left.* Westport, Conn.: Praeger, 1997.

Raymond, Gino. *France during the Socialist Years.* Brookfield, Vt.: Dartmouth, 1994.

Cristiani, Alfredo (1947–) *president of El Salvador*

Alfredo Cristiani Burkard was born on November 22, 1947 in San Salvador, El Salvador, the son of a wealthy businessman. Having enjoyed a privileged youth, he was educated at the American School in San Salvador before studying business administration at Georgetown University in Washington, D.C. Prior to 1980 Cristiani evinced little interest in politics and served as a mid-level executive in the family business. Here he displayed good analytical skills and was considered an effective manager. The turning point in his career came in 1980 when, as head of the Coffee Producer's Association, he was kidnapped and held hostage for two weeks by left-wing operatives of the Frente Farabundo Martí para la Liberación Nacional (FMLN). This was a violent guerrilla group aided and abetted by the neighboring Sandinista regime of Nicaragua, and it was determined to overthrow the existing government. Their excesses triggered a similar response from right-wing paramilitary forces under former army officer Roberto d'Aubuisson, who was suspected of many political murders. Cristiani, however, managed to negotiate his release safely, and thereafter he joined the right-wing Nationalist Republican Alliance (ARENA) Party. This initially consisted of former military officers, suspected death-squad adherents, and reactionary business elements. In 1984 d'Aubuisson ran for the presidency of El Salvador as the ARENA candidate, but he lost to the Christian Democrat (DC) nominee José Napoleón Duarte. He then stepped aside while Cristiani assumed the position of party head.

Given the unsavory public reaction to ARENA, Cristiani realized that the party needed a drastic change in image. Thereafter, he distanced himself from d'Aubuisson and all suspected death squad figures, while pledging moderate political and economic reforms for El Salvador. Surprisingly, he also declared his intention to both respect land redistribution efforts enacted by the Christian Democrats and commence peace negotiations with the rebels. By 1988 the Duarte administration was sustaining terrible economic conditions brought on by protracted warfare, and in legislative elections that year ARENA candidates won a majority in the legislature. Cristiani himself also won a seat and began positioning himself to run for the presidency. Over the next year he again championed moderate reforms, and he further pledged that the hated d'Aubuisson would have no place in his administration. His message resonated with the war-weary electorate, and in 1989 he defeated the DC candidate Fidel Chávez Mena by 54 percent to 36 percent. "I pledge to organize a government of national salvation and a major priority is to combat extreme poverty in the country," Cristiani announced. This was also the first instance in El Salvador's political history that power was transferred peacefully from one party to another.

True to his word, Cristiani immediately sent peace feelers to the FMLN. However, the rebels negotiated in bad faith, apparently biding their time, for in November 1989 they launched a surprise offensive that captured parts of San Salvador. Cristiani, displaying great courage and tenacity, took to the field with his troops and ordered air strikes against rebel-held enclaves in the city. Within days the guerrillas were contained and driven back to the jungles. It was a striking victory for the military, but Cristiani reopened diplomatic channels with his adversaries. Negotiations continued until November 1991, when the FMLN launched another failed offensive, but a cease-fire agreement was finally signed in Mexico City the following December. This act concluded El Salvador's bloody 12-year civil war, a conflict costing 80,000 lives and rendering another half-million people homeless. Peace was therefore greatly welcomed, and Cristiani became the nation's most popular politician.

In 1992 Cristiani enjoyed similar success in peacefully resolving a simmering border dispute with neighboring Honduras. More important, as an exponent of free-market economics, his reforms greatly revitalized the war-torn economy in less time than anticipated. By 1993 the gross national product was rising at an annual rate of 5 percent while inflation remained low. Thereafter, the nation's financial system was handed off to the private sector, while import tariffs were cut, price controls ended, and monetary policy kept on a tight leash. The ensuing increase in wealth confirmed the sagacity of ARENA's economic philosophy and strengthened the party's position in upcoming elections. Cristiani was forbidden by law to seek a second term. In 1994 he stepped down and was succeeded by another ARENA candidate, Armando Calderón Sol.

Memory of the internecine civil war died hard, however. In 1996 Cristiani survived an assassination attempt outside his business office. Four years later, in October 2000, he came under investigation for his possible role in the killing of six Jesuit priests during the 1989 offensive. The former president formally denied any culpability for the act, affirming that two soldiers had already been arrested and tried for the crime. Others expressed concerns that reopening the case would only open old wounds. In December 2000 a Salvadoran judge formally dropped all charges against Cristiani on the basis that the statute of limitations—10 years—had already expired. Thus the country was spared from revisiting one of the most painful chapters in its history.

Further Reading

Gomez, Guillermo A. "El Salvador after the Peace Accords: An Economic, Political, and Social Crisis."

Unpublished master's thesis, San Diego State University, 2001.

Sollis, Peter. "Power Alleviation in El Salvador: An Appraisal of the Cristiani Government's Social Program." *Journal of International Development* 5 (September–October, 1993): 437–58.

Spence, Jack, and Chapu Hepec. *Five Years Later: El Salvador's Political Reality and Uncertain Future.* Cambridge, Mass.: Hemisphere Initiatives, 1997.

Tulchin, J., G. Bland, and R. Meza. *The State of the Economy: Is There a Transition in El Salvador?* Boulder, Colo.: Lynne Rienner Publishers, 1991.

Wood, Elizabeth. *Forging Democracy from Below: Insurgent Transitions in South Africa and El Salvador.* Cambridge: Cambridge University Press, 2001.

D

Dalai Lama (1935–   ) *Tibetan spiritual leader*

Lhamo Dhondrub was born on June 6, 1935, to peasant villagers in Takster, Tibet. Tibet was then ruled by a Buddhist theocracy headed by a high priest, the Dalai Lama ("Ocean of Wisdom"), whose line had been enthroned since the 17th century. Following the death of the 13th Dalai Lama in 1933, a search was on to find his successor. Tibetan Buddhist precepts maintain that his reincarnation will be found in the form of a young child. After searching several years, the clergy came upon Lhamo and concluded, through various mystical tests, that he was the 14th Dalai Lama. The young child was then taken to the city of Lhasa to be enthroned under the name of Tenzin Gyatso. Over the next decade he completed an intense regimen of spiritual and religious training, consistent with his position as Dalai Lama—and as a bodhisattva. This was a Buddhist deity representing spiritual perfection and complete devotion to assisting all mankind. The new Dalai Lama successfully completed all his studies, and, despite his youth, he impressed many Western observers by his intellect, charm, and maturity.

Tibet sits astride the southern border of China, and for many years the country was allowed to exist as an autonomous region under the guise of Chinese "protection." This situation dramatically changed in 1950 when Communist Chinese forces overran the country with a view toward annexing it. The Tibetans, fierce mountain warriors, resisted dutifully but at length the Dalai Lama had little choice but to surrender. He cooperated with Chinese authorities solely upon the condition that Tibet would remain autonomous and that its culture would be respected. However, the ensuing occupation proved brutal and occasioned both the murder of Buddhist clergymen and the destruction of 6,000 temples. By 1959 the situation had grown so intolerable that the population rose en masse against the invaders. Chinese military forces cruelly suppressed the uprising and the Dalai Lama fled across 300 miles of mountainous terrain to India with only his family and 100 followers. There he gained political asylum and was allowed to form a government in exile. He has maintained a residence at Dharamsala ever since. Meanwhile, the Chinese government has forcibly resettled thousands of its citizens in Tibet, thus reducing the native population to minority status in its own country. Moreover, an estimated 1 million Tibetans have been murdered in a concerted attempt to forcibly assimilate the population and destroy their traditional culture, language, and society. It remains one of history's most repressive occupations.

Since entering exile, the Dalai Lama has roundly criticized the Chinese government for its inhumane excesses toward his people. Since 1959 he has traveled the world, speaking to sympathetic governments and soliciting aid for the estimated 100,000 Tibetans who have escaped to India and other countries. "We are not Chinese, never have been and never will be," he has stated. "We are a peaceful people. We want our freedom of religion." To this end he has called for civil disobedience and the prompt removal of Chinese forces from his homeland. However, at no point in his criticism of China has the Dalai Lama called for armed confrontation or active resistance to its rule. His insistence that a peaceful resolution be sought to the problem resulted in his receipt of the Noble Peace Prize in 1989.

Despite his visible international profile, the Dalai Lama has selflessly attended to the needs of the thousands of Tibetan refugees who continually trickle into India and elsewhere. Intent on preserving Tibetan culture, he has founded numerous agricultural settlements along with 80 Tibetan schools in Indian and Nepal. He has also overseen construction of 200 monasteries to perpetuate the unique Tibetan brand of Buddhism for future generations. He campaigns passionately for the independence of his homeland and in 1987 promulgated a five-point peace plan to resolve the crisis. This entailed Tibet's designation as a "nonviolent zone," an end to Chinese migration, restoration of democratic freedom and human rights, and the removal of all nuclear weapons and dump sites. But, true to his beliefs, the Dalai Lama still refrains from the use of violence. "One of the main points is kindness," he says. "With kindness, with love and compassion, with this feeling that is the essence of brotherhood, sisterhood, one will have inner peace. This compassion is the basis of inner peace." China, however, remains highly sensitive to the issue of Tibet and regards it as an internal matter of national sovereignty. In February 2002 the official Xinhua news agency called upon the Dalai Lama to stop criticizing China and return home. However, he flatly refuses to rule as a figurehead and continues working to achieve his goal, garnering support for his cause. In May 2002, an estimated 20,000 supporters turned out in rain-soaked Melbourne, Australia, to hear him speak about Tibet, among the world's other mounting crises. "I always believe the basic purpose of our life is happy life, happiness, joyfulness," he said, "Many problems occur because of a lack of knowledge and reality, too much expectation."

Further Reading

Ardley, Jane. *The Tibetan Independence Movement: Political, Religious, and Gandhian Perspectives.* New York: Routledge, 2003.

Blais, Genevieve. *The Dalai Lama: A Beginner's Guide.* London: Hodder and Stoughton, 2000.

Boyd, Helen M. *The Future of Tibet: The Government in Exile Meets the Challenge of Democratization.* New York: Peter Lang, 2002.

Goldstein, Melvyn C. *The Snow Lion and the Dragon: China, Tibet, and the Dalai Lama.* Berkeley: University of California Press, 1999.

Hilton, Isabel. *The Search for the Panchen Lama.* New York: W. W. Norton, 2001.

Levenson, Claude B., and Joseph Rowe. *Tenzin Gyatso: The Dalai Lama from Birth to Exile.* New York: Oxford University Press, 1999.

Sartman, Barry. "Resolving the Tibet Question: Problems and Prospects." *Journal of Contemporary China* 11 (February 2002): 77–107.

Tsering, Diki. *Dalai Lama, My Son: A Mother's Story.* New York: Compass Books, 2001.

D'Alema, Massimo (1949–) *prime minister of Italy*

Massimo D'Alema was born on April 20, 1949, in Rome, Italy, into a household whose members supported the Communists. He studied philosophy at the University of Pisa but failed to graduate. D'Alema subsequently channeled his energies into politics, joined the Communist Party of Italy (CPI) in 1968, and eventually served as secretary of the Communist Youth Federation. He also edited the party newspaper and published several highly respected books on political theory and reform. However, by the 1980s the Italian Communist Party began entering its own Eurocentric orbit in flexing its independence from the main organization headquartered in Moscow. As it gravitated toward democratic socialism and away from doctrinaire Marxist-Leninist principles, the CPI emerged as the biggest Communist Party outside the Soviet Union. D'Alema continued serving as a talented, highly driven operative and by 1983 he was on the Central Committee. By 1988 he rose to the rank of deputy within the Secretariat, the second-highest party post. In concert with a new general secretary, Achille Ochetto, D'Alema convinced the party to renounce Marxism-Leninism as its guiding ideology. After the Soviet Union's demise in December 1991, the Communists reaffirmed this trend by renaming themselves the Democratic Party of the Left (PDS). Meanwhile, D'Alema was elected to parliament by wide margins in 1994, signaling the acceptance of the PDS into the mainstream of Italian politics. That year he also became the party's general secretary, and he joined the "Olive Tree Alliance" between the PDS and progressive reformists under ROMANO PRODI. When Prodi became prime minister in 1996, PDS became a full member of the governing coalition and D'Alema chaired several parliamentary commissions dealing with electoral reform. Prodi's government collapsed in October 1998 when the hard-core communist Refoundation Party withdrew from the coalition, so President OSCAR LUIGI SCALFARO asked D'Alema to form a new government.

D'Alema was sworn in as prime minister on October 19, 1998, as part of the 56th government to lead Italy since 1945. It marked the first time in Italian political history that a former Communist Party official led the country and conservative elements, along with the Vatican, evinced the greatest alarm. D'Alema, however, had renounced the past and his cabinet included such conservative stalwarts as LAMBERTO DINI as foreign minister, CARLO CIAMPI as treasurer, and other pro-Western, pro-NATO officials. To these were added a sprinkling of environmentalists, socialists, and former communist officials, none of whom held sensitive or controversial posts. It was, all told, a dauntingly eclectic coalition with many competing interests, and seemingly unworkable. But D'Alema was convinced that his government could work. "An alliance between liberal-democrat, socialist and environmentalist forces does not seem to be an anomaly," he insisted. "This is a political coalition formed around a clear program." Henceforth, his leadership style was predicated upon cooperation among diverse elements rather than adherence to outdated ideological precepts.

In power, D'Alema pursued moderately leftist objectives, including electoral reform and job creation for southern Italy and Sicily, the nation's poorest regions. He sought to end bribery and corruption while also strongly opposing secessionist efforts by the conservative Northern League, based in Lombardy. He sought to expand the role of government in negotiations between management and labor, thereby promoting greater harmony. D'Alema adhered firmly to capitalist tenets, but he also sought new approaches in granting average citizens better access to investment opportunities and a bigger share of the national wealth. Furthermore, he paid a nod to such traditional socialist policies as using corporate taxes to develop jobs and new technology while at the same time granting employment opportunities to the young.

However, the political winds in Italy were shifting, abetted by the rise of ring-wing media magnate SILVIO BERLUSCONI. Conservatives began asking the electorate if they wanted more governmental regulations controlling their lives. D'Alema, a dour, unsmiling politico, also suffered badly in style when contrasted against the flamboyant, telegenic Berlusconi. In the April 2000 national elections, the PDS and its allies went down in defeat, and D'Alema conceded: "The point is, the country has lost faith in me." The surviving leftists scrambled to form a new coalition—even more unwieldy than before—and President Ciampi asked GIULIANO AMATO to form a new government. This was achieved over the protests of Berlusconi, who demanded new national elections.

D'Alema's defeat tolled the death knell for Italy's traditional leftist parties. He has since retired to private life, although he occasionally shows up at PDS rallies to decry the impending advance of globalism. But, though marginalized now, D'Alema played a pivotal role in transforming the Italian Communist Party from a cold war anachronism to a viable, mainstream organization.

Further Reading

Bufacchi, Vittorio, and Simon Burgess. *Italy since 1989: Events and Interpretations.* Basingstoke, England: Palgrave, 2001.

Cook, Linda, and Mitchell A. Orenstein. *Left Parties and Social Policy in Postcommunist Europe.* Boulder, Colo.: Westview Press, 1999.

Fouskas, Vassilis. *Italy, Europe, the Left: The Transformation of Italian Communism and the European Imperative.* Brookfield, Vt: Ashgate, 1999.

Gilbert, Mark, and Gianfranco Pasquino. *Italian Politics: The Faltering Transition.* New York: Berghahn Books, 2000.

Tambini, Damian. *Nationalism in Italian Politics, 1980–2000: The Stories of the Northern League.* New York: Routledge, 2001.

Deby, Idriss (ca. 1953–) *president of Chad*

Idriss Deby was born around 1953 in Fada village, Ennedi province, Chad, into an impoverished family of Zughawa shepherds. Chad was then a French colony, and it was among the world's poorest countries when it achieved independence in 1960. After completing his education, Deby attended to the military officer's school in N'Djamena, and upon graduating in 1976 he went to France to obtain a professional pilot's license. Back in Chad Deby served with the Forces Armée du Nord (FAN), which became closely associated with prime minister Hissene Habré. In June 1982 Deby helped orchestrate a coup that brought Habré to power, and he was promoted to commander in chief of Chadian armed forces. In this capacity, and assisted by French troops, he engaged Libyan forces contesting the mineral-rich Aozou Strip to the north. Deby enjoyed such success that the Libyans sued for peace, which garnered him the nickname "Cowboy of the Desert." Soon after Habré, who had begun to fear Deby as a potential rival, replaced him as chief of staff and sent him back to France for advanced military training. Habré also instituted a period of harsh suppression of internal dissent, which included arbitrary arrests and executions. Deby returned to Chad as Habré's security and defense aide, but by 1989 he began to fear for his own life. He soon fled to neighboring Sudan to meet up with other Chadian dissidents and helped form the Patriotic Movement of Salvation (MPS). This was an armed group, assisted by France and Libya, bent on the conquest of Chad. After some severe fighting, Deby was completely successful and Habré, after looting the treasury, escaped to Niger. Deby was in complete control of the country by December 2, 1990, and he suspended the assembly and instituted military law.

Having consolidated his power base, Deby declared an eventual transition back to democracy. In 1991 he allowed political parties to form again and, the following year, he authorized a national conference to hammer out a rational transitional process. By a 1993 charter the delegates were allowed to elect a prime minister while Deby retained the office of president and head of the armed forces for the rest of the transition. Continued debate and maneuvering resulted in a constitutional referendum, which was overwhelmingly approved by voters in March 1996. This allowed a president to run for two consecutive five-year terms, and Deby campaigned actively throughout the country. No less than 15 candidates were in line for his succession, but in 1996 Deby was returned to office with 69 percent of the vote. A second round of voting in January 1997 gave his MPS party an absolute majority of 63 seats out of 125 in the National Assembly. The process was deemed fair, but also characterized by a polarized vote pitting northern Chad against the south.

Nevertheless, Deby stated: "I am the president of all Chadians . . . any development effort is only possible in national unity."

Despite this veneer of democracy, Deby continued to rule Chad with an iron hand because the 1996 constitution places power almost exclusively in the hands of the executive branch to the detriment of the legislature. The lack of an independent judiciary is also viewed as an impediment to securing a system of balance of power. Consequently, opposition forces continue to be harassed and imprisoned without warning, while freedom of the press is also under severe restraint. Deby also cracked down on Islamic fundamentalists by dissolving all religious associations save for the High Council of Islamic Affairs, which is government-controlled. Furthermore, Chad remains a desperately poor nation, with chronic trade and budget imbalances. Deby still places a high priority on cooperating with the World Bank and International Monetary Fund (IMF), which have granted his regime numerous subsidies and loans. Of special concern to Chad is construction of an extensive, 650-mile oil pipeline to the Cameroon port of Kribi. Monied interests in the West overlooked Deby's poor human rights record and granted him $54 million to complete the project. Once finished, oil is expected to pump $2 to 3 billion into the impoverished Chadian economy.

On May 20, 2001, Deby was elected to a second five-year term. His margin of victory was 67 percent of the vote, but this has been disputed by an assortment of opposition leaders, who claim fraud. Deby responded by arresting and briefly detaining the six other candidates, who declare they will still challenge the results in Chad's constitutional court. Deby was nonetheless sworn into office on August 9, 2001.

Further Reading

Azevedo, Mario J. *Roots of Violence: A History of War in Chad.* New York: Gordon and Breach, 1998.

———, and Emmanuel U. Nnadozic. *Chad: A Nation in Search of Its Future.* Boulder, Colo.: Westview Press, 1998.

Burr, Millard. *Thirty Years' War: Libya, Chad, and the Sudan, 1963–1993.* Boulder, Colo.: Westview Press, 1999.

Nolutshungo, Sam C. *Limits of Anarchy: Intervention and State Formation in Chad.* Charlottesville: University Press of Virginia, 1996.

Dehaene, Jean-Luc (1940–   ) *prime minister of Belgium*

Jean-Luc Dehaene was born on August 7, 1940, in Montpellier, France, the son of Belgian parents. He grew up in Bruges, Belgium, and he received degrees from both the University of Namur and the Catholic University of Louvain. Although a native French-language speaker, he also became fluent in the other national language, Flemish (Dutch). In fact, Belgian national politics are largely defined by friction between these two competing groups. Dehaene took an early liking to politics and he gravitated toward the trade-union wing of the Christian Democratic Party (CVP). In this capacity he served as head of the party's youth division in 1967, and by 1972 he had become staff assistant to several government ministers. In 1987 he won a seat in parliament and formally joined the cabinet of long-serving prime minister Wilfried Martens as his deputy and minister of communications. Dehaene, though plump and jovial by nature, evinced singular determination to succeed and became widely known as the "Bulldozer." He was also an expert negotiator and compromiser, essential traits for a nation sharply divided linguistically and saddled with 14 small parties. Early on he became an advocate of devolution, namely, returning power from the central government to the provinces as a way of promoting ethnic peace. Dehaene continued functioning capably until the elections of December 1991, when the Martens government failed to assemble a coalition. Martens then resigned while Dehaene went on to cobble together an unlikely partnership between the CVP and the opposition Socialists. Dehaene was then sworn into office on March 7, 1992.

Belgium is a country splintered along many planes, and, to rule effectively, Dehaene had to placate, cajole, and assuage an assortment of ruffled feathers. He did so with such adroitness that he acquired a new nickname, the "Plumber," for his seemingly effortless ability to keep the political system afloat. He started off strongly by appointing three women to his cabinet, a first in Belgian politics. Among his earliest priorities was passage of new constitutional amendments that rendered the country a federal constitutional monarchy. This measure granted Walloon and Flemish regions more political autonomy in areas such as education and agriculture. They also established the direct election of regional and communal assemblies for the first time, completing the shift of power from the center. The reforms passed in 1993 with-

out ceremony, and they did keep the fractured polity functioning. They also confirmed Dehaene's reputation as a master politician and, in 1995, his seemingly unwieldy center-left coalition was reelected for another five-year term.

Another pressing issue for Belgium was its role in a continent dominated by the increasingly important European Union (EU). In 1994 Dehaene's leadership credentials made him a strong contender to succeed Jacques Delors as president of the European Commission. His nomination was approved by 11 European heads of state but was ultimately withdrawn after objections raised by British prime minister John Major that Dehaene was a "federalist." The position ultimately went to Italy's RO-MANO PRODI. In 1997 Dehaene was also obliged to make painful reductions in the national budget in order to qualify Belgium's entry into the Monetary Union. However, he remained fully wedded to the notion of a fully integrated European economy. Given the fact that Belgium had been overrun twice by hostile armies in the 20th century, the EU appears as a guarantor of peaceful relations for small nations such as his. "Considering that nationalism is resurfacing in various European countries, the initiated unification process is now more necessary than ever," he said. "Of course, in a united Europe there must be room for the cultural diversity of the various countries." He has also strongly favored contributing funds and technical assistance to the struggling democracies and economies of Eastern Europe to speed their assimilation and development. Above all, Dehaene believes that only through fostering a "European identity" can international tensions and future wars be avoided.

Dehaene remained in office by skillfully catering to and juggling the needs of competing Flemish and Wallonian interests. He succeeded impressively until June 28, 1999, when it was revealed that the government badly mishandled a case of dioxin-tainted animal products. Elections held that day severely punished the Christian Democrats, while the Liberals (conservatives) and environmental Greens registered marked gains. He then resigned from office and was replaced by GUY VERHOFT-STADT of the Liberals, who assembled a coalition without the CVP. This was the first time in 50 years that the Christian Democrats were not part of the government, and Dehaene subsequently resigned as head of the party as well. However, by October 1999 he resurfaced as chairman of the board of the S.A.I.L. Trust, a high-tech firm active in the global applications of language technology and artificial intelligence. "It is a wonderful challenge to be involved in an ambitious project that can achieve success well beyond national borders," he declared, "I am convinced that high-tech speech and language applications are the sector of the future in the information society."

Further Reading

Dick, Leonard. "Trials and Tribulations—Dehaene Keeps Belgium on Track," *Europe,* no. 355 (1996): 6–10.

Downs, W. "Federalism Achieved: The Belgian Elections of May 1995." *West European Politics* 19 (January 1996): 168–175.

Mudde, Cas. *The Ideology of the Extreme Right.* Manchester: University of Manchester Press, 2000.

Noppe, Jo. "The Parliamentary Activity of the Belgian and Dutch Prime Ministers: Comparison between the Martens VII, Dehaene I, and Lubbers III Administrations." *Res Publica* 42, no. 4 (2000): 521–545.

Vos, Louis. *Nationalism in Belgium: Shifting Identities, 1780–1995.* Basingstoke, England: Macmillan, 1998.

De Klerk, Frederik (1936–) *president of South Africa*

Frederik Willem De Klerk was born in Johannesburg, South Africa, on March 18, 1936, into an influential political family. His father was general secretary of the conservative Transvaal National Party, and several grandparents also served in parliament. De Klerk was actively involved in party youth activities, and he attended the Afrikaanse Studentebond, a school for future political leaders. In 1958 he obtained a law degree from Potchefstroom University, and he maintained a legal practice in Vereeniging for 20 years. De Klerk formally commenced his political career in 1972 by winning a seat in parliament, and he quickly rose to become president of the South African Senate in 1976. In both capacities he gained the reputation as a cautious but pragmatic conciliator, impeccably honest and forthright. All these qualities held him in good stead when President P. W. Botha appointed him to a succession of ministerial posts, including telecommunications, home affairs, environmental planning, and energy and education. His behavior proved competent, but conservative, and seem-

ingly in lock step with the apartheid regime then in power.

Since the early 1950s, South Africa's ruling National Party had been a bulwark of racial separation, whereby Africans and nonwhite minorities were segregated into national "homelands." Through this expedient the majority of the population was denied participation in governmental affairs and reduced to a body of cheap labor. However, since 1912 the African National Congress (ANC), founded outside of South Africa, had engaged in open resistance to the white regime. By the 1980s this escalated to ongoing guerrilla warfare that proved costly to both sides and was sapping the country of its resources. When world governments also imposed tight economic sanctions upon South Africa pending the disbandment of apartheid, economic pressure became another inducement for change. Still, the Botha administration refused to dismantle apartheid under any circumstances, and it adopted a siege mentality for many years. The impasse was finally broken in 1989, when Botha suffered a heart attack and elections were held for a new leader of the National Party. De Klerk was victorious after several rounds of voting, and he defeated candidates far more conservative than himself. Given the desperate straits that South Africa was in, he proved the right man at the right time.

There was nothing in De Klerks's prior record to suggest what would follow. In fact, he apparently concluded that apartheid was doomed and began taking steps to dismantle it. In August 1989 he proposed to visiting Zambian president Kenneth Kaunda that he mediate talks, and Botha resigned from office in a fit of rage. This removed a major obstacle to change. De Klerk was quickly appointed president by the parliament in September, and he finally affirmed his commitment to a change in racial policy. To that end he released several imprisoned members of the ANC, including, in February 1990, the most visible symbol of African resistance, NELSON MANDELA. The two men, never cordially disposed to each other, did eventually establish a working relationship out of a need to prevent further racial antagonism. In quick order, the government legalized the ANC and the Communist Party, and exiled leaders from both were allowed to return home. In May 1990 the first-ever negotiations with the ANC transpired, whereby it was agreed that apartheid would be lifted in exchange for a suspension of guerrilla activity. The following September, resigned to the inevitable, De Klerk finally opened the ranks of the National Party to all races. For his efforts, in 1993, he shared the Nobel Peace Prize with Mandela.

In 1994, South Africa experienced its first free national elections on the basis of one-man/one vote and, as predicted, the once-illegal ANC was swept to power under Nelson Mandela. But the National Party, with the help of many nonwhite votes, finished a strong second, and De Klerk resigned from the presidency to become deputy president. In this office he tried his best to accommodate ANC demands while still looking out for the interests of white constituents. In May 1996 he removed himself and his party from government in the interest of establishing a strong opposition. However, many whites never resigned themselves to the new political realities, and the National Party began splitting into left-and right-wing factions. On September 8, 1997, De Klerk tendered his resignation as party head and was replaced by Marthinus van Schlkwyk. "I am resigning because I am convinced it is in the best interest of the party and the country," he insisted. De Klerk has lived in relative obscurity ever since, but in October 1998 he threatened to sue the Truth and Reconciliation Commission for implying that he was culpable for several politically inspired murders. In the interest of preserving national harmony, the allegations were struck from the finished report. De Klerk then went on to compose his memoirs, in which he details his frustrations over negotiating with Mandela and avers that he served from the onset as a reformer—and ultimately slayer—of apartheid.

Further Reading

De Klerk, F. W. *The Last Trek—A New Beginning: The Autobiography*. London: Macmillan, 1998.

Glad, Betty, and Robert Blanton. "F. W. De Klerk and Nelson Mandela: A Study in Cooperative Transformational Leadership." *Presidential Studies Quarterly* 27 (Summer 1997): 565–621.

Mungazi, Dickson A. *The Last Defenders of the Laager: Ian D. Smith and F. W. De Klerk*. Westport, Conn.: Praeger, 1998.

Ottaway, David. *Chained Together: Mandela, De Klerk, and the Struggle to Remake South Africa*. New York: Times Books, 1993.

Sparks, Allison. *Tomorrow's Another Country: The Inside Story of South Africa's Negotiated Revolution*. London: Mandarin, 1995.

de la Rúa, Fernando (1937–) *president of Argentina*

Fernando de la Rúa Bruno was born in Córdoba on September 15, 1937, and he received his doctorate in law from the University of Córdoba. As a member of the Radical Civic Union, he joined the administration of President Arturo Illia in 1963 before pursuing a successful career in politics. Commencing in April 1973 he was elected repeatedly to the Senate, and in 1996 he became the first-ever elected mayor of Buenos Aires. As a politician, de la Rúa cultivated an image that was rather timid and boring, but also scrupulously honest and efficient. These qualities held him in good stead as mayor, in which position he cleared up a $600 million deficit into a surplus, and managed to expand city services. With this success under his belt, he easily won nomination as the Radical Party's presidential candidate in 1999.

In pursuit of his quest, de la Rúa was indirectly helped by the flamboyant incumbent, CARLOS SAÚL MENEM of the Justicialist (Peronist) Party, who was notorious for fast living, extravagance, and a hint of corruption. Menem had only recently been dissuaded from running for a third term—which would have required a constitutional amendment—and his last two years in office were buffeted by a severe recession. Thus his successor, Eduardo Duhalde, was left to face the voter's wrath. De la Rúa's calls for honesty in government and to corruption paid dividends on October 1999, when he was swept into power with 48.5 percent of the vote. To achieve a majority in parliament, the Radical Party also allied itself with the leftist Frepaso Party, thus creating the new Alianza coalition.

At the turn of the 21st century, Argentina is one of the world's richest countries. Presently it is the third-largest economy in all of Latin America after Brazil and Mexico. A spate of massive privatization under President Menem did spur job creation in the mid-1990s, but the economy took a downturn after 1998. However, months of fiscal mismanagement, when combined with the Asian and Russia economic disasters and a recession in neighboring Brazil, left the country on the edge of a precipice. By March 2000 an estimated 29 percent of the population lived in poverty while unemployment reached 14 percent. Worse, the national debt had soared to $145 billion and the country seemed posed to default on its obligations to the World Bank. It was against this backdrop that de la Rúa was sworn into office in December 1999. He assured his fellow Argentinians that "my government has a clear and simple strategy: growth, growth, and growth." It was widely believed that the recession had bottomed out and, as a sign of confidence in the country's ability to recover, the International Monetary Fund (IMF) granted Argentina an immediate $7.4 billion in credit.

De la Rúa immediately enacted strict austerity measures to bring the country's spending in line with its production. Consequently, the economy continued shrinking and, with it, the government was forced to cut salaries and social services further. The first year of de la Rúa's presidency was marred by deteriorating economic conditions and unemployment. These factors, in turn, began playing havoc in the social sector, as poverty and desperation were on the rise. In the spring of 2001 de la Rúa fired his economy minister and brought in Domingo Cavallo, who had been the architect of the impressive growth experienced under Menem. Naturally Cavallo was willing to impose the very fiscal policies that had worked so well previously. Most notable was pegging the peso to the U.S. dollar, which rendered the currency very stable and capped inflation. This time, the scheme backfired. The strong dollar made Argentinian products very expensive, so exports slumped and unemployment rose further. Citizens then began spending their pesos on cheap imported goods, greatly increasing the national debt. By the fall of 2001, the voters expressed their dissatisfaction with de la Rúa by granting control of the Chamber of Deputies to the opposition Perónists. This made passage of any meaningful legislation impossible without concessions.

Events came to a head that December. Unemployment had reached 18.3 percent, and the government responded with further pay cuts and additional tax hikes to service the public debt. The straw that broke the camel's back occurred when de la Rúa ordered a $1,000 limit on cash withdrawals to prevent a run on the banks. On December 19, 2001, widespread rioting and looting erupted around the country, occasioning several deaths, and the government declared a 30-day state of siege. A large, hostile crowd of unemployed Argentinians gathered outside the presidential palace, banging pots and calling for de la Rúa's ouster. The following day, the minister for the economy, Cavallo, resigned from the cabinet, which induced de la Rúa to shore up his flagging support by offering to form a coalition government. When the Peronists refused, the president likewise tendered his resignation on December 20, 2001. "I trust my decision will contribute to pacifying the country and maintaining the institutional continuity of the republic," he wrote. Soon after, the bland and well-intentioned de la Rúa was unceremoniously escorted to the roof of the presidential palace and evacuated by helicopter from the seething capital. He departed only halfway through his four-year term with his nation still reeling from economic chaos.

Further Reading

Brennan, James P., and Ofelia Painetto. *Religion and Nation: Politics, Economics, and Society in Twentieth-Century Argentina.* New York: St. Martin's Press, 2000.

Pang, Eul-See. *The International Political Economy of Political Transformation: Argentina, Brazil, and Chile.* New York: Palgrave, 2002.

Powers, Nancy R. *Grassroots Expectations of Democracy and Economy: Argentina in Comparative Perspective.* Pittsburgh: University of Pittsburgh Press, 2001.

Spektorowski, Alberto. *The Origins of Argentina's Revolution of the Right.* Notre Dame, Ind.: University of Notre Dame Press, 2002.

Tedecso, Laura. *Democracy in Argentina: Hope and Disillusionment.* London: Frank Cass, 1999.

Demirel, Süleyman (1924–) *president of Turkey*

Süleyman Demirel was born on October 6, 1924, in Islamokov, Isparta province, Turkey. After graduating from the Istanbul Technical University with a degree in civil engineering in 1948, he was sent to the United States to further his education. Once home he served as head of the state water board, and, in 1961, Demirel commenced his political career by joining the Justice Party (JP). By 1964 he was serving as party chairman and leader of the opposition in parliament. In February 1965 Demirel managed to defeat the budget of Prime Minister Ismet Inönü, prompting his resignation. New elections were held the following October and the JP gained an outright majority in parliament. Demirel thus gained appointment as the new prime minister, and he held it for six years. During his first tenure in office, he embarked on a program of gradual reform and modernization, which alienated many of his more traditionally minded constituencies. The nation was also engulfed in waves of political and social turbulence, including labor unrest and student radicalism. When military leaders concluded that Demirel could no longer maintain order, they intervened and forced his resignation on March 12, 1971.

Though deposed from power, Demirel had established himself as a force in Turkish politics. Thoughtful and articulate, he gained a well-deserved reputation for deal-making behind closed doors—an essential trait for crafting sometimes unwieldy political coalitions. This was never more evident than following the resignation of BÜLENT ECEVIT as prime minister in August 1974. Ecevit decided to call for early elections after his successful invasion of Cyprus. Not only did Demirel dash his opponent's expectations of easy victory, he also assembled a coalition of four small right-wing parties and returned to office in March 1975. Success proved short-lived, for two years later the Republican Party won the national elections and Demirel again relinquished power in June 1977. More deals were then struck, and by July 1977 he was back in office in another coalition effort. This untangled five months later following a vote of no confidence and Demirel served as head of the opposition in parliament until December 1979, when he headed yet another coalition. However, the country was enduring another spate of economic distress and social dislocation. Rather than risk spiraling instability, the military again intervened and removed Demirel from power a second time on October 12, 1980. By this time, high-ranking officers began questioning the utility of democracy for Turkey's continuing survival. Many felt that the country would be better served by imposition of an authoritarian regime and, accordingly, they banned all parties and political activity for 10 years.

Despite the prohibition on politics, Demirel actively brought together a new organization, the Grand Turkey Party, in May 1983. The military subsequently declared his activities illegal and he was imprisoned for several months, then released. Undeterred, Demirel continued working behind the scenes to establish yet another organization, the True Path Party (TPP), from which he served as unofficial chairman. The military finally lifted its ban on political activity in 1987 and Demirel returned to parliament as head of the TPP opposition. In October 1991 he rose to become prime minister for the seventh time and presided over the first coalition government in 12 years. However, after the sudden death of President TURGUT ÖZAL of the Motherland Party in April 1993, the National Assembly chose him to fill the vacancy and he resigned. Demirel was by now one of Turkey's most respected elder statesmen and he worked to continue its close ties to the United States and Western Europe. In October 1995 he faced a minor crisis when the current prime minister, TANSU CILLER, lost a vote of confidence and stepped down. However, new elections held the following December catapulted a new entity, the Islamic-based Welfare Party, into national prominence. Demirel was then forced by necessity to form a coalition with its chairman, NECMETTIN ERBAKAN, but he remained determined to preserve Turkey's traditional, secular approach to politics. "Secularism and modernism are required for civilization," he insisted. "This is the direction that [founding father] Ataturk showed us."

In any event, Erbakan's prime ministership proved of short duration, and he was forced from power in June 1997. Demirel's mastery of coalition dealing enabled diverse but antireligious elements to unite, thereby keeping the Welfare Party out of power. This deflecting of religious-based politics was probably his most important service to the country. And, despite his Western orientation, Demirel sought to improve relations with both Iran and Iraq, which raised eyebrows in the United States. He also initiated closer relationships with Poland and concluded an extensive trade agreement with Premier EMIL CONSTANTINESCU of Romania in April 1997. Demirel finally retired from office in May 2000, and he was replaced by Ahmet Necdet Sezer. This act concluded a political career spanning three decades, of which 12 were spent as prime minister and seven as president. In stepping down Demirel announced no plans for the future, but he nonetheless remains at the disposal of his nation.

Further Reading

Balkan, Nesecan, and Sungar Sauran. *The Politics of Permanent Crisis: Class, Ideology, and the State in Turkey.* New York: Nova Science Publishers, 2002.

Gruen, G. E. "Ambivalence in the Alliance: U.S. Interests in the Middle East and the Evolution of Turkish Foreign Policy." *Orbis* 24 (Summer 1980): 363–378.

Heper, Metin, and Sabri Sayari, eds. *Political Leaders and Democracy in Turkey.* Lanham, Md.: Lexington Books, 2002.

———, and M. Cinar. "Parliamentary Government with a Strong President: The Post-1987 Turkish Experience." *Political Science Quarterly* 11 (Fall 1996): 483–503.

Waxman, Dov. *Turkey's Identity Crisis: Domestic Discord and Foreign Policy.* Warwickshire, England: Research Institute for the Study of Conflict and Terrorism, 1998.

Deng Xiaoping (Teng Hsiao-p'ing; Deng Xiansheng) (1904–1997) *Chinese political leader*

Deng Xiansheng was born in Xiexing, Sichuan province, China, the son of wealthy landowners. He was fortunate enough to receive a good education locally and in 1920 he left for additional studies in France. There he encountered Zhou En lai (Chou En Lai), a future Chinese political luminary, and he joined the Chinese Communist Party (CCP). Having completed his education, Deng next ventured to Moscow for additional political training. He then returned home in 1927, having adopted the name Xiaoping ("little peace"). These were tumultuous times for China, as the country was girding for a political showdown between Nationalist forces under Jiang Jieshi (Chiang Kai-shek) and Communists under Mao Zedong (Mao Tse-tung). The Nationalists proved successful and forced Mao's ragged columns to endure the hardships of the legendary "Long March," but Deng distinguished himself as a military and political figure. In time he was looked upon as a trusted compatriot of Mao and a totally devoted Communist. Deng's stature rose while fighting the Japanese in World War II, and by 1949 he helped orchestrate the final Communist victory that drove Jiang's forces off the mainland to Taiwan. Mao proclaimed the People's Republic of China on October 1, 1949, while Deng functioned as a trusted regional party secretary and political commissar in southwestern China.

Once the Communists had consolidated their control over mainland China, Deng was summoned to Beijing to fulfill important national offices. He successfully discharged his duties, including all-important ideological litmus tests imposed on all party members by Chairman Mao, and, in 1955, he gained appointment to the CCP Politburo, the nation's central decision-making body. By this time Mao had abandoned orthodox Marxism-Leninism and embarked upon his disastrous "Great Leap Forward," whereby the economy faltered and several million people starved to death. For the first time, Deng openly questioned Mao's grasp of political wisdom, especially economics. "For the purpose of increasing agricultural production, any by-hook-or-by-crook method

can be applied," he reasoned. "It doesn't matter whether a cat is black or white so long as it catches mice." Such views were held as heretical by Mao and other ideological purists, and steps were taken to isolate Deng from political influence. By 1966 Mao had embarked on the Cultural Revolution, whereby radical elements and students were unleashed against pro-Soviet and perceived pro-capitalist leaders. Foremost among them was Deng, now arrested, condemned as a "capitalist in-roader," and sent off to a tractor factory for political "reeducation." Fortunately, through the intercession of his old friend Premier Zhou, Deng was not harmed, and, by 1973, he was released and partially rehabilitated.

The passing of China's old guard exacerbated tensions and factional rivalries. Deng, for his part and despite the danger it posed to him, remained stridently pro-capitalist in his economic outlook. Following the death of Mao in the fall of 1976, the radicals again asserted themselves, arrested Deng, and purged him a second time. However, this time they overplayed their hand. More traditional elements removed the radicals from power within months, and, by July 1977, Deng had been reinstated. Thereafter, he worked vigorously to arrest and punish Mao's remaining adherents in government, and he laid the platform for a new and revolutionary approach to economic reform. Deng had always been a staunch defender of the communist system, but he realized its limits when it came to managing the national economy. Therefore, with consummate practicality and great determination, he struck a political compromise that freed up the tremendous power of Western-style market economics while taking steps to ensure the supremacy of the Communist Party. It proved an unorthodox, highly pragmatic approach to reform, but dissenting conservatives quickly found themselves removed from power.

Deng's economic liberalization program, unveiled at the December 1978 Third Plenum of the CCP's Central Committee, was both farsighted and far-reaching. Officially labeled the "Four Modernizations," it was intended to completely overhaul and modernize China's agriculture, industry, science, and technology. More important, it signaled the death of Mao's brand of revolutionary-style orthodoxy forever. The new system embraced free markets, foreign investment, decentralized controls, greater emphasis given to production of consumer goods over traditional heavy industries, and a completely new outlook on national priorities. "It is a glorious thing to become rich," the diminutive leader declared. Consequently, from 1979 to 1997, the Chinese economy leaped ahead with an annual growth rate of 9 percent, doubling the gross national product every eight years. Deng also improved China's international standing by seeking closer ties to the United States, Japan, and the Soviet Union, all viewed at various times as arch adversaries. Deft negotiations with Great Britain also secured the wealthy British colony of Hong Kong once its century-long lease expired in 1997. The peaceful transfer of ownership ended one of the most glaring symbols of Western imperialism in China together with its humiliating legacy.

Releasing the pent-up economic energies of the Chinese people produced enormous wealth, but also unforeseen consequences. Unemployment, inflation, and social inequity, unthinkable in Mao's time, began making themselves felt and Chinese leaders became hard-pressed for quick solutions. Also, the rising tide of market forces triggered vocal demands for concurrent political freedom, something Deng clearly opposed. In the spring of 1989, massive protests occurred in Tiananmen Square in Beijing, as thousands of students and workers demonstrated for greater individual freedom. However, on June 4, 1989, Deng brutally unleashed military forces against the demonstrators, and many hundreds of deaths resulted. This single act forever branded Deng as a dictator in Western minds, but he remained determined to maintain Communist control over the country. This steely little man finally resigned from power in November 1989, although he continued on as a power broker behind the scenes. Curiously, despite the tremendous power he wielded as the "paramount leader," Deng never assumed any official titles. Nevertheless, he continually purged any or all opponents of his reform agenda, and, in 1992, the 14th Party Congress formally accepted Deng's plans to put in place a socialist market economy by the year 2000. Deng never lived to see this cherished goal come to fruition; he died on February 19, 1997. However, his protégé, JIANG ZEMIN (Chiang Tse-min), continues his legacy of advancing the free market in China. After Mao Zedong, Deng remains the most influential leader of 20th-century China, and the driving force behind its successful quest for modernization.

Further Reading

Barth, Kelley, ed. *Tiananmen Square Massacre.* San Diego, Calif.: Greenhaven Press, 2002.

Baum, Richard. *Burying Mao: Chinese Politics in the Age of Deng Xiaoping.* Princeton, N.J.: Princeton University Press, 1996.

Evans, Richard. *Deng Xiaoping and the Making of Modern China.* New York: Penguin Books, 1997.

Marti, Michael E. *China Rising: The Legacy of Deng Xiaoping.* Washington, D.C.: Brassey's, 2002.

Misra, Kalpana. *From Post-Maoism to Post-Marxism: The Erosion of Official Ideology in Deng's China.* New York: Routledge, 1998.

Shambaugh, David L., ed. *Deng Xiaoping: Portrait of a Living Statesman.* New York: Oxford University Press, 1995.

Yang, Benjamin. *Deng: A Political Biography.* Armonk, N.Y.: M. E. Sharpe, 1997.

Denktash, Rauf (1924–) *president of the Turkish Republic of Northern Cyprus*

Rauf Denktash was born on January 27, 1924, in Paphos, Cyprus, the son of a judge. Cyprus was then a British crown colony situated off the Turkish coast, and jointly populated by Greeks and Turks. He graduated from the English School in Nicosia in 1941 and briefly pursued a career in journalism. Fluent in English, he proved an articulate spokesman for the Turkish viewpoint concerning problems confronting the island. In 1944 he studied law in England and was called to the bar by 1947. He returned home the following year as a Crown prosecutor, and he also became an adviser to the governor's Constitutional Council. Over the next 15 years relations between the Greek majority and Turkish communities grew tense over the issue of unification with mainland Greece. This was a prospect that Denktash strongly opposed, and in 1958 he became president of the Federation of Turkish Associations of Cyprus and the Turkish Resistance Organization. As Great Britain granted Cyprus its independence in August 1960, there were continuous outbreaks of violence between Greeks and Turks. A new constitution was adopted that allowed for separate island legislatures, and Denktash was elected president of the Turkish assembly, but the arrangement proved unworkable. In January 1964 he arrived in London to help broker peace talks between Britain, Greece, and Turkey over the future of Cyprus. He also made several trips to the United Nations as an advocate for the Turkish position. However, in 1964 Cypriot president Archbishop Makarios III banned Denktash from returning and he spent several years in Turkey. He was allowed home four years later and was reelected president of the communal council. The council conducted bilateral negotiations with Greek Cypriots, but six years of bargaining failed to produce a solution.

The Cyprus impasse dramatically ended in 1974 when the National Guard, encouraged by the Greek military dictatorship, revolted against Makarios and tried reunifying Cyprus by force. This drew an immediate military response from Turkey, which invaded the northern third of the island and evicted 180,000 Greek residents living there. On February 13, 1975, the new Cyprus Turkish Federated State was proclaimed with Denktash as president of the assembly. He was formally elected to a five-year term the following year as head of the National Union Party. In this capacity he suggested that Cyprus should adopt a two-state federal solution toward eventual reunification, but the Greeks rejected it.

In 1981 Denktash was again elected to head the communal council, and two years later the Turkish Republic of Northern Cyprus was proclaimed. This ministate is only recognized by Turkey and, again, Denktash served as president. He remained an articulate spokesman for the island's Turkish community and unyielding in his demands for greater autonomy. Consequently, in 1990 and 1995 he was returned to office by large margins. In 1995 Greek Cyprus declared its intention to join the European Union (EU) whether the dispute with Turkey had been resolved or not. Denktash, backed by the Turkish government, countered by threatening to secure annexation by the mainland. The impasse continued, despite calls from Greek Cypriot president GLAFCOS CLERIDES for demilitarization, which Turks refused. Hostilities further escalated in January 1997 when the Greeks decided to buy long-range Russian antiaircraft missiles for their half of the island. These weapons posed a direct threat to Turkish civil and military aviation, and Turkey threatened to stop their deployment, even at the risk of war with Greece. At this juncture, Denktash and Clerides, both former acquaintances, decided to conduct the first face-to-face talks in three years. The two leaders presented an affable front, but no conclusive solution for resolving the 27-year-old division was reached. The Cypriots, fortunately, rescinded their decision to acquire missiles and they were ultimately deployed on Crete.

Since 1997 Denktash and Clerides have met repeatedly to negotiate an end to Turkish occupation of north-

ern Cyprus and secure its eventual reunification with the south. The Turks do not officially reject such a solution, but they want assurances of complete political autonomy in advance. Denktash continues to argue that the best solution remains a bizonal, bicommunal partnership state, which the Greeks have refused to accept. He also continues to serve as a popular elder statesman, and, in April 2000, he was reelected president by wide margins. Meanwhile, the latest round of UN-sponsored talks began in July 2002, and both sides evinced pessimism over prospects of success. To date the 77-year-old Denktash steadfastly rejects UN Security Council resolutions calling for the reunification of Cyprus into a single entity, along with the withdrawal of 40,000 Turkish troops and 100,000 Turkish settlers from the island. The EU has also weighed in with promises of millions of dollars in aid to both sides if a peaceful accord is concluded. "For us direct aid is acceptable, not aid given through Greek Cypriot channels," Denktash declared, "that is not acceptable." The crisis will undoubtedly reach new levels of anxiety in 2003 when Greek Cyprus is slated to join the EU, because Turkey promises to annex the northern third once they do.

Further Reading
Denktas, Rauf R. *Rauf Denktas at the United Nations: Speeches on Cyprus.* Huntington, England: Eothen Press, 1997.

Diez, Thomas. *The European Union and the Cyprus Conflict: Modern Conflict, Postmodern Union.* Manchester: Manchester University Press, 2002.

Green, Pauline, and Ray Collins. *Embracing Cyprus: The Path to Unity in the New Europe.* London: I. B. Tauris, 2002.

Leventis, Yioghos. *Cyprus: The Struggle For Self-Determination in the 1940s: Prelude to Deeper Crises.* New York: Peter Lang, 2002.

Richmond, Oliver P., and James Ker-Lindsay. *The Work of the United Nations in Cyprus: Promoting Peace and Development.* New York: Palgrave, 2001.

Dini, Lamberto (1932–) *prime minister of Italy*

Lamberto Dini was born on March 1, 1932, in Florence, Italy, and he pursued an economics degree at the University of Florence. He subsequently received a Fulbright fellowship to conduct graduate studies at the Universities of Michigan and Minnesota. In 1959 he joined the International Monetary Fund (IMF) in Washington, D.C., as an economist, and rose steadily through the hierarchy. Dini joined the executive committee of IMF by 1976, and three years later he returned home to serve as director general of the Bank of Italy. Universally respected as a competent bureaucrat and financier, Dini had also acquired the unflattering sobriquet of "the Toad" because of his taciturn, unsmiling demeanor. Moreover, he expressed no political aspirations and remained unassociated with any party or organization. All this changed in March 1994 following the election of media magnate SILVIO BERLUSCONI as prime minister. Viewed as a nonpartisan "technocrat," Dini was solicited to reform the economy and bring down the spiraling national debt. The colorless bureaucrat accepted the challenge and became reviled as Berlusconi's hatchet man. Over the next few months he adopted harsh policies that trimmed government expenditures, especially regarding pensions, medical assistance, and public spending. Dini successfully reduced Italy's deficits, but he remained one of the most unpopular figures in politics. However, worse was in store for Berlusconi, who, after being investigated on bribery charges, resigned from office in December 1994. It fell upon President OSCAR LUIGI SCALFARO to appoint an interim prime minister until national elections could be called. Not surprisingly, he chose Dini based on his reputation for honesty, efficiency, and because of his nonpartisan status. The appointment seemed acceptable to most parties and Dini was sworn in on January 26, 1995.

Dini realized his tenure would be limited, but he handled his time in office with diffidence and care. He selected a cabinet composed of fellow "technocrats," including a cross-section of academics, magistrates, businessmen, and former civil servants. He also outlined a multipoint plan of governance—each with specific, concrete objectives to pursue—until new elections transpired. These included continuing deficit reductions, giving greater access for all political parties to state media, and implementing pension reforms. He also resolved to root out bribery and corruption wherever possible, crimes that continued to undermine the foundations of Italian democracy. All told, Dini adopted an ambitious agenda for such a short span in office, but he typically saw it through to completion. "To dispel

misunderstanding," he lectured, "I confirm that the government will consider its duty exhausted as soon as the commitments taken on as essential of its program are exhausted."

Within months, Dini transformed his reputation from one of Italy's most hated politicians into one of its most respected. Supported by the majority of the center-left parties, and leading figures such as MASSIMO D'ALEMA and ROMANO PRODI, he fulfilled most of his stated goals. Foremost among these were negotiations to reduce state pensions, which were among the most generous in Europe and left Italy awash in a sea of red ink. More remarkably, he succeeded, in his usual competent manner, without raising much furor. In fact, his biggest critic proved to be Berlusconi, who vindictively acted as a political spoiler arranging in November 1995 a motion of no confidence against the government over its fiscal policies. Dini then decided to resign, but he agreed to oversee a caretaker administration until April 1996. He also founded a new centrist party, Italian Renewal, which campaigned on behalf of Romano Prodi's Olive Tree Alliance (Ulvio). General elections subsequently favored Prodi, who became the new prime minister. However, in a nod to Dini's reputation for solving problems, he gave the latter the portfolio of foreign minister.

In his new position, Dini confronted several unexpected crises. The most serious was the influx of illegal immigrants from North Africa and the capture of Kurdish freedom fighter Abdullah Ocalan. Turkey, which regarded Ocalan as a terrorist, demanded his immediate extradition to face trial. Dini refused to comply, as a trial in Turkey might entail the death penalty, something his government opposes. In May 2000 Dini also expressed support for a new "federal structure" to administer the European Union (EU) and achieve tighter political integration. He was subsequently retained as foreign minister in the administrations of Massimo D'Alema and GIULIANO AMATO, but left office when Berlusconi returned to power in April 2001. Since that time Dini has served as deputy speaker of the Italian senate and a member of the European constitutional convention. He remains widely respected in both capacities.

Further Reading

Ball, Martin J., and Martin Rhodes. *Special Issue on Crisis and Transition in Italian Politics*. Ilford, England: Frank Cass, 1997.

Bardi, Luciano, and Martin Rhodes. *Italian Politics: Mapping the Future.* Boulder, Colo.: Westview Press, 1998.

Bufacchi, Vittorio, and Simon Burgess. *Italy since 1989: Events and Interpretations.* Basingstoke, England: Palgrave, 2001.

Gilbert, Mark, and Gianfranco Pasquino. *Italian Politics: The Faltering Transition.* New York: Berghahn Books, 2000.

Locke, Richard M. *Remaking the Italian Economy.* Ithaca, N.Y.: Cornell University Press, 1997.

Diouf, Abdou (1935–) *president of Senegal*

Abdou Diouf was born on September 7, 1935, in Louga, northern Senegal, into a Serer Muslim household. He performed well as a student at the Lycée Faidherbe in St. Louis, and he was allowed to attended the University of Dakar to study law. Thereafter Diouf traveled to Paris, France, to obtain advanced degrees in political science from the Sorbonne and the University of Paris. Senegal at this time was a French colony, and agitation for independence was underway under the aegis of Léopold Sédar Senghor, future head of the Senegalese Socialist Party. Independence came in 1960, the same year that Diouf returned home to serve as a civil servant. He quickly established a reputation as an efficient administrator and filled a succession of increasingly prestigious posts within the government. In 1968 Diouf gained election to the parliament, where he caught the attention of Senghor, by now president. Impressed by his youth and ability, Senghor appointed Diouf minister of planning and industry. He thereafter acted as a close political ally, and it became apparent that Senghor was grooming him for possible succession. Accordingly, in 1970, the president convinced the parliament to create a prime minister's office, to which Diouf assumed at the age of 27. It was while acting in this capacity that Diouf expanded his reputation for efficiency, and he served as a spokesman for the nation's middle class and governmental technocrats. He also spent the next 10 years imposing Socialist Party controls on the national economy, although with much less success. Nonetheless, by 1980 Diouf was easily the most popular politician in Senegal after Senghor himself. When the aged president suddenly announced his resignation from the presidency that year, Diouf fulfilled a constitutional mandate to succeed him. It was

one of few peaceful transfers of power in African history to that date.

As president, Diouf strove to maintain his reputation for honesty and effectiveness and, despite his socialist background, he steered a course that was remarkably free from ideological precepts. In fact, Senegal's foreign policy became increasingly pro-Western, and Diouf frequently sided with conservative nations like Chad against radical regimes like Libya. This stance garnered him many friends in the West, particularly France and the United States, which assured the continuance of foreign aid. In 1985 Diouf also completed a highly successful term as head of the Organization of African Unity, pushed hard for the resolution of regional conflicts, and offered Senegalese troops as peacekeepers. His biggest foreign policy failure was in trying to resolve a simmering dispute with Gambia, a sliver of a country that almost completely bisects Senegal. In 1982 he encouraged a federation between the two states, known as Senegambia, but the arrangement collapsed in 1989.

Domestically, Diouf tried to deliberately cultivate the image of a democratic-minded statesman. Once empowered he even signed laws promoting creation of 14 new opposition parties. However, Diouf intended to maintain power all along, for this same legislation restricted opposition parties from acting as a coalition, and hence they remained badly divided. In national elections held in 1983, 1988, and 1993, the incumbent invariably won by large margins, especially against his long-standing adversary from the Senegalese Democratic Party, ABDOULAYE WADE. The 1988 election seemed especially fraught with voter irregularities, and when Wade publicly denounced the government, riots and large-scale protests erupted. Diouf thereupon cracked down and arrested opposition members, but these were eventually freed once order was restored. Thereafter, both Wade and Diouf negotiated their political differences to avert further unrest. Diouf, however, managed to have the Socialist-controlled parliament remove constitutional restrictions to two terms in office. And he subsequently reneged on a promise not to seek reelection in 2000. To the average Senegalese voter, Diouf looked unassailable in office and seemed to continually devise electoral schemes that ensured he remained there.

The turning point in Senegal's recent political history occurred during the 2000 national elections. The country, saddled with outdated socialist policies, was edging closer to economic collapse. As before, Diouf's major opponent was Wade, and results of the first round of voting in March gave the president more votes, but not enough to avoid a runoff. Mindful of the Socialist Party's long-standing grip on national politics, and weary of its growing insensitivity and corruption, Senegalese voters suddenly united in an effort for change. Closing ranks, they voted for Wade by over 60 percent, handing him the election. Diouf was surprised by the results, but he gracefully yielded the palm to his adversary. He thus became only the third elected African leader to peacefully concede power in four decades. Wade also proved magnanimous, for he appointed the former president as Senegal's representative at the European Union summit the following April. After 40 years of de facto one-party rule, democracy had finally triumphed in Senegal.

Further Reading

Dacosta, P. "Diouf's Tarnished Victory." *Africa Report* 38 (May–June, 1993): 49–51.

Detwiler, Joseph. "The Development of Liberal Democracy in Senegal and Botswana." Unpublished master's thesis, Ohio University, 1989.

Mortimer, Robert A. "Senegal's Role in ECOMOG: The Francophone Dimension in the Liberian Crisis." *Journal of Modern African Studies* 34 (June 1996): 293–307.

Schraeder, Peter J. "Senegal's Foreign Policy: Challenges of Democratization and Marginalization." *African Affairs* 96 (October 1997): 485–509.

Villalon, Leonardo A. "Democratizing a (quasi) Democracy: The Senegalese Election of 1993." *African Affairs* 93 (April 1994): 163–194.

Djukanovic, Milo (1962–) *president of Montenegro*

Milo Djukanovic was born in Niksic, Montenegro, on February 15, 1962. Montenegro is a small, mountainous state of 650,000 people on the coast of the Adriatic Sea. Populated mainly by Serbs, it enjoys a history of political independence going back to the Middle Ages. By the 20th century the state was nominally part of Yugoslavia, a nation comprised of six federal republics. When Djukanovic was born, Montenegro was ruled by the communist government of Josip Broz Tito, who welded that nation together by force in 1945. Despite appearances of socialist solidarity, deep-seated ethnic tensions among various groups bubbled not far beneath the surface. Djukanovic was educated at Titograd University, Podgorica, where he received an advanced degree in economics. He then joined the League of Communists of Yugoslavia to bolster his chances for political advancement. An astute politician who acquired the name "Milo the Blade" on account of his sharpness, Djukanovic rose to become part of the party's central committee, which subsequently renamed itself the Democratic Party of Socialists of Yugoslavia. In this capacity he came to the attention of Serbian leader SLOBODAN MILOŠEVIĆ who, in 1991, appointed Djukanovic prime minister of Montenegro. As the head of government, he became responsible for the day-to-day administration of national affairs.

After the death of Tito, Djukanovic espoused new views on democratic reform along with traditional stances on ethnic tolerance. However, Milošević's relentless persecution of Muslims and Albanians in the name of greater Serbia greatly accelerated Yugoslavia's bloody breakup. The two men formally parted during the winter of 1996–97, when Milošević, as president of the remaining Yugoslav states of Serbia and Montenegro, refused to recognize democratic trends in the latter. These crystalized in the fall of 1997 when Djukanovic defeated Momir Bulatovic—a nominal Milošević ally—for president of the tiny republic. This high office was responsible for representing Montenegro's interests in foreign affairs. It also gave him higher visibility for promoting Montenegro the international scene. Djukanovic brooked no delay adopting a divergent path from Serbia and began asserting Montenegro's traditional independence. He did this by degrees, however, for Serbs constitute the majority of people in his country and were themselves torn between allegiance to one or the other state. His position was greatly complicated when Western forces under NATO commenced a 78-day bombing campaign of Serbs in the Kosovo region. This came in response to Serbian aggression and atrocities against ethnic Albanians and Muslims, carried out at the behest of Milošević. However, the Serbs were humiliated in Kosovo and withdrew, while Milošević was removed from power in October 2000.

With the highly nationalistic Milošević indicted for war crimes by the international community, Djukanovic felt the time had come to fully assert Montenegro's sovereignty. Commencing in June 1999 he no longer recognized the army as an instrument of the Yugoslav federation. Later that year he also declared that Montenegro would adopt the German mark and discard the Yugoslavian dinar as its official currency. However, the new Yugoslav president, VOJISLAV KOSTUNICA, who assumed office in September 2000, opposed Montenegro's quest for independence. If anything, he strongly urged Djukanovic to settle the matter democratically through a public referendum.

Throughout most of 2001, Djukanovic agitated for national independence and claimed that his position reflected that of the majority of citizens. He did agree, however, that the process should be achieved at the ballot and not by decree. He further attempted to mollify critics by pressing for a modified form of sovereignty—an informal union between the two states that would include a common market and a common currency. "The first element is independence and international legal personality for both Serbia and Montenegro," he insisted. "The second element is our proposal for a union of two independent, internationally recognized states." A good indication of the divisive nature of this struggle was the April 2001 parliamentary elections. Djukanovic claimed popular support for independence, but his "Victory Belongs to Montenegro" coalition pulled only 42 percent of the vote. In contrast, the opposing "Together with Yugoslavia" forces gained 40.6 percent, which suggests a highly polarized electorate. The following May, Djukanovic, recognizing the broad lack of consensus about this issue, indefinitely suspended his long-anticipated referendum on statehood. The fate of tiny Montenegro hangs in the balance.

Further Reading

Calhoun, Steven C. "Serbia and Montenegro: The Struggle to Redefine Yugoslavia." *European Security* 9 (Autumn 2000): 62–86.

"Djukanovic, Milo." *Current Biography* (August 2001): 32–37.

Glenny, Misha. *The Fall of Yugoslavia: The Third Balkan War.* New York: Penguin Books, 1993.

Judah, Tim. *The Serbs: History, Myth, and the Destruction of Yugoslavia.* New Haven, Conn.: Yale University Press, 1997.

Pavlovich, Paul. *The Serbians: The Story of a People.* Toronto: Serbian Heritage Books, 1988.

Roberts, Elizabeth. "Montenegro-unraveling." *The World Today* 57, no. 4 (2001): 13–16.

Do Muoi   (1917–) *prime minister of Vietnam*

Do Muoi was born in Dong My, Thanh Tri district (Hanoi), Vietnam, on February 2, 1917. Vietnam was then a French colonial possession and Do, like many resentful youths, became embroiled in anticolonialist activities. In 1931, while serving as a house painter, he joined the anti-French Popular Front. His activities induced him to join the Vietnamese Communist Party (VCP) in 1939, for which he was arrested and sentenced to 10 years in prison. However, as World War II ended in August 1945, Do escaped and took up arms by enlisting in the Viet Minh of Ho Chi Minh. Do subsequently fought the French in his native Ha Dong province, rising by dint of good performance to the rank of brigadier general. The French were defeated by 1954 and departed from the northern half of the country, which became the Democratic Republic of Vietnam (DRV). Do continued on in the party as chairman of the People's Military and Administrative Committee in Hai Phong, and, by 1960, he had risen to the rank of vice premier. At this time Ho Chi Minh had embarked upon a war of unification with South Vietnam, an ally of the United States, and the ensuing war lasted with little intermission until 1975. Do, for his part, had quit the military altogether because of poor health, and he continued climbing up the party's hierarchy. He became closely associated with state-controlled economic agencies, becoming revered as a guardian of Communist Party policies and principles.

South Vietnam was conquered in 1975 and incorporated into the DRV. Do, because of his pristine ideological credentials, was then dispatched for the purposes of dismantling the region's capitalist system and substituting a socialist model. However, stark incongruities between the two systems could not be reconciled and the union failed dramatically. In fact, Do's rigid conformity to communist principles effectively ruined the South's economy. Over 35,000 private businesses were closed down, and the ensuing despair and deprivation induced 2 million Vietnamese to flee the country as "boat people." Of these an estimated 400,000 perished at sea. Nonetheless, Do was widely congratulated for his "success" in the former South, and his political star remained on the ascent. In 1980 he was appointed as chairman of the Council of Ministers, whose chief responsibility was to ensure party loyalty and expel dissenting party members. Five years later Do was elevated to full membership in the Politburo, the nation's highest decision-making body. On June 22, 1988, he capped 35 years of loyal service to the Communist Party by becoming prime minister of the DRV, largely because of his staunch adherence to party dogma. "I belong to the party and the people," he once explained. "The party and the people tell me what to do." His appointment also came at the expense of Vo Van Kiet, a known reformer, and it was regarded as a setback for political change.

By the mid-1980s the euphoria of military triumph faded and the economic realities of socialism had become manifest. In fact, Vietnam, already poor, was steadily sinking in terms of economic performance. This happened despite dramatic changes in neighboring China, which, under DENG XIAOPING, had fully embraced free-market capitalism. But Hanoi's leaders continued wallowing in traditional Communist Party orthodoxy. "Our party and our people will follow the way of socialism, of Ho Chi Minh," Do insisted, "as the sole correct way." The national economy trudged along, but the dominance of the Communist Party remained intact. Consequently, in 1991 Do replaced aging Nguyen Van Linh as secretary-general of the Communist Party, again thanks to his identification with conservative elements. This made him the highest-ranking and most influential politician in the land. Predictably, Do used his influence to maintain and enhance the political status quo, but by now even he began contemplating the advantages of a liberalized marketplace. To this end, he campaigned abroad for foreign investment, and he even sought to reestablish diplomatic relations with the former enemy, the United States. He was also instrumental in taking steps to heal the diplomatic rift between Vietnam and China, its gigantic northern neighbor. But, all told, Do's continuance in power confirmed the victory of traditionalists over reformers.

Do remained highly regarded as an incorruptible party idealist, but many began questioning his grasp of economic realities. The 80-year-old leader was also in declining health, so after a decade of pristine, if muddled, leadership, a search began to replace him. On June 3, 1998, Do formally resigned as party secretary in favor of LE KHA PHIEU, a former army general and a known political conservative. He was clearly relieved by the change, declaring, "I feel weak now and I really want to rest." Do nonetheless remained active in diplomatic activities as an elder statesman and political adviser. In February 2002 he was present to confer with visiting Chinese president JIANG ZEMIN, who congratulated him for helping normalize Sino-Vietnamese relations. Meanwhile, Do hoped that the two nations would continue along the path of friendly relations and fraternal brotherhood as espoused by Ho Chi Minh and Mao Zedong, their respective founding fathers.

Further Reading

Ho, Hue-Tam Tai. *The Country of Memory: Remaking the Past in Late Socialist Vietnam.* Berkeley: University of California Press, 2001.

Kenny, Henry. *Shadow of the Dragon: Vietnam's Continuing Struggle with China and the Implications for U.S. Foreign Policy.* Washington, D.C.: Brassey's, 2002.

Luong, Hy U. *Postwar Vietnam: Dynamics of a Transforming Society.* Lanham, Md.: Rowman and Littlefield, 2003.

Metzner, Edward P. *Reeducation in Postwar Vietnam: Personal Postscripts to Peace.* College Station: Texas A & M University Press, 2001.

Ninh, Kim Ngoc Bao. *A World Transformed: The Politics of Culture in Revolutionary Vietnam, 1945–1965.* Ann Arbor: University of Michigan Press, 2002.

Stern, Lewis M. "Vietnam's Eighth Party Congress: Renovated Organizations, Revised Statutes, Evolving Processes." *Asian Survey* 37 (May 1997): 470–481.

Dos Santos, José (1942–) *president of Angola*

José Eduardo Dos Santos was born in Luanda, Angola, on August 28, 1942, the son of a bricklayer. Angola had been a Portuguese colony since the late 15th century, although a war for independence sprang up in 1961. That year Dos Santos joined the Popular Movement for the Liberation of Angola (MPLA) and fled to the nearby Congo. After serving as an MPLA youth representative in Yugoslavia, he received a Soviet scholarship and ventured to Moscow's Patrice Lumumba University to study petrochemical engineering. In light of his military connections, he also received training in radar telecommunications. Do Santos returned home in 1970, where he fought for several years on the northern Cabinda front as a guerrilla. He performed well and, commencing in 1975, he began filling a number of important positions within the MPLA. In this capacity he came to the attention of President Antonio Agostinho Neto, who appointed him minister of foreign affairs following

Angolan independence in November 1975. However, success failed to usher in a period of peace. A competing guerrilla group, the National Union for the Total Independence of Angola (UNITA), under JONAS SAVIMBI, declared war on the MPLA, thereby initiating a prolonged, internecine civil war. This conflict became more and more of a cold war confrontation, as the MPLA received help from the Soviet Union and Cuba while the United States and South Africa assisted UNITA forces. Dos Santos was serving as deputy prime minister of Angola when Neto died suddenly on September 10, 1979. The MPLA central committee declared the 37-year-old former guerrilla president of the People's Republic of Angola 11 days later. He was then one of Africa's youngest heads of state.

Dos Santos inherited a dispirited country devastated by war and still in the throes of both civil war and postcolonial reconstruction. As such his policy inevitably revolved around economic development and military survival. Despite his revolutionary background, Dos Santos proved himself surprisingly pragmatic and politically moderate. He moved quickly to remove the more strident ideologues from positions of responsibility and he replaced them with trained technocrats and administrators. By 1988 he felt emboldened to ditch the last vestiges of centralized planning, and he fully liberalized Angola's economy by promoting small business and foreign investment. Dos Santos also closely adhered to rules established by the World Bank and International Monetary Fund and thereby Angola qualified to receive direct foreign aid.

In time the ongoing civil war against UNITA began to assume a surrealistic quality in a struggle long portrayed as a war between capitalism and communism. The government called in 50,000 Cuban soldiers to protect oil wells and refineries owned and operated by U.S. companies. This was to ensure the steady flow of oil revenues into Angola's struggling, capitalistic coffers. Events were further complicated when the government of South Africa, which was clinging to power in neighboring Namibia, sent troops and aircraft directly into the fray. The guerrilla war swayed back and forth over the next 15 years until 1990, when both Cuba and South Africa agreed to remove their forces. Thus situated, Dos Santos felt that time was ripe for political liberalization, and in 1990, he legalized the establishment of political parties. By 1992 a cease-fire had also been reached with Savimbi's UNITA forces, and both he and Dos Santos ran

for the presidency. Dos Santos won by 49.6 percent to 40.1 percent in relatively free and fair elections, but Savimbi claimed the results were rigged. Fighting then recommenced in earnest.

Fortunately for Dos Santos, the United States finally recognized his regime as legitimate, established diplomatic relations, and curbed the supply of weapons to UNITA forces. This brought Savimbi back to the negotiating table, and, in 1994, both men acceded to the Lusaka Accord, which called for a new cease-fire. Moreover, Savimbi recognized Dos Santos as the legitimate leader of Angola, while he was also tendered the vice presidency. The following year the UN Security Council called for deployment of 7,000 troops to monitor the cease-fire. However, Savimbi remained dissatisfied with political arrangements and his forces renewed fighting in 1997. Eventually they captured much of Angola's diamond mining district in order to sell the gems internationally to finance their war. Dos Santos, meanwhile, mobilized his country for total conflict, which led to further economic and social dislocation. He also assumed the roles of prime minister and head of MPLA to better coordinate national efforts. The result, however, remains at an impasse.

Surprisingly, in August 2002, Dos Santos declared his intention not to run for the presidency again. After 22 years in power he is apparently weary of the struggle and is looking forward to retirement. Angola, meanwhile, stumbles along, with the second-highest child mortality rate in the world and a quarter of its population living as refugees while a small clique of MPLA operatives who control the oil industry amass great fortunes. New elections have been postponed until late 2003.

Further Reading

Heywood, Linda A. *Contested Power in Angola, 1840s to the Present.* Rochester, N.Y.: University of Rochester Press, 2000.

Hodges, Tony. *Angola: From Afro-Stalinism to Petro-Diamond Capitalism.* Oxford: James Currey, 2001.

Le Billon, Philippe. "Angola's Political Economy of War: The Role of Oil and Diamonds." *African Affairs* 100, no. 398 (2001): 55–80.

Matloff, Judith. *Fragments of a Forgotten War.* New York: Penguin Books, 1997.

Messiant, Christine. "The Eduardo Dos Santos Foundation: Or, How Angola's Regime Is Taking Over Civil

Society." *African Affairs* 100, no. 399 (2001): 283–307.

Douglas, Denzil (1953–) *prime minister of St. Kitts and Nevis*

Denzil Douglas was born in St. Kitts and Nevis on January 14, 1953. These are two small islands in the eastern Caribbean populated by 43,000 people, principally the descendants of African slaves. Both isles were granted independence from Great Britain in September 1983, and they have had a parliamentary form of government ever since. Douglas attended local schools and subsequently studied medicine at the University of the West Indies. Having earned several degrees, he returned home to serve as president of the St. Kitts and Nevis Medical Association. Douglas also became politically involved by joining the St. Kitts and Nevis Labour Party (SKNLP). In 1989 Labour went down to its third straight defeat at the hands of the conservative People's Action Movement (PAM) under Prime Minister Kennedy A. Simmonds, and Douglas was nominated as party head. As such he spent the next six years as opposition leader in the National Assembly. However, a unique turn of events completely reversed the political fortunes of the island.

In September 1994 a large buried shipment of cocaine was uncovered on St. Kitts. Allegations of drug smuggling and gun running were made against the sons of the deputy prime minister, Sydney Morris, who belonged to PAM. He resigned from office shortly thereafter. This fact and a general rise in crime convinced many business and civic leaders that the islands were being increasingly drawn into the drug trade. Simmonds did little to address the problem, but he did arrange for Morris to serve as an adviser to the ministry of education, which Douglas denounced as "insensitive and callous." The majority of voters apparently agreed; during elections held on July 3, 1995, PAM was turned out of office and replaced by Labour. Consequently Douglas became the new prime minister.

During his campaign, Douglas had pledged to do everything in his power to fight street crime and combat the underground malignancies of money laundering and drug smuggling. He was also determined to overhaul existing law enforcement agencies, and he asked for British assistance to improve police functions. Douglas then moved rapidly to enhance the island's economy, and he redirected funding toward the fields of tourism, housing, education, and infrastructure. To facilitate additional growth, the prime minister supported St. Kitts and Nevis's membership in the Caribbean Community and Common Market (CARICOM), which promotes free trade and negotiates on its members' behalf with other trading blocs. This was undertaken to create a local free-trade zone to compete with those arising in North and South America. Furthermore, the Douglas administration effectively eliminated bureaucratic restrictions on trade, reduced the external tariff, and promoted free movement of people between member countries.

Despite his best efforts, by 1994 the economy of St. Kitts and Nevis had actually declined from 4.5 percent to 3 percent annual growth. This spurred Douglas to place greater emphasis on increasing tourism, the nation's biggest source of income, and he authorized construction of several new hotels. Sugar production is also essential to the well-being of the islands, but it had also registered declines owing to drought, transportation shortages, and labor unrest. Worse, in 1995 both islands suffered $100 million in damage from the ravages of two hurricanes. Fortunately the government worked closely with the business community to help rebuild, and authorities reduced or even abolished many company taxes. The net result was an impressive 5 percent increase in economic performance over the next few months. The public responded positively to Douglas's reforms and, in March 2000, they returned him to power with near-total control of the National Assembly.

Ironically, the biggest political challenge facing Douglas came from neighboring Nevis. Legislators from that island long complained of being dominated by St. Kitts and a movement arose for secession and independence. In October 1997, the assembly of Nevis voted unanimously for secession, contingent upon passage of a public referendum. Douglas was amenable to greater autonomy for Nevis, but he balked at secession. He therefore scheduled the referendum for August 10, 1997, which also coincided with the annual Culturama Festival on Nevis, when many island residents living abroad would be returning home. Whether or not this ploy succeeded is unproven, but the referendum went down in defeat after gathering 61.7 percent of the vote—less than the required two-thirds. Douglas has since called in a commission to investigate ways of improving relations between the two little islands.

Further Reading

Alexander, Robert J. *Presidents, Prime Ministers, and Governors of the English-Speaking Caribbean and Puerto Rico.* Westport, Conn.: Praeger, 1997.

Ashton, S. R., and David Killingray. *The West Indies.* London: Her Majesty's Stationery Office, 1999.

Premdas, Ralph R. *Secession and Self-Determination in the Caribbean: Nevis and Tobago.* St. Augustine, Trinidad and Tobago: University of the West Indies, 1998.

Thompson, Alvin O. *The Haunting Past: Politics, Economics, and Race in Caribbean Life.* Oxford: James Currey, 1997.

Douglas, Roosevelt (1941–2000) *prime minister of Dominica*

Roosevelt Douglas was born in Portsmouth, Dominica, on October 15, 1941, the son of a wealthy coconut grower. Dominica is a small Caribbean island halfway between Puerto Rico and Trinidad, and it was formally a British crown colony. Douglas was educated locally at the Dominica Grammar School and St. Mary's Academy before relocating to Canada. He received a diploma from the Ontario Agricultural School in 1963 but subsequently switched to political science while attending Sir George Williams University. The experience of college apparently radicalized his views, for he soon served as head of a black student organization. In 1969 Douglas was pursuing an advanced degree at prestigious McGill University when he became embroiled in a dispute with a professor over charges of racism. He then led a number of black students in occupying the Henry F. Hall building until forcibly evicted by police. Douglas found himself arrested, tried, and sentenced to two years imprisonment. However, he served only 18 months of his sentence before being deported back to Dominica in 1974.

Once home, Douglas immersed himself in leftist politics by founding the Popular Independence Committee. This group agitated for independence from Great Britain, which was achieved in November 1978. As a reward, he gained appointment to the island's government as a senator. The following year, Dominica was devastated by Hurricane David, and Douglas garnered further notoriety by formally inviting Cuban troops to assist in clean up operations. The government, eager for monetary assistance from the United States, promptly dismissed him from office. Douglas nevertheless continued pursuing active friendships and associations with the

governments of Cuba, Libya, and Iraq, which resulted in his banishment from the United States. Douglas also further solidified his radical credentials by directing the Libyan-based Mataba organization, which sponsored guerrilla movements throughout Africa. His maverick stance caused his popularity to soar at home, and between 1985–95, Douglas gained election as a Labour Party representative in parliament.

By 1994 Douglas had risen to head of the Dominica Labour Party (DLP), and the following year he became leader of the opposition in parliament. In 1998 he gained additional attention by questioning the controversial citizenship program initiated by the government in 1991. This practice allowed foreigners to obtain Dominica citizenship in return for a $35,000 cash investment. It proved a lucrative source of revenue to the nation's coffers, but Douglas decried how criminals were entering the country undetected. He continued serving as opposition leader until January 2000, when conservative prime minister Edison James unexpectedly called for new elections. However, after two decades of conservative rule, the electorate was ripe for a change and they handed Labour a narrow majority. Labour's ability to govern was further enhanced when the party entered into a coalition with the conservative Dominica Freedom Party, which made for a more balanced approach to governance. Hence, Douglas, who made political hay from his reputation as a left-wing gadfly, suddenly found himself elected prime minister.

Douglas now faced the problem of addressing long-standing issues aimed at improving access to education, youth training, and adequate health care and reducing the island's dependancy upon bananas, the principal export crop. He accordingly moved to enhance tourism, a usually reliable source of income, and secured arrangements to ensure the arrival of several new airlines to bring them. He also briefly rescinded the practice of selling Dominica passports for cash, although it was speedily resumed once abuses had been halted and better safeguards initiated. Furthermore, Douglas dropped his erstwhile intractable hostility toward the United States in an attempt to attract badly needed foreign investment. Canada has also welcomed the warming trend, and, in May 2000, Ottawa formally pardoned Douglas for his role in the student riots. On October 1, 2000, "Rosie" Douglas died of a sudden heart attack at home and he was succeeded by Pierre Charles, the former minister of communications and public works. His old seat was subsequently won by his nephew, Ian Douglas, which helped maintain Labour's narrow majority in parliament.

Further Reading

Andre, Irving W., and Gabriel J. Christian. *In Search of Eden: Dominica, the Travails of a Caribbean Mini-State.* Marlboro, Md.: Pond Casse Press, 1992.

Baker, Patrick L. *Centering the Periphery Chaos: Order and the Ethnohistory of Dominica.* Kingston, Jamaica: University of the West Indies, 1994.

Honychurch, Lennox. *Carib to Creole: A History of Contact and Cultural Exchange.* Roseau, Dominica: Dominica Institute, 2000.

Mars, Perry. *Ideology and Change: The Transformation of the Caribbean Left.* Detroit, Mich.: Wayne State University Press, 1998.

Dowiyogo, Bernard (1946–2003) *president of Nauru*

Bernard Dowiyogo was born on the Pacific island of Nauru in February 1946. This tiny enclave, the world's smallest nation, is only eight square miles in size and lies about 1,500 miles northeast of Papua-New Guinea. It is populated by 12,000 people, mostly Naurians, but also a small number of Chinese and Europeans. Toward the end of the 19th century, Nauru was occupied by Imperial Germany, which administered the island until the end of World War I. Thereafter, a protectorate was established by Great Britain, New Zealand, and Australia to jointly govern the isle. Nauru by that time had become famous for its phosphate deposits. For thousands of years, migrating birds used the island as a nesting place, and tons of their fossilized droppings yield high-quality phosphate for agricultural fertilizer. The Australians, in particular, were keen to avail themselves of this useful commodity and they efficiently strip-mined the island for several years. The ecological damage incurred was tremendous, and it deprived Nauru of its lush jungle vegetation. Worse, in 1942 the island was occupied by Japanese forces, who cruelly deported a large segment of its residents as slave labor. An estimated one-third of Nauru's population thus perished, and in 1947 it resumed its status as a protectorate under Australian care. In 1966 the island was granted self-rule, and two years later Nauru gained total independence.

Dowiyogo matured on Nauru and received his primary education there, but he went abroad for his advanced degrees. He completed his undergraduate work at Ballarat College, Victoria, Australia, and he subsequently obtained a law degree from the Australian National University. Once back home, he gained election to the island's 18-member parliament in 1973, and he has since gained notoriety as one of its longest-serving politicians. Nauru at that time did not have established political parties, but in 1976 Dowiyogo engineered a no-confidence vote among opposition leaders that brought down the presidency of Hammer DeRobert, who had led the country since 1968. He was then installed as the nation's second president, but Dowiyogo was also deposed by similar means two years later. Since that time he has occupied the highest office no less than six times, with his longest tenure commencing in August 1989, which marked the end of DeRobert's political career. Dowiyogo managed to remain in office for six productive years before losing again, this time to the machinations of Lagumot Harris in 1995. For such a tiny political electorate, Nauru's politics are fierce and partisan, with a high rate of presidential turnovers.

Dowiyogo returned to the political limelight in February 1997, when voters installed Kinza Clodumar as president, and he gained appointment as education minister. In 1998 Clodumar was removed from office, and Dowiyogo succeeded him. In this capacity, he oversaw Nauru's membership in both the Commonwealth of Nations and the United Nations in 1999. However, he was briefly superceded by Rene Harris on April 17 of that year before staging a political comeback in the April 2000 elections. Throughout his tenure in office, Dowiyogo has always acted upon his instincts as a committed environmentalist. In 1989 he appealed to the World Court for a landmark settlement against Australia for damage to the island's environment. Nauru won, and has since been awarded a $57 million settlement, payable in installments of $2.5 million over the next two decades. In exchange, the island forsook all similar claims against Great Britain, New Zealand, and other occupying powers. These funds will be used to rehabilitate damaged portions of the island, and to also restock it with plants and animals that formerly flourished there. Furthermore, the island's vaunted phosphate reserves are approaching exhaustion, and Dowiyogo enacted economic development plans to keep the population employed. He also paid particular attention to educational affairs, fearing that the lack of opportunity might initiate a "brain drain" of young talent away from the island. He is also keen to establish a small but viable tourist industry that will not pose further ecological damage to the island. Moreover, Dowiyogo has been outspoken on world environmental issues such as global warming, and for good reason. Nauru enjoys only a slight elevation above sea level, and rising waters threaten to swamp the tiny republic. In 1995 Dowiyogo also broke diplomatic relations with France over the issue of renewed nuclear testing in the South Pacific. In 2000 the government incurred international fame by receiving a boatload of Asian refugees previously denied entry by the Australian government. Nauru consequently received several generous aid packages in exchange for its cooperation.

In March 2001 Dowiyogo was hospitalized in Australia for health reasons when he was ousted for a sixth time. Apparently, parliament arranged a no-confidence vote over his inability to comply with Russian requests for information about specific bank accounts. Nauru has since become the site of a flourishing "offshore" banking industry, which has served to heighten fears of corruption and criminal money laundering. He was succeeded again by his closest competitor for power, Rene Harris, who presently remains in office. Dowiyogo died in Washington, D.C., on March 10, 2003.

Further Reading

McDaniel, Carl N., and John M. Gowdy. *Paradise for Sale: A Parable of Nature.* Berkeley: University of California Press, 2000.

Petit-Skinner, Solange. *The Naurians.* San Francisco: Macduff Press, 1981.

Weeramantry, C. G. *Naura: Environmental Damage under International Trusteeship.* New York: Oxford University Press, 1992.

Williams, Maslyn, and Barrie Macdonald. *The Phosphateers.* Melbourne: Melbourne University Press, 1985.

Drnovsek, Janez (1950–) *prime minister of Slovenia*

Janez Drnovsek was born on May 17, 1950 in Celje, Slovenia, then part of the Republic of Yugoslavia. He studied economics at the University of Ljubljana and received his doctorate from the University of Maribor in 1986. He also studied international finance in the United States, Spain, and Norway before returning home. In the course of this work he became fluent in English, French, German, Spanish, in addition to his native Serbo-Croatian, and he published widely on a number of money-related issues. Drnovsek commenced his political career in 1986 by gaining election to the Slovene parliament, and he subsequently served in the Yugoslav Assembly. That nation, consisting of six ethnically different republics, possessed a collective presidency drawn from constituent members and rotated on a regular basis. In April 1989 Drnovsek was elected president of Yugoslavia, where he served until May 1990. Aged but 39 years, he was also the youngest executive to occupy the office. By now the old communist system erected by Marshal Josip Broz Tito was crumbling, and Drnovsek called upon the parliament to allow pluralist, multiparty elections, release all political prisoners, and adopt a Western-style, free-market economy. Such reforms only hastened the onset of ethnic nationalism, and Yugoslavia disintegrated in a deluge of secessionism and civil war. Slovenia, eager to break with the past, declared its political independence on June 25, 1991, an act triggering an invasion by the Serb-dominated Yugoslav People's Army. However, Drnovsek, as president of Yugoslavia, bore a critical role in negotiating an end to the 10-day war and the army's withdrawal. Renewed fighting between other republics left Yugoslavia consisting only of Serbia and Montenegro.

For the first time in a thousand years, Slovenia, a tiny patch of mountainous terrain sandwiched between Austria and Hungary, was free of occupying armies. It quickly adopted a multiparty parliamentary system under President MILAN KUCAN. Drnovsek, meanwhile, had risen on his own to become president of the Liberal Democratic Party (LDP), which he also co-founded. In April 1992, when Prime Minister Lojze Peterle lost a vote of confidence, Drnovsek advanced to succeed him. In this capacity, he proved instrumental in increasing privatization and restructuring of the banking industry to conform with rigorous standards set by the European Union. EU membership also became a centerpiece of Drnovsek's administration, as was joining NATO. Such reforms incurred a degree of economic hardship, and in January 1993 Drnovsek retained his office but the LDP was forced into coalition arrangements with the rival Slovenian Christian Democrats and United List of Social Democrats. The prime minister nonetheless juggled national priorities and competing interests masterfully, preserved the alliance, and vigorously pursued his reform agenda. As a leader, Drnovsek proved methodical, uncharismatic, and proudly devoid of national vision. "People have demanded vision," he insisted. "I hate vision. The cemetery of history is full of visionaries."

Since achieving independence, Slovenia emerged as the wealthiest and most Western-looking of former Yugoslav republics. It also ended centuries of isolation by joining the United Nations, the International Monetary Fund (IMF), and the World Bank. Drnovsek was elected prime minister a third time in January 1997 after cobbling together a new coalition consisting of the LDP, the Slovene People's Party, and the Democratic Party of Slovene Pensioners. However, in April 2000 he lost a vote of confidence to Andrej Bajuk's Social Democrats and resigned from office. Fortunately, the LDP bounced back the following October, and Drnovsek resumed the prime ministership a fourth time under a new coalition. He remains one of Slovenia's most enduring and popular politicians. On June 22, 2002, the soft-spoken economist declared his intention to run for the presidency after Milan Kucan completed his final term in office that fall.

Drnovsek, after serving 10 years as prime minister—the second longest tenure in Europe after Iceland's DAVID ODDSSON—continues on as a pivotal political figure. In recognition of his success in guiding Slovenia's transition to democracy and capitalism, he has received a number of international awards, including honorary degrees from Boston University and Illinois Wesleyan University. Slovenia thrives under his enlightened, low-key leadership and is expected to join NATO and the EU by 2003.

Further Reading

Drnovsek, Janez. "Riding the Tiger: The Dissolution of Yugoslavia." *World Policy Journal* 17, no. 1 (2000): 57–63.

———. *Escape from Hell: The Truth of a President.* Martigny, France: Editions Latour, 1996.

Gow, James, and Cathie Carmichael. *Slovenia and the Slovenes: A Samm State and the New Europe.* London: Hurst and Company, 2000.

Harris, Erika. *Nationalism and Democratization: Politics in Slovakia and Slovenia.* Burlington, Vt.: Ashgate, 2002.

Sabic, Zlatko, and Charles Butkowski, eds. *Small States in the Post–Cold War World: Slovenia and NATO Enlargement.* Westport, Conn.: Praeger, 2002.

Dzurinda, Mikuláš (1955–) *prime minister of Slovakia*

Mikuláš Dzurinda was born on February 4, 1955, in Spisska Stvrtka, Czechoslovakia. He attended local schools before studying economics at the University of Transportation and Telecommunications in Zilina. After several years of serving with a research institute in Zilina, Dzurinda gained appointment as district directorate for the national railways in Bratislava. Around this time Czechoslovakia was undergoing the "Velvet Revolution" against communism. Prior to this, and through most of its history during the 20th century, that country had existed as a union between two distinct nationalities, Czechs and Slovaks, each of whom enjoyed unique languages, customs, and traditions. The two groups managed an uneasy alliance while under Russian domination, but when that was removed after 1989, Czechoslovakia began unraveling. The first free elections since the late 1940s were held in June 1990, whereby several competing parties participated, including the Christian Democratic Movement to which Dzurinda belonged. However, democracy could not placate centuries of hostility and mistrust between Czech and Slovak, so their formal union was dissolved. On January 1, 1993, Slovakia gained its political independence.

The first Slovakian prime minister was Vladimir Meciar, an ardent nationalist and authoritarian figure in the mold of prior communist leaders. His tenure was marked by Slovak being declared the country's only official language, a move that greatly upset the sizable Hungarian minority. Meciar also determined to maintain strict international neutrality by positing the nation as a "bridge between East and West." In terms of economic reforms, cronyism became the rule of law, and so-called privatization efforts were selectively enacted to reward political allies. The government also refused to reel in various traditional political and social subsidies, so that by 1998 the economy sputtered. Worse still, national health care and the educational services were also severely curtailed. Consequently, five opposition parties bonded together to found the Slovak Democratic Coalition with Dzurinda as their candidate. Though little known, he ran on a campaign stressing economic reform and an end to political favoritism. More important, Dzurinda promised to point Slovakia to the West, with the goal of securing membership in the European Union (EU) and NATO. Slovak voters, tired of Meciar's excesses, which included the political kidnapping of an

Mikuláš Dzurinda *(Embassy of the Slovak Republic)*

opponent's son, defeated the incumbent by a narrow margin. Having thrown together a coalition government, Dzurinda became prime minister on October 30, 1998.

The new leader assumed political office with very high expectations, for he represented a complete break with the traditional, heavy-handed Slovak politics as practiced by Meciar. Unfortunately, to shore up the tottering economy, he was forced to introduce tight austerity measures, including new taxes and a rollback of popular subsidies on energy, water, and some basic foodstuffs. These produced the expected results, but not without anticipated hardships. Dzurinda's economic minister, Brigita Schmognerova, became popularly derided as "Brutal Brigita" for her zeal in implementing tough measures. The public response was negative, and in January 2002 many members of Dzurinda's own party began calling for her resignation. However, he refused to dismiss her, noting that the economy had stabilized

and that the attending sacrifices had rendered Slovakia eligible for admission into the EU. And, in concert with the EU's insistence that minority rights be respected, Dzurinda passed legislation that gave the Hungarian language equal footing with Slovak. His reform measures have been well received abroad and, consequently, Slovakia has been moved up to the first tier of applicants for EU membership. In this manner Dzurinda placed his country on an even playing field with Poland, Hungary, and the Czech Republic, all of whom are vying for expanded economic and military ties to the West.

Under Dzurinda, Slovakia made even greater strides in accommodating Western military concerns. In 1991 it approved of U.S. military air strikes against Serbia and opened Slovak skies to U.S. aircraft. In the wake of the September 11, 2001, attack upon the World Trade Towers in New York City, Dzurinda again allowed NATO aircraft free access to Slovak airspace while they pursued the war against Afghanistan. Furthermore, as a sign of support for the United States, Dzurinda ventured to New York at his own expense to partake of the famous city marathon held there every fall. "I want to go to New York to show my solidarity with the people of this injured city," he beamed. All these moves were calculated to insure that Slovakia's application for NATO membership would receive priority consideration.

Having effectively repudiated the excesses of Meciar, Dzurinda has improved both the economic and political standing of Slovakia in relatively short time. These constitute impressive turns of events, considering that his nation has had little exposure to the workings of democracy. "The basic precondition for a successful fulfillment of tasks that stand ahead of us is political stability," he stated. "There is no time for artificial ideological conflicts."

Further Reading

Goldman, Minton F. *Slovakia since Independence: A Struggle for Democracy.* Westport, Conn.: Praeger, 1999.

Innes, Abby. *Czechoslovakia: The Short Goodbye.* New Haven, Conn.: Yale University Press, 2001.

Kernan, Bent. *Democratization in Eastern Europe with a Special Emphasis on Slovakia.* Colchester, England: University of Essex, 2000.

Leff, Carol S. *The Czech and Slovak Republics: Nation versus State.* Boulder, Colo.: Westview Press, 1998.

Shepherd, Robin H. E. *Czechoslovakia: The Velvet Revolution and Beyond.* New York: Macmillan Press, 2000.

E

Ecevit, Bülent (1925–) *prime minister of Turkey*

Ecevit Bülent was born in Istanbul, Turkey, on May 28, 1925, the son of a university medical instructor. He graduated from nearby Robert College in 1944 before receiving advanced degrees from Ankara University and the University of London. An exceptional linguist, Ecevit became fluent in English and also reads Sanskrit. He returned to Turkey in 1950 to work as a reporter for *Ulus,* a newspaper sponsored by the Republican People's Party (RPP). This is a political party with deep roots in Turkey's recent past, having been founded by the legendary Mustafa Kemal Atatürk—father of the modern, secular state. In 1957 Ecevit tested the political waters by being elected to parliament as an RPP member, and he served until a military takeover of the government, 1960–61. Ecevit then served in the Constituent Assembly tasked with drawing up a new constitution. By 1965 he had risen to secretary-general of the RPP and also served as labor minister in the government of Ismet Inönü, a political mentor. The military again intervened in 1971, and Ecevit resigned in protest. Though out of office, he obstructed the military's handpicked candidate for the presidency, thereby incurring both their wrath and a measure of popular support. His political courage and charismatic personality held him in good stead in 1974, when the RPP dominated elections that year. Consequently, Ecevit became Turkey's new prime minister.

Ecevit rose to power through a tenuous alliance with an Islamic splinter group that lasted only nine months. His most notable accomplishment was authorizing a Turkish invasion of Cyprus in July 1974 to prevent its annexation by Greece. The situation was greatly complicated by the fact both nations are members of NATO. Ecevit's invasion prompted wide condemnation by the international community, but it cemented his reputation as an ardent Turkish nationalist. His government coalition collapsed soon after, only to be swept back into power in December 1977. He left office again in October 1979 when the Justice Party came to power and both parties were then deposed by a third military intervention in September 1980. Ecevit was briefly jailed for political activities during this period, when he helped establish a new organization, the Democratic Socialist Party (DSP), and he also served as its chairman. In this capacity he more or less abandoned the RPP—the party of Atatürk—as too elitist and backward-looking. Instead, he concentrated on espousing causes closer to working-class concerns, including the right to strike. He effectively served as an opposition leader in parliament until the April 1999 elections, the DSP won 22.2 percent of the popular vote and he formed a coalition government—his third.

Ecevit resumed power at a difficult time in Turkey's recent history. Despite a long association with the West, his country possessed a relatively backward economy, being largely agrarian. This has rendered the country unsuited for membership in the European Union (EU), to which Turkey very much aspires. Accordingly, Ecevit has been forced to implement draconian fiscal measures to bring down runaway inflation and combat rising unemployment. To cement cooperation with the International Monetary Fund (IMF), the government next slashed subsidies to agriculture to preserve state finances. Ecevit has also enacted extensive pension reforms to extend the retirement age (it had been 43 years). Turkey has also overhauled banking laws and procedures in order to attract foreign investment. Consistent with EU requirements, military judges have been removed from state security courts to improve Turkey's human rights record. All these measures have since produced the desired results for Ecevit, as inflation has been checked, unemployment lowered, and Turkey's chance membership in the EU have risen. It would be the first predominately Muslim nation to join.

The biggest challenge facing Turkey at present is the issue of the Kurdish minority, an ancient people with long-standing claims to the southeastern part of the country. For many years the self-styled Kurdish People's Party (PKK) has waged an internecine guerrilla war for independence that has cost 37,000 lives. Ecevit staked out a position of no compromise with the Kurds and has stepped up military activities against them. In fact, when it became known that Abdullah Ocalan, the PKK leader, was training guerrillas in Syria, the prime minister mobilized several thousand troops on their respective border. The Syrian regime then deported Ocalan out of the country, and he was subsequently captured in February 1999 and returned for trial. A military court has since sentenced him to die, but Ecevit, a death penalty opponent, has not carried out the sentence. Such an action might jeopardize Turkey's entrance into the EU, which opposes the death penalty. Ironically, relations with neighboring Greece, long viewed as a potential enemy, have significantly improved. The catalyst for change was the devastating earthquake of August 1999, in which the Greek government offered humanitarian assistance. When that country was also hit by an earthquake the following month, Ecevit reciprocated, and both countries enjoyed a general thaw in relations. Greece also took the unprecedented step of supporting Turkey's admission into the EU, which should occur with the next decade given current economic trends.

Turkey is a nation quite sensitive to the issue of terrorism, and it immediately pledged cooperation with the United States following the World Trade Center attacks of September 11, 2001. Ecevit opened Turkish skies to American aircraft bombing Afghanistan and is the only Muslim country to have committed ground troops in the hunt for terrorists. In January 2002, Ecevit traveled to neighboring Bulgaria and secured pledges of support in the fight against Kurdish terrorists. "There should be wider cooperation between services," he noted. "We are sure that Bulgaria will pay the necessary attention to this issue." In exchange Turkey formally backs that nations' application for NATO membership. In February 2002, faced with the prospects of an American invasion of Iraq, Ecevit also pleaded with SADDAM HUSSEIN for resumption of UN weapons inspection teams. This, unfortunately, did not produce the intended result, and the Turkish leader conceded: "There is no change in Saddam's stance."

Unfortunately for Ecevit, his declining health and a lingering recession have turned the tables against his administration. On August 1, 2002, the parliament voted in favor of holding national elections that November, over the prime minister's objections. Specifically, Ecevit feels that election turmoil might interfere with Turkey's forthcoming entrance into the EU and, worse, public anger over the economic malaise might witness the rise of another Islamic-based government. Nonetheless, the motion for early elections passed on a 462 to 62 vote margin, which all but spells the end of Ecevit's 40-year political career. His government is therefore unlikely to survive until its term ends in April 2004, unless he can quell a mutiny in his own party. "We have to carry on until the end," the embattled official insisted. "At this stage, I am on top of my duties; I am obligated to be."

Further Reading

Kiniklioglu, Suat. "Bulent Ecevit: The Transformation of a Politician." *Turkish Studies* 1, no. 2 (2000): 1–20.

Kinzer, Stephen. *Crescent and Star: Turkey between Two Worlds.* New York: Farrar, Strauss, and Giroux, 2001.

Lovatt, Debbie, ed. *Turkey since 1970: Politics, Economics, and Society.* Basingstoke, England: Palgrave, 2001.

Pope, Nicole, and Hugh Pope. *Turkey Unveiled: A History of Modern Turkey.* Woodstock, N.Y.: Overview Press, 2000.

Secor, A. J. "Ideologies in Crisis: Political Cleavages and Electoral Politics in Turkey in the 1990s." *Political Geography* 20 (June 2001): 538–61.

Endara, Guillermo (1936–) *president of Panama*

Guillermo Endara Galimany was born on May 12, 1936, in Panama City, Panama. An accomplished student, he was educated at private academies in Argentina and Los Angeles, California, before attending the University of Panama. He graduated first in his class before studying law at New York University, and he returned home in 1963 to practice with the nation's foremost corporate law firm. He became politically active in 1968 by winning election to the National Assembly as a fervent supporter of dissident political leader Arnulfo Arias Madrid, a twice-deposed president. Arias was reelected to high office in 1971, but the military overthrew him a third time and Endara fled into exile. In 1988 both Arias and Endara founded the Authentic Panamanist Party to continue organized opposition, but the latter eventually switched sides to join and ultimately head the Liberal Authentic Party. In this capacity, Endara was chosen by the Democratic Alliance of Civic Action, a broad coalition of opposition groups, to run as their candidate in upcoming presidential elections. Panama was then under the one-man rule of General Manuel Noriega, a military strongman who had run the country since 1984. Noriega's handpicked candidate was Carlos Duque, a businessman with strong links to the military and the drug trade. However, to attract as broad a spectrum of voters as possible, Endara ran on a ticket with two vice presidential candidates, Ricardo Arias of the Christian Democratic Party and Guillermo Ford of the Nationalist Liberation Republican Party, in a three-way power-sharing arrangement. The tactic worked, and on May 7, 1989, Endara won the election handily, garnering 62.5 percent of the vote.

Endara's victory would seem to have announced democracy's return to Panama, but General Noriega had other ideas. Stung by the election, he summarily annulled it and installed another henchman, Francisco Rodriguez, as president. Angry citizens flocked to the streets in protest, and the general unleashed his goon squads, the so-called Dignity Battalions, against them. In one encounter, Endara was pulled from his motorcade and severely beaten. But the affable president-elect remained undeterred and unintimidated. "Noriega has to go," Endara declared from his bedside: "I won't back off one inch." The military responded with additional harassment, and at one point Endara was forced to take refuge in the papal embassy. By now it had become apparent that military force would be needed to rescue Panama's democracy, so on December 20, 1989, President George H. W. Bush authorized Operation Just Cause, the overthrow of Noriega. American forces brushed aside the general's supporters, while he himself took refuge in the papal embassy. There he surrendered and was whisked away to Miami to face charges of drug smuggling. Endara, meanwhile, was formally sworn into office while the invasion was underway. He next faced the unenviable task of rebuilding a country ruined by war and oppression.

One of Endara's first priorities was the disbandment of the Panamanian Defense Forces, which had so diligently propped up the Noriega regime. Thereafter, Panamanian security became entrusted to a national police force. But over the next five years, the administration also confronted a national economy contracting by 25 percent and unemployment rates approaching 50 percent. The nation, once a thriving international finance center, also suffered from a massive flight of capital, which further decimated the economy. To emphasize his country's plight, Endara embarked on a highly publicized hunger strike to garner international attention. Though ridiculed at first, the ploy had the desired effect and within a year the United States and other countries pledged $1 billion in aid. Endara and President Bush also signed several high-level treaties to combat drug smuggling and money laundering, which had only intensified after Noriega's fall. However, Panama's political and economic conditions continued unraveling. In April 1991, Endara dismissed all five Christian Democrats from his cabinet on the grounds that they were spying on him. This did little to enhance the viability of his fragile coalition, which began splintering well in advance of upcoming national elections.

By 1994, despite Endara's best efforts, Panama's economic and social distress remained prevalent. Unemployment, while improving, still hovered at 20 percent whereas crime and corruption remained endemic. The drug trade also flourished and occasioned a spate of expensive high-rise waterfront construction—with buildings paid for in cash. But worst of all was the public perception that Endara was floundering through his presidency, and his popularity ratings tumbled. On

September 1, 1994, he was soundly trounced by Ernesto Pérez Balladeres of the Democratic Revolutionary Party (DRP), the very organization that had previously supported Noriega. Humiliated, Endara resumed his successful legal practice and otherwise maintained a low public profile. In October 2001 a judicial court sentenced him to 18 months in prison for slandering a social security director. The sentence was later commuted, but Endara remained angry. "They are humiliating me," he complained. "After they condemn me they suspend the sentence, making it seem like I am a privileged person."

Further Reading

Elsenmann, R. "The Struggle against Noriega." *Journal of Democracy* 1 (Winter 1990): 41–46.

Furlong, William L. "Panama: The Difficult Transition towards Democracy." *Journal of Interamerican Studies and World Affairs* 35 (Fall 1993): 9–66.

Guevara Mann, Carlos. "Forsaken Virtue: An Analysis of the Political Behavior of Panamanian Legislators, 1984–1999." Unpublished Ph.D. dissertation, Notre Dame University, 2001.

Harding, Robert C. *Military Foundations of Panamanian Politics.* New Brunswick, N.J.: Transaction Publishers, 2001.

Perez, Orlando J. *Post-invasion Panama: The Challenges of Democratization in New World Order.* Lanham, Md.: Lexington Books, 2000.

Erbakan, Necmettin (1926–) *prime minister of Turkey*

Necmettin Erbakan was born in 1926 in the Black Sea port of Sinop, Turkey. At this time the country was ruled by the legendary Mustafa Kemal Atatürk, who grafted a Western-oriented, secular system onto his predominately Muslim country. He insisted that while religion is important, it must be strictly isolated from the political realm. This proved a unique approach to Middle Eastern governance and contributed significantly to Turkey's social and economic progress. Erbakan was educated locally and eventually attended the prestigious Istanbul Technical University. He graduated with honors in 1948 and subsequently earned a doctorate in mechanical engineering before completing postgraduate work at the Technical University in Aachen, Germany. Erbakan returned home in 1953 to teach engineering at the university, and, in 1968, he was voted president of the

Turkish Chamber of Commerce. However, Erbakan's outspoken stance on unrelated issues brought him into conflict with Prime Minister SÜLEYMAN DEMIREL, who forced him from office. In 1969 he next won a seat in the Grand National Assembly as an independent, and one year later Erbakan emerged on the national scene, heading the new National Order Party. This was the first political organization in modern Turkish history to demand greater recognition for Islam in secular affairs. In 1971 the military overthrew the government and all parties were banned. The following year Erbakan promulgated a new group, the National Salvation Party, which also exuded religious overtones. He railed against attempts at expanding Westernization and called for a spiritual reawakening. Although the government discouraged religion-based parties, the NSP received 12 percent of the vote in the 1973 national elections, rendering it a viable voting bloc in parliament. That year Erbakan also joined in a coalition arrangement with Prime Minister BÜLENT ECEVIT, which lasted until November 1974. The NSP then continued on as a coalition partner in a center-right government under Demirel. Erbakan remained a prominent figure in national politics until 1980, when the army overthrew Demirel and politics was again banned.

Erbakan's success with religion-based parties paralleled a regional trend toward Islamic fundamentalism. By the time political restrictions were lifted in 1983, he had established a third organization, the Welfare Party, which was extremely Islamist in outlook. In 1994 it established itself as a power to reckon with by winning 28 of 76 mayoral races, and the following year Welfare took a surprising 158 seats in parliament, becoming the biggest voting bloc. Erbakan, however, failed to form a government, and on July 8, 1996, he entered into coalition arrangements with TANSU CILLER of the True Path Party. Through this expedient he served two years as prime minister and Cillar functioned as foreign minister before the offices rotated. Erbakan's rise was viewed with some trepidation among Western countries, who were counting upon Turkey's friendly cooperation in the otherwise volatile Middle East. Once in power, he paid homage to greater Muslim solidarity throughout the region, and he cultivated closer economic and diplomatic ties with Libya, Iran, and Iraq. However, he dispensed with his prior anti-Western rhetoric about leaving NATO and breaking ties with Israel. In fact, Erbakan went on record as favoring Turkey's entry into the European Union (EU) and actually expanded economic ties to Israel. However, there remained the issue of Turkey's constitution and its stark demand for secularization. Apparently, on February 25, 1994, Erbakan made a speech criticizing the government for having schoolchildren recite nationalist slogans instead of verses from the Koran. He also then described opposition members of parliament as "infidels." The military, the self-appointed watchdog of secularization, regarded this as blatantly provocative and marked Erbakan as a seditionist. He further alienated the army by suggesting that the rebellious Kurdish minority in eastern Turkey should be granted more autonomy, another hot-button issue. Pressure then mounted on Erbakan for his resignation, especially following allegations of corruption. Accordingly, he withdrew from office in June 1997 and was replaced by a new prime minister, Mesut Yizal. By January 1998 the Welfare Party was also banned.

Erbakan spent the next three years in various courts denying any attempt to undermine Turkish secularism. Nevertheless, in September 2000 he was found guilty of sedition, sentenced to one year in prison, and banned from politics for five years. Erbakan's sentence was suspended through a general amnesty but, in March 2002, a court found him guilty of embezzling funds from the disbanded Welfare Party. He then received two years in prison and, if his appeal is overturned, he could be banned from politics for life. Turkey maintains its strict enforcement of secularization and keeps a vigilant eye on Islamic fundamentalist groups in the political arena.

Further Reading

Heper, Metin, and Sabri Sayari, eds. *Political Leaders and Democracy in Turkey.* Lanham, Md.: Lexington Books, 2002.
Levatt, Debbie, ed. *Turkey since 1970: Politics, Economics, and Society.* London: Palgrave, 2001.
Liel, Alin. *Turkey in the Middle East: Oil, Islam, and Politics.* Boulder, Colo.: Lynne Rienner Publishers, 2001.
Sayari, Sabri, and Yilmaz Esmer, eds. *Politics, Parties, and Elections in Turkey.* Boulder, Colo.: Lynne Rienner Publishers, 2001.
White, Jenny B. *Islamist Mobilization in Turkey: A Study in Vernacular Politics.* Seattle: University of Washington Press, 2002.
Yavuz, M. Hakan. *Islamic Political Identity in Turkey.* New York: Oxford University Press, 2003.

Estrada, Joseph (1937–) *president of the Philippines*

Joseph Marcelo Ejercito was born in Manila on April 19, 1937, the son of a government engineer. Like his father, he studied engineering at college for several years, then dropped out in favor of pursuing a career in the film industry. His family objected to using their name in such fashion, so he adopted the surname "Estrada" (Spanish for street). Estrada also went by the nickname "Erap," which means *pare,* or "friend" spelled backward in Tagalog. Despite his lack of theatrical training, Estrada took readily to film and, in a movie career spanning three decades, he starred in 50 feature films. In his films he was invariably cast as a commoner who fights crime and injustice out of a sense of moral outrage. Estrada never rose beyond a "B grade" actor professionally, but he endeared himself to a generation of poor Filipinos who closely identified with him. In time he began to act out his "Robin Hood" persona in politics. Here, Estrada carefully couched his appeal in keeping his distance from the cultural and commercial elites who traditionally dominated national politics.

Estrada commenced his political career in 1968 with a successful run for mayor of San Juan. He was reelected successively over the next 16 years and proved surprisingly effective in constructing the city's first high school, post office, and fire department. He next moved on to the Senate in 1987, remaining there six years. Beyond his usual calls to help the country's poor, he also championed the cause of removing U.S. military bases from the country. In 1992 Estrada's growing popularity convinced him to run for the vice presidency under the National People's Coalition banner. He won 33 percent of the national vote, mostly from poor and downtrodden regions, where residents viewed his candidacy as a chance for reform. In this capacity Estrada also chaired the Presidential Anti-Crime Commission at the behest of President FIDEL RAMOS, and he made several high-profile arrests connected to corruption and kidnapping. The former movie star functioned competently in his new role and garnered greater national support over the next six years. By 1998, Estrada felt ready for the limelight and announced his candidacy for the presidency. While campaigning he deliberately invoked his widespread public image as a charismatic crime fighter, and he reiterated familiar themes such as securing greater health care, housing, education, and employment for the struggling poor. He further promised to promote effective government, put an end to corruption, encourage political accountability, and support local autonomy. His was a message of hope, and, on May 11, 1998, Estrada's new National Filipino Masses party was swept into power with 46 percent of the vote. Much was expected of this swaggering screen idol, who was derided by the opposition as intellectually bankrupt and who was, in his private life, notorious for drinking, partying, and womanizing.

Once in power, Estrada was faced by seemingly insurmountable economic challenges. The economic crisis that wracked Asia through the late 1990s crippled the Philippine economy and its ability to generate new jobs. Worse, by 2000 the national debt had soared to a staggering $45 billion, and the interest payments alone amounted to more than government expenditures on education, health, and agriculture combined. Estrada also made a serious misstep politically by allowing the remains of former dictator Ferdinand Marcos to be buried at the national Heroes Cemetery in Manila. Public outrage induced wife Imelda Marcos to inter him elsewhere. Over the next five years Estrada did manage to pass a comprehensive package of social and governmental reforms aimed at improving tax collecting, ending pork-barrel legislation, and making government more effective. Some improvements have been registered overall, but Estrada himself came under increasing criticism for corruption and pandering to cronies—the exact charges he had leveled against opponents. In August 1999 Cardinal Sin of Manila organized a demonstration of 100,000 people in protest. Three months later a World Bank report alleged that 20 percent of the national budget was being lost to corruption, and the bottom fell out of Estrada's regime. The final act had begun.

In October 2000 the Philippine government underwent a profound crisis when a Senate investigative committee accused Estrada of accepting large sums of money from illegal gambling businesses. National protests mounted once the House of Representatives endorsed a bill of impeachment against the president in November 2000. The following month the Senate began formal impeachment proceedings against Estrada and, on January 20, 2001, the Supreme Court declared his office vacated. This move was occasioned by a demonstration of "People Power," when thousands took to the streets demanding the president's resignation. He was then succeeded by Vice President GLORIA MACAPAGAL-ARROYO. Despite mounting evidence, Estrada pro-

claimed his innocence and portrayed himself as a martyr. "What I am now I owe to the masses," he emoted, "so when I step down, I would like to be known as the president who championed the cause of the masses." His still-numerous supporters took to the streets in protest and by April 2000 a state of rebellion was declared. Estrada was nonetheless arrested and charged with graft and perjury. He is alleged to have amassed a fortune totaling $78 million, which is considered economic plunder and punishable by the death penalty. Estrada remains behind bars at a military prison awaiting his fate. Characteristically, perhaps, in January 2002 complaints were filed against him for having grown too friendly with the security detail guarding him and for hosting a lavish Christmas party with them. The curtain has yet to fall.

Further Reading

Coronel, Shelia S. *Investigating Estrada: Millions, Mansions, and Mistresses.* Manila: Philippine Center for Investigative Journalism, 2000.

"Estrada, Joseph," *Current Biography Yearbook* (2000): 178–181.

Hedman, Eva-Lotta E., ed. *Philippine Politics and Society in the Twentieth Century.* New York: Routledge, 2000.

Lande, Carl H. "The Return of 'People Power' in the Philippines." *Journal of Democracy* 12 (April 2001): 88–102.

Magno, Alexander P. "Philippines—Trauma of a Failed Democracy." *Southeast Asian Affairs* 28 (2001): 251–262.

Martinez, Manuel F. *A Political History of Our Time.* Parañaque City: MFM Enterprises, 1999.

Reid, Ben. "The Philippines, Democracy, Uprising, and the Contradictions of Neoliberalism," *Third World Quarterly* 22, no. 5 (2001): 777–793.

Eyadema, Gnassingbe (1937–) *president of Togo*

Gnassingbe Etienne Eyadema was born on December 26, 1937, in Pya, a village in northern Togo. He belonged to the minority Kabye tribe, which was among the most numerous groupings in the north. Eyadema proved more fortunate than most African children in receiving six years of elementary education, and he then joined the French colonial army in 1953. Eyadema saw widespread service in the employ of France, including wars in Indochina and Algeria. He distinguished himself in combat on several occasions, and he finally mustered out with a rank of sergeant. By that time, Togo, successively a German and French protectorate on the West African coast, had gained its independence in April 1960 under President Sylvanus Olympio. In 1963 Eyadema and a number of veteran Togolese soldiers petitioned that they be allowed to join the 150-strong national army, but Olympio refused. Accordingly, on January 13, 1963, Eyadema led a bloody coup in which the president was killed and Nicholas Grunitzky was installed. Consequently, he achieved rapid promotion in the newly constituted military, becoming chief of staff by 1969. Four years later another military coup deposed Grunitzky in favor of Colonel Kleber Dadjo, who within months was overthrown by Eyadema himself. The new leader then abolished the constitution, outlawed political parties, and ruled as a military dictator. Having consolidated power completely by 1969, Eyadema created a political party—the Assembly of the Togolese People (RPT)—and he declared the nation a one-party government. He has since remained in power over three decades, becoming the longest-serving head of state in Africa.

Under Eyadema's leadership, Togo has assumed all the dimensions of a military dictatorship. He rules by fiat in being backed overwhelmingly by two critical allies: the military and the business community. To this end, he has staffed all national security forces with members of his own Kabye tribe, especially those from his native village of Pya. He sees to it that they are regularly paid and fed, thus securing their loyalty. He has also enhanced his national image by promoting a cult of personality. Images of Eyadema permeate the countryside in the form of posters, pictures, or statues. He has also embraced free-market economic principles that keep the business, banking and commercial classes in his pocket. The president has further boosted his popular image by surviving a 1974 plane crash, which lent a miraculous aura to his regime.

Eyadema's control of the country is firm, but not absolute. Numerous opposition groups operating from neighboring Ghana have funneled money and arms into resistance movements and, in 1985, these orchestrated a concerted bombing campaign throughout the capital city of Lomé. The president responded by unleashing his military upon the populace. For several months thereafter, arrests, torture, and execution were commonplace. However, since the end of the cold war, two of Togo's most influential allies, France and the United States, have insisted on opening up the political process. Eyadema complied, but only sullenly and in such a manner as to ensure his grip on power. In 1991, following a wave of national strikes, the president agreed to formation of a conference to promote national reconciliation. However, this body had no sooner convened than it declared itself sovereign and began drafting a new constitution. Eyadema, predictably, cracked down with imposing force, jailing many opposition leaders and firing on peaceful demonstrators. Two years later renewed foreign pressure resulted in the first multiparty elections, which proved so fraudulent that the opposition boycotted them. Eyadema thus ran unopposed, garnering 96 percent of the vote. According to a Benin-based human rights group, the ruling party oversaw the execution of hundreds of people during the campaign.

Having mastered his splintered opposition, in 1998 Eyadema again allowed multiparty elections, and among his opponents was Gilchrist Olympio, son of the slain president. The incumbent was again declared the victor with 52 percent of the vote, which was sufficiently large enough to avoid a runoff. However, Eyadema's refusal to share power induced both the United States and the European Union (including France) to suspend foreign aid pending genuine and democratic political reform. This remains conjectural at best, considering Eyadema's absolute control of state media and security forces. However, a July 2000 meeting with French president JACQUES CHIRAC finally induced the former sergeant to pry open the political process in return for economic aid. Eyadema has since conferred with opposition leaders and pledged not to seek reelection when his current term expires in 2003. A minor flap occurred in August 2001 when Prime Minister Agbeyome Messan Kodjo suggested altering the constitution to allow Eyadema to run again, but this has since been squelched. Curiously, despite his reputation as a despot, Eyadema is favorably received by most West African countries, and, in July 2000, he took over as chairman of the Organization of African Unity (OAU). He was quick to remind fellow heads of state that in Africa "democracy moves along at its own pace and in its own way."

Further Reading

Decalo, Samuel. *Historical Dictionary of Togo.* Lanham, Md.: Scarecrow Press, 1996.

Ellis, Stephen. "Rumor and Power in Togo." *Africa* 63, no. 4 (1993): 462–476.

Houngnikpo, Mathurin C. *Determinants of Democratization in Africa: A Comparative Study of Benin and Togo.* Lanham, Md.: University Press of America, 2000.

Piot, Charles. *Remotely Global: Village Modernity in West Africa.* Chicago: University of Chicago Press, 1999.

F

Fahd bin Abdul Aziz al-Saud (1923–   )
king of Saudi Arabia

Fahd Ibn Abdul Aziz al-Saud was born in Riyadh, Saudi Arabia, in 1923. His father was King Ibn Saud, who founded that desert kingdom in 1932. A few years later the Arabian Peninsula was found to contain one-fourth of the world's known petroleum reserves, which made the ruling family extremely wealthy and influential throughout the Arab world. Fahd received a classical court education in Riyadh, and he stood third in line for succession to the throne behind elder brothers Faisal and Khalid. However, despite his conservative religious upbringing in the Wahhbi Muslim tradition, Fahd acquired something of a playboy image. He freely engaged in drinking, gambling, and womanizing throughout his youth, which made elders question his ability to rule. King Saud then sent his obdurate son abroad to the United States in 1945, where he witnessed the creation of the United Nations in San Francisco. Fahd was indelibly impressed by his visit, and thereafter he remained kindly disposed toward the United States. Fahd also represented the House of Saud during the coronation of Queen Elizabeth II of England. This global exposure apparently had the desired effect of curtailing Fahd's personal excesses, and in 1953, following the accession of Faisal to the throne, he gained appointment as Saudi Arabia's first education minister.

Fahd's early exposure to Western culture rendered him less conservative in political outlook than many contemporaries, and the policies he enacted were decidedly progressive and modern. As education minister he tapped into oil revenues to construct numerous schools and, for the first time, allowed Saudi girls to attend. Results were impressive, and between 1962 and 1967 Fahd was successively appointed minister of the interior and deputy prime minister. In this capacity he carefully oversaw national security, educational, and petroleum issues with considerable tact and foresight. King Faisal was assassinated in 1975 and was succeeded by Khalid, whereupon Fahd rose to become first deputy prime minister. As the new crown prince, he was also next in line to the throne. He assumed office during a boom period in Saudi Arabia's economic growth, as oil prices were high globally and the country raked in fantastic amounts of wealth. However, Fahd distinguished himself by careful planning and orderly economic progress to ensure that the benefits of oil revenue trickled down to enhance the lives of common Saudis. Their high standard of living ensured a stable regime at home. Fahd also excelled at inter-Arab diplomacy and gained a reputation as an effective mediator. He attended several high-level Arab summits in connection with the Palestinian question and promulgated the famous Fez Declaration of August 1981. This held that Israel must withdraw from Arab lands captured in 1967, and that a Palestinian state should be created, but took the unprecedented step of calling for diplomatic recognition of Israel—and hence its inherent right to exist. This approach was far too accommodating to more radical Arab regimes and was never adopted, but it established Fahd's credentials as a political moderate and a regional realist. He also played a leading role in helping to mediate the Iran-Iraq war and, in concert with the United States, marshaling money and weapons for Afghani freedom fighters during the Soviet occupation of their country. When Khalid died in 1982, Fahd finally ascended to the throne. In light of rising Islamic fundamentalist pressures, he also assumed a new title, "Custodian of the Two Holy Mosques," a direct reference to his role as protector of the shrines at Mecca and Medina.

Fahd came to power during a period of increasing political, religious, and economic instability. The 1990s were marked by a worldwide oil glut, with a commensurate cut in prices and declining revenues. The Saudi government was obliged to cut back on its generous policy of social spending and increase funding for national defense. In 1991 Iraqi dictator SADDAM HUSSEIN invaded neighboring Kuwait, which set off alarm bells in Riyadh and Washington that he might just as easily overrun the Saudi oil fields. Again, Fahd proved himself solidly in the Western camp, for not only did he allow United States troops onto Saudi soil for the first time but he also spent billions of dollars subsidizing the war against Iraq. However, since that time the nominally close ties between Saudi Arabia and America have been slowly undermined by undercurrents of religious extremism. One Saudi dissident, Osama bin Laden, used his personal wealth to finance a campaign of global terror against United States installations. On September 11, 2001, several of his followers hijacked airliners and destroyed the World Trade Center in New York City. The majority of the 19 hijackers involved were, in fact, Saudi nationals. Fahd has personally condemned the attacks but, this time, only hesitatingly allowed U.S. forces to mount operations against Afghanistan, where Bin Laden was known to be operating. The rise of Islamic fundamentalism is a threat to the Saudi throne, for it considers the government far too conciliatory toward the heathen West. Religious leaders have grown increasingly hostile to the moderate, modernistic governance that always characterized the Fahd regime. The king has also been in poor health for several years, and he delegates increasing responsibilities to his younger brother, Abdullah, the current crown prince. Whoever succeeds the elderly monarch will inherit a kingdom on the edge of a religious and regional precipice, with far less income—and scope for toleration—than previous rulers have enjoyed.

Further Reading

Dutton, Frederick G. *King Fahd of Saudi Arabia: The Man, His Work, and His Country.* Washington, D.C.: Hannaford Co., 1990.

Fandy, Mamoun. *Saudi Arabia and the Politics of Dissent.* New York: Palgrave, 2001.

Farsy, Fouad al-. *Custodian of the Two Holy Mosques: King Fahd Bin Abdul Aziz.* Guernsey, Channel Islands: Knight Communications, 2001.

Kechichian, Joseph A. *Succession in Saudi Arabia.* New York: Palgrave, 2001.

Rasheed, Madawi al-. "God, the King, and the Nation: Political Rhetoric in Saudi Arabia in the 1990s." *Middle East Journal* 10, no. 3 (1996): 359–372.

Falcam, Leo A. (1935–) *president of the Federated States of Micronesia*

Leo A. Falcam was born on November 20, 1935, on Pohnpei, one of four states that constitute the Federated States of Micronesia. This grouping consists of 607 islands spread over 2.5 million square miles of the Pacific Ocean. The other three states are Chuuk, Yap, and Kosrae. Micronesia was formerly known as the Caroline Islands, and host to various Spanish, German, and Japanese administrations throughout the 20th century. After World War II the islands became a United Nations Trust Territory of the Pacific under U.S. jurisdiction. Long and tedious negotiations then ensued before the islands gained political independence in July 1979 as the Federated States of Micronesia. A constitution was adopted in May 1979 that mandated an elected president and a unicameral legislature composed of 14 senators. However, in the absence of political parties, politics usually manifest along tribal lines, with chiefs frequently instructing their followers to vote as blocs. Micronesia also enjoyed a unique agreement with the United States, the so-called Compact of Free Association, which stipulated the leasing of military bases on the islands in exchange for rent and free immigration to the mainland.

Falcam was educated locally before completing his undergraduate work in sociology at the University of Hawaii, the first Micronesian citizen to do so. He subsequently attended the prestigious Woodrow Wilson School of Public and International Affairs at Princeton University. Once home, he chaired the Pohnpei delegation to the 1975 constitutional convention and subsequently served as its vice president. With independence gained, he functioned as the district administrator of his island state and also served as the first Micronesian liaison officer to the United States, 1983–84. Since then Falcam has distinguished himself as one of the island's most enduring civil servants, with a litany of public offices held. He was first elected to Congress in 1987 from Pohnpei, and remained in office over the next 12 years. On July 21, 1999, Falcam entered a presidential runoff against Jacob Nena and defeated him handily to become Micronesia's fifth elected president.

Once in office, Falcam's first priority was to cement the traditional close ties the islands maintained with the United States. This country remains Micronesia's greatest source of income and investment, and he spent considerable effort negotiating renewal of the Compact of Free Association. However, this entailed expanded performance of free markets and economic growth to facilitate self-sufficiency. Greater accountability of funding also remains an official concern. Falcam has largely complied with numerous demands and further curries American favor by lending its support to the United States in various UN debates. As a sovereign state, Micronesia has also expanded ties to Japan, Australia, and China, but its working relationship with the United States remains the foundation of its economic well-being.

On the domestic front, Falcam is challenged by encouraging economic growth while protecting and preserving the delicate ecological integrity of his charge. Because the bulk of the Micronesian economy derives from fishing, much attention is paid to selective granting of licenses to foreign fleets so as to preclude depletion of natural resources. He is also determined that Micronesia should assume a greater share of fishing activities and secured a $934,000 development grant to modernize equipment and management. An exponent of privatization, Falcam desires to eliminate government controls of the fishing industry and turn it completely over to the private sector. He also espouses similar intentions for the islands' tourism and agricultural industries, which

have lagged behind fishing in terms of profit and self-reliance.

Life on these tropic isles remains far from idyllic, however. Micronesia generally enjoys one of the Pacific's highest living standards, but unemployment is relatively high owing to sluggish job creation. Furthermore, in May 2000 Pohpei experienced an outbreak of cholera, which killed 20 people before a vaccination campaign was successfully enacted. The islands' close association with nature has also come under closer scrutiny, owing to the encroachment of man. In December 2000 marine biologists predicted continuing erosion of the Micronesian coastlines owing to the destruction of coral reefs through overfishing, pollution, and warming ocean temperatures. This last factor is a note of special concern, for warming trends mean higher sea levels, which threaten to engulf many of the tiny islands comprising Micronesia. Falcam has since called upon the United Nations to pay closer attention to ecological issues such as global warming. "Within the last several hundred years, the onset of industrialization and technological advance has created a multinational appetite for luxury and consumption that seems unquenchable," he warned, "but compelling scientific evidence tells us today that this headlong pursuit, if not moderated in the 21st century, threatens the lives of all our descendants and the very habitability of the planet that we so recklessly continue to abuse." It remains to be seen if this cogent and eloquent appeal for moderation will be heeded.

Further Reading

Haglegam, John. *Traditional Leaders and Governance in Micronesia.* Canberra: Australian National University, 1998.

Hanlon, David L. *Remaking Micronesia: Discourses over Development in a Pacific Territory, 1944–1982.* Honolulu: University of Hawaii Press, 1998.

"Leo A. Falcam—President of the Federated States of Micronesia." *Vital Speeches of the Day* 66, no. 24 (2000): 761.

Wuerch, William L. *Historical Dictionary of Guam and Micronesia.* Metuchen, N.J.: Scarecrow Press, 1994.

Fenech-Adami, Eddie (1934–) *prime minister of Malta*

Eddie Fenech-Adami was born in Birkirkara, Malta, on February 7, 1934. His homeland is a strategic island community located between Sicily and North Africa, with a history of settlements dating back to antiquity. For most of the 20th century, Malta was a possession of Great Britain, although self-rule was finally granted its inhabitants in 1947. Political independence was achieved in 1964, although the island has elected to remain part of the British Commonwealth of Nations. Under its present constitution, Malta is a parliamentary democracy in which an elected president serves as head of state, but an appointed prime minister is in charge of foreign affairs. This is determined by whichever party in parliament possesses a clear majority of seats.

Fenech-Adami studied economics and philosophy at St. Aloysius College, a Jesuit school, obtaining his bachelor's degree in 1955. He subsequently studied law at the Royal University of Malta and was admitted to the bar in 1959. Thereafter he found work within the Nationalist (Christian Democratic or PN) Party of Malta, and he served as assistant general between 1962–75. He joined parliament by taking the seat of a deceased member in 1969 and was first elected to that seat in 1971. Fenech-Adami was effective politically, though somewhat castigated by opponents for his dry, soft-spoken style. He nonetheless rose to become vice president of the European Union of Christian Democrats in 1979 while also functioning as the party's spokesman for labor and social services. From 1983 to 1987 Fenech-Adami assumed the role of opposition leader in parliament, and he stridently opposed the socialist policies of the incumbent Labour Party (LP) then in office. Maltese politics reached a critical turning point in the elections of May 1987, when the PN squeaked through with a 50.9 percent majority of votes. With a majority of seats in parliament, Fenech-Adami gained appointment as prime minister. He was also the first Christian Democrat to hold power after 16 years in opposition.

Fenech-Adami's tenure in office marked a turnaround in the island's political and economic landscape. For the next nine years, he focused single-mindedly upon his cherished goal of Maltese membership in the European Union (EU). He therefore commenced a rollback of socialist policies, especially government control of large segments of the economy. Consequently, more freedom was granted to the private sector, taxes were lowered, and foreign investment was sought. He also promised to increase, not cut, social services, based on optimistic predictions that economic growth would register 10 percent per year. Furthermore, Fenech-Adami

Edward Fenech-Adami *(Embassy of Malta)*

steered away from Malta's traditional nonaligned stance diplomatically by seeking closer economic and political ties with Western Europe and the United States. To this end, he ordered a crackdown on pro-Libyan terrorist groups on the island and also sought to stamp out political corruption. The PN's new agenda proved popular initially and the island's economy witnessed a flourishing of growth under a free-market stimulus. Fenech-Adami pursued his goal of joining the EU zealously. An important precondition for membership was imposition of a 15 percent value added tax (VAT) on all consumer goods, which would replace the usual customs duties. However, the electorate lost much of its enthusiasm for change, and, in the 1996, elections they granted the Labour Party 52 percent of the vote. Accordingly, Fenech-Adami stepped down to become leader of the opposition while the LP's Alfred Sant served as prime minister.

For the next two years Sant's administration attempted to roll back many of the previous reforms and reinstitute many of the previous socialist policies. His first undertaking was to withdraw the island's EU membership application. However, many of his economic austerity measures proved unpopular and seemingly compromised Malta's hard-won status among Western nations. Accordingly, in September 1998 new elections were called to decide the direction of the country. Fenech-Adami reiterated his uncompromising stance on EU membership to fully integrate the island into the booming economies of the West. The PN was then returned to power with a 51.81 percent majority and Fenech-Adami again gained the prime ministership.

Not surprisingly, the new administration continued unraveling many of the old socialist policies and set Malta irrevocably on the path toward EU membership. He reduced regulations on the private sector, emphasized foreign investment, and lightened the tax burden on companies and individuals. The banking industry has also been overhauled, new privacy laws enacted, and other steps taken to transform Malta from a service-oriented economy into a booming financial center. And the prime minister once again abandoned Malta's traditional neutrality in favor of currying Western ties. The island's formal application for EU membership has since been revived. Based upon current projections, it is most likely slated for approval in 2003.

Further Reading

Berg, Warren G. *Historical Dictionary of Malta.* Lanham, Md.: Scarecrow Press, 1995.

Boissevain, Jeremy. *Saints and Fireworks: Religion and Politics in Rural Malta.* Valletta, Malta: Progress Press, 1993.

Fenech, Dominic. "Malta." *European Journal of Political Research* 38, no. 3/4 (2000): 458–61.

Frendo, Henry. *Party Politics in a Fortress Colony: The Maltese Experience.* Valletta, Malta: Midsea Publications, 1991.

Fernández, Leonel (1953–   ) *president of the Dominican Republic*

Leonel Fernández Reyna was born in Santo Domingo, Dominican Republic, on December 26, 1953, and raised in New York City. As a result, he became fluent in both Spanish and English and fully versed in the cultural nuances of the United States. After attending an American high school he moved back to the Dominican Republic to study law at the Autonomous University of Santo Domingo. Fernández received a doctorate in law and in 1973 joined the newly formed Dominican Liberation Party (PLD) of President Juan Bosch. This initiated his lengthy career in politics, and he successively held numerous party posts. Fernández handled himself capably, and, in 1995, Bosch tapped him to serve as his PLD vice presidential running mate. Defeated that year, Bosch surrendered party leadership to Fernández, and two years later he emerged as the PLD candidate for the presidency.

The Dominican Republic had a long tradition of political instability and dictatorial rule. Affairs grew so violent in 1965 that U.S. president Lyndon B. Johnson dispatched troops to occupy the island and restore order. A new constitution, based upon the American model, was then instituted, which distributed political power into executive, legislative, and judiciary branches. The president is elected to a four-year term, much like his American counterpart, although he can run only once. However, the 1996 election proved volatile even by Dominican standards, owing to the racial composition of the contenders. Fernández of the PLD and Jacinto Peynado of the Christian Reformist Party (PRSC) were both Spanish in origin, but the third candidate, José Francisco Peña Gómez of the Dominican Revolutionary Party (PRD) was of African descent. This set off alarms in many quarters, for the Spanish-speaking Dominican Republic shares the island of Hispaniola with French-speaking Haiti, which is predominately black. The two nations have held relations that, both politically and racially, have been traditionally antagonistic. At once, rumors were circulated that Peña Gómez was actually a Haitian agent bent on merging the two nations. Fernández, for his part, ran a clean campaign and kept his message focused on economic reform, job creation, and social justice. The first round of voting produced no decisive majority for any candidate, although Peña Gómez did surprisingly well and garnered a slight majority of votes. At that juncture Peynado threw his weight behind Fernández, who was also supported by former presidents Bosch and JOAQUÍN BALAGUER, a legendary national figure. Apparently, the tactics of race-baiting worked. During the next round of voting on June 30, 1996, Fernández squeaked by Peña Gómez in garnering 51 percent of the vote, a sufficient margin to claim victory. At 42 he thus became the youngest elected president of the Dominican Republic and the first ever from the Dominican Liberation Party.

Though victorious, Fernández's tenure in office has been marred by seemingly insurmountable obstacles. His youthful appeal did not translate into a coattail effect, and consequently Congress remained in the hands of the PRSC. By combining their votes with that of the opposition PRD, they could effectively curtail any new legislation or judicial appointments by the new president. Fernández also faced a less tangible but equally difficult problem in the personage of Joaquín Balaguer, his erstwhile ally. He was a legendary politician with roots dating back to the dictatorship of Rafael Trujillo during the 1960s. Conservative and charismatic, Balaguer exerted a pronounced influence on national politics, even when out of office. Fernandez thus governed carefully by not giving offense to the island's senior politico, nor to his numerous cronies in the courts and military. Fortunately for the country, the new leader was determined to break with the past and its tradition of *caudillismo,* or strongman tactics.

Throughout his four-year tenure, Fernández struggled to put a halt to corruption, which, throughout the Dominican Republic, is rampant. He also embarked on large-scale efforts to promote an open market by privatizing large state-owned industries, such as the utilities, mining, and the national airline. He then sought to increase social spending for better schools, welfare and education to help eradicate the nation's grinding poverty. In June 1998 Fernández also attempted to mend fences with Haiti by becoming the first Dominican president to visit that nation since 1936. But overall his record was mixed, even if important gains were posted, and it did not prevent economic downturns during the 2000 election. On May 16 of that year, the PLD candidate Daniel Medina was defeated by Hipólito Mejía of the Dominican Revolutionary Party, who pledged less emphasis on market reforms and greater spending on social concerns. Fernández, meanwhile, was implicated in a corruption scheme involving misappropriation of $80 million in state funds. He has stridently denied the charges and attributes them to political enemies, but the former president only sullenly cooperated with investigating authorities. Curiously, the affair has only served to boost his national approval rating to 48 percent, higher than it was while he held office.

Further Reading

Gutierrez, Carlos M. *The Dominican Republic: Rebellion and Repression.* New York: Monthly Review Press, 1996.

Hartlyn, Jonathan. *The Struggle for Democratic Politics in the Dominican Republic.* Chapel Hill: University of North Carolina Press, 1998.

Sagas, Ernesto. *Race and Politics in the Dominican Republic.* Gainesville: University Press of Florida, 2000.

Spankos, Anthony P. "The Privatization of Citizenship, Race, and Democracy in the Dominican Republic and Brazil." Unpublished Ph.D. dissertation: University of Massachusetts, Amherst, 2000.

Wucker, Michele. "Democracy Comes to Hispaniola." *World Policy Journal* 13, no. 3 (1996): 80–88.

Finnbogadóttir, Vigdís (1930–   ) *president of Iceland*

Vigdís Finnbogadóttir was born on April 15, 1930, in Reykjavík, Iceland, the daughter of a civil engineer. Icelandic surnames are formed by joining either "dóttir" (daughter) or "sson" (son) to the father's first name, so that, for simplicity's sake, people are usually addressed by their given name. Vigdís was highly educated abroad at the University of Grenoble, the Sorbonne, and the University of Iceland, where she studied French, English, and theater. She returned home to teach French at a local secondary school while also pursuing her passion for the stage. In 1972 Vidgís became director of the Reykjavík Theater Company, where she mounted plays and translated numerous English productions into Icelandic. Basically apolitical, in 1961 and 1974 she organized demonstrations against the U.S. Navy base at Keflavík. In 1980, when presidential elections were scheduled for the summer, several friends challenged the tall, eloquent, intellectual to run for office. She did so on a lark, taking on three veteran male candidates for the office. Icelandic women to that point were notoriously subordinated in a male-dominated culture, and her campaign was initially viewed as a novelty. However, Vigdís campaigned seriously, impressing voters with intelligence and charm, and her popularity spread. When the election transpired on June 30, 1980, she won by amassing 33.8 percent of the vote. Vigdís thus became the first woman president elected to power in a Western republic. Her victory certainly gave Icelandic women a renewed sense of empowerment.

The Icelandic presidency is a largely ceremonial office, whose intent is to promote unity among the islanders. Vigdís, cultured, urbane, and fluent in several languages, was certainly well situated to perform her assigned role. She spent most of her time crisscrossing the island, shaking hands, and giving speeches. On occasion, she was also required to sign bills for the Althing, or legislature. If she vetoed one, it automatically was presented to the electorate in a national referendum. But Vigdís took a special interest in promoting Scandinavian culture abroad. In 1982 she embarked on an extensive traveling tour throughout the United States, which was favorably received. She then paid state visits to U.S. president Ronald Reagan, and later conferred with Britain's prime minister Margaret Thatcher to repair relations after the brief but emotional "Cod War" between their respective nations. Her performance abroad won Vigdís plaudits at home, and, in 1984, she won reelection unopposed.

Vigdís reveled in her role as cultural ambassador, but she also made serious attempts to improve working conditions for Icelandic women. In 1985 women staged an islandwide strike protesting pay inequities and other grievances. Vigdís announced her intention to observe the strike, but government leaders prevailed upon her to first sign a bill that would outlaw strikes by airline stewardesses. She did so only reluctantly and because such action might entail serious economic consequences for the entire island. Nonetheless, Vigdís consciously positioned herself as a symbol of growing equality between the genders. "My message to the girls of the world is this: get educated," she lectured, "never accept a shorter education than your brothers." The Icelandic president also set herself on the world's stage in October 1986, when she hosted disarmament talks between President Reagan and Soviet premier Mikhail Gorbachev. Two years later Vigdís won a landslide victory over her male opponent, and, in 1992, she ran unopposed for the presidency. Through it all she downplayed her newfound celebrity and steadfastly maintained, "The role of the president is to be a symbol for the nation of unity and identity."

Vigdís's popularity can be gauged by the fact that she remained four straight terms in office, a total of 16 years—the longest elected tenure in Iceland's modern history. Vigdís finally stepped down in August 1996 at the end of her fourth term and was replaced by Ólafur Ragnar Grimsson. Her political legacy lies in having elevated the ceremonial office of the presidency and endowing it with greater stature and symbolism than ever before. She also made an indelible impact on the Icelandic political landscape for advancing the cause of women's rights, particularly in the realm of public service. Thereafter she was invited to become chairperson

of the Council of Women World Leaders, which she fulfilled with her usual grace and style. Highly respected abroad and popular at home, Vigdís forever shattered the stereotype of passive Scandinavian women, and she serves as a role model for the rising generation of women political leaders everywhere.

Further Reading
Corgan, Michael T. *Iceland and Its Alliances: Security for a Small State.* Lewiston, N.Y.: Edwin Mellen Press, 2003.

Ellis, Jenny L. "Feminist Politics and the Women's Alliance of Iceland." Unpublished master's thesis, University of Colorado, Denver, 1993.

Koester, David. "Gender Ideology and Nationalism in the Culture and Politics of Iceland." *American Ethnologist* 22 (August 1995): 572–589.

Olafsson, Bjorn G. *Small States in the Global System: Analysis and Illustrations from the Case of Iceland.* Brookfield, Vt.: Ashgate, 1998.

Schneider, Edward. "Icelandic Women on the Brink of Power." *Scandinavian Studies* 64 (Summer 1992): 417–439.

Flores, Carlos (1950–) *president of Honduras*

Carlos Roberto Flores Facusse was born on March 1, 1950 in Honduras, the son of a wealthy newspaper publisher. His father, Oscar A. Flores, was politically active on behalf of the Liberal Party, and his newspaper, *El Pueblo,* became an unofficial party organ. However, this did not sit well with opposition leaders of the National Party, and, in 1956, the elder Flores found himself exiled to Costa Rica. Thoroughly chastised, he returned to Honduras several years later to commence a new publication, *La Tribuna,* which was decidedly noncommittal. Flores, meanwhile, attended American schools in Honduras, and he went on to study industrial engineering at Louisiana State University. He received his master's degree in 1973, took an American wife the following year, and returned to Honduras. There he served on the board of the Central Bank of Honduras for several years and also taught part time at the National University. In 1979 he assisted in founding *La Tribuna* and, following his father's death, he made it an unofficial mouthpiece for the Liberal Party. In 1982 the outspoken Flores was called upon to help draft a new constitution, badly needed since the end of military rule that year. Afterward he stood for a seat in the national congress as a Liberal Party candidate, and he was reelected three times. He came to the attention of President Roberto Suazo Córdoba, who appointed him to his cabinet, 1982–84.

By 1988 Flores felt that his national reputation merited a run for the presidency. He won the Liberal Party primary, backed by his own newspaper, but he subsequently lost to National Party candidate Rafael Leonardo Callejas by 50.9 percent to 43.1 percent. Four years later the Liberals returned to power through the aegis of Roberto Reina, and Flores resumed his legislative career. In 1993 he became president of the National Congress, the second most powerful post in Honduras. In this capacity Flores enacted reforms pertaining to civil service, the judiciary, and the military, all of which enhanced his national standing. In 1997 he again became the Liberal Party nominee for the highest office and campaigned on a neoliberal "New Agenda" platform. This called for greater financial assistance to low-income families (the majority of Hondurans are poor) for education, salaries that keep pace with inflation, and greater emphasis on privatizing inefficient state industries. Flores also pledged to help protect the nation's delicate ecology and also to promote ecotourism. Hondurans had heard such far-reaching promises before, but Flores was especially fortunate that his opponent was Nora Gunera de Melgar. She was the first women presidential candidate ever and widow of the military figure who had overthrown a military government in 1975. Flores beat her easily with 53 percent of the votes cast and was sworn in on January 27, 1998. Mindful of his obligations to the poor, he reiterated that "Honduras is a country that does not tolerate the misery of underdevelopment."

Flores had assumed office with an ambitious agenda for reform, but in October 1998 the country was staggered by the onset of Hurricane Mitch, one of the century's deadliest storms. It left over 5,000 people dead and 1.5 million refugees in its wake, along with damage estimated at $3 billion. His priorities now dramatically rearranged, Flores immediately adopted a more transparent process for relief funds to arrive and be accounted for. This anticorruption measure worked, and within months the country received and processed over $600 million in assistance. The government's newfounded success at coordinating massive national reconstruction was applauded internationally and encouraged Flores to resume his original agenda. This included judicial and penal reforms, creation of an anticorruption

commission, and establishment of a new independent supreme court. More important, he shepherded in new laws eliminating the position of army commander in chief, thereby ensuring civilian control of the military. Through this expedient Flores finally cemented the much-needed transition from military to civilian dominance in political affairs. He also advocated a big package of fiscal adjustments and privatization to make Honduras more attractive to foreign investors.

The Honduran constitution limits its president to one four-year term in office, and Flores made preparations to step down accordingly. Just hours beforehand, however, he raised eyebrows in Washington, D.C., by unilaterally extending diplomatic ties to FIDEL CASTRO's Cuba—these had been severed since 1961. Previously, in November 2001, Liberal Party candidate Rafael Pineda Ponce had been defeated by National Party nominee Ricardo Maduro Joest. Flores finally concluded his generally successful term in office on January 27, 2002, and Maduro succeeded him. The former executive has since resumed his career as a high-ranking adviser to the Liberal Party, and waxes proudly about his accomplishments in office. "People have learned to respect the constitution as a permanent guarantee of principles," he stated. "They have the conviction that the system works, that the government will respond to their expectations."

Further Reading

Karl, Terry L. *Central America in the Twenty-first Century: The Prospects for a Democratic Region.* Notre Dame, Ind.: University of Notre Dame Press, 1994.

Ruhl, Mark J. "Redefining Civil-Military Relations in Honduras." *Journal of Interamerican Studies and World Affairs* 38 (Spring 1998): 33–67.

Schulz, Donald E. *The United States, Honduras, and the Crisis in Central America.* Boulder, Colo.: Westview Press, 1994.

Waddell, Rick. *In War's Shadow: Waging Peace in Central America.* New York: Ivy Books, 1993.

Wolfson, Samuel P. "Past Performance and Future Viability of Honduran Political Parties." Unpublished master's thesis, University of Texas, Austin, 1977.

Flores, Francisco (1959–) *president of El Salvador*

Francisco Guillermo Flores Pérez was born in Santa Ana, El Salvador, on October 17, 1959, the son of a successful lawyer. He was educated abroad at the University of Massachusetts, Amherst, and also received a graduate degree in philosophy at World University, California. Intent upon broadening his global perspectives, Flores next visited India throughout the 1980s to study philosophy and mysticism, although he, like the majority of his countrymen, remains a practicing Catholic. He then rounded out the decade by lecturing at the Central America University and José Matías Delgado University. Flores commenced his political career in 1990, when he became a governmental adviser. Four years later he gained election to the National Assembly as part of the conservative National Republican Alliance Party (ARENA). Eloquent and forceful, Flores rose to become head of the ARENA congressional delegation and ultimately the assembly speakership. There he acquired a reputation for deflecting confrontation and building consensus. In 1998 Flores stole a march on the opposition by declaring his presidential candidacy months before rival parties had nominated theirs. He then waged a carefully worded, moderate campaign, which studiously avoided the polarizing rhetoric of past elections. The Salvadoran electorate responded positively to his centrist positions, and on March 7, 1999, he won a landslide victory with 52 percent of the vote. His nearest competitor, Facundo Guardado of the left-leaning Frente Farabundo Martí para la Liberación Nacional (FMLN) barely received 29 percent. Upon taking his oath of office on June 1, 1999, the 40-year-old Flores became the youngest president in all the Americas.

The fact that Flores obtained his quest with a minimum of controversy or bloodshed was a welcome departure from recent El Salvadoran politics. Since 1980 an internecine civil war had raged between various military-backed regimes and FMLN guerrillas. The former responded with repression of poor peasants and death squads to eliminate opponents to their rule. The FMLN, meanwhile, aided and abetted by the Marxist dictatorship in neighboring Nicaragua, commenced a bloody campaign of terrorism throughout the countryside. El Salvador grew so destabilized that the U.S. government intervened with money and military advisers to stave off what U.S. officials perceived as communist-inspired subversion. By the time fighting concluded on January 16, 1992, with the signing of a United Nations–backed peace accord, an estimated 75,000 civilians had died. The national economy was also in tatters while the plight of El Salvador's poor, who constitute the overwhelming majority of the population, had never been bleaker.

Flores inherited a nation that is among the poorest in Central America. An estimated 50 percent of the population live below the poverty line, while unemployment hovers around 30 percent. Such social dislocation and hardship has resulted in concomitant increases in crime rates, among the highest in Latin America. He therefore campaigned on a theme of addressing poverty and crime. To stimulate the economy, Flores aspires to supply loans to small and medium businesses, and to shore up El Salvador's crumbling national infrastructure. In November 2000 he also authorized its national currency, the colón, to be fixed to the U.S. dollar, a move calculated to lower interest rates and attract foreign investment. He also pledged to provide greater access to health care, housing, and education to improve the lot of most citizens. The government is further committed to remedying air and water pollution, which is extremely high and forms an increasing risk to the environment and national health. To fight crime, Flores brooked no delay in overhauling police administration and practices, including imposition of tougher sentencing and penal reform. Swift action on all these fronts is essential if El Salvador is to maintain its recently acquired political stability and allow democratic traditions to take root.

In terms of foreign relations, Flores has also been surprisingly active as a mediator. When tensions arose between Honduras and Nicaragua over simmering border disputes, in March 2001, he met with the presidents of both nations to diffuse the crisis. His intervention had the desired effect and the issue has since been referred to the International Court of Justice in The Hague. El Salvador's discomfiture has also been exacerbated by several devastating earthquakes throughout the spring of 2001. An estimated 1,000 lives were lost and another 1 million people were left homeless. Flores then took to the diplomatic front and issued an urgent request for aid from abroad. "I want to tell the residents of the capital that I am near you," he assured them, "maintaining a continuous alert with a monitoring operation." Flores is limited by the constitution to one term in office. Should his reform efforts exert positive effects on his beleaguered nation, there is a good chance his ARENA party will capture the presidency again in 2003.

Further Reading

Geyer, Georgie A. "The Amazing New 'Center' in Central America." *Washington Quarterly* 27 (Summer 1999): 197–222.

Spence, Jack, Mike Lanchin, and Geoff Thale. *From Elections to Earthquakes: Reform and Participation in Postwar El Salvador.* Cambridge, Mass.: Hemisphere Initiatives, 2001.

Stanley, William D. *The Protection Racket State: Elite Politics, Military Extortion, and Civil War in El Salvador.* Philadelphia: Temple University Press, 1996.

Wood, Elizabeth J. *Forging Democracy from Below: Insurgent Traditions in South America and El Salvador.* Cambridge: Cambridge University Press, 2001.

Fox, Vicente (1942–) *president of Mexico*

Vicente Fox Quesada was born in Mexico City on July 2, 1942, the son of a prosperous rancher. He was raised on the family's sprawling estate in the northern Mexican state of Guanajuato before attending the Universidad Iberoamericano. He also studied at the University of Wisconsin, Madison, acquiring fluency in English. By 1964 Fox had received his degree in business administration and was hired by the American firm Coca-Cola as a route salesman. Fox, who stands over six and a half feet tall, proved himself a dynamic, disciplined individual with an appetite for work and indomitable will to succeed. He rose steadily through the corporate ladder on competence alone, and, by 1975, he was the company's chief executive in Mexico. As a ranking corporate executive, Fox was routinely summoned to the Mexican presidential palace, in his own words, "so that we could hear a lot of foolishness." This experience and the mindless bureaucracy regulating business left him disillusioned, and he began entertaining political aspirations of his own. The turning point came in 1979 when, by virtue of his very success, Fox was slated to be transferred from Mexico City to Miami, Florida, as head of Coca-Cola's Latin American operations. Rather than leave his country, Fox quit and returned home to manage the family business of making cowboy boots and exporting vegetables. Shortly after, government mishandling of the economy led to a devaluation of the peso and the national economy sank. The hardships endured by Fox and many other struggling small businessmen convinced them that the government was hopelessly corrupt. They also believed that national reform was essential for survival.

Since 1929, Mexican national, state, and local politics had been dominated by the only legitimate political party, the Institutional Revolutionary Party, or PRI. It was a study in entrenched, political power, writ large. During a reign of power that lasted 71 years, the leftist-leaning PRI had become mired in corruption, yet unchallenged in the political field. This was due to a closely woven net of special interest groups that were manipulated to produce majorities during periodic national "elections." Numerous political killings and "disappearances" were also commonplace and went unpunished. So complete and far-reaching was the PRI's grasp, and so complete their overt skill at rigging elections, that the majority of Mexicans shrugged at any notion of change. Fox, however, was one among a handful of individuals willing to challenge the system head-on. The decision surprised many, even in his own family. "I never, ever thought I would be in politics," he confessed. "My father told us that nothing would offend him more, because only thieves and crooks go into politics here." Nonetheless, in 1988 Fox ran for congress as a member of the new, conservative National Action Party (PAN) and won. Three years later he made an unsuccessful bid at toppling the PRI governorship of his native Guanajuato and lost in an election tainted by widespread fraud. Undeterred, Fox resumed his quest for national office in 1995 and, thanks to a spate of election reforms recently initiated, he won handily. However, like many Mexicans, he remained distressed by the country's inherent economic instability. This was the product of both cronyism and mismanagement at the highest levels, along with fraudulent election practices that flaunted the will of the people. Having gained considerable skill in managing political campaigns, and gauging the country ripe for change, Fox announced his candidacy for president in 2000.

The tall, swaggering businessman cut a figure unlike any candidate Mexico had ever seen. He toured the country, resplendent in cowboy boots and Stetson hat, and vehemently denouncing the PRI for their institutionalized graft. And, unlike numerous PRI nominees before him, who were urbane and studied abroad, Fox portrayed himself as a son of Mexico, who was raised, educated, and conducted a successful business at home. Millions of disenchanted Mexicans, desperate for change, listened earnestly and rallied to his side. On July 2, 2000, they overwhelmingly delivered Fox the election, thereby ending the seven-decade dominance of the PRI. A corner had been turned in the history of Mexico, and the political landscape forever altered.

Fox, first and foremost a businessman, stressed the need for economic reform for Mexico to become more competitive in the emerging global market. He hoped to transform his nation, the United States, and Canada into a European-style free market with a common currency and free-ranging labor across international boundaries. One of his more controversial proposals would be the eventual opening of borders between the United States and Mexico, along with relaxed immigration procedures. He also sought to promote efficiency by eliminating bureaucracy, privatizing state-owned industries, and distributing government-sponsored loans to assist farmers and small businessmen. Fox then determined to open a new front on the war against drug trafficking, a problem of epidemic proportions. He authorized that the notoriously ineffective Federal Judicial Police be abolished and replaced with a new, American-style Federal Agency of Investigation. Finally, Fox extended his hand to the indigenous Indian peoples of the southern Mexican state of Chiapas, where armed rebellions had flared for nearly a decade. To placate the self-styled Zapatista movement, he closed down numerous army checkpoints, removed troops from the area, and granted greater rights and autonomy to Indian regions. And, as a hedge against future corruption, Fox championed new constitutional amendments that allowed the Mexican congress to impeach and remove any president guilty of political crimes. Public accountability had arrived with a vengeance.

The September 11, 2001, attacks on the World Trade Center immediately impacted U.S.–Mexican relations because of fear that terrorists were slipping into the country over their mutual border. Fox conferred closely with President GEORGE W. BUSH later that month and pledged his fullest cooperation in the fight against organized terror. "We have strengthened our mechanisms related to immigration so that we make sure that Mexican territory is absolutely not used by terrorists," he declared in an interview. But while marching in lock step with the United States on issues of global security, Fox is careful not to appear pandering to the Americans and to be "his own man." In February 2002, he visited Cuba to confer with aging dictator FIDEL CASTRO, with whom Mexico enjoys a long tradition of political and economic relations. He was also greatly pressured by his own party to meet with seven of Castro's leading opponents and press the issue of human rights upon them. Through such dialogue, Fox hopes that "Cuba would come closer to the standards of human rights and of democracy that day by day help make things more secure, not only in Latin America, but in the rest of the world."

Vicente Fox *(Embassy of Mexico)*

Further Reading

Ard, Michael J. *An Eternal Struggle: How the National Action Party Transformed Mexican Politics.* Westport, Conn.: Praeger, 2003.

Camp, Roderic Ai. *Politics in Mexico: The Democratic Transformation.* New York: Oxford University Press, 2003.

Gutman, Matthew C. *The Romance of Democracy: Compliant Defiance in Contemporary Mexico.* Berkeley: University of California Press, 2002.

Hernandez, Juan, ed. *Vicente Fox: Dreams, Challenges, and Threats.* Dallas: University of Texas Press, 1998.

Hodges, Donald L., and Daniel R. Gandy. *Mexico: The End of the Revolution.* Westport, Conn.: Praeger, 2002.

La Botz, Dan. "Mexico in Transition . . . to What?" *New Politics* 8 (Summer 2001): 108–21.

Rodriguez, Victoria E. *Women in Contemporary Mexican Politics.* Austin: University of Texas Press, 2003.

Teutli, Otero G. *The Mexican 2000 Presidential Election: Lectures.* Austin: University of Texas Press, 2000.

Franco, Itamar (1930–) *president of Brazil*

Itamar Augusto Franco was born on June 28, 1930, off the coast of Bahia, Brazil. However, he was raised in the state of Minas Gerais and considers himself a native. Franco earned a degree from the Juiz de Fora Engineering School in 1958, where he was elected president of the school debating club. By 1960 he evinced an interest in politics and twice ran unsuccessfully for the mayorship of Juiz de Fora. Franco persevered and, in 1966, he finally won as a candidate of the Brazilian Democratic Movement (PMDB), ushering in a period of public works construction and other major improvements. Good performance in office led to his reelection in 1972, and, two years later, he successfully stood for a seat in the national senate. Franco again performed admirably, and quickly established himself as an opponent of the prevailing military regime. He remained a senator for 15 years, demonstrating an uncanny ability to carry Minas Gerais by large margins. Largely for this reason, presidential aspirant FERNANDO COLLOR DE MELLO tapped Franco as his vice presidential running mate in 1989. It proved an odd choice, for the two men were intellectually and temperamentally poles apart. But with Franco on the ticket, as anticipated, Collor carried Minas Gerais and went on to win the election.

As vice president, Franco enjoyed an ambivalent relationship with his superior. The two men barely spoke and Franco was never consulted in major decisions. In 1992 Collor became ensnared by a corruption scandal and resigned from office while Franco became an interim executive. He was formally sworn in as president on December 29, 1992, whereby his limitations in high office became immediately apparent. Franco, a well-intentioned, scrupulously honest politician, was also a fiery nationalist who either attracted or repelled voters through unpredictable antics. His two-year tenure in office proved uneventful, save for a bizarre episode in which he convinced the German firm Volkswagen to resume construction of his favorite car, the outdated Beetle. The company obliged but ultimately canceled their decision after three years. The one positive decision undertaken by Franco was his selection of FERNANDO CARDOSO as finance minister, who, in this capacity, engineered the successful Real Plan for stabilizing the Brazilian economy. It worked spectacularly and Cardoso became both the most popular politician in the country and a leading candidate for president in October 1994. Franco was subsequently defeated by Cardoso in a bitter campaign, resenting that he did not receive credit for the Real Plan and that, in the tradition of Brazilian politics, he could not name his successor. Thereafter he treated the new executive with disdain bordering on contempt.

After leaving office in late 1994, Franco was magnanimously given an appointment as ambassador to Portugal and the Organization of American States (OAS). He served four years without distinction, save for his unlimited capacity for complaining, and, in 1998, he returned home to run for governor of Minas Gerais. Franco won handily and has since acquired one of the most quixotic reputations of any modern Brazilian politician. Still smarting over Cardoso's success, he assumed power during a time of fiscal retrenchment and staggering national debt. In January 1999, Franco summarily declared a 90-day moratorium on payments toward $8 billion owed the federal government. This act, coming on the heels of the Asian Currency Crisis, sent the national economy downward and the currency had to be devalued. In November Franco became aware of government plans to privatize the Furnas Cetrais Eletricas hydroelectric plant in Minas Gerais to help pay down the debt. Franco strongly opposes privatization of national assets and he threatened to change the course waters supplying it, declaring: "We will never hand over our rivers." Franco was further angered when Cardoso coasted easily to reelection in November 1999, and he took additional measures to underscore his displeasure. By June 2001 Brazil was suffering from one of its worse recorded droughts, which impeded electricity production and forced the government to ration power. Franco, however, legally challenged the plan, declaring he would take steps to protect the consumers of his state and keep the electricity flowing.

The headstrong and unpredictable Franco still retains a measure of popularity in Minas Gerais, probably more in spite of his erratic behavior than because of it. In 2000 he encouraged the Landless Peasants Movement to protest at a farm in Minas Gerais owned by President Cardoso's family. When he refused to assign state police to protect the property, Cardoso dispatched military forces to guard it himself. This, in turn, convinced the governor that he was the object of an impending military coup and he ordered the police to conduct military-style maneuvers. He also barricaded the governor's palace and begun comparing himself to Chile's ill-fated president Salvatore Allende. Whatever his motives, Franco's personal war has assumed the dimensions of a national soap opera. It may not have ruined the governor's reputation yet, but certainly adds nothing to his stature.

Further Reading

Abers, Rebecca. *Inventing Local Democracy: Grassroots Politics in Brazil.* Boulder, Colo.: Lynne Rienner Publishers, 2000.

Ames, Barry. *The Deadlock of Democracy in Brazil.* Ann Arbor: University of Michigan Press, 2001.

Samuel, David. *Ambassadors of the State: Federalism, Ambition, and Congressional Politics in Brazil.* New York: Cambridge University Press, 2002.

Tendler, Judith. *Good Government in the Tropics.* Baltimore: Johns Hopkins University Press, 1998.

Weyland, Kurt. "The Rise and Fall of President Collor and Its Impact on Brazilian Democracy." *Journal of Interamerican Studies and World Affairs* 35 no. 1 (1993): 1–37.

Frei, Eduardo (1942–) *president of Chile*

Eduardo Frei Ruiz-Tagle was born on June 24, 1942, in Santiago, Chile, into comfortable middle-class surroundings. He pursued civil engineering at the University of Chile and in 1968 ventured to Italy to study management procedures with the ENI group of Milan. He returned home as a specialist in hydraulics and eventually became a wealthy businessman. Frei first became interested in politics when he joined the Christian Democratic Party, to which his father, Eduardo Frei Montalva, belonged. In 1964 Frei campaigned on his father's behalf during the latter's successful run for the presidency, and his father remained in office until 1970. That fateful year Frei Montalva was succeeded by Socialist Party candidate Salvador Allende, who was brutally overthrown by the Chilean military in 1971. A new ruler, General Augusto Pinochet, imposed a right-wing dictatorship characterized by the "disappearance" of over 3,000 communists and dissenters. Frei, meanwhile, had been elected to the Senate in 1989, where he worked to defeat Pinochet's plebiscite for another six years in power. In 1990 Christian Democrat PATRICIO AYLWIN became the first democratically elected leader in two decades, while Frei continued on in the Senate. He rose

to party chairmanship in December 1992 with 70 percent of the vote by drawing largely upon the memory of his popular father. But Frei, in many respects, was an unlikely candidate for high office, being somewhat soft-spoken and shy. However, his candidacy was well received by the electorate, and on December 11, 1993, he succeeded Aylwin by garnering 64 percent of votes cast. Frei's victory also represented the first peaceful transfer of power from one leader to another in over two decades. "We will create the room and the opportunity for the poor and disadvantaged of this country to grow," he promised. "We will reach the 21st century as a developed nation with humanity and solidarity."

Though victorious, Frei realized that Chile's newfound democracy was still precarious, and the military maintained an ominous presence by hovering in the background. The price for returning democracy entailed making Pinochet and other military figures senators for life, hence immune from legal prosecution. But Frei also inherited a robust economy, growing at 6 percent per year, that gave him some leverage for addressing the nation's sizable poor community. He thus began a delicate balancing act with the middle and upper classes to assist the downtrodden. No dramatic programs were enacted, just better access to an increasing number of jobs and, occasionally, better wages. Throughout his single, six-year term, Frei did his best to alleviate poverty and was equally concerned with preserving and expanding the democratization process. In March 2000 he was succeeded by RICARDO LAGOS, the nation's first Socialist president since 1970, who assumed power without interference from the military. But before stepping down, Frei called for resumption of talks between human rights groups and military circles to resolve the fate of Chile's infamous "missing." He maintained that honest dialogue is the only way to preserve peace and promote national reconciliation.

Frei's tenure in office was basically successful and uneventful, save for one potentially explosive foreign episode. On October 16, 1998, General Pinochet, still a senator, was arrested in Britain on an international warrant issued from Spain. Spanish judges sought to try the former dictator for complicity in murder involving the lives of Spanish citizens who had vanished under his regime. This event sparked waves of anger in Chile, where Pinochet still commands great respect and popularity. Frei, regardless of his personal feelings, felt tremendous pressure to condemn what was held as an egregious slap at national sovereignty. "Would a Chilean court be allowed to start a trial for abuses that occurred under the Spanish authoritarian regime?" he asked, referring to General Francisco Franco. Frei formally protested Spanish claims to extraterritoriality over the next two years until the British government released Pinochet on January 11, 2000, for health reasons. The aged dictator returned home to thunderous applause from his supporters and quietly retired. Frei remained nonetheless deeply committed to expanding democracy throughout Latin America and, in November 1996, he hosted various heads of state, including Cuba's notorious FIDEL CASTRO, at a conference. "Today it's no longer possible to speak of two democracies," he insisted. "There is only one legitimate one, one that represents respect for human rights and is governed by the rule of the majority in sincere elections." All present, including Castro, then signed a statement declaring free elections, freedom of expression, and freedom of association as essential for democracy.

Frei has since returned to politics as a senator for life. In April 2001 he accompanied former president Andrés Zaldívar Larraín to Beijing, China, where they met with President JIANG ZEMIN. The Chinese executive then toasted his Chilean opposites, and he thanked them for their efforts in promoting the close ties presently enjoyed by their respective nations.

Further Reading

Haagh, Louise. *Citizenship, Labor Markets, and Democratization: Chile and the Modern Sequence.* New York: Palgrave, 2002.

Hawkins, Darren G. *International Rights and Authoritarian Rule in Chile.* Lincoln: University of Nebraska Press, 2002.

Munck, Geraldo. "Democratic Stability and Its Limits: An Analysis of Chile's 1993 Elections." *Journal of Interamerican Studies and World Affairs* 36, no. 2 (1994): 1–38.

Pollack, Marcelo. *The New Right in Chile, 1973–1997.* New York: St. Martin's Press, 1999.

Stechina, Viviana. "The Policy-Making Style of the Chilean Government of President Frei." *Ibero Americana* 30, no. 1 (2000): 31–52.

Fujimori, Alberto (1938–   ) *president of Peru*

Alberto Fujimori was born in Lima, Peru, on July 28, 1938, the son of Japanese immigrant farm workers. He was educated locally and raised as a Roman Catholic before attending the prestigious National Agrarian University. He received his degree there in agronomics before pursuing graduate studies at the University of Wisconsin, Madison. Fujimori then returned to Peru to teach at his alma mater for several years. He acquitted himself competently and was next appointed rector of his school and, subsequently, president of the Association of University Rectors. However, by 1988, the Peruvian economy experienced pronounced downturns and Fujimori, like many academics, sought greater public discourse on the nation's problems. Accordingly, he starred in a nationally televised talk show entitled "Getting Together," in which he came across as eloquent and well informed. Public reaction proved positive and, in 1990, to the surprise of many, the bespeckled former professor announced his candidacy for the presidency.

Fujimori's campaign, simply titled "Change 90," was unorthodox in many respects. First, he did not belong to any established party and deliberately fashioned himself as a protest candidate. Second, he flaunted his Japanese ancestry to underscore the fact he was unconnected to the political status quo. In fact, he claimed to be descended from samurai warriors and frequently campaigned in a kimono while brandishing a sword. Fujimori's status as a novice and his low-key campaign contrasted sharply with the lavish, high-visibility efforts of Mario Vargas Llosa, the political favorite. However, the opposition underestimated Fujimori's appeal to the majority of Amerindian voters, who traditionally felt alienated by the political process. They turned out in droves to hear him speak and show their support. In two rounds of voting in April and June 1998, he soundly defeated Vargas Llosa with 37 percent of the vote. Fujimori, inaugurated on July 28, 1990, thus became the first Peruvian head of state of Japanese descent.

The new leader inherited an economic and political morass. Fiscal mismanagement left Peru with staggering hyperinflationary rates of nearly 8,000 percent. Worse, the countryside was engulfed by a communist-inspired guerrilla group, the so-called Shining Path, who wreaked widespread terror. Security efforts were further compounded by the widespread drug trade inherent to the region. Peru enjoys the dubious distinction of harboring half the world's coca production, which is subsequently refined into cocaine and exported abroad. Murder and rampant corruption invariably follow in its wake. Fortunately for Peru, Fujimori proved decisive in implementing badly needed reforms. Intent on promoting free-market economics, he deregulated and decentralized business, slashed government operating costs, cut tariffs, and ordered state-owned utilities to raise their prices to profitable market rates. Consumers reeled under the inevitable price hikes and unemployment, but within a year soaring inflation rates had been reduced to single digits. Moreover, the government's aggressive embrace of privatization led to increases in efficiency that, when coupled with foreign investments, resulted in a 12 percent growth rate—the world's highest. Economically, it was a bravura performance and, in the 1995 election, Fujimori handily defeated Javier Pérez de Cuéllar, the noted former UN secretary-general, with 64 percent of the vote.

Fujimori proved less successful in respecting democratic institutions, and his brand of leadership came to be regarded as authoritarian. Angered by the slow pace of legislation, in April 1992 he dissolved the Peruvian congress and the judiciary, and he assumed emergency dictatorial powers. He then authorized a constituent assembly that rewrote the constitution, enabling him to run for a third term. Meanwhile, Peruvian security forces finally succeeded in crushing the Shining Path guerrillas by capturing their leader, Abimael Guzmán. In April 1997, rebels belonging to the militant Tupac Amaru faction captured the Japanese embassy, but all were later killed when military forces stormed it and freed the hostages. The war-weary public willingly overlooked Fujimori's dictatorial tendencies and welcomed the arrival of peace and prosperity. On April 9, 2000, they overwhelmingly reelected Fujimori over ALEJANDRO TOLEDO by 49 percent to 40.2 percent. It then appeared that Fujimori's political career—and legacy—were secure.

Unfortunately for Fujimori, he became ensnared in a major political scandal when security chief Vladimiro Montesinos was videotaped bribing an opposition member of Congress in 2001. Allegations of corruption then spread to the president, who was visiting Japan at the time. On November 20, 2001, Fujimori resigned from office and claimed diplomatic immunity. The Peruvian government has since charged him with complicity in several politically inspired murders and has issued a warrant for his arrest. However, because the respective countries lack extradition arrangements, Japan refuses to hand him over to Peruvian authorities. Fujimori presently resides in Japan, professing his innocence, and lecturing at Takushoku University in Tokyo. "I am no fugitive and hide from nobody," the former president insists. "I go out like every free citizen." The entire matter has been referred to Interpol, the international law enforcement agency.

Further Reading

Crabtree, John, and J. J. Thomas. *Fujimori's Peru: The Political Economy.* London: Institute of Latin American Studies, 1998.

Gorriti, Ellenbogen, Gustave. *The Shining Path: A History of Millenarian War in Peru.* Chapel Hill: University of North Carolina Press, 1999.

Klaren, Peter. *Peru: Society and Nation in the Andes.* New York: Oxford University Press, 2000.

McGhee, Douglas A. "From Demos to Democradura: Fujimorismo and Democracy in Peru." Unpublished Ph.D. dissertation, University of Utah, 2000.

Vargas Llosa, Alvaro. *The Madness of Things Peruvian: Democracy under Siege.* New Brunswick, N.J.: Transaction Pubs., 1994.

G

Gatti, Gabriele (1953–) *San Marino secretary of state*

Gabriele Gatti was born in San Marino on March 27, 1953. His country is among the world's tiniest, being situated in northern Italy about 100 miles north of Rome. Its total area is slightly under 20 square miles and hosts a population of 25,000 citizens. Curiously, San Marino can trace its founding back to 350 A.D., and the country also claims to be the world's oldest functioning republic. Its unwritten constitution was derived from statutes drawn up in 1660, which are still in force today. This legislation places administration of San Marino in the hands of the Grand and General Council of 60 members, while the appointed office of secretary of state functions more or less in the manner of a prime minister. San Marino enjoys close cultural, linguistic, religious, and economic ties with Italy, but otherwise the nation enjoys complete sovereignty and independence. As such it is the sole survivor of numerous small states that dotted the Italian Peninsula prior to national unification in the middle of the 19th century. Politically, San Marino has been alternately run and controlled by either a leftist coalition of Socialists and Communists or an awkward alliance between Socialists and Christian Democrats. The 1998 election gave rise to a new party, the Sanmarinese Progressive Party, which further splinters the polity of this micro-democracy.

Gatti studied literature and philosophy while in college, and he gained election to the Grand and General Council in 1978 as a Christian Democrat. In July 1985 he advanced to serve as party secretary-general. Up until then San Marino had been governed by a leftist coalition, which collapsed when the Communists withdrew after foreign policy disputes. The Socialists then countered by striking up an alliance with the Christian Democrats. Elections held on May 28, 1988 then gave the Christian Democrats a solid majority on the council, and Gatti gained appointment as secretary of state for foreign and political affairs. Ten years later voters again handed the conservatives a controlling majority, and Gatti continued as national leader. He expected to hold this position until the next round of elections in June 2003.

As a conservative, Gatti proved instrumental in adoption of policies favoring small businesses and private enterprise, including generous tax exemptions for up to 10 years. However, he is eager that San Marino be fully integrated into the greater Western European economy and pushed hard for admittance into the European Union (EU). The country has also sought greater economic freedom from Italy, and, in 1987, its central bank acquired the right to conduct business directly with international lending institutions, rather than through the Bank of Italy alone.

In terms of foreign policy, Gatti, has maintained San Marino's tradition of strict adherence to neutrality, which has kept it virtually free from war for 17 centuries. It nonetheless maintains consulates in over 50 countries and enjoys observer status at the United Nations, which it joined in 1992.

Further Reading

Duursma, Jorri. *Self-Determination, Statehood, and International Relations of Micro-states: The Cases of Liechtenstein, San Marino, Monaco, Andorra, and the Vatican City.* New York: Cambridge University Press, 1996.

Gaviria, César (1947–) *president of Colombia*

César Augusto Gaviria Trujillo was born on March 31, 1947, in Pereira, Colombia, the son of a coffee grower and occasional journalist working for the Liberal Party. He excelled as a student and graduated first in his class from the prestigious University of Los Andes in 1970 with an economics degree. That same year he commenced politicking at the age of 23 by winning a Pereira city council seat for the Liberal Party. Gaviria's reputation for competence spread and, in 1971, President Misael Pastrana Borrero appointed him assistant director of the National Planning Department. By 1974 he had won a seat in the House of Representatives, and the following year he gained appointment as mayor of his hometown. A new president, Julio César Turbay Ayala, then allowed Gaviria to serve as his vice minister of economic development, 1978–80. He subsequently resumed his legislative career in the Colombian congress, and he was elected by a bipartisan majority to the post of House president. Concurrently, Gaviria became active in the field of journalism, and he contributed many columns and commentaries to regional and national newspapers. In 1985 Gaviria helped orchestrate the successful campaign that brought Liberal Party candidate Virgilio Barco Vargas to the presidency, and he was rewarded with the post of finance minister. Here Gaviria made history by completely overhauling the creaking Colombian tax code, improving collection procedures, and exempting low-income citizens from filing income tax reports. In light of his impressive performance, Barco then named Gaviria minister of government. His most useful work was in convincing the M-19 guerrilla group to disarm while inviting several of its leaders to join the

government. In 1988, while Barco was out of the country, Gaviria assumed the duties of president and managed to negotiate the release of a kidnapped political candidate.

In February 1989, Gaviria resigned from the Barco administration to serve as campaign manager for Liberal Party candidate Luis Carlos Galán, who campaigning on a "get-tough" policy toward Colombia's notorious drug cartel bosses. For this reason Galán was brutally assassinated on August 18, 1989, and his family convinced Gaviria to take up the mantle and run for the party nomination. He did exactly that, and, in March 1990, Gaviria won the presidential election with a 47 percent plurality. Sworn into office on August 7, 1990, he became Colombia's youngest-ever executive officer. He assumed power at a time of mounting national apathy toward politics and escalating violence connected to the rising tide of drug trafficking.

Gaviria brooked no delay in tackling the crime problem and did so on a constitutional basis. Previously, the Colombian judicial system had grown so remiss that criminal drug smugglers had to be extradited to the United States for prosecution, which only intensified resistance to law enforcement. Gaviria countered by constitutionally ending this procedure and offered an amnesty to drug smugglers: if they surrendered and confessed their crimes, they would not be extradited abroad and would receive reduced sentences. This had the desired effect and many formerly intractable fugitives capitulated, notably Jorge Luis Ochoa of the notorious Medellín cocaine cartel. Colombia was also faced with ongoing insurgencies by armed left-wing guerrillas. Again, Gaviria convinced many of them to turn in their arms in exchange for amnesty, and allowed senior members to serve in government ministries. Such an approach did not placate every group, but a significant number of rebels did disarm and surrender. During his final year in office, the constitutional court ruled in favor of legalizing small amounts of hard drugs for personal use. Gaviria was aghast at the decision, and he immediately signed decrees outlawing possession of any drugs whatsoever. He also lent his weight to a constitutional amendment banning drug use, and he called upon church leaders, professionals, and student leaders to support it.

The Colombian constitution restricts presidents to a single term in office, and, in August 1994, Gaviria stepped down. Thereafter he was elected secretary-general of the 35-member Organization of American States (OAS), the world's oldest regional alliance. In his usual fashion, Gaviria completely overhauled the OAS infrastructure, slashing staffs by 30 percent and investing the savings into better narcotics control. He also worked hard to promote regional trade and economic liberalization in all the member states. In June 1999 Gaviria was reelected to another five-year term as head of the OAS, and he pledged to strive to deepen democratic values, human rights, integrated economies and to directly confront a new menace—international terrorism. In January 2002 he declared: "Our challenge is to maintain the political will to make the fight against terrorism a top hemispheric priority—beyond the emotional level, which is sometimes volatile and transitory." Gaviria is expected to remain head of the OAS until the summer of 2004.

Further Reading

Aviles, William. "Globalization, Democracy, and Civil-Military Relations in Colombia's Neoliberal State." Unpublished Ph.D. dissertation, University of California, Riverside, 2001.

Gaviria, César. "The Future of the Hemisphere." *Journal of Interamerican Studies and World Affairs* 39 (Spring 1997): 5–12.

Kline, Harvey F. *State Building and Conflict Resolution in Colombia, 1986–1994.* Tuscaloosa: University of Alabama Press, 1999.

Richani, Nazih. *Systems of Violence: The Political Economy of War and Peace: Colombia.* New York: State University of New York Press, 2002.

Tokatlian, Juan G. "Colombia at War: The Search for a Peace Diplomacy." *International Journal of Politics, Culture, and Society* 14 (Winter 2000): 333–362.

Gayoom, Maumoon Abdul (1937–)

president of the Maldives

Maumoon Abdul Gayoom was born in Malé, capital of the Maldives, on December 29, 1937, a son of the attorney general. His homeland consists of an attenuated series of 1,192 coral atolls scattered 300 miles southeast of India. Formerly a British possession, the Maldives acquired political independence in 1965, and three years later it abandoned a traditional Islamic sultanate in favor of a constitution that enshrines representative government. Gayoom was educated locally before attending Al-

Azhar University in Cairo, Egypt, where he majored in Islamic studies, philosophy, and law. After receiving an advanced degree from American University in Cairo, he proceeded to lecture at Abdullah Bayero College, Nigeria, before returning home in 1973. The following year Gayoom entered public service, eventually holding a succession of posts, including manager of the republic's shipping department and director of the telephone department. By 1974 Gayoom's competent performance landed him a position as special undersecretary within the prime minister's office. In this capacity he was sent abroad as deputy ambassador to Sri Lanka and, in 1976, as the Maldives's permanent representative to the United Nations. He returned the following year as minister of transport and, in 1978, Gayoom was nominated as a presidential candidate by the Citizen's Majlis, or parliament. In recognition of his competence as an administrator, he was reelected by wide margins in 1983, 1988, 1993, and 1998. In this way Gayoom has become

Maumoon Abdul Gayoom *(High Commission of the Maldives)*

renowned as one of Southeast Asia's most durable national figures.

Once in office, Gayoom distinguished himself for his activist style of leadership and commitment to democracy. He constantly visited the various atolls, attended public functions, and otherwise maintained high public visibility. His primary concern while in office has been expansion of the economy, for the Maldives remains one of the world's poorest nations. Fishing is the mainstay of the national economy, and he has taken steps to modernize the fishing fleet while simultaneously preserving these natural resources. He also greatly enhanced the Maldives as a region for tourism, which now comprises a significant portion of the gross national product. Consequently, related businesses such as banking, construction, and the airlines have all flourished as well. Other projects have been initiated to improve communication and transportation between the 20 groups of atolls comprising this disparate nation.

Despite Gayoom's accomplishments and his popular appeal, his tenure in office has been marked by no less than three coup attempts against him. Most have been minor efforts by individual military officers and easily diffused. However, the most serious attempt occurred in 1988 when a disgruntled businessman hired scores of armed Sri Lankan guerrillas as mercenaries. They stormed the island and chased the president into hiding. Gayoom, fortunately, managed to place a phone call to Indian prime minister Rajiv Gandhi, who hastily dispatched 1,000 elite paratroopers to restore order. However, the biggest problem confronting the Maldives is global warming. The melting polar ice caps have contributed to rising sea levels, which threaten to swamp many of the republic's smaller islands. In 1989, Gayoom hosted an international forum on global warming, and he has also addressed the United Nations Millennium Summit in September 2000. "We may lack in numbers; we may lack in material wealth; we may lack in technological development; in fact we may lack in many of the material criteria by which progress is measured in the present-day world," he lectured, "but my country, the Republic of Maldives, does not lack the courage to speak out freely according to its own convictions." For ceaseless efforts in promoting awareness of global warming, General Secretary KOFI ANNAN pronounced Gayoom the "godfather of environmental awareness."

Despite the Maldives's relative obscurity, Gayoom has also been active in international affairs. In 1985 his nation joined the South Asian Association for Regional Cooperation, and the country strives to secure designation of the Indian Ocean as a demilitarized "Zone of Peace." For this reason he has refused to lease Gan Island, a former British base, to any military power. Officially, the president pursues a neutral, nonaligned policy, but he also seeks close regional and economic ties to India, Sri Lanka, and the Arab states. He continues in office as a respected leader and diplomat until his present term expires in 2003.

Further Reading
Ahmad, Rizwan A. "The State and National Foundation in the Maldives." *Cultural Dynamics* 13, no. 3 (2001): 293–315.
Amsler, Kurt. *Maldives.* New York: Smithmark, 1995.
Ostheimer, John M. *The Politics of the Western Indian Ocean Islands.* New York: Praeger, 1975.
Royston, Ellis. *A Man for All Islands: A Biography of Maumoon Abdul Gayoom, President of the Maldives.* Singapore: Times Editions, 1998.

Gligorov, Kiro (1917–   ) *president of Macedonia*
Kiro Gligorov was born on May 3, 1917, in Shtip, Macedonia, then a part of the kingdom of Serbs, Croats, and Slovenes. He was initially educated at the Skopje Gymnasium, and went on to acquire a law degree from the University of Belgrade in 1938. He then worked as a banking attorney until the onset of World War II, when Yugoslavia was brutally occupied by German and Italian forces. Gligorov joined the League of Communists (Communist Party) in 1944 and fought in the resistance. The following year the Federal People's Republic of Yugoslavia was founded under Marshal Josip Broz Tito, and a dictatorship modeled on the Soviet style was imposed. From that point forward, Gligorov served as a trusted economic and financial adviser, and he held a succession of important governmental posts. From 1974–78 he served as president of the Assembly of Yugoslavia, while also teaching economics at the University of Belgrade. Curiously, despite his Communist Party background, Gligorov was a lively exponent of free-market economic principles. As early as 1965 he argued for liberalizing the state command economy, becoming the first government official of a communist state to do so. Tito, however, balked at such reforms, fearing that market forces might stimulate intense ethnic nationalism

that would spell the doom of Yugoslavia. It was not until the late 1980s, when Gligorov joined with reformist prime minister Ante Markovic, that his economic ideas were seriously scrutinized. But by then the country was reeling under the blows of militant nationalism, just as Tito had predicted.

By 1990 Yugoslavia was being torn asunder by feuding secessionist states, including Croatia, and Slovenia. These were ominous trends for the small Macedonian republic, which is very ethnically diverse and contains large numbers of Greeks, Albanians, and Bulgarians—none of whom hold great affection for the others. However, as one of Macedonia's elder statesmen, the moderately disposed Gligorov symbolized the republic's best hope for a peaceful transition to independence. To this extent, he spent most of 1989–90 advocating wholesale adoption of multiparty democracy and free-market economics. On January 25, 1991, Gligorov became the first freely elected president in Macedonia's long history. The problems accompanying independence were enormous, but the new executive remained fully cognizant of the difficulties before him. "In this part of the world it is difficult to find the true path between reason and emotion, myth and reality," he affirmed. "This is the burden of the Balkans which prevents us becoming truly European."

On September 8, 1991, the Macedonian public overwhelmingly ratified a referendum calling for separation from Yugoslavia and national independence. Thus was born the new republic of Macedonia, and Gligorov remained determined to maintain domestic tranquillity. It was a tall order, considering the explosive mix of nationalities and prolonged difficulties associated with switching to a capitalist economic model. Fortunately, the nation's new constitution circumvented many problems by enshrining the principles of human rights and civil rights for all citizens. Thus Macedonia, and Slovenia under MILAN KUCAN, became the only Yugoslavian republics to peacefully cede from the federation. This was in stark contrast to SLOBODAN MILOŠEVIĆ of Serbia and FRANJO TUDJMAN of Croatia, who embarked on wars of terror and "ethnic cleansing" to achieve their ends. At length the greatest threat to Macedonian stability came from the neighboring province of Kosovo. Serbian attempts to forestall succession by the province of Kosovo led to widespread violence and a flood of Albanian refugees into Macedonia. Territorial conquest was again driving the engines of ethnic hatred, and the Balkans verged on becoming a powder keg.

Gligorov, who gained reelection to a second five-year term in October 1994, was nearly killed by an assassin's bomb on October 3, 1995. He survived with the loss of an eye and managed to resume his responsibilities within months. But his primary concern was securing United Nations peacekeeping forces to patrol the border between Macedonia and Kosovo, and thus cap the escalating tendency toward violence. More than anything, he feared creation of a "Greater Albania," whereby the refugees would slice off parts of Macedonia and annex it to a united Kosovo and Albania. In June 1997 Gligorov parleyed with U.S. president BILL CLINTON and secured a pledge of 500 American soldiers to guard the border zone. Other UN troops would also be dispatched as an additional guarantee. "No one in the Balkans," he warned, "can remain impassive or quiet and peaceful and tranquil in terms of all the developments we have seen in Bosnia and the ones we're now seeing in Albania." In September 1995, Gligorov also diffused a long-standing dispute with his southern neighbor, Greece, which also did much to stabilize the region.

Gligorov was forbidden by law from serving more than two terms in office, so, in December 1999, he stood down and was replaced by BORIS TRAJKOVSKI. But even in retirement, he remains wary of events next door and calls for greater isolation of Albanian extremists. "The rebels have not learnt the lesson that such ideas—like greater Serbia and Greater Croatia—have collapsed," he declared in June 2001, "I am absolute about this, the idea of a Greater Albania cannot be realized."

Further Reading

Ackerman, Alice. *Making Peace Prevail: Preventing Violent Conflict in Macedonia.* Syracuse, N.Y.: Syracuse University Press, 2000.

Coutarelli, Marina-Lida. "Nationalism and Democracy: A Case Study of the Former Yugoslav Republic of Macedonia." Unpublished master's thesis, Oxford University, 1999.

Pettifer, James. *The New Macedonian Question.* New York: St. Martin's Press, 1999.

Roudometof, Victor. *The Macedonian Question; Culture, Historiography, Politics.* Boulder, Colo.: East European Monographs, 2000.

Vukmanovic-Tempo, Svetozar. *Struggle for the Balkans.* London: Merlin Press, 1990.

Goh Chok Tong (1941–   ) *prime minister of Singapore*

Goh Chok Tong was born in Singapore on May 20, 1941, to parents of Chinese descent. His father died while he was still young, and his mother supported him by working as a schoolteacher. Despite his poverty, Goh proved apt as a student and was allowed to attend the prestigious Raffles Institute. He graduated at the top of his class and subsequently studied economics at the University of Singapore. Goh received his bachelor's degree in 1964 and went on to obtain a graduate degree in development economics at Williams College in Massachusetts. He shortly after returned home to join the Singapore Civil Service as an economic planner and research economist. And, like many citizens of his background and training, he joined the People's Action Party (PAP), Singapore's leading political organization.

Singapore is a tiny island off the southernmost tip of the Malay Peninsula. It covers an area of only 240 square miles, yet its population of 3.5 million make it the most densely populated region on earth. The inhabitants are mostly Chinese in origin, but large communities of Malays and Indians are also present. Since obtaining its independence from Great Britain in 1965, Singapore has established itself as an economic powerhouse and, along with Taiwan, Hong Kong, and South Korea, is renowned as one of the four Asian "Little Tigers." This affluence came about due to the intelligent planning of Lee Kuan Yew, the nation's first prime minister, who placed great emphasis on social stability and economic planning. Singapore, lacking any natural resources, capitalized instead on the talents of its hardworking, highly skilled labor force, its mastery of electronics and communications equipment, and its intermediary role for transhipping products through Southeast Asia. Moreover, education is compulsory, crime almost nonexistent, and racial harmony well established. The government also remains committed to a "social compact" with its citizenry, and supports them with low-cost housing, free health care, and first-rate education. For all these reasons, tightly controlled Singapore remains one of the world's most impressive economic and social success stories.

Goh worked with the civil service for many years before transferring as managing director of the Neptune Orient Lines. His success caught the attention of Hon Sui Sen, Singapore's finance minister, who convinced him to run for office. In 1976 Goh did exactly that, and

he won a parliamentary seat for the PAP. His reputation as an effective technocrat propelled him through the party ranks, and he also held a succession of important governmental portfolios such as trade and industry minister. His good performance and youthful appeal convinced Prime Minister Lee Kuan Yew to appoint him first deputy prime minister and minister for defense in 1984. Goh was now formally in line to succeed Lee when he stepped down in November 1990. He was sworn in as the second prime minister in Singapore's history.

The accession of Goh marked a change in the government's leadership style. Whereas the traditional Lee was authoritarian and paternalistic toward his charge, Goh realized that younger Singaporeans wanted a greater say in the administration of their island, and he adopted a more "consensus approach" to governance. Unlike Lee, he consults with the public on all major issues through interviews and public gatherings. However, he still maintains a strictly conservative outlook with respect to social mores, and he promotes censorship of foreign publications or movies that militate against time-honored "Asian Values." In 1996 he oversaw establishment of a Tribunal for Maintenance of Parents, which can punish adults for neglecting to care for aged parents. Maintaining traditional respect for elders is strictly reinforced, in part to prevent them from becoming too high a burden on state revenues. Given the rapidly aging nature of Singapore's population, care for the old remains of critical importance to social stability. In 1997 Goh was easily reelected to a second term with 65 percent of the vote.

Singapore's boom period came to a perilous halt during the Asian financial crisis of 1997 and 1998. Trade and prices slumped during the regional recession, while debts and unemployment soared. However, the tiny citystate was well prepared with sufficient financial resources to bounce back, and Goh took immediate steps to revamp business and industry. His vision, the "New Singapore," now fosters globalization, entrepreneurial spirit, reduction of government's role in business, and promotion of a more risk-taking culture. He also seeks to wean Singapore away from its overwhelming dependence upon electronics and production in favor of more banking and finance. To further promote social stability, in August 2001 Goh announced the government's plan to give all citizens "shares" in the country, so as to more evenly distribute any budget surplus. However, he remains under increasing pressure from the West, particularly the United States, to reduce existing constraints against social activity and free speech. "I know some people want even greater freedom," Goh has said, "but where politics is concerned, I prefer to ease up slowly rather than open up with a big bang. We should, therefore, pump air into the political balloon slowly." He will be up for reelection in 2002.

Further Reading

Chong, Alan. *Goh Chok Tong, Singapore's New Premier.* Retaling, Jaya, Malaysia: Pelanduk Pubs, 1991.

Ho, Khai Leong. *The Politics of Policy-Making in Singapore.* Oxford: Oxford University Press, 2000.

Vasil, R. K. *Governing Singapore: Democracy and National Development.* St. Leonards, New South Wales: Allen and Unwin, 2000.

Mauzy, Diane K. *Singapore Politics under the People's Action Party.* New York: Routledge, 2002.

Mutalib, Hussin. "Illiberal Democracy and the Future of Opposition in Singapore." *Third World Quarterly* 21, no. 2 (2000): 313–342.

Worthington, Ross. *Government in Singapore.* Richmond: Curzon, 2001

Göncz, Árpád (1922–) *president of Hungary*

Árpád Göncz was born on February 10, 1922, in Budapest, Hungary. In 1939 he enrolled at Pazmany University to study law and acquired his degree in 1944. Hungary at that time was allied to Nazi Germany and Göncz was drafted into the army. However, he deserted, joined the underground resistance, and was wounded in action. After the war he became affiliated with the Independent Smallholders Party, a conservative landowners group, and he also edited their newsletter. However, after 1945 Hungary endured occupation by Soviet troops, and in 1948 they foisted a communist-style dictatorship on the country. Göncz subsequently withdrew from politics to work on farms and as a pipe fitter. A decade later, Hungarian resentment against Soviet repression resulted in the violent revolution of 1956. Göncz, a staunch anticommunist, participated fully in the fighting, which was brutally crushed by Soviet tanks and troops. He was thereupon tried in a secret court and sentenced to life imprisonment. This, however, proved a turning point in his intellectual life. Always interested in literature, he taught himself English and kept his sanity by translating famous American novels into Hungarian. Göncz was

released in 1963 under a general amnesty and, denied the ability to find anything but menial labor, he supplemented his income by continuing to translate. He took to writing creatively and ultimately composed six plays, several short stories, and a novel.

For many years, Göncz circulated among the underground literary movement, until the late 1980s, when the withdrawal of Soviet troops from Eastern Europe spelled the doom of communism. In 1988 he became a founding member of the Network of Free Initiatives and he later joined a new political organization, the Alliance of Free Democrats. Together with other groups they began agitating for Hungary's first freely held elections in 40 years, and in May 1990 Hungarians went to the polls. Victory was claimed by the center-right Democratic Forum, which nominated JOZEF ANTALL to the post of prime minister. However, in the interest of promoting unity and consensus, Antall reached across to the opposition and selected Göncz to serve as president. He was at that time Hungary's most famous writer and a living symbol of Hungarian nationalism and independence, so the nomination was well received.

The Hungarian presidency is largely a ceremonial post, and Göncz was variously sent abroad to promote Hungary's interests. In 1990 he ventured to the United States, where he was feted by President George H. W. Bush and, as head of the Hungarian National Writer's Association, also was entertained by several literary figures. At that time he received an honorary degree from the University of Indiana. Back home Göncz actively campaigned for the end to Hungarian membership in the Russian-dominated Warsaw Pact, which transpired after the Soviet Union's collapse in December 1991. Like most Hungarians of his generation, though, he was mindful of his small nation's inability to defend itself, and thereafter Göncz campaigned for Hungarian membership in NATO. On November 16, 1997, the entire issue was subjected to a public referendum, which overwhelmingly passed by 85 percent of votes cast. Hungary, along with former Warsaw Pact members Poland and the Czech Republic, had formally and finally cast their lot with Western Europe. Mindful of the responsibilities this carried, in June 1999 Göncz declared to President BILL CLINTON Hungary's determination to provide troops to serve as peacekeepers in war-torn Kosovo. "We are acting in accordance with our national interests and our obligations as allies in offering the greatest possible support to the international community acting for peace," he insisted.

On the home front, Göncz served as a voice for moderation and stressed a gradual approach to privatization to minimize social costs. He was also an outspoken critic of the Antall regime and frequently denounced its authoritarian tenor. On one occasion he flatly refused to sign papers dismissing the heads of state-run radio and television stations. Göncz's outspoken nature only endeared him further to the public, and, in June 1995, he was reelected to a second term in office. On June 7, 2000, he also received Germany's highest award, the Special Class of the Order of Merit of the Grand Cross, from President JOHANNES RAU. It was given in recognition of Göncz's efforts to promote progress and democracy in Hungary, German-Hungarian relations, and support for European cooperation. By the time he stepped down on May 3, 2002, in favor of Ferenc Madl, he was easily Hungary's most popular politician. In the course of his long literary career, Göncz has also received recognition and awards for his literary craft, and several of his plays have been staged abroad.

Further Reading

Anderson, Ruth M. and J. M. Anderson. *Barbed Wire for Sale: The Hungarian Transition to Democracy, 1988–1991.* Graham, Wash.: Poetic License, 1999.

Berend, Ivan T. and Gyorgy Ranki. *Studies on Central and Eastern Europe in the Twentieth Century: Regional Crises and the Case of Hungary.* Aldershot, England: Ashgate Variorum, 2002.

Göncz, Árpád. *In Mid-Stream: Talks and Speeches.* Budapest: Corvina Books, 1999.

Meusberger, Peter, and Heike Johns. *Transformations in Hungary: Essays on Economy and Society.* New York: Physica-Verlag, 2001.

Schmidt, Maria, and Laszlo G. Toth. *From Totalitarian to Democratic Hungary: Evolution and Transformation, 1990–2000.* Highland Lakes, N.J.: Atlantic Research and Publications, 2000.

González, Felipe (1942–) *prime minister of Spain*

Felipe González Márquez was born on March 5, 1942, in Seville, Spain, the son of a cattle rancher. He matured at a time when Spain was controlled by fascist dictator Francisco Franco, who ruled the country with an iron fist. Virtually no political activity or dissent was allowed, and transgressors were severely punished. González studied law at the University of Seville and the University of Leuven (Belgium) and he became involved in anti-Francoist activities. This brought him into the ranks of the illegal Spanish Socialist Worker's Party (PSOE) while he established a law practice in Seville, specializing in labor matters. González proved himself to be energetic, articulate, and forceful, so that by 1970 he had risen to executive secretary within the Seville branch of the PSOE. By 1974 he and other younger party members judged the time right to break with the party's traditional leadership, then exiled in France, and he became part of the Executive Commission. Within a year the boyish-looking González was voted secretary-general of the PSOE.

González, despite his leftist leanings, was no Marxist, and he insisted that rank-and-file members delete the term from the party's name—or he would resign. The bluff worked, the title changed, and González next worked to shift the party's ideology closer to the political center. These changes were propitiously timed; in 1975 Franco died, and the Socialist Party became legal. With González at its helm, they provided organized opposition to the newly elected government of Prime Minister Adolfo Suárez. By the 1980s the Spanish government had failed to stop economic decline and regional violence, so Suárez resigned. New elections were scheduled for October 1982 and the PSOE won 47 percent of the vote, whereupon King Juan Carlos I asked González to form a government. He thus became the first Socialist prime minister since 1939, and his peaceful ascent was also an important step in the transition to democracy.

As premier, González largely continued the moderate policies of his predecessors, much to the disappointment of more radical elements within his party. He fully supported Spain's economic integration into Europe, and he advocated membership in the European Economic Community, the forerunner of today's European Union (EU). In 1981 the Socialists had also railed against Spain's entry into NATO, which occurred in 1982, but by 1986 González urged retaining membership and put the issue up for a public referendum. The measure passed by a large margin, confirming the centrist sway of the new Socialist Party. It also signaled that Spain's traditional isolation from the rest of neighboring Europe had passed.

In time, González became Spain's most popular politician, and a symbol of democracy's final triumph. In 1986, 1989, and 1993, he was elected prime minister, although by successively declining margins. The problem was not so much Socialist policies, which were moderate and well planned, but rather events beyond González's control. By the mid-1990s, the economic boom began declining and unemployment was moving toward 20 percent. Furthermore, the prime minister's distinctly neoliberal economic policies created angry rifts among Socialists, and many broke off to form leftist parties of their own. The period was also characterized by mounting terrorist violence at the hands of Basque separatists. González, meanwhile, had apparently grown bored with domestic politics and was exerting more energy on the international scene. As national policy began to drift, so did his carefully crafted coalition with Basque and Catalan nationalist parties. But the most damaging aspect of his later tenure was the seemingly endless parade of scandals that surfaced. González was never implicated for engaging in financial impropriety, but several high-ranking ministers were accused and tainted the party with corruption. Worse, in 1994 the prime minister became peripherally linked with right-wing paramilitary forces suspected of executing 27 Basque terrorists. He denied any culpability, but the revelation cost him the support of his Basque allies, who withdrew from the coalition. In 1995 the Cortes, or national legislature, did not approve his budget, the first-ever rejected in the post-Franco era. González then called for new elections to be held in May 1996. When they were narrowly won by JOSÉ MARÍA AZNAR of the conservative Popular Party, 13 years of Socialist rule in Spain came to an ignominious end. However, González's administration marked a significant signpost on the road to Spanish democracy.

Disheartened, González resigned as head of the PSOE in June 1997, and he subsequently was called upon to testify in the corruption cases of several former ministers. However, his own stature as a leading European politician and diplomat remained intact. In April 2002 he agreed to join South African minister Cyril Ramaphosa in a United Nations fact-finding inquiry investigating the latest round of Israeli-Palestinian violence. According to high-ranking UN officials, both men were chosen because of the wide-ranging respect they command around the world.

Further Reading

Ferreiro, Jesus, and Felipe Serrano. *The Economic Policy of the Spanish Socialist Government, 1982–1996.* Leeds: University of Leeds, 2001.

Gillespie, R. "The Spanish General Election of 1996." *Electoral Studies* 15 (August 1996): 425–431.

González, Felipe. "European Union and Globalization." *Foreign Policy,* no. 115 (Summer 1999): 28–43.

Lancaster, Thomas D. *The Spanish Political System: An Institutional Approach.* New York: Oxford University Press, 2002.

Smith, W. Rand. *The Left's Dirty Job: The Politics of Industrial Restructuring in France and Spain.* Pittsburgh: University of Pittsburgh Press, 1998.

González Macchi, Luis (1947–   ) *president of Paraguay*

Luis González Macchi was born in Paraguay on December 13, 1947, the son of a government finance and labor minister. He studied labor law while attending the National University of Asunción and subsequently joined the Colorado Party in 1966. This party has dominated national politics since its inception in 1880. Over the next 20 years González held a succession of important posts within the Ministry of Justice and Labor. He decided to run for public office in 1993, and he first gained election to the Chamber of Deputies. An astute politician, González managed to have himself elected vice president of that body in 1994, and four years later he gained election to the Senate. González's legislative career climaxed in 1998 when he became president of that body.

González rose to prominence during an inauspicious period in Paraguay's stormy political history. Since 1954 the country had been under the control of General Alfredo Stroessner and, abetted by a power-sharing agreement with the Colorado Party, he ruled the country with an iron hand for nearly 50 years. In 1989, Stroessner was overthrown by General Andrés Rodríguez, who drew up a new constitution and placed the nation back on the path to democracy. Free elections were then resumed in 1993 when JUAN WASMOSY was elected the first civilian ruler in five decades and, in 1998, he was succeeded by Raúl Cubas Grau of the Colorado Party. The transition to civilian rule was basically peaceful, but in 1996 General Lino Oviedo led an attempted coup against Wamosy over widespread allegations of corruption. Despite close ties to the Colorado Party, the general was arrested and sentenced to ten years in prison. However, once Cubas, another party stalwart, became president in 1998, he freed the general and touted him as a vice presidential running mate. This move sparked a national uproar and the legislative branch began impeachment proceedings against Cubas. The crisis was further heightened in March 1999 when Vice President Luis María Argaña was assassinated, or so many came to believe, at the behest of General Oviedo. Paraguay's mounting instability prompted neighboring countries and the United States to apply pressure upon Cubas to resign, and, on March 28, 1999, he left office and fled to Brazil. The general also sought refuge in Argentina. González, as president of the Senate, was next in line for succession and he was immediately sworn into office.

González inherited a nation on the verge of political and economic collapse. His immediate task was to secure unity among his own Colorado Party, which was split between those seeking greater democracy and those still wedded to the notion of strong-man rule. This was eventually accomplished, but González took the process a step further by establishing a new "unity government" that included leftist opposition members in his cabinet. However, the ouster of Cubas, largely by mass demonstrations, had energized peasants, students, and union members, all of whom began flexing their newfound muscle at the government's expense. Many have since refused to join the "unity government" and instead are making demands of their own. Thus the Paraguayan polity remains splintered, beset by severe infighting, and increasingly ungovernable.

González also faced an economic crisis not of his own making. Brazil is Paraguay's largest trading partner, and when its currency was devalued in 2000, a major recession commenced. This had a severe impact on Paraguay's own tottering economy and contributed to the near cessation of trade activity. González has thus been forced to go against the very tenants of his party, which emphasizes state control of the national economy, and undertake privatization of leading state utilities such as water, power, and telephone service. He also hopes to interject some economic momentum through investments and loans for public works, agriculture, and industry. However, results are mixed and the gross national product continues declining. Worse, in February 1999, the United States revoked the country's trade certification because of widespread drug trafficking and money-laundering operations. Even FERNANDO HENRIQUE CARDOSO, the sympathetic president of Brazil, repeatedly called for Paraguay to resolve its numerous economic and political instabilities if it wants to remain part of the Mercosur trading alliance.

Unfortunately for González, his position is being eroded by a stream of new scandals. In March 2001 he reshuffled his cabinet in the wake of allegations that the president's official car was stolen overseas and smuggled into the country. On February 7, 2002, the national legislature charged González with responsibility for the disappearance and torture of two left-wing dissidents by state security forces under his command. Impeachment proceedings are being weighed against him and his political future now hangs in the balance.

Further Reading

Lambert, Peter, and R. Andrew Nicholson. *The Transition of Democracy in Paraguay.* New York: St. Martin's Press, 1997.

Powers, Nancy R. *The Transition to Democracy in Paraguay: Problems and Prospects.* Notre Dame, Ind.: University of Notre Dame Press, 1992.

Valenzuela, Arturo. "Paraguay: The Coup That Didn't Happen." *Journal of Democracy* 8 (January 1997): 43–56.

Vergara, Isaias. *Paraguayan Policy towards the New Organization of American States.* Virginia Beach, Va.: Regent University, 1997.

Whigham, Thomas, and Jerry W. Cooney. *A Guide to Collections of Paraguay in the United States.* Westport, Conn.: Greenwood Press, 1995.

Gordon, Pamela (1955–) *prime minister of Bermuda*

Pamela Gordon was born on September 2, 1955, in Hamilton, Bermuda. Her father, Dr. E. F. Gordon, was a Trinidad-born physician and a prominent civil rights activist for the island's Afro-Caribbean population. Furthermore, his legacy of left-wing populism is part of the Progressive Labour Party's (PLP) heritage, being one of Bermuda's two main political groups. Gordon never knew her father, for he died weeks before she was born. She was then raised by her mother and educated locally before becoming pregnant at 16. This would have ended the educational opportunities for most Bermuda women, but early on Gordon demonstrated her father's same headstrong qualities that characterized her later life. Enrolling in another school, she went on to attend Alma College in Ontario, Canada, and she subsequently received a master's degree in commerce from Queen's University, Ontario. Gordon then returned home to work successively as a restaurant manager and a hotel manager. She successfully fulfilled the last position despite lacking any experience in accounting. But it was while working in this capacity that Gordon became acquainted with Sir John Swan, Bermuda's current premier, and he prevailed upon her to join the conservative United Bermuda Party (UBP). She did so with relish and, because her father had been a noted liberal activist, her new political affiliation raised more than a few eyebrows.

Gordon's political career began in 1990 when Swan appointed her to the Senate. With charm and intelligence, she quickly established herself as a rising political force in the party. This was evinced in March 1992, when Swan made her minister of youth development. Bermuda by that time had been a British colony for more than four centuries, although by now it was considered a "dependent territory." That status brought advantages—islanders are exempt from income taxes and enjoy one of the highest per capita incomes in the world. In 1995 Swan placed the issue of independence from Great Britain before the public in a referendum. Not surprisingly, it was roundly defeated by 73 percent, and Swan felt compelled to resign. His replacement was David Saul, who then appointed Gordon his minister of environment, planning, and recreation. In October 1993, Gordon decided to test the political waters herself by winning a seat in the House of Assembly, representing Southampton West. It was a modest beginning, but auspicious events lay directly ahead.

In March 1997 Prime Minister Saul suddenly tendered his resignation over a minor scandal and the UBP scurried to find a suitable replacement. Under the parliamentary system, the head of the majority party also serves as the head of government. After much discussion, Gordon emerged as the uncontested candidate and she won unanimous approval as party leader. In this capacity she became Bermuda's first woman prime minister on March 27, 1997, and also its youngest. Like her father before her, she proved herself extremely strong-willed and outspoken on controversial issues. The UBP is conservative and extremely pro-business in outlook, so Gordon spent considerable time shoring up her support among the business community. She also dismissed out of hand any notion of Bermuda's independence, pointing out the economic plight of other Caribbean islands that chose that route. "Our sisters to the south taught

us not to do it," she maintained. Many conservative commentators compared her to Margaret Thatcher of Great Britain in both her conservative outlook and the steely resolve with which she pursued it. Gordon also shrugged off continuing comparison with her left-leaning father. "Although the philosophical way of how to get there may be a little different," she said, "the reality is that our position is the same. We want the best for Bermuda and Bermudians, and I would like to carry on that legacy because it is my intent."

Gordon continued in office for the next 18 months, when the next cycle of elections commenced. Her opponent was Jennifer Smith of the PLP, another woman politician of Afro-Caribbean descent. In November 1998, the PLP unexpectedly swept the contest, taking 26 house seats compared to the UBP's tally of 14. Gordon then stepped down as prime minister to serve as head of the opposition, where she remains today. But her brief tenure in office does not detract from the historic significance it represents for aspiring female politicians in Bermuda.

Further Reading

Benbow, Celia H., and Dale Butler. *Gladys Morrell and the Women's Suffrage Movement in Bermuda.* Bermuda: Writer's Machine, 1994.

Connell, John. *Bermuda: The Failure of Decolonization.* Leeds: School of Geography, University of Leeds, 1987.

Hodgson, Eva N. *Second-Class Citizens, First-Class Men, or, Great Men All Remind Us.* Bermuda: Writer's Machine, 1997.

Hunter, Barbara H. *The People of Bermuda: Beyond the Crossroads.* Oakville, Ontario: Carter and Carter, 1993.

Wade-Smith, Muriel. *Let Justice Flow: A Black Woman's Struggle for Equality in Bermuda.* Enumclaw, Wash.: Wine Press Publishing, 1999.

Gore, Albert, Jr. (1948–) *vice president of the United States*

Albert Gore, Jr., was born on March 31, 1948, in Carthage, Tennessee, the son of Albert Gore, Sr. His father was a near-legendary Democratic politician with more than 30 years of public service in the U.S. House of Representatives and Senate. Accordingly, Gore was raised in Washington, D.C., and educated at various elite prep schools before attending Harvard University in 1965. He obtained a bachelor's degree in politics, with honors, four years later. At that time Gore eschewed politics in favor of journalism. And, although he personally opposed the Vietnam War, he enlisted in the U.S. Army and served as a reporter on the *Stars and Stripes*. Discharged in 1971, he was an investigative reporter for the Nashville *Tennessean*. He enrolled at Vanderbilt University's School of Religion, and he subsequently attended Vanderbilt's law school. He then dropped out in 1976 to run for a seat in the U.S. House of Representatives from Tennessee.

Capitalizing on his famous family name, Gore easily won a contested primary, and he triumphed in the general election. A Democratic moderate, he seemed well attuned to the political tastes of his constituents and won reelection three more times. He also staked out reasonable and erudite positions on health care, the environment, nuclear disarmament and—what became his trademark issue—the rise of new technologies such as computers and the Internet. Gore then repeated his father's success by winning a seat in the U.S. Senate in 1984. Again, Gore distinguished himself in office, and by 1988 he took advantage of his growing national reputation by running for the presidency. He campaigned on traditional Democratic issues but was criticized for somewhat vague and vacillating stances. Gore nonetheless ran well throughout the South, his home base, but was beaten elsewhere by liberal nominee Michael Dukakis and withdrew from the campaign. Two years later he easily won reelection to the Senate, although in 1992 he declined to seek the presidency. Nonetheless, Gore continued to be an effective spokesman for mainstream and moderate policies. He also gained further renown by demonstrating ecological expertise in his book *Earth in the Balance: Ecology and the Human Spirit* (1992). Again, Gore strove for consensus between the needs for sustaining economic growth and preserving the planet's delicate environment. "We must make the rescue of the environment the central organizing principle for civilization," he stressed. The book was well received critically and enhanced his reputation.

The turning point in Gore's political fortunes came during the 1992 presidential election when candidate BILL CLINTON chose him as his running mate. This choice confounded the pundits. Rather than representing a geographical "balance," both men were Southerners and dedicated to pulling the Democratic Party back from its liberal fringes to the political center. Moreover, they were relatively youthful representatives of the "baby boomer" generation, and they projected a new political outlook. Gore handled himself well during debates with his Republican counterpart, Vice President J. Danforth Quayle, and his competence facilitated the ultimate Democratic victory over President George H. W. Bush. On January 20, 1993, Gore became the 45th vice president of the United States, among the youngest ever. The ensuing four years, however, were fraught with controversy and scandal relating to Clinton's finances and personal behavior, none of which affected Gore at this time. In 1996 the team went on to score another, albeit smaller, victory over Republican challenger Robert Dole. By 2000, the economy was in good shape, the Democrats enjoyed reasonably high poll ratings, and Gore seemed a likely candidate to succeed Clinton in the White House.

Unfortunately for the Democrats, Gore's political fortunes began unraveling. His usual "squeaky clean" image was badly tarred over revelations that, during the 1996 election, he had made illegal campaign calls from the White House. Gore admitted as much to the public—then insisted he had done nothing wrong. In September 1997, a congressional investigation of campaign fund-raising abuses again tarred Gore as a culprit in money illegally received from a Buddhist temple. Again, Gore apologized, but denied any culpability. Angry Republicans insisted that a special prosecutor be assigned to probe these allegations, but Democratic attorney general Janet Reno refused. Given the ongoing climate of scandal within Clinton's presidency, rocked continuously by investigations of Whitewater and Monica Lewinsky, her reticence only reinforced a growing sense of impropriety. Gore's campaign got off to a sound start when he handily defeated New Jersey senator Bill Bradley for the party nomination, and then went on to engage the Republican nominee, Texas governor GEORGE W. BUSH, the former president's son. His choice of Connecticut senator Joe Lieberman, the first Jewish-American to seek the vice presidency, was also a bold move, widely praised. But by the fall of 2000, polling was virtually in a dead heat, despite Gore's advantages of incumbency and a healthy economic climate. He was careful to distance himself from the scandal-plagued Clinton administration, and he declined to use the president on the campaign trail. Moreover, Gore's essentially wooden performance during three televised debates seemed to enhance growing perception of his inability to fulfill the highest office. When the election transpired that November, Gore won the popular contest by half a million votes, but lost in the electoral college to Bush by a razor-thin margin of three electoral votes. The last candidate to lose under similar circumstances was Grover Cleveland in 1888.

The most memorable moment of the 2000 campaign, and its most controversial, was the handling of affairs in Florida. The Democrats were plagued by faulty ballots in three heavily Democratic counties, while Ralph Nader, candidate of the Green Party, siphoned off 100,000 votes that might have otherwise gone to Gore. Worse, an earlier decision by Attorney General Reno to return Elián González, a young Cuban refugee, back to communist-controlled Cuba, had incensed the large Cuban community. They apparently decided to punish the Democrats by voting in overwhelming numbers for Bush. Still, and despite Republican expectations of easy victory, Bush prevailed only by 327 votes out of 6 million cast. Gore, who had initially conceded the night before, subsequently challenged statewide machine tabulations in court. A multiplicity of suits and countersuits dragged the process out over the next five weeks until the U.S. Supreme Court intervened and ordered all counting stopped. Contrary to popular opinions at the time, this decision did not alter the outcome of the election, for subsequent and numerous recounts by independent agencies all confirmed Bush's victory—albeit by the slightest of margins. Gore then gracefully accepted defeat and concluded 25 years of public service by retiring. "While I strongly disagree with the court's decision," he declared, "I accept it." Many Democrats, however, waxed angry over the final result and insist that they were illegally denied victory.

Since the election, Gore has maintained a low public profile and restricted his activities to teaching in Tennessee and at Columbia University, in New York. Given the controversy surrounding his defeat, many pundits believed that the Democrats were morally obliged to nominate him in 2004 for a rematch. But Gore made no commitment either way, although throughout 2002 he stumped for Democratic candidates in advance of congressional elections scheduled for fall. "Think about how you felt the morning after the Supreme Court decision in December," he implored. "Take that feeling you have inside and use it." After more soul searching, Gore apparently had second thoughts about running for the presidency again in 2004. With polls showing President Bush with a 60 percent approval rating, on December 15, 2002, he declared his intention not to be a contender.

"I personally have the energy and drive and ambition to make another campaign," he stated, "but I don't think that it's the right thing for me to do."

Further Reading

Ackerman, Bruce A. *Bush vs. Gore: The Question of Legitimacy.* New Haven, Conn.: Yale University Press, 2002.

Burdon, Barry C., ed. *Uncertainty in American Politics.* New York: Cambridge University Press, 2003.

Maraniss, David, and Ellen Nakashima. *The Prince of Tennessee: Al Gore Meets His Fate.* New York: Simon and Schuster, 2001.

Sabato, Larry. *Overtime! The Election 2000 Thriller.* New York: Longman, 2002.

Sammon, Bill. *At Any Cost: How Al Gore Tried to Steal the Election.* Lanham, Md.: Regnery Publishers, 2001.

Schneider, Jerrold E. *Campaign Finance Reform and the Future of the Democratic Party.* New York: Routledge, 2002.

Toobin, Jeffrey. *Too Close to Call: The Thirty-Six Day Battle to Decide the 2000 Election.* New York: Random House, 2001.

Gowda, H. D. Deve (1933–) *prime minister of India*

Shri Haradanahalli Dodde Deve Gowda was born on May 18, 1933 in Haradanahalli village, Karnataka state, southern India, into a farming or "backwards caste" family. Karnataka is also India's most technologically advanced state and the majority of people do not speak Hindu, one of 15 official languages. Gowda received a degree in civil engineering from Government Polytechnic and entered politics in 1953 by joining the Congress Party. In light of his agrarian background, he also became an outspoken advocate for poor farmers and the underprivileged. By 1962 Gowda had worked his way up to securing election to the Karnataka legislative assembly, where he served four consecutive terms until 1983. He then held the post of state minister of public works and irrigation until 1987, when he resigned in protest over inadequate funding. Gowda also strongly protested Prime Minister Indira Gandhi's state of emergency in 1975, a stance that resulted in his imprisonment. Released after 18 months, he then quit the Congress Party and joined the Janata Party, a moderately socialist political group. In 1980 he proved instrumental in reuniting it with a splinter faction, Janata Dal. He next gained election to the state parliament at Bangalore in 1991, again on the basis of lobbying on behalf of poor farmers, and in 1994 he rose to become party chairman. On December 11, 1994, Gowda assumed office as chief minister of Karnataka state. Two years later the Congress Party, which had ruled India for nearly 40 years, was badly defeated in national elections, and Prime Minister P. V. N. RAO resigned. The government then briefly passed into the hands of the Hindu nationalist Bharatiya Janata Party under ATAL BEHARI VAJPAYEE, who failed to cobble together a working coalition. Finally, the United Front, a broad coalition of 14 disparate parties, coalesced under the Janata Party banner and Gowda became the third prime minister in as many weeks on June 1, 1996. In light of the fact he neither came from the New Delhi political establishment nor spoke Hindi, Gowda was un-officially regarded as India's first "regional prime minis-ter." The post also proved to be his first national office.

Despite socialist leanings, Gowda embraced free-market economics and cultivated a pro-investment phi-losophy. This was essential for encouraging the growth of modernization in India, which is the world's largest democracy and second only to China in population. Un-fortunately for Gowda, India was at this time torn by increasing levels of ethnic tensions and outright hostili-ties between many of its several hundred groupings. Most especially, violence has grown arising from the hotly disputed status of the Muslim northern state of Kashmir, where extremists have agitated for indepen-dence or union with Pakistan through terrorism. The issue has been endemic ever since India acquired inde-pendence from Great Britain in 1947, and the nation has endured three wars and innumerable border skir-mishes with neighboring Pakistan, which covets Kash-mir. Gowda did his best to impose rule and discipline over both his country and his coalition, both of which seemed about to splinter at any moment. But he also enjoyed a reputation as an unsophisticated but crafty po-litical leader, and for a year the United Front kept its co-hesion. However, in April 1997, the Congress Party withdrew its support from the government, precipitating a crisis. Gowda was unable to repair the damage, sus-tained an unfavorable motion of no confidence, and re-signed after only a year in power. He was succeeded by a former prime minister, INDER KUMAR GUJRAL on May 18, 1997, and the United Front resumed control of the nation.

Since leaving high office, Gowda has continued as head of the Janata Party and a member of the opposi-tion. But political divisions run deep in India, and fac-tional fighting can even assume family dimensions. In February 2001 Gowda's wife was splashed with acid and injured by her nephew at their village temple. Police de-duce that the incident was motivated by the fact that the assailant's father, Basave Gowda—the former prime minister's brother—is a member of the rival Congress Party. Fortunately, she recovered from the attack. Gowda also retains a measure of international recognition befit-ting the former leader of the world's second-largest na-tion. In August 2001 he ventured to China at the behest of the Chinese People's Institute of Foreign Affairs, where he was feted by LI PENG, chairman of the National People's Congress Standing Committee. Li spoke highly of Gowda's attempts to promote Sino-India ties while in office and afterward. Gowda returned the compliment, and he stated that he hoped that the two countries would continue strengthening bilateral agreements and enhancing mutual trust and understanding.

Further Reading

Attar, Chand. *Prime Minister H. D. Deve Gowda: The Gain and the Pain (A Biographical Study)*. New Delhi: Gyan Publishing House, 1997.

Chadda, Maya. *Building Democracy in South Asia: India, Nepal, Pakistan*. Boulder, Colo.: Lynne Rienner Pub-lishers, 2000.

Gangoly, Sumit. "India in 1996: A Year of Upheaval." *Asian Survey* 37 (February 1997): 126–136.

Jai Janak Raj. *The Rise and Fall of Deve Gowda and the Constitutional Breakdown*. New Delhi: Regency Pub-lishers, 1997.

Jayal, Nivaja G. *Democracy in India*. New York: Oxford University Press, 2001.

Guei, Robert (ca. 1941–) *president of Côte d'Ivoire*

Robert Guei was born in Côte D'Ivoire (Ivory Coast) around 1941, although little else is known of his back-ground. His country was formerly a French colonial pos-session, which gained its independence in 1960 under legendary President FÉLIX HOUPHOUËT-BOIGNY. It has since acquired a well-deserved reputation for prosperity and political stability rarely seen on the African continent.

Guei apparently joined the French colonial army while a young man and received military training abroad. His career then became closely intertwined with the elite paracommando forces, the FIRPAC, in which he served as commander. By 1990 Guei's good performance resulted in promotion to military chief of Côte d'Ivoire. However, in December 1993 a new president, HENRI-KONAN BÉDIÉ came to the fore and tensions began to mount. Like Houphouët-Boingy, Bédié belonged to the Democratic Party of Côte d'Ivoire (PDCI), which had ruled the nation for 40 years. In 1995 Guei criticized Bédié for using army troops to suppress student unrest, a stance that led to his demotion. In 1997 Bédié removed him from the military altogether on the grounds that he was plotting a coup. Guei, meanwhile, struck up cordial relations with Alassane Ouattara of the opposition Republican Rally Party (RDR), which did little to endear him to the regime. Around this time the government had deployed parts of its army in the Central African Republic as part of a UN–sponsored peacekeeping force. Following the troops' return, however, President Bédié refused to pay them back wages. A crisis occurred in December 1999 when many soldiers mutinied. Bédié then promised to accede to their demands for the money, but the soldiers also began agitating for a return of Guei as general in chief. Violence and confusion ensued until December 24, 1999, when the former general announced that he was taking over the government. Bédié then fled the country for exile in France. It was Côte d'Ivoire's first coup since gaining independence in 1960.

Once in power, Guei attempted to assert political control and place his house in order. Many citizens, disillusioned by the corruption of the Bédié regime, initially welcomed the change. The general conferred with President CHARLES TAYLOR of Liberia and several UN representatives, assuring them that he would take steps to restore Côte d'Ivoire's democracy. Guei also sought to redirect the economy so as to promote greater reduction of its international debt load, payment of which consumed up to 40 percent of export earnings. Coffee and cocoa, the country's leading cash crops, had undergone a severe drop in price, which contributed to the sinking economy. Worse, recurring acts of rebellion by several garrisons over poor pay and political favoritism tested Guei's ability to control the country. "Acts of defiance and insubordination are unacceptable," he warned, "because a refusal to abide by the wishes of the public is refusal to accept the primary principles of democracy."

At length, Guei, under intense pressure from the international community, agreed to a new constitution to be passed by a public referendum in July 2000. This would be followed in close order by general elections that October. However, his former alliance with Ouattara also suffered a downturn when the proposed constitutional clause restricted high office to native-born citizens. This enraged Ouattara, who was born abroad, and his RDR Party began agitating against it. Consequently, in May 2000 Guei sacked eight RDR appointees from the government, heightening the sense of instability. Many opposition leaders then predicted that the general would put himself forward as a presidential candidate, thereby legitimizing his coup. This is exactly what Guei did. On October 22 he ran against PDCI candidate Laurent Gbagbo for the presidency. However, as votes were tabulated and it appeared that Guei had lost, his cronies stopped the process for two days, then announced that Guei had won with 52.7 percent of the vote. The entire process was condemned locally and internationally, and thousands of citizens flocked to the streets in protest. Many of these were Guei's own soldiers, who refused to fire on the crowds as ordered and, in fact, began mingling with them. Taking the hint for a speedy departure, Guei left suddenly for his native village of Gouessesso, where he remained in hiding. Gbagbo, meanwhile, was formally sworn in as president on October 26, 2001.

The removal of Guei from office was welcomed by the international community, but they remained uneasy over the prospect of future coups and insurgencies. Therefore, the European Union made national reconciliation a precondition for resuming foreign aid, which had been suspended. Accordingly, in December 2001, Gbagbo invited former president Bédié, opposition leader Ouattara, and deposed general Guei to a national reconciliation forum. A rapprochement has since been achieved between the feuding parties, economic aid has been restored, and domestic tranquillity has returned to the formerly prosperous nation.

Further Reading
Mundt, Robert. *Historical Dictionary of Côte d'Ivoire.* Lanham, Md.: Scarecrow Press, 1995.

N'Diaye, Boubacar. "A Comparative Analysis of Civilian Control Strategies: Botswana, Ivory Coast, and Kenya." Unpublished Ph.D. dissertation, Northern Illinois University, 1998.

Nneda, Ugochukwu I. "The Impact of African Traditions and Economic Policy Traditions in Economic Growth: The Colonial and Post-colonial Experience in Nigeria and Ivory Coast." Unpublished master's thesis, Auburn University, 2001.

Toungara, Jeanne M. "Ethnicity and Political Crisis in Côte d'Ivoire." *Journal of Democracy* 12 (July 2001): 63–73.

Zolberg, Aristide R. *One-Party Government in the Ivory Coast.* Princeton, N.J.: Princeton University Press, 1969.

Guelleh, Ismail Omar (1947–) *president of Djibouti*

Ismail Omar Guelleh was born in Dire-Dawa, Ethiopia, in 1947, and his family subsequently relocated to neighboring Djibouti. This tiny nation on the Horn of Africa was previously a French colonial possession until it achieved independence in 1977. Under French rule, the minority Afar group was favored over the majority Issa tribe, thereby sowing the seeds for future ethnic hostility. Guelleh, meanwhile, joined the French colonial administration in 1968 and rose to become police inspector. In 1975 he abandoned his post to take up the cause of national independence from France as a newspaper editor. Two years later, Guelleh was dispatched abroad to seek political and financial assistance from Libya and Somalia. His efforts were well received at home and, following independence in 1977, Guelleh gained appointment as President Hassan Gouled Aptidon's chief of staff. He occupied this post for the next 22 years, which gave him more national visibility than any other Djibouti politician. As such he became responsible for national security, and he steadily climbed the party hierarchy to prominence. By 1996 Guelleh was also serving as the Popular Rally for Progress Party (RPP) vice president, and he chaired numerous and important committees.

In 1977 President Aptidon, of the RPP, sought ethnic accommodation by appointing members of both ethnic groups to his government. Unfortunately, this move failed to placate deep-seated resentments between the competing groups. In the absence of French troops, who no longer garrisoned the countryside, fighting erupted and spread between rival ethnic gangs. In 1991 an Afar insurgency broke out under the auspices of the Front for the Restoration of Unity and Democracy (FRUD). Years of combat and bloody repression followed, so much so that France suspended foreign aid to its former colony. It was not until a constitutional referendum, held in December 1992, that moderate elements from both sides began banding together. By 1999 President Aptidon was old and in poor health; he tendered his resignation and called for new elections.

Guelleh was well positioned to succeed to the presidency. For years he had assumed greater and greater responsibility as the ailing Aptidon withdrew from public life, and he openly courted favor from both the military and the RPP. The fact that he was ethnic Issa also endeared him to the majority of voters. Elections were held on April 9, 1999, and Guellen won handily with 73.89 percent of the vote over Moussa Ahmed Iddris, who only polled 26.11 percent. He assumed office on May 7, 1999, as Djibouti's second president.

Despite Djibouti's small size, its strategic location at the mouth of the Arabian Gulf gives it considerable weight in regional affairs. For many years Guelleh tried to mediate the long-standing war between Ethiopia and its breakaway province of Eritrea, which deprived the latter of access to the ocean. Ironically, as the war continued, Djibouti reaped considerable profit as a neutral shipper and its principal port facilities underwent modernization and expansion. Ethiopian by birth, Guelleh favors that nation in talks, and he seeks greater economic and security ties with Addis Ababa. This is deemed essential for Djibouti's continuing existence, for neighboring Somalia has since laid claims to its territory. For this reason, Guelleh has also cultivated close military ties to France, which maintains a small garrison in the capital.

However, President Guelleh has enjoyed less success managing the economy. Djibouti is an arid, desert country with scattered rainfall. Consequently, it is dependent upon outside sources for important foodstuffs and other basic commodities. In 1995 an economic downturn, coupled with the expense of fighting the FRUD insurgency, contributed to a sagging economic picture. Income was down, the national debt soared, and Djibouti failed to meet payments on its national debt. Guelleh has since taken steps to revive the flagging economy, but unemployment continues hovering at 40 percent. Fortunately, the recent discovery of natural gas deposits offers the prospect of added revenue and could lessen Djibouti's dependence on foreign aid. Guelleh has also been active in placating the more moderate elements within the FRUD, inviting several members into the electoral process. Political stability also seems to have returned. On December 9, 2000, General Yacine Yabeh Galab, who had been dismissed by Guelleh, led a coup attempt against the government until army loyalists crushed it. On May 4, 2001, Guelleh also met with Eritrean president ISAIAS AFWERKI in an attempt to negotiate an end to hostilities with Ethiopia. In exchange Afwerki promised to stop aiding Afar rebels in the north and to promote political accommodation.

Further Reading

Alwan, Daoud A., and Yohanis Mibrathu. *Historical Dictionary of Djibouti.* Lanham, Md.: Scarecrow Press, 2001.

Cutbill, Catharine C. "A Post-colonial Predicament: Imagining Djibouti." Unpublished Ph.D. dissertation, University of Virginia, 1994.

"Djibouti." *The Courier,* no. 153 (September–October 1995): 14–31.

Saint Veran, Robert, and Virginia M. Thompson. *Djibouti, Pawn of the Horn of Africa.* Metuchen, N.J.: Scarecrow Press, 1981.

Schrader, Peter J. "Ethnic Politics in Djibouti: From 'Eye of the Hurricane' to 'Boiling Cauldron.'" *African Studies* 92 no. 367 (1993): 203–222.

Gujral, Inder Kumar (1919–) *prime minister of India*

Inder Kumar Gujral was born on December 4, 1919, in Jhleum, Punjab province, then part of British-controlled India. His family was politically active in anti-British demonstrations and he once organized a children's march at the age of 11. Gujral subsequently joined the Communist Party while attending the Forman Christian College, Hailey College of Commerce, and Punjab University, from which he obtained two doctorates. When Britain granted India independence in 1947, a violent upheaval developed between Muslims and Hindus in the north, resulting in creation of a new country, Pakistan. Because Gujral's family was of Hindu extraction, they fled and eventually settled in New Delhi. There Gujral quit the Communist Party and joined the more socialist-oriented Congress Party. An urbane, respected intellectual, he came to the attention of Prime Minister Indira Gandhi, who appointed him to various government ministries commencing in 1967. However, he protested

Gandhi's 1975 state of emergency, along with the mass arrests that followed, and he was fired from her cabinet. In 1976 Gujral was exiled politically, being sent as ambassador to the Soviet Union, where he remained four years.

After continued disagreement with the Gandhi family, Gujral quit the Congress Party in 1989 and joined a dissenting group, the Janata Party, which formed part of the larger United Front coalition. That year he stood for a seat in the upper house of parliament and became minister of external affairs in the administration of Prime Minister V. P. Singh. He returned to parliament the following year, but by 1996 served as minister of external affairs in the United Front coalition government of H. D. DEVE GOWDA. Here Gujral distinguished himself by promulgating the so-called "Gujral Doctrine," whereby India tried mending fences with its smaller neighbors and sought closer cooperation with them. This entailed enactment of water-sharing arrangements with Bangladesh and Nepal and, most important, an effort to lessen tensions with Pakistan, long viewed as a traditional enemy. Gujral managed to ease travel restrictions between the countries, strove for normalized diplomatic relations, and also initiated talks regarding their respective nuclear arsenals. The fact that Gujral was completely fluent in Urdu, the national language of Pakistan, and was himself a native Punjab, facilitated the crossing of this otherwise hostile cultural divide.

Gujral made impressive progress on all fronts until the Gowda administration collapsed after only 10 months in office. Apparently, the Congress Party felt that its needs were not being sufficiently addressed and withdrew from the United Front. The remaining coalition members cast about for a successor, and the scholarly, affable Gujral emerged as the most logical candidate, being well respected and having few political enemies. "I bow my head in all humility to the people of India and will to the best of my ability give them a clean government," he announced, "a government which serves them and attends to all their basic problems." He took the oath of office on April 21, 1997, amid speculation as to where his former communist leanings would take him. Fortunately, Gujral continued the free-market reforms of his predecessor and moved India away from its traditional, state-sponsored socialism. Gujral also made improved relations with Pakistan his highest foreign policy priority, and in May 1997 he met with Prime Minister MUHAMMAD NAWAZ SHARIF in the Maldives.

This represented the first face-to-face contacts between heads of state of the two countries in eight years, and they were cordially conducted. Consequently, a hotline was established between the two capitals and other meetings were arranged to encourage normalized relations. The foremost concern for both leaders was the ongoing crisis in Kashmir, a majority Muslim Indian province and site of a guerrilla war for independence. It remains a potential flashpoint between India and Pakistan.

Gujral had been in office only six months when his coalition suddenly unraveled. Apparently, one small member, the Tamil-based Dravida Munnetra Kazhagan (DMK), became tied to the 1991 assassination of Prime Minister Rajiv Gandhi. Other coalition members demanded that Gujral denounce the party and drop it from the alliance, but he refused. This led to wholesale defections from the United Front, and the prime minister resigned from office in November 1997. He oversaw a caretaker administration until spring 1998, when a new coalition emerged under ATAL BEHARI VAJPAYEE of the Hindu nationalist party Bharatiya Janata. Gujral has since returned to parliament as a leading opposition figure.

Further Reading

Atul, Kohli. *The Success of India's Democracy.* New York: Cambridge University Press, 2001.
Gopal, Niraja, ed. *Democracy in India.* New York: Oxford University Press, 2001.
Hansen, Thomas B., and Christophe Jaffrelot. *The BJP and the Compulsions of Politics in India.* New York: Oxford University Press, 2001.
Hasan, Zoya, ed. *Parties and Party Politics in India.* New York: Oxford University Press, 2002.
Leslie, Julia, and Mary McGee, eds. *Invented Identities: The Interplay of Gender, Religion, and Politics in India.* New York: Oxford University Press, 2000.

Gusmão, Xanana (1946–) *president of East Timor*

Xanana Gusmão was born on June 20, 1946, in Manatuto, East Timor (Timor Lorosae). His homeland, which forms the easternmost part of the Indonesian archipelago, had been a Portuguese colony for over 400 years. From 1615 the island of Timor itself was jointly ruled between Portugal and the Netherlands, who maintained West Timor as their own colony. East Timor is also distinct in being populated mostly by people of Papuan stock, not Malay, and while the western half of the island subscribes to Islam, East Timor is predominately Roman Catholic. Both halves endured a cruel occupation by Japanese forces in World War II, but while West Timor became part of the new nation of Indonesia, the eastern half reverted back to Portuguese control in 1946, the year of Gusmão's birth. He was educated locally and spent four years studying at a Jesuit seminary in the town of Dili. He subsequently performed three years of compulsory service with Portuguese colonial forces, whereby he absorbed the rudiments of military science, and he later worked as an administrator within the colonial regime. Things changed dramatically in 1975, however, when a left-wing coup toppled the Portuguese government, and its successors unilaterally declared all of its colonies free. East Timor's population, restive under colonial control, eagerly founded several political movements, of which the largest and most important was the Revolutionary Front of Independent East Timor (FRETILIN). After a brief civil war, FRETILIN proved successful and on November 28, 1975, East Timor declared its national independence under the aegis of President Francisco Xavier do Amaral.

East Timor's flirtation with independence proved fleeting, for in December 1975 President SUHARTO of Indonesia ordered a military invasion of the island. Over 10,000 troops suddenly descended upon the unsuspecting populace with great brutality. Atrocities were commonplace and an estimated 60,000 East Timorese died during the assault. Gusmão, fortunately, managed to survive the fighting and took to the hills as an insurgent. Joined by armed elements of FRETILIN, they then waged relentless guerrilla warfare against the invaders, who responded by rounding up and slaughtering thousands of innocent civilians. At this time Western powers like the United States blithely ignored such outrageous conduct simply because Suharto was staunchly anticommunist and viewed as an ally. Sporadic fighting, punctuated by wholesale massacres, continued unabated for the next 24 years, and an estimated 200,000 people were killed out of a total population of 750,000. By 1996 FRETILIN was almost spent as a fighting force, but its cause received additional impetus that year when José Ramos Horta and Bishop Carlos Belo won the Noble Peace Prize for their efforts on East Timor's behalf. Emboldened by the glare of international attention,

FRETILIN garnered new recruits and recommenced its long struggle toward independence.

In time, Gusmão acquired the reputation of a legendary commander, being both charismatic in command and calculating in battle. His luck expired in 1992 when he was captured and sentenced to life in prison. Fortunately, time and events were on East Timor's side. Mindful of the negative publicity the brutal occupation generated for Indonesia, a new president, BACHARUDDIN HABIBIE, began negotiations for a public referendum on independence. This transpired in August 1999 and passed by wide margins. However, angry pro-Indonesian militias went on a rampage to punish the population, massacring an estimated 10,000 people. Their excesses convinced the United Nations to finally intervene in force, and over 5,000 troops and police were dispatched to maintain order. Gusmão had been freed from prison in 1999 and was then under house arrest. He remained aloof from the prospect of holding political office, declaring he would rather be a pumpkin farmer or a photographer. "No, I do not want to become president," he said, "because if you look at almost every revolutionary struggle, the leaders who are there while in opposition become leaders of a new nation, and they have nothing more to give." However, he was unquestionably the favored candidate among the majority of East Timorese. On April 15, 2002, he ran as an independent among a field of 16 political parties, winning handily. On May 20, 2002, Gusmão was sworn into office as East Timor officially became the world's newest nation. Significantly, one of the dignitaries in attendance was MEGAWATI SUKARNOPUTRI, who had released Gusmão from prison, former U.S. president BILL CLINTON, and UN General Secretary KOFI ANNAN.

Gusmão assumed office amid much national rejoicing, for his 24-year struggle had finally prevailed. However, new contests lay before him. The occupation had gutted the nation, ruined the economy, and destroyed most of its infrastructure. The UN pledged billions of dollars in financial aid, but the bulk of reconstruction must be shouldered by the East Timorese people. Gusmão also pledged to seek foreign investment to help develop the island's offshore oil deposits, which could bring in billions of dollars in revenue within five years. More importantly, the president strongly encourages national reconciliation toward citizens guilty of collaborating with the occupiers. "The Indonesian people and the Timorese people have endured 24 years of difficult relations," he declared. "Today, we all agree that the strains in our dealings was a result of a historical mistake, which now belongs to history and the past." The nation—and people—of East Timor deserve no less.

Further Reading

Cox, Steve. *Generations of Resistance: East Timor.* London: Cassell, 1995.

Hill, Helen. *Stirrings of Nationalism in East Timor: Fretilin 1974–1978: The Origins, Ideologies, and Strategies of a Nationalist Movement.* Oxford, New South Wales: Oxford University Press, 2002.

Gusmão, Xanana. *To Resist Is to Win: The Autobiography of Xanana Gusmão.* Melbourne: Aurora Books with David Lovell Publishing, 2000.

Saul, Ben. "Was the Conflict in East Timor 'Genocide' and Does it Really Matter?" *Melbourne Journal of International Law* 2 (December 2001): 477–517.

Smith Michael G. *Peacekeeping in East Timor: The Path to Independence.* Boulder, Colo.: Lynne Rienner Publishers, 2002.

Tanter, Richard, and Stephen R. Shalom. *Bitter Flowers, Sweet Flowers: East Timor, Indonesia, and the World Community.* Sydney: Pluto Press Australia, 2001.

Guterres, Antonio Manuel de Oliveira

(1949–   ) prime minister of Portugal

Antonio Manuel de Oliveira Guterres was born on April 30, 1949, in Lisbon, Portugal, into a traditional Roman Catholic family. Portugal, which had been a republic since 1910, had long been ruled by a right-wing, authoritarian regime under Antonio de Oliveira Salazar, who established control in 1932. A left-wing coup in 1974 deposed the conservatives and instituted a new constitution establishing participatory, multiparty democracy. The constitution also mandated creation of a largely ceremonial office of president, a prime minister who headed the government and, thus, possessed real power, and a unicameral legislature, the Assembly of the Republic. Several parties exist in Portugal, but the main political contenders are the conservative Social Democratic Party (SDP) and the Portuguese Socialist Party (PSP), who have alternated power over the years. In practice, ideological differences between the two have grown slight, and national elections appear to be determined more by personalities than by issues.

As he matured, Guterres attended Lisbon University and acquired a degree in electrical engineering. At that time he became strongly attracted to the Socialist Party while working with the Catholic University Youth, and he joined the party in the wake of the 1974 revolution. He then became a ministerial assistant for Prime Minister MARIO SOARES, and, in 1976, he gained election to the assembly. After losing his seat in 1983, Guterres was reelected in 1985 and he also served as deputy to the assembly. The Socialists at that time had been turned out of power and were functioning as the opposition. In this capacity, Guterres demonstrated a flair for pragmatism that transcended ideology and he developed a following in both the left and moderate wings of the party. In 1992 Guterres was elevated to vice president of the Socialist International. However, the elections of October 1995 went decidedly against the Social Democrats, the Socialists were returned to power, and Guterres succeeded Cavaco Silva as prime minister.

Back in power after a decade of opposition, the Socialists held high hopes for their continuing political fortunes under Guterres. Like TONY BLAIR of Britain, he was youthful, telegenic, and smart. He was also practical enough not to tamper with the privatization policies of his conservative predecessor, under which inefficient state industries had been sold to the private sector. Consequently, when the economy began reviving a few months later, Guterres and the Socialists received the credit. A grateful electorate then returned him to office during elections held on October 10, 1999.

Again, the Socialists expected to solidify their gains at the national level and hold power for several years. However, Portugal's unsteady economic performance militated against their hopes. In fact, given the country's entrenched and largely unproductive bureaucracy, it is the least productive member of the European Union (EU). By 2001 the economy had contracted a full percentage point to 2.0 percent annual GNP and the business community began criticizing Guterres's performance. The prime minister was then forced to moderate his policy of promised wage increases to keep pace with inflation, as dictated by EU regulations, which alienated more strident members of his party. Worse, the Socialists were either unable or unwilling to modernize the bureaucracy. Consequently, citizens had to endure insufferable waits for promised medical services, long delayed verdicts from an inefficient judicial system, and a general sense that public services were failing. This last point was underscored in March 2001, when a bridge over the Douro River collapsed, killing 70 people. The disaster led to the resignation of Public Works Minister Jorge Coehlo, who had long been viewed as Guterres's likely successor.

The turning point in Socialist political fortunes under Guterres occurred in local elections held in October 2001. In light of the Socialists' failure to revive Portugal's economy, the opposition Social Democrats took 141 of 308 councils, while the left secured only 98. Guterres, humiliated by the results, felt compelled to leave office. "I requested this audience to present my resignation from the post of prime minister," the dejected leader told journalists on December 17, 2001. "This defeat is my defeat." Guterres also stepped down as general secretary of the Socialist Party and withdrew from politics altogether. His resignation sent the country into something of a tailspin, for new national elections were not scheduled until October 2003. President Jorge Sampaio had little recourse but to schedule elections for March 21, 2002, to choose a new prime minister. At that time the Social Democrats under José Manuel Durão Barroso roared back to power, taking 116 seats out of 230 in the legislature. This was just short of an absolute majority, so the conservatives formed a coalition with the right-wing Popular Party. At that time, President Sampaio asked Barroso for a new center-right government. In sum, it appears that the Socialists, who held power for six years, failed to enact badly needed institutional and economic changes. Resting on their laurels seemed the natural thing to do, but it ultimately cost them their mandate for office.

Further Reading

Magone, Jose M. *European Portugal: The Difficult Road to Sustainable Democracy.* New York: St. Martin's Press, 1997.

Manuel, Paul C. *Uncertain Outcome: The Politics of the Portuguese Transition to Democracy.* Lanham, Md.: University Press of Maryland, 1995.

Maxwell, Kenneth. *The Making of Portuguese Democracy.* New York: Cambridge University Press, 1995.

Ortiz Griffin, Julia, and William O. Griffen. *Spain and Portugal Today.* New York: Peter Lang, 2002.

Royo, Sebastian. *A New Century of Corporatism? Corporatism in Southern Europe: Spain and Portugal in Comparative Perspective.* Westport, Conn.: Praeger, 2002.

H

Habibie, Bacharuddin Jusuf (1936–)

president of Indonesia

Bacharuddin Jusuf Habibie was born on June 25, 1936, in Pare Pare, Indonesia, the son of a government agricultural minister. His father died while he was still young, and he was informally adopted by Suharto, a military officer residing nearby. Habibie excelled at mathematics in school, and he studied at the Bandung Institute of Technology. There he won a scholarship to pursue advanced aeronautics in Germany, and he subsequently attended the Technische Hochschüle of Aachen in 1956. Technically competent, Habibie went on to acquire his doctorate from the Aachen Institute in 1965, and for nearly a decade thereafter he worked as an aircraft engineer at Messerschmitt-Boelkow-Bluhm, rising to vice president. Habibie remained so employed until 1974 when SUHARTO, now Indonesia's dictator, invited him home to become a technical consultant.

Habibie relished the opportunity to serve with his longtime friend, and in 1978 he gained appointment as minister of research and technology. But, despite his distinguished background in engineering, he lacked the foresight and temperament for high office. Habibie sponsored numerous and ill-fated projects, invariably costing millions of dollars and profiting only himself and his immediate family, who controlled the various businesses involved. He squandered $2 billion alone in an ill-conceived attempt to foster an Indonesian aerospace industry, which led to production of only one airplane—a small passenger liner called the CN-235. They functioned poorly when built and were never fully deployed. Equally scandalous was his decision to foist 100 aging East German warships on the Indonesian navy without prior consultations. Once purchased, they were found to require up to $1 billion in repairs to make them combat-ready. Despite this steady stream of debacles, Habibie was determined to "leap-frog" over low-skill industries and initiate highly complex projects that Indonesia could scarcely sustain, let alone afford. He soon became the butt of public humor, especially considering his high-strung disposition and proclivity toward shrill, inane babbling. Nonetheless, Suharto's patronage made him unassailable for the time being, so he became closely identified with the corruption and cronyism of that regime. On a more positive note, Habibie was a devout Muslim, and, in 1990, he founded the Indonesian Association of Muslim Intellectuals.

The high point in Habibie's public career happened in the spring of 1998. The Indonesian economy, never sound, was hard-hit by the Asian financial crisis and began sputtering to a halt. This triggered a wave of public unrest, particularly among workers and students angered by the regime's repression. In March 1998, Suharto surprised critics when he suddenly and inexplicably appointed Habibie vice president. He appears to have done this more out of loyalty than expediency, for the minister was singularly unsuited and untrained for national leadership. Predictably, the move did little to foster either political calm or economic growth, and, on May 21, 1998, Suharto ended his 32 year reign by resigning. Habibie then assumed the presidency, although political insiders gave him almost no chance of surviving the internecine nature of Indonesian politics.

Once in power, the new president pledged to root out corruption, nepotism, and also restore democracy. He was never taken seriously on any count, but he surprised critics by completely overhauling the nature of Indonesian politics. In dismantling his mentor's authoritarian legacy, political prisoners were freed, the press unmuzzled, and multiparty democracy encouraged. More impressively, Habibie determined to end the protracted and costly occupation of neighboring East Timor, and he authorized the question of its independence to be placed on an islandwide referendum. "I was very much aware of the many irreversible decisions that I have to make which could be very counterproductive for my country," he explained, "and for the first time I was really alone." The new president seemed earnest and well-intentioned, but his liberalization of politics released long-simmering resentments against the government. Fighting broke out between Malay Muslims and Chinese Christians, and several students were killed by army units during antigovernment demonstrations. It was against this setting of spiraling communal violence that Indonesia's first free elections transpired in June 1999.

Predictably and because of prior associations with Suharto, Habibie and his Golkar Party were summarily swept from office. The new winners were MEGAWATI SUKARNOPUTRI, daughter of a famous national leader, and ABDHURRAHMAN WAHID, a near-blind Muslim cleric. Habibie, for his part, expressed no further interest in politics and pledged to resign in December 1999. "You know, if you are swimming and you are surrounded by sharks, you have to swim, otherwise you will be eaten," he stated, "and I am not going to be eaten by the shark." Accordingly, having left office as promised, Habibie relocated to Germany with a family fortune estimated at $80 million. In February 2002 he returned to Indonesia to be questioned as a witness by the Bulog (National Logistics Agency) about a multimillion dollar funding scandal. The eccentric former president was not implicated and he returned to Germany immediately after.

Further Reading

Bourchier, David, and Vedi R. Hadiz, eds. *Indonesian Politics and Society: A Reader*. New York: Routledge, 2003.

Ford, Michelle. "Continuity and Change in Indonesian Labour Relations in the Habibie Interregnum." *Southeast Asian Journal of Social Science* 28, no. 2 (2000): 59–88.

Heryanto, Ariel, and Sumit K. Mandal. *Challenging Authoritarianism in Southeast Asia: Comparing Indonesia and Malaysia*. New York: RoutledgeCurzon, 2003.

Kingsbury, Damien. "The Reform of the Indonesian Armed Forces." *Contemporary Southeast Asia* 22, no. 2 (2000): 302–321.

Liddle, R. William. "Indonesia's Democratic Opening." *Government and Opposition* 34 (Winter 1994): 94–107.

Manning, Chris, and Peter Van Diermen, eds. *Indonesia in Transition: Social Aspects of Reformasi and Crisis*. London: Zed, 2000.

Porter, Donald. *Managing Politics and Islam in Indonesia*. Richmond, England: Curzon, 2002.

Habyarimana, Juvénal (1937–1994)

president of Rwanda

Juvénal Habyarimana was born on March 8, 1937, in Gaziza, Gisenyi prefecture, Rwanda. His homeland was then a Belgian colony, and Brussels ruled by playing off long-standing rivalries between the region's two main ethnic groups, the majority Hutu and the minority Tutsi. Thus, Rwanda was increasingly predisposed toward social friction, resentment, and violence. Habyarimana, meanwhile, was educated locally, and he attended the College of St. Paul in neighboring Bukavu, Zaire (Congo). He subsequently studied medicine for a year at Lovanium University, Kinshasa, Zaire, before quitting to join the Officer's School at Kigali in December 1960. He graduated one year later with honors, and he was commissioned in the National Guard immediately following independence from Belgium. Rwanda was then ruled by President Gregoire Kayibanda, who promoted Habyarimana chief of staff in 1963, aged 28 years. The young officer performed well in his appointed role, and, in 1965, he advanced to minister of the armed forces and to major general by 1973. However, by now Rwanda was increasingly beset by economic problems that, in turn, stimulated violence between rival Hutus and Tutsis. When Kayibanda appeared incapable or unwilling to restore order, Habyarimana suddenly seized control in a bloodless coup on April 1, 1973.

Over the next two decades, Habyarimana proved himself one of Africa's most fleet-footed political survivors. He initially banned all political activity and ruled through a Committee for Peace and National Unity, staffed mostly by northern Hutus like himself. Once firmly in control his plan for a gradual return to democracy unfolded. In July 1975 Habyarimana announced creation of the National Revolutionary Movement for Development (MRND), which would serve as Rwanda's sole political party. A new constitution was then promulgated in December 1978, which enshrined both one-party rule and confirmed Habyarimana as president. National legislative elections were held in December 1983 with only MRND candidates present, and in December 1983 Habyarimana ran unopposed for the presidency. As the only candidate, he "won" by large margins, and was reelected a third time in December 1988. Through all these expedients Habyarimana imposed a façade of democracy upon his long-suffering people, but in reality his rule could never be seriously challenged. But while in office he also took steps to ease ethnic frictions by eliminating ethnic identity cards and promoting more harmonious relations.

Impetus for change in Rwanda originated from outside the country. By 1989 the national economy reeled from declining coffee prices (its main cash crop), while population pressures and soil erosion also contributed to rising instability. Consequently, Habyarimana was forced by the International Monetary Fund (IMF) to impose strict austerity measures, which eroded his support. But the biggest change came in September 1990 when, faced with increasing international pressure from lending countries, he finally acquiesced to true, multiparty elections. By then, however, it was too late. Beginning that year the Rwanda Popular Front (RPF), consisting of exiled Tutsis and moderate Hutus, conducted armed incursions into the country from neighboring Uganda. With military help from France the rebels were contained, but constant fighting drained the country of its vital resources. Ethnic tensions continued escalating after Habyarimana entered into peace talks with the RPF, and, in June 1991, political pluralism became a reality. Two years later a power-sharing arrangement was reached with the rebels and many leading rebel figures stopped fighting to join the government. Unfor-

tunately, a militant faction led by PAUL KAGAME refused to lay down its arms and, by 1993, his partisans were within reach of the capital.

Fighting continued sporadically over the next three years as Habyarimana scrambled to hang on to power. He finally reissued ethnic identification cards, restricted Tutsis to 7 percent of government posts available, and tried manipulating ongoing strife to his best advantage. In April 1994 Habyarimana attended talks in Dar-es-Salaam, Tanzania, concerning the spread of regional ethnic tensions. On April 6, he flew home together with Burundi president CYPRIEN NTARYAMIRA, who confronted from similar problems. As the aircraft approached Kigali, it was suddenly struck by an antiaircraft missile and brought down. Habyarimana and Ntaryamira both died instantly and their deaths sparked one of the greatest tragedies of the 20th century. The Hutu-dominated military blamed rebel forces for the deed and they went on a rampage, murdering half a million Tutsis and creating 1.2 million refugees. It was not until Kagame's RPF finally triumphed that peace returned to this war-ravaged land.

Further Reading

Adleman, Howard, and Astri Suhrke. *The Path of Genocide: The Rwanda Crisis from Uganda to Zaire.* New Brunswick, N.J.: Transaction Publishers, 2000.

Khan, Shaharyar M. *The Shallow Graves of Rwanda.* New York: I. B. Tauris, 2000.

Newbury, Catherine, and David Newbury. "A Catholic Mass in Kingali: Contested Views of the Genocide and Ethnicity in Rwanda." *Canadian Journal of African Studies* 33, nos. 2–3 (1999): 292–328.

Shalom, S. R. "The Rwanda Genocide." *Z Magazine* 9 (April 1996): 25–36.

Verwimp, Philip. "Development Ideology, the Peasantry, and Genocide: Rwanda Represented in Habyarimana's Speeches." *Journal of Genocide Research* 2, no. 3 (2000): 325–361.

Haider, Jörg (1950–) *Austrian politician*

Jörg Haider was born on December 26, 1950, in Bad Goisern, Austria. His parents were enthusiastic Nazis who supported Germany in World War II and transferred much of their political invective to their son. Haider, an excellent, hard-working student, attended the University of Vienna and received his law degree in

1973. He also became active in the Austrian Freedom Party (FPO), then a small organization espousing extreme right-wing views. At that time the party polled only around 9 percent in national elections. Haider took readily to politics, acquiring the reputation of a charismatic speaker and a skilled operator. By 1976 he served as secretary of the FPO in his native state of Carinthia, and three years later he stood for a seat in parliament. He became the youngest member in that body, and, in 1986, he became national chairman. In 1989 Haider next campaigned on a hard-line, anti-immigrant platform and won a surprisingly easy victory for the governorship of Carinthia. But Haider, even at this juncture, remained something of a political enigma, and few really understood what his views were, or how extreme they might be. These unknowns were dramatically answered in 1991, when he publicly praised Adolph Hitler's anti-Jewish and anti-immigrant policies. Austria, as Hitler's birthplace, was uncomfortable with its past relationship to Nazism. In 1986 revelations about President Kurt Waldheim's World War II career greatly embarrassed the nation, and the ensuing uproar forced Haider from office. However, the FPO, as avatars of hatred, now occupied a conspicuous niche on the Austrian political landscape.

Haider was unrepentant about his remarks, but the episode afforded him valuable lessons in tact. He then quietly set about rebuilding his political fortunes, and, in March 1999, the FPO won 42 percent of the votes in regional elections. Haider became governor of Carinthia a second time, again by stressing anti-immigrant themes and resistance to the European Union (EU). By now the Austrian people had grown restive under the political status quo and weary of the entrenched graft seemingly endemic to the mainstream People's Party and the Social Democrats. Prior to national elections held that fall, the FPO pledged to upend the old order and root out corruption, themes that found much popular approval. Haider's none-too-subtle strategy of tapping into public anger worked. On October 3, 1999 the FPO won an impressive 27 percent of votes cast, their largest tally to date. Their votes came largely at the expense of the People's Party under WOLFGANG SCHUESSEL, who now needed a coalition arrangement to stay in power. By February 2000, when talks with the opposition Social Democrats failed, he had no alternative but to approach the FPO as a partner. Thanks to Haider's political savvy—and clever manipulation of discontent—the far right finally established a foothold in government for the first time since World War II.

The inclusion of an extremist like Haider sent shockwaves around Europe, and many governments protested election of an individual whom they considered to be a pro-Nazi figure. Both Israel and the United States withdrew their ambassadors, while Austria's fellow EU members imposed economic sanctions. This, in turn, forced Schuessel and President THOMAS KLESTIL to assume the diplomatic offensive by downplaying Haider's actual role. After all, he was not included in the government and had even stepped down as head of the FPO. His retirement was probably a ploy to make the party appear more palatable to outsiders, and within months the sanctions were removed. But Haider, who reveled in the role of a lightning rod, refused to let the dust settle peacefully. In December 1999 he collected several hundred thousand signatures demanding that the Czech government relent from putting into operation a Soviet-era nuclear reactor at Temelin. The protest drew sharp criticism from Prime Minister MILOŠ ZEMAN, who eventually submitted to enhanced safety measures at the plant. In February 2002 Haider again raised hackles by personally visiting President SADDAM HUSSEIN, expressing sympathy for the Iraqi people, and demanding that UN sanctions be lifted. He then announced his decision to withdraw from national politics and the FPO altogether. "If the party thinks they are grown up enough and want to stand on their own two feet, then I do not want to be seen as interfering," Haider remarked, "I will concentrate on my role as governor of Carinthia." In this capacity he continues railing against the presence of foreigners in Austria, and the cultural baggage they carry. Haider openly scoffed at laws requiring signs in his province to be posted in German and Slovene, and he derided the Supreme Court justice who authorized them for having a Slavic surname. It remains to be seen if Haider can parley his racially tinged dogma into a viable political career or if he will remain simply Austria's most visible spokesman for the extreme right.

Further Reading

Heilbrun, Jacob. "A Disdain for the Past: Jorg Haider's Austria." *World Policy Journal* 17 (Spring 2000): 71–78.

Hobelt, Lothar. *Jorg Haider and the Politics of Austria, 1986–2000.* West Lafayette, Ind.: Purdue University Press, 2002.

Luther, Kurt R. "Austria: A Democracy under Threat from the Freedom Party." *Parliamentary Affairs* 53 (July 2000): 426–442.

Thompson, Peter. "Jorg Haider and the Paradoxical Crisis of Social Democracy in Europe Today." *Debatte* 8, no. 1 (2000): 9–22.

Wodak, Ruth, and Anton Pelinka, eds. *The Haider Phenomenon in Austria.* New Brunswick, N.J.: Transaction Publishers, 2002.

Hans Adam II (1945–   ) *prince of Liechtenstein*

Hans Adam Pius was born in Liechtenstein on February 15, 1945, a son of Franz Josef II, the ruling prince. His country, one of the world's smallest, is nestled between Switzerland and Austria amid the picturesque Alps. The breathtaking countryside, dotted with medieval castles, give it the appearance of a fairytale kingdom. Liechtenstein has existed as a principality since the 12th century, and it is the only surviving remnant of the Holy Roman Empire. Since 1921 it has functioned as a constitutional monarchy, although women were denied the right to vote until 1984. Wealthy and studiously neutral in its foreign relations, Liechtenstein also enjoys one of the highest standards of living in the world. It presently derives the bulk of its income from its role as a high-tech manufacturing and exporting center, and the country also serves as a center for large-scale international banking.

Hans Adam attended public schools at the insistence of his father, who wished that he maintain contact with his subjects. He subsequently received higher education at the Catholic Schotten Gymnasium in Vienna, Austria, 1956–60. In 1969 he received a degree in economics from the University of Switzerland. For nearly a decade thereafter, Hans Adam lived in luxurious splendor, and he oversaw family holdings worth an estimated $4 billion. He ascended to the throne following his father's death on November 13, 1989. Hans Adam enjoys hereditary rights as a prince, and usually functions outside the political mainstream as an impartial observer and adviser. He is folksy, unpretentious, and readily accessible, and he thus enjoys a great degree of popularity among the citizens of Liechtenstein, who are also his subjects.

As prince, Hans Adam sought to modernize his 300-year-old country and bring it more into line with 20th-century practices. For example, he was an outspoken proponent of giving women the right to vote, and he championed a public referendum granting them suffrage in 1984. He then urged his country to join the United Nations, which it did in 1990. Hans Adam also sought to update the antiquated criminal code with a new one, encouraged overhauling the existing tax codes, and supported imposition of an income tax. He has also drawn heavily on his background as a trained economist to insure that Liechtenstein continues to enjoy a highly diversified mix of business and technology.

Officially, Liechtenstein tows a neutral, nonaligned course in diplomacy, and it usually allows Switzerland to represent it in international dealings. However, in June 2001, Hans Adam filed a complaint against Germany with the UN's International Court of Justice. Apparently, during World War II Nazi Germany confiscated much of the family's holdings in Czechoslovakia. Afterward, the postwar German government donated the property, including castles and art works valued at $675 million, to the Czech government, without compensation to Liechtenstein. The prince is thus pressing for either monetary redress or return of the items seized. In addition, recent events have militated against Liechtenstein's reputation as a placid, storybook kingdom. A scandal erupted in November 1999, when members of the German intelligence community made it known that several banks in Liechtenstein routinely engage in the illegal practice of money laundering to assist criminal elements. Among their various "customers" were Colombian drug lords and Russian mafia dons. Hans Adam was not exactly stunned by the revelation, conceding that "the fight against white-collar crime has not been very efficient in the past, and that is perhaps putting it politely." Accordingly, a high-level Austrian prosecutor was brought in whose investigations resulted in the arrest of the deputy prime minister and two brothers of the chief justice. The parliament then passed sweeping legislation to assist foreign investigators to acquire banking information as well as to make available official reports of any shady transactions. The United States also weighed in with new regulations requiring that Liechtenstein alert the Internal Revenue Service of all customers who are American citizens—and apparently hiding assets there to avoid taxation. Thus Liechtenstein's traditional role as an international tax haven appears to have been downgraded.

Hans Adam has also enjoyed a stormy relationship with the national legislature over various reform issues. In July 2000 he demanded the right to nominate judges

Hans Adam II *(Permanent Mission of the Principality of Liechtenstein to the United Nations)*

to make them independent of the political process and, hence, less susceptible to outside influence. Failing this, he threatened to move out of the country entirely. Rather than lose their prince, voters passed the referendum by a wide margin. In February 2002, he again confronted the legislature with demands for constitutional reforms to maintain his hereditary powers. "The history of the 20th century unfortunately has all too many examples of self-styled democrats getting rid of a monarchy," he cautioned, "without the approval of the people, and then setting up a dictatorship." The issue as of yet remains undecided. Should a public referendum on the subject fail to pass, he is again threatening to leave his postcard kingdom for a more accommodating clime.

Further Reading

Duurama, Jorri. *Self-Determination, Statehood, and International Relations of Micro-States: The Cases of Liecht-enstein, San Marino, Monaco, Andorra, and the Vatican City.* New York: Cambridge University Press, 1996.

Lack, H. Walter, and Martin Walters. *A Garden for Eternity: The Codex Liechtenstein.* Berne: Switzerland, 2000.

Meier, Regula A. *Liechtenstein.* Santa Barbara, Calif.: ABC-Clio, 1993.

Moore, Russell F. *The Principality of Liechtenstein: A Brief History.* New York: Simmons-Boardman, 1960.

Hariri, Rafiq al- (1944–) *prime minister of Lebanon*

Rafiq Baha'uddin al-Hariri was born on November 1, 1944, in Sidon, Lebanon, the son of poor farmers. As a child he worked in the orchards and eventually accumulated enough money to attend the Arab University in Beirut. Hariri graduated in 1965 with a degree in economics and subsequently relocated to Saudi Arabia. He worked as a mathematics teacher in Jiddah for many years before founding his own construction company in 1970. Hariri proved himself an astute businessman and by 1978 he had bought out Ogen, a French firm. He also ingratiated himself with the Saudi royal family by constructing numerous palaces and luxury hotels on time and under budget. As a naturalized Saudi citizen, he eventually expanded his business empire to include construction, finance, and telecommunication, and, by 1980, he was one of the world's wealthiest men. At this time he started turning his attention back to Lebanon, then rocked by internecine civil strife and repeated Israeli invasions. As of 1982 his company began a massive reconstruction project to rebuild devastated Beirut, only to be interrupted by outbreaks of violence. Saudi Arabia then offered its services as a mediator and Hariri actively pursued peace negotiations. In 1989 he helped orchestrate the signing of the Taif Agreement, which ended the civil war and brought about a national entente. The following year he returned to Lebanon to assist rebuilding his shattered homeland.

Hariri used his great wealth to both facilitate business ventures and assist needy citizens. As early as 1984 he founded the Hariri Foundation, which dispensed millions of dollars to Lebanese students attending college. He also donated to institutions of higher learning and hospitals throughout the country. As a Sunni Muslim, Hariri was eligible to run for prime minister as that office was reserved only for members of his creed under Lebanon's sectarian division of government. He was also a unique candidate, not coming from the elite landed clan from which national leaders are traditionally drawn. And, in light of his charitable and philanthropic activities, he was also one of Lebanon's most popular figures. In October 1992 Hariri was elected prime minister in the administration of President ELIAS HRAWI, a Maronite Christian. Once in power he outspokenly criticized Israel for repeated incursions into southern Lebanon and, like Hrawi, generally towed the Syrian line in foreign policy. He also increased his reconstruction efforts by attracting billions of dollars in foreign investments, borrowing heavily, to restore Beirut to its prewar glory.

Hariri was first and foremost a billionaire tycoon, and he was soon criticized for contractual arrangements that enriched himself and his inner circle of friends. Moreover, he paid inordinate amounts of time and money resurrecting the moribund financial sector, while neglecting industry and agriculture. Hariri felt that once money began flowing through Lebanon, the rest of the economy would also grow. However, by 1994 Lebanon's gross national product declined, and the country remained billions of dollars in debt. These deficits, in turn, raised interest rates and contributed to the downward spiral. Once Hariri was accused of corruption he tendered his resignation to Hwari, which was refused. But by 1998, despite an impressive national facelift, the recession had not improved, and the prime minister came under increasing pressure to resign. When the new Syrian president, BASHIR AL-ASSAD, sacked many of Hariri's allies in Damascus, his political position in Lebanon was further compromised. The final straw proved the difficulties experienced in dealing with President EMILE LAHOUD, a former general, who was a more formidable opponent than the pliable Hwari. Hariri subsequently resigned as prime minister and was replaced by another Sunni Muslim, Salim al-Hoss.

Over the next two years Hariri continued to expand his business and telecommunications empire, all the while flaunting his personal relationships with such national leaders as JACQUES CHIRAC of France. By 2000 al-Hoss's administration had yet to improve the economy significantly and new elections were scheduled for the fall. Not surprisingly, Hariri used his media empire to promote his campaign for office, and he was resoundingly reelected prime minister. "We are facing a new era," he declared. "We call on everybody to show solidarity in order to restore our confidence in our country, our government, and our institutions." During his second term, Hariri displayed more independence from Syria than previously, but he remains too popular a figure for Damascus to remove. Hariri also has sought closer relations with the United States in his drive to help end the ongoing Israeli-Palestinian conflict. He pledged Lebanon's assistance in the war against global terrorism, but he then refused an American request to freeze the assets of Hezbollah, an Islamic-based guerrilla group based in southern Lebanon. Hariri insists that this organization conducts legitimate resistance toward Israeli aggression and, hence, its members are not terrorists. Despite this Syrian-inspired posturing, Hariri's business acumen is needed to help Lebanon out of its economic doldrums.

Further Reading

Dagher, Carole. *Bring Down the Walls: Lebanon's Postwar Challenge.* New York: St. Martin's Press, 2000.

Ellis, Kail C., ed. *Lebanon's Second Republic: Prospects for the Twenty-first Century.* Gainesville: University Press of Florida, 2002.

Khalifah, Bassem. *The Rise and Fall of Christian Lebanon.* Toronto: York Press, 2001.

Picard, Elizabeth. *Lebanon: A Shattered Country: Myths and Realities of the Wars in Lebanon.* New York: Holmes and Meier, 2002.

Saad-Ghorayel, Amal. *Hizbu'llah: Politics and Religion.* Sterling, Va.: Pluto Press, 2002.

Hashimoto, Ryutaro (1937–) *prime minister of Japan*

Ryutaro Hashimoto was born on July 29, 1937, in Tokyo, Japan, the son of a politician. His father, Ryogo Hashimoto, had been crippled since childhood by polio but overcame his difficulties and successfully ran for office in his home district. Eventually he rose to become health and welfare minister, a fact which inspired his son toward politics. Hashimoto himself graduated from elite Keio University in 1960 with a degree in political science. He then worked in a spinning mill for three years until his father died in 1963, and he successfully ran for his vacated seat in the House of Representatives. Like his father, he belonged to the Liberal Democratic Party (LDP), which had successfully dominated national politics since 1956. But, unlike many Japanese politicians, who are scrupulously conformist by nature, Hashimoto proved himself brash and loud—replete with slicked-back, jet black hair and Elvis-style sideburns. His unconventional style was apparently well received at home, for he gained reelection to parliament over 12 consecutive terms. In time he came to be regarded as one of the rising stars of the LDP and virtually assured a high rank within the party.

Recognition of Hashimoto's abilities came quickly and, commencing in the 1970s, he was tapped to fill a number of high-level ministerial positions. These included health and welfare minister (like his father), transportation minister, finance minister, and finally trade minister. In this last post Hashimoto confirmed his reputation as one of Japan's most unconventional statesmen. By 1994 Japan and the United States were headed for a trade war over the former's reluctance to import more American cars and spare parts. Japan's noncompliance proved so extreme that U.S. president BILL CLINTON threatened to initiate retaliatory trade measures. To circumvent this disruption, Hashimoto met repeatedly with his U.S. counterpart, Mickey Kantor, and he was decidedly confrontational and outspoken during intense negotiations. In the end, sanctions were averted after both sides compromised, and the contestants both walked away declaring "victory." But Hashimoto's resolve to stand up to the Americans enhanced his popularity both at home and within the LDP. Consequently, in September 1994 he was elevated to party head and became widely regarded as a possible contender for prime minister. He served as deputy prime minister until the resignation of Socialist premier TOMIICHI MURAYAMA, and he assumed the executive office as of January 11, 1996. The LDP had finally returned to power after a scandal-filled hiatus, but, given the volatile nature of Japanese politics, Hashimoto was the fourth prime minister in three years.

Much was expected of the new administration, as Japan was in dire straits. For nearly five consecutive years the country sank deeper and deeper into recession, and its economic problems were further exacerbated by the onset of banking and loan scandals. Hashimoto had nonetheless pledged to root out corruption and deregulate the economy, and he confronted a very tall order. He faced numerous scandals within his own party, and opposition leader Ichirio Ozawa led a sit-in at parliament that nearly closed down the government, but the Japanese public was willing to give him more time. The elections of October 1996 increased LDP's numbers in the Diet, and Hashimoto was easily reelected. He thus felt empowered to enact a sweeping stimulus and reform package, the so-called Big-Bang program, to eliminate regulatory barriers to make it easier for foreign companies to operate in Japan. He also tried tackling the national debt, which drove up interest rates and made the recession worse. In 1997 he took the politically courageous decision to raise the sales tax from 3 percent to 5 percent, coupled with deep cuts in government spending. However, what little progress these moves accomplished were erased by the Asian currency crisis of that year, and the national economy sputtered. On July 12, 1998, new elections brought LDP the loss of 17 seats in the upper chamber as if to underscore public displeasure with the government's performance. Consequently, to save face, Hashimoto resigned as prime minister on July 31, 1998, and he was replaced by another LDP stalwart, Keizo Obuchi. "As all politicians do," he reflected, "I will make, in my own heart, my own decision about my political future. I will make a decision that is reasonable in my own mind."

Hashimoto retained a measure of national popularity despite his resignation. In the spring of 2001 he was widely touted as a front-runner to replace outgoing prime minister YOSHIRO MORI, but he unexpectedly lost to another flamboyant contender, JUNICHIRO KOIZUMI. But the following year he was selected to head a group dispatched to China in commemoration of the 30th anniversary of normalized relations. This was a touchy assignment for such a strident nationalist, but Hashimoto was determined to succeed. "It is our responsibility to further promote the relationship so that our 30 years of efforts in the past will not be wasted," he stated.

Further Reading

Mishima, Ko. "The Changing Relationship between Japan's LDP and the Bureaucracy: Hashimoto's Administrative Reform Effort and Its Politics." *Asian Survey* 38 (October 1998): 968–989.

Nakano, Koichi. "The Politics of Administrative Reform in Japan, 1993–1998: Toward a More Accountable Government?" *Asian Survey* 38 (March 1998): 291–310.

Neary, Ian. *The State of Politics in Japan.* Malden, Mass.: Blackwell Publishers, 2002.

Reed, Steven R. *Japanese Electoral Politics: Creating a New Party System.* New York: Routledge, 2003.

Tipton, Elsie K. *Modern Japan: A Social and Political History.* New York: Routledge, 2001.

Zagorsky, Alexi V. "Three Years on a Path to Nowhere: The Hashimoto Initiative in Russo-Japanese Relations." *Pacific Affairs* 74 (Spring 2001): 75–93.

Hassan II (1929–1999) *king of Morocco*

Mouley Hassan was born on July 9, 1929, in Rabat, Morocco, the son of King Mohammed V. He was well educated at home before obtaining a law degree from the University of Bordeaux in France. At the time, Morocco was restive as a French colony, and both Hassan and his father were exiled to Corsica in 1955 for political activism. However, independence was achieved the following year and Hassan gained appointment as chief of staff of the armed forces. In this capacity he ruthlessly suppressed armed Riff uprisings in 1957 and 1959. In 1961 he ascended to the throne as Hassan II after the death of his father, becoming the 17th monarch of the Alawi dynasty. This lineage had ruled Morocco since the 1750s and, by claiming direct descent from the Prophet Mohammed, functioned both as caliphs (religious leaders) and zaims (national leaders). From the onset, Hassan proved determined to succeed at both. More inclined toward modernism than his father, he initially supported constitutional reforms in 1963, but growing instability at the hands of left-wing agitators induced him to clamp down on all dissent. After 1965 the king preferred ruling with an iron hand in order to maintain political stability. He introduced moderate reforms at his own pace and of his own choosing so as to ensure his own survival. For nearly four decades thereafter, Hassan proved himself one of the most skillfully adaptive players in this notoriously unstable part of the world.

Hassan proved popular with his subjects, but he had to endure two coups attempted by the military in 1971 and 1972. He narrowly escaped on both occasions, which lent his reign an air of *baraka* or blessedness, unique to Moroccan holymen. Hassan also used his role as supreme religious leader to deflect the rising tide of Muslim fundamentalism in the Arab world. In Moroccan politics, to assail the king—the "commander of the faithful"—is to assail God himself, so religious agitation found itself constrained by traditional political dynamics. This is not to say Hassan tolerated religious dissent or otherwise; he did not. In fact, he constructed a very effective secret police and ruthlessly crushed any or all

opposition to his reign, be they political or religious in nature. But he did his best to serve the interest of his subjects, made frequent public appearances to confer with tribal leaders, and evinced genuine concern for their well-being. Moreover, by virtue of his Western-style education, he enacted measures to improve the legal and political status of women; hence they were among the freest in the Arab world. Hassan may have been forced to walk a tightrope politically, but he always took definitive steps to garner public support for his regime. Consequently, during the numerous and violent social upheavals that characterized North Africa in the 1970s and 1980s, Morocco was relatively tranquil by comparison.

In 1975 Spain announced that it was withdrawing from the neighboring region of the Western Sahara, and Hassan quickly moved in to fill the vacuum. Hosting a 350,000-strong "Green March" of unarmed civilians, he annexed the northern half of this phosphate-rich province while Mauritania claimed the southern half. This occupation, however, inspired resistance in the form of the Polasario movement, which enacted a low-level guerrilla war for independence. Funded largely by Algeria, which also covets the region for itself, fighters resist Moroccan occupation to the present day. Hassan had much better success on the international scene by positioning himself as a moderate Arab and a diplomatic conciliator. Throughout his long tenure, he sponsored more Arab summits than any other regional leader, and he was instrumental in bringing Egypt and Israel together for peace talks in 1976. He enjoyed similar success with Libya and Chad in 1984. At times he also hosted meetings with such Israeli leaders as SHIMON PERES and YITZHAK RABIN. And, despite the derision it has brought from fellow Arabs, Hassan II cultivated very close ties with the Jewish state, formalized low-level relations, and allowed Jewish emigrants from Morocco to travel and return at will. During the 1991 Gulf War, Morocco was the only North African state to provide military troops as part of the allied coalition against Iraq. This was undertaken in spite of popular protests in favor of SADDAM HUSSEIN, but the act reconfirmed Hassan's intention to maintain a decidedly Western orientation in foreign policy.

Toward the end of his long reign, Hassan increasingly turned to religion as the bulwark of peace and stability in his country. To that end he constructed the Hassan II mosque in 1993, presently the world's tallest. In 1996 he also sponsored constitutional reforms creating a freely elected, bicameral legislature. When he died on July 23, 1999, he was the longest-serving head of state in the Arab world and among the most successful. His global significance may be gauged by the fact that U.S. president BILL CLINTON, French president JACQUES CHIRAC, Jordanian king ABDULLAH II, and Palestinian leader YASSIR ARAFAT attended his funeral. Hassan II was immediately succeeded by his son, enthroned as MOHAMMED VI, who remains dedicated to modernizing and liberalizing Morocco's political institutions. He is building upon on the national stability that remains his father's greatest legacy.

Further Reading

Abadi, Jacob. "The Road to Israeli-Moroccan Rapprochement." *Journal of North African States* 5 (Spring 2000): 27–54.

Hassan II, King of Morocco. *The Challenge: The Memoir of King Hassan II of Morocco.* London: Macmillan, 1978.

Hughes, Stephen D. *Morocco under King Hassan.* Reading, England: Ithaca, 2001.

Thobani, Akbarali. *Western Sahara since 1975 under Moroccan Administration: Social, Economic, and Political Transformation.* Lewistown, N.Y.: Edwin Mellen Press, 2002.

Zoubir, Yahia, H., and Daniel Volman, eds. *International Dimensions of the Western Sahara Conflict.* Westport, Conn.: Praeger, 1993.

Haughey, Charles (1925–) *prime minister of Ireland*

Charles Haughey was born on September 16, 1925, in Castlebar, County Mayo, Ireland, the son of a former Irish Republican Army (IRA) fighter. Though Ireland had won its independence by 1921, the six Protestant-dominated provinces constituting Northern Ireland are in British hands and serve as a continuing source of friction in Anglo-Irish relations. Haughey was raised in Dublin and educated locally before attending the University College, Dublin. He obtained a degree in communications and accounting by 1949, and then he established an accounting practice. However, Haughey, a colorful, head-strong personality, also made a fortune dabbling in real estate, and he cemented his rising political aspirations by marrying the daughter of a future taoiseach (prime minister). In 1953 Haughey won a seat on the Dublin city council as a member of the Fianna Fáil Party, where he remained two years. He next gained election to the Dail Eireann, the lower house of the Irish parliament, in 1957, while his father-in-law, Sean Lemass, was prime minister. Haughey was a born politician, and between 1960–64 he secured appointment to head the ministries of justice and agriculture, introducing many useful reforms. In 1966 he made a failed attempt for the party leadership, but he lost to Jack Lynch and subsequently served as his finance minister, 1966–70.

Haughey proved effective in office, but he had a propensity for dominating others and skirting controversy. In 1970, as finance minister, he became implicated in an arms smuggling plot with the IRA and was forced to resign. Though formally cleared by a court of inquiry, the charge proved damaging enough to sideline his career for nearly a decade. He nonetheless plied his influence behind the scenes to good effect. By 1979 he had rehabilitated his reputation sufficiently to become minister of social welfare during Lynch's second administration, 1977–79. Thereafter he challenged and defeated George Colley for the leadership of Fianna Fáil in 1979 and, a member of the majority party, he became prime minister. His shortcomings as a national leader were quickly manifested. Haughey proved unable to formulate effective responses to Ireland's mounting economic crisis beyond short-term, politically inspired fixes. There was also mounting tension with Great Britain over the violence in Northern Ireland, and he was particularly confrontational in his dealings with Prime Minister Margaret Thatcher. The country, however, had endured enough controversy, and in June 1981 Haughey was forced out of office by Garrett Fitzgerald. Considerable infighting persisted while Ireland's economic pulse weakened, but Haughey regained the executive office in March 1982. However, he subsequently lost the post the following November following revelations that he illegally authorized wiretaps of various political enemies.

Haughey remained in parliament and functioned as an influential force in party politics. Despite public notoriety, he managed a third triumphant comeback as taoiseach in 1987. By this time he demonstrated more flexibility in dealing with Britain over Northern Ireland. He also managed to remain in office four years before being brought down by another scandal in 1991. At that time it was reported that the prime minister had accepted $1.9 million in gifts from the boss of Ireland's biggest supermarket chain, stashing the money in off-shore banks to avoid taxes. He also managed to acquire his own personal island in the Atlantic. These revelations only spurred calls for his resignation as prime minister and as head of Fianna Fail, which transpired on January 30, 1992. Haughey, who for over a decade was one of Ireland's most formidable political figures, was again undone by his own capriciousness. His successor was AL-BERT REYNOLDS.

Over the past decade Haughey has lived in quiet retirement, having distanced himself from the political arena that he loved so much. However, his legal problems are unending. In July 2000, he appeared before a corruption tribunal to answer charges that he accepted, in one form or another, cash and gifts totaling upward of $15 million. He confessed to the magistrate that he felt "overwhelmed" by the allegations, but he offered no concrete rebuttal. In the spring of 2001 he was admitted to the hospital for a period of intensive care, at which point the presiding judge limited his inquiry to a few hours a week. Haughey is nevertheless charged with obstructing the original corruption inquiry, and proceedings against him have been delayed pending his full recovery.

Further Reading

Allen, Kieran, *Fianna Fáil and Irish Labour: 1926 to the Present.* London: Pluto Press, 1997.

Arnold, Bruce. *Haughey: His Life and Unlucky Deeds.* London: HarperCollins, 1993.

Collins, Aongus. *The Legend of Charlie Haughey.* Niwot, Colo.: Irish American Book Co., 1997.

Dwyer, T. Ryle. *Short Fellow: A Biography of Charles J. Haughey.* Dublin: Marino, 2001.

Keena, Colm. *Haughey's Millions: The Full Story of Charlie's Money Trail.* Dublin: Gill and Macmillan, 2001.

Havel, Václav (1936–) *president of the Czech Republic*

Václav Havel was born on October 5, 1936, in Prague, Czechoslovakia, the son of a wealthy real estate developer. He was raised in the lap of luxury and began writing at an early age. However, Soviet forces occupied Czechoslovakia at the end of World War II and in 1948 they engineered a communist takeover. Henceforth, Havel's family were regarded as "class enemies" and they were forced to perform menial labor. Worse, Havel himself was denied any opportunity to attend high school and worked many years as a lowly laboratory assistant. This, however, did not prevent him from taking courses at night school, and he eventually aspired to attend college. The authorities refused to allow him to study history, philosophy, or cinema, so he settled upon economics at the Czech University of Technology. Havel graduated in 1957 and then fulfilled two years of compulsory military service. Being interested in stage plays, he founded a regimental theater and subsequently applied to the Academy of Music and Fine Arts in Prague. He was again turned down, so he started writing books and screenplays while working as a stagehand. Havel soon established himself as one of the nation's most enterprising playwrights, and during the famous "Prague Spring" of 1968, he was conspicuous in agitating for greater creative and personal freedom. However, Soviet tanks crushed this liberalizing interlude in August 1968 and reimposed strict communist orthodoxy. Havel once again became an enemy of the state and was jailed repeatedly over the next two decades. In 1977 he joined hundreds of other Czech intellectuals in sponsoring Charter '77, a document insisting that citizens be accorded fundamental human rights. Havel was then promptly arrested again and sentenced to four years in prison. Previously, he had been offered several opportunities to leave the country, but Havel refused, declaring: "The solution of this human situation does not lie in leaving it." By 1989, moreover, the communist empire was crumbling throughout Eastern Europe. That year Havel was instrumental in helping found the Civic Forum, a group of former dissidents instrumental in fostering the so-called Velvet Revolution that forced Communist Party leader and premier Gustav Husak from office. On December 29, 1989, Havel, by now a world-famous dissident writer, was appointed interim president of Czechoslovakia by popular acclaim.

One of Havel's most pressing priorities was to meet with Soviet premier Mikhail Gorbachev and arrange the departure of 30,000 Russian troops from his homeland. This was successfully accomplished, and the parliament responded by reelecting him to a second two-year term on July 5, 1990. He then presided over a raucous legislature dominated by the right-wing Civic Democratic Party of VÁCLAV KLAUS and numerous Slovak nationalists. Working together, they managed to arrange Czechoslovakia's division into two new entities: Slovakia and the Czech Republic. Havel, who strongly opposed the move, resigned in protest, but he was then asked to accept the presidency of his native land. No other political figure in office was as trusted as this diminutive playwright. Disillusioned by politics, Havel reluctantly agreed and, on January 26, 1993, he became the first president of the Czech Republic.

Havel's subsequent tenure in office was rewarding and productive, but also stormy. He pushed hard for Czech admission into the European Union (EU) and also helped arrange its entry into the NATO alliance. However, the government of Prime Minister Klaus came under increasing scrutiny and criticism over recurring scandals that forced him from office in November 1997. Havel then appointed JOSEF TOSOVSKY, a prominent banker, to succeed him. Afterward, Havel and Klaus bitterly denounced each other over their differing perceptions of government. Specifically, Klaus strongly advocated quick adoption of free-market principles, while Havel insists on a "go-slow" approach to minimize social dislocation. Their estrangement continues to the present day. Havel's performance in office was also severely affected by the loss of his wife to cancer, and the removal of his own right lung to the same malady. Nonetheless, he remained as a symbol of moral and national authority by the majority of his countrymen. Over the objections of Klaus's party in parliament, he gained reelection to a second five-year term on January 20, 1998. Later that summer he replaced Tosovsky with MILOŠ ZEMAN of the Social Democratic Party, which garnered the biggest share of seats during legislative elections.

Toward the end of his political career, Havel became increasingly disillusioned by the rough-and-tumble nature of Czech politics. He has denounced its increasingly partisan nature and belittles contemporaries as essentially short-sighted and self-serving. In return, both Klaus and Zeman freely disdain the man who led their country down the path to freedom. In one of his final official acts, Havel met with German president JOHANNES RAU in June 2002 to diffuse a minor crisis over the infamous Beneš Decree of 1945. This act, which expelled 3 million ethnic Germans from Czechoslovakia after World War II, remains a sensitive issue and had forced cancellation of a state visit by Chancellor GERHARD SCHROEDER earlier that year. It also threatens to impede Czech entry into the EU, which is slated for 2004. Havel will have retired from office by then and, by his own admission, is eager to "read, study, and hopefully write."

Further Reading

Eyal, Gil. *The Origins of Post-communist Elites: From Prague Spring to the Breakup of Czechoslovakia.* Minneapolis: University of Minnesota Press, 2003.

Fawn, Rick. "Symbolism in the Diplomacy of Czech President Vaclav Havel." *East European Quarterly* 33, no. 1 (1999): 1–19.

Havel, Vaclav. *The Art of the Impossible: Politics as Morality In Practice; Speeches, Writings, 1990–1996.* New York: Alfred A. Knopf, 1997.

Keane, John. *Vaclav Havel: A Political Tragedy in Six Acts.* New York: Basic Books, 1999.

McRae, Robert G. *Resistance and Revolution: Vaclav Havel's Czechoslovakia.* Ottawa: Carleton University Press, 1997.

Pynsent, Robert B. "The Work of Vaclav Havel." *Slavonic and East European Review* 73, no. 2 (1995): 269–281.

Herzog, Chaim (1918–1997) *president of Israel*

Chaim Herzog was born on September 17, 1918, in Dublin, Ireland, the son of that country's chief rabbi. He subsequently accompanied his father to Palestine when the latter gained appointment as a senior spiritual leader. Herzog received a strict religious education and went on to attend numerous colleges back in England, most notably London University, from which he obtained his law degree in 1941. Shortly after Herzog tendered his services to the British army in World War II and passed through the prestigious military academy at Sandhurst. Herzog served as a tank commander in the elite Guards Armored Division until he was wounded, then he transferred his skills to military intelligence. He fought at Normandy in 1944, was among the first Allied soldiers to cross the Rhine River into Germany, and personally represented Field Marshal Bernard Montgomery in many postwar conferences. Afterward he resigned his commission and returned to Israel, then on the cusp of its war for independence with the Arabs. In this capacity he served as an intelligence officer with the Haganah, the underground military, until the war successfully concluded. Thereafter he was appointed chief of military intelligence by Prime Minister David Ben-Gurion in 1948. Over the next decade Herzog held numerous positions, including military attaché to the United States and head of the Israeli Defense Force (IDF) intelligence, before retiring in 1962. One of his last official acts was to predict the Arabs were preparing for a new war five years hence, which happened in 1967. Afterward Herzog became the first military governor of the newly acquired West Bank territory. He also served in the private sector as a radio commentator, and he won praise for his cool, concise analysis during the 1973 Yom Kippur War. Herzog then parleyed his military expertise into publishing a scathing appraisal of the war in which he blamed his good friend, Defense Minister Moshe Dayan, for the near disaster.

In August 1975 the dapper Herzog arrived in New York City as Israel's ambassador to the United Nations. At the UN, he performed his most dramatic service in the wake of the Soviet Union's attempt to have Israel expelled. Communist bloc and developing nations also succeeded in passing UN Resolution 3379, which equated Zionism (the return of Jews to Israel) with racism, which was roundly condemned by Western nations. However, it fell upon Herzog to dramatically address the assembly, denounce the resolution, and—waving it before the delegates—tear it up in his hands. Over the next three years he remained an eloquent representative of the Jewish state, which greatly enhanced his popularity at home. Herzog then returned to Israel in 1978 to campaign on behalf of the Labor Party. On the encouragement of friends, he stood for a seat in the Knesset (parliament) as a labor candidate in 1981, winning easily. Herzog by this time was one of the best-known and most trusted national figures in Israel, and, in March 1983, he was elected the sixth president of Israel on a secret ballot—by overwhelming margins.

In Israel, real political power rests with the prime minister, and the president's role is mainly ceremonial and symbolic. But Herzog's life experience made him perfectly suited for the role, being worldly, highly educated, and extremely conscientious. Israel at that time was undergoing profound political crises, beset by terrorism, diplomatic isolation, and religious bickering over the definition of who precisely was a "Jew." Herzog met the challenge with his accustomed verve and dedication. He gave numerous speeches reminding Israelis of their duty to the state and the need to refrain from arguments that divide them. For this reason he deeply deplored religious extremism with the same passion that he denounced terrorism. He also embarked on a national campaign to acquire and assimilate Jewish communities from Russia and Ethiopia, and he made full use of his credentials as Israel's goodwill ambassador abroad. Having been elected to an unprecedented second term in 1988, he became the first Israeli president to visit China.

He also made a visit to Germany and he sought to maintain good relations with Spain as it marked the 500th anniversary of expulsion of the Jews. Herzog also frequently visited the United States to shore up public support, and he sought to emotionally link Israel with Jewish communities across the globe.

Herzog died on April 17, 1997, at the age of 78. By turns soldier, politician, and diplomat, he never shirked responsibilities to his homeland, no matter how onerous or unpleasant. He also wrote numerous books on military history that were roundly praised for their objectivity, sagacity, and honesty. Gifted with intelligence and eloquence in equal measure, Herzog was an effective spokesman for the Jewish state during a trying period in its history. He was replaced in office by his nephew, EZER WEIZMAN.

Further Reading

Bordoff, Jason. "Israel's Labour Governments and the West Bank, 1967–1977: Domestic Politics and Foreign Policy." Unpublished M. Litt, University of Oxford, 1998.

Garfinkle, Adam M. *Politics and Society in Modern Israel.* Armonk, N.Y.: M. E. Sharpe, 1997.

Herzog, Chaim. *Living History: A Memoir.* New York: Pantheon Books, 1996.

———. *The Arab-Israeli Wars.* New York: Pantheon Books, 1983.

Perry, Dan. *Israel and the Quest for Permanence.* Jefferson, N.C.: McFarland, 1999.

Hosokawa, Morihiro (1938–) *prime minister of Japan*

Morihiro Hosokawa was born on January 14, 1938, in Kyushu, Japan, into a family well known for its traditional role as samurai warlords. His grandfather, Fumimaro Konoe, had been Japan's prime minister during the attack on Pearl Harbor in 1941, and he was later tried as a war criminal. His father, Morisada Hosokawa, also entered politics and rose to the rank of chief cabinet secretary. Hosokawa himself was raised in luxurious surroundings and attended prestigious Sophia University in Tokyo, studying political science. After graduating in 1963, and to the great distress of his parents, he chose to work as a humble reporter with *Asahi Shimbun,* the nation's second-largest newspaper. He finally followed his father's footsteps into politics in 1971 by becoming the youngest person ever elected to the upper chamber of the national Diet, or parliament. Hosokawa was reelected in 1977, and he held various ministry appointments within the Liberal Democratic Party (LDP). The LDP had dominated Japanese political life since 1956, and had acquired a reputation for growing corruption and complacency. Hosokawa tried serving as an agent for change, but he could not counter the entrenched interests characteristic of Japanese politics. Therefore, in 1983 he quit the Diet and ran for the governorship of Kumamoto province on Kyushu Island.

As governor, Hosokawa strove to positively impact the lives of average citizens, and he ended government opposition to lawsuits arising from the infamous Minamata (lead poisoning) disease scandal. Hosokawa was easily returned to office in 1986, but he grew disillusioned by the highly centralized nature of Japanese national administration and the endless bureaucracy it ladled upon local authority. As an example, he cited an instance concerning the relocation of a city bus stop. "To move the stop a few hundred meters I had to send a delegation to Tokyo," he said. "In Japan, you can't tie your own shoes without official permission." He therefore declined to run again in 1991, declaring: "Those who stay in power too long become corrupt." This philosophy was soon destined to become a political mantra.

In 1992 Hosokawa finally broke with the LDP, which he castigated as self-serving and hopelessly insensitive to change. He then founded the Japan New Party in an attempt to weed out corruption and offer the public an alternative to "politics as usual." Propelled by public discontent, events moved swiftly from there. In May 1993 the LDP posted a poor showing in elections for the powerful House of Representatives while Hosokawa's party captured 38 seats. This placed him within striking distance of forming a majority coalition without the LDP, an unthinkable prospect only months before. By dint of hard bargaining, Hosokawa accomplished exactly that, and his seven-party coalition finally ended 38 years of undisputed LDP control of government. On August 9, 1993, the 55-year-old politician was sworn in as Japan's youngest prime minister since his grandfather held the title at 48.

Hosokawa entered high office committed to political change and he took active steps to achieve it. First, he appointed a nontraditional cabinet that included the first female speaker of the house. He also presented dramatic reforms to the Diet that banned corporate donations to individual politicians, thereby ending the single largest source of corruption and influence buying. Internecine fighting erupted as politicians scrambled to preserve vested interests, but on the very last day of the parliamentary session, a watered-down version of Hosokawa's reform bill finally passed. Given the normally staid nature of Japanese politics, this represented change of a very high order. The prime minister had little time for rejoicing, as he next confronted mounting pressure from the United States to open Japan's markets to competition, thereby decreasing the one-sided trade imbalance. Hosokawa flatly refused to embrace any concessions that would deflate the already shaky economy, but he and President BILL CLINTON embraced certain vague reforms that temporarily diffused the issue. A retaliatory trade war between the world's two largest economies had been averted, if only for the time being.

For all his emphasis on reform, Hosokawa's administration was ultimately done in by a minor corruption charge. Opposition leaders revealed that, as governor of Kumamoto, he accepted a $1 million bribe from a leading trucking firm. Hosokawa responded that the "loan" was used to repair his ancestral home and that the money was repaid. However, he failed to produce the necessary documents and, not wishing to appear hypocritical, Hosokawa tendered his resignation on April 8, 1994, after a year in office. "I sincerely apologize to the people of Japan," he stated upon leaving. After additional infighting, the new prime minister proved to be TOMIICHI MURAYAMA, the first Socialist Party member to hold high office since 1938.

Further Reading

Christensen, Raymond V. "Electoral Reforms in Japan: How It Was Enacted and Changes It May Bring." *Asian Survey* 34 (July 1994): 589–606.

Field, N. "The Stakes of Apology." *Japan Quarterly* 42 (October–December 1995): 405–418.

Iritani, Toshio. "The Emergence of the Hosokawa Coalition: A Significant Break in the Continuity of Japanese Politics?" *Japan Forum* 6, no. 1 (1994): 1–7.

Masumi, F. "Political Reform's Path of No Return." *Japan Quarterly* 41 (July–September 1994): 254–262.

Reed, Steven R. *Japanese Electoral Politics: Creating a New Party System.* New York: Routledge, 2003.

Shinoda, T. "Japan's Decision Making under the Coalition Governments." *Asian Survey* 38 (July 1998): 703–723.

Houphouët-Boigny, Félix (1905–1993)

president of Côte d'Ivoire

Félix Houphouët was born in the village of Yamoussokro, Ivory Coast (Côte d'Ivoire), the son of a Boule chieftain. Ivory Coast being a French possession, he was educated locally at colonial schools. Houphouët subsequently attended medical school in Dakar, Senegal, and he graduated in 1925. Once home he commenced a successful medical practice and by 1940 had also established himself as a successful planter. Ivory Coast was then and remains the world's biggest cocoa producer, but French colonial practices routinely discriminated against African growers in favor of transplanted European ones. To combat such disparity, Houphouët founded the African Democratic Assembly (ADA) in 1950, one of the first anticolonial organizations on the continent. By 1945 he had expanded its activities into the Democratic Party of the Ivory Coast (PDIC) before gaining election to the French National Assembly. Around that time he also adopted the surname Boigny, which means "battering ram." Once in Paris he argued relentlessly against colonial exploitation, decisively ended the practice of conscripted labor in 1946, and he gained considerable notoriety at home. By 1950 the ADA was working in close association with the Communist Party, which authorized a series of crippling strikes. The result was a severe French crackdown upon dissent, and Houphouët concluded he had no further use for the Communists. Thereafter he worked closely with the more moderate Socialists, and he became a personal acquaintance of FRANÇOIS MITTERAND. Unlike many African contemporaries, Houphouët was a devoted francophile, equally at ease in his native village or in the salons of Paris. This did not detract at all from his reputation as one of the staunchest advocates of African independence. However, toward the end of the late 1950s, Houphouët-Boigny was also tapped to serve in several governmental ministries, and he continually demonstrated a willingness to become France's most reliable African ally. Not surprisingly, when the Ivory Coast gravitated toward independence in 1959, he was chosen as its first prime minister. On November 27, 1960, Houphouët-Boigny was elected the first president of Ivory Coast by 98 percent of votes cast. In 1986 he had the country officially renamed Côte d'Ivoire.

Over the next 33 years, Houphouët-Boigny proved himself to be one of Africa's most enduring politicians, a master of political compromise and adaptation. He easily won seven consecutive five-year terms in office, more than any African leader. Yet he owed his longevity to subtlety and paternalism, not crass manipulation and control. Early on he decided against promotion of multiparty democracy, fearful of the confusion such a system might produce. Therefore, he introduced political participation through the guise of one-party rule through the PDIC, which enjoyed popular roots dating back 20 years. Elections for executive and legislative offices were regularly held, even if those elected served only to perpetuate Houphouët-Boigny's rule. In terms of style, Houphouët-Boigny used charisma, blatant patronage, and minor political repression to entrench his position. Dissenters were arrested, but then usually released unharmed. He was also careful to give an impression of responsiveness to public demands, and he frequently met with chiefs, dignitaries, and average citizens to hear grievances. Also, to minimize any chances of a coup, the size of the military was always kept small, and French forces assumed the burden of national defense. But most of all, the regime was buoyed by the "Ivorian miracle," a period of economic growth unprecedented in West Africa. Houphouët-Boigny was a committed capitalist, and he invited foreign investment in at very favorable terms. This fact, coupled with good trade relations with France, resulted in two decades of spectacular prosperity and stability.

In terms of foreign relations, Houphouët-Boigny was firmly in the Western camp, and he railed against communist encroachment throughout Africa. He was also willing to establish a political dialogue with the apartheid regime of South Africa, to the consternation of many African leaders. Later on, he reluctantly broke off relations with Israel over events in the Middle East, but he then reestablished links with that nation—but also with the Soviet Union—to demonstrate impartiality. Côte d'Ivoire enjoyed enviable stability for an African nation, but declining economic fortunes in the 1980s increased political agitation for change. Perceiving the trend to democracy to be inevitable, Houphouët-Boigny finally authorized multiparty democratic elections in 1989—then held them quickly before the opposition consolidated itself. He won again by large margins. His only serious gaffe was the erection of the world's largest church in his native village of Yamoussoskro. Bigger than the Vatican, it cost an estimated $200 million when finished and Pope JOHN PAUL II arrived from Rome for its consecration. By the time Houphouët-Boigny died of cancer on December 10, 1993, he had ruled Côte d'Ivoire for three decades. He was greatly mourned as the father of his country, and for the peace and prosperity associated with his authoritarian-style of leadership. As an indication of his significance to France, his funeral was attended by President Mitterand and seven former premiers. The "Grand Old Man of Africa" was succeeded in office by HENRI-KONAN BÉDIÉ, then leader of the National Assembly.

Further Reading

Crook, Richard C. "Politics, the Cocoa Crisis, and Administration in Côte d'Ivoire." *Journal of Modern African Studies* 28 (December 1990): 649–70.

Ihdeuru, O. C. "The State of Maritime Nationalism in Côte d'Ivoire." *Journal of Modern African Studies* 32 (June 1994): 215–45.

Thompson, Virginia M. *West Africa's Council of the Entente.* Ithaca, N.Y.: Cornell University Press, 1972.

Toungara, Jeanne M. "The Apotheosis of Côte d'Ivoire's Nana Houphouët-Boigny." *Journal of Modern African Studies* 28, no. 1 (1990): 23–54.

Widner, Jennifer. "Two Leadership Styles and Patterns of Political Liberalization." *African Studies Review* 37 (April 1994): 151–75.

Howard, John (1939–) *prime minister of Australia*

John Winston Howard was born in Sydney, Australia, on July 26, 1939, the son of an auto mechanic. He was educated at the Canterbury Boys High School before attending the University of Sydney, where he pursued a law degree. After several years as a successful lawyer, Howard joined the Liberal (actually, conservative) Party and in 1974 he gained election to parliament. Blunt, unassuming, but exuding a pervasive sense of morality, Howard rose quickly up the party hierarchy. Prime Minister J. Malcolm Fraser appointed him minister for business and consumer affairs, wherein he proved instrumental in passing the Australian Trade Practices Act, which outlawed boycotts on businesses and trade unions. This gained him the ire of the leftist-leaning Labour Party, which tarred him, unsuccessfully, as an opponent of working-class people. Nonetheless, Howard's uncompromising conservative stand won him plaudits within the Liberal Party and in 1977 he became finance minister. By 1982 he was also serving as party deputy leader, a post he kept after Labour was swept back into power the following year. Howard experienced a downturn in political fortunes in 1987 when he led his party

into the national elections and lost badly, whereupon he was ousted from the leadership. But, over the next 13 years, Howard served as head of the opposition in parliament, gaining national standing and name recognition. In 1998 Howard was once again elected party leader and Liberal Party candidate for prime minister. In a carefully orchestrated campaign, he painted the Labour Party as out of touch with average people, but he also appealed to blue-collar workers by promising to increase social spending on their behalf. Australians, ready for a change, then swept the conservatives back into power by handing them 95 seats in the House of Representatives, their largest margin since 1944. Howard was then sworn in as Australia's newest prime minister.

As a philosophical conservative, Howard embraced the notion of free markets, deregulation, and privatization of inefficient state-owned industries. Therefore, he proposed selling the government's share of the Commonwealth Bank of Australia, along with Telstra, the national communications company. He then determined to overhaul the inefficient tax collection system, pass across-the-board tax cuts, and impose a national 10 percent sales tax on goods and services to make up for the loss. Howard also proved less than sympathetic toward reconciliation, whereby the rights of aboriginal peoples received a higher priority and consideration than before. However, the public at that time had become disenchanted by the tax scheme and, when new elections were called, it appeared that Labour might recapture national leadership. Howard's position was further complicated by the rise of the new One Nation Party under Pauline Hanson, which was nativist in outlook and highly anti-immigrant. Howard was widely criticized for not condemning Hanson's views strongly, as if he were lending tacit approval to her views, but he eventually repudiated them. Consequently, the Liberal Party coasted to another victory in the 1988 national elections, although their majority in parliament had been pared to only 10 seats.

Since winning a second term, Howard has finessed a number of controversial issues. Though a staunch monarchist, he called for a public referendum to drop Australia's status as a constitutional monarchy with the British Commonwealth. This entailed dropping Queen Elizabeth II as nominal head of the country, which the voters rejected by 55 percent. Australia did not declare itself an independent republic but the issue will likely surface again. International affairs also weighed heavily and unexpectedly upon Howard's agenda. The previous administration under PAUL KEATING placed greater emphasis on Australia's place within Southeast Asia, even at the expense of traditional allies like Great Britain and the United States. Howard pledged to reverse that stand, and in August 2000, he ordered the navy to intercept a freighter carrying Asian refugees and prevent it from landing in Australia. "We decide who comes to this country," Howard declared, "and the circumstances in which they come." He was widely criticized by the Labourites as racist, but his hard-line stand on asylum proved popular with the electorate. After the September 11, 2001, attacks on the World Trade Center in New York, Howard also pledged full cooperation in combating terrorism, and he committed Australian special forces (SAS) to the ground war in Afghanistan. The Labour Party under Kim Beazley was badly split by the issue, and, on November 11, 2001, the voters returned the Liberal Party to power with a slightly increased margin in parliament. Through it all, Howard waxed defiantly and stridently toward the left as he always had. "When you get to the people and you win a comfortable majority," he lectured, "you plainly have a mandate to implement policies and approaches that are consistent with your philosophy." Australian national policy thus remains firmly in the hands of Howard's conservative agenda until his anticipated retirement in 2003.

Further Reading

Barnett, David, and Pru Goward. *John Howard, Prime Minister.* New York: Viking, 1997.
Grattan, Michelle. *Australia's Prime Ministers.* Sydney: New Holland, 2000.
Manne, Robert. *The Barren Years: John Howard and Australian Political Culture.* Melbourne: Text Publishing, 2001.
Singleton, Gwynneth. *The Howard Government: Australian Commonwealth Administration, 1996–1998.* Sydney: University of New South Wales, 2000.
Suter, Keith. "Fear and Loathing on the Campaign Trail." *Contemporary Review* 280 (January 2002): 16–22.
Warhurst, John, and Marian Simms. *Howard's Agenda: The 1998 Australian Election.* St. Lucia: University of Queensland Press, 2000.

Hrawi, Elias (1925–   ) *president of Lebanon*

Elias Hrawi was born on September 4, 1925, in Zahle, Bekaa Valley, Lebanon. His family was traditionally Ma-

ronite Christian by faith and large landowners. Hrawi attended St. Joseph University in Beirut to study commerce, although he did not graduate. Instead, he made his reputation as an agricultural businessman and founded one of the first farming cooperatives in that country. Lebanon, which achieved political independence from France in 1943, is a highly stratified country, and it is distinctly divided between Christians, Sunni Muslims, and Shiite Muslims. However, political accord and harmony were maintained through a constitution guaranteeing that the president would always be a Maronite, the prime minister a Sunni, and the speaker of the Assembly a Shiite. Considering this potentially explosive situation, Lebanon functioned relatively well until it was drawn into the general turmoil of Middle Eastern politics and wars.

Hrawi initiated his political career in 1972, when he inherited political power from his brother and won his assembly seat. He proved himself politically adept and capable of working with either Christian or Muslim counterparts in the legislature. In 1980 President Ilyas Sarkis appointed him minister of public works, and he won plaudits for initiating many road and construction projects. However, since 1975 Lebanon had been at war with itself. The Palestinian issue, exacerbated by Israeli incursions into the country, fanned the flames of religious extremism among the Shiite community, which had increased in numbers since 1943. As a bloc they demanded more power in government, which the Christians were reluctant to hand over. Fighting then broke out between fundamentalist fighters and Christian militias, until Syrian president HAFEZ AL-ASSAD stepped in with 30,000 troops to restore order. This also made him a counterweight to Israeli forces stationed in south Lebanon and the de facto power broker for the rest of the country. It was not until 1989 that warring factions met in Taif, Saudi Arabia, and signed an agreement granting the Shiites greater leverage at the expense of the Christians. Peace was then seemingly restored to the war-torn country until November 22, 1989, when sitting president René Mouawad was assassinated. Hrawi, given his Maronite background and his demonstrated ability to work with Muslims, was nominated to succeed him two days later. He became Lebanon's 10th president since achieving independence, receiving 90 percent of votes cast in the parliament.

Once in office Hrawi pledged to "follow the same path that the martyred President Mouawad planned for national unity." But not everybody was pleased with the Taif Accord, especially Christian general Michel Aoun, the interim prime minister. Backed by his private army, he was angered because the agreement had failed to stipulate the removal of Syrian troops. He therefore refused to recognize Hrawi's authority, and he conducted protracted military efforts to drive the Syrians out by himself. But lacking support from the bulk of other militias, Aoun was himself defeated and driven into exile. Hrawi did nothing to assist his fellow Christian, so he lost considerable support among the Maronite community. He did, however, impress President Assad by his willingness to accommodate Syrian interests in Lebanon and constructive events began unfolding. First, Hrawi managed to secure the release of all Western hostages from religious militants, including several Americans, apparently with Assad's blessing. He also oversaw the disarming of most militias and their incorporation into a unified Lebanese army. The only exception was the Hezbollah, a militant Shiite guerrilla group in south Lebanon whom Assad wanted to carry on attacks against Israel. Hrawi readily complied and he refrained from using the army to disband them. He also displayed good business sense by appointing Sunni millionaire businessman RAFIQ AL-HARIRI as prime minister, which marked a return to traditional partnerships between Christians and Muslims.

Nominally, the Lebanese president is restricted to a single five-year term in office. However, Assad found Hrawi such a useful ally that, in November 1995, he secured from parliament an amendment to the constitution that allowed him three additional years in office. Again, this brought Maronite criticism that the president was little more than a Syrian puppet, but it insured continuing stability and continuity of policy. Under Hrawi's steady hand and conciliatory leadership, the country was finally and formally on the mend. When he stepped down from office on November 24, 1998, in favor of EMILE LAHOUD, the act represented Lebanon's first peaceful transfer of power in nearly 15 years.

Further Reading

Dagher, Carole. *Bring Down the Walls: Lebanon's Post-war Challenge.* Basingstoke, England: Palgrave, 2000.

Ellis, Kail C. *Lebanon's Second Republic: Prospects for the Twenty-first Century.* Gainesville: University Press of Florida, 2002.

Khalifah, Bassem. *The Rise and Fall of Christian Lebanon.* Toronto: York Press, 2001.

Picard, Elizabeth. *Lebanon: A Shattered Country: Myths and Realities of the Wars in Lebanon.* New York: Holmes and Meier, 2002.

Zisser, Eyal. *Lebanon: The Challenge of Independence.* London: I. B. Tauris, 2000.

Hu Jintao (Hu Chin-tao) (1942–) *president of China*

Hu Jintao was born in December 1942 in Shanghai, China, the son of a prosperous tea merchant. The onslaught of World War II induced his family to relocate to Jiangsu province, where he was raised in comparative luxury. However, by 1949 Mao Zedong's Communist Chinese Party (CCP) had conquered China and founded the People's Republic. In 1959 Hu entered Tsinghua University to study hydroelectric power and graduated with honors. He subsequently obtained an advanced degree from prestigious Quinghua University, Beijing, in 1964. By that time Mao's Cultural Revolution was in full flow, and Hu's career was sidetracked by political and ideological issues. By 1968 he transferred to remote Gansu province, where he worked as a junior hydroelectric engineer and won praise for overall competence. He also gained a reputation for displaying a near-photographic memory, so much so that local party boss Song Ping pronounced him the "walking map of Gansu." After a stint of service as Song's personal secretary, Hu transferred back to Beijing to head the Communist Youth League, 1982–85. He subsequently became party secretary of Guizhou, a poor southern province, which confirmed his status as one of the rising stars of the Communist Party. By 1988 Hu assumed a more sensitive assignment, that of party secretary in Tibet. That province had seethed with anti-Chinese sentiments ever since its annexation in 1950, and in 1988 protests spilled out onto the street. Hu reacted promptly by deploying 100,000 Chinese troops in the capital of Lhasa, who crushed the rebellion with great severity. The following year he quickly cabled congratulations to Beijing superiors for their handling of events at Tiananmen Square. For this loyalty he was roundly applauded by party purists and continued climbing up through the hierarchy.

In light of Hu's intelligence, grasp of political affairs, and ideological correctness, aging "paramount" leader DENG XIAOPING once declared him the most promising figure of his generation. This status was seemingly confirmed in 1992, when Hu gained admission to the powerful Standing Committee of the party's Politburo. This made him the seventh-most powerful man in China and privy to central decision-making processes for the entire country. His performance proved both cool and correct, and, in March 1998, the 55-year-old Hu advanced to vice president of China, and first vice chairman of the influential Central Military Commission the following year. He concurrently served as president of the Central Party School, which serves as a training ground for future cadres. His unprecedented rise also stoked suspicions that Hu has been designated heir apparent to succeed President JIANG ZEMIN as party head in the fall of 2002, and head of state in March 2003. However, given his continual deference and subservience to party seniors, liberal intellectuals derisively labeled him "grandson" for his consistent unwillingness to challenge elders about anything.

Hu was clearly being groomed for succession in October 2001 when he commenced his first five-nation European tour to become acquainted with heads of state, prime ministers, and business tycoons in Britain, Spain, France, Germany, and Russia. Resplendent in his two-piece suit and designer glasses, he impressed hosts with his geniality, charm, and intelligence, but the basic nature of the man remains enigmatic. Little else was revealed in the spring of 2002, when he paid his first state visit to the United States to meet President GEORGE W. BUSH. On April 30, 2002, he also became the highest-ranking Chinese official ever to visit the Pentagon, where he conferred with Secretary of Defense William Rumsfeld over the ongoing war on terrorism. The affairs was widely touted as successful, and Bush declared his willingness and ability to work with the future leader, but Hu's actual intentions remain impossible to divine. In talks touching upon human rights in China and the sensitive matter of Taiwan, he simply reiterated long-standing party dogma. Such rhetoric enhances his credentials as a loyalist, but otherwise obscures any indication of flexibility over future issues that might arise. Certainly, conservative elements in the CCP will expect him to stand up to the Americans on issues ranging from trade to Taiwan.

As expected, Hu was voted China's new president on March 15, 2003, and he pledged to "impose strict self-discipline, keep honest and clean in performing public duties, always maintain a modest, prudent, and industrious style of work, and work hard and selflessly night and day for the country and the people." The following day Wen Jiabao was appointed vice premier to replace outgoing ZHU RONGJI. Not surprisingly, Hu's mentor Jiang remains behind the scenes by assuming chairmanship of the Central Military Commission for the next five years. The new executive now confronts a nation in mounting distress over the widening gap between rich and poor, between city and countryside, and rising unemployment as state-owned industries lay off workers to become more competitive.

The nation's embrace of capitalism has enriched it financially but created vast social gulfs and inequities. Presently, China is experiencing large demonstrations in cities and the countryside protesting lack of work, high taxes, and bureaucratic corruption. To contain rising discontent, China must either do more economically or liberalize its political system and accommodate more freedom of expression. Thus far, party elders refuse such change as it threatens the hegemony of the CCP. It remains to be seen if the reticent Hu, representing the fourth generation of Communist Party leadership, will likewise prove as reticent toward change.

Further Reading

Ding, Yijiang. *Chinese Democracy after Tiananmen.* New York: Columbia University Press, 2002.

Finklestein, David M., and Maryanne Kivlehan. *China's Leadership in the Twenty-first Century: The Rise of the Fourth Generation.* Armonk, N.Y.: M. E. Sharpe, 2002.

Marti, Michael E. *China and the Legacy of Deng Xiaoping: From Communist Revolution to Capitalist Evolution.* London: Brassey's, 2002.

Saich, Tony. *Governance and Politics of China.* Basingstoke, England: Palgrave, 2001.

Tkacik, John, Joseph Fewsmith, and Maryanne Kivlehan. *Who's Hu? Assessing China's Heir Apparent, Hu Jintao.* Washington, D.C.: Heritage Foundation, 2002.

Wang, James C. *Contemporary Chinese Politics: An Introduction.* Upper Saddle River, N.J.: Prentice Hall, 2002.

Zhao, Hongwei. *Political Regime of Contemporary China.* Lanham, Md.: University Press of America, 2002.

Zhou, Jinghao. *Remaking China's Public Philosophy for the Twenty-first Century.* Westport, Conn.: Praeger, 2003.

Zheng, Yongnian. "The Politics of Power Succession in Post-Deng China." *Asian Journal of Political Science* 8 (June 2000): 13–32.

Hun Sen (1951–) *prime minister of Cambodia*
Hun Sen was born on April 8, 1951, in Cambodia's Kompong province, astride the Vietnamese border. He acquired only minimal education before being caught up in the revolutionary activities then sweeping Southeast Asia during the 1970s. At that time the United States was embroiled in a costly war with North Vietnam and it sought to expand the conflict by destroying communist sanctuaries in Cambodia. In March 1970 General Lon Nol overthrew the regime of Prince Norodom Sihanouk, precipitating an internecine civil war that lasted 30 years. In the course of the fighting Hun Sen join the ranks of the Communist Party of Kampuchea (PKP), more commonly referred to as the Khmer Rouge. By 1975 the Communist leader, Pol Pot, had driven Lon Nol out of the capital of Phnom Penh and established a brutal ideologically driven regime. Their political excesses included mass deportation of Western-educated Cambodians to forced labor campaigns, and the mass extermination of over 1 million people. Significantly, many of the older PKP members who had been trained in North Vietnam had also been singled out for extinction because of fears that they could not be trusted. This prompted Hun Sen to abandon Pol Pot and switch allegiance to the North Vietnamese as part of the new Kampuchean National Front for National Salvation. Increasing border tensions prompted the Vietnamese to invade Cambodia in 1978 and overthrow the Khmer Rouge, who resorted to guerrilla warfare. In 1979, Hun Sen was appointed minister of foreign affairs for Cambodia as part of the new Kampuchean People's Revolutionary Party. He managed to keep his head above the rising tide of civil war and factionalism, thereby becoming prime minister of Cambodia on January 14, 1985. At that time he was also the youngest premier in the world.

For nearly a decade, Hun Sen was preoccupied with ending the ongoing civil war against Pol Pot's guerrillas while also striving to gain recognition of his regime. He was especially determined to minimize the influence of China, which had proven a strong supporter of the Khmer Rouge. By the time Vietnamese troops finally returned home, Cambodia enjoyed diplomatic recognition with 30 developing countries. However, the United Nations refused to recognize his regime, along with most Western powers, which meant foreign aid sources remained unavailable. The only way such favor could be curried was by a comprehensive peace plan that included all warring factions except for the Khmer Rouge. On October 23, 1991, all sides agreed to a UN-sponsored cease-fire and adoption of a Supreme National Council until elections could be held. In 1993 the Cambodian people voted overwhelmingly in favor of the royalist party of Prince Sihanouk, whereupon four Communist-controlled provinces threatened to secede. A compromise agreement was then worked out whereby Sihanouk's son, Prince Ranariddh, and Hun Sen became dual prime ministers.

After four years of relative calm, Hun Sen staged a coup against Prince Ranariddh on July 7, 1997, which was widely denounced by the international community. However, he was now firmly in power and reminded onlookers that his socialist regime was the only viable alternative to another Khmer Rouge dictatorship. Moreover, in July 1998 a new power-sharing agreement was reached whereby the exiled prince would return as assembly president while Hun Sen continued on as the sole premier. This seemed to be the most viable solution for the exhausted country and, following the final surrender of the Khmer Rouge leadership in December 1998, three decades of bloody civil war had finally ceased.

In power Hun Sen is authoritarian by nature, but pragmatic with respect to policy and diplomacy. He inherited a country shattered by war and openly seeks foreign assistance to help rebuild it. For this reason, in May 1999 Cambodia was finally allowed entrance into the Association of Southeast Asian Nations (ASEAN), which promotes free trade and mutual economic assistance. Both Japan and the European Union (EU) have also pledged a resumption of foreign investment and aid. The regime has also been allowed to occupy Cambodia's seat at the United Nations. However, in February 2002 the forthcoming tribunal for former Khmer Rouge members incurred controversy when the UN, convinced that the human rights of the defendants would not be respected, withdrew its support. Hun Sen, who hates his former compatriots, is determined to prosecute them for war crimes, even at the risk of reopening old war wounds. However, his popularity seems assured. The first local elections, held in the spring of 2002, overwhelmingly endorsed the Cambodian People's Party by granting them 1,600 of the nation's 1,621 local councils. Hun Sen has repeatedly pledged to help establish an administrative framework for democracy in Cambodia but, apparently, in the time frame and manner that he sees fit.

Further Reading

Frieson, Kate G. *In the Shadows: Women, Power, and Politics in Cambodia*. Victoria, British Columbia: University of Victoria, 2001.

Heder, Stephen R. "Dealing with Crimes against Humanity: Progress or Illusion?" *Southeast Asian Affairs* 28 (2001): 129–41.

Hughes, Caroline. "Cambodia: Democracy or Dictatorship?" *Southeast Asian Affairs* 28 (2001): 113–28.

———. *The Political Economy of Cambodia's Transition, 1991–2001*. New York: Routledge, 2003.

Metha, Harish C. *Hun Sen: Strongman of Cambodia*. Singapore: Graham Brash, 1999.

Peou, Sorpung. *Cambodia: Change and Continuity in Contemporary Politics*. Aldershot, England: Ashgate, 2001.

Roberts, David W. *Political Transition in Cambodia, 1991–1999: Power Elitism, and Democracy*. Richmond, Va.: Curzon, 2001.

Ung, Loung. *First They Killed My Father: A Daughter of Cambodia Remembers*. New York: Perennial, 2001.

Hussein I (1935–1999) *king of Jordan*

Hussein Ibn Tala was born in Amman, Jordan, on November 14, 1935, the son of Crown Prince Talal. His family was descended from the traditional line of Hashemite kings, and also claimed close affiliation with the prophet Muhammad. Like HASSAN II of Morocco, Jordanian monarchs invoke this religious lineage to strengthen their claims to political legitimacy. Jordan at that time was a poor nation populated mainly by Bedouin tribesmen. Hussein attended private schools in Egypt and England, and received his military training at the prestigious Royal Military Academy at Sandhurst. He was present when his grandfather, King Abdullah, was assassinated by a Palestinian extremist on July 21, 1951, and the event indelibly scarred him. Hussein's father Tala then became monarch, although he was removed from the throne due to mental illness in 1953. Hussein then ascended the throne at the age of 17, though actual power was entrusted to a regency. From the onset, his reign was imperiled by numerous factors, including hostile neighbors, militant Palestinians comprising nearly half of Jordan's population, wars with Israel, and the usual palace intrigue. However, the young monarch proved himself gifted in terms of leadership, political realism, and overall astuteness. He almost always gauged the tenor of his people correctly, won their trust and admiration, and ended his days as the Middle East's longest-reigning leader.

Early on, Hussein perceived that the left-wing, pan-Arab nationalism espoused by Egypt's Gamal Abdul Nasser was a threat to his kingdom's existence. He therefore joined an ill-fated federation with neighboring Iraq until 1958, when a coup killed off the Iraqi royal family. Increasingly isolated in the Arab world, Hussein then turned to Great Britain and the United States for diplomatic and economic succor. By dint of charm, intelligence, and a telegenic personality, he convinced them of his moderate inclinations, and tendered his service as a loyal ally in this tumultuous region. By 1967, however, Arab nationalism had propelled Egypt, Syria, and Jordan into war with Israel, and the former were badly defeated. Hussein desperately tried to avoid armed confrontation, but he realized that unless he fought he might be overthrown by his own people. Consequently, Jordan lost the West Bank, the holy city of Jerusalem, and inherited thousands of Palestinian refugees. Their growing militancy was abetted by the Palestine Liberation Organization (PLO) under Chairman YASSER ARAFAT, who began flouting the king's authority. In time, Palestinian enclaves functioned as virtual states within a state, and fighters conducted guerrilla attacks against Israel from Jordanian soil. Knowing such behavior courted disastrous retaliation from Israel, Hussein moved on the PLO in September 1970 and, after hard fighting, evicted them from the country. He also engaged in a brief border war with Syria's president HAFEZ AL-ASSAD, which was only halted by American and Soviet diplomatic intervention. Hussein's expulsion of the PLO ruined his reputation throughout the Arab world, but he achieved his paramount goal: preservation of the Jordanian throne. To that end, in 1973 he declined participating in the costly Yom Kippur War against Israel and even warned Israeli prime minister Golda Meir of its approach. For many years thereafter, Hussein basically ignored his neighbors, clamped down on political dissent and religious extremism at home, and attended to domestic needs. Consequently, by the 1990s Jordan had experienced considerable economic growth, impressive levels of literacy, and much reduced poverty, all of which enhanced the king's popularity at home.

The next biggest threat facing Jordan proved to be the Iraqi invasion of Kuwait in 1991. The Gulf states, with whom Jordan enjoyed close relations, strongly condemned this overt aggression against a fellow Arab state. Hussein, however, was strangely noncommittal in his criticism, mainly because the bulk of his population, now about half Palestinian, strongly supported it. Several years elapsed before the rift with the Gulf states could be healed. However, Hussein remained in the forefront in mending fences with Israel and negotiated continuously for peaceful relations with the Jewish state and an equitable resolution of the Palestinian problem. On October 26, 1994, he signed a peace treaty with Israeli prime minister YITZHAK RABIN that brought condemnation from radical Arab group, but eased tensions in the immediate region. The king also relaxed his autocratic style of leadership and legalized the first multiparty elections since 1956. However, he was less successful in resolving the issue of the West Bank and creation of a viable Palestinian state, a problem that would be inherited by successors.

Hussein died of cancer on February 7, 1999, in Amman. Prior to his passing, he engaged in a public row with his younger brother, Crown Prince Hassan, whom he passed over in favor of his eldest son, now King AB-DULLAH II. His death was greatly lamented by the Jordanian people, for, throughout his long and turbulent lifetime, Hussein worked diligently to maintain the kingdom's independence despite coup attempts, wars, and murderous fanaticism. His determination to survive was equaled only by an unending quest for a legitimate peace with Israel and a better life for his own as well as the Palestinian people. In every respect this moderately disposed, reassuring figure remains the "father" of modern Jordan.

Further Reading

Bligh, Alexander. *The Political Legacy of King Hussein.* Portland, Oreg.: Sussex Academic Press, 2002.

Boulby, Marion. *The Muslim Brotherhood and the Kings of Jordan, 1945–1993.* Atlanta, Ga.: Scholar's Press, 1999.

Dallas, Roland. *King Hussein: A Life on the Edge.* New York: Fromm International, 1999.

Joffe, George, ed. *Jordan in Transition.* New York: Palgrave, 2002.

Massad, Joseph A. *Colonial Effects: The Making of National Identity in Jordan.* New York: Columbia University Press, 2001.

Ryan, Curtis R. *Jordan in Transition: From Hussein to Abdullah.* Boulder, Colo.: Lynne Rienner Publishers, 2002.

Hussein, Saddam (1937–   ) *president of Iraq*

Saddam Hussein was born on April 28, 1937, in the village of Tikrit, Iraq. Raised by a cruel stepfather, he ran away from home at the age of 10 and found refuge with a former military officer, who imbued him with a sense of duty and pan-Arab nationalism. In 1957 he relocated to Baghdad and joined the then-shadowy socialist Baath Party. Hussein proved adept at conspiracy making, and he participated in several failed coup attempts against the government. However, the Baath Party eventually seized power in 1969 and installed Hussein as chief of the state security apparatus. Hussein, in a careful and calculated manner, continually eliminated his opponents until July 17, 1979, the day he declared himself president of Iraq. He owed his rise to personal cunning, an intricate web of family alliances, and utter ruthlessness.

Hussein inherited a poor, relatively weak Middle Eastern country and was determined to enhance its world standing. He aggressively developed an impressive array of oil fields and petrochemical industries, then invested heavily in infrastructure, literacy, health programs, and—above all—arms purchases. Within a decade Hussein had transformed Iraq into a modern, industrialized state and a regional superpower. However, the Iranian Revolution in 1981 led to an insurgency among Shiite Muslims living within his boundaries, which threatened to tear the country apart. Hussein simply crushed these dissident elements, then followed up by invading Iran in 1980. This act precipitated a bloody eight-year standoff that consumed hundreds of thousands of lives. Among them were many Iraqi citizens of Kurdish descent, who rose in rebellion and were slaughtered by chemical weapons. By the time a United Nations–brokered cease-fire commenced in August 1988, Iraq was bloody but unbowed. Throughout that conflict, Hussein had been financially assisted by rich neighboring Gulf states, which feared the Iranians, but the money stopped with the war. Saddled by huge debts, Hussein then prevailed upon the oil-rich nation of Kuwait to both cancel its loans and raise the price of oil to increase Iraq's yearly income. When Emir JABER III refused, Hussein suddenly ordered his tanks south.

In August 1990 Saddam's army quickly overran Kuwait, which placed him directly astride the rich oil fields of Saudi Arabia. However, his aggression triggered unforeseen consequences when a coalition of Western and Arab powers, led by the United States, initiated military moves to oust him. The UN, meanwhile, issued

Resolution 600 calling for the immediate evacuation of Kuwait by Iraqi forces. Hussein, predictably, refused to budge. It was followed by Resolution 661, which imposed worldwide economic sanctions upon Iraq. Again, Hussein glowered in defiance. Finally, at the behest of U.S. president George H. W. Bush, Resolution 678 was passed, which authorized use of military force to remove the invaders. Operation Desert Storm commenced on January 17, 1991, with a scathing aerial bombardment of Iraqi installations. A month later, when Hussein still clung to his conquest, coalition forces numbering half a million men advanced into Kuwait, forcibly ejecting the Iraqis. Hussein's forces were completely overpowered, losing an estimated 50,000 men and most of their equipment. Allied losses in this lopsided engagement amounted to only 400 casualties. However, President Bush, wishing to comply with UN resolutions, was not authorized to remove Hussein from power and he stopped the advance. After the fighting concluded on February 28, 1991, Hussein was badly battered but still in control.

For a decade after the Gulf War, Hussein embarked on a deliberate program of obstructing UN-mandated weapons inspections. Inspectors were supposed to be allowed to comb the country looking for weapons of mass destruction (nuclear and chemical), but, after 1998, Saddam denied them entry. A spate of retaliatory bombings ensued, along with continued economic sanctions that brought Iraq to its knees economically, but Hussein waxed defiant before the world community. The events of September 11, 2001, however, finally broke the impasse. The World Trade Center disaster heightened the intolerance of the United States toward terrorist states such as Iraq, and, on January 29, 2002, President GEORGE W. BUSH denounced Iraq, Iran, and North Korea as "an axis of evil."

President Bush throughout the summer and fall of 2002 threatened to invade Iraq and topple the regime if Hussein did not immediately allow United Nations weapons inspectors back into the country. Hussein initially dug in his heels but, finding no support for his position internationally, he finally admitted the first UN teams in December 2002 after a four-year hiatus.

After several months of searching, the UN weapons inspectors' findings were "inconclusive." The membership of the UN was divided over the next course of action. A group of nations led by France, Germany, and Russia called for further inspections, while the United States, Britain, and others called for the use of force in disarming Iraq. On March 20, 2003, American and British and other coalition forces launched Operation Iraqi Freedom. Hussein was twice targeted by bombs in the three-week campaign and his conspicuous absence fueled speculation about his death. Nonetheless, the United States is offering $200,000 for information leading to his capture, while its troops are receiving packs of cards decorated with the portraits of Iraqi fugitive leaders—Hussein is on the ace of spades. The status of the former dictator remains unknown as of this writing, but President Bush maintains that since Hussein's regime ended, the dictator's fate is irrelevant.

Further Reading

Aburish, Said K. *Saddam Hussein: The Politics of Revenge.* London: Bloomsbury, 2001.

Bengio, Ofra. *Saddam's Word: The Political Discourse in Iraq.* Oxford: Oxford University Press, 2002.

Glad, Betty. "Why Tyrants Go Too Far: Malignant Narcissism of Absolute Power." *Political Psychology* 23 (March 2002): 1–37.

Hiro, Dilip. *Neighbors, Not Friends: Iraq and Iran after the Gulf Wars.* New York: Routledge, 2001.

Karsh, Efraim. *Saddam Hussein: A Political Biography.* New York: Grove Press, 2003.

Mackey, Sandra. *The Reckoning: Iraq and the Legacy of Saddam Hussein.* New York: Norton, 2002.

Mylorie, Laurie. *The War against America: Saddam Hussein and the World Trade Center Attack.* New York: Reagan Books, 2001.

I

Iliescu, Ion (1930–) *president of Romania*

Ion Iliescu was born on March 3, 1930, in Oltenita, southeastern Romania, the son of a railway worker. His father was an active Communist Party sympathizer, and he imbued his son with left-wing beliefs. In 1944, when Soviet troops occupied Romania, Iliescu joined the Union of Communist Youth. He then studied at the Bucharest Polytechnic Institute and Moscow State University, achieving advanced degrees in engineering. After rising to secretary of the Union of Communist Youth in 1949, Iliescu was allowed to join the Communist Party in 1953. For over a decade he steadily climbed up through the party apparatus, and by 1965 he was allowed to join the all-important Central Committee. However, that same year witnessed the ascent of Nicolae Ceauşescu, who eventually instituted the most repressive political regime in all of Eastern Europe. Iliescu initially admired and cooperated with Ceauşescu, who appointed him to the Central Committee in 1968 as a full member. However, Ceauşescu's dictatorship grew increasingly megalomanic, and Iliescu frequently found himself at odds with his superior. The full break came in 1971, when he contested Ceauşescu's attempts to introduce a Chinese-style "cult of personality." Iliescu was consequently demoted and designated a regional party secretary. Over the next 14 years, Ceauşescu demoted Iliescu three additional times, finally reducing him to director

of a publishing house. However, the Romanian economy, never strong, began sinking under the weight of excess state regulation, and distress triggered the first mass protests in Romanian history. Ceauşescu responded by sending in the secret police, which only further alienated his regime from the public. When fighting broke out in December 1989 the dictator tried leaving the country, but he was caught and executed. Iliescu soon appeared to fill the vacuum as head of the newly formed National Salvation Front. By that time he had been long-known as Ceauşescu's opponent and on December 26, 1989, the provisional government appointed him interim president. Communism had finally died in Romania, but no one could predict what would happen next.

Over the next several months, Iliescu made token attempts to reform both the economy and the political system of Romania, but in such a way as to insure his own survival. To that end he promised to dissolve both the Communist Party and the dreaded Securitate (police) but, finding them useful allies, he eventually reneged on both pledges. Moreover, having complete control over the state-run media gave him distinct advantages over political adversaries; therefore, in the first election under the new regime, held in May 1990, Iliescu was overwhelmingly elected president by 85 percent of votes cast. This triggered the onset of wholesale demonstrations in Bucharest. Iliescu bused in 10,000 miners who severely beat the demonstrators. They killed 21 people before Iliescu had made his point: he was firmly in charge.

Over the next four years Iliescu embarked on a gradual transformation of Romania toward a free-market economy and democratic pluralism. However, being imbued with egalitarian sensibilities and market-driven economic convictions, he determined to avoid the inevitable dislocation and hyperinflation of transition through graduated reforms. This deliberate slowness exasperated political adversaries, but he invariably relied on his former Communist Party allies for political support in the legislature, and his methods were invariably approved. As a result Romania suffered few ill effects while changing from communism to capitalism, and Iliescu appeared to be the only available leader who could promote change while maintaining a reasonable degree of order. National elections held in October 1992 confirmed this fact when he won by a convincing 62 percent of the vote. As president, Iliescu also conducted several high-profile trips abroad, and he signed numerous treaties affecting trade and relations with Yugoslavia, Hungary, Moldova, and Russia. However, Romania's economic picture slid from bleak to worse and stimulated public cries for faster change. When Iliescu refused to increase the pace of reform, or take active measures to combat widespread corruption, he lost the 1996 national election to EMIL CONSTANTINESCU of the Democratic Convention Party by 51 percent of the vote. This outcome represented the first peaceful transfer of power in modern Romanian political history.

Iliescu spent the next four years as a force in the Romanian Senate, where he agitated behind the scenes for a political comeback. In November 2000 he got his chance in the wake of Constantinescu's fumbled attempts at economic reform. Moreover, this time his adversary was Coreneliu Vadim Tudor, a far-right nationalist, who had previously alarmed Romania's minorities—Jews, Gypsies, and Hungarians—by expounding extreme views. Iliescu won a majority of ballots on November 26, 2000, but not enough to prevent a runoff. When this finally transpired on December 11, 2000, he was returned to office a third time by 67 percent of votes cast. "This vote was a categoric rejection of extremism, xenophobia, and totalitarian temptations," the former communist hard-liner declared. Since then Iliescu has worked to prepare Romania for entry into the European Union (EU) and the NATO alliance. To facilitate these ends, in June 2002 he refused to sign a proposed controversial journalism law that many Western observers perceived as a threat to freedom of the press.

Further Reading

Almond, Mark. "Romania since the Revolution." *Government and Opposition* 25 (Autumn 1990): 484–497.

Gallagher, T. "A Feeble Embrace: Romania's Engagement with Democracy." *Journal of Communist Studies and Transitional Politics* 12 (June 1996): 145–179.

Heifner, C. Joan. *Development of Civil Society in Romania: Nature and Direction.* Banbury: Drake, 2002.

Light, Duncan, and David Phinnemore. *Post-communist Romania: Coming to Terms with Transition.* New York: Palgrave, 2001.

Pop-Eleches, Grigore. "Romania's 'Politics of Dejection.'" *Journal of Democracy* 12 (July 2001): 156–169.

Tismaneanu, Vladimir. "Electoral Revolutions." *Society* 35 (November–December, 1997): 61–66.

Ingraham, Hubert (1947–) *prime minister of the Bahamas*

Hubert Alexander Ingraham was born in Cooperstown, Abaco Island, Bahamas, on August 4, 1947. His country forms an extended chain of small islands roughly 500 miles southeast of Florida and directly north of Cuba. Long a British colony, the Bahamas acquired self-rule on the parliamentary model in 1973, and since then politics have been dominated by two main parties: the Progressive Liberal Party (PLP) and the Free National Movement (FNM). As a nation, the Bahamas enjoys exceptionally fine weather, beautiful surroundings, and a high standard of living. Ingraham was educated locally in Cooperstown, although he subsequently trained as a lawyer. In 1976 he commenced his political career by joining the PLP, then dominant under Sir Lynden Pindling, and he rose swiftly through the hierarchy to become chairman. In this capacity Ingraham completely overhauled the PLP's numerous branches, and he helped orchestrate the party's landslide victory of 1977. That year he also joined parliament as a PLP member from Abaco. He won again in 1982 and was rewarded with an appointment as minister of housing and national insurance in the Pindling administration. However, Ingraham proved outspoken in his criticism of corruption within the government, and in 1986 he was dismissed. He subsequently joined the FNM in 1987, was reelected to parliament on an anticorruption platform, and, following the death of party chief Sir Cecil Whitfield, he advanced to party head. Ingraham's political fortunes crested in August 1992 when he defeated Pindling, his former mentor, thereby ending 25 years of PLP rule. Having pledged to increase the accountability of the government, fight corruption, and revitalize the economy, Ingraham was then sworn in as the Bahamas second prime minister.

Because tourism accounts for 72 percent of the gross national product, Ingraham focused much of his attention upon expanding and improving that industry. This was essential because in 1992 and 1999 the islands were hit by two devastating hurricanes that necessitated extensive structural repairs. Ingraham also moved to increase the efficiency of business by selling off several state-owned enterprises, such as hotels and banks. By encouraging an atmosphere of privatization and free enterprise, he managed to attract record amounts of foreign investment. To lower government expenditures, he next sponsored legislation that lowered the salaries of bureaucratic officials and legislators, which proved highly popular to the voters. Ingraham, who posits himself as a friendly, outgoing populist, ran for reelection in March 1997. His popularity can be gauged by the fact that the FMN captured 34 out of 49 seats in parliament.

A major problem confronting Ingraham, or for that matter, any Caribbean leader, remains the pervasive and ongoing illicit trade in drugs. This is an especially daunting proposition for the Bahamas, which gains a large share of its income from numerous and highly confidential "offshore banks." These are frequently used by gangs for large-scale laundering of drug money. Nonetheless, Ingraham initiated tighter restrictions on all banking procedures to identify and halt all illegal transactions. Furthermore, in 1995 he oversaw the arrest of several members of the island's leading business and political families on drug and weapons charges. He moved with alacrity because the bulk of illegal drugs are destined for the United States, which is also the overwhelming source of tourists. It is essential for the continuing security and prosperity of the Bahamas to maintain a strict vigilance over contraband trafficking.

Another problem endemic to the Caribbean is the growing numbers of economic refugees, especially from Cuba and Haiti. Ingraham embarked on an aggressive program to deny illegal aliens entry and to deport them swiftly once arrived. However, he realizes that poverty is at the root of such migration and, in February 2002, he urgently called upon fellow nations of the Caribbean Common Market (CARICOM) to increase aid and assistance to Haiti. "Failing that," he warned, "it's going to be a catastrophe." Another sticking point has been the Bahamas refusal to formally join the movement toward a Single Market Economy (SME). Ingraham simply cannot comply with provisions that would allow all members of the Caribbean community, especially the poorer ones, free and unfettered travel rights to his islands. "If and when the time comes for the Bahamas to accept full or limited membership of the SME," he added, "It is my hope and desire and expectation that sister CARICOM states will consider the issue of the Bahamas' membership in the SME with pragmatism and in the context of Bahamian reality." Ingraham ultimately hopes to loosen travel restrictions for university graduates and create a mobile workforce that will assist local businesses without inundating his country with undocumented workers.

Hubert Ingraham *(Embassy of the Commonwealth of the Bahamas)*

Further Reading

Craton, Michael, and Gail Saunders. *Islanders in the Stream: A History of the Bahamian People.* 2 Vols. Athens: University of Georgia Press, 1999.

Collinwood, Dean W., and Steve Dodge. *Modern Bahamian Society.* Parkersby, Iowa: Caribbean Books, 1989.

Hughes, Colin A. *Race and Politics in the Bahamas.* New York: St. Martin's Press, 1981.

Jenkins, Olga C. *Bahamian Memories: Island Voices of the Twentieth Century.* Gainesville: University Press of Florida, 2000.

Lightburn, Tiffany J. "When Diasporas Discriminate: Identity Choices and Anti-immigration Sentiment in the Bahamas." Unpublished Ph.D. dissertation, University of Michigan, 2000.

Ionatana Ionatana   (d. 2000)   *prime minister of Tuvalu*

Ionatana Ionatana was a native of Tuvalu, a chain of nine Pacific Ocean atolls located several hundred miles west of the larger Solomon Islands. Though populated by 11,000 inhabitants, as a whole the group comprises only 10 square miles of land with an average height of less than 20 feet above sea level. It also constitutes the fourth-smallest nation in the world after Vatican City, Monaco, and Nauru. Tuvalu had been a British protectorate in the late 19th century, and in 1916 it became a colony. Negotiations for independence commenced in the 1970s and in October 1978 Tuvalu was separated from Great Britain, although it remains part of the British Commonwealth. However, dissatisfaction with continuing ties with Britain remains a sore point with many inhabitants, and, in February 2000, there was momentum to leave the Commonwealth altogether and strike out alone as a republic. It is a curious display of political defiance for a tiny nation that has no established parties, and where family relations and personal alliances are the driving force behind politics.

Little is known of Ionatana's early life, although he enjoyed a long career as a civil servant and also served as minister of education and culture and minister of health, women, and cultural affairs. In April 1999 the sitting prime minister, Birkenibeu Paeniu, received a vote of no confidence from parliament and was removed from office. On April 27, 1999 Ionatana was elected in his stead and immediately formed a new cabinet. The new leader faced challenges endemic to running a small nation totally lacking in natural resources and dependent on foreign aid. The national economy subsists mainly on fishing license fees, fishing, and income from seamen who work on foreign ships. Worse, Tuvalu also faces the prospect of rising unemployment, as many workers have traditionally been sent to nearby Nauru to labor in the phosphate industry. With that resource's impending depletion, they will return home to look for work. Ionatana therefore labored carefully to manage and increase the holdings of the Tuvalu National Trust, which was established in 1987 with money from Australia, New Zealand, and Japan, to help balance the national budget. He was also active in licensing the island's "tv.com" Internet domain to a Canadian firm, which is expected to bring in an additional $20 million yearly. The selling of passports to wealthy tourists, along with the marketing of stamps, is also expected to increase national revenues. Finally, in September 2000 Ionatana guided Tuvalu's membership into the United Nations, where it became the world's 189th country. UN Secretary-General KOFI ANNAN was effusive in his praise for the tiny island nation. "At a time when many small states are embroiled in violent conflicts, Tuvalu has remained stable and serene," he announced. Annan also felt "confident that the voice of Tuvalu will prove to be an eloquent one in our family."

In March 2000 Tuvalu suffered the worse disaster in its brief history when a boarding house caught fire and 18 schoolgirls died because the building was locked. Ionatana ordered an immediate investigation of the cause and also replaced the door locks with a chain-link fence around the building. However, he insisted that it was necessary to protect young girls "from young men and young boys going after young women and girls, so we lock in the girls." He has since come under criticism by feminist groups charging discrimination for sequestering girls at night, while boys' dormitories remain unguarded. However, an even greater disaster facing Tuvalu, and many smaller island domains, is the question of global warming. In the late 20th century, the greenhouse effect, thought to be triggered from the exhaust emissions of advanced technological societies led to a melting of the polar ice caps. This, in turn, has caused the ocean levels to rise, which threatens to swamp low-lying islands throughout the world. Fortunately, in June 2000 Ionatana successfully negotiated a pact with New Zealand that would allow the population to resettle there en masse should Tuvalu sink beneath the waves.

Prime Minister Ionatana died suddenly of a heart attack on December 9, 2000, and Faimalaga Luka replaced him after a secret ballot in parliament in February 2001.

Further Reading

Connell, John. "Environmental Change, Economic Development, and Emigration in Tuvalu." *Pacific Studies* 22, no. 1 (1999): 1–20.

Geddes, W. H., et al. *Atoll Economy: Social Change in Kiribati and Tuvalu.* Canberra: Australian National University Press, 1982.

Levine, Stephen. "Constitutional Change in Tuvalu." *American Journal of Political Science* 27, no. 3 (1992): 492–509.

Macdonald, Barrie. *Cinderellas of the Empire: Towards a History of Kiribati and Tuvalu.* Miami, Fla.: Australian National University Press, 1982.

Taaki, Tauaasa, and Janaline Oh. *Governance in the Pacific: Politics and Policy in Tuvalu.* Canberra: Australian National University Press, 1995.

Izetbegovic, Alija (1925–) *president of Bosnia-Herzegovina*

Alija Izetbegovic was born in Bosanski Samac, Bosnia-Herzegovina, on August 8, 1926, into a devout Muslim family. Bosnia at that time formed part of Yugoslavia, a slapdash union of six ethnically differing republics created in the aftermath of World War I. Their recent political union did nothing to ease or erase centuries of ethnic and religious hostility among the three leading factions: Croats, Muslims, and Serbs. Nonetheless, Izetbegovic was raised and educated in Sarajevo, where he attended the First Real Gymnasium for Boys until 1943. For the ensuing two years he joined partisan forces under Josip Broz Tito to fight occupying German forces. After 1945 Tito installed a communist-oriented regime, but Yugoslavia remained essentially a confederation of six republics. In 1946 Izetbegovic was arrested and jailed for helping found the Young Muslims, a religion-based political organization created to counter the atheist, Marxist dogma of communism. After a short imprisonment, he was released, and in 1956 Izetbegovic studied law at the University of Sarajevo. He spent the next three decades serving as a company lawyer. However, Izetbe-

govic remained religiously inclined, and, in 1970, he authored a provocative pamphlet entitled *The Islamic Declaration.* In it he maintained: "There can be neither peace nor coexistence between the Islamic religion and non-Islamic political and social institutions." In 1980 he also penned *Islam between East and West,* which the government found impermissible and sentenced Izetbegovic in 1983 to 14 years in jail. He served only five years before being released in 1988, and the following year he proved a driving force behind creation of a Muslim political organization, the Party for Democratic Action. On December 20, 1990, Izetbegovic was elected the first president of the Bosnia-Herzegovina Republic at the age of 65.

By this time, Yugoslavia as a national entity was on the verge of collapse. The death of Tito in 1980 led to a general resurgence of ethnic tensions and the state began tearing itself apart. Serbia and Montenegro elected to remain united, but Slovenia, Croatia, Macedonia, and Bosnia-Herzegovina all declared their independence after 1991. However, because Bosnia is shared jointly among Muslims, Croats, and Serbs, none of whom particularly care to be dominated by the other, intense fighting erupted among them to carve out as much territory as possible. Here the ethnic Serbs were materially assisted by allies in neighboring Serbia under SLOBODAN MILOŠEVIĆ, and they quickly overran three-fourths of Bosnia. The Serbs also carried out the practice of "ethnic cleansing," whereby Muslims and Croats were systematically removed or killed to make room for new settlers. Atrocities against civilians and prisoners were widespread and well-documented. Internecine fighting continued well into 1994, with the Muslims, badly outnumbered and outgunned, taking a terrible toll. Izetbegovic, however, elected to remain in the besieged city of Sarajevo, where he made repeated appeals to the West for assistance. He also visited Iran and various states lining the Gulf of Arabia to solicit money and mujaheddins (religious fighters) to assist his cause. His efforts were well received by fellow Muslims, and in 1993 Izetbegovic received the King Faisal International Prize for Serving Islam. At this point, Western forces under NATO unleashed an intense bombing campaign against Serb military forces in Bosnia, which brought them to the peace talks held in Dayton, Ohio, in 1996. The so-called Dayton Peace Accords, a comprehensive settlement, was thereupon signed. This mandated that Bosnia-Herzegovina would be governed by a tripartite presidency equally shared among the three competing groups. Moreover, Bosnia would be formally partitioned into two entities, a Muslim-Croat federation and the Serb-dominated Republika Srpska. Thus ended one of the bloodiest civil wars of recent history.

On September 14, 1996, elections were held for the presidency of Bosnia-Herzegovina and Izetbegovic, having received the largest share of votes, was installed as the first sitting leader. However, he shared his office with Momcilo Krajsnik (Croat) and Kresimir Zubak (Serb) on a rotating basis that turned every eight months. It seemed an awkward arrangement, but peace had been restored to a shattered land. He was especially grateful to the United States for turning back the tide of Serbian aggression. "As supporters of freedom, we believe that it is the right and duty of every man and woman to resist violence," he affirmed. "In this resistance to violence, we justifiably expect the support and help of your great country." Once in office, Izetbegovic was inordinately occupied with the repatriation of prisoners and the settlement of nearly 1 million war refugees, the largest seen in Europe since World War II. Izetbegovic surrendered the chairmanship on October 15, 1998, although he still remained on the presidential board. He was reelected in 1998 and resigned from politics altogether in 2000 owing to poor health. In January 2002, Izetbegovic received treatment for a heart ailment at the King Faisal Specialist Hospital in Riyadh, Saudi Arabia. He is living out his retirement in Sarajevo.

Further Reading

Burg, Stephen L., and Paul S. Shoup. *The War in Bosnia-Herzegovina: Ethnic Conflict and International Intervention.* Armonk, N.Y.: M. E. Sharpe, 1999.

Chandler, David. *Bosnia: Faking Democracy after Dayton.* London: Pluto Press, 2000.

Izetbegovic, Alija. *Izetbegovic of Bosnia-Herzegovina: Notes from Prison, 1983–1988.* Westport, Conn.: Praeger, 2002.

Keane, Rory. *Reconstituting Sovereignty: Post-Dayton Bosnia Uncovered.* Burlington, Vt.: Ashgate, 2002.

Maghas, Branka, and Ivo Zanic. *The War in Croatia and Bosnia Herzegovina, 1991–1995.* Portland, Oreg.: Frank Cass, 2001.

Mahmutcehajic, Rusmir. *The Denial of Bosnia.* University Park: Pennsylvania University Press, 2000.

———. *Sarajevo Essays: Politics, Ideology, and Tradition.* Albany: State University of New York Press, 2003.

J

Jaber III (1926–   ) *emir of Kuwait*

Jaber al-Ahmed al-Sabah was born in Kuwait City on June 29, 1926, the son of reigning Sheikh Ahmad al-Jaber. Kuwait is a small kingdom on the northeastern coast of the Arabian Peninsula. A nominal British protectorate since 1899, it was granted full independence in November 1962 under the aegis of the Sabah family, to which Jaber belongs. Kuwait, topographically, consists entirely of parched desert but it is also rich, possessing some of the world's deepest oil reserves. Consequently, the ruling family has lavished considerable wealth upon its subjects, granting them one of the world's highest standards of living. Jaber was educated at the Mubarakiya School, Kuwait's first such institution, and he subsequently received private tutoring in English, science, and literature. As a member of the royal family, he was destined to work for the government and between 1949–59, he directed public security throughout the oil-bearing Ahmadi region of Kuwait. In 1959 he was elevated to head the finance department, whereby tight budgetary controls were imposed upon all sectors of the Kuwaiti government. Jaber was also heavily involved in foreign negotiations that culminated in the founding of the Organization of Petroleum Exporting Nations (OPEC) in 1960. In November 1965, following the accession of cousin Sabah III as emir, Jaber gained appointment as prime minister. Over the ensuing decade, as the aged emir's health declined, Jaber assumed more and more responsibility for running the country, which he did capably and with great tact. On January 31, 1977, Jaber became emir of Kuwait following the death of Salah III.

As emir, Jaber displayed all the paternalistic instincts and aptitude for politics inherent in a desert culture. Ruling by consensus, rather than decree, he always consults and negotiates with members of the ruling family before embarking on any major new policies. Such an approach to leadership places a premium on resolving disputes peacefully and amicably. Jaber also considers himself a champion of Arabic nationalism. As a member of the Arab League, he regularly contributes money and weapons to the Palestine Liberation Organization in its struggle with the Jewish state of Israel. He also dispatches generous assistance to poorer Arab nations throughout the region to cement goodwill relations. He is also carefully attentive to the needs of his subjects, upon whom the stability of Kuwait rests.

However, the great wealth of Kuwait, its thriving oil industry, and proximity to the Middle East have conspired in the recent past to upend or even destroy the kingdom. Being sparsely populated, Kuwait depends upon large contingents of foreign workers, most poor Palestinians, to work the oil fields. These workers, known as *bidoon,* or "stateless" Arabs, enjoy few political rights and cannot vote, regardless of how long they reside in the country. Such practices, combined with a tendency of rich Kuwaitis to look down upon poor Arabs, has generated more than a little resentment. Religion is also a matter of concern. Consistent with accepted Muslim beliefs, women are covered with scarves in public, and they cannot vote. Furthermore, while most Kuwaitis subscribe to the moderate Sunni sect of Islam, a small but long-established Shiite community also flourishes. This last group has proved susceptible to foreign influences, most notably the Iranian Revolution of 1979, which resulted in growing radicalization. Throughout the Iraq-Iran war, the royal family sent weapons and billions of dollars to Iraq to prevent Persian influence from overrunning the Gulf region. But growing disillusionment with the Salah family rule served as an outlet for politically inspired terrorism, and in May 1985 Jaber narrowly missed being killed by a suicide bomber. Finally there remains the question of neighboring Iraq. During medieval times, Kuwait was once part of that state, and, after 1962, various Iraqi regimes espoused territorial ambitions against their rich, weak neighbor. In August 1990 SADDAM HUSSEIN invaded and occupied Kuwait with a view toward its annexation, only to be driven out by a U.S.–led UN coalition six months later.

Since being restored to his throne in the spring of 1991, Jaber has made several determined moves to strengthen his regime against further Iraqi aggression. His is the only Arab country to enjoy close military and political ties to the United States, which is also an ally of Israel. Jaber has also taken steps to improve relations with both Jordan and Yemen, two states that vocally supported the Iraqi invasion. Furthermore, he encourages restoration of amity between the United States and Iran, two seemingly intractable enemies. "Establishing good relations between the US and Iran could contribute to stability in the region," he maintained, "and strengthen Kuwait's security too." Finally, in a much-needed nod to modernization, the emir promulgated legislation calling for women's suffrage and the right to run for public office. This last gesture, though welcomed by Western powers, has been reviled by conservative religious elements as an attack upon Muslim society. In September 2001, Jaber suffered a mild stroke and was flown to London for treatment. He has since recovered, but the 77-year-old emir is considered increasingly unfit for the strains of public life, and Shiekh Saad al-Abdullah al-Sabah, the reigning crown prince, stands in line to succeed him.

Further Reading

Dekhayel, Abdulkarim al-. *Kuwait: Oil, State, and Political Legitimation.* Reading, England: Ithaca Press, 2000.

Long, Jerry M. "The Politics of Religion and the Persian Gulf War, 1990–1991." Unpublished Ph.D. dissertation, Baylor University, 2001.

Mughni, Haya al-. *Women in Kuwait: The Politics of Gender.* London: Saqi, 2001.

Tetreault, Mary Ann. *Stories of Democracy: Politics and Society in Contemporary Kuwait.* New York: Columbia University Press, 2000.

———. "A State of Two Minds: State Cultures, Women, and Politics in Kuwait." *International Journal of Mid East Studies* 33 (May 2001): 203–220.

Zahlan, Rosemarie S. *The Making of the Modern Gulf States: Kuwait, Bahrain, Qatar, United Arab Emirates, and Oman.* Reading, England: Ithaca Press, 1998.

Jagan, Cheddi (1918–1997) *president of Guyana*

Cheddi Berret Jagan was born on March 22, 1918, in Port Mourant, British Guiana, the only English-speaking region of South America. His parents were poor indentured servants from India who worked the sugar fields and, as a child, Jagan assisted them. At length, he performed well as a student and was sent to attend Howard University in Washington, D.C. As a dark-skinned Indian, he encountered the racial discrimination then prevalent in America, and the experience indelibly seared him. Jagan subsequently studied dentistry at Northwestern University, Chicago, where he met and married Janet Rosenberg, a student nurse. Jagan then returned to British Guiana, where he established a successful dental practice at Georgetown. He and his wife also became politically active by organizing field-workers. The native population of British Guiana consists mostly of a majority black population descended from African slaves and a sizable Indian migrant community. As economic competitors, there was a long-standing enmity between them, but Jagan worked to overcome this antagonism for a common goal. By now a committed leftist, in 1950 he founded the People's Progressive Party (PPP) and assigned Forbes Burnham, a prominent black attorney, as his chairman. The first-ever elections under the new constitution, held in 1953, were a success for the PPP and he became speaker of the national legislature. In this capacity Jagan agitated for a strong Marxist-Leninist line, which greatly alarmed Prime Minister Winston Churchill back in Britain. Fearful that the colony might be lost to Communists, Churchill dispatched a military expedition that removed Jagan from office after only 133 days. Unrepentant, he continued his political activism, tried organizing mass civil disobedience, and was jailed for violating the state of emergency. The British then withdrew their troops and in 1957 the PPP won another round of elections. Jagan advanced to minister of trade and industry for the next four years while pressure mounted for national independence.

In 1961 the PPP again won resoundingly at the polls. This occurred under a new constitution intended to promote greater self-governance, and Jagan became prime minister. Again, he touted his usual Marxist line and actively cultivated close ties to the Soviet Union and Cuba's FIDEL CASTRO. His activities came to the attention of the U.S. government, which, in concert with Britain, enacted a campaign of economic destabilization to try to depose him. By 1964 massive strikes had paralyzed British Guiana and this, coupled with a growing sense of urgency, caused the PPP to lose the national elections that year. Burnham, who had split with the PPP and formed his own party, the People's National Congress (PNC), became the new prime minister. He led the colony toward independence in 1966, when it was officially renamed Guyana, and he remained in power until 1985. The form of government also changed from parliamentary to presidential. Jagan, meanwhile, functioned as both chairman of the PPP and leader of the opposition in parliament. However, Burnham's tenure in office was corrupt and authoritarian, and the country's economic situation worsened dramatically. When Burnham died in 1985 he was succeeded by another PNC candidate, Desmond Hoyte, who held high office until 1992. That year new elections finally brought the 70-year-old Jagan to power as president; his success capped an audacious 39-year climb to the top.

By the time Jagan ruled Guyana, the cold war had ended and Marxist-Leninist doctrine was irrelevant. He had previously discarded most of his firebrand rhetoric and frequently visited the United States to explain his position to various administrations. "I was a Gorbachev even before Gorbachev, in the sense of what we were doing and not adopting the traditional dogmas of Marxist parties," he insisted. He still opposed privatization as "recolonization," but his victory was nonetheless welcomed by the Americans as it put the hopelessly corrupt PNC out of office. Over the next five years Jagan solidified his credentials as one of the Western Hemisphere's outspoken champions of the poor, and he called upon wealthy nations for assistance. "The unjust economic order must be replaced by a just, new global human order for international and individual security and peace," Jagan affirmed. To that end, he proposed assembling funds from reduced arms spending, environmental taxes, and national investment to use in reducing worldwide poverty. He remained an outspoken critic of global inequity until his death from heart disease on March 6, 1997. Jagan remains highly regarded at home for assisting the downtrodden when it was not fashionable—and even dangerous—to do so. His funeral was attended by an estimated 170,000 people, one-seventh of Guyana's population. Jagan was succeeded in office by his vice president, Samuel Hinds.

Further Reading

Daniels, Gordon O. "A Great Injustice to Cheddi Jagan: The Kennedy Administration and British Guiana, 1961–1963." Unpublished Ph.D. dissertation, University of Mississippi, 2000.

Datt, Norman. *Cheddi B. Jagan: The Legend.* Pickering, Ontario: N. Datt, 1997.

Huntley, Eric L. *The Life and Times of Cheddi Jagan.* London: Bogle and L'Ouverture Press, 1994.

Jagan, Cheddi. *The West on Trial: My Fight for Guyana's Freedom.* New York: International Publishers, 1967.

Lakhan, V. Chris. *Cheddi Jagan: Selected Contributions on His Life and Legacy.* Windsor, Ontario: Summit Press, 1997.

Spinner, Thomas J. *A Political and Social History of Guyana, 1945–1983.* Boulder, Colo.: Westview Press, 1984.

Jagan, Janet (1920–) *president of Guyana*

Janet Rosalie Rosenberg was born in Chicago, Illinois, on October 20, 1920, the daughter of Jewish immigrants. She was educated locally and in Detroit, but in 1942 she enrolled at Cook County Hospital, Chicago, intent upon becoming a nurse. There she met her future husband, CHEDDI JAGAN, then studying dentistry at Northeastern University. The two fell in love and married over the objections of their respective families. In 1943 the couple relocated back to British Guiana, and Jagan felt distinctly unwelcome living as a white woman in a land dominated by dark-skinned Indian and Afro-Caribbeans. Whites had traditionally dominated the plantation hierarchy and it took several months for Jagan to make the adjustment. However, her efforts to assimilate were abetted by deep commitments toward helping the working poor. She also greatly lamented the fact that class politics were largely polarized along racial lines, pitting Indians against blacks. But she and her husband, committed Marxists, became actively involved in organizing field-workers and engaging in labor disputes as early as 1946. By 1950 they founded the People's Progressive Party (PPP) in which Jagan served as general secretary for two decades. That year she won a seat on the Georgetown City Council while also editing the party newspaper. These were heady times for young leftists, as British Guiana had been granted internal governance in preparation for independence. In 1953 a new constitution was adopted allowing for local elections, and the PPP took 17 out of 24 assembly seats. Jagan gained one of them, becoming the first woman in British Guiana to hold high office. Her husband served as speaker of the assembly, a fact that induced the British government to intervene and remove them from power. Both were subsequently jailed several months for political activism during a state of national emergency.

In 1957 new elections were held and, again, the PPP proved a dominant force. Jagan gained reelection to the legislature and was also appointed minister of labor, health and housing. She performed useful work over the next four years, until 1961, when her party won 20 of 35 available seats. This made her husband British Guiana's first PPP prime minister. Two years later she became minister of home affairs, but, in 1964, the PPP was beaten in national elections by its rival, the People's National Congress (PNC) headed by Forbes Burnham. This was accomplished with the help of the British and American intelligence services, who organized strikes that crippled the economy. Neither government wanted the Jagans to lead the only English-speaking region of South America into a communist orbit. Consequently, in 1966 Burnham led the country into independence under the new name of Guyana.

Jagan remained part of the political opposition for the next 30 years. The PPP, which formally described itself as a Marxist party in 1969, remained shut out of power, due mostly to the election machinations of the PNC. Jagan nonetheless continued serving within the party hierarchy as secretary of international affairs and executive secretary until 1992, when her husband finally won the presidency by defeating Burnham's successor, Desmond Hoyte. Jagan now became Guyana's first lady, although she continued serving in the legislature and also found time to author several children's books. When her husband died on March 6, 1997, she advanced to the post of prime minister, another first for women in Guyana, while Samuel Hinds became acting president. After lengthy discussion, it was decided that Jagan should be allowed to carry on her husband's legacy, and she was nominated as the party's presidential candidate. In December 1997 the PPP again outpolled Hoyte's PNC and the 77-year-old matron became the first female head of state in Guyana's history. She was also that country's first white head of state.

Jagan served only 20 months in office and they proved exceptionally stormy. Hoyte refused to recognize her political legitimacy and mobilized the highly polarized black electorate against her. In February 1998, her car was surrounded by protestors and stoned, although she emerged unscathed. When an independent audit of ballots by the Caribbean Community (CARICOM) concluded that the PPP had in fact won the election, Hoyte still refused to concede. Worse, in August 1999, Jagan suffered a heart attack after attending the Rio de Janeiro summit of leaders. "Despite the assurances that my condition is not life threatening," she explained, "I found that my energy and stamina have been seriously reduced." Tired of struggling, she tendered her resignation on August 9, 1999, and she was succeeded by her finance minister, BHARRAT JAGDEO. Hoyte and the PNC, meanwhile, steadfastly refused to recognize the legitimacy of the new administration. Jagan has promised to stay active in PPP affairs as the elder stateswoman of her adopted land.

Further Reading
Canterbury, Dennis C. "Politics and Social Forces in Guyana Working Class Development." Unpublished Ph.D. dissertation, State University of New York at Binghamton, 2000.

"Guyana." *The Courier,* no. 150 (March–April 1995): 30–51.

Levy, Ari. "A History of the Color Line in Guyana: Blacks, East Indians, and the Legacy of Colonialism." Unpublished master's thesis, Clark University, 1998.

Premdas, Ralph R. *Ethnic Conflict and Development: The Case of Guyana.* Brookfield, Vt.: Avebury, 1995.

Ramcharit, Paul H. "Socialism in Guyana: Analysis of Post-independence Policies." Unpublished master's thesis, Hamline University, 1992.

Jagdeo, Bharrat (1964–) *president of Guyana*
Of Indian descent, Bharrat Jagdeo was born in Unity Village, Demerara, British Guiana, on January 23, 1964. His small nation sits on the northern fringes of South America, sandwiched between Venezuela and Suriname, and is the only English-speaking country on the continent. Guyana was formerly a Dutch possession, but Britain acquired it in 1803 and maintained it as a colony until political independence arrived in 1966. It is generally regarded as one of the poorest nations in the Western Hemisphere. Jagdeo was educated locally at the Gibson Primary School and the Mahaica Multilateral School, performing well. In 1984 he received a scholarship to study economics at the Patrice Lumumba University in Moscow, from which he graduated in 1990. Once home, Jagdeo joined the leftist-oriented People's Progressive Party (PPP) and applied his expertise while holding governmental posts connected with economics. In 1993 he became junior minister of finance, and between 1992–97 also served as director of various banks. He gained a reputation for honesty and personal integrity. In 1995 Jagdeo gained appointment as senior minister of finance and it was here that he made indelible contributions to Guyana's floundering economy.

Early in his career, Jagdeo gained a reputation as a conciliator and consensus builder. Therefore, in drawing up a National Development Strategy, he gathered together various competing interests, such as labor unions, business leaders, and civic society, and he imbued them with a sense of the common good. Debt relief was his first, and most pressing, priority. By coordinating the efforts of 200 significant individuals in his nation, he reduced Guyana's skyrocketing national debt from $700 million to less than half that amount. He also facilitated increased output in the country's gold and bauxite mining sectors, which contributed to an overall yearly growth rate of 5 percent. The national inflation rate of 8 percent was also cut in half. He was widely hailed at home and abroad for his business acumen, and he did much to revive Guyana's reputation as a reliable source for overseas investment. Given the applause, when President JANET JAGAN retired from office because of poor health, Jagdeo succeeded her as Guyana's sixth president on August 11, 1999.

Once empowered, Jagdeo sought continuity by perpetuating the policies that had worked so successfully. This was done frequently over the objections of Desmond Hoyte, leader of the People's National Congress Party (PNP), who disputed the December 1997 election that brought Jagan to power. Consequently he also refuses to acknowledge Jagdeo's political legitimacy. Nonetheless, the young (36-year-old) president has continued his success in leading Guyana back from the brink. Despite a background in socialist economics, which champions state control over key sectors of the economy, Jagdeo has embraced free-market strategies. He has authorized the privatization of inefficient, state-run industries, and he has plowed the resulting profits back into housing, education, and health care. He further cemented his alliances with the unions and the private sector, doing his utmost to coordinate their interaction and promote greater economic prosperity. And, despite the protests of environmentalists, he plans to expand the exploitation of national resources such as minerals, fishing, and forestry. Unemployment still stands at 12 percent, a very high rate for such a small country, but all told Jagdeo has staged an impressive economic comeback. Consequently, in the national elections of March 19, 2001, the PPP was easily returned to power. Since then Jagdeo and opposition leader Hoyte have issued a joint statement pledging to cooperate in drafting a new constitution to promote greater political harmony.

Extensive oil deposits have been discovered recently off the northern coast of South America. Both Guyana and neighboring Suriname covet the prospects of additional revenues from oil but the prospect has led to considerable friction. In June 2000 a Canadian GCX oil rig leased by Guyana was chased by Surinamese gunboats out of a region claimed by Suriname. Jagdeo has since entered into negotiations with President RUNALDO VENETIAAN to resolve the dispute peacefully through joint exploration. More threatening is Venezuelan president HUGO CHÁVEZ's claim that the 1899 border settlement with Guyana is unsatisfactory and must be revised.

Chávez also complained about Jagdeo's willingness to lease a rocket launch site to an American company that lies only 25 miles from the Venezuelan border. Because stability is a prerequisite for continued foreign investment, Guyana—lacking an army or navy—must strive for peaceful and equitable resolution of these pressing matters.

Further Reading

Alfred, Clarence. *The Great Betrayal: A Historical Perspective and Lessons of Experience in Guyana's Political System.* Trinidad: S. A. Ibemerum, 1998.

"Guyana." *The Courier,* no. 150 (March–April 1995): 30–51.

Mars, Joan R. *Deadly Force: Colonialism and the Rule of Law: Explaining Police Violence in Guyana.* Westport, Conn.: Greenwood Press, 2002.

Morrison, Andrew. *Justice: The Struggle for Democracy in Guyana, 1952–1992.* Georgetown, Guyana: A. Morrison, 1998.

Ramcharit, Paul H. *Socialism in Guyana: Analysis of Post-independence Policies.* St. Paul, Minn.: Ramcharit, 1997.

Jammeh, Yahya (1965–) *president of* The Gambia

Yahya Jammeh was born on May 25, 1965, in the village of Kanilai, western Gambia, into a Jola Muslim family. The Gambia, a British colony until 1965, is a small sliver of land surrounded on three sides by neighboring Senegal, to which it shares great ethnic and religious similarities. Politically, the country—officially known as The Gambia—was unique for having one of Africa's true multiparty democracies and, under the aegis of President DAWDA JAWARA, among its most stable. Jammeh was educated locally before joining the National Gendarmerie in 1983. Adept as a soldier, he received a lieutenant's commission in 1989 and subsequently served with Jawara's presidential guards. Jammeh then transferred to The Gambia National Army in 1992 as a lieutenant and underwent military police training at Fort McClellan, Alabama. Though peaceful, the Jawara regime was extremely corrupt, and, on July 22, 1994, a group of dissenting officers under Jammeh approached the president to demand back wages. When this was refused, they disarmed the presidential guard and enacted a bloodless coup. Jawara fled the country after a five-man military council was established to rule in his place, chaired by Jammeh. Thus, aged but 30 years, he became one of the world's youngest heads of state.

Jammeh's ensuing rule was marked by a distinct dichotomy of events. On the one hand, he was merciless toward all political opposition. Once in power he suspended the constitution and outlawed any political activity. Opponents of his rule, even perceived ones, were harassed by the police and frequently arrested. In November 1994 a failed coup attempt against him resulted in the deaths of 50 soldiers. Furthermore, having promised the world community an early return to democratic institutions, he continually rolled back the date for allowing the transition. "If we don't want elections in the next 1,000 years," he thundered, "there will be no elections. We will make sure that those who want elections will go six feet deep and there's nothing anybody can do about it." Naturally, in the face of such despotism, the United States and Europe cut off all of The Gambia's foreign aid. The ensuing economic crisis made Jammeh reconsider his position and he announced new elections within four years. Continuing foreign pressure reduced this to two years, although with the caveat that no political parties could be organized until within three months of the scheduled date. This had the effect of loosening up international investments, and Jammeh moved swiftly and deliberately to shore up his political support.

Although political parties were forbidden, Jammeh sponsored a public organization called the 22 July Group, which possessed all the trappings of a political party. As such it had free access to state-controlled media, which was also favorably disposed toward the regime. But Jammeh managed to deliver on his earlier pledge to address the great material deficiencies of The Gambia. Throughout his 25 years in office, Jawara had failed to construct so much as a single school. Jammeh, by contrast, erected 16 such buildings, along with a new hospital, an international airport, and the first television station. The nation's first university had also been established upon his instructions. He also ordered work done on The Gambia's long-neglected infrastructure, and many roads were either repaired or built. In 1996, with elections approaching that fall, Jammeh resigned from the military so that he could run as a civilian leader of the Alliance for Patriotic Re-orientation and Construction Party (APRC). On September 26, 1996, Jammeh successfully ran against three other contenders, "officially" garnering 56 percent in a very flawed electoral process. Critics railed, but Jammeh became The Gambia's second freely elected leader. Subsequent elections for the National Assembly also delivered 33 of 45 seats to the victorious APRC, which served to consolidate his rule over the country.

In light of recent events, both the United States and the European Union (EU) resumed their flow of foreign aid to The Gambia. Jammeh effectively routed it into the economy, which grew by an estimated 4 percent yearly. The president also authorized selling off government-owned enterprises such as hotels, telecommunications, and electrical utilities. The Gambia has since become active in many regional organizations and security arrangements. Jammeh was one of few politicians to support an American proposal for an All-African peace-keeping force, and in 1999 Gambian soldiers were dispatched to Guinea-Bissau. However, when the regime weathered another unsuccessful coup attempt in January 2000, the president cracked down on dissident ethnic elements. The government further responded by removing many senior military officers of Mandinka or Fula background and replacing them with Jola. For all his ham-fisted tendencies, Jammeh has reduced the pervasive corruption afflicting The Gambia in installing a measure of stability and prosperity to his state. National elections held on October 19, 2001, confirmed these facts when the president was reelected with 52.9 percent of the vote in an election with a very high voter turnout. This time the process was judged free and fair by international observers, which lends Jammeh's regime the political legitimacy it has always craved.

Further Reading

Hughes, Arnold. *The Gambia: Studies in Society and Politics.* Birmingham, England: University of Birmingham, 1991.

———. "'Democratization' under the Military in Gambia, 1994–2000." *Journal of Commonwealth & Comparative Politics* 38 (November 2000): 35–43.

"The Gambia." *The Courier,* no. 142 (November–December 1993): 13–31.

Saine, Abdoulaye. "The Gambia's Foreign Policy since the Coup, 1994–1999." *Commonwealth and Comparative Politics* 38 (July 2000): 73–88.

Schroeder, Richard A. *Shady Practices: Agroforestry and Gender Politics in The Gambia.* Berkeley: University of California Press, 1999.

Wiseman, John R. "The Gambia: From Coup to Elections." *Journal of Democracy* 9 (April 1998): 64–76.

Jawara, Dawda (1924–) *president of The Gambia*

Dawda Kairaba Jawara was born on May 16, 1924, in Barajally, Gambia, the son of wealthy Muslim farmers. Educated at nearby Christian schools, he won a scholarship to Achimoto College, Gold Coast (Ghana), in 1948, where he remained a year. Jawara subsequently attended Glasgow University, Scotland, intent upon becoming a veterinarian. He graduated with honors in 1953, and he later completed postgraduate studies at the Royal College of Veterinary Surgeons. When Jawara returned home in 1954 he was Gambia's only trained animal doctor, and he plied his trade skillfully. "There's not a cow in The Gambia that does not know me personally," he once boasted. In 1955 he also converted to Christianity, adopting the name David. While working in the wilderness of Africa's smallest colony, he became struck by the vast disparity of wealth between the countryside and the cities. This prompted him to found the Protectorate People's Society in 1959 to address the lack of basic human services among the poor. The following year it was renamed the People's Progressive Party (PPP) and, as party head, Jawara entered politics. He won a seat in the newly elected National Assembly and also gained appointment as minister of education. In 1962 he led the PPP to a sweeping national victory and became the colony's first prime minister. In this capacity Jawara also led Gambia to political independence from Great Britain on February 18, 1965—now known officially as The Gambia—while retaining a British-style parliamentary system for governance. That year he also reconverted back to Islam, and in 1966 Queen Elizabeth knighted him for service to the British Commonwealth.

In power, Jawara reigned as one of Africa's longest-serving heads of state. Yet he accomplished this solely by adhering to the democratic process, ushering in a period of growth and political stability rarely seen in western Africa. For many years, The Gambia was Africa's sole example of a flourishing, multiparty system. In 1970 Jawara further demonstrated his commitment to free elections by placing adoption of a republic-style system to a public referendum. It passed by wide margins, and on April 24, 1970, Jawara became The Gambia's first president. As a politician, he invariably embraced a moderate stance on most issues and discouraged political or religious extremism. He was also fiscally responsible, and so, through most of the 1970s, the country was free of national debt. However, global economic problems in the 1980s resulted in austerity measures, which in turn generated political discontent. In July 1981, while Jawara was visiting Britain, a group of disenchanted military officers staged a coup. This was subsequently suppressed by troops from neighboring Senegal, and Jawara was soon restored to power. Despite the magnitude of destruction involved, and the deaths of 600 citizens, the president proved surprisingly magnanimous. Those coup leaders arrested received fair trials and, though condemned to death, were never executed. Most were eventually released.

The experience of rebellion underscored The Gambia's relative military weakness. In February 1982 Jawara joined a new confederation, Senegambia, headed by ABDOU DIOUF. Because The Gambia is only 30 miles wide and juts several hundred miles through the center of Senegal, the union seemed natural, but Jawara steadfastly refused to surrender his economic independence. The union finally unraveled in 1989, once Diouf removed troops from The Gambia to Senegal's hotly contested border with Mauritania. But in 1992, as an indication of his continuing popularity, Jawara was overwhelmingly re-elected to the presidency for a fifth term. By then he had been in control of The Gambia for three decades.

Jawara's placid handling of national events came to a violent and unexpected ending on July 22, 1994, when a group of military officers headed by Captain YAHYA JAMMEH suddenly stormed the capital. The president was quickly sequestered aboard a U.S. Navy warship laying offshore and moved thence to Dakar, Senegal. Because of the breakup of the confederation, President Diouf felt no compulsion to assist Jawara this time, and he spent the next eight years living in England. The victors promptly suspended the constitution and all political activity. Western nations condemned the coup as undemocratic, but Gambians shrugged it off because, after three decades in power, the previous regime had grown helplessly corrupt. However, in December 2001 President Jammeh declared an amnesty for Jawara and invited him home. On June 1, 2002, the former leader did exactly that, and he arrived at Banjul on a regularly scheduled airliner. A small group of loyal supporters greeted the aged president, who was then whisked away by security forces to his home in Banjul. He remains

thus disposed, legally free but surrounded by military troops, a situation that supporters consider tantamount to house arrest.

Further Reading

Hughes, Arnold. "'Democratization' under the Military in The Gambia, 1994–2000." *Commonwealth and Comparative Politics* 38 (November 2000): 35–52.

Saine, Abdoulaye S. M. "The Coup d'etat in The Gambia, 1994: The End of the First Republic." *Armed Forces and Society* 23 (Fall 1996): 97–112.

Sallah, Tijan M. "Economics and Politics in The Gambia." *Journal of Modern African Studies* 28, no. 4 (1990): 621–648.

Wiseman, John A. "The Gambian Presidential and Parliamentary Elections of 1997." *Electoral Studies* 6, no. 3 (1987): 286–288.

Yeebo, Zaya. *State of Fear in Paradise: The Military Coup in The Gambia and Its Implications for Democracy.* London: Africa Research and Information Bureau, 1995.

Jiang Zemin (Chiang Tse-min) (1926–   )
president of China

Jiang Zemin was born in Yangzhou City, west of Shanghai, on August 17, 1926, the son of a teacher. However, when an uncle was killed fighting on behalf of the Chinese Communist Party (CCP), his father gave him to relatives as an heir. Jiang subsequently studied at an American missionary school and gained admittance into Jiaotong University in Shanghai. That city was then experiencing cruel occupation by Japanese forces prior to World War II, and he participated in anti-Japanese activities. Jiang himself joined the Communist Party in 1946 and the following year he received a degree in electrical engineering from Jiaotong. However, in 1949 the Communists under Mao had finally conquered the country and renamed it the People's Republic of China. Under these circumstances, Jiang's prior reputation as the son of a fallen revolutionary martyr held him in good stead.

Early on Jiang showed potential as a manager, and, commencing in 1950, he was entrusted with running a number of state-owned enterprises. By 1955 he was judged competent enough to learn abroad and that year he transferred to the Stalin Automobile Factory in the Soviet Union. Jiang returned to China five years later and spent nearly a decade working as a mechanical engineer and director of a power plant. By 1978 he had advanced to the First Ministry of Machine Building as an adviser, and he held down a succession of increasingly significant positions. He enjoyed a good reputation for getting results and this fact, combined with politically correct behavior, landed him a slot in the CCP Central Committee, one of the party's most important governing bodies, in 1983. Two years later Jiang's political capital was further enhanced by his appointment as mayor of Shanghai, a city that served as a window to the West. He labored incessantly to upgrade the city through foreign investment, and his efforts helped lead to construction of many modern hotels and the city's first modern golf course. In 1987 he was further rewarded by becoming part of the CCP Politburo, the handful of politicians that actually runs China, and he also served as secretary-general of the Central Committee. It was while acting in this capacity that the notorious Tiananmen Square Massacre took place in June 1989, whereby 15,000 students and protestors were killed by army troops. Jiang, despite his affinity for Western-style economic reform, enhanced his reputation as a party loyalist by defending the action. Consequently, aging leader DENG XIAOPING handpicked Jiang to replace him as chairman of the Central Military Committee in November 1989. Since March 1993 he has also held the largely ceremonial post of president of China. Jiang thus currently shares power with LI PENG as premier and ZHU RONJI as vice premier.

Jiang currently oversees the world's most populous nation. China can claim over 1 billion inhabitants, but the population's sheer size militates against its painful climb out of poverty. It was precisely for this reason that Jiang was chosen to lead. More than any other leader of his generation, he displayed remarkable ability to adapt Western-style economic reforms and practices to Chinese ways. Moreover, he is fluent in four languages, is telegenic, and considered extremely worldly and cosmopolitan for a Communist leader. He frequently travels abroad promoting Chinese viewpoints, and, in 1995, he became the first Chinese leader to visit the United States in over a decade. Most important, while embracing capitalism economically, he is determined to maintain the traditional tight controls over dissent, religious activities, and political discourse. For this reason he quickly cemented close working relations with party bureaucrats and leading military figures to shore up his position in the party. This is to guard against ideological "purists" who oppose further lessening of state control over the economy.

China's survival as a nation is synonymous with economic growth. Jiang, therefore, is active in soliciting foreign investment and promoting reform of unproductive state industries. The country has made impressive strides toward modernization, but it faces the impossible task of feeding its growing population with inefficient state farms. Thus the country is undergoing a profound period of privatization to increase both efficiency and profits. But China's development has not proved uniform. The coastal regions now sport a dazzling array of ultramodern cities, the product of foreign investment and vast government spending, but this was achieved at the expense of the poorer hinterland. In fact, China's cities have become the targets of one of the largest mass migrations in human history, with millions of poor and unemployed workers cramming themselves into the cities to find work. With them have come corresponding rises in crime, drug use, and other social ills that the Chinese government has always dealt with harshly. Political corruption, a traditional Chinese malady, is also increasing, and it is punishable by death. This crackdown, in turn, has generated criticism from Western powers, particularly the United States—China's biggest trading partner—but Jiang is unapologetic for refusing to moderate social controls. Human rights thus remains a pressing issue between the two nations and their respective leaders.

China's economic rise has also abetted its role as a regional superpower. Great Britain was cognizant of this, and, in July 1997 arranged for the peaceful return of Hong Kong, the last British outpost of empire in Asia, to the mainland. The Communist regime also looks askance at close American ties with Taiwan, which they regard as a renegade province. Despite the presence of American forces in the area, Jiang has threatened the use of force against Taiwan should that government make any steps toward political independence. China has also been quick to defend its territorial sovereignty. In February 2001, an American reconnaissance plane on patrol was accidentally rammed by a Chinese fighter off the coast of Hainan Island and forced to land there. The damaged craft and its crew were immediately interred for several days while the government demanded a formal apology from the United States. President GEORGE W. BUSH, while refusing to apologize for routine intelligence gathering, did diffuse the situation by declaring his "sorrow" over the affair, especially the loss of the Chinese pilot involved. However, since the September 11, 2001, attack upon the World Trade Center in New York, Jiang has pledged complete cooperation in the war against terror. Consequently, he has not protested the presence of U.S. forces in neighboring Afghanistan, and he seeks American help in containing Muslim extremism throughout western China. Prior to Bush's first state visit to China in February 2002, the government was keen on releasing several religious dissidents as a concession in an exercise of "smile diplomacy."

Jiang relinquished the presidency in the spring of 2003 to HU JINTAO. Jiang leaves behind a mixed legacy of impressive financial growth and technical modernization, but also a nation under increasing social stress and continuing political repression. Progress was also achieved at the price of great environmental damage. It remains to be seen if the Chinese Communists can survive the free-market reforms they so willingly embrace without allowing commensurate personal liberties to flourish. There is also the question of political infighting. Jiang has long raised accusations of financial corruption against Premier Li and in February 2002, it was made known that electronic listening devices had been found on the president's American-built plane. Rather than blame the United States, Jiang publicly castigates Li and his allies in military intelligence for the bugs' placement.

Further Reading

Dickson, Bruce J. *Red Capitalists in China: The Party, Private Entrepreneurs, and Prospects for Political Change.* New York: Cambridge University Press, 2003.

Fewsmith, Joseph. *China since Tiananmen: The Politics of Transition.* Cambridge: Cambridge University Press, 2001.

Gilley, Bruce. *Tiger on the Brink: Jiang Zemin and China's New Elite.* Berkeley: University of California Press, 1998.

Lam, Willy Wo-Lap. *The Era of Jiang Zemin.* New York: Prentice Hall, 1999.

So, Alvin V., ed. *China's Developmental Miracle: Origins, Transformations, and Challenges.* Armonk, N.Y.: M. E. Sharpe, 2002.

Tien, Hung-mao. *China under Jiang Zemin.* Boulder, Colo.: Lynne Rienner Publishers, 2000.

Tsai, Kellee S. *Back-Alley Banking: Private Entrepreneurs in China.* Ithaca, N.Y.: Cornell University Press, 2002.

Unger, Jonathan. *The Nature of Chinese Politics: From Mao to Jiang.* Armonk, N.Y.: M. E. Sharpe, 2002.

John Paul II (1920–) *pope*

Karol Josef Wojtyla was born on May 18, 1920, in Wadowice, Poland, the son of a devoutly Catholic army pensioner. Wojtyla lost his parents and elder brother at an early age, which deepened his spiritual convictions and propelled him toward a religious vocation. He studied theology and theatrics at Jagiellonian University until 1939, when the Nazi conquest of Poland closed all learning institutions. Thereafter he worked under forced labor in a quarry, but in his spare time Wojtyla participated in underground theater activities, and he saved several Jewish acquaintances by hiding them. Because of his spiritual convictions, Wojtyla also studied religion in an underground seminary. In 1946 he was formally ordained as a priest in the Roman Catholic Church at Krakow. He worked briefly in France ministering to working-class youths and Polish refugees before attending the Pontifical Angelicum University in Rome. Wojtyla proved himself an accomplished scholar of the church, and in 1958 he was consecrated auxiliary archbishop of Krakow. In 1964 he became a full archbishop, and three years later Pope Paul VI elevated him to cardinal. The turning point in Wojtyla's life occurred in September 1978 following the deaths of Paul VI and John Paul I. That fall he was summoned to the College of Cardinals in Rome to elect a new pontiff and, on October 22, 1978, he became the 263rd pope, John Paul II. In so doing, he became the first non-Italian pope since 1523, and the first pontiff of Slavic extraction.

In many respects the accession of John Paul II marked a watershed event in the history and ideology of the Roman Catholic Church, which claims over 1 billion adherents worldwide. He was both proud of his Polish heritage and stridently anticommunist. Thus situated, the pope served as a symbol of Polish nationalism and resistance to Soviet domination. And, unlike previous pontiffs, Pope John Paul II was a man of the world. With the media as his most important ally, he circled the globe to reach fellow Catholics, reminding them of their spiritual obligations to Christ and castigating totalitarian regimes for abusing human rights. Millions flocked to hear his message. The pope also condemned the material excesses of capitalism and called for greater efforts on behalf of the world's poor, oppressed, and

John Paul II *(Apostolic Nunciature in the United States)*

ity against godless communism, he played a direct role in the collapse of the Warsaw Pact and, ultimately, the Soviet Union.

John Paul's role as spiritual guide of the Roman Catholic Church, and the encyclicals he authored, proved no less controversial. A staunch theological conservative, he repeatedly railed against the rise of materialism, overt sexuality, and birth control among Catholics. He also firmly opposes euthanasia and the death penalty, in addition to the ordination of women. But his biggest triumph was in deflating the spiritual capital of the so-called revolutionary theology of Central and South America, which mandated social change at any cost—even violence. The pope condemned such practices as heretical and contrary to the teachings of Christ. Thereafter, members of the clergy were ordered to separate themselves from politics and concentrate on the spiritual needs of their charges. He also strongly re-iterated and codified traditional stances against abortion, contraception, and other forms of birth control—which place him at odds with many in his own church. The pope also formally apologized for the church's traditionally antagonistic stance toward Judaism, along with the anti-Semitism this engendered. However, he also affirmed his support for creation of a Palestinian state in the interest of promoting regional peace and justice. The pope also tendered reconciliation toward the Orthodox, or Eastern Church, which deviated from Rome in the 11th century, and the Egyptian Coptic Church, which splintered off in the fifth century.

Despite old age and the onset of Parkinson's disease, the 81-year-old pontiff shows no sign of slowing down on his global mission. In January 2002, he convened an interfaith gathering of world leaders at Assisi, Italy, birthplace of St. Francis, to condemn violence committed in the name of religion. The assembly was held in the wake of the September 11, 2001, attack on the World Trade Center in New York, and the gathering included several ranking Muslim clerics, Buddhists, and Jews. "It is essential, therefore, that religious people and communities should in the clearest and most radical way repudiate violence," he affirmed. "There is no religious goal which can possibly justify the use of violence by man against man." In his sunset years, John Paul has determined to mend fences with the Islamic faith, especially in light of recent events. For this reason, in May 2002 he became the first Christian ever to pray in the Umayyad Mosque in Damascus, Syria. On the scientific front, the pope has

alienated. His 1979 visit to Poland was marked by a national celebration in that "officially" atheist nation, and he urged Poles to renew their faith, reject tyranny, and agitate for greater personal freedom. John Paul's visit electrified the nation and lent greater impetus to the Solidarity movement that ultimately toppled the Communists in 1989. Soviet authorities in Moscow clearly feared the pope's moral authority, and, in 1981, the KGB managed to stage an assassination attempt carried out by Mehmet Ali Agca, a Turkish terrorist. John Paul, though severely injured, completely recovered, and he later visited Agca in his cell, forgiving him. The pope's high visibility on nearly 30 worldwide trips, with his stirring call to faith and action, rendered him one of the most effective and dynamic players of the cold war. Millions thronged to hear him wherever he spoke. By marshaling the moral and spiritual forces of Christian-

also warned against the rapidly advancing field of genetic engineering and manipulation. "The achievements of medicine and biotechnology can sometimes lead man to think of himself as his own creator, and to succumb to the temptation of tampering with the 'tree of life,'" he warned. "It is also worth repeating here that not everything that is technologically possible is morally acceptable." Even in his declining years, John Paul II remains a potent symbol for peace, social justice, and spirituality in a world dominated by materialism and violence. He remains an outspoken champion of the dignity of mankind.

Further Reading

Flynn, Raymond. *John Paul II: A Personal Portrait of the Pope and the Man.* New York: St. Martin's Press, 2001.

Hofmann, Paul. *The Vatican's Women: Female Influence at the Holy See.* New York: St. Martin's Press, 2002.

Legrand, Catharine. *John Paul II: Chronicle of a Remarkable Life.* New York: Dorling Kindersley, 2000.

Linker, Damon. "The Papacy in a Secular World." *Current,* no. 427 (November 2000): 23–31.

Reese, Thomas J. *Inside the Vatican: The Politics and Organization of the Catholic Church.* Cambridge, Mass.: Harvard University Press, 1996.

Weigel, George. *Witness to Hope: The Biography of Pope John Paul II.* New York: Cliff Street Books, 1999.

Wistrich, Robert S. "The Vatican and the Shoah." *Modern Judaism* 21 (May 2001): 83–110.

Zagacki, Kenneth S. "Pope John Paul II and the Crusade against Communism: A Case Study in Secular and Sacred Time." *Rhetoric & Public Affairs* 4 (Winter 2001): 689–710.

Jospin, Lionel (1937–) *prime minister of France*

Lionel Robert Jospin was born in Paris on July 12, 1937, the son of an activist in the French section of the International Workers (or Communist) Party. This imbued him with an affinity for left-wing politics and policies throughout most of his life. Jospin was educated in Paris and in 1956 he studied political science at the Institut d'Etudes Politiques in Paris. He also became politically active by joining the student union, which protested French military activity in Algeria. However, the Soviet Union's brutal invasion of Hungary in 1956 forced Jospin to reevaluate his communist sympathies, and two years later he joined a more moderate leftist group, the Union de la Gauche Socialiste. After several years of conducting social work, he attended the Ecole Nationale d'Administration, which groomed students for government service. He also completed a spell of mandatory military service in Germany by 1965, when he found employment with the Ministry of Foreign Affairs. Jospin served competently in this capacity until 1970, when he assumed a teaching position at the Paris-Sceaux University of Technology, remaining there for the next 11 years. And though interested in politics, Jospin never contemplated a life in public office until 1971, when the Socialist Party was resurrected. The bookish professor moved rapidly up the party's hierarchy, and, by 1981, he helped Socialist Party candidate FRANÇOIS MITTERRAND concoct his successful campaign strategy. That year Mitterrand won the French presidency, decisively ending over two decades of conservative rule.

Jospin subsequently held a succession of important positions in the socialist administration. He was by turns a member of the National Assembly from Paris and Haute Garonne, and he also claimed a seat in the European Parliament. In 1988, Mitterrand appointed Jospin his minister of national education, and, under his direction, an audacious program of reform was enacted. Throughout his tenure seven new universities and hundreds of new classrooms were added. In 1992 he returned to the Ministry of Foreign Affairs as a minister without portfolio, and the following year he was elevated to the party's executive bureau. The Socialists by that time were gearing up for the 1995 presidential elections, but they were divided by numerous scandals. Therefore, when Jospin announced his candidacy for that office, given his sterling credentials for efficiency and integrity, he won the endorsement of his party by an almost unanimous vote. That year the presidency was won by JACQUES CHIRAC, the conservative mayor of Paris. However, in 1997, when Chirac called for national elections ahead of schedule, the Socialists won a clear majority in parliament; therefore, Jospin was invited to become prime minister. This is the second most powerful political office in France.

Once installed, Jospin acquired a fairly impressive record of creating and passing legislation—frequently over the objections of President Chirac. He introduced laws to cut the national work week from 39 to 35 hours by 2002, and he championed transferring the burden of health insurance from workers to companies and wealthier individuals. He also managed to undo some highly anti-immigrant policies enacted by the conservatives. However, Jospin—contrary to party precepts—is less given to dogma on economics, and he embraced the notion of privatization and the selling off of inefficient government industries. In fact, in his first 18 months in office, he liquidated more state properties than Chirac had done in the previous 24. The French economy rebounded in consequence and posted very strong returns throughout 1998. Given his performance in office and his national popularity, Jospin was considered the Socialist's best chance of unseating Chirac in the spring 2002 elections.

The Socialists seemed well placed and buoyed for victory in 2002. The conservatives were in disarray and reeling from a number of scandals within the Chirac regime. In January 2002, damaging photos were released of the president associating with Didier Schuller, long a fugitive from justice on charges of corruption. Chirac had previously denied ever knowing the man, and his Rally for the Republic Party (RPR) scrambled to come up with an explanation. Unfortunately for Jospin, the French economy was gripped by the global recession of 1999 and has remained sluggish. Jospin was also recently rebuffed by the highest national court when the judges ruled that his bill allowing greater autonomy for the island of Corsica was unconstitutional. Through it all, Jospin seemed self-assured, and he used foreign events to deflect attention away from the poorly performing economy. After the September 11, 2001, attacks on the World Trade Center in New York, he vocally supported the ongoing war against terrorism. However, he condemned President GEORGE W. BUSH's simplistic approach to world politics, and he addressed growing European unease about the direction of the war. "We hope the United States does not give in to the strong temptation of unilateralism," he warned. "We cannot reduce the problems of the world to a single dimension of the struggle against terrorism, despite its pressing importance, nor rely on the preponderance of military means." His stance brings into sharper focus the ideological differences between himself and Chirac, and heightened the impending confrontation in the nation's polls, held on May 5, 2002. However, during the first round of voting, the unexpected dramatically happened. Jospin finished a close third behind JEAN-MARIE LE PEN of the far-right National Front, ending his chances for the presidency. "I assume responsibility for this defeat," he conceded, "and I will draw from conclusion by withdrawing from politics after the end of the presidential elections." The dejected Socialist then found himself in the unsavory position of endorsing the conservative Chirac to keep Le Pen from attaining power. This final act apparently concluded Jospin's long and distinguished political career. His resignation leaves the French left badly tattered and scrambling for a leader with sufficient stature to replace him.

Further Reading

Clift, Ben. "The Jospin Way." *Political Quarterly* 72 (April–June 2001): 170–179.

Cole, Alistair. "French Socialists in Office: Lessons from Mitterrand to Jospin." *Modern and Contemporary France* 7, no. 1 (1999): 71–87.

Drake, Alfred. *Intellectuals and Politics in Post-war France.* Basingstoke, England: Palgrave, 2002.

Gordon, Philip H., and Sophie Meunier. *The French Challenge: Adapting to Globalization.* Washington, D.C.: Brookings Institute, 2001.

Guyomarch, Alain. *Developments in French Politics.* New York: Palgrave, 2001.

Orlow, Dietrich. *Common Destiny: A Comparative History of the Dutch, French, and German Social Democratic Parties, 1945–1969.* New York: Berghahn Books, 2000.

Jugnauth, Anerood (1930–) *prime minister of Mauritius*

Anerood Jugnauth was born on March 29, 1930, in La Caverne, Mauritius, the son of planters. His homeland, an island 500 miles off the coast of Madagascar, is considered part of Africa, although the population consists mainly of immigrants from India. Jugnauth, both Indian and Hindu by descent, was educated locally and attended law school in London. He was called to the bar in 1954, but he returned home to commence practicing. He evinced no interest in politics until 1963, when he joined the Independence Forward Bloc movement and won a seat in the Legislative Assembly. From this base Jugnauth helped negotiate Mauritius's independence from Great Britain. In 1967 Sir Seewoosagur Ramgoolan, the nation's first prime minister, appointed him minister of state development. However, Jugnauth, who proved more radically disposed than Ramgoolan, disagreed over economic policy and left office. He resumed his law practice until 1971, when he joined a new organization, the Militant Mauritius Movement (MMM), a socialist-oriented opposition group founded by Paul Berenger. Jugnauth proved himself an astute politician and by 1974 had risen to party president. Two years later he gained election to parliament and served as head of the opposition. He remained so disposed until the elections of June 11, 1982, when the MMM, in concert with the Mauritius Socialist Party (PSM), won all 60 seats in the assembly. They ousted Ramgoolam's Labour Party from power and Jugnauth was installed as the country's second prime minister.

In office, Jugnauth retracted much of his radical rhetoric about socialism and basically pursued the same pro-business policies as his predecessor. However, this caused discontent among the MMM's more strident members and the coalition began breaking up. Therefore, on March 28, 1983, Jugnauth launched a new organization on his own, the Mauritian Socialist Movement (MSM) and new elections were called. Jugnauth proved victorious while Berenger and the MMM were removed from power. He was subsequently reelected by popular margins in 1987 and 1991. His general policy became one of diversifying the island's economy away from sugar exports and toward industry and tourism. He also desired to transform Mauritius into a service-based economy by opening the country to serve as a base for numerous offshore banks and financial services. Jugnauth's overall success can be gauged by the fact that by 1990 Mauritius was one of the richest countries in sub-Saharan Africa. However, critics accused him of autocratic tendencies and corruption, especially regarding the flourishing drug trade. Jugnauth stridently denied all allegations of pandering to criminals, and he attributed two failed assassination attempts in 1988 and 1989 to his suppression of the drug trade. "I have felt that my life has been in danger ever since I launched a national crusade against the drugs mafia," he insisted, "I have received death threats both from abroad and from Mauritius." Another pet project of his was transforming Mauritius, a member nation within the British Commonwealth—and therefore symbolically under the British monarchy—into an independent republic. He tried for many years to have a constitutional amendment passed to that effect, but not until 1993 was the measure adopted. But by 1995 the populace had tired of 13 years of MSM rule, and they overwhelmingly elected Dr. Navinchandra Ramgoolam, son of the first prime minister, into office.

For five years Jugnauth continued on as head of the opposition, until September 17, 2000, when the MSM returned to power with a new alliance. He continued ruling without controversy until February 2002, when allies in parliament sponsored a new antiterrorist bill allowing police to detain suspects for longer periods without charging them. President Angidi Chettiar, required to sign the legislation into law, resigned in protest. The bill remains pending until Jugnauth can find a new president more pliable to his wishes. Jugnauth also remains committed to expanding trade and diplomatic contacts with other nations. In July 2002 he visited Beijing, China, to confer with President JIANG ZEMIN and Premier ZHU RONGJI over improving bilateral relations, cultural contacts, and international cooperation. At that time Jugnauth also congratulated his hosts for their successful entry into the World Trade Organization. Mauritius continues on as an island of stability and prosperity and as one of the few African nations to successfully embrace multiparty democracy.

Further Reading

Dommen, Edward, and Bridget Dommen. *Mauritius: An Island of Success: A Retrospective Study, 1960–1993.* Oxford: James Currey, 1999.

Erikson, Thomas H. *Common Denominators: Ethnicity, Nation-Building, and Compromise in Mauritius.* Oxford: Berg, 1998.

Fletcher, R. Lee. "Globalism, Regionalism, and the State: The Case of Mauritius in the Indian Ocean Region." Unpublished master's thesis, Baylor University, 2001.

Jugnauth, Aneerood. *A Man, a Mission, a Vision: Selected Speeches of Sir Anerood Jugnauth.* Beau Basin, Mauritius: Gold Hill Publications, Ltd., 1994.

Shillington, Kevin. *Jugnauth: Prime Minister of Mauritius.* London: Macmillan, 1991.

Juncker, Jean-Claude (1954–) *prime minister of Luxembourg*

Jean-Claude Juncker was born in Redange-sur-Attert, Luxembourg, on December 9, 1954, the son of a steel worker. His country is unique in being one of the smallest nations on earth, but also one of the richest. Luxembourg has existed as a principality since the Middle Ages, and it has successfully fended off repeated attempts at annexation by its two powerful neighbors, France and Germany. In 1921 Luxembourg established a duty-free customs union with its third neighbor, Belgium, which has since served as the prototype for today's European Union (EU). Because the country suffered two bouts of German occupation during the 20th century, it has been an outspoken proponent of promoting European cooperation. In 1948 the country was also one of the founding members of the North Atlantic Treaty Organization, or NATO. Luxembourg is currently a hereditary constitutional monarchy, with a grand duke as head of state and a 60-member Chamber of Deputies that serves as the representative body. National politics have been dominated by the center-right Social Christian Party (PCS), although they sometimes rule in concert with one of three smaller leftist parties.

Juncker performed well as a student, and, in 1979, he received a law degree from the University of Strasbourg. Fluent in French and German, he was well prepared for a career in politics, and that year he joined the Christian Social Youth Organization of the PCS as president. In that capacity he gained recognition for effi-

ciency and the ability to make important decisions. Juncker was then promoted to parliamentary secretary to gain greater exposure to the inner machinations of national politics. In 1984 he was elected to the Chamber of Deputies for the first time, and further enhanced his reputation as a far-sighted economic analyst. Juncker gained reelection in 1989, at which point the government of Prime Minister Jacques Santer invited him aboard. He served as minister of both labor and finance with distinction, and was reappointed following the landslide PCS victory of 1994. That year the youthful, fast-rising minister was also elected head of his party. Juncker had previously demonstrated his financial acumen in 1989, when he gained appointment as a governor of the World Bank and, six years later, as governor of the International Monetary Fund (IMF). He consistently displayed mastery of the complexities inherent in modern banking and international finance. In 1992, the parliament approved the Maastrict Treaty, which became the foundation stone for creating the European Union. On January 26, 1995, Santer stepped down as prime minister to become president of the European Commission, which governs the European Union. Juncker then succeeded him, becoming the youngest head of state within the EU.

Juncker's tenure in office has been marked by a continuation of conservative policies that served his party so well since 1945. Luxembourg's small and relatively defenseless state has ingrained within its policymakers a tradition of cooperation and conciliation, and this manifests in Juncker's boundless enthusiasm for EU membership. In 2000 Luxembourg met the requirements for admission to the European Monetary Union, which mandates replacing the national currency, the franc, with the new euro. Most Luxembourg citizens have no quarrels about dropping their visible symbol of national sovereignty and they consider it a trade-off for greater economic cooperation. "I think there can be no Luxembourg view, because in the Union people should practice dual patriotism," Juncker stated. "To us this means a Luxembourg and a European patriotism."

Juncker also oversaw a dramatic reorientation of the national economy. Luxembourg was previously a leading exporter of high-quality steel, but worldwide declines in that industry prompted him to nudge the country toward more service-oriented activities. Luxembourg enjoys a long-established tradition of serving as a center of banking and finance, and the country is thus well situated

Jean-Claude Juncker *(Embassy of Luxembourg)*

to make the transition. However, given the rise of international crime, and the influx of drug cartel money into Luxembourg's highly secretive banks, the country has been criticized for lax supervision of depositors. Wishing to heed his neighbor's requests, Juncker sponsored legislation calculated to modify the country's strict confidentiality laws, thereby making it easier to conduct judicial investigations of investment sources. However, the prime minister remains determined to retain Luxembourg's traditional low tax rate, for it draws investments from more heavily taxed members of the EU.

Luxembourg under Juncker has also been a vocal proponent of the Eurocorps, an armed peacekeeping force drawn from military establishments across Europe. The country, by necessity, maintains a small standing army, and, in 1995, Luxembourg soldiers were among the first troops committed to Yugoslavia as part of the International Protection Force. Luxembourg presently enjoys the enviable position of low inflation, low unemployment, and quite possibly the highest standard of living in the world. If Juncker can maintain these idyllic conditions, his continuation as prime minister is virtually assured.

Further Reading

Baille, Sasha. *The Seat of the European Institutions: An Example of the Small State Influence in European Decision-Making.* Florence: European University Institute, 1996.

Barteau, Harry C. *Historical Dictionary of Luxembourg.* Lanham, Md.: Scarecrow Press, 1996.

Majerus, Pierre, and Marcel Majerus. *The Institutions of the Grand Duchy of Luxembourg.* Luxembourg: Ministry of State, Press, and Information Service, 1986.

Newcomer, James. *The Nationhood of Luxembourg: Eight Essays on the Grand Duchy.* Echternach, Luxembourg: Editions Phi, 1998.

Osborn, Alan. "Prime Minister of Luxembourg Jean-Claude Juncker." *Europe* (March 1999): 10–13.

Juppe, Alain (1945–) *prime minister of France*

Alain Marie Juppe was born on August 15, 1945, in Mont-de-Marsan, France, the son of prosperous farmers. He proved adept academically and attended a number of elite service academies, including the Ecole Nationale d'Administration, a breeding ground for future politicians. Conservative by nature, he struck up an abiding relationship with JACQUES CHIRAC in the 1970s, and he converted him to the principles of American-style free-market economics. In 1976 both he and Chirac founded a new party, the neo-Gaullist Rally for the Republic (RPR), although Juppe twice ran unsuccessfully for parliament. He nonetheless served under Chirac when the latter became mayor of Paris in 1978, gaining a reputation as a super-efficient "technocrat." In March 1982 Juppe was elected to parliament as an RPR candidate and two years later he also stood for a seat in the European Parliament. He rose to become secretary of RPR in July 1988 while holding down various positions within the Paris municipal government. Juppe rose to party president in 1994, and he also served as foreign minister in the administration of Prime Minister EDOUARD BALLADUR (then cohabitating with Socialist president FRANÇOIS MITTERRAND). Juppe again distinguished himself for his keen intellect and grasp of administrative detail, becoming one of the respected administrators in France. Nobody was more aware of this than Chirac, who, after finally winning the presidency in 1995, appointed Juppe his prime minister.

Juppe assumed office fully intending to overhaul French economic practices. However, it proved his misfortune that the nation was saddled by sluggish markets and high unemployment. He nonetheless embarked on strict austerity measures intending to qualify France for entry into the single European currency (euro) by 1999. Cutbacks in health care, education, and unemployment benefits were all enacted, which triggered a sharp response from students, workers, and trade unionists. In fact, the sheer number of protestors in the streets had not been seen since the great student rebellions of 1968. A series of crippling strikes in the fall of 1994 also nearly paralyzed the country. But Juppe, seen now as a cold, calculating figure detached from the concerns of average people, continued plying his cuts. In retrospect he failed to convince the electorate that his measures, however painful in the short term, would soon produce beneficial results for the entire nation. In 1996 he set his sights on rolling back France's employment protection laws, among the most stringent in the world, despite unemployment levels of 12.8 percent. The decisive moment occurred in the spring of 1997 when Chirac made the ill-advised decision to call for elections a year before they were due. He hoped the move would sacrifice a few seats in parliament, but otherwise reaffirm the legitimacy of his reform-minded administration. However, both Chirac and Juppe underestimated the extent of voter disenchantment over reform. The coalition of Socialists and Communists gained a clear and unexpected monopoly in parliament, forcing Juppe to resign as prime minister. "The people have spoken. Their decision is sovereign. We all respect it," he conceded, "I wish good luck to those who will now govern France." The call for early elections was certainly a blunder on Chirac's part, but the conservatives needed a convenient scapegoat and Juppe was singled out for punishment. He lost his position as RPR chairman and was effectively exiled from national politics. His successor was longtime Socialist leader LIONEL JOSPIN, who entered into an unsavory cohabitation with Chirac.

For many years Juppe served as the mayor of Bordeaux, which office he first assumed in 1995, and he quietly worked at rehabilitating his political reputation. In retrospect, his austerity measures, ruthlessly pressed, hurt the RPR in the short term, but they improved the overall economy within months. France consequently qualified in time for the new Euro currency. In August 1998 Juppe was investigated for alleged payroll abuses while working in the 1970s as the Paris finance director, but he has since been cleared. In June 2002 he gained appointment as chairman of the newly created Union for the Presidential Majority (UMP), an umbrella group of conservative interests aimed at promoting unity among the French right. In this capacity, the steely intellectual convinced Chirac to appoint the affable Jean-Pierre Raffarin to succeed Jospin in the wake of the hugely successful spring 2002 elections. Having distanced himself from his prior reputation as the country's least-popular prime minister, speculation remains that Juppe is positioning himself to run for the presidency of France in 2007—with Chirac's blessing. The first step in that direction is to become leader of the majority faction in parliament and thereby give his UMP greater national visibility and viability.

Further Reading

Bensaid, Daniel. "Neo-Liberal Reform and Popular Rebellion." *New Left Review,* no. 215 (1996): 109–116.

Elgie, Robert. *The Changing French Political System.* Ilford, England: Frank Cass, 1999.

Levy, Jonah D. "Partisan Politics and Welfare Adjustment: The Case of France." *Journal of European Public Policy* 8 (April 2001): 265–285.

Northcutt, Wayne. "Alain Juppe's Two-Year Descent into Hell: The Re-emergence of the Left in France in the 1997 Legislative Elections." *Contemporary French Civilization* 22, no. 1 (1998): 89–105.

Shields, J. "Europe's Other Landslide: The French National Assembly Elections of May–June, 1997." *Political Quarterly* 68 (October–December 1997): 412–424.

K

Kabbah, Ahmad Tejan (1932–) *president of Sierra Leone*

Ahmad Tejan Kabbah was born in the village of Pendemba, Kailahun district, in eastern Sierra Leone. That nation, previously a British protectorate and colony, acquired a unitary constitution and multiparty political system in 1951. However, mounting domestic demands for independence crested in April 1961, when Sierra Leone joined the British Commonwealth as its newest member. A democratically elected presidency under Siaka Stevens came to power in 1967, but his long-serving regime proved corrupt, maintained by rigged elections. Stevens finally retired from office in 1985, and thereafter national government degenerated into a series of coups and counter-coups. The year 1992 also witnessed creation of the Revolutionary United Front (RUF), which waged a ruthless guerrilla insurgency over the next decade. In 1996 the latest self-serving despot, Valentine Strasser, was overthrown by Julius Maada Bio, who then placed the country back on a transitional path toward democracy.

Kabbah, born a Muslim, was nonetheless educated at Catholic Missionary Schools in Freetown, where he excelled. He subsequently received degrees in law and economics at the University College, Wales, where he met and married his wife. Kabbah then returned home in 1954, and he joined the Sierra Leone People's Party (SLPP) to work as an administrator. He was district commissioner in each of the country's four regions before becoming secretary to both the Ministry of Education and the Ministry of Trade and Industry. Throughout the 1970s, Kabbah next held a succession of important posts while working outside Sierra Leone as part of the United Nations Development Programme. In this post he served as representative to Lesotho, Tanzania, Uganda, and Zimbabwe, all the while gaining a reputation for efficiency and honesty. Kabbah was summoned home by the Bio administration in 1991, where he applied his expertise in helping draft a new constitution. In light of his sterling credentials and national popularity, the SLPP nominated him as their candidate for the presidency. He then defeated his leading opponent, John Karefa Smart of the United National People's Party, by a 59.9 percent margin. Kabbah became president on March 29, 1996, the first civilian leader to hold power in four years.

Though well-intentioned, Kabbah's tenure in office has been marred by intermittent civil strife. He initially sought a government of national unity by establishing a large cabinet staffed by various ethnic representatives. He also entered into peace talks with the RUF leadership under Foday Sankoh to curtail further bloodshed. To this end he dismissed all South African mercenaries fighting on his behalf and recruited the services of Nigerian troops. However, on May 25, 1997, Kabbah was overthrown by Major Johnny Paul Koroma and fled to Guinea. There he appealed to the international community for a force to overthrow Koroma and restore his democratically elected regime. Consequently, various West African countries belonging to the Economic Community Monitoring Group (ECOMOG) raised an army that invaded Sierra Leone in February 1998. They disposed of the Koromo regime, which failed to gain diplomatic recognition from a single country, and reinstalled Kabbah on March 10, 1998.

Once back in power, Kabbah reassembled his government, but he also declared a state of national emergency. This enabled him to hold 1,500 civilians and members of the armed forces suspected of complicity in the coup in detention without being charged. Furthermore, Sankoh, the RUF leader, had been arrested in Nigeria on arms violations and repatriated to Sierra Leone. However, in January 1999, rebel forces successfully stormed Freetown, forcing Kabbah to flee a second time. They released hundreds of former soldiers. Intense fighting then spread throughout the countryside, consuming hundreds of lives. The rebels committed unspeakable atrocities against unarmed civilians and also scored a major propaganda success when they managed to kidnap several hundred UN peacekeepers. They owed their success to access to the country's diamond fields, whose yield was used to purchase weapons and supplies. Nigerian forces charged with protecting the fields were subsequently accused of collaborating with the rebels for a percentage of the profits. Kabbah nevertheless stepped up peace negotiations, and, on November 10, 2000, the RUF leadership agreed to a cease-fire and to disarm. New elections were announced for February 2001, but these were postponed a year owing to continuing unrest in the countryside. To preclude any chance that Foday Sankoh will stand any chance of winning the election, Kabbah determined to detain the former rebel leader in captivity until after the May 2002 elections.

As a further hedge against fighting, in February 2002, British prime minister TONY BLAIR visited Sierra Leone and pledged that Britain would supply troops to help maintain order in this former colony. Instead of incurring resentment, the citizens of Sierra Leone enthusiastically greeted the Europeans as saviors. The country now hosts one of the largest UN peacekeeping forces ever deployed in Africa. By serving as a stabilizing force, they allow President Kabbah to finally address the busi-

ness of mending his war-ravaged country. His efforts were abetted on May 19, 2002, when he coasted to an easy reelection victory over rebel candidate Pallo Bangura, winning with 70.6 percent of votes cast, while the Sierra Leone People's Party also swept parliament, carrying 83 of 112 seats.

Further Reading
Abdullah, Ibrahim. "Bush Path to Destruction: The Original Character of the Revolutionary United Front/Sierra Leone." *Journal of Modern African Studies* 36, no. 2 (1998): 203–235.
Adebajo, Adekeye. *Building Peace in West Africa: Liberia, Sierra Leone, and Guinea-Bissau.* Boulder, Colo.: Lynne Rienner Publishers, 2002.
Ferme, Marianne C. *The Underneath of Things: Violence, History, and Everyday in Sierra Leone.* Berkeley: University of California Press, 2001.
Hinton, Samuel S. *University Student Protests and Political Change in Sierra Leone.* Lewiston, N.Y.: Edgar Mellen Press, 2002.
Hirsch, John L. *Sierra Leone: Diamonds and the Struggle for Democracy.* Boulder, Colo.: Lynne Rienner Publishers, 2001.
Lord, David. *Paying the Price: The Sierra Leone Peace Process.* London: Conciliation Press, 2000.

Kabila, Joseph (b. ca. 1968–1972) *president of the Democratic Republic of the Congo*
Joseph Kabila was born between 1968 and 1972, although the circumstances surrounding his birth are obscure. His birth place is variously described as either eastern Congo or Tanzania. Kabila's father was LAURENT DESIRE KABILA, founder of a Marxist-oriented guerrilla group, who had his son educated in Tanzania. The younger Kabila subsequently received his military training in neighboring Rwanda around 1995, and he joined his father in the struggle to overthrow Congo's long-lived dictator MOBUTU SESE SEKO. His homeland, then known as Zaire, is a vast expanse of land roughly the size of Western Europe and home to 50 million people. It is renowned for the vast amounts of mineral wealth within its borders, including diamonds, copper, uranium, oil, timber, and coffee. However, this former Belgian colony, which won its independence in 1960, remains one of the most poverty-stricken countries in the world. The corruption of the Mobutu regime, coupled with lengthy

wars and civil strife, have impoverished the Congolese people and ruined the economy. Its history since independence remains one of Africa's saddest postcolonial sagas.

Rebel forces led by the elder Kabila succeeded in ousting Mobutu in 1997, whereupon Joseph ventured to China for advanced military training. As events proved, his father's regime was just as corrupt and oppressive as that of the despot it replaced, and it generated further unrest. To solidify his position among his own military, Kabila then summoned his son back to the newly renamed Democratic Republic of the Congo in August 1998 to serve as his chief of staff. In this capacity the younger Kabila was sent to the front to fight against the armies of Rwanda, Uganda, and Burundi, which invaded the Congo to seize some of its fabulous mineral resources. In the course of the fighting, three other nations—Zimbabwe, Namibia, and Angola—all contributed forces on behalf of the government. Three indigenous rebel groups also pitched in and resisted Kabila's rule. The situation became hopelessly mired in a military and diplomatic stalemate while the elder Kabila and his cronies systematically enriched themselves at public expense. The younger Kabila, meanwhile, acquired a reputation as a reliable soldier, if somewhat shy and soft-spoken. In all likelihood, he would have never been appointed heir by his extroverted, outgoing father.

On January 16, 2001, the elder Kabila was gunned down by his own security forces. Joseph Kabila then returned from the front to the capital at Kinshasa, where he conducted high-level meetings with representatives from his allies. On January 26, 2001, he was then formally sworn in as the new president of the Democratic Republic of the Congo. He thus became one of the youngest heads of state in modern world history. Kabila's glaring youth and inexperience prompted many onlookers to deduce that he was unqualified to lead the nation. For one thing, he was fluent in English and Swahili but not French, the official language. Worse, many feared he would simply serve as a puppet figure controlled by his father's former associates. To everybody's surprise, Kabila quickly dismissed his father's old cabinet, swore in a new one, and distanced himself further from his father's policies by calling in UN peacekeeping forces. As president, Kabila's first priority is to secure peace, followed by the quick removal of all foreign troops. He therefore sought to resurrect the 1999 Lusaka Accord, which all sides had signed then summarily ignored.

However, the young leader proved determined to make a difference. "The most important thing I can do for my country is to end this war," he declared. "The future is bright for the Congo if the Congolese people will take this opportunity, sit down, talk to each other."

Within months of taking office, Kabila visited the United States, Belgium, and France to solicit diplomatic support. He also conferred with heads of the World Bank and International Monetary Fund (IMF) to offer assurances that the DRC would meet its financial obligations. He also tried reviving the stalled Lusaka Accord to remove all foreign elements from the country. In October 2001, members of the Congolese government, the six foreign armies, and the three rebel factions assembled in Addis Ababa, Ethiopia, for renewed peace talks. Progress was made but no accord could be reached. The biggest stumbling block remains Rwandan president PAUL KAGAME, who refuses to move troops out until his security concerns have been addressed. He is especially leery of the presence of extremist Hutu militia, or Interahamwe, who carried out the infamous 1994 genocide in Rwanda. Kabila, however, is adamant about their departure, and he warned: "whether Rwanda likes it or not, its troops will leave the Democratic Republic of the Congo." In January 2002 the beleaguered president arrived in Lusaka, Zambia, to address a Southern African Development Community summit. It is anticipated that, having matured somewhat as a statesman, Kabila can revive the peace initiative before ongoing violence destabilizes the entire region. Otherwise, the six foreign armies in question, ally and invader alike, will continue plundering the countryside, enriching themselves at Congo's expense.

Further Reading

Amphas-Mampoua. *Political Transformation of the Congo.* Durham, N.C.: Pentland Press, 2000.

Mwakikagile, Godfrey. *Africa after Independence: Realities of Nationhood.* Huntington, N.Y.: NOVA Science Publishers, 2001.

Nzongola-Ntalja. *Resistance and Repression in the Congo: Strengths and Weaknesses of the Democracy Movement.* London: Zed, 2002.

Reyntjens, Filip. "Briefing: The Democratic Republic of Congo, From Kabila to Kabila." *African Affairs* 100, no. 399 (2001): 311–317.

Turrer, Thomas. "The Kabila's Congo." *Current History* 100, no. 646 (2001): 213–219.

Kabila, Laurent (1939–2001) *president of the Democratic Republic of the Congo*

Laurent Desire Kabila was born on November 13, 1939, in Shaba, Katanga province, Belgian Congo, part of the important Luba ethnic group. Although little is known of his youth, he was apparently educated in France, where he enthusiastically embraced Marxism. Kabila returned home in 1960 following Congo's independence, and he was elected to the Assembly of North Katanga. Thus situated, he became an outspoken proponent of Patrice Lumumba, the nation's first prime minister. Lumumba was patently pro-Soviet in outlook, and in 1961 he was assassinated by a group of military officers headed by MOBUTU SESE SEKO. Army troops then chased Kabila and other Communist sympathizers into the bush where they coalesced into a guerrilla force. They fought government forces over the next few years and, in 1965, were joined by noted Argentine revolutionary Ernesto "Che" Guevara. However, Guevara openly questioned both Kabila's abilities and his commitment to revolution, so he quit the insurgents within months. Nonetheless, by 1967 Kabila had founded the People's Revolutionary Party (PRP) and carved out an enclave on Lake Tanganyika, in distant Kivu province. There the rebels supported themselves by killing elephants, trading in ivory, and gold mining. They also received occasional help and funding from China and Cuba. But the PRP rebels gained international notoriety in 1975 when they kidnapped two American students and one Dutch researcher for ransom. Mobutu, now firmly in control of the country, which he renamed Zaire, was sufficiently provoked to order troops into the region. By 1975 Zaïrean forces induced the rebels to relocate inside Tanzania, where they regrouped.

From his bases in Tanzania, Kabila continued his struggle against the highly corrupt Mobutu regime. He had since met and forged close ties to two East African personalities, PAUL KAGAME of Rwanda, and YOWERI MUSEVENI of Uganda, who figured prominently in subsequent events. For the rest of the 1970s and well into the next decade, Kabila waged his one-man war against Mobutu, and he enjoyed increasing success owing to dissatisfaction with the regime. However, he disappeared from public view for the next 15 years and did not reemerge until 1996. That year an uprising of the Banyamulenge, ethnic Tutsi tribesmen living in Zaire, further strained government resources. Kabila's PRP fighters amalgamated them into the ranks of the newly created

Alliance of Democratic Forces for the Liberation of Congo (AFDL) and the struggle greatly expanded. By now the internal rot of Mobutu's government became painfully apparent. His soldiers, unpaid for months, simply ransacked villages they were supposed to defend and fled before the rebels. Kabila, who had promised his countrymen he would put an end to corruption and oppression, was greeted as a liberator by local populations. Events crested on May 17, 1997, when Kabila's forces stormed the capital of Kinshasa, and Mobutu fled the country. After concluding his 30-year vendetta against the government, Kabila declared himself president and renamed Africa's third-largest country the Democratic Republic of the Congo. "My long years of struggle were like spreading fertilizer on a field," he emoted, "but now is the time to harvest."

Having been promised much, the Congolese people held high expectations for Kabila's regime. They had been so impoverished by Mobutu's blatant kleptocracy that any change was tantamount to improvement. Another encouraging sign was the fact that Kabila had long since eschewed Marxism in favor of free-market economics. And, in fairness, it must be conceded that the rebels inherited a nation on the verge of collapse, with a ruined infrastructure and more than 200 bickering ethnic groups. However, as events unfolded Kabila continually reneged on promises to rewrite the constitution and hold new elections. This suppression of political activity was supported by South African president NELSON MANDELA, who viewed it as necessary to secure an orderly transition to democracy. More ominously, and like Mobutu before him, Kabila, his immediate family, and most trusted allies were growing rich off the fat of the land. To common Congolese, very little had changed.

In time, Kabila was roundly criticized by Western nations for obstructing a UN investigation into the murders of 100,000 Hutu refugees near Rwanda, ostensibly by his Tutsi cohorts. However, in 1998 Kagame and Museveni suddenly turned against him, allegedly for aiding and abetting Hutu rebels. They fomented rebellions throughout the eastern part of the nation and Kabila required troops from Angola, Namibia, and Zimbabwe to stay in power. Thus a new continental war was unleashed that exacerbated the people's miseries, and Kabila's regime began losing support. Discontent was rife, and, not surprisingly, he was suddenly murdered by a bodyguard on January 16, 2001. His son, General JOSEPH KABILA, then stepped in to succeed him.

Further Reading

Boya, Odette M. "Contentious Politics and Social Change in Congo." *Security Dialogue* 32 (March 2001): 71–85.

Reyntjens, Filip. "Briefing: The Democratic Republic of the Congo: From Kabila to Kabila." *African Affairs* 100 (April 2001): 311–17.

Rosenblum, P. "Kabila's Congo." *Current History* 97 (May 1998): 193–99.

Schatzberg, Michael G. "Beyond Mobutu: Kabila and the Congo." *Journal of Democracy* 8 (October 1997): 70–84.

Weiss, Herbert. "Civil War in the Congo." *Society* 38 (March–April 2001): 67–71.

Kagame, Paul (1957–) *president of Rwanda*

Paul Kagame was born in Gitarama prefecture, central Rwanda, in October 1957, of Tutsi tribal origins. His homeland is a small, landlocked enclave in East Africa, bordered by Burundi, Tanzania, Uganda, and the Democratic Republic of the Congo. A German protectorate until 1916, Rwanda was administered by Belgium for most of the 20th century. However, in doing so Belgians showed preference to the minority Tutsi tribe at the expense of the poorer but more numerous Hutu. Resentment and outbreaks of violence between the two groups was pandemic. In 1959 a rebellion by rampaging Hutu forced thousands of Tutsi to flee to neighboring Uganda, including Kagame and his parents. Although Rwanda subsequently gained its independence from Belgium in 1962, Kagame was raised and educated in a refugee camp. At length, the excesses of Ugandan dictator Milton Obote induced him to join the National Resistance Army under YOWERI MUSEVENI, which succeeded in toppling the government in 1986. Consequently, Kagame was rewarded with a rank of chief of military intelligence in the new Ugandan army. Despite the honor, he desired to return to Rwanda to redress the long-standing grievances of his Tutsi tribe. In 1987 Kagame founded the Rwandan Patriotic Front (RPF), a guerrilla force with military and financial backing from Museveni. The group conducted a low-intensity guerrilla war against the regime of Rwandan president JUVÉNAL HABYARIMANA while Kagame received military training in the United States. However, when several ranking leaders of the RPF were killed in action, Kagame returned home to assume command in person.

The turning point in Rwanda's political fortunes occurred on April 6, 1994, when Habyariyama—a Hutu—was killed in a mysterious plane crash. His death was ascribed to RPF forces and triggered a sudden and deadly uprising against citizens of Tutsi ancestry, who were hunted down by Hutu militiamen and slaughtered. An estimated 800,000 people were killed in a matter of weeks, while millions of refugees stampeded into Uganda. Kagame took advantage of the confusion by invading Rwanda and routing the Hutu militiamen. His victorious capture of Kigali, the national capital, caused an estimated 2 million Hutu to flee into the Democratic Republic of the Congo. This proved one of the largest and most spontaneous mass exoduses ever recorded. However, Kagame was willing to be magnanimous and on July 2, 1994, he established a government comprised of both Hutus and Tutsis. In fact, President PASTEUR BIZIMUNGU and Prime Minister Faustin Twagiramungu were both Hutu in origin. However, Kagame, a Tutsi, was installed as vice president and defense minister. In this capacity he controlled the Tutsi-dominated military and, hence, wielded the actual authority. For this reason many Hutu refugees in the Congo refused to come home, fearing reprisal. The various militia elements among them also began regrouping to renew their struggle.

Kagame, Bizimungu, and Twagiramungu formed an uneasy alliance over the next six years, but at least the killing stopped. However, in March 2000, Bizimungu resigned as president after the Tutsi-controlled parliament began investigating him on charges of corruption. Kagame then stepped into the void and, on April 17, 2000, he was overwhelmingly elected by a joint session of parliament to succeed him. He thus became the first Tutsi president to hold power since Rwanda gained its independence in 1962. Unlike many contemporaries, Kagame displayed exceptional qualities as a leader. He studiously abstains from alcohol and smoking and imposes tight military-style discipline on himself. He has since proved unyielding in his determination to promote national reconciliation between Tutsis and moderate Hutus. However, he campaigns actively against the Hutu Interahamwe (militiamen) who committed Rwanda's infamous genocide and, in 1997, he dispatched his troops into the Congo to help oust LAURENT KABILA. He has since conferred with JOSEPH KABILA, Laurent's son, but refuses to withdraw his troops until all Hutu militia units have been disbanded. Kagame has also endured a spate of friction with Museveni of Uganda, his erstwhile ally. Both have accused the other of harboring rebels, and their forces fought for possession of the Congo town of Kisangani in May 2000. But dependable allies in this region of Africa are hard to procure, so the two men agreed to meet and mend fences. On February 14, 2002, Kagame and Museveni signed an accord in the border town of Kabale, pledging to expand military and political contacts between their respective nations. They also reconfirmed their commitment to resumption of normal relations and the pursuit of greater stability throughout their region.

Further Reading

Barnett, Michael W. *Eyewitness to Genocide: The United Nations and Rwanda.* Ithaca, N.Y.: Cornell University Press, 2002.

Jefremovas, Villia. *Brickyards to Graveyards: From Production to Genocide in Rwanda.* Albany: State University of New York Press, 2002.

Kagame, Paul. "My Side of the Story." *West Africa,* no. 4236 (June 12, 2000): 15–18.

Khan, Shaharyar M. *The Shallow Graves of Rwanda.* New York: I. B. Tauris, 2000.

Mamdani, Mahmood. *When Victims Become Killers: Colonialism, Nativism, and the Genocide in Rwanda.* Princeton, N.J.: Princeton University Press, 2001.

Neuffer, Elizabeth. *The Key to My Neighbor's Home: Searching for Justice in Bosnia and Rwanda.* London: Bloomsbury, 2002.

Ottaway, M. "Africa's New Leaders: African Solution or African Problem?" *Current History* 97 (May 1998): 209–213.

Kalam, Abdul (1931–) *president of India*

Abdul Pakir Jainulabdeen Abdil Kalam was born on October 15, 1931, in Dhanushkodi, India, the scion of a strict Muslim family. This placed him somewhat at odds with the rest of the nation, which is predominately Hindu. Kalam proved adept as a student and in 1950 won admittance to St. Joseph's College in Tiruchirappalli to study aeronautical engineering. He graduated with honors in 1958 and found work at the Madras Institute of Technology. Despite a Muslim background and devotion to his creed, Kalam mixed easily with people of other backgrounds, and he further distinguished himself by remaining a life-long vegetarian and teetotaler. He

was also skilled in his chosen field and fired by personal beliefs that India must acquire self-sufficiency in rocketry and other advanced technology to gain world respect. His government eventually shared his point of view and, in 1962, he helped create the nation's first rocket laboratory at Thumba. Commencing in 1963, when Kalam successfully launched India's first successful missile, the nation embarked on development of sophisticated space and weapons technology. Despite the expense associated with such devices, and the fact that one-third of India's 1 billion people live in squalor, national pride prevailed. In fact, over the next two decades India endured armed confrontations with China and neighboring Pakistan, which lent greater impetus to their regional arms race. Kalam's fortunes crested in July 1980 when Prime Minister Indira Gandhi appointed him head scientist of India's missile development program. In this post he supervised construction and launching of the SLV-3, India's first satellite launch vehicle, which finally placed it on a par with the United States, the Soviet Union, and China. Kalam then became popularly touted in the press as India's "Missile Man."

For all his skill at engineering, Kalam also acquired a degree of notoriety as a nonconformist, being somberly dressed while his silver hair was kept long and unkempt. And, while never forsaking his devotion to Islam, he also became conversant in Hindu religious scriptures and considers himself "200% Indian." But above all, Kalam wished to convey his dream of developing India's potential. "We must think and act like a nation of a billion people, and not like that of a million people," he insists, "Dream, dream, dream!" Kalam realizes the nation needs to address the pressing problems of poverty and needs to facilitate greater access to education. For years he spoke out in favor of a grassroots revolution, one possessing a single-minded determination for catapulting India into the ranks of the developed world. Kamal also remains unabashedly nationalistic. His missile program closely paralleled India's successful attempt to acquire nuclear weapons and, to his mind, promoted greater security with Pakistan and China. In May 1998 he also orchestrated highly publicized underground nuclear tests, which were widely condemned abroad but underscored Indian resolve. For his daring vision and unflinching commitment to national security, Kamal received the Bharat Ratna—India's highest civilian award—in 1997.

Throughout his long and distinguished scientific career, Kamal evinced no interest in politics. Therefore, eyebrows were raised in the spring of 2002 when he suddenly emerged as a candidate for the Indian presidency. This office is largely ceremonial, although its duties include choosing the party from which the next prime minister will originate. The incumbent executive, Kocheril Raman Narayanan, was slated to retire and fractious coalition parties needed a unifying figure they could agree upon. Kamal, one of the most visible personalities in the country—and a man above partisan reproach—suited this perfectly. He easily won endorsements from the Hindu nationalist party of Prime Minister ATAL BIHARI VAJPAYEE and the opposition Congress Party. His opponent was Lakshmi Sahgal, an 87-year-old freedom fighter who was nominated by the Communist Party. On July 18, 2002, Kamal won easily with 87 percent of the vote and was sworn in as president seven days later. He is the 12th person to hold that office and only the third Muslim to do so.

Kamal assumed his role during a tumultuous period in India's modern history. Tensions with neighboring Pakistan have increased over a religion-based civil war in Kashmir province, and India has sustained terrorist attacks from Muslim fundamentalists. These acts sparked tremendous indignation from the majority Hindu population, and nearly 1,000 Muslims died in sectarian violence. The accession to office of Kamal, a practicing Muslim, is anticipated to exert a calming effect. He is strongly committed to secularism in this badly divided nation, and also extended his hand in friendship to the Muslim leadership of Pakistan. But more than anything, Kamal remains the purveyor of great dreams for his country, and he sees a brighter future ahead. India faces a litany of vexing and seemingly insurmountable problems over the next few decades, but Kamal places great faith in education, national unity, and religious harmony. "We should not give up and we should not allow the problem to defeat us," he affirmed. "Great dreams and great dreamers are always transcended." It is a message worth heeding.

Further Reading

Abdul Kalam, A. P. J. *Wings of Fire: An Autobiography.* Hyderabad, India: Universities Press, 1999.

Hasan, Zoya, ed. *Parties and Party Politics in India.* New York: Oxford University Press, 2002.

Matinuddin, Kamal. *The Nuclearization of South Asia.* Oxford: Oxford University Press, 2002.

SarDesai, Damodar R., and Raju G. C. Thomas. *Nuclear India in the Twenty-first Century.* New York: Palgrave, 2001.

Sarkar, Sumit. *Beyond Nationalist Frames: Postmodernism, Hindu Fundamentalism, History.* Bloomington: Indiana University Press, 2002.

Varshney, Ashutush. *Ethnic Conflict and Civic Life: Hindus and Muslims in India.* New Haven, Conn.: Yale University Press, 2002.

Kalpokas, Donald *prime minister of Vanuatu*

Donald Kalpokas Masike was born on the island of Lelpa, New Hebrides, in 1943. His homeland comprises an extensive archipelago of 80 islands located 1,300 miles northeast of Australia. It constitutes a landmass of 5,700 square miles and a population totaling 189,000, mostly of Melanesian descent. Throughout most of the 20th century the New Hebrides was jointly administered by France and Great Britain. The islands acquired political independence in 1980 and have since renamed themselves Vanuatu. Presently, it is a republic governed by a 52-seat parliament, the Representative Assembly, which is elected every four years and chooses a prime minister from the majority party or coalition. Commencing in 1971 and for two decades thereafter, political control rested in the hands of Walter Lini, architect of the New Hebrides National Party. He was a legendary politician of considerable longevity, and a power to be reckoned with whether in office or out.

Kalpokas was educated on Efate Island, but he subsequently attended the King George IV school in the Solomon Islands. He received advanced training at the Ardmore Teachers Training College in New Zealand before studying educational administration at the University of the South Pacific, Fiji. There he met Walter Lini, a fellow student, and the two struck up cordial relations. Once back home, Kalpokas became politically active during the period leading up to independence. He founded the New Hebrides Cultural Association in 1971, which later reorganized itself as Lini's New Hebrides National Party. Six years later it was renamed the Vanuatu Party (VP) and, during the first elections held in 1979, it garnered 26 of 39 available seats. Among the victors was Kalpokas, who now represented North Efate. In this capacity he worked with Lini, Vanuatu's first prime minister, and he received a cabinet appointment as minister of education. However, in 1983

Kalpokas resigned his office to protest the firing of a deputy prime minister and put forward a no-confidence motion in parliament against Lini. This was defeated, but many months passed before the rift healed between the two men.

By 1991, many VP members felt that Lini, in poor health, could neither lead his party nor the country effectively. That August the parliament elected Kalpokas party leader, and two months later a no-confidence motion was passed against Lini. Kalpokas became prime minister in his stead. However, Lini vindictively forsook the unity that had propelled his party to power by splitting off and forming a new faction, the National Union Party (NUP). In December 1991 new elections were held and the NUP joined with the Union of Moderate Parties (UMP) to form a coalition government. Kalpokas and the VP were subsequently voted out of office in favor of Korman Maxime Carlot.

The ramifications of the 1991 elections remain felt to this day. Overnight Vanuatu changed from a relatively stable two-party system to a multiparty system based upon coalition rule. Given the highly volatile nature of the archipelago's polity, this has translated into a high turnover rate for prime ministers. In fact, Vanuatu enjoys a reputation for almost total political anarchy. Kalpokas, meanwhile, retained his seat in parliament and served as a member of the opposition until January 1998, when new elections were held. Allegations of corruption had been leveled against the UMP prime minister Serge Vohor, and on March 6, 1998, the VP was swept back into power when Kalpokas arranged a political union with his former friend Lini and the NUP. He served until November 1999 but resigned to avoid the censure of a no-confidence vote. Kalpokas was then replaced by the present prime minister, Barak Sope. But, in April 2001, he resumed his high political visibility by becoming parliamentary speaker.

During his brief tenure in office, Kalpokas concentrated on the area of his specialty, education. He promulgated a master plan that would imbue Vanuatu's school children with marketable skills in an increasingly technological age. He also sought to reinstate a governmental watchdog organization, the Ombudsman, which was canceled by Vohor after revelations of scandal. Moreover, in light of Vanuatu's status as an exporter of crops, he strongly advocated creation of a Pacific Free Trade Area in June 1999 to enhance the island's prospects for trade. Kalpokas, as one of Vanuatu's longest-serving politicians, is well positioned to resume the office of prime minister whenever the VP garners the next working majority. But whoever occupies that office, he will inherit a fractious polity, a declining economy, and the perils of leading a very small nation in a very large and increasingly complex global economy.

Further Reading

Miles, William F. S. *Bridging Mental Boundaries in a Postcolonial Microcosm: Identity and Development in Vanuatu.* Honolulu: University of Hawaii Press, 1998.

Premdas, Ralph R. *Politics and Government in Vanuatu: From Colonial Unity to Post-colonial Disunity.* Saskatoon: University of Saskatchewan, 1989.

Steeves, Jeffrey S. "Vanuatu: The 1991 Elections and Their Aftermath." *Journal of Pacific History* 27 (October 1992): 217–229.

Tephac, Philip. *Chiefly Power in Southern Vanuatu.* Canberra: Australian National University, 1997.

"Vanuatu." *The Courier,* no. 149 (January–February 1995): 30–47.

Wittershim, Eric. *Melanesian Elites and Modern Politics in New Caledonia and Vanuatu.* Canberra: Australian National University, 1998.

Karadzic, Radovan (1946–) *president of the Republic of Srpska*

Radovan Karadzic was born in Montenegro, Yugoslavia, in 1945, to Serbian parents. He relocated to the Bosnia-Herzegovinian capital of Sarajevo sometime in the 1950s, where he studied to become a psychiatrist. Yugoslavia was then a tightly controlled Communist dictatorship ruled by Marshal Tito (Josip Broz), who felt that authoritarianism was necessary to prevent the six constituent republics from fighting each other for territory. After his death in 1980 Yugoslavia experienced the very surge of ethnic and regional nationalism that Tito had feared and predicted. Foremost among the agitators were the Serbians, who wished to create "Greater Serbia" by annexing the Serb-dominated portions of Bosnia-Herzegovina and who oppressed the Albanians in Kosovo. By 1990 Karadzic, an ardent Serb nationalist, founded and headed the Serbian Democratic Party (SDS) in Bosnia to achieve those exact ends. In concert with Serbian leader SLOBODAN MILOŠEVIĆ, he intended to cajole, threaten, or take by force all adjoining lands coveted by his people. Prior to this, Karadzic functioned within a multinational coalition in Bosnia headed by Muslim leader ALIJA IZETBEGOVIC until November 1991. That month the SDS organized a referendum for Serb-dominated areas over the issue of partition. When the measure passed overwhelmingly, the Serbian regions of Bosnia-Herzegovina declared independence as the new Republic of Srpska. Karadzic, as nominal head of the SDS, then declared himself president.

Given traditional antipathies of Serbs against Muslims and Croats, any warfare that erupted was likely to be both savage and merciless. On the same day independence was declared, Bosnian Serb forces, assisted by volunteers from Serbia itself, launched an all-out assault upon Muslim and Croatian regions of the republic. Fighting proved internecine and, worse, the Serbs instituted a concerted policy of "ethnic cleansing," whereby undesirable groups of people were either forcibly removed from their homes or killed outright. Torture, murder, and sexual abuse became commonplace occurrences. Karadzic, meanwhile, basked in the light of his success, much to the horror of the West. Gloating and vindictive, he repeated time-honored assertions that Serbs cannot live peacefully with other people and required their own region. His policies reached their logical conclusion in July 1995, when Serbian forces massacred an estimated 5,000 Muslim men at Srebrenica. This was the single-largest atrocity committed in Europe since 1945 and it mobilized world opinion against the Serbs.

Karadzic ignored repeated warnings from the United States and United Nations to curtail his aggression, and the war continued. Consequently, in the spring of 1995, NATO aircraft commenced a three-month long bombardment of Serbian and Bosnian positions in an attempt to halt further advances. The Serbs withstood this grueling punishment with impressive stoicism, but in the end they were forced to concede. The United States then attempted a diplomatic solution when leaders of the three contending factions arrived in Dayton, Ohio, and signed peace accords, which stipulated that Bosnia would be divided into two independent republics, one reserved for Serbs and the other for Muslims and Croats. As part of the agreements, Serbs relinquished control of all Muslim and Croat territory not designated theirs by the Dayton Accords, and they withdrew. Moreover, a NATO-led Stabilization Force (SFOR) would hereafter patrol the region to keep the contestants separated. The solution proved workable, but it came too late for the estimated 200,000 Muslim slaughtered by Serbs, or the 1 million refugees they generated.

Defeat did little to diminish Karadzic's standing among his people, for in elections held latter that year he was unanimously reelected head of the SDS. This was despite the fact that the United Nations War Crimes Tribunal indicted him for crimes against humanity on June 27, 1996. The United States then applied intensive diplomatic pressure, coupled with threats of renewed hostilities, to have Karadzic step down as president of the Republika Srpska. He only sullenly complied and was also forced out as head of the SDS in December 1995. His replacement was the more moderate Serb figure, BILJANA PLAVSIC. Since his removal, Karadzic has ignored all summonses to appear before the War Crimes Tribunal at The Hague, Netherlands. He scoffs at the notion, insisting: "If The Hague was a real judicial body I would be ready to go there to testify or to do so on television, but it is political body that has been created to blame the Serbs." Meanwhile, SFOR units in Bosnia-Herzegovina have been authorized to arrest Karadzic should they encounter him. He proved elusive, so twice in the spring of 2002, allied forces made two concerted efforts to trap him at suspected hangouts. But the wily Karadzic avoided capture and even mocked the impotence of his pursuers through published letters. "I have made thousands of new friends, about whom my pursuers do not know," he exclaimed. "Perhaps they left us in Bosnia so that the whole of it can be ours one day." Karadzic presently remains at large, the most wanted fugitive from justice in the world.

Further Reading

Bellamy, Alex J. *Kosovo and International Society.* New York: Palgrave, 2002.

Bose, Sumantra. *Bosnia after Dayton: National Partition and International Intervention.* New York: Oxford University Press, 2002.

Colevic, Ivan. *Politics and Identity in Serbia.* New York: New York University Press, 2002.

Malesevic, Sinisa. *Ideology, Legitimacy, and the New State: Yugoslavia: Serbia, and Croatia.* Portland, Oreg.: Frank Cass, 2002.

Moon, Paul. *The Shadow of Radovan Karadzic: An Investigation of a War Criminal.* Palmerston, New Zealand: Campus Press, 1998.

Karamanlis, Constantine (1907–1998)

president of Greece

Constantine Karamanlis was born on March 8, 1907, in Proti, Macedonia, then part of the Ottoman Empire. The son of a schoolteacher, he attended the University of Athens through the help of friends, and he obtained his law degree in 1932. Karamanlis then tested the political waters by gaining election to parliament as part of the conservative Populist Party. Karamanlis, like many conservatives, originally supported the Greek monarchy, which was restored after a failed military coup in 1935. He gained reelection the following year but the government was overthrown by the military and Karamanlis declined to accept any positions in a military regime. Events worsened after 1941 when German forces conquered Greece, and, over the next four years, Karamanlis studiously avoided politics. However, he stood for a seat in parliament in 1946 and Prime Minister Constantine Tsaldaris subsequently appointed him minister of labor. His task centered on securing the resettlement of thousands of refugees fleeing from the Greek civil war, 1946–49. During the next six years he also held a succession of important ministerial posts until the death of Prime Minister Alexander Papagos in 1955. Karamanlis, by dint of his reputation as an honest and efficient administrator, was then appointed prime minister by King Paul. At that time he was Greece's youngest executive officer.

Karamanlis's ascension to high office in 1955 initiated one of the most remarkable and productive political careers in Greek political history. Cognizant of his country's economic and diplomatic weakness, he founded the National Radical Union, a conservative party devoted to economic development, and he forged closer ties to the Western European community. This stance earned him praise from the United States, which feared the rising influence of communism in the Aegean, and resulted in higher levels of foreign aid. By 1960, however, Karamanlis was engulfed by a potentially violent situation over the island of Cyprus. The population, divided between Greeks and Turks, seemed on the verge of a civil war that also threatened to involve Greece and Turkey in armed confrontation. However, Karamanlis devised an effective compromise that mandated a Greek president and a Turkish prime minister for the island, so Cyprus acquired independence from Great Britain and war was averted. Consequently, the National Radical Union won the 1961 elections easily, although Kara-

manlis was angered by the army's manipulation of the vote. After charges and countercharges between the prime minister and George Papandreou of the opposition Center Union, Karamanlis resigned from office in May 1963. He then entered self-imposed exile in Paris, but his uninterrupted eight years in office was considered unprecedented at that time.

In 1967 the Greek political system was upended by a military coup, which Karamanlis roundly criticized from abroad. When the colonels were themselves toppled by public unrest over their botched takeover of Cyprus, Karamanlis was cordially invited back to Greece by the interim government as prime minister. In this capacity he took dramatic steps to undue the ethos of dictatorship and restore Greek democracy. Foremost among essential conditions was insistence upon military subordination to civilian authority. Next came the future of the monarchy, which did little to oppose the colonels and was finally abolished by public referendum in December 1975. Karamanlis, having founded the New Democracy Party (ND), led it to victory that fall and the following year he instituted a new constitution. This mandated creation of a republic with a presidency that possessed strong executive powers to rein in the military, and the referendum passed overwhelmingly. Karamanlis was content to remain prime minister, and even with reduced power, but he remained the de facto leader of Greece. In 1977 the ND again prevailed in national elections, but their position steadily declined following the onset of economic difficulties. By 1980 the opposition Panhellenic Socialist Movement under ANDREAS PAPANDREOU assumed power, and Karamanlis resigned from office.

The aging patriarch had lost none of his public appeal, however, and he subsequently served as president of Greece in 1981–85 and 1990–95. By the time he finally resigned from office, Karamanlis concluded 60 years of sterling service to the Greek nation. He died in Athens on April 8, 1998, hailed as the savior of Greek democracy. Karamanlis had firmly cemented his nation to the European Union (EU) and NATO, ended its traditional isolation, and elevated it to the center stage of European affairs. His only conspicuous failure was peaceful resolution of the Cyprus problem, which remains unresolved to this day. Nonetheless, by his judicious reform of government institutions, he remains the architect behind Greece's democratic system. This constitutes his most enduring—and endearing—legacy. Karamanlis was the most influential Greek statesman of the 20th century.

Further Reading

Close, David. *Greece since 1945: Politics, Economy, and Society.* New York: Longman, 2002.

Kaloudis, George S. *Modern Greek Democracy: The End of a Long Journey?* Lanham, Md.: University Press of America, 2000.

Kartakis, E., ed. *Constantine Karamanlis in Thought and Action.* Athens: Roes Publications, 1990.

Peckham, Robert S. *National Histories, National States: Nationalism and the Politics of Place in Greece.* New York: I. B. Tauris, 2001.

Pettifer, James. *The Greeks: The Land and the People since the War.* London: Penguin, 2000.

Woodhouse, Christopher M. *Karamanlis, The Restorer of Greek Democracy.* New York: Oxford University Press, 1983.

Karimov, Islam (1938–) *president of Uzbekistan*

Islam Karimov was born in Samarkand, Uzbekistan, on January 30, 1938, the son of laborers. Uzbeks are ethnically related to Turks and share a similar language, customs, and traditions. At that time this landlocked nation in Central Asia was a Communist republic within the Soviet Union. As such, virtually every aspect of personal and economic life was closely regulated by Moscow, and Islam, the national religion, was severely curtailed. Karimov attended the local high school before entering the Central Asian Polytechnic Institute at Tashkent, where he studied mechanical engineering. Intent upon improving his political future, he also joined the Communist Party in 1964. Karimov soon dropped engineering to serve as an economic adviser within the Uzbek government, and he worked for the State Planning Commission until 1983. That year he drew closer to the centers of power by becoming the minister of finance and a deputy to the Uzbek Supreme Soviet. Karimov, who enjoyed a reputation for political cunning, next supplanted the corruption-tainted Rafik Nishanov as head of the Uzbek Communist Party in 1989. He was now literally in charge of the entire nation. However, as the Soviet Union began unraveling in 1991, Karimov quickly consolidated his power base. A conservative by nature, he initially supported the coup attempt against Premier Mikhail Gorbachev in August 1991, then quickly changed sides. By December he declared Uzbek's independence from Moscow, and he or-chestrated his election for the presidency of the new republic, winning 94 percent of eligible votes. As subsequent events proved, wily Karimov became one of a handful of former Communists deft enough to survive under totally changed circumstances.

As president, Karimov is a strong executive saddled with a weak legislature, the Oliy Majlis. He spent the next five years in office shoring up political support and introduced badly needed economic reforms, but at a snail's pace to insure stability. He remained unapologetic about his authoritarian leadership and reluctant to embrace either free markets or free elections. "A firm hand is needed in today's explosive situation," he declared, "and the people Uzbekistan will not accept Western-style democracy because of their history and national character." To underscore this belief, in March 1995, he authored a referendum that extended his five-year presidential term to seven years. To nobody's surprise, it passed by 99.6 percent of the votes. Western observers deemed the results both inevitable and questionable.

Despite tight controls, Karimov's regime has been rocked by the rise of Islamic fundamentalism endemic to Central Asia. In fact, religious guerrillas, seeking to oust his secular state and replace it with an Islamic republic, were trained at the behest of Taliban-controlled Afghanistan. In February 1999 the capital of Tashkent was rocked by a series of bombings that killed several people. Karimov consequently unleashed his security forces, who collared several suspects, some brutally, and bound them over for trial. Wishing to set an example, Karimov insisted that the first six defendants receive the death penalty. However, the entire episode forced him to call for regional security forces to cooperate in the fight against terrorism. He has since called upon Russia and his fellow Central Asian republics to contribute, but results are mixed. Kyrgyzstan, for example, has struggled with Islamic extremists for years, and Karimov criticized President ASKAR AKAYEV for alleged laxity in suppressing them. The heightened sense of security has also enabled him to crack down on political dissent unrelated to religion. On January 9, 2000, Karimov was overwhelmingly reelected president by a margin of 91.9 percent. The United States openly characterized Uzbekistan's electoral practices as neither free nor fair and has been one of the regime's biggest critics.

American complaints about Karimov have been largely muted in the wake of the September 11, 2001, terrorist attack upon the World Trade Center in New

York. President GEORGE W. BUSH determined to remove the Taliban regime by force and he appealed to Uzbekistan for use of several airbases. Karimov, sensing an advantage, readily complied the following October and he was showered with numerous promises of aid in return. The Taliban were effectively eliminated that winter, but the Uzbek government wished the American military presence to remain as a hedge against possible Russian expansion into the region. "Our two governments have decided to establish a qualitatively new relationship based on a long-term commitment to advance security and regional stability," Karimov stated. Karimov has thus posited himself as a key American ally in this very strategic theater, and he won high praise for cooperating in the war against terrorism, but otherwise his old habits die hard. On January 29, 2002, he sponsored another referendum extending his term in office from five to seven years and he secured it by 91 percent of the vote. Western observers and human rights groups condemned the vote as failing to meet standards of fairness, and they dismiss it as Karimov's latest ploy to hang on to power.

Further Reading

Karimov, I. A. *Uzbekistan on the Threshold of the Twenty-first Century.* Richmond, England: Curzon, 1997.

Kurzman, Charles. "Uzbekistan: The Invention of Nationalism in an Invented Nation." *Critique* 15 (Fall 1999): 77–98.

Levitin, Leonid, and Donald S. Carlisle. *Islam Karimov, President of the New Uzbekistan.* Vienna: Grotec, 1995.

Luong, Pauline J. "After the Breakup: Institutional Design in Transitional States." *Comparative Political Studies* 33 (June 2000): 563–593.

Melvin, Neil. *Uzbekistan: Transition to Authoritarianism on the Silk Road.* Amsterdam: Harwood Academic, 2000.

Meyer, Karl K. *The Dust of Empire: The Race for Mastery in the Asian Heartland.* New York: PublicAffairs, 2003.

Rumer, Boris Z. *Central Asia and the New Global Economy.* Armonk, N.Y.: M. E. Sharpe, 2000.

Karzai, Hamid (1957–) *prime minister of Afghanistan*

Hamid Karzai was born in Kandahar, southern Afghanistan, on December 24, 1957. His father, Abdul Ahmad Karzai, was chief of the Popolzai tribe, a constituent part of the larger Pashtun-speaking majority. He also served as a senator in the Afghan parliament before the overthrow of King ZAHIR SHAH in 1973. Karzai was educated in the national capital of Kabul, then attended graduate school in Simla, India, where he acquired fluency in English. He returned to Afghanistan to partake in tribal affairs until 1979, when the Soviet Union mounted a full-scale invasion of that country. In 1983 Karzai fled to Quetta, Pakistan, where he served as a liaison in getting money and weapons to assist the Mujahideen (holy warriors) in resisting Soviet occupation. It was here that he first came to the attention of the United States. By 1989 Communist forces had been driven out and replaced by a loose coalition of Mujahideen warlords under President Burhanuddin Rabbani. Karzai, who by this time has acquired a reputation as a dapper, engaging diplomat, gained appointment as deputy foreign minister in 1992. However, incessant fighting and civil war occasioned the rise of a new group, the Taliban ("Students of Religion"), who were fanatical adherents of militant Sunni Islam. By 1996 the Taliban effectively controlled 90 percent of the country and invited Karzai to serve as their ambassador to the United States. However, Karzai, convinced that the Taliban was being infiltrated and controlled by Arab elements, declined. In 1998 he left the country again for Quetta with his aged father, who railed against Taliban excesses. The following year Karzai's father was murdered outside a mosque, presumably at the hands of a Taliban assassin. This prompted the former diplomat to formally oppose the fanatical regime in Kabul, and in 2000 he made a secret trip to the United States. Appearing before a congressional committee, he lambasted the Western powers for completely abandoning Afghanistan after the Soviet withdrawal.

Karzai languished in relative obscurity until after the September 11, 2001, terrorist attack on the World Trade Center in New York. This event was widely viewed as the handiwork of Saudi expatriate Osama bin Laden, who had masterminded a worldwide network of global terrorism based in Afghanistan. When the Taliban refused to extradite him to the United States, President GEORGE W. BUSH commenced a relentless air war to drive them from power. In concert with ground forces supplied by the Northern Alliance, a Tajik-based resistance group, the Taliban were driven out of the country by December 2001. It then became a question of occupying

Afghanistan with United Nations forces and reinstalling some kind of functioning government. Buoyed by success, the Allied coalition began casting around for a potential candidate to serve as an interim head of state.

On December 22, 2001, a council of Afghan elder statesmen meeting in Bonn, Germany, elevated Karzai to the post of prime minister. He was supported by the Americans mainly because of his fluency in English, military connections with the Central Intelligence Agency dating back to the Soviet invasion, and his reputation for political moderation. In October of that year, Karzai had slipped into southern Afghanistan to rally Pashtun resistance to the Taliban and to organize a Loya Jirga, a traditional council of elders, to succeed them. However, this region was also a Taliban stronghold, and Karzai's followers were attacked and nearly overrun before being rescued by American air power. He subsequently helped to negotiate the surrender of Kandahar to coalition forces, although two of his aides were killed by errant American bombs. With the Taliban toppled and Karzai, backed by Western military force, tentatively in control, an important crossroad had been reached: For the first time in 23 years the guns have fallen silent and a process of national reconstruction has begun. "Looking around us," he told his eager audience in Kabul, "it is all too clear that Afghanistan has been physically and emotionally devastated. We all pray that this day will mark the end of the long dark night of conflict and strife."

Karzai inherits a country that has been almost totally gutted by war. Roads, bridges, and the national infrastructure have all been destroyed. Only about 6 percent of the population in this rugged, mountainous territory enjoy basic commodities such as running water or electricity. The region is also suffering from one of the worst droughts in recent memory, which has reduced most of the population to near starvation. Worse still, two-thirds of adult Afghans remain illiterate, while half their children are chronically malnourished. A further 3,000 people are also crippled annually by the many land mines inundating the countryside. Karzai faces a near impossible task of holding his country together while attracting sufficient foreign aid, estimated at $15 billion over 10 years, to rebuild the country. He is also tasked with assigning 5,000 UN peacekeepers to enforce the rule of law and to discourage the reemergence of local warlords. "If you abandon us in the middle of the road somewhere," he cautioned his allies, "there's a good chance that Afghanistan will become unstable again, and these bad guys will find a space here again." The race to deliver food and basic services to a long-suffering populace has just begun.

National restoration and reconciliation is also proving more difficult to achieve than anticipated. On February 17, 2002, Abdul Rahman, the newly appointed aviation and tourist minister, was assassinated on board a plane at Kabul's airport. The suspects, all disgruntled former members of the Northern Alliance, have been rounded up and charged with the murder. "There is no doubt what happened and that's why we made that strict, strong decision to announce and arrest them," Karzai stated. "There will not be any lenient hand here." Hopes are pinned upon the new prime minister's tact in handling his unruly countrymen. If he can placate warring factions, then peace and democracy might take root in that desolate, devastated land. He is also keenly interested in promoting regional peace and stability. During a February 2002 visit to Tehran, Karzai implored both Iran and the United States to restore diplomatic relations and national dialogue. His efforts at promoting national reconciliation paid handsome dividends on June 14, 2002, when the Loya Jirga formally voted him president of the transitional government by 1,292 votes out of 1,575 cast—an 82 percent approval rating. Karzai must now hammer out the final nature of the new Afghanistan government with the various power factions comprising the Loya Jirga. He then faces the tall order of rebuilding a nation shattered by war, religious discord, and feuding ethnic rivalry. It is an imposing order to fulfill, but Karzai waxed supremely confident. "Thank you for your trust, you make me honored," he emoted. "I thank God and I hope that I can serve my mujahid nation and my religion and my country."

Further Reading

Asad, Amirzada. *The Politics and Economics of Drug Production on the Pakistan-Afghanistan Border: Implications for a Globalized World.* Burlington, Vt.: Ashgate, 2003.

Goodson, Larry P. *Afghanistan's Endless War: State Failure: Regional Politics, and the Rise of the Taliban.* Seattle: University of Washington Press, 2002.

Griffiths, John C. *Afghanistan: A History of Conflict.* London: Andre Deutsch, 2001.

Marsden, Peter. *The Taliban: War and Religion in Afghanistan.* London: Zed Books, 2002.

Nojumi, Neamatollah. *The Rise of the Taliban in Afghanistan: Mass Mobilization, Civil War, and the Future of the Region.* Basingstoke, England: Palgrave, 2001.

Rashid, Ahmed. *Taliban: Militant Islam, Oil, and Fundamentalism in Central Asia.* New Haven, Conn.: Yale University Press, 2001.

Roberts, Jeffrey J. *The Origins of Conflict in Afghanistan.* Westport, Conn.: Praeger, 2003.

Kasyanov, Mikhail (1957–) *prime minister of Russia*

Mikhail Mikhailovich Kasyanov was born on December 8, 1957, in Solntsevo, the Soviet Union. He attended courses at the Moscow Automobile and Highway Construction Institute before training as an engineer with the All-Union Project and Research Institute of Industrial Transport in the late 1970s. By 1981 Kasyanov transferred to the foreign economics relations department of the State Planning Committee (or Gosplan) in Moscow, which originated the famous "five-year plans" guiding Soviet national development. After completing advanced studies with the State Planning Committee, he decided to pursue economics, specializing in foreign relations. Industrious and driven, he rose to section head of foreign economic relations by 1990. Kasyanov then held successive economic advisory posts, culminating in his appointment as deputy minister of finance in 1995. By now the Soviet Union had dissolved and had been succeeded by the Commonwealth of Independent States, of which Russia was the largest member. However, the transition from a socialist command economy to a free-market capitalist one proved extremely difficult, and the long-suffering Russian people girded themselves for a protracted spell of hardship and deprivation.

As deputy minister, it fell upon Kasyanov to facilitate the sale of Russia's aging and notoriously inefficient state-owned and operated industries. This was done to allow private investment and entrepreneurship to take hold and flourish. However, the administration of President BORIS YELTSIN proved particularly inept at regulating business, so the national currency (ruble) tumbled in value. By 1998 the situation was critical and it became Kasyanov's unpleasant duty to renegotiate Russia's staggering foreign debt at more favorable terms. But, fluent in English and highly competent, he accom-

plished exactly that and kept the nation from defaulting on payments. In fact, Russia's economy was so mired down that he renegotiated the national debt no less than twice in one year. Nonetheless, through his efforts Russia's economy remained solvent and eligible for continuing aid from the World Bank and the International Monetary Fund (IMF). By dint of his exceptional performance, Kasyanov advanced to minister of finance in May 1999, and he was now responsible for the economic health of the entire country. He scored a particularly impressive triumph in February 2000 by convincing the London Club of Creditors to forgive Russia of $32 million in debt.

The turning point in Kasyanov's career occurred following the resignation of President Yeltsin in December 1999. He was succeeded by VLADIMIR PUTIN, a former intelligence operative, who named the 42-year-old Kasyanov first deputy prime minister. On May 17, 2000, the Russian Duma confirmed his nomination and he officially become prime minister. Kasyanov's rise is significant because it consolidated a trend in Russian politics toward a younger, less dogmatic generation of political leadership. In his official capacity, Kasyanov became tasked with creating, in his own words, "an efficient government, something that Russia has never enjoyed in its history." The nation suffers from endemic corruption at all levels of administration, while many senior ministers are pawns of large companies and vested interests. Large-scale bribery, in effect, has become a second coin of the realm. It is Kasyanov's unsavory task to root out such practices, even at the risk of angering some of Russia's biggest and most influential tycoons. "I know a lot of businessmen and well-known entrepreneurs," he boasted, "but I don't have any concrete ties to any particular financial-industrial group." Nevertheless, changes here will certainly test his reformist credentials to the limit. Fortunately, he is backed by President Putin, who is himself determined that big business will pay its fair share of taxes and cease influence-buying at public expense. Failure means that the economy will continue dragging along, with the full potential of the Russian people never realized.

In addition to financial considerations, Kasyanov has also shouldered responsibility for representing Russian interests abroad. In March 2002 he paid an official state visit to the Democratic Republic of Vietnam, a former Soviet ally. In Hanoi, he signed several trade agreements and also announced that the Russian navy will be pulling out of the leased Cam Ranh Bay facility by July, two years ahead of schedule, for economic reasons. The following June he was also required to make face-saving statements in the wake of destructive soccer riots during a game between Russia and Japan in Moscow. Consequently, he expressed doubts as to Russia's ability to host the European World Championship in 2008. "Will Russia have the right to aspire to host such events if we see more of the same?" he asked. "It was hooligans who caused the tragedy."

Further Reading

Goldman, Marshal I. *Lost Opportunity: Why Economic Reforms in Russia Have Not Worked.* New York: W. W. Norton, 1994.

Smith, Kathleen E. *Mythmaking in the New Russia: Politics and Memory during the Yeltsin Era.* Ithaca, N.Y.: Cornell University Press, 2002.

Treisman, Daniel. *After the Deluge: Regional Crises and Political Consolidation in Russia.* Ann Arbor: University of Michigan Press, 1999.

Zasoursky, Ivan. *Media and Power in Post-Soviet Russia.* Armonk, N.Y.: M. E. Sharpe, 2002.

Zimmerman, William. *The Russian People and Foreign Policy: Russian Elite and Mass Perspectives, 1993–2000.* Princeton, N.J.: Princeton University Press, 2002.

Katsav, Moshe (1945–) *president of Israel*

Moshe Katsav was born in Yazd, Iran in 1945, to parents of Sephardic Jewish ancestry (namely, Jews born in Muslim countries). His family migrated to the young state of Israel in 1951 and settled briefly in an immigrant camp for Jews from around the world. In this manner, young Katsav became fluent in Hebrew, English, Arabic, and Farsi (Persian). He matured in the shoddy settlement town of Kiryat Malachi and passed through the Ben-Shemen Agricultural School by 1964. Two years of military service followed, after which he found work as a newspaper reporter. Around this time Katsav enrolled at Hebrew University of Jerusalem, becoming the first resident from Kiryat Malachi to do so. While studying for his bachelor's in economics and history he also joined the conservative Likud Party before graduating in 1972. Previously, in 1969, Katsav also acquired distinction for briefly becoming mayor of Kiryat Malachi and Israel's youngest mayor. He successfully ran again in 1974 and remained in office until 1981. That year he won a seat in the Knesset (parliament) and served on various committees. One of Katsav's highest personal priorities was lobbying for better government services and funding for impoverished settlements like his hometown.

Though nondescript and low-key by nature, Katsav was undeniably competent and through the 1980s he advanced through the Likud hierarchy. He filled several ministerial positions in the governments of Menachem Begin and YITZHAK SHAMIR, especially minister of transportation. In this capacity, Katsav was responsible for enhancing Israel's transportation network, which was notoriously shoddy and accident-prone. By 1991 he also successfully negotiated a deal with the Soviet Union for direct flights between the two countries. However, within a year an economic downturn allowed the return of the Labour Party under YITZHAK RABIN, and Shamir stepped aside as party head. Katsav ran to succeed him but was defeated by BINJAMIN NETANYAHU. In November 1996 Rabin was assassinated by an Israeli extremist and new elections made Netanyahu prime minister. Katsav, now serving as minister of Israeli-Arab affairs and closely allied to Netanyahu, continued opposing the Oslo Peace Accords signed by Rabin, which Likud perceived as threatening to Israeli security. However, Katsav proved more flexible toward the Israeli-Arab population than his predecessors, and in 1997 he became the first Jewish statesman to mark ceremonies commemorating the 1949 massacre of Arabs at Kafr Kasim. In 1998 he also expressed outrage that a poll of Israeli high school students favored limiting the civil rights of Israeli Arabs. "I am angered and deeply concerned by this kind of attitude," he insisted. "Israel's Arabs are still citizens, although I know a minister's statement is not enough to solve the problem."

By 1999 Netanyahu's administration, beset by a poor economy and mounting terrorist attacks, was voted out of office in favor of Labour's EHUD BARAK. Katsav, meanwhile, continued on in relative obscurity as a Knesset member until July 2000, when President EZER WEIZMAN, implicated by a scandal, resigned. The Israeli president is largely a ceremonial officer, one imbued with the task of promoting national and political unity. Likud nominated Katsav as their candidate, while Labour chose Nobel–prize winning statesman SHIMON PERES. Peres, given his experience and global visibility, was considered a shoo-in over his colorless, mild-mannered opponent, but after three ballots Katsav emerged victorious on a 63 to 57 vote. The upset proved embarrassing to Barak, and it was considered to be a protest registered over his seemingly lenient approach toward Palestine Liberation Organization (PLO) chief YASSER ARAFAT. On August 1, 2000, Katsav became the eighth president of the Jewish state, and only the second of Sephardic origin. He is also the first executive born in an Islamic country.

Like most Likud members, Katsav evinces hard-line positions against Arab terrorism, which has recently escalated to include suicide bombings. But he also waxes less stridently than many contemporaries. In December 2001 he tried allowing Arafat to conduct his traditional visit to Bethlehem for Christmas, but he was blocked. In January 2002 he next proposed establishing a "buffer zone" between Jews and Palestinians to curtail further violence. "We should certainly put up a barrier fence that would decrease or block this unbearable ease of penetration of terrorists and vehicles," he explained, "I am convinced that the scope of terrorists attacks will dramatically decrease." However, his notion of a physical barrier is strongly opposed by fellow right-wingers out of fear that it might serve as the initial border of a Palestinian state. Furthermore, that same month Katsav attempted to visit the West Bank town of Ramallah to address the Palestinian Legislative Council and propose a cease-fire, but Prime Minister ARIEL SHARON refused to let him go. Katsav thus continues in office, one of the few moderate voices in the Likud conservative bloc. He will be up for reelection in 2005.

Further Reading

Arian, Alan, David Nachmias, and Ruth Amir. *Executive Governance in Israel.* Basingstoke, England: Palgrave, 2002.

Jones, Clive, and Emma Murphy. *Israel: Challenges to Identity, Democracy, and the State.* London: Routledge, 2001.

Marshall, Edgar S. *Israel: Current Issues and Historical Background.* New York: Nova Science, 2002.

Mendilow, Jonathan. *Ideology, Party Change, and Electoral Campaigns in Israel, 1965–2001.* Albany: State University of New York Press, 2003.

Shindler, Colin. *The Land Beyond Promise: Israel, Likud, and the Zionist Dream.* New York: I. B. Tauris, 2002.

Keating, Paul (1944–) *prime minister of Australia*

Paul John Keating was born on January 18, 1944, in Sydney, Australia, the son of a boilermaker. His father was a staunch adherent of the Australian Labour Party (ALP), the nation's oldest, and he transmitted many of these values to his son. Keating quit school at 15 to enter the workforce and continued his education by taking evening classes. And, thanks to his father, he became enamored of the ALP and a member of its youth wing. Keating clerked at the Sydney city council for many years and also managed a rock group in his spare time, but in October 1969 he won a seat in parliament from Blaxland. Aged but 24 years, he was the youngest member of the House of Representatives, and he managed to retain his seat until 1996. He quickly gained the reputation as a brash young man but also an able politician. This was confirmed in 1975 when Prime Minister Gough Whitlam appointed him minister of the Northern Territory at the age of 31. However, a few weeks later Labour was tossed out of office by new elections, and Keating settled into the role of an opposition member. Aggressive and brandishing a decidedly barbed tongue, he excelled in the role and garnered national attention. In March 1983, when Labour returned to power under the aegis of Robert Hawke, Keating gained appointment as the administration's federal treasurer.

Keating's role as treasurer constituted the defining moment of his political career for it established him as a force in Australian politics. Although he lacked training as an economist, he fully supported conservative, free-market principles. To that end he made strong moves to deregulate national finances and allowed the Australian dollar to float. Exchange controls were also removed and he endorsed laws allowing foreign banks to operate in Australia. In 1986 he also won some significant tax reforms, including various cuts aimed at stimulating the economy. However, by this time Australia was experiencing a serious economic downturn while the national debt skyrocketed. The ALP government managed to stave off defeat in the July 1987 elections but Keating, from the right wing of the party, was determined to stand up to the unions. He managed to hold down wage increases to tame inflation, and the economy, although soft, did not worsen. He also served as point man for increased privatization of such government-controlled assets as the National Bank and Quantas Airlines. In April 1990, Keating's good performance resulted in his appointment as deputy prime minister. However, within a year he challenged Hawke for the party's leadership and initially lost. Keating thereupon resigned from office and, after several months of backroom machinations, he finally wrested the prime minister's office from Hawke in December 1991. "I would like to start 1992 with a cohesive and comprehensive plan to push Australia," he insisted. "I've got a good idea already of what should be in that plan, but I want to tie it all together and make sure we have got it right."

As prime minister, Keating embraced three touchstone issues throughout his administration. The first was better land rights and genuine reconciliation with Australia's Aboriginal population. The second was casting off the final vestiges of colonialism by transforming Australia from a constitutional monarchy within the British Commonwealth to a federal republic. His third and most controversial stance was recognition that Australia should downplay its traditional reliance upon Western Europe in favor of closer ties with the burgeoning economies and societies of Asia. His policies were basically embraced by Labour supporters but they remained unpopular with the public at large. Aside from better treatment of Aboriginals, he failed to muster sufficient support to enact the others. Nonetheless, Keating remained an active, aggressive campaigner, and in March 1993 he handily defeated John Hewson of the Liberal (conservative) Party by playing off fears about proposed tax increases.

Despite his success, Keating was increasingly viewed as an arrogant individual beset by moral rectitude. He maintained that it was always better to do what was right than do what was popular, and remained convinced of his political infallibility. But, despite a record of solid accomplishment, Keating was increasing defined by his vitriolic personality, which did little to improve poll numbers. By February 1996 his luck had ended and national elections were swept by JOHN HOWARD and the Liberal Party. This defeat ended 13 years of Labour rule and Keating, noting the magnitude of his unpopularity, quit politics altogether to pursue teaching and business interests.

Further Reading

Carew, Edna. *Paul Keating: Prime Minister.* Sydney: Allen and Unwin, 1992.

Edwards, John. *Keating: The Inside Story.* New York: Viking, 1996.

Gordon, Michael. *A True Believer: Paul Keating.* St. Lucia: University of Queensland Press, 1996.

Grattan, Michele. *Australian Prime Ministers.* Sydney: New Holland, 2000.

McCarthy, G., and D. Taylor. "The Politics of the Float: Paul Keating and the Deregulation of the Australian Exchange Rate." *Australian Journal of Politics and History* 41, no. 2 (1995): 219–238.

Kérékou, Mathieu (1933–   ) *president of Benin*

Mathieu Kérékou was born in Koufra, northern Dahomey, on September 2, 1933, a member of the Bariba tribal group. Dahomey was at that time a French colony sandwiched between Ghana and Nigeria, and it did not achieve political independence until August 1960. The son of a former soldier, Kérékou was educated at primary and secondary schools in Mali and Senegal. He then joined the French colonial army and attended the Officers School at Fréjus, France, before transferring to the Dahomey national army in 1961. Kérékou proved an active and attentive soldier, and he gained appointment as aide-de-camp to President Hubert Maga. However, Dahomey became wracked by corruption and instability, and over the next decade the military intervened six times to restore order. Kérékou, commanding an elite paratroop unit, distinguished himself in several coups, and by 1968 he was chairman of the Revolutionary Military Council. That year he also ventured to France to further his education, but by the time he returned, in 1970, Dahomey was gripped by yet another political crisis. The presidency was then shared by three men on a rotating basis, and their competition left the economy reeling. On October 27, 1972, Kérékou participated in his final coup by overthrowing President Ahomadegbe and seizing control. Having the full support of the military, he next arrested all high-ranking government officials and charged them with corruption. Kérékou then assumed the powers of the presidency, the prime ministry, and the ministry of defense. Moreover, all offices within his new regime were staffed solely by military officers under the age of 40.

The new president was determined to break from all previous political traditions. He began espousing a Marxist-Leninist approach toward government, which entailed the nationalization of all schools, banks, and oil companies. Furthermore, control of these institutions became highly centralized in the hands of the government. Kérékou also proved himself to be something of a cultural nationalist, for he strove to expunge foreign influence, particularly French, from education and culture. However, a unique feature of the regime was its commitment to local participation in government. Kérékou authorized creation of revolutionary committees down to the village, town, and commune levels, along with district and provincial councils. Eventually their number topped 1,500 and they granted citizens a sense of interaction and fellowship with the government that had been previously lacking. By 1975 Kérékou felt emboldened enough to rename his country the People's Republic of Benin, the latter a reference to the powerful empire that existed in the region in the 16th century.

Kérékou's socialist regime may have centralized his control over the country, but it also gutted the economy. Declines in the balance of trade and productivity, accompanied by a rise in inefficiency, all translated into hardship for teachers, civil servants, trade unionists, and students. The nation was wracked by protests throughout 1975, and Kérékou withdrew from the capital to direct affairs from an army barracks at Cotonou. That year he also weathered an unsuccessful coup attempt by disgruntled army officers. However, Kérékou's grip on Benin remained firm as ever, and he increased his revolutionary reputation by expanding diplomatic and economic ties with unsavory regimes such as Libya. This, in turn, induced France and the United States to eliminate foreign aid completely. The ensuing hardships occasioned many protests and a severe crackdown by security forces. On the surface it appeared that Benin had become simply the latest in a long line of petty African dictatorships.

By 1990 it was apparent that Benin's experiment with socialism had failed and Kérékou, showing considerable pragmatism, formally ditched Marxism-Leninism as an official ideology. He then embarked on a course toward pursuit of free markets, privatization, and a liberalized economy. On February 25, 1990, he also summoned a national council to discuss the prospect of political reform. This body suddenly declared itself sovereign, and suspended the existing constitution. Kérékou surprisingly agreed to their demand for creating multiparty democracy. Thus his country, which again renamed itself the Republic of Benin, became the first African nation to restore popular democracy through

civilian action. In March 1991 Kérékou was defeated by Nicéphore Soglo in open elections and voluntarily stepped down. He also publicly apologized for the previous excesses of his regime and was pardoned by Soglo.

By March 1996 the austerity measures imposed by Soglo to meet IMF standards created much dissension, and Kérékou was reelected to the presidency with 52.2 percent of the vote. As proof of his enduring popularity he again defeated Soglo on March 13, 2001, by a margin of 45.4 percent, although the opposition claimed widespread fraud. Nonetheless, Kérékou continues in power as a controversial figure who has dominated the political life of Benin for more than three decades. As such he remains one of Africa's most enduring heads of state.

Further Reading

Allen, Christopher. *Democratic Renewal in Africa: Two Essays on Benin.* Edinburgh: University of Edinburgh, 1992.

Houngnikopo, Mathuria C. *Determinants of Democratization in Africa: A Comparative Study of Benin and Togo.* Lanham, Md.: University Press of America, 2001.

———. "The Military and Democratization in Africa: A Comparative Study of Benin and Togo." *Journal of Political and Military Sociology* 28, no. 2 (2000): 210–229.

Magnusson, Bruce A. "Democratization and Domestic Insecurity: Navigating the Transition in Benin." *Comparative Politics* 33 (January 2001): 211–231.

Strandsbjerg, Camilla. "Kerekou, God, and the Ancestors: Religion and the Conception of Political Power in Benin." *African Affairs* 99, no. 396 (2000): 395–415.

Khalifa, Hamad bin Isa al- (1950–) *king of Bahrain*

Hamad bin Isa al-Khalifa was born in Bahrain on January 20, 1950, the son of ruling emir Isa bin Sulman al-Khalifa. His family presently constitutes the only ruling authority for the nation, and it has served in that role since the 19th century. In contrast to the large states making up the Persian Gulf region, Bahrain consists of 80 small islands off the coast of Saudi Arabia. It is populated by 630,000 people, divided unequally between adherents of Sunni and Shiite Islamic sects. In view of its small size and vulnerability, Bahrain had been a British protectorate since 1861, but the country achieved political independence in August 1971 under a parliamentary form of government. Initially, this included an elected National Assembly, but the emir dissolved it in August 1975 in favor of a 16-member cabinet headed by a prime minister. Bahrain is also part of the oil-rich exporting consortia OPEC and, as such, it enjoys one of the highest standards of living in the world. Oil revenues are carefully lavished upon the populace, who enjoy free access to education and health care.

Hamad was educated in Bahrain before attending the noted British military academy at Sandhurst. He also took courses at the U.S. Command and General Staff College at Fort Leavenworth, Kansas, and he is a qualified helicopter pilot. He returned to Bahrain to observe the traditional, paternalistic patterns of leadership exercised by his father. This included the calling of public assemblies, or Majlis, whereby any citizen, regardless of his social standing, can meet with and directly petition the ruler for redress in civil matters. This long-standing tribal practice insures that citizens enjoy direct contact with their leaders, but by the end of the 20th century it could not satiate demands for greater democracy and freedom. Bahrain's transition to a modern society was consequently difficult and not without severe disruptions. A major factor in civil unrest was that the ruling Khalifa family subscribes to the Sunni branch of Islam, which has a traditional antipathy for the Shiite majority in Iran. The Sunni constitute the majority of the population in Bahrain. The group's antagonism was further exacerbated following the Iranian Revolution of 1979 and the rise of Muslim fundamentalism. Many Shiite extremists received paramilitary training in Iran, and they returned home to initiate terrorist activities in hopes of fomenting a religious revolution. Hamad, now installed as head of state security, was called on to restore order and maintain the family's control of power. Given the radical nature of the opposition, and the violent rioting they engendered, order was maintained with a heavy hand. Nonetheless, the country continued on its path toward greater freedom, a trend accelerated by the passing of the emir on March 7, 1999.

Hamad inherited a complicated morass that called for balancing traditional social and religious conservatism with modern political institutions. This has proven to be a delicate juggling act for Hamad, who has been genuinely committed to granting women the right to vote. His stance, however well-intentioned, brought him the derision of most Islamic clerics and engendered further unrest. But he also extended a hand to his Shiite majority, allowing them to join the military for the first time, and he released several hundred political prisoners. The emir then confronted the inherent instability of the Persian Gulf region, including friction with Iraq, Iran, and Qatar. Bahrain supported Iraqi strongman SADDAM HUSSEIN during his eight-year conflict with Iran, but the country later condemned his occupation of Kuwait. This move forced him to secure closer ties to the U.S. military, which bases its 5th Fleet in his country. Bahrain enjoyed stormy relations with Iran, which ruled the island kingdom up through the 18th century, and diplomatic relations grew strained over the issue of Shiite extremism. However, the election of the more moderate president MOHAMMED KHATAMI calmed tensions considerably, and, in August 1999, Hamad became the first emir to visit Iran in several decades. Relations with the tiny nation of Qatar, however, remain problematic. Both countries have claimed various islands in the Gulf, and at one point Qatar's military evicted Bahrain's workers from territory by force. Despite recent diplomatic overtures, the two nations remain at an impasse over this issue.

Hamad, however, kept his promise to encourage democracy and equal rights. In May 2000 he announced that municipal elections would be held for the first time in early 2001, with legislative elections shortly thereafter. That September he also appointed a new council, which included the first women and non-Muslims. His reform efforts crested on February 15, 2002, when Hamad proclaimed himself king at the head of a new constitutional monarchy, and he officially renamed his country the kingdom of Bahrain. Moreover, women are now formally allowed to participate and run for public office for the first time. In a region where civil and human rights are largely stifled by religious tradition, Hamad's embrace of modernity was welcomed by Western countries, particularly the United States, its largest trading and defense partner. "We are keen to resume democratic life as soon as possible," he insisted, "for the glory of Bahrain, its prosperity and development."

Further Reading

al-Khalifa, Hamad Bin Isa. *First Light: Modern Bahrain and Its Heritage.* New York: Kegan Paul, 1994.
———, and Michael Rice, eds. *Bahrain through the Ages.* New York: Kegan Paul, 1993.

Lawson, Fred H. *Bahrain: The Modernization of Autocracy.* Boulder, Colo.: Westview Press, 1984.

Mapp, H. V. *Leave Well Alone! Where Oil Shapes Dynasties and Destinies.* Southend, England: Prittle Brook Publications, 1994.

Zahlan, Rosemarie S. *The Making of the Modern Gulf States: Kuwait, Bahrain, Qatar, the United Arab Emirates, and Oman.* Reading, England: Ithaca Press, 1998.

Khalifa, Isa bin Sulman al- (1933–1999)

emir of Bahrain

Isa bin Sulman al-Khalifa was born on June 4, 1933, in al-Jasra, Bahrain, the son of Sheikh Sulman bin Hamad al-Khalifa. His country, a chain of small islands in the western Persian Gulf adjacent to the Saudi Arabia coast, was a poor and underpopulated area whose principal activity was pearl diving. Nonetheless, Bahrain entered into defensive arrangements with Great Britain in 1861 to protect it from the Ottoman Empire and neighboring Iran, both of whom coveted the region. Khalifa, meanwhile, was educated by private tutors brought in from England and Egypt, and in 1953 he represented his father during the coronation of King Faisal II of Iraq. Three years later he became head of the Manama city council after disturbances with the local Shiite majority. The sheikh then appointed him crown prince and heir apparent in January 1957, and he played increasingly important roles in daily governance as his father's health failed. Following the death of Sheikh Sulman, Khalifa was installed as head of state on December 16, 1961. In terms of administration, he presided over the al-Khalifa family council, which served as the governmental inner circle and dispensed oil profits among family members and key allies. And, as a traditional sheikh, Khalifa was responsible for holding weekly public assemblies called Majlis, whereby average citizens approached him with petitions and grievances. In this manner Bahrain's leaders kept in close contact with their subjects, addressed their needs, and demonstrated their concern with paternalistic care.

Britain formally withdrew from the Persian Gulf region in 1971, and Bahrain declared its independence on August 15 of that year. Khalifa thus assumed the new title of emir. Previously, he had appointed a 12-member Council of State to assist in ruling and, in 1971, he transformed it into a sitting cabinet. By 1972 Council members were charged with promulgating a new constitution, which included an elected National Assembly, the region's first. This body convened in December 1973 but arrangements proved unwieldy and Khalifa dissolved it in August 1975. He kept it suspended for the rest of his reign. After 1979 the emir also faced imminent dangers from the new Islamic Republic of Iran. Iran and Bahrain both share predominately Shiite Muslim majorities, while the Al-Khalifa family is from the Sunni branch of Islam. Sunnis in Bahrain traditionally enjoyed better access to jobs and education, and the poorer Shiites, apparently at the behest of Iran, became more militant. Over the next two decades they staged violent protests and called for the imposition of a strict Islamic republic. Khalifa, who sought to bring Bahrain into a more moderate, Western-oriented orbit, resisted their machinations with equal force. "If they hit you with one bullet, you hit them, with a hundred," he reasoned. "Then people respect you." His heavy-handed approach to social control worked. Despite Iranian subterfuge and instigation, Shiite unrest was contained. Religious discontent became a pressing matter of national security during the 1980–88 Iran-Iraq War when Khalifa sided firmly with SADDAM HUSSEIN, providing millions of dollars in economic assistance. However, throughout the 1991 Gulf War, he demonstrated his loyalty to the West by allowing use of Bahrain's facilities for the campaign to free Kuwait. His support won plaudits from the United States, which also stations its 5th Fleet there. But in 1995–1996 Bahrain was rocked again by violent Shiite agitation and demands for reconstituting the National Assembly. Khalifa, feeling his position threatened, kept the 1973 constitution suspended but did order formation of a 30-member advisory council as a token of reform.

In terms of domestic policy, Khalifa proved instrumental in modernizing Bahrain and making it one of the world's wealthiest nations. He was cognizant that the islands lacked the oil resources of neighboring states like Qatar and Kuwait, so he embarked on diversifying the service sector economy, primarily banking. During his reign no less than 60 "offshore" banks and 20 commercial banks were established, transforming this former pearl diving enclave into a financial and transportation center. Khalifa also proved himself disposed toward a more moderate interpretation of Islam than many of his neighbors. Though a practicing Sunni, he allowed women to drive, work, and receive public education.

They enjoy a status that makes them among the most liberated females in the Arabic world. The emir remained a valuable Western ally in the Persian Gulf region until his death in Manama on March 6, 1999. By Gulf standards he was a strict, authoritarian figure, and ruthless in the imposition of order, but he displayed a strong sense of benevolence toward his subjects. Invariably, he ruled with a view toward improving their lot. Khalifa's popularity was amply demonstrated at his funeral when the cemetery was crammed with 10,000 grieving subjects while the funeral route was lined by another 50,000. He was succeeded by his son, HAMAD BIN ISA AL-KHALIFA.

Further Reading

Dabrowski, Karen. *Bahrain Briefing: The Struggle for Democracy, December 1994–December 1996.* London: Colourmast, 1997.

Lawson, Fred H. *Bahrain: The Modernization of Autocracy.* Boulder, Colo.: Westview Press, 1989.

Mapp, H. V. *Leave Well Alone! Where Oil Shapes Dynasties and Destinies.* Essex, England: Prittle Brook Publications, 1994.

Nakhleh, Emile A. *Bahrain: Political Development in a Modernizing Society.* Lexington, Mass.: D. C. Heath, 1976.

Zahlan, Rosemarie S. *The Making of the Modern Gulf States: Kuwait, Bahrain, Qatar, the United Arab Emirates, and Oman.* Reading, England: Ithaca Press, 1998.

Khamenei, Said Ali (1939–) *supreme leader of Iran*

Said Ali Khamenei was born in the city of Meshed, Iran, in 1939, to a family of Islamic scholars. He commenced religious training at an early age and in 1948 was sent to Naiaf, Iraq, for advanced studies. In time Khamenei became fluent in Arabic and Turkish, and he distinguished himself as a religious writer and translator. By 1958 he had settled in the holy city of Qom, Iran, becoming a disciple of Ruhollah Musavi Khomeini, a noted cleric and a harsh critic of Shah Reza Pahlavi's authoritarian regime. Khamenei apparently shared those beliefs, for, in 1963, he was arrested for protesting the shah's Western-oriented reforms. He nonetheless continued with his religious agitation, despite repeated internments, and, in 1968, he was briefly exiled to the remote province of Balushistan. Following his release, Khamenei resumed his revolutionary activities, which crested in 1979 when large-scale public demonstrations forced the shah into exile. The Iranian Revolution had commenced, and Khamenei was well-placed to serve at the forefront of events.

Despite his relative lack of seniority among the Islamic clergy, Khamenei enjoyed a close and abiding relationship with Ruhollah Khomeini, who in 1979 was elevated to the rank of *ayatollah,* or "supreme leader." The religious militants ruling Iran then imposed a strict Islamic dictatorship upon the country, severely restricting press and personal freedoms and relegating women to second-class status. As a close confidante of the Ayatollah, Khamenei evinced vocal support for radical Islam, and he founded the Islamic Republican Party to formally empower the theocracy. His highly visible profile culminated in his election to the presidency on October 2, 1981, which further confirmed his status as Khomeini's favorite. However, radical dissidents in Iran resisted the imposition of religious rule, and, at one point, Khamenei was severely injured by a bomb blast. He nonetheless continued as a reliable ally of hard-line religious elements and doctrines. However, in the field of foreign policy, Khamenei moderated his stance somewhat and sought friendly relations with most countries. He even extended an olive branch to the United States, heretofore regarded as the "Great Satan," on the basis of mutual respect and reciprocity. However, his criticism of America's ally, Israel, proved unrelenting and fierce. Recently, his support of Palestinian suicide bombers has all but insured that full normalization of relations with most Western powers will remain unattainable.

After Khomeini died in 1989, the 80-member Council of Islamic Experts chose Khamenei to succeed him. As Ayatollah, he enjoys complete authority over all religious and political matters, and he maintains the regime's insistence on religious and moral purity. But he also sought accommodation with leading moderate reformers such as President ALI RAFSANJANI. In fact, like his predecessor, Khamenei strove for conciliation among warring factions within the ruling elites. He certainly did not oppose the need for international financing to help reconstruct Iran's economy, shattered by its 1980–88 war with Iraq. But he insisted on defining the character of the Iranian Revolution, which he interprets as fundamentally anti-Western. Thus blue jeans, Hollywood movies, soda, and all the trappings of American-style society were rigidly proscribed. He also undertook moves to make the university system adhere more closely to Islamic principles, and he endorsed widespread censorship of newspapers, books, and films. These positions notwithstanding, Khamenei was elected to a second term as president on August 16, 1985.

By 1997 the Iranian public wearied of Islamic extremism, and that year they defeated Khamenei's choice for the presidency, Ali Akbar Nateq-Noori, in favor of MOHAMMED KHATAMI, a noted reformer. A protracted cat-and-mouse game began between those wishing for greater liberty and conservative elements who do not. Khatami, reelected by a landslide vote in June 2001, has enjoyed minor success in loosening up the intellectual arena, but in other matters he remains checkmated by the all-powerful clergy. Thus the reformist-oriented parliament remains on a collision course with the Ayatollah and his Council of Guardians. Nor has Khamenei's distrust of the United States diminished with time. He condemned the September 11, 2001, attack on New York's World Trade Center, but he also criticized the ensuing American war in Afghanistan. President GEORGE W. BUSH, meanwhile, denounced Iran, in concert with Iraq and North Korea, as an "axis of evil" as these three powers seek to develop weapons of mass destruction. Khamenei, fearing a strong American military presence on his border, has recently lashed out at the Americans, warning that Iran will fight if attacked. "They are violent, but this imposition of violence or expression of violence cannot help America achieve its aims and succeed," he declared. "America is the most hated regime in the world." His conservative allies have since renewed their grip on domestic policy, and, in June 2002, the Guardian Council rejected a bill designed to end torture for obtaining prisoner confessions as "un-Islamic." The Supreme Leader of Iran remains locked in a power struggle with President Khatami over the future direction of the country.

Further Reading

Brumberg, Daniel. *Reinventing Khomeini: The Struggle for Reform in Iran.* Chicago: University of Chicago Press, 2001.

Downes, Mark. *Iran's Unresolved Revolution.* Burlington, Vt.: Ashgate, 2002.

Gieling, Saskia. "The Marjaliya in Iran and the Nomination of Khamenei in December 1994." *Middle Eastern Studies* 33 (October 1997): 777–788.

Katouzian, Homa. *Iranian History and Politics: The Dialectic of State and Society.* New York: Routledge Curzon, 2003.

Nabavi, Negin. *Intellectuals and the Senate in Iran: Politics, Discourse, and Dilemma of Authenticity.* Gainesville: University Press of Florida, 2003.

Tarock, Adam. "The Muzzling of the Liberal Press in Iran." *Third World Quarterly* 22 (August 2001): 585–602.

Vahdat, Farzin. *God and Juggernaut: Iran's Intellectual Encounter with Modernity.* Syracuse, N.Y.: Syracuse University Press, 2002.

Khamtay Siphandone (1924–) *president of Laos*

Khamtay Siphandone was born on February 8, 1924, in the southern Laotian province of Champasak. Laos is a small, landlocked nation in Southeast Asia sandwiched between several larger neighbors, including Thailand, Vietnam, and China. A former French colony, it became integrally involved in the wars of the 20th century, including Japanese occupation, but especially Communist-inspired anticolonial movements culminating in the Vietnam War. Following independence in 1954, Laos was ruled by a constitutional monarchy and the United States strongly supported the government during struggles against Communist guerrillas, the Pathet Lao. However, the country was overrun by December 1975 and a new nation, the Lao People's Democratic Republic, was proclaimed. This remains a Communist dictatorship run as a one-party state under the Lao People's Revolutionary Party (LPRP). The government consists of a National Assembly of 99 members, which appoints both a president and a 12-member Council of Ministers to govern national affairs. Laos is also one of the world's poorest nations, where the vast majority of its 5.4 million people live on earnings of around $1 per day. Worse, it has a very high infantry mortality rate, the average life expectancy is around 50 years, and nearly 80 percent of the workforce is occupied in agricultural production.

Like many Laotian youths, Khamtay became caught up in revolutionary activities fired by nationalism surrounding the anticolonial movement. By 1954 he had risen to chief of staff of the Lao People's Liberation Army with a view toward overthrowing the monarchy. He led the insurgent forces through two decades of incessant warfare, which included heavy American bombing, and worked his way up the party hierarchy. After victory was achieved in December 1975, Khamtay was rewarded with an appointment as minister of defense. By 1988 the elder cadre had either retired or been removed, and Khamtay again advanced to serve as party secretary, the next in line to succeed Kaysone Phomvihane, the sitting president. Kaysone was a lifelong friend and trusted associate of Khamtay, so his choice was not surprising. On August 15, 1991, Khamtay was appointed president by the National Assembly. Unlike many of the revolutionary generation, the new leader, while fixed in his political beliefs, proved far more flexible with respect to economic policy. Following the breakup of the Soviet bloc that year, and the loss of the financial aid it provided, dramatic reforms became a national priority to jump-start the economy.

Khamtay's rise witnessed the retirement of additional "old guard" politicians from within the LPRP whose only reaction to national problems was to evoke ideology. Previously, President Kaysone had introduced the "New Economic Mechanism" in 1986, which called for the phased introduction of free-market economics. Khamtay, similarly disposed, was active in its implementation and enlargement. In 1991 he also shepherded through a new constitution, one which guaranteed the protection of private property, previously unthinkable in a Marxist-Leninist society. The new constitution was adopted to attract foreign investment, in which Thailand, a former adversary, has proven the leader. Khamtay also continued his policy of pragmatism abroad and expanded cordial relations with many formerly estranged countries. Foremost among these was the United States, which had bombed Laos repeatedly during the Vietnam War, and now demanded help in retrieving the remains of lost servicemen. Laos gladly complied and, in exchange, the country has received millions of dollars to assist in fighting the drug trade. After several years of decline, especially in the wake of the 1997 Asian currency crisis, the Laotian economy is slowly rebounding. The government now faces a new problem arising from the influx of money, namely, corruption. Part of these illegal earnings have stemmed from the illegal logging of Laotian rain forests, and the government has cracked down to prevent further injury to the nation's ecology.

For all its progress in instituting free-market reforms, Laos remains among the last doctrinaire Marxist-Leninist regimes in the world. The government is committed to the continuance of one-party rule (although the hammer-and-sickle symbols have been replaced by a Buddhist temple) and the political repression this entails. Elections are tightly controlled, voting is mandatory, and party-approved politicians usually gain office by voting margins of 99 percent. Khamtay himself is a secretive figure with a reputation for authoritarian politics, and he has ordered severe crackdowns on political dissent. In 2000 this resulted in a bombing campaign throughout the capital of Vientiane, and groups of exiles have also stirred up violence along the Thai border. However, following the February 2002 national elections, he exclaimed: "The people are pleased to have only one party, and have always had faith and trust in the party." The 77-year-old Khamtay's tenure in office is slated to expire in 2004. Given the Laotian penchant for electing younger politicians, there is a good chance he will be succeeded by a new generation of leadership—and thinking.

Further Reading

Butler-Diaz, Jacqueline. *New Laos—New Challenges.* Tempe: Arizona State University Press, 1998.

Evans, Grant. *The Politics of Ritual and Remembrance: Laos since 1975.* Honolulu: University of Hawaii Press, 1998.

Simms, Peter. *The Kingdom of Laos: Six Hundred Years of History.* Richmond, England: Curzon, 1999.

Stuart-Fox, Martin. *A History of Laos.* Melbourne: Cambridge University Press, 1997.

———. *Historical Dictionary of Laos.* Lanham, Md.: Scarecrow Press, 2001.

Tanabe, Shigeharu, and Charles F. Keyes. *Cultural Crisis and Social Memory: Modernity and Identity in Thailand and Laos.* Honolulu: University of Hawaii Press, 2002.

Khatami, Mohammed (1943–) *president of Iran*

Mohammed Khatami was born in Ardakan, Yazd province, Iran, in 1943, the son of a prominent Muslim cleric. He was educated at home by his father before studying theology at the religious city of Qom in 1961. Khatami subsequently attended the University of Esfahah, majoring in philosophy, and in 1970 he received a graduate degree in education from the University of Tehran. For a Shiite cleric, Khatami is extremely worldly and speaks German, English, and Arabic. Furthermore, unlike many contemporaries, he is soundly versed in the nuances of Western religion and political philosophy. He has authored several books on the interaction of Islam with the modern world.

By 1979 Iran was convulsed by a fundamentalist Islamic revolution that deposed Shah Mohammed Reza Pahlavi and installed Ruhollah Musari Khomeini as the *ayatollah,* or supreme leader. Khatami was initially sympathetic toward the revolution, although he grew increasingly wary of its doctrinaire excesses. In 1980 he was elected to the Majlis, or national assembly, which brought him to the attention of the ruling clerics. The urbane and intellectual Khatami then gained appointment as minister of culture and Islamic guidance, and he proceeded to put his personal stamp on the revolution. Unlike many hard-liners, Khatami was liberal in his cultural leanings, and he did much to encourage freedom of expression in film and media. This stance irritated many conservatives, who demanded and obtained his resignation in 1992. Khatami then served as a cultural adviser to President ALI RAFSANJANI, another celebrated moderate, and he also headed the national library.

By 1997, Iran arrived at a crossroads. The high birth rate rendered the young the majority voting public and they were impatient for change. The state-run economy was also sluggish and failed to produce new jobs fast enough. Khatami, sensing this discord, announced his decision to run for the presidency by championing political liberalization, women's rights, and freedom of expression. He was particularly strident in denouncing the government's practice of censorship. "When we speak of freedom we mean the freedom of the opposition," Khatami lectured. "It is no freedom if the only people who agree with those in power and with their ways and means are free." Such outspoken views brought him criticism from conservative clerics, but his moderation resonated among the young, trade unionists, and disenchanted elements within the Iranian polity. On May 23, 1997, the smooth-talking cleric was swept into power with 69 percent of the vote in this, the first freely held elections since the 1979 revolution. The elections firmly repudiated hard-line religious rule and underscored the need for social and political reforms nationwide. The following August Khatami again displayed his determination for change by appointing both moderates and women to his cabinet. Furthermore, legislative elections held in May 2000 delivered 80 percent of the seats to reform-minded candidates. Unfortunately for Khatami, his office is relatively weak and easily overruled by the supreme religious leader. The entrenched conservatives have since resorted to judicial acts to close down reformist publications, and hundreds of journalists, activists and students have been jailed. In the face of such stiff resistance Khatami's reform agenda has made little progress. Nor have his efforts to liberalize the state-controlled economy met with success and, consequently, Iran still experiences slow growth and job creation. The lackluster economy, rising unemployment, and social unrest threaten to unhinge the nation's stability, and the president therefore stridently urges reforming the private sector.

Despite his inability to overcome theological obstructionism, Khatami remains Iran's most popular political figure. On June 9, 2001 he was reelected to the presidency by the even larger margin of 77.4 percent, which adds an even public mandate for change. This was especially true respecting foreign relations. "The Islamic Republic of Iran has no intention of hostilities with any country or anybody," he declared. Accordingly, Khatami made the first friendly overtures to Western Europe in nearly two decades. Officially, however, the United States remains the "Great Satan" and a pariah to the Islamic republic. But, in the wake of the September 11, 2001, destruction of the World Trade Center in New York, Khatami openly expressed sympathy for America and condemned the use of terror. Moreover, despite religious objections, Iran muted its criticism of the ensuing American campaign against the Taliban regime in Afghanistan. That December, before a gathering of thousands of students at Tehran University, Khatami also urged conservative clerics to respect the views of opposition reformers. He unequivocally warned that failure to heed the legitimate will of the people is creating a mood of disillusionment and despair. Furthermore, in January 2002, Khatami officially pardoned Hossein Loqmanian, a reform member of parliament who had been jailed for denouncing Iran's conservative judiciary branch. His arrest and incarceration heightens the ongoing struggle between reformists and conservatives that, as yet, remains unresolved. The U.S. government has responded favorably to such gestures but overall relations between the two countries remain tense. In January 2002 President GEORGE W. BUSH's assertion that Iran, in concert with Iraq and North Korea, constitutes an "axis of evil," drew a sharp riposte from the nominally neutral Khatami.

Addressing the nation, he said that the "recent, unfounded assertions, which are insulting to the Iranian people" were uncalled for. He then implored his countrymen to assemble in large numbers during a scheduled anti–U.S. demonstration that coincided with the 23rd anniversary of the Iranian Revolution. Khatami nonetheless remains the best hope for peaceful change in Iran and the resumption of its place among the community of nations. He continues as a moderate and effective counterweight to the arch-conservative clerics under Ayatollah SAID ALI KHAMENEI.

Further Reading

Abdo, Geneive. *Answering Only to God: The Dangerous Road to Democracy in Iran.* New York: John Macrae, 1993.

Arjoman, Said Amin. "Civil Society and the Rule of Law in the Constitutional Politics of Iran under Khatami." *Social Research* 67, no. 2 (2000): 283–301.

Brumberg, Daniel. *Reinventing Khomeini: The Struggle for Reform in Iran.* Chicago: University of Chicago Press, 2001.

Clawson, Patrick. *Iran under Khatami: A Political, Economic, and Military Assessment.* Washington, D.C.: Washington Institute for Near East Policy, 1998.

Fischer, Michael M. *Iran: From Religious Dispute to Revolution.* Madison: University of Wisconsin Press, 2003.

Khatami, Muhammed. *Hope and Challenge: The Iranian President Speaks.* Binghamton, N.Y.: Binghamton University Press, 1997.

Mafinezam, Alidad. *The Intellectual Bases of the Khatami Phenomenon in Iran.* New York: Columbia University Press, 1999.

Souresrafil, Omid. *Revolution in Iran: The Transition to Democracy.* London: Pluto, 2001.

Kim Dae Jung (1925–) *president of South Korea*

Kim Dae Jung was born in South Cholla province, Korea, on December 3, 1925, the son of farmers. He was educated at the Mokpo Commercial High School and found work as a newspaper editor. Korea at that time was annexed to the Japanese Empire, which ruled it ruthlessly until 1945. After that, the peninsula was divided into a communist northern half under Soviet tutelage and a southern half supported by the United States. In June 1940 communist North Korea invaded the South, precipitating the Korean war, 1950–53. Kim was captured by North Koreans and he was almost killed, but he managed to escape. After the war he resumed his education by attending Kunkook University, Korean University, and Kyunghee University, ultimately earning advanced degrees in economics. By 1960, however, the course of South Korean politics, characterized by severe authoritarian rule, had left him disillusioned. Liberal by nature and a fiery orator, he became politically active by joining the Democratic Party in 1960 and he gained national notoriety as an outspoken critic of the government.

In 1971 Kim's strident opposition activism led to his candidacy for the presidency against strongman Park Chung Hee. His calls for greater social and economic liberalization were well received by students and the working class, and he gained 46 percent of the popular vote; not enough to win, but sufficient to cement his reputation as a national dissident. However, his strident condemnation of government policies resulted in jailings, beatings, kidnappings, a death sentence, and at least one bungled assassination attempt. But Kim, a devout Catholic, refused to be silenced. In 1987 he ran again against former general ROH TAE WOO, but he split the opposition vote with KIM YONG SAM and lost again. Kim then opposed Roh in the 1992 presidential elections, and he failed once more. It was not until his fourth attempt, in December 1997, against Lee Hoi Chang, that the outspoken economist won a narrow election with 40.3 percent of the vote. His victory marked a turning point in South Korea's political history: for the first time since 1948 the government party had been turned out of power. After enduring years of hardship in the name of freedom, Kim wrapped his presidency in the mantle of moral authority.

Kim's victory occurred against an inauspicious backdrop. The Asian currency crisis was in full swing and the national economy began entering a period of deep recession. A bailout by the International Monetary Fund was estimated at $60 billion, which would have required great sacrifice by the Korean populace. Kim nonetheless imposed the austerity measures required, and he embarked upon ambitious structural reforms. Previously, South Korea enjoyed robust growth as the world's 11th largest economy and became known, along with Singapore, Taiwan, and Hong Kong, as one of the four "Little Tigers." But new government policies were enacted to encourage greater accountability, especially respecting loans, which had been granted indiscriminately. A bigger issue facing Kim was the question of political retribution. Many Koreans demanded that those responsible for three decades of authoritarian rule and political oppression be punished. Kim, however, sought national reconciliation, and he quickly pardoned Roh Tae Woo and others for their excesses. However, after he campaigned on a pledge to fight corruption, he has been embarrassed by a number of scandals close to his administration. In January 2002, his brother was arrested on suspicion of receiving bribes, which prompted several ministers to also resign. "I cannot help but feel shock and apologize to the people," Kim said. "I am sorry for corruption involving senior officials and even former and current presidential staff."

The hallmark of Kim's tenure in office was the thaw in relations with North Korea, which still technically remains at war with the South. He launched his vaunted "Sunshine Policy" of constructive engagement with his communist equivalent KIM JONG IL, with whom he met for the first time in June 2000. Their dialogue allowed citizens of the South to hold reunions with northern family members, send mail, even listen to North Korean radio broadcasts. Northerners can also cross the border for similar reasons. Such simple acts were previously outlawed and, given the tortured history of the peninsula, it proved a bold stroke in personal diplomacy. Consequently, in October 2000 Kim received the Nobel Peace Prize.

For all Kim's good intentions, Northeast Asia remains a potential tinderbox. Kim Jong Il continues to supply advanced missiles to despotic regimes around the world and has only stopped production of nuclear weapons so as to receive food shipments from the West. All this changed in the wake of the September 11, 2001, attack on the World Trade Center. President GEORGE W. BUSH proved far less accommodating to dictatorships like North Korea, and he insists upon proof that the regime has abandoned development of missiles and other weapons before aid is released. Furthermore, he denounced North Korea, along with Iraq and Iran, as an "axis of evil," with which the Americans are going to deal with directly. To forestall the possibility of renewed war, Kim conferred with Bush in February 2002, pledging his support for the war against terrorism. He also highlighted the advantage of continuing dialogue with Pyongyang and stated that he hopes to resolve national differences peacefully. In the December 2002 presidential elections Kim lost to ROH MOO HYUN.

Further Reading

Dudley, William. *North and South Korea*. San Diego, Calif.: Greenhaven Press, 2003.

Kang, David C. *Crony Capitalism: Corruption and Development in South Korea and the Philippines*. Cambridge: Cambridge University Press, 2002.

Kim Dae Jung. *A New Beginning: A Collection of Essays*. Los Angeles: Center for Multiethnic Transnational Studies, 1996.

Kim, Samuel S., ed. *Korea's Democratization*. New York: Cambridge University Press, 2003.

Kim, Sunhyuk. *The Politics of Democratization in Korea: The Role of Civil Society*. Pittsburgh, Pa.: University of Pittsburgh Press, 2001.

Moon, Chung-in. "The Kim Dae Jung Government's Peace Policy toward North Korea." *Asian Perspective* 25, no. 2 (2001): 177–198.

Kim Il Sung (1912–1994) *president of* *North Korea*

Kim Sung Ju was born on April 15, 1912, in the village of Pyongan-namdo, Korea, into a peasant family. Korea had since been annexed to the Japanese Empire and was cruelly administered. The ensuing resentment pushed many Koreans into anti-Japanese activities, which triggered even greater oppression in return. Kim was expelled from school, apparently because of his membership in a Communist youth organization, and his family eventually fled to Manchuria in 1925. There Kim completed his education and also joined the Chinese Communist Party. He fought the Japanese as a guerrilla for many years until 1941, when enemy action forced him into the Soviet Union. Though interred, he continued his political education at the Soviet party school in Khabarovsk, and he was allowed to join the Red Army. His service record in World War II is unknown, but, by 1945, he had risen to the rank of major and was assigned to Soviet occupation forces in the Far East. These troops garrisoned the northern half of the Korean Peninsula until 1948, when the North Korean's People's Republic was established. Kim by this time had changed his name to Kim Il Sung, after a noted anti-Japanese guerrilla, and he was installed as premier.

Soviet troops were withdrawn from North Korea in 1948, as were American forces from South Korea. However, Kim came into possession of large numbers of modern tanks and other military equipment, and he spent the two years preparing for what became his lifelong ambition: the forced unification of both Koreas under his command. With the backing of Soviet dictator Joseph Stalin, Kim launched his army southward on June 25, 1950, an act that precipitated the Korean War, 1950–53. His army was nearly successful, but it was finally evicted by U.S. forces acting under a United Nations mandate. Communist Chinese soldiers also intervened, so that by 1953 the war had become stalemated and an armistice was signed that June. Kim's gamble at national unification had failed, and his country was completely devastated by fighting. However, once faced with the daunting prospect of rebuilding his shattered land, he proved surprisingly resolute and resilient. He installed a hard-line Stalinist dictatorship with himself as premier, rounded up and executed all perceived opponents, and began a carefully orchestrated cult of personality around himself. This reached fantastic extremes, and soon the countryside was littered with larger-than-life-size statues of the dictator. He also espoused an indigenous version of socialism that he styled *Juche,* or "self-reliance." This required the long-suffering Korean people to make even greater sacrifices on Kim's behalf, but he quickly transformed North Korea into the world's largest garrison state. By 1972 the national constitution was also revised and he was installed as president. In this capacity, and running as the sole candidate, he was formally "reelected" in 1982, 1986, and 1990.

Kim never abandoned his maniacal obsession to unify Korea, and over the years he engineered a series of international crises to destabilize South Korea. These efforts entailed assassination attempts, airline bombings, armed incidents and infiltration along the demilitarized zone, and capture of the American vessel USS *Pueblo.* Age only honed Kim's craftiness and determination. Despite the yawning rift between the Soviet Union and China, he remained on good terms with both nations, and he played them off against each other when it suited him. Hostilities with South Korea escalated throughout the 1980s, however, and the South Korean navy engaged and sunk several North Korean miniature submarines

crammed with commandos on board. But by the 1990s, the specter of a militant, heavily armed North Korea achieved a new urgency. Kim, in contravention of world opinion and flouting respect for international law, began a dangerous game of nuclear brinkmanship by developing his own atomic weapons. This was followed by a crash program to build nuclear-tipped missiles that could reach as far east as Japan. He undertook these costly and controversial measures at a time when military expenditures already consumed 25 percent of the national budget. Worse, the state-controlled economy and agricultural sector broke down, resulting in widespread famine and death by starvation. But the wily Kim had achieved his goal when the United States, eager to avoid a nuclear showdown, persuaded the North Koreans to abandon their nuclear projects in return for food and other forms of aid. Thus it fell to Kim's bitter ideological enemy to help sustain his regime.

Kim died in Pyongyang on July 8, 1994, one of the most brutal and repressive dictators of the 20th century. And, despite the winds of change sweeping through Eastern Europe, Russia, and even China, North Korea remains entombed as the world's sole surviving Stalinist state. Even in death, Kim broke all the political conventions associated with Marxism by nominating his son, KIM JONG IL, to succeed him. North Korea thus became the first Communist country to be ruled by a family dynasty.

Further Reading

Hunter, Helen L. *Kim Il Song's North Korea.* Westport, Conn.: Praeger, 1999.

Lanksov, A. N. *From Stalin to Kim Il Sung: The Formation of North Korea, 1945–1960.* New Brunswick, N.J.: Rutgers University Press, 2002.

Lee, Hy-sang. *North Korea: A Strange Socialist Fortress.* Westport, Conn.: Praeger, 2000.

Seiler, Sydney. *Kim Il-Song, 1941–1948: The Creation of a Legend, the Building of a Regime.* Lanham, Md.: University Press of America, 1994.

Suh, Dae-sook. *Kim Il Sung: The North Korean Leader.* New York: Columbia University Press, 1995.

Kim Jong Il (1943–) *National Defense Commission chairman of North Korea*

Kim Jong Il was born in a Soviet camp near Khaborovsk, Siberia, on February 15, 1942. His father, KIM IL SUNG, was a leading guerrilla who fought with the forces resisting Japanese occupation of his country. Korea had been absorbed into the Japanese Empire in the early 20th century, and it was cruelly administered. The younger Kim spent his early days as a refugee and after World War II was educated at various schools in Pyongyang and China. In 1948 Kim Il Sung was installed as North Korea's communist dictator, backed by Soviet troops. In 1950 he led an ill-fated invasion of South Korea, then an American sphere of influence, precipitating the Korean War, 1950–53. The conflict ended in stalemate three years later along the 48th Parallel, and the two halves of this beleaguered nation still remain technically at war.

As the son of North Korea's leader, Kim was well educated and carefully indoctrinated into the cult of personality surrounding his father. He graduated from Kim Il Sung University in 1960, with degrees in political science and economics, and he also attended aviation school in East Germany. Kim then commenced a long but successful climb up the party hierarchy. He was initially employed with the Department of Organization and Guidance of the Central Committee of the Korean Worker's Party, and, in this office, he directed numerous plays and films glorifying his father's rule. His tendency for quixotic behavior was never more apparent than in 1973, when he orchestrated the kidnapping of his favorite South Korean actress and her film producer husband. They were transported to Pyongyang as "guests" and forced to make Communist Party propaganda films until escaping in 1986. Kim, meanwhile, continued acquiring a national reputation and, after 1980, when he became leader of the Communist Party's central committee, his portraits were publicly displayed alongside his father's. Just as Kim Il Sung was hailed as the "Great Leader," the son became popularly—and officially— known as the "Dear Leader." To further cement this state deification, their birthdays were also heralded as national holidays. But despite a reclusive nature, the younger Kim wielded great influence with state security forces, and he has been linked to several terrorist acts directed against South Korea. The most notorious of these were the 1983 bombing of a South Korean delegation in Burma, which killed 17 people, and the 1987 downing of a Korean Airlines plane, with the loss of 115 passengers and crew.

On July 8, 1994, Kim Il Sung died and was succeeded by his son. Thus North Korea became the first Communist-led regime to embrace a family dynasty. He also inherited the world's last-surviving Stalinist dicta-

torship, and a nation skirting the edge of catastrophe. The collapse of the Soviet Union and the Warsaw Pact after 1991 left the country marooned without sponsors to bail out its notoriously inefficient economy. Collectivized agrarian communes again failed to produce sufficient food and, compounding these hardships, the country sustained several years of serious flooding. The ensuing food shortages led to the deaths of several thousand people while an entire generation of children endured malnutrition. Given North Korea's intense xenophobia and diplomatic isolation, the country had almost no leverage in appealing for global assistance beyond blackmail. During the early 1990s the elder Kim initiated a military arms buildup, including construction of long-range missiles that threatened to destabilize the entire region. North Korea also acquired a nuclear reactor and was taking steps to develop its own nuclear arsenal. The United States, Japan, and South Korea, anxious to deter development of such technology and, with it,

Kim Jong Il *(Getty Images)*

the possibility of war, offered food and financial assistance in exchange for a halt to production. Kim Jong Il had little recourse but to continue with these coercive policies, which, in effect, kept his supposed enemies at bay—while encouraging them to prop up his ailing regime.

Fortunately, the election of South Korea's KIM DAE JUNG in 1997 led to a period of fence mending between the two regions. The two Kims met for the first time in 1998 and signed accords allowing for limited freedom of movement across their heavily armed border. The U.S. government had previously encouraged such detente to diffuse tensions on the peninsula, but such accommodation ended with the September 11, 2001, destruction of New York's World Trade Center. President GEORGE W. BUSH, angered by Kim Jong Il's willingness to export missiles and other advanced military technology abroad to other rogue regimes, summarily ceased all foreign aid until international inspectors are allowed in the country. Furthermore, in January 2002 he denounced North Korea, Iraq, and Iran as an "axis of evil," and he warned them against acquiring weapons of mass destruction. Bush intimated that failure to comply meant that the Americans might eliminate these regimes in order to preempt any chance of another terrorist attack. Kim, meanwhile, celebrated his 59th birthday the following month amid carefully orchestrated celebrations. The Worker's Party, the cabinet, and military leaders thereupon "evinced their pledge to become absolute adherents and implementers of Kim Jong Il's ideas and politics and hold him in high esteem with loyalty, having ardent worship of him." North Korea remains the most repressive, dangerous, and unpredictable dictatorship in the world. Kim Jong Il, the "Dear Leader," is also among the most enigmatic despots in modern world history, whose epitaph may yet be written in blood.

Further Reading

Akaha, Tsuneo. *The Future of North Korea.* London: Routledge, 2001.

Cha, Victor D. "Korea's Place in the Axis." *Foreign Affairs* 81 (March–June, 2002): 79–92.

Dudley, William. *North and South Korea.* San Diego, Calif.: Greenhaven Press, 2003.

Jeon, Jei Guk. "North Korean Leadership" Kim Jong Il's Balancing Act in the Ruling Circle." *Third World Quarterly* 21 (October 2000): 761–780.

Lee, Han S. *North Korea: The Politics of Unconventional Wisdom.* Boulder, Colo.: Lynne Rienner Publishers, 2002.

Oh, Kong Dan. *Korea Briefing, 1997–1999: Challenges and Changes at the Turn of the Century.* Armonk, N.Y.: M. E. Sharpe, 2000.

Park, Hy-Sang. *North Korea: A Strange Socialist Fortress.* Westport, Conn.: Praeger, 2001.

Kim Young Sam (1927–) *president of South Korea*

Kim Young Sam was born on December 20, 1927, in Koje-gun, South Kyongsang province, Korea, the son of a wealthy fisherman. His homeland then formed part of the Japanese Empire, and it was cruelly occupied. Korea was subsequently freed after World War II, although it remained divided between the American-administered south and the Communist-controlled north. Kim performed well in local schools, so he enrolled at the prestigious Seoul National University in 1950. However, within months North Korean forces attacked South Korea, precipitating the Korean War, 1950–53, and Kim spent several months working as secretary to President Syngman Rhee. After the war he acquired a bachelor's degree in philosophy and began his political career in 1954 by winning a seat in the National Assembly from Pusan. As an indication of his local popularity, Kim was consecutively reelected up through 1979. He was then the youngest member of the Korean government and quickly established himself as an outspoken dissident. Originally a member of the Liberal Party, Kim quit in 1960 after President Rhee tried modifying the constitution to prolong his term in office, and he joined the Democratic Party. South Korea then reverted to a military dictatorship over the next three decades, and Kim waxed outspokenly in his denunciation. He was forcibly removed from the legislature in 1979 by General Chun Doo Hwan, an act that triggered national protests and riots, but was forbidden from participating in politics. Nevertheless, Kim operated with other dissidents behind the scene and helped found the New Korean Democratic Party (NKDP). He partly accomplished this by staging a widely covered 23-day hunger strike that led to his release, and the ban on political activity was lifted. He also remained strident in his calls for the liberalization and democratization of South Korea.

In 1987 Kim ran for the presidency as head of the NKDP, although he lost to General ROH TAE WOO when opposition forces failed to unite and split the vote three ways. By 1992, the various parties had mended their differences and coalesced under a new organization, the Democratic Liberal Party (DLP), with Kim at their head. In this capacity he ran for the presidency of South Korea on December 18, 1992, and he won, defeating KIM DAE JUNG and Chung Ju Yung by 42 percent of votes cast. Kim's victory was important; it marked the first time in three decades that power was finally transferred to a civilian leader. And, after 40 years as a leading dissident, he declared with much justification: "Democracy comes to Korea just as surely as the dawn brings the morning."

Previously, Kim campaigned upon a strict reformist agenda, intending to end political corruption facilitated by the traditional relationships between politicians with *chaebol,* large national conglomerates. As such he instituted drastic and badly needed reforms of the political system. Kim ordered all ranking civil servants to reveal the extent of their personal fortunes, and he also clamped down on the underground economy by banning anonymous financial transactions. By mid-1993 over 1,000 ranking bureaucrats and politicians where either fired or forced into retirement. Kim, mindful of Korea's recent past, also purged the military of high-ranking, politically minded senior officers. To that end, he placed both Chun Doo Hwan and ROH TAE WOO on trial for corruption and treason charges. He also took careful, deliberate steps to commence a rapprochement with aging North Korean dictator KIM IL SUNG. All these contributed to an early approval rating of nearly 90 percent—unprecedented for a Korean leader.

Kim's undoing, however, proved to be the economy. Due to high-level mismanagement and insider machinations, the national debt soared upward to $150 billion, which drove interest rates up and strangled business. Thus Korea, previously one of Asia's "Four Tigers," slid dangerously toward insolvency. In 1997 all of Asia was rocked by the currency crisis, which nearly brought all regional economic growth to a halt. Kim scrambled to get the economy back on track, but, in October 1997, it was revealed that he had accepted campaign money from the giant Hanbo conglomerate, the very form of graft he had railed against. Corruption proved to have very long tentacles, and in May 1998 the president's son, Kim Hyun Chul, was also arrested, charged with tax evasion and acceptance of bribes. The growing sense of corruption, which underscored the nation's mounting economic malaise, severely undercut Kim's ability to deal with pressing national issues. "I am wholly responsible for the foreign currency crisis," he confessed.

Fortunately for Kim, the Korean constitution forbids presidents from seeking a second term in office, so he stepped down, and the 1998 elections were won by his reformist competitor KIM DAE JUNG. His defeat is significant, as it marked the first peaceful transfer of power from one civilian to another. Kim has since been reviled for his inability to revitalize Korea's economy and for having engaged in scandals. However, his reforms made possible the transition from authoritarianism to democracy, which has since expanded and consolidated its hold upon South Korea.

Further Reading

Cotton, James, ed. *Politics and Policy in the New Korean State: From Roh Tae Woo to Kim Young Sam.* New York: St. Martin's Press, 1995.

Hahm, Sung Duek, and Kwang Woong Kim. "Institutional Reforms and Democratization in Korea: The Case of the Kim Young Sam Administration." *Governance* 12, no. 4 (1999): 479–495.

Kil, J. "The Kim Young Sam Government's Unification Policy: Phase Two." *Korea and World Affairs* 18 (Fall 1994): 473–485.

Yang, Jae-jin. "The 1999 Pension Reform and a New Social Contract in South Korea." Unpublished Ph.D. dissertation, Rutgers University, 2001.

Yoon, S. "South Korea's Kim Young Sam: Government Political Agendas." *Asian Survey* 36 (May 1996): 511–522.

Kiriyenko, Sergei (1963–) *prime minister of Russia*

Sergei Maksimovich Kiriyenko was born on July 26, 1963, in Sukhumi, Georgia, the son of a Jewish father and a Ukrainian mother. His family then relocated to Gorky (now Nizhny Novgorod), about 250 miles east of Moscow, where he attended the Institute of Water Transport Engineering. Eager to enhance career and political prospects, Kiriyenko joined the Komsomol (Communist Youth League) while employed at the Krasnoye Sormovo shipyard as a foreman and youth leader. However, he gradually evinced interest in banking and in 1991 Kiriyenko gained admission to the Academy of National Economy, just prior to the Soviet Union's collapse. He witnessed firsthand the folly of the old command-economy system and eagerly embraced free-market approaches to Russia's economic dilemma. In January 1994 Kiriyenko and several associates founded Bank Garantiya, a private institution created for selling off vast government-owned assets to the private sector. Mindful of the social dislocation such transitions occasion, the bank also siphoned off part of its profit to assist local pension funds. Kiriyenko acquired a reputation as an excellent businessman, and he rose to become head of Norsi, a large petroleum refinery in Nizhny Novgorod. It was while acting in this capacity that he came to the attention of Boris Nemtsov, the radical governor of the Nizhegorodskaya region, who was himself devoted to an expanding free market. The two men struck up an abiding relationship, and when Nemtsov was appointed minister of fuel and energy by President BORIS YELTSIN in May 1997, Kiriyenko accompanied him to Moscow as his deputy minister.

No one could have predicted what happened next. Kiriyenko served with his customary efficiency and in November 1997 he supplanted Nemtsov as minister of fuel and energy. As such he became closely identified with a political group known as the "Young Reformers." However, by 1998 the national economy was in such dire straits that President Yeltsin scrambled for a dramatic gesture to assure the long-suffering Russian people that he was striving for reform. On March 23, 1998, he inexplicably fired his entire cabinet, including Prime Minister VIKTOR CHERNOMYRDIN, a cautious but consistent reformer. Kiriyenko, the 34-year-old political neophyte, then suddenly found himself thrust upon the national stage as the new first deputy prime minister. The move was roundly criticized; many politicians viewed the young man as lacking experience. Indeed, if he were confirmed by the lower house of parliament (the Duma), he would be next in line to succeed the ailing Yeltsin. Communists in the Duma pointed to the nomination as proof of the president's declining powers of judgment. Yeltsin, however, stuck by his choice. When the Duma twice rejected Kiriyenko because of his inexperience and blind faith in market reforms, the president nominated him once again. This set the stage for a political showdown: under the Russian constitution, if the Duma rejects an executive appointment three times, the

legislature is then dissolved and new elections held. Rather than risk losing control, the Communists and their allies finally relented on a secret ballot and, on April 24, 1998, Kiriyenko became the youngest-ever prime minister of Russia. "Today's vote clearly shows that none of us needs great upheavals," the young man exulted, "and we all need a great Russia." It was widely hope that the young reformer could revitalize this moribund situation.

Unfortunately, Kiriyenko inherited a nation on the brink of economic collapse. State employees had not been paid for many months, and striking workers in the strategic coal industry only increased the nation's discomfiture. The young leader was expected to initiate new budget cuts and monetary reforms to jumpstart the ailing economy and put money back in people's hands. By June 1998 Kiriyenko had submitted a 25-point plan to overhaul the creaking tax collection system and other long-standing malaises. But the situation had become so critical that by August the government announced a 90-day moratorium on debt repayments to Western creditors. "The financial market has practically ceased to exist," Kiriyenko told legislators. "Social tension is growing in society, which naturally is not helpful to stabilization." On August 23, 1998, Yeltsin again surprised onlookers by dismissing his entire cabinet, including Kiriyenko. When Chernomyrdin failed to gain reappointment as prime minister from the Duma, he was replaced by Yevgeny Primakov. Kiriyenko's tenure in high office, five months, is the shortest in Russian history.

Since leaving Moscow, Kiriyenko has served the administration of VLADIMIR PUTIN as presidential envoy to the Volga Federal District, and he also chairs the Russian State Committee on the Destruction of Chemical Weapons. In June 2002 he visited Germany to confer with his NATO counterparts, and he pressed for addition funding to cleanup ex-Soviet chemical dumps. "The weapons are being kept in metal containers that are rusting," he warned. "That is why, as experts say, there remain 10–12 years to dispose of chemical weapons." Once Kiriyenko has acquired greater national exposure at home and international recognition abroad, perhaps he will assume high office again.

Further Reading

Aslund, Anders. *Building Capitalism: The Transformation of the Soviet Bloc.* New York: Cambridge University Press, 2002.

Isham, Heyward. *Russia's Fate through Russia's Eyes: Voices of a New Generation.* Boulder, Colo.: Westview Press, 2001.

Goldman, Marshall I. *Lost Opportunity: Why Economic Reforms in Russia Have Not Worked.* New York: W. W. Norton, 1994.

Novikova, Nina. "Political Order and Economic Change: The Impact of Political Decisions on Economic Reforms in the Transition to a Market Economy in Russia." Unpublished master's thesis, Johns Hopkins University, 1993.

Simes, Dimitri K. "Russia's Crisis, America's Complicity." *National Interest* 54 (Winter 1998–1999): 12–22.

Skidelsky, Robert J. *Russia's Stormy Path to Reform.* London: Social Market Foundation, 1995.

Klaus, Václav (1941–   ) *prime minister of the Czech Republic*

Václav Klaus was born on June 19, 1941, in Prague, Czechoslovakia, the son of an economist. He studied economics and international trade at the Prague School of Economics, graduating in 1963. After working several years at the Ministry of Finance, Klaus ventured abroad to pursue graduate work in Italy and the United States. In 1969 he studied six months at Cornell University, New York, where he became a disciple of Milton Friedman's economics of free trade. He returned home to a nation that had been invaded by Soviet troops and was now saddled by a government espousing strict Communist Party orthodoxy. Klaus, outspoken and abrasive in his defense of free markets and clearly out of synch with authorities, was fired from the Ministry of Finance and sent to work at the Czechoslovak National Bank. He remained so employed until 1989, when he joined the newly formed Civic Forum of noted dissident playwright VÁCLAV HAVEL. This broad-based coalition began agitating for an end to communism in Eastern Europe and precipitated the so-called Velvet Revolution, which peacefully brought down the regime of Gustav Husack. Havel was installed as president and Klaus, in recognition of his economic expertise, gained appointment as Czechoslovakia's first non-communist finance minister in 40 years.

Once in office, Klaus began pressing hard for a complete transformation of Czechoslovakia from a socialist command economy to one based entirely upon free-market principles. This entailed selling off state-owned industries in the interest of privatization. He was also determined to return to their previous owners over 100,000 properties and businesses confiscated by the Communists. His plan was approved by the parliament in March 1991, but the stridency with which he pursued it put Klaus on a collision course with Havel, who favored a less radical, more gradual approach to transition. This fissure, which gradually assumed the dimensions of a personal feud between the two men, culminated with the splitting of Civic Forum into a new group, the conservatively minded Civic Democratic Party (CDP). Klaus became party chairman and, in this capacity, he advanced to deputy prime minister of Czechoslovakia in October 1991. By June 1992, national elections gave the CDP a parliamentary majority and Klaus was installed as prime minister. He governed at the head of a four-party center-right coalition that would completely dominate national politics for the next five years.

One of the first items on Klaus's agenda was the breakup of Czechoslovakia into two sovereign entities, the Czech Republic and Slovakia. President Havel denounced the move as divisive and premature, but the "Velvet Divorce" went smoothly on January 1, 1993. In fact it remains one of the few peaceful dissolutions of a state in recent European history. For the next four years, Klaus went on to orchestrate the "Czech miracle," whereby the national economy soared faster and further ahead than any of its Central European neighbors. The prime minister also determined to reorient his country toward Western Europe and sought full integration into the European Union (EU). But, ever the free trader, he railed continually about incessant bureaucracy and controls upon free markets, and he advocated a "velvet revolution in Brussels" to curtail the EU's trend toward centralization. "Entering the European Union is a problem for us," he stated, "because we are importing more regulation, more controls, more licensing, more interventionism." The country is slated to be up for entry in 2004. But by June 1996 the Czech economy began slowing down and the CDP lost ground to Havel's Social Democratic Party (SDP). Klaus nevertheless withstood the backlash and assembled a minority coalition to continue as prime minister. But clearly the magic was gone.

The next two years were unproductive for Klaus, now a lame-duck prime minister beset by a worsening economy and declining standards of living. In November 1997 he resigned from office in the wake of a party financing scandal and was succeeded by MILOŠ ZEMAN of the SDP. Klaus still retained a measure of national popularity and arranged for Zeman to lead the country while he became parliamentary speaker and head of the opposition. Caustic and outspoken as ever, he excelled in that role and, during the June 2002 national elections, Klaus remained a viable contender for high office. However, the Czech voters saw otherwise, and they returned the Social Democrats to power with 30 percent of the vote. The new prime minister was Vladimir Spidla, a dour 51-year-old historian with none of his opponent's panache for controversy. How much this loss reflects the unpopularity of free-market economics, or simply discontent over Klaus's abrasive style of leadership, is unknown.

Further Reading

Eyal, Gil. *The Origins of Postcommunist Elites: From Prague Spring to the Breakup of Czechoslovakia.* Minneapolis: University of Minnesota, 2003.

Klaus, Vaclav. *Liberty and the Rule of Law.* Washington, D.C.: The Heritage Foundation, 1999.

———. *Renaissance: The Rebirth of Liberty in the Heart of Europe.* Washington, D.C.: Cato Foundation, 1997.

Saxonberg, Steven. "Vaclav Klaus: The Rise and Fall and Re-emergence of a Charismatic Leader." *Eastern European Politics and Societies* 13 (Spring 1999): 391–419.

Stegmaier, Mary Ann. "Voting Behavior during Economic and Political Transitions: The Last of Post-communist East Central Europe." Unpublished Ph.D. dissertation, University of Iowa, 2001.

Stein, Eric. *Czecho/Slovakia: Ethnic Conflict, Constitutional Fissure, Negotiated Breakup.* Ann Arbor: University of Michigan Press, 2001.

Klestil, Thomas (1932–) *president of Austria*

Thomas Klestil was born on November 4, 1932, in Vienna, Austria. He was raised in poverty with four other siblings, but he managed to attend the University of Vienna. In 1957 he obtained his doctorate in economics and worked for the Department of Economic Coordination two years later. Fluent in English, he took a post with the Austrian embassy in Washington, D.C., in 1962, remaining there four years. After a stint working as secretary to Chancellor Josef Klaus back in Vienna,

Klestil settled down in Los Angeles in 1969 to found the Austrian consulate there. He came home in 1974 and spent the next four years bringing various United Nations organizations into Vienna. Klestil next served as Austria's ambassador to the UN from 1978 to 1982, and then as ambassador to the United States, 1982 to 1987. He finally returned home for good in 1987, a career diplomat with an outstanding resumé and record of success. Although Klestil had never entertained political ambitions, in 1992 friends prevailed upon him to run for the presidency as the conservative People's Party (OVP) candidate. In 1983 Austria's reputation was sullied by revelations about President Kurt Waldheim's World War II service record and Klestil, a highly respected diplomat, strongly condemned Austria's Nazismitten past. His message of contrition resonated with voters, and, in July 1992, he was elected by 56.9 percent of the vote, the largest tally ever posted by a presidential candidate.

The Austrian presidency is largely a ceremonial post used to promote national unity, but Klestil transformed it into an activist ambassadorship-at-large. He was highly visible on the international scene, represented Austrian interests abroad, and argued for greater integration of Eastern European countries. He also strongly pushed for Austria's inclusion into the European Union, even at the expense of its traditional neutrality. Taking the process a step further, he openly advocated membership in the NATO military alliance to complete the integration process. He met constantly with European counterparts, traveling as far away as China and Iran to promote goodwill and trade. One of his most moving acts was appearing before the Israeli Knesset and formally apologizing for Austria's role in the Holocaust. "We Austrians are enthusiastic Europeans and will remain so," he declared. "There is a firm commitment of Austrians to never again be seduced by nationalism and extremism." Klestil's fellow citizens were apparently pleased with his performance, and, in July 1998, he was easily reelected with 63.5 percent of votes cast, the highest total ever.

Klestil's skill at promoting diplomatic harmony was never more strongly tested than in the wake of the 1999 national elections. That fall the far-right Freedom Party gained enough seats to warrant inclusion in a coalition government. However, JÖRG HAIDER, a right-wing extremist spouting pro-Nazi sentiments, was regarded as a pariah by the rest of Europe. Many heads of state within the EU threatened Austria with sanctions if Haider and his Freedom Party joined the government. By February 2000 talks with the opposition Social Democrats had broken down, and Chancellor WOLFGANG SCHUESSEL had no recourse but to unite with Haider to stay in power. This move sparked waves of protests across Europe, and many nations, including the United States, withdrew their ambassadors. Klestil, meanwhile, assumed the diplomatic offensive, reassuring leaders that Haider's role was minimal and that punitive sanctions were arbitrary and unfair. "In my opinion a procedure at the community level would be preferable because the accused member would be given an opportunity to respond to fears before any measures were taken against this member," he reasoned. "It should also be in the interests of the European Union to develop such a mechanism as soon as possible to find a way out of the present situation." Fortunately, calmer heads prevailed and by the fall of 2000 all EU reprisals against Austria had been lifted.

Klestil continues as one of Austria's most popular and effective national figures. Ever mindful of past excesses, on New Year's Day 2001 he reminded his fellow citizens that Austria's political establishment should work together for the common good and not regard people with opposing viewpoints as enemies. He also refocused his energies upon a personal priority—expansion of the EU toward the East and strengthening ties with the young democracies found there. In April 2002 the energetic president met with his Macedonian counterpart, BORIS TRAJKOVSKI, to confer about improving relations with southeastern European countries. "Austria is committed for inclusion of new states in the EU," he insisted, "especially states from the Balkans." Through all these expedients, Klestil has successfully restored Austria's image at home and abroad. The tenure of this exceptionally gifted diplomat is due to expire in July 2004.

Further Reading

Bischof, Gunter, Anton Pelinka, and Ruth Wodak. *Neutrality in Austria.* New Brunswick, N.J.: Transaction Publishers, 2001.

Bischof, Gunter, Anton Pelinka, and Michael Gehler. *Austria in the European Union.* New Brunswick, N.J.: Transaction Publishers, 2002.

Heinisch, Reinhard. *Populism, Proporz, Pariah: Austria Turns Right: Austrian Political Change, Its Causes and Repercussions.* New York: Nova Science, 2002.

Steininger, Gunter B., and Michael Gehler, eds. *Austria in the Twentieth Century.* New Brunswick, N.J.: Transaction Publishers, 2002.

Thaler, Peter. *The Ambivalence of Identity: The Austrian Experience of Nation-Building in a Modern Society.* West Lafayette, Ind.: Purdue University Press, 2001.

Klima, Viktor (1947–) *chancellor of Austria*

Viktor Klima was born on June 4, 1947 in Vienna, Austria, into a family strongly tied to Austrian socialism. He carried many of these political values over to college, where he studied business and computer science at the Vienna Technical Institute and the University of Vienna. There he joined the Social Democratic Party in 1966 and was also active in its youth division. After graduating Klima found employment as an economist with the Austrian Mineral Oil Administration (OMV), where he remained two decades. He started out as a consultant and business manager and ended up as head of the company's personnel office and board of governors by 1990. However, his close links with the Social Democrats held him in good stead when Chancellor FRANZ VRANITZKY appointed him minister of transport and state industry in April 1992. In this capacity Klima became the point man for large scale privatization of many state-run businesses, and he was an outspoken proponent of private enterprise. He remained so situated until January 1996 when Vranitzky shuffled his cabinet and Klima became finance minister. He performed useful work in bringing the nation's monetary and fiscal policies in line with admission to the European Monetary Union—the adoption of a single currency that would eliminate monetary borders. Klima was also charged with hammering out a budget with the SDP's coalition partners, the conservative People's Party (OVP, or Christian Democrats), which was successfully accomplished. In this manner Klima oversaw cuts in government expenditures and social services consistent with Austrian membership within the European Union (EU). However, neither he nor Vranitzky had much success reforming the Austrian banking industry, which is deeply rooted in government control. When Vranitzky failed to merge the two largest national banks into a single entity, he suddenly resigned and Klima succeeded him on January 28, 1997. He was generally viewed as more charismatic, energetic, and tougher in negotiating than his veteran mentor.

Klima assumed power during a period of national uncertainty for Austria. The country had embraced a strict neutral foreign policy ever since it reacquired independence from Soviet occupation in 1955. However, with the end of the cold war in 1991, political pressure was growing for Austria to reach out and fully integrate itself within the Western European economy. Klima did not dispute this trend. He saw it as inevitable, and Austria formally joined the European Union in 1995. But he thereafter declined to join the NATO military alliance, preferring to keep the country compliant with its traditional neutrality. "Austria will not become a member of any military bloc," he cautioned.

However, Klima's biggest political challenge was on the domestic front. For several years the ultra-right nationalist Freedom Party of JÖRG HAIDER had made consistent inroads and was garnering more and more of the popular vote. In 1996 they acquired 28 percent of the votes cast, and Haider's repeated warnings about EU dominance and the flood of immigrants it would bring resonated effectively among working-class Austrians. Klima thus became obliged to renegotiate his coalition with the conservative People's Party to maintain his SDP-OVP coalition in power. Moreover, he excoriated the Freedom Party for its thinly veiled admiration of Nazism, and he characterized it as a "party which is always against something but never actually for anything, which plays on fears, seeks out scapegoats, and has a sloppy relationship to the issue of national socialism." By 1998 Klima was forced to shoulder additional burdens as president of the EU for six months. Again, he performed with his usual dash and reiterated his determination to lead Austria down the path of enhanced international trade and greater political transparency. But, like Vranitzky before him, he remained bedeviled with deregulation of banking and other industries, whose compliance proved sullen at best.

Despite his best efforts, Klima could not forestall the continuing popularity of Haider's Freedom Party. Elections held in October 1999 bore this out when the SDP and the Freedom Party gained the majority of votes at the expense of the OVP. This forced Klima into the predicament of forming a coalition with Haider to stay in power. He blanched at the prospect, however, and refused. It then fell upon President THOMAS KLESTIL to form an OVP/FP coalition under Vice Chancellor WOLFGANG SCHUESSEL, and Klima resigned from power on February 4, 2000. Thereafter he quit politics altogether and sought employment in the corporate world. In July 2000 Klima joined the German auto-manufacturing firm Volkswagen as head of their Argentine operations. He accepted this post despite the fact he does not speak Spanish, and he was coached in it by his daughter-in-law, a Spaniard. "I didn't want to do what other retired politicians do; find cushy advisory jobs," Klima insisted. "It's going to be a fascinating challenge. I am the first former prime minister to go into the auto industry."

Further Reading

Bischof, Gunter, and Anton Pelinka. *Austria in the European Union.* New Brunswick, N.J.: Transaction Publishers, 2002.

Guttamn, Robert J. "Viktor Klima." *Europe* 378 (July–August 1998): 11–14.

Heinisch, Reinhard. *Populism, Proporz, Pariah: Austria Turns Right: Austrian Political Change, Its Causes and Repercussions.* New York: Nova Science, 2002.

Thaler, Peter. *The Ambivalence of Identity: The Austrian Experience of Nation-Building in a Modern Society.* West Lafayette, Ind.: Purdue University Press, 2001.

Thornton, Robert J. *Austria and Switzerland at the Crossroads.* Bethlehem, Pa.: Martindale Center for the Study of Private Enterprise, 2000.

Kocharyan, Robert (1954–) *president of Armenia*

Robert Setrakovich Kocharyan was born in Nagorno Karabakh, then part of Azerbaijan, on August 23, 1954. This Armenian-dominated region was also a republic within the greater Soviet Union. He attended the Yerevan Polytechnical Institute in 1981, eventually obtaining degrees in electrical engineering. Kocharyan, eager to advance his career prospects, also joined the Communist Party. He quit two years later to join the Karabach Committee of Nagorno Karabakh, dedicated to freeing it from Azerbaijan control. In this capacity he organized paramilitary forces and commenced military action against Azeri troops. His actions were greatly abetted by the collapse of the Soviet Union in August 1991, whereby Armenia and Azerbaijan both declared their political independence. In August 1992 Azeri forces mounted a full-scale offensive in order to keep Nagorno Karabakh, but Kocharyan successfully countered it. At length Armenian forces occupied the disputed region, comprising 20 percent of Azerbaijan's territory, before a cease-fire was reached. Kocharyan consequently emerged as a national war hero, and he gained election to the Supreme Council in Armenia, a nation to which he technically never belonged. In 1996 the grateful residents of Nagorno Karabakh also elected him president of their tiny republic.

In 1997 Kocharyan's immense popularity resulted in President Levon Ter-Petrosyan appointing him prime minister of Armenia. For many months he toiled incessantly, assisting areas flattened by the devastating 1988 earthquake, encouraging tax reform, and fighting political corruption. However, the unresolved fate of Nagorno Karabakh remained a sensitive national issue, with many calls for complete annexation. Ter-Petrosyan learned this the hard way when he sponsored a European peace plan that mandated withdrawing from the disputed region and further negotiations. Demands for the president's resignation then resounded through the national legislature, with Kocharyan leading the charge. The political turmoil induced Ter-Petrosyan to resign on February 3, 1998, and he was immediately replaced by the hero of Nagorno Karabakh. Seeking the stamp of legitimacy to his office, Kocharyan called for new elections, scheduled for later that spring, and he ran against three well-established candidates. Not surprisingly, on April 9, 1998, Kocharyan coasted to an easy victory over former Communist Party boss Karen Demirchyan. He thus became the second freely elected president in Armenian history.

Besides his wartime reputation, Kocharyan won on a campaign promising to completely overhaul the economy and bureaucracy, which retained the heavy-handed sluggishness of their recent Communist past. He pledged to embark on free-market reforms, privatization of state-owned industries, and introduction of small business loans to encourage creation of new industries and jobs. An ardent nationalist, Kocharyan also called for closer ties with the global Armenian diaspora, and he promoted a system of dual citizenship. Finally, he called for creation and maintenance of a strong, well-disciplined military to preserve Armenia's security and independence. Armenians everywhere harbor vivid memories of Turkish atrocities in the early 20th century and are determined never to let it happen again. For this reason, while Kocharyan curries close diplomatic ties with Georgia, Iran, and other Islamic republics, he wants Turkey to admit responsibility for the deaths of 1.5 million Armenians. This is a precondition

of better relations; however, to date, the Turks have yet to comply.

Despite marked improvement in Armenia's economic picture, the country still suffered from political instability. On October 27, 1999, the legislature was attacked by gunmen who killed several high-ranking government ministers. Continuing unrest led to a legislative attempt to impeach Kocharyan in April 2000, whereupon the enraged president dismissed his prime minister and defense minister. In a televised address to the nation, Kocharyan explained: "Political games have become a way of life within the executive, while at the same time the economic problems are snowballing." Having sacked his leading political adversaries, Kocharyan has since enjoyed relative political stability and, with it, heightened popularity. He remains highly regarded as a smart, tough national figurehead.

The most elusive goal in Kocharyan's agenda is a final settlement of the Nagarno Karabakh question. He wants independence for the disputed region, and, he seeks broad international consensus in doing so. Consequently, in April 2001, both Kocharyan and Azeri president HEYDAR ALIYEV met in Key West, Florida, to negotiate possible solutions. The talks, brokered by France, Russia, and the United States, held high hopes for success, but as yet they remain deadlocked. Aliyev wants the region returned to Azerbaijan in exchange for more autonomy, but Kocharyan adamantly refuses to compromise. However, both sides are tantalized by the prospect of up to $1 billion in regional aid should a peace treaty be signed, so future negotiations are scheduled. Curiously, the two leaders have conferred on the subject more than 15 times without result.

Further Reading

Astourian, Stephen H. *From Ter-Petrosian to Kocharian: Leadership Change in Armenia.* Berkeley: University of California Press, 2000.

Bremmer, Ian, and Cory Welt. "Armenia's New Aristocrats." *Journal of Democracy* 8 (July 1997): 77–92.

Libaridian, Gerard J. *The Challenge of Statehood: Armenian Political Thinking since Independence.* Waterford, Mass.: Blue Crane Books, 1999.

Masih, Joseph R., and Robert O. Krikorian. *Armenia at the Crossroads.* Amsterdam: Harwood Academic Publishers, 1999.

Tololyan, Khachig. *Elites and Institutions in the Armenian Transnation.* Oxford: Oxford University Press, 2001.

Kohl, Helmut (1930–) *chancellor of Germany*
Helmut Kohl was born on April 3, 1930, in Lud-
wigshafen, Germany, into a conservative Roman
Catholic household. As a youth he became active in the
Christian Democratic Union (CDU), which was formed
after World War II. During the final stages of World War
II he was drafted into the military and spent several
weeks in a training camp before being discharged. Germany at that time had been conquered by the Allies and
divided into a western section dominated by the United
States and an eastern section controlled by the Soviet
Union. Kohl, fortunate enough to reside in West Germany, studied law at the University of Frankfurt, and in
1958 he obtained his doctorate in history from the University of Heidelberg. He found work in an industrial association while concurrently rising up the hierarchy of
the CDU. In 1959 Kohl first gained election to the
Rhineland-Palatine legislature (his home state), and he
was continually reelected over the next decade. By 1969
Kohl had demonstrated both political and leadership
abilities, and that year he became prime minister of
Rhineland-Palatine. He remained in that post up
through 1975, presided over an efficient government,
and enacted many necessary reforms. Success whetted
his appetite for national politics and, after CDU defeats
in 1969 and 1973 general elections, his party anointed
him their new chairman.

In 1976 Kohl ran as the CDU candidate for chan-
cellor, but he was defeated by long-standing incumbent
Helmut Schmidt of the Social Democratic Party (SPD).
He lost, but only after garnering the highest percentage
of votes that the CDU had received since 1957. He
thereafter served as opposition leader in the Bundestag,
West Germany's lower house, over the next six years.
Kohl's historic chance occurred in October 1982 when
the Free Democrats, who ruled in partnership with the
SDP, suddenly bolted from their coalition. Chancellor
Schmidt therefore received a procedural vote of no confidence, and resigned from office. Kohl was elected in his
place, becoming the youngest chancellor in West Germany's history. Seeking political legitimacy, he then
called for elections in 1983 and won a majority. He
would occupy West Germany's highest office for the next
16 years.

Kohl initially presided over a Germany torn between its commitments to NATO and the West and its
burning desire for reunification with Communist East
Germany. Given the ravaging that the Soviet Union endured at German hands in World War II, this prospect
seemed unlikely. Kohl, however, firmly posited himself
as a loyal NATO ally, and he supported President
Ronald Reagan's politically charged decision to deploy
Pershing II and cruise missiles on German soil to
counter new Soviet missiles. But he also held continuous
talks with Soviet officials over the prospect of eventual
reunification. Furthermore, to placate any fears from
France and other neighboring countries, Kohl always
couched his arguments in the context of integrating Germany deeply into the economic and political fabric of
Western Europe. He was determined to demonstrate
that the new Germany would never again be a threat to
its neighbors.

Kohl was easily reelected chancellor in 1987 and,
two years later, with the rise of Mikhail Gorbachev in
Russia, a new political equation presented itself. Gorbachev was willing to entertain the notion of a unified
Germany, with certain safeguards. However, following
the 1989 collapse of communism in the Eastern Europe,
events took on a life of their own. The Berlin Wall, the
hated symbol dividing East and West Germany, was suddenly torn down by the people, and Kohl hastily assured
the Russians that there was no danger. A panicky Gorbachev then phoned the chancellor and demanded to
know if the disorder threatened Russian personnel with
violence. Kohl assured him it did not and, consequently,
Russian tanks did not intervene. "Therefore it was really
a stroke of luck," he maintained years later, "and I am
grateful to Gorbachev in particular for this, that he believed us, especially me, and not the KGB." Thereafter,
when the Soviet Union began transporting its troops out
of East Germany, the West German government provided money and logistical support to assist. He also
prevailed upon Gorbachev to accept that a reunited Germany would remain a member of NATO, as a further
safeguard against territorial ambitions. On October 3,
1990, Germany was formally reunited and held elections
as a single nation for the first time in over 40 years. Kohl
and the CDU were easily returned to power, whereupon
he focused his attention upon defining Germany's role in
a new Europe devoid of cold war divisions.

In addition to German unification, Kohl also
strongly advocated greater European integration. For
many years he championed the Maastricht Treaty,
signed in 1991, which would integrate national
economies through use of a single currency, the euro.
Germany, as Europe's biggest and most robust economy,

was well positioned to serve as the "engine of prosperity" and pull the others along. In 1995 he also became the first leader since 1945 to deploy troops outside of Germany, when several hundred were dispatched to Bosnia to serve as peacekeepers. This action was consistent with Kohl's belief that a unified Germany was obliged to play a greater and more visible role on the international stage. However, reunification with East Germany posed great difficulties, since that country was broke, saddled with obsolete technology, and experiencing high levels of unemployment while transitioning to capitalism. The ensuing economic slump could not be remedied in time for elections held in September 1998, and Kohl was defeated by SDP candidate GERHARD SCHROEDER.

Kohl left office with the enviable reputation as the "unification chancellor," and his historical efficacy seemed secure. In terms of longevity, he was in office longer than any other Germany chancellor save Otto von Bismark (1871–90), and he wielded decisive effects upon the destiny of his nation. However, in 1999 Kohl became embroiled in controversy by defying the law and refusing to name donors of over $1 million in illegal campaign funds. The scandal forced him to resign as head of the CDU, although he retained a seat in parliament. Kohl remained something of a pariah to his party until June 2002, when he made a speech at the CDU convention in Frankfurt, signaling his return to the political arena as an adviser. "We have German unity and now we need more European unity," he said. "The two belong together." He also castigated Chancellor Schroeder for doing nothing to address the nation's unemployment, and he called upon fellow conservatives to rally together and elect Edmund Stoiber the new leader of Germany.

Further Reading

Clemens, Clay. "A Legacy Reassessed: Helmut Kohl and the German Party Finance Affair." *German Politics* 9 (August 2000): 25–50.

———, and William E. Paterson. *The Kohl Chancellorship*. Portland, Oreg.: Frank Cass, 1998.

Helms, Ludger. "Is There Life after Kohl? The CDU Crisis and the Future of Party Democracy in Germany." *Government and Opposition* 35 (Autumn 2000): 419–438.

Honeghan, Tom. *Unchained Eagle: Germany after the Wall.* New York: Pearson Education, 2000.

Prowe, Diethelm, "Kohl and the German Unification Era." *Journal of Modern History* 74 (March 2002): 120–139.

Pulzer, P. "Luck and Good Management: Helmut Kohl as Parliamentarian and Electoral Strategist." *German Politics* 8 (August 1999): 126–140.

Koirala, Girija Prasad (1925–) *prime minister of Nepal*

Girija Prasad Koirala was born in the Indian state of Bihar, on the Nepalese border, in 1925. Nepal is a small, mountainous nation sandwiched between two giants: China and India. Though very scenic in appearance and home to Mount Everest, the world's highest peak, it remains one of the world's most desperately poor nations. Koirala's father was a revolutionary who fought the ruling Rana family, in power in Nepal since 1846, then fled to India to evade arrest. Back home, two of Koirala's elder brothers also helped found the Nepali Congress Party (NCP) in 1950. Koirala himself matured in India and grew politically active while campaigning for Indian independence from Great Britain in 1947. Three years later he returned to Nepal and participated in the revolution of 1950, which finally overthrew the Ranas and installed the Tribhuvan line of kings. In 1960 the royal family banned all political parties and Koirala was imprisoned seven years. He then fled to India, becoming head of the NCP while in exile. Fortunately, in 1990 mass protests and international pressure forced King Birenda to restore multiparty democracy, and that November a new constitution was adopted. This called for a bicameral legislature headed by a prime minister. Koirala subsequently came home in 1991 to run in the first general elections ever held and he won a seat in parliament. In light of his reputation as one of Nepal's senior and most durable political figures, Koirala was then appointed prime minister and managed to hold on to power for three years. He did this by breaking away from the collective-style domination of an earlier generation of party leaders and establishing effective one-man leadership.

Nepalese politics are noted for their volatility, and Koirala held the prime ministership several times in his lengthy career. After resigning as head of the government in 1994, he returned to prominence again in 1998 as head of an NCP–Marxist-Leninist Party coalition, which collapsed in a matter of months. Koirala nonetheless gained election as head of the NCP Party. The following year he also supported fellow NCP member K. B. Bhattari, another veteran politico, as prime minister. However, within months Koirala roundly criticized Bhattari for corruption and sponsored a no-confidence vote that forced his resignation in March 2000. He then defeated a younger challenger, Sher Bahadur Deuba, to remain party head, and, in doing so he gained appointment as prime minister by King Birendra on March 20, 2000. "As the new prime minister," he said, "my priorities will be to maintain law and order, eradicate corruption, and good governance."

Unfortunately, Koirala did not have long to savor his victory. Since 1996 Nepal has been wracked by an armed Maoist insurrection, intent upon replacing the constitutional monarchy with a communist-style dictatorship. Fighting has claimed over 2,400 lives since the revolt began in the countryside, and Koirala was forced to redirect scanty resources toward fighting the rebels. In April 2000 he activated the National Defense Council, consisting of himself, the defense minister, and the head of the Royal Nepalese Army, to enact new and more effective security policies. This move also brought military units into the fray, which are better trained and equipped for fighting than the regional police. But Koirala's position was further compromised by the tottering Nepalese economy. Bureaucratic corruption is endemic, and the country suffered from years of economic mishandling. Consequently the government has sustained losses of revenue, development funding from abroad, and a corresponding drop in the gross national product. Koirala's perceived inability to resolve the Maoist problem and revive the economy led to a no-confidence vote in January 2001, which he survived. However, the following February he became personally tainted by changes of corruption when it was revealed that his office illegally leased an aircraft from an Austrian aviation firm. Koirala denied any wrongdoing, although the base of his political support began eroding.

On June 1, 2001, Nepal endured a shocking event at the core of its government. Crown Prince Dipendra, distraught over a failed romance, shot and killed King Birendra, Queen Aishwarya, and seven other members of the royal family before killing himself. The void was then filled by the surviving Prince Gyanendra, who was proclaimed king. The Maoists, wishing to take advantage of the confusion, continued their deadly attacks against police and civilians. The country was spinning out of control and Koirala, sensing the futility of his position, finally tendered his resignation on July 19, 2001. "I decided to resign to protect democracy, solve national problems, and maintain unity within my own party," he warned. "If all political parties do not confront the crisis united, the country will face an even graver situation in the future." His prediction proved painfully accurate.

In July 2001 Sher Bahadur Deuba replaced Koirala as prime minister. He also enjoyed little success fighting the guerrillas; on February 17, 2002, they launched their biggest attack ever, killing 129 soldiers and policemen. Four days later the prime minister asked for, and received, a three-month extension of the nationally imposed state of emergency throughout Nepal.

Further Reading

Baral, Lok Rai. "Nepal in 2000: Discourse of Democratic Consolidation." *Asian Survey* 41 (January–February, 2001): 138–142.

Bhattarai, Dinesh. "Nepal: Changing Political Economy." *International Journal of Commerce and Management* 11 (Summer 2001): 50–65.

Chadda, Maya. *Building Democracy in South Asia: India, Nepal, Pakistan.* Boulder Colo.: Lynne Rienner Publishers, 2000.

Hutt, Michael. *Nepal in the Nineties: Versions of the Past, Visions of the Future.* New Delhi: Oxford University Press, 2001.

Mishra, Chaitanya. "Nepal: Five Years Following the Social Summit." *Contributions to Nepalese Studies* 27 (January 2000): 1–23.

Parajulee, Ramjec P. *The Democratic in Nepal.* Lanham, Md.: Rowman and Littlefield, 2000.

Koizumi, Junichiro (1942–) *prime minister of Japan*

Junichiro Koizumi was born in Yokosuka, Japan, on January 8, 1942. His father, Junya Koizumi, was a noted member of the Liberal Democratic Party (LDP), which has dominated Japanese politics since the end of World War II. Koizumi himself attended prestigious Keio University in Tokyo, and he graduated with an economics degree in 1967. Fluent in English, he subsequently studied at the London School of Economics until his father died in 1968. He thereupon quit school, returned to Japan, and unsuccessfully ran for his father's seat in the Diet (parliament). Koizumi then became a secretary under Takeo Fukuda, a future prime minister, and, in 1972, he gained election to the Diet as an LDP member. Over the next two decades he held a succession of important party and ministerial posts, including minister of health and welfare minister of posts and communications. Koizumi gained notoriety for his unconventional stances on many sensitive issues, such as privatizing the much-vaunted Japanese postal service. In 1995 he felt emboldened to run as the party's nominee for prime minister, but he was defeated by RYUTARO HASHIMOTO. Two years later Koizumi again garnered national attention for refusing the traditional stipend awarded to senior politicians after 25 years in office—at a time when national deficits were soaring. In 1998 he led another insurgent attempt to run as prime minister and lost again, this time to KEIZO OBUCHI. Obuchi died two years later while in office and was succeeded by another old party hand, YOSHIRO MORI. It was LDP politics as usual and this, coupled with a mounting sense of economic crisis, proved just the opportunity Koizumi had been waiting for.

For over a decade Japan's famous booming economy had been sliding deeper and deeper into recession. One reason for continuing decline was the LDP's inability or unwillingness to make fundamental changes to the established economic order. Mori clearly lacked the fortitude to overhaul the bureaucracy that served him so well, so his national popularity fell precipitously. When it appeared that the LDP might lose control of the country altogether, Koizumi challenged Mori for the prime ministership. He campaigned on a theme of "Change the Liberal Democratic Party, Change Japan," which resonated with Japanese voters. In truth, the nation had grown weary of the same old institutionalized politics and politicians. The flamboyant Koizumi was greatly assisted by his decidedly unorthodox approach to politics. In a land where conformity is king, he wore colorful outfits, made outlandish remarks, and kept his hair long and unkempt. Furthermore, he promised to implement painful but necessary measures to restart the economy, such as broad-based cuts in borrowing and spending, and privatizing the entrenched postal bureaucracy. On April 24, 2001, Koizumi handily defeated the more mainstream Ryutaro Hashimoto by a margin of two to one, and he was sworn in as Japan's newest prime minister, the 10th in only 12 years. "People in the private sector are prepared to cope with and accept

Junichiro Koizumi *(Embassy of Japan)*

change," he declared. "What is lacking is political and administrative will."

Once in office, Koizumi enhanced his reputation for doing the unexpected by appointing a cabinet that contained five women—more than any previous administration. Among them was Makiko Tanaka, the outspoken daughter of a former prime minister and the first woman to be inducted as Japan's foreign minister. He also began agitating for structural change in the way Japan conducts business to make it more competitive and accountable. Koizumi also advocated the untraditional stance that female offspring of the imperial household ought to be allowed to occupy the nation's throne. He then caused a stir in China and Korea by becoming the first Japanese prime minister since World War II to pay homage at Yakusuni Shrine, where the ashes of several war criminals are enshrined. Realizing the vital importance of maintaining good relations overseas, Koizumi moved quickly to repair the damage and, during a visit to South Korea, he profusely apologized for "the pain and sorrow that Japan inflicted on the Korean people under Japanese colonial rule." Moreover, in the wake of the September 11, 2001, destruction of New York's World Trade Center, Koizumi reaffirmed his support for the United States in the war against international terrorism. He backed his words up with action by deploying three Japanese warships to the Middle East, despite constitutional prohibitions against using military force. President GEORGE W. BUSH has since established a close personal relationship with the unconventional prime minister, and he has conferred with him twice in Washington, D.C. Koizumi reciprocated by fully embracing Bush's notion that Iran, Iraq, and North Korea constitute an "axis of evil" and should be dealt with by force, if necessary.

For all Koizumi's bluster and determination to break with the past, the Japanese economy remains stalled. More ominously, the onset of an American recession triggered an overall worsening trend toward spiraling deflation, with rising national debts and unemployment. In February 2002 President Bush visited the beleaguered prime minister in a show of solidarity, and he urged the recalcitrant Japanese bureaucracy to embrace badly needed economic reforms. "Now the path that we can tread in terms of fiscal and monetary policy is very narrow," Koizumi cautioned, "but we will keep a careful watch on the current economic situation and we will take decisive steps, if necessary, to prevent financial unrest and halt the deflationary spiral." In the face of continuing economic stagnation, Koizumi's popularity has plummeted. His political security—and Japan's—rest upon his ability to turn events around. Foreign considerations have also weighed heavily upon his domestic actions. In August 2002 he declined to appear at the annual ceremony outside the Yasukuni war shrine, dedicated to Japanese victims of World War II, including convicted war criminals. Rather than incur the wrath of China and Korea, Koizumi instead attended a ceremony marking the surrender of Japan to the United States in August 1945. "During the war, our country inflicted great damage and pain to the people of many countries, especially in Asia," he said. "As the representative of this nation's people, I again reflect deeply and express humble condolences to those who lost their lives." To underscore his sincerity, in August 2002 Koizumi announced his intention to visit North Korea, becoming the first Japanese prime minister ever to do so.

Further Reading

Graham, Jeff, and Syed Javed Masood. *Japan—Change and Continuity*. Richmond, Va.: Curzon, 2002.

Hayes, DeClan. *Setting Sun: The Decline and Fall of Japan, Inc.* Boston: Tuttle Pub., 2002.

"Koizumi, Junichiro." *Current Biography* (January 2002): 67–73.

Lam Peng Er. *Can Koizumi Carry Out Japan's Needed Reforms?* Singapore: National University of Singapore, 2001.

Lincoln, Edward L. "Japan in 2001: A Depressing Year." *Asian Survey* 42 (January–February, 2002): 67–80.

Neary, Ian. *The State of Politics in Japan*. Malden, Mass.: Blackwell Publishing, 2002.

Reed, Steven R., ed. *Japanese Electoral Politics: Creating A New Party System*. New York: Routledge, 2003.

Tamamoto, Masaru. "A Land without Patriots: The Yasukuni Controversy and Japanese Nationalism." *World Policy Journal* 18 (Fall 2001): 33–41.

Kok, Wim (1938–) *prime minister of the Netherlands*

Wilem "Wim" Kok (pronounced Koch) was born in Bergambacht, Netherlands, on November 29, 1938, the son of a carpenter. His nation is among Europe's most prosperous, and unique for having reclaimed about one-fourth of its land from the sea. In fact, through use of innumerable dikes to keep the ocean back, nearly half the nation rests below sea level. The Netherlands is also one of the most densely crowded nations, but this does not distract it from enjoying one of the highest standards of living in the world. National government in this constitutional monarchy rests in a bicameral legislature and the leader of the majority party is appointed prime minister. However, the Netherlands system differs from most in relying upon a system of proportional representation, that is, each party automatically gains seats in direct proportion to the vote received in each election. This approach renders the Dutch polity predisposed toward coalition rule, with its inherent sense of give and take, so most policies tend to be mainstream while consensus is widespread. Curiously, for most of the 20th century, Dutch national politics had been controlled by parties steeped in either Catholic or Protestant religious affiliation. It was not until the 1990s that this traditional, religion-based dominance was broken.

Kok attended business school before joining the Netherlands Federation of Trade Unions. He was to spend over two decades with the agency, rising to chairman in 1973. A skilled arbiter and negotiator, he also headed the European Trade Confederation from 1979 to 1982. Kok's political fortunes heightened in 1986 when he gained election to the Second Chamber of the States General and also became head of the Labor Party. In consequence of the 1989 elections, Labor formed a coalition with the Christian Democratic Appeal Party, wherein Kok served as minister of finance and deputy prime minister under RUUD LUBBERS. In this office Kok gained national renown for his austere, simple ways, devoid of the showy ostentation associated with most politicians. However, elections held in August 1994 finally placed the Labor Party within striking distance of taking the reins of government. They then formed a coalition with two other moderate parties (all three under the "Purple Banner" indicating their diversity) and Kok became the new prime minister. It was a landmark election in the history of Dutch politics; for the first time since 1917, traditional religious parties had been excluded from power.

For a decade prior to Kok's election, the usual spritely Dutch economy had endured its share of qualms. Growth had stagnated and unemployment rose, mostly due to the high-tax, generous welfare policies of Dutch governments. Kok realized the acute need to make the Netherlands more competitive in a global economy and, more important, better able to carry its own weight in the forthcoming European Monetary Union (EMU). "We know that it is sometimes difficult to compete, but it is better to be competitive and to have a good performance than just be protected," Kok insisted, "because protectionism leads to laziness and to a lack of modernization." He then utilized all his negotiating tact in convincing fellow Labor members that it was time to reevaluate their slavish devotion to perpetuating the welfare state. Accordingly, benefits were cut and eligibility tightened. Taxes were also slashed to stimulate growth. Consequently, and in contrast with bigger neighbors like France and Germany, the Dutch national economy zoomed out of recession within months and posted an impressive 4 percent growth rate. The voters responded favorably to such dramatic improvement and, in May 1998, they overwhelming returned Kok and the Labor Party back to power. None of this could have been possible without the level-headed judgment of Kok, a

longtime union leader who balanced the welfare or workers against national well-being. In his quiet and typically unpretentious way, he arrived at the correct formulation for change.

The Netherlands, despite its embrace of conservative economic policies, remains very liberal socially. In 1996, as it drew closer to integrating itself within the economic, social, and environmental guidelines of the European Union (EU), the country endured mounting criticism for a lax attitude toward drugs. In fact, the country sports some of the most liberal approaches to drug control in the world, and use of marijuana is legal. But, eager to placate his neighbors, the Kok government agreed to tighten up controls on recreational drugs to discourage smuggling into fellow EU nations. However, more work is needed along these lines. In February 2002, the government conceded that an estimated 25,000 drug couriers passed through Schiphol International Airport and only 1,200 were apprehended. Kok then requested new legislation to heighten security measures and facilitate hiring more police and customs officials at the airport. In April 2001 the Netherlands further established itself on the cutting edge of liberal policies by legalizing euthanasia for terminally ill patients—the first country in the world to do so.

Despite the sometimes controversial legislation associated with his administration, Kok remains one of the most successful and popular European politicians of his generation. He has struck up close relations with another left-of-center reformer, TONY BLAIR of Britain, and together the two men have called on fellow heads of state for greater private investment and the establishment of an integrated European research effort to spur innovation. But Kok, based on his political instincts, did so gingerly. "I learned over the years that its better to not exaggerate how far you can tell other Europeans how to do things," he cautioned. He has also signaled his impending retirement from public office as of the May 2002 elections. His handpicked successor is the Labor Party's Ad Melkert, who, if elected, will inherit the most robust economy of the otherwise lackluster EU. However, Kok's government collapsed on April 16, 2002, when his cabinet resigned en masse over a report condemning the Netherlands' failure to prevent a tragic massacre during the war in Bosnia. On May 16, 2002, new elections were handily won by JAN PETER BALKENENDE of the Christian Democrats, the first time they held power, or even a share in government, since 1994.

Further Reading

Andeweg, R. B., and Galen A. Irwin. *Dutch Government and Politics*. Basingstoke, England: Macmillan, 1993.

Hendriks, Frank, and Theo A. J. Toonen. *Polder Politics: The Reinvention of Consensus Democracy in the Netherlands*. Aldershot, England: Ashgate, 2001.

Mudde, Cas. *The Ideology of the Extreme Right*. New York: Manchester University Press, 2000.

Rochon, Thomas R. *The Netherlands: Negotiating Sovereignty in an Independent World*. Boulder, Colo.: Westview, 1998.

Snels, Bart. *Politics in the Dutch Economy: The Economics of Institutional Interaction*. Brookfield, Vt.: Ashgate, 1994.

Konaré, Alpha (1946–   ) *president of Mali*

Alpha Oumar Konaré was born in the town of Kayes, Mali, on February 2, 1946, the son of a schoolteacher. At that time his nation was a French colonial possession known as French Sudan. The region acquired self-rule in 1956 and complete independence on September 22, 1960, although in temporary union with neighboring Senegal. The so-called Federation of Mali lasted only a year before Senegal left and Mali declared itself an independent republic. However, the first freely elected leader, President Modibo Keita, proved despotic and, in 1968, he was overthrown by a military officer, Moussa Traoré. Under Traoré's aegis, Mali was transformed into a tightly controlled, one-party state, and he remained firmly at the reins until deposed by a coup in March 1991. The new leader, Amadou Toumany Touré, then installed himself as a transitional figure until democratic elections, the first in 30 years, could be held.

Despite growing up in relative poverty, Konaré proved himself an apt student, and, in 1969, he graduated with honors from the Ecole Normal Supérieure in Kayes. He subsequently studied history and geography for two years before becoming head of the national Institute of Human Science. Konaré next attended the University of Warsaw, Poland, from which he obtained his doctorate in history in 1975. Returning home he joined several international organizations, and in 1978 the Traoré regime appointed him minister of youth, arts, and culture. Konaré resigned two years later to protest government oppression, and he resumed teaching and also became actively involved with underground democracy movements. In this capacity he helped found the National Democratic and Nation Front in 1986, along with two opposition newspapers. In 1991 Konaré became active in the Alliance for Democracy in Mali (ADEMA), which organized student strikes against the government. By the time free elections were resumed in 1992, he enjoyed greater national stature than any politician in the country. In May 1992, Konaré swept the field clear of eight other candidates, winning 69 percent of the vote in what foreign observers held to be free and fair elections. He was then sworn in as Mali's second elected president on June 8, 1992. Ironically, Touré, who overthrew the hated Traoré regime and set the country on a path toward democracy, was a former student of Konaré's.

At the time of Konaré's election, Mali was reeling from over two decades of corruption and economic mismanagement. The national treasury was empty and political stability problematic at best. The country was also beset by a severe drought that devastated pastoral regions of his largely desert nation. However, Konaré implemented a dramatic agenda intent upon liberalizing the economy, expanding the free market and private sector, and bringing Mali in line with guidelines established by the International Monetary Fund (IMF) and the World Bank. The results were surprisingly successful. Not only did Mali successfully meet all its debt obligations, it also experienced a boom in various sectors of the national economy. The country is now second only to Egypt in terms of cotton exports, and it has risen to become Africa's third-largest gold producer. Western donor nations applauded such a performance and rewarded Konaré with $63 million in IMF loans. Nor had the prime minister neglected affairs on the political front. Mali remains a one-party state officially, but Konaré sought to expand civil society by initiating local elections at the county and township levels. Such practices grant Mali citizens a sense of participation and input into the governance of their daily lives. Konaré has also revived the long-established tribal practice of yearly public gatherings, now called Forum for Democratic Consultation, whereby citizens can directly address their concerns to the government. Western nations, particularly the United States, hailed Konaré's commitment to capitalism and democracy. Their pleasure was underscored in October 1999 when Secretary of State Madeleine Albright paid an official state visit to reaffirm American support and approval. In 1997 Konaré was also returned to office in an election judged to be free and fair, garnering 95.5 percent of the popular vote.

Konaré has also proved himself adept at resolving local disputes. In 1992, Mali was threatened by violent unrest from the Tuareg, a nomadic people in the northernmost reaches of the country. However, the government granted the tribe greater autonomy in their region, and peace has been restored. Konaré then sought to raise Mali's international visibility through United Nations peacekeeping efforts in West Africa. His country's troops have been dispatched to quell a number of regional disputes, and Konaré himself visited Liberia's despotic president CHARLES TAYLOR, entreating him to respect democracy and freedom of the press. Mali itself boasts over 40 newspapers and an equal number of radio stations. Given Konaré's personal commitment to democracy, he will not challenge constitutional limits by seeking a third term in office in 2002. "Democracy has given us social dialogue as a method of government," he stated. "With participation and transparency we have managed to limit the ethnic tensions that tear at so many African countries and avoid the waste that has ruined so many others." For all these reasons Konaré has been hailed as a model for promoting the growth and ethos of democracy in Africa.

Further Reading

Bingen, R. James. *Democracy and Development in Mali.* East Lansing: Michigan State University Press, 2000.

Brenner, Louis. *Controlling Knowledge: Religion, Power, and Schooling in a West African Muslim Society.* Bloomington: Indiana University Press, 2001.

Drisdelle, Rheal. *Mali: A Prospect of Peace?* Oxford: Oxfam UK and Ireland, 1997.

Konaré, Alpha O. "Memory on the March." *Revue Noir,* no. 2 (September 1991): 2–3.

Seely, Jennifer C. "A Political Analysis of Decentralization: Coopting the Tuareg Threat in Mali." *Journal of Modern African Studies* 39 (September 2001): 499–525.

Kostov, Ivan (1949–   ) *prime minister of Bulgaria*
Ivan Kostov was born in Sofia, Bulgaria, on December 23, 1949. His country had an established monarchy through the first half of the 20th century until 1946, when Soviets forces induced 10-year-old King SIMEON II to flee to the West. Bulgaria then became part of the So-

viet Union's Warsaw Pact and among Russia's staunchest allies. From 1954 to 1989, the country was headed by Communist strongman Todor Zhikov, who ruled it with an iron fist. Following the breakup of the Soviet empire in 1989, Zhikov came under increasing pressure to accept multiparty democratic elections and he refused. Meanwhile, an umbrella coalition of dissenting groups, the Union of Democratic Forces (UDF) was formed and Zhikov summarily resigned in November 1989. Democracy had returned to this erstwhile Soviet stalwart with a vengeance.

Kostov attended the Karl Marx Higher Institute of Economics, from which he graduated in 1974. Following an additional spate of graduate work, he acquired a doctorate in economics from the Technical University of Sofia in 1984. Kostov subsequently taught there for many years until the impending fall of the Communist regime in 1989 induced him to become politically active. Kostov first ran for office in 1990, when the Bulgarian Socialist Party (BIP, the former Communists) gained a slight majority. He then served as a finance minister during a short-lived UDF-BIP alliance, and he was responsible for introducing market-centered economic reforms. These policies engendered some social dislocation and a wave of strikes that brought the government down. Afterward, Bulgaria became hostage to a steady succession of failed coalitions. As the nation drifted politically, its economy experienced rising unemployment and inflation rates, and a dwindling gross national product. However, the badly splintered UDF lost again to the Socialists during 1994 elections, at which point Kostov was elected party chairman. His first goal was to impose order and discipline on a fractious coalition by bringing 20 disparate parties into line. Kostov also determined to increase the party's appeal in the countryside, previously a Socialist Party stronghold, which he finessed with considerable skill for an amateur politician. Consequently, the UDF became much more formidable at the polls. And, as the party's nominee, Kostov campaigned to fight crime, end corruption, and seek Bulgaria's admission into the European Union (EU) and NATO. His success was apparent during the February 1997 national elections, when the UDF outpolled the Socialists and took a clear majority in parliament. The following May he became Bulgaria's newest and youngest prime minister.

Once installed, Kostov faced the unenviable task of bringing Bulgaria back from the brink of economic collapse. But again he championed liberalizing the economy, privatizing inefficient state industries, and in every way promoting a free-market economy. "Our country finally has the chance to head down the road to economic prosperity," he warned. "This is a unique chance because it is the last one." Bulgaria's economy rebounded soon after, although unemployment lingered at 18 percent while living standards remained abysmally low. In the face of such uneven performance, the Kostov administration survived no less than four votes of no confidence in three years. Moreover, the prime minister was accused of selectively privatizing business to assist political allies, which did little to endear him to the electorate.

Kostov enjoyed greater success abroad, where Bulgaria completely reversed its previous reputation as a loyal ally of Moscow. The new government was irrevocably committed to closer ties to the West, and Kostov pushed strongly for integration into the EU and NATO. This despite the fact that NATO leadership failed to allow Bulgaria into the first wave of expansions in July 1997. It was not until March 1999 that NATO reconsidered Bulgaria's eligibility following the opening of Bulgaria's skies to NATO aircraft during the bombing campaign against Yugoslavia. His support proved crucial in speeding up the process of NATO admission and, in January 2002, Turkish prime minister BÜLENT ECEVIT visited Bulgaria and pledged to champion its admission. It is still pending but Bulgaria slated for acceptance.

Unfortunately, Kostov's diplomatic triumphs resonated less strongly at home owing to a lackluster economy. In April 2001, Simeon Borislov Saxe-Coburggotski—the former king SIMEON II—suddenly announced his candidacy for prime minister. He had returned to Bulgaria in 1996 after a 55-year absence, and he carried with him a reputation for honesty and freshness. These were qualities that the Bulgarian electorate—weary of having to chose between the UDF and the Socialists—appeared to appreciate. On July 1, 2001, the former king won half the seats in the 240-seat assembly and was declared prime minister. Kostov took the loss stoically. "We have taken a lot of unpopular decisions and also made mistakes," he reflected. "We wanted the voter to pay a higher price than he was prepared to pay." Beyond surrendering the government, Kostov also resigned as head of the UDF Party in favor of Ekaterina Mikhailova, a close aide.

Further Reading

Anguelov, Zlatko. *Communism and the Remorse of an Innocent Victimizer.* College Station: Texas A & M University Press, 2002.

Bell, John D. *Bulgaria in Transition: Politics, Economics, and Culture after Communism.* Boulder, Colo.: Westview Press, 1998.

Dimitrov, Vesselin. *Bulgaria: The Uneven Transition.* London: Routledge, 2001.

Ganev, Venelin I. "The Dorian Gray Effect: Winners as State Breakers in Post-communism." *Communist and Post-communism* 34 (March 2001): 1–26.

Paskaleva, Krassimira. *Privatization, Regional Development and Democratization in Bulgaria.* Atlanta: Georgia Institute of Technology, 1996.

Kostunica, Vojislav (1944–) *president of Yugoslavia*

Vojislav Kostunica was born on March 24, 1944, in Belgrade, Yugoslavia, the son of a respected Serbian jurist. Within a year the People's Federal Republic of Yugoslavia was created by Marshal Josip Broz Tito, who imposed a centralized Communist regime. The new nation comprised six republics: Macedonia, Slovenia, Croatia, Bosnia-Herzegovina, Serbia, and Montenegro, each controlled by a different ethnic group. Kostunica studied at Belgrade University Law School, graduated in 1966, and eventually received his doctorate there in 1974. Having specialized in constitutional theory, he taught there for several years until he criticized Tito for making constitutional changes that he deemed unfair to fellow Serbs. Kostunica then lost his position and subsequently found work at the Institute for Social Science, and then the Institute for Philosophy and Social Theory. Kostunica became a respected authority in the field of constitutional law, and he also edited and published articles for various scholarly journals. Tito died in 1980 and, by 1989, Eastern Europe was in the throes of discarding Communist ideology altogether. That year Kostunica founded the Democratic Party to help perpetuate the notion of democracy throughout Yugoslavia. However, by 1992 all that remained was a union between Serbia and Montenegro—the other four republics had either declared their independence or were about to. Thereafter, he renamed his organization the Democratic Party of Serbia (DSS) in 1992. But Kostunica also remained, first and foremost, a Serb nationalist.

With the breakup of the Yugoslav Federation came a series of territorial wars between competing republics. The biggest aggressor proved to be Serbia, which, under the direction of SLOBODAN MILOŠEVIĆ, embarked on territorial expansion against Croatia and Bosnia-Herzegovina. The struggle was internecine and marked by savage atrocities, which finally induced the NATO military alliance to intervene directly. Kostunica, as a nationalist, generally supported attempts by RADOVAN KARADZIC to carve out an enclave in the Albanian-dominated Serbian province of Kosovo, but he railed against the practice of ethnic cleansing. In the spring of 1999 NATO aircraft bombed Serb positions and the attack ground to a halt. Thereafter, Kostunica, who was nominally allied to Western policies, became decidedly anti-American in outlook. But defeat also loosened the grip of Milošević on power and by the summer of 2000 a 19-group coalition, the Democratic Opposition, drafted Kostunica to run against him. He had never held public office before, was untainted by corruption, and presented a fresh face to the war-weary voters of Serbia. The bookish, low-key professor seemed an unlikely candidate to run against the charismatic dictator, but at that time he represented the best chance for peace.

The decisive Yugoslavian election was held on September 24, 2000, and Kostunica was widely predicted to have secured 55 percent—a clear majority. However, Milošević's allies on the voting commission insisted that he won the majority of votes, though only 48.22 percent and not enough to prevent a runoff election in October. The Serbian people, sensing that the election was about to be rigged, staged massive demonstrations in Belgrade on October 5, 2000. Kostunica then appeared before parliament. "Good evening, liberated Serbia," he exclaimed, "Serbia has hit the road of democracy and where there is democracy there is no place for Slobodan Milošević." Surprisingly, the former dictator agreed and abruptly concluded his 11-year reign of terror. Considering the formidable police state to be surmounted, it was a bravura performance by Kostunica and his opposition consorts. He was formally sworn in as president on October 7, 2000.

Since taking office, Kostunica has tried maintaining the façade that Yugoslavia, now reduced to Serbia and Montenegro, is a smoothly functioning country. In fact, from the onset he has been at odds with the Serbian prime minister, Zoran Djindjic—a former ally—who is extremely pro-Western in outlook. Kostunica projects a much more moderate and gradual approach to international affairs and economic liberalization, and the two leaders disagree sharply over issues of import to the nation. For example, Djindjic was eager to hand Milošević over to the War Crimes Tribunal at The Hague, but Kostunica blanched at the thought of turning over a fellow Serb to foreigners. Many months passed before Milošević was finally arrested and deported. This deliberation led to opposition charges that Kostinica was coddling war criminals. The ensuing power struggle now threatens to upend the ruling 18-party coalition, but in June 2002, Djindjic raised the ante by dismissing 21 deputies from the DSS on the grounds of absenteeism. Kostunica countered by calling the move worthy of Milošević himself. It remains to be seen if the two leaders can reconcile their differences, or finally dismiss the notion of a successor state to the long-dead Yugoslavian Federation.

Further Reading

Binder, David. "The Yugoslavian Earthquake." *Mediterranean Quarterly* 12 (Winter 2001): 11–21.

Cigar, Norman L., and Sonja Biserko. *Vojislav Kostunica and Serbia's Future.* London: Saqi Books, 2001.

De Krnjevic-Miskovic, Damjan. "Serbia's Prudent Revolution." *Journal of Democracy* 12 (July 2001): 96–111.

Macgregor, Douglas A. "The Balkan Limits to Power and Principle." *Orbis* 45 (Winter 2001): 93–110.

Sofos, Spyros. "Yugoslavia: The Day After." *Mediterranean Politics* 6 (Autumn 2001): 103–111.

Kravchuk, Leonid (1934–) *president of Ukraine*

Leonid Kravchuk was born on January 10, 1934, in Velykvi, Ukraine, the son of peasants. Since 1922 Ukraine had been forcibly joined to the Soviet Union, where it experienced Stalinist police-state oppression and the forced collectivization of agriculture. These sufferings were further compounded by the German invasion of June 1941, which totally devastated the region. Kravchuk's father was killed in combat, and, after the war, he worked in the fields to assist his family. However, the young man performed well in school and in 1958 he graduated from Taras Shevchenko Kyiv University, Kiev, with degrees in economics and political science. He also joined the Communist Party to further enhance his prospects of success. Over the next 30 years Kravchuk labored within the party hierarchy and, by 1989, he assumed responsibilities as secretary of ideology in the Central Committee of the Ukranian Communist Party. He then advanced to full Politburo member the following year, a move which greatly enhanced his influence. It could not have occurred at a more propitious time.

By 1991, the Soviet Union was in its final death throes. Prior to this, Krachuk more or less surrendered to the inevitable and began making allowances for greater democracy and multiparty participation in Ukraine. This liberal stance did little to endear him to superiors in Moscow, but it greatly enhanced his popularity at home. But Kravchuk remained a loyal Communist, long after it had become unfashionable to be so. In fact, between 1989 and 1991, he worked ceaselessly at reforming the party in order to save it. He was unable to stem the rising tide of nationalism in Ukrainian politics, and he decided to finally climb on board. "I have not come from being a Communist to being a nationalist," he emoted, "but to be more precise, from being a Communist to a democrat." Kravchuk remained active in Communist Party affairs, especially after his election to the Supreme Rada (parliament) of Ukraine in 1989 and, being a skillful politician, he was appointed speaker in July 1990. In this capacity he was working to found a party branch independent of Moscow when the failed coup against Soviet premier Mikhail Gorbachev took place in August 1991. Kravchuk delayed condemning the action for several days until its failure was clear, then he finally quit the Communist Party altogether. Consequently, as speaker, he facilitated the peaceful transfer of Ukraine to democracy. To confirm this fact, presidential elections were then scheduled for December 1991.

Kravchuk was by this time the most popular politician in Ukraine and a symbolic figure of its burgeoning independence from Moscow. Therefore, on December 1, 1991, he defeated five other candidates by winning 61.6 percent of votes cast in the first free election in Ukraine's long history. "Only free citizens can make a free state," he announced at his inaugural. However, the new president faced an extremely complicated task of presenting his country's credentials to the world. He quickly forged new economic and diplomatic links to former Soviet states in Eastern Europe, and he also sought diplomatic recognition for the nation. Kravchuk also took a hard-line toward the new Russian president, BORIS YELTSIN, over three issues of significance to his homeland. The first was

the status of the Crimea, a traditional Russian region that had been ceded to the Ukraine by Stalin, and was now of significant economic value. Kravchuk refused to hand it back, although to diffuse tensions he relaxed statutes requiring use of the Ukrainian language for Russian residents. Next came the fate of the 300-ship Black Sea Fleet, which, after much negotiation, was evenly divided between Russia and Ukraine. Not wishing to become a major sea power, Kravchuk then sold his half back to Russia in exchange for cancellation of long-standing debts. A final, more contentious issue, was the fate of several hundred nuclear-tipped missiles still on Ukrainian soil. Kravchuk negotiated an agreement with U.S. president BILL CLINTON over the destruction of the missiles, after which it was agreed the warheads would be shipped back to Russia. All told, by 1994 Kravchuk's clever and sometimes hardball diplomacy put the new nation on a solid footing, diplomatically speaking.

Unfortunately, Kravchuk had far less success reordering and restructuring the Ukraine's economic order, and in such a manner as to minimize social dislocations that threatened stability. In fact, through his tenure in office, unemployment soared, productivity dropped, and inflation hit 170 percent. Part of the problem was his compromise approach to economics, which embraced a measure of privatization, but also clung to state-run businesses. By the time new elections were called on July 26, 1994, his popularity was at an all-time low. Hence, Kravchuk, the erstwhile career Communist turned nationalist, lost to LEONID KUCHMA, a one time Soviet missile manufacturer, who promised to seek closer relations to Russia. Kravchuk nonetheless remains active in politics, and, in 1994 and again in 1998, he won reelection to the parliament as a Social Democratic Party (SDP) candidate representing the Terebovlia district.

Further Reading

Kuromiya, Hironki. *Kuchma, Krachuk, and Ukrainian Nation Building: An Essay.* Washington, D.C.: National Council on Soviet and East European Research, 1995.

Kuzio, Taras. "Kravchuk to Kuchma: The Ukrainian Presidential Election of 1994." *Journal of Communist Studies and Transitional Politics* 12 (June 1996): 117–144.

———, and Paul J. D'Anieri. *Dilemmas of State-Led Nation-Building in Ukraine.* Westport, Conn.: Praeger, 2002.

Wolczuk, Kataryna. *The Moulding of Ukraine: The Constitutional Politics of State Formation*. New York: Central European University Press, 2001.

———. "Precedentalism in Ukraine: A Midterm Review of the Second Presidency." *Democratization* 4 (Fall 1997): 152–171.

Kucan, Milan (1941–) *president of Slovenia*

Milan Kucan was born in Krizevci, Slovenia, on January 14, 1941, the son of a teacher. His country then belonged to a six-republic Balkan federation called Yugoslavia. However, Slovenia differed from its neighbors by enjoying long-established relations with Western countries, especially Italy and Austria, which straddle its northern borders. It also differed by possessing a population that is relatively heterogeneous and largely devoid of the ethnic strife for which Balkan states are notorious. After 1945 Yugoslavia was ruled by Marshal Josip Broz Tito, who instituted a ham-fisted Communist regime to keep all six republics tightly in line. Highly centralized by design and authoritarian in tenor, Tito's government nevertheless managed to keep the federation functioning coherently until he died in 1980. His passing was marked by an escalating rise of deep-seated antagonisms. These, in turn, essentially spelled doom for this unwieldy amalgamation of national hatreds.

Kucan received his primary education in Mursaka Sobata in 1963, and he subsequently pursued a law degree at the University of Ljubljana. Living in a Communist state meant that political fortunes were tied to close association with the party apparatus. Like many ambitious youths, Kucan joined the party-sponsored Youth Association at an early age, and, in 1969, he gained election as its president. His good performance brought him to the attention of party elders, who allowed him to join the Central Committee of the Slovene Party. After holding a succession of party-related positions, Kucan also won election to the Slovene parliament in 1978, in which he also served as president. By 1982 Kucan was respected enough to become one of Slovenia's two representatives in the Presidency of the League of Communists of Yugoslavia, the country's top decision-making body. Four years later Kucan became president of the Slovene Communist Party, in which he came under increasing pressure from Serbian elements to recentralize the Yugoslavian state. Kucan refused and, in fact, he agitated for greater autonomy and democracy within the republics. His ef-

forts crested in April 1990 when he helped organize the first-ever multiparty elections held in Slovenia. In recognition of his endless pursuit of national rights, Kucan was elected the first president of his republic.

By January 1990, the impending breakup of the Soviet empire held dire implications for Yugoslavia's federation and Kucan sought expanded autonomy for his republic. When the Serbian-dominated Yugoslav legislature refused, the Slovene delegation walked out, thereby dissolving the country. Kucan then announced his determination to secede from the federation. This triggered a sharp response from SLOBODAN MILOŠEVIĆ, the president of Yugoslavia, who mobilized military forces to invade the breakaway region. A short 10-day border war ensued but the Slovenes proved victorious and on June 21, 1991, Slovenia declared its independence. The European Community was quick to extend diplomatic recognition to the new country, and the United States followed suit in June 1992. Kucan's artful juggling of politics and diplomacy rendered him a national hero as—for the first time in its long history—Slovenia was a free country. The hated Communist Party was abolished and a new political organization, the Party of Democratic Renewal, emerged with Kucan at its head. Consequently, in the first postindependence elections held in 1992, he was reelected to the presidency by 64 percent of the popular vote. The following year Pope JOHN PAUL II also dignified Kucan by making him a papal knight with the Medal of the Order of St. Pius.

As president, Kucan strove ceaselessly to integrate Slovenia with Western Europe, especially by joining the European Union (EU) and NATO. His country, being relatively coherent by Balkan standards, easily made the transition from a state-controlled economy to a free market, and it has posted an impressive annual growth rate of 4 percent a year. This was stronger than most Western European countries enjoyed and contributed significantly to their decision to admit Slovenia in 2005. The NATO leadership was also impressed by Slovenia's performance, and Slovenia was slated for membership in 2002, the first Balkan state so admitted. "We are an ancient European nation, even though our state is just 10 years old," he explained in 2001. "By joining the EU and NATO, we'll return to the Western civilization we were wrenched from half a century ago." Having once again proved his mastery of high-stakes diplomacy, Kucan gained reelection in November 1997 by a margin of 56 percent. That year he also railed against Milošević's persecution of Muslims and ethnic Albanians in Kosovo and Bosnia-Herzegovina, calling for greater emphasis on human rights throughout his region.

As part of the Balkan region, Slovenia has had to mend fences with some of its less fortunate neighbors, especially neighboring Croatia. Being essentially landlocked, Slovenia needs access to the Adriatic Sea, and, in July 2001, Kucan personally met with Croatian president STJEPAN MESÍC to negotiate a secession of territory. Talks proved successful and their mutual boundary was readjusted elsewhere as compensation. The two leaders also agreed to jointly manage and fund the Krsko nuclear power plant essential to both countries. Under Kucan's tutelage, Slovenia remains one of the few bright spots in an otherwise bleak Balkan landscape. It remains a model for other Eastern European countries to emulate.

Further Reading

Fink Hafner, Danica, and John R. Robbins. *Making a New Nation: The Formation of Slovenia.* Brookfield, Vt.: Dartmouth, 1997.

Gow, James, and Cathie Carmichael. *Slovenia and the Slovenes: A Small State and the New Europe.* London: Hurst and Company, 2000.

Harris, Erika. *Nationalism and Democratization: Politics of Slovakia and Slovenia.* Aldershot, England: Ashgate, 2002.

Ramet, Sabrina P. "The Slovene Success Story." *Current History* 97 (March 1998): 113–19.

Sabic, Zlatko, and Charles J. Burkowski. *Small States in the Post-Cold War World: Slovenia and NATO Enlargement.* Westport, Conn.: Praeger, 2002.

Kuchma, Leonid (1938–) *president of Ukraine*

Leonid Danylovich Kuchma was born on August 8, 1938, in Chaikine, Ukraine. This country, situated between Poland and Russia, has long been a Russian sphere of influence and, since 1922, an integral part of the Soviet Union. Furthermore, it enjoyed a historic reputation as the regional breadbasket and was entrusted with many strategic defense industries. In 1954 the Russians also transferred the southern region of the Crimea to the Ukraine, ostensibly as a gift but actually to prevent the return of millions of Crimean Tartars. Following the collapse of the Soviet Union in 1991, the Ukraine freed itself of Russian domination, and it began treading the perilous road toward national independence.

Kuchma attended Dnepropetrovsk State University and obtained his degree in mechanical engineering by 1960. Thereafter he served as a highly skilled engineer and manager of the Soviet design bureau at Dnepropetrovsk and he subsequently transferred to the Soviet space launch facility at Baikonur, Kazakhstan. A successful manager, in 1986 Kuchma transferred back to Dnepropetrovsk to direct the world's largest missile factory. He then commenced his political career in 1990 by being elected to the Ukrainian parliament. There Kuchma gained national attention by strongly denouncing Soviet mismanagement of state and national affairs, especially the tottering economy, and his maverick sense of defiance catapulted him into the national limelight. Once independence was achieved in 1991, Kuchma served as prime minister in the administration of President LEONID KRAVCHUK, the Ukraine's first democratically elected leader. In 1993 he resigned from office over policy differences with Kravchuk, and he served as president of the Ukrainian Union of Industrialists and Entrepreneurs. This organization served as a political base for Kuchma's successful presidential bid on July 19, 1994. His victory over Kravchuk also signaled the first peaceful transfer of power in Ukrainian history.

The new president faced an immediate economic crisis that threatened a national meltdown. Production was slowing, unemployment was rising, and, worst of all, rampant hyperinflation was approaching 8,000 percent a year! Kuchma countered by introducing radical legislation aimed at privatizing 80 percent of state-owned monopolies, introducing a new national currency, reducing of taxes and state budgets, and in every way resuscitating the moribund national economy. "The people of the Ukraine have decided to put the economy right," he declared, "And we are prepared to bear the cost of adjustment." Unfortunately, majority control in the national legislature remained in the hands of former Communists, and they successfully thwarted or slowed Kuchma's necessary reforms. Consequently, the Ukraine fell further and further behind European states like Poland and Romania, who fully embraced free-market economics.

In 1996 Kuchma, angered by the slow pace of reforms, sought to circumvent legislative obstructionism by authorizing a public referendum aimed at broadening the powers of the presidency. This was undertaken to break the deadlock surrounding his economic agenda. The public approved the measure and Kuchma inherited greater authority to dictate change, but political resistance to change remained entrenched. The Ukraine did register some marginal economic improvements, but the pace of privatization fell far behind intended goals. The government also resorted to strong-arm tactics to enforce tax collection. In August 1998, 2,200 regional and business leaders were held hostage after a mass meeting with the Cabinet of Ministers until they agreed to pay off a third of their debts that month. However crude, it convinced the International Monetary Fund (IMF) that Ukraine was serious about reform and they continued financial aid. Moreover, the Ukrainian electorate, especially the sizable bloc of ethic Russians residing in the eastern part of the country, chose to overlook the nation's sputtering economy. Unlike previous leaders, the tough-talking Kuchma, who spoke Russian better than he did Ukrainian, was a man of action. On October 31, 1999, he was soundly reelected to office with 57.7 percent of the vote.

Kuchma's handling of international diplomacy proved far more adept and productive. Mindful of the Ukraine's traditional role as a "younger brother" to neighboring Russia, he sought a close political concord with President BORIS YELTSIN. This was undertaken despite pronounced Western fears that the country was falling back into its pro-Russian orbit. Several issues were of immediate concern to both leaders, and foremost among these was the disposition of the once-mighty Black Sea Fleet, moored at Crimea. Both sides claimed these valuable warships, but intense discussions peacefully resolved the issue, and the fleet was divided up between them. The two leaders also struck an accord concerning Russian purchase of Ukrainian-generated electricity, and, in 1997, they crowned their efforts by signing a 10-year treaty of friendship and cooperation. However, Kuchma counterbalanced his deferential treatment of Russia by seeking close and abiding ties with the West, particularly the United States. After considerable negotiations with President BILL CLINTON, he agreed to scrap the vast arsenal of nuclear weapons inherited from the old Soviet Union—sweetened by receipt of $500 million to assist in their destruction. Presently Kuchma remains dogged by legislative opposition to his various reforms, but he is nonetheless running for a third five-year term in office on March 31, 2002. He seems confident of victory, as his For a United Ukraine Party presently polls far ahead of two well-known opposition candidates.

Further Reading

Birch, Sarah. *Elections and Democratization in Ukraine.* New York: Macmillan Press, 2000.

Kuzio, Taras, and Paul D'Anieri, eds. *Dilemmas of State-Led Nation-Building in Ukraine.* Westport, Conn.: Praeger, 2002.

Matsuzato, Kimitaka. "All Kuchma's Men: The Reshuffling of Ukrainian Governors and the Presidential Election of 1999." *Post-Soviet Geography and Economics* 42 (September 2001): 416–440.

Moroney, Jennifer P., and Taras Kuzio. *Ukrainian Foreign Security Policy: Theoretical and Comparative Perspectives.* Westport, Conn.: Praeger, 2002.

Wilson, Andrew. *The Ukrainians: Unexpected Nation.* New Haven, Conn.: Yale Nota Beta, 2002.

Wolchik, Sharon L., and Vladimir A. Zviglyanich. *Ukraine: The Search for National Identity.* Lanham, Md.: Rowman and Littlefield, 2000.

Wolczuk, Kataryna. *The Moulding of Ukraine: The Constitutional Politics of State Formation.* New York: Central European Press, 2001.

Zaborsky, Victor. "The 'New President' of Ukraine: Reforming the Government, Facilitating Arms Exports." *World Affairs* 163 (Winter 2001): 123–128.

Kumaratunga, Chandrika (1945–) *president of Sri Lanka*

Chandrika Bandaranaike Kumaratunga was born in Columbo, Ceylon, on June 29, 1945, into a family steeped in national politics. Hers is a large island nation of 20 million people that lies off the southern coast of India. Ceylon had been part of the British Empire since 1815, although it gained political independence in May 1948 and renamed itself Sri Lanka. Since 1978 it has operated under a French-style parliamentary system, whereby a strong president appoints a prime minister and works in conjunction with a unicameral legislature. The population is representative of the region, with followers of Hinduism, Buddhism, Islam, and Christianity all present. Ethnically, the majority of people are Sinhalese, but at least 17 percent are Tamils with close cultural ties to the Indian subcontinent. Friction between these two groups has dominated political events on the island since independence, when official government policies favored Sinhalese culture and language over Tamil. Widespread violence erupted in the 1980s and

Chandrika Kumaratunga *(Embassy of Sri Lanka)*

rapidly escalated into a war of liberation at the behest of the Tamil Tigers, who seek an independent homeland in the northern part of the island. Deep-seated ethnic strife remains a seemingly permanent fixture of everyday Sri Lankan life.

The Bandaranaikes enjoy the reputation as one of Sri Lanka's preeminent political families. Chandrika's father, Solomon W. R. D. Bandaranaike, served as the nation's prime minister between 1956–59, when he was assassinated. Her mother, the equally strong-willed SIRIMAVO BANDARANAIKE, succeeded him in office, becoming the world's first female prime minister; she was repeatedly returned to office from 1960–65, 1970–77, and in 1994. Chandrika's brother Anura Bandaranaike, also served as a cabinet minister at various times throughout his political career. Chandrika was therefore predestined for a life of public service.

She was well educated abroad at the University of Paris, where she obtained a Ph.D. in developmental economics. In 1976 she returned home to serve as a United Nations consultant while also lecturing at universities in India and England. She also served as managing editor of a daily newspaper until 1985. However, public service carried a heavy price. In 1959 she witnessed her father being gunned down, and in 1978 her husband Vijaya Kumaratunga, a leading actor, also died before her eyes. Violence, however, only deepened her personal and political convictions to run for office and seek peaceful solutions to Sri Lanka's problems. In 1990 she proved instrumental in helping found the People's Alliance Party (PA), which swept parliamentary elections in 1993. The following year she became her mother's heir apparent, who again was made prime minister in June 1994. However, during the ensuing presidential campaign of that fall, the opposition candidate, Gamini Dissanayake, was assassinated by Tamil extremists, and Kumaratunga found herself arrayed against his widow. On November 9, 1994, she polled an impressive 64 percent of the vote, becoming Sri Lanka's first female president. Her victory also ended the 17-year reign of the opposition United National Party (UNP).

Throughout her tenure in office, Kumaratunga was preoccupied by a single, burning issue: the Tamil Tigers and their campaign of terror. She originally hoped to obtain a cease-fire by offering the Tamils greater autonomy in their part of the island and in January 1995 the fighting temporarily stopped. However, the rebels used this interval to consolidate and regroup their forces before fighting resumed. The regular Sri Lankan military has fought the Tigers incessantly, but it has proved unable to contain them. The ongoing conflict has cost 61,000 lives, including several ranking ministers killed by suicide bombers. Despite her inability to squelch the insurgency, Kumaratunga's political capital proved as durable as her mother's, and, on December 21, 1999, she was reelected to a second term as president. She managed this only after being wounded by an assassination attempt that cost her an eye. Another suicide bomber unsuccessfully struck outside her office in January 2000, although 12 people were killed. The ongoing campaign of terror served to harden opposition to Tamil demands, and the UNP–controlled parliament refused to consider any of the president's constitutional amendments that would grant them autonomy. Kumaratunga's support from the war-weary population began ebbing, and, in October 2001, she called for early elections. The PA party was badly defeated, but the president maintained power by cobbling together an awkward alliance of several small parties. This entailed creation of a jumbo-sized cabinet of 44 ministers, with portfolios distributed among the supporting groups. Naturally, such an arrangement of competing interests did little but promote national disharmony. Furthermore, as soon as one disgruntled coalition member pulled out, Kumaratunga was forced to seek out and sign on with another. In light of this political distress, a no-confidence vote was about to be called in parliament when the president dissolved the legislature, calling for new elections. On December 5, 2001, her party was totally defeated and Ranil Wickremesinghe of the UNP became prime minister. The Tamil Tigers have since signaled their interest in a ceasefire, and Wickremesinghe has asked representatives from Norway to serve as intermediaries during scheduled peace negotiations.

Further Reading

Balasingham, Adele. *The Will to Freedom: An Inside View of the Tamil Resistance.* Mitcham: Fairmax, 2001.

Krishna, Sankaran. *Post-colonial Insecurities: India, Sri Lanka, and the Question of Nationhood.* Minneapolis: University of Minnesota Press, 1999.

Sabaratam, Lakshmanan. *Ethnic Attachments in Sri Lanka: Social Change and Cultural Conformity.* New York: Palgrave, 2002.

Schaffer, Howard B. "The Sri Lankan Elections of 1994: The Chandrika Factor." *Asian Survey* 35 (May 1995): 409–426.

Shastri, Amita. "Sri Lanka in 2001: The Year of Reversals." *Asian Survey* 42 (January–February, 2002): 177–182.

Sivarajah, Ambalavanar. *Politics of Tamil Nationalism in Sri Lanka.* Denver, Colo.: Academic Books, 2000.

Kwasniewski, Aleksandr (1954–) *president of Poland*

Aleksandr Kwasniewski was born in Bialogard, Poland, on November 15, 1954. Poland, which disappeared as a national entity in 1795 after being partitioned by Prussia, Austria, and Russia, only reemerged as an indepen-dent nation in 1918. It was then overrun by Russian troops during World War II, who instituted a Communist-style dictatorship and incorporated it into the Warsaw Pact. However, the crumbling Soviet Union withdrew from Eastern Europe in 1989, an act which unleashed long-suppressed democratic impulses. In 1990 former Solidarity Union leader LECH WALESA became the first Polish head of state not a member of the Communist Party in over four decades. His rise heralded a new dawn in Eastern Europe.

As a young adult, Kwasniewski studied economics at the University of Gdansk, but he quit to become a member of the Polish United Worker's (Communist) Party in 1977. For individuals harboring political ambitions, membership in the ruling elite was essential for success. In this respect, Kwasniewski proved almost too successful. His rise up the party hierarchy was meteoric and undoubtedly due to his intelligence, self-discipline, and personal drive. In 1989 he gained enough stature to

Aleksandr Kwasniewski *(Embassy of Poland)*

be chosen as a negotiator for the government with Solidarity during transitional talks. The following year Kwasniewski co-founded the new Social Democratic Party of the Republic of Poland, which contained many former Communists. In 1991 he also gained a seat in the Sejm, or national assembly, where he worked on various committees. Deft maneuvering gained him appointment as chairman of the Sejm's Constitutional Committee, which garnered the young man national exposure. By 1995 Kwasniewski judged that public sentiment had swung away from Lech Walesa and he decided to challenge him for the presidency. In several televised debates, the charismatic, telegenic former Communist accused Walesa of being "a man of the past." Apparently, a majority of voters agreed and in the ensuing elections of December 23, 1995, Kwasniewski triumphed, winning 51.7 percent of the vote. Furthermore, he had become Poland's second freely elected executive, confirming that nation's successful transition to democratic rule. "Let us not allow the divisions that were so sharp in the generations of our grandfathers and fathers to burden endlessly our common future," he lectured. "I believe that we can overcome divisions, that we can look for whatever it is that unites the Poles and organize the Poles for great and necessary deeds."

Given Kwasniewski's previously sterling Communist credentials, his victory was greeted with trepidation by the West, the United States in particular, which feared he would place the country back in a pro-Russian orbit. Surprisingly, the new leader unequivocally aligned himself with Walesa's pro-Western diplomatic and economic policies. These included a dramatic restructuring of the economy from state controls to free markets, complete privatization of government-owned industries, and a climate conducive to foreign investment. These changes, once implemented, unleashed the pent-up resolve of Poles to improve their lifestyle. The national economy rebounded by leaps and bounds, becoming the fastest growing of all former Soviet satellites. Such good economic performance greatly abetted Kwasniewski's next highest priority for Poland, membership in the European Union (EU) and NATO. EU membership will in all likelihood be achieved by 2005, based on current predictions of growth. NATO membership, however, happened much faster. Poland boasts one of the largest and most modern military establish-

ments of the former Warsaw Pact nations, and it possesses a fine martial tradition. NATO authorities were duly impressed, and in 1999, Poland, along with Hungary and the Czech Republic, were inducted into the alliance. "Poland for the first time in a thousand years found itself in the same military-political bloc as Germany, its biggest neighbor," the president trumpeted. His fellow Poles also applauded Kwasniewski's success, and on October 8, 2000, they returned him to power with 53.9 percent of the vote.

Despite his formal alignment with the West, Kwasniewski was painfully aware of traditional Russian insecurities about foreign encroachment. Poland's membership in NATO placed a powerful military alliance on Russia's doorstep and triggered an intense diplomatic chill between the two nations. Normal relations with his giant neighbor were essential for regional stability and security, so in January 2002 he invited Russian premier VLADIMIR PUTIN for high-level talks. Both men, former Communists, vowed to put their respective national pasts behind them and work for greater harmony. "Whenever there were attempts to divide Europe, be it for political reasons, or religious, or economic reasons, it resulted in wars and conflicts," Kwasniewski declared, "Europe, by its very nature, because of its common roots, values, and common legacy over 1,000 years of history, has to be treated in an integrated way." The two leaders also agreed to create a committ resolving the complex problems confronting the for allies. Kwasniewski is also eager to see both Russia and Ukraine join the EU and NATO as a logical progression of the new world order. Poland, meanwhile, continues to bask in the welcome light of a thriving economy and newfound friends.

Further Reading

Bell, Janice. *The Political Economy of Reform in Post-communist Poland.* Northampton, Mass.: Edward Elgar, 2001.

Castle, Marjorie, and Ray Taras. *Democracy in Poland.* Boulder, Colo.: Westview Press, 2002.

Cordell, Karl. *Poland and the European Union.* New York: Routledge, 2000.

Jasiewicz, Krysztof. "Dead Ends and New Beginnings: The Quest for a Procedural Republic in Poland." *Communist and Post-communist Studies* 33 (March 2000): 101–123.

Millard, Frances. "Presidents and Democratization in Poland: The Roles of Lech Walesa and Alexander Kwasniewski in Building a New Polity." *Journal of Communist Studies and Transitional Politics* 16 (September 2001): 39–62.

Orenstein, Mitchell A. *Out of the Red: Building Capitalism and Democracy in Post-communist Europe.* Ann Arbor: University of Michigan Press, 2001.

Pienkos, Donald E. "The 1995 Polish Presidential Election: A Step toward Normalcy." *Polish Review* 42, no. 4 (1997): 395–430.

Szczecbink, Aleks. "Explaining Kwasniewski's Landslide: The October 2000 Polish Presidential Election." *Journal of Communist Studies and Transitional Politics* 17 (December 2001): 78–102.

L

Lagos, Ricardo (1938–   ) *president of Chile*
Ricardo Lagos was born in Santiago, Chile, on March 2, 1938, the son of middle-class parents. In 1960 he obtained a law degree at the University of Chile, and he subsequently received a doctorate in economics from Duke University in 1966. For several years thereafter he taught at the University of Chile, and he also served as its attorney and secretary-general. Lagos had always professed a left-wing bent to his politics, and he struck up a close association with Chile's Socialist Party. In 1970, following the election of the country's first Socialist president, Salvador Allende, Lagos was under consideration for a high-ranking ambassadorship. However, when Allende was overthrown by the military in September 1973, Lagos fled to the United States and taught several years at the University of North Carolina. In 1976 he tendered his services as an economist to the United Nations, and finally returned home two years later. Chile was then under the firm control of General Augusto Pinochet, who had installed a ruthless, right-wing dictatorship. The leading hallmark of his regime was the suppression of left-wing politics and the disappearance of thousands of dissidents. Nonetheless, Lagos defiantly helped organize a protest group, the Alliance for Democracy, and he then later founded the Party for Democracy (PPD), which agitated for an end to Pinochet's dictatorship. In 1988 national demands for a plebiscite on Pinochet's regime resulted in a return to multiparty democracy. Lagos himself caused quite a stir on national television in 1988, when he boldly accused the general of gross human rights violations to his face.

In 1989 Lagos ran for the Chilean Senate and failed, but newly elected president PATRICIO AYLWIN of the Concertación coalition appointed him education minister. In 1993 Lagos felt emboldened to run for the presidency itself, but his long-established left-wing credentials hurt him and he lost the primaries to EDUARDO FREI. Frei went on to become Chile's second freely elected president, and he appointed Lagos minister of public works. In this capacity he shed his prior reputation as an ardent Socialist in favor of that of a competent technocrat. By 1999 national polls established him as one of Chile's most respected politicians and he mounted a third try for the presidency. His opponent was Joaquín Lavín, a former associate of General Pinochet, and in the first round of elections both men polled evenly. Lagos went on to campaign for left-wing and Communist voters to good effect, and in January 2000 he narrowly defeated Lavín by 51 percent to 48.7 percent. A pivotal moment in Chile's tortured political history had been reached: for the first time in 30 years a Socialist had been returned to the country's highest office.

From a political standpoint, Lagos had shed most of his hard-left ideology and proved himself to be a

Ricardo Lagos *(Embassy of Chile)*

moderate Socialist leader. His inauguration speech was therefore conciliatory, and his centrist platform did nothing to polarize the nation's polity further. However, he was adamant in addressing the gross disparity of wealth that characterized Chile's social climate. "We must end the two Chiles," he lectured, "No longer can we accept an unjust nation where the rich live comfortably while too many people live in poverty." But, like TONY BLAIR of Britain, Lagos sought the vaunted "Third Way," a functional alternative to the excesses of capitalism and the failed policies of socialism. He placated the fears of the business community while promising to enhance worker's rights and wages. Lagos also pledged to increase access to health care, unemployment insurance, and better education. It was a decidedly liberal agenda, but one grounded in the realities of Chile's political establishment and resources. Lagos was determined to avoid Allende's mistakes—and fate.

Lagos also had to deal with a major skeleton from the nation's recent past. In October 1998 General Pinochet was arrested in Britain and about to be extradited to Spain. Chile's right wing was in an uproar, but events were allowed to run their course and, once the tottering dictator was released in March 2000 and returned home, Lagos let the entire episode pass quietly. This brought him renewed criticism from his own left wing for failing to prosecute the general and his atrocious human rights record. This long-time opponent of Chile's infamous dictator has since skirted the legal battle of whether or not the general can be put on trial at home. The instability that this would potentially produce is apparently not worth going forward with prosecution.

Unfortunately for Lagos, Chile's national economy, for many years the most robust in South America, has been buffeted by events abroad. Both the Asian currency crisis and the Argentinian recession have conspired to slow its growth, thereby increasing concerns of a general economic slowdown. Despite his best efforts, Lagos has also failed to dent the high unemployment rate, estimated at 12 percent—and rising. This lackluster performance translated into sagging popularity for Lagos and his center-left coalition—by July 2001 they had sunk to only 44 percent. Elections held on December 16, 2002, confirmed this fact when the conservative Independent Democratic Union (UDI) of Joaquín Lavín gained strength in both houses of the legislature. Lagos's Concertación coalition still kept control of the lower house, but with only a six-seat majority. This will make governance all the more difficult, and in all likelihood he will be required to make greater concessions to the Christian Democrats, his largest coalition partner, to keep them in the fold. Meanwhile, it is anticipated that the newly invigorated right wing will nominate Lavín to oppose Lagos when his term expires in 2005.

Further Reading

Barr-Melej, Patrick. *Reforming Chile: Cultural Politics, Nationalism, and the Rise of the Middle Class*. Chapel Hill: University of North Carolina Press, 2001.

Borzutzky, Silvia. *Vital Connections: Politics, Social Security, and Inequity in Chile*. Notre Dame, Ind.: University of Notre Dame Press, 2002.

Ffrench-Davis, Ricardo. *Economic Reforms in Chile: From Dictatorship to Democracy*. Ann Arbor: University of Michigan Press, 2002.

Hite, Katharine. *When the Romance Ended: Leaders of the Chilean Left, 1965–1998.* New York: Columbia University Press, 2000.

Leon-Dermota, Ken. *—and Well Tied Down: Chile's Press under Democracy.* Westport, Conn.: Praeger, 2003.

Paley, Julia. *Marketing Democracy: Power and Social Movements in Post-Dictatorship Chile.* Berkeley: University of California Press, 2001.

Lahoud, Emile (1936–   ) *president of Lebanon*

Emile Lahoud was born in Baabdat, Lebanon, on January 10, 1936, the son of a noted army officer and national politician. Lebanon is a small country situated at the eastern fringes of the Mediterranean Sea, where it shares common borders with Syria and Israel. Its present government can be traced back to a constitution first adopted in 1943, which mandates a president, a prime minister, and a unicameral legislature. However, the disparate ethnic and religious composition of Lebanon required further finessing to make the arrangement work. At that time it was decided that the president would be a Maronite Christian, the prime minister a Sunni Muslim, and the speaker of the assembly a Shiite Muslim. Through this arrangement, it was hoped that the three leading groupings, who shared a long history of antagonism, could live in peace. This system worked for many years but broke down after 1970 when the Shiites, who now comprised the majority of the population, demanded more power. The Christians refused to comply and an internecine civil war commenced that lasted for 15 years. Complicating affairs was the presence of large numbers of Palestinian refugees from Israel and, after 1976, a large force of Syrian troops. In 1982 Israeli forces also mounted an invasion of south Lebanon and their troops remained garrisoned there for the next 15 years. The bloodletting in Lebanon proved intermittent and savage until a new political formula, the 1989 Taif Agreement, was agreed upon and civility restored to public life. By this point the outnumbered Christians had little choice but to surrender some power.

Lahoud, a Maronite Christian, was educated at the Broummana High School before attending the Military College in 1956. He subsequently studied at the Dartmouth Naval Academy in England, and he returned home with a commission in the small Lebanese navy. By 1970 he had become transportation chief to the army's 4th Division, and three years later he took command of

Yarze. Lahoud rose to colonel in 1980 and by 1983 he was chief of military affairs in the Ministry of National Defense. As a major general, Lahoud next served as a deputy under General Michel Aoun, a leading Christian warlord, until his ill-advised confrontation with Syrian forces in 1989. Many Christians, including Lahoud, supported the Syrian presence, and he resigned his post. Later that year Prime Minister Salim al-Hoss promoted Lahoud to full general and tasked him with rebuilding the shattered Lebanese national army. To everybody's surprise, he accomplished just that, reconstituting professionalism and stamping out religious factionalism. By 1998, the presidential term of ELIAS HRAWI was scheduled to end and he needed a successor that would satisfy both the Maronite Christians and Syrian president HAFIZ AL-ASSAD, the de facto power broker in Lebanon. Lahoud, based on his record, character, and distaste for factionalism, was unanimously approved by the National

Emile Lahoud *(Embassy of Lebanon)*

Assembly. "I have few promises, many tasks, and much hope," he stated, "I will try my best to be the example in every aspect called for by duty, requested by the law, and made inevitable by responsibility." On November 24, 1998, he became president, representing Lebanon's first peaceful transfer of power in almost three decades.

Lahoud faced a major task resurrecting a nation that was devastated by civil war. The economy and infrastructure still lay in ruins and worse, from a nationalist standpoint, the southern portion of the country was still occupied by Israeli troops and their puppet force, the Southern Lebanese Army (SLA). The president embarked on an ambitious scheme for reconstruction and public works. This entailed heavy government borrowing to jump-start the economy, which in turn led to skyrocketing deficits. However, the industrious Lebanese people, no longer at each other's throats, pitched in together and the nation started reviving. Peace had been achieved only through a political accommodation laid out through the 1989 Taif Accord. Henceforth, the office of the Christian presidency surrendered some of its powers to the Sunni prime minister and Shiite speaker. But the arrangement did not deter Lahoud from reaching out to all elements within Lebanon's diverse polity, be they Maronite, Sunni, Shiite, or Druze, and instilling a sense of national pride and reconciliation. The tenuous peace he inherited remains intact, although it remains hostage to other events in the Muslim world.

Lahoud has had less success with the religious zealotry of Hezbollah, a Shiite guerrilla group, which had declared a holy war against Israel and Israeli invaders in Lebanon. For eight years they waged a costly low-intensity conflict, losing hundreds of fighters, but also killing scores of Israelis and SLA soldiers. At length Israeli president EHUD BARAK decided to end his country's 15-year occupation of south Lebanon and Israeli forces withdrew in 2000. Lahoud, as a nominal Syrian ally, welcomed the development, and he has since invited Hezbollah to join his government of unity. Fighting has subsided but, in January 2002, Elie Hobeika, a noted Christian warlord, was killed by a car bomb. His was the first death in Lebanon since 1994, and Lahoud was quick to blame his assassination on "foreign elements," a veiled accusation against Israel. And, despite growing demands from Christian groups that Syrian troops leave the country, Lahoud, who places nationalism over religion while rendering matters of state, insists that they remain. After the September 11, 2001, destruction of

New York's World Trade Center, Lahoud also assured President GEORGE W. BUSH of his determination to cooperate in the fight against terrorism. However, the Lebanese government refused to freeze the assets and bank accounts of Hezbollah, insisting that they are a resistance group that exists to counter Israeli aggression, not terrorists.

Further Reading

Dagher, Carole. *Bring Down the Walls: Lebanon's Post-war Challenge.* Basingstoke, England: Palgrave, 2002.

Hamzeh, A. Nizar. "Lebanon's Islamicist and Local Politics: A New Reality." *Third World Quarterly* 21 (October 2000): 731–760.

Khalaf, Samir. *Civil and Uncivil Violence in Lebanon: A History of the Internationalization of Human Contact.* New York: Columbia University Press, 2002.

Khalifah, Bassom. *The Rise and Fall of Christian Lebanon.* Toronto: York Press, 2001.

Rabil, Robert G. *Embattled Neighbors: Syria, Israel, Lebanon.* Boulder, Colo.: Lynne Rienner Publishers, 2003.

Zisser, Eyal. *Lebanon: The Challenge of Independence.* London: I. B. Tauris, 2000.

Landsbergis, Vytautas (1932–) *president of Lithuania*

Vytautas Landsbergis was born on October 18, 1932, in Kaunas, Lithuania, the scion of a family steeped in nationalist sentiment. His father had fought for independence from Russia, 1918–20, and against the Nazis in World War II. Lithuania had previously acquired its freedom in 1932, only to lose it eight years later when Russian forces annexed it to the Soviet Union. This act ushered in half a century of political and cultural oppression. As a young man Landsbergis expressed interest in music, and he studied at the Lithuanian Conservatory in Vilnius. He eventually earned his doctorate there and began a distinguished career as a musicologist specializing in national composition. This placed him at odds with Soviet authorities, who actively suppressed any manifestation of Lithuanian culture in order to eliminate it. However, Landsbergis displayed no interest in politics and was content to record albums and publish articles, which kept him out of jail. The turning point in his life—and his country's—happened in 1988 with the founding of the dissident party

Sajudis, or "The Movement." This collection of intellectuals and nationalists began pressing for complete independence from the Soviet Union. It was a dangerous proposition to question the Communist authority under the best of circumstances, and Landsbergis, as a Sajudis member, urged restraint and more cautious moves toward autonomy. But by February 1989, when the Soviet Union embraced reforms under Premier Mikhail Gorbachev and began crumbling, Lithuanians became more vocal in their demands. Landsbergis himself conceded the trend as irreversible, and he gained national renown as a vocal proponent of greater cultural and political freedom.

By the fall of 1989, the Soviets consented to multiparty democratic elections in Lithuania, and the Sajudis swept the parliament. By February 1990 they nominated Landsbergis to be Speaker of the House, and in effect president of the nation. In this capacity he took up the cause of independence at the highest levels while his homeland seethed with nationalistic fervor. On March 12, 1990, despite repeated warnings from Moscow, Landsbergis had parliament formally declare severance of all ties to the Soviet Union. The angry Russians then established an economic blockade and dispatched troops and tanks into the country. Landsbergis, knowing that he dealt from a position of weakness, tried diffusing the situation by offering to rescind the declaration in exchange for a removal of troops. Negotiations then continued as tensions escalated on both sides. The crisis occurred on January 13, 1991, when Soviet tanks and troops suddenly seized the Lithuanian television headquarters and 14 demonstrators were killed. The clampdown continued without abatement until August 1991, when a failed Communist coup against Gorbachev led to the dissolution of the Soviet Union. Immediately Lithuania asserted its complete independence, only this time with formal recognition from Russia.

Landsbergis continued as president of the nation, although his relative lack of political skills became manifest. Despite growing economic distress and rising unemployment, he spent the bulk of his time abroad, touting himself as the "father of the nation." Nevertheless, he was successful in securing Lithuania's membership in the United Nations, and he also proved instrumental in formulating the Baltic Council in concert with neighboring Estonia and Latvia. He also displayed considerable grit for derailing nationalist efforts

intending to deny citizenship to non-Lithuanian-speaking residents, mostly Russians who remained as residents. Nevertheless, by 1992 economic conditions remained bleak and parliamentary elections were dominated by the former Communist Party. Landsbergis issued dire warnings about the trend, but in February 1993 he himself was ousted as president by former Communist Algirdas Brazauskas. At this juncture the Sajudis broke up into feuding factions, and Landsbergis ended up heading the new Conservative Party. Again, he pandered to nationalist sentiments, and, by 1996, the Conservatives recaptured control of parliament. Landsbergis, however, declined to assume the presidency and chose to remain as speaker of parliament. In this position he strongly advocated membership in both the European Union (EU) and the NATO military alliance. However, in new elections held in October 2000, the Conservative Party was badly trounced, retaining nine seats out of 70, and Landsbergis stepped down as speaker. He continues as a member of parliament.

Though his political career has become somewhat marginalized, Landsbergis remains outspoken about events pertaining to Lithuanian sovereignty. During memorial services marking the 10th anniversary of the January 1991 massacre, he demanded that all ex-Soviet officials responsible be arrested and brought to trial. "This is a topic for The Hague Tribunal," he insisted, "the Soviet army was carrying out aggression and international crime." He then called upon the governments of Russia, Belarus, and Ukraine to track down the 42 suspected leaders of the incident and bring them to justice.

Further Reading

Ables, Dana M. "Lithuania, Dissent, and the Drive for Independence." Unpublished master's thesis, South West Texas State University, 1990.

Chelminski, R. "Lithuania's Freedom Fighter." *Freedom Review* 24 (March–April 1993): 34–38.

Landsbergis, Vytautas, and Anthony Packer. *Lithuania, Independent Again: The Autobiography of Vytautas Landsbergis.* Seattle: University of Washington Press, 2000.

Lane, A. T. *Lithuania: Stepping Westward.* London: Routledge, 2001.

Trapans, Arveds. "Averting Moscow's Baltic Coup." *Orbis* 35 (Summer 1991): 427–440.

Lebed, Aleksandr (1950–2002) *Russian politician*

Aleksandr Ivanovich Lebed was born on April 20, 1950, in Novocherassk, the famous Cossack region of the Soviet Union. His father, an ironworker, had once been imprisoned three years for being late to work, which filled young Lebed with a hatred for tyranny. A pugnacious, combative youth, he originally wanted to be a fighter pilot, but injuries received in his many fights disqualified him. He thereafter joined the elite Soviet paratroop service, from which he graduated in 1973. Lebed proved himself a natural leader and rose steadily through the ranks. He fought in Afghanistan, 1981–82, as a battalion commander and was highly decorated, but he became disillusioned over the incompetence and deceptions inherent under communism. "For politically unreasonable and unacceptable decisions, soldiers always paid with their lives, their bones and their blood," he angrily reflected. "Those who start wars know in advance that neither they nor their children will ever participate in them. No, they stir up the flames of war for us, the cattle." In 1985 Lebed was promoted to colonel and he assumed command of the elite Tula Airborne Division. He had declared, as a professional soldier, his willingness to die in defense of the country. Instead, for the next six years he was primarily occupied with harshly repressing fellow citizens in Georgia, Azerbaijan, and other republics of the rapidly disintegrating Soviet Union. The crucial moment in his destiny—and Russia's—occurred in August 1991 when Communist hard-liners detained Premier Mikhail Gorbachev. BORIS YELTSIN, president of the Russian Republic, then rallied democratic elements outside the parliamentary White House to oppose them. Lebed received orders to storm the White House with his paratroopers, but he refused. Instead, he took a column of tanks to parliament and tendered his services to Yeltsin. The coup attempt failed within hours and order was restored. Yeltsin publicly thanked the gutsy, gravel-throated general for his assistance, and he promoted him to command the 14th Russian Army in Moldavia. Curiously, Lebed's feeling about democracy remained somewhat opaque—he was far more concerned with the country's survival than its political system.

Once again, Lebed found himself in the middle of sectarian fighting. Moldavia had previously declared its independence from Russia, and strife ensued between secessionist elements and Russian immigrants in the Trans-Dneister region. Lebed, while intervening on behalf of fellow citizens, eventually brokered a cease-fire with the new Moldovian regime in July 1992. This was one of the few success stories for the military that year, and Lebed became one of the most popular leaders in the Russian Federation. But he continued railing against graft and incompetence at the highest levels of government and grew especially alarmed by the state of the Russian army, now undertrained, underpaid, and underequipped. Lebed also entered a contretemps with Defense Minister Pavel Grachev over alleged corruption, was accused of harboring Napoleonic ambitions, and concluded 25 years of service by resigning in June 1995.

Lebed's fierce personal demeanor, coupled with his ready willingness to tackle entrenched interests, made him an ideal populist politician. In 1995 he stood for a parliamentary seat in the Duma (lower house of parliament) from the Tula district, winning handily. The following year he decided to run for the presidency as a candidate of the Congress of Russian Communities Party. In May 1996 he finished a strong third, but not well enough to participate in the final runoff between Yeltsin and a surprisingly strong Communist challenger, GENNADI ZYUGANOV. Lebed despised Communists, so he threw his political support behind Yeltsin, who coasted to an easy victory that July. For having saved the president a second time, Lebed gained appointment as his secretary of the National Security Council, the nation's top military adviser. In this capacity he negotiated with Aslan Maskhadov to bring an end to the embarrassing war in the breakaway region of Chechnya, spurred on by Muslim separatists. It proved a painful decision for a nationalist like Lebed, but as a soldier he realized how Russia's enfeebled condition precluded any chance of victory. The move also greatly angered Yeltsin, now critically ill with heart disease, and Lebed publicly remonstrated for him to step down. This defiance proved the last straw, and, on October 22, 1996, he was fired as national security adviser. "I was a black sheep in my herd," Lebed waxed philosophically. "It was only a matter of time before they sacked me." However, the general had lost none of his immense national standing, and he went on to found his own party, Honor and Motherland. Growing politically ambitious, he ran for the governorship of Krasnoyarsk, Siberia, defeating Yeltsin's handpicked candidate. Lebed put the local business leadership on notice that their corrupt ways had ended, and several high-profile arrests followed. Lebed then became widely touted as a presidential contender for the year 2000, but he decided not to run. Instead, the former general continued making life difficult for criminals and Communists in Krasnoyarsk until April 28, 2002. That day the former general was riding in a helicopter when it struck a utility pole and crashed, killing him. Russia had lost one of its few remaining heroes, and President VLADIMIR PUTIN ordered a formal investigation into the accident. Since then, Lebed's younger brother, Alexei Lebed, has announced his candidacy to succeed the late hero as governor.

Further Reading

Elletson, Harold. *The General against the Kremlin: Alexander Lebed; Power and Illusion.* London: Warner, 1998.

Lebed, Aleksandr. *General Alexander Lebed: My Life and My Country.* Washington, D.C.: Regnery Publishers, 1997.

Phillips, R. "Aleksandr Lebed: Soldier, Statesman, President?" *World Affairs* 159 (Winter 1997): 109–113.

Radkevich, Stanislaus, and Michel Vale. "Lebed." *Russian Politics and Law* 37 (July–August 1999): 58–65.

Simonsen, S. G. "Going His Own Way: A Profile of General Aleksandr Lebed." *Journal of Slavic Military Studies* 8, no. 3 (1995): 528–546.

Lee Teng-hui (1923–   ) *president of Taiwan*

Lee Teng-hui was born on January 15, 1923, in Sanchih, Taiwan, the son of a landlord. Taiwan had been part of the Japanese Empire since 1895, and he attended local schools with Japanese students. Lee proved himself adept scholastically, and he was allowed to attend the prestigious Kyoto Imperial University to study agriculture. World War II interrupted his endeavors in Japan, however, and, in 1946, he returned to Taiwan to enroll at National Taiwan University. Lee acquired his bachelor's degree in agricultural economics in 1948, taught the subject for four years, and in 1952 gained entry to Iowa State University to undertake graduate work. He obtained his master's degree a year later and returned home to work as a government agronomist. Lee then held a succession of private and government posts, and, in 1964, he ventured back to the United States to pursue his doctorate at Cornell University, New York. He graduated with honors four years later and resumed his work as an agricultural economist back on the island.

In 1949 Taiwan, located approximately 100 miles off the south China coast, became the last stand of the forces of General Jiang Jieshi (Chiang Kai-shek) after fleeing the mainland Communists. Here they foisted their Kuomingtang (KMT), or Nationalist Party, on the ethnic Taiwanese population as a one-party dictatorship. But in 1972 the general's son, President Chiang Ching-kuo, became acquainted with Lee and appointed him minister without portfolio—and the youngest such official in his administration. The two men subsequently struck up an abiding relationship and Chiang began grooming him for possible succession. By 1978 Lee had risen to mayor of Taipei, a post at which he distinguished himself by efficient governance and construction of much-needed public works. In 1981 he became governor of Taiwan, signaling another advance toward the office of president. Three years later the KMT–dominated National Assembly, at Chiang's behest, made Lee his vice president and in direct line to succeed him. Over the next four years, as the president's health began failing, Lee assumed more and more executive authority and ruled in his name. By this time Lee also enjoyed more than a decade of national visibility, becoming one of the most trusted political figures on the island. When Chiang died in 1988, Lee formally succeeded him as president of Taiwan. He thus became the first native Taiwanese to serve as executive, and the first executive to hold advanced college degrees.

Prior to his passing, Chiang had embarked on liberalizing the otherwise staid political process by allowing for a political opposition and granting greater rights to native Taiwanese. Lee fully intended to expand upon these practices, which provoked strong reactions from the KMT's old guard. Nonetheless, Lee established his credentials as a popular leader, and, in 1990, the National Assembly overwhelmingly elected him to fill out a four-year term. In return, the president sacked numerous legislators who had been appointed to seats in 1949 and granted free elections in 1991. That year the KMT dominated the national agenda but an opposition group, the Democratic Progressive Party (DPP), had also registered gains. Taiwan's political system was slowly opening up.

Senior leaders within the KMT worried that their privileged status was waning, a fact confirmed by Lee's decision, in 1996, to hold free, direct elections for the presidency of Taiwan. This move won him plaudits at home and abroad, but it deeply angered the Chinese Communists in Beijing, who viewed Taiwan as a rebellious province, and who interpreted such steps as a move toward independence. This they were foresworn to stop, and throughout the fall of 1996 the Communists staged naval war games off the island's straits. But far from being intimidated, Taiwanese voters overwhelmingly endorsed Lee, making him the first democratically elected Chinese leader in over 4,000 years. China was also deeply angered by the decision of the United States to grant Lee a visa so as to attend his class reunion at Cornell in 1995. He thus became the first Taiwanese leader to ever visit America, even if in an unofficial capacity. Lee reveled in his unpopularity with the mainlanders, but, whereas he enjoyed antagonizing them, he never officially endorsed independence in office. Nonetheless, in July 1999 he caused another uproar by declaring that China/Taiwan relations should be conducted on a "state-to-state" basis, which again led to bitter denunciations and more threatening war games.

Lee declined to run for the presidency in 2000 and he stepped aside to let democracy render its verdict. Astonishingly, the contest was won by CHEN SHUI-BIAN of the PDP, an act which ended half a century of KMT dominance on Taiwan. Lee then further antagonized his party during legislative elections in the fall of 1991 by campaigning for the new Taiwan Solidarity Union, and party leaders summarily expelled him as head of the KMT. Lee countered that party leaders were getting too cozy with mainlanders for his taste. "Taiwan and the People's Republic of China are two countries," he declared in May 2002. "This is a reality." Lee's legacy as the driving force behind Taiwan's flourishing democracy is assured. Now in his 80th year, he remains a respected elder statesman, and a local political legend in his own right.

Further Reading

Chao, Linda. *Some Implications of the Turnover of Political Power in Taiwan.* Stanford, Calif.: Hoover Institution, 2002.

Dickson, Bruce, and Jianmin Zhao. *Assessing the Lee Teng-hui Legacy in Taiwan's Politics.* Armonk, N.Y.: M. E. Sharpe, 2002.

Fuh-sheng, Hsieh. "Whither the Kuomindong?" *China Quarterly* 168, no. 1 (2001): 930–943.

Ross, Robert S. "The 1995–1996 Taiwan Strait Confrontation: Coercion, Credibility, and the Use of Force." *International Security* 25 (Fall 2000): 87–123.

Ho, Khai Leong. "Prime Ministerial Leadership and Policy Making Style in Singapore: Lee Kuan Yew and Goh Chok Tong." *Asian Journal of Political Science* 8 (June 2000): 91–123.

Shambaugh, David, ed. *Contemporary Taiwan.* New York: Oxford University Press, 1998.

Wu, Hsin-hsing. "Taiwan-Mainland China Relations Under the Leadership of Lee Teng-hui." *Asian-American Review* 14, no. 2 (1996): 115–146.

Leghari, Sardar (1940–   ) *president of Pakistan*

Sardar Farooq Ahmed Khan Leghari was born on May 2, 1940, in Choti Zerim, Punjab province, Pakistan, the son of the chief of the Baluch Leghari tribe and a noted political activist. Pakistan was then part of British India and it obtained independence in 1947 only after a frightful loss of life during massive population transfers between Pakistan and India. Leghari was educated locally before attending Atchison College in Lahore, from which he received a bachelor's degree in 1958. He subsequently attended Oxford University in England, and, by 1963, he had obtained his master's in economics. Leghari returned to Pakistan in 1964 and he joined the civil service in his native state. In 1973, following the death of his father, he inherited considerable feudal estates and also became chief of the Leghari tribe. He then resigned from the civil service and joined the Pakistan People's Party (PPP) as joint secretary of the Dera Ghazi Khan district. Leghari demonstrated his political skills by winning a seat in the Pakistani senate in August 1975, where he came to the attention of Prime Minister Zulfikar Ali Bhutto, founder of the PPP. Leghari next gained appointment as minister of production in the Bhutto cabinet, and, in March 1977, he was also elected to the National Assembly. However, massive protests over allegations of election rigging induced General Zia ul-Haq to intervene and arrest Bhutto in July 1977; he was subsequently executed by military authorities. Leghari, meanwhile, remained staunchly loyal to his prime minister and endured four years of prison before being released in 1981.

After General Zia died in a plane crash in August 1988, Pakistani authorities began reintroducing democratic rule. The following November BENAZIR BHUTTO, the late prime minister's daughter, won the national election, becoming the first woman to lead a predominately Muslim country. Leghari, meanwhile, won seats in both the National Assembly and the Punjab Assembly, but he lost his bid to serve as prime minister of that province to MIAN MUHAMMAD NAWAZ SHARIF of the Pakistan Muslim League (PML). Given Leghari's support of her father, Bhutto consequently assigned him the portfolio of minister of water and power. An internecine power struggle then erupted between Bhutto and Sharif that nearly paralyzed the government over the next two years. To prevent a national collapse, President Ghulam Ishaq Khan, citing Bhutto's incompetence and corruption, dismissed her from the prime minister's office in August 1990. The following October Sharif's party won a majority in the parliament and he became prime minister. Leghari retained his assembly seat, however, and for the next two years he assisted Bhutto as fellow leader of the opposition in parliament.

By April 1993, President Khan had stripped Sharif of his office for precipitating a constitutional crisis, and he called for new elections. Leghari, given his pristine reputation, was then appointed to serve as an interim prime minister until October 1993, when the issue would be decided by the ballot. The PPP secured a slight plurality and Bhutto again became prime minister. Leghari then joined her cabinet a second time as foreign minister. He served in this capacity briefly before running for the vacated office of president, and, on November 13, 1993, Leghari narrowly defeated Wasim Sajjad of the PML. He thus became Pakistan's eighth president and would serve five years. Despite his prior and long-standing alliance with Bhutto, the new executive was determined to refrain from partisan politics. His resolve clearly manifested itself in November 1996 when, citing the corruption of the second Bhutto administration, he dismissed her from office and called for new elections in February 1997. Not surprisingly, her old adversary Sharif was swept back into power with his own self-serving agenda. Enjoying a majority in parliament, he amended the constitution to prevent the Pakistani president from removing the prime minister from office. Leghari, realizing that the game was finally up, officially lent his support to the measure.

Leghari remained president of Pakistan until the fall of 1997, when a constitutional row developed between Sharif and the supreme court. When Sharif's five appointments to that body were summarily dismissed, Leghari and Sajjad Ali Shah, the chief justice, his allies on the bench, removed Ali Shah in turn. The ensuing confrontation all but crippled the government's ability to

rule for two months, so Leghari resigned as president on December 2, 1997. He then relocated back to Lahore to found a new political party, the Millat, which aimed to secure much-needed economic, social, and constitutional reform. Leghari also resumed his place in the National Assembly for several years, and, in June 2002, he was dispatched to Egypt as President PERVEZ MUSHARRAF's personal envoy. In Egypt, he conferred with Prime Minister Atef Obeid and discussed, among other things, Pakistan's tense relations with India over events in neighboring Kashmir. "It is very important that we deal with the problems in a civilized manner," Leghari reasoned, "and if we cannot start talking to each other, there will be no progress."

Further Reading
Akhtar, Rai Shakil. *Media, Religion, and Politics in Pakistan.* Karachi: Oxford University Press, 2000.

Amin, Shahid M. *Pakistan's Foreign Policy: A Reappraisal.* New York: Oxford University Press, 2002.

Ganguly, Sumit. *Conflict Unending: India-Pakistan Tensions since 1947.* New York: Columbia University Press, 2001.

Newbury, Paula R. *Judging the State: Courts and Constitutional Politics in Pakistan.* Cambridge: Cambridge University Press, 2002.

Weiss, Antia M., and S. Zulfigar Gilani. *Power and Civil Society in Pakistan.* Oxford: Oxford University Press, 2001.

Le Kha Phieu (1931–) *secretary-general of Vietnam*

Le Kha Phieu was born in Dong Khe, Thanh Hoa province, Vietnam, on December 27, 1931. His country was then a French colonial possession, and had been since 1893. Vietnam, however, is an ancient culture with ancient antipathies. Between 111 B.C. to 939 A.D. it waged a thousand-year war of independence from China and remained determined to throw off any foreign yoke that cared to descend upon it. Following a brief Japanese occupation in World War II, Vietnamese resistance coalesced around Ho Chi Minh and his Communist Party. These engaged in a ruthless war of liberation against France, which tried reasserting control of its former colony in 1945. Millions died before the Communists, or Viet Minh, defeated the French in 1954. Thereafter Vietnam was partitioned into a Communist-dominated north and an ostensibly democratic south backed by the United States. However, Ho Chi Minh remained determined to unify the nation at any cost, so between 1964–74, he waged an internecine guerrilla war against America. The Vietnamese took staggering losses, yet the presence of 500,000 American troops, backed by air power, could not defeat the wily insurgents. The United States withdrew after 1973 and within two years North Vietnamese forces had completely subdued South Vietnam. For the first time in a century the nation was free of foreign domination.

Phieu hailed from a region of Vietnam noted for revolutionary activity, and, in June 1949, he joined the Communist Party to fight the French. Adept as a soldier, he was culled from the ranks to attend the Vietnamese Military Academy, and he subsequently saw service as a regimental commander. As the fighting intensified and spread to neighboring Cambodia and Laos, Phieu shouldered additional administrative duties as deputy chief commissar of central Vietnam, and he also gained promotion to major general. By the time fighting ceased in 1975, Phieu was a lieutenant general and, having risen through the ranks under combat, among the military's most respected senior leaders. After the war he also assumed additional responsibilities as chief of political council for the Vietnamese People's Army (PAVN), his field of responsibility, ideology and indoctrination. Phieu had also acquired considerable influence within the ranks of the party, and he served with the Central Committee throughout the 1980s. His political career crested in 1994 when he joined the Politburo, which issues executive decisions for the party and, hence, the entire country. Possessed of an excellent military reputation and pristine Communist credentials, Phieu was chosen to succeed the elderly DO MOI as secretary-general of the Communist Party, the country's highest office. He did so on December 29, 1997, representing a resurgence of conservative political orthodoxy.

Phieu assumed power at an inauspicious period in Vietnam's economic development. The nation had enjoyed a period of rapid growth during the early 1990s owing to the great influx of foreign investment. However, the onset of the Asian currency crisis in 1998 led to an economic slowdown for the entire region and periods of stagnation. In contrast to China, which has embraced free-market capitalism while maintaining social controls, the stodgy Vietnamese leadership exemplified by Phieu remains wedded to outdated notions of state control. As such, Phieu has enacted policies that were the complete antithesis of the remedies needed to sustain the growth of Vietnam's tiny industrial base. The country's problems are further compounded by the fact that it has a relatively high birth rate, but not the means of creating new jobs for listless young people. Consequently, Vietnam is experiencing social dislocations usually associated with more advanced Western nations: crime, drug addiction, and rising social violence. However, Phieu scowled at the notion of economic and structural reform. His solution was to simply squelch dissent and demand greater ideological training for the young. Throughout his tenure in office, the former general simply confronted new problems with old dogma, an approach that virtually assured continuance of Vietnam's hardships. Where economic restructuring was allowed it was incremental and implemented in such a fashion so as not to upset the party's political dominance. These proved halfway measures at best. Having bested two Western powers in their lifetime, the aging rulers of Vietnam, and their arcane ideology, were in a losing battle against a new and more implacable foe: modernity.

By 2000 most foreign investment had dried up in the face of corruption and seemingly impenetrable bureaucratic red tape. Worse, the International Monetary Fund (IMF), whose advice for reform had been rejected in the past, began insisting upon changes to assure the availability of future loans. Within a year, the country's ruling elite realized the need for new blood at the highest levels of governance. On April 22, 2001, the Communist Party demanded Phieu's resignation in favor of 61-year-old Nong Duc Manh, a known reformer. Manh represents a new generation of leaders who did not fight in the wars of the past century and were not saddled by its intellectual baggage. Phieu had also come under criticism for using military intelligence to spy upon party members, which did little to endear him to the leadership. Still, the old general was allowed to perform some symbolic functions. In September 2001 Phieu made one his few sojourns outside the country by visiting China and conferring with Premier LI PENG. A joint statement was then issued announcing expanded economic and trade ties between the former adversaries.

Further Reading

Bui, Tin. *From Enemy to Friend: A North Vietnamese Perspective on the War.* Annapolis, Md.: Naval Institute Press, 2002.

Gilbert, Marc J. *How the North Won the Vietnam War: New Interpretations.* New York: Palgrave, 2002.

Ho, Hue-Tam Tai. *The Country of Memory: Remaking the Past in Late Socialist Vietnam.* Berkeley: University of California Press, 2001.

Kenny, Henry. *Shadow of the Dragon: Vietnam's Continuing Struggle with China and the Implications for U.S. Foreign Policy.* Washington, D.C.: Brassey's, 2002.

Luong, Hy V., ed. *Postwar Vietnam: Dynamics of a Transforming Society.* Lanham, Md.: Rowman & Littlefield, 2003.

Metzner, Edward P. *Reeducation in Postwar Vietnam: Personal Postscripts to Peace.* College Station: Texas A & M University Press, 2001.

Templer, Robert. *Shadows and Wind: A View of Modern Vietnam.* New York: Penguin Books, 1999.

Thayer, Carlyle A. "Vietnam in 2001: The Ninth Party Congress and After." *Asian Survey* 42 (January–February 2002): 81–89.

Le Pen, Jean-Marie (1928–) *French politician*

Jean-Marie Le Pen was born on June 20, 1928, in La Trinité-sur-Mer, France, the son of a fisherman. He lost his father while young and received a Jesuit education before fighting with the French underground in World War II. In the Resistance he came to despise the Communists who dominated the resistance movement. Afterward Le Pen pursued law at the University of Paris while also becoming closely associated with right-wing causes and student groups. A noted brawler, he dropped out in 1953 by volunteering as a paratrooper in the famous French Foreign Legion. He fought briefly in Indochina and returned home to join the right-wing Poujadist protest movement of small, antitax shopkeepers. Le Pen rose rapidly through the ranks and, in January 1956, he was elected to parliament, becoming the youngest member to serve. Here Le Pen strongly denounced President Charles de Gaulle's efforts to disengage from Algeria, scene of a desperate war of liberation from France. Le Pen quit parliament to rejoin his paratroop outfit in North Africa, served with distinction, but became tainted by allegations of torturing Algerian prisoners. Le Pen then resumed his parliamentary career in 1958, lost his seat two years later, and spent over a decade in political isolation.

In 1972 Le Pen reappeared on the political scene at the head of a new party, the National Front. This was an umbrella organization of various right-wing constituencies, all united in their hatred for immigrants, Communists, and especially the vacillating policies of traditional conservative parties. Le Pen demonstrated considerable skill as a rabble-rousing demagogue, and he publicly articulated his right-wing views. His most recurring theme was the forced expulsion of France's sizable North African immigrant community. "Massive immigration has only just begun," he warned followers. "It is the biggest problem facing France, Europe, and probably the world. We risk being submerged." At first the National Front performed poorly in national elections, but the rise of FRANÇOIS MITTERRAND in 1981, and his liberalization of immigration policies, energized the radical right. Le Pen vocally addressed rising tides of crime with xenophobic populism, and he proffered his candidacy as an alternative to politics as usual. Commencing in 1988, he gathered 14.4 percent, the largest right-wing vote ever registered. Even left-wing officials like EDITH CRESSON began parroting his demand for leaving "France for the French," additional proof that views of the far right in France had become politically respectable.

In 1998 elections, the National Front again registered 15 percent of the vote, representing about 4 million voters. However, by this time Le Pen's grip on the party was slipping and his second-in-command, Bruno Megret, launched a bid to oust him. It failed and Le Pen angrily kicked him out of the party, afterwhich he founded his own movement. Le Pen's sometimes outrageous behavior also tarred him as a committed racist and anti-Semite. In 1987 he characterized the Nazi extermination of Jews as a mere "detail of history"—illegal under French law—and he was sued for promoting anti-Semitism. But Le Pen always managed to come back by hammering away at his inevitable themes of anti-immigration, law and order, and pulling France out of the European Union. In 1996 he paid a personal visit to Iraqi dictator SADDAM HUSSEIN and demanded an end to UN sanctions against that country. France at that time was also experiencing a serious economic downturn, and elections that year handed Le Pen held 15 percent of the vote, a slight increase. Then, in 1998, he assaulted a female Socialist candidate and was suspended from politics for two years. The National Front remained a source of concern for many politicians, but few took the blustery

Le Pen as anything but a marginal candidate. Everything changed in May 2002.

In the spring of 2002 the prospect of an electoral showdown between incumbent president JACQUES CHIRAC and his Socialist prime minister LIONEL JOSPIN was greeted by French voters with yawns. Le Pen was again expected to finished a distant third but—shockingly—he finished a strong second, displacing Jospin from the race. "It's a big defeat for the two main candidates," he trumpeted. "The chances of me winning the second round don't depend on me but on the French electorate, the French people's desire to rip out the decay that is hitting our country." Le Pen may have scored the National Front's best showing ever at 17 percent, but his success galvanized disillusioned left and centrist figures into action. On May 1, 2002, an estimated 1 million protestors turned out in the streets while Jospin endorsed the heretofore unthinkable tactic of campaigning for the conservative Chirac. On May 6, 2002, Chirac easily crushed Le Pen's fourth presidential bid by amassing 80 percent of the vote. "Lies have been told about us, lies have been told about me, and I have been made into a figure of caricature," an angry Le Pen exclaimed while explaining his demise.

Le Pen, now past 70, has probably conducted his last bid for the French presidency. Without his charismatic and inflammatory leadership, the ultimate fate of the National Front, which he created and led for three decades, remains problematic. However, Le Pen certainly made history as the "marginal" candidate who lifted far-right politics from obscurity and reduced the once mighty French left to impotency. Rarely has national rage been so artfully channeled into a viable political movement.

Further Reading

Arnold, Edward, ed. *The Development of the Radical Right in France: From Boulanger to Le Pen.* New York: St. Martin's Press, 2000.

Blerich, Erik. *Race Politics in Britain and France: Ideas and Policy Making since the 1960s.* New York: Cambridge University Press, 2003.

Davies, Peter. *The Extreme Right in France, 1789 to Present: From De Maistre to Le Pen.* New York: Routledge, 2002.

———. *The National Front in France: Ideology, Discourse, and Power.* New York: Routledge, 1999.

———. *The Routledge Companion to Fascism and the Far Right.* New York: Routledge, 2002.

DeClair, Edward G. *Politics on the Fringe: The Case of the French National Front.* Durham, N.C.: Duke University Press, 1999.

Liberia-Peters, Maria (1941–) *prime minister of the Netherlands Antilles*

Maria Philomena Peters was born on May 20, 1941 on Curaçao, Netherlands Antilles, the daughter of a construction foreman. Her homeland consists of a group of six small islands located in the Central Caribbean and north of the Venezuelan coastline. Long a Dutch colonial possession, the Antilles served as an important oil refinery station throughout most of the 20th century. It sports a highly varied population, ethnically speaking, with those of Dutch, Spanish, and English stock living alongside the descendants of African slaves. Liberia-Peters was educated locally, and she attributes her work ethic to strict parents, who instilled in her virtues of discipline and resolve. "In order to make progress in life you have to work," she stated. "Don't be ashamed of any work, as long as your conscience can bear it." In 1958 she left home to attend the Normal Training School for the Teaching of Children in Emmen, the Netherlands, graduating four years later. Commencing in 1962, Peters served as head teacher in several public schools, rising to supervisor of Roman Catholic Schools for Early Childhood Education. In 1972 she returned to the Netherlands for an advanced degree in pedagogics from the University of the Netherlands. Once back she met and married Niels Liberia, a civil servant. Liberia-Peters then joined the National People's Party (NPP), a conservative organization, and began agitating on educational issues. In 1974 she acquired her first taste of political activism by organizing the Steering Committee for Women's Organizations. Success here prompted her to run for public office, and, in 1975, she won a seat on the Curaçao island council. In this capacity she was subsequently appointed to the Executive Council of the island government by Queen Beatrix of the Netherlands.

In 1982 Liberia-Peters ran for a seat in the Staten, or legislature for the Netherlands Antilles, and won. The coalition regime then in power assigned her additional duties as the minister of economic affairs before being voted out in 1984. However, Liberia-Peters had favorably impressed her colleagues as a conciliator and consensus-builder, and that year she was asked to form a new coalition government. She thus became the

Netherlands Antilles' first female head of state, and she remained in power for two additional years. Her biggest struggle at this time was adjustment following Royal Dutch Shell's decision to close their giant refineries on Curaçao and Aruba. These facilities accounted for nearly 20 percent of all jobs in the entire Netherlands Antilles and their departure would have struck a disastrous blow to the local economy. Liberia-Peters moved quickly and worked out an agreement with the Venezuelan firm PDSVA to manage both refineries. The majority of jobs remained on the islands.

One of Liberia-Peters's unsavory tasks as prime minister was imposition of a 10 percent income tax to buoy up a new national fund. It was created as a hedge against any future economic emergencies. However, the move resulted in the election of Don Martina of the left-wing New Antilles Movement (NAM) in 1986, and Liberia-Peters stepped down to serve as head of the opposition. She held this post until 1988, when the NPP made a political comeback and she again served as prime minister. Her second administration lasted four years, near the end of which she sponsored a referendum on Curaçao's independence from the Antillean Federation (Aruba having departed in 1986). When it was soundly defeated, Liberia-Peters resigned for the second and last time. New elections resulted in Susanne Camelia-Rower of the NAM becoming the Netherlands Antilles' second female prime minister. Since 1992 Liberia-Peters has served as head of the opposition in parliament. One of her significant goals remains creation of a Caribbean bloc to protect and enhance the region's small economies, especially in light of the North American Free Trade Agreement (NAFTA). She feels that, "If everybody bundles up together maybe something good will happen."

Further Reading

James, Conrad, and John Perivdaris, eds. *The Cultures of the Hispanic Caribbean.* Gainesville: University Press of Florida, 2000.

Lynch, Edgar. *Know Your Political History: St. Maarten, Saba, St. Eustatius.* Philipsburg, St. Maarten: House of Nehesi Publishers, 1999.

Marshall, Nelson. *Understanding the Eastern Caribbean and the Antilles.* St. Michaels, Md.: The Anchorage Publishers, 1992.

Peters, Donald C. *The Democratic System in the Eastern Caribbean.* New York: Greenwood Press, 1992.

Sedoc-Dahlberg, Betty, ed. *The Dutch Caribbean: Prospects of Democracy.* New York: Gordon and Breach, 1990.

Li Peng (Li P'eng) (1928–) *prime minister of China*

Li Peng was born in Chengdu, the capital of Sichuan province, China, in October 1928, the son of Communist parents. His father was an early martyr of the Chinese Communist movement, having been executed by Nationalist troops in 1930. Li was consequently adopted by a close relative, Zhou En Lai, the future prime minister, and raised in a Communist household. In 1945 he joined the Communist Party and enrolled at Yan'an Institute of Natural Science, where he studied electricity. Three years later Li was sent to the Moscow Power Institute, becoming part of the Soviet-trained elite that would one day run the country. He returned to the People's Republic of China in 1957 and commenced working on various hydroelectric power plants. Early on Li established himself as an efficient, if colorless, technocrat with pristine family ties to the party's old guard. This connection held him in good stead throughout the violent Cultural Revolution, during which, unlike many Russian-trained specialists, he was protected by the influence of his adopted father Zhou. This violent upheaval crippled the Chinese economy and brought scientific progress to a near standstill, but by the late 1970s DENG XIAOPING, a radical reformer, had come to power. Meanwhile Li, who touted a more traditional, conservative life, continued rising up the party ranks with positions of increasing responsibility. Between 1979 and 1981 he served as vice minister and minister of the electric power industry, and, four years later, he rose to minister of the State Education Committee. In 1988 his political fortunes rose again when he was appointed vice prime minister, which made him third in command after Prime Minister Zhao Ziyang and President JIANG ZEMIN.

China at this period was undergoing tremendous social and economic reforms at the behest of Chairman Deng, who embarked upon a radical restructuring of China's centrally planned socialist economy. Free markets and capitalism became the watchword of the day, and the nation experienced explosive periods of growth for many years. However, conservatively minded Li frequently railed against such free-wheeling reforms and, while agreeing that change was necessary, espoused the need for a more cautious pace. This brought him in direct conflict with superiors like Deng and Zhao, but the very reforms they championed brought about an unfortunate and unforeseen chain of events.

In March 1988, Li succeeded Zhao as prime minister of China. His rise coincided with increasing student unrest about the lack of academic freedom on campus. In May 1989 events culminated in a mass protest in Tiananmen Square, Beijing. The students reiterated their call for political freedoms that paralleled economic ones and pleaded with Li to address the crowd. Li and other conservatives, however, wasted no time marshaling military units for a final showdown. On the night of June 3, 1989, Chinese troops stormed into Tiananmen Square by force, killing several thousand students. The event was broadcast live and brought worldwide condemnation of the Communist regime. However, Li, now the most reviled man in China, had made his point. Reform, if allowed at all, would be dictated by the Communist Party.

To underscore his determination to maintain Communist Party orthodoxy, in April Li ventured to Moscow to meet with Soviet premier Mikhail Gorbachev. His was the first visit by a Chinese official in 30 years and signaled a new period of better relations between the two Communist giants. However, Li expressed reservations about Gorbachev's reforms in Russia, and he declared that China would pursue its own destiny. Li's fear about the unbridled pace of reform proved correct: within a year the Soviet Union had collapsed. This political catastrophe induced Chinese conservatives to redouble their determination to brake the pace of economic and educational reforms, which have since proceeded at much slower rates. However, in 1992 the National People's Congress forced Li to publicly denounce hard-line elements with the Communist Party for their obstructionism.

Li's association with the Tiananmen massacre, however, had not diminished his ability to force through important works in 1992. The most notable of these was the flooding of the famous Three Gorges to make way for new hydroelectric dams. Given the history associated with this region, it is a tragic loss to China and the world. Li's remaining tenure in office was successful, if unspectacular, and, in March 1998, he obeyed the 10-year limit in office by stepping down in favor of ZHU RONGJI. The advancement of Zhu, a known advocate of reform, represents a setback for conservative forces trying to hinder the pace of reform. Li, meanwhile, has since gained appointment as president of the National People's Congress. He thus remains the second-most-powerful politician in China after President JIANG ZEMIN. In March 2001 he used his position to condemn widespread corruption and graft, insisting that they threaten the very existence of China, and he also promised to enact tough new measures to combat them. In April 2002, Li was also dispatched to Japan, where he conferred with Prime Minister JUNICHIRO KOIZUMI on the 30th anniversary of the establishment of diplomatic relations between the two Asian powers. He pledged continuing cooperation with Japan on economic matters, and he assured business leaders that the huge and growing Chinese economy was an unprecedented opportunity, and not a threat, to the rest of Asia. Li Peng is slated for retirement in 2003.

Further Reading

Chang, Gordon G. *The Coming Collapse of China.* London: Random House Business, 2001.

Fewsmith, Joseph. *China since Tiananmen: The Politics of Transition.* Cambridge: Cambridge University Press, 2001.

Hutchings, Graham. *Modern China: A Companion to Rising Power.* London: Penguin, 2001.

Leung, Pak-Wah. *Political Leaders of Modern China, 1840–2001: A Biographical Dictionary.* Westport, Conn.: Greenwood Press, 2002.

Saich, Tony. *Governance and Politics in China.* Basingstoke, England: Palgrave, 2001.

Lipponen, Paavo (1941–) *prime minister of Finland*

Paavo Tapio Lipponen was born in Turtola, Finland, on April 23, 1941. Finland is a small republic on the Baltic Sea, sandwiched between Russia and Sweden. It previously formed part of Czarist Russia until 1919, when independence was won under a democratic constitution. Nonetheless, Finland's proximity to Russia and its successor state, the Soviet Union, weighed heavily on all foreign policy considerations. The country was forced to cede land to Soviet dictator Joseph Stalin following a bitter war in 1940, and, after World War II, Finland remained studiously neutral. It has since paid careful heed to the overarching concerns of its giant neighbor. Presently, the country is administered by a French-style parliamentary system, whereby a president and a prime minister share power and deal with a unicameral legislature, the

Eduskunta. Several political parties, representing a wide spectrum of beliefs, are present but no group has dominated the legislature since 1945. Consequently, the government is predisposed to coalition rule by several allied groupings. This, in turn, has resulted in a relatively high turnover in heads of state for an otherwise stable Scandinavian nation. Nonetheless, the Finnish people are well educated, highly skilled, and industrious. They also enjoy one of the world's highest standards of living.

Lipponen attended the University of Finland, where he obtained a master's degree in political science in 1965. Afterward he worked as a journalist until 1967, when he joined the Social Democratic Party (SDP). Lipponen rose rapidly through the party hierarchy, and he served as a special political adviser to the prime minister, 1979–82. He gained election to the parliament in 1983, remaining there four years. Afterward Lipponen sought to expand his horizons by working for the Helsinki city council in 1985–95, and he also headed the Finnish Institute of International Affairs, 1989–91. Two years later, by dint of good performance, he was elected

Paavo Lipponen *(Embassy of Finland)*

head of the SDP, and, in March 1995, he campaigned for a new seat in parliament. That year the party did better than anticipated, despite a lingering recession, and the SDP won the largest share of seats. As party leader, Lipponen became prime minister at the head of a broad ("Rainbow") coalition of five disparate parties. "The government will move forward," he announced, "sustained by the legacy of its predecessor. We can look forward to the future with optimism."

As head of the government, Lipponen displayed exception skill at juggling the various priorities of his coalition partners, yet always managing to deliver coherent national policies. His popularity was further abetted by the buoyant Finnish economy, which made impressive gains over the next five years. Lipponen's primary concern was national debt reduction to lower interest rates and thereby stimulate further growth. He accomplished this by refusing to cut taxes until the deficits were markedly below the yearly gross national product. This was done over the objections of conservatives in his coalition, but it had the effect of reducing Finland's debts and enhancing its international credit standing. The government also settled upon a "full employment" approach to grow out of recession and, consequently, by 1999, the 17 percent unemployment rate had been reduced to single digits. Overall, Lipponen's steadfast governance of the Finnish economy was well received, and, on March 21, 1999, the SDP was returned to office with 51 seats. He thus enjoys the longest-serving coalition government in Finnish history.

Lipponen's handling of foreign affairs was also a study in caution. Finland has traditionally maintained a neutral stance toward Russia and the pursuit of friendly relations with her giant neighbor remains a top priority. Previous agreements with the Soviet Union forbade Finland from joining any military alliances and, for this reason, Lipponen is one of few Western leaders who declines to seek NATO membership. The placement of a mighty Western alliance on the northern doorsteps of Russia is viewed as too destabilizing and an affront to good relations. As a sign of commitment to previous understandings, in 1992 Finland renewed its pledge to refrain from military alliances. This agreement was to be automatically renewed at five-year intervals unless annulled by either government. However, security arrangements have not precluded Finnish membership in the European Union (EU), which has been pursued vigorously. In fact, the Finnish economy is so sound, and its democratic traditions so firmly established, that the country was among the very first Scandinavian nations invited to join. Lipponen hopes that Finland's economic integration, with its mandated end to public support of the agricultural sector, will reduce deficits further and help preserve the generous welfare state now in place.

The most daunting problem confronting Lipponen at present is the prospect of building a fifth nuclear reactor. This is a project passionately opposed by leftists and the environmentally minded Green Party in his coalition, but his support is also a litmus test for his conservative allies as well. "If Europe begins to invest in imported natural gas, as appears to be the case, prices will eventually go up," he reasoned. "This is why Finland needs a new reactor. Our goal is a diversification of the energy resources we use." On May 24, 2002, parliament approved construction of Finland's fifth nuclear reactor by a vote of 107-92. Through its construction, Lipponen hopes to curtail Finland's dependency on Russia, which presently supplies 70 percent of the nation's electricity. Lipponen's diverse coalition apparently surmounted infighting over such divisive issues and prevailed.

Further Reading

Arter, David. "The March 1995 Finnish Election: The Social Democrats Storm Back." *West European Politics* 18 (October 1995): 194–205.

Jussila, Osmo, Seppo Hentila, and Jukka Nevakiri. *From Grand Duchy to a Modern State: A Political History of Finland since 1809.* London: Hurst and Company, 1999.

Kasekamp, Andres. "Radical Right-Wing Movements in the North-East Baltic." *Journal of Contemporary History* 34 (October 1999): 587–631.

Tiilikainen, Teija. *Europe and Finland: Defining the Political Identity of Finland in Western Europe.* Brookfield, Vt.: Ashgate, 1998.

Ylikangas, Heikki, Petri Karonen, and Martti Lehti. *Five Centuries of Violence in Finland and the Baltic Area.* Columbus: Ohio State University Press, 2001.

Lubbers, Ruud (1939–   ) *prime minister of the Netherlands*

Rudolphus Franciscus Marie Lubbers was born on May 7, 1939, in Rotterdam, the Netherlands, son of a wealthy engineer and factory owner. His family also possessed a strong Roman Catholic background. Lubbers attended the Jesuit-led St. Canisius College, Nijmegen, and the Netherlands College of Economics, Rotterdam, where he focused upon monetary matters. After graduating in 1962, Lubbers joined the family firm, Lubbers Hollandia Engineering Works, as codirector, becoming one of the wealthiest men in the Netherlands. Lubbers had also joined the left-leaning Catholic People's Party (KVP) in 1964 and first gained election by winning a seat on the Rijnmond Council of Rotterdam. Three years later the young man became minister of economic affairs in the Labor administration of Joop den Uly. In 1977 he failed to gain a similar post in the new center-right government of Andreas van Agt; instead he was elected to the lower house of parliament as a KVP member. Here he served as chairman of the newly formed Christian Democratic Appeal (CDA), an umbrella group of various Catholic and Protestant interest groups. Lubbers proved himself adept as a politician, particularly in his seemingly endless ability to formulate new and better ideas while discussing them, and, in 1978, he rose to become leader of the CDA in parliament. In November 1982, Prime Minister Agt suddenly resigned and Lubbers, as party head, cobbled together a new center-right coalition. He thus became, at the age of 43, the Netherlands' youngest prime minister to that date.

Lubbers' idealism was always tempered by pragmatism, and he proved himself a master of political improvisation. Dutch proportional representation in the system of government is naturally conducive to coalitions and compromise, but Lubbers took this to new extremes with his uncanny ability to work with any group—on any issue. Over the next 12 years he crafted governments consisting of center-right and then center-left groups, usually in tandem. His first administration, 1982–86, was characterized by extreme austerity budgets aimed at reigning in the country's traditionally generous social welfare state. This was accomplished to halt the rising national debt, itself brought about by the economic slowdowns of the decade. Said cuts proved painful and were publicly derided as the "Ruud Shock." Lubbers also made the courageous but politically unpopular decision to deploy American cruise and Pershing II missiles on Dutch soil to counter new Soviet weapons. Lubbers thus incurred the wrath of many unions and social organizations long accustomed to the public dole, but the Dutch economy posted impressive gains. In 1996 Lubbers was returned to office for a second term. He continued as before—trimming the welfare state, balancing the budget, and restoring long-lost confidence in government and other public institutions. To that end he also helped author the 1991 Maastricht Treaty, which paved the way for greater economic integration within the rapidly forming European Union (EU). In September 1989 Lubbers won an unprecedented third term, making him the longest-serving Dutch prime minister in history. Though the CDA had lost seats in the house, the prime minister again demonstrated flair for coalition politics by aligning himself with the opposition Labor Party.

Lubbers decided against running for a fourth term in 1992, possibly anticipating an appointment to succeed Jacques Delor as head of the European Commission. His absence, unfortunately, wielded disastrous effects upon the CDA's political fortunes. The public was ready for a change, and that year they decisively elected WIM KOK's Labor Party into power, eliminating Christian Democrats from government for the first time since 1945. It proved a sour note with which to conclude 12 years of political success, but Lubbers was determined to find work on the international stage. However, he was thwarted in his goal of heading the European Commission owing to opposition from German chancellor HELMUT KOHL. Lubbers next embarked on a campaign to become NATO's secretary-general, but this was vetoed by the United States, on the grounds of lack of qualifications. Lubbers then withdrew from politics altogether to teach at the University of Tilberg. He remained in obscurity until October 2000 when United Nations Secretary-General KOFI ANNAN personally named him high commissioner for refugees (UNHCR). He achieved this by beating out Jan Pronk, Prime Minister Kok's handpicked candidate. Lubbers thus became responsible for orchestrating deliveries of food, shelter, and medicine to the world's 14 million refugees, along with an additional 21 million displaced within their own homelands. He was undaunted by the task and established himself as an energetic spokesman for refugees around the world. In January 2002 he visited war-torn Chechnya to personally oversee UN relief efforts for 150,000 people. He also urged the Russian government to downsize military forces in the region and replace them with Chechen police officers. "We hope real solutions will come that mean people can go home," he insisted. "They are too scared." The following April Lubbers also appeared in Pakistan to assist in the resettlement of 250,000 Afghan refugees huddled there. He remains one of Europe's best-known, best-liked, and most durable political figures.

Further Reading

Andeweg, R. B., and Galen A. Irwin. *Governance and Politics of the Netherlands.* New York: Palgrave, 2002.

DeVries, Jouke, and Kutsal Yesilkagit. "Cove Executives and Party Policies: Privatization in the Netherlands." *West European Politics* 22, no. 1 (1999): 115–137.

Hendriks, Frank, and Theo A. J. Toonen, eds. *Polder Politics: The Re-invention of Consensus Democracy in the Netherlands.* Burlington, Vt.: Ashgate, 2001.

Noppe, Jo. "The Parliamentary Activity of the Belgian and Dutch Prime Ministers: A Comparison between Martens VIII, Dehaene I, and Lubbers III Administrations." *Res Publica* 42, no. 4 (2000): 521–545.

Srinivsanm, K. "The Lubbers II Cabinet and the Quest for Perfection." *Round Table* 346 (April 1996): 149–177.

Lucinschi, Petru (1940–) *president of Moldova*

Petru Lucinschi was born in Floresti, Moldova, in 1940. Moldova, also known as Bessarabia, had been part of Romania until 1940, when it was acquired by the Soviet Union. Moldova then became the second-smallest of many Soviet republics. Lucinschi was educated at the State University in Chisinau, the national capital, and he subsequently studied at the High Party School in Moscow. His background and interpersonal skills prepared him for a career as a ranking Communist Party functionary. Lucinschi advanced steadily through the party hierarchy and, in 1989, he became first secretary of the Moldovan Communist Party Central Committee. His good behavior culminated in appointment as secretary of the Soviet Communist Party Central Committee in Moscow, directly within the inner circles of power. However, once the Soviet government collapsed in August 1991, parliament proclaimed its independence as the new Republic of Moldova. Lucinschi then returned home and successfully ran for the local legislature. The following year he served as Moldova's ambassador to the new Russian Federation, and, in 1993, he returned to parliament as its chairman. Lucinschi gained reelection to parliament in March 1994 and began aspiring for the highest office in the land. Parliament at that time was controlled by the Agrarian Democratic Party (ADP), which consisted of mostly former Communists, from whom Lucinschi broke in 1995. The following year he gathered enough signatures to run as an independent and prevailed in a three-way race against ADP candidate Mircea Snegur and Communist Vladimir Voronin. A runoff was held on December 1, 1996, and Lucinschi decisively defeated Snegur by 54 percent to 46 percent of the vote. Thus, on January 15, 1995, he became Moldova's second freely elected leader. "I shall be a president who shall not divide people into good and bad," Lucinschi proclaimed: "I shall be a president for all."

The new president faced a multiplicity of obstacles that would have daunted the most astute and farsighted politician. Moldova, with the possible exception of Albania, remains Europe's poorest nation. Small and landlocked, it is surrounded by giant neighbors, including the Ukraine and Romania, and is largely devoid of natural resources. The region is endowed with fine weather and rich soil, making it a leading exporter of fruit and wine, but little else. The country also remains very much a hostage to its former Soviet past. The population is linguistically and ethnically Romanian, although a sizable Russian-speaking population also exists. Tensions over the prospects of rejoining either Romania or Russia, and the recriminations this might hold for respective native speakers, are rife. Since March 1992 there has also been an ongoing civil war in the tiny Russian-speaking region of Trans-Dniester, which is seeking independence. Fighting between Moldovan troops and Russian militia has resulted in about 700 deaths and the conflict is as yet unresolved. There are also recurrent fears that Romania harbors territorial ambitions for its old province and might try to annex it outright.

An even bigger headache remains the national economy, which has contracted one-third in gross national product since the fall of the Soviet Union. Lucinschi has tried repeatedly to initiate a concerted strategy of privatization of inefficient state-owned industries, but he has been thwarted at every step by a Communist-controlled legislature. Consequently, the International Monetary Fund (IMF) withheld development loans from Moldova for failing to implement full-scale privatization. The national economy is further saddled with a foreign debt approaching $1.1 billion, which hinders economic growth. To counter all this political deadweight, in May 1999 Lucinschi authorized a nonbinding referendum to strengthen the office of the presidency at the legislature's expense, thereby reducing its propensity for deadlocking badly needed reforms. The measure passed, but so few people cared to vote that parliament immediately questioned its validity, declaring it null and void. The future of Moldova's economy remains at an impasse pending wide-ranging constitutional and structural reforms.

Lucinschi's inability to pass reforms induced him not to seek a second term. Not surprisingly, during national elections held on February 26, 2001, the still-viable Communist Party won just over 50 percent of the vote, giving them effective control of the government. Political pundits attribute the results to simmering anger over market reforms that have left the majority of Moldovans in extreme poverty. On April 7, 2001, Lucinschi surrendered power to his former adversary Vladimir Voronin, who promises to expand state control over key sectors of the economy. The former president waxed philosophical over his lackluster term in office. "We have managed to expand ties with many countries and international organizations," he reflected, "initialed a base political treaty with Romania, drafted a similar document with Russia, and we are solving problems of demilitarization on the state border with Ukraine." However, Lucinschi regrets not having been able to resolve the ongoing Dniester conflict or improve the living standards of his country.

Further Reading

Brezianu, Andrei, and John Woronoff. *Historical Dictionary of the Republic of Moldova*. Lanham, Md.: Scarecrow Press, 2000.

Dima, Nicholas. *Moldova and the Transdnestr Republic: Russia's Geopolitics toward the Balkans*. Boulder, Colo.: Wiley, 2001.

Dawisha, Karnen, and Bruce Parrott. *Democratic Changes and Authoritarian Reactions in Russia, Ukraine, Belarus, and Moldova*. New York: Cambridge University Press, 1997.

King, Charles. *The Moldovans: Romania, Russia and the Politics of Culture*. Stanford, Calif.: Hoover Institute Press, 2000.

Lowenhardt, John, Ronald J. Hill, and Margot Light. "A Wider Europe: The View from Minsk and Chisinau." *International Affairs* 77 (July 2001): 605–621.

Quinland, Paul D. "Moldova under Lucinschi: The First Two Years." *Romanian Civilization* 9, no. 2 (2000): 3–26.

Lukashenko, Alyaksandr (1954–)

president of Belarus

Alyaksandr Lukashenko was born in Vitebsk Oblast, Belarus, on August 30, 1954. His country, an important military and economic crossroads since medieval times, then formed part of the Soviet Union. It is a small stretch of land, landlocked, and surrounded by Poland to the west, Ukraine to the south, Russia to the east, and Latvia and Lithuania to the north. Ethnically, Belarus enjoys close cultural and linguistic ties to Russia, and the majority of its population is bilingual. However, following the collapse of Soviet communism in August 1991, the country declared itself an independent republic, but its capital of Minsk performs similar functions for the new Commonwealth of Independent States. In March 1994 Belarus finally discarded its last trappings of Soviet government by adopting a new, democratic constitution calling for a president, a national assembly, and a supreme court. As with most of the newly freed and former Soviet republics, it was widely anticipated that Belarus would seek closer political and economic ties to the West.

Lukashenko was educated at the Mohylev Pedagogical Institute and the Belarussian Agricultural Academy. After a brief stint teaching and two years military service as a border guard, he was appointed manager of the Gorodets State Farm in Mohylev in 1987. Three years later he gained appointment as a deputy in the Belarussian Supreme Soviet, or assembly. In this position Lukashenko gained notoriety for advocating closer ties to the Soviet Union, then in its death throes, and he cast the only dissenting vote against establishing its successor, the Commonwealth of Independent States. The country was then led by Stanislaus Shushkevich, a former nuclear scientist, who tried implementing Western-style economic reforms. However, his efforts to improve the sinking Belarus economy and standard of living was thwarted by corruption. Lukashenko, meanwhile, managed to have himself appointed chairman of the Interim Parliamentary Anticorruption Committee and, through this office, he helped drive the well-intentioned Shushkevich from power. Having made a name for himself hunting down corrupt politicians, and gauging the rising discontent from the muddled national economy, Lukashenko decided to run for the presidency in 1994. He was an outspoken, flamboyant campaigner, and unabashedly favorable toward the late Soviet Union—and the stability it represented. His call for a firmer hand on the tiller resonated with the voters of Belarus, and, on June 23, 1994, he was overwhelming elected by 80 percent of the voters. Lukashenko thus became Belarus's first freely elected president.

No sooner had Lukashenko taken command than he took deliberate steps to enhance the power of his office. In 1996 he demanded and received sweeping constitutional reforms that strengthened the presidency and extended its term from five to seven years. He then summarily dissolved parliament, replacing it with a Soviet-style legislature that rubber-stamped his dictates as warranted. In this manner Lukashenko went on to pack the Supreme Court with his cronies, thereby further tightening his grip on power. Worse, his tenure in office began manifesting all the trappings of the former Soviet Union. The state security apparatus retains the name and badge of the former KGB and operates with identical impunity. Opposition groups were muzzled, beaten, and arrested, and several prominent critics suddenly "disappeared." From an economic standpoint, it was also a return to the good old days. Lukashenko reinstated tight centralized control over key sectors of the flagging economy, which, in turn, led the International Monetary Fund (IMF) to withhold developmental loans. The renewed emphasis on controls also led to a near collapse of the private sector, as up to 30 percent of the nation's entrepreneurs have relocated to Russia. Belarus remains an economic quagmire, with sluggish growth and steadily declining living standards. However, Lukashenko's control over political events remains almost absolute. During the September 11, 2001, elections, he "officially" received 75.6 percent of the vote, a tally which was roundly decried by the United States and other Western observers.

Nor was Lukashenko hesitant to act upon his pro-Russian political leanings. He campaigned on a platform calling for closer ties to the country's giant neighbor and has taken several steps to integrate their national economies. By 1998 Belarus and Russia had all but done away with borders, sharing a single currency and identical tax and customs measures. A bilateral agreement mandating closer military and political cooperation has also been signed. Moreover, Lukashenko remains oblivious to mounting criticism heaped on his authoritarian regime by Europe and the United States. "In the next year and a half," he exulted, "Belarus and the West and NATO will have not only normalized dialogue but shown the world how civilized people relate to each other when they live in the same house, which is Europe." For helping to drag Belarus back into the past, and keep it there with the heavy hand of state-sponsored political repression, Lukashenko has cemented his reputation as Europe's latest dictator.

Further Reading

Balmaceda, Margarita M., James I. Clem, and Lisbeth L. Tarlow. *Independent Belarus: Domestic Determinants, Regional Dynamics, and Implications for the West.* Cambridge, Mass.: Harvard University Press, 2002.

D'Amato, Erik. "Belarus—Lukashenko Tightens His Grip." *Euromoney,* no. 390 (October 2001): 84–92.

Feus, Kim. *The EU and Belarus.* London: Kogan Page, 2002.

Karbalevich, Valerii. "The Belorussian Model of Transformation: Aleksandr Lukashenko's Regime and the Nostalgia for the Soviet Past: An Attempt at Analysis." *International Journal of Sociology* 31 (Winter 2001–2002): 7–38.

Korosteleva, Elena, and Rosalind J. Marsh. *Contemporary Belarus: Between Democracy and Dictatorship.* Richmond, Va.: Curzon, 2002.

Popov, Igor. "Belarus Under Lukashenko." *Contemporary Review* 250 (January 2002): 22–31.

Riach, David A. "Themes in Belorussian National Thought: The Origins, Emergence, and Development of the Belorussian 'National Idea.'" Unpublished Ph.D. dissertation, Carleton University, 2001.

Lula da Silva, Luiz Inácio (1945–   )
president of Brazil

Luiz Inácio Lula da Silva was born on October 27, 1945, in Garahuns, Pernambuco, Brazil, the son of an impoverished stevedore. He endured a childhood of grinding poverty and only became literate at the age of 10. In 1969 Lula da Silva joined the Metallurgist Trade Union, and by 1975 he was voted president. In 1980 he founded the left-wing Worker's Party, which posted successively impressive tallies in state and local elections. In 1986 Lula was elected to the federal congress from the state of São Paolo by the largest margin in Brazilian history. He was then a fiery radical who agitated for closing the ever-widening gap between rich and poor. In 1989 he felt emboldened to run for the presidency and narrowly lost. In 1994 and 1998 he ran again, only to lose to incumbent FERNANDO HENRIQUE CARDOSO. However, in 2002 Cardoso surrendered his office, and Lula ran against four other opponents. No candidate received a majority, but a runoff gave Lula 61 percent of the votes cast making him Brazil's first leftist president in 40 years. He is also the country's first chief executive of a humble background.

Lula was inaugurated on January 2, 2003, with such leading socialist presidents as Cuba's FIDEL CASTRO and Venezuela's HUGO CHÁVEZ in attendance. "I am not the result of one election," he declared at the swearing-in ceremony. "I am the result of history." The new president has toned down his typically radical rhetoric and pledged to work with the International Monetary Fund to keep Brazil from defaulting on its national debts. This has entailed some belt-tightening measures and new taxes, which have occasioned some protest. Upon taking office, he was immediately faced with a strike by his old trade union, which is demanding wage increases. In addition, Lula faces the prospect of a sinking economy and lowered national expectations, but he insists that his agenda remains assisting Brazil's impoverished majority. "These reforms are not for the benefit of some [while hurting] others," he informed an uneasy Congress. "They are for us to see if we can transform our nation into a developed country that conquers the place it should already have occupied in this globalized world."

Further Reading

Eakin, Marshall C. *Tropical Capitalism: The Industrialization of Belo Horizonte, Brazil.* New York: Palgrave, 2002.

Lopez, Carlos T. *Brazil at a Crossroads: An Evaluation of the Economic, Political, and Social Situation.* New York, Peter Lang, 2002.

M

Macapagal-Arroyo, Gloria (1947–)
president of the Philippines

Gloria Macapagal was born in Manila, the Philippines, on April 5, 1947, the daughter of a leading politician. Gloria's father, Diosdado Macapagal, served as president of the Philippines from 1961–65, and the experience of living in the Malacañang Palace indelibly impressed her with a sense of power and civic responsibility. She graduated from the Assumption Convent as class valedictorian and subsequently studied at Georgetown University, Washington, D.C. Macapagal subsequently finished her bachelor's degree at Assumption College before returning to the Philippines for graduate study. She then obtained a master's in economics at Ateneo de Manila University and a doctorate in macroeconomics at the University of the Philippines. She also married prominent attorney José Miguel Tuason Arroyo.

Macapagal-Arroyo commenced her public career in 1986 when she served as undersecretary of trade and industry in the administration of President Corazon Aquino. Young, ambitious, and technically competent, she felt inspired to run for office in 1992, and won election to the Senate. Her successful reelection three years later confirmed her status as a rising star of Filipino politics. In 1998 Macapagal-Arroyo successfully ran for the vice presidency of the country and won a term of office

under the victorious presidential candidate, JOSEPH ESTRADA. In this office she also served as his secretary of social welfare and development, which further enhanced her reputation as a benefactor of the nation's poor. However, Estrada was rapidly overtaken by charges of widespread corruption and impeachment proceedings were begun against him. Macapagal-Arroyo, however, guilefully waited until it was apparent that Estrada's presidency could not be salvaged before resigning from his cabinet. When the beleaguered president refused to leave, more than 200,000 Filipinos took to the streets of Manila, demanding his resignation on January 19, 2001. Furthermore, having lost the support of key police and military figures, Estrada finally stepped down and the Supreme Court declared his office vacant. Macapagal-Arroyo then moved swiftly to fill the void, becoming the nation's second woman president within a decade on January 20, 2001. She has since served as the most popular politician in the Philippines in continuing her father's populist legacy.

Macapagal-Arroyo came to power when the Philippines was still reeling from the Asian currency crisis. Productivity was down, unemployment was up, and, worse, the national currency was buffeted by turmoil surrounding Estrada's resignation. However, within five months of taking office, and drawing upon her experience as a trained economist, she implemented a comprehensive blueprint for reviving the moribund economy, reducing unemployment, and attacking poverty. The heart of this campaign centers upon privatizing inefficient state-run industries, putting an end to widespread corruption, and attracting foreign investment. As a committed Catholic who carries a Bible on her person every day, she is also committed to mitigating the sufferings of the poverty-stricken. However, Estrada's support also runs deep among the poor, to whom he catered politically, and in May 2001 a mass demonstration outside the presidential palace turned violent and had to be repressed by force. In a move calculated to demonstrate her resolve to remain in office, Macapagal-Arroyo declared the capital in a "state of rebellion," which authorized the use of military forces to restore order. But future unrest hinges upon the outcome of Estrada's trial for political plunder, in which he faces the death penalty. The prospects of an acquittal also disturbs most constitutional scholars, as he never resigned the presidency and may take to the streets demanding it back.

A bigger challenge facing Macapagal-Arroyo is the ongoing Muslim insurrection in the jungles of the southern Philippines. The rebellion is spearheaded by the Abu Sayyaf ("Bearer of the Sword") guerrilla group, which is intent upon founding an independent Islamic republic. For several years they waged a campaign of terrorism and kidnapping, killing several hostages. Repeated bombings and assassinations have also been linked to their secession efforts. However, their connection to Osama bin Laden's al-Qaeda terrorist organization induced President GEORGE W. BUSH to proffer military assistance to help stamp out the guerrillas. In January 2002, Macapagal-Arroyo made headlines at home by accepting Bush's offer and allowing American troops back on Philippine soil for the first time in a decade. However, she was adamant that they will be used for training purposes only and that all fighting is to remain in the hands of the Philippine army. "We are not fighting Islam," she cautioned, "we are fighting terrorism." The following month she visited New York to attend the World Economic Forum, where she railed against "the handmaiden of terrorism, poverty." The diminutive president then called upon rich nations for greater assistance in helping the world's poor. Macapagal-Arroyo is presently buoyed by an economic growth rate of 3.7 percent—stronger than expected. Nonetheless she declined to run for reelection in 2004.

Further Reading

Bankoff, Grey, Kathleen Weekley. *History, State, and National Identity in the Philippines.* London: C. Hurst, 2000.

Carrion-Buck, Maria Rosa N., Ma Lourdes Brillantes, and Antonio T. Barcelo. *Gloria Macapagal-Arroyo: Continuing the Legacy of Principled Leadership.* Parañaque: Seagull Philippines, 2000.

Hedman, Eva-Lotta E. *Philippine Politics and Society in the Twentieth Century: Colonial Legacies, Post-colonial Trajectories.* New York: Routledge, 2000.

Kang, David C. *Crony Capitalism: Corruption and Development in South Korea and the Philippines.* Cambridge: Cambridge University Press, 2002.

Labrador, Mel C. "The Philippines in 2001: High Drama, a New President, and Setting the Stage for Recovery." *Asian Survey* 42 (January–February, 2002): 141–49.

Nadeau, Kathleen M. *Liberation Theology in the Philippines: Faith in a Revolution.* Westport, Conn.: Praeger, 2002.

Mahdi Mohammed, Ali (1940–) *president of Somalia*

Mohammed Ali Mahdi was born at Mogadishu, Somalia, in 1940, a scion of the Abgal subclan of the larger Hawiye grouping. Somalia was then an Italian colony about to be captured by the British. It remained under a United Nations mandate for many years until achieving independence in July 1960. Ali Mahdi, as part of the Abgal community that constitutes the regional merchant class, was raised in a commercial environment and initially trained for business. However, he received teacher training courses in Somalia, and he subsequently underwent community health training in Egypt and Italy between 1963 and 1966. He then returned home to serve as director of malaria research until 1969, when the government was overthrown by General Mohamed Siad Barre. The new leader instituted a brutal and corrupt regime for his own benefit, an act which induced Ali Mahdi to become politically active in opposition groups. He was then arrested and the experience of prison imbued him with caution. Ali Mahdi thereafter served as a businessman and operated a plush hotel for foreigners in Mogadishu. By 1990 Siad Barre's policies had become unbearable, and Ali Mahdi signed a petition protesting such excesses. The general responded by issuing an arrest warrant, and he fled the country for

Italy. In Rome he established an office for the opposition United Somali Congress (USC), and he channeled funds back home for guerrilla fighters. By 1991 the Hawiye-based USC fighters brought the war to the nation's capital, and Siad Barre fled Somalia for his life. The movement next tried establishing order through an interim president to serve as a symbol of national unity, pending formation of an actual government. Mahdi, viewed by six guerrilla groups as the best compromise candidate, was then drafted to serve as acting executive of the new Somali Salvation Alliance. He was sworn into office on August 18, 1991, declaring "in the name of God Almighty to work without fear or favor in the interests of the Somali people."

No sooner had Mahdi occupied his office than he ran afoul of USC chairman MOHAMMAD FARAH AIDID, a fellow Hawiye. Unlike Mahdi, who had almost no following outside of Mogadishu, Aidid commanded an army of several thousand fighters. And, like many other factional leaders, he was angered that Mahdi was nominated for high office without consulting him. Aidid expressed his dissatisfaction by attacking the regime's supporters in the capital. Mahdi's forces fought back tenaciously, and a new Somali civil war commenced in earnest.

Unlike most African countries, which are badly divided along tribal and linguistic lines, Somalis all belong to the same ethnic grouping, speak the same language, and subscribe to the same moderate Sunni branch of Islam. Worse, as fighting spilled out into the countryside, many warlords took advantage of the situation by carving out their own personal enclaves. Somalia was then hit by a prolonged drought and severe starvation, and, in December 1992, President George H. W. Bush committed U.S. forces to restore order and distribute food to the populace. The prospect of such powerful allies greatly heartened Mahdi, as did the thousands of United Nations peacekeeping troops that followed. Unfortunately, even this formidable array could not remove rival militias from the streets of Mogadishu, and pitched battles between warlords and peacekeepers erupted. In 1994 Mahdi participated in peace talks held at Nairobi, Kenya, to form a government of national reconciliation, but to no avail. By 1997 Aidid, who had also styled himself "president," died of wounds received in fighting after the Westerners pulled out. Mahdi's term in office also expired that year, and no candidate was forthcoming to succeed him. The sorry situation of competing warlords, aided and abetted by clan rivalry and black marketing, continues to this day.

Despite his ineffectiveness as Somalia's president, Mahdi continues on as a prominent national politician. In 1999 he admitted that the overthrow of Siad Barre in 1991 had achieved nothing and said he further feared that the formalization of new regional administrations might prevent Somalia from ever again functioning as a national entity. Nonetheless, in April 2000 he appeared in neighboring Djibouti to attend peace talks with 100 other clan leaders. To date, little of substance has been resolved and Somalia continues on as a nation without a viable government—or leader. It remains one of Africa's most enduring tragedies.

Further Reading

Besteman, Catherine L. *Unraveling Somalia: Race, Violence, and the Legacy of Slavery.* Philadelphia: University of Pennsylvania Press, 1999.

Dool, Abdullah. *Somalia: A Creative Political Philosophy for the New Somali Generation.* London: Horn Heritage Publications, 2000.

Farah, Nuruddin. *Yesterday, Tomorrow: Voices from the Somali Diaspora.* New York: Cassell, 2000.

Jacquin-Berdal, Dominique. *Nationalism and Ethnicity in the Horn of Africa: A Critique of the Ethnic Interpretation.* Lewiston, N.Y.: Edwin Mellen Press, 2003.

Lang, John B. "Somalia: A Story of Centralization's Devastation of a Segmented Society." Unpublished master's thesis, Creighton University, 1999.

Peterson, Scott. *Me against My Brother: At War in Somalia, Sudan, and Rwanda.* New York: Routledge, 2000.

Major, John (1943–) *prime minister of Great Britain*

John Major was born on March 29, 1943, in Merton district, London, the son of a circus acrobat and small businessman. In 1954 hardship forced his family to relocate to Brixton, a poor working-class neighborhood. Major, while a good student, disliked school and he dropped out at 16 to work. He spent several years as a laborer and several months on the public dole while unemployed. This experience convinced him that Britain's paternalistic approach to societal problems only perpetuated poverty. However, he eventually became a clerk at the Standard Chartered bank, one of England's biggest, and he rose by sheer talent to bank chairman's assistant. By 1968 he had joined the Conservative Party, or Tories, and gained election on the Lambeth Borough Council. Success here only whetted his appetite for national politics and, in 1979, following two failed attempts, Major won a seat in the House of Commons from Huntingdonshire in east central England. That year also marked the rise of Margaret Thatcher as prime minister, and their two political careers became inextricably linked.

Commencing in 1980, Major experiencing a rapid rise to the top of Tory politics. After a stint as parliamentary secretary, he became party whip in 1984, which gave him much greater national exposure. It was also in this capacity that he came to Prime Minister Thatcher's attention at a party, where he successfully debated economics with the "Iron Lady" and made a good impression. After serving several more capable years as undersecretary of social security, where he evinced great concern for the poor, Major advanced to chief secretary of the treasury. He took a staunchly conservative line on public expenditures, insisting that "People must understand that if they have jam today, they may not be able to afford butter tomorrow." However, the turning point in Major's career occurred in July 1989, when Thatcher suddenly tapped the affable young man, relatively unknown outside of party circles, to serve as foreign secretary. This thrust Major into the national limelight for the first time, and the following October Thatcher reassigned him as Chancellor of the Exchequer, the head of the national treasury. Here Major called upon his considerable skills as a former banker and, in May 1990, he drew up the 1991 fiscal budget that featured—in the Thatcherite tradition—high interest rates to combat inflation. However, he also differed from Thatcher in being favorably disposed toward closer ties to European Union members, which many Conservatives viewed as threatening to national sovereignty. But Major, by dint of his smooth interpersonal style, managed to diffuse most critics and, in October 1990, he facilitated Britain's entry into the Exchange Rate Mechanism (ERM) of the European Monetary System. This was the first step toward adopting a single, European currency.

Britain, meanwhile, continued to experience high unemployment and low productivity, facts that bore heavily upon Prime Minister Thatcher's popularity ratings. After being challenged as party head, she unexpectedly concluded her 11-year administration by stepping down. A power struggle ensued to succeed her, and Major, chosen as heir apparent, eventually defeated two strong contenders to become Tory leader. On November 27, 1990, he then presented his credentials to Queen Elizabeth II as the youngest British prime minister to serve in the 20th century up to that date. He was also one of very few British executive officers to have never attended college. In view of his intelligence, demonstrated political skills, and status as heir to the Thatcher legacy, much was expected of him. Unlike his confrontational predecessor, however, Major strove for party unity. He appointed opponents Douglas Hurd and Michael Heseltine to his cabinet. And, despite his erstwhile conservative credentials, Major was in fact a centrist politician with neither the flair nor the fire of Margaret Thatcher.

Once in office, Major's first task was to oversee Thatcher's policy toward SADDAM HUSSEIN's invasion of Kuwait. In the spring of 1991 British forces played a conspicuous role in the ensuing Gulf War and its victorious conclusion. With this victory in hand, Major next sought political legitimacy by calling for elections in April 1992. Surprisingly, even though the polls indicated a Labour victory, the Tories were completely successful. Over the next five years, Major grappled with a sagging national economy, growing resistance toward integration with the European Union (EU), and elusive prospects for peace in Northern Ireland. The Irish Republican Army (IRA) let their discontent over peace talks be known when they exploded a bomb within 40 feet of 10 Downing Street—Major's office. Nevertheless, by 1994 significant ground was covered, which laid the foundations for the IRA's unprecedented cease-fire. In 1993 Major also proved instrumental in securing Parliament's ratification of the Maastricht Treaty, which laid the groundwork for greater European integration. Nonetheless, Conservative Party opposition to Britain's entry into European monetary union proved unrelenting and politically embarrassing to Major, who, in a show of force, resigned as party leader in July 1995. He then ran against a single candidate, was reelected by wide margins, and was thus strengthened in his ability to formulate and implement EU policy. But the Tories remained dogged by a balking economy and, by 1997, Major's poll ratings were at 20 percent—the lowest ever recorded for a modern prime minister. His Labour opponent this time was TONY BLAIR, a dynamic, telegenic personality who contrasted sharply with the dour, businesslike persona of the Tory leader. After 18 years of conservative rule, the nation was apparently ready for a change. The ensuing election of May 1997 was a debacle for the Tories and Major summarily re-signed as both prime minister and head of the party. He was replaced by William Hague and has since avoided the limelight. Though ultimately unsuccessful from a policy standpoint, Major still enjoys one of the most meteoric climbs to power in modern British political history.

Further Reading

Blair, Alasdair. "Understanding the Major Governments." *Contemporary British History* 15, no. 1 (2001): 115–122.

Cowley, Philip, and John Garry. "The British Conservative Party and Europe: The Choosing of John Major." *British Journal of Political Science* 28, no. 3 (1998): 429–479.

Doey, Peter. *The Major Premiership: Politics and Policies under John Major, 1990–97.* New York: St. Martin's Press, 1999.

Holmes, Martin. *John Major and Europe: The Failure of a Policy, 1990–7.* London: The Bruges Group, 1997.

Major, John R. *John Major: The Autobiography.* London: HarperCollins, 1999.

Reitan, Earl A. *Tory Radicalism: Margaret Thatcher, John Major, and the Transformation of Modern Britain, 1979–1997.* Lanham, Md.: Rowman and Littlefield, 1997.

Malielegaoi, Tuilaepa (1946–) *prime minister of Samoa*

Tuilaepa Sailele Malielegaoi was born in Lape Village, Western Samoa, in 1946. His homeland consists of a chain of two large and seven small volcanic islands lying 1,500 miles north of New Zealand. To the east is another island, American Samoa, whose inhabitants are ethnically related, but is a separate entity. The population presently totals 230,000, which is largely of Polynesian descent. The islands became a German protectorate in 1899. During World War I they were occupied and administered by New Zealand. In 1946 Western Samoa became a United Nations trust territory and measures for internal governance were systematically introduced, culminating in the constitution of 1960. Two years later Western Samoa became the first independent Pacific island nation, and, in July 1997, it officially renamed itself Samoa to distinguish itself from American Samoa. The islands are administered by a prime minister, who is chosen from a legislative assembly, the Fono. Prior to 1991

voting and political office were reserved for holders of chiefly titles, or *matai*. This system by its very nature excluded all women and most younger men. Universal suffrage has since been granted, but all candidates for the Fono still require *matai* status.

Malielegaoi was educated at the Marist Brothers' St. Joseph College on Latopa before attending St. Paul's College in Auckland, New Zealand. He subsequently studied economics at the University of Auckland, receiving master's degrees in accounting and economics. Upon reaching adulthood, he also assumed the *matai* title Tuilaepa. Malielegaoi returned home and occupied public service positions in the administration of Tofilau Eli Alesana, a legendary Samoan politician and founder of the Human Rights Protection Party (HRPP), the island's largest. Malielegaoi, meanwhile, was authorized to represent his island at various international conferences, and, in 1981, he gained election to the Fono. There he advanced his reputation through the party hierarchy and in 1988 the position of finance minister was tendered to him. But his career reached an important turning point in 1981 when the office of deputy prime minister was conferred. In this office he struck up a close association with the aging Alesana, and he assumed more and more of the island's daily administration during periods of incapacity. When Tofilau could no longer fulfill his duties in November 1998, the Fono elected Malielegaoi to succeed him.

The accession of Malielegaoi represents something of a generational change in Samoan politics because of his relative youth. As such he is considered somewhat headstrong and independent in dealing with elders, traits held unfavorably by a society that prizes deference and seniority. Nonetheless, his grounding in economics left him with a better grasp of Samoa's place in the world economy than others of his contemporaries. "We put in place our fiscal and monetary policies which focused on ensuring that we have discipline in our own budgetary management," he insisted. "We are very confident that this will bring additional impetus to the economy." Malielegaoi continued Tofilau's policy of privatizing government owned assets, especially Polynesian Airlines, the national carrier, which had been poorly administered and awash in debt. He also adamantly pursued diversification of Samoa's economy to lessen its reliance upon agriculture. This constitutes an important and traditional part of the island's overall economy, but as a whole it is too susceptible to typhoons and other natural disasters. Malielegaoi therefore intends to place greater emphasis upon fishing and tourism, and he has argued for funding to develop the necessary infrastructure, especially hotels, to support the latter. He also maintains friendly relations with various Japanese interests throughout Samoa, for they constitute the largest single source of foreign aid.

Malielegaoi's administration has proven by and large popular, but, in July 1999, it weathered a blistering scandal when Luagalau Levaula Kamu, the minister of public works, was assassinated. This was Samoa's first politically inspired killing. The circumstances surrounding his death appeared even more suspicious because, at the time of his death, he was investigating allegations of corruption and bribery in high places. Two former governmental ministers have since been charged with the murder, although Malielegaoi was not implicated. Nonetheless, the stain of corruption lingered, and in elections held on March 3, 2001, the governing HRPP lost 12 seats. This brought its total representation down to 23, but, by deft maneuvering, Malielegaoi managed to bring several newly elected Fono members into his ruling coalition, preserving his stay in office. "It should be noted that quite a few independent candidates are our supporters," he beamed. Malielegaoi managed to stave off defeat, but his mishandling of the corruption investigation led to the biggest threat to HRPP dominance in 19 years of rule.

Further Reading

Field, Michael. *Mau: Samoa's Struggle for Independence.* Auckland: Polynesian Press, 1991.

Lawson, Stephanie. *Tradition versus Democracy in the South Pacific: Fiji, Tonga, and Western Samoa.* New York: Cambridge University Press, 1996.

Meleisea, Malama. *Change and Adaptation in Western Samoa.* Christchurch: University of Canterbury, 1992.

Olson, M. D. "Regulating Custom: Land, Law, and Central Judiciary in Samoa." *Journal of Pacific History* 32 (September 1997): 153–180.

Tuimaleali'fano, Morgan. "Titular Disputes and National Leadership in Samoa." *Journal of Pacific History* 33 (June 1998): 91–104.

Mandela, Nelson (1918–) *president of South Africa*

Rolihlala Dalibhunga Mandela was born on July 18, 1918, in Mvezo, Transkei, South Africa, a member of the influential Thembu tribe. His father was a tribal chief's counselor who died while Mandela was still a child, and he was raised by a tribal regent. This had a profound effect on the young man, as did being educated at a nearby Methodist school. Thereafter he adopted the name Nelson and became deeply imbued with Christian sensibilities. Mandela entered Fort Hare College in Alice in 1938, which was then South Africa's only institute for higher learning that accepted black Africans. There he became active in student unrest over racial inequities and was expelled in 1940. Returning to Transkei, he relocated to Johannesburg to avoid a traditional arranged marriage and worked in a gold mine. Again, the stark mistreatment of black Africans by the white establishment seared his conscience and he became obsessed by notions of social justice. To that end, after studying law at the University of Witwatersrand, he cofounded the Youth League of the African National Congress (ANC) in 1944 and rose to its presidency in 1950. Despite his growing political radicalism, Mandela studiously distanced himself from Communists while also entreating Indian activists to present a united front against racial discrimination. His cause received greater impetus after 1948, when the all-white National Party took control of parliament and enacted a program of strict racial separation, which came to be reviled as apartheid.

In 1952, Mandela and Oliver Tambo established the first all-black legal service in South Africa while the ANC commenced a campaign of passive civil disobedience. Consequently, thousands of ANC sympathizers were arrested, including Mandela, who was banned from attending future meetings. He countered by devising the "M-Plan," which established small cells of underground activists who could escape police detection. In 1956 Mandela was arrested and charged with treason but, after a trial lasting five years, he was cleared for lack of evidence. In 1960 his political fortunes changed in the wake of the so-called Sharpeville Massacre, whereby police shot and killed a number of peaceful demonstrators. This act convinced Mandela that passive resistance had failed, and he was tasked by the ANC to form a military wing, Umkhonto wa Sizwe ("Spear of the Nation"), to conduct guerrilla warfare. Mandela was captured shortly afterward in 1962, convicted of inciting workers to strike, and received a sentence of five years in prison. When incriminating documents surrounding his guerrilla activities later surfaced, his sentence was revised to life imprisonment. Mandela nonetheless took the opportunity to defend himself in court, declaring: "I cherish the ideal of a democratic and free society in which all persons live together in harmony and with equal opportunities. It is an ideal I hope to live for and to achieve. But if needs be, it is an ideal for which I am prepared to die." Mandela spent the next 27 years behind bars, cruelly confined to a seven-by-seven foot cell, restricted to writing and receiving one letter every six months, and breaking rocks for days on end. "In prison, you come face to face with time," he maintained. "There is nothing more terrifying."

Fortunately for Mandela and the anti-apartheid movement, his sacrifice was not forgotten. Instead, Mandela was transformed into a living symbol of injustice and the fight against racial oppression. In 1982 a worldwide campaign began pressuring the South African regime to release him, and governments backed their words with economic sanctions. Because of his mounting global celebrity, Mandela was transferred from a high-security prison to more comfortable surroundings in Capetown. South African president P. W. Botha repeatedly offered to release Mandela if he would renounce violence, but he continually refused. But the rise of a new white leader, FREDERIK W. DE KLERK, served to accelerate the tempo of events. Realizing that apartheid was doomed, De Klerk began releasing political prisoners unconditionally in 1989, and, on February 2, 1990, Mandela was finally freed. His emergence was greeted by throngs of cheering supporters as the end of apartheid was at hand. In 1991 Mandela was elected chairman of the ANC and, after a triumphant tour of Europe and North America, he engaged De Klerk in talks about the post-apartheid government. Discussions were tense, and the two leaders never became friends, but results were constructive and apartheid slowly unraveled. Mandela had considerably less success dealing with Zulu chief MANGOSUTHU BUTHELEZI, whose tribal-based Inkatha Freedom Party violently attacked ANC workers and interests. Mandela also ended up divorcing his second wife, Winnie Mandela, who had formed a political base of her own in his absence, and who was later convicted of complicity in the kidnapping and murder of a local youth. By 1993 negotiations were concluded and South Africa's first free multiparty, multiracial elections were slated for April 27, 1994. On that historic occasion, the 75-year-old Mandela proved the overwhelming favorite with 62 percent of votes cast. "Never, never, and never again shall it be said that this beautiful land will again experience the oppression of one by another," he declared at his inaugural. He thus became the first black African to serve as president of South Africa. Previously, in 1993, Mandela shared the Nobel Peace Prize with De Klerk for finally slaying the dragon of apartheid.

The most distinguishing characteristic of Mandela's tenure in office, and of the man himself, was his deeply ingrained magnanimity. Despite nearly 30 years behind bars, the tall, gaunt leader evinced no bitterness toward his captors and chose instead to remain focused upon addressing present needs. South Africa, while wealthy, possessed dramatic disparities of wealth, and the government began a deliberate campaign to provide free education and basic services to its impoverished African majority. The country then commenced a slow but gradual transformation toward a completely integrated, multiracial democracy. Mandela also endorsed the "Truth and Reconciliation Commission," which encouraged perpetrators of violence and oppression to come forward, confess their crimes publicly, and be absolved. Through such expedience a bloody, race-based civil war was averted. But Mandela was no socialist, and he allowed the capitalist, free-market economy to thrive and even toured the world to attract foreign investors. After being diagnosed with prostate cancer, he voluntarily stepped down in June 1999 and was succeeded by THABO MBEKI. Since that time he has visited other countries, given speeches, and otherwise basked in his celebrity as the most significant African political figure of the 20th century. "We have confronted the prophets of doom," Mandela insists. "We have become a miracle nation."

Further Reading

Deluca, Anthony R. *Gandhi, Mao, Mandela, and Gorbachev: Studies in Personality, Power, and Politics.* Westport, Conn.: Praeger, 2000.

Duke, Lynne. *Mandela, Mobutu, and Me: A Bittersweet Journal of Africa.* New York: Doubleday, 2003.

Frueh, Jamie. *Political Identity and Social Change: The Remaking of the South African Social Order.* Albany: State University of New York Press, 2003.

Harvey, Robert. *The Fall of Apartheid: The Inside Story from Smuts to Mbeki.* New York: Palgrave, 2001.

Mandela, Nelson. *Long Walk to Freedom: The Autobiography of Nelson Mandela.* Oxford: Oxford University Press, 1996.

Sampson, Anthony. *Mandela: The Authorized Biography.* New York: Vintage Books, 2000.

Manley, Michael (1924–1997) *prime minister of Jamaica*

Michael Norman Manley was born on December 10, 1924, in St. Andrews, Jamaica, heir to an illustrious political legacy. His father, Norman Washington Manley, gained renown as a distinguished attorney, founded the People's National Party (PNP) in 1938, campaigned for Jamaican independence, and served as the island's first prime minister, 1955–62. Manley himself, a light-skinned person of color, followed his father's footsteps by attending elite schools in Jamaica prior to studying at McGill University in Montreal. In 1943 he volunteered for service in the Royal Canadian Air Force, and, after 1945, he gained admittance to the prestigious London School of Economics. Manley graduated in 1948 with degrees in economics, but afterward he sought employment as a journalist at home. He also joined the PNP's executive committee in 1952 and helped organize the bauxite and sugar workers. These activities cemented his credentials as a leftist firebrand, and, in 1962 Manley, also gained appointment to the Senate. By 1967 he won a seat in the House of Representatives, and two years later he replaced his ailing father as chairman of the PNP. As a campaigner Manley was blunt, brash, and dynamic, attributes that helped secure the PNP's island-wide victory in 1972 and his own appointment as the new prime minister. He had campaigned on a promise of sweeping change—and was determined to carry it out.

In office, Manley lived up to his reputation as a radical reformer. Having inherited an economy saddled by 20 percent unemployment, he began a crash program of public works projects to get people working. Then, intent upon installing his vision of "democratic socialism," he authorized free education, better health care for the poor, and over 40,000 new housing units. And, to squarely address the gross disparities of wealth in Jamaica, Manley pushed through laws aimed at improving working conditions for women and unions, instituting land reform, and eliminating illiteracy. He also antagonized American business interests by boosting the price of bauxite—Jamaica's biggest export—and establishing close relations with Cuba's FIDEL CASTRO. Manley also sought to lead a new movement of nonaligned nations to counter what he stridently viewed as imperialism and exploitation of the poor. His reforms did, in fact, improve the daily lives of average Jamaicans, but he almost bankrupted the country. Nonetheless, in 1976 he ran against the conservative Jamaica Labour Party (JPL) and won handily. Manley was clearly the man of the hour, but the excesses of his first term haunted him throughout his second. By 1980 unemployment hovered at 30 percent, the nation was saddled by a $4 billion national debt and nearly bankrupt. He turned to the International Monetary Fund (IMF) for loans, but at the cost of imposing severe austerity measures to shore up the economy. Manley's popularity then dropped, despite his refusal to subscribe to further IMF conditions. In 1980 JPL candidate Edward Seaga ran a strong pro-business campaign against a setting of spiraling distress. Over 700 people were killed in politically related violence before the JPL won decisively and Manley was defiantly turned out of office. "We lost because we challenged the power of the Western economic order," he snarled to supporters, "and for that I am unrepentant."

Manley continued in parliament as opposition leader, and his comeback bid was defeated in 1983. However, by 1988 Seaga's mismanagement of the economy left Jamaica in terrible straits, and the PLP again swept the national elections. Manley was sworn in to power for his third term, but this time he eschewed the fiery rhetoric of free-market principles. In fact, he was especially keen on mending fences with the United States, which he previously excoriated, and visited President George H. W. Bush to endorse his proposed North American Free Trade Act (NAFTA). Manley, now a committed capitalist, thereafter promoted growth and prosperity by cultivating the small business sector and attracting foreign investment. But, although moderating his views, he continually railed against the growing disparity between rich and poor nations, a stance that won him several international awards. He also authored eight books on the subject of international poverty and its causes. In 1990 Manley was diagnosed with cancer and he decided to step down from office on March 15, 1992. In one of his last acts as prime minister, he attended the 1994 national elections in South Africa, which ended the apartheid regime there. When Manley died in St. Andrews on March 7, 1997, he concluded 40 years of conscientious—and sometimes controversial—service to Jamaica. In doing so, he became something of a minor political legend among residents of developing countries, and is fondly remembered by the Jamaican political establishment. He was succeeded in office by Percival J. Patterson of the PLP.

Further Reading

Henke, Holger W. "Foreign Policy and Dependency: A Comparative Study of the Manley and Seaga Governments in Jamaica, 1972–1989." Unpublished Ph.D. dissertation, University of the West Indies, Mona, 1996.

Keith, Nelson W., and Novella Z. Keith. *The Social Origins of Democratic Socialism in Jamaica.* Philadelphia: Temple University Press, 1992.

Levi, Darrell F. *Michael Manley: The Making of a Leader.* Athens: University of Georgia Press, 1990.

Payne, Anthony. *Politics in Jamaica.* New York: St. Martin's Press, 1995.

Shirley, Girvan G. "From Unity and Confrontation to Pragmatism and Cooperation: A Case Study of Jamaica's Developmental Strategy from 1972 to 1992." Unpublished Ph.D. dissertation, Georgia State University, 2001.

Masire, Quett (1925–   ) *president of Botswana*

Quett Ketumile Joni Masire was born on July 23, 1925 in Kanye, capital of the British protectorate known as Bechuanaland. As part of the minority Bangwaketse tribe, he was raised as a herdsman before he was allowed to attend school. Masire excelled academically and, in 1948, he studied teaching at the Tigerkloof Institute in South Africa. Two years later Masire returned home and founded the Seepapitso Secondary School, the first such institute on the Bangwaketse Reserve, and thereafter he served as headmaster. In 1957 Masire acquired a Master Farmer's Certificate from the colonial government and went on to prosper in agriculture. The following year he also became a reporter for the protectorate newspaper, which brought him into contact with prominent tribal and political figures throughout the territory. Foremost among these was Seretse Khama, who cofounded the Democratic Party with Masire in 1961. Previously, Masire had won election to the Bangwaketse Tribal Council, and he translated his experience into helping the Botswana Democratic Party (BDP) as its chief organizer. This was a deliberately moderate party intending to secure broad-based support from such diverse elements as tribal chiefs and white businessmen. He proved spectacularly successful, and, during elections to the protectorate Legislative Assembly in 1965, the BDP won 28 of 31 seats. Masire himself was also elected and he acted as a negotiator with Great Britain in talks to secure independence. On September 30, 1966, the protectorate severed its ties to Britain and declared itself the new Republic of Botswana, with Seretse as president and Masire as vice president.

Botswana was then one of the world's poorest nations, but in 1967 Vice President Masire also acquired portfolios as minister of finance and development planning. He served as a farsighted technocrat with a knack for promoting economic growth. In fact, for many years thereafter, Botswana registered annual growth rates of 13 percent—among the world's highest. He accomplished this by avoiding centralized government planning, unlike neighboring socialist states, and instead concentrating instead on economic pluralism and foreign investment. In addition to the usual tourism and agriculture aspects of development, Masire proved keen to develop and regulate the thriving mining and mineral export business. Thanks to his diligence, Botswana continues today as the second-largest exporter of diamonds after South Africa. The vice president also saw that a certain percentage of all profits were plowed back into either education or infrastructure development. Nor did he neglect such vital services as health care, housing, or communications. Furthermore, Masire earned a well-deserved reputation for honesty and integrity, and he became widely respected despite his minority status. When Seretse died in July 1980, the National Assembly cast secret ballots for his successor, and Masire was unanimously endorsed. He was formally sworn in as Botswana's second president on July 21, 1980.

For nearly two decades, Masire cemented his reputation as one of the most moderate and successful leaders of sub-Saharan Africa. His country was thriving, its multiparty politics were stable, and its press was entirely unfettered. Consequently, the soft-spoken administrator was reelected by wide margins in 1984, 1989, and 1994. In terms of foreign policy, Masire also showed a flair for diplomacy and realism lacking in many contemporaries. He openly endorsed the cause of majority rule in South Africa, but with qualifications. Sharing a long border with the powerful apartheid regime to the south, Masire maintained correct but cool relations, and he steered Botswana clear of the national liberation struggle developing there. He therefore forbade the militant African National Congress (ANC) from establishing guerrilla bases in Botswana, although the South African army occasionally made armed forays in search of arm caches and guerrilla cells. The presidency of

NELSON MANDELA and the end of apartheid in 1994 have since resulted in cordial relations. More significantly, in 1995 Botswana was removed from the list of nations receiving foreign aid and actually began donating money to finance the International Monetary Fund (IMF). "Help us to help ourselves," Masire lectured his benefactors, "and the more you help us the sooner you will get rid of us."

Masire remained highly regarded for his astute leadership, and, in 1989, he received the Africa Prize for Leadership for the Sustainable End of Hunger. This was partially on account of his adroit handling of a severe drought in Botswana, 1983–84, in which not a single citizen died. On March 23, 1994, he bequeathed the presidency to FESTUS MOGAE, who inherited one of the most prosperous and corruption-free nations in Africa. Botswana remains a model of economic development for the Third World, and testimony to Masire's leadership qualities.

Further Reading

Acemoglu, Daron, and Simon Johnson. *An African Success Story: Botswana.* London: Centre for Economic Policy Research, 2002.

Good, Kenneth. *The Liberal Model and Africa: Elites against Democracy.* New York: Palgrave, 2002.

Morton, Barry, Jeff Ramsay. *The Making of a President: Sir Ketumile Masire's Early Years.* Gaborone, Botswana: Puta Press, 1994.

Motzafi-Haller, Pnina. *Fragmented Worlds, Coherent Lives: The Politics of Difference in Botswana.* Westport, Conn.: Bergin and Garvey, 2002.

Wells, Jason M. "A Threshold of Independence? The Case of Botswana." Unpublished master's thesis, University of Missouri, Columbia, 2000.

Mbasogo, Teodoro (1942–) *president of Equatorial Guinea*

Teodoro Obiang Ngueme Mbasogo was born in Acoa-Kam on mainland Equatorial Guinea, on June 4, 1942. This tiny territorial enclave on the West African coast is sandwiched between Cameroon and Gabon. It had been ruled as a Spanish colony since 1844 and received political independence in October 1968. The first president, Francisco Macias Nguema, was democratically elected, but he catered almost exclusively to his fellow Fang tribesmen. The ensuing resentment culminated in a failed coup attempt in 1969, and Nguema countered by installing a brutal dictatorship. Arrests, torture, and murder of perceived political opponents became almost institutionalized. For a decade Equatorial Guinea was run as a personal fiefdom as, in 1973, a new constitution was adopted that made Nguema president for life. He continued ruling with an iron hand until August 1979, when a military coup overthrew his regime and, like so many of his victims, he faced a firing squad.

Mbasogo had been educated locally before attending the Saragossa Military Academy in Spain in 1963. Two years later he returned home, where, as President Nguema's nephew, he served in the territorial guard. Mbasogo proved a competent and loyal soldier to the regime, so his advancement through ranks and in responsibility proved rapid. He gained promotion to lieutenant colonel in 1975 and, with it, command of Fernando Po island and Playa Negra Prison. Mbasogo played a conspicuous role in state repression until the spring of 1979, when the president ordered his brother executed. The young soldier then played his hand carefully and, on August 3, 1979, he orchestrated a military coup that toppled Nguema. The former head of state was also summarily tried for genocide, murder, treason, and corruption before being unceremoniously put to death. The change in government was initially welcomed by the citizens of Equatorial Guinea for Mbasogo had promised them, and the world, an early return to free elections and democracy. However, their trust was sadly misplaced.

In practice, Mbasogo's regime proved every bit as repressive as his uncle's. As chairman of the Supreme Military Council, he suspended the constitution, banned political activity, and terrorized dissenting elements. Opposition groups fled en masse to neighboring countries, where they organized and brought international pressure on the regime to reform. Mbasogo consequently embarked on a gradual reintroduction to multiparty democracy, but at a snail's pace. A new constitution adopted in 1982 promised democratic elections after a seven-year transition period. However, in 1987 he declared the country a one-party state and his Democratic Party for Equatorial Guinea (PDGE) the only legal political agent. Two years later, in a massively rigged election boycotted by all opposition groups, Mbasogo was elected president by 99 percent of the vote. Over the next decade the government paid increasing lip service to democratic reforms, but only to add a veneer of legitimacy to its brutal reign. In 1991 a new constitution was adopted with carefully crafted measures to stifle political dissent. It included measures that forbade citizens from running for office if they had been absent from the country for more than 10 years—which most of the exiled opposition leaders certainly had. In 1993 elections were held for the House of People's Representatives, again fraudulently conducted and boycotted by the opposition. Moreover, the process was marked by the systematic beating, detention, and arrest of opposition candidates. Mbasogo could not be seriously challenged under such conditions, so in a second round of presidential elections held in February 1996, he won a second seven-year term with 97.7 percent of the vote. This outcome only lent greater credence to the dictator's ominous mantra of "Our President, Today, Tomorrow, and Forever." However, this race did witness the presence of four minor opposition parties, who "officially" polled only 2.1 percent of the vote. International observers declared the entire process extremely flawed and plagued by irregularities. Mbasogo waxed philosophically over Western protests, insisting: "This idea that there has been a climate of intimidation doesn't correspond to concrete reality." In March 1999 multiparty legislative elections were held that, to no surprise, yielded 75 of 80 seats to the ruling PDGE.

For many years Equatorial Guinea enjoyed the dubious distinction of being one of Africa's poorest nations. However, the discovery of oil-rich deposits off the coast in 1996 gave the regime a new source of revenue with which it could perpetuate itself. However, Mbasogo needs foreign expertise and investment capital to fully exploit these resources, and so, by March 2001, he proceeded to announce a "great effort to democratize the county." He then met with U.S. State Department officials and business executives to assure them of the improving human rights record in Equatorial Guinea. That fall Mbasogo also conferred with Malaysian president MAHATHIR MOHAMAD about the prospects of emulating that country's economic success and its system of wealth distribution. These changes have done little to alleviate the sufferings of Equatorial Guineans, deprived of free elections since 1968, and in the grasp of one of Africa's most ruthless and maniacal dictatorships.

Further Reading

Cusack, Igor. "Nation-Builders at Work: The Equatoguinean 'Myth' of Bantu Unity." *Nationalism and Ethnic Politics* 7, no. 3 (2001): 77–97.

Fegley, Randall. *Equatorial Guinea: An African Tragedy.* New York: P. Lang, 1989.

Klitgaard, Robert E. *Tropical Gangsters.* New York: I. B. Tauris, 1991.

Liniger-Goumaz, Max. *Historical Dictionary of Equatorial Guinea.* Lanham, Md.: Scarecrow Press, 2000.

Sundiata, I. K. *Equatorial Guinea: Colonialism, State Terror, and the Search for Stability.* Boulder, Colo.: Westview Press, 1990.

Mbeki, Thabo (1942–) *president of South Africa*

Thabo Mbeki was born in Mbewuleni, Transkei province, South Africa, the son of political activists. South Africa, a wealthy former English colony, had become dominated politically by the white-oriented National Party since 1948. Their policies were racially based in nature and included the practice of apartheid, a physical separation of blacks, whites, and mixed-race peoples. This unsavory practice gave rise to the African National Congress (ANC), which rose to combat apartheid and promote political freedom for the majority African population. By 1990 international isolation prompted white rulers to hold secret discussions with the ANC about a peaceful transition to majority rule. This became a reality in May 1994, when free multiparty and multiracial elections swept the ANC into power and NELSON MANDELA became president. A new constitution has since been adopted that mandates creation of a National Assembly which, in turn, appoints a president. The senior executive oversees the daily administration of national affairs, can dissolve the parliament with members' approval, and serves for no more than two consecutive five-year terms. Given the traditions of violence and racial animosity, South Africa's transition to majority rule has been amazingly peaceful and successful. However, apartheid's most enduring legacy, the gross disparity of income between races, remains unresolved. Despite 10 years of ANC rule and reform, white income remains 10 times higher than black, and black joblessness remains stuck at a staggering 40 percent.

Mbeki was educated locally, but he became imbued with a sense of political activism through his parent's activities. He joined the outlawed ANC at the age of 14, and, in 1959, he was expelled from school for leading a student strike. Mbeki then joined the South African Communist Party after his father was arrested and sentenced to life in prison for political activity. In 1962 he was ordered out of the country for his own safety by the ANC and Mbeki ended up in England. There he studied economics at the University of London and received his master's degree from the University of Sussex. Following a brief stint of military training in the Soviet Union, Mbeki returned to Africa as part of the ANC's widespread diplomatic offensive. He traveled and lectured throughout Nigeria, Botswana, Mozambique, and Zambia—the so-called Frontline states—recruiting members and mobilizing world opinion against the apartheid regime. In this capacity Mbeki gained the reputation of an accomplished diplomat and party intellectual, who forsook confrontation in favor of consensus and cooperation. Consequently, in 1985 he was promoted to the ANC's National Executive Committee, and four years later participated in secret talks with President FREDERIK W. DE KLERK, president of South African. Mbeki finally returned home in 1990 after almost 30 years in exile, and, in 1993, he succeeded long-serving Oliver Tambo as head of the ANC. He then further distinguished himself by helping orchestrate the country's first multiparty elections in 1994. Thereupon he served as deputy president in a government of national unity under NELSON MANDELA. Mbeki subsequently gained election as president of South Africa and, on June 16 1999, he was sworn in as that nation's second freely elected president.

As president, Mbeki has labored to address the gross disparity in yearly income and living standards that divides black and white citizens. As such he walks a constant tightrope between ANC radicals, who demand confiscation of white property and immediate redistribution of wealth, and conservative business elements, mostly white, who manage the national economy. Mbeki, fortunately, draws upon years of experience as a diplomat and negotiator in dealing with such extreme positions. He has continued Mandela's policy of channeling state funds to provide basic services such as affordable housing, electricity, and clean water to the majority poor population. However, this is achieved without the imposition of state controls on the economy, as dictated by traditional ANC ideology. He has also overseen the integration of the ANC's guerrilla forces into the standing national army, creation of a multiracial civil service and national police, and erection of 500 rural clinics to assist children and pregnant women.

Mbeki has since come under some criticism, at home and aboard, for problems not entirely of his making. The recent trend toward political repression in neighboring Zimbabwe has threatened to upend regional stability, but Mbeki has been curiously restrained toward the former guerrilla leader ROBERT MUGABE. He has since come under increasing pressure from international investors to cut off South African power supplies to Zimbabwe, which would bring its economy to a halt within days. Mbeki, however, insists on "constructive engagement" with that regime to encourage better behavior. A bigger storm was brewing at home in the form of the current AIDS epidemic, which is widespread among black communities and growing. Curiously, he is somewhat reluctant to discuss the matter publicly and, during his February 2002 state of the union address, he failed to even mention it. Opposition leaders lambast him for indulging in what they see as denial and arrogance toward a ticking time bomb. Nonetheless, Mbeki simply retorted that the government will conduct "a proper review of its health policies and ensure that all elements of its work that bear on

Thabo Mbeki *(South African Consulate General)*

the health of our people are properly synchronized and co-ordinated." He then reiterated the need to end poverty throughout South Africa and appealed to more citizens to volunteer their efforts to help the poor. Ex-president Mandela also went on record denying a rift had developed between himself and the government over its AIDS policy and expressing confidence that the government was doing everything in its power to address the problem.

Further Reading

Beinart, William. *Twentieth-Century South Africa.* Oxford: Oxford University Press, 2001.

Frueh, Jamie. *Political Identity and Social Change: The Re-making of the South African Social Order.* Albany: State University of New York Press, 2002.

Graybill, Lyn S. *Truth and Reconciliation in South Africa: Miracle or Model?* Boulder, Colo.: Lynne Rienner Publishers, 2002.

Jacobs, Sean, and Richard Culand, eds. *Thabo Mbeki's World: The Politics and Ideology of the South African President.* London: Zed Books, 2003.

Johnson, R. W. "Mugabe, Mbeki, and Mandela's Shadow." *National Interest* 63 (Spring 2001): 59–75.

Landsberg, Chris. "Promoting Democracy: The Mandela-Mbeki Doctrine." *Journal of Democracy* 11, no. 3 (2000): 197–221.

Mathebe, Lucky. *Bound by Tradition: The World of Thabo Mbeki.* Pretoria: University of South Africa, 2001.

Vale, Peter C. J. *Security and Politics in South Africa: The Regional Dimension.* Boulder, Colo.: Lynne Rienner Publishers, 2003.

McAleese, Mary (1951–) *president of Ireland*
Mary Leneghan was born on June 27, 1951, in Ardoyne, West Belfast, Northern Ireland, into a stolidly Catholic household. This put them at odds with the majority of Northern Ireland residents, who are strongly Protestant. She matured during a period that has come to be known as "The Troubles," characterized by bloody violence between the two sects. The issue was whether Northern Ireland was to remain part of the United Kingdom, or would rejoin the Republic of Ireland to the south. Leneghan's family bore the full brunt of such infighting; her deaf brother was roughed up by Protestant militants, and their house repeatedly burned. Consequently, the family relocated to Rostrevor in County Down, which enjoys a higher percentage of Catholics. She subsequently attended Queen's University in Belfast to study law, and she was called to the bar in 1975. The following year she married Martin McAleese and also became professor of criminal law at Trinity College. McAleese proved adept in her profession and, in 1987, she became director of legal studies at Queen's University. Curiously, she succeeded another Catholic stalwart, MARY ROBINSON. In 1994 McAleese rose to become the first female pro vice chancellor at that school. She also acquired the reputation as a staunchly conservative Catholic who opposed abortion and the liberalization of divorce laws.

McAleese's political career commenced in 1997, following the resignation of Mary Robinson, who was the eighth president of Ireland and the nation's first woman executive. She decided running for the office even though, as a resident of Northern Ireland, she could not legally vote in the Irish republic. Among her opponents were Mary Banotti of Fine Gael, also a member of the European Parliament, and Dana Rosemary Scallon, a rock singer. Now a candidate of the conservative Fianna Fáil Party, McAleese espoused both pro-Catholic and nationalist positions on the issue of Northern Ireland and stated her support for eventual reunification with the six Protestant counties. However, she steadfastly opposes violence, and denounces guerrilla activities by the outlawed Irish Republican Army (IRA). "I am not anti-British. I am an Irish nationalist," she declared. "The situation in Northern Ireland never justified the spilling of one drop of blood." Consistent with her stand, she conducted several clandestine meetings with GERRY ADAMS, head of Sinn Féin, political wing of the IRA, to discuss reunification efforts. A smear campaign then unfolded, suggesting McAleese entertained greater sympathy for Sinn Féin objectives than previously admitted, but when former taoiseach (prime minister) AL-BERT REYNOLDS campaigned on her behalf, McAleese won with 59 percent of the vote. "I want us to share as a nation the adventure of this, the most dynamic country in Europe, heading into that new millennium," she announced. "It will mark, I believe, the true age of the Irish because I believe we are an unstoppable nation, now very definitely in our stride." McAleese was then sworn in as Ireland's ninth president on November 11, 1997, and its second female executive. She was also the first native of Northern Ireland—and hence a British subject—to serve as president of Ireland.

The Irish presidency is basically a ceremonial office intended to promote national unity, but it carries im-

Mary McAleese *(Department of Foreign Affairs, Dublin)*

portant responsibilities such as formally appointing the prime minister, signing legislation into law, and calling for new elections. However, MARY ROBINSON had previously elevated the office into a high-profile bully pulpit for global issues, and McAleese followed the trail she blazed. Having campaigned on a platform of "Building Bridges," her first priority was promoting peace between Catholics and Protestants throughout Northern Ireland. She also determined to represent Ireland's interests abroad, especially after the dramatic transformations of the 1990s. Her country, previously an economic backwater, now emerged as the "Celtic Tiger" of Europe, a center for high-tech industries with one of the most robust economies in Europe. However, McAleese was especially distraught over the September 11, 2001, destruction of New York's World Trade Center, which took the lives of several Irish citizens. "This National

Day of Mourning is a very special opportunity for us all to show solidarity with our brothers and sisters in the United States of America," she lamented, "May God guide us through these troubled times." McAleese's tenure in office expires in 2004. Until then she continues promoting Irish reunification through legal means. "The greatest salute to the memory of all our dead, and the living whom they loved, would be the achievement of agreement and peace," she said.

Further Reading

Crotty, William, and David E. Schmitt. *Ireland on the World Stage.* New York: Longman, 2002.

Dixon, Paul. *Northern Ireland: The Politics of War and Peace.* New York: Palgrave, 2001.

Finnegan, Richard B., and Edward T. McCarron. *Ireland: Historical Echoes, Contemporary Politics.* Boulder, Colo.: Westview Press, 2000.

McAleese, Mary. *Love in Chaos: Spiritual Growth and the Search for Peace.* New York: Continuum, 1999.

McCarthy, Justine. *Mary McAleese, The Outsider: An Unauthorized Biography.* Dublin: Blackwater Press, 1999.

Menem, Carlos Saúl (1930–) *president of Argentina*

Carlos Saúl Menem was born on July 2, 1930 in Anillaco, La Rioja province, Argentina, the son of Syrian immigrants. He was raised a Muslim but subsequently converted to Roman Catholicism at an early age. Menem attended the University of Cordoba, from which he obtained his law degree in 1955. By this time he developed strong affinities for President Juan Perón and his "Peronist Party," especially following the military coup of 1956. Menem himself was jailed briefly for supporting the deposed president, and, in 1957, he established the Peronist Youth Party of La Rioja province. For many years thereafter he supported himself through legal practice, but when the military dictatorship concluded in 1973, Menem ran as the Peronist candidate for governor of his home province. He won handily, but in 1976 the military again intervened to evict Eva Perón from the presidency and Menem was arrested again. He endured five years of incarceration before being released in 1981. Two years later civilian rule was finally restored in the wake of the disastrous Falkland Islands War with Britain, and, in 1983, Menem was again elected governor of La

Rioja Province. Four years later he was reelected an unprecedented third time with 63 percent of votes cast, which established him as a potential contender for the presidency.

By 1989 President Raúl Alfonsín of the Radical Party had all but run the Argentine economy into the ground. Hyperinflation was running at 6,000 percent, while the national debt mushroomed perilously. The energetic Menem, who deliberately cultivated a macho image as a race-car and sports enthusiast—with a fondness for beautiful women—contrasted sharply with the dour, rumpled-looking Alfonsín. On May 14, 1989, the Argentine voters, desperate for change, elected Menem president by 47 percent of the popular vote. He thus became the first avowed Peronist to hold high office since 1976. This was also the first time since 1928 that political power shifted peacefully from one party to another. The national outlook was so grave that Menem was sworn into office on July 8, 1989, five months ahead of schedule.

A principal tenant of Perón's "corporate state" politics entailed lavish government expenditures on the poor and unions, from which Menem had derived his core popular support. However, the new president realized that these policies were potentially ruinous under the present circumstances and, in true Menem style, he threw his ideological baggage overboard and began anew. He now embraced a radical neoliberalism and enacted a program of strict anti-Peronist economic measures. These included pegging the peso to the U.S. dollar to tame inflation, cutting government subsidies and spending to the bone, rolling back the government payroll, and place increasing emphasis upon privatization, or the selling off of state-run enterprises. Like a gambler on a roll, Menem beat the odds. Inflation rapidly declined to single digits within a year, unemployment dwindled, and the economy recovered a healthy beat. However, this was achieved by inflicting considerable hardship upon public employees and union households, which were his greatest source of support.

Buoyed by popularity polls, Menem wasted no time in mending fences with the military, which loomed in the background as a potential coup threat. To obtain their loyalty, he unceremoniously pardoned 300 military officers accused of human rights violations during the military regime of the 1970s. He also performed similar favors for those generals disgraced by the Falklands War. In a simi-

lar vein, Menem reversed Argentina's traditional non-aligned role by seeking cordial relations with the United States, and he even managed to reestablish diplomatic relations with Great Britain for the first time since 1981. He then went on to assert what he believed was Argentina's role as a leader in Latin American affairs by sponsoring creation of Mercosur, a South American Common Market. On the downside, there was nothing subtle about Menem's crass leadership style. He routinely ignored Congress and ruled by decree, packed the Supreme Court and other agencies with allies, and, in 1995, had the constitution revised to allow him to run for a second consecutive term, if reduced from six to four years. Argentinians had lost none of their fascination for their flashy populist, and in 1995 he was easily reelected.

Menem's record of success slowly unraveled during his second administration. The nation suffered from the worldwide recession and his popularity declined as unemployment rose. Worse, Menem and several associates were implicated in a plot to sell illegal weapons to Croatia and Ecuador, while corruption and nepotism grew rampant. He also tried, and failed, to acquire sufficient votes to change the constitution again and run for a third term. In October 1999 the public had apparently wearied of Menem's controversial, headline-grabbing antics, and they chose the staid mayor of Buenos Aires, FERNANDO DE LA RÚA, over the Peronist candidate Eduardo Duhalde by a landslide. Menem then stepped down, although he did not rule out again running for the highest office in 2003. The fact that in June 2001 he was indicted for illegal arms sales did nothing to diminish his ardor, nor did the imposition of house arrest. Menem has apparently lost none of his panache or appetite for controversy. "Despite all the lies, despite all the defamations, I will return to be president of Argentina," he confidently predicted. Menem withdrew from a runoff presidential election slated for May 2003.

Further Reading

Escude, Carlos. *Foreign Policy Theory in Menem's Argentina*. Gainesville: University Press of Florida, 1997.

McSherry, J. Patrice. "Strategic Alliance: Menem and the Military-Security Forces in Argentina." *Latin American Perspectives* 24 (November 1997): 63–92.

Morrell, Martin V. "Menemism: Persistence and Change in Argentine Politics." Unpublished master's thesis, Johns Hopkins University, 1996.

Smith, William C. "State, Market, and Neoliberalism in Post-transition Argentina: The 'Menem' Experiment." *Journal of Interamerican Studies and World Affairs* 33 (Winter 1999): 45–83.

Zagorski, Paul W. "Civil-Military Relations and Argentine Democracy: The Armed Forces under the Menem Government." *Armed Forces and Society* 20 (Spring 1994): 423–437.

Meri, Lennart (1929–) *president of Estonia*

Lennart Meri was born in Tallinn, the capital of Estonia, on March 29, 1929, the son of a diplomat. Estonia is a small enclave nestled on the southern shore of the Baltic Sea between Finland and Russia. It had been dominated by foreign powers since medieval times, but, in 1918, it acquired political independence from the Russian Empire. Just prior to World War II Estonia was reannexed by the Soviet Union, which installed a brutal Communist regime. The long-suffering Estonian people found their national culture and religious rights suppressed and they chafed in silence until the late 1980s, when Soviet president Mikhail Gorbachev embarked upon political liberalization for the various republics. Following the collapse of the Soviet Union in August 1991, Estonia immediately declared its independence from Moscow and the following year a new constitution was introduced. The government consists of a president and a national assembly, the former to be chosen by whichever party or coalition could muster a majority of votes. The first elections, held in October 1992, validated Estonia's complete repudiation of its former Communist past.

Meri was educated at schools in Tallinn until forced to accompany his family to Siberian exile in 1941. They were repatriated in 1946 and Meri attended Tartu University in Tallinn, where he majored in history. In 1953 he headed the literature department of the Vanemuine Theater, and subsequently he worked for the national radio station as an editor. At various times between 1963 and 1978, Meri also served as an editor at Tallinnfilm Studios, and several of his books, published abroad, received awards. He entered politics in the wake of Gorbachev's political thaw in 1985 as a senior official with the Estonian Writer's Guild, and he was also active in the Popular Front of Estonia and the Estonian Heritage Society, all of which agitated for greater cultural autonomy from Russia. In 1990 he was appointed to the Council of Estonia, which governed the national congress, and in 1992 Meri was named ambassador to Finland. At that point his credentials as an Estonian nationalist were well established, and he decided to run for high office. On October 5, 1992, he outpolled former Communist Arnold Ruutel in parliamentary voting, becoming the nation's first freely elected leader in 70 years. Meri owed his success largely because, unlike many senior Estonian figures, he was never part of the hated Communist regime.

Once installed, Meri wasted no time renouncing Estonia's Soviet past and, with it, the moribund economic policies then in place. Privatization was enacted with a vengeance, and the bulk of all inefficient state-owned industries were sold off to foreign investors. Tight monetary policies inflicted some distress in terms of unemployment, but also reduced a soaring 1,069 percent inflation rate to 29 percent by 1995. The government also developed close ties with Scandinavian banking firms for loans and foreign investment. Diplomatically, Meri moved energetically to integrate Estonia into the Western fold by applying for membership in the European Union (EU). Economically, Estonia roared ahead, meeting the closely prescribed conditions for EU membership in record time. Presently, it is slated to join in 2003. The good performance of Estonia's economy also paid dividends for Meri's Fatherland Union Party, and, in September 1996, he again defeated Ruutel in a close race decided by the electoral college.

Estonia has always lived in the shadow of its giant neighbor, Russia, and the two nations enjoy uneasy relations. Despite the collapse of the Soviet Union in 1991, there remained the question of thousands of Russian troops still stationed on Estonian soil. Meri clearly wanted them to leave, but newly elected President BORIS YELTSIN first sought assurances that the rights of Russian retirees living in Estonia would be respected. Meri endured considerable public criticism for signing such an accord in August 1994, but the Russians withdrew as requested. However, old frictions were revisited when the Estonian government imposed strict language requirements on all inhabitants and, consequently, many retired Russians have had trouble acquiring full citizenship. Furthermore, the Russian government was highly upset when Meri openly sought to join NATO. This would place a powerful military alliance right on the Russian border, but Meri viewed membership as a hedge against future Russian aggression. Other border tensions ensued when Russian towns, strapped for cash, proved unable to pay Estonia for water and sewage treatment across the border and were cut off. All told, many more years of readjustment will be necessary before Estonia's people can put their oppressive Soviet interval behind them.

In August 2001, Meri, having championed the cause of Estonian independence, and then having led his emerging nation for a decade, declined to run for a third term. He was succeeded by his old adversary Ruudel, who pledged not to go back on the progress made in redefining Estonian national identity. It remains one of the greatest success stories of the post–cold war era.

Further Reading

Anderson, Erik A. *An Ethnic Perspective on Economic Reform: The Case of Estonia.* Brookfield, Vt.: Ashgate, 1999.

Panagiotor, R. A. "Estonia's Success: Prescription or Legacy?" *Communist and Post-Communist Studies* 34 (June 2001): 261–278.

Smith, David J. *Estonia: Independence and European Integration.* London: Routledge, 2001.

Steen, Anton. *Between Past and Future: Elites, Democracy, and the State in Post-Communist Countries.* Brookfield, Vt.: Ashgate, 1997.

Vogt, Henri. "The Utopia of Post-Communism: The Czech Republic, Eastern Germany, and Estonia after 1989." Unpublished Ph.D. dissertation, Oxford University, 2000.

Mesić, Stjepan (1934–) *president of Croatia*

Stjepan (Stipe) Mesić was born in Orahovica, Croatia, on December 24, 1934. His country, a small territory resting on the Adriatic Sea between Italy and Bosnia-Herzegovina, then constituted part of a six-republic federation called Yugoslavia. The region was occupied by German troops during World War II and Mesić's parents joined partisan forces to resist them. Afterward, Yugoslavia came under the iron rule of Josip Broz, Marshal Tito, who instituted a centralized communist regime over all the republics. For three decades Croatia functioned more or less peaceably, but after 1971 long-suppressed nationalist impulses began surfacing. Tito's Communist Party harshly cracked down on dissenters, but following his death in 1980, pressure for multiparty elections mounted. These materialized in April 1990

when Yugoslavia formerly broke apart and a nationalist group, the Croatian Democratic Community (HDZ), took control of the legislature. That year also saw the rise of the country's first elected president, FRANJO TUDJMAN, who remained in office until his death in 1999. His tenure corresponded with an internecine Balkan conflict that claimed the lives of more than 250,000 people.

After World War II Mesić finished his primary education and ultimately received a law degree from Zagreb University. Like many of his countrymen, he became caught up in the rise of Croatian nationalism that crested during the late 1970s, was arrested, and served time in jail. Afterward, he joined Tudjman's HDZ nationalists as its secretary, and he subsequently served as Croatia's first prime minister within the federation. In this capacity he collided head-on with SLOBODAN MILOŠEVIĆ, the president of Serbia, who was determined to exert greater centralized control over the republics. In response, Croatia declared its independence on December 5, 1991, and the following year Mesić became Speaker of the parliament. However, Tudjman's rule had grown very despotic and, like Milošević, he was quick to exploit ethnic tensions for his own gain. He provoked the country's Serbian minority to rebel, thereby providing him an excuse to expel 200,000 citizens. Tudjman also unleashed the Croatian army during the three-way struggle to carve up Bosnia-Herzegovina. These excesses induced Mesić to quit the HDZ altogether, and, by 1997, he had founded the Croatian Independent Democrats (HNS) Party as a moderate counterweight to rabid nationalism. He then announced his candidacy for the presidency following Tudjman's death in 1999, and, on January 27, 2000, Mesić won with 56.2 percent of the vote. After being sworn in the following February, he immediately sought national reconciliation by inviting former Serbian refugees to return home. "We want all Croatia to become a truly democratic society," he declared. "We are committed to strengthening all of the institutions of the rule of law."

Early in his administration, Mesić sought to correct despotic tendencies in the Croatian government by seeking a more pronounced division of powers between the executive and judicial branches. He has since called upon the legislature to abandon the strong semi-presidential system in favor of a parliamentary one, with inherent checks and balances between the executive, legislature, and judiciary. Mesić is also firmly committed to realigning Croatia with the West and desires economic integration within the European Union (EU). Thereafter he seeks membership in NATO and he has fulfilled preliminary steps by joining the Partnership for Peace program, which grants observer status to members at the annual NATO parliament. But continuing Balkan tensions must also be addressed. In July 2001 Mesić conferred with Slovenian president MILAN KUCAN to iron out long-standing border disputes. Slovenia subsequently acquired a strip of land allowing it access to the Adriatic, while their mutual border was readjusted elsewhere as compensation. The two leaders also achieved concord over joint management and funding of the Krsko nuclear power plant in Slovenia.

Other Balkan disputes have not been so amicably settled. Since the 1999 war in Bosnia-Herzegovina ended, Croatia has been pressured by the United Nations to cooperate with the International War Crimes Tribunal in The Hague. Mesić indicated his willingness to testify against Milošević at his trial. "I will be very pleased to testify—although it will be of no benefit to him," he stated. Mesić has also publicly denounced his predecessor's willingness to oppress and expel Croatian Serbs, and has arrested several ranking Croatian military officers accused of war crimes. Speaking on the 10th anniversary of national independence, he expressed sorrow over Croatia's complicity. "Some might say that a great day of celebration is not the right day to voice such reflections," Mesić lectured, "but I say every day, even a day of celebration, is the right day to speak the truth." None of this soul-searching has resonated well with Croatia's sizable number of nationalists, and, in October 2001, they mustered 30,000 marchers in Zagreb to protest what they view as Mesić's "treason." The erstwhile tractable president admonished them, saying that while democracy encourages protest, calls for overthrowing the government should not be allowed.

Further Reading

Bartlett, William *Croatia: Between Europe and the Balkans.* New York: Routledge, 2002.

Goldstein, Ivo. *Croatia: A History.* Montreal: McGill-Queen's University Press, 1999.

Judah, Tim. "Croatia Reborn." *New York Times Review of Books* 47 (August 10, 2000): 20–24.

Malesevic, Sinisa. *Ideology, Legitimacy, and the New State: Yugoslavia, Serbia, and Croatia.* London: Frank Cass, 2001.

Malovic, Stjepan. *The People, Press, and Politics of Croatia.* Westport, Conn.: Praeger, 2001.

Tanner, Marcus. *Croatia: A Nation Forged in War.* New Haven, Conn.: Yale University Press, 2001.

Meta, Ilir (1969–) *prime minister of Albania*

Ilir Meta was born in Skrapar, Albania, on March 24, 1969. Albania had been a territory within the Ottoman Empire for nearly 400 years by the time independence transpired in 1912, making it the only European nation with a largely Muslim population. It was liberated from Axis powers late in World War II and in 1948 an independent Communist state under Enver Hoxha was established. This turned out to be one of the most xenophobic, isolationist regimes of modern times, as the hard-line Hoxha severed relations with the Soviet Union and Yugoslavia, and Communist China became his principal ally. After these ties were renounced in the 1970s, Albania was virtually cut off from the world. It was not until the 1980s that a new leader, RAMIZ ALIA, slowly opened up his nation to the rest of Europe. The fall of the Soviet Union in 1991 also prompted Albania to hold its first free elections in four decades, and over the next eight years a succession of Socialist Party and Democratic Party prime ministers held office. Albania thus became the very last Eastern European nation to embrace structural reforms and a free-market economy. Worse, in 1996 the country was rocked by revelations of a pyramid scheme that defrauded thousands of citizens of their life savings. This triggered widespread unrest and turmoil, with nearly 2,000 people killed. Albania was further buffeted by the 1999 Serbian-led campaign of "ethnic-cleansing" in neighboring Kosovo that unleashed a flood of 450,000 refugees. Despite moves toward economic modernization and greater democratization, Albania remains Europe's poorest and most potentially unstable nation.

Meta was educated at the Economic Faculty of Tiranë University, where he also served as an amateur weight lifter. He became politically active soon after by joining the Young Albanian Euro-Socialist Forum. Although never a Communist, he joined the newly revamped Socialist Party in 1991, and the following year he gained election as deputy chairman. Meta was also repeatedly elected to the Albanian parliament from Skrapa, and, in 1996, he became the party's secretary of foreign relations. In this post he struck up cordial relations with Prime Minister Pandeli Majko, who became his political mentor. In 1999 Meta was elected head of the Socialist Party at a time of deepening regional and economic crises. When the government under Majko felt it had lost the nation's confidence to lead, Meta was tapped to serve as the new prime minister on October 27, 1999. At the time of his appointment he was Europe's youngest head of state.

As prime minister, it was essential that Meta move quickly to restore civilian faith and trust in elected officials and shore up public support for his administration. He therefore brooked no delay in firing the ministers of public economy and state, who were long suspected of issuing fraudulent gas and oil licenses in exchange for kickbacks. He then took steps to improve the police and increase their professionalism, again to win the public's approval. To facilitate law enforcement, he also prevailed upon the parliament to overhaul the judiciary system, streamline procedures, and severely punish lawyers for taking bribes, an entrenched practice. An equally pressing problem for Albania was the question of national infrastructure. Private automobiles has been outlawed for nearly 40 years and most roads were primitive and strewn with potholes. Meta actively courted foreign investments and loans to build and repair the nation's transportation network, which is primitive and lags far behind most European states. Moreover, he was also quick to implore the long-suffering citizens of Albania to tighten their belts another notch, for the cost of such badly needed improvements could only mean higher taxes. Through all these expedients Meta aspired to increase the Albanian standard of living, which remains rather poor, even by Balkan standards. He sought the goal of eventual admittance into the European Union (EU) for all the economic benefits such integration would bring. He also wants Albania to join NATO, when eligible.

Meta came to power just as the cauldron of ethnic and regional tensions was boiling over. Serbian aggression in Kosovo resulted in a large influx of refugees but, in neighboring Macedonia, enclaves of Albanians began agitating for annexation to a "Greater Albania." Meta has formally renounced any intention of acquiring Macedonian territory, which would put his country on a collision course with its southern neighbor, Greece. "Greater Albania is a project that doesn't exist even in our minds," he declared. "Our priority is to leave behind our historical backwardness and start closing the gap between Albania and the rest of Europe." Meta therefore assured the Greek government that Albanian citizens of Greek descent would be treated fairly and, moreover, all national textbooks would be expunged of negative references to Greece. In exchange, Prime Minister Costas Simitis promised to issue millions of visas to willing Albanian workers, and he worked to secure financial investment for its cash-strapped neighbor.

For all Meta's good intentions, he could not surmount the belligerent nature of Albanian politics. In September 2001 Socialist Party rival Fatos Nanos accused the prime minister of corruption and incompetence. Moreover, the Albanian economy, though prodded, failed to live up to expectations. Therefore, in January 2002, Meta resigned from office. He was replaced by the veteran Pandeli Majko, who secured votes from competing factions—but only on the condition that Meta be excluded from any cabinet position.

Further Reading

Biberaj, Elez. *Albania in Transition; The Rocky Road to Democracy.* Boulder, Colo.: Westview Press, 1999.

Bieber, Florian, and Zhidas Daskalovski, eds. *Understanding the War in Kosovo.* Portland, Oreg.: Frank Cass, 2003.

Murati, Teuta. "The Emergence of the Albanian Nation: The Effect of Nationalism on Politics and Society." Unpublished master's thesis, East Stroudsburg University, 2000.

Schwander-Sievers, Stephanie, and Bernd J. Fischer. *Albanian Identities: Myth, Narrative, and Politics.* London: C. Hurst, 2000.

Vaughn-Whitehead, Daniel. *Albania in Crisis: The Predictable Fall of the Shining Star.* London: Edward Elgar Pubs., 1999.

Vickers, Miranda, and James Pettifer. *Albania: From Anarchy to a Balkan Identity.* New York: New York University Press, 2000.

Milošević, Slobodan (1941–) *president of Yugoslavia*

Slobodan Milošević was born in Pozarevac, Serbia, on August 20, 1941, the son of schoolteachers. His country then constituted part of the six-republic federation of Yugoslavia ("Southern Slavs") in conjunction with Croatia, Bosnia-Herzegovina, Macedonia, Montenegro, and Slovenia. This arrangement proved somewhat of an unholy alliance, for the Balkans simmered with centuries-old hatreds based on differing religions and ethnicities. However, after 1945 the federation was seized by Josip Broz, Marshal Tito, who installed a tightly regulated communist-style dictatorship. Peace and a degree of prosperity were maintained until Tito's passing in 1980, at which point the presidency of Yugoslavia was rotated among candidates from each of the republics. However, 40 years of communist rule could not constrain traditional antipathies, and, by 1991, the nation had broken up into four component parts, with the rump "Yugoslavia" consisting of Serbia and Montenegro. Much anguish and bloodshed ensued for nearly a decade before the issue of a "Greater Serbia" was settled by force.

Milošević attended the University of Belgrade, where he received a law degree in 1964. A competent administrator, he held a number of executive positions in banking and management before joining the Serbian Communist Party Central Committee in 1982. Milošević then commenced a steady climb up through the state and national hierarchy. By 1986 he was head of the state party apparatus and, hence, the nominal head of Serbia. It was in this capacity that Milošević first became aware of long-smoldering Serbian nationalism as a potential tool for his own advancement. Serbs living in neighboring Kosovo had been coming under increasing friction from their Albanian consorts, and Milošević began orchestrating mass rallies and demonstrations on their behalf. Soon he was able to command half a million demonstrators in the streets of Belgrade, and his outspoken defense of Serbian rights throughout the Balkans enhanced his national political standing. He was also ruthlessly despotic, and he used state security forces to suppress political dissenters of every stripe. By 1990 Serbia experienced great internal pressure for free elections, and that summer Milošević ran as a candidate of the newly renamed Socialist Party of Serbia (formerly Communist). Given his inflammatory demagoguery, and the willingness of Serbs to assert their national strength, he won the presidency by 65 percent of the vote. Fanning the flames of ethnic animosity played directly into his agenda and set the stage for the tragedies that followed.

Yugoslavia was by this time in tatters, so Milošević embarked on an ambitious scheme to recentralize it under direct Serbian control. This led to brief but violent frontier wars with Slovenia and Croatia throughout 1991, whereupon both nations ceded from the federation. They were soon joined by Macedonia and Bosnia-Herzegovina, and Yugoslavia had disintegrated save for a political union between Serbia and Montenegro. Having failed to solidify Serbia's political dominance, Milošević then determined to establish "Greater Serbia" by annexing Serbian enclaves in neighboring states to the homeland. Between 1991 and 1995 he orchestrated a bloody campaign of "ethnic cleansing" in neighboring Bosnia-Herzegovina, whereby the Muslim population was relocated by force or, in many instances, massacred outright. Not wishing to be left out, the Croats under FRANJO TUDJMAN also attacked Bosnia with equal ferocity. Serbian aggression was abetted by a slow Western response, and it was not until 1995 that the United Nations compelled, by a combination of economic sanctions and threat of military force, all warring parties to sign the Dayton Peace Accord. This split Bosnia up into two ethnic enclaves under a single administration, but otherwise denied it to Serbia. But the conflict nonetheless had advanced Milošević's political career and, on April 17, 1992, he was widely reelected for a second term as president of Serbia. He also continued cracking down on political dissent.

In July 1997 Milošević managed to have himself elected president of Yugoslavia, seeing that the Serbian constitution restricted presidents to two terms. He was faced with domestic discontent over economic hardships and political repression, but he predictably smothered all opposition forces. Worse, in 1998 he began aiding Serbian rebels fighting for an independent Kosovo, who were committing many atrocities against ethnic Albanians. This latest aggression drew a sharp response from the West, and in March 1999, NATO air forces began a concerted, three-month bombing campaign against Serbian troops. On May 27, 1999, the UN International War Crimes Tribunal also indicted Milošević for genocide—he is the first sitting head of state thus charged. Milošević eventually abandoned the Serb conquest of Kosovo in exchange for peace, but he publicly reveled in his newfound reputation as a war criminal. Serbia, however, was reeling from heavy damage and economic sanctions, and new elections were called for September 24, 2000. Milošević did his best playing the ethnic hatred card, but a new leader, VOJISLAV KOSTUNICA won handily. The former dictator demanded a runoff election and refused to step down until mass protests throughout Belgrade forced him from office on October 5, 2000. His 13-year reign of terror had come to an unceremonious end.

Despite his indictment for war crimes, Milošević remained a free man until April 1, 2001, when he was surrounded at his home and arrested after a 26-hour standoff with police. The following June he was handed over to the UN War Crimes Tribunal in The Hague, Netherlands, for trial. He is charged with responsibility for the deaths of tens of thousands of non-Serbs during "ethnic cleansing" campaigns, as well as the forced deportation of 800,000 refugees from Kosovo. In all he faces 66 criminal counts. During pretrial motions, however, Milošević refused to recognize the authority of the court, and pleas of "not guilty" were entered on his behalf. "I would like to say to you that what we have just heard, this tragic text, is a supreme absurdity," he railed at the judge. His trial commenced in February 2002 and is expected to last upward of two years. Milošević faces life imprisonment if convicted on any single charge.

Further Reading

Bieber, Florian, and Zhidas Daskalovski, eds. *Understanding the War in Kosovo.* Portland, Oreg.: Frank Cass, 2003.

Cigar, Norman L., and Paul Williams. *Indictment at the Hague: The Milosevic Regime and Crimes of the Balkan War.* New York: New York University Press, 2002.

Cohen, Lenard. *Serpent in the Bosom: The Rise and Fall of Slobodan Milosevic.* Boulder, Colo.: Westview Press, 2000.

Gow, James. *The Serbian Project and Its Adversaries: A Strategy of War Crimes.* London: C. Hurst, 2002.

Naimark, Norman M., and Holly Case, eds. *Yugoslavia and Its Historians: Understanding the Balkan Wars of the 1990s.* Stanford, Calif.: Stanford University Press, 2003.

Scharf, Michael P. *Slobodan Milosevic on Trial: A Companion.* New York: Continuum, 2002.

Sell, Louis. *Slobodan Milosevic and the Destruction of Yugoslavia.* Durham, N.C.: Duke University Press, 2002.

Mitchell, James (1931–) *prime minister of St. Vincent and the Grenadines*

James Fitz Allen Mitchell was born on March 15, 1931, on the island of Bequia, one of 32 islands constituting St. Vincent and the Grenadines. This Caribbean archipelago was previously governed as a British colony from 1833 to 1960. He was educated at the St. Vincent Grammar School before studying agriculture at the Imperial College of Tropical Agriculture in Trinidad and the University of British Columbia. Mitchell then went to obtain a graduate degree in history from the University of Toronto before returning home to work as a government agronomist in 1958. Over the ensuing decade he also served as a teacher, an editor with the British Ministry of Overseas Development, and found time to write several books on Caribbean agriculture. St. Vincent and the Grenadines, meanwhile, was wending its way toward political independence. It achieved self-governance from Great Britain in 1962 under a government with a premier and a unicameral legislature, the House of Assembly. In 1966 Mitchell decided to run for the legislature as a member of the Saint Vincent Labour Party (SVLP) and succeeded. He was then appointed minister of trade, production, labor, and tourism in the administration of Robert Milton Cato, the island's senior politician and founder of the SVLP. However, Cato's authoritarian style alienated Mitchell, and, in 1972, he quit the party to run as an independent. The legislature became deadlocked, equally divided between the SVLP and the People's Political Party (PPP), and Mitchell, as a nonaligned member, was selected as a compromise candidate to become premier. He served as premier for two and a half years before being ejected in a no-confidence vote. In October 1979 St. Vincent and the Grenadines acquired formal independence from Great Britain and would henceforth be administered by a prime minister instead of a premier. Mitchell, wishing to signify his own political independence, also founded the New Democratic Party (NDP) that same year.

The SVLP continued dominating the island's politics and national agenda until 1984 when, in the wake of revelations of scandals and corruption, the NDP swept the elections. Mitchell, as party head, was immediately proclaimed the new prime minister. Over the course of three more elections spanning 16 years, he replaced Cato as the island's most senior and respected politician. He also became the longest-serving head of state within the English-speaking Caribbean and a familiar sight at many regional economic gatherings.

Unlike many former Labour Party members, Mitchell was an economic liberal who embraced free-market economics at the expense of traditional state controls. In office he invoked reforms that sold off inefficient government-owned businesses, and he cultivated a better climate for foreign investment. His leadership was badly needed, as St. Vincent and the Grenadines is among the poorest nations in the Western Hemisphere. His reform effort centered on weaning the nation away from its dependency on bananas, the principal cash crop. While lucrative, this industry is subject to the whims of nature and suffers severely from tropical storms. Lately, the country has also enjoyed preferential treatment from the European Union (EU), out of fear that the island could not compete with larger growers in Central and South America. This has proved a source of friction with the United States, which advocates free trade, and which is appealing the legality of such preferences. Mitchell, therefore, has been keen to pay increased attention to development of tourism as an alternative source of income. New hotels and their accompanying infrastructure were built, the national airport upgraded, and, by 1993, tourism finally overtook cash crops as a source of foreign exchange.

In addition to domestic concerns, Mitchell has also been at the forefront of promoting stability and cooperation throughout the Caribbean. To that end he has championed creation of the Regional Constituent Assembly, which forged closer links with St. Vincent, St. Lucia, Dominica, and Grenada. He was also instrumental in securing St. Vincent's membership in the Caribbean Community and Common Market (CARICOM), another organization promoting free trade. Nor has Mitchell been shy about asserting St. Vincent's authority and interests abroad. He applauded American efforts to restore democracy to Haiti, and then allocated personnel for a multinational peace force. However, Mitchell did not want to be seen to be too beholden to the United States, and he spent his last years in office opposing the militarization of the Caribbean. He thus canceled joint maneuvers with American forces. On August 20, 2000, Mitchell relinquished the post of NDP leader in favor of the minister of agriculture, Arnhim Eustace, who subsequently succeeded him as prime minister on October 27, 2000. However, rather than retire from public life, the veteran politico remained in the new cabinet as senior minister. In light of his conspicuous devotion to public service, spanning three decades, Mitchell also received a knighthood from the British Crown in 1995.

Further Reading

Brana-Shute, Gray. "An Eastern Caribbean Centrist: Interviewing Prime Minister James F. 'Son' Mitchell." *Caribbean Review* 14, no. 4 (1985): 27–29.

Mitchell, J. F. *Caribbean Crusade.* Waitsfield, Vt.: Concepts Publications, 1989.
———. *Guiding Change in the Islands: A Collection of Speeches, 1986–1996.* Waitsfield, Vt.: Concepts Publications, 1998.
———. *A Season of Light: A Series of Messages on Development.* Waitsfield, Vt.: Concepts Publications, 2001.
"St. Vincent and the Grenadines." *The Courier,* no. 148 (November–December 1994): 37–56.

Mitchell, Keith (1946–) *prime minister of Grenada*

Keith Mitchell was born on November 12, 1946, in St. George, Grenada, a small Caribbean island situated south of St. Vincent and the Grenadines. Great Britain acquired it as a colony in 1763, and political independence was not granted until 1974. The island then acquired its own parliamentary system featuring a prime minister and a bicameral legislature. Politically, Grenada was initially dominated by the leftist Grenada United Labor Party (GULP) until 1979, when it was deposed by the extremist New Jewel Movement of Maurice Bishop. Bishop then installed a communist-style People's Revolutionary Government, aided and abetted by Soviet and Cuban troops and material support. However, Bishop was himself overthrown and murdered in another coup in 1983, during which several hundred American medical students were taken hostage until the United States military intervened to restore order and expel the foreigners. An important corner was thus turned in the island's political history; Grenada again fully embraced democratic institutions. A multiparty system has flourished ever since, although fractious island politics has entailed a rapid turnover of prime ministers.

Mitchell was educated locally before attending the University of the West Indies, Barbados, in 1968. He graduated with a degree in mathematics and taught several years before winning a scholarship to Howard University in Washington, D.C. Further study at American University culminated in a Ph.D. in mathematics and statistics by 1979, and Mitchell spent several years teaching at Howard University. However, following the American invasion, he returned to Grenada to assist the rebuilding process. In 1984 he joined the conservative New National Party (NNP), won a seat in parliament, and successively gained appointment as minister of works, communications, public utilities, civil aviation, and energy. However, he experienced a falling-out with the party's senior leadership and, in 1989, he was elected head of the NNP. In 1990 Mitchell failed to organize a vote of no confidence against Prime Minister Herbert Blaize and was further badgered by allegations of corruption. Government then passed to a new organization, The National Party (TNP), which Blaize founded, and Mitchell waited five years in opposition before economic troubles brought the administration down. He then ran for prime minister in 1995, promising to repeal the income tax and create new jobs for young people. His message of hope and moderation sat well with Grenada's electorate, and he became prime minister that February.

As a conservative leader, Mitchell advocated greater reliance upon a free-market economy and creation of a better business climate to attract foreign investment. However, rather than focus on the small business level, he was forced to address long-neglected issues such as improving the infrastructure of roads and water works. He also intended to give tourism a boost by authorizing construction of major new hotels and establishment of the service industries necessary to administer them. Within months unemployment dropped from a record high of 30 percent to half that amount, but it still remained sizable for such a small island economy. Unfortunately, Mitchell enjoyed even less success in trying to stimulate the agricultural sector, with its traditional reliance upon exporting bananas and coconuts. The abolition of the income tax, while welcomed by voters, also forced the government to shift revenue incomes to international sales taxes, which discourages trade. Mitchell's uneven handling of the economy prompted two close aides and a government minister to defect to the opposition in December 1998. This prompted constitutionally mandated elections to be held 18 months ahead of schedule. But the ensuing interval of six weeks proved insufficient for other parties to organize themselves properly. Consequently, in January 1999 Mitchell's NNP captured 89 percent of the vote and all 15 seats in parliament, effectively eliminating the opposition. "I honestly believe it's a turning point in the history of Grenada," he boasted. "People are tired of the old-style politics of vicious attacks on person and family and they are ready to take the country into a new era." Mitchell's is also the first Grenadian administration elected to two successive terms in office.

On the diplomatic front, Mitchell has been an outspoken proponent of the Caribbean Community and Common Market (CARICOM) and its drive to achieve a single-market regional economy. In 1997, he ventured to neighboring Guyana to help smooth relations between feuding African and East Indian factions who were disrupting the country. He has also cultivated closer ties with Cuba's FIDEL CASTRO and hopes to impart much of its developmental expertise to his island—while promoting democracy abroad. He has similarly pledged close cooperation with the United States in the ongoing fight against drug smuggling, which has reached epidemic proportions and threatens national stability. The global economic downturn occasioned by the September 11, 2001, destruction of New York's World Trade Center hit Grenada's tourist sector particularly hard. In February 2002 Mitchell announced that all governmental ministers would take a 10 percent cut in salary as part of an overall spending reduction strategy.

Further Reading

Bartilow, Horace A. "Institutional Politics in IMF Debt Reductions: The Case of Jamaica, Grenada, and Guyana." Unpublished Ph.D. dissertation, State University of New York, Albany, 1995.

Brizan, George. *Grenada, Island of Conflict*. London: Macmillan, 1998.

Meeks, Brian. *Caribbean Revolutions and Revolutionary Theory: An Assessment of Cuba, Nicaragua, and Grenada*. Jamaica: University of the West Indies Press, 2001.

Schoehals, Kai P. *Grenada*. Santa Barbara, Calif.: ABC-Clio, 1990.

Thorndike, Tony. *Grenada: Politics, Economics, and Society*. Boulder, Colo.: Lynne Rienner Publishers, 1985.

Mitterrand, François (1916–1996) *president of France*

François-Maurice-Adrien-Marie Mitterrand was born on October 26, 1916, in Jernac, western France, into a middle-class Catholic household. He attended the University of Paris during the 1930s to study politics and evinced right-wing sympathies. Mitterrand enlisted in the army in 1939 and was captured during the Battle of France in May 1940. However, he escaped after three attempts, made his way home, and subsequently served in the Nazi-controlled Vichy French government.

Ostensibly, Mitterrand used this as a cover for his activities in the French underground resistance. He entered politics after the war in 1946 and was elected to the National Assembly as deputy with a small right-wing party. An astute political operator, he then joined the government as minister of veteran affairs in 1947 and for the next 11 years held numerous ministerial slots in different administrations. The turning point in his career came in 1958 when he vocally opposed the return of General Charles de Gaulle to power under the Fifth Republic. Thereafter Mitterrand drifted more and more into an ideologically ambiguous, left-leaning orbit. For opposing de Gaulle, he lost his seat in the National Assembly, but within months won election to the Senate, a less powerful chamber. By 1962 Mitterrand regained his deputy's seat in the National Assembly and solidified his credentials as an anti-Gaullist. However, he realized that for left-wing parties to win a national election, he needed to formulate an unholy alliance between the moderate Socialists and hard-line Communists. The melding of competing and frequently hostile leftist interests became the cornerstone of his ensuing election strategy. Thus armed, Mitterrand challenged de Gaulle in 1965, won 45 percent of the vote, and established himself as a force in national politics. However, a long struggle to the top awaited him.

Three years after his narrow loss, the student-worker upheavals of May–June 1968 alienated left-wing parties from mainstream politics, and the conservatives won legislative elections resoundingly. It was not until 1971 that Mitterrand again stitched together his left-wing constituents into a new and invigorated Socialist Party (PS). In 1974 he contested the presidency with Gaullist candidate Valéry Giscard d'Estaing, and he lost the runoff vote by a single percentage point. This placed the combined Socialists and Communists within striking distance of victory, but the Communists, who distrusted Mitterrand and felt they were being used to advance his personal agenda, withdrew from the coalition in 1977. This, however, made the PS appear more palatable to mainstream French voters. The economy was also slipping deeper and deeper into recession. In May 1981 Mitterrand ran again against Giscard d'Estaing and won a historic upset over the Gaullists. Legislative elections the following month also gave the Socialists a majority in parliament. Both events marked the end to 23 years of conservative rule, and Mitterrand was sworn as France's first Socialist executive.

The united left-wing parties were jubilant over the extent of their victory and Mitterrand, as a conciliatory gesture, appointed four Communists to ministries in his cabinet. He thereupon embarked on an ambitious program of Socialist-oriented reforms. These included nationalization of several large banks and industries and passage of the so-called Deffere Law, which dismantled the old, centralized mechanism for governance and doled out greater power to local authorities. Furthermore, the work week was reduced to 39 hours, the minimum wage raised, and 100,000 public sector jobs created. The death penalty was also abolished and abortion legalized. These changes were initially greeted with enthusiasm, but they triggered growing budget deficits, higher inflation, and more joblessness. His plan to integrate Catholic schools into the public school system was also met by fierce resistance. Faced with declining popularity polls, Mitterrand suddenly and unexpectedly did an about-face on economics, embraced free-market liberalism, and cut government and social spending resoundingly. Some of his strident ideological allies sensed a sellout, but the change came too late to save the Socialist majority in parliament. By 1986 the conservatives were swept back into power, and Mitterrand was forced into "cohabitation," a unique power-sharing agreement with JACQUES CHIRAC of the Neo-Gaullist Rally for the Republic Party (RPR). In this manner Chirac, as prime minister, was responsible for domestic policy, while President Mitterrand directed his efforts toward foreign policy. The conservatives then implemented fiscal measures that improved the economy by 1988 but Mitterrand, known to friend and foe alike as the "Old Fox," proved the chief beneficiary. That year he soundly defeated Chirac for the presidency, resumed his majority in parliament, and ended cohabitation with the right. Endowed with another seven-year term in office, he now became the longest-serving French head of state since Napoleon III.

Mitterrand, despite his avowed preference for left-wing policies, proved decidedly conservative in terms of foreign policy. He established cordial working relations with conservative U.S. president Ronald Reagan, and he supported his controversial decision to deploy cruise and Pershing II missiles in Europe to foil new Soviet weapons. Again, leftists collectively groaned and also complained of Mitterrand's increasingly regal presidency. He then established close military ties to NATO, which had been broken by de Gaulle in the

1960s, and, in 1991, he committed French combat forces to the Gulf War against SADDAM HUSSEIN. Mitterrand also proved firmly committed to European integration and championed the 1991 Maastricht Treaty that established a common currency and a unified banking system. He also cultivated a close personal and political rapprochement with German chancellor HELMUT KOHL, further eroding centuries of hatred and mistrust between the two neighbors. However, by 1991 France was still saddled with a sour economy and, in an attempt to add new gloss to the Socialist Party, he appointed EDITH CRESSON as France's first woman prime minister. The result proved disastrous, and within months she was replaced by another party stalwart, PIERRE BEREGOVOY. Two years later the RPR captured control of parliament, and Mitterrand endured another round of cohabitation, this time with EDOUARD BALLADUR. In 1994 the public was also startled by accusations that Mitterrand had actually collaborated with the German-controlled Vichy government during World War II, a serious charge that he vehemently denied. The following year Mitterrand was diagnosed with prostate cancer and declined to seek a third term in office. After 14 years of Socialist rule, the public was ready for change and Chirac's conservatives came roaring back to capture both the presidency and parliament. The Socialist experiment, which had begun on such a promising note, ended just as dramatically.

Mitterrand died in Paris on January 8, 1996. After de Gaulle, he is probably the most significant French political leader of the 20th century. However, students of history and political science are at a loss to decipher this enigmatic figure or the seemingly contradictory policies he pursued. But, unquestionably, by edging the Socialists and their allies closer to the middle, he gave them a victory that might have otherwise proved unattainable.

Further Reading

Cole, Alastair, *François Mitterrand: A Study in Political Leadership.* London: Routledge, 1997.

Cook, Linda J., and Mitchell A. Orenstein. *Left Parties and Social Parties in Post-Communist Europe.* Boulder, Colo.: Westview Press, 1999.

Friend, Julius W. *The Long Presidency: France in the Mitterrand Years, 1981–1995.* Boulder, Colo.: Westview Press, 1998.

Morray, J. P. *Grand Disillusion: François Mitterrand and the French Left.* Westport, Conn.: Praeger, 1997.

Tiersky, Ronald. *François Mitterrand: A Political Life.* New York: St. Martin's Press, 2000.

Utley, R. E. *The French Defense Debate: Consensus and Continuity in the Mitterrand Era.* New York: St. Martin's Press, 2000.

Miyazawa, Kiichi (1919–) *prime minister of Japan*

Kiichi Miyazawa was born on October 8, 1919, in Tokyo, Japan, the son of a politician. He proved an exceptional student and, being fluent in English, visited the United States in 1939. Miyazawa subsequently attended the Law School of Imperial University in Tokyo, graduating in 1941, and he was assigned to the finance ministry. An efficient worker, he became the minister's personal secretary in 1949, and, two years later, he returned to the United States as a delegate to the San Francisco peace conference that ended the American military occupation of Japan. Miyazawa remained thus disposed until 1953, when he gained election to the House of Councillors, the largely ceremonial upper chamber of the Japanese Diet (parliament), where he remained until 1965. In 1955 Miyazawa also joined the newly formed Liberal Democratic Party (LDP), which was to dominate national politics for four decades. In 1967 Miyazawa took his father's seat in the lower body, the House of Representatives, which wields real political power. There he was tapped to serve three separate stints as director of the Economic Planning Ministry, and he also held portfolios as minister of international trade and industry, along with that of foreign minister, 1970–76. By this time Miyazawa had favorably impressed his peers by dint of intelligence and hard work, and he was viewed as a potential candidate for prime minister. However, his career was seriously sidetracked in 1988 when, as finance minister in the administration of Noboru Takeshita, a scandal involving one of his closest aides forced his resignation on December 9, 1988. However, he bounced back in February 1990 by winning his former seat, and he came to control the largest faction within the LDP. By November 1991 the party was looking to replace unpopular Prime Minister Kaifu Toshiki, and Miyazawa was voted both party leader and head of state.

Miyazawa's tenure in office coincided with one of the worse economic recessions in Japanese history, and he was hard-pressed to please nationalists, economists, and his largest trading partner, the United States. His specific challenge was to open up the country's markets to American goods without giving the appearance of caving in. Miyazawa was certainly not willing to risk a confrontation with the powerful rice lobby, so imported food was ruled out immediately. In January 1992 he held a personal meeting with President George H. W. Bush in Tokyo and agreed to allow greater importation of American cars and parts. This was a superficial expedient at best, and had been tendered before, but it diffused any chance of a trade war for several months. Miyazawa enjoyed considerably less success in another emotionally charged issue: return of the Kurile Islands. This territory had been seized by the Soviet Union in 1945, which flatly refused to hand it back. Following the collapse of that entity in December 1991, Miyazawa applied renewed pressure upon newly elected Russian president BORIS YELTSIN, and he also dangled the prospect of badly needed financial aid as an incentive. But the Russians, equally as nationalistic as the Japanese, were unyielding. The issue remains a sticking point in their diplomatic relations.

One of the biggest successes of Miyazawa's administration, one holding profound changes for the nation, was his insistence that Japan assume its rightful place in world affairs. Since 1945, the postwar constitution specifically forbade the deployment of military forces overseas. Miyazawa decried Japanese timidity over its reluctance to contribute troops during the 1991 Gulf War with Iraq, which directly threatened its economic well-being, and he demanded change. On June 15, 1992, the Diet passed a peacekeeping operations bill that allowed such deployments, provided they were part of a larger United Nations effort. The following September 1,800 troops were sent to Cambodia, the first time Japanese troops were deployed abroad since 1945.

Miyazawa had little time to enjoy success, for in 1993 his administration was rocked by another bribery scandal involving a close aide. The economy also failed to perform as anticipated, and in lower house elections held in 1993, the LDP lost its majority for the first time since coming to power in 1955. Consequently, Miyazawa resigned from office on August 9, 1993. Despite his disgrace, he remained a highly respected economic troubleshooter, and in August 1998 Prime Minister KEIZO OBUCHI appointed him finance minister. He was also retained by Obuchi's successor, YOSHIRO MORI. The Japanese economy was then in the throes of a deep recession, brought about largely by the issuing of

bad loans. Miyazawa certainly appreciated the gravity of the situation more than his political counterparts, for in March 2001 he predicted dire consequences. With candor unusual for a Japanese minister, he declared that urgent structural reforms were necessary to handle Japan's national debts, then the highest in the developed world. "The nation's finances are now abnormal, in a state relatively close to collapse," he declared, "We have to create a healthy economy instead of just trying to sound positive with words." As yet his advice remains unheeded, and Japan's once surging economy remains in the doldrums.

Further Reading

Edstrom, Bert. *Japan's Evolving Foreign Policy Doctrine: From Yoshida to Miyazawa.* New York: St. Martin's Press, 1999.

Hayes, Dedan. *Japan, the Toothless Tiger.* Rutland, Vt.: Charles E. Tuttle, 2001.

Kim, Young C. "Japanese Policy towards China: Politics of the Imperial Visit to China in 1992." *Pacific Affairs* 74, no. 2 (2001): 225–242.

Michitoshi, T. "Miyazawa Kiichi: A Statesman on Trial." *Japan Quarterly* 39 (January–March 1992): 6–16.

Neary, Ian. *The State and Politics in Japan.* Oxford: Polity, 2002.

Mkapa, Benjamin (1938–) *president of Tanzania*

Benjamin Mkapa was born in Ndanga, Tanganyika, on November 12, 1938, and he attended Catholic missionary schools. His country, a former German protectorate on the African east coast, was acquired by Great Britain in 1918 and administered as a colony. After World War II it became a United Nations trust territory under British control and in 1954 the first political party was organized under Dr. Julius Nyerere. Tanganyika gained complete independence in December 1961 with Nyerere as its first president, and the country was promptly renamed Tanzania. The mainland state was also joined by two predominately Muslim islands offshore, Zanzibar and Pemba, and the three regions constitute the United Republic of Tanzania. It is governed by a president and a unicameral legislature, the National Assembly. Nyerere, who ruled the country from 1962 to 1985, was well intentioned but saddled his nation with a sweeping economic reorganization called *ujaama,* an African variation of state socialism. Under this regimen, the government controlled virtually every aspect of political, social, and economic life. It nearly drove the country into bankruptcy and is now regarded as a conspicuous failure; consequently, Nyerere's immediate successor, ALI HASAN MWINYI, began a slow dismantling process. However, unlike most newly liberated countries in Africa, Tanzania has enjoyed relative peace and stability, undoubtedly because all 130 tribes speak Swahili, the national language. The government has also never been overthrown by a military coup. However, Tanzania remains one of Africa's poorest nations.

Mkapa attended Makere University College in Kampala, Uganda, where he majored in English. After fulfilling stints with civil and foreign service agencies, he became managing editor of two newspapers. It was in this capacity that he caught the attention of President Nyerere in 1974, who appointed him press secretary. A succession of mid-level bureaucratic positions then followed, interrupted by attendance at Columbia University in New York, where Mkapa studied international relations. He subsequently served as High Commissioner to Canada, 1982–83, and ambassador to the United States, 1983–84. Around this time he also joined the Revolutionary Party (CCM), Tanzania's only legal political entity, and he began advancing up the party hierarchy. In 1985 Mkapa successfully ran for a seat in the National Assembly and gained reelection in 1990. With his star in the ascent, and as a political protégé of the aging Nyerere, Mkapa was well positioned to assume national leadership at the highest levels. In 1995 he became Mwinyi's handpicked successor to run in the first multiparty elections held since 1962. On October 29, 1995, Mkapa garnered 61.8 percent of the vote in a free and fair election marred only by procedural errors and delays. He thus became Tanzania's third president in three decades of CCM rule.

Mkapa inherited a country still saddled with an inefficient socialized economy and replete with central planning and collectivized agriculture. Its citizens were poor, getting poorer, and their plight made Tanzania all the more dependent on foreign aid. Corruption was also widespread and Mkapa had pledged to curtail it. In January 1996 he appointed a special commission to fully investigate all irregularities, which forced several high-ranking officials from office. However, his biggest challenge remained the economy. He thereupon scuttled CCM's cherished notions of state controls and ushered

in a new age of free-market economics, privatization, and free enterprise. Under this scheme large, inefficient state industries were put up for sale and farmland, previously owned by the government, was parceled out to poor farmers. Mkapa has also been active in personal diplomacy, visiting potential donor nations, and soliciting funding and loans. As a sign of sincerity, in 1996 he oversaw establishment of a multilateral debt fund to help the nation service its $1.1 billion debt. Mkapa's brand of fiscal discipline and face-to-face contact apparently worked, for by 2000 he managed to acquire $2 billion in foreign aid. In light of his success, and real growth registered by the Tanzanian economy, Mkapa breezed to victory in the October 29, 2000 elections, winning 71.7 percent of the vote.

Tanzania has a long-established tradition of political activism throughout East Africa and Mkapa sought to expand that role. He worked closely with presidents YOWERI MUSEVENI of Uganda and DANIEL ARAP MOI of Kenya to sign the East Africa Cooperation Treaty in 1999, which signals a new era in better relations. Such concord is greatly needed, for the region still suffers from the social upheavals in Rwanda and the flood of refugees this engendered. Worse, in August 1998 a bomb destroyed the U.S. embassy in Dar es Salaam, the handiwork of Saudi-born terrorist Osama bin Laden. Mkapa has since pledged to help the United States fight international terrorism. But, however accommodating, the president is quick to resist what he considers economic coercion from rich Western powers. In February 2002 he rejected calls by the European Union to impose sanctions on neighboring Zimbabwe, and he declared that Tanzania would also resist such moves. "Developed countries and donors did not decide how Tanzanians can attain their independence; they decided on their own," he stated. "In that same vein foreign powers will not be allowed to dictate how Tanzania can develop, defend, and protect its independence." He then likened the 2002 European Union (EU) meeting in Brussels to the infamous 1884 conference in Berlin, Germany, whereby Africa was formally partitioned into colonies by various European powers. In August 2002, Mkapa also facilitated peace talks between the Burundi government and rebel leaders in Dar es Salaam to conclude a nine-year civil war that has killed an estimated 200,000 citizens. "Each and every gun must be silenced," the president insisted, "and each and every machete sheathed."

Further Reading

Askew, Kelly M. *Performing to the Nation: Swahili Music and Cultural Politics in Tanzania.* Chicago: University of Chicago Press, 2002.

Kebede, John A. *The Changing Face of Rural Policy in Tanzania.* London: Minerva, 2000.

Mkapa, Benjamin W. *Building a Vision: President Benjamin W. Mkapa of Tanzania.* Dar es Salaam: SARDC, 1995.

Neumann, Roderick P. *Imposing Wilderness: Struggles over Livelihood and Nature Preservation in Africa.* Berkeley: University of California Press, 2002.

Sadleir, Randal. *Tanzania: Journey to Republic.* New York: Radcliffe Press, 2000.

Mobutu Sese Seko (1930–1997) *president of Zaire*

Joseph Desire Mobutu was born on October 14, 1930, in Lisala, Belgian Congo, the son of a cook. He also belonged to the Bengala people, who were the traditional source of manpower for the Belgian colonial army. Mobutu attended various missionary schools before being expelled for violence, and he joined the military in 1949. He had risen to the rank of sergeant major when discharged in 1956, and he then worked as a journalist. However, Mobutu, like many African nationals, resented the discriminatory practices of the Belgians and he joined the National Congolese Movement under firebrand leftist Patrice Lumumba. The Belgian Congo obtained its independence in June 1960 and Lumumba, now president, appointed Mobutu secretary of state for national defense. In this capacity he squelched several mutinies, and he won the loyalty of officers through bribes and political favors. By 1961 an ongoing power struggle between President Lumumba and Prime Minister Joseph Kasavubu erupted into violence. Mobutu, who criticized Lumumba for soliciting help from the Soviet Union, sided with Kasavubu. He had Lumumbu arrested and turned over to the prime minister, following which he was murdered. By this time Mobutu had secured the military's allegiance and was the de facto ruler of Congo. He tolerated Kasavubu and a new premier, Moise Tshome, for several more years before overthrowing both in 1965. Mobutu then installed himself as absolute ruler for the next 32 years.

In power, Mobutu proved himself to be one of the most astute and ruthless dictators of the 20th century.

By March 1966 he had abolished the legislature and ruled by decree, establishing an elaborate system of spoils and graft that perpetuated his power for three decades. In fact, wholesale graft became the coin of the realm. Mobutu quickly availed himself of Congo's rich mineral resources and allowed Western interests to mine them, provided he received a percentage of the profits. He also made similar allowances for his network of cronies, military and civilian alike. To further concentrate power in his hands, Mobutu outlawed all political parties except for his own, the Popular Movement of the Revolution, of which he was chairman. Worse, by 1970 he embarked on a Stalin-like cult of personality whereby his photograph was distributed around the country and the state-controlled media sang his praises at every opportunity. Another facet of his strategy was "Africanization" of the country, whereby Congo was renamed Zaire, and all citizens were forced to abandon Western-style clothing and Christian names for their indigenous counterparts. Pursuant to this creed, the president unmodestly styled himself Mobutu Sese Seko, "the rooster that leaves no hen intact." Through all these expedients, not the least of which were the loyalties he purchased, Mobutu amassed a personal fortune estimated at $5 billion. By dint of institutionalized theft on an unprecedented scale, Zaire functioned as the world's biggest "kleptocracy."

Another reason for Mobutu's longevity was his foreign policy. Beholden to no ideology of his own, he positioned himself as stridently anticommunist to win favor among Western powers. France and the United States, in particular, slipped him millions of dollars in aid, most of which he siphoned off for personal use. In return, Mobutu allowed the CIA and Western mercenaries to train Jonas Savimbi's UNITA forces against the neighboring socialist regime in Angola. But Mobutu's excesses and oppression aroused considerable resentment, and in 1977 and 1978 he required French military assistance to suppress large-scale rebellions. The Zairean people, though residing in one of Africa's richest lands, were reduced to abject poverty while Mobutu lived in grotesque splendor.

The turning point in Mobutu's fortunes derived from the end of the cold war. Hereafter, Western powers began demanding that he allow multiparty elections. The dictator only sullenly complied and by 1995 new presidential and legislative elections were scheduled for the following year. However, these never had a chance to transpire. Mobutu had earlier threatened ethnic Tutsis living in the eastern reaches of Zaire with mass expulsion, so they joined an ongoing rebellion commanded by LAURENT DESIRE KABILA, a former Lumumba ally. The badly paid and trained Zairean army crumbled before this renewed onslaught, and by May 1997 the insurgents had reached the outskirts of Kinshasa. Mobutu, meanwhile, lacked any popular support to halt the rebels, who were greeted as liberators. His traditional benefactors, France and the United States, also declined to extend help. He thereupon fled the country on May 16, 1997, ending 32 years of corrupt despotism. Kabila subsequently proclaimed himself president and renamed Zaire the Democratic People's Republic of the Congo. The aging despot did not have long to enjoy his ill-gotten gain, for he died of prostate cancer in Rabat, Morocco, on September 7, 1997. Mobutu remains one of the longest-lived and most notoriously self-enriching tyrants in African history.

Further Reading

Duke, Lynne. *Mandela, Mobutu, and Me: A Bittersweet Journal of Africa.* New York: Doubleday, 2003.

Kelly, Sean. *America's Tyrant: The CIA and Mobutu of Zaïre.* Lanham, Md.: American University Press, 1993.

Mwakikagile, Godfrey. *Africa after Independence: Realities of Nationhood.* Huntington, N.Y.: Nova Science Publishers, 2001.

Schatzberg, Michael G. *Mobutu or Chaos: Zaïre's Friendly Tyrant.* Philadelphia, Pa.: Foreign Policy Research, 1990.

Wrong, Michela. *In the Footsteps of Mr. Kurtz: Living on the Brink of Disaster in Mobutu's Congo.* New York: HarperCollins, 2001.

Young, Crawford. *The Rise and Decline of the Zaïrean State.* Madison: University of Wisconsin Press, 1985.

Mogae, Festus (1939–) *president of Botswana*
Festus Gontebanye Mogae was born in Serowe, Botswana, on August 21, 1939. Botswana is a large, landlocked nation in southern Africa, bordered by South Africa, Namibia, and Zimbabwe. In 1885 it became a British protectorate under the name of Bechuanaland, and remained so administered until 1961, when a native legislative council was established. This body prevailed upon Great Britain to allow a gradual transition to self-rule and, following the creation of numerous political parties, the new nation of Botswana was born in September 1966. In a strictly political sense, the country is exceptional in being one of few multiparty democracies extant on the African continent. The constitution allows for a president, who is limited to two consecutive five-year terms, and a unicameral national assembly. Another senior advisory body, the House of Chiefs, consists of tribal leaders drawn from each of the eight major ethnic groupings, and it deals specifically with cultural affairs. Botswana also enjoys a long tradition of stable government uninterrupted by military coups, and a peaceful transference of power. Moreover, endowed with mineral resources, including diamonds, it also enjoyed consistent economic growth at a time when most African economies were struggling.

Mogae completed his basic education locally, then went on to obtain a degree in economics from Oxford University in England. He subsequently attended the University of Sussex for his master's degree in developmental economics in 1970. Mogae then returned home to work within the ranks of the government bureaucracy, and he held various posts under the Ministry of Finance and Development. An astute manager, he also worked for the International Monetary Fund (IMF), the World Bank, and various other Commonwealth lending institutions. His good performance brought him to the attention of President QUETT MASIRE of the Botswana Democratic Party, who appointed him a permanent secretary in 1982. He held this post for a decade until becoming minister of finance and development planning. By 1992 the Masire regime was under attack in the face of allegations of scandal, which forced the vice president from office. Mogae, by virtue of his sterling reputation, was selected to fill his office and Masire began grooming him for succession. The president then announced his own resignation in January 1998, and, on March 23 of that year, Mogae replaced him as Botswana's third president.

Mogae's accession was viewed with relief by members of the BDP, for it was anticipated he could heal the rifts that had developed during Masire's rule. Accordingly, he worked to smooth ruffled feathers, appointed members of various factions to his cabinet, and restored party harmony in short order. On October 16, 1999, the BDP was overwhelmingly elected to power in parliament, thereby assuring Mogae's continuation as president. Once in office, he carried out the successful policies that had distinguished his predecessors. Mogae's tasks were greatly simplified in that he inherited a prosperous nation with a stable electorate and a growing economy. The world recession of the late 1990s had hit Africa particularly hard, however, and Botswana underwent a period of relatively slow growth. Mogae, by virtue of his training as an economist, was able to anticipate and plan for such contingencies. He outlined his National Development Plan in February 1997, which called for sustained economic growth through diversification and greater emphasis on private sector activity. This strategy managed to stimulate modest job creation, but not enough to significantly reduce the 21 percent unemployment rate. Mogae then turned to foreign investment to pick up the slack and, thanks to the healthy mineral extraction industry, he initiated a number of joint partnerships with foreign corporations.

Botswana is also fortunate in having friendly relations with all of its neighbors. It had previously served as a front line state throughout the ongoing struggle against apartheid in South Africa but, following the election of NELSON MANDELA, it established full and cordial relations. Mogae also maintained Botswana's membership in the 12-nation South African Development Community and the Southern African Customs Union, which coordinates development activities and promotes duty-free trade. However, of late the country faces an unparalleled challenge in the form of a rampant AIDS epidemic. Botswana enjoys the melancholy distinction of having the world's highest infection rate, and the deadly disease increasingly strains social and governmental services. On November 7, 2000, Mogae addressed the national parliament, declaring: "The killer disease has raised the national human toll to nightmarish proportions." He concedes that AIDS is responsible for at least half of all natural deaths occurring in Botswana and pledges greater government intervention in education and prevention to stem the tide. Under such dire circumstances he has also welcomed assistance from abroad in the manner of discount drugs and educational materials. More controversial was Mogae's support for a long-delayed media bill that places control of press affairs in the hands of the public affairs minister and levies heavy fines for "faulty journalism." Naturally, the press and media community are crying foul and express fears of a government attempt to reduce press freedom.

Further Reading

Good, Kenneth. *The Liberal Model of Africa: Elites against Democracy.* New York: Palgrave, 2001.

Motzafi-Haller, Pnina. *Fragmented Worlds, Coherent Lives: The Politics of Difference in Botswana.* Westport, Conn.: Bergin and Garvey, 2002.

Samatar, Abdi Ismail. *An African Miracle: State and Class Leadership and Colonial Legacy in Botswana Development.* Portsmouth, N.H.: Heinemann, 1999.

Wells, Jason M. "A Threshold of Independence? A Cultural Evaluation of Civil Society in an African Democracy: The Case of Botswana." Unpublished master's thesis, University of Missouri, Columbia, 2000.

Wiseman, John A. "The Slow Evolution of the Party System in Botswana." *Journal of Asian and African Studies* 33 (August 1998): 241–265.

Mohamad, Mahathir (1925–   ) *prime minister of Malaysia*

Datuk Seri Mahathir bin Mohamad was born on December 20, 1925, in Alor Setar town, Kedah state, Malaysia, the son of schoolteachers. Malaysia occupies the southern half of the Malayan Peninsula and the northern third of the island of Borneo. It had been administered as a British colony since the 19th century and incrementally gained independence between 1957 and 1963. The Chinese-dominated island of Singapore was originally part of this union, but it broke away in 1965. Ethnically, Malaysia remains a highly stratified society, with poor Malays comprising the bulk of the population, balanced off by far wealthier Chinese and Indian minorities. The last two groups were imported by the British as laborers and have since dominated the business community's upper strata. There exists considerable resentment and tensions between them. The country is further polarized along religious lines, with Islam forming the majority sect, seconded by Buddhism, Christianity, and others. Malaysia is theoretically headed by a king, who is elected every five years by nine ruling sultans. However, actual power is entrusted to a prime minister and a bicameral legislature, consisting of a Senate and a House of Representatives. Several political parties have been functioning in Malaysia since independence, but overwhelming dominance belongs to the ethnic-oriented United Malays National Organization (UMNO).

Mahathir attended local Islamic schools before attending the Sultan Abdul Hamid College in Alor Setar. He subsequently studied medicine at the University of Singapore and worked as a government doctor for many years until opening a private practice in 1957. While at school he gained a reputation as an outspoken, ruthless debater with a brusque demeanor far different from most of his compatriots. In 1964 Mahathir commenced his political career by winning a seat in the lower house. An astute politician, he soon gained election to the Supreme Council of UMNO, an elite body that formulated party policy. As a member, Mahathir established his credentials as a leading spokesman for Malay nationalism, and he agitated for greater rights at the expense of the Chinese. In 1969 he authored an inflammatory book entitled *The Malay Dilemma,* which codified his radical views on race and led to his expulsion from the party. However, mounting social unrest culminated in anti-Chinese riots, and in 1971 the government enacted many affirmative action programs originally espoused by Mahathir. The following year he was welcomed back to UMNO and continued his rise up the party hierarchy. Mahathir was made deputy prime minister in 1976, which virtually assured his succession to the highest seat of power. This transpired in 1981, when he became the first person of common origin to serve as prime minister.

Mahathir has since established himself as Malaysia's longest-serving head of state, with impressive election victories in 1982, 1986, 1990, 1994, 1998, and 2000. His rule has also flirted with controversy, owing to an authoritarian style of governance. Early on, Mahathir posited himself as a Malay nationalist, and he continued his program of expanding economic and political opportunities for the impoverished majority. Nor was he above tangling with royal authority. In 1983 he challenged the king's constitutional power to veto government legislation and lost—but not before obtaining the legislatures right for an override. In 1987 he felt sufficiently imperiled by opposition forces to invoke the Internal Security Act, through which a hundred Islamic fundamentalists, Chinese nationalists, and party adversaries were summarily jailed. He also called upon fellow Malays to reject their colonial past and "Look East" for inspiration. Specifically, Mahathir sought to emulate the Japanese and South Korean models of economic expansion and become economically self-sufficient. More important, he called upon his fellow countrymen to reject Western cultural values, such as democracy and freedom of the press, as "anti-Asian." The Malaysian economy experienced sustained growth for many years until the Asian currency crisis of 1997, following which the prime minister attributed the country's declining performance to "Western conspiracies." He then enacted austerity measures to conform with debt reduction guidelines of the International Monetary Foundation (IMF) and the World Bank, and, by August 1999, Malaysia had declared its recession over.

Despite his sometimes ethnocentric tenor, itself the product of a colonial upbringing, Mahathir enjoys a reputation as a senior Asian statesman of impressive political longevity. His approach to human rights and freedom of the press has sometimes alarmed and upset the United States, and, in 1998, Vice President AL GORE publicly upbraided him for past repression. But, despite his Islamic background, Mahathir is strongly anti-fundamentalist and has come out strongly in support for America's war against terror. In February 2002 he addressed the World Economic Forum in New York, site of the World Trade Center disaster, and dwelt upon the problems relating to religion and security. "I find that they understand better after the explanation that Islam is a religion of peace and that Islam does not promote terrorism," he stated. "We do not sympathize with them but it is important to understand why these people resort to such actions." Mahathir then called upon industrialized nations to help address the vast social inequalities between rich and poor, for poverty and despair, he believes, lie at the heart of terrorism. Slated for retirement soon, Mahathir's confrontational policies did achieve his stated goal of granting fellow Malays a greater share of the national prosperity. This, and not his controversial outbursts, will be his greatest legacy. As if to underscore his unpredictable behavior, on June 23, 2002, Mahathir suddenly announced his resignation as head of the National Front coalition during a nationally televised gathering of the party faithful. "Why?" he declared to horrified party members. "I have decided. It's been a long time." Pandemonium ensued backstage until the senior party officials convinced the 77-year-old leader to stay on. Officials of the fundamentalist Islamic opposition dismissed the entire episode as a staged event to generate sympathy—and votes—for the head of state.

Further Reading

Barlow, Colin, and Francis Loh Kok Wah, eds. *Malaysian Economics and Politics in the New Century.* Northampton, Mass.: Edward Elgar Pub., 2003.

Case, William. "Malaysia's Resilient Pseudodemocracy." *Journal of Democracy* 12 (January 2001): 43–57.

Hilley, John. *Malaysia: Mahathirism, Hegemony, and the New Opposition.* London: Zed, 2001.

Gunn, Geoffrey C. *New World Hegemony in the Malay World.* Trenton, N.J.: Red Sea Press, 2000.

Jones, David M. "What Mahathir Has Wrought." *National Interest* 59 (2000): 101–112.

Khoo Boo Teik. *Paradoxes of Mahathirism: An Intellectual Biography of Mahathir Mohamad.* New York: Oxford University Press, 1995.

Nasr, Seyyed Vali Reza. *Islamic Leviathan: Islam and the Making of State Power.* New York: Oxford University Press, 2001.

Shome, Tony. *Malay Political Leadership.* Richmond, England: Curzon, 2001.

Verma, Vidhu. *Malaysia: State and Civil Society in Transition.* Boulder, Colo.: Lynne Rienner Publishers, 2002.

Mohammed VI (1963–) *king of Morocco*

Sidi Mohammed Ben al-Hassan was born in Rabat, Morocco, on August 21, 1963, the son of reigning King HASSAN II. He belongs to the Alaoui dynasty, which traces its history back over 22 rulers and also claims descent from the prophet Muhammed. More recently, Morocco had been a French protectorate since 1912, and it achieved independence in 1956. Mohammed's father was installed as king in 1961 and he ruled for 38 years. His tenure on the throne was characterized by arbitrary action and suppression of political opponents, but also modest trends toward liberalization. Morocco's government is presently a constitutional monarchy, whereby the hereditary king presides over parliament and either approves or vetoes legislation it sends him. The country also hosts one of the few multiparty democracies in the Arab world, with 28 parties present. Given its close proximity to France and Spain, Morocco is the most Westernized of all Muslim countries, and therefore religiously and politically somewhat more moderate than most. For several years it has been rocked by the rise of Islamic fundamentalism, but nothing on the scale that is terrorizing neighboring Algeria. The country also enjoys a small but thriving economy and currently boasts three-fourths of the world's known phosphate reserves. Presently, it also exercises military and political control over the Western Sahara to the south, although the fate of this region awaits United Nations adjudication.

Mohammed was educated at various Muslim academies as a youth, and in 1981 he received his bachelor's degree from the Royal College. He subsequently attended the College of Law in Rabat and, fluent in French, he acquired his doctorate from the University of Nice–Sophia Antipolis, France, in 1993. He then returned home to complete a stint of military service, after which Hassan II appointed him a divisional commander in the Royal Army. Unlike his media-conscious father, Mohammed kept a low profile publicly, but privately he gained notoriety as a playboy who enjoyed fast cars and nightclubs. He also distinguished himself by expressing interest in social issues, poverty in particular, and he familiarized himself with the problem. On July 23, 1999, King Hassan died suddenly, whereupon Mohammed was suddenly thrust into the public limelight. Because the position of king demands that successors be married, the young leader quickly took a bride whose name remains unknown. On July 30, 1999, he also addressed his nation for the first time, declaring an amnesty for 46,000 political prisoners detained by his father. From the onset of his reign the new king, installed as Mohammed VI, continued and accelerated his father's trend toward modernity and moderation.

Mohammed VI's determination to redress past grievances manifested itself in August 1999, when he announced the creation of an independent commission to investigate political "disappearances" and arrange monetary compensation to the families. He also invited several leading dissidents, such as Abraham Serfaty, back to the homeland. The king then fired his father's longstanding minister of the interior, Driss Basri, who had an unsavory reputation for violently suppressing political opposition. In the spring of 2000 the king took the unprecedented step of introducing a program of political reforms to improve the social status and legal rights of women. These included raising the minimum age for marriage from 15 to 18, allowing polygamy only with the permission of the first wife, and equalizing the division of family assets during divorce. Islamic fundamentalists were enraged by the changes and protested loudly, claiming they threatened traditional Muslim values. However, the legislation passed easily, making Moroccan women among the freest in the Muslim world. In October 2001, upon the second anniversary of his accession, the king called upon Morocco to become a modern, democratic state "based on civic freedoms and human rights."

More than anything, King Mohammed wishes to affirm his commitment to greater democracy. He publicly pledged to support the multiparty system, the rule of law, and individual rights. King Mohammed also differed from his father by extensively touring the nation, especially the poorer Rif district, which he promised to aid. By expanding help to the poor, the king determined to break the traditional monopoly enjoyed by Islamic fundamentalists and their numerous charitable associations. All these liberalizing moves were applauded by the West, which sought expanded trade and political ties to the regime. However, King Mohammed made clear his sympathies for the Palestinian cause, and, in January 2002, he roundly criticized Israel for its enforced confinement of Palestine Liberation Organization chairman YASSER ARAFAT within the West Bank town of Ramallah. Mohammed also accused Prime Minister ARIEL SHARON of "torpedoing" the peace process and "undermining the very foundations of dialogue and negotiation." He has since endured a chill in relations with Spain over the issues of fishing and illegal immigration, and diplomatic deadlock over the issue of the Western Sahara. Accordingly, a summit scheduled for December 2001 was suddenly called off and the Moroccan ambassador to Spain recalled home for "consultations."

Further Reading

Bourqia, Rahma, and Susan G. Miller. *In the Shadow of the Sultan: Culture, Power, and Politics in Morocco.* Cambridge, Mass.: Harvard University Press, 1999.

Hart, David M. *Tribe and Society in Rural Morocco.* Portland, Oreg.: Frank Cass, 2000.

Howe, Marvine. "Fresh Start for Morocco." *Middle East Policy* 8 (June 2001): 59–66.

Maghraovi, Abdeslam. "Monarchy and Political Reform in Morocco." *Journal of Democracy* 12, no. 1 (2001): 73–86.

Waltz, Susan E. *Human Rights and Reform: Changing the Face of North African Politics.* Berkeley: University of California Press, 1995.

Moi, Daniel arap (1924–) *president of Kenya*

Daniel arap Moi was born in the village of Kuriengwo, Kenya, on September 2, 1924, a member of the minority Kalenjin tribe. Kenya, occupying a large swath of land on Africa's east coast, had previously been administered as a British colony, although agitation for independence began in the wake of World War II. Moi attended various missionary schools before graduating from the Kapsabet Teacher Training College in 1945. He then taught for several years, rising to headmaster of the Government African School in 1954. The following year Moi ran as a representative in the transitional Legislative Council and has held public office ever since. In 1960 he was chosen to attend the Lancaster House Conference in London, which laid the groundwork for Kenyan independence and its first constitution. The country became sovereign in 1963 under the aegis of Jomo Kenyatta and his Kenya African National Union Party (KANU). He also served as a powerful symbol of national unity in this otherwise divided country, where tribalism was rife. Moi, however, felt slighted by the political dominance of the Kikuyu tribe, and he went on to found the Kenya African Democratic Union (KADU) in 1961. After several minor administrative posts, Moi dissolved KADU in the interest of national unity and rejoined KANU. Kenyatta subsequently appointed him minister of home affairs with control of the national police. He served well, and in 1967 Kenyatta made him vice president to replace Oginga Odinga, recently ousted for corruption. At that time Kenya seemed rooted in democratic practices, although after 1969 it officially became a one-party state. KANU thus became the only legal outlet for political expression. As the aging Kenyatta grew less capable of leading, Moi also assumed greater responsibility for administering the country. He then officially succeeded Kenyatta following his death on August 22, 1978. He has since become the nation's longest-serving president, running unopposed in 1979, 1983, and 1988, and winning contested elections in 1993 and 1997.

Initially, Moi appeared to embrace Kenyatta's democratic leanings and initiated the *Nyaya*, or "footsteps" program, to continue his policies. This entailed renewed emphasis on promoting nationalism at the expense of tribalism, gradual replacement of foreign workers with native Kenyans, and a market economy. Moi also pledged to root out corruption, initiated large-scale land reforms, and even hinted at legal acceptance of a multiple party system. However, by 1981 Moi had dramatically altered his approach to governance and placed increasing trust in an entourage of corrupt cronies. Patronage and blatant favoritism now became hallmarks of his administration. Worse, whenever dissent spilled into the streets, it was brutally repressed by the national police. Moi, himself a businessman with vast holdings nationwide, continued to enrich himself at public expense. Soon he gained a reputation for being among Africa's most corrupt politicians, and among its most cunning.

In 1981 dissident elements within the Kenyan air force tried to overthrow Moi's regime, but they were defeated by loyalist units. He used the unrest as a pretext for wholesale repression, and he further consolidated his control over his ministers and KANU, in which he serves as party head. By 1986 Moi's machinations had reduced the National Assembly to a rubber-stamping apparatus, and he used it to eliminate the offices of attorney general and controller general. This opened the door to even further widespread fraudulence and domestic unrest. Shootings, disappearances, and murder were becoming commonplace. Criticism of Moi's despotism in the West, moreover, remained muted, simply because he pursued a largely pro-Western foreign policy throughout the cold war. After 1991, with the collapse of the Soviet Union, the European Union and the United States began applying economic pressure on Kenya to allow multiparty elections. Moi only grudgingly complied, and in December 1992 he overcame a very scattered opposition to win with 36 percent of the vote. In December 1997 he again squeaked by with a 40 percent plurality. The entire election process only demonstrated Moi's mastery of tribal manipulation, and the procedure underscored his determination to remain in power.

Fortunately for the people of Kenya, Moi has stated his intention to stand down before the next round of presidential elections, slated for 2002. His successor will inherit a nation demoralized by oppression and among the very poorest in Africa, owing to widespread graft and gross economic mismanagement. Nonetheless, in February 2002, Moi urged Western donors to shun favoritism when giving financial aid to developing nations. "Although Kenya has been pursuing true democratic ideals and had been peaceful," he proclaimed in mock surprise, "She has been subjected to foreign aid embargo, yet some other war-torn African countries and others mired in conflicts had been given financial aid." He thereupon called for an end to "double standards" when determining foreign aid, and cordially invited foreign investors to boost Kenya's sagging economy. Meanwhile, Moi's political legacy seems secure. In addition to being Kenya's longest-serving politician, according to Amnesty International he has also enjoys one of the worst human rights records of recent times. He is slated to step down from power in December 2002, and he hopes new elections will make Uhuru Kenyatta, son of the nation's first president, his successor.

Further Reading

Adar, Korwa G. "Assessing Democratization Trends in Kenya: A Post-mortem of the Moi Regime." *Journal of Commonwealth and Comparative Politics* 38 (November 2000): 103–131.

Brown, Stephen. "Authoritarian Leaders and Multiparty Elections in Africa: How Foreign Donors Help to Keep Kenya's Daniel arap Moi in Power." *Third World Quarterly* 22, no. 5 (2001): 725–739.

Moi, Daniel A. *Which Way, Africa?* Nairobi: Government Press, 1997.

Morton, Andrew. *Moi: The Making of an African Statesman.* London: Michael O'Mara, 1998.

Mwakikgaile, Godfrey. *Ethnic Politics in Kenya and Nigeria.* Huntington, N.Y.: Nova Science Publishers, 2001.

Watson, Mary Ann. *Modern Kenya: Social Lives and Perspectives.* Lanham, Md.: University Press of America, 2000.

Molné, Marc Forné (1946–) *Executive Council president of Andorra*

Marc Forné Molné was born in La Massana, Andorra, on December 30, 1946. Andorra is one of Europe's most unusual countries, and among the world's smallest. It has existed as a principality since 1278, and it is jointly governed by its larger neighbors, France and Spain. Until 1993 Andorra lacked an executive leader and was ruled by a General Council, in concert with the president of France and the bishop of Urgel, Spain. Its inhabitants consist of native Andorrans, who speak Catalan, and a large proportion of French and Spanish immigrant workers. Women were not allowed to vote or hold office until 1970. Throughout the 1980s, at the urging of France and Spain, Andorra was requested to draw up a constitution of its own for better self-governance. However, its integration into Western Europe was incremental at best. Talks concerning membership with the European Union (EU) were delayed until 1986, and Andorra was not a signatory to the Universal Declaration of Human Rights until 1988. By that time, trade unions and political parties were also allowed for the first time. In 1993 the notion of national independence under a constitution came before the public in a referendum passed by 74 percent of the vote. This mandated continuing governance under an executive council, but headed by a president. Significantly, the dual ruler arrangement with Spain and France remained in place, although thereafter it applied only to defense and foreign policy. The constitution also preserves political power in the hands of native Andorrans, but guarantees the rights of citizenship for long time foreign residents. The first general elections, held in December 1993, made Oscar Ribas Reig of the National Democratic Party (AND) Executive Council president, and he held it until being deposed by a vote of no-confidence in November 1994. His successor was Marc Forné Molné of the newly founded Liberal Union Party (UL).

Molné trained as a lawyer and worked with a family law firm until the 1970s. He did not seek political office until 1993, when he gained election to the Executive Council. That year he also founded the UL party, a center-right organization with conservative overtones. By 1994 Andorra was experiencing a mounting national deficit, and the government of Ribas Reig sought to address the problem by implementing a national income tax—the nation's first. However, Andorra enjoys an established reputation as a low-tax haven, and Ribas Reig's government fell victim to a no-confidence vote on November 25, 1993. Forne was then elected to take his place based on his long opposition to broader taxation.

Once in office, Molné sought to engage Andorra more closely with the outside world, and he took steps to attract greater trade and investment. An important step occurred in July 1993, when Andorra joined the United Nations as its 184th member. The country enjoys a long tradition of peaceful coexistence and neutrality, and the following year it signed the Nuclear Non-Proliferation Treaty, which forbids possession of chemical, nuclear, or biological weapons. Because national defense arrangements are entrusted to France and Spain, Andorra does not maintain an army per se, only a small color guard which is trotted out for ceremonial functions. "My country has the intention to continue to contribute to initiatives such as these in order to express our solidarity with the actions for peace of the United Nations," Molné declared in October 1999. Curiously, Andorra generally lacks formal diplomatic representation abroad, with ambassadors in France and Spain only. The country's ambassador to the United Nations in New York also serves as its ambassador to the United States.

Molné has also taken careful steps to increase Andorra's economic survival in an age of growing international integration. The country remains largely agricultural, but he has emphasized attracting tourism, its concomitant service industry, and also financial institutions. Given Andorra's strict confidentiality laws, banking has become a source of some anxiety with France and Spain, for they fear such secrecy foments criminal money laundering. Molné also adamantly refuses to impose an income tax to sustain national growth. Instead, he relies upon an annual levy from foreign workers and an import tax for goods brought into the country. Generally, Andorrans are the most undertaxed people in Europe, and they pay only a small fee for telephone and electrical service. The nation has since entered into negotiations for membership in the EU, contingent upon Andorran efforts to suppress cigarette smuggling, a serious revenue loss to other nations. Overall, the voters remain content with Molné's brand of moderate leadership. In 1997 and again in 2001 they returned him to office with an absolute majority of UL seats in the Executive Council, thereby assuring continuation of his policies. Andorra's ultimate integration into the greater community of Western nations seems thereby assured.

Further Reading

Armengol Vila, Lidia. *Approach to the History of Andorra.* Perponinya: Institut d'Estudis Andorran, 1989. *Country Review: Andorra, 2001.* Houston, Tex.: CountryWatch.Com, 2000.

Duursma, Jorri. *Self-Determination, Statehood, and International Relations of Micro-states: The Cases of Liechtenstein, San Marino, Monaco, Andorra, and the Vatican City.* New York: Cambridge University Press, 1996.

Rogatnick, Joseph H. "Little States in a World of Powers: A Study of the Conduct of Foreign Affairs by Andorra, Liechtenstein, Monaco, and San Marino." Unpublished Ph.D. dissertation, University of Pennsylvania, 1976.

Taylor, Barry. *Andorra.* Santa Barbara, Calif.: ABC-Clio, 1993.

Monteiro, Antonio Mascarenhas (1944–)
president of Cape Verde

Antonio Mascarenhas Monteiro was born on São Tiago, Cape Verde islands, on February 16, 1944. His country, a 10-island archipelago 300 miles west of Senegal, then constituted part of the Portuguese Empire, and it had been ruled continuously from Lisbon since 1460. In the wake of World War II an independence movement emerged in nearby African colonies and within Cape Verde itself. In 1956 the African Party for the Independence of Guinea-Bissau and Cape Verde (PAIGC) crystallized under Amilcar Cabral, who continued agitating for self-rule until his assassination in 1973. The following year the Portuguese government was toppled and all its African possessions, including Cape Verde, acquired political independence. Its first president was Aristides Pereira, who sought an eventual political union with Guinea-Bissau. However, after a failed coup attempt by mainland factions, Cape Verdeans broke with PAIGC and founded their own entity, the African Party for the Independence of Cape Verde (PAICV). Over the next decade, Pereira ruled capably as leader of a one-party state, although he also laid the groundwork for one of Africa's first multiparty elections. Under its present constitution, Cape Verde is ruled by an elected president, who appoints a prime minister and works in conjunction with a national assembly. Moreover, to avoid polarizing the electorate, all presidential candidates are forbidden from belonging to established political parties. Pereira and the PAICV remained in control of Cape Verde's political destinies until February 1991, when they were defeated by the new Democratic Movement Party (MPD).

Monteiro was educated locally before relocating to Portugal to attend the Universities of Lisbon and Coimbra. In 1974 he transferred as a law student to the Catholic University of Louvain, Belgium, where he graduated three years later. Monteiro had previously been a member of the Marxist-oriented PAIGC in 1967, but he broke with them over ideological issues. Once back home in 1977, he pursued a legal career, specializing in international law. That year he also gained appointment as secretary-general of the parliament, which he held for 10 years. In 1980 Monteiro's good performance resulted in his becoming president of the Supreme Court. In this capacity, he gained political stature by attending international symposiums on human rights, and he represented his nation in the Organization of African Unity. (OAU). Monteiro then declared his candidacy for the presidency in September 1990, after Cape Verde officially became Portuguese Africa's first multiparty democratic state. In this en-

deavor he was backed by the newly formed MPD, which declared its support and campaigned on his behalf. In February 1991 he was victorious, with 73.5 percent of the vote, and was duly sworn in as the nation's second freely elected president. "The people elected me because I was the candidate that represented democracy," he exclaimed, "and this is the important factor that made the difference."

One of Monteiro's first chores in office was promulgating a new constitution that formally declared the Second Republic. It drew heavily upon his legal education, and the document officially dedicated Cape Verde to the principles of human rights, equality, and democracy. Otherwise, Monteiro has been fully occupied with developing the economic infrastructure of his islands. Volcanic in origin, they are sparsely vegetated with only about 10 percent of the land arable, and even this is often subject to severe drought conditions. Consequently, Cape Verde remains one of the world's poorest nations, almost entirely dependent upon outside aid to survive. For this reason, Monteiro and his predecessors were attentive toward keeping the nation's debt-servicing costs as low as possible to demonstrate fiscal responsibility. This, in turn, has assured a steady influx of loans and grants from abroad that keep the population fed and the economy afloat. Cape Verde's principal source of income is from exporting crops, chiefly bananas, coffee, and pineapples. However, nearly half of all arable land is consumed by sugar cane production, used mostly in the manufacture of local alcoholic beverages. The government wishes to curtail this activity and divert a greater percentage of land usage to production of cash crops. In 1993, Monteiro also oversaw creation of a free-enterprise zone to encourage foreign investment. Overall, Cape Verde remains one of Africa's few truly democratic states, albeit desperately poor and in constant need of foreign assistance.

In 1996 Monteiro ran unopposed for the presidency and was reelected by 80 percent of votes cast. However, he declined to seek a third term in January 2001 and he supported the candidacy of another MPD candidate, Carlos Veiga, the sitting prime minister. However, after a decade in opposition, the much-maligned PAICV came roaring back to win a majority of seats in the parliament and José Maria Neves replaced Monteiro as the new president. A month later he himself was succeeded by another veteran PAICV official, Pedro Pires.

Further Reading

Guilford, Mary Alice. "Rainfed Farmers and Rural Development in Cape Verde, 1950–1992." Unpublished Ph.D. dissertation, Boston University, 1999.

Lobban, Richard A. *Cape Verde: Crioulu Colony to Independent Nation.* Boulder, Colo.: Westview Press, 1995.

Mayer, Jean. "Development Problems and Prospects in Portuguese-speaking Africa." *International Labour Review* 129 (July–August, 1990): 459–479.

Shaw, Caroline S., comp. *Cape Verde.* Santa Barbara, Calif.: ABC-Clio, 1991.

Whann, Christopher A. "The Political Economy of Cape Verde's Foreign Policy." *Africana Journal* 17 (1998): 40–50.

Morauta, Mekere (1946–) *prime minister of Papua New Guinea*

Mekere Morauta was born in Kukipi Village, Gulf province, Papua New Guinea, in 1946. His homeland is part of a large island located directly north of Australia, rich in natural resources such as minerals, gold, and oil. It is also home to 4.7 million people, who speak an estimated 800 different languages. Papua New Guinea was a German colony by the end of the 19th century, but, after 1918, it passed into Australian hands as a League of Nations mandate administered by that country. Parts of northern Papua New Guinea endured brutal Japanese occupation during World War II, but Australia maintained its control during the postwar period. However, by 1964 the first steps toward political independence were achieved through creation of a national parliament, the House of Assembly. In September 1975 Papua New Guinea achieved political independence as a constitutional monarchy under the British Crown, and as a British Commonwealth nation. The government is organized along parliamentary lines whereby the party with the largest number of seats appoints a prime minister. However, the island's polity is fractious and volatile, with members of different parties repeatedly supporting other candidates at whim. In fact, the notion of political allegiance is still somewhat alien to Papua New Guinea, where most personal loyalties are to a chief, a clan, or a region. Consequently, none of the country's prime ministers elected since 1975 has completed a full five-year term. When governments are able to be formed, they are invariably coalitions of competing interests, temporarily allied to each other. The net result is an extremely rapid turnover of politicians from high office and, from a policy standpoint, general instability.

Morauta was educated locally and in Port Moresby, the national capital, before attending the newly founded University of Papua New Guinea. Having briefly studied at Flinders University, Australia, he returned home and graduated in 1970 with a degree in economics. Morauta then held a series of important government posts, commencing as a researcher with the Department of Labour. In time he rose to become the first native-born secretary in the Department of Finance, a post usually occupied by Australians. By 1983 Morauta was president of the PNG Banking Corporation, where he served nearly a decade. In consequence of his good performance there, he was knighted by Queen Elizabeth II in 1990. He then served as head of the Central Bank until 1994, when he opened a successful private business. Morauta first aspired public office when he ran for and was elected to parliament in 1997 as an independent. Shortly thereafter Prime Minister Bill Skate of the People's National Congress Party appointed him minister of fisheries, although Skate himself resigned from office in July 1999. Morauta then demonstrated his skills at political bargaining when he gained the support of the People's Democratic Movement Party (PDM) and was elected the country's newest prime minister on an amazing 99 to 5 vote.

Morauta came to office at a difficult period in Papua New Guinea's history. The economy was in tatters after decades of mismanagement and the national currency, the kina, had plummeted to only 40 cents to the U.S. dollar. Worse, inflation was running at 22 percent while political corruption was widespread. Morauta was determined to follow the closely prescribed program for economic reform laid out by the International Monetary Fund (IMF) and World Bank. These called for an increased emphasis upon privatization of inefficient state-owned industries, such as the PNG Banking Corporation and Air Niugini, the national carrier. Morauta placed both up for sale, which signaled that Papua New Guinea was becoming more receptive to outside investment and free-market economics. Within a year inflation had dropped by half and the economy showed some signs of reviving. The international banking community was also pleased and they authorized continuing financial assistance. The Australian government under Prime Minister JOHN HOWARD alone pledged $195 million in aid, along with increased technical assistance.

Unfortunately, the pace of Morauta's reforms became mired in unrelated events that rocked the country. In March 2001, when the government announced plans to cut expenditures by reducing the army's size by one-third, many soldiers took up arms and rioted. These were then joined by thousands of student demonstrators, angered by the selling off of national assets to foreign investors. On June 25, 2001, riots erupted in Port Moresby and were put down by force, leaving three students dead. However, Morauta managed to quell military unrest by stalling his budget cuts, and his efforts were further buoyed in August 2001 when a peace deal was reached with dissidents on the island of Bougainville, who had been in a state of rebellion for 10 years. The pact, which must be approved by two-thirds of the parliament, grants Bougainville greater autonomy and the possibility of independence at a later date. Thus a terrible civil war, which claimed 20,000 lives, came to a negotiated end. However, the problem of a mutinous soldiery revisited the nation in March 2002, when mutineers took over several barracks at Wewak. However, Morauta dismissed the problem as an internal military issue unrelated to the issue of budget cuts. He therefore intends to revive the sputtering national economy with a stiff dose of austerity measures, and he hopes to be the first prime minister to complete a full term in office.

Further Reading

Billings, Dorothy K. *Cargo Cult as Theater: Political Performance in the Pacific.* Lanham, Md.: Lexington Books, 2001.

Chin, James. "Papua New Guinea in 2001: Election Fever Begins." *Asian Survey* 42 (January–February, 2002): 150–155.

Dinnen, Sinclair. *Law and Order in a Weak State: Crime and Politics in Papua New Guinea.* Honolulu: University of Hawaii Press, 2001.

Dorney, Sean. *Papua New Guinea: People, Politics, and History since 1945.* Sydney: ABC Books, 2000.

May, R. J. *State and Society in Papua New Guinea: The First Twenty-five Years.* London: C. Hurst, 2001.

Nelson, Hank. "Crises of God and Man: Papua New Guinea Political Chronicle, 1997–99." *Journal of Pacific History* 34 (December 1999): 259–264.

Standish, Bill. "Papua New Guinea in 1999–2000." *Journal of Pacific History* 36 (December 2001): 285–300.

Mori, Yoshiro (1937–) *prime minister of Japan*
Yoshiro Mori was born on July 14, 1937, in remote Ishikawa prefecture, western Japan, the son of a politician. During World War II his mother died and his father was sent abroad to fight, so he was raised by his grandparents. Afterward, his father served as mayor of Neagari, as his grandfather had, and it stimulated Mori's interest in politics. Mori subsequently attended prestigious Waseda University, where he joined the debate society and proved himself a skillful orator. He also encountered and befriended Noboru Takeshita and KEIZO OBUCHI, both future prime ministers. Mori, who was endowed with an impressive physique, also developed a taste for rugby and has remained an avid sportsman ever since. He graduated in 1960 and sought work as a newspaper reporter, but two years later he became secretary to a member of the House of Representatives. Gregarious by nature and adept at forging consensus, an essential Japanese trait, Mori first ran for office in 1969 and won a seat in the lower house as an independent. Shortly thereafter the majority Liberal Democratic Party (LDP) in parliament prevailed upon the burly young man to join their ranks. He commenced a slow but steady rise through the party hierarchy, acquiring a reputation as an expert backroom deal-maker.

Over the next three decades, Mori successively filled a number of significant positions, both within the government and his party. These culminated in his 1998 appointment as party secretary-general, which placed him only a step behind Prime Minister KEIZO OBUCHI. However, in April 2000, Obuchi was suddenly felled by a stroke and Mori advanced to succeed him. Only then were facts about this impressive, sports-loving politician better known. In 1988 he had apparently been implicated in a bribery scandal that eventually brought down the Takeshita administration. In 1992 he also accepted suspicious donations from a large trucking firm, ostensibly in return for political favors. Corruption and politics are old bedfellows in Japan, and Mori's apparent licentiousness was not deemed unusual for a bureaucrat of his stature. But the new leader, while well versed in local politics, lacked meaningful experience in dealing with international diplomacy and complex world issues. Furthermore, he exhibited an alarming penchant for verbal gaffes and speaking off-the-cuff at inopportune times. This garnered little attention during the backroom machinations for which he was renowned, but as head of state his behavior and pronouncements were subject to national and even global scrutiny. Mori also had the misfortune of running Japan while the nation suffered through its worse recession since World War II.

In office, Mori was well-intentioned but quickly established a reputation for clumsiness. In May 2000, he casually remarked to a group of Shintoist politicians that "Japan is a divine nation with the emperor at its core, and we want the people to recognize this." The press and public recoiled over such sentiments, as they harkened back to the pre–World War II days when the emperor was enthroned as a god and became a living symbol for militarism. Mori refused to apologize for his choice of words, insisting that they had been misinterpreted. "It is a matter of course that I, as prime minister, strictly uphold and respect the sovereign power, which resides with the people and freedom of religion," he emoted. The following July he referred to his nation by the outmoded word "kokutai," which again dates back to the prewar period and is closely associated with emperor worship and militarism. This sparked renewed discomfort among wartime survivors, and the comment confirmed Mori's predilection for shooting himself in the foot. His popularity had also declined precipitously to 19 percent by that point, the lowest in years for a national figure, and he called for early elections. The LDP subsequently lost 38 seats in the lower house, but it managed to remain in power through a three-party coalition. Mori, for better or for worse, was allowed to remain prime minister.

Mori's numbers continued sinking alongside the moribund economy, and his personal behavior seemed to underscore a general inability to lead. On November 21, 2000, he barely survived a vote of no confidence over his lackluster performance. Then, on February 9, 2001, upon receiving news that an American submarine had accidentally rammed and sank a Japanese vessel carrying high school students, he decided to finish a round of golf before issuing a statement. But the turning point in Mori's political fortunes happened that spring when three of his closest ministers resigned because of monetary scandals. This only tarred the inept administration with an air of corruption, and, on April 18, 2001, Mori withdrew from office after only 11 months in power. "I decided to resign because I felt we need to start over with fresh members in order to regain the people's trust," he

sullenly declared. At that point his popularity ratings stood at 9 percent, the lowest ever recorded for a prime minister. Mori continued as a member of parliament, and, in February 2002, he conferred with Russian foreign minister Igor Ivanov in Tokyo. He discussed with him establishing closer working relations with the Central Asian republics, especially Afghanistan.

Further Reading

Hayes, Lewis. *Introduction to Japanese Politics.* Armonk, N.Y.: M. E. Sharpe, 2001.

Nisigari, Celine. *Japan's Road to Popular Empowerment: The Story So Far.* Chicago: Adam Press, 2000.

Schwartz, Frank J. *Advice and Consent: The Politics of Consultation in Japan.* Cambridge: Cambridge University Press, 2001.

Reed, Steven R. *Japanese Electoral Politics: Creating a New Party System.* New York: Routledge, 2003.

Sims, R. L. *Japanese Political History since the Meiji Restoration, 1868–2000.* Basingstoke, England: Palgrave, 2001.

Tipton, Elsie K. *Modern Japan: A Social and Political History.* New York: Routledge, 2001.

Moscoso, Mireya (1946–) *president of Panama*

Mireya Elisa Moscoso Rodríguez was born on July 1, 1946, in Panama City, Panama, the daughter of a teacher. Her country, part of an isthmus connecting Central and South America, was settled by Spain in 1513 and became part of Colombia after 1821. Independence was acquired in 1903 with the help of the United States, which aspired to build a strategic canal that connected the Atlantic and Pacific Oceans. This was accomplished in 1914, and since then Panama had endured an uneasy alliance with its powerful northern neighbor. In 1977 military strongman General Omar Torrijos signed an agreement with President Jimmy Carter to transfer ownership of the canal by December 1999. Control of the country then passed to another dictator, Manuel Noriega, who ruled ruthlessly until overthrown by U.S. military forces in 1989. Democracy was finally restored to Panama and in 1994 Ernesto Pérez Balladares of the Democratic Revolutionary party (PRD) came to power. He served for five years, albeit amid continuing economic crises that undercut his attempts at reform. However, in 1999, after attempting to amend the constitution to allow him to run for a second term, he was succeeded by Mireya Moscoso, the first female president of Panama.

Moscoso attended Catholic schools in Panama City, and in 1968 she entered politics as an assistant to President Arnulfo Arias, who had been elected twice before. The following year he was driven from office by a military coup and she followed him into exile in Florida. In 1969 Moscoso married Arias, 45 years her senior, thereby cementing her political fortunes to his legacy. She then studied interior design at the Miami Dade Community College, receiving her degree in 1974. Arias died in 1988 and the following year, after General Noriega had been deposed by President George H. W. Bush, she returned to Panama and helped found the Arnulfista Party (AP) in honor of her husband. In May 1994 she attempted to run for the presidency against Pérez Balladares, and lost after receiving a credible 29 percent of the vote. Thereafter she consolidated her support within the party, and she gained national attention for leading the effort to defeat constitutional reforms sought by Pérez Balladares that would allow him a second consecutive term in office. Moscoso then survived a primary challenger to become the AP's presidential candidate in the May 1999 elections. Surprisingly for a macho-dominated society, she defeated Martín Torrijos, son of the general, with 37.8 percent of the vote. Moscoso was then sworn into office on September 1, 1999, amid high expectations for political and economic reforms. "From now on we are in charge of our own destiny," she trumpeted. "We don't want a divided country, we want a unified nation."

Though victorious, the new president faced serious opposition in the 72-seat parliament, where her party controlled only 14 seats. The majority belonged to the vengeful PRD, which was foresworn to block any or all of her badly needed initiatives. Previously, Moscoso campaigned on a pledge to reverse some of the privatization trends initiated by Pérez Balladares. The government did in fact suspend the sale of state-owned industries, and also raised some agricultural tariffs. However, her moves to undo all prior reforms were successfully blocked and never passed. Panama remains in serious economic difficulty with high unemployment, high government expenditures, and mounting national debt. Worse, once the United States handed over the Panama Canal in December 1999 as promised, Washington ceased paying millions of dollars of rent to the government. The exodus of long-established and wealthy American companies associated with operating the canal also led to a general decline in revenues. And, due to treaty provisions, the United States retained the right to intervene militarily if access to the canal was deemed threatened. In October 2000 guerrillas from neighboring Colombia attacked a Panamanian village, raising the specter that their activity might trigger an American response. Accordingly, Moscoso conferred with Colombian president ANDRÉS PASTRANA to discuss better border controls. Meanwhile, the country remains mired in a recession with unemployment at 12 percent and a general poverty rate of 35 percent.

Three years into her administration, Moscoso has yet to deliver on any major campaign initiatives and the political deadlock is beginning to prompt rumors of a coup against the government. Such matters have well-established precedent in Panama's political history, and Moscoso's own husband was deposed three times in this manner. Her own administration has come under strong criticism from the national press, and she countered by signing a bill that effectively muzzles journalists for slandering public officials. However, such controls do little to counter growing perception that Moscoso, while well-intentioned, is simply too inexperienced to handle the complex and difficult issues facing the country. In the face of rising unemployment, poverty, and declining social services, she has until general elections scheduled for 2004 to turn events around. Otherwise, her party will inevitably pay the price for unfulfilled expectations.

Further Reading

Furlong, William L. "Panama: The Difficult Transition towards Democracy." *Journal of Interamerican Studies and World Affairs* 35, no. 3 (1993): 19–66.

Gardner, Jace. A. "Emergent Panama: A Nation and Canal in Transition." Unpublished master's thesis, University of Central Oklahoma, 1998.

Harding, Robert C. "The Military Foundation of Panamanian Politics: From the National Police to the PRD and Beyond." Unpublished Ph.D. dissertation, University of Miami, 1998.

Perez, Orlando J. *Post-invasion Panama: The Challenges of Democratization in the New World Order.* Lanham, Md.: Lexington Books, 2000.

Scranton, Margaret E. "Panama's First Post-transition Election." *Journal of Interamerica Studies and World Affairs* 37 (November 1995): 69–101.

Mosisili, Pakalitha (1945–) *prime minister of Lesotho*

Pakalitha Mosisili was born in Qacha's Nek, Lesotho, on March 14, 1945. Lesotho is a small, landlocked nation in the heart of southern Africa, previously known as Basutoland. It has its origins as a bastion against Zulu encroachment during the 19th century, and in 1868 it became a British protectorate. But, having lost its most fertile lands to the neighboring Orange Free State, Lesotho's sizable population has been forced to eke out a marginal existence through farming. This is a difficult task, given the mountainous terrain, and excessive farming has greatly reduced the quality of arable land available. Lesotho therefore remains one of the poorest and most underdeveloped regions on the African continent. In addition to economic deprivation, it is also politically unstable, with a history of coups and countercoups against the government. Lesotho finally gained its independence from Britain in 1966 as a constitutional monarchy that immediately went awry. In 1986 a military dictatorship was established under Mesting Lekhanya, who dethroned King Moshoeshoe II and installed his 27-year-old son Letsie III. In 1991 Lekhanya himself was removed in a coup, and the new junta placed Lesotho back on the path to democracy. Elections held in 1993 brought the Basotholand Congress Party (BCP) under Nstu Mokhele into power, who reinstalled King Moshoeshoe on the throne and managed to rule capably until 1998. That year he announced his retirement due to health reasons.

Mosisili attended the University of Lesotho for many years, where he obtained three degrees in education. He then taught there for a decade between 1972 and 1983 before teaching at three South African universities, 1983–93. Previously, he joined the BCP in 1967 and was a stalwart supporter of the party over the next 30 years. In 1993 he gained election to the National Assembly, and he also held the minister of education portfolio. In February 1995 Prime Minister Mokhele appointed him deputy prime minister with a view toward eventual succession. However, that year both men walked out of parliament to form a new association, the Lesotho Congress for Democracy (LCD), in which Mosisili served as deputy leader. Still in majority control, the aging Mokhele then granted Mosisili additional portfolios of home affairs and local government, until his retirement from office in 1998. New elections were consequently held and on May 23, 1998, and the LCD won a landslide victory, taking 79 of 80 parliamentary seats. Mosisili was then sworn in as the new prime minister.

The size and scope of the LCD's impressive victory led immediately to charges of voter fraud by the three opposition parties. Mosisili, wishing to curry favor with all his people, agreed to have South African vice president THABO MBEKI investigate and certify the results. This was done accordingly, but it failed to assuage government critics, who orchestrated large demonstrations and called for Mosisili's resignation. This he was not prepared to do. By September 1998, once protests grew violent, he invited South African troops to restore order and serve as peacekeepers. However, the opposition reacted violently to the invasion, and several pitched battles were fought. By the time Mosisili agreed to new elections within 18 months and agreed to withdraw all foreign troops, 60 people had died. It proved an inauspicious debut for the new prime minister, who had yet to confront Lesotho's staggering economic problems, including an unemployment rate approaching 50 percent.

Due to the poor farming conditions and scanty levels of industrialization present, Lesotho's leading export is its workers. Well educated and disciplined, many residents labor in South African mines, farms, and industry, and the wages they send home constitute up to 45 percent of Lesotho's annual gross national product. The nation also derives considerable income from the Lesotho Highland Water Project, which supplies South Africa with year-round supplies of freshwater. However, Mosisili seeks to expand economic opportunity at home by encouraging South African firms to relocate through a package of tax incentives and duty-free access to European Union markets. Through all these expedients, some economic gains have been registered in this hard-pressed land, and, in January 2001, the LCD majority in parliament returned Mosisili to a second five-year term. His prospects for greater influence were greatly bolstered in October 2001, when a key party figure defected and founded the new Lesotho's People's Congress Party. Mosisili responded with a call for new elections, and the LCD gained 18 new seats. Even with this new strength, a handful of sitting members declined to announce whether they would remain within the LCD or not. "Everyone has a right to choice and I think the opposition will help strengthen democracy in this country," he observed. "The country needs men and women of strong characters who would take the country to greater heights." With new elections slated for May 2002, the prime minister sought to extend his control over parliament even further and pass new legislation essential to the continuing welfare of his impoverished state.

On June 5, 2002, the LCD won a resounding victory, taking 77 out of 80 contested seats in the 120-seat parliament. Mosisili was then sworn in for his second five-year term, declaring, "The government faces a daunting task, but we are optimistic that we will pull through."

Further Reading

Copeland, David B., and Tim Quinlan. "A Chief by the People: Nation versus State in Lesotho." *Africa* 67, no. 1 (1997): 27–61.

Ferguson, James. *The Anti-politics Machine: Development, Democratization, and Bureaucratic Power in Lesotho.* New York: Cambridge University Press, 1990.

Franklin, Anita. *Land Law in Lesotho: The Politics of the 1979 Land Act.* Brookfield, Vt.: Aldershot, 1995.

Lemon, Anthony. "Lesotho and the New South Africa: The Question of Incorporation." *Geographic Journal* 162, no. 3 (1996): 263–373.

Weisfelden, Richard F. *Defining National Purpose: The Roots of Factionalism in Lesotho: A Thesis.* Cambridge, Mass.: Harvard University Press, 1997.

Mswati III (1968–   ) *king of Swaziland*

Crown Prince Makhosetive was born in Swaziland on April 9, 1968, the 68th son of King Sobhuza II. Swaziland is a small, mountainous enclave surrounded by South Africa and Mozambique. It was founded by the Ngwane people during the last half of the 18th century and in 1902 it became a British protectorate. Swaziland remains Africa's last absolute monarchy, although a constitution, adopted after independence in September 1968, allows for some deliberative bodies and minor political activity. Foremost among these are the *tinkhunda*, or local councils, whose members are drawn from various chieftains. These, in turn, select 40 members to the parliament, subject to the king's approval. The sovereign also appoints half the members of the 20-seat Senate. But these remain advisory bodies only; throughout the 20th century, Swaziland has undergone a general centralization of political power toward the king and his bureaucrats. His word, literally, is law. This practice, in turn, has alienated many tribal chieftains, who feel that the new system undercuts their traditional authority and way of life. Nonetheless, King Sobhuza II was considered an illustrious monarch who ruled Swaziland from 1921 to 1982, and he did much to cement constructive relations with South Africa, thereby preserving his nation's independence.

Makhosetive was attending a private school in England when his father died, and he immediately returned home. Though he was crown prince in line for the succession, the country was subsequently ruled by regents over the next four years. Opponents to the new king in the Liqoqo, or King's Council, tried purging that body of members sympathetic to the new monarch, but these were then dismissed by Queen Ntombi, his mother. Rather than risk further infighting before the crown prince reached the age of 20, the youngest he could be legally enthroned, Makhosetive was crowned Mswati III on April 25, 1986, two years in advance. It was anticipated that the young man would be awkward and easily influenced, but the new monarch proved surprisingly adept at palace intrigue. Within months he disbanded the Liqoqo and dismissed his prime minister. He also ordered the arrest of several members of the royal family viewed as obstructionist, and charged them with treason, but they were eventually pardoned. Mswati III also faced a growing surge for popular, multiparty democracy and, as a concession, he appointed Sotsha Diamini, a former unionist and activist, as prime minister. Short of that, however, he refused to abandon any of his traditional rights and privileges.

After several years in power, Mswati still faces numerous challenges to his authority and the well-being of Swaziland. Foremost among these is pervasive corruption, which saps economic strength and threatens the political stability of the country. Offending politicians and police officials have since been arrested, tried, and punished, but as late as January 2000 the king identified poverty and corruption as the nation's leading ailments. Also, he has been forced to acknowledge the growing pro-democracy movement in Swaziland by appointing a constitutional review commission to draft a new document. However, and perhaps not unexpectedly, the commission consisted only of royal family members who would naturally be averse to any dramatic changes. Their report is still pending. The monarchy has also endured run-ins with the free press, and arrested several journalists for slandering the royal family. Against this backdrop, it would appear that Swaziland's embrace of the 21st century will prove hesitating and incremental at best. Success hinges on maintaining a successful balancing act between tradition and change.

Mswati III has also come under closer scrutiny than most traditional monarchs for his personal lifestyle. As king, he is entitled to nine wives for sole purpose of creating large numbers of offspring, but his third consort, Queen LaMbikiza (Sibonnelo Mngomezulu), has proven controversial. A totally modern woman, she flouts the closely prescribed and traditional roles ascribed to Swaziland wives. LaMbikiza is, in fact, a practicing attorney and active in children's and women's issues. The queen has also generated considerable criticism from more traditional segments of society by declaring that it is perfectly acceptable for a young girl to wear pants in public. King Mswati III, meanwhile, seems too preoccupied with his eight other wives to notice. Of more pressing concern is the rampant AIDS epidemic in Swaziland, where an estimated 30 percent of the adult population is infected. To prevent its further spread, in November 2001 the king announced renewal of the traditional chastity rite of *umchwasho,* which forbids sexual relations for unmarried women under the age of 17. However, when it was revealed that his newest wife is only 17 and had been living in the royal palace for some time, young Swazi women protested by flinging their traditional blue and yellow chastity tassels at the palace steps. The king has since apologized for his indiscretion, and levied the fine of one cow against himself.

Given the ongoing tug-of-war between tradition and modernization in Swaziland, it remains to be seen how the young and somewhat impulsive monarch can adapt to changing times. The continuation of the royal line, the well-being of his people, and the very independence of Swaziland all hang in the balance.

Further Reading

Abiodun, Onadipe. "Overhauling the Feudal Regime in Swaziland." *Contemporary Review* 269 (December 1996): 296–302.

———. *Swaziland's International Relations and Foreign Policy: A Study of A Small African State in International Relations.* New York: P. Lang, 1990.

Gillis, D. Hugh. *The Kingdom of Swaziland: Studies in Political History.* Westport, Conn.: Greenwood Press, 1999.

Ginindza, Z. R. *King Mswati 111: A Pictorial Biography of the New King of Swaziland.* Swaziland: Macmillan Swaziland National Pub. Co., 1986.

"Swaziland." *The Courier,* no. 147 (September–October 1994): 18–38.

Mubarak, Hosni (1928–) *president of Egypt*

Hosni Mubarak was born in the Nile Delta village of Kafr El-Meselha on May 4, 1928, the son of a judicial bureaucrat. Egypt had been a British protectorate since 1914 and an independent monarchy under British protection since 1922. British troops were withdrawn following World War II, but in 1952 the monarchy was overthrown by nationalists under Abdul Nasser and a republic proclaimed. Presently, the country is governed by a president who is nominated by one-third of the National Assembly, approved for candidacy by two-thirds, and formally elected through a national referendum. For many years the National Democratic Party (NDP) was the only legal outlet for political expression, although in 1977 opposition parties were finally legalized. One significant exception is the Muslim Brotherhood, a religion-based organization given to fanaticism, terror, and the imposition of radical Islamic policies. Egypt, as the largest Arab country in the world, is also the most influential and among the most Westernized. Since 1978 it has been one of only two Arab countries to enjoy full diplomatic relations with the Jewish state of Israel, and its impact on events throughout the Middle East remains significant. It also enjoys close ties with the United States and, despite some internal instability, serves as a trusted regional ally.

Mubarak was well educated locally and he was one of a handful of students chosen to attend the prestigious National Military Academy. He graduated in 1949 and proceeded on to the fledgling Air Force Academy, winning his wings. Mubarak subsequently served there for two years as a flight instructor before serving as a regular military pilot. He performed well, and, in 1964, he was selected for a year of study at the famous Frunze General Staff Academy in the former Soviet Union. Mubarak then returned home and held a succession of increasingly important military posts, including air force chief of staff in 1972. The fine performance of the Egyptian air force during the 1973 Yom Kippur War with Israel was viewed as his handiwork, and he became a national hero. Consequently, in April 1975 President

Anwar Sadat appointed him vice president, and he played a pivotal role in brokering the Camp David peace accords between Egypt and Israel in 1978. Two years later Mubarak enhanced his political standing by becoming vice chairman of the NDP party, which made him Sadat's chosen heir. Following Sadat's assassination at the hands of Muslim extremists on October 6, 1981, Mubarak became president by parliamentary action. The following October his position was confirmed in a national referendum with 98 percent of the vote. Since then, Mubarak has been consistently reelected in 1987, 1993, and 1997, making him the longest-serving Egyptian head of state in recent times, and among the most popular.

In contrast to the showy ostentation of Sadat, Mubarak is viewed as a modest, competent technocratic—if somewhat dull. However, consistent with his military background, he exudes both iron discipline and an unflagging will in directing affairs of state. Throughout his long tenure in office, national security and stability have become the lynchpin of his agenda, thanks to the murderous activities of the outlawed Muslim Brotherhood. This fanatical organization is responsible for the deaths of several ranking politicians, numerous tourists, and Coptic Christians. Their self-avowed goal remains the violent overthrow of the secular Egyptian government and imposition of the strict Islamic code of law. Mubarak, himself the object of a botched assassination attempt in 1995, has responded with brutal force and remains determined to squelch such activity, especially as attacks on foreigners endanger the country's flourishing tourist industry. Consequently, thousands of extremists have been routinely rounded up and imprisoned. These tough measures have produced the desired results, and by 2000 violent attacks on tourists and officials were largely curtailed. Mubarak then responded in kind by releasing several thousand detainees from prison. Stability has been preserved, but a strong undercurrent of religious fanaticism remains.

Another essential priority of the Mubarak administration is economic solvency. Like Sadat, he has embraced a program of privatization to sell off inefficient state-owned industries to attract foreign investment. His efforts are further buoyed by the treaty with Israel, which guarantees a $1 billion annual subsidy from the United States. The government has also aggressively embarked on reducing bureaucracy and government regulations.

Consequently, inflation is modest, the national debt is shrinking, and some growth has been achieved. However, the national economy only totters on, and it is scarcely equal to the task of creating new jobs to absorb the exceptionally high birth rate, which adds 1.2 million new citizens every year. Because national and social stability are at stake, Mubarak's goal is to transform Egypt from its tourist and subsidy-dependent economy to one of export-driven growth. But the task remains enormous. Problems relating to national self-sufficiency will in all likelihood evade Mubarak during his remaining time in office, and they will have to be addressed by his successors.

Egypt's greatest impact on world affairs remains international diplomacy. The country was highly ostracized for recognizing Israel in 1978, and it took years of fence mending before Mubarak could convince fellow Arab states to resume normal relations. This has been for the most part accomplished, but continuing upheavals between Israel and the Palestinian Authority under YASSER ARAFAT remain a potential flash point in the Middle East. Attacks on Jewish settlers and civilians have always drawn predictable and costly Israeli retribution, which threatens regional stability. Mubarak has roundly criticized Israel for its continuing occupation of lands seized in the 1967 war, including Jerusalem, but he has repeatedly offered Egyptian mediation to resolve the issue. The problem has become even more pressing as fighting and terrorism between the two sides escalated throughout 2001. In March 2002, while on a state visit to Washington, D.C., Mubarak again reiterated his call for mediated talks. "We have to do whatever we can with the administration here to bring the two parties together," Mubarak said. "They should sit down whether they like it or not." The beleaguered president also affirmed his support for the American fight against global terrorism in the wake of the September 11, 2001, destruction of New York's World Trade Center. However, Mubarak has strongly urged the United States to desist from a military campaign to oust Iraqi dictator SADDAM HUSSEIN for risk of further alienating the Muslim world. "We have to be very careful there—very, very careful," he warned President GEORGE W. BUSH at a White House ceremony. Bush responded by praising Mubarak for his efforts to arrange a badly needed Israeli-Palestinian summit. All told, the Middle East remains a simmering cauldron of hatred and extremism that has yet to be defused. Mubarak's ability to juggle strategic priorities, and sooth extreme religious impulses, may very well define his political legacy—and that of his nation.

Further Reading

Alterman, John B. "Egypt: Stable, but for How Long?" *Washington Quarterly* 23, no. 4 (2000): 107–118.

Fahmy, Ninette S. *The Politics of Egypt: State-Society Relationship*. Richmond, Va.: Curzon, 2001.

Hassan, Sana. *The Struggle for Coptic Equality: Christian Egypt versus Muslim Egypt*. New York: Oxford University Press, 2002.

Hill, Enid. *Discourses in Contemporary Egypt: Politics and Social Issues*. New York: American University in Cairo Press, 2000.

Kienle, Eberhard. *A Grand Delusion: Democracy and Economic Reform in Egypt*. New York: I. B. Tauris, 2001.

Murphy, Caryle. *Passion for Islam: Shaping the Modern Middle East: The Egyptian Experience*. New York: Scribner, 2002.

Wickham, Carrie R. *Mobilizing Islam: Religion, Activism, and Political Change in Egypt*. New York: Columbia University Press, 2003.

Mugabe, Robert (1924–   ) *executive president of Zimbabwe*

Robert Gabriel Mugabe was born in Kutama, Southern Rhodesia, on February 21, 1924, the son of a carpenter. His country was then a British colony, although in 1965 it unilaterally declared its independence under Prime Minister Ian Smith. The new regime, which now called itself Rhodesia, was characterized by white minority rule that excluded African blacks from any political participation. Whites also monopolized most of the arable land in this fertile, food-producing region. However, discontent with white rule led to the rise of two distinct liberation movements. The first, the Zimbabwe African People's Union (ZAPU) fell under the aegis of JOSHUA NKOMO. The second was the Zimbabwe African National Union (ZANU), a direct competitor for political and military laurels. Together, the two movements waged a ruthless guerrilla war against Smith's white minority government, aided and abetted by sanctions imposed by most of the world's nations. By 1979 Rhodesia's situation had grown desperate and the government entered into negotiations with rebel leaders to seek a peaceful transfer of power. The ensuing Lancaster House Agreement settled the issue by easing Smith out

of power, while ZANU president Robert Mugabe became the nation's first black prime minister on April 18, 1980.

Mugabe had been educated at various mission schools and by 1941 had begun work as a teacher. He subsequently earned an advanced degree at Fort Hare University, South Africa, in 1951 before returning home for work at various government schools. In 1957 Mugabe migrated to newly independent Ghana to teach at St. Mary's College, and there he became exposed to the nationalist writings of Kwame Nkrumah and HASTINGS KAMUZU BANDA. After returning home in 1961, he entered politics by joining the outlawed ZAPU party under Nkomo, with whom he experienced a falling out. Mugabe then helped found the competing ZANU organization in 1964, which led to his arrest and nearly a decade behind bars. Released under a general amnesty, Mugabe hastily relocated to Mozambique, where he rose to become commander in chief of the Zimbabwe National Liberation Army (ZANLA), an accomplished guerrilla force. In this capacity he enjoyed an uneasy alliance with Nkomo's ZAPU forces. However, victory over the white minority finally transpired by April 1980, and Mugabe was installed as prime minister of the newly renamed Republic of Zimbabwe.

Despite his victory, Mugabe was initially conciliatory toward whites, and he allowed 20 seats to be reserved for them in the new House of Assembly. Nor did he make any immediate moves to confiscate property from white farmers, who controlled the majority of the land. This despite promises made to his own fighting men that he would do so. However, friction between himself and Nkomo persisted, especially following the national elections of June 1985, and a dramatic gesture of reconciliation became necessary. In 1987 he allowed the ZANU and ZAPU factions to merge on a national basis, and Nkomo was installed as vice president. However, the 20 seats set aside for the white minority were abolished, and Mugabe discarded the position of prime minister in favor of executive president. This move centralized power more directly under his control, although it heightened tensions between his regime and the white business community and Nkomo's allies. A worsening economic climate brought events to a climax in 1988, when fighting broke out between the two former guerrillas, and Nkomo was forced to flee the country. Thereafter Mugabe consolidated his rule under the aegis of a one-party socialist state governed by the Zimbabwe

African Union–Popular Front (ZANU-PF), which he also heads. Nkomo subsequently was allowed to return and serve as a senior minister. However, Western donor nations insisted that the political process be opened up to allow a legal opposition. Sullenly and only reluctantly, Mugabe complied.

In 1996 Zimbabwe experienced its first multiparty elections and Mugabe was overwhelming reelected in an uncontested race. However, as the nation's economic condition continued to worsen, he resorted more and more to mob rule in order to maintain power. Part of this entailed encouraging armed bands of military veterans to seize white-owned property by force, and frequently murdering the owners. In this manner some 1,700 farms out of a total of 4,526 have been illegally seized by force. Political opponents were also rounded up, detained, and in some instances killed by roving gangs of ZANU-PF supporters. Such behavior brought international condemnation, especially from the British Commonwealth, to which Zimbabwe belongs. The turning point in Mugabe's political fortunes came with the presidential election held in March 2002. Though warned repeatedly of impending sanctions from British prime minister TONY BLAIR, Mugabe waxed defiant and unleashed his strong-arm tactics against Morgan Tsvangirai's Movement for Democratic Change (MDC). "Go to Hell," he insisted, "Why should they poke their pink noses in our business?" On March 13, 2002, the election was roundly criticized by independent observers, who claimed that thousands of MDC supporters were denied the right to vote through violence, intimidation, or outright theft. Mugabe nonetheless claimed victory with 52 percent of the vote and was sworn in for another six years in office. However, the 78-year-old dictator still faces a restive population, a sinking economy, and growing global isolation, which may yet upend the political situation in Zimbabwe. If Commonwealth sanctions are indeed applied, they can serve only to worsen a 60 percent unemployment rate, a 112 percent inflation rate, and accelerate the trend toward economic collapse. Nonetheless, recent electoral success has emboldened the aging despot to implement his radical land distribution scheme at the expense of white farmers. "We set ourselves an August deadline for the redistribution of land and that deadline stands," he insisted. Still, 60 percent of white farmers continue defying eviction notices, apparently hoping for a reprieve from the courts—or possibly the nation's erratic leader himself.

Further Reading

Blair, David. *Degrees in Violence: Robert Mugabe and the Struggle for Power in Zimbabwe.* New York: Continuum, 2002.

Chan, Stephen. *Robert Mugabe: Life of Power and Violence.* Ann Arbor: University of Michigan Press, 2003.

Johnson, R. W. "Mugabe, Mbeki, and Mandela's Shadow." *National Interest* 63 (Spring 2001): 59–75.

Meredith, Martin. *Our Votes, Our Guns: Robert Mugabe and the Tragedy of Zimbabwe.* New York: Public Affairs, 2002.

Moyo, Sam. "The Political Economy of Land Acquisition and Redistribution in Zimbabwe, 1990–1999." *Journal of Southern African Studies* 26, no. 1 (2000): 5–28.

Rotberg, Robert I. "Africa's Mess, Mugabe's Mayhem." *Foreign Affairs* 79, no. 5 (2000): 47–61.

Sithole, Masipula. "Fighting Authoritarianism in Zimbabwe." *Journal of Democracy* 12, no. 1 (2001): 160–169.

Smith, Ian Douglas. *Bitter Harvest.* London: Blake, 2001.

Mulroney, Brian (1939–) *prime minister of Canada*

Martin Brian Mulroney was born on March 20, 1939, in Baie Comeau, Quebec, Canada, the son of an electrician. He was raised in that province's bilingual culture, obtaining natural fluency in both English and French. After completing his secondary education, Mulroney received his bachelor's degree in political science from St. Francis Xavier University, Nova Scotia, in 1959. He subsequently received a law degree from Laval University, Quebec, in 1964. While a student he became active in the Progressive Conservative Party, and struck up cordial relations with Prime Minister John Diefenbaker, serving as an unofficial adviser. Thereafter he settled in Montreal to work for the city's largest law firm, specializing in labor issues. He soon acquired the reputation as a sharp-tongued, tough-bargaining attorney, and in 1974 he was tapped to serve with the Cliche Commission, charged with investigating corruption and violence in Quebec's construction industry. The entire event was televised and Mulroney, by dint of his telegenic looks and dynamic presentation, gained national attention. Growing ambitious, he next sought the leadership of the Progressive Conservative Party, despite that fact he had never held public office. He was easily defeated by veteran Joe Clark and returned to Quebec to run an American-owned ore company. Mulroney rose to company president before returning to politics in 1983 and making a second bid to lead the Conservatives. He finally defeated Clark on the third ballot, becoming the first bilingual head of the party and thus well positioned to win traditionally Liberal Quebec over to the Conservative column. That year Mulroney also won his first election by gaining a seat in the House of Commons from Nova Scotia. With the economy sinking and public discontent with Liberals rising, Canada seemed poised for big changes.

On September 4, 1984, Mulroney led the Progressive Conservatives in one of the biggest upsets of Canadian political history. Not only did he defeat incumbent prime minister John Turner, but his party gained a record 211 seats in the House of Commons. This included 58 seats captured in Quebec, putting an end to Liberal dominance there. The new leader then embarked on an ambitious agenda that included greater liberalization of the economy, enhanced stature for Quebec as a "distinct culture," and closer political and economic ties with the United States. However, his most pressing priority was bringing Quebec into the 1982 constitutional agreement for better governance. That province, surrounded by of English-speaking Canadians, has long felt that its identity and language were imperiled. Thus was born the Lake Meech Accord, which Mulroney fashioned to placate francophone fears, induce Quebec to sign the 1982 Constitution, and promote a more closely knit federation. At length the majority of provinces signed on to the Lake Meech Accord, but the legislatures of Manitoba and Newfoundland, resenting what they considered "preferential treatment" toward the French, refused to adopt it. This arrangement, upon which Mulroney had staked much of his political capital, finally died in June 1990. Quebec, in turn, starting making loud noises about possible secession from Canada. A subsequent attempt, the Charlottetown Agreement, was also defeated in 1992. These failed efforts at reform, coupled with several high-profile corruption cases and a soft economy, led to dismal poll ratings for Mulroney.

Another pressing issue with Mulroney's administration was passage of the Free Trade Agreement with the United States, which promised to eliminate tariffs and stimulate greater prosperity. However, Mulroney failed to reckon with long-standing Canadian suspicions about perceived domination of their economy by their southern neighbor and the Liberals turned the 1988 election into a national referendum. Mulroney, persuasive and articulate as ever, was fully up to the challenge, for he viewed this legislation as important to Canada's well-being as that of Lake Meech. A national debate ensued, and on November 21, 1988, the Conservatives swept the election again. This was the first time since the early 20th century that the party had won two consecutive elections. Furthermore, Mulroney's return from the brink, having sustained some of the lowest popularity ratings in Canadian political history, seemed nothing short of miraculous.

Mulroney's second administration proved far less successful than his first, however. He was still dogged by lackluster economic performance, high unemployment, and a growing perception of pandering to the United States. The turning point in his political fortunes came in repealing a hidden 11 percent business tax from consumer goods, then replacing it with a highly visible 7 percent goods and service tax (GST). He then compounded his unpopularity in December 1992 by committing Canada to NAFTA, the North American free trade agreement with the United States and Mexico. This convinced many Canadians that their jobs would be lost to low-wage workers farther south. Consequently, Mulroney's numbers had sunk to 20 percent by spring. Rather than lead the party into a third election, he decided to resign from office on February 24, 1993, and appointed KIM CAMPBELL as Canada's first female prime minister. This novel expedient did not produce the results anticipated, and in 1993 the Progressive Conservative Party was nearly eliminated from parliament by the Liberals under JEAN CHRÉTIEN.

The recent loss was an unprecedented political debacle, and many politicians blamed Mulroney personally for the rout. He thereupon quit politics altogether to work in private industry. In 1995 the government and the Royal Canadian Mounted Police charged him with accepting millions of dollars in kickbacks from a lucrative airline deal, and he swiftly countersued. On January 6, 1997, both accusing agencies issued an apology to the former prime minister and settled out of court. Mulroney continues working in the private sector to the present day. His native province still remains grateful for his services, and in May 2002 he received the prestigious Order of Quebec with the title grand officer.

Further Reading

Cross, William, ed. *Political Parties, Representation, and Electoral Democracy in Canada.* New York: Oxford University Press, 2002.

De Clercy, Cristine. "Leadership and the Manipulation of Uncertainty." Unpublished Ph.D. dissertation, University of Western Ontario, 2001.

Mulroney, Brian. *Where I Stand.* Toronto: McClelland and Stewart, 1983.

Savoie, D. J. *Thatcher, Reagan, Mulroney: In Search of a New Bureaucracy.* Pittsburgh, Pa.: University of Pittsburgh, 1994.

Sutton, J. "Canada at the End of Mulroney's Prime Ministership." *Round Table* 326 (April 1993): 147–152.

Velk, Tom. *Brian Mulroney and the Economy: Still the Man to Beat.* Montreal: McGill University Press, 2000.

Muluzi, Bakili (1943–   ) *president of Malawi*

Bakili Muluzi was born on March 17, 1943, in the Machinga district of southern Nyasaland into a Muslim household. His country had been a British protectorate since 1891, although the wake of World War II witnessed the first stirrings of national independence. After 1953 Nyasaland and Southern Rhodesia were joined together in a political union that lasted only a decade. Many nationalist leaders, including Dr. HASTINGS KAMUZU BANDA, agitated for complete political independence, and in July 1964 Nyasaland was transformed into the new Republic of Malawi. Banda, in recognition of his efforts, became the first president, but after 1966 he declared the country a one-party state controlled by the National Congress Party (MCP). In practice he ruled with a heavy dictatorial hand. After 1971, Banda had the National Assembly declare him "President for Life." Malawi endured his personal brand of political oppression until 1992, when a movement for multiparty democracy, spearheaded by the Catholic Church, forced a public referendum on the subject. In June 1993 the issue of multiparty democracy passed overwhelmingly, and Banda relented. In May 1994 the president, one of the world's oldest heads of state, became one of four candidates for the leadership of Malawi.

Muluzi was well educated by African standards, and he attended both Huddersfield College of education in England and the Thirsted Technical College in Denmark. He subsequently returned home to serve as a clerk in the colonial service and, following independence, had risen to serve as the government's court clerk. Muluzi's good performance resulted in his appointment as principal of the Nasawa Technical College, and, in 1975, Banda allowed him to take a seat in parliament. As a member of the MCP, he rose rapidly through the party hierarchy, and he joined the Banda administration as junior minister of youth and culture. By 1977 he had become secretary of the party and also received promotion to minister without portfolio. Muluzi was one of Banda's most trusted advisers by 1982, but that year the two men had a falling out, and he was demoted to minister of transport and communication. This signaled an end to Muluzi's political aspirations, for he quit the government to work as a private businessman. Here he was startlingly successful and by 1992 had reentered politics as a force behind the movement for greater democracy. The following year he also founded the United Democratic Front Party (UDF) and declared his candidacy for the presidency. Malawi's first multiparty elections were held on May 17, 1992, and Muluzi, with 47.3 percent of the vote, was declared the winner.

The new president's first task on taking office was to seek national reconciliation for decades of oppression. He declared a general amnesty for political prisoners and also closed three prisons notorious for human rights abuses. Muluzi also commissioned an official inquiry into the deaths of several opposition leaders during Banda's administration, which led to six arrests. In 1996, with further nudging from the government, Banda publicly apologized for the "pain and suffering" that characterized his rule, although he remained unindicted. Having addressed the past, Muluzi faced an even greater challenge tackling the present, for Malawi's economy and economic infrastructure were essentially gutted by years of misrule. Having run on a platform pledging democratic reform, an end to grinding poverty, and increased social services, Muluzi's first step was to jolt the moribund national economy back to life. He achieved this by embracing free-market reforms and imposing strict fiscal discipline, in line with International Monetary Fund (IMF) and World Bank guidelines. Eventually, this strong dose of austerity registered gains in Malawi's gross national product and the country qualified for international loans and development grants. In light of his success, Muluzi was reelected president on June 17, 1999, by 52.4 percent of the vote, although this came amid charges of irregularities.

Despite Muluzi's accomplishments, Malawi remains one of Africa's poorest nations, beset by poverty and corruption. In January 2002 he was formally advised by British prime minister TONY BLAIR that improved governance and better fiscal accountability were essential if Malawi were to receive continuing British aid. The IMF also weighed in, demanding that the government cut spending, arrest corrupt officials, and improve the lot of working Malawians. That month the government of Denmark, a large contributor to Malawi's international aid, also cut off funding completely until drastic reforms were implemented. This sparked an angry response from Muluzi, who accused Western powers of meddling in African affairs by using aid money to influence political events. "We are poor, yes, but we are a sovereign state and nobody should teach me how to run this country," he lectured. However, the National Democratic Alliance Party (NDA) has publicly declared it would oppose any constitutional amendments that would permit Muluzi to run for a third term in office. In addition to the loss of international aid, the long-suffering people of Malawi are beset by widespread famine due to drought. "The food situation is a national emergency and disaster," Muluzi declared. "I urge all our international cooperating partners to come to our rescue and help alleviate the situation." Such aid, however, remains contingent upon stamping out corruption and bringing government spending in line with annual incomes. The issue remains unresolved.

Further Reading

Cullen, Trevor. *Malawi: A Turning Point.* Edinburgh: Pentland Press, 1994.

Fields, Karen. *Revival and Rebellion in Colonial Central Africa.* Portsmouth, N.H.: Heinemann, 1997.

Harrigan, Jane. *From Dictatorship to Democracy: Economic Policy in Malawi, 1964–2000.* Burlington, Vt.: Ashgate, 2001.

Kaspin, Deborah. "The Politics of Ethnicity in Malawi's Democratic Transition." *Journal of Modern African Studies* 34 (December 1995): 595–620.

Muluzi, Bakili, Yusuf Juwayeyi, and Mercy Makhambera. *Democracy with a Price: The History of Malawi since 1900.* Oxford: Heinemann, 1999.

Sindima, Harvey J. *Malawi's First Republic: An Economic and Political Analysis.* Lanham, Md.: University Press of America, 2002.

Von Doepp, Peter. "The Survival of Malawi's Enfeebled Democracy," *Current History* 100 (May 2001): 232–237.

Murayama, Tomiichi (1924–) *prime minister of Japan*

Tomiichi Murayama was born on March 3, 1924, in Oita, Japan, the son of a fisherman. Coming from a poor family, he acquired only a primary education before having to work. He completed his secondary education by attending night school, and by 1942 he had been accepted to the prestigious Meiji University. There he encountered Marxism and became a socialist. He graduated two years later with a degree in political science and was drafted into the army. After World War II, Murayama became active in union organizing and eventually served as secretary of the Oita Prefectural Government Employees Union. He also joined the Japanese Socialist Party and commenced his political career by winning a local seat in the Oita City Assembly in 1955. He subsequently finished three terms with the Oita Prefectural Assembly before moving to the House of Representatives (parliament) in 1972. Two years later Murayama became secretary of the Oita Socialist Headquarters, a post he held for seven terms. Reticent and sporting trademark bushy eyebrows, he proved something of a retiring figure, even by Japanese standards. Murayama, however, was totally committed to his constituents and held true to his personal motto, "Remain always with the people and learn from them." After two decades of holding power, he became president of the newly renamed Social Democratic Party of Japan (SDPJ) in September 1993. Murayama initially declined such distinction, but he later accepted out of a sense of obligation to his peers.

By the summer of 1994 the usually raucous state of Japanese politics was even more fractured. A caretaker administration under Tsutomu Hata had recently resigned after only a few months in power, and the search was on for a new prime minister. At this point the leadership of the Liberal Democratic Party (LDP), which dominated Japanese politics since 1955 but had lost power recently due to incessant scandals, began bargaining with the SDPJ leadership. The Socialists had not led the country since 1947 and were unlikely to do so outside of a coalition arrangement. The LDP and the SDPJ were traditional adversaries, but both wanted power and a deal was struck. An arrangement emerged whereby the LDP held 15 of 22 of the most important ministerial posts while Murayama became prime minister. It was an unholy alliance at first glance, but Murayama reasoned that the policy gap between parties had narrowed over the years and a coalition was possible. Accordingly, on June 29, 1994, the 70-year-old Socialist was sworn into office. Public expectations held that the coalition would collapse under the weight of its own incongruities.

From the onset, Murayama's coalition proved almost untenable. He studiously steered a middling course that angered most extreme elements among the Socialists, especially his refusal to condemn the practice of dispatching military forces abroad with United Nations peace-keeping efforts. Many held this activity unconstitutional. The prime minister also nudged his party toward closer relations with the United States, less diffidence toward North Korea, and cutbacks in welfare benefits, which further estranged the party. At length, the biggest task confronting Murayama was simply retaining power. His erstwhile LDP allies also grew disenchanted when he opposed imposition of a new 3 percent consumption tax to counter growing budget deficits, brought on by a stubborn recession. But the prime minister refused on the basis that it would hurt average citizens. "The kind of government that we should be striving for is not one that assumes that the state and industry come first," he admonished critics. For all his inability to craft a coherent national policy, Murayama did shine in one distinct area: foreign policy. Since the end of World War II, Japan's national policy was to deny any wrongdoing for the horrors and bloodshed unleashed in neighboring countries like China and Korea. When apologies did materialize, they were kept deliberately ambiguous to save face. However, on August 28, 1995, Murayama broke ranks with the wall of silence and offered genuine contrition. That morning, the 50th anniversary of Japan's surrender, he met with reporters outside his residence and offered sincere regrets for "mistaken national policy" and "colonialism and aggression." The majority of Japanese concurred with his attempts at reconciliation, but right-wing nationalists bristled over any admissions of guilt. Such candor is rare in Japanese national figures, and certainly unexpected from a modest individual like Murayama. It proved the finest moment in his long public career, and a personally courageous decision.

Murayama's caretaker regime finally collapsed on January 11, 1996, after 561 days in power. Apparently, he resigned under pressure from fellow leftists, long tired of coexisting with their LDP adversaries. More internal wrangling finally allowed RYUTARO HASHIMOTO of the LDP to replace him. That fall Murayama also stepped down as head of the SDPJ and resigned from politics, a respected senior statesman. He came out of retirement in November 2001 by flying to China and meeting with President JIANG ZEMIN. The occasion was the 30th anniversary of normalized relations between their respective countries, and both men hailed trends toward expanding trade, business contacts, and good neighborly relations.

Further Reading

Beer, Lawrence W. *From Imperial Myth to Democracy: Japan's Two Constitutions, 1889–2001.* Boulder, Colo.: University Press of Colorado, 2002.

Hayes, Louis D. *Japan and the Security of Asia.* Lanham, Md.: Lexington Books, 2001.

Maswood, Javed, Jeffrey Graham, and Hideaki Miyajima, eds. *Japan: Change and Continuity.* New York: Routledge, 2002.

Wakamiya, Yoshibumi. "Jury Still Out on Murayama Cabinet." *Japan Quarterly* 43 (April–June, 1996): 137–145.

Wilson, Sandra, ed. *Nation and Nationalism in Japan.* New York: RoutledgeCurzon, 2002.

Musa, Said (1944–) *prime minister of Belize*

Musa Wilbert Said was born in San Ignacio, British Honduras, on March 19, 1944, of partly Palestinian heritage. His homeland had been a British colony since the 19th century, although the first moves toward political independence surfaced in 1950. That year the People's United Party (PUP) was founded under George Price, who remained a dominant force in local politics for 30 years. In 1973 formal opposition also arose in the guise of the United Democratic Party (UDP). Political independence for British Honduras transpired in 1981 and the country renamed itself Belize. It is governed by a British-style parliamentary system whereby the party with a majority of seats in the legislature appoints a prime minister. National leadership has fluctuated between the two leading parties for 20 years, although in

August 1998 the PUP scored a major upset by winning 26 of 29 seats in the House of Representatives.

Said was educated locally and in the capital of Belize City before attending Manchester University in England. There he studied law until 1966, when he was called to Gray's Bar Inn, London, to practice. Said then returned home in 1967 to serve as a circuit magistrate and Crown counsel. In 1970 he also commenced a private legal practice with the law firm of Musa and Baldermos, and he joined the PUP in 1974. Said began his political career that year with an unsuccessful bid for parliament, but Prime Minister George Price recognized his abilities and appointed him to the Senate. It was at this point Said embarked on what became his trademark issue, increasing political participation within the party and nation as a whole. His populism paid off in 1979 when he finally gained election to parliament from the Fort George Division and, hence, qualified for a ministerial portfolio. Said quickly gained successive appointments as minister of education, attorney general, and minister of economic development. In concert with other leading politicians, he also worked actively on behalf of national independence, and was chosen to negotiate with Britain and Guatemala over the issue. In 1984 the PUP was heavily defeated at the polls, and Musa was elected party chairman in consequence. Here he sought to infuse the party with newer, younger leadership and reiterated his theme for expanded voting franchise. In 1996 George Price, now an elder statesman, finally stepped down as party leader, and Said was chosen to replace him. In national elections held in August 1998 the PUP was returned to power handily and Said, as party head, became the nation's third prime minister.

Said came to power at a difficult time in Belize's short history as the Caribbean region was gripped by a deep recession. He had campaigned on a platform dedicated to new jobs and new homes, and wasted no time abolishing the 15 percent value-added tax (VAT) to stimulate the economy. "The urgent task at hand is to raise income and productivity for sustainable growth," he declared, "while also securing human development and social equality for all." He then embarked on a strategy involving tightly directed government spending and renewed emphasis on private sector investment. Belize, naturally saddled with a small economy, is also heavily reliant upon tourism as a major source of revenue. Said, however, was determined to increase the scope of the growing ecotourism trade, while still insuring protection and preservation of the nation's fragile ecology. He also sought to establish Belize's credentials as a Caribbean financial center of note, and, in 1998, he pushed through legislation authorizing the nation's first "offshore banking" sector.

In terms of foreign policy, Said exudes a decidedly left-wing slant, and he has espoused numerous and controversial causes such as a Palestinian homeland and a close, working relationship with Cuba's aging dictator, FIDEL CASTRO. However, he is also heavily engaged in negotiations with neighboring Guatemala over the issue of border controls and national sovereignty. This was not achieved without some friction as Guatemala has long-standing claims on Belize as its territory, which has induced the British government to retain a small garrison as a hedge against aggression. It was not until 1993 that both nations achieved concord respecting border disputes, but violent incidents have occurred as recently as 2001. That December both Belize and Guatemala invited the Organization of American States to finally arbitrate this century-old issue. Moreover, Said, as head of the Caribbean Common Market and Community (CARICOM), has been forced to acknowledge the need to combat increased crime throughout the region. "The threat of trans-boundary organized crime to the Caribbean is real," he remarked. "We must be diligent to attack the causes of crime as vigorously as we address the curtailment of criminal activities." Said has since entreated heads of the 14-member alliance to push for tightened security for better control of the war against drug trafficking.

Further Reading

Ergood, Bruce. "Belize: An Introduction." *Latin American Research Review* 26 (Summer 1991): 257–266.

McKillop, Heather I. *Salt: White Gold of the Ancient Maya.* Gainesville: University Press of Florida, 2002.

Peedle, Ian. *Belize: A Guide to the People, Politics, and Culture.* Brooklyn: Interlink Books, 1999.

Stove, Michael C. "Caribbean Nation, Central American State: Ethnicity, Race, and National Formation in Belize, 1798–1990." Unpublished Ph.D. dissertation, University of Texas at Austin, 1994.

Young, Alma H., and Dennis H. Young. "The Impact of the Anglo-Guatemalan Dispute on the Internal Politics of Belize." *Belizean Studies* 18, no. 1 (1990): 11–35.

Museveni, Yoweri Kaguta (ca. 1944–   )

president of Uganda

Yoweri Kaguta Museveni was born in Ntungamo, southwestern Uganda, around 1944, the son of a cattle rancher. Uganda, a small, landlocked country in East Africa, had been a British protectorate since 1894 and, with its sizable Asian (Indian) middle class, among the most prosperous of the empire. It finally obtained independence in October 1962 under Dr. Milton Obote. Museveni was fortunate is securing a good elementary and secondary education, and in 1966 he attended the University of Dar Es Salaam, Tanzania. He graduated with a degree in economics and political science in 1970 and returned home to work as a research assistant in the Obote administration. He served in this office until Obote was overthrown by a military coup orchestrated by General Idi Amin Dada. Museveni then fled to Tanzania where he helped organize the Front for National Salvation (FRONASA), a guerrilla force intending to overthrow Amin. An internecine conflict waged for several years, but his FRONASA fighters distinguished themselves by their strong military discipline and restraint towards civilians. This contrasted sharply with the behavior of Amin's troops, who were reviled for their cruelty and brutality. In 1979, assisted by Tanzanian troops, Museveni's forces finally overthrew Amin, who fled to Saudi Arabia. After several interim administrations, Obote was then returned to power. Museveni, for his part, secured an appointment as minister of defense.

In December 1980, Obote was reelected president through blatantly rigged elections. Museveni protested such fraudulence, and joined opposition leaders in Tanzania. There he helped organize the National Resistance Army (NRA), intent upon deposing his former benefactor. As before, this entailed several years of savage guerrilla warfare, but Museveni's soldiers were kept on a short leash and seldom implicated in atrocities toward civilians. In July 1985 Obote was overthrown by General Basillo Okello, who reached an accord with most resistance groups. However, Museveni continued fighting and soon gained control of the countryside. On January 26, 1986, victorious NRA forces captured the capital of Kampala, signifying an end to hostilities. For 15 years Uganda had been ravaged by political oppression, murderous armies, and the loss of 400,000 lives. Museveni now inherited a country on the brink of collapse and a national economy that barely functioned. He was installed as president of a provisional government in February 1986 and set about the task of national reconstruction. "No one can think that what is happening today, what has been happening in the last few days, is a mere changing of the guard," he declared. "This is a fundamental change in the politics of our country."

Though trained as a socialist, Museveni quickly embraced free-market economics and embarked on a path toward privatization and foreign investment. He readily assented to the closely prescribed conditions set forth by the International Monetary Fund (IMF) and the World Bank, which led to infusions of badly needed foreign capital. Within a few years, Museveni's fiscal discipline paid immediate dividends: inflation was tamed, the national debt was reduced, and the annual GNP averaged 6 percent growth. Furthermore, he formally invited back all the Indian entrepreneurs who had been exiled by Amin, which further boosted the economy. In time, lending countries in the West hailed Uganda as a model of economic development for the rest of Africa. Museveni also endeared himself to the populace by declaring education free and compulsory for all Ugandan children. He aggressively confronted the AIDS epidemic sweeping Africa with intense educational and preventative programs so that Uganda enjoys one the continent's lowest infection rates. In light of Museveni's positive contributions to national rehabilitation, presidential elections were held on May 9, 1996, and he was returned to power with 74 percent of the vote.

For all his good intentions, Museveni has frowned upon multiparty democracy and views it as contributing to lingering ethnic and religious hostility among Uganda's many different tribes and sects. Therefore, despite intense pressure from the West, he has only sullenly and slowly allowed political participation. His attitude is much less an attempt to maintain a hold on power than it is a desire to prevent a return to the internecine horrors of the last two decades. Museveni shrugged off criticism that he was at best a benevolent despot, and he maintained that he would reintroduce democracy when he alone deemed it feasible. This transpired in June 2000, when a public referendum to maintain the present "no-party" system was overwhelmingly approved by 90.7 percent. A second round of presidential elections was held on March 12, 2001. Museveni, in a process judged free and fair by outside observers, handily triumphed with 69.3 percent of votes cast. With his political future secure, he turned increasingly toward issues of regional security.

Following the January 2001 assassination of the Congo's president, LAURENT KABILA, Museveni pledged to remove all Ugandan troops fighting alongside rebel troops there. In February 2002, he also conferred with Rwandan president PAUL KAGAME over the issue of the mutual harboring of rebels, and they reconfirmed their commitment toward normal relations and bilateral border discussions. Museveni continues in office as one of Uganda's most effective leaders and among the most popular. It remains to be seen if he can transcend his distaste for multiparty democracy and restore political freedom to his long-suffering people.

Further Reading

Clark, John F. "Explaining Ugandan Intervention in Congo: Evidence and Interpretation." *Journal of Modern African Studies* 39 (June 2001): 261–288.

Furley, Oliver. "Democratization in Uganda." *Commonwealth & Comparative Politics* 38, no. 3 (2000): 79–102.

Museveni, Yoweri. *Sowing the Mustard Seed: The Struggle for Freedom and Democracy in Uganda.* London: Macmillan, 1997.

Watt, David, Rachel Flanary, and Robin Theobald. "Democratization or Democratization of Corruption? The Case of Uganda." *Commonwealth & Comparative Politics* 37, no. 3 (1999): 37–64.

Tripp, Aili Mari. *Women and Politics in Uganda.* Madison: University of Wisconsin Press, 2000.

Young, Cranford. "Uganda under Museveni: What's Africa's Problem?" *Africa Studies Review* 44, no. 2 (2001): 207–211.

Musharraf, Pervez (1943–) *president of Pakistan*

Pervez Musharraf was born in New Delhi, India, on August 11, 1943, the son of a career diplomat. His Sunni Muslim family relocated to the newly created Islamic country of Pakistan following the partitioning of Hindu-dominated British India in 1947. Musharraf then accompanied his father to Turkey as a youth, where he spent several years and became fluent in Turkish and English. After being further educated at several Christian academies in Pakistan, he gained admittance to the Pakistan Military Academy in 1961, and he was commissioned as an artillery lieutenant three years later. Never an outstanding student, Musharraf quickly gained the reputation of a studious, consummate professional officer with no avowed interest in politics. This proved a curious happenstance, for the Pakistani military has played a crucial role in shaping the political landscape of that nation. Since 1947 it had overthrown democratically elected governments twice and was usually looked upon as a source of national stability during crisis periods with its enormous neighbor, India.

Musharraf served with distinction in two wars against India and rose rapidly through the command structure. After several tours at the Royal College of Defense Studies in England, he was elevated by Prime Minister NAWAZ SHARIF to chairman of the Joint Chiefs of Staff Committee on April 9, 1999. Musharraf was undoubtedly a capable officer and well suited for the role, but Sharif apparently selected him because he originates from an Urdu-speaking background and not the Punjabi class dominating the Pakistani officer corps. As such, he was viewed as incapable of establishing a possible power base within the military. However, the Sharif regime, while democratically elected, proved intrinsically corrupt and, furthermore, as the national economy soured in the late 1990s, a period of social instability ensued. From a military standpoint, Sharif was also viewed as bowing to pressure from the United States in ordering the withdrawal of Pakistani forces from the disputed Kashmir region. When it became known to the prime minister that Musharraf had criticized him privately, he took steps to remove him. On October 12, 1999, Sharif dismissed Musharraf from his post while he was flying home from a mission to Sri Lanka. Furthermore, he forbade the general's plane from landing at Karachi airport, despite being very low on fuel. When they learned of the apparent rift, soldiers loyal to Musharraf seized the airport and allowed the general to land. Musharraf then promptly declared himself the de facto ruler of Pakistan and he ordered Sharif's arrest, which was immediately done. Given the corruption and incompetence of the civilian government, many Pakistanis welcomed a return to military rule. The nation's Supreme Court also sanctioned the coup as legal, but it mandated a three-year limit for army control before returning to democracy.

Musharraf had no sooner taken control than he addressed his nation, vowing to return Pakistan to democracy after an indeterminate period. "I would like to move away from the sham democracy we have had in Pakistan," he declared. "I want a true democracy." He also affirmed the necessity of restoring economic growth to a nation threatened by one of the world's highest birth rates. However well-intentioned, his move against the Sharif regime was roundly condemned by Western countries, particularly the United States and Great Britain, which cut off military aid. His rise was also viewed with great skepticism by India. New Delhi feared an escalation of tensions over Kashmir and the rise of Muslim fundamentalism that it fomented. Musharraf, however, simply proceeded to implement the desired changes, including overhauling the nation's tax structure, countering the rise of sectarian violence between Sunni and Shia Muslims, and establishing a timetable for democracy. Little noticed at the time was Pakistani support for the radical Islamic regime in neighboring Afghanistan, the Taliban, who were known to harbor terrorists allied to Saudi exile Osama bin Laden. In fact, Pakistan was one of only three nations, along with Saudi Arabia and the United Arab Emirates, to extend the Taliban diplomatic recognition. But, given Pakistan's traditional antipathy for Iran, which also sought to wield influence in Afghanistan, no real changes were anticipated in this field.

The events of September 11, 2001, changed everything, placing Musharraf at the epicenter of global events. The destruction of New York's World Trade Center was linked to bin Laden's al-Qaeda terrorist network and, when the ruling regime refused to hand him over to the United States, President GEORGE W. BUSH initiated military action. Given the geography of Afghanistan, this required use of Pakistani air space to conduct long-range bombing runs from the Persian Gulf. The Americans leaned heavily upon Musharraf for such access, despite the fact that many Pakistanis were sympathetic to both the Taliban and bin Laden. Thus the general commenced a hazardous balancing act between accommodating the United States and assuaging the violent trend toward Islamic fundamentalism at home. This support caused an outbreak of demonstrations against the government, but all were constrained by force and they eventually dissipated. In return for such essential cooperation, President Bush promised to cancel up to $3 billion in Pakistani debts, and he also undertook other measures to bolster the shaky Pakistani economy. By December 2001 the Taliban had been driven from power, and coalition forces under the United States began occupying the country. However, that month Muslim extremists turned their wrath against India with an attack

upon its parliament that killed several officials. The government of ATAL BIHARI VAJPAYEE was naturally indignant, and thousands of troops massed along the Pakistani border in preparation for war. This confrontation promised the gravest of consequences, for both India and Pakistan possess viable nuclear arsenals. Fortunately, deft diplomacy by the United States defused the crisis. South Asia remains one of the world's most critical flashpoints.

Musharraf, true to his word, promised to return Pakistan back to democracy with new elections scheduled for the fall of 2002. At that time a new civilian prime minister will be selected, but he himself will remain president for an additional five years to ensure a stable transition. Musharraf has also taken addition steps to closely regulate Pakistan's flourishing religious schools (*madrasas*), long seen as a recruiting ground for Muslim extremists, and, in March 2002, he announced the expulsion of all foreign students, including Arabs, Afghans, and North Africans. His regime is also determined to crack down on religious terrorism and upward of 2,000 known radicals have been arrested and detained. It remains to be seen if Pakistan can weather the tide of religious extremism and resume democratic politics, but Musharraf, the quiet military professional, has secured his place as a pivotal American ally in the international war against terrorism. "There's a very thin line between bravery and cowardice," he noted. "I am scared, certainly, but I am a believer in destiny—in my own destiny and therefore that gives me more courage." It was a bravura performance by a leader previously reviled as a minor military despot.

Further Reading

Arif, Khalid M. *Khaki Shadows: The Pakistan Army, 1947–1997.* Oxford: Oxford University Press, 2000.

Baxter, Craig, and Charles H. Kennedy, eds. *Pakistan 2000.* Karachi: Oxford University Press, 2001.

Ganguly, Sumit. *Conflict Unending: India-Pakistan Relations since 1947.* Oxford: Oxford University Press, 2002.

Mahmood, Sohali. *The Musharraf Regime and the Governance Crisis: A Case Study in the Government of Pakistan.* Huntington, N.Y.: Nova Science, 2001.

Matinuddin, Kamal. *The Nuclearization of South Asia.* Oxford: Oxford University Press, 2002.

Shah, Aqil. "Democracy on Hold in Pakistan." *Journal of Democracy* 13 (January 2001): 67–75.

Uk Heo, and Shale A. Horowitz, eds. *Conflict in Asia: Korea, China-Taiwan, and India-Pakistan.* Westport, Conn.: Praeger, 2002.

Weaver, Mary Ann. *Pakistan: In the Shadow of Jihad and Afghanistan.* New York: Farrar, Straus, and Giroux, 2002.

Mwinyi, Ali Hassan (1925–) *president of Tanzania*

Ndugu Ali Hassan Mwinyi was born on May 8, 1925 in Kivure, Tanganyika, to Muslim parents of Zanzibari extraction. At this time both Tanganyika and Zanzibar, an offshore island, were administered as a British protectorate. After completing his secondary education on Zanzibar, Mwinyi attended the University of Durham, England, to train as a teacher. He graduated in 1944 and returned home to work at a primary school and the Zanzibar Teacher Training College, 1954–61. After additional advanced studies in England he became principal of the college in 1964. Mwinyi also became politically active around this time by joining the Afro-Shirazi Party, which agitated for independence from Great Britain. When this occurred in 1963 Mwinyi gained appointment as secretary to the minister of education on Zanzibar. The following year this island and Tanganyika were joined into a new federated state called Tanzania. However, it was not until 1970 that Mwinyi came to the attention of President Julius Nyerere, who successively appointed him minister of state and minister of health. Mwinyi performed useful services in both capacities, and, in November 1975, he was promoted to minister of home affairs. He served in that office for the next two years until January 23, 1977, when a scandal involving police forces attached to his bureau induced him to resign. He then served as Tanzania's ambassador to Egypt, 1977–82.

By 1983 Mwinyi was back in Zanzibar, which enjoyed a great deal of autonomy from the mainland and had its own executive officers. Following a stint of service as minister of state there, he replaced Aboud Jumbe as president in January 1984. His biggest task was restoring calm to the island, then wracked by secessionist fervor, and he also oversaw a return to prosperity by liberalizing the marketplace. Mwinyi by this time had accrued an outstanding reputation for efficiency, honesty, and modesty, traits that undoubtedly led to his selection as vice president of Tanzania in April 1984. That year Ny-

erere also announced his impending resignation and when his handpicked successor, Edward Sokoine, was killed in a car crash, Mwinyi was tapped as Tanzania's new president on August 15, 1985. He was confirmed in the post by the National Executive Committee of the Chama Cha Mapindzui Party (CCM), then Tanzania's only legitimate political organization. It was also believed that Mwinyi would perpetuate Nyerere's policy of fostering socialist-oriented programs. "I think I should make it clear that Tanzania is aiming at becoming a socialist country," he declared to his countrymen.

Unfortunately, Mwinyi inherited a nation on the verge of economic collapse. The government-oriented policies of Nyerere drained the treasury of funds while the closely controlled command economy performed sluggishly. Confronted with a malaise of this magnitude, Mwinyi brooked no delay in ditching the CCM's socialist theory in favor of free-market economics. He liberalized the economy, privatized many state-owned industries, and attracted foreign investment. In order to secure funding from the International Monetary Fund (IMF) he also adopted strict austerity guidelines to control inflation and reduce the national debt. These policies angered more strident members of the CCM, but the economy soon posted marked improvement. Concurrently, Mwinyi also initiated a strong campaign to stamp out corruption in government, which won him plaudits from the populace and the wrath of bureaucrats. Nyerere, who continued as head of the CCM, did not interfere as his life's work was dismantled, and this tacit support further eliminated resistance to change. At the end of his five-year term, Mwinyi had turned Tanzania around, and, on November 3, 1990, running as the sole candidate for president, he was reelected by 95.5 percent of votes cast.

Mwinyi's accomplishments in his second term were equally impressive. In March 1991 he established a commission to explore the possibility of establishing the nation's first multiparty government and results were encouraging. He also relentlessly pursued the pervasive corruption inherent in the political culture, and, in 1994, a massive tax evasion scandal by leading government officials was uncovered. Mwinyi, long regarded as impeccably honest, was not implicated in the affair, and he continued enjoying public support. However, his influence on party affairs was waning, and by 1994 he lost control of spending. This, in turn, forced him to break with the IMF and forego further economic assistance for the time being. By 1995 he was forbidden by the Tanzanian constitution to seek a third term. On October 29, of that year he was replaced by BENJAMIN MKAPA in the nation's first multiparty elections. Mwinyi has since lived in retirement as an elder statesman, emerging from time to time to address national issues. In July 2000 he served as chairman of the national advisory board on HIV/AIDS, and he called for greater emphasis on disease prevention. The malady is raging in Tanzania and threatens to infect 25 percent of the population by 2015.

Further Reading

Coldham, Simon. "Land Tenure Reform in Tanzania: Legal Problems and Perspectives." *Journal of Modern African Studies* 33 (June 1995): 227–242.

Kaiser, Paul J. "Structural Adjustment and the Fragile Nation: The Demise of Social Unity in Tanzania." *Journal of Modern African Studies* 34, no. 2 (1996): 227–237.

Obichere, Boniface I. "Tanzania at the Crossroads, From Nyerere to Mwinyi." *Journal of African Studies* 14, no. 3 (1987): 84–88.

Sadleir, Randal. *Tanzania: Journey to Republic.* New York: Radcliffe Press, 2000.

Shariff, Ahmed. "Politics and Policy in Africa: A Case Study of Tanzania's Transition to Democracy." Unpublished Ph.D. dissertation, Indiana University, 1998.

N

Nabiyev, Rakhman (1930–1993) *president of Tajikistan*

Rakhman Nabiyev was born on October 5, 1930, in Dushanbe, then capital of the Tajik Soviet Socialist Republic. This region was created in 1929 by separating it from neighboring Uzbekistan and, consistent with the Soviet policy of divide and conquer, cultivating among the populace a greater sense of ethnic distinctiveness from the rest of Central Asia. Nabiyev was educated locally and in 1954 he graduated from the Tashkent Institute of Irrigation and Agricultural Mechanization. He worked there as an instructor for four years and by 1960 had joined the Tajik Communist Party as head of the agricultural department. Nabiyev proved himself an astute political operator and served on the party's Central Committee until 1971, when he gained appointment as minister of foreign affairs. By 1983 he emerged as first secretary of the Tajik Communist Party and de facto leader of his nation. Nabiyev's rule was characterized by the usual Soviet combination of brutal repression and mounting corruption, conditions that prompted the new reform-minded premier, Mikhail Gorbachev, to remove him in 1985. Nabiyev was then replaced by longtime rival Kakhar Makhkamov, who proved every bit as despotic. By 1990 economic conditions in the republic had worsened, and civil unrest became manifold. Makhkamov responded by calling in Soviet troops to restore order, which they accomplished with great brutality. This act fueled an unexpected nationalist resentment both against Moscow and Makhkamov. Worse, during the August 1991 coup attempt against Gorbachev by hard-line Communist elements, he voiced his support for the insurgents. Once the coup unraveled, however, popular protests resulted in Makhkamov's resignation. On August 31, 1991, the Tajik Soviet (legislature) then declared itself independent of the ailing Soviet Union, renaming itself Tajikistan. They also suspended the Communist Party pending further investigation of its role in the aborted coup.

Nabiyev, who had since renounced his Communist membership, now headed the Tajik Socialist Party, composed mostly of former Communists. However, he was viewed as the only political figure capable of maintaining order during a dangerously unpredictable period. And, despite Nabiyev's prior reputation as an old-line party boss, he committed himself to moderate democratic change. Accordingly, the legislature appointed him interim president of Tajikistan, pending national elections. When these took place on November 24, 1991, Nabiyev won easily with 58 percent of votes cast. However, the opposition then charged the government with rigging the election and another spate of civil unrest ensued. Islamic groups proved particularly obdurate, and that month they stormed the legislature, taking hostages.

Nabiyev then offered to form a government of "national reconciliation" that included several opposition figures in his cabinet. This bought only a temporary peace, for, behind the scenes, radical reformers and conservative elements began arming themselves and preparing for all-out war. Opposition forces particularly resented Nabiyev's previous role as a slavish devotee to the Communist Party, the corruption this engendered, and his well-deserved reputation for drunkenness and brutality.

In May 1992 civil war commenced between pro- and anti-Nabiyev forces in the southern part of the country. By September, the Islamic militias had again taken the legislature and, on September 7, 1992, they captured Nabiyev as he tried to flee. His captors then forced him to appear on television at gunpoint, whereby he announced his resignation from office. "It was purely and simply a coup," he later asserted. "I had no choice but to sign the resignation statement they gave me. If I hadn't, dozens would have died." The former executive was then released, but he proceeded straight to his home region of Khodjent and began recruiting supporters. Nabiyev then led an offensive that recaptured Dushanbe in October, but he was forced back the following month. This reverse finally convinced Nabiyev that he lacked the popular support necessary to rule Tajikistan, and he withdrew from politics altogether. "My people have chosen me, but I am ready to resign if that will bring peace," he declared. His second resignation had no influence on the course of events; after additional fighting, he was succeeded by former Communist EMOMALI RAKHMONOV in December 1992. The pro-Communist forces then entrenched themselves in power, but Nabiyev deliberately kept a low public profile. On April 11, 1993, he died of natural causes in Dushanbe, little mourned.

Further Reading

Akiner, Shirin. *Tajikistan: Disintegration or Reconciliation?* London: Royal Institute of International Affairs, 2001.

Abdullaev, Kamoludin, and Catherine Barnes. *Politics of Compromise: The Tajikistan Peace Process.* London: Conciliation Resources, 2001.

Jonson, Lena. *The Tajik War: A Challenge to Russian Policy.* London: Royal Institute of International Affairs, 1998.

Khudonazarov, Davlat. *Tajikistan: Tragedy and Prospects, Perspectives of a Democratic Leader.* Washington, D.C.: George Washington University, Elliott School of International Affairs, 1993.

Meyer, Karl E. *The Dust of Empire: the Race for Mastery in the Asian Heartland.* New York: PublicAffairs, 2003.

Tajbakhsh, Shahrbanu. *The Bloody Path of Change: The Case of Post-Soviet Tajikistan.* New York: Harriman Institute, Columbia University, 1993.

Najib, Mohammad (1947–1996) *president of Afghanistan*

Sayid Mohammad Najibullah was born in August 1947 in Kabul, Afghanistan, a member of the influential Pashtun tribe. His father was a government official who had previously served as a trade commissioner and diplomat. Najibullah was educated locally at the Habibiya Lycée, where he excelled as a student, and subsequently gained admission to the University of Kabul Medical School. Before graduating he became politically active by joining the People's Democratic Party of Afghanistan (PDPA), or Communist Party. There he met and befriended Babrak Karmal, a future prime minister. By this time Najib had shortened his name to indicate his disavowal of Islam, and he functioned as Karmal's bodyguard and editor of the party newspaper. His burly physique and ruthless demeanor also garnered him an appropriate nickname, "the Bull." Najib was active in antigovernment activities and was twice imprisoned. However, the Communists successfully overthrew King Mohammed Zahir Shah in 1973 and installed Mohammad Daud in his place. By July 1977 Karmal had united various feuding factions within the PDPA and they overthrew Daud's regime. Najib, for his role, was granted a seat on the Central Committee. The PDPA further consolidated power in a second coup on April 27, 1978, and Najib gained promotion as a member of the Revolutionary Council. However, party rule in Afghanistan proved fractious, and in July 1978 he was dispatched out of the country as ambassador to Iran. Najib then moved to Eastern Europe for an indeterminate period of time, apparently to improve communications with KGB officials in the Soviet Union. Accordingly, when Soviet troops invaded Afghanistan in December 1979 and installed Karmal as prime minister, Najib also arrived back home as head of KHAD, the Afghan secret police.

The ensuing Russian occupation of Afghanistan proved to be one of the cold war's turning points. Incredibly cruel and brutal, it stimulated the rise of Islamic fundamentalist guerrilla groups throughout the country-side, abetted by covert military aid from the United States. Najib, as head of state security forces, bore full responsibility for the imprisonment, torture, and murder of thousands of dissidents. But, try as they may, the Communists proved unable to contain this religion-based resistance, or Mujahideen, and resistance continued spreading. After seven years, when Karmal proved unable to impose some semblance of order upon national affairs, the Soviets engineered his overthrow in a bloody coup and installed the highly efficient Najib as president on May 4, 1986. In this capacity he mitigated the socialist policies of his predecessor and made moves to reconcile Islam and a liberalized market economy with his regime. He also sponsored a new constitution that allowed multiparty democracy and enshrinement of religion at the center of state affairs. The Mujahideen, however, refused to negotiate and fighting intensified.

Najib's fate was sealed by concurrent developments within the Soviet Union. A new premier, Mikhail Gorbachev, sought to allay Western charges of aggression and he commenced gradually removing 120,000 Russian soldiers from Afghanistan. The withdrawal was completed by February 1989, ending a decade of failure to bring Afghanistan into the Communist fold. However, Moscow did arrange for $300 million of monthly military aid to support Najib, and this enabled his forces to fight the Mujahideen factions to a draw. However, the crumbling Soviet Union could not shoulder this economic burden indefinitely, and in 1991 Moscow agreed with Washington to cut off assistance to both sides. Najib consolidated his positions. He did a masterful job playing his enemies off one another, but in the end his regime lacked sufficient popular support. The Mujahideen, sensing complete victory, simply refused to negotiate. On April 15, 1992, the guerrillas had all but surrounded Kabul, and Najib resigned from office and attempt to flee to India. However, his escape was foiled by one of his erstwhile allies, and he immediately sought refuge in a United Nations compound. After a decade of power, "the Bull" was finally cornered.

Over the next four years competing guerrilla factions waged civil war over control of Afghanistan, while Najib remained a helpless onlooker. In 1996 a new player, the Islamic fundamentalist Taliban ("students of religion") captured Kabul and most of the countryside. Disregarding the nuances of diplomacy, on September 27, 1996, they stormed the UN compound, arrested

Najib and his brother, and summarily hung them in public. This act initiated another five years of religion-based hostility and oppression in that war-ravaged land.

Further Reading
Bradsher, Henry S. *Afghan Communism and Soviet Intervention.* New York: Oxford University Press, 1999.
Corwin, Phillip. *Doomed in Afghanistan: A UN Officer's Memoir of the Fall of Kabul and Najibullah's Escape.* New Brunswick, N.J.: Rutgers University Press, 2003.
Galeotti, Mark. *Afghanistan: The Soviet Union's Last War.* Portland, Oreg.: Frank Cass, 2001.
Maley, William. *The Afghanistan Wars.* New York: Palgrave, 2002.
O'Balance, Edgar. *Afghan Wars: 1839 to the Present.* London: Brassey's, 2002.

Nakamura, Kuniwo (1946–) *president of Palau*

Kuniwo Nakamura was born in Koror, the capital of Palau, in 1946. Palau is an archipelago of 300 small volcanic islands situated 500 miles east of the Philippines and 600 miles north of Indonesia. They are populated by 20,000 people of Polynesian, Melanesian, and Malayan stock, with small pockets of Filipinos and Japanese also present. In the late 19th century, Palau was successively administered by Spain and Germany, who christened them the Caroline Islands. After World War I, Palau passed to the Japanese, who ruled the islands as a colony until September 1944, when they were stormed by U.S. military forces. After World War II Palau became a United Nations Strategic Trust Territory under American supervision. In this capacity the United States oversaw the educational, economic, and political development of the islands while simultaneously maintaining military basing rights. The Americans spent lavishly on the infrastructure and on the local economy, so that Palau enjoys one of the Pacific's highest standards of living. However, after 1965 there rose a political groundswell to end Palau's Trust Territory status in exchange for full independence. Thereafter, the movement toward sovereignty hinged upon passage of the Compact of Free Association with the United States, which allowed free trade and free movements between the two nations. In 1981 a constitution was adopted by public referendum, which called for a president, a judiciary, and a legislative assembly. However, because the United States wished to preserve its basing rights, yet would neither confirm nor deny the presence of nuclear weapons on its naval vessels, the compact failed to pass by the mandated 75 percent of the popular vote. Between 1982 and 1994 Palau tried six times to approve this legislation, but opposition to nuclear weapons proved intransigent, and it failed to garner the three-quarters vote necessary for passage.

Nakamura matured on Palau, and he subsequently earned a degree in economics from the University of Hawaii. He then served as a teacher and an economics adviser to the U.S. administration on Palau. Nakamura tested the political waters in 1975, when he won election to the district legislature from Koror. That year he also secured a seat in the Congress of Micronesia. Nakamura was active during the 1979 constitutional convention, and the following year he was elected to the first national congress as a senator. He subsequently gained reelection in 1984, and four years later advanced to vice president. In 1992 Nakamura announced his candidacy for president and ran against Johnson Torbiong, defeating him by a razor-thin 134-vote margin.

As president, Nakamura focused on three goals: independence, economic expansion, and transparency in government. He very much wanted to usher in the age of Palau's independence, but realized he could not muster the 75 percent necessary for approval. Therefore, he championed lowering the approval threshold to a simple majority and placed it before the public as a referendum. In this manner the nuclear provision was easily overridden, and, on October 1, 1994, the Compact of Free Association with the United States was approved and signed. Palau thus became an independent republic and in December 1994 it joined the United Nations. Three years later it also joined the International Monetary Fund (IMF), thereby qualifying for loans and developmental grants.

One of the benefits of the compact with the United States was a promise of $100 million in aid over a 15-year period in exchange for 50 years of basing rights. Nakamura has determined to spend and invest this capital wisely, mostly for improved infrastructure and roads. Through enlargement of the private sector, he hopes to end the population's traditional dependence upon the government as a source for jobs. He also signed a new minimum wage bill, an ethics-in-government bill to promote more honest governance, and restrictions upon the illegal use of government vehicles for private business.

He strongly opposed legislation promoting creation of "offshore banking" out of fear that it might attract criminal money-laundering activity. Failing this, in December 1999 Nakamura championed a National Banking Review Commission to oversee and regulate the banking environment as closely as possible.

Nakamura also maintained a high international profile through his participation in the United Nations South Pacific Forum, summoned to discuss sea level changes, fishing regulation, and regional security. He has also been an outspoken proponent of the Free Trade Area, which would allow free trade between 14 island countries in the region. Nakamura's tenure in office was generally successful, but he declined to seek a second term. On November 7, 2000, he was succeeded by Thomas E. Remengesau, who pledged to continue his predecessor's policies of economic expansion and diplomatic engagement.

Further Reading

Aldrich, Robert C., and Ched Myers. *Resisting the Serpent: Palau's Struggle for Self-Determination.* Baltimore, Md.: Fortkamp Pub. Co., 1990.

Leibowitz, Arnold W. *Embattled Island: Palau's Struggle for Independence.* Westport, Conn.: Praeger, 1996.

Nakamura, Mamoru. *Palau's Transition to Democracy and New Relationships in the Pacific Community.* Salem, Oreg.: Willamette University, 1990.

Rosenberg, Erica. *Paradise Lost? Environmental Prospects and Politics in the Republic of Palau.* Madison, Wis.: Greenlife Society, 1996.

Wilson, Lynn B. *Speaking to Power: Gender and Politics in the Western Pacific.* New York: Routledge, 1995.

Nawaz Sharif, Mian Muhammad (1949–)
prime minister of Pakistan

Mian Muhammad Nawaz Sharif was born on December 25, 1949, in Lahore, Pakistan, the son of a major industrialist. He was well educated, having attended the Government College of Lahore and Punjab University Law College. Sharif originally worked for his father's iron foundry, Ittefaq, until 1972, when it was nationalized by Prime Minister Zulfikar Ali Bhutto. Thereafter, the Sharif and Bhutto families became intense political adversaries. However, the plant was returned to the family in 1975 by General Mohammad Zia-ul-Haq, who arrested Bhutto and ultimately executed him for corruption two years later. Sharif entered politics in 1981 at the behest of General Zia, who appointed him finance minister of Punjab province. In this office, he pushed for modernizing the provincial economy by liberalizing the free market while also improving the socioeconomic conditions of rural areas. Sharif performed so well that by 1985 he was elected to the post of chief minister of Punjab, becoming the youngest of four provincial executives. He also represented a new breed of Pakistani politician, hailing from the commercial sector and not the traditional landed gentry. The turning point in his career came in 1985, when General Zia died in a plane crash and BENAZIR BHUTTO, daughter of the late prime minister, came to power together with the Pakistan People's Party (PPP). Three years later Sharif was elected to the national assembly representing the Pakistan Muslim League, a coalition of conservative groups that fiercely opposed the Bhutto regime.

In time a bitter dispute developed between Prime Minister Bhutto, stationed in Islamabad, and Punjab chief minister Sharif, headquartered at Lahore. They spent the next two years trying to unseat each other and a general paralysis set in. At length President Ghulam Ishaq Khan dismissed the government and called for new elections to be held in October 1990. Sharif, now head of a 10-party coalition called the Islamic Democratic Alliance, beat the PPP in general elections and became prime minister. Exploiting his entrepreneurial skills, Sharif embarked on a program of national modernization and deregulation. He dismantled the old-style command economy and liberalized the market place by inviting foreign investors to establish operations while he set about selling off inefficient, state-run businesses. He also lifted controls on foreign currency exchange and promoted extensive privatization, which resulted in increased financial assistance from the World Bank and the International Monetary Fund (IMF). However, Sharif was also determined to make the prime minister's office immune from presidential interference, and his machinations triggered a constitutional crisis with President Khan. After continuous legal wrangling, the military stepped in and they forced both Sharif and Khan from office in July 1993.

New elections held in October 1993 placed Benazir Bhutto and the PPP back in power. She managed to deprive Sharif of his Punjab power base, and he was forced to serve as head of the opposition in parliament. However, she was dismissed a second time by President Fa-

rooq Leghari on November 5, 1996, and new elections were announced. The elections proved just the opportunity that Sharif and the PML had been waiting for, and in February 1997 they drove Bhutto and the PPP completely out of office. He became prime minister a second time with comfortable majorities in parliament and—this time—was determined to enact far-reaching constitutional reforms. "We have become a laughingstock where every time the president and prime minister are fighting one another," he argued. "This must now come to an end." Sharif then legislated two amendments that forbade the president from dismissing the prime minister, which easily passed. Thus invigorated, he next sought to consolidate power by moving against the judiciary. He refused to allow the Supreme Court to appoint five of its own judges. In the wrangling that followed both the head of the Supreme Court and President Leghari resigned in December 1997 rather than perpetuate a crisis. On the international scene, Sharif also caused consternation in June 1998 when he allowed Pakistan's first-ever nuclear tests in response to similar Indian maneuvers. This action brought on a spate of international economic sanctions that nearly bankrupted the country. However, it was in confronting the military, a traditional power center in national politics, that Sharif finally overplayed his hand.

In light of mounting national instability, Jehangir Keramat, a former army chief, proposed that the army should have a greater voice in governance. Sharif dismissed the notion out of hand. In July 1999 he further estranged the generals by ordering Army Chief of Staff PERVEZ MUSHARRAF to withdraw his forces from the Indian side of the disputed province of Kashimir. When the general proved reluctant to comply, he tried and failed to have Musharraf replaced. On October 12, 1999, the prime minister was himself suddenly overthrown in a bloodless coup and placed under arrest. He was then tried for corruption and sentenced to life in prison. However, in March 2001 Sharif was released and exiled for 10 years to Saudi Arabia, where his family runs and maintains an extensive steel mill. General Musharraf, meanwhile, is determined to avoid a return to political instability and he has summarily warned both Bhutto and Sharif not to return to Pakistan under pain of arrest.

Further Reading

Amin, Tahir. "Pakistan in 1994: The Politics of Confrontation." *Asian Survey* 35 (1995): 140–147.

Bray, John. "Nawaz Sharif's New Order in Pakistan." *Round Table* 318 (September 1998): 179–190.

Kux, Dennis. *The United States and Pakistan, 1947–2000: Disenchanted Allies.* Washington, D.C.: Woodrow Wilson Center Press, 2001.

Samad, Y. "The Military and Democracy in Pakistan." *Contemporary Southeast Asia* 3, no. 3 (1994): 189–201.

Syed, Anwar H. "Pakistan in 1997: Nawaz Sharif's Second Chance to Govern." *Asian Survey* 38 (February 1998): 116–126.

Nazarbayev, Nursultan (1940–) *president of Kazakhstan*

Nursultan Abishevich Nazarbayev was born in the village of Chemolgan, Kazakhstan, on July 6, 1940, the son of mountain shepherds. At that time Kazakhstan was a constituent state within the Soviet Union, and the second largest republic after Russia. It is also one of the most ethnically diverse, with over 140 different tribes and groupings present, including a large proportion of Russians. Unlike its fellow Central Asian republics, Kazakhstan is unique in being blessed with abundant natural resources, especially oil, and enjoys the most developed economy in the region. As with all Soviet republics, political ambitions were closely tied to membership in the Communist Party, and Nazarbayev joined in 1962. He also acquired an advanced degree in metallurgy and worked several years at the Karaganda Metallurgical Combine as an economist until 1969. That year Nazarbayev began his successful climb up the party hierarchy and by 1984 he was chairman of the Kazakh Council of Ministers. However, his fortunes greatly accelerated in 1989 when Soviet premier Mikhail Gorbachev appointed him head of the Kazakh Community Party in the wake of anti-Russian rioting. The following year he assumed the newly created post of president of Kazakhstan at a time when the entire Soviet infrastructure was crumbling. In this office, Nazarbayev distinguished himself by carefully juggling ethnic demands for independence with his own inclination for continuing reliance upon Russia for economic and security reasons. The fall of the Soviet Union in 1991 did not alter these perceptions although, in December of that year, he ran unopposed as Kazakhstan's first freely elected president.

Once in office, Nazarbayev initiated a leadership style that can best be described as authoritarian. He did so, however, more for pragmatic reasons than as a quest for political power. Cognizant of the extreme ethnic tensions in his state, and that friction between Kazakhstan's two largest groups, Kazakhs and Russians, could tear the country asunder, Nazarbayev has kept political and social processes on a tight leash. He seemed to gauge the political temperament of his countrymen realistically when he declared: "The path from totalitarianism to democracy lies through enlightened authoritarianism." As such he authorized creation of a rubber-stamp legislature, the People's Assembly, to force through desired regulations. Accordingly, in April 1995, members passed a referendum to extend Nazarbayev's rule until the year 2000. As an indication of his popular support, it passed by 93 percent of votes cast.

As president, Nazarbayev has been overtly concerned with the survival of Kazakhstan as a national entity. He therefore deliberately cultivated close ties with non-Soviet Russia, and his was the first Central Asian republic to join the newly created Commonwealth of Independent States (CIS) with Russia, Ukraine, and Belarus. He has also repeatedly warned his countrymen against extreme xenophobia, and he has worked to improve the working and living conditions of Russians in his republic. Concurrently, Nazarbayev has also worked to curry favor with the United States, Western Europe, and regional powers like Iran, in an attempt to attract foreign investment and trade. Nazarbayev may have fondness for tight political control, a legacy of Kazakhstan's Soviet past, but he has fully embraced free-market economics and the selling off of inefficient, state-owned industries. He has also taken deliberate steps to ensure Kazakhstan's nonaligned stance in world affairs. After the Soviet Union's collapse, his nation inherited a huge arsenal of nuclear missiles and bombs but he determined to remodel it as a nuclear-free state and signed the Nuclear Nonproliferation Treaty in 1995. In this manner some 1,040 warheads were transferred back to Russia. He has also been extremely active in developing Kazakhstan as an oil-producing state, which promises an influx of millions of dollars annually. It has since been revealed that the country possesses some of the world's largest-known oil reserves, which bodes well for continuing economic development. The citizens of Kazakhstan seem to appreciate Nazarbayev's efforts, for in January 1999 they returned him to office by 79.8 percent of the vote.

The events of September 11, 2001, further thrust Kazakhstan into the international limelight. Nazarbayev soundly denounced the destruction of the World Trade Center and immediately offered President GEORGE W. BUSH access to airfields and other facilities to prosecute the war against terrorism. Consequently, in December 2001 he concluded a successful meeting in the American capital, whereby new and important economic pledges were signed. Nazarbayev's present term in office expires in 2006. However, he faces increased calls for greater democracy at home, including formation of a new political opposition, Democratic Choice. In February 2002, his prime minister, Kasymzhomart Tokayev, also resigned to protest official foot-dragging on political reform, and he was replaced by a long-standing Nazarbayev ally, Imangali Tasmagambetov. It remains to be seen if this aging, if enlightened, despot, will continue in office for the rest of his term.

Further Reading

George, Alexander. *Journey into Kazakhstan: The True Face of the Nazarbayev Regime.* Lanham, Md.: University Press of America, 2001.

Gokay, Bulent. *The Politics of Caspian Oil.* Basingstoke, England: Macmillan, 2001.

Luong, Pauline J. *Institutional Change and Political Continuity in Post-Soviet Asia: Power, Perceptions, and Pacts.* New York: Cambridge University Press, 2002.

Meyer, Karl E. *The Dust of Empire: the Race for Mastery in the Asian Heartland.* New York: PublicAffairs, 2003.

Nazarbayev, Nursultan. *My Life, My Times, of the Future.* Northamptonshire, England: Pilkington Press, 1999.

Nazpary, Joma. *Post-Soviet Chaos: Violence and Dispossession in Kazakhstan.* Sterling, Va.: Pluto Press, 2002.

Netanyahu, Binyamin (1949–) *prime minister of Israel*

Binyamin Netanyahu was born on October 2, 1949, in Jerusalem, Israel, the son of a Jewish medieval scholar. He was partly educated in the United States and returned to Israel to fulfill his military service. This included several years in the Sayeret Matkal (elite commandos), 1967–72, after which he obtained an advanced degree from the Massachusetts Institute of Technology in 1976. That year his elder brother Yonatan was killed during the daring rescue of Israeli hostages from Entebbe, Uganda. Netanyahu then resumed his life as an Israeli citizen and founded the Jonathan Foundation, which seeks to study and combat terrorism, in honor of his brother. In time Netanyahu gained notoriety as a forceful and articulate spokesman for Israeli security issues. Therefore, in 1982 he was selected as deputy chief to the Israeli embassy in Washington, D.C., where he became something of a media celebrity. Two years later he performed similar work for Israel at the United Nations in New York. By 1988 Netanyahu's reputation for toughness led to his appointment as deputy foreign minister in the YITZHAK SHAMIR administration. That year he also won his first election by winning a seat in the Knesset (parliament) as a member of the conservative Likud Party. In this capacity he attended the 1991 Madrid Middle East Peace Conference and many subsequent peace talks in Washington. Throughout the 1991 Gulf War, when Israel was pelted by Iraqi Scud missiles, Netanyahu again appeared nightly on various news shows and enhanced his reputation as a staunch defender of the Jewish state. His popularity ratings at home soared accordingly.

As a politician, Netanyahu also proved a strong advocate of electoral reform and he helped devise legislation allowing for direct election of prime ministers by popular vote. By 1993 he felt ready to challenge the leadership of Likud and conducted a masterful political and personal campaign to acquire it. On March 24, 1993, Netanyahu scored a stunning upset by defeating David Levy, war hero ARIEL SHARON, and Benny Begin, son of Menachem Begin, for the mantle of command. Netanyahu's rise also signaled a sea change in Likud's approach to the peace process. Heretofore, the older generation of leadership was willing to exchange Israeli-held Palestinian land for peace. However, Netanyahu, in concert with other conservatives and religious factions, felt this approach directly threatened Israeli security. Moreover, they questioned the validity of a viable Palestinian state for the first time and sought other, less comprehensive solutions.

After three years in strident opposition, the turning point in Netanyahu's political fortunes—and Israel's—followed in the wake of Prime Minister YITZHAK RABIN's assassination in November 1995. New elections were scheduled for May 1996, and Likud availed themselves the opportunity to run on a "Peace though Security" platform. The party vocally decried ongoing territorial concessions to Chairman YASSER ARAFAT of the Palestine Liberation Organization (PLO). Tensions were certainly heightened throughout this period by a spate of Palestinian terrorist attacks, which only underscored Likud's position. Accordingly, on May 29, 1996, Netanyahu was elected the eighth prime minister of Israel by direct vote. His margin over the veteran SHIMON PERES was less than 1 percent, but he became both the youngest man to hold high office and the first native-born Israeli to do so. His rise was greeted with trepidation around the world, and fears arose that renewed Israeli intransigence would scuttle the 1993 Oslo Peace Accords. Nonetheless, Netanyahu waxed defiant and promised no accommodation with PLO aspirations "until Arafat arrests terror suspects and increases cooperation with Israeli security forces."

Over the next three years Netanyahu conducted a scorched-earth approach to peace negotiations with the PLO, which triggered an endless cycle of terrorist attacks and swift retaliation. However, he did withdrew Israeli forces from Hebron and other settlements in concert with the 1998 Wye River Memorandum, and he awaited a concomitant reduction in terrorism and hostility from the Arabs. None was forthcoming and the violence continued. After three years of fruitless negotiations and bloodshed, it appeared that Likud's strong-armed approach to peace talks had failed. Netanyahu was also embroiled in a personal scandal involving misappropriating state funds, although he was never indicted. On May 17, 1999, he was turned out of office by the Labor Party under EHUD BARAK. Netanyahu subsequently resigned from both the Knesset and the Likud leadership to assume the role of a public gadfly. He has roundly criticized Barak and his successor, fellow Likud member ARIEL SHARON, for their perceived softness in dealing with the Palestinians. In the spring of 2002, following the onset of deadly suicide bombings throughout Israel, Netanyahu orchestrated a party vote that rejected any consideration of a Palestinian state—a direct rebuke to Sharon. He has also called for the outright expulsion of Arafat and the dismantling of his Palestinian Authority as a precondition for further negotiations. "I'm against the Palestinians having their own army, air force, and an opportunity to forge alliances with neighboring states hostile to Israel," he insisted. "The terrorist regime of Arafat must be removed from the political arena." In May 2002 he declared his intention to run against Sharon for prime minister in the next general election, slated for 2003.

Further Reading

Broder, Jonathan. "Netanyahu and American Jews." *World Policy Journal* 15 (Spring 1998): 89–98.

Karsh, Efraim. *From Rabin to Netanyahu: Israel's Troubled Agenda*. Portland, Oreg.: Frank Cass, 1997.

Kaspit, Ben, and Ilan Knfir, and Ora Cummings. *Netanyahu: The Road to Power*. Secaucus, N.J.: Carol, 1998.

Lochery, Neill. "The Netanyahu Era: From Crisis to Crisis." *Israel Affairs* 6 (Spring–Summer 2000): 221–37.

Ron, James. *Frontiers and Ghettos: State Violence in Serbia and Israel*. Berkeley: University of California Press, 2003.

Shindler, Colin. *Israel, Likud, and the Zionist Dream: Power, Politics, and Ideology from Begin to Netanyahu*. New York: I. B. Taurus, 1995.

Niyazov, Saparmurad (1940–) *president of Turkmenistan*

Saparmurad Niayzov was born in Turkmenistan in May 1940. His country lay within the Russian sphere of influence since 1886, and in 1924 it became a republic of the Soviet Union. Unlike other Central Asian republics, Turkmenistan is somewhat small, underpopulated, and desperately poor. For many years it was more or less ignored by the Communist Party in Moscow and, consequently, received little priority in terms of economic development. The majority of the population are ethnic Turkmen, who are Muslim and speak a Turkish dialect, although a sizable Russian population is also present.

Little is known of Niyazov's early years, but he apparently joined the Communist Party in 1962. From then he went on to attend the Leningrad Polytechnical Institute, where he obtained degrees in engineering physics. Niyazov then returned home to hold a number of technical positions, but in 1970 he commenced his climb through the party's ranks. By 1980 he served as first secretary of the Ashkhabad City Party Committee, and he gained a reputation for efficiency and ruthlessness. These traits held him in good stead in 1984 when he became an instructor within the Organizational Party Work Department, which brought him to the attention of Premier Mikhail Gorbachev. Gorbachev was intent upon removing moribund party members and replacing them with fresh, new blood, so in 1985 he appointed Niyazov first secretary of the Communist Party of Turkmenistan. This also conferred full membership in the Central

Committee back in Moscow. In October 1990, a new constitution was adopted that allowed for creation of Turkmenistan's first president, and Niyazov garnered 98.3 percent of the vote in an uncontested election. He was serving in this capacity in August 1991, when the failed coup against Gorbachev transpired. Niyazov, firmly wedded to the notion of authoritarian rule, refused to condemn it.

The Soviet Union collapsed in 1991, but the rise of democracy and multiparty elections failed to materialize in Turkmenistan. In fact, Niyazov, as an old party hand, militated against such trends. Consequently, it was not until 1992 that a post-Soviet constitution was finally adopted that put in place executive, legislative, and judicial branches of government. In June of that year Niyazov was again elected president while running unopposed, and, in January 1994, he oversaw the passage of a public referendum extending his tenure until 2002. However, in his most blatant move against democratization, Niyazov had the constitution altered in December 1999, and he now rules the nation as "president for life."

Despite a veneer of democratic rule, outlined by the constitution, Turkmenistan still functions with all the trappings of a Soviet-style state. The government has clamped down on all political expression and dissent, and state security forces routinely harass and arrest potential opponents. The biggest transgressor, however, remains Niyazov, who, to perpetuate his influence, has embarked on a cult of personality worthy of Joseph Stalin. In fact, his image is the most numerous image reproduced in public: it adorns classrooms, posters, and even the currency. Moreover, the countryside is littered with golden, larger-than-life statues of the ubiquitous Niyazov, who has also adopted the ceremonial title of "Turkmenbashi" or "leader of all Turkmen." His image and influence is pervasive and permeates schools, businesses and all political activities within this one-party state.

Having secured his power base at home, Niyazov has striven to be an effective broker in defining and representing Turkmenistan's interests abroad. Knowing his is the smallest and least powerful of all Central Asian republics, he has sought to shore up traditional economic and security ties with the new Russian Federation, without being smothered by them. To that end, he steadfastly refuses to join the Commonwealth of Independence States (CIS), which he views as a threat to national sovereignty. Moreover, more than any country in the region, he has sought close working relationships with

Turkey and especially Iran, which itself hosts a large Turkmen population. Consequently, Iran is Turkmenistan's largest investor and source of foreign revenue. Niyazov is also committed to pursuing a staunchly neutral foreign policy, especially with respect to neighboring Afghanistan. He has long overlooked a lucrative drug-smuggling trade across his borders, and he is widely suspected of having made a fortune facilitating the transit of illegal heroin to the West. Worse, in the wake of the September 11, 2001, attack upon New York's World Trade Center, the despotic "president for life" offered his sympathy to the United States, but refused to allow Washington access to airfields or airspace. In view of the radical Taliban's collapse, he has since allowed humanitarian airlifts to take place from Turkmenistan's soil.

Niyazov continues as one of the world's most repressive dictators, and among its most quixotic. In December 1999, he announced that the creation of political parties would not be permitted before 2010, until after the "political conscience" of his fellow Turkmen has been more perfectly developed.

Further Reading

Akbarzadeh, Shahrom. "The Political Shape of Central Asia." *Central Asian Survey* 16, no. 4 (1999): 517–42.

Dailey, Erika, Jeri Laber, and Alexander Petrov. *Human Rights in Turkmenistan.* New York: Helsinki Watch, 1993.

Hyman, Anthony. *Power and Politics in Central Asia's New Republics.* London: Research Institute for the Study of Conflict and Terrorism, 1994.

Meyer, Karl E. *The Dust of Empire: The Race for Mastery in the Asian Heartland.* New York: PublicAffairs, 2003.

O'Hara, Sarah L. "Agriculture and Land Reform in Turkmenistan since Independence." *Post-Soviet Geography and Economics* 38 (September 1997): 430–445.

Turkmenbashy, Saparmyrat. *Independence, Democracy, Prosperity.* New York: Noy Publications, 1994.

Nkomo, Joshua (1917–1999) *vice president of Zimbabwe*

Joshua Nkomo was born on June 19, 1917, in the Semokwe Reserve, Matabeland, then a British protectorate called Southern Rhodesia. His father was a prosperous cattle rancher, lay preacher, and member of the Kalanga tribe. Nkomo received his primary education at a missionary school and subsequently attended the Tjolotjo Government School and the Jan Hofmeyer School in South Africa. He returned in 1945 and worked for Rhodesian Railways as the colony's first African social worker. Intent on receiving greater education, in 1951 he obtained his bachelor's degree by correspondence from the University of South Africa. Africans at this time, though constituting the overwhelming majority of Rhodesia's population, were marginalized politically and powerless to influence the course of national affairs. Nkomo, like many Africans of his generation, resented the racially discriminatory practices of European settlers, and it spurred him to become politically active. He proved himself effective at union organizing and later joined the African National Congress (ANC), a leading nationalist organization. In 1959 Rhodesia banned the ANC and Nkomo was forced to flee to England, where he established a party office. He returned two years later to head a new organization, the National Democratic Party, and he continued agitating for an end to colonial rule. When the government banned his newest entity, Nkomo abandoned pacifism and founded the Zimbabwe People's Union (ZAPU) as a formal guerrilla group. By this time he had become celebrated for his massive girth and height and his fierce opposition to white rule, yet he remained distinguished by a willingness to settle accounts through negotiation.

Despite revolutionary leanings, Nkomo was conservative and cautious by nature, traits which aggravated younger, less patient members of ZAPU. Foremost among them was ROBERT MUGABE, who broke away to form a splinter force of his own, the Zimbabwe African National Union (ZANU). In 1965 Rhodesia declared its independence from Great Britain and installed a minority white regime under Ian Smith. Nkomo forcefully protested the move, was arrested, and spent a decade either behind bars or in close confinement. He was released under a general amnesty in 1974, as the guerrilla war began picking up momentum, yet he was still willing to discuss a peaceful transition to majority rule. However, Nkomo faced stiff competition from the more radical Mugabe and his competing ZANU group, which continued waging war. As the conflict unfolded, ZAPU operated at home with aid from the Soviet Union, whereas ZANU was based in Tanzania, assisted by China. There was considerable hostility between the two factions and little in the manner of military coordination. It was not until 1976 that both groups held talks and formed the

Patriotic Front against the Rhodesian government. By 1980 their combined guerrilla movements had prevailed and, through negotiations, the Lancaster House Accords led to creation of a new country, Zimbabwe. After successfully concluding a 30-year struggle, Nkomo felt he rightly deserved to be the first president.

No sooner were national elections scheduled than additional friction between Nkomo, as the senior nationalist figure, and Mugabe, who controlled the largest military force, began anew. Elections held in 1980 were decided along tribal lines, and Nkomo lost badly. Mugabe was then created prime minister, although he assembled a reconciliation government by appointing Nkomo a cabinet minister. However, by 1982 Nkomo had been ejected from government on the grounds that he was planning an insurrection, and fighting between the factions ensued. In 1985 Nkomo lost another round of national elections because he still lacked the large population base that Mugabe enjoyed. A five-year impasse ensued until 1987, when their respective parties were merged into a one-party state, and Mugabe appointed Nkomo minister without portfolio. In 1990 the national constitution was then revised, and Mugabe became president while Nkomo served as one of two vice presidents. He served loyally in that capacity over the next six years, reemerging as a spokesman for African nationalism. In 1997 Nkomo, citing poor health, resigned from office. He died of prostate cancer in Harare on July 1, 1999. Hailed as Umdala Wethu ("Our Old Man"), Nkomo was a founding father of Zimbabwe and, for a half a century, a leading player in the war against colonialism.

Further Reading

Bond, Patrick, and Masimba Manyanya. *Zimbabwe's Plunge: Exhausted Nationalism, Neoliberalism, and the Struggle for Social Justice*. London: Merline, 2002.

Johnson, Vernon D. *Racial Formation in Zimbabwe*. New Brunswick, N.J.: Transaction Publications, 1995.

Kriger, Norma J. *Guerrilla Veterans: Symbolic & Violent Politics in Zimbabwe, 1980–1987*. New York: Cambridge University Press, 2003.

Nhema, Alfred G. *Democracy in Zimbabwe: From Liberation to Liberalization*. Oxford: African Books Collective, 2002.

Nkomo, Joshua. *Nkomo, The Story of My Life*. London: Methuen, 1984.

Schwartz, Richard. *Coming to Terms: Zimbabwe in the International Arena*. New York: I. B. Tauris, 2001.

Noboa, Gustavo (1938–) *president of Ecuador*

Gustavo Noboa Bejarano was born in the coastal Ecuadorian city of Guayaquil in 1938. He spent most of his life either attending college or administering one, including the noted Catholic University. Bookish, bespectacled, and apolitical, he never joined any political party, although his views closely mirror those of Christian Democrats. Moreover, his ascension to the presidency of Ecuador was almost accidental. Prior to 1978, the country was ruled by an oppressive military junta who, under intense international pressure, finally restored civilian rule. After a series of peaceful elections, Abdala Bucaram rose to the presidency on a platform of social reforms in 1996. But, in view of a declining economy, he reneged on all his promises to the poor, mostly indigenous Indians, and widespread civil unrest resulted. The national congress then removed Bucaram on February 6, 1997, and, in the May 1998 elections, Jamil Mahuad came to the fore. Noboa, a political neophyte, was tapped as his vice president. Though intent upon social reforms, Mahuad was simply overwhelmed by inflation and a sagging economy. To stabilize the situation, he announced plans to link the national currency, the sucre, to the U.S. dollar. Unfortunately, this triggered fears of devaluation that would wipe out the savings of indigenous peoples, driving them further into poverty. On January 21, 2000, a huge protest march by Indians descended on the national capital of Quito, at which the military intervened to remove Mahuad from office. The international community strongly protested the return of military rule and threatened economic sanctions; therefore, they stepped aside and allowed the national congress to appoint the scholarly Noboa as president on January 24, 2000.

By default Noboa had assumed the unenviable task of sorting out a country in the midst of an economic meltdown. The native population, already poor, had been reduced to grinding poverty through the loss of jobs while teachers, policemen, and hospital workers remained unpaid for months. Worse yet, Noboa pegged the sucre to the dollar as planned, which brought back a measure of stability but doubled the price of most consumer goods. Fortunately for the country, the scholarly president enjoys a reputation for honesty and integrity at a time when recent polls show most Ecuadorians in favor of abolishing the government altogether! This fact, coupled with radicalization and mobilization of the Indians under radical leader Antonio Vargas, made any plan conceived by Noboa and passed by the legislature a perilous undertaking, indeed.

Despite protests and violence, Noboa enforced the requisite austerity measures to prove to the International Monetary Fund that Ecuador was serious about reform. This brought about a welcome infusion of emergency aid from abroad that shored up the tottering economy and currency. "Ecuador is immersed in the worse crisis of its history," he lectured the public, "I will proceed to implement decisions that cannot be postponed in order to return to the normalcy of everyday life." Stiff doses of economic medicine included a doubling of fuel prices and a tripling of transportation fares, both of which spurred major protests from the angry populace. Inflation, which had been at 90 percent, the highest in South America, suddenly began coming down. But in February 2001, violence over price hikes began spiraling out of control and Noboa declared a state of emergency. Furthermore, in light of the very political instability that brought him to power, he began urging Congress to adopt a package of constitutional changes that would grant the executive office greater authority. He also feels the country would be better served by a bicameral legislature instead of the single chamber now in existence. Such changes might very well thwart future outbreaks of political deadlock and hasten political response to check social unrest.

Amazingly, 18 months into Noboa's administration, the Ecuadorian economy has recovered a healthy beat. In fact, it is presently expanding at 5 percent a year, making it the fastest growing in South America. Better yet, inflation has been tamed and unemployment, once 16 percent, has dropped to 10 percent. All this good news has led to a corresponding decline in protest, which has virtually disappeared. But having gained economic stability, Noboa wants to insure the return of sustainable growth. He is therefore adamant, over the objection of environmentalists, that a new oil pipeline be built to increase petroleum exports. If all these plans and reforms proceed apace, then the scholarly president will be well positioned for reelection, which is slated for October 2002. The measures he enacted were unpopular when unveiled, but they have ushered in badly needed economic growth and prosperity. It will fall upon future generations of politicians to insure that the nation's economic well-being receives the highest possible priority, and thus avoid repeating this recent brush with disaster.

Further Reading

Isaacs, Anita. *Military Rule and Transition in Ecuador, 1972–1992.* Basingstoke, England: Macmillan in Association with St. Anthony's College, Oxford, 1993.

Little, Paul E. *Amazonia: Territorial Struggles on Perennial Frontiers.* Baltimore: Johns Hopkins University Press, 2001.

Martin, Pamela. *Globalization of Contentious Politics: The Amazonian Indigenous Rights Movement.* New York: Routledge, 2003.

Roos, Wilma. *Ecuador in Focus: A Guide to the People, Politics, and Culture.* New York: Interlink Books, 1997.

Torre, Carlos de la. *Populist Seduction in Latin America: The Ecuadorian Experience.* Athens: Ohio University Center for International Studies, 2000.

Norodom Ranariddh (1944–) *prime minister of Cambodia*

Prince Norodom Ranariddh was born on January 2, 1941, in Phnom Penh, Cambodia, the son of prince and future king NORODOM SIHANOUK. Cambodia was then administered as a French colony, and members of the royal family were inevitably educated abroad. Ranariddh received a law degree from the University of Aix-en-Provence in 1967 and he taught several years on the Faculty of Law in Phnom Penh until 1970. He returned to France shortly after, obtaining his doctorate in law from the University of Aix-Marseille, and he conducted constitutional research until 1983. That year he returned to Southeast Asia to participate in national politics.

Throughout the last half of the 20th century, Cambodia served as a remote battlefield of the cold war and was the scene of some of history's most grisly atrocities. His father had been installed as king in the 1950s, and he orchestrated a delicate balancing act against Vietnamese Communists, homegrown Maoist guerrillas, and incursions by U.S. forces. By 1975 the radical, Chinese-sponsored Khmer Rouge had shot their way into power under the aegis of Pol Pot, who soon executed 1.5 million people—one-fourth of the population. However, growing border tensions with Vietnam, recently victorious in its own struggle with the United States, prompted an invasion. Thus Communist forces allied with the Soviet Union began fighting those supported by China. The Vietnamese prevailed and established the new People's Republic of Kampuchea, while Western powers and the United Nations demanded a withdrawal. This did not transpire until 1991, at which point Ranariddh reentered the political life of his country. Previously, he had settled in Bangkok, Thailand, where he maintained the offices of the national United Front for an Independent, Neutral, Peaceful and Cooperative Cambodia (FUNCINPEC). This group was composed of former Cambodian loyalists who wished to see King Sihanouk restored to the throne. For his part, being the king's son, Ranariddh was a natural choice to lead FUNCINPEC, and in 1992 he was elected president. Once the Vietnamese departed in October 1991, the United Nations moved in to monitor free elections and facilitate a cease-fire between warring Cambodian factions. Foremost among these was the Cambodian's People's Party (CPP) under HUN SEN, a former Khmer Rouge operative who broke with Pol Pot and became an ally of Vietnam. Much infighting and squabbling transpired before elections could be held in May 1993 to decide the future of Cambodia and the nature of its government.

The new elections revolved around a showdown between the royalists under Ranariddh and the socialists under Hun Sen. However, sentiments for the royal family still ran strong, and FUNCINPEC easily won the election, taking 58 of 120 seats in the new National Assembly. The CPP, by contrast, captured only 51 seats, while the Khmer Rouge, still armed and menacing the countryside, boycotted the process. Naturally, Ranariddh claimed victory as Cambodia's new prime minister, but Hun Sen raised objections to his legitimacy and claimed voter fraud. However, to preclude any possibility of a new civil war, a power-sharing arrangement was devised allowing Ranariddh to serve as first prime minister and Hun Sen as second prime minister. It was an unholy alliance between two mutually hostile factions, but violence was averted for the time being. On September 21, 1993, a new constitution was also adopted, declaring war-ravaged Cambodia a constitutional monarchy and again enthroning Norodom Sihanouk.

For three years Ranariddh and Hun Sen maintained an uneasy truce while they secretly jockeyed behind the scenes for greater power. In 1996 the prince helped found the National United Front to link various parties in a concerted effort to oust the CCP. Hun Sen, however, seems to have been better prepared for renewed struggle, for in July 1997 CPP forces attacked FUNCINPEC facilities and supporters, forcing Ranariddh to flee the country. "The honeymoon has really ended," the former prince declared. "To run a country this way does not work." Hun Sen then unilaterally declared himself first prime minister and appointed his consort, Ung Huot, to serve as the second. The United Nations was also undecided as to which leader possessed political legitimacy, and for many years Cambodia's seat in the General Assembly remained empty. Eventually, once Ranariddh was willing to recognize Hun Sens' authority, he returned to Cambodia. He thereupon served as president of the National Assembly, which post he currently holds today. But his efforts to unify the opposition met with a serious reverse in May 2002, when his brother, Prince Norodom Chakrapong, established a splinter group of his own. This threatens to split the opposition vote in next year's general elections, which almost certainly assures the continuance of CPP's dominance. "The Royalists continue to split and Hun Sen continues to control," Ranariddh stated. "If I were Hun Sen I would keep playing golf."

Further Reading

Gotte, Evan R. *Cambodia after the Khmer Rouge: Inside the Politics of Nation Building.* New Haven, Conn.: Yale University Press, 2002.

Hughe, Caroline. "Cambodia: Democracy or Dictatorship?" *Southeast Asian Affairs* 28 (2001): 113–128.

Peou, Sorpong. "Cambodia in 1997: Back to Square One?" *Asian Survey* 38 (January 1998): 69–75.

———. *The Political Economy of the Cambodian Transition.* Richmond, England: Curzon, 2002.

Un, Kheang, and Judy Ledgerwood. "Cambodia in 2001: Toward Democratic Consolidation?" *Asian Survey* 42 (January–February, 2002): 100–107.

Norodom Sihanouk (1922–) *king of Cambodia*

Norodom Sihanouk was born on October 31, 1922, in Phnom Penh, Cambodia, a son of Prince Norodom Suramarit. Cambodia was then administered as a French colonial possession. Sihanouk was educated locally and in Vietnam, when he was suddenly tapped by the French to succeed his grandfather on the throne in April 1941. At the age of 18, the young king was viewed as politically naïve, gullible, and plausibly more receptive to French wishes. Cambodia was subsequently occupied by victorious Japanese troops, who allowed the French administration to remain in place. When the Japanese finally retreated in March 1945, they encouraged Sihanouk to seek independence from France. This he did adroitly, proving himself to be a master of political intrigue, although always in the interest of preserving his nation. At first the French scoffed at his demands and Sihanouk, judging the moment premature, mitigated his stance and vetoed several attempts by the legislature to initiate moves toward independence. But Sihanouk awaited the outcome of the ongoing Indochina War between France and Communist forces in North Vietnam. When the French were decisively defeated in 1954, Sihanouk again pressed his demands for independence, which transpired the following year. In 1955 the king judged the political winds of Southeast Asia to be shifting, so he abdicated in favor of his father, founded the People's Socialist Community, and became prime minister. He ruled in this capacity until 1960, when his father died, and he was reinstated as king.

Throughout the 1960s Southeast Asia was ablaze in a new war between Communist North Vietnam and the United States. Sihanouk, acknowledging the relative weakness of his small country, adopted a neutralist stance and, by doing so, tread a perilous tightrope. He refused American foreign aid after 1963 and allowed the North Vietnamese to use Cambodian territory to infiltrate troops into South Vietnam—provided they did not support Cambodian Communists. This tactic angered the United States, which wanted the infiltration routes closed, and, in 1970, Washington engineered a coup by General Lon Nol. The general quickly overthrew the government while the king was visiting Beijing, and he allowed the Americans to bomb the Communists. What Sihanouk had feared most had finally happened: his nation now embarked on a period of destabilization. He nevertheless founded a government in exile while the Chinese Communists funded a Cambodian guerrilla group, the Khmer Rouge. Led by Pol Pot, they succeeded in toppling Lon Nol in 1975, and the king returned home after a five-year absence. However, Pol Pot began implementing a radical regime of mass deportation and cultural cleansing, pursued so brutally that 1.5 million Cambodians—one fourth of the population—were murdered. Pol Pot's rule is generally regarded as one of the most horrific atrocities of the 20th century, and rivals the European Holocaust in scope. When Sihanouk protested such tactics he was placed under house arrest. Worse, in 1978 the Khmer Rouge started attacking Vietnamese troops along the border, which prompted a full-scale invasion. Sihanouk fled back to Beijing in 1979, where he orchestrated an unlikely but broad-based alliance by royalist and Khmer Rouge forces to oppose their traditional enemy. A decade of intense guerrilla warfare ensued and by 1989 the Vietnamese had had enough and withdrew from Cambodia. In their place they left HUN SEN, a former Khmer Rouge operative turned ally, as prime minister of the new Kampuchean People's Republic.

In 1992 Sihanouk returned to Cambodia to install a new constitutional monarchy and oversee new elections. These were overwhelmingly won by his son, NORODOM RANARIDDH, who became prime minister, while Hun Sen, angered over the voting process, was allowed to serve as second prime minister. As king, Sihanouk tried restoring stability to Cambodia's polarized polity, but he failed. By July 1997 the tenuous truce broke down and Hun Sen's forces drove both Sihanouks out of the country. The king and his son were allowed to return once they recognized Hun Sen's legitimacy as Cambodias sole prime minister. Since then Sihanouk strives to serve as a symbol of national unity for all his people, although he is determined to prosecute former Khmer Rouge leaders for crimes against humanity. In August 2001 he signed legislation setting up a United Nations–directed tribunal to arrest and sentence all war criminals. "About the judgment and condemnation of those Khmer Rouge arch criminals, I don't have any objection," Sihanouk declared. "I will respect the final decision of the government and parliament." The king is now back, securely on his throne, and grateful to Chinese benefactors who supported him for nearly two decades. In June 2002 he paid a visit to Beijing, personally thanked China for its assistance, and stated his wish that friendship between their respective countries, honed by three decades of adversity, will last forever. Sihanouk himself should be acknowledged as one of the most astute political survivors of Southeast Asian history, and one whose longevity in power reflects, in equal measure, stubbornness in adversity and flexibility when dealing from a position of weakness.

Further Reading

Gottesman, Evan R. *Cambodia after the Khmer Rouge: Inside the Politics of Nation Building.* New Haven, Conn.: Yale University Press, 2002.

Lizee, Pierre. *Peace, Power, and Resistance in Cambodia: Global Governance and the Failure of International Conflict Resolution.* New York: St. Martin's Press, 2000.

Osbourne, Milton E. *Sihanouk: Prince of Light, Prince of Darkness.* Honolulu: University of Hawaii Press, 1994.

Peou, Sorpong, ed. *Cambodia: Change and Continuity in Contemporary Politics.* Burlington, Vt.: Ashgate, 2001.

Sihanouk, Norodom. *My War with the CIA: The Memoirs of Prince Norodom Sihanouk.* New York: Pantheon Books, 1973.

Note, Kessai (1950–) *president of the Marshall Islands*

Kessai H. Note was born on the island of Airok, Republic of the Marshall Islands, on August 7, 1950. His homeland consists of a volcanic chain of 29 coral atolls, that is, ridges that have formed along the edges of submerged volcanos, located 1,000 miles northeast of Papua New Guinea. The population is estimated in excess of 65,000, the majority of whom are of native Micronesian stock. The Marshalls were originally claimed by Spain, but in 1885 they were sold to Germany as a protectorate. They then passed into Japanese ownership after World War I, and during World War II they were captured by U.S. forces. In 1947 the United Nations designated the Marshalls a Trust Territory of the Pacific Islands under American supervision. The most notable events over the next decade were a series of 67 atomic bomb tests that obliterated several atolls and rendered others unliveable. Since 1959 the island of Kwajalein has also been used as a missile testing ground. By the 1970s the Marshalls exhibited growing pressure for independence from the United States, and in May 1979 they adopted their own constitution. This document mandated creation of a national assembly or Nitijela, from which a president would be chosen. In 1986 the islands also ratified a Compact of Free Association with the United States, which allows free migration of natives to the mainland in exchange for military bases. To date, rental money from Washington remains the largest source of national income.

Note was educated locally at the Marshall Islands High School and he subsequently attended the Vudal College in Papua New Guinea. He then returned home to serve as a government economist until 1979, when he gained election to the newly created Nitijela. Shortly after Note was also appointed to the presidential cabinet, where he held the portfolios of minister of resources and development, minister of the interior, and minister of transportation. In 1988 Note gained election as speaker of the assembly, where he remained 12 years, and he also presided over two constitutional conventions. His opportunity to lead came in the wake of the November 1999 elections whereby the opposition United Democratic Party (UDP) trounced the government party in legislative elections. This convinced the sitting president, Imata Kabua, who was also a traditional *iroijlapap,* or paramount chief, to decline to seek another term. On January 3, 2000, Note was then elected president by the assembly. His rise is significant in that he was the first president of commoner origin.

Once in office, Note announced his determination to pursue anticorruption policies, and, in May 2000, he established a task force for the purpose of investigating allegations leveled against government members. He also pledged to respect the independence of the judiciary branch, unlike his predecessor, who removed four sitting justices from the bench. However, his greatest challenge remains developing the islands' economic base. Presently, the Marshall Islands subsists largely on the export of coconuts, which was greatly affected by declining world prices. Note decided better results would be achieved by placing greater emphasis on tourism and selling off fishing licenses to international companies. Traditionally, however, the biggest source of national income was the United States and its leasing of military bases. With the end of the cold war, fewer bases are required and the country has suffered a corresponding decline in revenue. Consequently, Note has been forced to conduct widespread economic restructuring to develop homegrown industries and incomes. "We will restructure, rebuild, and restore the dignity of the country's institutions," he noted. "We will advocate discipline and transparency in all sectors of government."

The most conspicuous target of Note's anticorruption drive has been former president Kabua. To preempt the government from pursuing his case further, in January 2001 Kabua had his former minister of education, Justin DeBrum, introduce a motion of no confidence against the Note administration. Ostensibly, this was done in response to the government's failure to renegotiate land rental payments with the United States for the missile range on Kwajalein Atoll. Fortunately, the motion was defeated 19 to 14, and the corruption investi-

gations continue apace. Another pressing point for many islanders involves reparations from the Americans for atomic tests held between 1946 and 1958. The Marshall Islands has received $100 million in compensation thus far for populations that were forcibly relocated from Bikini and Enewetak atolls, both of which remain contaminated. More controversial was Note's decision to establish full diplomatic relations with the Republic of China (Taiwan), which caused the People's Republic of China to sever all ties with the Marshall Islands. However, the Americans vetoed a proposed visit to the islands by the Taiwanese navy as a violation of the compact's defensive agreements. Note has also gone on record as opposing an American scheme for developing a nuclear waste storage facility. It remains to be seen if his administration can deflect policies desired by the Americans while developing his nation's ability to secure financial independence from them as well.

Further Reading

Bryan, E. H. *Life in the Marshall Islands.* Honolulu, Hawaii: Bernice P. Bishop Museum, 1972.

De Jonge, Alice. *The Constitution of the Marshall Islands: Its Drafting and Current Operation.* Kensington: University of New South Wales, 1993.

Hezel, Francis X. *Strangers in Their Own Land: A Century of Colonial Rule in the Caroline and Marshall Islands.* Honolulu: University of Hawaii Press, 1995.

Mason, Leonard. "A Marshallese Nation Emerges from the Political Fragmentation in American Micronesia." *Pacific Studies* 13, no. 1 (1989): 1–46.

Runeborg, Ruth E. *The Marshall Islands: History, Culture, and Communication.* Honolulu, Hawaii: East-West Center, 1980.

Ntaryamira, Cyprien (ca. 1955–1994) *president of Burundi*

Cyprien Ntaryamira was born around 1955 in Burundi, a member of the majority Hutu clan. His tribe constitutes one of two major ethnic divisions in that nation, the other being the minority Tutsi. As in neighboring Rwanda, national politics had been dominated by friction and violence between the two groupings ever since the 17th century. Burundi is also one of Africa's poorest and most densely populated countries; it contains some 6 million inhabitants crammed into a region the size of New Hampshire. For many years it was also ruled by

Belgium as a colony, and Belgians institutionalized discrimination on behalf of the minority Tutsi to ensure their rule. After Burundi gained independence in the early 1960s Ntaryamira apparently trained as an agricultural engineer. But one of the first explosions of violence occurred in 1965 after Hutu soldiers attempted to overthrow the Tutsi monarch and thousands of people were slain. An even bigger upheaval was triggered in 1972 when a violent coup failed to topple the dictator Michel Micombero, and Ntaryamira sought refuge among fellow Hutus living in Rwanda. He remained in exile for the next 11 years while an estimated 50,000–200,000 Hutus and Tutsis were killed in sectarian violence. Ntaryamira returned home in 1983, when he joined the Foreign Ministry under President Jean Baptiste Bagaza. Committed to democratic ideals, he also helped found the opposition Front for Democracy in Burundi (FRODEBU) to oppose the only legal party, Bagaza's Union for National Progress (UPRONA). In 1987 Bagaza was suddenly deposed by General PIERRE BUYOYA, and further fighting ensued. It was not until June 1, 1993, that Buyoya was defeated in a fair election by Melchior Ndadaye of FRODEBU and democracy was restored. One of the new executive's first acts was to appoint Ntaryamira as minister of agriculture.

It was hoped that Ndadaye's peaceful accession would promote a period of national reconciliation in Burundi. Pursuant to that lofty goal, the new president appointed several Tutsis to his cabinet and also named one as prime minister. He even invited the disgraced Bagaza back to Burundi under a general amnesty. This proved a fatal mistake, for on October 21, 1993, Bagaza led a bloody coup against the government, and Ndadaye died after only three months in power. Street fighting between rival groups then commenced anew and it was not until the following spring that the National Assembly chose Ntaryamira as the new president. He was sworn in on February 5, 1994.

It was hoped that the new president would be able to usher in peace and and harmony between the Hutu and Tutsi peoples. In April 1996 Ntaryamira flew to nearby Tanzania to attend a summit meeting with various leaders from Central Africa to discuss ways of diffusing regional tensions. On April 6, 1994, Ntaryamira boarded a plane for Kigali, Rwanda, with President JUVÉNAL HABYARIMANA, a fellow Hutu. As they approached the airport, a missile suddenly streaked up from the ground and struck their craft, destroying it.

Thus Burundi lost two presidents in the span of only six months. Worse, the sudden deaths of the two executives threw both Burundi and Rwanda into chaos and destruction, as rival Hutus and Tutsi blamed each other for the attack. Literally thousands of people were summarily killed before the violence subsided in this, one of the worst atrocities of the 20th century. But Burundi's fragile political process righted itself eventually, and, on April 6, 1994, Ntaryamira was succeeded by Vice President Sylvestre Ntibantunganya.

Further Reading

Hale, Aaron Z. "The Socio-Political Implications of Environmental Degradation: The Case of Burundi." Unpublished master's thesis, Humboldt State University, 2001.

Lemarchand, Rene. *Burundi: Ethnocide as Discourse and Practice*. New York: Cambridge University Press, 1998.

Longman, Timothy P. *Proxy Targets: Civilians in the War in Burundi*. New York: Human Rights Watch, 1998.

Nyankanzi, Edward L. *Genocide: Rwanda and Burundi*. Rochester, Vt.: Schenkman Books, 1998.

Reyntjens, Filip. *Burundi: Prospects for Peace*. London: Minority Rights Group, 2000.

Nuhayyan, Zayid bin Sultan al- (ca. 1917–   )
president of the United Arab Emirates

Zayid (or Zayed) bin Sultan al-Nuhayyan was born in Abu Dhabi around 1917, the son of Sultan Zayid al-Nuhayyan, head of the Al Bu Falah division of the larger Bani Yas tribe. His father came to rule this impoverished desert sheikdom by murdering his brother, and he was in turn murdered by a younger sibling. Young Zayid was raised in the desert among the bedouins and inculcated in their most cherished values of physical bravery, generosity, and mediation of disputes. This qualities all held him in good stead in the early 1940s when his brother, Sheikh Shakhbut, appointed him governor of al-Ain province. This was a strategic oasis region for Abu Dhabi, owing to its considerable water supplies, and it was coveted by neighboring Saudi Arabia and Oman. However, Zayid formed a strong alliance of bedouin tribes and managed to stave off Saudi advances and bribes for several years. He was active in developing the region's irrigation system, and he also constructed the first elementary schools. By 1960 oil had been discovered in Abu Dhabi, which promised considerable income for this poor region, but Sheikh Shakhbut was reluctant to lavish any of his newfound wealth on his subjects for fear of compromising traditional Arab values. Zayid, fortunately, strongly disagreed with his older brother and pushed for improved social conditions to circumvent the rise of either Islamic or Marxist radicalism. Great Britain, which provided military forces to defend the lower gulf area, was alarmed by Shakhbut's conservatism and London helped arrange Sayid to overthrow his regime in 1966. His ascension marked a turning point in the affairs of the Persian Gulf.

As emir, Zayid continued the policies that made him so popular as governor. While skillfully developing and exploiting the natural resources of his realm, he remained attentive to the needs of his people, particularly in the fields of health, education, and social services. "Money is of no value unless it is used for the benefits of the people," he preached. The emir was also quick to invite foreign companies and investors into Abu Dhabi, which became renowned for its freewheeling entrepreneurial spirit. By 1968, however, the British announced their intention to quit the Gulf altogether and entrust regional security to existing nations. For Zayid, this meant placing his kingdom at the tender mercies of much larger powers, a prospect he was not willing to endure. Therefore, through deft negotiations, in 1971 he managed to bring Abu Dhabi, Dubai, Sharjah, Ras at Khaimah, Ajman, Umm al-Qaiwain, and Fujairah into a mutual defensive and economic alliance called the United Arab Emirates (UAE). This entity is governed by a Supreme Council drawn from each of the participating emirates, and they elect a president to lead them. An executive-appointed Council of Ministers and a Federal National Council are also present to assist and advise. There are presently no political parties in the UAE, and Zayid has served as the only president since 1971.

Under Zayid's aegis, the UAE has transformed itself from a collection of essentially feudal desert kingdoms into a modern state with one of the world's highest standards of living. Oil revenue has all but eliminated the need to levy taxes, and most social services are free to citizens. Part of Zayid's success is his skill at compromise and judicious applications of tribal generosity. Neighboring Dubai, a traditional rival to Abu Dhabi, was initially a difficult partner to deal with under the federation scheme, but the president's willingness to expend funds from his own coffers to assist modernization efforts has kept them in the fold. His modern and moderate outlook has also given him considerable standing in the Arab world at large. Zayid has also been an outspoken proponent of various Arab issues, and has given generously to the Palestinian cause. During the Iran-Iraq War of the 1980s, he offered his services as a mediator and also served as the Gulf Cooperation Council spokesman. However, during SADDAM HUSSEIN's ill-fated seizure of Kuwait in August 1990, he allowed Western coalition powers access to UAE bases and airspace and supported the military efforts that followed. Since then he has moderated his stance toward Iraq and urged an end to sanctions.

Zayid, now approaching his 86th year, has been in poor health, and, in 2000, he required surgery and hospitalization in the United States. However, as the father of the UAE, his triumphant return was greeted as a national holiday and the aging ruler retains the gratitude of his subjects. Consequently, on December 2, 2001, he was reelected president of the federation for another five years, although real authority is being parceled out to younger subordinates. After the September 11, 2001, attack on New York's World Trade Center, Zayid signed comprehensive legislation authorizing a crackdown on money laundering by terrorist organizations and organized crime. This is reputedly the first time that his nation has infringed upon its freewheeling business image. All told, for three decades the UAE has flourished under the leadership of this barely literate, but astutely diplomatic, desert leader.

Further Reading

Al-Abed, Ibrahim, and Paula Casey-Vine. *Chronicle of Progress: 25 Years of Development in the United Arab Emirates.* London: Trident Press, 1999.

Kechichian, Joseph A. *A Century in Thirty Years: Shaykh Zayed and the United Arab Emirates.* Washington, D.C.: Middle East Policy Council, 2000.

Lienhardt, Peter, and Ahmed Al-Shahi. *Shaikhdoms of Eastern Arabia.* New York: Palgrave, 2001.

Morris, Claude. *The Desert Falcon: The Story of H. H. Sheik Zayed Bin Sultan al Nahiyan, President of the United Arab Emirates.* London; Morris International, 1974.

Van Der Meulen, Hendrik. "The Role of Tribal and Kinship Ties in the Politics of the United Arab Emirates." Unpublished Ph.D. dissertation, Fletcher School of Law and Diplomacy, 1997.

Zahlan, Rosemarie S. *The Making of the Modern Gulf States: Kuwait, Bahrain, Qatar, the United Arab Emirates, and Oman*. Reading, England: Ithaca Press, 1998.

Nujoma, Sam (1929–) *president of Namibia*

Sam Daniel Shafishuna Nujoma was born in Etunda village, Ovamboland, South-West Africa, on May 12, 1929. He belonged to the Ovambo, the largest ethnic group in the remote northern region of that colony. Originally a German possession, it passed into British hands during World War I and was ultimately administered by the apartheid-oriented regime of South Africa as Namibia. After herding goats for several years Nujoma managed to receive rudimentary education at a Finnish mission in the capital of Windhoek, and he went on to serve as a sweeper with the South African Railways. It was while working in this capacity in 1957 that Nujoma became politically active by organizing rail workers within the Ovamboland People's Organization (OPO). The South African government running the colony begun imposing strict apartheid regulations over Namibia, which entailed physical separation between blacks and whites. This meant that many blacks were summarily forced to leave their homes in Windhoek and commute vast distances to work. Again, Nujoma was at the forefront of protests, which turned bloody in 1959, and the following year he exiled himself to Tanzania. He would not return home for 30 years. While abroad Nujoma helped organize the South-West Africa People's Organization (SWAPO) to support independence from South Africa. In 1966 they commenced active guerrilla warfare against South African troops, which lasted 23 years. It was not until 1988 that a United Nations deal could be brokered for a peaceful settlement. This entailed the removal of South African troops from the former colony in exchange for Cuban troops departing Angola. In 1989 Nujoma then returned home to run in the first freely held elections and, not surprisingly, SWAPO candidates took 57 percent of votes cast. He was then appointed Namibia's first democratically elected president, and the country formally declared its political independence on March 21, 1990.

For all the bloodshed and rancor associated with Namibia's long struggle for freedom, its transition to democracy proved surprisingly peaceful. Nujoma himself established a conciliatory tone by appointing several whites to his cabinet and calling upon fellow Namibians to forget the past and concentrate on rebuilding the nation. "Memories of bitter and long years of conflict, racial hatred, and deep distrust among us Namibians must be buried forever," he declared. Needless to say, such an approach won him high praise from his former enemies and from democracies around the world. Moreover, Nujoma proved himself a pragmatist in office. Though nominally socialist in outlook, he discarded long-held ideological beliefs in favor of a free-market economy and political pluralism. As such SWAPO peacefully shares power with the Democratic Turnhall Alliance (DTA) and several other smaller parties. The nation's economy slowly began rebounding, and, in December 1994, Nujoma was returned to power with 76 percent of the vote by a grateful electorate.

Rebuilding the Namibian economy has entailed a delicate balancing act for Nujoma, as decades of apartheid rule rendered an entire generation of black citizens bereft of meaningful education or skills. Thus he has been forced to rely heavily on the white merchant class, without appearing to appease them. However, with African unemployment rates still hovering at 40 percent, a gradual redistribution of wealth seemed inevitable. Nujoma nonetheless adheres to a policy of stimulating the private sector as a source of job creation. Consequently, Namibia enjoys one of the best economies in Africa, with a strong growth rate and very low inflation. In many respects it has become a model for the rest of developing Africa. The only blot on Nujoma's otherwise meritorious record came in November 1998, when he supported constitutional changes that would allow him to hold office for a third term. This was accomplished in December 1999 when SWAPO won 76.8 percent of the vote in elections judged to be free and fair.

In terms of foreign affairs, Nujoma has been active in promoting closer ties to South Africa, once his former foe, and President NELSON MANDELA responded by erasing an $800 million debt. He also intervened with troops to assist President LAURENT KABILA of the Democratic Republic of the Congo in the late 1990s. However, his biggest challenge came in establishing close ties with Angolan president JOSÉ EDUARDO DOS SANTOS in his struggle against the UNITA rebels of the late JONAS SAVIMBI. In February 2002 he met with dos Santos at a wreath-laying ceremony at Oihole in southern Angola.

"All the sacrifices that have been made are not in vain," Nujoma said. "UNITA bandits will be crushed and peace and stability will be fully restored." For his own part, Nujoma has begun to feel his age and the 72-year-old leader recently declined to seek a fourth term in office after 2004. "It has never been my intention to serve again, because I am too old," he conceded. "I have to give way to young people, but I will remain in the party leadership and work with the young people because they move fast and I'm no longer able to move fast." Namibia, fortunately, remains a highly touted example of economic growth and political moderation for developing nations around the world. For his role in creating that status, Nujoma's political and historical legacy seem secure.

Further Reading

Cooper, Allan D. *Ovambo Politics in the Twentieth Century.* Lanham, Md.: University Press of America, 2001.

Forrest, Joshua B. *Namibia's Post-Apartheid Regional Institutions: The Founding Year.* Rochester, N.Y.: University of Rochester, 1998.

Hearn, Roger. *UN Peacekeeping in Action: The Namibian Experience.* Commack, N.Y.: NOVA Science Publications, 1999.

Leys, Colin, and Susan Brown. *Histories of Namibia: Living through the Liberation Struggle.* London: Merlin, 2001.

Nujoma, Sam. *Where Others Wavered: The Autobiography of Sam Nujoma.* London: Panaf Books, 2001.

O

Obasanjo, Olusegun (1935–) *president of Nigeria*

Olusegun Obasanjo was born at Abeokuta, Ogun state, Nigeria, on March 6, 1935, a Christian member of the sizable Yoruba tribe. Nigeria, a large country on Africa's west coast, is the most populous nation on that continent and among the most diverse. It is home to at least 250 different languages and dialects, and almost evenly divided between adherents of Christianity and Islam. Nigeria had been a British protectorate since 1900, but political independence transpired in October 1960. Long regarded as one of Africa's most promising countries, it quickly degenerated under an endless succession of military coups. Meanwhile, Obasanjo excelled at the Baptist Boys High School near his home but, as his family was too impoverished to send him to college, he joined the military to complete his education. Adept as a soldier, he trained in England as an engineering officer, and he saw additional duties with the Indian army and as a United Nations peacekeeper. During the Nigerian civil war, 1967–69, he commanded an infantry division with distinction, and he was allowed to accept the surrender of rebel forces in Biafra. A turning point in his career occurred in 1976 when he became a lieutenant general and commander in chief of the armed forces. That year a coup eliminated General Murtala Muhammad, the nominal head of state, and Obasanjo was se-

lected to succeed him. Much to the surprise of fellow countrymen, the general dutifully placed Nigeria back on the path to civilian rule, which was accomplished in 1979. He thus became the first African general to ever relinquish power peacefully. Soon after, Obasanjo retired from active service to run a pig farm, although he was a frequent critic of ongoing military regimes. In 1995 he was arrested by General SANI ABACHA and sentenced to death, although he was released three years later when Abacha died suddenly. Obasanjo then agreed to run as a civilian as a candidate of the People's Democratic Party, and, in February 1999, he became the first freely elected Nigerian leader in 15 years. "It is my determination to run an open, fair, and transparent government throughout the period of my mandate," he promised.

Obasanjo inherited a nation dispirited by years of tyranny and misrule. The economy and national infrastructure were in ruins and the country's various ethnic groups, forced to compete for an ever-shrinking slice of the pie, had begun settling their differences in the streets. Moreover, Nigeria under the Abacha regime had become a pariah state, cut off from the British Commonwealth and subject to international sanctions. Obasanjo's ascendancy confirmed for many that the nation had turned a corner and was mending. He sacked the heads of many inefficient, state-owned utilities, and he also removed all military officers appointed to

Obuchi, Keizo (1937–2000) *prime minister of Japan*

Keizo Obuchi was born on June 25, 1937, in Nakanojo, Japan, the son of a prosperous yarn mill owner. His father also enjoyed a lengthy career in parliament while his older brother became mayor of Nakanojo. Obuchi himself failed three times to gain entry into Tokyo's Imperial University, so in 1958 he began attending the equally prestigious Waseda University. He graduated four years later with a bachelor's degree in English literature. In 1963 Obuchi conducted a world tour, including the United States, where he met Attorney General Robert F. Kennedy. He then returned to Japan shortly after his father's death and successfully ran for his seat in the lower house of the national Diet (parliament) representing Gumma district. At the age of 26, he was one of the country's youngest politicians and a member of the Liberal Democratic Party (LDP), which had controlled the national agenda since 1955. As an individual, Obuchi was cut in the classic mold of a traditional Japanese politician; quiet, self-effacing, and outwardly not very ambitious. But more important, he proved highly capable at consensus-building within his party, which remains an essential characteristic for success in Japanese politics. In this manner, Obuchi rose quietly but steadily through the ranks of the LDP over the next 30 years. His success was due in no large measure to patronage from his friend and mentor, Prime Minister Noboru Takeshita. Takeshita by this time had resigned from public office, but he remained a force to be reckoned with behind the scenes as the "shadow shogun."

By 1991, Obuchi had reached the lofty position of secretary-general within the LDP, which is generally regarded as the next step before becoming prime minister. He rose to party vice president in 1994 and two years later campaigned strongly for RYUTARO HASHIMOTO throughout national elections. Hashimoto won, and as prime minister he appointed Obuchi minister of foreign affairs in 1997. However, by that time the nation was suffering from economic doldrums, and, in 1998, the Japanese electorate punished the LDP by eliminating their majority in the upper chamber. Hashimoto consequently resigned from office and the fight was on to choose his successor. The nondescript Obuchi, because of seniority, was considered third in a three-way race for premier, and not given much chance to succeed. Critics saw him as timid, lackluster, and derided his bland demeanor as one befitting "Mr. Ordinary." Two younger candidates were viewed as much more dynamic in the public eye, and more capable of making the tough decisions necessary to lead the nation out of recession. However, they did not figure on party elder Takeshita, who, behind the scenes, favored Obuchi. Nor could the minister's proclivity for forging consensus around his candidacy be ignored. A minor civil war erupted in parliament over the succession dispute, but at length the quiet, dignified Obuchi prevailed and he took the reigns of government on July 12, 1998. "Mr. Ordinary" had triumphed at last.

Obuchi rose to power during Japan's worst economic crisis in 50 years. The nation's financial institutions were crumbling under the weight of nearly $1 trillion in bad loans while unemployment had reached 4 percent—astronomical by Japanese standards. Worse, the ongoing recession played havoc with neighboring Asian economies as well, and the entire region began buckling. Confronted with a malaise of such magnitude, Obuchi displayed decisiveness that belied his prior timidity. "I have a strong sense that without courage today, there is no tomorrow," he lectured parliament, "Mark my words on it." He then appointed the outspoken KICHII MIYAZAWA, a former prime minister, as his finance minister. Next, Obuchi vowed to spend an additional $70 billion to jump-start the economy, on top of the $100 billion already pledged by the previous administration. This flew in the face of conventional political wisdom, as the Japanese government has a long-established aversion toward deficit spending. He also embarked on a program to reduce personal tax rates from 65 percent to 50 percent and corporate rates from 46 percent to 40 percent. "This is the first step to put the Japanese economy on a recovery orbit within a couple of years," he insisted. Obuchi subsequently tackled other controversial issues such as adoption of the prewar Hinomaru (rising sun flag) and Kimigayo (national anthem) as national symbols. He also lent his weight to legislation allowing the buildup of Japanese military and naval forces with a view toward deploying them abroad. This was an emotional issue and one that the national constitution forbade at the time.

The initial results of Obuchi's massive deficit spending were encouraging, and, by the spring of 2000, the economy had apparently stabilized. However, he did not have long to savor his success. On April 2, 2000, Obuchi suffered a massive stroke. He lay in a coma for six weeks before finally passing away on May 14,

2000. His successor was another LDP stalwart, YO-SHIRO MORI.

Further Reading
Hayes, Declan. *Setting Sun: The Decline and Fall of Japan, Inc.* Boston: Tuttle Publishing, 2002.
Lincoln, Edward J. "Japan in 2000: The Year That Could Have Been but Was Not." *Asian Survey* 41 (January–February 2001): 49–60.
McCormack, Gavan. *The Emptiness of Japanese Affluence.* Armonk, N.Y.: M. E. Sharpe, 2001.
Muramatsu, Michio, and Farrukh Iqbal. *Local Government Development in Postwar Japan.* Oxford: Oxford University Press, 2001.
Park, Cheol Hee. "Factional Dynamics in Japan's LDP since Political Reform: Continuity and Change." *Asian Survey* 41 (May–June 2001): 428–461.
Reed, Steven R. *Japanese Electoral Politics: Creating a New Party System.* New York: Routledge, 2003.

Oddsson, David (1948–) *prime minister of Iceland*

David Oddsson was born in Reykjavík, Iceland, on January 17, 1948, the son of a doctor. Iceland is a rocky island between Norway and Greenland and its parliament, the Althingi, is among the world's oldest, having been established by Vikings in A.D. 930. It was controlled by Denmark until June 1944, and has since been ruled by a parliamentary form of government. This includes the Althingi, now a bicameral body, and a prime minister who is appointed from the largest party or coalition in power. Traditionally, the Icelandic economy revolves around fishing, its principal export, and the nation remains very sensitive to international politics that might affect its ability to carry on that trade.

Oddsson was educated locally and he also attended the University of Iceland, graduating with a law degree in 1976. While holding several clerking positions, he also established himself as a minor playwright and author. Oddsson commenced his political career in 1973 when he joined the conservative Independence Party (IP) as a youth director. After several turns as the manager of a health insurance fund, he secured his first political office in 1980 by being elected to the Reykjavík City Executive Committee. Two years later he became mayor of Reykjavík while also working his way up the ranks of the IP. In 1989 Oddsson gained election as party vice chairman and two years later he replaced Thorsteinn Palsson as chairman. That year he was also elected to the Althingi during a major shift in parliamentary power. In April 1991 the IP registered strong gains during an economic recession and entered into a coalition with the left-wing party. In this manner Oddsson was sworn in as prime minister on April 30, 1991, and has held the position for over a decade. In 1995 and 1999 the IP won increasingly larger margins in parliament. Therefore, he became one of Europe's longest-serving heads of state.

Oddsson rise to power coincided with the island's declining economic fortunes and he resolved it was time for a change. Unlike most Scandinavian countries, where left-leaning, big-spending Social Democrats rule, Iceland has a particularly conservative bent to its politics. This fact was manifested in Oddsson's determination to completely liberalize the traditional state-run economy. He accomplished this by selling off inefficient, state-owned businesses and lowering taxes on

David Oddsson *(Embassy of Iceland)*

profits. The result was a fourfold increase in Iceland's purchasing power and proved so successful that the extensive social benefits of this traditional welfare state remained almost unscathed. However, the retirement age was raised by two years to 67. Nonetheless, in his 10 years in power, Iceland has enjoyed 5 percent annual growth per year, low inflation, and an unemployment rate so small that Polish workers have been brought in to augment the workforce. However, fishing remains the island's largest employer and a topic of continuing concern. Oddsson, like many Icelanders, is interested in joining the European Union (EU) for all the trade advantages it would convey. However, the islanders fear this would come at the expense of opening up Iceland's waters to European fishing fleets as required by treaty. Rather than surrender control of this traditional natural resource, the IP—and most of the population—would rather not join the EU. "You can be a fine European without giving up sovereignty," Oddsson reasoned. Nonetheless, the government continues its liberalization trends in banking and telecommunications in the event that Iceland does one day join.

Despite its ambivalence toward the EU, Iceland under Oddsson has fully embraced membership in NATO, and it seeks close military, trade, and political ties to the United States. In 1991 he raised the ire of many left-wing groups by signing a separate security agreement with Washington above and beyond what was required by NATO. Thus the United States maintains a sizable base and a relatively high profile on the island. Conversely, Iceland's relations with the former Soviet Union were strained, especially over the issue of the Baltic states. When they began seeking independence in the spring of 1991, Oddsson declared Iceland's diplomatic recognition of Estonia, the first nation to do so, which prompted Moscow to recall its ambassador. Having called for complete independence for the Baltic nations, recognition for Latvia and Lithuania also followed promptly. "The events that took place in Europe less than a decade ago radically transformed the political landscape in the continent," Oddsson affirmed. "If we fail to seize this magnificent opportunity to consolidate democracy throughout the continent, generations to come will be astonished and shocked at our performance." Oddsson's current tenure in office expires in 2003; having solidified his party's standing as the largest in Iceland, his return to power at that time seems probable.

Further Reading

Corgan, Michael. *Iceland and Its Alliances: Security for a Small State.* Lewiston, N.Y.: E. Mellen Press, 2003.

Einhorn, Eric S. *Modern Welfare States: Scandinavian Politics and Policy in the Global Age.* Westport, Conn.: Praeger, 2003.

Karlsson, Gunnar. *Iceland's 1100 Years: The History of a Marginal Society.* London: C. Hurst, 2000.

Kristinsson, Gunnar H. "The Icelandic Parliamentary Election of 1996." *Electoral Studies* 10, no. 3 (1991): 262–266.

———. "Parties, States, and Patronage." *West European Politics* 19, no. 3 (1996): 433–457.

Lacy, Terry G. *Ring of Seasons: Iceland, Its Culture and History.* Ann Arbor: University of Michigan Press, 2000.

Olafsson, Bjorn G. *Small States in the Global System: Analysis and Illustrations for the Case of Iceland.* Brookfield, Vt.: Ashgate, 1998.

Ogi, Adolf (1942–) *president of Switzerland*

Adolf Ogi was born in Kandersteg, canton Berne, Switzerland, on July 18, 1942. Switzerland is a strategically located country in the heart of Europe that began coalescing toward nationhood in 1291. However, it was not until 1815 that its present boundaries were fixed by international treaty, along with a federal government that pledges itself to maintain strict neutrality. Politically, Switzerland is ruled by the Federal Assembly, which consists of a 46-seat Council of States and a 200-member National Council elected from the 26 cantons nationwide. The main executive body is a seven-member Federal Council, from which a president and vice president are nominated for one-year terms. These posts are largely ceremonial, although, like a prime minister, their role is to channel and direct debate among fellow members. However, Switzerland is unique among Western democracies in that major legislation adopted by the Federal Assembly must be approved publicly through the referendum process to become law. Of late, this has produced some surprising results relative to traditions of neutrality and separation from the rest of Europe. And, despite some ethnic tension between the four major linguistic groups—French, German, Italian, and Romansch—Swiss politics are a study in caution and cordiality. Power is shared between four major parties and invariably takes the form of a coalition government. As a rule, change comes rather slowly to this mountainous land, and only after painstaking introspection and consensus building. This stability has contributed to the fact that the Swiss enjoy one of the world's highest standards of living, and that Switzerland hosts some of the world's largest banks and multinational corporations.

Ogi was educated locally before studying economics at the Ecole Supérieur de Commerce in La Neuveville and the Swiss Mercantile School in London. Commencing in 1963, he then formed a close association with national sports groups and successively served as director of the Swiss Ski Association, the World and European Committee of the International Ski Federation, and Intersport Schweiz Holding AG. Ogi also began his political career by joining the Swiss People's Party (SVP) in 1978, and he gained election to parliament the following year. After heading various military and sports commissions he was elected to the Federal Council in 1987. As such, in 1993 he rotated to the position of president for the first time and held it a year before heading other committees. In 1999 Ogi became vice president of the Federal Council, which again placed him in line for a stint at the presidency. In 2000 he commenced his second term as Switzerland's highest executive officer.

Because the Swiss economy runs well, the overriding concerns of national politics center mostly around the country's traditions of neutrality and separation. In light of the changing face of Europe, this can be cause for considerable debate and discord. Formation of the European Union (EU) threatens to place the Swiss economy at a trade disadvantage, but the prospects of closer integration with the outside world remain daunting. In 1992 voters decisively turned down a referendum that would have granted Swiss entry into the European Economic Area (EEA), the first step of association within the EU. However, under Ogi's aegis, Switzerland became party to several other bilateral agreements to remove trade barriers and enhance air and road links to prevent the country from becoming completely isolated. Furthermore, Ogi is confident of Switzerland's eventual admission into the EU, and he predicts preliminary discussions for membership will commence sometime in 2003. In a similar fashion, Swiss voters only reluctantly joined the International Monetary Fund (IMF) and World Bank in 1992, and they did not join the United Nations until the spring of 2002—and then only by a very narrow margin. The government has also been cool toward membership in NATO, which many feel threat-

ens the time-honored practice of neutrality. But in light of emerging collective security arrangements, the Swiss did sign on to the limited Partnership for Peace program, and in November 2000 they allowed the first joint NATO exercises to be held on Swiss soil. Swiss troops have also been employed as UN peacekeepers in Kosovo and Bosnia for the first time, so change is in the wind.

In 1996, the normally placid Swiss polity was shaken by allegations that the country profited by collaborating with Nazi Germany during World War II. Apparently, the government had purchased $500 million of Nazi gold, some of which was appropriated from Jewish Holocaust victims. Consequently, the Swiss government started examining the provenance of several dormant bank accounts from that period, and it also established a $1.2 billion fund to settle accounts with Jewish groups and Holocaust survivors.

After an uneventful but relatively constructive year in office, Ogi stepped down in December 2000, and the Federal Assembly elected Moritz Leuenberger as president. In February 2001, he announced his intention to serve as a member of the International Olympic Committee (IOC) with the backing of the Swiss Olympic Federation, of which he is honorary president.

Further Reading

Banaszak, Lee Ann. *Why Movements Succeed or Fail: Opportunity, Culture, and the Struggle for Woman Suffrage.* Princeton, N.J.: Princeton University Press, 1996.

Butler, Michael. *The Making of Modern Switzerland, 1848–1998.* Basingstoke, England: Macmillan, 2000.

Chevallaz, Georges A. *The Challenge of Neutrality: Diplomacy and the Defense of Switzerland.* Lanham, Md.: Lexington Books, 2001.

Fossendal, Gregory A. *Direct Democracy in Switzerland.* New Brunswick, N.J.: Transaction Publishers, 2001.

Gstohl, Sieglinde. *Reluctant Europeans: Norway, Sweden, and Switzerland in the Process of Integration.* Boulder, Colo.: Lynne Rienner Publications, 2002.

Omar, Mohammad (ca. 1962–   ) *religious leader of Afghanistan*

Mohammad Omar is believed to have been born around 1962 in the province of Uruzgan, Afghanistan, a farmer's son. Intent upon becoming a mullah (Islamic clergyman), he studied in the local religious school as a *talib* (student) until 1979, when Soviet troops invaded to prop up a failing Communist regime. Omar, like many tribesmen comprising the population, was outraged and joined the armed resistance as a Mujahideen (holy warrior). He fought well as a sniper but apparently lost his right eye to Soviet shrapnel, and it was sewn shut. By 1989 the Soviets had withdrawn in defeat while various bands of Mujahideen, armed by the United States and Arab countries, coalesced under various warlords. An intense civil war then ensued for control of the country, wreaking havoc on the already tottering infrastructure. Omar, seeing the destruction arise from competing militias, founded his own, the Taliban (literally, "students of religion") in 1994. He imbued members with a strict sense of Islamic fundamentalism and inspired them to rid the nation of infidels and nonbelievers. Inspired by such religious fervor, Taliban forces fought ferociously, sweeping steadily northward from their main base at Kandahar and capturing the national capital of Kabul, along with 90 percent of the countryside. The war-weary population initially greeted the newcomers as heroes for restoring order and behaving properly toward noncombatants. But, as a harbinger of things to come, Omar's first deed was ordering the public execution of former president MOHAMMAD NAJIB in a soccer stadium on September 27, 1996.

Once in control, Omar assumed the religious title "Commander of the Faithful" with a view to creating the world's purest Islamic state. Compulsory practices entailed mandatory beards for men and denying women education and forbidding them from leaving their homes. Kites, music, movies, and any other form of entertainment judged not to be "Islamic" were outlawed. Public execution of criminals and Koranic amputation of limbs also became prevalent. Omar subsequently extended his strict orthodoxy to further ends. In the spring of 2001 he ordered the destruction of ancient Buddhist statues at Bamiyan, which had stood for over a thousand years. The number of dead brought international condemnation and underscored the fanaticism of his regime. He also instituted the death penalty for foreigners trying to convert Muslims to other faiths. But for all the terrible authority Omar wielded, which was absolute, he remained reclusive, rarely seen in public, and almost never venturing outside his base at Kandahar. Physical descriptions that survive suggest a tall, imposing figure, resplendent in black turban and shawl, and whose single remaining eye casts a baleful glare. Grizzled warriors apparently wilted before the moral and religious authority of this hard-line Islamic cleric.

But of all Omar's transgressions, none proved worse than his apparently cordial relationship with Saudi millionaire refugee Osama bin Laden, whom he befriended while fighting the Soviets. Bin Laden, espousing an inveterate hatred for the West, especially the United States, used his wealth to prop up the Taliban financially. He also brought in numerous Arab mercenaries to form a personal army, al-Qaeda, to wage a holy war, or jihad, against perceived enemies. It has since been rumored that Omar and bin Laden intermarried with women from their respective families, further strengthening their bonds. But over the years, and apparently with Omar's blessings, bin Laden used Afghanistan as an impregnable base to stage terrorist attacks against the United States. On September 11, 2001, several of bin Laden's men staged history's most infamous act of terror by hijacking airliners and crashing them into New York's World Trade Center and the Pentagon. Several thousand deaths resulted and spurred President GEORGE W. BUSH to retaliate. Specifically, the Americans demanded that Omar immediately turn bin Laden over—or face the consequences. The mullah defiantly refused, declaring the request insulting to Islam. "Half my country was destroyed by 23 years of war," he averred. "If the remaining half is destroyed trying to save bin Laden, I am ready." Last minute appeals were made by representatives of the Pakistani government, nominal allies of Omar, but to no avail. Accordingly, in October 2001 American air power was unleashed against Taliban and al-Qaida forces throughout Afghanistan. Within two months Omar's seven-year reign of terror had disappeared under a hail of bombs and missiles. He departed Kandahar a refugee in his own country and amid the rubble of his own intransigence. Messianic Omar remains a fugitive at large, one of the world's most wanted criminals, and he is presumed to be hiding among the local population of his native southeastern Afghanistan. He is also the object of an intensive manhunt by U.S. Special Forces, sometimes in appalling terrain. In May 2002 a taped interview, purportedly made by Omar, surfaced in Arab capitals. He denied any complicity for the events of September 11, but otherwise he spoke defiantly. "There were reasons behind these great deeds," Omar reasoned. "America should seek to remove these reasons—and it knows them well—so that such accidents do not reoccur."

Further Reading

Bergen, Peter L. *Holy War, Inc.: Inside the Secret World of Osama bin Laden.* New York: Free Press, 2001.

Gohari, M. J. *The Taliban: Ascent to Power.* Karachi: Oxford University Press, 2000.

Griffin, Michael. *The Taliban Movement in Afghanistan.* Sterling, Va.: Pluto Press, 2001.

Hafez, Mohammad W. *Why Muslims Rebel: Repression and Resistance in the Muslim World.* Boulder, Colo.: Lynne Rienner Publishers, 2003.

Kaplan, Robert D. *Soldiers of God: With Islamic Warriors in Afghanistan and Pakistan.* New York: Vintage Books, 2001.

Marsden, Peter. *The Taliban: War and Religion in Afghanistan.* New York: Zed Books, 2002.

Skane, Rosemarie. *The Women of Afghanistan under the Taliban.* Jefferson, N.C.: McFarland, 2002.

Orban, Viktor (1963–) *prime minister of Hungary*

Viktor Orban was born in Szekesfehervar, Hungary, on May 31, 1963. Hungary entered the 20th century as part of the dual Austro-Hungarian Empire, but after World War I it became an independent republic within greatly reduced borders. Hungary supported Nazi Germany during World War II and was subsequently occupied by Soviet forces after 1945, who instituted a dictatorship modeled on that of the Soviet Union. This triggered a violent but unsuccessful revolt in 1956, but the regime of Janos Kadar subsequently embarked on some cautious political and economic liberalization. In 1990, with the Soviet Empire in near-collapse, Hungary took the first steps toward multiparty democracy and the following year the Hungarian Democratic Freedom Forum took power. However, the economy tumbled while transforming itself from one subject to a central planning to one ruled by the free market, and in 1994 the Hungarian Socialist (former Communist) Party was swept back to power. Curiously, the Socialists did little to undo badly needed reforms and the economy revived, but elections held in May 1998 brought a new organization, the Federation of Young Democrats–Hungarian Civic Party (Fidesz) to power. This event accelerated the pace of change completely.

As a youth, Orban studied law at the Eotvos Lorand University, and, in 1987, he became cofounder of the Fidesz Party. He was stridently anticommunist at a time when such a stance was inherently dangerous. During the 1989 reburial of Imre Nagy, who led the failed 1956 rebellion, Orban demanded the immediate withdrawal of Soviet troops from Hungary. "If we believe in our own strength," he declared, "we will be able to put an end to the Communist dictatorship." He has since acquired—and reveled in—his reputation as a brash, impulsive, and outspoken young man. In 1990 Orban first won election to parliament, and he was reelected in 1994. That year he also became party chairman of Fidesz, although the party fared poorly in national elections. Orban realized that, to win nationally, he must transform his charge from a youth-oriented movement and broaden its appeal to that of a mainstream organization. Moving quickly and confidently, he accomplished just that and by 1998 Fidesz was well positioned to challenge the Socialists for dominance. In the first round of voting in May 1998, the Socialists won 32.2 percent to 28.2 percent, but a runoff was required. However, power decisively shifted back to Orban three weeks later during the second round and, in concert with the Independent Smallholders Union, Fidesz took control of the government. Orban was then sworn in as prime minister on June 18, 1998.

Once in power, Orban wasted no time renouncing Hungary's communist past. He accomplished this by aggressively pursuing the country's membership in NATO; along with Poland and the Czech Republic, Hungary was approved for membership in March 1999. He backed up his request with action, and allowed NATO warplanes free access to Hungarian airspace during the bombing campaign in Kosovo. Orban was also committed to joining the European Union (EU), and he instituted the structural and economic changes necessary to qualify. Presently, Hungary is slated to join in 2004. On the domestic front, Orban continued the same liberalization policies that the Socialists had maintained, and the Hungarian economy continues humming along at 4 percent a year. More important, unemployment has dropped to 6 percent and inflation to only 7 percent, giving Hungary the most productive economy in Central Europe. In another slap at the Communists, a centerpiece of Orban's administration was creation of a new political museum, the House of Terror, which is dedicated to all those tortured by the Communist secret police. "Its been documented that as many as 100 million died under Communist tyrannies around the world since 1917," he declared. "The House of Terror is a tribute to all those who suffered." The Socialists, fuming as the opposition, merely portray the museum as Orban's latest public relations stunt to enhance his already controversial reputation.

Orban's strident nationalism also does not sit well with many of his Central European neighbors. When Hungary was partitioned in 1920, two-thirds of its land and one-third of its population ended up in Slovakia and Romania. For this reason, Orban stridently advocates greater rights for the Hungarian diaspora, possibly with a return of the lost territories. He made headlines for failing to criticize Austrian chancellor WOLFGANG SCHUESSEL for including the far-right Freedom Party within his government. He also raised eyebrows by attending the funeral of Croatian strongman FRANJO TUDJMAN, although he did so from a shared belief that strong leadership is necessary to help nations overcome a repressive heritage. Thanks in large measure to Orban's virile leadership, Hungary has in fact triumphed over its past and emerged as a model of political stability, and a worthy addition to NATO and the EU. Although present polls indicate a tight race, in April 2002 the 38-year-old Orban seemed well situated to become the first Hungarian prime minister to serve consecutive terms since the days of communism. However, on April 21 the Fidesz accumulated only 49 percent of the vote, not enough to form a majority in parliament. That fell upon Socialist candidate Peter Medgyessy to perform in concert with the Liberal Party. "We were many but we were not enough," Orban subsequently conceded.

Further Reading

Anderson, Ruth M., and J. M. Anderson. *Barbed Wire for Sale: The Hungarian Transition to Democracy, 1988–1991.* Graham, Wash.: Poetic License, 1999.

Berend, T. Ivan, and Gyorgy Ranki. *Studies in Central and Eastern Europe in the Twentieth Century: Regional Crises and the Case of Hungary.* Burlington, Vt.: Ashgate, 2002.

Braun, Aurel, and Zoltan D. Barany. *Dilemmas of Transition: The Hungarian Experience.* Lanham, Md.: Rowman and Littlefield, 1999.

Fitzmaurice, John. *Politics and Government in the Visegrad Countries: Poland, Hungary, the Czech Republic, and Slovakia.* New York: St. Martin's Press, 1998.

Schmidt, Maria, and Laszlo Gy. Toth, eds. *From Totalitarianism to Democratic Hungary: Evolution and Transformation, 1990–2000.* Boulder, Colo.: Social Science Monographs, 2000.

West, Barbara A. *The Danger Is Everywhere! The Insecurity of Transition in Postsocialist Hungary.* Prospect Heights, Ill.: Waveland Press, 2002.

Özal, Turgut (1927–1993) *president of Turkey*

Turgut Özal was born on October 13, 1927, in Malatya, Turkey, the son of a minor bank official. He distinguished himself academically and gained admittance to the Istanbul Technical University in 1946 to study electrical engineering. There he met and befriended SÜLEYMAN DEMIREL, a future benefactor and prime minister. Özal graduated four years later and found work with the Office of Electrical Research in Ankara. However, a defining moment in his life occurred in 1954, when he visited the United States for graduate studies. The young man was immensely impressed by America, and he thereafter expressed a lifelong admiration. Following his return to Turkey he served with the State Planning Organization and also taught mathematics at the Middle Eastern Technical University. Özal commenced his climb to power in 1966 when Demirel, now prime minister of Turkey, appointed him a technical adviser. He performed capably in that role until March 1971, when a military coup deposed Demirel and dismissed all his ministers. Özal then returned to the United States and found work as an adviser with the World Bank, 1971–73.

Özal returned to Turkey in 1973 once the military had restored democracy, and he found success as an entrepreneur. By 1979 he again curried favor with Demirel, back in power as prime minister, and was appointed his economic adviser. Turkey was then wracked by a poor economy and mounting social unrest, and the military again intervened in September 1980 and tossed Demirel out of office a second time. However, they requested Özal to remain in office as the nation's economic adviser and help sort the country out. It was in this capacity that Özal orchestrated indelible changes in Turkish national affairs. He was a vigorous adherent of free-market principles and was determined to dismantle the government's old-fashioned command-style economy and centralization. The ensuing "economic earthquake," as it came to be known, involved transforming Turkey from a home market into an exporting nation. This entailed slashing subsidies, selling off inefficient state-owned industries, and devaluating the currency. These changes induced a period of high prices and strikes, but they were backed by the military and order prevailed. Within months, the economy posted marked improvements and the 100 percent inflation rate dropped rapidly to single digits. The military regime was pleased by Özal's performance and they installed him as deputy prime minister and minister in charge of the economy. However, he proved reluctant to install adequate controls on the financial sector, and in July 1982 a national banking scandal defrauded thousands of citizens and prompted his resignation.

Once the military finally restored democracy in April 1983, Özal felt he had acquired sufficient national stature to run for high office. To that end he founded the centrist Motherland Party and in November 1983 he became the first civilian prime minister elected in three decades. As before, Özal focused his attention on improving Turkey's economic health, revitalizing and modernizing its industry, and also pressing for closer economic ties to Europe. In 1987 he was reelected prime minister by wide margins. The following year he became the first Turkish head of state in two decades to visit Greece, long held as a traditional enemy, where he sought to improve relations. Turkey's overall economic picture did improve, but Özal's reputation became sullied by charges of corruption and nepotism. Consequently, over the next six years his popularity ratings slipped to single digits, and he thought it imprudent to run as party leader. However, the Motherland Party and its allies still enjoyed a majority in parliament. Consequently, on October 31, 1989, they elected Özal Turkey's eighth president. This is largely a ceremonial office, but it does influence the conduct of foreign affairs. However, the opposition gained rapidly in the 1991 election, Özal lost his majority, and his rival Demirel became prime minister. The two men had since parted company, and Demirel was sworn to oust Özal from the presidency, but when the opposition failed to assemble a coalition, Özal was allowed to remain in office.

From an international standpoint, Ozal performed crucial work throughout the 1990–91 Gulf War crisis.

Although Turkey is a nominally Muslim country, he allowed United States forces to use airbases to evict Iraqi dictator SADDAM HUSSEIN from Kuwait, and he also shut down Iraqi oil pipelines running through Turkey. This boycott cost billions of dollars and did little to promote his popularity at home, but Özal's international stature soared, and President George H. W. Bush lauded him as an invaluable ally in the otherwise turbulent Middle East. His services also resulted in renewed financial aid from America, Japan, and Saudi Arabia, and the Turkish military was rewarded with its pick of new equipment. Ozal did not have long to revel in his new status. He died suddenly on April 17, 1993, following a whirlwind tour of the newly freed Central Asian republics. He was succeeded in office by Demirel while TANSU CILLER became Turkey's first female prime minister. But by this time, Turkey's economic and societal landscape had been forever altered and placed on a path toward the 21st century. Özal succeeded as a singular force behind the modernization and secularization in his country.

Further Reading

Aral, Berdal. "Dispensing with Tradition? Turkish Politics and International Security: The Özal Decade, 1983–1993." *Middle Eastern Studies* 37 (January 2001): 72–88.

Dagi, Ihsan D. "Human Rights, Democratization, and the European Community in Turkish Politics: The Özal Years, 1983–1987." *Middle Eastern Studies* 37 (January 2001): 17–40.

Heper, Metia, and Sabri Sayari, eds. *Political Leaders and Democracy in Turkey.* Lanham, Md.: Lexington Books, 2002.

Sofos, Spyros S. "Reluctant Europeans? European Integration and the Transformation of Turkish Politics." *South European Society and Politics* 5 (Autumn 2000): 243–260.

White, Jenny B. *Islamist Mobilization in Turkey: A Study in Vernacular Politics.* Seattle: University of Washington Press, 2002.

P

Paisley, Ian (1926–) *Northern Ireland politician*

Ian Kyle Paisley was born on April 6, 1926, in Armagh, Northern Ireland, the son of a Baptist minister. Like his father, Paisley was intensely religious and drawn to church work. He was ordained by his father at the age of 20 and founded his own Free Presbyterian Church of Ulster. This placed him within the militant, fundamentalist wing of Protestantism, and quite at odds with the Catholic minority living in Northern Ireland. In fact, friction between the two creeds formed the basis of Northern Irish political life and ideology. Paisley soon established himself as an effective and articulate spokesman for the Protestant cause, stridently intolerant toward Catholics, and denouncing any attempt by the British government to seek accommodation with them. Locally, his views have since become either reviled or renowned as "Paisleyism." In 1962 he flew to Rome to protest the Second Vatican Council, and the following year he vehemently disparaged lowering Belfast city hall's flag following the death of Pope John XXIII. By 1969 a movement for Catholic civil rights had erupted, which occasioned violent clashes with the police and armed Protestant paramilitary units. Paisley, while never directly connected to vigilantes, did nothing to discourage them and he also attacked Prime Minister Terence O'Neill's attempted reconciliation with the Republic of Ireland. By

1970 Paisley had become politically, as well as theologically, active, and he secured a seat in the Northern Ireland parliament. He subsequently gained election to the Parliament at Westminster and the Northern Ireland Assembly, consistently and vocally opposing any or all attempts at power-sharing with Catholics. Paisley, moreover, played no favorites, and he cast a suspicious eye upon his erstwhile Protestant allies, the Unionists and Order of Orange. He has gone on record viewing these groups as vacillating and too willing to compromise with the "enemy." His dissatisfaction with other Protestants induced him to found his own party, the ultramilitant Democratic Unionist Party, in 1971.

Paisley always reveled in his role as an anti-Catholic bigot, and he built up a tremendous political following around it. Tall and imposingly built, he delivers evangelical sermons with the subtlety of a thunderstorm. His unique melding of politics and Protestantism is well received by large portions of the community, who fear assimilation if absorbed into the Irish republic. Northern Ireland, which consists of six counties separated from the rest of the island in the 1920s, has a long tradition of Protestant agitation and loyalism toward Great Britain. The Catholic minority living there bore the brunt of their abuse, principally discrimination and intimidation, and they responded by embracing the equally violent Irish Republican Army (IRA). This group vows to unite Northern

Ireland to the republic by force, a prospect that Paisley and Protestant militants vow to oppose at any cost.

Despite sectarian polarity surrounding political life in Northern Ireland, the governments of Britain and Ireland have since taken positive steps toward dialogue and reconciliation. In 1985 Paisley bitterly denounced the Anglo-Irish agreement, which established a joint secretariat staffed by both countries, and which also granted Ireland the ability to raise issues of governance. In April 1998 both sides concocted the Good Friday Agreement, whereby Northern Ireland acquired its own assembly, including Catholic representation from Sinn Féin, political wing of the IRA. Paisley and his following were naturally outraged by this development, and he was elected to the assembly as an obstructionist. He then excoriated DAVID TRIMBLE, the leading Protestant negotiator, for betraying his country. The outspoken cleric was also elected to the European Parliament representing Northern Ireland, and in 1988 he was forcibly removed for protesting an address there by Pope JOHN PAUL II.

For all their stridency, it appears that Paisley and his militants are on the wrong side of history. The Good Friday Agreement is presently stalled over the IRA's reluctance to ground its arms as promised, which, in turn, has forced the Protestants to threaten a walkout. But both sides remain pledged to continue their dialogue, which, by Northern Ireland's standards, is unprecedented. Paisley himself appears to be growing increasingly marginalized by the entire process. In May 2002 he was summoned before the Saville Inquiry, convened to investigate abuses during the "Bloody Sunday Massacre" of January 30, 1972, in which 13 civilians were killed by British troops. It was convened at the behest of Prime Minister TONY BLAIR after hearing appeals from families of the victims. Paisley initially and angrily refused to comply, but he eventually showed up after being threatened with a contempt citation. In the dock he denied any and all knowledge of the affair. All told, Paisley remains unrepentant and unapologetic for his behavior as the head of Northern Ireland's militant Protestant wing. "All I can say is that I'll not be changing," he insists. "I will go to the grave with the convictions I have."

Further Reading

Bruce, Steve. *God Save Ulster: The Religion and Politics of Paisleyism.* New York: Oxford University Press, 1986.

———. "Fundamentalism and Political Violence: The Case of Paisley and Ulster Evangelicals." *Religion* 31 (October 2001): 387–406.
Daughtrey, Mary M. "Paisleyism in Northern Ireland: Its Intellectual Antecedents, Development, and Constituency." Unpublished Ph.D. dissertation, Temple University, 2000.
Edwards, Ruth D. *The Faithful Tribe: An Intimate Portrait of the Loyal Institution.* London: HarperCollins, 2000.
Nic Craith, Mairead. *Cultural & Identity Politics in Northern Ireland.* New York: Palgrave Macmillan, 2003.
Paisley, Rhonda. *Ian Paisley, My Father.* Hants, England: Marshall Pickering, 1988.

Panday, Basdeo (1933–) *prime minister of Trinidad and Tobago*

Basdeo Panday was born on May 25, 1933, in Princes Town, Trinidad, of East Indian descent. Trinidad and Tobago form a small, two-island Caribbean republic just off the coast of Venezuela. Long a British colony, Trinidad and Tobago gained their independence by 1962, and in 1976 they adopted a British-style parliamentary system. This entails appointing a prime minister from whichever party controls the most seats or can form a viable coalition government. Despite its small size, Trinidad and Tobago are among the Caribbean's most industrialized nations, and they are also a leading oil exporter. However, roughly a quarter of the population of 1.1 million people still live at the poverty level, which exacerbates tensions between citizens of African and Indian descent. In fact, rivalry between the two has also dominated national politics, with blacks voting largely for the People's National Movement (PNM) and Indians supporting a variety of opposition parties. Trinidad and Tobago thus possess one of the world's most polarized electorates, and political deadlocks are not easily resolved.

Panday was educated locally before proceeding to Great Britain for further study. Between 1960 and 1965 he received degrees in drama from the London School of the Dramatic Arts, law from King's Inn, and economics from London University. When Panday returned home in the late 1960s he began his political career by serving as a union activist and legal adviser. Arrested several times for organizing strikes in the sugar industry, he joined the Democratic Labor Party (DLP) in 1971 to oppose the black-dominated policies of the PNM. By 1976 Panday felt compelled to establish the new United Labor Front (ULF), which attracted many former DLP members. That year the party won 10 seats in the 36-seat parliament, and Panday was installed as opposition leader. He concurrently served as president of the sugar union, where he remained until 1995. In 1986, in an attempt to wrest more votes from the PNM, Panday merged his party with others to form the new National Alliance for Reconstruction (NAR), and he gained appointment as external affairs minister. Internal tensions then resulted in his expulsion, but Panday went on to found yet another group, the United National Congress (UNC), whereby he reclaimed his role as opposition leader. The turning point in his career happened during elections held in November 1995, when the UNC finally won enough seats to form a coalition government. Thus Panday became Trinidad and Tobago's first prime minister of Indian descent.

Ever since taking office, the Panday administration has been preoccupied with matters pertaining to race. Blacks accused his regime of granting positions and favors exclusively to the Indian community at their expense. The prime minister, however, countered with appeals for national unity and pledges that his is a government of all the people. The other major issue remains the economy, which was on the upswing when he took power and continues to grow. To maintain this favorable outlook, Panday advocated a consensus in decision making, and a closer partnership between government, business, and labor. He also intends to diversify agriculture, increase oil production, and lower corporate taxes to stimulate additional growth. Another major problem that has been thrust on the government is that of drug interdiction. As offshore islands, Trinidad and Tobago are ideal transhipment points for smuggling illegal substances to the United States, and that government has offered Panday additional law enforcement resources to counter criminal activity. Panday has also been active in promoting the Caribbean Community (CARICOM), which supports regional free trade, and the Association of Caribbean States, which is headquartered on Trinidad. Through all these expedients, especially the influx of energy revenues, he hopes to raise the standard of living on the islands to that of neighboring Barbados.

Panday was easily reelected to a second term on December 11, 2000, with a slight majority of one seat in parliament. However, throughout his second term, his administration was tainted by allegations of corruption and graft. Political support within the UNC party began to wane, so Panday called for new elections in October 2001, four years ahead of schedule, to shore up his support. However, the unexpected result was an 18 to 18 seat tie between the UNC and PNM! The constitution mandates that, in the event of a draw, the president of Trinidad and Tobago would end the impasse by selecting the new prime minister. Prior to this move, both Panday and his adversary, Patrick Manning, agreed to honor whomever was selected. However, President Arthur Robinson, an old political adversary of Panday, chose Manning to succeed him. An enraged Panday, despite his previous pledge, cried foul and set up an "alternative" government. The impasse has continued into the spring of 2002, with Manning sworn in but unable to convene parliament because Panday refuses to appoint a speaker of the house. Panday has also demanded new presidential elections in July. The continuing rivalry between African and Indian communities on Trinidad and Tobago appears as intractable as ever, with deleterious results for both.

Further Reading

Cudjoe, Selwyn R. *Basdeo Panday and the Politics of Race.* Wellesley, Mass.: Calaoux, 1997.

Meighoo, Kirk P. "Politics in Trinidad and Tobago, 1956–2000: Towards an Understanding of Politics in a 'Half-Mark' Society." Unpublished Ph.D. dissertation, University of Hull, 2000.

Mungsinghe, Viranjini. *Callaloo or Tossed Salad? East Indians and Cultural Politics of Identity in Trinidad.* Ithaca, N.Y.: Cornell University Press, 2001.

Ramadar, Frankie B. *Race Relations in Trinbago: Afro and Indo-Trinbagonians and Basdeo Panday.* Brooklyn, N.Y.: Caribbean Diaspora Press, 1997.

Regis, Louis. *The Political Calypso: True Opposition in Trinidad and Tobago, 1962–1987.* Gainesville: University Press of Florida, 1999.

Walker, Judith Ann. *Development Administration in the Caribbean: Independent Jamaica and Trinidad and Tobago.* New York: Palgrave, 2002.

Panic, Milan (1929–) *prime minister of Yugoslavia*

Milan Panic was born on December 20, 1929, in Belgrade, Yugoslavia, the son of Serbian parents. His father died during his infancy and he worked from an early age to support his family. During World War II he served as a courier for the anti-Nazi resistance and was particularly thrilled by the sight of American aircraft bombing German positions in Belgrade. But by 1945 Yugoslavia had come under the domination of Marshal Josip Broz Tito, who imposed a Communist dictatorship upon the six republics comprising that country. Panic, restive under the restraints of communism, obtained his bachelor's degree from the University of Belgrade in 1955, and he managed to escape to Germany the following year. There he completed a graduate degree in science at the University of Heidelberg, and finally emigrated to the United States in 1956. Having settled in Southern California, Panic supported himself by working at various chemical companies while also pursuing a graduate degree at the University of Southern California. On December 7, 1960, he felt emboldened to start his own company, the International Chemical and Nuclear Corporation (ICN) with only $200 and a washing machine rigged as a centrifuge in his garage. What followed was an American success story.

An incredibly driven individual, Panic soon established ICN as one of the nation's leading chemical manufacturers. He pioneered new drugs for various diseases while continually plowing the profits back to acquire competing interests. By 1991 he had purchased 21 companies valued at $170 million. Moreover, ICN now employed over 6,000 people, with annual sales of half a billion dollars. Once the cold war ended, Panic orchestrated ICN's global reach by founding subsidiary offices in countries previously behind the Iron Curtain. Foremost among these was a joint partnership with Galenika, Yugoslavia's largest drug manufacturer. The merger was entirely successful, highly profitable—and sweet revenge for this former refugee from communism. His efforts were particularly appreciated because Yugoslavia (now consisting of only Serbia and Montenegro) was currently the subject of broad-based United Nations economic sanctions. These sanctions stemmed from a Serbian-led war of aggression against neighboring Croat and Muslim states, especially Bosnia-Herzegovina, which commenced in April 1992. However, to forestall further sanctions and possibly have them lifted, Serbian president SLOBODAN MILOŠEVIĆ and Yugoslavian president Dobrica Cosic formally invited expatriate Panic to return home and serve as prime minister of Yugoslavia. Panic, who never turned down a challenge, was eager to

leave a mark on his homeland and, after being assured by President George H. W. Bush that his American citizenship would not be compromised, he was sworn into office on July 14, 1992. "This is a peace mission. I know I am going on a pirate ship," he insisted, "but if I become captain the pirate ship will be turned into a peace ship."

Many diplomats looked upon Milan as a face-saving stooge for Milošević and other Serbian nationalists. By the summer of 1992 the new Balkan war had killed an estimated 50,000 people and created 1.5 million refugees. However, Panic quickly asserted his independence from Milošević and roundly condemned Serbian actions. This won him plaudits from the Western press, but exerted no influence on events closer to home. However, he was sincere in his efforts to have a cease-fire declared in Bosnia-Herzegovina, followed by the prompt withdrawal of Serbian forces fighting there. "I have no tolerance for the old Yugoslavia," he told reporters. "My responsibility to the Yugoslav people is do what I can do best: bring democracy here, put peace together, and start the economic recovery." Such rhetoric simply rebounded off Milošević and his henchmen, who continued escalating attempts to carve out a "Greater Serbia" at the expense of neighboring states. At length Panic decided he had no recourse but to challenge Milošević for the presidency of Serbia in December 1992. He campaigned vigorously on a platform to end the war and economic sanctions against Serbia. However, because Milošević enjoyed complete control of state media and the entire electoral process, the result proved an exercise in futility. Milošević was declared the winner by 20 points, at which juncture the federal parliament overwhelmingly passed a no-confidence measure against Panic. He consequently resigned on December 20, 1992, after six months as prime minister, concluding one of the more quixotic episodes of the ongoing Balkan tragedy.

Panic returned to the United States to resume his business operations. His tenure at the helm of ICN proved equally controversial, and in 1998 the Securities and Exchange Commission investigated him over trading violations involving company stock. By June 2002 irate shareholders had grown disenchanted enough to take control of the board of directors and demand his resignation. Panic then decided to voluntarily step down as chairman and chief executive after 40 years of leadership. "There are better things to do than fight, and I am 72," Panic conceded. "It's time for me to consider doing something else."

Further Reading

Andrejevich, M. "The Radicalization of Serbian Politics." *RFE/RL Research Report* 2 (March 26, 1993): 14–24.

Bellamy, Alex J. *Kosovo and International Society.* New York: Palgrave, 2002.

Colevic, Ivan. *Politics of Identity in Serbia.* New York: New York University Press, 2002.

Malesevic, Sinsia. *Ideology, Legitimacy, and the New State: Yugoslavia, Serbia, and Croatia.* Portland, Oreg.: Frank Cass, 2002.

Zolo, Danilo. *War, Law, and Global Order.* New York: Continuum, 2002.

Papandreou, Andreas (1919–1996)
prime minister of Greece

Andreas Georgios Papandreou was born on February 5, 1919, on the island of Chios, Greece, the son of a prominent liberal politician and future prime minister. He studied law at the University of Athens in 1936, but his vocal opposition to the dictatorship of General Ioannis Metaxas led to his arrest and exile to the United States. There Papandreou continued his education, receiving his Ph.D. from Harvard University, and he was also commissioned an officer in the U.S. Navy. After World War II Papandreou returned to academia and taught variously at the University of Minnesota, Northwestern University, and the University of California, Berkeley, for two decades. It was during this period that his intellectual outlook acquired a decidedly "leftist" slant, and he espoused great sympathy toward socialist policies. In 1959 he returned to Greece to serve as chairman of the Center of Economic Research, and he renewed his Greek citizenship. In 1962 he commenced his political career by being elected a deputy for the Center Union Party, of which his father, George Papandreou, was head. When his father became prime minister in 1964, Papandreou gained appointment as minister to the prime minister. However, in April 1967 the Greek military overthrew the regime and he was arrested. An international campaign by fellow academics resulted in his release soon after, and Papandreou resumed his teaching career abroad in Stockholm, Sweden, and Toronto, Canada. He nonetheless stridently denounced the military regime and founded the Panhellenic Liberation Movement (PAK) in exile as a protest.

Papandreou returned to Greece in 1973 after the junta had fallen, and he set about founding a new political party, the Panhellenic Socialist Movement (PASOK) with himself as chairman. This was the first socialist party in Greek history and it gained 15 seats during elections held in November 1974. The next round of elections in November 1977 confirmed its growing appeal, and PASOK gained additional seats to emerge as principal opposition to the New Democratic Party. Papandreou also served as a populist opponent of the establishment and campaigned endlessly for change. His message apparently resonated with voters, and, on October 18, 1981, PASOK swept the parliament, taking 173 seats for an outright majority. On October 21, 1981, Papandreou was sworn in as the country's first avowedly socialist prime minister.

Previously, Papandreou had campaigned on an anti-American, anti–NATO platform, and pledged to rid the nation of all foreign military facilities. However, once in office he mitigated his stance, if not his rhetoric, and allowed the Americans to renegotiate their leases for additional money. He was also highly angered by the failure of NATO to stop Turkey's takeover of the island of Cyprus in 1974, especially as Greece and Turkey are both members of the same military alliance. He therefore struck out on his own diplomatically, and called for creation of a "nuclear-free zone" in the Balkans and northern Europe. This placed him at odds with prevailing NATO strategy, and Papandreou further ruffled members' feathers by seeking better relations with the Soviet Union. But PASOK's biggest changes transpired on the domestic scene. Papandreou championed women's rights, worker's rights, and greater benefits within a redefined welfare state. His success can be gauged by the election of 1985, when he was returned to power with increased margins. However, his popularity tumbled in the wake of a much-publicized divorce and dalliance with a former airline stewardess half his age. He was further hurt by a declining economy and a long-standing financial scandal that forced three of his ministers to resign. Apparently, Papandreou's populism and anti-Americanism were wearing thin with the polity, for on June 18, 1989, they turned PASOK out of office altogether.

In 1991 Papandreou faced serious embezzlement charges over his dealings with Greek-American banker George Koskotas and the Bank of Crete. However, he was acquitted the following year and, although suffering from intermittent health problems, determined to run again for high office. Typically, he accused the New

Democratic Party of orchestrating his demise though false charges, and he demanded new elections. When these transpired in October 1993 Greek voters handed PASOK another landslide victory. Papandreou's third term in office proved unspectacular and barely productive, as he remained dogged by heart problems. He nevertheless found the time to engage in some scandal-making headlines when he appointed his young mistress to be chief of staff. But by January 1996 Papandreou's health had declined precipitously, and he resigned from office. The flamboyant leader, reviled in the United States as the "bad boy of NATO," died on June 23, 1996. He was among the most controversial and charismatic Greek politicians of his day, and a recognized scholar. PASOK fortunes were then handed to the former industry minister, COSTAS SIMITIS.

Further Reading

Bantimaroudis, Philemon. "Western Media Portrayals vs. Historical Assessments: The Framing of Andreas Papandreou." Unpublished Ph.D. dissertation, University of Texas, Austin, 1999.

Close, David. *Greece since 1945: Politics, Economy, and Society.* New York: Longman, 2002.

Kalaitzidis, Akis, and Nikolaos Zaharidas. "Papandreou's NATO Policy: Continuity or Change?" *Journal of the Hellenic Diaspora* 23, no. 1 (1997): 105–116.

Kazamias, A. "The Quest for Modernization in Greek Foreign Policy and Its Limitations." *Mediterranean Politics* 2 (Fall 1997): 71–94.

Kitroeff, Alexander. "Andreas G. Papandreou: A Brief Political Biography." *Journal of Hellenic Diaspora* 23, no. 1 (1997): 7–32.

Pastrana, Andrés (1954–) *president of Colombia*

Andrés Pastrana Arango was born in Bogotá, Colombia, on August 17, 1954, the son of Misael Pastrana, a former president. Colombia gained independence from Spain in 1819, and since then its national politics have been dominated by either the Liberal Party (LP) or the Conservative Party (PC). The nation enjoys good natural resources and a relatively advanced economy that have endowed it with one of Latin's America's highest standards of living. However, since the 1970s Colombia's stability and national viability have been upended by the twin specters of guerrillas and drug lords. Two communist-inspired groups, the Revolutionary Armed Forces of Colombia (FARC) and the smaller but equally vicious National Liberation Army (ELN) have waged a ruthless, internecine bush war that has claimed 60,000 lives. Despite several concerted military campaigns against them and millions of dollars in military assistance from the United States, the fighting shows no sign of abatement. Equally ominous is the rise of various drug cartels trafficking in illegal cocaine. Colombia enjoys the dubious distinction of being the world's largest producer of coca leaves, the raw material from which cocaine is manufactured and exported abroad, principally to the United States. The cartels themselves are highly organized, utterly ruthless, and woven deeply into the national political and social fabric. Their great wealth—an estimated $4 billion per year—enables them to bribe cooperating officials, while their firepower enables them to assassinate others. Not infrequently, the guerrillas offer the cartels protection in exchange for money and thus the two evils sustain each other. Colombia remains a nation under siege and teetering on the brink of chaos.

As a member of Colombia's elite ruling class, Pastrana was highly educated at private schools before attending the Colegio San Carlos de Bogotá and the Colegio Mayor Nuestra Señora del Rosario Law School. In 1978 Pastrana also received an advanced degree from the Harvard University Center for International Affairs. Once home, he began a high-profile career in national media and cohosted several popular television news shows. In 1988 he translated his public reputation into a viable political career by being elected to the Bogotá city council. That year he was also kidnapped by the Medellín drug cartel for ransom, but he eventually escaped. Afterward Pastrana became a vocal proponent for tough action against the drug lords, and he gained election as Bogotá's mayor. In 1991 he followed up his success by gaining election to the Senate and becoming head of the PC, and three years later Pastrana was tapped to serve as the PC presidential candidate. He narrowly lost to PL candidate ERNESTO SAMPER, and afterwards released tapes that linked Samper to the drug lords. In 1998 Pastrana again ran for president against PL candidate Horacio Serpa and a noted independent, Noemí Sanín. The PC party finished a close second in the first round of voting, but it clinched the election in a runoff on June 19, 1998. Pastrana was then sworn in as the first conservative president in more than a decade.

Pastrana had campaigned on the theme of cracking down on drugs and securing a negotiated peace with the guerrillas. "We must all unite around the supreme objectives of reaching peace, reactivating the economy, and achieving social justice," he promised. Accordingly, he met with the leaders of both movements in 1998 and established a demilitarized jungle enclave for both movements in exchange for a cease-fire. For the first time in 30 years the guns fell silent, if only temporarily. That October Pastrana also became the first Colombian president to visit the United States in 23 years and he conferred with President BILL CLINTON over increased aid to combat drugs. The result was a $280 million package to assist poor Colombian farmers to switch from coca production to other crops. Another area of concern was the national economy, which was in a deep recession.

Despite the best of intentions, Pastrana enjoyed no success in achieving his objectives. The drug trade continues to flourish, the economy remains stalled, and the guerrillas have since relaunched their violent campaign against the government. On March 4, 2002, they killed Martha Catalina Daniels, a noted senator, at which point Pastrana called off the truce and all peace talks. The attackers, he noted, "will not intimidate us with their cruel acts and their demented behavior." Again, the United States stepped in with additional money and advisers, but the guerrillas remained deeply rooted in the countryside, sheltered by impoverished peasants. Nonetheless, their sanctuary has been revoked and regular units of the Colombian military now comb the Switzerland-sized regions for enemy activity. Still, the guerrillas still manage to strike back hard. On March 19, 2002, they assassinated Archbishop Duarte Cancino outside his church after a wedding. The Colombian public, weary of such excesses and fed up by lack of success, booed Pastrana during the archbishop's funeral services. "We will not rest until we find and punish the material and intellectual authors of this atrocious crime against the life and faith of Colombia," he declared. Forbidden by the constitution to seek a second term, the beleaguered president is scheduled to leave office in August 2002.

Further Reading

Berquist, Charles W. *Violence in Colombia, 1990–2000: Waging War and Negotiating Peace.* Wilmington, Del.: SR Books, 2001.

Hoskin, Gary, and Gabriel Murillo. "Colombia's Perpetual Quest for Peace." *Journal of Democracy* 12 (April 2001): 32–45.

Richani, Nazih. *Systems of Violence: The Political Economy of War and Peace in Colombia.* Albany: State University of New York Press, 2002.

Ruiz, Bert. *The Colombian Civil War.* Jefferson, N.C.: McFarland, 2001.

Safford, Frank, and Marco Palacios. *Colombia: Fragmented Land, Divided Society.* Oxford: Oxford University Press, 2001.

Sanchez, Gonzalo, and Donny Meertens. *Bandits, Peasants, and Politics: The Case of 'La Violencia' in Colombia.* Austin: University of Texas Press, 2001.

Patasse, Ange-Félix (ca. 1937–) *president of the Central African Republic*

Ange-Félix Patasse was born in Paoua, in the northwestern part of the French colony of Ubangi-Shari, around 1937. This is a landlocked region of Central Africa, bounded by Chad to the north, the two Congos to the south, Sudan to the east and Cameroon to the west. Its population of 3.5 million people is divided up among some 60 different ethnic and linguistic groups, but the two most important groupings are the Sara to the north and the Yakoma to the south. In 1960 Ubangi-Shari achieved its independence from France and was renamed the Central African Republic (CAR). However, it still shares close cultural and economic ties to France, and French remains the official language of government. CAR's first president, David Dacko, established one-party rule under his Mouvement d'évolution sociale de l'Afrique, (MESAN) but the country endured a spate of coups and countercoups over the next 30 years. Between 1976 and 1979, sitting president Jean-Bedel Bokassa declared himself emperor and renamed his domain the Central African Empire. Consequently, it was not until 1981 that a new constitution was approved that allowed for multiparty democracy, which in practice turned out to be a sham. That year a leading general, André Kolingba, gained election to the presidency, where he remained until 1993. In 1993, the first really democratic elections transpired and civilian rule was finally restored.

Patasse, a member of the Sara group, was educated locally and went on to study at the Higher School of Tropical Agriculture in Paris, France. From 1959 to 1965 he then worked in the CAR Department of

Agriculture before assuming various agricultural and developmental positions within the government. In 1976 Bokassa briefly appointed him prime minister before declaring himself emperor, and Patasse was briefly jailed in 1979 before the republic was restored with French assistance. The following year he became a presidential candidate under the Mouvement pour la Libération du Peuple Centrafricaine (MPLC) against Dacko and lost with a respectable 38.1 percent of votes cast. In 1981 Dacko was overthrown by Kolingba, and Patasse was accused of plotting a coup against him. He spent the next 10 years exiled in Togo and did not return home until 1992, when foreign pressure forced the holding of multiparty elections. His opponents were Dacko, Kolingba, and seven other minor candidates. In September 1993 Patasse was elected to high office by 52.47 percent of the vote and was sworn in the following October.

Patasse inherited a nation dispirited by years of oppression and misrule. The countryside lay in ruins, the schools had been closed for several years, and the deeply entrenched civil service was on strike over back wages owed. His first priority thus became rebuilding the CAR's economy and communications infrastructure to afford some semblance of normalcy. However, Patasse has been beset by ingrained corruption, made especially evident when a French associate was arrested for absconding with 75 million francs in an embarrassing banking scandal. Over the ensuing decade, the civil service has been both strident and militant in demanding—and generally receiving—more and better wages. This proved another staggering liability for the CAR to shoulder as an estimated 95 percent of its annual income is spent on civil servants. But central to all economic reforms is the CAR's continuing reliance upon France for funds and technical assistance. For many years the French government maintained a sizable military garrison as a hedge against Libyan aggression in Chad, but as that threat dissipated, so too did the troops. Of late, Patasse has been hard-pressed to secure additional funding and help from France and Europe, pending reform of the civil service, the agricultural sector, and greater emphasis on privatization to satiate the requirements of the International Monetary Fund (IMF) and World Bank.

By far, the single greatest obstacle to peace and prosperity in the Central African Republic is the military. A northern Sara, Patasse is on uneasy terms with his army, which is overwhelmingly recruited from southern Yakoma tribesmen. This has resulted in repeated coup attempts and mutinies over the years that he has served in office. As late as May 28, 2001, when a group of disgruntled soldiers fired on the presidential palace, the CAR has remained in turmoil and unable to focus its energies on more pressing problems. Kolingba, a former president and leading military figure, apparently backed the coup through the simple expedient of seeking to rule again. The rebellion was eventually crushed by troops loyal to Patasse, but numerous government officials, including former army chief François Bozize and former defense minister Jean-Jacques Demafouth, were arrested and put on trial in February 2002. The basic source of instability, beyond ethnic rivalry, is lack of pay owing, again, to the large civil service that readily consumes most available funding. Until a solution is created to either integrate the armed forces with other groups or establish better funding procedures to keep them paid, the military remains a wild card in the CAR's quest for stability and prosperity.

Further Reading

Derriennic, Yann, and Amy Pine. *Trip Report for the Central African Republic.* Cambridge, Mass.: Abt Associates, 1994.

Giles-Vernick, Tamara. *Cutting the Vines of the Past: Environmental Histories of the Central African Rain Forest.* Charlottesville: University Press of Virginia, 2002.

Karan, Mark E. *The Dynamics of the Sango Language Spread.* Dallas, Tex.: SIL International, 2001.

Madison, Wayne. *Genocide and Covert Operations in Africa, 1993–1999.* Lewiston, N.Y.: Edwin Mellen Press, 1999.

Webb, Raymond P. "State Politics in the Central African Republic: An Original Study." Unpublished Ph.D. dissertation, University of Wisconsin, Madison, 1990.

Patterson, Percival James (1935–) *prime minister of Jamaica*

Percival James Noel Patterson was born in St. Andrew, Jamaica, on April 10, 1935, the son of a farmer. His homeland is the Caribbean's third-largest island, nestled 90 miles south of Cuba and 100 miles west of Haiti. Its inhabitants are largely African, descended from slaves brought in to work the sugar fields. Though originally colonized by the Spanish, Jamaica became a British colony in 1655 and did not acquire independence for nearly three centuries, until 1962. Since then it has functioned under a British-style parliamentary system, with a bicameral legislature and a prime minister appointed from the party with the majority in power. Jamaican politics traditionally oscillate between the conservative-leaning Jamaica Labour Party (JPL) and the left-leaning People's National Party (PNP) and has been dominated by several strong, charismatic personalities. The most notable among these was MICHAEL MANLEY, son of Norman Manley, the island's first prime minister. His loss of the 1980 election ushered in almost nine years of conservative rule and forms the backdrop for which "P. J." Patterson rose to national prominence.

Patterson completed his primary education near home and won a scholarship to attend Calabar High School, where he excelled in academics. He subsequently studied English at the University of the West Indies and received his bachelor's degree in 1958. That year he became politically active by joining the PNP as a party organizer. In 1960, however, he gained admittance to the prestigious London School of Economics, where he studied law and political science. Patterson graduated in 1963 and returned to Jamaica, where he found work within the PNP as a member of various councils. Thereafter he enjoyed a long and distinguished climb up the party hierarchy. In 1970 he was elected to the House of Representatives and also served as PNP vice president, which further heightened his national stature. It was while in this office that he caught the attention of Prime Minister MICHAEL MANLEY, who appointed him to various ministerial positions, including those of industry and tourism and vice prime minister. In 1980 Jamaicans rejected the left-wing politics and stance of Manley and the PNP, choosing instead Edward Seaga of the JLP. Patterson consequently lost his seat in parliament and briefly resumed his legal career before eventually being reelected and emerging as opposition leader. When Manley recaptured the prime minister's office in 1989, Patterson again resumed his role as vice prime minister, although the outbreak of a major scandal, in which he was not personally involved, prompted his resignation in 1991. Nonetheless, when poor health forced Manley himself from office in March 1992, Patterson was elected by the party to succeed him. He was then the nation's first prime minister whose parents were both of African descent.

Patterson came to power at a time when Jamaica was undergoing severe economic distress. Inflation was 73 percent, unemployment was rising, and the gross national product sputtered. He responded by enacting a much-needed infrastructural overhaul to better integrate Jamaica into the world economy. Despite his socialist beliefs, free-market economics and privatization became the order of the day. Many inefficient state-owned and state-run industries, such as the national airline, were put up for sale, and with good effect. By 1993 inflation had dropped to only 17 percent, the economy showed signs of reviving, and Patterson saw fit to capitalize on his success by calling for early elections. "With creativity, discipline, determination, and hard work," he preached, "we will enter the 21st century as a strong nation." On March 30, 1993, Patterson received his largest margin ever and returned to power with additional seats in parliament. It was an impressive performance from a politician who, unlike the charismatic Manley and others before him, was a decidedly low-key and soft-spoken character.

Over the next four years Patterson continued focusing on the economy, while simultaneously confronting two other pressing issues: violence and drugs. Jamaica has a long and turbulent history of street fighting in association with politics, and Patterson hired more police, instituted curfews, and cracked down on hooliganism. However, he enjoyed less success in combating illegal drugs, which are pervasive and whose money has corrupted large parts of Jamaican society. It was not until May 1997 that an agreement was reached with the United States to allow its federal agents to pursue known smugglers on Jamaican soil. Furthermore, in October 2000 it was revealed that several police officers had bugged Patterson's phone in an attempt to thwart his enforcement efforts, and the opposition JLP has called for Scotland Yard to head any investigation. However, Patterson continued as an efficient technocrat, and, on December 18, 1997, he was returned to power with 56 percent of votes cast. He thus became the first Jamaican prime minister to serve three consecutive terms. The 66-year-old Patterson ran for a fourth term in October 2002, although the PNP was behind in the polls. However, on October 17, 2002, the PLP was resoundingly returned to power, capturing 35 seats in the 60-seat parliament. Patterson thus began his record fourth consecutive term as prime minister. "The message that we must derive," he declared to cheering supporters, "is that all of us must work in unity in order to build a better Jamaica."

Further Reading

Bertram, Arnold. *P. J. Patterson: A Mission to Perform.* Kingston, Jamaica: AB Associates and Supreme Printers and Publishers, 1995.

Dunn, Leith L., and Alicia Mondesire. *Poverty and Political Coherence: The Case of Jamaica.* Ottawa: North-South Institute, 2002.

Edie, Carlene J. *Democracy by Default: Dependency and Clientelism in Jamaica.* Boulder, Colo.: Lynne Rienner Publishers, 1991.

Hewan, Clinton G. *Jamaica and the United States Caribbean Initiative: Showpiece or Failure?* New York: Peter Lang, 1994.

King, Stephan A., Barry T. Bays, and Rene P. Foster. *Reggae, Rastafari, and the Rhetoric of Social Control.* Jackson: University Press of Mississippi, 2002.

Munroe, Trevor. *Renewing Democracy into the Millennium: The Jamaican Experience in Perspective.* Kingston, Jamaica: University of the West Indies Press, 1999.

Waller, Judith Ann. *Development Administration in the Caribbean: Independent Jamaica and Trinidad and Tobago.* New York: Palgrave, 2002.

Paz Zamora, Jaime (1939–) *president of Bolivia*

Jaime Paz Zamora was born on April 15, 1939, in Cochabamba, Bolivia, the son of an army general. He received a Catholic upbringing and earned a degree in philosophy from the seminary of Villa Allende in Córdoba, Argentina. Intent upon joining the clergy, Paz Zamora later studied at the Catholic University in Louvain, Belgium. He subsequently returned home sometime in the mid-1960s to teach sociology at San Andreas University in La Paz, and he also became politically active by joining the Christian Democratic Party. However, left-wing politics, long suppressed, were currently in vogue throughout Latin America, and Paz Zamora shifted allegiance to the newly founded Movement of the Revolutionary Left (MIR) around 1971. This was a radical organization far to the left of more mainstream Marxist parties, and it immediately drew the ire of the military regime under General HUGO BANZER. MIR members were summarily rounded up and persecuted, while Paz Zamora took his political activism underground. Luck deserted him in 1974 when he was caught and imprisoned. Bolivia at this time was rocked by economic dislocation and social upheavals, and Paz Zamora, once released from prison in 1978, began evolving into a national figure. Upon his urging, MIR became a coalition partner with the more moderate Democratic and Popular Union (UDP), and he also stood as its candidate for the vice presidency. In June 1980 he was apparently elected vice president along with Hernán Siles Suazo of the National Revolutionary Movement (MNR), who became president. But the military forbade either from taking office. In fact, their politics were viewed as too left of center to be tolerated, and that year Paz Zamora miraculously survived a mysterious plane crash that killed several leading MIR figures.

By October 1982 international pressure forced the military to surrender power, and the authorities finally recognized Siles Suazo and Paz Zamora as the legitimate winners of 1980. Fortunately, Paz Zamora had since eschewed his fiery leftist rhetoric in favor of more centrist policies and he remained in office until December 1984. Thereafter, Paz Zamora resigned in order to stand for the June 1985 presidential elections. He subsequently placed third and lost to his uncle, Víctor Paz Estenssoro of the MNR. Thereafter he served many years as head of opposition forces in parliament. The turning point in Paz Zamora's political fortunes happened during the presidential elections of May 1989. Once again he finished third with 20 percent of the votes. But, because no candidate finished with a majority of votes, the Bolivian constitution mandates that the national assembly must chose the executive. Paz Zamora then struck up an unlikely alliance with General Banzer of the far-right Democratic National Action Party (AND), and he was elected president at the head of a right-left coalition on August 6, 1989. "I will fight against the threat from drug trafficking, while preserving the sovereignty, development, and well-being of our people," he promised. Significantly, Paz Zamora's ascent was only made possible by his denunciation of his past radical ideology and his embrace of free-market liberalism. In return, AND members were granted several important ministries within the administration.

Paz Zamora inherited a nation on the verge of economic collapse. He needed to implement dramatic reforms, and quickly. He thereupon attracted foreign investment in the country's strategic mining industry and privatized inefficient state-owned corporations like the national airline. The economy eventually rebounded, but his austerity measures increased the suffering of poor households that comprise the majority of the population. Paz Zamora also had to make difficult choices regarding ongoing suppression of the coca trade. The United States applied great economic and diplomatic pressure on Bolivia to allow U.S. Special Forces to come in and train the Bolivian military for crop eradication. The president did so only reluctantly, fearing that this move would be interpreted as a sellout of national sovereignty. The arrival of U.S. personnel was, in fact, highly unpopular in public and political circles, so much so that, when finished with their task, they were asked to leave by the Bolivian military. Paz Zamora then completed his four years in office without further controversy. He had partially restored Bolivia's economy back to solvency, although amid charges from the left wing that he had abandoned his principles. Popular perceptions were even less flattering: public opinion held that the MIR/AND coalition facilitated the biggest rise of drug-related corruption in Bolivia's history. Consequently, during the 1993 elections the MIR/AND coalition was defeated by an opposition candidate, Sanchez de Lozada of the MNR.

Though out of high office, Paz Zamora sought to maintain a high international profile. In 1993 he served as a member of the international peace commission sent to investigate Indian unrest in Chiapas, Mexico. However, Bolivia's national malaise continued multiplying, with high unemployment and rising crime becoming familiar fixtures of everyday life. In June 2002 Paz Zamora staked out his position as the MIR candidate in general elections that year but, a month before the contest, the former executive polled only a distant third. Bolivia still enjoys the dubious distinction of being Latin America's poorest nation.

Further Reading

Conaghan, Catherine M. *Democracy That Matters: The Search for Authenticity, Legitimacy, and Civic Competence in the Andes.* Notre Dame, Ind.: Notre Dame University Press, 1994.

———. *Unsettling Statecraft: Democracy and Neoliberalism in the Central Andes.* Pittsburgh: University of Pittsburgh Press, 1994.

Crabtree, John, and Laurence Whitehead. *Towards Democratic Viability: The Bolivian Experience.* New York: Palgrave, 2001.

Dunkerly, James. *Political Transition and Economic Stabilization: Bolivia, 1982–1989.* London: University of London, 1990.

Urioste, Fernandez de Cordova, Miguel. *Bolivia: Reform and Resistance in the Countryside (1982–2000).* London: University of London, 2001.

Peres, Shimon (1923–   ) *prime minister of Israel*
Shimon Persky was born on August 21, 1923, in Volozhin, Poland, and his family emigrated to the British-controlled mandate of Palestine in 1931. There he legally changed his name to Peres and studied at the Ben-Shemen agricultural school. Peres became active in Jewish underground movements, intent upon resurrecting the long-lost state of Israel. He rose to a prominent position in the Hagganah, the clandestine militia, and he came to the attention of David Ben-Gurion, who became his political mentor. When the war for Israeli independence broke out in 1948, Ben-Gurion tasked Peres with purchasing arms for the embryonic Israeli Defense Force (IDF). By 1949 he was serving as director of the Defense Ministry's procurement division, with important links to the United States and France. Peres performed capably, and, by 1953, he was director-general of the Defense Ministry. His most important work was in forging close links with the French military establishment and obtaining highly sophisticated weapons. This factor proved essential for obtaining a quick victory over Egyptian forces in the 1956 Sinai campaign. He subsequently laid the groundwork for Israel's nuclear weapons industry by obtaining a French nuclear reactor. By this time Peres enjoyed a reputation as a highly efficient technocrat and, in 1959, he was elected to the Knesset (parliament) as a member of the left-wing Mapai faction.

Over the next four decades, Peres successfully navigated the treacherous waters of Israeli politics, although he never won a single national election. Internecine party wrangling brought him to within striking distance of Labor Party leadership in 1974, but he narrowly lost to his long-standing rival YITZHAK RABIN. Thereafter, Rabin appointed him minister of defense, and Peres proved instrumental in overhauling the Israeli military after the near-calamitous 1973 Yom Kippur War. By 1977 a major corner was turned in Israeli politics, when

Labor lost power for the first time in 29 years to the conservative Likud Party. Peres subsequently replaced Rabin as party head, and he served as opposition leader to Menachem Begin's policies, especially the ill-fated 1982 invasion of southern Lebanon. Elections held two years later proved something of a national stalemate, and a power-sharing agreement was arranged between Labor and Likud: thereafter, Peres would serve as prime minister for two years at which point the post rotated to Yitzhak Shamir. It was during his first tenure as prime minister that Peres gained renown—or notoriety—for his willingness to reach a meaningful peace agreement with the Palestinians. This entailed high-level contacts with Israel's nemesis, YASSER ARAFAT of the Palestine Liberation Organization (PLO), and discussion of a possible Palestinian homeland on the West Bank. By 1992 Peres had lost the party's mantle to Rabin again, who went on to become prime minister. But Peres retained his forceful presence as a behind-the-scenes negotiator and, in 1993, his efforts culminated in the Oslo Peace Accord. For these efforts Peres, Rabin, and Arafat shared the Nobel Peace Prize in 1994.

The prospects of Middle Eastern peace was abruptly shattered on November 4, 1995, when Rabin was assassinated by an Israeli extremist. Peres succeeded him as prime minister, pledging to continue dialogue with the Palestinians. However, a spate of suicide bombings increased apprehensions, and in February 1996, Peres was narrowly defeated by Likud candidate BINYAMIN NETANYAHU, who refused to trade land for peace. This defeat also cost Peres his party leadership and he was replaced by EHUD BARAK, who defeated Netanyahu in 1999. Worse, in July 2001 he lost a contest for the presidency, a largely ceremonial post, to relative newcomer MOSHE KATSAV. Peres nonetheless continued as a prominent elder statesman and opposition leader. When Barak subsequently lost to hard-liner ARIEL SHARON in February 2002, a national unity government was formed with Peres serving as foreign minister. Again he voiced his determination to negotiate with Arafat and did not discount the possibility of an eventual Palestinian state—something Likud is sworn to prevent. As such, he is uniquely positioned to be criticized on the left for being part of a right-wing government, while lambasted by the right for being perceived as soft on terrorism. But while Peres disagrees with Sharon over national peace policy, he prefers not to topple the government by leaving it and elects to keep his high national profile.

Peres maintains that it is better to remain in the government and attempt to influence its policy than "to sit in parliament and make speeches." His opinion apparently carries some weight. On June 24, 2002, when the government presented him with a proposed fence map that claimed a fifth of the West Bank territories, he threatened to resign immediately if it were adopted. It was quickly scuttled. Peres insisted "there is no need to declare a security zone which includes 22 percent of the West Bank—it is clear that this is a political change, a wink toward a political change, in contravention of all existing agreements." Peres remains the longest-serving member of the Israeli Knesset and a major player in the ongoing Middle East peace process.

Further Reading

Golan, Matti. *Shimon Peres: A Biography.* New York: St. Martin's Press, 1982.

Keren, Michael. *Professionals against Populism: The Peres Government and Democracy.* Albany: State University of New York Press, 1995.

Peres, Shimon. *Battling for Peace: A Memoir.* New York: Random House, 1995.

———. *For the Future of Israel.* Baltimore, Md.: Johns Hopkins University Press, 1998.

Varadi, Max. "The Peres-Shimon Axis." *Rivista di Studi Polici Internazionale* 68 (July–September, 2001): 415–421.

Pérez, Carlos Andrés (1922–) *president of Venezuela*

Carlos Andrés Pérez was born on October 27, 1922 in Rubio, Venezuela, the son of a small businessman. He became politically active while still a teenager and in 1939 his family relocated to Caracas. There he studied law at the Universidad Central de Venezuela, but soon dropped out in favor of pursuing politics. He quickly became a protégé of Rómulo Betancourt and joined his Democratic Action Party (AD) as a youth organizer to promote democracy and social reforms. In 1945 Betancourt became head of a revolutionary junta and chose Pérez as his personal secretary, but three years later the group was overthrown by a military coup. For a decade Pérez alternated between jail in Venezuela and exile in Costa Rica, and he did not return home until after the overthrow of dictator Marcos Pérez Jiménez in 1958. When Betancourt was elected to the presidency that year, Pérez followed him into high office by holding a number of important ministerial positions over the next 15 years. In 1962 he singularly distinguished himself as minister of the interior by violently quashing Cuban-sponsored guerrilla groups. Pérez by this time had acquired the reputation as a charismatic leader and a vigorous campaigner for the AD. When Betancourt resigned from office owing to poor health, he officially endorsed Pérez's candidacy for president. Not surprisingly, Pérez, known affectionately by his initials as CAP, won a resounding victory by garnering 49 percent of the popular vote in December 1973.

Pérez came to office at a fortuitous time in Venezuelan history. Thanks to the recent Arab oil embargo against the West, petroleum prices skyrocketed and brought the country billions of dollars in revenue. Pérez decided to capitalize on this trend by nationalizing the oil industry and buying out U.S. and foreign interests. This move branded him as something of a left-wing populist in Western circles, but the effort was well received at home. Furthermore, Pérez took advantage of increased revenue to spend lavishly on new social programs, greater national infrastructure and, in short, all the trimmings of an advanced industrialized society. He also raised eyebrows abroad by conducting an activist foreign policy and constantly lecturing advanced nations on their obligation to assist poorer ones. But, however well intentioned, Pérez's ambitious reforms stalled from their sheer magnitude. Accountability was poor, billions of dollars were wasted, and the national debt blossomed. In the end, even his erstwhile ally Betancourt denounced his policies. Pérez was forbidden by the constitution from seeking a second term and would have to wait at least a decade before doing so. Given the unpopularity of his national programs, the AD handily lost the national elections of 1978 to Luis Herrera Campins of the Christian Democrats.

For a decade Pérez remained a vocal part of the opposition, decrying what he viewed as mishandling of the nation's assets. In 1988 he commenced his second campaign for the presidency by promising to expand democracy to include the first elections ever held for mayors and governors (previously, these were appointed). That December Pérez won a second five-year term in office—the first in Venezuelan history—but much had changed in 10 years. First, he mitigated some of his strident left-wing views and embraced the free-market model of economic growth. He also mended fences with the United States and sought to ally Venezuela with it diplomatically. However, the 1990s were a bust period for the economy and Pérez was forced to embark on severe austerity measures to keep the nation solvent. In 1991, the difficulties that these steps engendered proved so extreme that riots broke out across the country. Worse, in 1992 Pérez had to endure two attempted military coups against his regime. But the final blow was delivered in May 1993, when the president was officially indicted for embezzlement of public funds. Pérez then suffered the indignity of impeachment by the Senate and was formally removed from office—elections resulted in Rafael Caldera becoming the next president. He also lost his membership in the AD Party. The following year Pérez was sentenced to house arrest in light of his advanced age, and there he waited the outcome of events. In May 1996 the Supreme Court found Pérez guilty of misusing public funds, but he was acquitted of the more serious embezzlement charge.

Pérez's impeachment did little to diminish his appetite for politics, and he vowed to return to the public arena and clear his name. Nonetheless, in April 1998 a judge again charged him with illegal enrichment by spiriting away untold millions of dollars in foreign banks. However, in November 1998 Pérez was elected to the Senate representing the new Apertura (Opening) Party. As a senator, he now enjoyed immunity from additional investigations. Yet, Pérez has since left Venezuela under a cloud and he divides his time between the Dominican Republic and the United States. On April 5, 2002, the national prosecutor's office issued formal extradition orders against the former flamboyant president on charges of corruption. His whereabouts to date remain unknown.

Further Reading

Baburkin, Sergei, et al. "The 1992 Coup Attempts in Venezuela: Causes and Failure." *Journal of Political and Military Sociology* 27, no. 1 (1999): 141–154.

Ewell, J. "Debt and Politics in Venezuela." *Current History* 88 (March 1989): 121–124, 147–149.

Perez-Linan, Anibal S. "Crisis without Breakdown: Presidential Impeachment in Latin America." Unpublished Ph.D. dissertation, University of Notre Dame, 2001.

Tarver Denova, Hollis M. *The Rise and Fall of Venezuelan President Carlos Andrés Perez: An Historical Examination.* Lewiston, N.Y.: Edward Mellen Press, 2001.

Tulchin, Joseph S., and Gary Bland, eds. *Venezuela in the Wake of Radical Reform*. Boulder, Colo.: Lynne Rienner Publishers, 1993.

Persson, Goran (1949–) *prime minister of Sweden*

Goran Persson was born in Vingaker, Sweden, on January 20, 1949. Sweden has been a constitutional monarchy throughout most of its modern history, and in 1971 it unified both houses of the Riksdag, the traditional legislature, into a unicameral body. From this body a prime minister is selected from the majority party in parliament, or from a coalition of parties. Like most Scandinavian states, Swedish politics are dominated by a concern to perpetuate a generous welfare state, and since 1932 the Social Democratic Party (SAP) has been the dominate national force. Their stated goals are economic prosperity, social security, full employment, and political equality. Over the years they have largely delivered on their pledge. Other groupings, such as the Moderate Conservative Party (M), the Christian Democrats (KDS), and others have exerted less influence as a whole, although they have been called on as coalition partners. As a rule, Swedes are renowned for unspectacular, "middle-of-the-road" pragmatism, and they have devised a working compromise between state socialism and free-market capitalism. The result is a robust economy and one of the world's highest standards of living, albeit with tax rates approaching 50 percent. Sweden is also famous for its precision-oriented industrial sector, which manufactures cars, airplanes, and medical equipment of the highest quality.

Persson completed his secondary education and went on to study chemistry and politics at the University College of Obrero. However, in 1971 he left school to become politically active in the SAP as a youth organizer, and he taught economics, mathematics, and social studies at various high schools. In 1979 Persson gained election to the parliament as a SAP member, and he subsequently held down a number of successively important ministerial portfolios. In 1991 the Social Democrats were temporarily turned out of office, but Persson continued distinguishing himself as a member of various party and governmental committees. When SAP was returned to power in 1994 he became finance minister. In this office, Persson gained national standing for reducing the excesses associated with the Swedish welfare

state without compromising it. His political fortunes crested in March 1996 when he gained appointment as chairman of the Social Democrats. That month he also succeeded INGVAR CARLSSON as prime minister.

Persson came to power mindful of the 1994 elections, which were among the worst his party ever endured, forcing them to rule as a coalition. Judging the time ripe for change, he immediately embarked upon fine-tuning the welfare state in order to preserve it. He thereupon cut government expenditures to reduce the national debt, and outsourced many jobs traditionally associated with the public sector. Hard-core leftists in the SAP howled in protest, but many in the engineering and high-technology sectors applauded this new emphasis on frugality. The economy, somewhat sluggish, made marked improvements, and, in September 1998, he was successfully reelected prime minister for the next four years.

The two most pressing issues in Swedish politics today are far more concerned with foreign policy than domestic economics. Like Switzerland, Sweden has maintained its reputation for neutrality and thus escaped the ravages of numerous wars and conflicts. However, the end of the cold war in 1991 and the ongoing formation of the European Union (EU) left the country with some stark choices. After much deliberation, it was decided that Sweden should break with past tradition by joining the EU in 1995, so as not to be disadvantaged in terms of trade. This was done only reluctantly, however, for the country simultaneously rejected the notion of joining the European Monetary Union (EMU) to replace the krona with the euro as currency. Furthermore, unlike Denmark, Iceland, and Norway, Sweden also balked at the prospect of joining the NATO military alliance out of concern for traditional nonalignment. However, Persson has prevailed upon his countrymen to join the less binding Partnership for Peace program, and Sweden has committed military forces abroad to serve as UN peacekeepers.

In January 2002, Persson also became the president of the EU, a post that is occupied on a rotating basis among the 15-member states. As president, he has stressed what he calls the "Three Es": enlargement of the membership to include Eastern European countries, greater emphasis on protecting the environment, and full employment. On this last note, Persson and the SAP insist that EU's commitment to the free market and economic growth should coincide with a higher living standard and better wages for all its workers. "The most important thing for me is that our presidency is regarded as professional and that we are seen as a competent player in the EU," he maintained. However, based on Sweden's own lack of enthusiasm for EU membership (only 37 percent favor it), he is studiously avoiding such contentious issues as political integration and the possible loss of sovereignty. Persson is also unique among contemporaries by paying attention to Russia, out of concern that the presence of such a rich, powerful alliance on that nation's doorstep might prove destabilizing for the country. Throughout the rest of his six-month tenure as president, Persson remains committed to engaging Russia by extending increased technical and financial assistance. In consequence of his handling of the EU presidency, Persson's political rating is at an all-time high of 61 percent and he has announced his candidacy for a third term in office. As such he remains well situated to continuing SAP's legacy as the dominating force in Swedish politics when national elections transpire in the fall of 2002.

Further Reading

Einhorn, Eric S. *Modern Welfare States: Scandinavian Politics and Policy in the Global Age.* Westport, Conn.: Praeger, 2003.

Gstohl, Sieglinde. *Reluctant Europeans: Norway, Sweden, and Switzerland in the Process of Integration.* Boulder, Colo.: Lynne Rienner Publishers, 2002.

Hadenius, Stig. *Swedish Politics during the 20th Century: Conflict and Consensus.* Stockholm: Swedish Institute, 1999.

Malmborg, Michael af. *Neutrality and State-Building in Sweden.* Basingstoke, England: Palgrave, 2001.

Miles, Lee. *Sweden and the European Union Evaluated.* New York: Continuum, 2000.

Swenson, Peter. *Capitalists against Markets: The Making of Labor Markets and Welfare States in the United States and Sweden.* New York: Oxford University Press, 2002.

Plavsic, Biljana (1930–) *president of Republika Srpska*

Biljana Plavsic was born on July 7, 1930 in Tuzla, Bosnia-Herzegovina, the daughter of a biologist. Her republic constituted as one of six such entities comprising the Federal Republic of Yugoslavia. Being of Serbian extraction, she was also culturally quite different from the Croatians and Muslims residing in that region. Plavsic attended Zagreb University, Croatia, from which she obtained a science degree in around 1956. That year she began teaching biology at Sarajevo University, and she also studied in the United States under a Fulbright scholarship. A competent scientist, Plavsic eventually served as dean of the university biology department. Despite Yugoslavia's communist orientation, she never joined the Communist Party and held aloof from politics. However, once Yugoslavia began breaking up under the strain of ethnic separatism in 1990, she helped to found the Serbian Democratic Party (SDS) in Bosnia-Herzegovina. This group proved a reservoir of long-suppressed nationalism, which held that Serbs could not live in peace with their neighbors. Moreover, they required a "Greater Serbia" of their own, implying that Serbs needed to expand territorial holdings in Bosnia-Herzegovina at Croat and Muslim expense. The tempo of events greatly accelerated in April 1992 when RADOVAN KARADZIC became president of the newly proclaimed Republika Srpska. This act commenced a bloody three-year civil war that witnessed atrocities in Europe on a scale not experienced since World War II.

Plavsic was by then vice president of the Republika Srpska. She acquired that post through her ardent support of Serbian nationalism and concerted efforts by military forces under Karadzic to drive Muslims and Croats from coveted lands. "There are 12 million Serbs in the former Yugoslavia," she trumpeted. "We can afford to lose six million on the battlefield." Plavsic was not directly involved with the practice of "ethnic cleansing," namely, the forced removal or mass murder of undesirable elements, but she did not object to it either. However, the United Nations certainly found the practice despicable, and from August to October 1995 they launched a concerted aerial offensive to drive the Serbians away from their ill-gotten gains. At length the Serbs relented and their government dispatched representatives to Dayton, Ohio, to sign a comprehensive peace accord. This divided Bosnia-Herzegovina into two separate entities under one government. However, Plavsic and other hard-liners railed against the treaty, and she went so far as to accuse Serbian president SLOBODAN MILOŠEVIĆ, who supported the peace process, of betraying the Bosnian Serbs. Another treaty provision also insisted upon the removal of Karadzic as president, as he had been formally charged with war crimes by the International War Crimes Tribunal. He stepped down from office to become an international fugitive, and, on May 19, 1996, Plavsic was appointed president to succeed him. Her position was confirmed by a national election held the following September.

Plavsic was initially viewed in the West as little more than Karadzic's stooge, but events proved otherwise. Despite her ardent nationalism, the former biologist was a realist and sensitive to the sufferings of her people. Accordingly, on July 2, 1997, she made a televised address and formally accused Karadzic and his cronies of reaping windfall profits through the black marketing of cigarettes and gasoline. These accusations energized Karadzic's supporters in parliament and they refused to dissolve that body and call for new elections as requested. At length, the Serbs split up, divided between Karadzic's supporters in the southern city of Pale and Plavsic's followers centered upon Banja Luka. However, the president enjoyed the support of thousands of heavily armed NATO peacekeepers, who provided her with money and also confiscated weapons caches intended for a coup attempt against her. The West's sudden embrace of this erstwhile Serbian nationalist, known locally as the "Iron Lady," seemed unusual, but she proved the only Serbian leader willing to uphold the Dayton Accords. Plavsic also parted company with the SDS and founded her own party, the Serbian National Association, to oppose them. However, she had apparently underestimated the resentment against her for turning against Karadzic, still a popular figure. In September 1998 a new round of national elections brought the SDS firmly back in control, and Plavsic was forced from office in favor of the ultranationalist Nikola Poplasen. The former president retained her seat in parliament until December 2000 before withdrawing from politics altogether.

There was worse news in store for Plavsic. In 2000 the UN International War Crimes Tribunal formally accused her with nine counts of genocide and other human rights violations dating to her years as vice president, 1992–95. In January 2001 she surprised critics by voluntarily surrendering for arraignment at The Hague, and she entered pleas of not guilty. The following September Plavsic was released from detention and allowed to returned home, pending assurances that she will return for her trial when so summoned. On December 16, 2002, the "Iron Lady" appeared in court and stunned onlookers by dramatically confessing to crimes against humanity. By pleading guilty to one charge of persecution, other charges, including genocide, were dropped. "I have made

no deal about the length of my sentence, nor did I want any such thing," she blithely declared. "What do 10 years of prison mean to me? For me it is a life sentence." On February 28, 2003, she was sentenced to 11 years in prison.

Further Reading

Bieber, Florian, and Zhidas Daskalovski, eds. *Understanding the War in Kosovo.* Portland, Oreg.: Frank Cass, 2003.

Bose, Sumantra. *Bosnia after Dayton: Nationalist Partition and International Intervention.* New York: Oxford University Press, 2002.

Clark, Wesley K. *Waging Modern War: Bosnia, Kosovo, and the Future of Combat.* Reading, Mass.: Perseus, 2001.

Keane, Rory. *Reconstituting Sovereignty: Post-Dayton Bosnia Uncovered.* Burlington, Vt.: Ashgate, 2002.

Magas, Branka, and Ivo Zanic. *The War in Croatia and Bosnia-Herzegovina, 1991–1995.* Portland, Oreg.: Frank Cass, 2001.

Ron, James. *Frontiers and Ghettos: State Violence in Serbia and Israel.* Berkeley: University of California Press, 2003.

Shatsmiller, Maya. *Islam and Bosnia: Conflict Resolution and Foreign Policy in Multi-ethnic States.* Montreal: McGill-Queen's University Press, 2002.

Portillo Cabrera, Alfonso (1954–) *president of Guatemala*

Alfonso Portillo Cabrera was born in Guatemala in 1954, the son of a teacher. He matured at a time of increasing social strife and war in his country, one of the most beautiful in Central America. In fact, Guatemala has known little beyond varying degrees of oppression since it gained independence from Spain in the 1820s. The 20th century has only enhanced its reputation for brutality and bloodshed. To begin with, Guatemala is among the most inequitable societies in the world, whereby 2 percent of the population controls 70 percent of the land. The bulk of the population, Mayan-speaking Indians, continue to live a hardscrabble existence through subsistence farming. The paths of injustice and poverty intersected in 1960 with the rise of several left-wing guerrillas groups, popularly supported by the rural population. The military responded with a brutally ruthless campaign of extermination and, between the two extremes, nearly 200,000 people lost their lives or disappeared. Subsequent investigations by human rights commissions attribute most of the bloodshed to right-wing security forces known as the EMI. A fragile peace accord between the rebels and the government had been reached in 1996, but never fully implemented. Guatemala remains a seething cauldron of social discontent, where 75 percent of the population lives in poverty and the majority of poor Indian children are malnourished.

As Portillo matured, he was initially sympathetic to left-wing movements in college, where he studied law and economics. He then worked as a university professor both at home and in Mexico, and he identified his political beliefs as corresponding to that of a leftist social democrat. Portillo has since admitted that in 1982, while teaching at the Guerrero Autonomous University of Mexico, he had a violent encounter with two men and killed both. He then fled the country to escape prosecution, but the episode would hold him in good stead later on. In 1995 Portillo joined the right-wing Guatemalan Republic Front Party (FRG) at the behest of former dictator Efraín Ríos Montt, who ran the country in 1982–83. During his short tenure in office, Ríos Montt had been severely criticized for an atrocious human rights record, but as head of the nation's powerful military and paramilitary forces, he has never been prosecuted. Whatever his prior feelings about leftist doctrines, Portillo accepted Ríos Montt's invitation to run as the FRG candidate for the presidency in 1996. He then ran an impressive campaign, losing to Álvaro Arzú of the National Advancement Party (PAN) by only 30,000 votes. Undeterred, Portillo spent the next four years lampooning his adversary's inability to implement the very peace accord he signed with the rebels. The political violence continued unabated and he campaigned on a strict law-and-order ticket. Recalling his own brushes with killing in Mexico, Portillo's posters proclaimed: "If he can defend himself, he can defend you and your family." The message resonated with the war-weary public, and, in December 1999, Portillo roundly defeated PAN candidate Oscar Berger by 69 percent of votes cast. He was sworn on January 14, 2000.

Portillo had run a populist campaign, promising to distance himself from the military, which had traditionally run Guatemala. He was especially keen on confronting the economic elites, and he promised to raise taxes, increase the minimum wage, and reduce protective import tariffs. Accordingly, he had three military officers, charged with the killing of Roman Catholic bishop Juan José Gerardi, arrested and brought to trial. In another attempt to break with the bloody past, in December 2001 Portillo managed to have monetary compensation paid to families of 226 victims who were killed by security forces in 1982. However, Portillo has not completely freed himself of Ríos Montt, who is president of Congress and who greatly influences all national legislation passed. For example, while he appointed half of his cabinet with close associates, as was expected, the remaining half went to allies of Ríos Montt. He has also been unable—or unwilling—to disband the dreaded presidential security force, the EMI, which was responsible for many political murders. Portillo, meanwhile, has also assured international investors like the United States that he will fully implement all terms of the 1996 peace accord, but to date only about one-third of the desired legislation has been approved. Final passage has now been pushed back to 2004, although the truce appears to be holding. The 36-year struggle finally appears to have been laid to rest.

In the spring of 2002 Portillo faced his biggest political hurtle to date when a group of 40 businessmen, known as the Civic Movement for Democracy, demanded that both President Portillo and Vice President Juan F. Reyes surrender political immunity and be brought to trial on corruption charges. Apparently, both men have maintained four companies and 13 bank accounts in neighboring Panama for the purpose of siphoning off millions of dollars from illegal sources. But Portillo strenuously denied any wrongdoing and waxed defiant. "This president is going to stand firm and not be frightened off," he declared. "The political show that they are putting on demonstrates that they have been hurt by the historic changes we have made." It remains to be seen if Portillo's controversial nonperformance will allow him to serve out his full term in office.

Further Reading

Cameron, Maxwell. "Self-Coups: Peru, Guatemala, and Russia." *Journal of Democracy* 9 (January 1998): 125–139.

Chase, Christopher, and Susanne Jonas. *Globalization on the Ground: Postbellum Guatemala, Democracy, and Development.* Lanham, Md.: Rowman and Littlefield, 2001.

McCleary, Rachel M. *Dictating Democracy: Guatemala and the End of Violent Revolution.* Miami: University Press of Florida, 1999.

Nelson, Diane M. *A Finger in the Wound: Body Politics in Quincentennial Guatemala.* Berkeley: University of California Press, 1999.

Shillington, John. *Grappling with Atrocity: Guatemalan Theater in the 1990s.* Cranbury, N.J.: Fairleigh Dickinson University Press, 2002.

Premadasa, Ranasinghe (1924–1993) *president of Sri Lanka*

Ranasinghe Premadasa was born on June 23, 1924, in the Kehelatte slum district of Columbo, Ceylon, part of the low-born Hinaya, or washermen's caste. He was also, by ethnicity, part of the Sinhalese majority dominating the island. Premadasa was educated at St. Joseph's College in Columbo and briefly worked as a journalist. He also took to politics at an early age and agitated for independence from Great Britain through the 1930s, a stance for which he was imprisoned. Ceylon gained its independence in 1948, and two years later Premadasa won a seat on the Columbo Municipal Council. Hard working and efficient, he rose to become mayor of that city by 1955. Premadasa had initially joined the Ceylon Labour Party in 1948, but, in 1955, he switched over to the more conservative United National Party (UNP). In 1960 he captured a seat in the House of Representatives, but lost it subsequently when new elections were called four months later. He did not return to office until 1965, and he served in the interim as party whip in parliament. Premadasa had since gained recognition for his firm commitment to grassroots organizing and services to the poor, which enhanced his appeal as a government official. To that end, he successfully served in the ministries of local government and information and broadcasting after 1968. However, the UNP was swept from power two years later and Premadasa garnered additional luster to his reputation as head of the opposition. He also served on a constitutional board, which finally dropped the island's colonial title of Ceylon and substituted a new name, the Republic of Sri Lanka.

In 1977 the UNP's political fortunes were reversed under the leadership of Junius. R. Jayewardene, who became prime minister. Premadasa then held his usual parliamentary functions while holding down several important ministries. He also found time to serve with the Parliamentary Select Committee, tasked with revising the national constitution in 1978. Through this expedient, Sri Lanka was to be headed by a president and a prime minister with lesser powers. That year Jayewardene became the island's first president and Premadasa his prime minister—a position he held for a decade. In this post he was charged with confronting two major guerrilla movements: the Communist-inspired Janata Vimukti Peramuna (JVP) and the Liberation Tigers of Tamil Eelam (LTTE). The latter was a separatist ethnic movement, based in the north and west of the island, which demanded a separate homeland for Tamils. Premadasa managed to isolate and crush the JVP insurgents within a year, but the Tamil Tigers proved elusive and full of fight. They resisted so well that in 1987 the Sri Lankan government invited several thousand troops from mainland India to help restore order. Premadasa, an ardent nationalist, strongly opposed this move, however. He softened his stance only when party officials promised the presidency in 1988. As fighting continued, the prime minister was also responsible for several programs intended to uplift and assist the poor. Premadasa thus oversaw the construction of several thousand low-cost homes across the island, and he also initiated a program of subsidies to needy families. However, the necessity of addressing the Tamil problem was underscored in August 1988, when the prime minister narrowly escaped a bomb blast in his office.

After recovering from injuries, Premadasa campaigned for the island's highest office in December 1988 and won, defeating the veteran SIRIMAVO BANDARANAIKE. He also became the first member of his caste to wield executive authority. Premadasa had previously promised to initiate talks with the Tamil Tigers and press for the removal of Indian troops from Sri Lanka. He also sought to improve the island's overall economy by attracting foreign investments and reviving the tourist industry, which had suffered because of Tamil violence. But above all he renewed his commitments to alleviate the island's grinding poverty. Premadasa, however, was autocratic by nature, and opponents accused him of abusing power, corruption, and incompetence. In fact, he proved ruthless toward dissenting opinions, and, in 1991, he took measures to curb press freedoms. These attributes culminated in a sudden attempt by parliament to impeach the president in September 1991, but the measure was ultimately rejected, Afterward seeing how peace talks with the Tamil separatists had failed, Premadasa turned increasingly to military force to resolve the crisis. The army subsequently won some resounding victories over rebel forces in the field, but the insurgents countered with an increase in suicide bombings. On May 1, 1993, they struck directly at the president as he was making preparations to review the annual May Day parade. Premadasa, his bicycle-riding assailant, and a dozen innocent bystanders all died instantly, the latest victims of a bloody and seemingly intractable conflict.

Further Reading

Horst, Josine van der. *Who Is He, What Is He Doing: Religious Rhetoric and Performances in Sri Lanka during R. Premadasa's Presidency (1989–1993).* Amsterdam: Vu University Press, 1995.

Keerawella, G., and R. Samarajiva. "Sri Lanka in 1993: Eruptions and Flows." *Asian Survey* 34 (February 1994): 168–174.

Oberst, R. C. "A War without Winners in Sri Lanka." *Current History* 91 (March 1992): 128–131.

Matthews, Bruce. "Sri Lanka in 1989: Peril and Good Luck." *Asian Survey* 30 (February, 1990): 144–150.

Singer, Marshal. "Sri Lanka in 1991: Some Surprising Twists." *Asian Survey* 32 (February 1992): 168–174.

Préval, René (1944–) *president of Haiti*

René Préval was born in Port-au-Prince, Haiti, on January 17, 1943, the son of a government minister. Haiti, a former French colony, is located on the western third of the Caribbean island of Hispaniola, which it shares with the Dominican Republic. It achieved its independence by defeating Napoleon's army in 1803 and ever since has been ruled by a succession of failed democracies or brutal dictatorships. The trend crested in 1957 when the Duvalier family rose to power and remained entrenched for 30 years. Both François "Papa Doc" Duvalier and his son, Jean-Claude "Baby-Doc," used a privately raised militia, the Tonton Macoutes ("Boogeymen") to suppress all opposition and ran the island like a personal fiefdom. "Baby-Doc" was finally forced out of office in February 1986, and the following year a new constitution was approved by public referendum. This mandated a bicameral legislature, consisting of a Senate and a Chamber of Deputies, and a president elected by popular vote. That officer, in turn, appoints a prime minister from a sitting member of the majority party in parliament. It was not until 1990, however, that democracy was formally restored by the election of JEAN-BERTRAND ARISTIDE. By then, Haiti enjoyed the unenviable reputation as the poorest country in the Western Hemisphere and one of the poorest in the world. It has also one of the most inequitable distributions of wealth ever recorded, with 10 percent of the population controlling 90 percent of the national wealth. And, because with 7 million people it is also one of the world's most densely populated nations, the island's ecology has suffered severely due to soil erosion and deforestation. Haiti, formerly a food exporter, is now forced to import foodstuffs to survive, and the country remains totally dependent upon outside assistance to survive.

In 1963 the Duvalier regime forced Préval's family into exile, and he subsequently studied agronomics in Belgium. After operating a bakery in New York City for several years, he returned to Haiti in 1982 and struck up cordial relations with Jean-Bertrand Aristide, a former Catholic priest turned radical activist. The two men then clandestinely worked to overturn the existing political order, which was accomplished with the election of Aristide to the presidency in December 1990. The new leader was apparently impressed with Préval's political mettle, for, despite his lack of experience, he appointed him prime minister. When the government was overthrown by the military in September 1991, Préval followed Aristide into exile. It was not until 1995 that U.S. forces evicted the military dictatorship and reinstalled Aristide as president. Because the constitution forbids presidents from holding consecutive terms in power, Préval was then tapped to succeed Aristide in the December 1995 elections. These were the first open and honest elections in Haiti's tortured political history and, although only 28 percent of the public chose to participate, Préval beat out 14 other candidates to win with 87.9 percent of votes cast. His success also marks the first time in Haitian history that power passed peacefully from one regime to another.

Préval inherited a country in terrible economic shape. Years of misrule by the military and economic sanctions by other nations had all but ruined the agricultural sector, which had plunged nearly 50 percent since 1991. The island's minuscule industrial sector had also been hit hard. To revitalize the economy, Préval differed from Aristide in one major respect: he was a man of action. Whereas the former was reluctant to impose International Monetary Fund (IMF) and World Bank austerity measures to forestall inflation, Préval did so gladly. The result was a temporary upswing in social distress, but the economy revived and Haiti soon qualified for loans and other forms of financial aid. Aristide had also balked at privatizing the island's notoriously inefficient state-run industries to attract foreign investment, but Préval did so willingly. It was this eagerness to embrace free-market practices that apparently drove a wedge between the two men. Aristide, still highly popular with the majority of Haiti's poor masses, began marshaling his forces against the new president. Their party, the Organisation Politique Lavalas (OPL), subsequently split into two factions behind their respective leaders.

In 1997 the Préval administration suffered from accusations that recent Senate elections had been rigged, and Prime Minister Rosny Smarth, a trusted ally, resigned in protest. Over the next three years, Préval was consequently unable to get either a budget or legislation through parliament, which cannot convene without a prime minister. Worse still, three of Préval's candidates for that office were summarily rejected by the Senate, most likely at the behest of Aristide allies. In frustration, Préval dissolved parliament once its current term expired and resorted to rule by decree. This, however, imperiled the flow of aid from the United States, which insisted on a complete participatory democracy. The impasse continued despite Aristide's grip on Haiti's politics, and, during the November 2000 elections, the majority of parties boycotted the process. The ever-popular Aristide then clinched the election with 91.7 percent of the vote, although only about one-third of the electorate cared to participate. Préval, forbidden by law to run for a second consecutive term, ironically was replaced by the man he succeeded.

Further Reading

Fatton, Robert. *Haiti's Predatory Republic: The Unending Transition to Democracy.* Boulder, Colo.: Lynne Rienner Publishers, 2002.

Garrison, Lynn. *Voodoo Politics: The Clinton-Gore Destruction of Haiti.* Los Angeles: Leprechaun Publishing Group, 2000.

Rhodes, Leara. *Democracy and the Role of the Haitian Media.* Lewiston, N.Y.: Edwin Mellen Press, 2001.

Slotsky, Irwin P. *Silencing the Guns in Haiti: The Promise of Deliberative Democracy.* Chicago: University of Chicago Press, 1999.

Wucker, Michelle. *Why the Cocks Fight: Dominicans, Haitians, and the Struggle for Hispaniola.* New York: Farrar, Strauss, and Giroux, 1999.

Primakov, Yevgeny (1929–) *prime minister of Russia*

Yevgeny Maximovich Primakov was born in Kiev, Ukraine, on October 29, 1929, and raised in Tiblisi, Georgia. He grew up in Stalinist Russia and his father inexplicably disappeared while he was a child. Primakov attended the Institute of Oriental Studies in Moscow, where he studied Arabic and graduated in 1953. He subsequently attended Moscow State University in pursuit of a doctorate in economics, which was granted in 1956. Primakov's performance was impressive enough to warrant membership in the Communist Party by 1959, and in 1962 he served as a correspondent with the state newspaper *Pravda.* And, because his job entailed lengthy deployments overseas to various national capitals, it has long been speculated that Primakov enjoyed connections to the dreaded Soviet secret police, the KGB. He was repeatedly deployed throughout the Middle East throughout the height of the cold war, becoming personally acquainted with such leading figures as HOSNI MUBARAK of Egypt, King HUSSEIN I of Jordan, MUAMMAR QADDAFFI of Libya, and SADDAM HUSSEIN of Iraq. In all his assignments, Primakov performed satisfactorily, and in 1977 he was made director of the Institute for Oriental Research. By 1985 he had been promoted to director of the prestigious Institute of World Economics and International Relations. That same year Mikhail Gorbachev had become premier of the ailing Soviet Union, fully intending to reform it. Primakov proffered his services as an ally, and by 1988 he had risen to chairman of the Council of the Union, a senior parliamentary body. It was in this office that he repeatedly visited Iraq in 1990 and conferred with Saddam Hussein over his seizure of neighboring Kuwait. He tried unsuccessfully to obtain a peaceful withdrawal of Iraqi forces, which were ultimately evicted by United Nations forces in the spring of 1991. The following August Gorbachev endured a failed coup by Communist extremists, and by December 1991 the Soviet Union voted itself out of existence.

By the spring of 1992 Russia was ruled by President BORIS YELTSIN and Primakov became one of the few old-time Communist operatives to survive the transition to democracy. He remained as head of the new Foreign Intelligence Service, successor to the KGB, becoming the first civilian to run the agency in 70 years. By 1996, however, Russian attempts at economic liberalization had sputtered, taking the country into a deep, recessionary tailspin. Yeltsin, facing difficult elections that summer, felt politically imperiled, so he fired his Western-leaning foreign minister, Andrei V. Kozyrev, and appointed Primakov in his place. He was expected to stand up to the West and shore up support from the nationalists and Communists dominating the Duma, or parliament. Primakov performed exactly as directed, playing to nationalist sentiments and leaving many U.S. officials pondering if Russia was drifting back into an anti-American orbit. However, Primakov proved refreshingly candid in his personal dealings, and he struck up a cordial relations with Secretary of State Madeleine Albright. A major sticking point between the two superpowers remained the issue of Iraq, which refused to allow UN weapons inspectors into the country as per the terms of the 1991 peace settlement. This resulted in a spate of aerial bombings, which Primakov vehemently protested—ostensibly out of principle, but more likely because Iraq owes Russia $7 billion for weapons.

By March 1998 Russia was in deeper economic doldrums than before, and Yeltsin surprised the world by suddenly firing his entire staff, including Prime Minister SERGEI KIRIYENKO, who had only held the post for six months. However, when the Communist-controlled Duma refused to reappoint the reform-minded VIKTOR CHERNOMYRDIN, Yeltsin avoided a constitutional crisis by nominating Primakov instead. This placated many of the hard-line Communists, and he was sworn in without further delay. In light of the nation's precarious health he warned onlookers that "I'm not a magician. Don't judge this government by its first hundred days." The economy only clanked along as feared, but Primakov enjoyed better success in prosecuting several businessmen for corruption. In time he became the most popular politician in Russia, with higher poll numbers than Yeltsin, and Primakov became touted as a probable contender to succeed him. Largely for this reason, Primakov was fired as prime minister on May 12, 1999, after a year in power. Yeltsin apparently wanted to retain more power over who would succeed him.

Since his dismissal, Primakov has served as chairman of the new Fatherland–All Russia Coalition. He was expected to declare his candidacy for the presidency, but inexplicably withdrew his nomination in February 2000. He apparently grew disenchanted with politics altogether, and he also resigned as chairman. "I will not enter any party," he jested. "It's quite enough that I used to be a member of the Politburo." After July 2000, the newly victorious candidate, VLADIMIR PUTIN, appointed him president of the Chamber of Commerce and Industry and he has resumed his familiar routine of high-stakes negotiating on behalf of Russian interests. In June 2002 he conferred with Belorussian president ALYAKSANDR LUKACHENKO over their countries' relations. "I do not think that our relations have become so tense that they need regulation," he insisted. "There are some rough points that can be smoothed over today."

Further Reading

Lipman, Masha, and Michael McFaol. "Managed Democracy in Russia: Putin and the Press." *Harvard International Journal of Press/Politics* 6 (Summer 2001): 116–127.

Fawn, Rick, and Stephen White, eds. *Russia After Communism.* Portland, Oreg.: Frank Cass, 2002.

Lynch, Allen C. "The Realism of Russia's Foreign Policy." *Europe-Asia Studies* 53, no. 1 (2001): 7–31.

Lynch, Dov. "Walking the Tightrope: The Kosovo Conflict and Russia in European Security." *European Security* 8 (Winter 1999): 57–83.

Simes, Dimitry K. "Russia's Crisis and America's Complicity." *National Interest* 54 (Winter 1998–1999): 12–22.

Tsitkilov, P. I. "The 243 Days of Eugenii Primakov." *Russian Politics and Law* 38, no. 2 (2000): 34–52.

Prodi, Romano (1939–) *prime minister of Italy*

Romano Prodi was born on August 7, 1939, in Reggio Emilia, Italy, and he graduated from the University of Bologna in 1961 with a degree in economics. Intent on an academic career, he subsequently undertook advanced studies at the London School of Economics and Harvard University before returning home to teach. For many years he served as professor of economics and industrial policy at the University of Bologna, becoming well respected through numerous books and publications. Prodi also demonstrated interest in politics by joining the Christian Democrats (DC), who had dominated Italian politics since 1946. His fine reputation and political contacts led to an appointment as minister of industry in the government of GIULIO ANDREOTTI, 1978–79, and in 1982 he also assumed control of the Institute for Industrial Reconstruction (RI). This was a large conglomeration of state-owned firms, which had proved inefficient and were awash in debt. Nonetheless,

Prodi managed to turn the institution around and post profits through radical restructuring and privatization of unproductive sectors. However, his efforts were resisted by the government of Prime Minister SILVIO BERLUSCONI, and he retired from the board in July 1994. Prodi then resumed teaching, although his attention turned increasingly to political office. Disenchanted by the entrenched conservatism of the DC, he founded the Olive Tree Party (Ulivo) in February 1995, an umbrella alliance between the Democratic Party of the Left (PDS) under MASSIMO D'ALEMA and a smattering of minor leftist and centrist organizations.

Early in 1996 the government of LAMBERTO DINI resigned and new elections were called. Prodi, who had never previously run for public office, decided to campaign as the Olive Tree candidate. In his accustomed low-key style he conducted a nationwide bus tour on behalf of progressive interests, promising to usher in a new Italian "renaissance" if elected. He made a point of mingling with people and listening to their concerns. By comparison, his opponent, the telegenic Berlusconi, stomped around on a private jet while his media companies continually sang his praises. In the end, it was the personal touch that mattered. On April 21, 1996, the Olive Tree Party beat the conservatives by five points in national elections and President OSCAR LUIGI SCALFARO asked Prodi to form a government. He did so and was sworn in as Italy's 55th prime minister since World War II on May 17, 1996.

The Prodi regime was historically significant, for it represented the first time governmental power was shared by Socialists and former Communists. Intent on reaching the long-sought "historic compromise" with the left, Prodi brought many left-wing officials into his cabinet to establish broad-based consensus. He was also careful to select efficient conservatives such as CARLO AZEGLIO CIAMPI as finance minister for ideological balance. However, in practice, Prodi was firmly in the conservative camp. He determined to sell off inefficient state industries, lower taxes, and promote free-market economics, despite howls of protest from his Communist allies. In fact, budgetary discipline and fiscal restraint became the hallmarks of his administration. More than anything, Prodi wished to reduce the burgeoning national debt and place Italy in line for joining the single European currency (euro) by 1999. This entailed wholesale cuts in the nation's generous welfare programs to lessen expenditures. Over the next two years he suc-

ceeded, the debt was reduced, and the economy thrived. However, Prodi overstepped his bounds in 1998 when he tried reforming the pension system, something his leftist allies firmly opposed. When the Communist Refoundation Party managed to defeat his annual budget by a single vote, Prodi tendered his resignation from office. He was replaced by another left-wing stalwart, D'Alema, in October 1998.

Prodi's good performance in office, combined with his sterling academic record, made him an ideal candidate for the presidency of the European Commission. He assumed that post in September 1999, replacing Jacques Santer of Luxembourg, whose cabinet resigned after allegations of corruption. Once installed, he outlined his vision of an economically integrated democratic Europe that stretched from Ireland to the Black Sea. In practice this required coordinating the national policies of 15 constituent states, with contingencies for allowing as many as 13 new members from Eastern Europe. "For the first time since the Roman Empire we have an opportunity to unite Europe," he insisted. However, his juggling of national priorities—sometimes at the expense of EU objectives—proved awkward and Prodi appeared overwhelmed by the task. In November 2001 he was criticized for insisting that only single, coherent foreign policies will keep the EU from irrelevance. But various nations within the union reserve the right to conduct their own foreign policy if it is in their interest to do so. In fact, EU commissioner Chris Patten maintains that a single foreign policy is too idealistic to demand at present and, hence, is unattainable. However, the former professor ignores his critics and continues to demand that Europe speak with one voice. "Germany, France, the UK, and Italy have no voice if they remain alone," Prodi states.

Further Reading

Agnew, John A. *Place and Politics in Modern Italy.* Chicago: University of Chicago Press, 2002.

Fabrini, Bergio, and Mark Gilbert. "When Cartels Fail: The Role of the Political Class in the Italian Democratic Transition." *Government and Opposition* 35 (Winter 2000): 27–49.

Ginsberg, Paul. *Italy and Its Discontents: Family, Civil Society, State, 1980–2001.* London: Allen Lane, 2001.

McCarthy, Patrick. "Italy: A New Language for a New Politics?" *Journal of Modern Italian Studies* 2, no. 3 (1999): 337–357.

Mudambi, Ram, and Pietro Navarra. *Rules, Choice, and Strategy: The Political Economy of Italian Electoral Reform.* Northampton, Mass.: Edward Elgar, 2001.

Putin, Vladimir (1952–) *president of Russia*

Vladimir Vladimirovich Putin was born in Leningrad (now St. Petersburg), Russia, on October 1, 1952, the son of a shop foreman. Russia at that time was a constituent republic within the greater Soviet Union, a Communist-controlled dictatorship established in 1922 after the Russian Revolution. A merciless, militaristic police state, the Soviet Union collapsed under the weight of its own tyranny and bureaucratic incompetence in 1991, when the new Russian Federation was proclaimed. Two years later, following adoption of a new constitution, it emerged as a strong centralized republic with an elected president and a bicameral legislature consisting of a lower house, or Duma, and an upper chamber, the Federation Council. Russia, as a geographic entity, is the largest country in the world and spans 11 time zones from Europe to Asia. However, it remains one of the poorest and most underdeveloped of all developed nations, despite the startling advances of Soviet science under communism. Its political parties frequently betray strong authoritarian inclinations, while corruption is rife and law enforcement both spotty and selective. Freedom of the press and media also remains conjectural. In truth, despite casting off the chains of oppression a decade ago, Russia remains a tottering giant. The country is possessed of an impressive array of nuclear weapons, yet saddled by an economy performing far below expectations or capacity. World peace and stability may very well hinge on its ability to catch up to the West and deliver better standards of living to the stoic and long-suffering Russian people.

Putin was raised in a communal apartment in Leningrad, where he was secretly baptized into the outlawed Greek Orthodox Church. Early on he acquired a reputation as a quiet, studious individual, poker-faced and not much given to frivolity. However, young Putin possessed a determination to both succeed and excel, and he was able to attend the prestigious High School 281 for honor students. He performed adequately, mastered the Russian martial art of *sambo* (a combination of judo and wrestling), and he also played Western rock music as the school's unofficial deejay. While a student, Putin was personally inspired by numerous spy movies, and

after graduating he tendered his services to the Soviet KGB, the notorious state security apparatus. The young man was unceremoniously told to pursue a law degree first, and he subsequently studied economics at Leningrad State University, obtaining a Ph.D. in 1975.

After graduating, Putin was accepted into the elite ranks of the KGB and received further training at the Red Banner Institute of Intelligence, acquiring fluency in German. After fulfilling routine assignments in Russia, he was thereupon posted on active duty in East Germany in 1985 to recruit new agents and acquire Western technical information. The Soviet Union by that time was experiencing liberal reforms under the aegis of Mikhail Gorbachev, and in 1989 the Berlin Wall came down, Germany was united, and Soviet forces departed Eastern Europe. In 1990 Putin accepted a job teaching international affairs at Leningrad State University with his old professor, Anatoly Sobchak, a leading liberal

Vladimir Putin *(Getty Images)*

reformer. The following year he resigned from the KGB to become involved in politics and served as Sobchak's aide once the latter was elected major of newly renamed St. Petersburg. Here Putin gained a reputation as the "Gray Cardinal," who was soft-spoken and kept a low profile, but worked wonders getting results from the famously lethargic Russian bureaucracy. He was also intensely loyal to his mentor and, when Sobchak was voted out of office in 1996, Putin resigned as deputy mayor. However, word of Putin's performance came to the attention of ailing president BORIS YELTSIN, who invited him to join his "inner circle." Putin complied and became deputy chief administrator at the Kremlin and also director of the new state intelligence arm, the Federal Security Service (FSB). His good performance, partially traced to the fact that Putin neither smokes nor drinks, resulted in his appointment as secretary of the Security Council, a senior advisory body to the president. In August 1999 Yeltsin, who had sacked five prime ministers in only 17 months, appointed the neophyte Putin to fill the office. He was then virtually unknown to the Russian people, but nonetheless conducted himself with the quiet efficiency for which he became renowned. Suddenly, on New Year's Eve, 1999, Yeltsin resigned as president on account of poor health and Putin, still relatively little known, was appointed his acting successor.

In accordance with the Russian constitution, new elections were to be held on March 26, 2000, for a new president. During this interval Putin, who lacked prior political experience, campaigned on time-honored themes of national unity and strength. So strongly did he appeal for greater law enforcement that many liberals, cognizant of his intelligence service background, began fearing him as potentially antidemocratic. However, the Russian electorate responded favorably to his message of strength, and he gained election with 52.6 percent of the popular vote. On May 7, 2000, Putin was sworn in as Russia's first freely elected president in its 1,100-year history. Once installed, he faced the unenviable task of sorting out national priorities, all of which were pressing. Like Yeltsin, he sought closer ties to the West and peaceful relations with the United States, so he convinced the Duma to authorize Russian participation in the START II arms reduction treaty. He also alerted Western Europe that, while Russia would not obstruct the eastern expansion of NATO, it watched such events carefully and expected close consultation in advance. However, his biggest challenges remained domestic, especially the

ongoing war against Muslim rebels in the province of Chechnya. By giving the military a free hand to deal with the insurgents harshly, he incurred some criticism from the West, but he also solidified his support at home. The rebels soon buckled under this renewed pressure, agreed to peace talks, and most fighting has stopped. But Putin, like Yeltsin before him, had less success in curtailing the rise of organized crime and political corruption. "Corruption in law enforcement exists in other countries, not just in Russia," he insisted, "but in Russia, it has reached a magnitude where the government can't ignore it." He was also largely stymied by the sluggish, unresponsive Russian economy, and in the spring of 2002 he authorized major tax cuts for small businesses to generate both capital and new jobs.

Despite his reputation for reticence, Putin differed from previous Russian leaders in his accessibility. He would frequently approach common citizens on the street for advice, and he even submitted to an unprecedented televised question-and-answer session. Through such expedients he tried to demonstrate that the Russian government, for all its fabled indifference, was attempting real change. However, Putin's reputation for openness was hurt in the wake of the submarine *Kursk* disaster, when the government was slow to accept either blame for the accident or offers of Western help. He was also criticized, at least initially, for offering former president Yeltsin an amnesty to protect him from prosecution over corruption charges, although this was probably the price he had to pay for succeeding him.

The destruction of the World Trade Center in New York on September 11, 2001, cast Russia's role as a strategic American partner in an entirely new light. He was the very first head of state to telephone condolences to President GEORGE W. BUSH, and he pledged his total cooperation in the international war against terrorism. This meant granting the Americans access to Russian airspace as they flew men and equipment into Tajikistan and Uzbekistan, an unthinkable act during the cold war years. The mere presence of sizable American forces in Central Asia, long a coveted Russian sphere of influence, is convincing proof that the cold war is forever laid to rest. Moreover, Putin authorized the deployment of Russian special forces for the war in Afghanistan, again acting in concert with American troops there. Russian cooperation in this sphere has been absolutely essential and Putin has demonstrated strong resolve to overcome past animosity and act like a trusted ally. This, in turn, forces the United States and the West to pay greater heed to Russian security concerns, such as NATO expansion, and also guarantees quicker and more favorable response to requests for economic assistance. How ironic that the 50-year-old Putin, the calm, unobtrusive world leader, and formerly a member of an oppressive police state agency, is committed to leading Russia into the unknown reaches of political freedom—and its rightful place among the community of nations.

Further Reading

Brown, Archie, and Liliia F. Shevtsova. *Gorbachev, Yeltsin, and Putin: Political Leadership in Russia's Transition.* Washington, D.C.: Carnegie Endowment for International Peace, 2001.

German, Tracey C. *Russia's Chechen War.* New York: Routledge, 2003.

Hewspring, Dale R., ed. *Putin's Russia: Past Imperfect, Future Uncertain.* Lanham, Md.: Roman and Littlefield, 2002.

Hyde, Matthew. *Putin's Federal Reforms and Their Implications for Presidential Power in Russia.* Essex, England: University of Essex, 2000.

Kagarlitsky, Boris. *Russia under Yeltsin and Putin: Neo-liberal Aristocracy.* Sterling, Va.: Pluto Press, 2002.

McFarl, Michael. *Russia's Unfinished Revolution: Political Change from Gorbachev to Putin.* Ithaca, N.Y.: Cornell University Press, 2001.

Nichols, Thomas M. *The Russian Presidency: Society and Politics in the Second Russian Republic.* Basingtoke, England: Palgrave, 2002.

Putin, Vladimir. *First Person: An Astonishingly Frank Self-Portrait by Russia's President.* London: Hutchinson, 2000.

Rose, Richard. *Elections without Order: Russia's Challenge to Vladimir Putin.* New York: Cambridge University Press, 2002.

Sawka, Richard. *Russian Politics and Society.* New York: Routledge, 2002.

Q

Qaddafi, Muammar (1942–) *Libyan head of state*

Muammar Qaddafi was born in Sitre, Libya, in 1942, into the Qadhdhafa, an Arabized Berber tribe. Libya, formally part of the Ottoman Empire, was then an Italian colony on the point of being subdued by British forces during World War II. In 1951 the United Nations declared Libya an independent monarchy under King Idris, who ruled conservatively, denied women the right to vote until 1963, and banned all political activity. Libya, fortunately, was well endowed with numerous oil fields, and the country soon became a major energy exporter, primarily to Western Europe. Furthermore, mindful of security arrangements, the king invited Britain and the United States to establish numerous military bases and airfields. In September 1969 a group of young military officers engineered a bloodless coup while King Idris was away receiving medical treatment, and the Libyan Arab Republic was proclaimed.

Qaddafi was fortunate among Berbers for having received rudimentary education and, a bright student, he attended various primary and secondary schools. While at the Seb'a Preparatory School in 1956, he became profoundly influenced by the politics of Egypt's Gamal Abdul Nasser, who preached a militant form of pan-Arabic unity. Qaddafi readily took up the cause, and he was consequently expelled from school in 1961. He then reenrolled in a school at Misrata and forged links with other like-minded students. This became the nucleus of the Free Unionist Officers Movement, dedicated to overthrowing the reactionary monarchy. Qaddafi subsequently attended the Libyan Military Academy in 1965, and he performed well enough to merit advanced study in England. He returned in 1966 and took additional courses at the University of Benghazi before being commissioned with the signal corps. Qaddafi served with little notice until September 1, 1970, when his Free Unionist Officers Movement suddenly took action and toppled King Idris from power. Within weeks, the little-known Qaddafi emerged as head of the newly appointed Revolutionary Command Council (RCC). He then embarked on a quixotic quest to transform Libya into a modern socialist state with decidedly Islamic overtones.

Having eliminated potential rivals from the RCC, Qaddafi moved quickly to solidify his control of the country by stoking the fires of anti-Western sentiment. He accomplished this by closing the British and Americans military bases, nationalizing foreign oil firms, and expelling Italian and Jewish settlers. Consistent with his strict Islamic vision, he also banned alcohol and nightclubs, and he made the Islamic Koran the inspiration for state policy. However, Qaddafi was no religious fanatic, but rather a socialist modernizer with a strict Berber background. He diverted oil money from the national coffers to construct housing and improve agriculture, and he also granted women a degree of equality rare in the Arab world. The average Libyan citizen, mostly poor, did in fact prosper from Qaddafi's redistribution of wealth, although it alienated the country's middle class, and many fled the country. Between 1976 and 1979, Qaddafi codified his political beliefs in a three part publication called the *Green Book,* which outlined his "Third Way" between the material extremes of capitalism and the godless tyranny of communism.

In the field of foreign affairs, Qaddafi earned the well-deserved reputation of a pariah who supported terrorists on a seemingly random basis. Intent upon unifying the Arab world into a single entity, he negotiated failed unions with Egypt, Syria, and other Arab countries. Thereafter, he applied direct military force to conquer the strategic northern part of neighboring Sudan, which brought a sharp response from the French army. He also dispatched the *mathaba* ("revolutionary committees") abroad to harass and assassinate Libyan opponents living in exile. But his biggest miscalculation was confronting the United States over free passage through the Gulf of Sidra, which he claimed as national waters, in 1981. When this resulted in several aircraft shot down, Qaddafi apparently authorized the bombing of a Berlin disco, in which several Americans were killed. At that juncture, President Ronald Reagan unleashed air and naval units in April 1986, which targeted Qaddafi and bombed his residence. The erratic leader escaped serious injury but was apparently intent upon revenge. In 1988 Libyan agents apparently planted bombs on Pan Am Flight 103, which exploded over Lockerbie, Scotland, killing all on board. This sabotage resulted in severe economic and diplomatic sanctions from the United Nations and the United States, until the suspected agents were turned over for trial. Qaddafi refused for many years, but once the sanctions had their intended effect and began dragging Libya's economy down, he relented. On January 31, 2001, a Scottish court sitting in the Netherlands found one defendant, Abd al-Baset Ali Muhammed al-Megrahi, guilty and sentenced him to life imprisonment. The other defendant was acquitted and, in return for Libyan compliance, the sanctions were lifted. Great Britain also reopened its embassy, but relations with the United States remained frozen.

Libya and the United States experienced a small thaw in relations following the September 11, 2001, destruction of the World Trade Center in New York. Qaddafi publicly condemned the act and declared that the United States had a right to defend itself by attacking the Taliban regime in Afghanistan. This was followed by frank talks in London between the State Department and Musa Kusa, Qaddafi's head of external intelligence. In addition to terrorism, the question of reparations to the families of those lost on Flight 103 were discussed. Because of Qaddafi's own difficulties with rising Islamic fundamentalism at home, and his increasing isolation abroad, future negotiations might result in the first American ambassador to reside at Tripoli in 30 years.

Further Reading

El-Kikha, Mansour O. *Libya's Qaddafi: The Politics of Contradiction.* Gainesville: University Press of Florida, 1997.

Qaddafi, Muammar. *Escape to Hell and Other Stories.* London: Blake, 1999.

St. John, Ronald B. *Libya and the United States: Two Centuries of Strife.* Philadelphia: University of Pennsylvania Press, 2002.

Stanik, Joseph T. *El Dorado Canyon: Reagan's Undeclared War with Qaddafi.* Annapolis, Md.: Naval Institute Press, 2002.

Tremlett, George. *Gaddafi: The Desert Mystic.* New York: Carroll and Graf, 1993.

R

Rabin, Yitzhak (1922–1995) *prime minister of Israel*

Yitzhak Rabin was born on March 1, 1922, in Jerusalem, Palestine, then administered as a British protectorate. His parents had emigrated from Russia as Zionists, intent on reconstituting the state of Israel after two thousand years. Rabin was initially educated at an agricultural school, but he soon displayed an interest in military life. Around 1940 he joined the Palmach, a commando-style unit attached to the underground Jewish army, or Haganah. With this group he fought for the British during World War II by conducting clandestine operations against Vichy French forces in Syria and Lebanon. Rabin subsequently bore a distinguished role in the 1948 Israeli War for Independence. The following year he served as a military representative during peace talks on Rhodes and commenced a distinguished climb up the military hierarchy. In 1953 he passed through the British Staff College and by 1967 he had risen to chief of staff within the Israeli Defense Force (IDF). It was here, in planning the decisive Six-Day War against Egypt, Syria, and Jordan, that Rabin made his greatest contribution to Israeli security. The hostile armies were surprised by a preemptive strike and routed with the loss of the Sinai Peninsula, the Golan Heights, the West Bank of the Jordan River, and the holy city of Jerusalem. Rabin, a gruff, blunt-talking individual, suddenly found himself a national hero. He was rewarded with the post of Israeli ambassador to Washington, D.C., in 1968, where he remained five years. During this period he represented his country's interests well and secured increasing amounts of military assistance from the administration of President Richard M. Nixon.

Rabin returned to Israel in March 1973 to begin a career in politics with the Labor Party and won a seat in the Knesset (parliament). However, that fall Israel was badly surprised in the costly Yom Kippur War, which later forced the resignation of Prime Minister Golda Meir. Beforehand, she appointed Rabin as her minister of labor, and from this position he was chosen as the next prime minister on June 3, 1974. Rabin enjoyed peerless credentials as a war hero and he was also the first native-born Israeli, or *sabra,* to lead the nation. The next three years were characterized by intense shuttle diplomacy with the United States that hammered out a peace agreement with Egypt in 1975; henceforth, Israel returned the Sinai Peninsula in exchange for diplomatic relations. It was a coup for both sides and an important first step toward lasting peace, but in 1977, when it was uncovered that Rabin's wife kept an illegal bank account in the United States, he resigned from office. Thereafter, leadership of the Labor Party passed over to his longtime rival SHIMON PERES, whom Rabin had narrowly bested three years earlier.

Rabin remained a political outcast until 1984, when Labor and the conservative Likud Party arranged a power-sharing agreement between Shimon Peres and YITZHAK SHAMIR. Rabin, as the country's most celebrated soldier, received the portfolio of defense minister. Around this time relations with Palestinians living in the West Bank deteriorated into the violence and terrorism of the uprising called the *intifada*. Rabin then cracked down heavily with armed force, which greatly enhanced his reputation for toughness in dealing with the Arabs. However, he realized that the military occupation of southern Lebanon was futile, so he skillfully withdrew Israeli forces. Rabin's reputation by this time had again eclipsed Peres, and he successfully ran for prime minister in 1992. He had campaigned on a pledge of finally ending the Palestinian conflict, and that year he entered into secret negotiations with YASSER ARAFAT of the Palestine Liberation Organization (PLO). These talks culminated in the September 1993 signing of the Oslo peace accord in Washington, D.C., which stipulated PLO recognition of Israeli's right to exist in exchange for a Palestinian homeland. In 1994 Rabin also signed a separate agreement with King HUSSEIN I of Jordan, normalizing relations between their respective nations and demilitarizing the border. He also extended a palm toward Syrian president HAFAZ AL-ASSAD, promising a complete withdrawal from the Golan Heights in exchange for diplomatic recognition. For all these constructive activities Rabin shared the 1994 Nobel Peace Prize with Arafat and Peres.

Despite his skill as a negotiator, Rabin's willingness to trade land for peace angered many Israelis, who frequently booed and heckled the prime minister at public gatherings. On November 4, 1995, after Rabin addressed a peace rally in Tel Aviv, he was suddenly shot and killed by a 27-year-old Jewish extremist. His funeral was massive and attended by over 80 heads of state, including President BILL CLINTON, Egyptian president HOSNI MUBARAK, and King HUSSEIN I of Jordan. He was succeeded in office by his perpetual rival, Shimon Peres. Rabin will always be remembered as the valiant warrior who forsook violence and favored negotiations to advance the cause of peace.

Further Reading

Inbar, Efraim. *Rabin and Israel's National Security.* Baltimore: Johns Hopkins University Press, 1999.

Karpin, Michael I., and Ina Friedman. *Murder in the Name of God: The Plot to Kill Yitzhak Rabin.* London: Granta, 2000.
Kurzmna, Dan. *Soldier of Peace: The Life of Yitzhak Rabin.* New York: HarperCollins Publishers, 1998.
Rabin, Yitzhak. *The Rabin Memoirs.* Berkeley: University of California Press, 1996.
Sprinzak, Ehud. "Extremism and Violence in Israeli Democracy." *Terrorism and Political Violence* 13 (Autumn–Winter 2000): 209–236.

Rafsanjani, Ali (1934–) *president of Iran*

Ali Akbar Hashemi Rafsanjani was born in 1934 to a family of prosperous farmers in Rafsanjan, Iran. He underwent religious training at an early age and in 1948 he arrived in the holy city of Qom to receive advanced theological training in the Shia branch of Islam. There Rafsanjani studied under and befriended Ruhollah Khomeini, a noted cleric and sworn adversary of Shah Mohammed Reza Pahlavi. Khomeini was exiled for antigovernment activities in 1961, and thereafter Rafsanjani served as his conduit for antigovernment activities at home. Like his mentor, the young cleric bitterly opposed the Shah's so-called White Revolution, an attempt to introduce widespread Western-style reforms into this deeply conservative Islamic culture. His activities resulted in periodic bouts of imprisonment and torture, which only increased his determination to resist. By 1979 the Shah's regime collapsed from popular discontent, and Khomeini returned from exile to be installed as the ayatollah, or supreme religious leader. Rafsanjani, given his prior association with the new leader, thus became an influential member of the inner circle of theocratic power. By February 1979 he had helped found the Islamic Republican Party and also served in the new Revolutionary Council. Through all these expedients, Rafsanjani allowed the clerics to consolidate power over the country and install some semblance of stability. He also proved himself adept politically, and in 1980 he became speaker of the Iranian Majlis (parliament).

Though the clerics had seized the reins of government, they inherited a country on the brink of economic collapse. Production was down, inflation was rising, and the national debt ballooning. Worst of all, in 1980 Iraqi dictator SADDAM HUSSEIN took advantage of their perceived weakness to launch an all-out invasion. The ensuing conflict lasted eight years and cost the Iranians nearly

1 million dead. In July 1988 the ailing Khomeini appointed Rafsanjani commander in chief of the armed forces with a view toward achieving a final victory. However, Iraq's military establishment was receiving financial and technical assistance from the West and Arab Gulf states, and Rafsanjani concluded that protracted fighting would only endanger the Iranian Revolution. By July 1988 both he and President ALI KHAMENEI prevailed upon the ayatollah to agree to a cease-fire, even though the latter characterized it as taking poison. With peace at hand, the clerics could focus their attention on rebuilding their nation's shattered economy and reintegrating it back into the global community.

In June 1989 Khomeini died and he was succeeded by Khamenei, while Rafsanjani gained the presidency. In this office, his role, previously shady, exhibited more and more a pronounced trend toward pragmatism and conciliation. He strongly advocated liberalizing the economic sector, and he also pushed for additional rights for women, especially in higher education. And, speaking as a senior cleric, he did not hesitate to denounce the more ideological members of the ruling body for resisting necessary reforms. In 1989, because of Iran's overall weakness, Rafsanjani formally ended his country's role as the guardian of the Persian Gulf. Thereafter he embarked on a new policy of pursuing cooperative strategies with neighboring states. He also reestablished diplomatic relations with Great Britain and extended overtures to the United States, previously denounced as the "Great Satan." During the 1990 Iraqi invasion of Kuwait, Iran remained neutral but fully complied with international sanctions against Saddam Hussein. However, the clerics enjoyed less success in improving economic conditions, and consequently, in June 1993, Rafsanjani was reelected president, but by lesser margins than previously. He nonetheless continued challenging more conservative members on issues of popular culture, such as Western movies and blue jeans, and he was viewed abroad as a mitigating influence upon religion. However, the economic crisis, made worse by a high birth rate and a burgeoning, youthful population, continued throughout his second term.

In August 1997 Rafsanjani stepped down as president and was succeeded by MOHAMMED KHATAMI, another leading reformer. In May 2000 he also resigned his seat in the Majlis, apparently to protest continuing conservative resistance to badly needed reform. Rafsanjani then became chairman of the Expediency Council, which serves as a mediating body between the constitutional council and the parliament. Rafsanjani roundly condemned the September 11, 2001, attack on the World Trade Center in New York, but he railed against American military action against Afghanistan's Taliban regime. In January 2002, when President GEORGE W. BUSH characterized Iran as part of a global "axis of evil," along with Iraq and North Korea, his remarks drew a quick response from Rafsanjani. "If America attacks Iran it will be stuck in such a quagmire that it will find it hard to get out," he declared at Friday prayers. "Our weapons technology is not as sophisticated as yours, but we are armed with a more powerful weapon: faith and love of martyrdom." However, with a strong U.S. military presence next door, Rafsanjani felt moved to reiterate his goodwill toward America, provided it was reciprocal. "If America drops its bullying as well as its imperialist policies, the Islamic Republic of Iran is ready to cooperate with that country."

Further Reading

Fischer, Michael M. *Iran: From Religious dispute to Revolution.* Madison: University of Wisconsin, 2003.

Hermann, R. "From Economic Crisis to Legitimation Crisis: The Era Khamenei/Rafsanjani in the Islamic Republic of Iran." *Orient* 35, no. 4 (1994): 541–564.

Karbassian, Akbar. "Islamic Revolution and the Management of the Iranian Economy." *Social Research* 67, no. 2 (2000): 621–640.

Milani, Mohson M. "The Evolution of the Iranian Presidency: From Bani Sadr to Rafsanjani." *British Journal of Middle Eastern Studies* 20, no. 1 (1993): 83–97.

Sarabi, Farzia. "The Post-Khomeini Era in Iran: The Election of the Fourth Islamic Majlis." *Middle East Journal* 48 (Winter 1994): 89–108.

Schahgaldian, Nikola B. "Iran After Khomeini." *Current History* 89, no. 544 (1990): 61–64, 82–84.

Rainier III (1923–) *head of state of Monaco*

Rainier Louis Henri Maxence Bertrand de Grimaldi was born in Monaco on May 31, 1923, the only male heir of Count Pierre de Polignac and Princess Charlotte. His grandfather, Louis II, was then hereditary head of state, and part of Europe's longest-serving monarchy. Monaco is today a principality on the southern coast of France, and the world's second-smallest country after the Vatican

City. However, it is imbued with a rather dark and seamy past. It was founded in 1297 by the Grimaldi dynasty, initially a band of enterprising pirates, who have been empowered ever since. Though independent, it enjoys close economic and political ties to France. However, the country was increasingly destitute until 1860, when gambling—banned throughout most of Europe—was formally introduced. It has since become a haven for tax refugees and high-rolling criminals, in addition to the usual parade of glittering aristocrats seeking lavishly priced gratification. Monaco operated as an absolute monarchy until 1911, when it adopted its first constitution. Subsequent amendments in 1962 formally eliminated the divine right of kingship, and established joint rule between the prince and an 18-member National Council that can veto any pending legislation. Monaco remains basically apolitical, but a single party, the National and Democratic Union, does exist and has dominated national events since 1962. This tiny enclave of wealth, a little less than a square mile in size, is also among the richest countries in the world, and its inhabitants pay no taxes.

Rainier was educated at various private schools in England and Switzerland before attending the University of Montpellier in France. Possessed of a scholarly bent, he despised gambling and lived modestly for a prince. In 1944 he joined the Free French Army as an officer and fought with distinction in the closing phases of World War II, being highly decorated. In April 1950 he advanced to the throne shortly before the death of Louis II, becoming the 31st leader of the Grimaldi line. Unfortunately, Rainier's accession coincided with a difficult period in Monaco's history. Though neutral during the recent war, it had gained a degree of notoriety for collaborating with the Nazi occupiers of France, which naturally engendered resentment from its larger neighbor. Worse, tourism and gambling revenues were declining owing to the rise of gambling casinos elsewhere. However, Prince Rainier, while young, was a monarch on a mission. "I would like to be remembered as the person who corrected and got rid of the bad image and bad legend of Monaco," he stated. His first task was to break the nation's traditional dependancy on gambling, and all the shady characters, jewel thieves, and undesirables it attracted. Hereafter, Rainier placed great emphasis on construction, tourism, banking, and real estate development. His success can be judged by the fact that Monaco now sports one of the most impressive waterfronts along

the Riviera, and that gambling presently accounts for only 15 percent of national revenues.

An inescapable legacy of Rainier's reign was his marriage to American actress Grace Kelly. Through prior agreement with France, Monaco remains independent unless its monarchs fail to produce a male heir, at which point the nation reverts to French control. Now a reigning prince, Rainier was immediately pressured to marry as soon as possible. In May 1955 he encountered Kelly while at the Cannes Film Festival and the two fell in love. Kelly was a particularly suitable choice for the dashing prince, being equally young, beautiful, and staunchly Roman Catholic. Theirs was a storybook wedding that captured the world's imagination and placed Monaco on the cover of every tabloid in circulation. As a public relations stunt, their union also revived Monaco's reputation as a playground for the rich and famous, which then led to increases in tourism, gambling, and the like. Rainier's relationship with Kelly, while by no means perfect, was stable and produced three jet-setting children, Caroline, Stephanie, and the long-sought-after male heir, Albert. Tragically, Princess Grace, as she became officially known, died in a car accident on September 14, 1982, and Rainier mourned her passing for several years. His children have also enjoyed the controversial reputations associated with the superrich.

Presently, Rainier is awaiting retirement, pending the marriage of Prince Albert. However, he remains active in national affairs and is determined to clean up Monaco's sometimes clouded reputation. In June 2000 a French parliamentary investigation concluded that secrecy laws surrounding Monaco's banking industry were conducive to criminal money laundering. Moreover, investigators cited the principality's refusal to cooperate fully with the inquiry and suggested punitive measures be taken. Rainier, sensitive to national sovereignty issues, sought to minimize French intervention by agreeing to several reforms that brought Monaco's financial procedures more in line with the rest of Europe. Furthermore, several suspicious accounts were frozen, pending investigation of their owners. In 1997 Rainier also celebrated the 700th anniversary of Grimaldi rule in Monaco, and he now spends most of his time as a doting grandfather. He is expected to retire as soon as Prince Albert, who has courted some of the most glamorous women in Europe, is married and ready to succeed him. Monaco, meanwhile, soldiers on as an international playground for the well-heeled.

Further Reading

Bourgne, Marc. *The History of Monaco.* London: Dargaud, 1997.

Duursma, Jorri. *Self-Determination, Statehood, and International Relations of Micro-states: The Cases of Liechtenstein, San Marino, Monaco, Andorra, and the Vatican City.* New York: Cambridge University Press, 1996.

Edwards, Anne. *The Grimaldis of Monaco.* New York: William Morrow, 1992.

Glatt, John. *The Ruling House of Monaco: The Story of a Tragic Dynasty.* London: Pratkus, 1998.

Kirk, Cori. *Lost in Royalty: An Intimate Account of Monaco.* Victoria, British Columbia: Millenia Press, 1998.

Rakhmonov, Imomali (1952–) *president of Tajikistan*

Imomali Rakhmonov was born in Dangara, Tajikistan, on October 5, 1952, a member of the influential Kulyab clan. Tajikistan had long been the crossroads of Asia, and at one time or another was heavily influenced by a host of Persian, Greek, Arab, Turkish, Mongolian, and Afghan invaders. It entered the Russian sphere of influence by 1868 and became part of the Soviet Union in 1924. Tajikistan is a heavily mountainous region, long-regarded as "the roof of the world." Its people are tough and resilient by nature, and they are severely divided along clan and family lines. Even seven decades of communism did little to ameliorate traditional hostilities, which were dormant and percolating below the surface of political affairs. It is also a rather poor country, with the largest agricultural sector, the lowest educational levels, and the highest infant mortality rate of the six Central Asian "stans." Tajikistan presently has a population of 6 million, the majority of whom are Muslim Tajiks or Uzbeks, but the populace also includes an influential minority of highly skilled Russians. Political independence was achieved in September 1991 under RAKHMON NABIYEV, but this did little to improve the country's basic situation. All told, Tajikistan is poor, economically underdeveloped, and caught between the tides of modernity and Islamic fundamentalism.

As a young man, Rakhmonov attended Lenin State University in Dushanbe, where he majored in economics. He then completed his tour of military service before joining the Communist Party and holding numerous low-level jobs. A competent organizer, Rakhmonov had risen to state farm director by 1988, and four years later he was elected chairman of the Culvert regional government committee. By this time the Soviet Union was in its death throes and the Tajikistan Party was torn between conservative elements, who sought close relations with Russia, and reformists, who sought independence. Nabiyev was subsequently elected president of Tajikistan in November 1991, but widespread accusations of voter fraud led to massive demonstrations. Fighting between former Communists and Liberals, assisted by the newly formed Islamic Renaissance Party, then erupted, and nearly 50,000 died before order was restored in the capital. Rakhmonov, meanwhile, being closely associated with Kulyabi paramilitary forces and the disgraced ex-president Nabiyev, managed to have himself appointed chairman of the Taijikistan Supreme Soviet in December 1992. He has ruled the country with an iron fist ever since.

Once installed, Rakhmonov sought political legitimacy by holding presidential elections and also sponsoring a public referendum to approve a new constitution. Significantly, Tajikistan was the last of the former Soviet republics to ditch its communist-inspired constitution. This document called for creation of a strong executive president, and a rubber-stamp assembly, the Oily Majli. On November 6, 1994, Rakhmonov won a contested field with 58 percent of votes cast while the new constitution was approved by 90 percent. However, many opposition groups boycotted the entire process because they had not been privy to the decision-making process. Nonetheless, Rakhmonov's first task as leader was to seek an end to the civil war fought by Tajik rebels based in neighboring Afghanistan. With Iranian mediation, a cease-fire was arranged by December 1994, although its terms are enforced by a large Russian garrison of "peacekeepers" dispatched by Moscow. These troops have proven critical to the ongoing stability of the country, and in April 1999 Rakhmonov signed a 25-year basing agreement to keep them at hand.

As a ruler, Rakhmonov has been extremely authoritarian by nature. His regime has banned most opposition parties, limited press freedom, and generally violated the spirit and letter of human rights agreements. However, he did manage to bring to the country some semblance of peace and stability. Violence and political turmoil still exist, and in April 1997 the president was nearly killed in a grenade attack, but the overall truce appears to be holding. On November 6, 1999,

Rakhmonov was reelected with 97 percent of the vote, which opponents say is a suspicious number by its sheer scope. Furthermore, during parliamentary elections to fill a newly created bicameral legislature, Rahkmonov's party won 45 out of 63 seats, thereby insuring his complete control of national affairs.

Despite the unsavory nature of Tajikistan's government, after the September 11, 2001, attack on New York's World Trade Center, Rahkmonov determined to demonstrate his worthiness as an ally to his biggest critic: the United States. The following November he pledged full cooperation with America in its war against Afghanistan, and he allowed U.S. military forces complete access to two airfields. He has long suffered from attacks by the Taliban regime, along with receiving thousands of refugees fleeing the fighting, and he welcomed the opportunity to rid himself of this unruly neighbor. "It is no secret that we have supported the Northern Alliance for six or seven years," he declared, "and we will support them now." Allies are extremely difficult to find in this remote part of the world; consequently, in March 2002 the American ambassador to Tajikistan personally thanked Rakhmonov. Furthermore, he pledged to support the regime with food aid and educational assistance as necessary.

Further Reading

Abdullaev, Kamoludin, and Shahram Akbarzadeh. *Historical Dictionary of Taijikistan.* Lanham, Md.: Scarecrow Press, 2002.

Fatoev, Saidmurod. *President Emomali Rakhmonov.* London: London and Flint River Editions, 1998.

Gleason, Gregory. "Why Russia Is in Tajikistan." *Comparative Strategy* 20 (January–March 2001): 77–90.

Kiasatpour, Soleiman M. "Regime Transition in Post-Soviet Central Asia." Unpublished Ph.D. dissertation, University of California, Riverside, 1998.

Lynch, Dov. Russian *Peacekeeping Strategies in the CIS: The Cases of Moldova, Georgia, and Tajikistan.* New York: St. Martin's Press, 2000.

Meyer, Karl E. *The Dust of Empire: The Race for Mastery in the Asian Heartland.* New York: Public Affairs, 2003.

Ramgoolam, Navinchandra (1947–)

prime minister of Mauritius

Navinchandra Ramgoolam was born on Mauritius on July 14, 1947, the son of Sir Seewoosagur Ramgoolam,

a future prime minister. His nation is a collection of small islands located almost 500 miles east of Madagascar in the Indian Ocean. Originally uninhabited, Mauritius was colonized by the Dutch and French before passing into British hands after 1810. The island economy was then deeply committed to the sugar trade, manned by African slaves, but when slavery was outlawed in 1835, the British brought indentured servants from India to work the fields. Consequently, today Hindus form the majority of the island's population in this nominally African nation. Mauritius gained independence in 1968 as a parliamentary democracy, although in 1992 the constitution was amended to change the form of government into a republic within the British Commonwealth. Government thus consists of a president with ceremonial functions, a prime minister who holds real authority, and a National Assembly. Mauritius is also unique among African nations in possessing both a functioning economy and a very high standard of living. Its success is even more remarkable considering the vast array of people and cultures encompassed: Indians, Africans, Europeans, and a smattering of Chinese. English and French are the official languages of government, but newspapers are published in several languages. In many respects tiny Mauritius is a microcosm of humanity and an economic model for the rest of the developing world.

Ramgoolam was educated locally before studying medicine at the Royal College for Surgeons in Dublin, Ireland. He also studied law at the London School of Economics and returned home to complete his medical residence in the capital of Port Louis. In 1991 Ramgoolam commenced his political career by joining the Mauritius Labor Party (MLP) and winning a seat in parliament. Capitalizing on his reputation as the son of Sir Seewoosagur Ramgoolam, the nation's first prime minister (1968), he entered the contest for high office in 1995. His opponent was Sir ANEROOD JUGNAUTH of the Mauritius Socialist Party (PSM), who had been prime minister since 1982. For many years his administration had been dogged by allegations of corruption, and the public seemed ready for a change. In November 1995 a motion to mandate instruction in Oriental languages was defeated, prompting Jugnauth to call for new elections. However, Ramgoolam had engineered an alliance between his own MLP and the Mauritius Militant Movement (MMM), and elections held that December gave the coalition 60 of 62 seats. Ramgoolam was subsequently sworn in as the island's third prime minister, while MMM founder Paul Berenger became vice prime minister.

As head of a center/left coalition, Ramgoolam was called upon to juggle competing priorities and faced some tough decisions. He settled upon designing policies that would create jobs and prosperity while simultaneously addressing issues of social inequity. And, having campaigned to end corruption, he fired his finance minister in August 1996 for falsely enhancing the annual budget. However, Ramgoolam's most pressing problem was paring down the island's civil service, which was entrenched, accounted for many high-paying jobs, and annually drained the public coffers. To placate his coalition partners he did not reduce the size of the bureaucracy, but he found it more expedient to cancel a 15 percent pay increase promised by the previous administration. Ramgoolam had better success expanding the island's agricultural sector, which is overwhelmingly skewed toward sugar production. In 1998 the island was rocked by a severe drought that cost $160 million in lost revenues; the prime minister responded by discouraging the production of tea in favor of more sugar and overhauling the structure of agricultural production from inefficient, small-plot farmers to larger farms. Ramgoolam also encouraged greater industrialization in textile manufacturing, electronics, and software. Tourism and its attendant service industries were also enhanced over the next four years, so that the island's economy grew at an annual rate of 6 percent. "I want to make Mauritius the tiger of the Indian Ocean," he promised.

Ramgoolam's main shortcoming in office was in failing to placate more strident members of the MMM coalition. Once Vice Prime Minister Berenger became his most vocal critic, Ramgoolam demanded and obtained his resignation in June 1997. MMM subsequently left the government altogether, and the Labor Party was forced to carry on without them. In September 2000 the MLP faced off against a new coalition of the MSP and MMM under Jugnauth and Berenger. To facilitate their union, they had agreed that, if victorious, Jugnauth would serve as prime minister for three years and would be succeeded by Berenger—the first non-Hindu leader—for the remaining two. The strategy proved fortuitous, for the coalition swept the election, taking 54 of 62 seats. On September 14, 2000, Ramgoolam, who retained his own seat in parliament, re-

signed as prime minister. He will continue in office as leader of the opposition.

Further Reading

Dabee, Rajen, and David Greenaway. *The Mauritian Economy: A Reader.* Basingstoke, England: Palgrave, 2001.

Dommen, Edward, and Bridget Dommen. *Mauritius: An Island of Success; A Retrospective Study.* Oxford: James Currey, 1999.

Eriksen, Thomas H. *Common Denominators: Ethnicity, Nation-Building, and Compromise in Mauritius.* Oxford: Berg, 1998.

Fletcher, R. Lee. "Globalism, Regionalism, and the State: The Case of Mauritius and the Indian Ocean Region." Unpublished master's thesis, Baylor University, 2001.

Miles, William F. S. "The Politics of Language Equilibrium in a Multilingual Society: Mauritius." *Comparative Politics* 32, no. 2 (2000): 215–230.

Ramos, Fidel (1928–) *president of the Philippines*

Fidel Valdez Ramos was born on March 18, 1928, in Lingayen, the Philippines, the son of a career diplomat. He was raised in comparative luxury and attended private schools before being admitted to the U.S. Military Academy, West Point, in 1946. He graduated in 1950 and went on to command a detachment of American troops during the Korean War one year later. In 1952 he enrolled at the University of Illinois, where he obtained a degree in civil engineering. Ramos then remained in the ranks of the Philippine military where, in 1970, he led a contingent of troops during the Vietnam War. After his return in 1972, Ramos accepted command of the newly created Philippine Constabulary, a quasi-military national police force created by dictator Ferdinand Marcos. It was created ostensibly to deal with ongoing rebellions by Communists and Muslim insurgents, but in reality the force was designed to harass opponents of the regime. Curiously, Ramos was the dictator's second cousin, and he readily accepted the post. For the next 13 years he directed the activities of the constabulary, which acquired a poor reputation for respecting human rights. In 1985 Marcos then rewarded Ramos by elevating him to chief of staff of the Philippine armed forces. However, that year also marked the assassination of Senator Benigno Aquino by the military and the rise of his wife, Corazon, as an opposition figure. A national election was held on January 17, 1986, and both Aquino and Marcos claimed victory. Ramos, along with the rest of the military, were suddenly caught in the middle of a succession dispute. Despite his prior association with the dictator, Ramos apparently experienced a change of heart and he convinced the generals to support Aquino's claim to victory. This decision proved decisive, and in February 1986 Marcos fled the islands. Democracy had finally returned to the Philippines.

In exchange for this display of support, Aquino appointed Ramos to serve as her minister of defense. She, like most of her countrymen, was apparently willing to forgive the general for his long tenure with the Philippine Constabulary. In this office, Ramos proved his continuing loyalty to the administration by quashing no less than seven coup attempts by disgruntled military officers. He also completely overhauled the constabulary, tightening discipline and eliminating corruption. Ramos also took corrective measures to address the long-standing rebellion by the New People's Army in the southernmost islands. Having deduced the cause of the insurrection as economic, and not political, he stepped up financial measures to combat rural poverty and the rebellion eventually subsided. Ramos's capable and competent handling of various assignments eventually gave rise to his reputation as "Steady Eddie." In December 1991, when Aquino's mandated single term in office concluded, he declared his candidacy for the highest office. Aquino also endorsed her defense minister for president.

As a professional military officer, Ramos was not closely associated with any political party, so he initiated his own: the United People Power Movement. This consisted of mostly stockbrokers, company executives, and other elites, but Ramos campaigned vigorously throughout the land. The presidential field was hotly contested by six other candidates, and when the election was held on May 11, 1992, Ramos won a plurality with 23.5 percent of the vote. Congressional investigations concluded that a significant degree of voter fraud was present, but not enough to alter the outcome. Ramos's success is significant for several reasons: it represented the first peaceful transfer of power since 1965; he was the first military figure to attain the presidency; and he was also the first Protestant elected in this predominately Catholic nation. Over the next six years Ramos presided over an impressive period of economic growth and prosperity, and he

took dramatic steps to increase the amount of electricity available to the nation. Ramos also had good success in ending a rebellion by the Moro Islamic Liberation Front in Mindanao by granting the region more autonomy. By 1998, toward the end of his six-year tenure, the Philippines was wracked by the Asian currency crisis and the economy tumbled, but Ramos retained his otherwise high approval ratings. On May 11, 1998, he was succeeded by Vice President JOSEPH ESTRADA, who inherited a country more prosperous and stable than it had been in decades.

Ramos began a new life as a private citizen, but in January 2001, he was suddenly thrust back into the national limelight. Estrada was about to be impeached for corruption and the Supreme Court declared the presidency vacant. This allowed Vice President GLORIA MACAPAGAL-ARROYO to claim the executive office, but initially she enjoyed little support from the military. On January 20, 2001, Ramos, clad in his blue polo short and running shoes, jogged from his house to military headquarters at Camp Aguinaldo. There he prevailed upon commanders not to interfere with the massive anti-Estrada demonstrations accompanying Macapagal Arroyo's occupation of the presidential palace, which transpired peacefully. Thus, for the second time in his life, Ramos insured that the Philippine military upheld the rule of law and the democratic process.

Further Reading

Kirk, Donald. *Looted: The Philippines after the Bases.* New York: St. Martin's Press, 1999.

Sheridan, Greg. *Tigers: Leaders of the New Asia-Pacific.* St. Leonards, New South Wales: Allen and Unwin, 1997.

Riedinger, Jeffrey. "The Philippines in 1994: Renewed Growth and Contested Reforms." *Asian Survey* 35 (February 1995): 209–217.

Villacerta, Wilfrido. "The Curse of the Weak State: Leadership Imperatives from the Ramos Government." *Contemporary Southeast Asia* 16 (June 1994): 67–93.

Youngblood, Robert L. "President Ramos, the Church, and Population Policy in the Philippines." *Asian Affairs* 25 (Spring 1998): 3–20.

Rania al-Abdullah (1970–) *queen of Jordan*

Rania al-Yasin was born on August 31, 1970, in Kuwait City, Kuwait, the daughter of a Palestinian doctor. Her family had relocated from their home in the West Bank in search of a better life, and Rania was raised in a middle-class environment. She also received a Western-style education, becoming fluent in English, and in 1991 she graduated from the American University in Cairo, Egypt, with a degree in business administration. However, that same year the Iraqi invasion of Kuwait induced her family to move to Jordan, where she soon found work as a bank teller. She subsequently worked for Apple Computers in Amman, where in 1993, Rania was introduced to Prince Abdullah bin al-Hussein, son of King HUSSEIN I of Jordan. The two fell in love and were married on June 10, 1993. Now a princess and part of the royal household, Rania determined to take an active role in promoting the causes she held very dear. "I personally do not think that getting married to a prince and having the title of 'princess' bestowed upon me overnight makes me deserving of it," she insists. "It is something I feel I should earn by contributing positively to society." As the daughter of immigrants, Rania was acutely aware of the poverty gripping the majority of Palestinians as they arrived in Jordan as refugees fleeing various wars with Israel. Refugees currently constitute one-third to one-half of Jordan's population. Therefore, in 1995 Rania founded the Jordan River Foundation to help poorer citizens supplement their incomes through participatory projects. As the mother of three children, she also proved outspoken in matters pertaining to early childhood development. More than anything, the young princess prided herself in maintaining and cultivating a "common touch."

As King Hussein's son, Prince Abdullah was a member of the royal family but he was not directly in line for succession to the throne. The reigning crown prince was Hussein's younger brother, Hassan bin Tallal. However, this situation changed unexpectedly in January 1999 when the king, who had been in the United States receiving treatments for cancer, grew angry at his brother's excesses. Two weeks before his death, he suddenly advanced Abdullah as heir to the throne in Hassan's place. On February 7, 1999, he was crowned ABDULLAH II of Jordan, while his young wife was enthroned as Queen Rania al-Abdullah. This changed her life markedly, for she suddenly was a sovereign head of 6 million people. Given the quicksilver nature of Middle Eastern politics, and growing Islamic fundamentalism against women in government, it seemed a daunting proposition for the former bank clerk. However, Rania possessed an intellect

and steely resolve that belied her Hollywood starlet looks. Given her high visibility in the Arab world, she was determined to make a difference.

One of the first controversies confronted by the new queen was the subject of child abuse. This had long been a taboo subject in Jordanian society, and there was not even a proper word describing the practice. However, to combat this silence and the abuse it perpetuates, she founded Dar al-Aman (Home of Safety), the first such facility in the Middle East, in August 2000. The queen also proved outspoken on another taboo subject—honor killings—whereby female members of a family can be legally murdered by male relatives for engaging in premarital sex. This stance put her on a collision course with more conservative religious elements, who have never subscribed to the notion of women as equals. Nonetheless, Rania remains a practicing Muslim and freely defends both her faith and the subordinate role it assigns to women. "We, as a country, give women the right to choose whether they want to wear the veil or not," she affirmed. "From the Western perspective, I think a lot of people believe the veil symbolizes backwardness. In reality, that's not the case." But, when the Jordanian legislature twice rejected legislation to outlaw honor killings, the queen authorized a sizable women's march in protest. Rania remains a thoroughly modern woman in a region beset by medieval attitudes.

The king and queen of Jordan have since been accepted around the world as the best-liked and best-looking royal couple since Prince Charles and Princess Diana of England. They have been received by heads of state and literally besieged by the media in London, Paris, and Washington, D.C. Rania herself has been variously hailed as beautiful, intelligent, stylish, and in every sense the modern Arab woman. But neither monarch can escape the painful realities of the Middle East for long. In the fall of 2001 she visited the American Red Cross national headquarters to demonstrate sympathy for victims of the World Trade Center disaster. In May 2002, when a spate of deadly suicide bombings induced Israeli occupation of numerous Palestinian towns, Rania characteristically organized and led a march in protest. Apparently, the action struck a particular chord with the queen, for one of the settlements taken—Tulkam—is her family's ancestral home. The first lady of Jordan continues as the outspoken champion of women's and children's rights and a better future for the Palestinian people.

Further Reading

Brand, Laurie A. *Women, the States, and Political Liberalization: Middle Eastern and North African Experiences.* New York: Columbian University Press, 1998.

Joffe, George, ed. *Jordan in Transition.* New York: Palgrave, 2002.

Massad, Joseph A. *Colonial Effects: The Making of National Identity in Jordan.* New York: Columbia University Press, 2001.

Ryan, Curtis R. *Jordan in Transition: From Hussein to Abdullah.* Boulder, Colo.: Lynne Rienner Publishers, 2002.

Shukri, Shiria J. A. *Arab Women: Unequal Partners in Development.* Brookfield, Vt.: Avebury, 1996.

Rao, P. V. N. (1923–   ) *prime minister of India*

Pamulaparti Venkata Narasimha Rao was born on June 28, 1921, in Hyderabad, Andhra Pradesh state, India, the son of a successful farmer and landowner. Being a brahmin, the highest social caste, he was eligible for higher educational opportunities denied most Indians. Rao took degrees from Osmania University, Hyderabad, Bombay University, and Nagpur University, where he acquired a well-deserved reputation as a linguist. In fact, Rao became fluent in English, French, Persian, Arabic, Spanish, and three distinct Indian dialects. As a young man he actively participated in the independence movement from Great Britain, and he also worked as a journalist. It was not until 1957 that he pursued politics by winning a seat in the Andhra Pradesh legislature, which he held for the next 22 years. In 1971 Rao became chief minister of his state and three years later he resigned from local politics to serve as secretary of the Congress Party under Prime Minister Indira Gandhi. This initiated his long association as a political ally to the Gandhi dynasty, which lasted two decades. Gandhi certainly appreciated his loyalty during this turbulent period in India's history, and in 1980 she appointed the soft-spoken scholar her foreign minister. Rao initially protested this promotion, as he detested traveling and socializing, but he fulfilled his duties well. In 1984 Gandhi made him minister of home affairs, shortly before her assassination by Sikh bodyguards. This act triggered nationwide riots and Rao was heavily criticized for failing to impose order quickly. However, the new prime minister, Rajiv Gandhi, retained him in high office by conferring portfolios of defense minister and human resources

minister on him. When Gandhi was himself assassinated on May 21, 1991, the Congress Party scrambled to find a successor who was dynamic, charismatic, and widely known. Rao was none of these, yet he became the next party head because of his lack of political ambition and the enemies that accompany it. Though ill and on the verge of retirement, he was sworn in on June 21, 1991, the first prime minister to hail from a southern state.

Previously, Rao had been somewhat derided for his soft-spoken manner, his bookish inclinations, and decidedly boring personality. Nobody could have anticipated what would have happened next. India was then on the verge of economic collapse and was selling off gold reserves to raise money. Worse yet, the national debt had reached $71 billion while inflation was at 17 percent and climbing. Rao acted with surprising swiftness and decisiveness by jettisoning the Gandhi legacy of socialist/state control policies and instituting free-market reforms. These included liberalizing the economy, selling off state-owned and operated assets, and attracting foreign investment. "This government is committed to removing the cobwebs that come in the way of rapid industrialization," he declared. "We will work towards making India internationally competitive." Rao drastically overhauled the way India conducted business and, in concert with some austerity measures, he acquired results. Within months the economy turned around and in October 1991 the International Monetary Fund granted Rao $1.8 billion in loans for additional development. On the diplomatic front, Rao's first priority was to repair diplomatic relations with the United States, which had fallen into disarray during the Gandhi years. In 1993 he also signed an accord with neighboring China to reduce troop levels along the border and restore peace to the Himalayas. That same year the prime minister faced a vote of no confidence and survived easily. Too easily, it turned out.

Rao enjoyed decidedly less success addressing the rise of sectarian violence in India, especially between the Hindu majority and the Muslim minority. In late 1992 Hindu extremists burned down Ayodhya mosque, an act precipitating hundreds of deaths. Rao was roundly criticized for failing to anticipate the violence or halt it once it commenced. Fighting also flared up in the northernmost province of Kashmir, where Muslims constitute the majority and have been agitating for union with neighboring Pakistan. Sikhs in Punjab state also violently protested what they considered affronts to their religion at the hands of Hindu followers. Rao tried earnestly to ameliorate the tearing of India's social fabric, but results were slow in coming. Worse, in 1996 his administration was rocked by a scandal touching several high-ranking ministers. Elections held that May handed the Congress Party its worst defeat ever, and Rao was compelled to resign from office. His successor was H. D. DEVE GOWDA of the United Front.

Rao remained titular head of the Congress Party until late in 1996, when he finally withdrew from politics over allegations of political bribery. The gravity of the charges increased with the passage of time and, on September 29, 2000, he became the first former prime minister convicted of corruption charges. He was charged with making payouts to the Jharkland Mukti Morcha, a rival party, in exchange for favorable votes during the 1993 no-confidence motion. The following month he was fined and sentenced to three years in prison, but in March 2002 another court overturned his conviction for lack of evidence. The former head of state has since resumed his life of quiet retirement.

Further Reading

Adams, J. "Reforming India's Economy in an Era of Global Change." *Current History* 95 (April 1996): 151–157.

Ganguly, Sumit. "India in 1991: A Year of Upheaval." *Asian Survey* 37 (February 1997): 126–136.

Jenkins, R. "The Contrived Democratization of Indian Democracy: Regionalization, Social Change, and the 1996 General Election." *Democratization* 3 (Winter 1996): 501–516.

Raman, A. S. "Prime Minister Rao of India." *Contemporary Review* 259 (October 1991): 183–189.

Rubinoff, Arthur G. "Missed Opportunities and Contradictory Policies: Indo-American Relations in the Clinton-Rao Years." *Pacific Affairs* 69 (Winter 1997): 500–519.

Rasmussen, Anders (1953–) *prime minister of Denmark*

Anders Fogh Rasmussen was born on January 26, 1953 in Jutland, Denmark, the son of farmers. He became politically active in high school by joining the youth wing of the Venstre (Liberal, actually conservative) Party in 1970. He first stood for a seat in the Folketing (parliament) in 1973 at the age of 20, and he was defeated. However, in 1978 Rasmussen was appointed to fill a va-

cated Liberal seat there, becoming the youngest member of that body. Concurrently, Rasmussen attended Aarhus University and acquired his master's degree in economics by 1978. Staunchly conservative in his younger days, Rasmussen published widely on the excesses of Denmark's comprehensive welfare state, which promoted, to his mind, a "slave mentality." He was repeatedly returned to the Folketing over the next two decades, chaired a number of important committees, and in 1985 gained appointment as Venstre' deputy chairman. Two years later Rasmussen became minister of taxation, which he held for five years straight—a Danish record. As of December 1990 he also assumed the portfolio of minister of finance, and he represented Denmark in negotiations that produced the 1991 Maastricht Treaty for greater economic integration. In November 1992 a minor flap ensued about an investigative report—initiated by Rasmussen—that criticized his reporting of affairs to parliament, and he resigned. He remained Venstre's policy spokesman in the Folketing until March 1998, when the post of party chairman was tendered. After 25 years of solid and noncontroversial service in politics, Rasmussen finally positioned himself to run for prime minister in November 2001.

For the previous eight years, Danish politics had been dominated by the Social Democratic Party under Prime Minister POUL NYRUP RASMUSSEN (no relation). The country had basically prospered under his leadership, but the polity began showing wariness over the issue of immigration. One group, the nationalistic Danish People's Party, began vocally campaigning for the removal of immigrants as a threat to the continuance of Denmark's culture. Such extremism was roundly denounced by the Social Democrats, but Rasmussen seized upon it, seeking to draw greater distinction between Venstre and his opponents. "There is a minority of young immigrants who don't accept the values on which Danish society is built," he observed, "who refuse integration, and who commit serious crimes." However, Rasmussen had by now radically mitigated his approach to welfare state politics, and he came to embrace and defend them. Fear of dismantling social benefits was the issue that brought Poul Nyrup Rasmussen to power in 1994, and this time the Liberals would not repeat their mistake. And, like role model TONY BLAIR of Britain, Rasmussen made his greatest pitch for voters in the middle of the spectrum. After eight years of rising taxes and lenient immigration controls, Danish voters seemed ripe for change. Accordingly, on November 20, 2001, the Social Democrats endured their biggest defeat since 1920, being reduced to 52 seats while the Liberals scored 56. This placed Rasmussen in range of a coalition with the 16-seat Conservative Party, and he was sworn in as Denmark's new prime minister on November 27, 2001.

As promised, Rasmussen proffered new and tighter restrictions on Denmark's burgeoning immigrant community. Henceforth, new residents were obliged to wait seven years before receiving the full range of benefits. They were also forbidden from bringing family members into the country beforehand, and they had to learn the national language. However, Rasmussen was careful to couch his policies in terms acceptable to European Union guidelines for such issues, and he rejected the Danish People's Party call for outright expulsion. This puts his administration at odds with Pia Kjaersgaard, DPP chairperson, who holds the third-largest majority in parliament. Immigration reform was thus instituted, but in a more palatable fashion than many nationalists would have preferred. Rasmussen's rise to power also coincided with Denmark's turn as head of the European Union, in which he served as president for six months. Rasmussen, a fervent EU supporter, endorses the notion of admitting Eastern European countries into the fold once they acquire rudiments of a free-market economy and human rights. However, expansion is directly threatened by the issue of farm subsidies paid out to member nations and many countries, like Germany, are on record as opposing excessively high subsidy payments to their neighbors. Nonetheless, the new president stands firm in his support for expansion. "I have one big and very clear ambition, that we succeed in deciding on enlargement of the European Union," he said. "This is really the most important political decision of my generation and it would be a failure of historic dimensions if we failed to make that decision." Rasmussen surrendered the EU presidency in December 2002, although he is expected to remain prime minister until new elections are called in November 2005.

Further Reading

Branner, Hans, and Morten Kelstrup. *Denmark's Policy towards Europe after 1945: History, Theory, and Options.* Odense: Odense University Press, 2000,

Einhorn, Eric S. *Modern Welfare States: Scandinavian Politics and Policy in the Global Age.* Westport, Conn.: Praeger, 2003.

Fitzmaurice, John. *Politics in Denmark.* New York: St. Martin's Press, 1981.

Flyvbjerg, Bent. *Rationality and Power: Democracy in Practice.* Chicago: University of Chicago Press, 1998.

Miller, Kenneth E. *Friends and Rivals: Coalition Politics in Denmark, 1901–1995.* Lanham, Md.: University Press of America, 1996.

Tonra, Ben. *The Europeanization of National Foreign Policy: Dutch, Danish, and Irish Foreign Policy in the European Union.* Aldershot, England: Ashgate, 2001.

Rasmussen, Poul (1943–) *prime minister of Denmark*

Poul Nyrup Rasmussen was born in Esbjerg, Denmark, on June 15, 1943, the son of laborers. Denmark is the only Scandinavian country on the European landmass and is strategically located at the entrance to the Baltic Sea, north of Germany. It became a constitutional monarchy in 1849 and it is governed by a prime minister and a unicameral legislature, the Folketing. The prime minister is appointed by the king or queen, from the parliamentary party with the most seats, but since 1901 Denmark has been unique in being controlled by a coalition of parties, with no one group in the ascent. This has resulted in a system of governance that prizes bargaining and consensus between various interests to obtain—and keep—a working majority. Denmark also employs a system of proportional representation, which means any party gaining at least 2 percent of the national vote is eligible for representation in the Folketing. Consequently, the polity is divided up between ten viable parties. Denmark is also fortunate in possessing one of the world's highest standards of living and, like all Scandinavian states, it maintains a generous welfare state for its citizens.

Despite his working-class origins, Rasmussen attended Copenhagen University and received a master's degree in economics there in 1962. He also became politically active by joining the youth wing of the moderately leftist Social Democratic Party. Upon graduating, Rasmussen served as an economist with the National Labor Confederation, and in 1986 he became director of a worker's retirement fund. He gained election to parliament in 1988 with the Social Democrats and, by dint of his youth and dynamism, quickly gained appointment as the party vice chair. At that time the sitting party leader,

Anker Joergensen, was criticized for his abrasive style of leadership and inability to enlarge the party's appeal. In April 1992 the Social Democrats elected Rasmussen, who demonstrated a keen ability to work with diverse elements, as party head to replace him. The timing proved fortuitous, for the following year a conservative government under Poul Schluter resigned over a scandal. Rasmussen, as head of the largest party in the Folketing, was given a chance to form a coalition government. With consummate skill, he crafted together an alliance of three parties: his own Social Democrats, the Christian Democrats, and the Center Democrats. In 1994 he won his first contested national election, and the Social Democrats began their first majority coalition government since 1982.

Rasmussen came to power at a time of economic prosperity, but recent developments at home portended trouble ahead. Namely, in May 1992, Danish voters soundly rejected the Maastricht Treaty, which called for a common defense and foreign policy and a common currency for Europe. It was a major defeat for the European movement. However, Rasmussen, an impassioned believer in European integration, made passage of this act the centerpiece of his administration. He had the treaty revised to placate Denmark's nervousness over surrendering sovereignty, resubmitted the measure in June 1993, and it passed. Thereafter he concentrated on the economy, which grew at an annual rate of 3 percent, with 7 percent unemployment and an inflation rate of 2 percent. It was an impressive performance, but credit for success began to be undermined by the potentially divisive issue of immigration. Various right-wing groups had begun sounding the tocsin against the continuing arrival of foreigners and the Social Democrats, who favor immigration, struggled to respond. The issue struck hard at the left wing, and during elections held in March 1998 the Social Democrats clung to power only by aligning themselves with the Radical Liberal Party, which granted them a majority of only one seat.

Over the next four years, Rasmussen was generally successful in leading the country, although Denmark's notoriously independent streak began asserting itself again at the international level. On September 28, 2000, voters soundly rejected adoption of the euro as the nation's single, integrated currency by 53 percent. Rasmussen countered by pledging to resubmit the scheme, once certain ambiguities had been worked out. However, the issue of immigration again came to the fore at the be-hest of the far-right Danish People's Party. In the wake of the September 11, 2001, attack on the World Trade Center in New York, conservatives began calling for an outright ban on immigration to prevent the arrival of possible terrorists. Rasmussen, sensing a potential crisis, sought to capitalize on his high approval ratings by calling for national elections in October, five months ahead of schedule. "The world is not the same," he maintained. "In these times of uncertainty, security has to be ensured, increased cohesion and solidarity are needed, Denmark must not be split." However, his call went unheeded. On November 21, 2001, the right-leaning Liberal Party under ANDERS FOGH RASMUSSEN (no relation), which pledged to tighten immigration, won a convincing majority. The far-right Danish People's Party also registered increased appeal, winning 22 seats, its largest margin ever. Prime Minister Rasmussen had little recourse but to tender his resignation to Queen Margrethe, which he did the following day. His departure marks the end of 10 years of Social Democratic rule, and the first time since 1920 that the Liberals have held more seats.

Further Reading

Bjugan, Ketil. "The 1998 Danish Parliamentary Elections: Social Democrats Muddle through to Victory." *West European Politics* 22 (January 1999): 172–179.

Flyjerg, Bent. *Rationality of Power: Democracy in Practice.* Chicago: University of Chicago Press, 1998.

Jorgensen, Henning. *Consensus, Cooperation and Conflict: The Policy-Making Process in Denmark.* Northampton, Mass.: Edward Elgar, 2002.

Lundvall, Bengte-Ake. *Innovation, Growth, and Social Cohesion: The Danish Model.* Northampton, Mass.: Edward Elgar, 2002.

Miller, Kenneth E. *Friends and Rivals: Coalition Politics in Denmark, 1901–1995.* Lanham, Md.: University Press of America, 1996.

Ratsiraka, Didier (1936–) *president of Madagascar*

Didier Ratsiraka was born in Vatomandry, Madagascar, on November 4, 1936, a member of the Cotiers, or coastal tribes. His homeland is the world's fourth-largest island, located 240 miles off the coast of East Africa. It remains one of the world's poorest nations and is inhabited by an ethnically diverse population numbering

16 million. Worse, there is long-standing antipathy between the majority coastal tribes, or Cotiers, and the interior clans, or Merinas. Madagascar became a French possession in 1896, and for nearly a century France's colonial administration favored the Mervinas over the Cotiers. This only served to heighten existing tensions that spilled over once Madagascar became an independent republic in 1960. The first president, Philbert Tsiranana, ruled until 1972 when he was overthrown by a popular coup. A series of military leaders then ensued until a government was finally established in June 1975. Currently, Madagascar's constitution provides for a strong executive president and a bicameral legislature consisting of a Senate and a National Assembly. A prime minister is also appointed by the president who then assigns the members of a cabinet of ministers. And, despite a stormy relationship with its former colonial master, the island maintains close economic and cultural ties to France.

Ratsiraka was educated on Madagascar before attending the Lycée Henry IV in Paris, France. He subsequently joined the French navy, was allowed to pass through the Ecole Navale (French naval academy), and also graduated from the Ecole Supérieure de Guerre Navale with degrees in engineering. Ratsiraka then transferred to the Malagasy navy as a captain in 1963. In 1972 he was also directed to serve as the government's naval attaché in Paris. When President Tsiranana was overthrown by the military that year, he was replaced by General Gabriel Ramanatsoa. Ratsiraka then found himself appointed foreign minister, and in this capacity he also orchestrated the removal of all French military and naval bases from the island. Moreover, he was especially impressed by a visit to the People's Republic of China in the fall of 1972. By 1975 continuing unrest forced General Ramanatsoa to resign, but his replacement, Colonel Richard Ratsimandrava, was assassinated after only six days in power. Consequently, a military directorate appointed Ratsiraka president in June 1975. The following December a new constitution was passed by 94 percent of the vote, which confirmed his appointment as president for the next seven years.

Ratsiraka, a fiery nationalist and a committed socialist, ruled Madagascar with little interruption for 17 years. He completely reoriented the nation's priorities toward closer relations with China and the Soviet Union, and he broke off relations with Madagascar's closest trading partner, South Africa. Furthermore, he completely overhauled the previous free-market economy with a centrally directed nationalist one, and in the process nearly ruined it. By the mid-1980s he moderated his stance and returned to free-market practices, and he also cultivated favor with the International Monetary Fund (IMF) and World Bank for loans and investments. Overall, as the economy sputtered and growth slowed, Ratsiraka's popularity likewise faltered, although he remained extremely popular among his fellow Cotiers. In 1992 popular unrest forced him to allow a referendum on multiparty democracy, which passed by a large margin, and which also reduced the length of his terms to four years. That November Ratsiraka then lost the election to a challenger, Albert Zafy, who won by 45 percent to 29 percent in the first round of voting, and by an impressive 66.7 percent during the second round, held on February 10, 1993. Ratsiraka then stepped down until January 1997, when he defeated Zafy by a razor-thin margin, gaining 50.71 percent of votes cast.

Ratsiraka ruled during the next four years with little controversy, and he improved ties with the West by increasing a trend toward economic liberalization and privatization. In an attempt to smooth over continuing ethnic tensions, in March 1998 he sponsored a new constitutional referendum that divided the island into six autonomous provinces under a new federal arrangement. The measure narrowly passed by 50.96 percent and its effect upon future governance remains unknown. In December 2001 Ratsiraka ran against a new candidate, Marc Ravalomanana, and the two men garnered 40.9 percent and 46.2 percent of the vote, respectively. The plurality necessitated a runoff in March 2002, but Ravalomanana, fearing election fraud, upstaged his adversary by declaring himself president and seizing the capital of Antananarivo. However, the 67-year-old Ratsiraka refused to step down, especially as his popularity runs deep in the countryside. Throughout the spring of 2002 his supporters effectively blockaded the capital, attempting to starve the opposition into surrendering. "I don't want my name to be soiled," the president defiantly insisted, "I don't want people to say that Ratsiraka is a deserter, that he is one who allowed a horde of neo-fascists and Nazis, as they are often called, to vassalise our children and our children's children." The Organization of African Unity has since been called in to attempt arbitration but the three-month-old impasse remains in play, and Madagascar continues without a head of state.

Further Reading

Allen, Philip M. *Madagascar: Conflicts of Authority on the Great Island.* Boulder, Colo.: Westview Press, 1995.

Brown, Mervyn. *A History of Madagascar.* Princeton, N.J.: Markus Wiener Publications, 2001.

Gow, Bonar A. "Admiral Didier Ratsiraka and the Malagasy Socialist Revolution." *Journal of Modern African Studies* 35, no. 3 (1997): 409–439.

Marcus, Richard. "Madagascar: Legitimizing Authority." *Current History* 100 (May 2001): 226–231.

Sharp, Leslie A. *The Sacrificed Generation: Youth, History, and the Colonial Mind in Madagascar.* Berkeley: University of California Press, 2002.

Rau, Johannes (1931–) *president of Germany*

Johannes Rau was born on January 16, 1931, in Wuppertal-Barmen, Germany, the son of a businessman turned Protestant minister. He absorbed his father's intense religiosity and initially worked as a sales representative for Protestant publishing houses. Consistent with his pacifist leanings, Rau joined the German People's Party in 1952 to oppose resurrecting the German army for NATO. In 1957 he switched over to the more mainstream Social Democratic Party (SPD), becoming associated with its right wing. As a member Rau campaigned against tendencies toward Marxism in the party, and he also opposed alliances with the environmentalist Green Party, which he considered extremist. Rau himself proved something of a folksy, nondogmatic campaigner, and in 1958 he won a seat in the North Rhine–Westphalia assembly. He was consistently reelected over the next four decades and acquired a national reputation for dominating political affairs in his native state. By 1967 Rau had risen to chairman of the state SDP chapter, and he also served as mayor of Wuppertal. In 1978 he gained election as minister-president of North Rhine–Westphalia, and among his most notable accomplishments was the opening of six new universities. Through such popular expedients Rau became the most popular SDP politician in Germany, despite its lack of success against the Christian Democratic Union of Chancellor HELMUT KOHL. In 1987 the SDP nominated Rau as its candidate for the chancellory, although he spent inordinate time placating warring factions within his own party. But despite his popularity at home, the SDP was still viewed as too left-leaning in most of Germany and it lost handily to Kohl. None of this reflected badly on Rau,

and in 1994 he carried the SDP banner during elections for the federal presidency. Again, he lost to the more conservative Roman Herzog of the CDU, but only by narrow margins. In May 1999 he finally triumphed by becoming president over two female candidates. Rau was sworn into office on July 1, 1999, becoming the first German executive since World War II to serve in the newly reunified capital of Berlin.

Rau brings to office nearly 50 years of successful political activity, and he basks in his reputation as a consensus builder. His personal dictum for approaching contentious issues is: "To reconcile, not divide." It is a useful philosophy to apply to his position, as the German presidency is largely ceremonial and symbolic of national unity. And, true to his moralistic precepts, Rau unhesitatingly tackled several ticklish political issues. He had long been a political ally and friend of Israel, and in February 2000 he addressed the Israeli Knesset to atone for Germany's role in the Holocaust. "I ask forgiveness for what Germans have done—for myself and my generation, for the sake of our children and children's children, whose future I would like to see at the side of the children of Israel," he declared. "We will not allow xenophobia, racism, and nationalism to establish them-

Johannes Rau *(Embassy of the Federal Republic of Germany)*

selves again in Europe." Closer to home, and mindful of Germany's Nazi past, he faced rising tides of right-wing nationalism and extremism. Rau nonetheless stated that he was grateful to be German, but not proud. "In my view, one cannot be proud of this," he stated. "One is proud of what one has achieved oneself." His comments raised hackles among nationalists, who demanded his immediate resignation. Rau's national standing increased.

Domestic issues continue to dominate Rau's political agenda. In June 2002 he signed legislation allowing continued immigration of skilled foreign workers into Germany, again over the protest of conservative groups. The latter have vowed to appeal the issue in the Supreme Court and the matter will undoubtedly resurface in national elections slated for fall 2002. That same month he also visited the Czech Republic to confer with President VÁCLAV HAVEL and smooth over some ruffled feathers. Relations between the two countries soured recently over Czech refusal to void the Beneš Decree of 1945. This legislation expelled 2.5 million ethnic Germans after World War II, and led Chancellor GERHARD SCHROEDER to cancel his scheduled visit to Praguein. This remains an emotional sore point between the two nations. Finally, Rau takes a rather long view of economic trends, and he has warned colleagues about the pitfalls of globalization. "An unregulated globalization could deepen the gap between the rich and the poor," he affirmed. "We need regulations to secure the freedom of people worldwide and politics must take care that the freedom of the global market doesn't damage the freedom of people." Rau then called on the international community to establish mechanisms for assisting developing nations to handle debt, and for wealthy nations to open their markets to products from developing nations. This pious president will be up for reelection in 2004.

Further Reading

Collins, Stephen D. *German Policy-Making and the Eastern Enlargement of the European Union during the Kohl Era.* New York: Manchester University Press, 2002.

Gellner, Winand, and John D. Robertson, eds. *The Berlin Republic: German Unification and a Decade of Changes.* Portland, Oreg.: Frank Caas, 2003.

Haar, Roberta N. *Nation States as Schizophrenics: Germany and Japan as Post–Cold War Actors.* Westport, Conn.: Praeger, 2001.

Muller, Jan-Werner, ed. *German Ideologies since 1945: Studies in the Political Thought and Culture of the Bonn Republic.* New York: Palgrave, 2002.

Oswald, Franz. *The Party That Came in from the Cold War: The Party of Democratic Socialism in United Germany, 1989–2002.* Westport, Conn.: Praeger, 2002.

Umbach, Maiken, ed. *German Federalism: Past, Present, Future.* New York: Palgrave, 2002.

Rawlings, Jerry (1947–) *president of Ghana*

Jerry John Rawlings was born on June 22, 1947, in Accra, Ghana, the son of a Scottish pharmacist and a Ghanaian woman from the Ewe tribe. His country is located on the African west coast, and it is bounded by Togo, Burkina Faso, and Côte d'Ivoire. Its 18 million people speak an estimated 75 languages and dialects, but English remains the official language of government. Ghana was one of the first African countries to remove the shackles of English colonial rule in March 1957, although governance has since alternated between elected civilians and military dictatorships. With few exceptions, and until very recently, both have proven extremely corrupt and inefficient. Ghana is rich in mineral resources and agriculture, and its economy is heavily dependent upon exports, principally gold, diamonds, and cocoa. For this reason it is susceptible to price fluctuations on the world market, usually with political ramifications at home.

Rawlings was well educated by Ghanaian standards, having passed through the Achimota School in 1966. He subsequently attended the Ghana Military Academy at Teshie, where he trained as a jet pilot. Once he earned his wings, Rawlings gained a reputation as one of the nation's best pilots, and in 1978 he advanced to flight lieutenant. But the young officer also developed a passion for politics, coupled with a deep sense of outrage over the blatant corruption of General Frederick Akuffo's military regime. In concert with other young officers, he staged an unsuccessful military coup on May 15, 1979, and he was arrested. During his trial, Rawlings defended himself adroitly and openly attacked the ruling clique in power. This made him something of a national hero, and, on June 4, 1979, he was freed by a group of junior officers who subsequently overthrew the regime. Akuffo and seven other leaders were then arrested and summarily executed by Rawlings's newly-installed Armed Forces

Revolutionary Council, although he promised to reinstate democracy soon. Surprisingly, he kept his word, and, on July 10, 1979, Dr. Hilla Limann was elected president. Over the next few months Limann proved unable to improve the Ghanaian economy, which was declining, and Rawlings openly criticized him. He was then ordered out of the service as punishment and briefly jailed. However, when it became clear that Limann was unable to enact badly needed economic reforms, Rawlings staged a second coup on December 31, 1981. He was now installed as the head of a seven-man Provisional National Defense Council (PNDC), which suspended the constitution, dismissed the assembly, and outlawed political parties. This time Rawlings made no mention of returning civilians back to power any time soon. At the time, most Ghanaians did not seem to care.

Rawlings commenced his political career as a charismatic revolutionary, imbued with Marxist zeal and dogma. He quickly instituted state controls on the economy, enacted harsh measures to stamp out corruption, and adopted an anti-Western stance. However, within two years the economy sank even lower and the young officer, mindful of the suffering this engendered, abruptly altered his approach. His new outlook included free-market reforms, privatization, and a call for foreign investment. The Ghanaian economy suddenly rebounded after years of poor performance, and Rawlings further cemented his ties to the West by conforming to austerity measures outlined by the International Monetary Fund (IMF) and World Bank. However, he continued to rule the country as a one-party state through his National Democratic Congress Party (NDC). It took a combination of Western economic pressure and mounting domestic agitation before he acceded to multiparty elections in 1991. A new constitution was then promulgated by referendum in April 1992, and the following November Rawlings was elected to a four-year term as president. He did this over the objections of the opposition, who claimed the process was rigged and staged a boycott.

Rawlings continued ruling Ghana with an iron hand along with good economic progress until 1996, when new national elections were scheduled. This time the opposition parties had coalesced under a single candidate, Dr. John Kufour of the New Patriotic Party (NPP). Despite his authoritarian tendencies, Rawlings had lost none of his appeal to the nation's impoverished masses, and in 1996 he defeated his challenger with 57.2

percent of the vote in elections judged free and fair by international observers. The vote granted Rawlings the political legitimacy he sought, and he said: "Let us all, no matter what our differing opinions and party loyalties, work toward our common goal, which is the prosperity and well-being of all Ghanaians." Rawlings further declared that he would respect the constitutional limits by not seeking a third term in 2000. Again, the charismatic leader proved as good as his word and in December 2000 the contest devolved upon John Atta Mills, his chosen successor, and John Kufour. After two decades of rule under the NDC, and recent economic downturns, the country seemed ripe for change, and Kufour and his NPP were swept to power with 56.6 percent of the votes. The new president was officially sworn in on January 7, 2001. Rawlings retired as a goodwill ambassadorial post at the United Nations for one year. His legacy of having successfully restored democracy to Ghana after 20 years of uncontested rule seems secure, although Kufour has pledged establishment of a committee to investigate human rights abuses following the 1981 coup.

Further Reading

Askakae, Bedu. *Ghana in Search of Political Changes: Ghanaian Attitudes in the Present Time in Ghana.* New York: Vantage Press, 2000.

Dzorgbo, Dan-Bright S. *Ghana in Search of Development: The Challenge of Governance, Economic Management, and Institution Building.* Brookfield, Vt.: Ashgate, 2001.

Gyimah Boadi, Emmanuel. "A Peaceful Turnover in Ghana." *Journal of Democracy* 12, no. 2 (2001): 93–117.

Hutchful, Eboe. *Ghana's Adjustment Experience: The Paradox of Reforms.* Oxford: James Currey, 2002.

Osei, Akwasi P. *Ghana: Recurrence and Change in a Post-Independence African State.* New York: P. Lang, 1999.

Saine, Abdoulayes. "The Soldier-Turned-Presidential Candidate: A Comparison of Flawed Democratic Transitions in Ghana and Gambia." *Journal of Political and Military Sociology* 20, no. 2 (2000): 191–209.

René, Albert (1935–   ) *president of the Seychelles*
France Albert René was born on November 16, 1935, in the Seychelles, an archipelago consisting of 115 small islands located 1,000 miles east of Tanzania in the Indian

Ocean. The principal island is Mahé, which hosts the majority of the population, now estimated at 80,000. Previously a French possession, the Seychelles passed into British hands after 1814, and in 1903 it became a Crown colony. Located at the crossroads of several important trade routes, its population reflects a mixed racial heritage that is part European, African, and Asian. As the islands gravitated toward greater internal rule, elections were held in 1974, and James Mancham of the Seychelles Democratic Party (SDP) was acknowledged as the de facto island leader. The Seychelles gained its independence from Great Britain in 1976 and was governed by a constitution crafted through political negotiations. However, within three years the political order was completely upended by a military coup, and thereafter the course of national events revolved around one individual.

René was educated on the islands before traveling to England and attending St. Mary's College in Southampton and King's College in London. There he first became exposed to the tenants of Marxism, which shaped and formulated his subsequent political views. René completed his studies as a lawyer in 1957 and he returned home to help organize the first labor union in 1964. That same year he founded the Seychelles People's United Party (SPUP), which is extremely socialist in its orientation. Elections held in 1974 were overwhelmingly favorable toward Mancham's SDP, but René and the SPUP, which received only two seats out of 15, accused the opposition of voter fraud. In 1976, after independence had been achieved, Mancham was installed as president and René, as head of the opposition, became prime minister. However, this coalition arrangement only lasted about one year. On June 5, 1977, when Mancham was away in England at a conference, militant members of the SPUP overthrew the government and installed René as president, although he disavowed any relationship with the plotters. Once installed, René suspended the legislature and drafted a new constitution in 1979, which mandated a president and a nation assembly, elected every five years. The Seychelles also became a one-party state, with the SPUP the only legal outlet for political expression.

René, true to his socialist precepts, began remodeling the island along command-economy lines. He also initiated new programs such as education, health care, and sanitation, which were then in great need. However, these activities proved highly unpopular with seg-

ments of the polity associated with Mancham and the SDP, and several coup attempts were thwarted. The most notorious of these involved mercenaries from South Africa, and René had to be rescued by troops dispatched from Tanzania. Henceforth, René's regime began looking more and more like a communist dictatorship, with a strong military and police force to keep the population under control, and a secret police to stifle dissent. In terms of foreign policy, the Seychelles also formed close ties with such pariah nations as Libya, North Korea, and Cuba. The islands also became part of the nonaligned movement, keeping its distance from both the United States and the Soviet Union. Beginning in the 1980s, René further aggravated relations with the West by declaring the islands a nuclear-free zone and requiring all warships in its waters to declare if atomic weapons were present. The government also began agitating for the removal of American and British military facilities from the remote island of Diego Garcia, which the Seychelles claims. Consistent with the realities of a one-party dictatorship, René ran as the sole candidate in the 1984 and 1989 elections and won by wide margins.

For all his repressive tendencies, René did improve the Seychelles economy, and through the 1980s it enjoyed one of the highest per capita incomes in Africa. However, by the time the cold war ended in 1991, the island experienced increasing foreign pressure to allow free elections and multiparty democracy. René complied, and in 1993 a new constitution was adopted. In this new atmosphere, basic freedoms were restored to the public, and the government started transitioning back to free-market economics. René's new party, the Seychelles People's Progressive Front (SPPF) won decisively, defeating Mancham's SDP and a newcomer, Wavel Ramkalawan of the United Opposition Party (UOP). René enjoyed similar success in 1998, convincing proof of the president's durability and appeal as a politician. On September 3, 2001, René won an unprecedented sixth term in office with 54 percent of votes cast, which underscored his reputation as a fixture on the political landscape of the Seychelles. "The vote shows that the Seychelles people are confident in me, my party and my program, and have believed in what I said," he told his supporters.

Further Reading

Ellis, Stephen. "Africa and International Corruption: The Strange Case of South Africa and Seychelles." *African Affairs* 95 (April 1996): 165–197.

Franda, Marcus F. *Quiet Turbulence in the Seychelles.* Hanover, N.H.: American Universities Field Staff, 1979.

Hatchard, John. "Re-establishing a Multi-party State: Some Constitutional Lessons from the Seychelles." *Journal of Modern African Studies* 31, no. 4 (1993): 601–612.

Mancham, James R. *In the Seychelles: Democracy on the Horizon.* Washington, D.C.: Heritage Foundation, 1990.

Ostheimer, John. *The Politics of the Western Indian Ocean Islands.* New York: Praeger, 1975.

Reynolds, Albert (1932–) *prime minister of Ireland*

Albert Reynolds was born on November 3, 1932, in Rooseky, County Roscommon, an impoverished region of western Ireland. He was partly educated at Summerhill College, Sligo, but quit to pursue business interests. After clerking in several firms, Reynolds opened a chain of dance halls in the early 1960s and made a fortune. He followed this up by establishing a pet food manufacturing company and became a millionaire. Reynolds commenced his political career by securing election to the Longford Chamber of Commerce in 1974, and gaining a seat in the national parliament, the Dail Eireann, in June 1977, as part of the conservative Fianna Fáil Party. Within two years he had struck up an abiding relationship with fellow legislator CHARLES J. HAUGHEY and helped to establish him as party leader and taoiseach (prime minister). He was rewarded with appointments as minister for post and telegraph and minister for transport within the Haughey administration. Reynolds, however, lost his posts in June 1981 when Fianna Fáil was defeated in national elections by Garret Fitzgerald of the rival Fine Gael Party. Haughey came roaring back the following year, however, and Reynolds next served as his minister of industry and commerce and minister of finance. By 1991, unfortunately, Haughey's administration had become indelibly stained by numerous scandals and Reynolds felt that the party would be better off without him. He tried, unsuccessfully, to challenge his mentor for the leadership of Fianna Fáil in November 1991 and was dismissed from the cabinet. But by February 1992 Haughey was out of power, resigning over an imbroglio concerning illegal wiretaps. After some internecine deliberations, Reynolds was appointed his suc-

cessor and he was sworn in as prime minister on February 11, 1992.

Reynolds, once in office, sought to distance himself from his controversial predecessor and proceeded to remove all of Haughey's appointments from his cabinet. Such a thorough house-cleaning was unprecedented in Irish politics, but it enabled Fianna Fáil to rule with an untarnished slate. Reynolds, meanwhile, turned his attention to a matter of pressing importance. As a businessman, he appreciated Ireland's relative poverty better than most politicians, and he strongly felt that closer integration with Europe was the solution. Therefore, he ardently championed the 1991 Maastricht Agreement, which had to be approved by a public referendum. The vote, held in June 1992, was a sweeping success and kept the movement toward European unification alive. Reynolds enjoyed another striking success in his dealing with the Northern Ireland issue. This was a continuing sore point between Ireland and Great Britain and helped to embitter the ongoing violent guerrilla war between the infamous Irish Republican Army (IRA) and Protestant paramilitary groups. Reynolds was willing to confer closely with British prime minister JOHN MAJOR, and, on December 15, 1993, they issued the Downing Street Declaration. This protocol laid the foundation for an eventual ceasefire between feuding Catholic and Protestant factions, and in 1994 the IRA officially consented to stop fighting, which further enhanced the prospects for peace.

But try as he might to avoid them, Reynolds was ensnared in several controversies of his own. The first involved an ongoing judicial investigation of the beef-processing industry and illegal favors purportedly received from the government. Reynolds, as a meat packing plant owner, was suspected of being involved and was accused as such by his coalition partners, the Progressive Democrats. These strains brought down the government in November 1992, and Reynolds only survived by striking an alliance with the Labour Party under Dick Spring. Next came a civil case involving a pregnant 14-year-old girl who sought to travel to England for an abortion, and Reynolds found himself funding her appeal to the Supreme Court. This move angered many of his conservative allies in this staunchly Catholic country, but Reynold felt he had no choice. "It is not the function of government to conduct moral crusades," he reasoned, "I do not want to preside over a police state." Worse, a public uproar ensued when the Reynolds-appointed president of the High Court, Harry Wheelan, delayed the extradition of a priest accused of child abuse to Northern Ireland, ostensibly to placate the church hierarchy. When Reynolds failed to come up with a sufficient explanation for this tardy response, Spring pulled Labour out of the ruling coalition and the government collapsed on November 17, 1994. Subsequent machinations made JOHN BRUTON the new taoiseach, while Reynolds was replaced by BERTIE AHERN as Fianna Fáil leader.

Reynolds remained in the Dail Eireann for several more months, but by 1995 his business acumen was sought and he gained appointment to the Board of Governors of the European Investment Bank and similar postings within the World Bank and the International Monetary Fund. In March 1998 he made an attempt at a political comeback by running for the Irish presidency, but he lost to MARY ROBINSON. Reynolds has since remained active in the realm of international finance.

Further Reading

Burns, Mike. "Albert Reynolds." 335 *Europe* (April 1994): 7–12.

Collins, Stephen. *The Power Game: Ireland under Fianna Fail.* Dublin: O'Brien Press, 2001.

Cullen, Paul. *With a Little Help from My Friends: Planning Corruption in Ireland.* Dublin: Gill and Macmillan, 2002.

Kavanagh, Ray. *Spring, Summer, and Fall: The Rise and Fall of the Labour Party, 1986–97.* Dublin: Blackwater Press, 2001.

Ryan, Tim. *Albert Reynolds: The Longford Leader: The Unauthorized Biography.* Dublin: Blackwater Press, 1994.

Robinson, Mary (1944–   ) *president of Ireland*

Mary Teresa Winifred Bourke was born on May 21, 1944, in Ballina, County Mayo, Ireland, the daughter of two medical doctors. A Catholic and an exceptional student, she attended the predominately Protestant Trinity College and then King's Inn before being admitted to the bar in England in 1967. She subsequently pursued an advanced law degree at Harvard University in 1969, and she came home to become the youngest professor of law at Trinity College. That same year she entered politics as a Labour Party candidate and was elected to Senad Eireann, the Irish senate, becoming the youngest-ever member to serve. In 1970 she met and married Nicholas Robinson, a Dublin attorney and a Protestant. By this time Robinson had acquired a well-deserved reputation for bucking trends and blunt outspokenness. These proved two characteristics that ultimately defined her public career and beyond. As senator, Robinson established her credentials as a liberal and a feminist by championing women's rights. She fought stridently to ensure greater access to abortion, contraception, and to make divorce legal. In 1985 she broke with the Labour Party over the Anglo-Irish Agreement of that year, which she protested was achieved without consulting the Protestant Unionists, who would be directly affected. She nonetheless was reelected to the Senate as an independent until 1990, when Labour tapped her to serve as a candidate for the upcoming presidential election. This was a largely ceremonial post and neither Fianna Fáil nor Gael Fine made it a priority campaign, especially seeing that the former party had monopolized the office for most of the 20th century. However, Robinson viewed the office as a springboard for greater national visibility and she toured the country vigorously, speaking to constituents and proffering herself as an alternative to "politics as usual." The public was clearly ready for a change, for on November 7, 1990, she became Ireland's first female president, with 44 percent of the vote. Her success was all the more impressive considering her lack of association with any party or interest group.

Once sworn in, Robinson used her office as a bully pulpit to advocate those positions and issues most pressing to her. These included greater tolerance between Catholics and Protestants, recognition of women's contribution to Irish history and culture, and reconnecting with the Irish diaspora living in other lands, most notably the United States. She further demanded international recognition that the so-called Irish potato famine was a grave injustice to her people, bordering on genocide. Robinson also visited Queen Elizabeth II of England in May 1993, becoming the first Irish executive to meet an English head of state. Robinson then proved highly active in the testy negotiations among the Irish republic, the United Kingdom, and Northern Ireland, the site of an ongoing guerrilla war conducted by Protestant paramilitaries and the Irish Republican Army. Robinson roundly condemned the violence of both sides, but she unhesitatingly met with GERRY ADAMS, head of Sinn Féin (the IRA's political wing) to emphasize the need for continuing dialogue. By the time her seven-year term expired in 1997, Robinson had completely redefined the

Irish presidency through activism and advocacy. She had also emerged as an international spokesperson for human rights.

As president, Robinson maintained her highly visible stature by visiting various countries in distress. From Somalia to Rwanda, she toured and witnessed the horrific consequences resulting from clan warfare and genocide, and she pushed the United Nations into direct relief actions. The usually staid UN bureaucracy had never before encountered such energy and enthusiasm, and on September 12, 1997, UN Secretary-General KOFI ANNAN tendered Robinson the post of High Commissioner for Human Rights. For Robinson, it was a dream come true. She toured the world constantly, lecturing and berating various governments for their violations of human rights. Her penchant for upsetting the status quo was never more apparent—or effective. China, Russia, and the Congo all felt her wrath, as did the United States for its ongoing war against Afghanistan's Taliban regime. Robinson roundly condemned the September 11, 2001, destruction of New York's World Trade Center as an atrocity, but she urged the Americans to interrupt their bombing campaign to allow food supplies to reach refugees. She also criticized the detention of numerous Taliban and terrorist prisoners at Guantánamo, Cuba. "The buildings that were destroyed on September 11th can be replaced," she affirmed. "But if the pillars of the international system are damaged or demolished, they will not be so easy to restore." The Americans were infuriated by such remarks and they worked behind the scenes, apparently in concert with other nations, to deny Robinson an extension of her UN term. Somewhat disillusioned, she then announced her resignation from the United Nations effective in September 2002. To many governments, she will not be missed. But for many developing nations, Robinson elevated their plight, poverty, and injustice to the world's stage with her blunt and uncompromising brand of criticism. As she strenuously maintained in June 2002, "When I leave this office I will be looking for ways to try to create political will, to give more resources to developing countries to try and build up their own capacity in human rights."

Further Reading

Bresnihan, Valerie. "The Symbolic Power of Ireland's Presidential Robinson." *Presidential Studies Quarterly* 29, no. 2 (1999): 250–262.

Brown, A., and Y. Galligan. "Views from the Periphery: Changing the Political Agenda for Women in the Republic of Ireland and Scotland." *West European Politics* 16 (April 1993): 165–189.

Gallagher, M., and M. March. "Republic of Ireland Presidential Election, 7 November, 1990." *West European Politics* 14 (October 1991): 169–173.

Horgan, John. *Mary Robinson: A Woman of Ireland and the World.* Niwot, Colo.: Roberts Rinehart, 1998.

Siggins, Lorna. *Mary Robinson: The Woman Who Took Power in the Park.* Edinburgh: Mainstream, 1998.

Rodríguez, Andrés (1923–1997)

president of Paraguay

Andrés Rodríguez Pedotti was born on June 19, 1923, in Borja, Paraguay, a farmer's son. Intent upon a military career, he enrolled at the Marshal Francisco Solano López Military Academy in 1942 and was commissioned an army lieutenant four years later. In this post he met and befriended Alfredo Stroessner, another ambitious officer, and supported him in a 1954 coup that toppled President Federico Chávez. This act initiated an iron-fisted dictatorship lasting 35 years, and one in which Rodríguez served as Stroessner's right-hand man. As such, it became his responsibility to enforce the generalissimo's will and policies among the largely impoverished masses. Foremost among these was cultivation of a highly profitable black-market trade and international smuggling that Stroessner realized was unstoppable, and therefore resolved to regulate to his own advantage. Rodríguez proved particularly adept at manipulating the heroin and cocaine trade, so that by the late 1980s he had amassed a personal fortune approaching $1 billion. Stroessner's grip on power seemed absolute, but by 1989 he was clearly ailing and his well-financed cronies quietly bickered among themselves as to who should succeed him. Rodríguez, in true military fashion, simply preempted the competition on the night of February 2, 1989, by staging a coup that ousted the hated dictator, who fled to Brazil. Thus departed the Western Hemisphere's longest-serving tyrant. Having consolidated control, Rodríguez had himself sworn in as president on February 4, 1989.

The new regime, and the manner in which it assumed power, had all the trappings of a typical Latin American banana republic. And, because he was Stroessner's partner in oppression for more than 30 years, little was expected from Rodríguez except the usual rubber-stamp theatrics. However, the change was met by wild celebrations and outpourings of gratitude toward the new leader. Rodríguez, no matter what his original intentions were, apparently harbored second thoughts over what to do next. He thereupon decided to salvage his own reputation—and that of Paraguay's—by instituting complete and meaningful democratic reforms. To the astonishment of opposition leaders, the government suddenly released political prisoners, relaxed long-standing press restrictions, legalized all political parties except the Communists, and even invited dissidents living in exile to return home. The result was a jaw-dropping surge in Rodríguez's popularity rating, unprecedented and unexpected from a man so closely identified with a hated dictatorship. And, for the first time in 30 years, the government took active steps to combat the flow of illicit drugs, even to the extent of inviting American narcotics officials and crop eradication airplanes to assist. But the final shoe that dropped came with the announcement of free and open presidential elections, scheduled for May 1, 1989. Democracy had finally made its belated but welcome appearance in Paraguay.

Rodríguez had given considerable thought to his newfound role as a democrat, and he scheduled early elections for two reasons. The first was to capitalize on his immense popularity with the public. The second was to prevent the opposition for having sufficient time to properly prepare and organize. The ensuing election proceeded with military precision, and Rodríguez won 74 percent of the popular vote, with the remainder scattered among seven opposition candidates. "Today we begin the transition on the road to democratic government," he announced. "We promise our people we will carry Paraguay on a bright path to its destiny of greatness and happiness." Now armed with the veneer of political legitimacy, Rodríguez then embarked on a number of badly needed reforms to alleviate Paraguay's crushing poverty. He ushered in privatization and economic liberalization to free up the marketplace. This move won him plaudits from the International Monetary Fund (IMF), and an influx of financial aid rolled in. The long-moribund Paraguay economy, previously based on wholesale smuggling, thus began reviving. Rodríguez further burnished his image by declaring an end to torture, restoring human rights, adopting a new constitution, and removing the military from politics. His only conspicuous failure was an attempt at land redistribution, for 1 percent of the population owns 80 percent of the land. He determined to leave resolution of this intractable problem to his successors.

Under the terms of a new constitution adopted in 1992, the Paraguayan executive was forbidden from seeking a consecutive term. Therefore, in 1993 Rodríguez voluntarily stepped down from office, the first Paraguayan head of state to do so. Moreover, his successor, JUAN WASMOSY, became the first elected civilian to rule the nation in five decades. Rodríguez then retired as a senator for life, with legal immunity, to the privacy of his personal mansion. The residence was built steadily over the years and is said to rival Versailles in scale. Rodríguez died of cancer in New York City on April 21, 1997. Whatever his prior reputation as a despot and accessory to repression, Rodríguez merits recognition for placing Paraguay on the road to democracy—to the applause of his compatriots.

Further Reading

Abente Brun, Diego. *Stronismo, Post-Stronismo, and the Prospects of Democratization in Paraguay.* Notre Dame, Ind.: University of Notre Dame Press, 1989.

Lambert, Peter, and R. Andrew Nicholson. *The Transition to Democracy in Paraguay.* New York: St. Martin's Press, 1997.

Roett, R. "Paraguay after Stroessner." *Foreign Affairs* 68 (Spring 1989): 124–142.

Turner, Brian. "Community Politics and State-Peasant Relations in Paraguay." Unpublished Ph.D. dissertation, Tulane University, 1992.

Vergara, Isaias M. *Paraguayan Policy towards the New Organization of American States.* Virginia Beach, Va.: Regent University Press, 1997.

Rodríguez, Miguel Angel (1940–) *president of Costa Rica*

Miguel Angel Rodríguez Echeverría was born on January 9, 1940, in San José, Costa Rica. His small homeland, sandwiched between Panama and Nicaragua, was founded as a Spanish colony in 1562, and gained political independence in 1821. Like most Central American states, Costa Rica has an agrarian-based economy, but it greatly differs from others by also possessing strong democratic traditions. In fact, the country held the region's first free elections in 1890, and a brief civil war fought in 1949 cemented the present political system in place. This practice entails direct election of the president for a single four-year term, along with a Legislative Assembly. The Costa Rican president is rather weak compared to similar offices in Latin America, as he depends upon the parliament to originate and pass all legislation. Moreover, several autonomous governmental agencies exist that routinely circumvent presidential authority or control. Costa Rican politics traditionally fluctuate between two major groupings; the left-wing National Liberation Party (PLN) and the conservative United Social Christian Party (PUSC). The former came to power under the aegis of José Figueres Ferrer, who won the civil war of 1949, while the latter is centered upon the legacy of Rafael Calderón Guardia, who lost. The net result of active politics, high literacy rates brought about by compulsory education, and modern health care give Costa Rica one of the hemisphere's highest standards of living, and among its most stable political environments.

Rodríguez attended the University of Costa Rica, majoring in law and economics. He subsequently studied at the University of California, Berkeley, where he obtain a doctorate in economics in 1966. Once home he commenced teaching at the University of Costa Rica before gaining appointment as director of the National Planning Office. As a member of PUSC, he also acquired the position of chief of staff in Costa Rica's central bank. When his party was turned out of office after 1970, Rodríguez focused his attention on developing his own meat and dairy business. By 1987 he felt emboldened to run for party chairman, but he lost to RAFAEL CALDERÓN, who went on to win the presidency. However, Rodríguez managed to gain election to the National Assembly that same year, and in 1991 he advanced to president of that body. This position greatly enhanced his national standing, and in 1993 Rodríguez ran for the presidency again, only to lose to José María Figueres by 2 percent of votes cast. In 1998 he made his third attempt and finally succeeded, winning by 46.8 percent of the vote over PLP's José Miguel Corrales Bolanos. The PUSC also won a majority of seats in the Assembly, which further tightened their hold on government. Consistent with Costa Rican politics, however, the appearance of strength was illusionary.

Rodríguez had campaigned on a theme of fiscal austerity to rein in government spending and bring down both the national deficit ($3.6 billion) and the high interest rates this generated. He sought to achieve this by giving greater emphasis to privatization of the telecommunications and energy sectors. However, by May 1999, he withdrew this legislation in the face of massive social protests. Rodríguez then turned to enhancing the new and growing field of ecotourism. Costa Rica contains some of the most extensive rain forests anywhere, replete with many rare and exotic animals. He therefore took steps to increase access to these areas, but in such a manner that the ecology would not be threatened. Fortunately for the PUSC, the economy turned in good performances throughout 1999 and into 2000, with growth rates of 3 percent and unemployment running at 5.7 percent. This makes Costa Rica the envy of Central America, and the government has been forced to expel economic refugees and illegal aliens from Nicaragua who are looking for work. And, because of a rise in drug trafficking across Costa Rican soil, in December 1998 Rodríguez also concluded a 10-year cooperation treaty with the United States that allows American troops to conduct joint operations with Costa Rican security forces. Costa Rica does not have a standing army, having abolished it after the revolution of 1949.

Though his tenure in office was generally successful, Rodríguez was frustrated by his inability to get the legislation he wanted passed quickly and without a struggle. The very weak nature of the Costa Rican presidency ensures that this problem will continue. Therefore, in May 2001 he strongly advocated overhauling the present system in favor of a more parliamentary form of governance. In this arrangement the cabinet would be approved by a simple majority in the Assembly, which would also have a fixed schedule to either pass or reject legislation. He felt such reforms would thus ensure "that decisions are made within a reasonable time while improving congressional accountability to the public and presidential accountability to the legislative branch." Rodríguez's term in office expires as of May 2002. In February his designated successor Abel Pacheco, failed to win a decisive majority over PLP candidate Rolando Araya and faced a runoff election. This impasse resulted from the strong showing by Otton Soils of the newly formed Citizen's Action Party, which, although it garnered only 26.3 percent of the vote, forced the runoff—the first in 50 years. But on April 8, 2002, Pacheco won handily with 58 percent of the vote, assuring continuing Conservative rule in Costa Rica.

Further Reading
Booth, John A. *Costa Rica: Quest for Democracy.* Boulder, Colo.: Westview Press, 1998.
Daling, Tjabel. *Costa Rica: A Guide to the People, Politics, and Culture.* Brooklyn: Interlink Publications, 2002.
Lehoucq, Fabrice E. *Stuffing the Ballot Box: Fraud, Electoral Reform, and Democratization in Costa Rica.* New York: Cambridge University Press, 2002.

Roh Moo Hyun (1946–   ) *president of South Korea*
Roh Moo Hyun was born on August 6, 1946, to a poor peasant family in a small farming village in Kimhae on the southeast coast of Korea. Roh attended Busan Commercial High School on scholarship, and after graduating, he found work with a fishing net company. Aspiring to be a lawyer but unable to afford college because of his low-paying jobs, he decided to study for the bar exam on his own. Ten years later, in 1976, Roh passed the bar on his fourth attempt and proceeded to make a comfortable living as a tax attorney.

A turning point in Roh's career occurred when he was asked to defend several students who had been arrested for possessing banned books, then detained and tortured for nearly two months under South Korea's then-dictator Chun Doo Hwan. This incident inspired Roh to become a human rights lawyer and consequently one of the leaders of the Democratic Citizens Council, a prodemocracy movement, in 1985. In 1987, Roh participated in the June Struggle demonstrations, which called for direct presidential elections. In September of that year, Roh was arrested in a labor protest at Daewoo Shipbuilding and spent three weeks in prison, causing him to lose his license to practice law.

With his legal practice shut down, Roh entered politics in 1988, winning election to the National Assembly as a member of a prodemocracy party. However, he only held the seat for one term after losing in the 1992 election and also lost a bid for mayor of Pusan in 1995. In 1998, Roh tried again for the National Assembly, this time from Seoul, and won a two-year term. In 2000, Roh returned to Pusan to run for the National Assembly and lost once again.

After the latter defeat, Roh's supporters created a fab club called Rohsamo, which means "People who love Roh Moo Hyun," that included a website. The disillusioned Roh, who had considered quitting politics, was buoyed by a groundswell of support generated by Rohsamo and in particular the website that resulted in Roh's rise in the Millennium Democratic Party. In December 2002, Roh narrowly defeated opposition leader Lee Hoi Chang for the presidency. In the months since the election, Roh has made it clear that he is different than past South Korean presidents. He has called for a more equal partnership with Washington and bluntly questioned the U.S. policy of pressuring North Korea over its nuclear program. During the campaign, he said he would not "kowtow" to the United States on the issue of North Korea. "We do not want North Korea's collapse," Roh said recently.

Further Reading
Clifford, Mark, and Ihlwan, Moon. "Korea: The Politics of Peril," *Business Week* (February 24, 2003).
Wehrf, George. "Behind the Wheel," *Newsweek* (March 3, 2003).

Roh Tae Woo (1932–   ) *president of South Korea*
Roh Tae Woo was born on December 4, 1932, near Taegu, Korea, the son of a minor civil servant. He excelled academically and was admitted into the prestigious Kyonbuck High School, where he met and befriended Chun Doo Hwan. When the Korean War broke out in June 1950, he joined the army and was sent to attend the Korean Military Academy. After graduating, Roh served as a distinguished soldier and in 1959 he passed through the U.S. Special Forces School at Fort Bragg, North Carolina. As a general he commanded the famous Korean Tiger Division during the Vietnam War, and he subsequently led the First Division, stationed at the capital of Seoul. In this capacity, he did not intervene when Chun Doo Hwan, himself a general, staged a coup that killed President Park Chung Hee on December 12, 1979. The event caused protests throughout the land, and in 1980 forces loyal to Chun killed an estimated 200 protesters at Kwangju. Neither Roh nor his troops were implicated in the massacre but, through his close association with Chun, he became indelibly stained by it. In August 1980 Chun declared himself president and rewarded Roh, who had retired from the military, with numerous cabinet posts. In 1983 he was tasked with heading the Seoul Olympic Organizing Committee, which oversaw the successful Olympic Games held there in 1988. By this time Roh was widely acknowledged as

the second-most powerful man in South Korea, and seemingly Chun's handpicked successor. These suspicions were confirmed in June 1987, when the former general declared his candidacy. However, on June 29, 1987, Roh went on national television and demanded that the Chun regime release all political prisoners, reform the constitution to allow the president to be elected by a direct vote, and institute complete freedom of the press. Failure to comply immediately meant that Roh would withdraw his nomination as the Democratic Justice Party's candidate. President Chun was so nonplussed by this display of independence that the changes were met. The stage was now set for South Korea's first free election.

The pressure of increased democracy in South Korea had been growing for some time, so it is not known if Roh and Chun were at odds over the issue, or simply cooperating for greater gain as they always had. Nonetheless, the die had been cast in favor of direct elections and Roh campaigned vigorously across the country. His efforts were abetted by the two opposition candidates, KIM YOUNG SAM and KIM DAE JUNG, who refused to unify their efforts under a single banner and split the opposition vote. Consequently, on December 16, 1987, the Koreans elected Roh their new executive with 37 percent of votes cast. The new president was then sworn in for a five-year term on February 25, 1988, marking Korea's first peaceful transition of power in its 3,000-year history. A new era in national politics was born.

As president, Roh distinguished himself in two distinct spheres: diplomacy and democratization. In the former, he pursued a policy called Northern Diplomacy, or Nordpolitik, which was meant to extend South Korea's diplomatic relations among countries of the Communist world. North Korea was an obvious exception to this, but embassies were rapidly established in Poland, Hungary, Czechoslovakia, Bulgaria, Romania, and Mongolia. In June 1990 Roh was also introduced to Soviet premier Mikhail Gorbachev in Washington, D.C., which ended four decades of diplomatic nonrecognition between the two nations. Moreover, close economic ties to another Communist giant, the People's Republic of China, were also aggressively pursued, with concomitant increases in trade. However, Roh's efforts at domestic reforms were hindered by the National Assembly, which was bitterly divided among several opposition parties. Undaunted, Roh dropped another bombshell in January 1990 when he invited the Reunification and Democratic Party and the New Democratic Republican Party to close ranks with his own DJP. The result was a new organization, the Democratic Liberal Party, which was broad-based and now enjoyed majority control. The consensus it engendered was also unprecedented, and thereafter the National Assembly acted more in concert with the president's agenda.

Ron left office without incident on February 25, 1993, and he was replaced by Kim Young Sam. However, the arrival of new freedom did little to dissipate anger over the 1980 Kwangju incident, and both Roh and Chun were increasingly assailed in the press. By 1995 public pressure induced President Kim to arrest both men and try them for murder and corruption. To Koreans accustomed to leaders escaping justice, it was the "trial of the century." In August 1996 Roh was sentenced to 22 years in prison, while Chun received a death sentence. However, on December 22, 1997, newly elected president Kim Dae Jung, wishing to foster national unity, ordered both men released. Roh has since lived as a private citizen, and in June 2000 he revisited China to encourage the Korean government to continue investing in that country.

Further Reading

Bedeski, Robert. *The Transformation of South Korea: Reform and Reconstruction in the Sixth Republic under Roh Tae Woo.* New York: Routledge, 1994.

Cotton, James, ed. *Korea under Roh Tae Woo: Democratization, Northern Policy, and Inter-Korean Relations.* New York: St. Martin's Press, 1995.

Rugova, Ibrahim (1944–) *president of Kosovo*

Ibrahim Rugova was born on December 2, 1944, in Istok, Kosovo, the son of a shopkeeper. His father and grandfather were executed by Communist partisans in January 1945, but he was allowed to be raised by family members. Rugova completed his secondary education in neighboring Peja by 1967, and he subsequently attended the University of Prishtina. He graduated with a degree in literature in 1971, then conducted a year of graduate work in Paris at the Ecole Pratique des Hautes Etudes. Rugova obtained his doctorate in Albanian literature from the University of Prishtina in 1984. He quickly established himself as an authority on the subject, and in 1988 was elected to the prestigious Kosova Writers Association. In time this organization became the locus of anti-Serbian activity. Rugova had previously been a member of the Communist Party, the only legitimate avenue for advancement in Yugoslavia, but he was expelled for criticizing the Serbian constitution. He did not formally express an interest in politics until December 1989, when he gained election president as of the Democratic League of Kosovo (LDK). This was the noncommunist party in Kosovo's history, and many hoped that it would be a stepping stone toward ultimate independence.

However, by 1989 Yugoslavia was crumbling from ethnic tensions, and that year President SLOBODAN MILOŠEVIĆ of Serbia removed Kosovo's autonomous status and began filtering in armed troops and Serbian settlers to displace the Albanians. Increased friction led inevitably to fighting, but Rugova, as leader of the LDK, instigated only passive resistance. In fact, the Albanians in Kosovo opted for independence peacefully, and on July 2, 1990, they elected their own parallel government within the province. However, Milošević was firm in his commitment toward building a "Greater Serbia." In 1999 he ordered Serbian troops to commence a campaign of "ethnic cleansing" to forcibly remove or kill all Albanians living in Kosovo. This aggression gave rise to the Kosovo Liberation Army (KLA), a guerrilla force that routinely attacked Serbian police and civilian forces. The fighting also drew a sharp response from the United Nations and from NATO warplanes, which bombed Serbians forces back to their own border. During this interval Rugova appeared on television with Milošević to appeal for a halt to the bombing, although he was apparently being held hostage at the time. But the Serbs withdrew as demanded and Kosovo became a UN protectorate. With Rugova now at the helm, he took initial steps at providing the province with a government. His pacifist stance, for which he was highly criticized by fellow Albanians, was beginning to pay off.

In 1998 Rugova had been easily reelected president of Kosovo, although this was merely symbolic because the Serbs actually controlled the province. In October 2000 the LDK won 58 percent of votes cast in the first internationally sponsored elections. However, it was not until March 2002 that the Skupstina (parliament) formally elevated the bookish professor to president by a vote of 88 to 31. "We will work to build a society of tolerance, understanding, and reconciliation to integrate ethnic minorities into the political, economic, and social life of Kosovo," he pledged. As a compromise measure, Bajram Rexhepi of the rival Democratic Party of Kosovo also became prime minister. Furthermore, three Albanians were assigned eight government ministries while the minority Serbs received control of two. This arrangement cleared three months of legislative gridlock and enabled the government to address more pressing needs of education, public health, and poverty relief. "We will work jointly for a free, democratic, peaceful, prosperous, and independent Kosovo," Rugova said. However, the United Nations insists that all these measures signify Kosovo's autonomy within Serbia, and not its independence. The final political and legal status of the province remains pending.

In February 2002 Rugova again made headlines by volunteering to appear at the War Crimes Tribunal at The Hague to testify during Milošević's trial. During his appearance, bedecked in his trademark glasses and silk scarf, the former writer described how Serbian oppression and aggression forced the Albanian population into defending itself with arms. Furthermore, he accused Milošević of responsibility for the deaths of 900 Albanians and expulsion of another 800,000 in 1999. The two former adversaries then engaged in a heated exchange as to exactly what happened. The impact of Rugova's testimony cannot be gauged at this time, but the Albanian view of the recent events in Kosovo has been finally heard.

Further Reading

Cigar, Norman L., and Paul Williams. *Indictment at the Hague: The Milosevic Regime and Crimes of the Balkan War.* New York: New York University Press, 2002.

Duijzings, Gerlachus. *Religion and the Politics of Identity in Kosovo.* New York: Columbia University Press, 2001.

Waller, Michael, and Kyril Drezov. *Kosovo: The Politics of Delusion.* London: Frank Cass, 2001.

S

Said, Qaboos bin al- (1940–) *sultan of Oman*
Qaboos bin Said was born in Salalah, Oman, on November 18, 1940, the only son of Sultan Said Bin Taymur. Oman is one of the oldest unified states on the Arabian Peninsula, having been ruled by the current Al Bu Said dynasty since 1744. It is strategically located at the mouth of the Strait of Hormuz, which controls access to the Persian Gulf, and through which most of the world's oil supplies must pass. As in all Persian Gulf states, oil is Oman's leading source of revenue, but its reserves are dwarfed by those of neighboring Saudi Arabia and the United Arab Emirates. It is also a Muslim state, but the prevailing sect is neither Sunni nor Shiite, but rather Ibadi, a surviving remnant from the early Khawari Islamic schism. Politically, Oman remains an absolute monarchy without a written constitution, although several elected councils and advisory bodies do exist.

Qaboos was educated in the family palace, although he subsequently attended the Royal Military Academy at Sandhurst, England. He then spent several months in West Germany while serving with a Scottish regiment before returning home in 1965. However, his father, Sultan Taymur, was suspicious of Qaboos's intentions, and confined him under house arrest. Such behavior only reinforced the sultan's reputation for erratic, reactionary behavior. Although oil had been discovered in Oman in 1964, he refused to allocate funding to assist his desperately poor subjects, preferring instead to prop up the military. Several leading Omanis exiled themselves in protest over such shortsighted policies, and Qaboos began organizing a coup against his father with British help. On July 23, 1970, this was accomplished bloodlessly, and Sultan Taymur was himself exiled to a posh residence in England. Once installed as the eighth sultan of his line, Qaboos brooked no delay in addressing the numerous and pressing problems confronting his regime. Foremost among these was a Communist-inspired rebellion in distant Dhofar province, astride the Yemeni border. Qaboos initially tried negotiating with the Popular Front for the Liberation of Oman, but he was forced to employ military means. In addition to his own sizable army, he recruited large numbers of mercenaries from Iran, Pakistan, and Jordan, so that by 1980 the rebellion had been effectively stamped out. Thereafter, the young sultan focused on alleviating the suffering of his people with a view toward modernization. What followed was a model of careful development that transformed Oman from a backward, medieval kingdom into a modern, efficient state.

As money poured in from the export of oil, Qaboos invested millions of dollars in his national infrastructure. Roads, schools, and free housing were all constructed for the benefit of the citizenry. Equal strides were made in the areas of health care, education, and communication. Consequently, Oman enjoys one of the world's highest standards of living and an extremely stable political environment. Unlike Sunni and Shiite Muslims, the Ibadi sect is not prone to radicalism, and Qaboos's farsighted spending policies have precluded any opportunity of it arising. Moreover, the sultan is acutely aware of Oman's dependancy on oil, and he is determined to diversify national assets. In 2000 he initiated the nation's first gas liquefaction plant, declaring: "We have no choice but to develop the domestic economy so oil will be left with a limited share in the national income, as it is a depletable source on which we should not depend on [for] our development." By 2002 it is his intention to have natural gas contribute at least 15 percent to Oman's overall gross national product.

In a region known for extremism, Oman under Qaboos has also served as an island of relative calm. A determined moderate, he is the only Arab leader to open diplomatic relations with the Jewish state of Israel besides Egypt. His foreign policy, while pan-Arabic, is also decidedly pro-Western, and he has openly curried favor with the United States. To this end, during the 1990–91 Gulf War with Iraq, Qaboos was one of several Arab leaders to extend basing rights to American and coalition forces during the liberation of Kuwait. The sultan also ended Oman's traditional isolation by exchanging ambassadors with all Arab states, and in 1981 he helped found the Gulf Cooperation Council to facilitate smooth regional relations.

For all his Western leanings, Qaboos has frowned on democratic practices and harbors few pretensions toward lessening his absolutism. However, perhaps as a nod to the inevitable, in 1996 he promulgated the Basic Statute of State, which defines for the first time on paper the organs and guiding principles of Oman. The following year he sanctioned creation of the Majlis ash-Shoura, an elected advisory body, in which women are allowed to serve. Furthermore, in the wake of the September 11, 2001, destruction of New York's World Trade Center, the sultan called for international efforts to eradicate global terrorism and ensure global stability. Qaboos, throughout his 32-year reign, has proven himself to be an extremely shrewd, benevolent leader. He continues to serve as a voice for moderation and reason in an otherwise hostile and volatile part of the world.

Further Reading
Allen, Calvin H., and W. Lynn Rigsbee. *Oman under Qaboos: From Coup to Constitution, 1970–1996.* London: Frank Cass, 2000.
Owtram, Francis. *A Modern History of Oman: Formation of the State since 1920.* London: I. B. Tauris, 2002.
Riphenberg, Carol J. *Oman: Political Development in a Changing World.* Westport, Conn.: Praeger, 1998.
O'Reilly, Marc J. "Omanibalancing: Oman Confronts an Uncertain Future." *Middle East Journal* 52 (Winter 1998): 70–85.
Zahlan, Rosemarie S. *The Making of the Modern Gulf States: Kuwait, Bahrain, Qatar, the United Arab Emirates, and Oman.* Reading, England: Ithaca Press, 1998.

Saleh, Ali Abdullah (1942–) *president of Yemen*

Ali Abdullah Saleh (or Salih) was born in the village of Bayt al-Ahmar, North Yemen, on March 21, 1942, into the Sanhan tribe, itself a part of the powerful Hashid tribal grouping. Yemen, which occupies the southwestern corner of the Arabian Peninsula, is the most populous nation of the region. Its 17 million inhabitants are uniformly Arab by ethnicity, and Shiite by religion, but they are widely divided along tribal lines. Compared to other oil-producing nations on the peninsula, it is also the poorest, with oil having been discovered only in the 1980s. Yemen was technically part of the Ottoman Empire until 1918, when the Rassid dynasty was established. This was a religion-based leadership drawn from among the Zaidi imams, who had branched off from mainstream Shiites, and they ruled the country until being disposed in 1962. At that point two new countries emerged: North Yemen, which was tribally based and traditional, and South Yemen, which was dominated by Marxist ideology. Relations between them were predictably uneasy and characterized by sporadic fighting. But, after nearly three decades of bloodshed, the two countries were finally unified as the Republic of Yemen in May 1990.

Saleh received only a Koranic education before he enrolled in the tribal forces belonging to the Hassid dynasty. In 1958 he joined the regular army and supported the 1962 coup. Saleh proved himself a brave and accomplished soldier and thereafter rose steadily through the ranks. Having proved instrumental in the rise of Colonel Imbrahim al-Hamdi to power in 1974, he drew closer to the centers of power and four years later, following the assassination of President Hussein al-Ghashami in June 1978, he gained appointment to the temporary council of the presidency. Through deft maneuvering and the elimination of possible rivals, Saleh emerged as president of North Yemen in July 1978, and he was subsequently confirmed by the People's Constituent Assembly. There was nothing in Saleh prior's career to suggest an aptitude for politics, but once empowered he proved himself a master of conciliation and compromise. This approach was essential in a country spilt along tribal lines, where individual sheiks commanded considerable military strength within their own territory. Having consolidated his regime through national consensus, Saleh turned to the most important item on his agenda: unity with South Yemen. Again, Saleh was tactful and conciliatory in his dealings, and he even allowed Marxists to share power within his government. The result was creation of the newest Arab state on May 22, 1990. A brief civil war erupted in 1992, but this was put down and the country has enjoyed a measure of stability rarely experienced in its long history.

Saleh also extended his pragmatic approach to world diplomacy. He established close political and economic ties with the Soviet Union, a willing benefactor, but he was also keen on keeping channels open to the United States and the West. Saleh was also an outspoken proponent of Arab unity, and he cultivated close ties with Saudi Arabia and other Arab states. "The Republic of Yemen will be a factor for stability and security in the Arabian Peninsula and the Gulf region," he maintained, "and a strong bastion for the Arab nations, the Arab League, and Joint Arab action." However, his support for the Palestinian cause proved unrelenting, and he roundly criticized Egypt and Jordan for maintaining diplomatic ties to the Jewish state of Israel. Saleh lent strong support to Iraq throughout its long war with Iran, and he also looked favorably upon SADDAM HUSSEIN's seizure of Kuwait in 1990. This stance brought him nothing but enmity from the United States and Great Britain, and a near cession of trade and diplomatic contact. It also led to the expulsion of some 300,000 Yemeni nationals from Saudi Arabia, where they had been employed in the oil fields. But Saleh had firmly established his credentials as an Arab nationalist, which did much to bolster his appeal at home. On September 23, 1999, he was overwhelmingly reelected as president by 96.3 percent in Yemen's first democratic contest. "Democracy and the peaceful succession of power is considered by all our people to be the correct and civilized choice which cannot be reversed," Saleh declared. He continues as the longest-serving Arab ruler after Libya's MUAMMAR QADDAFI.

Despite his long-standing tussle with the United States over Israel, Saleh's pragmatism was again prevalent over the issue of terrorism. The destroyer USS *Cole* was attacked in a Yemeni port in October 2000 by adherents of Osama bin Laden, the Saudi terrorist mastermind, and Saleh quickly allowed the FBI and other investigative bodies into the country. In the wake of the September 11, 2001, destruction of the World Trade Center, Saleh publicly announced his support for President GEORGE W. BUSH's war against international terrorism. He was then allowed to visit Washington, D.C., to sign an antiterrorism agreement and to receive $150 million in foreign aid. This agreement subsequently resulted in attacks by the Yemeni army against al-Qaida terrorist strongholds in the Republic of Yemen. However, in the wake of Israel's renewed offensive against the Palestinian Authority in the spring of 2002, Saleh again renewed his calls for action against the Jewish state, and he condemned Arab nations that sustain diplomatic relations with Tel Aviv.

Further Reading

Carapio, Sheila. *Civil Society in Yemen: The Political Economy of Activism in Modern Arabia.* New York: Cambridge University Press, 1998.

Day, Stephen W. "Power Sharing and Hegemony: A Case Study of the United Arab Republic of Yemen." Unpublished Ph.D. dissertation, Georgetown University, 2001.

Halliday, Fred. *Revolution and Foreign Policy: The Case of South Yemen, 1967–1987.* Cambridge: Cambridge University Press, 2002.

Saif, Ahmed A. *A Legislature in Transition: The Yemeni Parliament.* Burlington, Vt.: Ashgate, 2001.

Schmitz, Charles P. "State and Market System in South Yemen." Unpublished Ph.D. dissertation, University of California, Berkeley, 1997.

Sharif, Abdu H. "Weak Institutions and Democracy: The Case of the Yemeni Parliament." *Middle East Policy* 9 (May 2002): 82–93.

Salinas de Gortari, Carlos (1948–   ) *president of Mexico*

Carlos Salinas de Gortari was born on April 3, 1948, in Mexico City, the son of a government minister. As a member of the Mexican elite, he was educated at private schools before attending the National Autonomous University of Mexico. Salinas excelled academically, and he subsequently gained admittance to Harvard University, obtaining a doctorate in economics by 1978. He then returned to accept several positions within the Center for Monetary Studies of Latin America. When one of his former professors, Miguel de la Madrid, became president in 1982, he invited Salinas to work in the national treasury as an economic planner. Salinas excelled in the role, and de la Madrid then allowed him to serve as director of the Institute of Political, Economic, and Social Studies. The institute was created by the Institutional Revolutionary Party (PRI) which had dominated national events since its founding in 1929. Salinas, as usual, handled himself adroitly, and he forcefully advocated modernizing the moribund Mexican economy. He stressed doing so even at the risk of offending entrenched political interests, which dominated the PRI. In 1987 de la Madrid endorsed Salinas as his political successor and he became the party's presidential candidate for the upcoming national elections. However, Mexico was gripped by serious economic problems and suffered from high unemployment, drug corruption, and violence. Furthermore, the PRI was traditionally adept at manipulating vote totals; consequently, its candidates for office always won by large margins. However, in 1988 discontent proved so rife that Salinas scraped by with only 50.2 percent of votes cast—meaning that he probably lost to Cuauhtémoc Cárdenas of the left-wing National Democratic Front. Cárdenas himself was formerly a PRI operative, but parted company, protesting the party's conservative stances on social and economic policies. Nevertheless, the scant margin of Salinas's victory was a serious political setback for the PRI, whose candidates usually won by 76 percent, and it compromised his legitimacy. Worse, the party failed to win two-thirds of seats in the national congress, hence the new president started off in a very weakened condition.

Despite these setbacks, Salinas determined to forge ahead with desperately needed economic reforms. These included, most essentially, the dismantling of Mexico's traditional reliance on government control of key sectors of the economy, especially oil and copper production. Accordingly, foreign investors were invited in and many old and inefficient industries were sold off. Salinas also broke new ground by helping negotiate the North American Free Trade Agreement (NAFTA) with the United States and Canada. This act sounded the death knell to Mexico's economic nationalism and state-sponsored protectionism. The changes wrought entailed a stiff dose of medicine for the ailing economy, and they led to increases in unemployment and business failures. The political ramifications for the PRI's grip on power became increasingly obvious when the governorship of Baja California was seized by the opposition National Action Party (PAN) in 1989. Worse, on January 1, 1994, the Native American population of Chiapas rebelled in protest against poverty and oppression. Rather than resort to force to quell the violence, Salinas opened a dialogue with the Zapatista Army of National Liberation to save face. Two months later the PRI sustained another telling blow when Salinas's handpicked successor, Luis Donaldo Colosio, was assassinated while campaigning in Tijuana. The prospects of increasing social instability forced U.S. president BILL CLINTON to intervene and prop up the peso before it collapsed. Things had stabilized by August 1994, and PRI again prevailed when ERNESTO ZEDILLO won in the nation's freest elections to date. At first glance it appeared Salinas had concluded a successful presidency and that Mexico had completed its transition to free-market economics. He left office regarded as one of Mexico's most popular executives.

By December 1994, the Salinas legacy began unraveling. Because of poor management and heavy borrowing, the economy collapsed and the peso lost half of its value in only a month. This triggered a massive flight of capital from the country and a two-year recession. The former president's reputation was further battered when his brother Raúl was implicated in the assassination of the PRI's deputy leader José Francisco Ruiz Massieu. Anger increased when it was revealed that Raúl had accumulated a fortune estimated at $80 million in Swiss bank accounts, all misappropriated from the government. With popular ferment roundly blaming Salinas for a massive economic meltdown and family corruption, President Zedillo ordered him out of the country in March 1995. Salinas has since set up residency in Ireland, where he is safe from prosecution, as that country lacks an extradition treaty with Mexico. He nonetheless stridently maintains his innocence and has blamed Zedillo for the economic woes of the country. In June 1999 the disgraced former president visited Mexico for the first time in four years and appeared on national television. "I am not going to deny that there were insufficiencies, that errors were committed," he admitted. Since then Salinas has remained in exile, tarred by allegations of corruption and mismanagement, but as yet still unindicted.

Further Reading

Brophy-Baerman, M. "Economics and Elections: The Mexican Case." *Social Science Quarterly* 75 (March 1989): 125–135.

Centeno, Miguel A. "After the Fall: The Legacy of Carlos Salinas." *Mexican Studies* 13, no. 1 (1997): 201–14.

Hamm, Patricia H. "How Mexico Built Support for the Negotiation of the North American Free Trade Agreement Targeting the American Diaspora in the United States." Unpublished Ph.D. dissertation, University of California, Irvine, 2001.

Morris, S. "Corruption and the Mexican Political System." *Continuity and Change* 20 (June 1999): 623–643.

Russell, Philip L. *Mexico under Salinas.* Austin, Tex.: Mexico Resource Center, 1994.

Samper, Ernesto (1950–) *president of Colombia*

Ernesto Samper Pizano was born on August 3, 1950, in Bogotá, Colombia, into a family of industrialists. He was well educated locally and obtained his doctorate in judicial and economic science from Javeriana University in 1973. Samper subsequently received a second doctorate in economics from Columbia University, New York, in 1979. At various times between 1974 and 1981 he also served with the Economic Research Center at the Bank of Colombia. In 1981 Samper founded the Institute for Liberal Studies, a policy think tank associated with the Liberal Party (PL), one of Colombia's two main political organizations. That year he also served as presidential campaign coordinator for Alfonso López Michelson, and by 1982 he had risen to the post of secretary of the PL. There he proved instrumental in moving the party toward neoliberal models of economic development. Following a stint as Colombian ambassador to the United Nations, Samper commenced his political career at home by gaining a seat on the Bogotá city council in 1984. He followed this up two years later by being elected senator and then gaining the party chairmanship in 1987. By 1990 Samper's political stock had risen to the point where he became a serious contender for the presidency,

although he eventually yielded the palm to another PL candidate, CÉSAR GAVIRIA. This occurred after a harrowing assassination attempt by Colombian drug lords in May of that year. Samper was critically injured but survived, and President Gaviria appointed him minister of economic development and ambassador to Spain. In May 1993 he returned home to run again for the Colombian presidency, and the following spring he emerged as the PL's candidate. On June 19, 1994, he defeated his Conservative Party (PC) opponent, ANDRÉS PASTRANA, in a runoff vote with 50.41 percent. He accepted the presidential sash on August 7, 1994.

Public expectations were high for Samper, as the Liberals held commanding majorities in both houses of the national congress. He was determined to enact badly needed structural reforms to the nation's economy, but with a view toward mitigating their effects upon the nation's lower classes. "Our problem is that we have applied neoliberal models without taking appropriate measures to cushion their social impact," he warned. However, from the onset the administration was continually sidetracked by allegations of misbehavior. No sooner had Samper assumed power than the PC charged him with accepting $3 million in campaign funds from the Cali drug cartel, a charge he vehemently denied. Colombia by now had become headquarters for the ultraviolent international cocaine trade which, along with numerous guerrilla insurgencies, contributed to a growing sense of national destabilization. The PC's accusations were eventually retracted, but they established a pattern that stalked Samper throughout his tenure in office.

Samper had campaigned on a broad platform to create 1.5 million new jobs, extend better rights to women, contain guerrilla activities, and suppress the drug trade. However, the economy remained stalled in recession, further aggravated by labor unrest and strikes. Samper enjoyed limited success establishing dialogue with several insurgent groups opposing the government, but others proved intransigent and unleashed costly terrorist attacks. Samper's inability to cope with this litany of problems made attracting foreign investors unsuccessful and this, in turn, fueled the economic downturn. The United States was especially angered by the president's lack of progress in combating the drug trade and, suspecting official collusion, Congress refused to certify Colombia's compliance. This left President BILL CLINTON no recourse but to cancel Samper's entry visa, and he was forbidden from entering the country.

Closer to home, new allegations of drug connections surfaced in 1995, and Samper found himself scrutinized by a congressional investigation. He emerged unscathed, but calls were made for his resignation. Samper refused, even though in 1996 he was formally accused of electoral fraud and illegal enrichment. The vicious cycle of accusation and denial infringed on his ability to effect much-needed legislation, and Colombia's economy continued declining. Political unrest and chronic violence were further exacerbated by a 13 percent unemployment rate. Worse, in March 1998 guerrilla attacks coincided with congressional elections, killing 18 people and lowering participation to 30 percent. By summer most voters concurred with PC candidate Andrés Pastrana that Samper had lost control of events and, on June 21, 1998, they elected the first Conservative government in a decade. Samper, disgraced by his questionable behavior and lackluster performance, lost credibility within the PL and resigned from public life.

Further Reading

Aviles, William. "Institutions, Military Policy, and Human Rights in Colombia." *Latin American Perspectives* 28, no. 1 (2001): 31–55.

Crandall, Russell C. "The Eagle and the Snowman: U.S. Policy towards Colombia during the Presidential Administration of Ernesto Samper (1994–1998)." Unpublished Ph.D. dissertation, Johns Hopkins University, 2000.

———. "Explicit Narcotization: U.S. Policy toward Colombia during the Samper Administration." *Latin American Politics and Society* 43 (Fall 2001): 95–105.

Kada, Naoka. "Politics of Impeachment in Latin America." Unpublished Ph.D. dissertation, University of California, San Diego, 2002.

Kauf, Phillip D. "Presidential Effectiveness and the Mass Media in Colombia: A Study Conducted during the Administration of Ernesto Samper Pizano, 1994–1997." Unpublished Ph.D. dissertation, University of Miami, 1998.

Sassou-Nguesso, Denis (1943–) *president of the Republic of the Congo*

Denis Sassou-Nguesso was born in the town of Edou, Owando district, Congo, in 1943. Congo was then a French colony on the west coast of Africa and surrounded by Gabon, Cameroon, and the Democratic Republic of the Congo. It gained independence from France in August 1960 and elected its first president, Abbe Fulbert Youlou, the following year. However, the country oscillated between civilian and military rule over the next three decades. National politics have been dominated by numerous Marxist-oriented parties, but the most significant of these is the Congolese Worker's Party (PCT), which held sway in four different administrations. The nation is further divided along ethnic lines, through which many groupings north and south share long traditions of antipathy. Agriculture and forestry have long characterized the national economy, but the discovery of oil, especially offshore, has led to a general increase in revenues. French remains the official language of government.

Sassou-Nguesso passed through primary schools before attending a teacher's college. However, he soon became caught up in radical youth movements then sweeping the country before joining the French army in 1961. Within a year he was back home as an elite paratrooper and rose successively through ranks and responsibility. In 1975 President Marien Ngouabi appointed the young officer minister of defense while he also served as vice president of the PCT military committee. Following Ngouabi's assassination in 1977 a new president, Joachim Yhombi-Opango, came to power with policies less sympathetic to Marxist dogma than the PCT. The party then overthrew him in February 1979 and appointed Sassou-Nguesso to head a provision committee to lead the country. The following month the party formerly installed him as the new president of the Republic of the Congo. Despite his Marxist leanings, Sassou-Nguesso was pragmatic in his approach to leadership and economics. He steered a neutral course in terms of foreign policy and fully embraced a liberalized, market economy. Results were mixed but his control of party affairs remained firm, so in 1984 and 1989, Sassou-Nguesso was reelected to the party chairmanship and presidency without dissent.

Following the fall of the Soviet bloc in 1991, the Congo came under increasing Western pressure to allow for multiparty democracy. Sassou-Nguesso only grudgingly complied and elections were held in 1992. In the elections, the opposition Panafrican Union for Social Democracy (UPADS) won handily, and Pascal Lissouba defeated the incumbent president with 61 percent of votes cast. Sassou-Nguesso resigned and the PCT tried entering into a coalition arrangement with UPADS, but ideological differences proved insurmountable. In concert with another group, the Union for Democratic Renewal (URD) under Bernard Kolelas, the opposition militias took to the jungle to commence a low-intensity civil war. For four years combat between the three sides slowly escalated until the capital of Brazzaville became a battleground. However, in October 1997 forces loyal to Sassou-Nguesso captured the entire city, forcing President Lissouba to flee the country, and the former dictator reclaimed his office. The civil war had cost some 10,000 lives and displaced 3 million residents.

Having seized the reins of power again, Sassou-Nguesso wasted no time appealing for a unity government and invited all Congolese exiles to return. He also promised democratic elections at an unspecified time in the future, once stability and prosperity had been restored. The PCT's success was due partly to military assistance from France, apparently in exchange for an extraction monopoly over oil exports. Lissouba, it seems, was too willing to share that industry with United States companies, and thus he lost any chance of French aid. His support for UNITA rebels in neighboring Angola was also shortsighted, for the regime there dispatched troops to assist Sassou-Nguesso. Over the next five years, Congo experienced a slow and painful reconstruction process. However, as promised, the general introduced a new constitution in January 2001 that was overwhelmingly approved by public referendum. The document extended the president's term in office from four to seven years and stripped away parliament's ability to impeach him. On March 16, 2002, the long-awaited presidential election transpired with Sassou-Nguesso, as the incumbent, holding every advantage in terms of funding and media control. However, he lacked a credible opposition: all leading figures boycotted the process out of what they characterized as widespread fraud. Furthermore, his old adversaries Lissouba and Kolelas were both in exile and banned from running owing to strict new residency laws passed the previous year. Sassou-Nguesso therefore piled up an impressive victory tally of 89 percent over four lesser candidates. "My dear countrymen, through this important process, which took place in an exemplary climate of serenity and tranquillity," he maintained, "you have affirmed your strong desire to live in a united, free, democratic and peaceful Congo." In the absence of viable political opposition, or the ability of parliament to remove him, Sassou-Nguesso is slated to remain in office until 2009.

Further Reading

Amphas-Mampoua. *Political Transformation of the Congo.* Durham, N.C.: Pentland Press, 2000.

Bazenguissa-Ganga, Remy. "The Spread of Political Violence in Congo-Brazzaville." *African Affairs* 98, no. 390 (1999): 37–54.

Clarke, John F. "Democracy Dismantled in the Congo Republic." *Current History* 97 (May 1998): 234–237.

———. "The Neo-colonial Context of the Democratic Experiment of Congo-Brazzaville." *African Affairs* 101, no. 403 (2002): 171–192.

Decalo, Samuel. *Historical Dictionary of Congo.* Lanham, Md.: Scarecrow Press, 1996.

Gauze, Rene. *The Politics of Congo-Brazzaville.* Stanford, Calif.: Hoover Institution Press, 1973.

Martin, Phyllis. *Leisured Society in Colonial Brazzaville.* New York: Cambridge University Press, 1995

Savimbi, Jonas (1934–2002) *Angolan rebel leader*

Jonas Malheiros Savimbi was born in Munhango, Moxico province, Angola, on August 3, 1934, the son of a railway worker and a member of the influential Ovimbundu tribe. Portugal then administered Angola as a colony, and when its African-born citizens received any education at all, it was to further their careers in servitude. However, Savimbi was more fortunate than many contemporaries in being allowed to attend missionary schools and completing his secondary education. Extremely bright as a student, in 1958 he won a full scholarship from the United Church of Christ to study medicine full-time at the University of Lisbon. Savimbi studied only a few months in Portugal before becoming involved in the anticolonial fervor then sweeping Angola, and his close association with radical student groups forced him to leave. He subsequently completed his education at the University of Lausanne in Switzerland, obtaining an advanced degree in political science by 1965. Soon after he visited the People's Republic of China to learn the art of guerrilla warfare. Savimbi also demonstrated considerable skill as a linguist: fluent in three African dialects, he went on to master Portuguese, French, and English. Furthermore,

Westerners who came to know Savimbi personally ascribed to him a brilliant mind saddled by a mercurial disposition.

Savimbi had originally posited himself as a Maoist and briefly flirted with radical groups like the Popular Union of Angola. However, he found this organization to be too heavily dominated by one ethnic group, and in 1966 he founded the National Union for the Total Independence of Angola (UNITA). As leader, he returned home and helped orchestrate a low-intensity guerrilla war against Portuguese troops. Despite his pleas for a political movement that was national and would transcend tribalism, he secured support largely from his own Ovimbundu kinsmen of central Angola. He was joined in the conflict by several other competing movements, especially the Marxist-oriented People's Movement for the Liberation of Angola (MPLA) under Agostinho Neto. Fighting continued intermittently until 1974, when the Portuguese government was overthrown by a left-wing coup. The Portuguese regime promptly withdrew its troops from Angola, which declared its independence. Savimbi, as leader of UNITA, then emerged from the bush country to sign an interim agreement with the MPLA for a peaceful transition to civilian rule. However, when it became apparent that the Soviet-supported MPLA was willing to substitute Portuguese overseers with Soviet ones, Savimbi withdrew from talks and recommenced fighting in 1975. Africa's longest and most costliest civil war had begun.

For the next 27 years, Savimbi and UNITA proved to be the bane of the Angolan government and people. Initially, his struggle was cast as simply a continuation of the cold war in Africa, especially after 60,000 Cuban troops and Soviet advisers arrived in Angola to prop up the MPLA. This, in turn, induced Western powers like the United States to ship millions of dollars of covert aid to UNITA and maintain the armed struggle against communism. Furthermore, to counter Cuban influence, the apartheid regime of South Africa also committed regular forces to combat. In 1986 Savimbi's political fortunes and global reputation crested during a White House visit with U.S. president Ronald Reagan, who touted the swaggering guerrilla, heavily bearded and sporting his perennial beret, as a freedom fighter. Furthermore, the former Maoist now posited himself as an ally of capitalism, fully committed to democracy and free-market economics. Consequently, American support enabled UNITA to overrun most of the Angolan countryside, but MPLA forces managed to cling to the cities. By 1988 an agreement was reached whereby both Cuba and South Africa would remove their forces from the region. Four more years of fighting convinced MPLA president JOSE DOS SANTOS to allow for multiparty elections, which were further abetted after the 1991 collapse of the Soviet Union. Savimbi then ran for the presidency of Angola in free and fair elections and narrowly lost. However, the disgruntled guerrilla refused to accept defeat at the polls and returned to the jungles to wage war. A UN–brokered cease-fire was reached in 1994 whereby Savimbi would have served as vice president, but he disagreed with the terms at the last minute and resumed fighting.

Once the Soviet Union ceased to exist in 1991, MPLA renounced socialism and embraced free-market economics. This brought Angola into the Western camp, and military aid to UNITA rebels dried up. However, Savimbi had overrun the diamond-producing regions of the country and kept his movement going through illegal sales. The MPLA also struck back, reclaiming vast tracts of countryside, but it proved unable to eradicate the rebels completely. It was not only an intense battle on February 22, 2002, when Savimbi was killed, that the war-torn nation could entertain any notions for peace. Devoid of their charismatic leader and faced with dwindling stocks of weapons and recruits, the UNITA rebels formally signed a peace agreement on April 7, 2002. The survivors were then offered the choice to either lay down their arms or be incorporated into the national army. Savimbi's personal 27-year war cost Angola dearly. Once touted as the richest nation in Africa, it now numbers among the world's poorest. An estimated 1 million people died in the struggle, 4 million were displaced by fighting, and the countryside remained strewn with millions of unexploded land mines. Appreciably, Savimbi's death was greeted with rejoicing in the streets of Angola, for it signaled the end of Africa's longest and most costly conflict.

Further Reading

Bridgland, Fred. *Jonas Savimbi: A Key to Africa.* Sevenoaks: Coronet, 1988.

Ciment, James. *Angola and Mozambique: Postcolonial Wars in South Africa.* New York: Facts On File, 1997.

Gleijeses, Pero. *Conflicting Missions: Havana, Washington, and Africa, 1959–1976.* Baltimore: Johns Hopkins University Press, 2002.

Heywood, Linda M. *Contested Power in Angola, 1840s to the Present.* Rochester, N.Y.: University of Rochester Press, 2000.

Matloff, Judith. *Fragments of a Forgotten War.* New York: Penguin Books, 1997.

Windrich, Elaine. *The Cold War Guerrilla: Jonas Savimbi, The U.S. Media, and the Angolan War.* New York: Greenwood Press, 1992.

———. "The Laboratory of Hate: The Role of Clandestine Radio in the Angolan War." *International Journal of Cultural Studies* 3 (August 2000): 206–218.

Scalfaro, Oscar (1918–) *president of Italy*

Oscar Luigi Scalfaro was born on September 9, 1918, in Novara, northern Italy, the offspring of a devout Catholic family. He received a law degree from the Catholic University Sacro Cuore, Milan, before the end of World War II, and he participated in the antifascist Catholic Action organization. In 1946 Scalfaro stood for a seat in the postwar National Assembly as a Christian Democrat (DC), and he helped design a new constitution transforming Italy from a monarchy to a republic. By 1948 he had won a seat in the Chamber of Deputies, a position he held without interruption until 1992. Scalfaro then assumed a number of governmental and ministerial positions within several administrations. Throughout his long tenure in office, he also established himself as a political moderate, untainted by the familiar specter of corruption. In fact, Scalfaro openly campaigned throughout his political career for greater morality in Italian politics, a message that resonated louder and louder throughout the scandal-wracked 1990s. In 1987 he was approached by President Francesco Cossiga to form a new government as prime minister, but he declined. Instead, he hung on to his deputy's seat and in 1992 he rose to occupy the speaker's chair. Scalfaro, by dint of his unimpeachable reputation as a senior statesman, longevity in office, and all-around political savvy, constituted an ideal candidate for the presidency in April 1992. However, a parliamentary row developed between conservatives and leftists, which stalemated the nomination process for 10 days and 16 ballots. The impasse continued until Judge Giovanni Falcone was murdered by Mafia hit men, an act that infuriated the public. This also terminated the leading candidate for president, GIULIO ANDREOTTI, who was suspected of having close ties to organized crime. But it proved just the catalyst Scalfaro needed, and on May 24, 1992, he was elected by an almost unanimous vote. The endorsement of a conservative candidate by so many leftists was unprecedented and a good indication of Scalfaro's reputation for personal integrity.

The Italian presidency is a largely ceremonial post, but the office enjoys critical powers of formally appointing the prime minister, dissolving the assembly, and calling for national elections. Scalfaro, despite his long association with the Christian Democrats, was no ideologue and even displayed a streak of independence. One of his first tasks was to appoint a new prime minister and he nominated Socialist GIULIANO AMATO, like himself an outsider untainted by charges of corruption. Together they began a concerted attack upon the Mafia in Italian political life. Organized crime at this juncture had sunk its tentacles deep into the Italian polity and threatened the republic's very survival. Accordingly, in March 1993 Scalfaro refused to sign legislation that would have protected high-ranking members of the government from criminal investigation; subsequently, many officials lost their positions. Within months one of these victims implicated Scalfaro in a scandal, and the minister went on the national airwaves to denounce what amounted to a smear campaign against him. However, when public unease over corruption in high office continued, the president called for new elections.

One unforeseen result was the rise of SILVIO BERLUSCONI, a media magnate who scorned Italy's traditional parties and ran as an independent. As prime minister, he proved to be frequently at odds with Scalfaro, who insisted on greater transparency by public figures. Berlusconi, a shady operator by nature, would hear none of it, and he rekindled speculations about the president's previous association in a scandal. Worse, he openly derided Scalfaro as the aged guardian of the "First Republic," a reference to the 1946 government, implying that he represented an antiquated order in Italian politics. Berlusconi also strenuously criticized the president's strict interpretation of constitutional law, which circumvented enactment of many of his electoral reforms. Such changes, the president held, only served to help Berlusconi. For three years an antagonistic tug of war ensued at the highest levels of government, but Scalfaro's reputation held him in good stead. Berlusconi's allegations proved harmless and, in fact, he was turned out of office in January 1995 and replaced by LAMBERTO DINI. The president's reputation, however, emerged from the fray unscathed.

Scalfaro continued serving as president of Italy until May 15, 1999, when he stepped down in favor of CARLO AZEGLIO CIAMPI. He had presided through one of Italy's most turbulent political periods, yet persistently lent an air of dignity and decorum to his office. His departure also marked the end of an era—Scalfaro was the last of the 1946 generation to wield political influence. Nonetheless, he left the presidency a more influential office than when he obtained it and, to a large degree, helped restore public confidence in national institutions. Though retired, Scalfaro still makes his presence felt on the international scene. In September 2000 he conferred with Chinese president JIANG ZEMIN in Zhongnanhai over trade and other related issues.

Further Reading

Agnew, John A. *Place and Politics in Modern Italy.* Chicago: University of Chicago Press, 2002.

Bedani, Gino, and B. A. Haddock. *The Politics of Italian National Identity: A Multidisciplinary Perspective.* Cardiff: University of Wales, 2000.

Bull, Martin J., and Martin Rhodes. *Special Issue on Crisis and Transformation in Italian Politics.* Ilford, England: Frank Cass, 1997.

Catena, Gene A. "The Dynamics of Institutional Reform in Contemporary Italian Politics." Unpublished master's thesis, Indiana University, 1992.

Gilbert, Mark, and Gianfranco Pasquino. *Italian Politics: The Faltering Transition.* New York: Berghahn Books, 2000.

Schluter, Poul (1929–) *prime minister of Denmark*

Poul Holmskov Schluter was born on April 3, 1929, in Tønder, Denmark, the son of a merchant. He joined the Conservative Party in 1943 and served as chairman of the youth organization. Schluter subsequently attended the Universities of Copenhagen and Aarhus, where he obtained his law degree in 1957. He maintained a law practice until 1964, when he successfully stood for a seat in the Folketing (parliament). A skilled politician and consensus builder, he rose rapidly through the party hierarchy and in 1974 was tapped to serve as

party chairman. Schluter, as a conservative, appeared somewhat out of synch with the rest of Denmark's polity, which had long traditions of control by liberal Social Democrats. Given the uniquely consensual nature of Danish politics, and its close adherence to the politics of a traditional Scandinavian welfare state, it seemed unlikely that any conservative could become prime minister or, if elected, would hold power for long. However, by 1980 Denmark was experiencing profound economic distress and voters were looking for an alternative. When Social Democratic prime minister Anker Jorgensen proved unable to resolve the crisis and resigned from office Schluter, who controlled the largest non-Socialist bloc in parliament, was asked to form a new government. He thereupon cobbled together a four-party center-right coalition government, and he was sworn in as prime minister on September 19, 1982. His was the first Conservative Party administration since 1901.

As prime minister, Schluter's first priority was reducing the national debt. He achieved this by paring back some of the extravagant social benefits of Denmark's generous welfare state, along with corporate taxes. Moreover, he abolished Denmark's long-standing system of wage and price hikes, pegged to the inflation rate, which further drove up the debt. "We don't intend to abolish the welfare state," he argued, "but we will have to adjust it severely to what is within our economic capacity." Within months, the Conservative policies worked as intended. The national debt, which once stood at 11 percent of the gross national product, was reduced by half. For the first time in 30 years, Denmark also achieved a positive trade balance with the rest of Europe, and with it a strengthened, stabilized currency. The dramatic adjustments these improvements necessitated did not please everybody within the fragile four-party coalition, but Schluter became renowned for his sense of pragmatism and willingness to compromise. His political skills only abetted his economic success, and he remained in office for 11 years, longer than any Danish prime minister of the 20th century.

Having confronted domestic issues, Schluter also had to grapple with international tensions. His most pressing problem remained Denmark's role in NATO, which many regarded with some ambivalence. Rather than be a small country in a very big alliance, leftist elements argued that neutrality would be the saner course to pursue. To that effect, the Social Democrats managed to enact legislation advising all ships entering Danish waters that nuclear weapons were prohibited. This flew in the face of American and British naval policy, whereby captains of warships could neither confirm nor deny the presence of such devices. Schluter, a strong NATO proponent, could not resolve the issue in parliament so he called for snap elections in May 1988 to resolve the impasse. When results proved less than decisive, he fashioned a compromise that placated the peace lobby while also accommodating his NATO allies. Schluter faced even greater opposition over Denmark's entry into the European Community, and in 1989, the conservatives lost half their representation in the European Parliament over the issue. In 1992 voters also rejected the 1991 Maastricht Treaty strengthening the European political union, although they have elected to remain within the EC.

Schluter continued in office until January 1993, when his administration was brought down by an immigration scandal. A judicial inquiry revealed that the prime minister had covered up an illegal policy of blocking visas for relatives of Sri Lankan refuges living in Denmark. This action, in turn, formed part of a larger Conservative plan to halt the flow of asylum seekers from all countries. Embarrassed by these revelations, Schluter resigned and was replaced by POUL NYRUP RASMUSSEN of the Social Democratic Party. In retrospect, Schluter enjoyed an impressive run in office and bequeathed to Denmark a measure of prosperity and fiscal responsibility it heretofore never enjoyed. He retired a respected senior statesman, and in 1994 gained election to the European Parliament as vice president, where he remained until 1999.

Further Reading

Beck Jorgensen, Torben. *From Agency to Department and Back Again: Contradictory Developments in Danish Public Administration.* London: London School of Economics, 1997.

Borre, Ole, and Jorgen Goul Andersen. *Voting and Political Attitudes in Denmark: A Study of the 1994 Elections.* Oakville, Conn.: Aarhus University Press, 1997.

Fitzmaurice, John. *Politics in Denmark.* New York: St. Martin's Press, 1981.

Flyvbjerg, Bent. *Rationality and Power: Democracy in Practice.* Chicago: University of Chicago Press, 1998.

Miller, Kenneth E. *Friends and Rivals: Coalition Politics in Denmark, 1901–1995.* Lanham, Md.: University Press of America, 1996.

Schroeder, Gerhard (1944–) *chancellor of Germany*

Gerhard Schroeder was born on April 7, 1944, in the town of Mossenburg, Lower Saxony, Germany. Throughout most of its history, Germany consisted of a collection of over 300 small, disunified states, each with its own king, prince, and dynasty. It was not united into a single political entity until 1870 under the guidance of Chancellor Otto von Bismarck, the architect of modern Germany. However, in the wake of World War II, the country was again divided into two competing halves. West Germany, with its capital at Bonn, became aligned with the Western democracies while East Germany, governed from Berlin, functioned as part of the Soviet bloc. The country remained partitioned until October 1990 when reunification suddenly became feasible, following the withdrawal of Russian troops from Eastern Europe. Germany is currently governed by a federal arrangement of 16 states. The head of the government is a chancellor who rules in concert with a bicameral legislature, consisting of an upper house (Bundesrat) and a lower house (Bundestag). The chancellor is chosen from the party that holds a majority of seats in the Bundestag, or can form a coalition with other parties. Germany enjoys a well-deserved reputation as the economic engine that pulls the rest of Europe along, and is renowned for its high-quality automobiles, technology, and optical equipment. Moreover, its citizens enjoy one of the world's highest standards of living, backed by a generous welfare state. Since 1945 the nation has also renounced its militaristic past, and the deployment of German forces outside of the country has been forbidden under the constitution. However, in the wake of recent world events, this and many other national priorities will undoubtedly be up for review.

Schroeder was born shortly after his father was killed in World War II, and his mother worked as a cleaning lady. To overcome a hardscrabble existence, he quit high school to work as a china shop salesman and took correspondence courses at night. In this manner Schroeder was eventually admitted into Göttingen University, where he studied law. At that time Schroeder became active in left-wing politics by joining the Young

Socialists wing of the Social Democratic Party (SDP). After serving on various party committees, he gained election to the Bundestag in 1980. Six years later Schroeder returned to his home state of Lower Saxony where, after two attempts, he was elected premier in 1986. As premier he gained the reputation as a media-savvy populist, one who was not particularly beholden to party ideology. This ambiguous stance alienated many strident Social Democrats, but it also enabled Schroeder to posit himself as a political moderate. After three successful terms as state premier he felt ready to challenge HELMUT KOHL of the Christian Democratic Union, who had served as Germany's chancellor for 16 years. On September 27, 1998, Schroeder defeated Kohl by a wide margin, the first time an incumbent leader had been defeated since 1945, and a clear signal that Germany was ready for change.

Schroeder, however, was scarcely an instrument of change. Though forced into a coalition government with the more radical Green Party, he paid lip service to the environment, and pledged to phase out nuclear power, but he otherwise charted a very centrist course. In fact, many of his positions were far friendlier to the business community than many in his party would have preferred. In many respects, Schroeder patterned himself after U.S. president BILL CLINTON and British prime minister TONY BLAIR, being young, attractive, a good talker, and surrounded by liberal/leftist cohorts, but essentially a centrist in practice. As the largest economy in Europe, Germany has an inordinate leadership role to play in the European Union, and Schroeder, while careful to monitor Germany's best interests, has been a powerful supporter of integration. In fact, the most radical proposal he has undertaken has been easing restrictions upon immigration to Germany, making it easier to apply for citizenship. He also restored some minor welfare cuts made by Kohl.

Events in the wake of the September 11, 2002, attack on New York's World Trade Center have greatly tested Schroeder's ability to act as a valuable American ally. He strongly endorsed President GEORGE W. BUSH's war against international terrorism, and he further tendered his support by offering, for the first time in nearly 50 years, 4,000 German combat troops. This ensued, however, only after an agonizing vote by the coalition-controlled parliament. His Green allies, sworn opponents of military adventurism, reluctantly decided to support the chancellor rather than see his government collapse.

Gerhard Schroeder *(Embassy of the Federal Republic of Germany)*

On November 17, 2001, the final tally was only 336 votes in favor, a scant two more votes than a simple majority. "Through this contribution the united and sovereign Germany meets its growing responsibility in the world," Schroeder trumpeted. "This decision shows that when things get serious, this coalition sticks together." Still, it had been a close call, and the Greens underscored their determination to resist any attempt by Schroeder to use German troops in an American-sponsored attack against Iraq. Schroeder had little recourse but to reiterate this position to President Bush, and he has called for restraint in proceeding in the absence of United Nations sanctions. The entire issue of war and peace had sorely jolted the SDP/Green coalition, and in a manner viewed unimaginable only a few years before. Fortunately, Schroeder found a rallying point in President Bush's saber-rattling toward Iraq. Elections held on October 23, 2002 returned the Red/Green Alliance to power, but with a razor-thin majority of only nine seats. The Green Party posted its best showing over, garnering 8 percent of the vote, and is demanding greater influence in governmental affairs. Thus the SDP is in a very weakened position, and its ability to maintain a coalition is questionable. It remains to be seen if, under Schroeder's ambiguous leadership style, they can jointly govern the country while maintaining Germany's newfound obligations abroad.

Further Reading

Allen, Christopher S. *Nations and Regions in the European Union.* Cambridge: Cambridge University Press, 2001.

Gellner, Winand, and John D. Robertson, eds. *The Berlin Republic: German Unification and a Decade of Changes.* Portland, Oreg.: Frank Cass, 2003.

Heneghan, Tom. *Unchained Eagle: Germany after the Wall.* London: Reuters, 2000.

Larres, Klaus. *Germany since World War II: From Occupation to Unification and Beyond.* Oxford: Oxford University Press, 2001.

Oswald, Franz. *The Party That Came Out of the Cold War: The Party of Democratic Socialism in United Germany, 1989–2000.* Westport, Conn.: Praeger, 2002.

Tewes, Henning. *Germany, Civilian Power, and the New Europe: Enlarging NATO and the European Union.* Basingstoke, England: Palgrave, 2002.

Wolfgang Schüessel *(Hopi Media, Vienna)*

Schuessel, Wolfgang (1945–) *chancellor of Austria*

Wolfgang Schuessel was born in Vienna, Austria, on June 7, 1945. Austria previously formed part of the Hapsburg Empire, one of the dominating forces of Central European history. However, it was reduced to a landlocked republic after World War I within greatly reduced borders. In 1938 Austria was annexed to Nazi Germany by Adolph Hitler, who was himself Austrian, but after 1945 it was reestablished by the Allied powers. Military occupation of Austria ended in 1955 on the condition that neutrality become the cornerstone of its foreign policy. The country is presently governed under a parliamentary system consisting of a bicameral legislature, the Nationalrat and the Bundesrat, and a president who holds largely ceremonial duties. Among these, however, is appointing the chancellor—the real head of government—from the largest party or coalition in parliament. Since 1945 national politics have been dominated by either the right-leaning People's Party (ÖVP) or the left-leaning Social Democratic Party

(SDP), although a handful of extremist smaller parties also exist. Austria is today a highly evolved technological state, with a splendid cultural past that embraces figures like Ludwig von Beethoven, that enjoys a very high standard of living. Yet it still struggles to emerge from underneath the shadow of neutrality, and, more distant still, the specter of its past involvement with Nazism.

Schuessel passed through Vienna's Schottengymnasium, from which he graduated in 1963. He subsequently attended the University of Vienna, and in 1968 obtained a doctorate in law. Soon after Schuessel gravitated toward politics, and he joined the ÖVP. He soon landed a job as the party secretary in parliament and went on to hold the post of general secretary within the Austrian Economic Federation. In 1989 he was made minister of economic affairs in the government of Chancellor FRANZ VRAN-ITZKY, and six years later gained election as chairman of the ÖVP. As chairman he continued holding down various ministerial portfolios until July 1998, when Schuessel became president of the Council of the European Union, which Austria joined in 1995. The nation did so only reluctantly, out of fear of being swamped by a tide of foreign immigrants looking for work, and Schuessel unsuccessfully lobbied for a 10-year waiting period before permitting the unrestricted movement of workers. The October 1999 national elections also held unforeseen results for Austria when the far right Freedom Party of JÖRG HAIDER gained as many seats as the People's Party. The Social Democrats had acquired more seats, but they were still short of an absolute majority. Schuessel, as head of the ÖVP, faced the stark choice of either entering into a coalition with the much-detested Haider, or becoming the opposition minority in parliament. After much soul searching, he decided upon the former, and he was sworn in as chancellor on February 4, 2000.

The inclusion of a right-wing, ostensibly pro-Nazi party in the Austrian government sent shock waves throughout Europe. Israel and the United States recalled their ambassadors for consultation while the 15-member EU imposed economic sanctions on Austria. However, Schuessel was determined to demonstrate that he could control the Freedom Party, and both he and Haider signed statements renouncing Austria's Nazi past and reaffirming its commitment to human rights. Foremost among these was the proper treatment of minorities, and Schuessel was quick to point out that Austria equals or exceeds most EU nations in this respect. By September 2000 most of the sanctions had been lifted. Schuessel, meanwhile, wanted Austria to fully partake of the new, emerging Europe and hinted that his nation should revise its traditional stance on neutrality. He also stated his desire to seek NATO membership. He affirmed: "The old clichés—Lippizaner, Mozart chocolate balls, and neutrality—are no longer applicable in the complex reality of the 21st century." Given Austria's general diffidence toward joining the EU in 1995, and its continuing reluctance to part with the cherished ideals of neutrality, much time may pass before it participates in any military alliance or collective security arrangement.

In January 2002 the Schuessel government faced its first serious crisis when Haider's Freedom Party protested the scheduled opening of the Temelin nuclear power plant in the neighboring Czech Republic. This Soviet-style installation, only 40 miles from the Austrian border, has repeatedly been shut down for technical reasons. Fears of a Chernobyl-type disaster prompted the far right to collect 915,000 signatures against its continuation. Failing this, they threaten to veto Czech membership in the EU when a vote is scheduled in 2004. Moreover, Haider also expressed his determination to leave the coalition and call for early elections if Schuessel did not formally join the protest. However, the Czechs regard the plant as safe and they resent what they consider Austrian interference over a domestic matter. The matter is presently unresolved and its political resolution will test Schuessel's diplomatic skills to their utmost.

Further Reading

Bischof, Gunter, and Anton Pelinka. *Austria in the European Union.* New Brunswick, N.J.: Transaction, 2002.

Forrester, M. *Inside Austria: The Sellout of a Country.* New York: Vantage Press, 1999.

Pelinka, Anton. *Austria: Out of the Shadow of the Past.* Boulder, Colo.: Westview Press, 1998.

Pick, Hella. *Guilty Victim: Austria from the Holocaust to Haider.* New York: I. B. Tauris, 2000.

Thaler, Peter. *The Ambivalence of Identity: The Austrian Experience in Nation-Building in a Modern Society.* West Lafayette, Ind.: Purdue University Press, 2001.

Serrano, Jorge (1945–) *president of Guatemala*

Jorge Antonio Serrano Elías was born on April 26, 1945, in Guatemala City, Guatemala, the son of a government minister. He studied industrial engineering at the University of San Carlos, and he also pursed advanced degrees in economic development at Stanford University. After graduating, Serrano prospered as a businessman, and in 1975 he converted to evangelical Protestantism, a distinction in this heavily Catholic nation. In 1983 he struck up cordial relations with another Protestant national figure, President Efrain Ríos Montt, a former general who ruled Guatemala, 1982–83, and Serrano proffered his services as president of the Council of State. However, the military ousted Ríos Montt in 1983 and made preparations for democratic elections within two years. Serrano then formed his own Solidarity Action Movement (MAS) among business and conservative interests, and he ran as a candidate, placing third. He again stood for the presidency in 1989, this time against Ríos Montt, who led in the polls. However, because the new 1985 constitution forbade figures associated with military coups from holding high office, Ríos Montt was disqualified and the election was won by Christian

Democrat Mario Vinicio Cerezo. Conservative support then gradually shifted over to Serrano by the next election. On January 6, 1991, he defeated Jorge Carpio Nicolle of the National Centrist Union with 68 percent of votes cast. However, because only one-third of the electorate bothered to participate in what many considered a futile exercise, Serrano's legitimacy proved somewhat fleeting. Nonetheless, he was inaugurated on January 11, 1991, becoming the first elected Guatemalan president to peacefully succeed another. He was also the first Protestant head of state to serve in a Latin American country.

Serrano had campaigned on a platform promising dramatic reform of the national economy, which was floundering. He therefore embarked on a neoliberal course of privatization of government-held assets and less interference in free-market practices. Serrano also sought to reduce government regulations, enhance exports of nontraditional commodities, and establish what he deemed a "social pact" between business and labor. To stimulate better economic growth in Central America and the free flow of goods, he also sought reinvigoration of the Central American Economic Integration Treaty by eliminating tariffs and other obstacles to free trade. Furthermore, Serrano went to great lengths to establish friendly relations with neighboring Belize, whose territory Guatemala claimed as its own. Under Serrano, Guatemala finally granted diplomatic recognition to the former British colony.

Equally pressing to Serrano was settlement of Guatemala's 20-year-old guerrilla insurgency. Grinding poverty, gross inequities in wealth and land distribution, and discrimination against the native Mayan population facilitated growth of disparate guerrilla groups in the 1960s. By 1982 these coalesced under the Guatemalan National Revolutionary Union (URNG), which waged a low-intensity war against the government. The military responded brutally, killing an estimated 200,000 people and acquiring one of the worst human rights records in the world. Serrano had pledged to enter peace negotiations with the rebels in Oslo, Norway, but no breakthroughs occurred. Fighting persisted without interruption through his administration, and Serrano refused to condemn the military for its violent oppression of dissent.

By May 1993, Serrano's economic reforms had improved prospects for the business classes, but it inflicted pain upon poor households and union families. Rising discontent led to waves of crippling strikes and demonstrations, which, when combined with guerrilla activity, threatened to destabilize the government. On May 25, 1993, Serrano suddenly suspended both Congress and the courts, apparently with the military's approval. This usurpation was met with a chorus of condemnation from the United States and the European Union, both of which suspended all economic aid. Worse, the ploy failed to intimidate long-suffering peasants, now joined by prominent businessmen, who continued protesting the coup. João Baena Soares, secretary-general of the Organization of American States, then arrived to declare the diplomatic isolation facing Guatemala if Serrano retained power. Within three days the army concluded the president's rule was untenable and they ordered him out of the country. He subsequently fled for Panama on June 1, 1993, and five days later Congress reconvened and appointed a human rights activist, Ramiro de León Carpio, to succeed him. For the past decade Guatemala has repeatedly requested the extradition of Serrano from Panama for corruption, but that government refuses compliance, citing the lack of proper evidence. Serrano's career has since cast doubts on the ability of future Protestant evangelicals to hold high office in Latin America.

Further Reading

Chase-Dunn, Christopher, Suzanne Jonas, and Nelson Amaro, eds. *Globalization on the Ground: Postbellum Guatemalan Democracy and Development.* Lanham, Md.: Rowman and Littlefield, 2001.

Grandin, Grey. *The Blood of Guatemala: A History, Race and Nation.* Durham, N.C.: Duke University Press, 2000.

Jonas, Suzanne. *Of Centaurs and Doves: Guatemala's Peace Process.* Boulder, Colo.: Westview Press, 2000.

McCleary, Rachel M. *Dictating Democracy: Guatemala and the End of Violent Revolution.* Gainesville: University Press of Florida, 1999.

North, Liisa L., and Alan B. Simmons. *Journeys of Fear: Refugee Reform and National Transformation in Guatemala.* Montreal: McGill-Queens University Press, 1999.

Sezer, Ahmet (1941–) *president of Turkey*

Ahmet Necdet Sezer was born on September 13, 1941, in Afyon, Turkey, the son of a schoolteacher. He received his undergraduate degree in law from the University of Ankara in 1958. After serving briefly as a judge, he fulfilled his term of military service at the Land Force Academy, and he was subsequently a supervisory judge at the High Court of Appeals in Ankara. Sezer then returned to the university to obtain his master's degree in law, graduating in 1978. Having practiced law for several years, he rose to the High Court of Appeals in March 1983, and five years later won laurels by being elected chief justice of the Constitution Court on January 6, 1998. As a jurist, Sezer firmly embraced the rule of law, and his opinions were frequently more liberal than government or military authorities would have preferred. He enjoyed sterling credentials for modesty, intellectual clarity, and devotion to the principles of secularism that formed the basis of modern Turkey. Furthermore, as a jurist he urged repeal of many of the country's restrictive speech laws, and he criticized the 1982 constitution, inspired by the military, as being undemocratic. For all these reasons, in the spring of 2000 he emerged as a candidate for the nation's presidency. At that time Prime Minister BÜLENT ECEVIT was in a quandary over who should succeed outgoing incumbent SÜLEYMAN DEMIREL. Ecevit, whose ruling coalition was shaky owing to a poor economy, wanted to avoid a prolonged nomination battle that highlighted his weakness. After failed attempts at compromise, Sezer's name was advanced since he proved the only candidate around whom coalition and opposition parties could unite. His nomination passed on the third ballot—over the objections of conservatives—and he was sworn in as Turkey's 10th president on May 16, 2000.

In many respects, Sezer was an unusual candidate for high office. He lacked political connections and his professional experience was restricted to jurisprudence. However, he was the first Turkish executive to originate from outside either parliament or the military, the traditional sources of senior national leadership. As such, Sezer owed no political favors and lacked political enemies. Moreover, this pristine judicial avatar played no favorites and enforced laws as they were intended. He served as a fully committed democrat intent upon enhancing political freedom. His emphasis dovetailed with Turkey's strong desire to join the European Union (EU), which mandated strong democratic safeguards as a prerequisite for membership. Sezer made his intentions known from the onset. "Our country, which cannot remain inward-looking, has to become integrated with the values of civilization embraced by the European Union," he announced in his inaugural address.

"Our success in the areas of supremacy of the law and democracy will enhance our respectability in the community of modern nations." The Turkish presidency is largely symbolic, but it carries tremendous weight in moral authority and national symbolism. Therefore, given his democratic mind-set, Sezer's tenure heralded a new era for the principle of personal freedom in Turkey.

Once installed, Sezer immediately put his political philosophy into action. He advocated relaxing stringent anti-Kurdish language laws, aimed at repressing the large Kurdish minority, for they violated precepts established by EU membership. "Although everybody knows that freedom of thought is vital to democracy, we have not been able to overcome obstacles that keep us from establishing it," Sezer maintained. "Allowing people to hold opinions is not enough. They must be able to speak freely." And, despite his overwhelmingly Western orientation, the former judge also extended freedom of expression to Islamic fundamentalist parties, whose very existence is contrary to the secular principles of Turkish governance. Hence, Sezer made repeated calls on parliament to enact democratic reforms, "not because the European Union wants them but because these are changes that our people deserve."

In his role as moral arbiter, Sezer has alienated the political establishment through noncompliance. He has especially angered Prime Minister Ecevit by twice vetoing legislation inspired by the military permitting the government to fire thousands of civil servants deemed too sympathetic toward Islamic law or the Kurds. In April 2002, Sezer also vetoed an amnesty bill that would have entailed the release of Mehmet Ali Agca, the man who shot and nearly killed Pope JOHN PAUL II. A month later he went on record opposing new media laws allowing the government to censor any television show or computer site they deemed contrary to Turkish spiritual or family values. Sezer then appealed to the Constitutional Court for its repeal lest "the public's right to receive true and unbiased news will be damaged." The outspoken president has firmly established himself as a watchdog for individual rights in Turkey. His first term of office will expire in 2007.

Further Reading

Alexander, Catharine. *Personal States: Making Connections between People and Bureaucracy in Turkey.* New York: Oxford University Press, 2002.

Balkan, Nesecan, and Sungar Sauran. *The Politics of the Permanent Crisis: Class, Ideology, and State in Turkey.* New York: Nova Scientific Publishers, 2002.

Cornell, Erik. *Turkey in the 21st Century: Opportunities, Challenges, Threats.* Richmond, England: Curzon, 2001.

Kinzer, Stephen. *Crescent and Star: Turkey between Two Worlds.* New York: Farrar, Straus, and Giroux, 2001.

Olson, Robert W. *Turkey's Relations with Iran, Syria, Israel, and Russia, 1991–2000: The Kurdish and Islamist Questions.* Costa Mesa, Calif.: Mazda Publishers, 2001.

Swankland, David. *The Alevis in Turkey: The Emergence of a Secular Islamic Tradition.* New York: Routledge Curzon, 2003.

Shamir, Yitzhak (1915–) *prime minister of Israel*

Yitzhak Yizernitsky was born on October 15, 1915, in Rujenoy, eastern Poland (now Belarus), the son of a small businessman. He attended local Jewish schools and briefly attended Warsaw University before migrating to the British-controlled mandate of Palestine in 1935. There he labored as a construction worker while attending Hebrew University in Jerusalem, and he also changed his name to Shamir ("Hard Rock" in Hebrew). Shamir's family was Zionist in orientation, that is, intent upon resurrecting the ancient state of Israel by wresting it away from the Arabs. To this end he joined the Irgun, an underground guerrilla force that meted out revenge to Arabs for attacks on Jews. They also attacked the British military when possible. Following the onset of World War II, most Jewish underground leaders decided to cooperate with the British in the fight against Nazism. However, Shamir subscribed to an ultraviolent faction that split off from Irgun to form a new group, known by its acronyms as Lehi. Members held that British imperialism was as great an obstacle to Israel as the Nazis, and they continued targeting the British. When the leader of Lehi, Avrahim Stern, was killed in battle, Shamir eventually succeeded him and planned the deadly 1946 bombing of the King David Hotel in Jerusalem. In his long career as a guerrilla, Shamir was captured twice and escaped twice, the second time from an internment camp in Eritrea. By the time he returned home in 1948, Israel had won its war of independence.

To this day, Shamir remains unapologetic about his clandestine, violent past.

As a civilian Shamir tried adapting to the business world, but in 1956 he joined Mossad, the Israeli secret service, as a European operative. He served in this office for over a decade and did not finally opt for a career in politics until 1970, at the age of 58. That year he joined the conservative Herut Party of Menachem Begin, his former Lehi commander, and three years later won a seat in the Knesset (parliament). By 1977 Herut had coalesced with other conservative parties to form Likud, and they swept the long-dominant Labor Party from power for the first time. Shamir then served as speaker of the Knesset, where he vocally opposed the 1979 Camp David Peace Accords with Egypt. Shamir, like many conservatives, rejected the notion of land for peace and felt that returning the Sinai Peninsula to Egypt threatened Israeli security. He was further angered by the dismantling of Jewish settlements in the Gaza Strip. When the treaty came up for a vote, he simply abstained. In 1979, Shamir replaced noted soldier Moshe Dayan as foreign minister, despite his lack of training in diplomacy. He nonetheless applied himself vigorously until Begin suddenly announced his retirement in August 1983. Subsequent elections proved a draw between Labor and Likud and a power-sharing agreement was reached in the guise of a national unity government. Henceforth, SHIMON PERES became prime minister for 25 months before the office rotated to Shamir, who acted as vice premier and minister of foreign affairs. Relations between the two sides were tense because Peres believed in trading land for peace while Shamir strongly opposed it.

Shamir was retained as prime minister at the head of a new Likud coalition in March 1990, which was cobbled together from various religious parties. He reluctantly agreed to peace talks with Palestinian leader YASSER ARAFAT in Madrid in October 1991, but he steadfastly refused to halt construction of Jewish settlements in the occupied West Bank. This greatly increased tensions with the United States, which was asked to subsidize such activity. Moreover, the Palestinians responded with a violent *intifada*, or uprising, which targeted civilian settlers in employing terrorism. These actions prompted the Israelis to respond in kind, which greatly increased Middle East tensions. However, in the 1991 Gulf War against SADDAM HUSSEIN, Shamir showed great restraint by not retaliating when Iraqi Scud missiles were launched at Israel, killing several citizens. Weeks later Secretary of State James Baker arrived in Tel Aviv to personally thank Shamir for his cooperation. Likud seemed buoyed by the victory in the war, but in January 1992 several religious parties withdrew from the coalition, and accused Shamir of being "soft" on the Arabs. New elections were called for June 1992, but Likud was trounced by Labor under YITZHAK RABIN. Shamir then returned to the Knesset as head of the opposition, but he subsequently yielded his chair to a young newcomer, BINYAMIN NETANYAHU. In June 1996 he concluded 60 years of service to the Jewish state by retiring from office. Shamir had served longer as prime minister than any Israeli leader since David Ben-Gurion.

Though a private citizen, Shamir remained an outspoken critic of Netanyahu, the peace process, and especially the 1993 Oslo Peace Accords establishing a quasi-independent Palestinian state. In January 2001 he campaigned for Likud candidate and former general ARIEL SHARON, although he remains pessimistic about the prospects of lasting peace and Israeli security. "I don't think Arafat thinks about peace, he never thought about peace," Shamir maintains. "Unfortunately, we have to be very, very strong now."

Further Reading

Diskin, Abraham. *The Last Days in Israel: Understanding the New Israeli Democracy.* Portland, Oreg.: Frank Cass, 2003.

Doron, G. "Labor's Return to Power in Israel." *Current History* 92 (January 1993): 27–31.

Eisenberg, L. Z. "Passive Belligerency: Israel and the 1991 Gulf War." *Journal of Strategic Studies* 15 (September 1992): 304–329.

Hadar, Leon T. "The Israeli Labor Party: Peacemaker of Likud II?" *Journal of Palestinian Studies* 21 (Spring 1992): 80–95.

Shamir, Yitzhak. *Summing Up: An Autobiography.* New York: Little, Brown, 1994.

Stellman, Henri. "Israel: The 1992 Election and After." *Parliamentary Affairs* 46, no. 1 (1993): 121–132.

Sharon, Ariel (1928–) *prime minister of Israel*

Ariel Sharon was born on September 9, 1928, at Moshav Kfar Malal, a Jewish farming community in British-ruled Palestine, to Russian immigrant parents. His parents were also devout Zionists, that is, adherents of Judaism who believed Jews must return to the Middle East to reclaim the state of Israel. As more Jews migrated to Palestine throughout the early 20th century, friction with Arabs already living there began rising. Sharon initiated his military career while a high school student by joining the Haganah, an underground Jewish army, and he prepared for an anticipated conflict. This occurred in 1948, when the state of Israel was declared and all-out war erupted. Sharon distinguished himself in combat and, while badly wounded, commenced a celebrated rise up the army's hierarchy. In fact, he greatly distinguished himself in all four of Israel's wars, 1948–73, gaining the reputation of a highly effective soldier. Sharon was also criticized for his sometimes brash and arrogant leadership, which frequently bordered upon insubordination. Nonetheless, he was Israel's most effective combat strategist and utterly ruthless toward Arab and Palestinian opponents. For many years he enjoyed a close and unsavory association with Unit 101, an elite commando-type formation dedicated to retaliatory strikes against the enemy, including civilians, for attacks upon Israel. Furthermore, he was outspoken in his beliefs that lands seized by Israel during the 1967 war ought to be annexed outright to the Jewish state for historical and strategic reasons. Sharon remains a man admired, hated, and feared by many people on both sides of the Arab-Israeli dispute.

Despite his military celebrity, Sharon had accrued too many enemies and too much controversy to be nominated as army chief of staff. He then resigned and entered the realm of politics, and in December 1973 won election to the Knesset (parliament) as a member of the far-right Likud Party. Two years later he gained appointment as a special adviser on security affairs under Prime Minister YITZHAK RABIN. In 1977 Sharon accepted the portfolio of minister of agriculture under Prime Minister Menachem Begin. In this post he gained much notoriety by formulating plans to increase Israeli settlement activity on occupied Arab land along the west bank of the Jordan River. In 1981 Begin appointed him minister of defense, and he was actively engaged in combating Palestinian Liberation Organization (PLO) terrorists based in neighboring Lebanon. Repeated attacks on Jewish settlements continued, however, and, therefore, in 1982 he orchestrated a massive invasion of southern Lebanon to evict PLO fighters under YASSER ARAFAT. However, on September 15, 1982, when he also allowed Lebanese Christian militia to enter Palestinian refugee camps, a massacre ensued. When a government commission found

Ariel Sharon *(Cris Bouroncle—Pool/Getty Images)*

percent of votes cast. Once empowered, Sharon commenced his predictable policy of tough retaliation against Arab terrorism, which only heightened tensions and drove the PLO and other organizations to new extremes. The wave of attacks, now abetted by young suicide bombers, crested on March 29, 2002, when 27 Israelis were killed at a restaurant on Passover eve. Sharon responded with Operation Defensive Shield, a military occupation of known terrorist strong points along the West Bank. At one point, Israeli tanks besieged Arafat in his own headquarters, literally holding him prisoner. This move sparked much outrage in the Arab world, already angry at the United States for the war in Afghanistan, which prompted President GEORGE W. BUSH to demand a complete Israeli withdrawal. Sharon simply pointed out that he was responding to terrorism in the same manner that the United States was doing in their struggle against Osama bin Laden. In April 2002, Secretary of State Colin Powell flew to Israel to confer with Sharon and press demands for a complete Israeli withdrawal and resumption of peace talks. The Israeli army made a few token withdrawals from a number of cities, but by and large they continued mopping-up actions against PLO enclaves. As a military man, Sharon is determined to insure Israeli security, even if it incurs world condemnation. He also announced his determination to attend any peace conference that the United States is likely to broker, provided that the PLO and the Arab states agree to show up. However, he no longer considers Arafat to be a legitimate leader capable of acting as a peace partner and he feels that other Palestinian leadership should be found. "I will only shake hands with Arafat after a complete peace settlement," the 72-year-old Sharon insisted.

him partly at fault, Sharon resigned as defense minister in 1983. For the next two decades he served in various capacities with a number of far-right coalition governments, touting a hard line against Arab terrorism and demanding increased Jewish settlement of captured land. He was, and continues to be, the most forceful voice and symbol for Israeli security and survival.

The turning point in Sharon's political career transpired in the fall of 2000, when he visited the Wailing Wall in Jerusalem, a site sacred to the Jewish people. However, the site sits astride the Dome of the Rock, the third holiest shrine in Islam, and, outraged by this action, Arafat declared an *intifada* (uprising) against Israeli occupation. Over the next five months, street clashes became part of the escalating cycle of violence, and Prime Minister EHUD BARAK, unable to stem the violence, called for new elections in the spring of 2002. Sharon then ran for prime minister as the Likud candidate, touting his well-established credentials for law and order. On February 6, 2002, the Israeli populace, seeking greater security, elected Sharon their new prime minister by 62

Further Reading

Benn, Aluf. "Last of the Patriarchs." *Foreign Affairs* 81 (May–June 2002): 64–78.

Goodspeed, Michael. *When Reason Fails: Portraits of Armies at War: America, Britain, Israel, and the Future.* Westport, Conn.: Praeger, 2002.

Rabil, Robert G. *Embattled Neighbors: Syria, Israel, Lebanon.* Boulder, Colo.: Lynne Rienner Publishers, 2003.

Sharon, Ariel. *Warrior: The Autobiography of Ariel Sharon.* New York: Simon and Schuster, 2001.

Tal, Yisra'el. *National Security: The Israeli Experience.* Westport, Conn.: Praeger, 2000.

Warshof, Jason. "Ariel Sharon at the Picklefish." Unpublished master's thesis, Johns Hopkins University, 2001.

Zetouni, Sigalit, and Jordan Miller. *Sharon: Israel's Warrior-Politician.* Chicago: Academy Chicago Publishers, 2001.

Shevardnadze, Eduard (1928–) *president of Georgia*

Eduard Amvroslyevich Shevardnadze was born in Mamati, Georgia, on January 25, 1928, the son of a schoolteacher. Georgia, an ancient country located on the shores of the Black Sea, has endured several conquerors throughout history, but its inhabitants remain fiercely independent. Following a long association with the Russian empire, in 1921 Georgia became a republic within the Soviet Union. For many years thereafter it gained renown as one of the most politically corrupt states within that entity. Its controversial reputation was further abetted by the fact that Joseph Stalin, the Soviet Union's notorious dictator, was Georgian by descent.

Shevardnadze was well educated at various Communist Party schools at the behest of his older brother, who was an influential party functionary. After receiving his degree in history from the Kutaisi State Pedagogical Institute, he joined the party in 1948 and helped administer the local Komsomol, or Communist Youth League. By 1960 Shevardnadze began a spectacular climb through the party hierarchy. He gained his highest degree of notoriety in 1964 as Georgia's minister of internal security, and he commenced a determined crackdown upon the region's celebrated corruption. He was extremely successful in curing excesses, and by 1978 Shevardnadze had become a nonvoting member of the Soviet Politburo in Moscow, the nation's highest decision-making body. It was while serving in this capacity that Shevardnadze came to the attention of Secretary-General Mikhail Gorbachev, who was seeking like-minded reformers. He then appointed Shevardnadze Soviet foreign minister in July 1985, despite his apparent lack of experience. Happily, Shevardnadze proved charming, astute, and efficient in diplomatic circles, and he helped implement a number of radical reforms. He arranged an extensive arms control agreement with the United States, ended the decade-old Soviet war in Afghanistan, and withdrew Soviet forces from Eastern Europe. When conservative elements bitterly denounced

him in December 1990, Shevardnadze resigned, warning of the possible return of tyranny. The failed Communist coup attempt against Gorbachev in August 1991 signaled the coming collapse of the Soviet Union. Shevardnadze then returned to his native Georgia, well regarded in the West as the man who helped bring an end to Soviet-backed communism in Europe.

Georgia had declared its independence in March 1991 under President Zviad Gamsakhurdia, whose authoritarian style plunged the nation into civil war. After heavy fighting toppled the regime, Shevardnadze, which had been regarded as a pariah owing to his long service to the Communist Party, was elected chairman of the governing State Council. This made him the de facto president of Georgia, a position confirmed by national elections held the following October. Once installed, Shevardnadze's first task was to curtail secessionist activity in various border districts. In September 1993 he personally flew to Abkhazia to direct military operations against the rebels and was nearly killed. Thereafter and with great reluctance, Shevardnadze was forced to turn to Russia for military assistance. The rebellion was eventually contained, but Georgia was then forced to enter the Commonwealth of Independent States (CIS) along with Russia, Ukraine, and Belarus. Russian troops did not finally leave Georgian soil until October 1999. Relations between the two former partners remain correct but very cool.

On the domestic front, Georgia has been plagued by the familiar problem of endemic corruption, despite adoption of a new constitution in 1995 mandating a strong executive president and new presidential elections, in which Shevardnadze won 80 percent of the popular vote. He was also confronted with the daunting tasks of running a balanced budget, reducing unemployment, and improving living standard for all Georgians. Shevardnadze continues as Georgia's most popular elder statesman, but his April 2000 reelection as president was marred by irregularities. This fact, and the failure to curb corruption, has triggered a number of demonstrations calling for his resignation. They culminated in November 2001, when Zurab Zhvania, speaker of parliament, resigned in protest. Apparently, the citizens of Georgia are looking for younger and more vigorous leaders to prosecute the war against crime. Shevardnadze, for his part, still enjoys considerable stature abroad and close relations with Western leaders. In September 2001 he declared that the United States would be granted open access to Georgian airspace and could make use of several air bases while prosecuting the war against terrorism in Afghanistan. In return, he welcomed the arrival of 200 American special forces, who are being deployed to train the Georgian military in antiterrorist techniques. However, the president cautioned his American counterparts that Georgia would not participate in any actions involving a unilateral U.S. strike against Iraq. He nonetheless hopes that the United States will remain a key player in developing a strategic gas and oil pipeline network in Georgia to neutralize Russian influence. Shevardnadze is expected to remain in office through 2005, although his inability to reduce crime may yet force an early resignation.

Further Reading

Ekedahl, Carolyn M., and Melvin A. Goodman. *The Wars of Eduard Shevardnadze.* Washington, D.C.: Brassey's, 2002.

Geyer, Georgia Anne. "Conversations with Eduard Shevardnadze." *Washington Quarterly* 23 (Spring 2000): 55–66.

Lang, David M. *A History of Modern Georgia.* Richmond, England: Curzon, 2001.

Palazhchenko, Pavel. *My Years with Gorbachev and Shevardnadze: The Memoirs of a Soviet Interpreter.* University Park, Pa.: Penn State University Press, 1997.

Shevardnadze, Eduard A. *The Future Belongs to Freedom.* London: Sinclair-Stevenson, 1991.

Tsekvava, Tengiz. "Georgia's Main Economic Events during the First 10 Years of Independence." Unpublished master's thesis, Williams College, 2001.

Shipley, Jenny (1952–) *prime minister of New Zealand*

Jenny Robson was born on February 4, 1952, in Gore, New Zealand, the daughter of a Presbyterian minister. She failed her university entrance exams and consequently enrolled at Christchurch Teachers' College. After teaching four years, she married Burton Shipley, a farmer, in 1976, and stopped working to raise two children. However, Shipley had previously joined the conservative National Party (NP) in 1975, and she sought out grassroots community service positions to gain political experience. She quickly established a reputation as a thinking, articulate candidate, possessed of bulldog-like tenacity. Shipley drew on these qualities in 1987, when she won a seat in the unicameral legislature, the

House of Representatives, as an NP member. By dint of personality and competence she rose steadily through the party's ranks. When the National Party regained power under JIM BOLGER in 1990, Shipley joined his cabinet as minister of social affairs. In that office she gained considerable notoriety for her single-minded determination to implant a conservative agenda on the time-honored generous New Zealand welfare state. This entailed a complete overhaul of the welfare system, including deep cuts, demands for greater personal responsibility, and a six-month hold on unemployment benefits. In consequence, protestors burned her in effigy while she cemented her reputation as a hard-line, no-nonsense conservative. In fact, her guiding principle in politics was summed up by a personal dictum, "I would rather do what's right than what's popular." To reduce public controversy, however, Bolger transferred Shipley to the Ministry of Public Health where, again, she plied her ax to cutting expenditures to the bone. Henceforth she demanded that all hospitals streamline procedures and turn a profit although, as a concession to the women's lobby, she authorized free distribution of birth control pills. Her tightfisted policies again incurred a degree of public displeasure, and in 1996 Bolger shifted her to the Ministry of Transportation. All the while, Shipley reveled in her reputation as the "toughest man in the ministry."

By 1996 The NP was in power only because of a coalition arrangement with the far-right New Zealand First Party of Winston Peters. Not only did this adversely affect NP poll ratings, but it also upset stalwarts like Shipley, who believed the party had surrendered too many principles to stay in power. With dissatisfaction growing over Bolger's performance, Shipley waited until he left the country to enact a minor coup. She gathered sufficient signatures in support and presented them to the prime minister upon his return. Bolger knew he had been outmaneuvered. He resigned and, on December 8, 1997, Shipley became the first female prime minister in New Zealand's history. Peters of New Zealand First was upset at the sudden change of leadership, but Shipley typically stood her ground. He tried to leave the coalition and offered his services to the Labour Party of HELEN CLARK, but she declined. Peters had no recourse but to continue with the ruling coalition and Shipley remained in office. Curiously, her appearance seems somewhat belated, as New Zealand became the first country to allow women to vote in

1893. "I hope I've won this task on my merit," she declared. "If it means that other young women in New Zealand will aspire to be the best that they can be, I'll feel very pleased."

As prime minister, Shipley continued the conservative, cost-cutting measures for which she was reviled. She advocated creation of a new, one-stop unemployment agency for job seekers, a simplification and reduction in taxes, and a new "community wage," whereby welfare recipients performed community service for their benefits. Shipley was also totally committed to the free market, and she sought out foreign investments, urged greater privatization, and promoted liberalizing the national economy. In terms of foreign policy, Shipley continued the tradition of close relationships with neighboring Australia and paid a state visit to Prime Minister JOHN HOWARD. She also sought to reestablish close links with the United States, although she did not revoke the popular ban on nuclear weapons in New Zealand waters. Finally, in December 1997 she committed New Zealand forces to Papua New Guinea as peacekeepers and mediators in the recent civil war there.

Shipley prided herself on her personal brand of non-compromise toughness, and she survived two close votes of no confidence. But apparently she pursued the dismantling of New Zealand's social policy too vigorously for a majority of voters. On November 27, 1999, the NP lost to Labour's HELEN CLARK, who became the first elected female prime minister in New Zealand's history. Shipley continued as head of the National Party and leader of the opposition until October 2001, when she was ousted from the party leadership—ironically, during a trip out of the country. She was replaced by the former finance minister Bill English.

Further Reading

Ahdar, Rex J., and John Stenhouse. *God and Government: The New Zealand Experience.* Dunedin, New Zealand: University of Otago Press, 2001.

Boston, Jonathan. *Left Turn: The New Zealand General Election of 1999.* Wellington, Victoria: University Press, 2000.

Grant, A. K., and Tom Scott. *Corridors of Paua: The Story of New Zealand's Decline in World Leadership.* Christchurch, New Zealand: Hazard Press, 1996.

Henderson, Anne. *Getting Even: Women MPs on Life, Power, and Politics.* Pymble, New South Wales: HarperCollins, 1999.

Miller, Raymond. *New Zealand: Government and Politics.* New York: Oxford University Press, 2001.

Simeon II (1937–   ) *prime minister of Bulgaria*

Simeon Borisov Saxe-Corburggotski was born on June 16, 1937, in Sofia, Bulgaria, the son of King Boris III and Queen Giovanna. His father died under mysterious circumstances in May 1943, and he was enthroned at the age of nine. Real power, however, was entrusted to a regency under Prince Kyril, his uncle. Toward the end of World War II Bulgaria was occupied by Soviet troops, and in September 1944 Communist sympathizers staged a coup that overthrew the regency. Bulgarian Communists solidified their grip on power in September 1946 by passing a referendum abolishing the monarchy and establish a people's republic. All royal estates were confiscated while Simeon and his family fled into exile in Egypt. He was educated there until 1951, when his family relocated to Spain. By 1957 Simeon had passed through the Lycée François in Madrid, and he visited the United States to attend the Valley Forge Military Academy. He returned to Spain in 1959 to study business and law privately and eventually established an international consulting business. The former monarch was exceptionally well trained to handle such matters, being fluent in English, Spanish, French, German, and Italian, as well as his native tongue. Over the years he also maintained close contact with the Bulgarian expatriate community, and he watched events in his Communist-controlled homeland closely.

Following the collapse of the Soviet Union in 1991, Communist regimes throughout Eastern Europe were dismantled in favor of democracy. That year Bulgaria sponsored a referendum to either restore the monarchy or institute a republic. This represented a glimmer of hope for Simeon, who never abdicated and wanted to return home. "If they want a republic, then I shall be a loyal citizen," he told reporters, "but if they want a monarchy, then I can guarantee that all national forces, every trend of political thought will be given the opportunity to express their views." The voters chose a republic, so Simeon remained sidelined until May 1996, when he visited Bulgaria for the first time in 50 years. His motorcade was greeted by thunderous applause, and the enthusiasm displayed by the crowds convinced him to establish permanent residence. In 1998 he received additional good news when the Constitutional Court restored all his family's property. Accordingly, Simeon relocated back to Sofia in January 2001 amid rumors he intended to reclaim the throne. "It is premature to answer this, but if the Bulgarian people want me, it is not a question of my being willing," he explained, "it is my duty."

The overwhelming response to Simeon's arrival prompted him to declare his candidacy for Bulgaria's presidency in February 2001. However, a court torpedoed this idea by citing his failure to meet the country's strict residency requirement. Undeterred, the former monarch next established the National Movement for Simeon II, which he hoped would springboard like-minded candidates into parliament. This, too, was struck down by the courts for technical reasons, so he allied himself with two existing organizations, the Party of Bulgarian Women and the Oborishte Party for National Revival. The alliance enabled him to run for prime minister in the June 2001 national election. Simeon's opponent was IVAN KOSTOV of the conservative Union of Democratic Forces (UDF), which had bungled Bulgaria's transition to a free-market economy. Rampant corruption and unemployment resulted, both of which Simeon pledged to fight. His message appealed emotionally to the Bulgarian electorate. On June 17, 2001, they handed him 120 of 240 seats in parliament. Kostov, previous Bulgaria's youngest executive officer, acquired but 51 seats and resigned. The mandate was unmistakable, and, on July 24, 2001, the former king Simeon II was sworn in as the country's new prime minister. Having never relinquished his royal title, he also became the first former Eastern European monarch to resume authority.

Once in office, and drawing upon his skills as a successful entrepreneur, Simeon authorized steps to increase the pace of privatization, namely, selling off state-owned concerns to private buyers. He also embarked on the twin goals of ending Bulgaria's traditional isolation by joining the European Union (EU) and NATO. He consolidated his political base by converting the National Movement for Simeon II into a national party. "This is not a technical formality but the beginning of the renovation of our country, which I aim at," he announced. "Only a party with units all over the country and open to as many members as possible will guarantee the success of the National Movement values." For all his good intentions, Bulgaria still faces a rocky road on its transition to modernity. The government has been criticized for its failure to improve the economy and has since imposed unpopular price increases on heating and electricity. In addition to enduring public criticism, Simeon has forcibly adjusted to the realities of working 16 to 18 hours a day. "This is not a job I dreamt of doing," he confessed, "but it's a great honor to be doing it, especially when so many believe in me. I feel obliged to do it."

Further Reading

Barany, Zoltan. "Bulgaria's Royal Elections." *Journal of Democracy* 13 (April 2002): 141–155.

Bell, John P. *Bulgarian Transition: Politics, Economics, Society and Culture.* Boulder, Colo.: Westview Press, 1998.

Dimirov, Vesselin. *Bulgaria: The Uneven Transition.* London: Routledge, 2001.

Ganev, Venelin I. "Preying on the State: Political Capitalism after Communism." Unpublished Ph.D. dissertation, University of Chicago, 2000.

Giatzidis, Emil. *An Introduction to Post-Communist Bulgaria: Political, Economic, and Social Transformations.* Manchester, England: Manchester University Press, 2002.

Knupffer, George. *King Simeon II of the Bulgarians.* London: Monarchist Press, 1969.

Simitis, Costas (1936–) *prime minister of Greece*

Constantine (Costas) Simitis was born on January 26, 1936, in Athens, Greece, the son of an attorney. Greece, long heralded as the cradle of Western civilization and democracy, endured a spotty political record in the 20th century. Between 1940 and 1974, it suffered from intermittent right-wing military juntas, which overthrew democratically elected governments. It was not until 1974 that democracy was restored through the election of ANDREAS PAPANDREOU of the left-wing Panhellenic Socialist Movement (PASOK). Unfortunately for Greek economic and political development, the charismatic Papandreou was a leftist demagogue intent on alienating both NATO, to which Greece belonged, and the European Union (EU), to which it hoped to secure membership. Add to this constant friction with nearby Turkey, a former enemy and fellow NATO member, and the eastern Aegean seemed ripe for turmoil.

Simitis was educated abroad, having studied law and economics at the University of Marburg, Germany, and the London School of Economics. In 1961 he returned home to commence a legal practice and also became politically active by founding a research society intent on criticizing the prevailing juntas. Military resentment forced him to flee the country in 1967, but he continued with his antigovernment activities while in exile. In 1974, following the return of democracy, Simitis came home to help found PASOK, and he subsequently held several ministerial portfolios. And, unlike the fiery Papandreou, he gained renown as an inconspicuous, low-key figure, but also highly efficient. In time he clashed repeatedly with Papandreou over his strident anti-American, anti-Western stances. Their differences mounted, and in 1995 he resigned from the government in protest. However, when Papandreou fell ill in the spring of 1996, reform elements within PASOK induced Simitis to run for party leadership. On January 22, 1996, he was simultaneously elected chairman and prime minister of Greece.

The rise of Simitis occasioned a complete overhaul of many of Papandreous's policies and placed Greece on a path toward closer European integration. Conciliatory and a consensus builder by nature, he appointed many of his former adversaries to high posts within his government to placate them. He also slowly but firmly began a process of moving PASOK to the center of political affairs, while avoiding major ruptures with his party or the opposition New Democracy Party (ND).

The biggest changes mounted by Simitis transpired in the realm of economics. Henceforth, his government enacted legislation to promote a free-market atmosphere with increased privatization of state-run industries. The result was an increase in national growth while inflation fell to only 4 percent by 1998. Simitis is also determined to tackle the sprawling and fabulously inefficient Greek bureaucracy by trimming 15,000 jobs and thereby cutting government spending. Furthermore, to accommodate smoother transition to a single European currency, the government has imposed austerity measures to bring the national debt in line with EU guidelines. Greece, long castigated as Europe's poorest economy, has consequently registered periods of impressive growth. The usually volatile Greek electorate seems to appreciate the foresight of their nondescript prime minister; in June 1996 and April 2000 he was reelected to office by wide margins. Simitis also managed to secure the selection of Greece as host of the 2004 World Olympics and, following European criticism of a sluggish start, he appointed a new 48-member cabinet in October 2001. This is the largest such cabinet in Greek history and includes some of the youngest and most reform-minded politicians in the nation. "This government marks a new era," Simitis confidently proclaimed.

A major obstacle facing any Greek leader is the issue of Turkey, long viewed as a traditional enemy. Early in Simitis's tenure, a dispute over two minor islands threatened to escalate into war between these two NATO partners. However, the prime minister adopted a very calm and rational approach in negotiating with his Turkish counterparts, and the crisis subsided. The issue of missiles on Cyprus was another volatile flash point and the Turks were again threatening war, but Simitis deflected the problem by having them installed on the island of Crete instead. As a sign of their continuing thaw, when Turkey was hit by a destructive earthquake in August 2000, Simitis offered humanitarian assistance for the first time in recent history. A month later, when Greece was struck by a quake, the Turks reciprocated in kind. Tensions persist over military arrangements arising from EU membership, but the two adversaries seem inextricably bound to follow the road to normal relations.

In the wake of the September 11, 2001, destruction of New York's World Trade Center, Simitis was quick to offer sympathy and pledges of assistance to President GEORGE W. BUSH. He then paid an official state visit to the White House in January 2002, where Bush lauded the bookish prime minister for his efforts and the decision to deploy Greek forces abroad. "We will take part in the international peace corps in Afghanistan," he declared, adding, "It's necessary to cooperate in the fight against terrorism worldwide because there are also terrorist groups in all the Balkan countries, and we think this must be controlled." Simitis is presently up for reelection in 2004 and, given the steady improvement in Greece's economy and international standing, his return to office seems assured.

Further Reading

Close, David H. *Greece since 1945: Politics, Economy, and Society.* Harlow, England: Longman, 2002.

Kaloudis, George S. *Modern Greek Democracy: The End of a Long Journey?* Lanham, Md.: University Press of America, 2000.

Karakatsanis, Neovi M. *The Politics of Elite Transformation: The Consolidation of Greek Democracy in Theoretical Perspective.* Westport, Conn.: Praeger, 2001.

Lavdas, Kostas A. *The Europeanization of Greece: Interest Politics and the Crisis of Integration.* New York: St. Martin's Press, 1997.

Peckman, Robert S. *National Histories, Natural States: Nationalism and the Politics of Place in Greece.* New York: I. B. Tauris, 2001.

Smith, Jennifer (1947–) *prime minister of Bermuda*

Jennifer Meredith Smith was born in Bermuda in 1947, the daughter of a bartender. Artistically inclined, she attended the University of Pittsburgh to earn an associate's degree and returned home in 1970. She became something of a political cause cèlébre when customs agents inexplicably confiscated several books they considered to be banned. When subsequent investigations proved her books were not on any official banned list, she wrote a scathing newspaper article protesting censorship in Bermuda. In response the board governing the list of banned books summarily added her titles to the list. However, Smith's defiance brought her to the attention of the Progressive Labour Party (PLP), one of Bermuda's two formal political organizations, and leaders convinced her to run as a candidate in 1972. The locale they chose, St. George's, was a United Bermuda Party (UBP) stronghold, but such was Smith's notoriety that she lost by a mere 79 votes. Afterward, she contented herself with artistic and dancing pursuits, and she also served as a political writer and commentator. In 1976 Smith again stood for election in St. George's as the PLP candidate and lost again by 50 votes. After a stint as a copywriter with the Bermuda Broadcasting Company, she ran again in 1980 and lost. However, her aplomb in the face of adversity finally paid off when she gained appointment to the Senate, the first female member in Bermuda's history. She was reappointed in 1983 and the following year attended the John F. Kennedy School of Government Program at Harvard University. Smith lost another attempt to win the St. George's seat in 1985, but she finally prevailed in 1989 after 15 years of effort.

Once in the House of Representatives, Smith proved her skill as a legislator by becoming the first woman to serve as a committee chair. She gained reelection in 1993 and was chosen by the PLP leadership to serve as a deputy leader. After party chairman Frederick Wade died in August 1996, Smith was chosen to succeed him, thus becoming the first woman to lead the opposition. Two years later she was tapped to run for the prime minister's office. The incumbent was Pamela Brown of the UBP, who, like Smith, was of African descent. How-

Jennifer Smith *(Embassy of Bermuda)*

ever, because the two parties catered to distinctly white and black constituencies, there existed a strongly racial undertone to the ensuing contest. And, because the PLP largely mirrored the 65 percent black majority population, they held an electoral advantage. On November 9, 1998, Smith made history by becoming the first elected woman premier in Bermuda history. The PLP accomplished this by taking an unprecedented 26 House seats, compared to only 14 by the opposition. Her victory also ended one of the longest political reigns in Bermuda's history, for the UBP had been undefeated in Bermudian politics since its creation in 1968.

Once in power, Smith had to tread the racial divide that underscores Bermuda politics. The business class is largely white and descended from plantation owners who settled on the island in the 17th century. Her Labour's constituents, meanwhile, make up most of the island's workforce and union membership. But Smith soon established herself as a conciliator and consensus seeker, and she sought to assuage the fears of the business community. However, some hard choices had to be made. In April 2000 she sponsored a bill that required businesses to report the racial composition of their workforce on a yearly basis. The PLP hoped it would reveal and root out racism, but the UBP felt it was the first step toward hiring quotas. The legislation stalled in the Senate and was not enacted. The following November Smith faced a leadership challenge from Arthur Hodgson, her own environment minister, and she survived by 81 votes to 35. "I am very pleased the delegates have once again placed their faith in me and I intend to complete the job I was elected to do to carry out the comprehensive policies of the PLP," she trumpeted. In May 2002, Hodgson sponsored legislation that would establish a register of expatriate workers. This system would allow Bermudians to scrutinize the job qualifications of 25 percent of the island's workforce. However, Smith opposed the measure, insisting it "smacked of Nazism," and it died in committee. She continues to serve as prime minister of an island community enjoying one of the world's highest standards of living, but whose citizens have yet to achieve racial accord.

Further Reading

Ahiakpor, James C. W. *The Economic Consequences of Political Independence: The Case of Bermuda.* Vancouver, British Columbia: Fraser Institute, 1990.

Brown, C. Walton. "Race and Party Politics in Bermuda." *Commonwealth and Comparative Politics* 27, no. 1 (1989): 103–126.

Connell, John. *Bermuda: The Failure of Decolonization.* Leeds, England: School of Geography, University of Leeds, 1987.

Manning, Frank K. *Bermudian Politics in Transition: Race, Voting, and Public Opinion.* Hamilton, Bermuda: Island Press, 1978.

Royle, Stephen A. "Economic and Political Prospects for the British Atlantic Dependent Territories." *Geographic Journal* 161 (November 1995): 307–322.

Soares, Mario (1924–) *president of Portugal*

Mario Alberto Nobre Lopes Soares was born on December 7, 1924, in Lisbon, Portugal, the son of a prominent liberal activist. He was educated at his family's private school and went on to to attend the Classical University in Lisbon and the Law School of the Sorbonne, Paris. Soares inherited much of his father's bel-

ligerency toward the right-wing authoritarian regime of Antonio de Oliveira Salazar, who overthrew the Portuguese republic in 1926. In the course of his lifetime, he would be jailed 12 times for antigovernment activity, and exiled twice. Yet, Soares would not be silenced and in 1964 he helped found the clandestine Portuguese Socialist Action, which laid the groundwork for resurrecting the long-dead Portuguese Socialist Party (PSP). He accomplished this during his four-year exile in France, 1970–74. However, in April 1974 the government of Portugal was overthrown by military forces under General Antonio de Spinola, and the country commenced a slow transition back to democracy. Soares, who by this time had achieved a cult following among left-wing circles, came home to adoring crowds of thousands, and he became the interim government's first foreign minister. In this office he laid the legal groundwork for granting independence to all of Portugal's Africans possessions, including Angola, Guinea-Bissau, and Mozambique. In April 1975, his PSP carried the first national elections in 50 years by taking 116 seats out of 250 in the national assembly. Soares was now well situated to exert a mitigating effect upon the excesses of Portugal's revolution.

Though Portugal clearly entered a leftist orbit, Soares carefully negated the influence of the Portuguese Communist Party, which evinced an old-style, Stalinist subservience to Moscow. Specifically, he wanted to thwart any attempts to gain control of the state media or the economy. Their increasing influence, and a failed coup attempt by General Spinola, convinced Soares to quit the government by July 1975. Thereafter he held public rallies in favor of democracy and freedom—not ideological tyranny. Eventually, moderate factions within the Armed Forces Movement supported Soares in his call for elections to create a new body, the Constituent Assembly, which transpired in July 1976. That year the PSP solidly trounced the Communists, winning 107 out of 263 seats in the assembly. As party head, Soares became the first civilian prime minister since 1974 and the first Socialist to hold high office.

Despite his leftist orientation, Soares proved no ideologue and he enacted policies that were decidedly conservative in outlook. Foremost among them was admission into the European Economic Community, predecessor to today's European Union (EU). He realized that Portugal, possessing the poorest and most backward economy in Western Europe, could only rise by drawing closer to its richer neighbors. The prime minister was also determined to end Portugal's dependency on its former colonial market by seeking greater self-sufficiency at home. He also reassured Western powers within NATO that Portugal remained a trusted ally in any dealings with the Soviet Union. Such posturing infuriated the Communists under Alvaro Cunhal, and they worked to undermine leftist support for the administration. Soares nonetheless served as prime minister from 1976 to 1978 and in 1983–84, when an economic downturn—brought on by necessary austerity measures—led to the rise of a Social Democratic Party (PSD) government under ANIBAL CAVACO SILVA. The Socialists were badly defeated, and Soares resigned as head of the PSP. It appeared to most onlookers that his political career had ended.

In 1986 Soares surprised pundits by running for the presidency of Portugal, even though recent polls placed his popularity at only 8 percent. Nonetheless, he sought to mend fences with his old coalition of leftists, including Cunhal's Communists, to deny the PSD a clean sweep of the government. The strategy worked, even though Cunhal advised his cohorts to "close their eyes and vote for Soares." On March 3, 1986, he defeated Diogo Freitas do Amaral by 49 percent to 46 percent, becoming the first freely elected civilian president in 60 years. The presidency is largely a ceremonial office, but Soares used it as a bully pulpit to consolidate and strengthen Portugal's fledgling democracy. To that end he helped institute informal town meetings, and he encouraged citizen participation and dialogue in politics. Through such tactics Soares became a thoroughly trusted public figure, and in 1991 he was easily reelected for another five-year term by 70 percent of the vote. He resigned in 1996 owing to constitutional restrictions against three consecutive terms in office, and he was replaced by another Socialist, Jorge Sampaio.

Since leaving office, Soares continues to serve as a well-known senior statesman. In September 1998 he was tapped to serve with a United Nations mission to Algeria, where he pronounced both the Islamic guerrillas and the government guilty of human rights abuses. He also voiced concerns over the American campaign against Taliban guerrillas after the September 11, 2001, destruction of New York's World Trade Center. "I condemned the use of chemical and biological weapons and terrorism," he maintained, "but I think that fighting terrorism does not mean dropping bombs on defenseless people or destroying a country like Afghanistan, which deserves to be respected."

Further Reading

Goldey, D. B. "Notes on Recent Elections: The Portuguese General Elections of October 1995 and Presidential Election of January 1996." *Electoral Studies* 16 (June 1997): 245–266.

Grayson, George W. "Portugal's New Link with Europe." *Current History* 85, no. 514 (1986): 373–376, 393.

Janitschek, Hans. *Mario Soares: Portrait of a Hero.* New York: St. Martin's Press, 1986.

Sablosky, Juliet A. "Transformational Party Influences on the Formation of the Portuguese Socialist Party." *Portuguese Studies Review,* 5, no. 1 (1996): 48–58.

Syrett, Stephen. *Contemporary Portugal: Dimensions of Economic and Political Change.* Brookfield, Vt.: Ashgate, 2002.

Stoltenberg, Jens (1959–) *prime minister of Norway*

Jens Stoltenberg was born on March 16, 1959, in Oslo, Norway. His homeland forms the western portion of Scandinavia and once sustained a long political union with neighboring Sweden. However, the independent-minded Norwegians began pressing for their own country, which was granted in 1905. Norway was nominally neutral in world affairs but, after a painful occupation by Germany during World War II, it has since asserted itself on the global stage as a mediator. Norway is currently the world's second-largest exporter of oil after Saudi Arabia, and among the richest nations in the world. Like all Scandinavian countries, it employs high taxes and a generous welfare state to ensure basic human services for all its inhabitants. Norway remains a constitutional monarchy, but the king or queen is restricted to ceremonial functions only. Real power rests in the hands of the prime minister, who is chosen from the largest party or coalition holding power in the Storting, or parliament. Because Norway employs a system of proportional representation, numerous small parties are present in addition to the two main rivals, the Labor Party (Social Democrats) and the Christian Democrats. Norwegian politics are therefore very fractious and, it being nearly impossible for a given party to seize an outright majority of seats, coalition government is almost inevitable. Women are also more prominent in national politics in Norway than in any other country in the world. In addition, Norway leads in allocating funds for poorer nations of the world.

Stoltenberg joined the International Union of Socialist Youth while in school, and from 1985 to 1989 he served as vice president. Having joined the Labor Party in 1990, he rapidly climbed through the ranks owing to his intelligence, hard work, and persuasive manner. In 1994 Prime Minister GRO HARLEM BRUNDTLAND tendered him the portfolio as minister of trade and energy, and he subsequently served as finance minister under THORBJOERN JAGLAND. In this office he supported the decision to invest at least half of the annual petroleum income in a permanent fund for future generations to enjoy. In 1993 Jagland resigned owing to a poor showing by the Labor Party, and KJELL BONDEVIK of the Christian Democrats came to power. Stoltenberg, meanwhile, emerged as the head of the opposition in parliament, which further enhanced his national visibility. Bondevik lost a vote of confidence in March 2000 and left office, so Stoltenberg, having replaced Jagland as party chairman, was then asked to form a new government.

Norway is a domestically tranquil country, rich and with a relatively booming economy. Therefore, the biggest areas of contention are generated from the outside. Norway has rejected two referendums on joining the European Union (EU) because this entailed opening up Norwegian waters to other fishing fleets. Cheaper agricultural products from abroad were also to have been allowed into the country. The result was a 1994 defeat for the effort, in stark contrast to similar votes in Denmark, Finland, and Sweden. However, while in office Stoltenberg worked to convince his countrymen of the advantages conferred by membership, especially free trade. "We want to take more global responsibility," he declared, "and in Europe we want as close a relationship as possible." This issue remains unresolved and still pending. Equally contentious is the matter of NATO. Norway was one of the charter members in 1949, and it had fulfilled more than its obligations and expenses. However, it has since expressed wariness over any expansion eastward, especially fearing how this might alienate and destabilize Russia. Norway considers good relations with Russia as essential to its own well-being, and Oslo has urged caution. Less contentious is the deployment of Norwegian forces abroad as UN peacekeepers, whose numbers are higher in proportion to those of any other country. Norwegians troops have kept a high profile in such dangerous regions as Bosnia, and the gov-

ernment is further committed to mediating regional disputes such as those afflicting Israel and Palestine, Myanmar, and Sri Lanka.

There is very little revolutionary about Norwegian politics in general, but a turning point may have been reached in the October 2001 elections. Stoltenberg enjoyed high marks personally, but his Labor Party has sustained shrinking numbers since the late 1970s. During the most recent campaign, the conservative coalition led by Bondevik promised lower taxes, more emphasis on privatization, better delivery of social services, and use of the vast oil surplus revenues for current expenditures. Though still supportive of the welfare state, most Norwegian voters supported the call for lower taxes, and on October 10, 2001, they dealt Labor its biggest defeat ever, dropping the party from 65 to 22 seats. "It became clear today that a majority in parliament wants a change," a philosophical Stoltenberg declared as he turned in his resignation. Thus Bondevik was reinstated as Norway's conservative prime minister, capping a trend toward right-wing politics that seems to be sweeping the old Social Democratic domains of Scandinavia.

Further Reading

Chrisyensen, Tom. *Structure, Culture, and Governance: A Comparison of Norway and the United States.* Lanham, Md.: Rowman and Littlefield Publishers, 1999.

Gsthol, Sieglinde. *Reluctant Europeans: Norway, Sweden, and Switzerland in the Process of Integration.* Boulder, Colo.: Lynne Rienner Publishers, 2002.

Heider, Knut. *Norway: Center and Periphery.* Boulder, Colo.: Westview Press, 2000.

Rommefvedt, Hilmar. *The Rise of Parliament: Studies in Norwegian Parliamentary Government.* Portland, Oreg.: Frank Cass, 2003.

Shaffer, William R. *Politics, Parties, and Parliaments: Political Change in Norway.* Columbus: Ohio State University Press, 1998.

Suchocka, Hanna (1946–) *prime minister of Poland*

Hanna Suchocka was born on April 3, 1946, in Plezew, Poland, the daughter of pharmacists. She received a strict Roman Catholic upbringing and pursued a law degree from Poznan University. Suchocka graduated with honors in 1968 and was invited to teach at the university, but she refused to join the atheistic Communist Party. "I wanted to have the freedom to go to church because I was authentically raised in this," she insisted. "It was not for show. It was real." In 1969, however, she joined the Democratic Party, a less strident associate party of the Communists, and returned to school. By 1975 she had obtained her doctorate in constitutional law from Poznan University, and over the next few years also pursued advanced studies at the Institute of Public Law, Heidelberg, Germany, and Columbia University, New York. As a professional scholar and devotee of the fine arts, Suchocka became fluent in English, French, and German.

Suchocka entered politics in 1980 in being elected to the Sejm (lower house of parliament) as a Democratic Party member. Poland was then experiencing anticommunist unrest spearheaded by the Solidarity labor union under LECH WALESA, of which Suchocka was a member. Displaying the independence that became her trademark, she voted against the imposition of martial law in 1981 and three years later opposed government moves to make Solidarity illegal. Such defiance made her a pariah with the Communist regime and she was expelled from parliament and stripped of her party membership. Suchocka remained out of politics until 1989, when Communist governments in Eastern Europe were crumbling, and she was reelected to the Sejm as part of the pro-Western, pro-capitalist Civic Committee. Free to speak her mind, Suchocka became widely respected for her conservative stances on social issues like abortion, which she wanted controlled but not criminalized. In October 1991 she was reelected as part of a new group, the Democratic Union, which agitated for immediate liberalization of the old command-economy system. The recent elections, however, were the first held in 50 years, and the Sejm became saddled by no less than 29 disparate parties. Coordinating and forming coalition governments out of such a bickering mass proved nearly impossible, and no leader emerged who could maintain power for more than a few months. In desperation, parliament unexpectedly turned to Suchocka as a symbol of national unity. She was widely respected for her intelligence and command of constitutional law and her low-key approach to problem-solving made few enemies, which made her a natural choice. After some initial hesitation, the former law professor became Poland's first woman prime minister on July 8, 1992. She was also the only second woman to head a European government after Great Britain's Margaret Thatcher.

Suchocka came to power as Poland was experiencing severe economic recession. Previous administrations badly mishandled the transition from communism to capitalism, and the country reeled from high inflation and growing unemployment. The prime minister was nonetheless determined to shepherd the transition along and she imposed both industrial restructuring and a severe austerity budget to win financial assistance from the International Monetary Fund (IMF). This resulted in a wave of crippling national strikes by miners, but the government stood firm and by 1993 inflation fell from 500 percent to 32 percent. Poland's exports also climbed, making it the first Eastern European economy to post a profit. In August 1992 she also obtained a parliamentary victory that amended the constitution and allowed her to implement economic reforms by decree. However, Suchocka encountered increasing resistance owing to the speed of her efforts. In March 1993 the Sejm rejected her attempt at mass privatization, and it passed the following month only after being watered down. Suchocka by this time was easily the most popular politician in Poland, with approval ratings of 75 percent. However, this did not translate into popularity for her programs. Most Poles were not ready to sacrifice the relative security they enjoyed under communism for the uncertainties of the free market. Accordingly, on May 26, 1993, she failed to survive a motion of no confidence by a single vote. Subsequent elections that fall led to control of parliament by former Communists, and Suchocka was replaced by Waldemar Pawlak of the Polish Peasants Party.

Suchocka retained her seat in parliament, serving as a member of the opposition until 1994, when she founded a new party, the Freedom Union, presently Poland's third-biggest political grouping. In 1997 she also secured appointments as attorney general and minister of justice in a new coalition government. The following year she issued an arrest warrant against Helena Wolinska, Poland's chief military prosecutor, who was responsible for sentencing people during Stalinist show trials during the 1950s. However, when the leftist coalition returned to power in 2000, Suchocka lost her governmental posts and resumed her parliamentary career as a member of the opposition.

Further Reading

Bell, Janice. *The Political Economy of Reform in Post-Communist Poland.* Northampton, Mass.: Elgar, 2001.

Castle, Marjorie, and Ray Taras. *Democracy in Poland.* Boulder, Colo.: Westview Press, 2002.

Simpson, Peggy. "An Update of the Polish Election: What Did It Do for Women?" *Journal of Women's History* 6 (Spring 1994): 67–75.

Szczerbiak, Aleks. *Poles Together? The Emergence and Development of Political Parties in Post-Communist Poland.* New York: Central European University Press, 2001.

Wiatr, J. "The Dilemmas of Reorganizing the Bureaucracy in Poland during the Democratic Transformation." *Communist and Post-Communist Studies* 28 (March 1995): 153–160.

Suharto, Thojib (1921–) *president of Indonesia*

Thojib N. J. Suharto was born on June 8, 1921, in the village of Kemusua, central Java, the son of an impoverished rice farmer. Indonesia was then a Dutch colony, and to escape poverty Suharto joined the colonial army. However, when the Japanese invaded Indonesia in 1942 he switched sides and commanded a local police force. After Japan had been defeated in World War II Japanese troops withdrew, but not before leaving behind caches of weapons for their Indonesian allies. Thus armed, Suharto and his compatriots successfully resisted the returning Dutch for three years, until the independent Republic of Indonesia was proclaimed in 1949. The first president, Sukarno, established a military dictatorship in 1957 while Suharto advanced through the military's ranks. By 1963 he had become a major general. The turning point in his career occurred on September 30, 1965, in the wake of an aborted communist coup. Suharto acted promptly and ruthlessly, crushing the rebellion and killing an estimated 300,000 Chinese migrants supporting the rebellion. This made the heretofore unknown general a national hero, and in March 1966 he formerly usurped authority from Sukarno, becoming Indonesia's second president.

For the next 32 years, Suharto continued as Asia's longest-serving dictator. No mere despot, he originated the concept of the "New Order," a comprehensive national strategy for expanding the national economy while simultaneously preserving power and enriching his family and cronies. To accomplish this, Suharto dismissed Sukarno's most trusted advisers and hired new, American-trained technocrats to embark on a systematic program of modernization. Industries were built, high-

ways constructed, and sweeping projects to end illiteracy were successfully enacted. These were boom times for Indonesia as oil became the nation's largest export and prices were at an all-time high. During his tenure poverty was reduced 50 percent nationally, an impressive achievement. On the foreign front, Suharto also changed directions by discontinuing the anti-Western policies of his predecessor. He reestablished friendly relations with the United States, made peace with Malaysia, rejoined the United Nations, and supported anticommunist efforts throughout Southeast Asia. By 1985 Suharto's success could be gauged by the fact that Indonesia, once the world's largest rice importer, had become agriculturally self-sufficient.

The Indonesian people paid a heavy price for this success. Suharto had adopted a political system that projected the veneer of democracy, without ever allowing a genuine opposition to develop. In fact, one of his first official acts in 1966 was to outlaw criticism of the government. Consequently, Suharto was reelected president every five years—without an opponent—for three decades. All dissent was also ruthlessly crushed, including students, Communists, and Islamic fundamentalists. Moreover, in 1975 Suharto embarked on his own little war of aggression when he suddenly annexed the former Portuguese colony of East Timor, precipitating an internecine guerrilla war that lasted until 2002. He simply and summarily ignored the storm of international protest and accusations of human rights abuses. Near the end of his regime, the public was also weary of the blatant nepotism shown toward family members and allies. Declining oil prices had led to a scaling back of several welfare programs, but Suharto's control appeared secure until 1995, when the Asian currency crisis precipitated a severe economic recession. Inflation, the national debt, and unemployment all rose precipitously while students and workers took to the streets in ever-increasing numbers. In 1996 the president had MEGAWATI SUKARNOPUTRI, a high-profile opposition figure and daughter of Sukarno, removed from the Indonesian Democratic Party, an act that triggered mass rioting. By March 1998 events had spun beyond Suharto's ability to control. In poor health, the embattled despot suddenly concluded 32 years in power by abdicating in favor of his vice president, BACHARUDDIN JUSUF HABIBIE, on May 21, 1998. The news was greeted with delirious rejoicing in the streets, and an important page had been turned in Indonesia's history.

Once deposed, the full extent of Suharto's corruption was revealed: his personal and family worth was estimated at around $45 billion. In August 2000 he was formally charged with misusing charitable funds and ordered to stand trial. However, the court subsequently decided that the former president, having suffered three strokes in 1999, was unfit and charges were dropped. This resulted in violent protests throughout the capital, and the aged dictator was then sentenced to house arrest. He remains in declining health, closely watched. Suharto was especially upset when his youngest and favorite son, Huto Mandala Putri ("Tommy") was formerly charged with orchestrating the murder of a judge who had sentenced him in a corruption case in March 2002.

Further Reading

Challis, Ronald. *Shadow of a Revolution: Indonesia and the Generals.* Stroud, England: Sutton, 2001.

Elson, R. E. *Suharto: A Political Biography.* Cambridge: Cambridge University Press, 2001.

Forrester, Geoff, and Ronald J. Mary. *The Fall of Soeharto.* Bathurst, New South Wales: Crawford House, 1998.

Hanna, Jun. *Military Politics and Democratization in Indonesia.* New York: Routledge, 2003.

Kingsbury, Damien. *Power Politics and the Indonesian Military.* New York: RoutledgeCurzon, 2003.

Van Klinken, Gerry. "The Battle of History after Suharto: Beyond Sacred Dates, Great Men, and Legal Milestones." *Cultural Asian Studies* 33, no. 3 (2001): 323–350.

Vatikiotis, Michael R. *Indonesian Politics under Suharto: The Rise and Fall of the New Order.* New York: Routledge, 1998.

Sukarnoputri, Megawati (Soekarnoputri)

(1947–) *president of Indonesia*

Dyah Permata Megawati Setyati Sukarnoputri ("daughter of Sukarno") was born on January 23, 1947, in Indonesia, then struggling against the Dutch for independence. Her father, Achmed Sukarno, led the successful rebellion that culminated in the founding of the Republic of Indonesia in 1948. He then instituted a successful, if autocratic, rule intent on uniting the 13,667 constituent islands into a coherent nation. Sukarno was overthrown by one of his generals, SUHARTO, in 1965, and he died three years later under house arrest. Mega-

wati ("Cloud"), meanwhile, briefly attended Padjadjaran University to study agriculture and psychology, but she subsequently dropped out to marry and raise her children. She displayed no interest in politics until 1987, when friends encouraged her to run for parliament with the Indonesian Democratic Party (PDI). This was one of two opposition parties tolerated by Suharto and his Golkar organization, but with the economic downturn of the late 1980s and early 1990s, there were increasing cries for his removal. By 1993 Megawati quietly and unobtrusively rose to become chairman of the PDI, and in this position she began speaking out against the government's repression and nepotism. Her family name brought her immediate national attention, so much so that in June 1996 Suharto orchestrated a party coup within the PDI to have her replaced. Violent protests resulted that further heightened her political appeal. Suharto countered in 1997 by refusing to allow Megawati to run for office in 1997, which further angered supporters and elevated her to a symbol of popular resistance. Throughout early 1998 Megawati began calling for Suharto's immediate resignation, and he finally capitulated that May. He was replaced by Vice President BACHARUDDIN JUSUF HABIBIE, who promised free and open elections in June 1999. For the long-suffering Indonesian people, a corner had been turned.

Megawati, by dint of her father's enduring legacy, was well placed to win the presidential contest on a popular basis. However, Indonesia, a predominately Muslim country, entertains long-standing sentiments against women in political office, especially among conservative religious elements. Megawati easily won the first series of elections in June 1999, while her closest contender, ABDURRAHMAN WAHID of the Islamic-based National Awakening Party, came in second. However, when members of another Muslim organization, the United Development Party, refused to cast their votes for a woman, they went over to Wahid's column en masse, handing him the election on a vote of 373 to 313. This unexpected loss caused public dismay and outbursts of violence, but Megawati appeared on television and appealed for calm. "For the unity of the nation I call upon the people of Indonesia to accept the results of the election," she urged. The following day parliament installed her as Indonesia's first woman vice president.

Wahid's leadership proved very erratic, and in February 2001 he was censored by parliament for a financial scandal. The aged cleric, nearly blind, then approached the army to have the legislature dissolved but the military refused. In August 2001 they removed Wahid from office altogether and he was replaced by Megawati. To date she had been known for her modest behavior and lack of assertiveness in public, which some onlookers attribute to political canniness. However, in the wake of the September 11, 2001, destruction of New York's World Trade Center, Megawati was suddenly thrust on the scene as a world leader of note. Aghast at the destruction, she was among the first heads of state to visit Washington, D.C., to confer with President GEORGE W. BUSH about the war on terrorism. The issue of terrorism remains a dicey proposition for her, as Indonesia is the world's most populous Muslim nation and many factions are openly sympathetic to terrorists such as Osama bin Laden. Given the fragile nature of her coalition in parliament, Megawati has decided to tread lightly against suspected terrorist cells at home, lest she be turned out of office. In April 2002 she visited India to confer with President ATAL BEHAN VAJPAYEE and she called for a terror-free Asia. "Asia can and must be developed into a terror-free zone by institutionalizing and practicing tolerance, imposing fair treatment to all and by maintaining democracy," she declared. The following month she accompanied former president BILL CLINTON and UN General Secretary KOFI ANNAN to Dili, capital of East Timor, where they observed the inauguration of Xanana Gusmão as East Timor's first president. This concluded a 24-year guerrilla war against Indonesian occupation, and her presence was roundly criticized by veterans of that conflict. Megawati, a nationalist like her father, had originally opposed granting the region independence, but she gracefully acknowledged the new political reality and laid a wreath at a cemetery containing the remains of 3,000 Indonesian soldiers killed in battle. Back home she made a televised address in June 2002 calling for more death sentences for drug dealers. "For those who distribute drugs, life sentences and other prison sentences of dozens of years are no longer sufficient," she admonished. "No sentence is sufficient other than the death sentence." Megawati's tough stance and high international profile apparently sits well with the electorate, for a recent public opinion poll gives her a favorable rating of 53 percent, higher than when she was first elected.

Further Reading

Bourchier, David, and Vedi R. Hadiz, eds. *Indonesian Politics and Society.* New York: Routledge, 2003.

Budhiman, Arief. "Indonesia: The Trials of President Wahid." *South East Asian Affairs* 28 (2001): 145–158.

King, Dwight Y. *Half-hearted Reform: Electoral Institutions and the Struggle for Democracy in Indonesia.* Westport, Conn.: Praeger, 2003.

Malley, Michael S. "Indonesia in 2001: Restoring Stability in Jakarta." *Asian Survey* 42 (January–February 2002): 124–133.

McIntyre, Angus. *In Search of Megawati Sukarnoputri.* Clayton, Victoria: Monash University Press, 1997.

Porter, Donald. *Managing Politics and Islam in Indonesia.* Richmond, England: Curzon, 2002.

Ziv, Daniel. "Populist Perceptions and Perceptions of Populism in Indonesia: The Case of Megawati Soekarnoputri." *South East Asia Research* 9 (March 2001): 73–88.

T

Tandja, Mamadou (1938–) *president of Niger*
Mamadou Tandja was born in Maine-Soroa, Niger, in 1938, a member of the Kanouri tribal grouping. Niger, which is West Africa's largest county, lies directly below Libya and Algeria and shares much of its desert climate. It was once part of the French Empire but gained political independence in 1960 along with most of the French West African Federation countries. Since then, governance in Niger has been undertaken by a series of inept civilian leaders and oppressive military regimes. Numerous tribal rebellions, particularly the Tuareg uprising in the barren north, have all contributed to a climate of political instability. This unfortunate situation has only exacerbated Niger's reputation as one of the world's poorest nations, surpassed only by Sierra Leone. A mere 29 percent of school-age children receive education; consequently, Niger possesses one of the lowest literacy rates in the world. Moreover, health services are rudimentary at best, which in turn has helped to fuel a costly AIDS epidemic. In light of all these deficiencies, Niger has become completely dependent upon foreign aid to survive and has only recently returned to democratic, multiparty elections.

Tandja was educated locally before attending military academies in Madagascar and Mali throughout the 1950s. As a colonel, he participated in the 1974 coup that toppled President Hamani Diori, and his successor,

General Seyni Kountche, rewarded him with appointment as prefect of the Tahoua and Maradi regions. Highly talented and driven, Tandja also served as ambassador to Nigeria and minister of the interior. A noted black mark on his otherwise credible career involved the 1990 massacre of several Tuareg protestors by army troops, which sparked a violent, five-year upheaval. Tandja, as interior minister, was responsible for their suppression, which was harshly carried out. In 1991 Tandja resigned from the army and joined the National Movement for the Society in Development (MNSD), for many years Niger's only legitimate political party. As a member he ran for president in 1993 and lost by a narrow margin to Mahanane Ousmane. He tried again in 1996, only to lose to President Ibrahim Bare Mainassara, who subsequently lost his life in a military coup on April 9, 1999. His successor, Major Daouda Mallam Wanke, then buckled under international economic pressure to allow democratic elections, which transpired in November 1999. Niger at that time was bankrupt, its coffers were empty, and the civil service had not been paid in months. Tandja campaigned on a pledge to restore lost wages, raise living standards, and restore democracy. This might prove a tall order for any ambitious politician, but the former officer enjoyed a national reputation as "the working chief" for his honesty and work ethic. During a runoff held on December 22, 1999, Tandja garnered an impressive 60 percent of votes cast, making him the new president of Niger. "This victory is the victory of all Nigerien people, of democracy, and of political, social, and institutional stability for a new beginning," he promised. The MSND party also received a majority of seats in the unicameral parliament, which will facilitate passage of impending legislation. But most important of all, Tandja's rise heralds the nation's long-awaited return to democracy.

Tandja inherited a country dispirited by years of mismanagement and misrule, and essentially bankrupt. The sheer lack of money has prevented paying the civil service or the military, both of which have been prone to strikes and mutinies. However, because little can be accomplished in the absence of political stability, Tandja wisely extended an olive branch to opposition politicians, and he appointed several of them to his cabinet. But now that democracy has been restored, France, Japan, and the European Union have resumed sizable levels of foreign aid. Now able to pay off the bureaucracy and military, the country has restored some basic human services, such as health care and national security. Tandja also used this opportunity to invite foreign corporations to Niger to explore for and invest in mineral extraction. Furthermore, to prevent the possible rise of fundamentalism in this predominately Muslim country, Tandja has discussed the possibility of implementing the *sharia,* or Koranic law, in the northernmost provinces. Otherwise, he remains committed to keeping Niger a secular state.

A persistent problem facing the government of Niger is its inability to collect taxes. This is largely the fault of an underground economy with neighboring Nigeria that is estimated to comprise as much as 50 percent of all economic activity. Tandja, who like Nigerian president OLUSEGUN OBASANJO is a former military officer, is thus naturally committed to better regulation of border trade, and he has asked his counterpart for cooperation. The president has also been actively involved in regional diplomacy and has completed state visits to Burkina Faso, Liberia, Nigeria, and Libya to solicit additional aid. He had an especially fruitful interview with French president JACQUES CHIRAC in January 2000, and he assured the latter: "In Niger we will assure that no coups happen, and it's simple: we will serve the people; we will strive to pay all our teachers and work to ensure that our resources are used to help resolve our problems." Tandja's ability to transform rhetoric into reality is

as yet untested, but should he succeed, it will mean a new and better life for his long-suffering compatriots.

Further Reading

Charlick, Robert B. *Niger: Personal Rule and Survival in the Sahel.* Boulder, Colo.: Westview Press, 1991.

Davis, John V., and Aboubacar B. Kossomi. "Niger Gets Back on Track." *Journal of Democracy* 12 (July 2001): 80–88.

Decalo, Samuel. *Historical Dictionary of Niger.* Lanham, Md.: Scarecrow Press, 1997.

Lund, Christian. *Law, Power, and Politics in Niger: Land Struggle and the Rural Code.* New Brunswick, N.J.: Lit Verlang, 1998.

Miles, William F. *Hausaland Divided: Colonialism and Independence in Nigeria and Niger.* Ithaca, N.Y.: Cornell University Press, 1994.

Stoller, Paul. *Le Maître fou: Embodiment, Politics, and the Post-colony in Niger.* Evanston, Ill.: Northwestern University Press, 1995.

Taufa'ahau Tupou IV (1918–) *king of Tonga*

Crown Prince Siaosi Taufa'ahau Tupoulahi was born in Tonga on July 4, 1918, a son of reigning Queen Salote Tupou III. Tonga consists of 160 small islands situated approximately 1,000 miles northeast of New Zealand, and they are inhabited by people of Polynesian stock. It was the only Pacific region never colonized by Europeans, although Tonga acquiesced to British protection in 1899. Independence from Great Britain was finally obtained in 1970, and it remains part of the British Commonwealth. Its people deeply religious and traditionally oriented, Tonga remains the Pacific's only hereditary kingdom. The prevailing mode of government, first established in 1875, is a constitutional monarchy that closely reflects its aristocratic, deeply stratified social system. At the top is the king, who possesses veto power over all legislation that may be passed. He is assisted in decision making by an Executive Council, which consists of the Privy Council and all cabinet members. The final body is the Legislative Assembly, a unicameral body that is either appointed by the king or chosen from among the island's 33 noble families. There are no political parties and, presently, only nine commoners can be elected directly to parliament. Tonga itself is devoid of natural resources, so agriculture forms the backbone of its economy and ongoing attempts are being made to diversify. Part of this entails undertaking various money-making schemes, the results of which are thus far mixed. However, a large segment of national income derives from Tongans living abroad who send their earnings home.

Crown Prince Siaosi was educated locally before becoming the first Tongan to attend college abroad. He studied at Newington College and the University of Sydney, Australia, and obtained several law degrees. Following his return home, the queen appointed him to several ministerial positions within her cabinet. These included education, health, agriculture, and foreign affairs. In his various capacities, the prince helped introduce fundamental changes in Tonga, including establishing the first high school and teacher training college. Tonga consequently enjoys one of the region's highest literacy rates. The prince also took steps to diversify the economy by founding the broadcast commission, a major hotel chain, and a government newspaper. Following the death of his mother, the prince was enthroned as King Taufa'ahau Tupou IV on July 4, 1967. He thus continues a royal line that reaches back to 1875, when the present form of government was established.

The king's main concern since being enthroned is the economy. Due to Tonga's lack of exportable resources, he has been eager to embrace a number of money-making schemes to diversify the economy. The most successful has been the importation of squash, a valuable export crop for the Japanese market, which reaped a windfall until prices fell in 1999. Less profitable were plans to turn Tonga into the world's biggest tire dump, along with swapping sugar for uranium to construct the island's first nuclear power plant. This quest for overseas investors with ideas has resulted in at least one embarrassing scandal for the king. In October 2001 it was revealed that millions of investment dollars had apparently been swindled by a secret account raised and maintained by selling passports to Hong Kong residents fleeing China. Several governmental ministers, including the deputy prime minister and justice minister, resigned in consequence. This embarrassing affair has only added more fuel to the island's growing democracy movement with rising demands for more transparency and greater accountability by government.

A more notorious scheme unfolded in November 2000. Because Tonga's population is entirely Polynesian and untouched by immigration, it is an ideal genetic pool for researching the cause of certain genetic diseases.

That month an Australian biotechnical firm affirmed an interest in assembling a DNA database of Tonga's people in return for royalties accrued from successful medicines that might result from the study. The king was willing to cooperate, as was the government, but word of the experiment caused a public uproar and the project folded. Despite his penchant for harebrained schemes, Tupou IV remains in good favor with his subjects. The king refrains from an opulent lifestyle and is also a lay preacher in the Wesleyan Church, which dominates the island's religious life. But he has firmly opposed any movements toward participatory democracy, or a new constitution that would allow more commoners into the parliament. Such changes will probably not transpire until the impending accession to the throne of his son, Crown Prince Tupouto'a, the current defense and foreign minister. He is viewed as much more liberally disposed than his father, and he will probably orchestrate the requisite reforms necessary to expand the voting franchise. Nevertheless, Tonga soldiers on as a quixotic, scheme-ridden little kingdom, secure in its present identity but increasingly buffeted by the realities of 21st-century global affairs. King Tupou's 25-year reign establishes him as one of the world's longest-serving monarchs, and among its most popular.

Further Reading

Campbell, I. C. "The Emergence of Parliamentary Politics in Tonga." *Pacific Studies* 15, no. 1 (1992): 77–97.

Eustis, Nelson. *The King of Tonga: A Biography.* Adelaide, South Australia: Hobby Investment, 1997.

Ewins, Rory. *Changing Their Minds: Tradition and Politics in Contemporary Fiji and Tonga.* Christchurch, New Zealand: Macmillan Brown Center for Pacific Studies, 1998.

Gailey, Christine W. *Kinship to Kingship: Gender Hierarchy and State Formation in the Tungan Islands.* Austin: University of Texas Press, 1987.

Kerry, James E. "Tonga's Pro-Democracy Movement." *Pacific Affairs* 67 (June 1994): 242–262.

Lawson, Stephanie. *Tradition versus Democracy in the South Pacific: Fiji, Tonga, and Western Samoa.* New York: Cambridge University Press, 1996.

Taya, Maaouya (1943–   ) *president of Mauritania*
Maaouya Ould Sid' Ahmed Taya was born in the Atar region of Mauritania in 1943. His homeland, a former

French colony, occupies a broad stretch of land in the middle of northern West Africa, and constitutes part of the Sahara Desert. In fact, Mauritania is at the confluence of two distinct regions of the African continent: the Arabic-speaking north (Maghreb) and sub-Saharan black Africa. The religion practiced is uniformly Islamic, but tensions between racial groups traditionally defines national politics and constitutes a source of continuing hostility. The core of the problem is that the Arab and Berber (Moorish) minorities continue to dominate the majority (70 percent) black Fulbe and Wolof compatriots. In fact, black slavery was widespread and remained in effect until officially outlawed in 1981. Mauritania is also one of the world's poorest nations. It is nearly two-thirds desert and uninhabitable by anyone but nomads. It gained independence from France in 1960 under President Moktar Ould Daddah, but within four years had been transformed into a one-party state. Daddah was overthrown in July 1978, an act that initiated a long period of military rule. National politics has been further complicated by long-standing friction with both Polisario rebels in Western Sahara and the neighboring nation of Senegal.

Taya joined the military as a young man and eventually served as an aide to President Daddah. In 1976 he commanded Mauritanian forces during the ill-fated attempt to seize Western Sahara from Morocco. The Polisario guerrillas, aided and abetted by Algiers, mounted stiff and effective resistance and Daddah's inability to successfully resolve the issue resulted in his being toppled. Taya was among the members of the military clique that removed him, and he was rewarded with a seat on the ensuing Military Council. He subsequently served as minister of defense in the regime of President Mustapha Salek and later rose to army chief of staff. In this position he orchestrated removal of President Mohammed Khouna Ould Haidalla in 1983. This was done more for economic than personal reasons, for the Haidalla regime was apparently corrupt and unable to restore the national economy to growth. Taya then ruled as an undisputed military dictator for nearly a decade, and he grappled with the familiar problems of a sagging economy, restive neighbors, and racial strife. However, by 1992, increasing domestic pressure from within and without the country finally forced the Taya government to accede to multiparty elections, the first in three decades.

On January 17, 1992, presidential elections were held between Taya and his Democratic and Social Republic Party (DSRP) and four other candidates. This was the first multiparty election ever held in an Arabic state, but, given his tenure in office and complete control of the media, the former military chief easily garnered 62.7 percent of the vote. The opposition declared fraud and proceeded to boycott the ensuing legislative elections held in March 1992, whereby DSRP swept the field, winning 67 of 79 seats. Now seemingly legitimate, Taya continued ruling with an iron hand, compiling a dismal human rights record and doing little to ameliorate racial hostilities between blacks and Arabs. In January 1991 he sponsored a new constitution by public referendum, which passed, despite charges of election rigging, by a wide margin. This document mandates presidential terms of six years and greatly strengthens the executive branch at the expense of the legislature and the judiciary. On December 12, 1997, presidential elections were again held between Taya and four opposition candidates, including the first-ever black African candidate. Not surprisingly, Taya once again coasted to victory, this time claiming 90 percent of votes cast. Opposition leaders, not surprisingly, characterized the entire process as a masquerade.

Taya's rule, while authoritarian by nature, has been severely compromised by the difficulties traditionally besetting Mauritanian society. Open warfare between Arabs and blacks escalated in 1988, and Taya immediately purged the military of most non-Arab personnel. Two years later Senegalese guest workers were viciously attacked by Arabs, forcing 15,000 to flee. In retaliation, Senegalese nationals attacked Mauritanian shopkeepers throughout Senegal, forcing 100,000 to return home. Taya was also slow to confront the slavery issue, despite continuing international criticism, and it remained a legal practice to own black slaves until 1981. Charges persist to this day that slavery still exists in more remote corners of the country. Another serious misstep occurred in 1991 when Taya supported the invasion of Kuwait by Iraqi dictator SADDAM HUSSEIN. As late as February 2002, a group of Mauritanian expatriates sued Taya in a Belgian court on charges of genocide and human rights violations. Taya, however, continues in power unabated, although in December 2000 he announced that proportional representation would be introduced in the next round of legislative elections to insure black representation. He further pledges that state funding and access to media would be made available to all legitimate parties.

Further Reading

Cotton, Samuel. *Silent Terror: A Journey into Contemporary African Slavery.* New York: Harlem Rivers Press, 1998.

N'Diaye, Boubacar. "Mauritania's Stalled Democratization." *Journal of Democracy* 12 (July 2001): 88–96.

Ould-Mey, Mohameden. *Global Restructuring and Peripheral States: The Carrot and Stick Approach in Mauritania.* Lanham, Md.: Littlefield Adams Books, 1996.

Pazzanita, Anthony G. "Political Transition in Mauritania: Problems and Prospects." *Middle East Journal* 53, no. 1 (1999): 44–58.

Ruf, Urs Peter. *Ending Slavery: Hierarchy, Dependency, and Gender in Central Mauritania.* Bielefield, Germany: Transcript Verland, 1999.

Taylor, Charles (1948–) *president of Liberia*

Charles McArthur Taylor was born in Liberia on January 28, 1948, a member of that nation's Americo-Liberian elite. In fact, Liberia is the only African country founded by the United States for the repatriation of former African slaves back to the continent. Established in 1847, it remains Africa's oldest republic. Traditionally, politics were dominated by the 50 or so families who could claim American heritage, and they wielded power over the vast majority of indigenous peoples. The Liberian constitution also harkens back to its U.S. heritage, and it mandates a popularly elected president and a bicameral legislature composed of a Senate and a National Assembly. In 1971 the existing order was partially upended by President William Tubman, who sought to end the practice of economic and political privilege. Reforms were continued under his successor, William Tolbert, whose blatant corruption also sparked a popular uprising. Tolbert was subsequently murdered by troops under Sergeant Samuel Doe, who shot his way into power in 1980. Doe then suspended the constitution, outlawed political parties, and instituted a brutal, corrupt regime of his own. For nearly a decade the Liberian people endured Doe's oppression, while numerous Liberian exiles fled to neighboring countries to start an armed opposition. A protracted and bloody civil war commenced in December 1989, which resulted in the death of Doe and the rise of a new and equally brutal regime.

Taylor was educated locally and attended Bentley College, Massachusetts, in pursuit of a degree in education. Though nominally associated with the Americo-Liberian elite, he proved sympathetic toward the average Liberian and came to detest the corruption and nepotism of the Tolbert administration. After graduating in 1977, Taylor worked as a mechanic in Boston for three years until Doe installed himself as the country's new leader. Much exhilarated, Taylor returned to Liberia, where he became head of Liberia's General Services Agency. He served in this office until 1983, when charges of embezzling $900,000 surface, and he fled back to Massachusetts. Taylor was subsequently arrested on an international warrant and briefly imprisoned, but he escaped and made his way back to Africa. There he helped found the National Patriotic Front of Liberia (NPFL) for the sole purpose of overthrowing Doe. He commenced his campaign on Christmas Day, 1989, and within a few months NPFL forces had overrun most of the country. On August 30, 1990, Doe was caught and executed, but a bloody impasse continued over control of the capital city of Monrovia. Taylor rejected any calls for a power-sharing arrangement and declared himself president, but international pressure began mounting for multiparty elections. The guerrilla chief relented, and on July 19, 1997, he was formally elected president at the head of his newly formed National Patriotic Party (NPP) with 75 percent of votes cast in elections deemed to be free and fair. Voters appear to have harbored no illusions as to the nature of their candidate, but he seemed the one most capable of restoring order to this badly divided land. By the time Liberia's civil war concluded that year over 200,000 people, mostly civilians, had died. Moreover, 1 million refugees had to be resettled and the countryside lay in ruins.

In practice, Taylor's rule has proven to be as brutal and corrupt as previous administrations. He has done little or nothing to alleviate suffering in the countryside, which remains devoid of electricity. Moreover, having grown suspicious of the men under his command, he has resorted to the practice of hiring heavily armed foreign mercenaries to enforce his will. To strengthen personal allegiances, he next awarded lucrative contracts in the gold, diamond, and lumber industries to his friends within the ruling clique. Taylor also obtains a large part of his annual income by supporting rebel groups in neighboring countries who control several diamond-producing regions. The Revolutionary United Front (RUF) in Sierra Leone is particularly indebted to him for continuing assistance while other groups routinely make incursions against Guinea from Liberian soil. Taylor's willingness to support such activities has rendered

Liberia a pariah nation in West Africa, and a threat to regional stability. Consequently, the United Nations imposed economic sanctions and an arms embargo. Foreign aid also continues to plummet and the country, with an annual income of $65 million, remains saddled by a national debt approaching $2.5 billion.

Taylor's excesses have spurred the growth of an indigenous resistance movement, the Liberians United for Reconciliation and Democracy, or LURD. They seem to represent various interests groups, all united in their loathing of the Taylor administration. Sporadic fighting commenced in 1999 but the Liberian military, hurt by the arms embargo, has failed to contain the well-armed insurgents. On February 8, 2002, they struck suddenly at Kley Junction, just 22 miles from the capital, and Taylor declared a national state of emergency. The rebels promise to continue fighting until Taylor either steps down or is killed. Meanwhile, the United States, formerly Liberia's closest ally, has made no effort to assist. It remains to be seen if Taylor can defeat this seemingly popular uprising, or else suffer the grisly fate of dictators before him. Meanwhile, Liberians continue toiling under the threat of war, famine, disease, and poverty.

Further Reading

Adebajo, Adekeye. *Liberia's Civil War: Nigeria, ECO-MOG, and Regional Security in West Africa.* Boulder, Colo.: Lynne Rienner Publishers, 2002.

Cain, Kenneth L. "The Rape of Dinah: Human Rights, Civil War in Liberia, and Evil Triumphant." *Human Rights Quarterly* 21 (May 1999): 265–308.

Clapham, Christopher S. *African Guerillas.* Bloomington: University of Indiana Press, 1998.

Ellis, Stephen. *The Mask of Anarchy: The Destruction of Liberia and the Religious Dimensions of an African Civil War.* New York: New York University Press, 2001.

Harris, David. "From 'Warlord' to 'Democratic' President: How Charles Taylor Won the 1997 Liberian Elections." *Journal of Modern African Studies* 37, no. 3 (1999): 431–456.

Than Shwe (1933–   ) *prime minister of Myanmar*
Than Shwe was born in Kyaukse, central Burma, on February 2, 1933. Burma at that time was part of the British Empire and did not gain full political independence until January 1948. It is the largest country of Southeast Asia, nestled between Bangladesh, India, China, and Laos. The population is overwhelmingly Burmese in composition, although several distinct minority groups are present. Burma experienced its first democratically elected prime minister when U Nu assumed power in 1948, but he proved unable to maintain control of various competing elements. By 1958 he was forced to call upon the military for assistance and in March 1962 General Ne Win toppled his administration altogether. Thereafter Burma fell under the aegis of a socialist-oriented Revolutionary Council, which imposed a unique blend of Marxism and Buddhism on the country. Burma also became a one-party state under the Burmese Socialist Party Program (BSPP), the sole legitimate outlet for political expression. In 1974 a new constitution was ratified, which established rule in the form of a Council of State under a chairman and a Council of Ministers, from whose ranks a prime minister is selected. Provisions were also made for a People's Assembly, but this body was dissolved in 1988, the same year that the military-run State Law and Order Restoration Council (SLORC) was instituted. The following year Burma was also renamed Myanmar. However, by 1990 international pressure mounted for multiparty elections, which were overwhelming won by the National League for Democracy (NLD). Unfortunately, the ruling clique in charge evinced no disposition to return to civilian rule. The election was ignored and the junta remained in power.

Than graduated from high school and worked as a post office clerk before joining the military in 1953. A decade later he attended the Central Institute of Political Science while still a commissioned officer, and he was groomed for national leadership. Than proved himself adept as a military administrator, and by 1985 he had become the army's deputy chief of staff. In 1988 General Ne Win suddenly resigned from power and it appeared that Burma would return to democracy, but these hopes were dashed by the coup that installed the SLORC. Than himself gained appointment as vice chairman of that body and, on April 23, 1992, following the retirement of General Saw Maung, Than became chairman of the SLORC and de facto prime minister of Myanmar.

Once in office, Than curried favor with the outside world by releasing several political prisoners—with one critical exception. This was AUNG SAN SUU KYI, head of the NLD, and an outspoken critic of military rule. After a decade of political agitation, she remained under house arrest for 19 months until May 2002, despite her celebrity

Olusegun Obasanjo *(Nigerian Information Service)*

political office since 1985. He also pledged to reduce the size of the army and to cultivate a renewed sense of civility. "I believe that there is a great need for moral and spiritual regeneration within our society," Obasanjo maintained.

Once in power, the former general immediately turned to revitalizing the agriculture sector, which for many years was a mainstay of the economy and made Nigeria self-sufficient. Unfortunately, previous regimes had rendered Nigeria almost entirely dependent upon oil for revenues. Because world energy prices were slumping, the money available to the government declined alarmingly, and Obasanjo was forced to curb his agricultural ambitions. He was also faced with eradicating widespread corruption and the challenge of equitably distributing the nation's wealth among all its ethnic groupings. These intertribal relationships were further complicated when the largely Muslim-dominated north imposed the strict Islamic legal code, or *sharia,* on all its inhabitants. This move sparked riots from the sizable

Christian community and a general exodus southward. Obasanjo himself has tribal problems of his own, mainly from his own Yoruba clan, for failing to support the candidacy of fellow tribesman Chief Awowolo in 1979. Despite his best efforts, the nation remains a tinderbox of ethnic tensions and religious discontent. Worse, his failures have sparked rumors that the military is once more ready to seize power and stave off further instability.

After three years in office, Obasanjo's reforms have failed to produce the desired results. In fact, his inability to spark economic growth and new jobs seemed to have signaled the end of civil society, for violence is increasingly endemic. Since 1999, an estimated 10,000 Nigerians have died violently, either in clashes with the police or against each other. This is a toll that far exceeds those endured during any of the previous military regimes. Events seemed to crest in the spring of 2002 when a massive explosion in Lagos killed nearly 1,000 people and led to further disorders. Obasanjo also decided to sever relations with the International Monetary Fund (IMF) as he felt the austerity measures they demanded would incite further unrest. However, Obasanjo, a born-again Christian, remains as unflappable as ever. In March 2002 he announced his intention to stand for the presidency in 2003. "I have decided that it is best that I make myself available as a presidential candidate," he announced. This declaration was made against a backdrop of escalating tension and killings between disparate tribal and religious factions. On April 22, 2003, Obasanjo was reelected president of Nigeria.

Further Reading

Aborisade, Oladimeji, and Robert J. Mundt. *Politics in Nigeria.* New York: Longman, 2002.

Adinoyi-Ojo, Onukaba. *In the Eyes of Time: A Biography of Olusegun Obasanjo.* New York: Africana Legacy Press, 1997.

Khalid, Mansour, ed. *Africa through the Eyes of a Patriot: A Tribute to General Olusegun Obasanjo.* New York: Kegan Paul, 2001.

Maier, Karl. *This House Has Fallen: Nigeria in Crisis.* London: Penguin, 2002.

Obasanjo, Olusegun. *In God's Time: The Building of a Democratic Nation.* San Diego, Calif.: Hampton Court Pub. Ltd., 2001.

Ojo, Bamidele A. *Problems and Prospects of Sustaining Democracy in Nigeria.* Huntington, N.Y.: NOVA Science, 2001.

as a Nobel Peace Prize recipient. More pressing was the question of ethnic unrest and rebellions. For many years the junta routinely conscripted forced labor work on national infrastructure, and minorities were frequently the object of such abuse. Many of these took to arms and commenced guerrilla operations in the jungles until General Khin Nyunt, a progressive moderate, began peace negotiations. However, as a rule, Myanmar suffers from terrible human rights abuses, and both the United States and the European Union have severed all economic aid. China has since stepped in to fill the void, although amid opposition charges that the generals have reduced Myanmar to that of a vassal state. As the country is run by generals, military expenditures account for roughly half of the annual gross national product and, consequently, education, health care, and welfare programs have all suffered. Worse, the junta turns a blind eye to Myanmar's thriving drug culture, and heroin exports constitute a large part of the underground economy. All told, after 12 years in power, the junta has done little for Myanmar other than to perpetuate its own survival. In 1997 it instituted the cosmetic change of renaming its ruling body the State Peace and Development Council (SPDC).

Time, however, is running against the military, for the weight of globalization is prompting much-needed reforms. The ruling clique is beset by aging leaders and Than is hard-pressed to find young military officers with the same commitment to the existing order. There is also a reputed split between Generals Khin Nyunt and Maung Aye, Than's probable successors, as one is more internationally oriented while the other is more traditionally xenophobic. Furthermore, Myanmar is under increasing pressure from the United States and the United Nations to begin a dialogue with Aung San Suu Kyi and the opposition NDL. In April 2000 UN representative Razali Ismail arrived in Myanmar to prod such talks along, with little results. Apparently, the generals running the country have developed a "siege mentality" and are digging in their heels in the face of both international criticism and domestic pressure for change. Whatever path events may follow is unknown, but the generals have also begun secret negotiations with the NDL for a possible transition to democracy a few years hence. Than, for his part, is holding up the rear guard against inevitable change and couches his praise for military rule in Burmese nationalism. But it would appear that Myanmar's days as one of Asia's last military dictatorships are numbered.

Further Reading
Fink, Christiana. *Living Silence: Burma under Military Rule.* London: Zed, 2001.
Mawdsley, James. *The Heart Must Break: The Fight for Democracy and Truth in Burma.* London: Century, 2001.
Reynold, Andrew, Alfred Stephan, Zaw Oo, and Stephen Levine. "How Burma Could Democratize." *Journal of Democracy* 12 (October 2001): 95–109.
South, Ashley. *Mon Nationalism and Civil War in Burma.* Richmond, Va.: Curzon, 2001.
Tucker, Shelby. *Burma: The Curse of Independence.* London: Pluto, 2001.

Thani, Hamad bin Khalifa al- (1950–)
emir of Qatar

Hamad bin Khalifa al-Thani was born in Doha, Qatar, in 1950, a son of Sheikh KHALIFA BIN HAMAD AL-THANI. Qatar is located on a peninsula that juts into the Gulf of Arabia, and it abuts Saudi Arabia, the United Arab Emirates, and Bahrain. Formerly part of the Ottoman Empire, it became a British protectorate in 1916 and remained thus until Britain withdrew its military forces from the Persian Gulf region in 1971. The al-Thani family has a long-established reputation as traditional rulers, and their status was confirmed by the British. Presently, Qatar is ruled under a written constitution that provides for an emir, who also acts as prime minister, and an appointed Advisory Council. Prior to 1939, Qatar was a very poor region, supported by fishing and pearling, but the discovery of oil transformed it into one of the world's richest countries. The al-Thani family continues to invest billions of dollars in the welfare of its citizens, who enjoy free housing, education, and health care. Water and electricity are also provided free of charge. Qatar also maintains one of the best-equipped, best-trained military establishments in the region, although its relatively small size mandates close defensive ties to larger Western powers.

Sheikh Hamad was educated locally and he received his military training at the Royal Military Academy, Sandhurst, England, in 1971. The following year he returned home as a general and became Qatar's commander in chief. Hamad was no paper soldier; as commander of an armored brigade, he transformed it into one of the best all-Arab units of the Gulf region. In light of his success, he was next promoted to defense minister and crown prince to succeed the sitting emir, his father. In time Hamad also established himself as an influential family member, who replaced younger rivals on the family-dominated Advisory Council. He also successfully curbed the extravagant tendencies of family members and other high officials. However, Sheikh Khalifa was an extremely conservative individual and reluctant to invest in Qatar's burgeoning oil industry or economic infrastructure. His lackadaisical approach to the problems of modernity threatened to destabilize the country. On June 27, 1995, Hamad overthrew his father in a bloodless coup while the latter was vacationing in Switzerland. The new ruler had since cultivated close ties with Great Britain and the United States, who immediately recognized his new regime.

Unlike his father, the Western-trained Hamad proved himself a progressive with a flare for implementing dramatic change. He immediately adopted a more open style of leadership, and he allowed limited criticism of his regime in the press and media, something rarely seen in an Arab country. Moreover, he has authorized various committees to draw up a new constitution for Qatar, one prompting a popularly elected National Assembly. Pursuant to the ruler's liberal vision, Qatar is also one of three Gulf states that allows women to both vote and run for public office. To this end, Hamad appointed the nation's first female deputy minister in 1998. The emir has been active in economic planning, especially given Qatar's complete dependence on oil. As early as 1989 he advocated diversifying the economy with enhanced industrial and agricultural sectors. He also pushed through plans to tap into Qatar's vast reserves of natural gas offshore, one of the world's largest. Through such expedients he hopes to lessen the impact of fluctuating oil prices, which were extremely unstable through the 1990s. More than any other Gulf leader, Hamad has pursued close economic ties to various Western powers, and he works closely with them to ensure steady and stable extraction of hydrocarbon resources.

Under Hamad, Qatar has also acquired a reputation for independence in its foreign policy. Qatar roundly supported Iraqi dictator Saddam Hussein during his drawn-out conflict with Iran, but promptly opposed his seizure of Kuwait in August 1990. Not only did Hamad allow American-led coalition forces to operate from Qatar's airfields, he also committed armored elements of his army to combat, which fought with distinction. His is also one of very few Arab states to enjoy cordial relations with the Jewish state of Israel and the government has concluded business arrangements to sell Israel natural gas. However, in light of recent Palestinian violence, he faces increasing Arab pressure to break such ties. Qatar enjoys more predictable relations with neighboring states as part of the Gulf Cooperation Council (GCC). Through its aegis a long-standing boundary dispute with Saudi Arabia was settled peacefully in 1999. However, Hamad has been unsuccessful in settling ownership of the oil-rich Hawar islands that are also claimed by Bahrain, and in 1994 he referred his case to the International Court of Justice in The Hague for arbitration. The nation is also forging ahead with political reforms. In March 1999 Qatar held its first elections for the new Municipal Council. On April 29, 2003, Qatar's first permanent constitution was enacted. This latest development and the onset of democratic elections will greatly assist Qatar's quest for modernity in a changing world.

Further Reading

Anscombe, Frederick F. *The Ottoman Gulf: The Creation of Kuwait, Saudi Arabia, and Qatar.* New York: Columbia University Press, 1997.

Crystal, Jill. *Oil and Politics in the Gulf: Rulers and Merchants in Kuwait and Qatar.* New York: Cambridge University Press, 1995.

Muhlbock, Monika F. "The Social and Political Reforms in Qatar under Khalif B. Hamad al Thani." *Hemispheres* 14 (1999): 115–120.

Rathwell, Andrew, and Kirsten Schulze. "Political Reform in the Gulf: The Case of Qatar." *Middle Eastern Studies* 36 (October 2000): 47–57.

Zahlan, Rosemarie S. *The Making of the Modern Gulf States: Kuwait, Bahrain, Qatar, the United Arab Emirates, and Oman.* Reading, England: Ithaca Press, 1998.

Thani, Khalifa bin Hamad al- (1932–   )
emir of Qatar

Khalifa bin Hamad al-Thani was born in 1932 at Rayyh, Qatar, a son of Hamad, emir of the al-Thani dynasty. Since 1916 Qatar had been jointly administered as a British protectorate, although the ruling family enjoyed wide latitudes on domestic issues. It was then a poor, sparsely populated region of the Arabian Peninsula, apparently of little consequence. Khalifa was educated by private tutors and eventually rose to serve as minister of education. His father died in 1947 and, after some internal family wrangling, his cousin, Ahmad bin Ali al-Thani, was chosen emir in 1960. As a concession to Khalifa, he assumed the post of finance minister and played key roles in developing Qatar's burgeoning oil industry. In 1968 he became president of the Provisional Federation Council among various Persian Gulf states, created because of Great Britain's impending withdrawal from the region. Qatar gained its independence in 1971 and on February 22, 1972, Khalifa bloodlessly deposed his cousin while he was on a hunting trip in Iran. The coup enjoyed wide support at home owing to the emir's lavish lifestyle, combined with fears that he would appoint his son as heir at Khalifa's expense. Now emir, he proved himself an enlightened reformer of exceptional foresight. He summarily stopped the family practice of reserving one-quarter of the national oil revenues for its own use, and he returned the monies to the treasury. He also instituted a 20-member advisory council to assist in ruling the emirate. However, Khalifa also shored up his position by appointing 10 of his closest relatives to hold the 15 cabinet ministries, thereby insuring close cooperation. The Qatari constitution also allowed him to rule by decree in most matters, and his turn of mind was autocratic. In view of the rising tide of secular and religious unrest throughout the Gulf region, Khalifa also outlawed unions and political parties as of 1976. But he enjoyed considerable success modernizing the bureaucracy, expanding the scope of agriculture, and developing new industries. Through his efforts Qatar subsequently attained one of the world's highest standards of living.

As head of state, Khalifa pursued decidedly pro-Western polices and was on friendly terms with both the United States and Great Britain. He supported Iraq in its war against Iran, 1980–88, and supplied billions of dollars in financial assistance. To shore up stability in the region, he also played a leading role in establishing the Gulf Cooperation Council (GCC) in 1981. In 1991 Khalifa further demonstrated his loyalty to the West by supporting the United States campaign to eject SADDAM HUSSEIN's Iraqi forces from Kuwait. That year the aging monarch began entrusting daily governing activities to his heir apparent, Crown Prince HAMAD BIN KHALIFA AL-THANI, who had also served as defense minister since 1977. This proved his undoing.

On June 22, 1995, Khalifa was suddenly overthrown and deposed by Hamad while on a trip to Switzerland. Apparently, the ruling elites had grown restless under his conservative brand of leadership, especially with respect to economic reform. His family was also alarmed by his growing fondness for liquor and his opulent palace lifestyle. Great Britain, the United States, and Saudi Arabia apparently supported the change and quickly recognized Hamad as the new emir. Khalifa, however, was angered by the coup. He refused to recognize his son's legitimacy and marshaled his personal finances, estimated at $3 billion, to win the throne back. He began touring Arab capitals soliciting political and military support, and he vocally opposed Hamad's independent foreign policy, which included cordial relations with Iran, Iraq, and Israel. Within weeks Hamad confronted some minor coup attempts against him. All failed and the emir countered by attempting to freeze his father's bank accounts and recovering what amounted to stolen state funds. In the end, father and son were finally reconciled. Khalifa was allowed to return to Qatar in November 1996 as a senior statesman, having renounced all intentions to the throne. He lives in splendid retirement at his many palaces. However, he will be remembered as Qatar's first modern ruler whose 23-year reign brought prosperity and modernity to his nation of desert dwellers. As a leader, Khalifa always evinced great interest in the people's well-being, and he supervised development of its government, social services, and economy. Hamad, meanwhile, continues as the ruling emir of Qatar.

Further Reading

Abdelkarim, Abbas, ed. *Change and Development in the Gulf.* New York: St. Martin's Press, 1999.

Crystal, Jill. *Oil and Politics in the Gulf: Rulers and Merchants in Kuwait and Qatar.* New York: Cambridge University Press, 1995.

Mulboch, Monika F. "The Social and Political Change Qatar under Khalifa b. Hamad al Thani." *Hemispheres* 14 (1999): 115–120.

Uthman, Nasir M. *With Their Bare Hands: The Story of the Oil Industry in Qatar.* New York: Longman, 1984.

Zahlan, Rosemary S. *The Making of the Modern Gulf States: Kuwait, Bahrain, Qatar, the United Arab Emirates, and Oman.* Reading, England: Ithaca Press, 1998.

Thorbjoern, Jagland (1950–) *prime minister of Norway*

Jagland Thorbjoern was born on November 5, 1950, in Drammen, Norway, the son of farmers. He matured in the woodlands of Buskerud county, absorbing many of the deep-seated values associated with the Norwegian countryside. He also developed close affinity for social issues that were hallmarks of the Labor Party, and he joined their youth division while at the University of Oslo. By 1973 Thorbjoern headed the local Labour Youth League, rising to executive secretary of the national board. Two years later he commenced his political career by winning a seat on the county council of Buskerund. In this capacity Thorbjoern cemented his reputation in the Labor Party by defending such traditional policies as generous welfare state programs, retirement pensions, care for the elderly, and support for public education. Thorbjoern's activism also secured his political base in the county and in 1985 he gained election to the Storting (parliament) as a Labor candidate. At that time government was controlled by HARLEM GRO BRUNDTLAND, one of Norway's most successful political figures. Bruntland was then weaning Labor away from its radical, hard-line elements and replacing them with younger, less dogmatic members. Thorbjoern came to her attention in 1986, and she appointed him a parliamentary committee secretary. He performed well and the following year was advanced to party secretary. In practice, Thorbjoern acquired the reputation of a skillful consensus builder, a trait considered essential for bringing the party's many factions together. On October 25, 1996, Brundtland suddenly stepped down as prime minister a year before scheduled elections. This was apparently done to give Thorbjoern, her anointed successor, a year to consolidate his political base nationwide.

Thorbjoern was no radical, and he determined to pursue and enhance the moderate agenda of his predecessor. He embarked on programs to strengthen the economy, maintain state pensions, and encourage investment. "There is now certainly scope for reform in the Norwegian economy," he stressed. "I want to exploit this for extensive investment in further education." However, Thorbjoern generally opposed trends toward privatization of government-owned industries and pensions systems. As a Labor stalwart, he felt strongly that government had a role to play in guaranteeing basic social services, especially to those societal elements in distress.

Norway, however, seemed to be on a collision course with the rest of Europe in the realm of economic integration. As persuasive as Brundtland was, in 1994 the public rejected joining the European Union (EU) by 52.4 percent. Many citizens were wary of EU regulations requiring the nation to open up its territorial waters to other fishing fleets and to allow cheaper foreign agricultural products to compete with homegrown commodities. Such possibilities endangered traditional Norwegian attachments to the sea and the land, making EU membership unsavory. Moreover, Norway, as the world's third-largest oil exporter, was quite richer than its neighbors. Many felt an economic union meant the country would ultimately subsidize poorer countries. All told, despite Thorbjoern's strong preference for membership in the EU, he lacked a popular mandate to pursue it. He enjoyed greater success advancing traditional Labor themes such as nuclear disarmament, and he also dispatched Norwegian troops as peacekeepers to the Middle East and Bosnia. But Brundtland, a tough act to follow politically, cast a long shadow over his administration, and Thorbjoern failed to generate much voter enthusiasm. Elections held in the fall of 1997 confirmed this when Labor failed to improve its standing and, in fact, suffered minor losses. He interpreted such lackluster results as a referendum on his administration and resigned. KJELL BONDEVIK succeeded him on October 17, 1997.

Thorbjoern remained head of the opposition until March 2000, when Bondevik lost a vote of confidence and stepped down. A new Labor leader, JENS STOLTENBERG, assumed the mantle of command and appointed Thorbjoern his foreign minister. He once again stated his preference for joining the EU, just as Switzerland and Iceland were negotiating to do so. "We are facing new international realities," he warned. "When Iceland thinks, we must dare to do so." Unfortunately, by October 2001 the conservatives under Bondevik resumed power, and Thorbjoern left the ministry. He served as Labor chairman for several more weeks, amid cries for new and younger leadership. Tensions between him and Stoltenberg resulted in spells of exhaustion and, on February 4, 2002, Thorbjoern stepped aside as party chairman. "I see that the combination between hard work and tremendous focus on my person was too demanding over time," he declared. "As party leader, I must take responsibility for getting this party out of a destructive personal conflict so that the party's energy can be used to win back the confidence we have lost." Thorbjoern has since been replaced by Stoltenberg, although he retains his seat in parliament as an opposition member.

Further Reading

Christensen, Tom. *Structure, Culture, and Governance: A Comparison of Norway and the United States.* Lanham, Md.: Rowman and Littlefield, 1999.

Geyer, Robert. *The Uncertain Union: British and Norwegian Social Democrats in an Integrating Europe.* Brookfield, Vt.: Amebury, 1997.

Gstohl, Sieglinde. *Reluctant Europeans: Norway, Sweden, and Switzerland in the Process of Integration.* Boulder, Colo.: Lynne Rienner Publishers, 2002.

Moses, Jonathan W. *Open States in the Global Economy: The Political Economy of Small State Macroeconomic Management.* New York: St. Martin's Press, 2000.

Shafter, William R. *Politics, Parties, and Parliaments: Political Change in Norway.* Columbus: Ohio State University Press, 1998.

Tito, Teburoro (1953–) *president of Kiribati*
Teburoro Tito was born at Tabiteaua North, Kiribati, on August 25, 1953. His homeland consists of 33 coral atolls scattered across 3 million square miles of Pacific Ocean, adjacent to Tuvalu and the Marshall Islands. However, total land mass amounts to only 250 square miles, about the size of New York's Manhattan Island. Many of the isles are also only a few feet above sea level and therefore potentially threatened by tides and ocean levels. In 1892 the region became a British protectorate known as the Gilbert and Ellice Islands Colony. They were seized by Japan in 1942 and the following year, Betio (Tarawa) Island witnessed one of World War II's most horrific amphibious battles between Japanese and American forces. After the war, the Gilberts reverted to British rule and in 1957 the British exploded their first hydrogen bomb on Christmas Island. However, by July 1979 there was strong pressure for increasing autonomy and the newly renamed Kiribati (minus Tuvalu, which separated in 1975) became an independent nation within the British Commonwealth. Its present constitution largely reflects the prevailing native culture, which is based on discussion, compromise, and consensus. Governance is in the hands of a unicameral legislature, the National Assembly (Maneaba Ni Maungatabu) which draws its inspiration from the traditional center of village

life, the Maneaba. From the ranks of the legislature up to four candidates are drawn to run for president (beretitenti), who is then elected by the assembly. Island politics are generally dominated by either the Christian Democratic Unity Party (CDUP) or the Gilbertese National Progressive Party (GNPP). Kiribati is also presently one of the Pacific's poorer regions, whose economy is dominated solely by the export of copra, or dried coconut meat.

Tito was well educated at various missionary schools on Tabwiroa before enrolling at the University of the South Pacific in Fiji. There he received a bachelor's degree in science in 1977, and in 1981 he also studied statistics at the Papua New Guinea Administrative College. He then returned to Kiribati to join the Civil Service and also served within the Ministry of Education, 1980–82. Tito commenced his political career by being elected as a CDUP member of the National Assembly in 1987, and he quickly established himself as an opposition leader. In this office he proved an outspoken critic of government waste and mismanagement. Tito gained reelection to the assembly in 1991 and continued rising in national stature owing to his confrontational, nontraditional approach to politics. These methods alienated more conservative elements in the assembly, but it established him as a leader of repute. In May 1994, the government of President Teannaki Teatao suffered a vote of no confidence and resigned. After several rounds of secret balloting within the assembly, Tito emerged as Kiribati's third president on September 30, 1992, by a wide margin. He was also reelected in November 1998 for a second term with 52 percent of votes cast.

As president, Tito openly attacked what he considers elitism in Kiribati politics, and he has pushed for measures that will expand the role of the average citizen. "As people become more politically aware, it will be much more difficult for politicians to stand up and make promises," he insists. "A better pattern of governing will develop, which reflect the fundamental values of Kiribati culture." However, given the slender economic resources that the islands are saddled with, any Kiribati administration is going to be absorbed by a need for diversification. Traditionally, Kiribati is highly dependent upon two major sources of revenue: coconuts and foreign earnings mailed home from citizens working abroad, usually on Nauru. Consequently, Tito has placed greater emphasis on tourism and granting foreign fishing licenses to raise additional capital. His efforts received a genuine boost during the millennium celebrations, for Kiribati straddles several time zones, and the year 2000 arrived there first. Tourism has since increased overall, but the islanders still remain dependent on foreign aid to augment their meager means. Tito has asked for additional funding to upgrade airports, shipyards, and ports to better facilitate trade and communication between constituent islands. In 1999 Kiribati joined the United Nations.

However, the biggest challenge facing Kiribati, and for that matter many small Pacific microstates, is the issue of rising sea levels. Since 1999 several low-lying atolls have been lost and many others are periodically swamped by storms. Tito, in conjunction with the leaders of Tuvalu and Nauru, has approached the government of Australian prime minister JOHN HOWARD to secure Australia's more rigid adherence to the 1999 Kyoto agreement on global warming gases. Australia is presently the biggest regional emitter of so-called greenhouse gases, which heat up the atmosphere, forcing the ice caps to melt, and thereby causing ocean levels to rise. Howard, however, steadfastly refuses, as strict compliance to the Kyoto Accords would cost an estimated 90,000 jobs. The impasse will cost Kiribati and others much more if a reduction in greenhouse gases is not forthcoming. However, in October 2001 the Australian government awarded Kiribati several million dollars for accepting boatloads of Iraqi refugees who were denied entrance into the country. In view of the dire need for funding, Tito readily accepted the offer. He will be up for reelection in 2004.

Further Reading

Macdonald, Barrie. *Cinderellas of the Empire: Towards a History of Kiribati and Tuvalu.* Miami, Fla.: Australian University Press, 1982.

————. *Governance and Political Process in Kiribati.* Canberra: Australian National University, 1996.

Sabatier, E., and Ursala Nixon. *Astride the Equator: An Account of the Gilbert Islands.* Oxford: Oxford University Press, 1978.

Uriam, Kambatik. *In Their Own Words: History and Society in Gilbertese Oral Tradition.* Canberra: Journal of Pacific History, 1995.

Van Trease, Howard. *Atoll Politics: The Republic of Kiribati.* Christchurch, New Zealand: University of Canterbury, 1993.

Toledo, Alejandro (1946–) *president of Peru*

Alejandro Toledo was born in Cabana, a small village in the Andean highlands of Peru. His parents were sheepherders, the descendants of Indians, who constitute 80 percent of the country's population. The plight of Peruvian Indians is particularly desperate, and Toledo grew up in a shack without running water or electricity. Nonetheless, he proved an extremely bright student and was allowed to enroll in high school. There two American Peace Corps volunteers encouraged him to study in the United States after graduating, and in 1962 he attended the University of San Francisco to study economics. Very focused, his good grades won him a fellowship from the Ford Foundation, after which he gained admittance to prestigious Stanford University. Toledo did well academically, and he received a Ph.D. in economics. He then completed a stint teaching at Harvard University before moving back Peru in 1994. Back home he founded the Perú Posible party and ran for the presidency against the incumbent ALBERTO FUJIMORI. Toledo conducted an ethnically oriented campaign, calling upon fellow Indians to feel pride in their heritage and vote for change. However, Fujimori won resoundingly, although his second term in office sowed the seeds of his own political denouement.

In 2000 Toledo decided to run against Fujimori again, especially after allies in Congress altered the constitution to permit him a third term. Again, Toledo declared his pride in his Indian heritage, but this time he carefully remodel his campaign to attract broader-based appeal. In april 2000 Toledo finished second, close enough to require a runoff that May. But, during this interval, Toledo's supporters cited growing awareness of widespread voter fraud by Fujimori's well-placed political operatives. The challenger then asked the Peruvian high court to postpone the election, but he was denied. Consequently, on May 23, 2000, five days before the election, Toledo struck his tent and boycotted the process. Fujimori went on to win his third term in office while thousands of Toledo's supporters took to the street in protest. His victory proved short-lived, however. By November a series of scandals erupted that induced Fujimori to resign from office and flee to Japan. An interim government was then installed until new presidential elections could be held in April 2001. Toledo acquired the most votes but was obliged to face a runoff against former president Alán García Pérez (1985–90). Campaigning on a platform to install a "market economy with a human face," Toledo won 53 percent of the vote on June 3, 2001. He thus became the first Peruvian president of Indian descent. However, the Peru Posible Party only captured 26 percent of the seats in congress, so the new president was forced to work with an entrenched opposition.

Once empowered, Toledo faced the enormous task of addressing the nation's acute poverty. "Together we share a dream that Peru be a more just country with more jobs, social justice, and without corruption," he proclaimed. "I want to open my arms to all people of all bloods to construct a Peru for all." This will prove to be an extremely tall order, as 54 percent of the population lives below the poverty line, with 17 percent of these in extreme poverty. Such gross deprivation and hopelessness have spawned two violent and radical guerrilla movements, the Shining Path and Tupac Amaru, who were only recently suppressed. Therefore, the new leader promised to establish an agrarian bank, reduce the national debt, fight corruption, and reform the judiciary. He commenced on a high note by replacing all military officers appointed by Fujimori to the defense and interior ministries with civilians. Furthermore, Toledo is also committed to reducing Peru's notorious role in the drug trade by discouraging cultivation of coca, from which cocaine is derived and shipped to the United States. "My country does not ask for alms but investment to substitute those cocaine-producing crops with agricultural products, which can give an added value to the agriculture, both for the domestic market and for the exports," he said. Toledo also called upon neighboring South American presidents to suspend purchases of offensive military weapons to save money and redirect it toward their own poor.

To date, Toledo has made scant progress delivering upon his many promises. The moribund economy grew a modest 3.9 percent in 2001, but the government has been slow providing new jobs and wage increases to assist the average Peruvian. Consequently, because of mounting impatience for change, his approval rating has dipped to only 25 percent. This was one reason why U.S. president GEORGE W. BUSH visited Peru in March 2002 as a show of support for the nation's successful transition to democracy. Ominously, three days before he arrived, a terrorist bomb exploded outside the U.S. embassy in Lima, killing nine people and injuring 40. No group claimed responsibility, but Peruvian authorities fear this attack might signal a resurgence of activity by the Shining Path guerrillas. It would appear that the eradication of poverty in Peru is more essential than ever if its fragile democracy is to survive and thrive.

Further Reading

Gorriti Ellenbogess, Gustavo. *The Shining Path: A History of the Millenarian War in Peru.* Chapel Hill: University of North Carolina, Press 1999.

Herz, Monica, and Joao Pontes Nogueira. *Ecuador vs Peru: Peace Making Amid Rivalry.* Boulder, Colo.: Lynne Rienner Publishers, 2002.

Klaren, Peter J. *Peru: Society and Nationhood in the Andes.* New York: Oxford University Press, 2000.

Roberts, Kenneth M. *Deepening Democracy: The Modern Left and Social Movements in Chile and Peru.* Stanford, Calif.: Stanford University Press, 1999.

Schonwalder, Gerd. *New Ways of Making Politics: Popular Movements, the Left, and Local Government in Peru.* University Park: Pennsylvania State University Press, 2002.

Tosovsky, Josef (1950–   ) *prime minister of the Czech Republic*

Josef Tosovsky was born on September 28, 1930 in Nachod, Czechoslovakia. He attended the Prague School of Economics and received his degree in 1973. Tosovsky commenced his financial career with the Czechoslovak State Bank, which, under the Communist government, was closely controlled by the state apparatus. Between 1977 and 1980, he visited France and Great Britain to study Western banking practices, and he became convinced of the superiority of free-market economics. His appointment as head of the London branch of the Zivnostenska Banka in 1984 gave him additional opportunity to inculcate the nuances of free trade, and he began questioning the viability of the command-economy system. Thus, by the time the Communist government of Czechoslovakia was peacefully overthrown in November 1989, Tosovsky had a well-deserved reputation as an opposition leader. Soon after he struck up cordial relations with dissident playwright VÁCLAV HAVEL, the new president, who appointed him governor of the Czechoslovakian State Bank. As governor he also acquired a favorable reputation abroad, and he served as a governor in the International Monetary Fund (IMF). In 1993 Czechoslovakia divided into two separate entities, the Czech Republic and Slovakia. The separation proved peaceful and the Czechs enjoyed political stability through the presence of two strong-willed executives, Václav Havel as president and VÁCLAV KLAUS as prime minister. For the next few years the nation also enjoyed unprecedented economic growth and was viewed by many as a model for privatization and economic liberalization.

The Czech bubble finally burst in 1995. Inflation reached 10 percent a year, while the banking system, which had routinely absorbed bad loans, suffered cash shortages. Once banks began failing, the economy sputtered, and Tosovsky squarely blamed Prime Minister Klaus for failing to adequately regulate financial centers. Worse, in November 1997 it became known that Klaus had acquired a secret Swiss bank account worth $5 million. This money apparently came in the form of contributions from his Civic Democratic Party supporters in return for political favors, and the revelations forced the combative Klaus to resign from office. Reform-minded President Havel now faced a difficult situation. A strong proponent of privatization, he realized that the next round of national elections would probably be won by the opposition Social Democrats (former Communists) who looked askance at the practice and would probably stop it. Havel needed to find an interim leader who would support the drive toward privatization, yet pass muster with various leaders of his coalition. On December 16, 1997, he nominated Tosovsky, a banker with no political background, to serve as prime minister. The choice proved fortuitous as the urbane executive was not associated with any party, untouched by scandal, and could be counted on to support free-market reforms. Despite objections from Klaus, Tosovsky was sworn in to office on the following day. "I have accepted the post of government head for a transitional period," he announced, "to pave the way for early legislative elections."

The new prime minister realized he had only six or seven months before new elections arrived, and he determined not to preside over a mere caretaker government. In January 1998 he passed the Banking Act, which restricted banks from holding more than 15 percent of any nonfinancial business. It also prevented bankers from sitting on the boards of these industries in a move to stop insider trading. He next orchestrated the breakup and sale of the four largest banks in the country in an effort to attract foreign investors. Concurrently, Tosovsky took measures to restore public confidence in government by reforming the rules of party finance and making officials more accountable. By the time elections took place in July 1998, much useful ground had been covered for facilitating privatization. As predicted, the Social Democrats were swept into power, and Tosovsky resigned in favor of a new prime minister, MILOŠ ZEMAN.

After leaving office, Tosovsky returned as governor of the Czech National Bank. He resigned on November 3, 2000, to become chairman of the Financial Stability Unit of the Bank of International Settlements in Basel, Switzerland. He timed his departure so as to grant President Havel a chance to appoint his successor before a new law, designed to grant more government control over banking issues, took effect on January 1, 2001. Curiously, the statute was drawn up by their mutual antagonist Václav Klaus. Moreover, the appointment of Zdenek Tuma as the new bank governor also drew the ire of President Zeman, who refused to endorse him and referred the entire issue to the constitutional court.

Further Reading

Bodo, Robert S. "The Czecho-Slovak Division in Midst of European Integration." Unpublished master's thesis, Harvard University, 1996.

Innes, Abby. *Czechoslovakia: The Short Goodbye.* New Haven, Conn.: Yale University Press, 2001.

Kopecky, Petr. *Parliaments in the Czech and Slovak Republics: Party Competition and Parliamentary Institutionalization.* Burlington, Vt.: Ashgate, 2001.

Krause, Kevin D. "Accountability and Party Competition in Slovakia and the Czech Republic." Unpublished Ph.D. dissertation, University of Notre Dame, 2000.

Orenstein, Mitchell A. *Out of the Red: Building Capitalism and Democracy in Post-Communist Europe.* Ann Arbor: University of Michigan Press, 2001.

Trajkovski, Boris (1956–) *president of Macedonia*

Boris Trajkovski was born in Strumica, Macedonia, on June 25, 1956. Landlocked Macedonia was then a constituent state of the six-republic federation of Yugoslavia, to which it belonged since the end of World War II. As such it was governed by a communist-style dictatorship and regarded as the poorest region of the federation. Following the death of Marshal Tito (Josip Broz) in 1980, Yugoslavia experienced increasing separatist pressures from the distinct ethnic minorities composing it. Consequently, the first multiparty elections were held in

December 1990, and a new Macedonian national assembly was then divided up between various parties, including ex-Communists. Macedonia did not originally seek separation from the Yugoslavian federation, but once the latter splintered along ethnic lines the nation had no choice. On September 9, 1991, political independence was confirmed by a public referendum, and two months later a new constitution was adopted establishing Macedonia as a republic. Now it is governed by a popularly elected president, who presides over a national assembly. In contrast with its northern neighbors, Macedonia's transition to democracy proved uneventful, but its domestic tranquillity was soon upended by fighting in neighboring Kosovo. A mass influx of refugees resulted, and this potentially pitted the majority Macedonian population against its sizable (21 percent) Albanian minority.

Unlike the vast majority of Macedonians, who conform to the Eastern, or Greek Orthodox Church, Trajkovski was born into a Methodist household. As such he

Boris Trajkovski *(Embassy of the Republic of Macedonia)*

attended the University of St. Cyril and Methodius in Skopje, where he studied business law. Trajkovski is also distinguished in being fluent in English, and he is a longtime member of the Macedonian American Friendship Association. As a conservative, he became a member of the Internal Macedonian Revolutionary Organization (VMRO), a center-right party. He first entered politics in 1997 by working as an official in the mayor's office at Kisela Voda. Within a year he attracted the attention of VMRO officials, who appointed him deputy minister of foreign affairs. In this position he was quick to criticize NATO for paying too much attention to the ongoing crisis in Kosovo, while ignoring the dangers the tensions there posed to Macedonia. Two years later Trajkovski felt emboldened to run for the presidency under the VMRO banner and won in the second round of voting. This was accomplished by attracting the support of the country's ethnic Albanian sector, to which he was politically indebted. Trajkovski then replaced KIRO GLIGOROV in November 1999, representing the first of a new generation of political leaders born after World War II. Mindful of Yugoslavia's ongoing strife, he declared: "I will not allow ethnic hatred, chauvinism, and intolerance to destroy the stability of the country."

As president, Trajkovski faces the problem of invigorating the moribund Macedonian economy, which is primarily based upon agriculture and mineral exports. Progress is essential for Macedonia has determined to enter the European Union (EU) once it has developed to requisite levels. Trajkovski also wishes to enhance national security by becoming a full-fledged member of NATO, Meanwhile, given the volatility of the Balkan region, he has been careful to seek good relations with all his former Yugoslavian consorts, along with neighboring Greece and Bulgaria. Trajkovski is also firmly committed to a platform that enshrines continuing democracy and human rights. "I believe that we will succeed in making Macedonia a stable and prosperous democratic country with a high level of respect for human rights and freedoms," he insisted, "and a high standard of living for all citizens."

The biggest crisis facing Trajkovski's administration proved not of his own making. When Serbian dictator SLOBODAN MILOŠEVIĆ instituted repressive measures against the majority the Albanian population of the province of Kosovo in 1999, the ensuing combat forced an estimated 300,000 Albanian refugees to migrate to Macedonia. Under pressure from the West, the border was opened to them, but discontent gave rise to a guerrilla-inspired separatist movement. This happened following a February 2001 treaty between Macedonia and Yugoslavia, which fixed their respective borders at Albanian Kosovo's expense. Armed refugees then began attacking Macedonian police and security forces within their sector, which prompted a harsh response from the government. NATO leaders subsequently feared that if fighting destabilized Macedonia, the conflict might spill over to Greece or Bulgaria, further fanning the flames of ethnic hatred. However, despite much criticism from hard-liners within his own party, Trajkovski went easy on the guerrillas and initiated peace talks with them. In August 2001 a treaty was signed with the separatists requiring them to disarm and disband in exchange for a complete amnesty. A contingent of 4,500 NATO troops, neutral as far as the rebels were concerned, would be established to facilitate their surrender. Furthermore, Trajkovski approached the National Assembly to authorize greater local autonomy for regions of the country dominated by ethnic Albanian majorities. The truce currently holds and, in January 2002, parliament passed the requested legislation. In return for helping to diffuse a potential disaster, the European Union has pledged to give Trajkovski millions of dollars in financial and technical assistance. Macedonia is thus well positioned to recover from its recent crisis, and NATO has already begun to downsize its presence in the country.

Further Reading

Ackermann, Alice. *Making Peace Prevail: Preventing Violent Conflict in Macedonia.* Syracuse, N.Y.: Syracuse University Press, 2000.

Cowan, Jane K. *Macedonia: The Politics of Identity and Difference.* London: Pluto, 2000.

Fackler, Deon J. "The Albanian Question in Macedonia and Its Implications for Balkan Stability." Unpublished master's thesis, University of Washington, 1997.

Pettifer, James. *The New Macedonian Question.* Basingstoke, England: Palgrave, 2001.

Roudometof, Victor. *The Macedonian Question: Culture, History, Politics.* Boulder, Colo.: East European Monographs, 2000.

Trimble, David (1944–) *first minister of Northern Ireland*

William David Trimble was born on October 15, 1944, in Belfast, Northern Ireland, into a middle-class Protestant family. He studied law at Queen's University in Belfast, graduated in 1968, and was admitted to the bar of Northern Ireland the following year. However, he did not engage in legal practice, preferring instead to serve as a lecturer in law at Queen's University, where he remained until 1990. Northern Ireland compromises six counties mandated to remain under British rule as a Protestant-dominated enclave in 1920. The South's refusal of similar status led to establishment of an independent Republic of Ireland in 1922. Catholics, who comprise the minority in the north, have been frequently discriminated against and remain the objects of harassment and murder. The Irish Republican Army (IRA), a guerrilla group, is determined to forcibly unite Northern Ireland with the Irish republic. Their activities, coupled with the rise of Protestant militarism, have left the province awash in sectarian violence and death.

Trimble first became politically active when he joined Vanguard, an extreme Protestant umbrella group determined to deny Catholics civil rights or participation in government. However, by 1978 he gravitated toward the Ulster Unionist Party (UUP), another hard-line group less disposed toward violence. As honorary secretary of the UUP, Trimble acquired a well-deserved reputation for loyalism to the Protestant cause and his abject refusal to deal with the IRA, whom he branded as terrorists. Like many Unionists, he strongly denounced the 1985 Anglo-Irish Agreement, which allowed Catholics a minor voice in provincial governance. In 1990 Trimble won election to Parliament from Upper Bann, where he worked stridently against further accommodation with either Catholics or the Irish republic. His strident opposition to compromise made him a permanent fixture in the Protestant Orange Order and its numerous rallies and marches through Catholic neighborhoods. By 1993, the tempo of peace talks between Britain, Ireland, and the IRA increased with the Downing Street Declaration, which allowed Sinn Féin, the political arm of the IRA, to participate in future talks. Such concessions infuriated the militant Protestants, and in 1995 Trimble's stridency against compromise resulted in his election as leader of the UUP. Because of his established opposition to negotiations, Trimble's presence in upcoming negotiations was viewed as a blow to the peace process.

The turning point in Northern Ireland peace talks occurred in 1996, when U.S. senator George Mitchell managed to persuade all the feuding parties to establish a viable dialogue. Trimble initially balked, but he finally relented at the urging of John Hume, leader of the Social Democratic and Labour Party, a moderate Catholic party. Trimble, however, utterly refused to have any direct contact with GERRY ADAMS, who represented Sinn Féin at the talks. Intense discussions lasted fruitlessly for two years until British prime minister TONY BLAIR established a deadline of April 9, 1998, at which point the effort would end. The urgency to reach accord was underscored by a spate of violent deaths, but it was not until April 10—17 hours after the deadline—that a decision was finally reached. Under the terms of the so-called Good Friday Agreement, Northern Ireland was to remain a British province, but governed by its own assembly. Furthermore, Catholics could now run for office, and closer economic and cultural links with the Irish republic were also encouraged, although claims to the province were renounced. The plan was overwhelmingly passed in both Ireland and Northern Ireland, and it represented the best prospect for peace yet devised. Trimble, for his part, was then elected first minister of Northern Ireland, but many of his former associates in the Orange movement considered him a traitor. In 1998 both he and Hume were awarded the Nobel Peace Prize.

To further promote chances for peace, Trimble finally met with Adams over the prospects of the IRA decommissioning its weapons. This was the first time that Protestants from the north and Catholics from the south had met face to face since 1922. The two men refused to shake hands, but Sinn Féin went on record as supporting IRA disarmament. However, over the ensuing four years the IRA consistently balked at the prospect of laying down its arms. Moreover, concessions were made by the UUP and Orangemen to stop marching through Catholic neighborhoods, provoking violent confrontations. By 2000 the Good Friday Agreement appeared all but dead, and at one point Trimble resigned as first minister because of the IRA's recalcitrance. That March he was only narrowly reelected first minister, which also underscores Loyalist discontent with his peace efforts. Sectarian violence continues between Catholics and Protestants throughout Northern Ireland. In July 2002 a large riot was directed against the police when they tried to stop Orangemen from marching through Catholic neighborhoods, and Trimble condemned the instigators. "The injuries that have been inflicted on the police cannot be supported," he declared, "and we hope there's no more incidents of this nature." The bloody impasse continues.

Further Reading

Cochrane, Feargal. *Unionist Politics and the Politics of Unionism since the Anglo-Irish Agreement.* Cork, Ireland: Cork University Press, 2001.

Godson, Dean. *Himself Alone: The Life of David Trimble.* London: HarperCollins, 2000.

Mac Ginty, Roger. *Guns and Government: The Management of the Northern Ireland Peace Process.* New York: Palgrave, 2002.

McDonald, Henry. *Trimble.* London: Bloomsbury, 2001.

Neuheiser, Jorg, and Stefan Wolff. *Peace at Last? The Impact of the Good Friday Agreement in Northern Ireland.* New York: Berghan Books, 2002.

Nic Craith, Mairend. *Culture and Identity Politics in Northern Ireland.* New York: Palgrave Macmillan, 2003.

Reynolds, Andrew. "A Constitutional Pied Piper: The Northern Irish Good Friday Agreement." *Political Science Quarterly* 114, no. 4 (1999–2000): 613–637.

Trovoada, Miguel (1936–) *president of São Tomé and Príncipe*

Miguel Anjos da Cunha Trovoada was born on December 27, 1936, on São Tomé Island. His homeland, in concert with the neighboring island of Príncipe, then constituted a colony with the Portuguese Empire. São Tomé and Príncipe had first been settled by Portugal in the late 15th century as a staging area for the colonization of West Africa. As such they were inhabited mainly by African slaves, imported to work the sugar fields, and European overseers. Over time the two cultures blended into a large, Portuguese-speaking creole population. It is Africa's second-smallest nation after the Seychelles Islands, and is dominated by an agrarian-based, export economy. São Tomé and Príncipe acquired local autonomy in 1973, but the following year they gained political independence after leaders of a left-wing coup in Portugal renounced all colonial possessions. The country's first leader was Dr. Manuel Pinto da Costa, who was an East German–trained economist and head of the exiled Movement for the Liberation of São Tomé and Príncipe (MLSTP). As such he imposed a strict socialized economic order on the island, nearly ruining it. After 15 years of political disenchantment, popular pressure forced the government to accept a new constitution in 1989 along with multiparty elections. The system of government makes provision for a legislative assembly, a president, and a prime minister. However, in a potentially ruinous oversight, the constitution allows two ways of filling the latter office: the prime minister is either elected by the popular vote or appointed by the president; however, there also exists a clause mandating that the selection come from whichever party holds sway in parliament. This inherent contradiction has encouraged continuing political instability on the islands, and a frequent change of governments.

Trovoada was educated locally and in Angola, and in 1957 he gained admittance to the University of Lisbon. There he met and befriended Da Costa and together they helped found the MLSTP in exile. In 1961 Trovoada set up a political office in Gabon to solicit aid to secure independence for all of the Portuguese colonies. For the next 15 years he served as the party's foreign affairs representative and in 1972 the movement received recognition from the Organization of African Unity (OAU). Trovoada then returned home after the 1974 Portuguese revolution, whereupon Da Costa, the nation's first president, appointed him prime minister.

Trovoada enjoyed a stormy relationship with Da Costa, and the two disagreed over the extent of socialism needed in São Tomé and Príncipe. Their differences resulted in Trovoada's dismissal from office in 1979 and exile in Paris. However, as economic conditions on the island worsened, and the MLSTP was forced to accept multiparty elections, Trovoada returned home and ran for the presidency after Da Costa resigned. On March 3, 1991, he defeated several challengers by an impressive 81 percent of votes cast and was sworn in as São Tomé and Príncipe's second president. Once installed, Trovoada was tasked with cleaning up the economic mess left behind by his predecessor. Consistent with guidelines established by the International Monetary Fund (IMF) and World Bank, he set about shrinking the government bureaucracy, establishing free-market principles, and liberalizing various sectors of the state-controlled economy. The economy responded only sluggishly, unfortunately, being overwhelmingly dependent upon cocoa exports and beset by declining world prices. Consequently, in 1994 Trovoada's Democratic Convergence Party (PCD) lost additional seats in the National Assembly. On August 15, 1995, both the president and his prime minister, Carlos da Graca, were overthrown in a bloodless coup, only to be restored shortly after. Also, adversarial relations with various individuals led to the appointment and reappointment of no less than six prime ministers over the years. But, despite his lackluster performance in office, Trovoada ran again for the presidency, and, on June 30, 1996, he trounced Da Costa by 52 percent to 48 percent. His victory seemed to seal the fate of Marxist-style socialist rule as practiced by his mentor.

By the late 1990s, the economy of São Tomé and Príncipe began reviving under free-market reforms, but the nation still remains overwhelmingly committed to agricultural exports. In fact, the islands have been beset by corruption, poor planning, and economic stagnation ever since they achieved independence. Only the recent discovery of significant offshore oil deposits holds the promise for additional revenues. The islands also remain greatly dependent upon foreign aid and international donors for assistance, which has led to some curious in foreign policy. In 1997 Trovoada, without consulting the National Assembly, recognized the government of Taiwan. Although this resulted in severance of relations with mainland China, Taiwan gratefully supplied the islands with increased amounts of aid. In 2001 Trovoada had served the constitutionally mandated limited of two consecutive terms and prepared to step down. Elections held in July 2001 made Fradique Melo de Menezes, a wealthy cocoa exporter, the new president with 65 percent of the vote.

Further Reading

Eyzaguirre, Pablo B. "Small Farmers and Estates in São Tomé, West Africa." Unpublished Ph.D. dissertation, Yale University, 1995.

Hodges, Tony, and Malyn Newitt. *São Tomé and Príncipe: From Colony to Microstate.* Boulder, Colo.: Westview Press, 1988.

Mayer, Jean. "Development Problems and Prospects in Portuguese-Speaking Africa." *International Labour Review* 129 (July–August 1990): 459–479.

Seibert, Gerhard. *Comrades, Clients, and Cousins: Colonialism, Socialism, and Democratization in São Tomé and Príncipe.* Leiden, Netherlands: Leiden University, 1999.

Shaw, Caroline S. *São and Príncipe.* Santa Barbara, Calif.: ABC-Clio, 1994.

Tudjman, Franjo (1922–1999) *president of Croatia*

Franjo Tudjman was born on May 14, 1922, in Veliko Trgoviste, Croatia, the son of a landlord. He was a

Communist sympathizer in his youth and during World War II sided with Josip Broz, Marshal Tito against both German invaders and their Croatian fascist allies, the Ustashe. After the war Tito welded the six republics of Yugoslavia into a Communist-dominated federation. Tudjman, having distinguished himself as a soldier, remained in the army and rose steadily through the ranks. By 1960 he was the military's youngest general, but Tudjman decided to quit the service in 1961 and pursue history. For the next six years he directed the Institute for the History of the Labor Movement of Croatia, and in 1965 he also received his doctorate in history from the University of Zadar. Around this time Tudjman had also grown dissatisfied with the Serbian-dominated Communist Party, and he began speaking out on behalf of Croatian rights. Such political deviance was not allowed, and in 1972, 1981, and 1984, he was sentenced to prison for antiparty activities. This only stoked the fires of nationalism, and Tudjman's historical writings sought to expunge Croatians for their alleged atrocities during World War II. This garnered him condemnation from Serbian intellectuals, but he was fast becoming a national spokesman for long-suppressed Croatian nationalist sentiments. Once his passport was restored in 1987, he ventured abroad to solicit support and funding from Croatian emigrés. In 1989, when the rapidly crumbling Yugoslavian Federation hosted its first free elections, Tudjman and his ultranationalist Croatian Democratic Union (HDZ) won handily. In 1990 parliament named him the first president in Croatian history, an act that set his nation on a collision course with Serbia—and history.

Croats and Serbs have a long history of mutual antipathy and Tudjman, like SLOBODAN MILOŠEVIĆ of Serbia, was not above fanning the flames of ethnic hatred to advance his agenda. When Croatia declared its independence from Yugoslavia on June 25, 1991, it triggered an internecine civil war with Serbia, which sought to claim large tracts of Serb-dominated land for itself. Backed by the Serb-dominated Yugoslavian army, the Croatian Serbs attacked Croatian settlements in an effort to expand. Tudjman, although his forces were being roughly handled in the field, sought international recognition—and military assistance—from abroad. Germany was the first nation to recognize the breakaway republic and the Germans began supplying their old ally with the latest in weapons. Heavy fighting between 1991–92 resulted in the capture of 30 percent of Croatia's territory, but Milo-

šević erred grossly by expanding the conflict into neighboring Bosnia-Herzegovina. This gave Tudjman's forces time to consolidate, rearm and retrain. In 1995 they committed a surprise offensive against the Serbs of Krajina and Western Slavonija, who were promptly driven out. Tudjman proved as adept an exponent of "ethnic cleansing" as Milošević, for an estimated 450,000 Serbian refugees were forcibly removed from their homes and deported. By the time the Dayton Peace Accords were finally signed among Croatia, Serbia, and Bosnia-Herzegovina, Tudjman had achieved most of his stated goals: an independent state with very few Serbs living within its boundaries. For his ruthlessness in securing Croatian survival in the bloody Balkan conflict, he was easily reelected president by direct vote in August 1992 and October 1997.

Despite his success in waging war, Tudjman was widely criticized abroad for authoritarian tendencies. The press was severely restricted, media was closely controlled by the state, and political dissent barely tolerated. His regime deliberately concentrated all power in the hands of a small oligarchy, especially members of his own family, who profited immensely. Moreover, he directed the historical rehabilitation of the fascist Ustashe regime of 1940–45 by reintroducing its currency, adopting its flag, and reinterring its soldiers with military honors. Tudjman was also careful to cultivate cooperative foreign relations, and in October 1996 Croatia gained admittance to the Council of Europe, and the following year he won support from the World Bank and the International Monetary Fund (IMF). The influx of foreign investment, coupled with adoption of a new, free-market economy, gave the national economy a boost and helped stabilize the situation at home. By the time Tudjman died on December 11, 1999, his dream of an independent Croatia had become a reality, but not a single head of state from the European Union attended his funeral. He continues to be hailed as the father of his country, but the voters grew less enchanted by his political legacy. On January 27, 2000 they elected STJEPAN MESIĆ their new president, who campaigned on a platform of not only celebrating independence but also bequeathing democracy to his people.

Further Reading

Bass, W. "The Triage of Dayton." *Foreign Affairs* 77 (September–October 1998): 95–108.

Lukic, Reneo. "Serb-Croat Relations after the Political Changes in Croatia and Serbia." *Etudes internationales* 32 (September 2001): 525–543

Miller, Robert F. "Tudjman's Victory: Croatia, the U.N., NATO, and the United States." *Nationalist Papers* 25, no. 3 (1997): 501–514.

Tanner, Marcus. *Croatia: A Nation Forged in War.* New Haven, Conn.: Yale University Press, 1999.

Uzelak, Gordana. "Franjo Tudjman's Nationalist Ideology." *East European Quarterly* 31, no. 4 (1997): 449–472.

Tutu, Desmond (1931–) *South African religious leader*

Desmond Mpilo Tutu was born on October 7, 1931, in Klerksdorp, Transvaal, South Africa, the son of a schoolmaster. He aspired to study medicine but, because his family could not afford medical school, he settled upon a teaching career. Like many Africans in race-conscious South Africa, Tutu was raised in relative poverty and squalor, conditions that led to his contracting tuberculosis as a child. He missed nearly two years of school while recuperating, but his life indelibly changed by becoming acquainted with Father Trevor Huddleston. Huddleston, a white Anglican missionary, opposed South Africa's racial policies, and he brought Tutu books along with encouragement to study. Such kindness induced Tutu to seriously consider joining the clergy, although he finally decided to pursue teaching. He graduated from the Bantu Normal School in 1954 just as the South African regime began enforcing its rigid policies of racial separation, apartheid. This entailed creation of distinct "homelands" for resident black Africans, along with decidedly inferior social services and standards of living. Tutu taught under such unequal conditions until 1958, when he finally resigned in disgust and joined the Anglican church as a minister. After passing through the theological college in Johannesburg in 1961, he quickly acquired the reputation as a feisty, outspoken cleric, full of energy and defiance. The following year he gained admittance into the prestigious University of London for graduate study, where he took his wife and four children. The relative freedoms enjoyed there only underscored Tutu's determination to affect change at home after returning in 1968. "I am not interested in picking crumbs of compassion thrown from the table of someone who considers himself to be my master," he once told reporters, "I want the full menu of rights."

Tutu spent several years catering to his poverty-stricken charges until 1976, when he penned an open letter to Prime Minister John Vorster, demanding the dismantling of apartheid and the "homelands" system. In light of his excellent theological precepts, he was also made bishop of Lesotho that year. From this new and more visible pulpit, Tutu solidified his credentials as one of the most strident critics of the apartheid government. In 1977 he delivered the funeral oration at the burial of Steve Biko, an antigovernment activist who died in police custody. But rather than seek revenge, Tutu insisted upon change through nonviolent protest. He was also keen to couch his criticism of apartheid in biblical scripture and thus he appealed to all Christians of conscience, white and black alike. "If Christ returned to South Africa today he would almost certainly be detained under the present security laws," he emoted, "because of his concern for the poor, the hungry, and the oppressed." In 1980 Tutu ventured abroad to castigate Western countries for propping up the oppressive regime, and he demanded imposition of economic sanctions against South Africa. He proved particularly hostile to U.S. president Ronald Reagan's policy of "constructive engagement," which he considered a euphemism for "friendly persuasion." Consequently, Tutu's visa was revoked and he was not allowed out of the country for several years. Nonetheless, his ceaseless efforts to seek justice through nonviolence impressed world leaders, and in 1984 he received the Nobel Peace Prize. Shortly after, he gained election as bishop of Johannesburg, the second highest-ranking position in the Anglican church. The following year he advanced to archbishop of Cape Town, making him the senior Anglican cleric in South Africa. Tutu was also the first black African so honored.

Apartheid finally unraveled on April 27, 1994, when the white government allowed free, multiracial elections that resulted in NELSON MANDELA becoming president. Mandela, who had been released from prison through the intercession of President FREDERIK W. DE KLERK, appointed Tutu chair of the new Truth and Reconciliation Commission. This body was convened to collect evidence from both the victims and enforcers of apartheid, exact confessions, and promote national healing. The hearings were emotionally charged and acrimonious, testing Tutu's peacemaking abilities to their utmost. However, this public airing of grievances, and acts of contrition by many white security officers, has contributed to the growing sense of calm and normalcy characterizing South Africa's fledgling democracy. Tutu has since retired from active church work, having been sidelined by surgery for prostate cancer in 1999. However, he remains on the sidelines, outspoken as always, and quick to point out shortcomings in the South African government's attempt to end poverty. "People can wake up in the squalor of Khayelitsha and work in the heart of all the affluence of Cape Town," he angrily declared, "and at the end of the day leave that and return to that squalor." In June 2002 Tutu also angered Jewish lobbies around the world by calling for an end to apartheid-like conditions in Palestine, and for imposition of trade sanctions against Israel. He has been denounced for deliberately ignoring acts of terrorism against the Jewish state, and he subsequently conceded that "Israel is certainly more democratic than most of its neighbors."

Never one to skirt controversy, the diminutive, energetic Tutu remains South Africa's leading moral authority, and a spokesman for those desperately in need.

Further Reading

Battle, Michael. *The Wisdom of Desmond Tutu.* Louisville, Ky.: Westminster John Knox Press, 2000.

Christie, Kenneth. *The South African Truth Commission.* New York: St. Martin's Press, 2000.

Deegan, Heather. *The Politics of the New South Africa: Apartheid and After.* New York: Longman, 2001.

Mungazi, Dickson A. *In the Footsteps of the Masters: Desmond M. Tutu and Abel T. Muzorewa.* Westport, Conn.: Greenwood Press, 2000.

Pieterse, Hendrik J. C. *Desmond Tutu's Message: A Qualitative Analysis.* Boston: Brill, 2001.

Tutu, Desmond. *No Future without Forgiveness.* London: Rider, 2000.

U

Ulufa'alu, Bart (1950–   ) *prime minister of the Solomon Islands*

Bartolomew Ulufa'alu was born in 1950 on the Malaita Island village of Alite'e. Malaita is one of 900 islands and coral atolls that constitute the Solomon Islands, a large volcanic chain lying east of Papua New Guinea and northeast of Australia. They are also home to over 80 distinct cultures and linguistic groups. The Solomons had been known by European explorers since 1568, although they were not colonized until the late 19th century. Rivalry between Germany and Great Britain resulted in most of the Solomons accepting a British protectorate in 1893. The largest island, Guadalcanal, was also the site of some of World War II's most intense fighting between Japanese and U.S. forces in 1942. The islands were devastated by the wartime battles, which subsequently gave rise to a popular movement among islanders to rid themselves of colonialism. Independence, however, was not granted until July 1978. The Solomons, as part of the British Commonwealth, are governed by the usual Westminister parliamentary system. This consists of an elected parliament, from which a prime minister is chosen and who, in turn, selects a cabinet. Unfortunately, the islands' polity is beset by deep-seated linguistic and cultural fissures, and the very notion of "party" denotes rather loose connotations. In fact, members frequently change party affiliation in the course of a year and,

hence, no single party has been able to rule consistently for any length of time. Coalition governments are thus the norm in the Solomons, and there is a considerable turnover of candidates in each election. As such the islands are rife with political instability, which in turn further exacerbates ethnic rivalries and tensions.

Ulufa'alu was educated at various village and missionary schools before attending the University of Papua New Guinea in Port Moresby. There, he established his reputation for radical politics and outspokenness on issues of importance. Ulufa'alu was active in various student movements and organizations, and back home he helped organize the first labor union in the Solomons. He entered the political arena in 1976 as a protégé of Solomon Mamaloni, a legendary politician who served three terms as prime minister. Ulufa'alu served as parliamentary member from East Honiara until 1983, when he joined the administration as finance minister. He served in exemplary fashion, and is still regarded as one of the nation's best accountants. However, he left politics in 1983 to set up a consulting firm and, in 1993, he unsuccessfully ran for a seat in Aoke, Malaita. Ulufa'alu enjoyed better luck in 1997 and was elected to the parliamentary opposition from Aoke. Mamaloni was by that time besieged by allegations of fiscal mismanagement, and the dissatisfaction it incurred set the stage for a new coalition government. In July 1997 a parliamentary ballot for a new prime minister was held and Ulufa'alu won by a mere two votes. He thereupon formed a new coalition under the rubric Alliance for Change.

Since taking office, Ulufa'alu has been preoccupied with ethnic animosity that has spilled over into violence. His background as a person of Malaitan extraction further complicated an already delicate situation. Due to internal migration among the island chain, a large number of Malaitans have settled on Guadalcanal seeking work. This move is deeply resented by the resident natives of Guadalcanal, who fiercely resist granting the newcomers any land rights. Tensions between the two erupted into violence, with one faction forming the Malaita Eagle Forces (MEF) and the other the Isatambu Freedom Fighters (IFF). The instability is further fed and aggravated by events on the neighboring island of Rabaul, which is seeking independence from Papua New Guinea. As fighting intensified, with the loss of about 80 lives, Ulufa'alu was forced to declare a state of emergency in July 1999. The British Commonwealth then intervened by directing a Fijian high official to conduct negotiations between the warring factions while police contingents from Fiji and Vanuatu arrived to help restore order.

As of February 2000, fighting persisted and the government was forced to outlaw membership in either rebel group. But on June 5, 2000, members of the MEF managed to storm Guadalcanal's capital of Honiara and place the prime minister under house arrest. They held Ulufa'alu for four days, demanding his resignation for failing to help fellow Malaitans. He was finally released unharmed after negotiations with government mediators and the promise of a vote of no confidence against the administration by parliament. On June 14, 2000, Ulufa'alu resigned in anticipation of the vote and over the next two weeks a transition government headed by Ade Adefuye of Nigeria ruled the nation. An extraordinary session of parliament then convened for the purpose of selecting a new prime minister, and June 30, 2000, Mannasseh Sogavare was elected by 23 votes to 21. The new leader immediately declared his intention to seek peace with the rebels while continuing his predecessor's basic policies. "My government is committed to bring the Solomon Islands into national unity and reconciliation," he insisted.

Further Reading

Dinnen, Sinlair, I. Scales, and A. J. Regan. *Solomon Islands: Ethnic Tensions and Regional Identities*. London: C. Hurst, 2001.

Finin, Gerard A., and Terrance Wesley-Smith. *Coups, Conflicts, and Crises: The New Pacific Way?* Honolulu, Hawaii: East-West Center, 2000.

Huiding, Edward. *Guardians of Marovo Lagoon: Practice, Place, and Politics in Maritime Melanesia*. Honolulu: University of Hawaii Press, 1996.

MacNeill, Ian. *Sweet Horizons: A History of the Solomon Islands*. St. Kilda West, Australia: Acland Press, 2000.

White, Geoffrey. *The Discourse of Chiefs: Notes on a Melanesian Society*. Honolulu, Hawaii: East West Center, 1995.

Uribe, Álvaro (1952–) *president of Colombia*

Álvaro Uribe Vélez was born on July 4, 1952, in Medellín, Colombia, the son of a rancher. He was an excellent student and in 1978 obtained his master's in political science from the University of Antioquia. Uribe subsequently pursued graduate studies at Harvard University, and in 1998 he was to win a Simon Bolívar Fellowship to teach at Oxford University. A capable young bureaucrat, Uribe was drawn to public service, and in 1976 he headed Medellín's real estate department. After six years of effective work in other fields, he was elected mayor in 1982 and distinguished himself by initiating greatly needed public works. In 1986 he successfully stood for a seat in the Senate and was reelected by wide margins four years later. Uribe gained further renown after becoming governor of Antioquia in 1995, where he effectively reduced the government payrolls, increased services to the poor and underprivileged, and oversaw a massive road construction program. He was also intolerant of crime and took steps to thwart the rising cocaine trade for which his city is infamous. This led to the death of his father in 1983 at the hands of the Revolutionary Armed Force of Colombia (FARC) rebels, along with several assassination attempts. But Uribe survived, becoming more determined than ever to fight drug dealers—and the Marxist guerillas supporting them.

Colombia by now had endured 38 years of guerrilla warfare at the hands of the FARC, a violent group bent on overthrowing the existing political order whose terrorist activities have claimed 38,000 lives. Moreover, FARC deliberately cultivates close times to the drug trade, which provides money in exchange for military protection. In 1998 President ANDRÉS PASTRANA was elected on a peace platform to initiate negotiations with the insurgents, and he even offered them a demilitarized refuge the size of Switzerland. However, talks proceeded fruitlessly for four years amid a spate of bombings, kidnappings, and assassinations, which made the administration look both weak and inept. Uribe, nominally a member of the Liberal Party (PL), had long established his credentials as an efficient administrator, and in 2002 he returned from Oxford declaring his candidacy for the presidency. Seeking bipartisan support, he ran as an independent and solicited support from both Liberals and Conservatives. In February of that year the guerrillas struck close to home, killing several people in the national capital of Bogotá, and kidnapping a female senator. These acts only spurred Uribe's candidacy, and his campaign touted a law and order platform marked by the slogan "Firm Hand, Strong Heart." In fact, it is his stated goal to crack down on drug lords, the leftist guerrillas who support them, and right-wing paramilitary vigilantes who have also committed atrocities. "The main proposal is security with democracy, security for all Colombians," he promised. "I will protect all Colombians regardless of whether attacks come from guerrillas or paramilitaries." His message of toughness, including closer military ties to the United States, proved popular with the war-weary populace. It also exposed him to tremendous danger, for he survived no less than 17 assassination attempts. Nonetheless, on May 27, 2002, Uribe garnered 53 percent of the vote, a clear majority precluding the necessity of a runoff. His closest rival, Liberal candidate Horacio Serpa, received only 32 percent.

Uribe, a diminutive bespeckled technocrat, who looks more at home behind a lectern than as a commander in chief, notified the guerrillas that they can expect the worse from his administration. In concert with President GEORGE W. BUSH, he will be enacting "Plan Colombia," a concerted effort by both governments to crush the insurgency and eliminate drug dealers. This entails the presence of American Special Forces for training purposes, modern helicopters and other equipment, plus creation of two specially trained rapid deployment brigades. Furthermore, Uribe is planning to arm and enroll more than 1 million civilians into an active constabulary to assist the military where possible and patrol the streets in their absence. This is an ambitious plan, underwritten by $440 million in U.S. aid, and the biggest challenge the wily FARC has faced in its bloody history. Success also depends on regional cooperation from countries such as Peru, which has known ties to the drug trade and often tolerates FARC guerrilla bases on its territory. In July 2002 the president-elect met with Venezuelan president HUGO CHÁVEZ to better coordinate their national security efforts. Uribe has also asked the United Nations to broker possible negotiations with the rebels, but these will be pursued only if FARC ceases its terrorism. Failing that, the government's response will be solely a military one.

Uribe took his oath of office on August 7, 2002, and he serves one constitutionally mandated four-year term. It is his earnest desire, and that of Colombia's people, that he leave the country in safer and sounder condition than when he found it. "There is only one path," Uribe maintains, "to work with affection for all our compatriots." The continuing viability of Colombia as a nation hinges upon his ultimate success or failure. To underscore the urgency of his task, on August 7, 2002, during Uribe's inauguration, rebels forces launched a surprise attack during the ceremony, killing 21 people. But far from being intimidated, the new executive remains strongly resolved to eradicating the insurgency. Once in power, he declared a "state of unrest" that allowed him to impose a new war tax and expand the security forces. "Now it is up to you and me," Uribe told his generals, "to work to obtain results."

Further Reading

Buscagalia, Edgardo. *War and Lack of Governance in Colombia: Narcos, Guerrillas, and U.S. Policy.* Stanford, Calif.: Hoover Institution, 2001.

Clawson, Patrick. *The Andean Cocaine Industry.* New York: St. Martin's Press, 1996.

Crandall, Russell. *Driven by Drugs: U.S. Policy toward Colombia.* Boulder, Colo.: Lynne Rienner Publishers, 2002.

Rochlin, James F. *Vanguard Revolutionaries in Latin America: Peru, Colombia, Mexico.* Boulder, Colo.: Lynne Rienner Publishers, 2002.

Ruiz, Bert. *The Colombian Civil War.* Jefferson, N.C.: McFarland, 2001.

V

Vajpayee, Atal Behari (1926–   ) *prime minister of India*

Atal Behari Vajpayee was born in Gwalior, central India, on December 25, 1926, the son of a Hindu scholar and schoolteacher, who was also a member of the ranking Brahmin caste. As a country, India dominates the southern part of the Asian continent, and is home to over 1 billion people. The population is widely divided along linguistic and ethnic lines, with 17 official languages (out of actually 600 spoken). The majority religion is Hindu, which imposes a strict, hereditary caste system upon society, and largely determines their social status. However, roughly 11 percent of the population also subscribes to Islam (nearly 100 million people), which makes India one of the largest Muslim nations in the world. Great Britain colonized India in the mid-18th century and administered it as a crown colony until 1947. That year the subcontinent was roughly partitioned into majority Hindu and Muslim sectors (the basis for present-day India and Pakistan), although sectarian violence flared and took thousands of lives before boundaries were fixed. By 1950 India had adopted a modified parliamentary system that includes a president, prime minister, and bicameral legislature consisting of a Council of States (Rajya Lok) and a House of the People (Lok Sabha). India is presently the world's largest democracy and boasts over 100 political parties, although the principal contenders for power are the centrist Congress Party (CP), the right-wing Indian People's Party (BJP), and the left-wing United Front (UF). Given the fractured nature of the Indian polity, parties rarely rule as a majority and instead seek out partners to govern as a coalition.

As a Brahmin, Vajpayee was able to obtain an excellent education by Indian standards. However, as a teenager he joined the secret National Voluntary Service (RSS), a Hindu nationalist organization agitating for independence from Britain. After spending some time in jail, he subsequently attended Victoria (now Laxmibai) College, and he ultimately acquired a master's degree in political science from Dayanand Anglo-Vedic College. Vajpayee channeled his Hindu nationalism into a journalistic career by editing the RSS newsletter for many years. In 1957 he became head of the new Jana Sangh Party, and he gained election to the House of the People. Five years later Vajpayee was elected to the Council of States, and he served as an opposition member of parliament. In 1975 Prime Minister Indira Gandhi had him arrested during her "state of emergency" against political foes. He was then released to serve as foreign minister until 1980, when he founded the Hindu-oriented BJP party. In 1996 the BJP came close to holding a majority of seats in parliament, and Vajpayee was tapped to serve as prime minister, provided he could find suitable coalition partners. He failed and was forced from office 13 days later. However, new elections held in 1998 catapulted the BJP into the majority, and Vajpayee once again became prime minister. Further elections the following year made him the first Indian prime minister to be sworn in three times since Jawaharlal Nehru. He had since earned a reputation as a master parliamentarian who possesses great skills as a conciliator and consensus builder.

Throughout his tenure in office, Vajpayee has nervously walked a tightrope on several sensitive issues. The first has been India's role as a nuclear power. In May 1998, he decided to flex his country's muscles by authorizing three nuclear tests that were roundly condemned by the world community. Many felt that India, one of the world's poorest countries, would be better off spending money on social programs. These detonations also prompted Pakistan, with whom India has fought three wars, to schedule tests of its own. However, the prime minister was unapologetic. "The decision to carry out these tests was guided by the paramount importance which we attach to national security," he declared. The United States was less impressed and imposed certain technological sanctions on India, which did little to improve relations. The next biggest issue facing Vajpayee, and indeed all of India, was the issue of Hindu extremism. The prime minister himself enjoyed roots as a Hindu nationalist, but has since moderated his stance and distanced himself from more extreme elements within the BJP. The appearance of neutrality was essential, for tensions and hostility between Hindus and Muslims has escalated, especially in the distant state of Kashmir, astride the Pakistani border. In 1999 tensions rose to a point at which Pakistani president PERVEZ MUSHARRAF ordered an invasion of the Kargil region. Vajpayee reacted firmly but cautiously with an increased military presence, which seems to have dissuaded the Pakistanis from advancing farther. Given the traditional antipathy between these two heavily armed nations, the possibility of a nuclear confrontation remains a real possibility.

The September 11, 2001, destruction of New York's World Trade Center only heightened the sense of regional crisis. Vajpayee roundly condemned the act and openly applauded the American war in Afghanistan against Taliban extremists, who were also suspected of arming Kashmiri terrorists. This point was brought home dramatically on December 12, 2001, when a Muslim suicide squad stormed into India's parliament with guns and hand grenades, killing 12 people. Vajpayee singled out Pakistan for providing logistical support to the attackers and mobilized thousands of soldiers on the border. Musharraf denied any culpability for the attack, but both sides seemed braced for all-out war. Fortunately, the United States and other countries managed to keep peace intact, although tensions remain high. Relations were further strained in February 2002, when Muslim extremists stormed and burned an Indian train in Gujarat state, killing 60 people. Enraged Hindus then attacked Muslim villages, leading to the worst sectarian violence in years and at least 800 deaths. Through it all, Vajpayee, the former nationalist, has served as a voice of moderation. He condemned the violence on both sides and has urged restraint by all parties, especially hard-line elements with the BJP. "This insanity cannot be allowed to continued," he declared to a Muslim audience. "The poison of religious violence must be stopped."

In a larger sense, Vajpayee also appealed to neighboring Southeast Asia for greater cooperation in fighting terrorism, ocean piracy, drug smuggling, and religious fanaticism, all of which have the potential for destabilizing the region. He also cautioned his neighbors not to ignore or discount India's security concerns by mere virtue of its vast size. "India's belonging to the Asia Pacific community is a geographical fact and a political reality," he stated. "It does not require formal membership of any regional organization for its recognition or sustenance." The continuing sectarian crises will undoubtedly test the political resiliency of the world's largest democracy for years to come. India's stability also continues to be threatened by ongoing Muslim unrest in Kashmir and Jammu, and Vajpayee places the blame squarely on the Pakistani government. In August 2002, during celebrations marking 55 years of independence from Great Britain, the prime minister accused President Pervez Musharraf of turning a blind eye to terrorist infiltration of India. However, he also struck a conciliatory chord with the residents of the disputed provinces. "I want to assure the people of Jammu and Kashmir that if there have been mistakes, we will correct them," Vajpayee insisted. "There will be discussion on the demand to give greater powers to the state." However, he stridently rules out any attempts at separatism, thereby ensuring continuation of religious strife for the foreseeable future.

Further Reading

Atal, Yogesh. *Mandate for Political Transition: Re-emergence of Vajpayee.* Jaipur: Rawat Publications, 2000.

Gangly, Sumit. *Conflict Unending: Indo-Pakistan Tensions since 1947.* New York: Columbia University Press, 2002.

Jayal, Niraja G., and Sudha Pai. *Democratic Governance in India: Challenges of Poverty, Development, and Identity.* Thousand Oaks, Calif.: SAGE, 2001.

Kux, Dennis. "India's Fine Balance." *Foreign Affairs* 81 (May–June 2002): 93–106.

Menon, Nivedita. *Gender and Politics in India.* Oxford: Oxford University Press, 2001.

Nanda, B. R. *Pan-Islamism, Imperialism, and Nationalism in India.* Oxford: Oxford University Press, 2002.

Venetiaan, Runaldo (1936–) *president of Suriname*

Runaldo Ronald Venetiaan was born on June 18, 1936, in Paramaribo, Dutch Guiana, one of South America's smallest colonies. He was educated locally and subsequently obtained his doctorate in mathematics from the University of Leiden, the Netherlands, in 1964. Venetiaan spent many years teaching math in Paramaribo until 1973, when he was appointed minister of education. He held that post until 1980 and was reappointed in 1987. His homeland, meanwhile, had since gained independence in 1976 as Suriname, although it had enjoyed basic tenets of self-governance since 1945. In 1980 civilian rule was overthrown by Desi Bouterse, a local military figure, who ruled Suriname with an iron fist until 1987. The following year Ramsewak Shankar was elected president for a five-year term by the National Assembly, but in December 1990 he too was ousted by Bouterse. Venetiaan, a man of stubborn conviction, refused to step down as education minister and was forcibly removed from office. New elections were then scheduled for September 1991. By the terms of the Suriname constitution, all presidential candidates must be confirmed by a two-thirds vote in the National Assembly. When no individual received this tally, a People's Assembly, drawn from parliament and all the district and regional councils, was summoned for another vote. Venetiaan was a candidate for the New Front, well known and respected for his work as education minister and untainted by either corruption or violence. On September 6, 1991, the People's Assembly passed his

nomination of a vote of 645 to 166. "I have to assume that by choosing me as president the people have made it clear that they want no military influence in politics," he insisted. "My first concern is to make sure that the people in the military understand this."

Venetiaan inherited a country on the brink of economic and political collapse. Bouterse's rule and that of those who followed him ran up the national debt, which raised interest rates and stalled economic growth. But over the next five years Venetiaan worked assiduously at revaluing the currency, lowering inflation, restoring the health care system, and reducing a government payroll that employed 45 percent of the workforce. He accomplished this through austerity measures that required a measure of pain for the lower and middle classes but eventually restored Suriname to solvency. The nation was also disrupted by an ongoing guerrilla war with the Jungle Commando commanded by Ronnie Brunswijk, a former Bouterse ally. In May 1992 Venetiaan proved instrumental in negotiating the Kourou Accord, which established a cease-fire with Bush Negro tribes in the interior. However, many citizens resented the hardships endured in the name of economic recovery and, following elections in 1996, the National Assembly nominated JULES ALBERT WIJDENBOSCH as president. Venetiaan had nonetheless made history as the first Surinamese president to complete his full five years in office.

The Wijdenbosch administration was characterized by a free-spending approach to governance, and the national debt exploded again. This led to rising prices and a slumping economy while the ever-ambitious Bouterse, now heading the Millennium Combination, hovered ominously in the background. Elections held in May 2000—a year ahead of schedule due to massive protests—returned Venetiaan's New Front coalition to power. "The crisis is big and deep," he explained. "The Wijdenbosch government has left the country with huge problems." After three months of negotiations with other parties, Venetiaan was sworn into his second presidential term on August 12, 2000. Over the past two years he basically repeated his prior performance in office, reducing expenditures to lower the debt and interest rates. He also determined to patch up relations with the Netherlands for economic assistance that had been promised—then withheld. A major sticking point between the two nations was the murder of 15 political dissidents in December 1982. This act was presumably done at the instigation of Bouterse, who also faces drug charges leveled by a Dutch court. He has since been sentenced in absentia to 11 years in prison, but the political establishment, including Venetiaan, declines to extradite him for fear of a coup. The Bush Negro tribes, deep in the interior, have also resumed their guerrilla activities and Surinamese officials routinely confiscate caches of weapons. "I think the police and the army are alert enough to handle any danger," Venetiaan proclaimed, "so it is not right to start panicking." But, as a precaution, the president announced joint military maneuvers with a contingent of Dutch marines in May 2002 amid speculation that Bouterse might be forcibly arrested. Meanwhile, Venetiaan has moved ahead in tackling other problems and conferred with Guyanan president BHARRAT JAGDEO over cooperation in the field of offshore oil exploration. He is expected to remain in office until 2005.

Further Reading

Brana-Shute, Gary. "Suriname: A Military and Its Auxiliaries." *Armed Forces and Society* 22 (Spring 1996): 469–485.

Dew, Edward M. *The Trouble in Suriname, 1975–1993.* Westport, Conn.: Praeger, 1994.

Hoefte, Rosemarijn, and Peter Neel. *Twentieth-Century Suriname: Continuities and Discontinuities in a New World Society.* Kingston, Jamaica: KITLU Press, 2001.

Sedoc-Dahlgberg, Betty Nelly. *The Dutch Caribbean: Prospects for Democracy.* New York: Gordon and Breach, 1990.

West-Duran, Alan, ed. *Blacks in the West Caribbean: A Reference Guide.* Westport, Conn.: Greenwood Press, 2002.

Verhofstadt, Guy (1953–) *prime minister of Belgium*

Guy Verhofstadt was born on April 11, 1953, in the town of Dendermonde. Belgium is a small country situated between France, Germany, and the Netherlands. Although smaller than Switzerland, it has long been regarded as the "Cockpit of Europe" because of its geographic location at the crossroads of traditional invasion routes, and the country has served as the site of many historic battles, such as Waterloo. The Belgian population is sharply divided between the Flemish (Dutch-speaking) north and the Walloon (French-speaking) south, although German speakers are also present in small numbers. It has been ruled as a constitutional monarchy since 1830 and administered by a prime minister and a bicameral legislature consisting of a Senate and a House of Representatives. Like all parliamentary systems, the prime minister is drawn from the party in parliament that has either the most seats or can form a coalition government with other parties. Belgium employs a system of proportional representation that enables even small parties to be seated in parliament if they gain enough votes. However, politics are traditionally divided between the Christian Democrats, the Socialists, and the Liberals. The far-left Green Party and the far-right Vlaams Blok have also made inroads during recent elections. Economically, Belgium is highly advanced, highly industrialized, and enjoys one of the world's highest standards of living. However, because the northern, Flemish-speaking region is roughly twice as rich as the southern, Walloon section, this dichotomy remains a source of considerable friction between them.

Verhofstadt majored in classical studies while in high school, and he developed an interest in Italian culture and opera. In 1975 he graduated from the Rijksuniversiteit with a law degree and moved directly into politics by joining the Liberal (actually conservative) Party. Prior to this, he was active in campus affairs as head of the student Liberal Party, and by 1977 he was serving as secretary to Willy De Clerq, a senior politician of note. Verhofstadt proved himself a quick study in the art of political machination, and by 1982 he was head of the Flemish Liberal Party (which, like all parties, has a Walloon equivalent) at the age of 29. This established him as one of Europe's youngest and most promising politicians. His vocal admiration for British prime minister Margaret Thatcher led opponents to deride him as "Baby Thatcher," owing to his strident belief in free-market economics. From 1985 to 1988 he served in a coalition government as vice prime minister and state budget minister. Twice, in 1991 and 1995, Verhofstadt was called upon by the Liberals to form a coalition government under his aegis, but he was unable to muster the necessary partners. It would appear his political views were then too strident and inflexible to bargain with competing interests. Verhofstadt then took a year off from politics to reside in Italy, where he gained an appreciation for the art of compromise and an awareness of ecology as a political issue. He returned to Belgium a more seasoned, realistic politician than when he left.

In 1997 the Christian Democrats, who had dominated Belgian politics for most of the century, were under close scrutiny for corruption. When a cover-up involving the existence of the toxic substance dioxin in cattle feed surfaced, the government resigned and new elections were held. Surprisingly, the conservative Liberals, the Socialists, and leftist Green Party did rather well, and Verhofstadt managed to craft a coalition among them. His success represented the first time in 41 years that the CD had not been part of the government, even as a coalition partner. More significantly, it was also the first time that the radical Greens had been brought into a viable coalition government, and only the second time in the 20th century that the Liberals claimed the prime ministership. Better prepared now for compromise, Verhofstadt embarked on a program of renewed emphasis on free markets and liberalization of the economy but also, to placate the Greens, he vowed to phase out nuclear power within 15 years. All three parties were determined to stamp out the corruption that had brought down the previous administration and threatened national stability.

Verhofstadt has been uniformly successful in ruling Belgium over the past three years. The economy is booming, and the Flemish and Wallonian parts of the country are in close accord over national affairs. He enjoyed a generally productive terms as president of the European Union (EU), whose chair is open on a rotating basis. Given the nation's small size and catastrophic experience in two world wars, Belgium remains keen on membership in NATO, and the country also seeks closer economic integration by joining the European Monetary Union (EMU). However, one possible point of contention is the rise of right-wing sentiments among the lower classes, and the backlash against immigrant workers this has engendered. In March 2002 the Belgian parliament chose to deny voting rights to non-EU residents in Belgium, even through most of the 15-nation union does in fact accord them such rights. The vote caused considerable strain among the prevailing coalition, as the Socialists and Greens support such rights, while Verhofstadt and his Liberals staunchly oppose them. However, the prime minister is slated to give up his seat as EU president to Spanish prime minister JOSÉ MARÍA AZNAR in 2002. Prior to doing so, he has encouraged his successor to place greater emphasis on social concerns, including workers' rights and education, to narrow the gap between rich and poor nations. "I would call this ethical globalization a triangle of trade, cooperation, and the prevention of conflicts," he insisted. "We need a global, ethical approach to issues such as the environment, working conditions, and monetary policy."

Further Reading

Cook, Bernard. *Belgium: A History.* New York: Peter Lang, 2002.

Fitzmaurice, John. *The Politics of Belgium: A Unique Federation.* London: C. Hurst, 1996.

"Guy Verhofstadt—Belgium's Prime Minister." *The Economist* 361 (October 20, 2001): 52–57.

Lewis, Richard. *The Example of Belgium.* Durham, N.C.: Duke University Press, 1996.

Timmermans, Arco. *High Politics in the Low Countries. Functions Effects of Coalition Agreements in Belgium at the Netherlands.* Burlington, Ut.: Ashgate, 2003.

Vos, Louis, and Kas Deprez, eds. *Nationalism in Belgium: Shifting Identities, 1780–1995.* New York: St. Martin's Press, 1998.

Vieira, João (1939–) *president of Guinea-Bissau*

João Bernardo Vieira was born on April 27, 1939, in Bissau, capital of Portuguese Guinea, a tiny sliver of land sandwiched between Guinea and Senegal. He trained as an electrician but became politically active by 1960 by joining the African Party for the Independence of Guinea and Cape Verde (PAIGC) under noted revolutionary Amilcar Cabral. This was a socialist guerrilla movement dedicated to the overthrow of the colonial regime. Fighting started in 1961 and Vieira quickly established himself as a commander of ability. Known as "Nino," Vieira's fighters eventually overran most of the countryside. After spending some time receiving advanced military training in China, he returned home to accept appointment as vice president of the party war council. As fighting ground on, Vieira was elevated to Secretary-General of PAIGC and also president of the People's National Assembly. Cabral had been assassinated in 1973 and was succeeded by his brother, Luis Cabral, a far less charismatic and skillful leader. By the time independence was achieved in 1974, PAIGC was already beset by internal power struggles. A major factor proved to be resentment toward mixed-race, light-skinned Cape Verdeans, who dominated the party leadership at the expense of mainland black Africans. Vieira, meanwhile, served as head of the military and in 1978 he succeeded Francisco Mendez as prime minister. At this time Cabral sacked Vieira from his military post, feeling he had grown too popular and too powerful. He then staged constitutional reforms that would enhance presidential powers at the expense of the prime minister. By 1980 Guinea-Bissau was also in the throes of a painful economic crisis, so Vieira judged the moment right for a coup. On November 14, 1980, military forces loyal to him arrested Cabral, and he proclaimed himself the new executive.

Once in power, Vieira suspended the constitution, dissolved the national assembly, and ruled through a nine-member revolutionary council consisting entirely of black Africans. He then paid the usual homage to the socialist policies of his predecessors, but he was intent upon changing them. However, over the next five years Vieira grappled with consolidating his control of government and weathered at least four coup attempts. All were defeated and by 1985 he was finally in a position to jettison the discredited economic policies of PAIGC. He worked closely with the World Bank and the International Monetary Fund (IMF) to impose austerity measures at home and thus receive financial aid from abroad. The national currency was also devalued by 41 percent to reduce inflation, which caused considerable social unrest, but led to an improved economic climate. Guinea-Bissau was still officially a one-party state, and in June 1989 Vieira ran unopposed for the presidency and was easily reelected for another five years. However, by this time the cold war was winding down and Guinea-Bissau came under international pressure to allow for multiparty democracy. The president feared that such a move would only serve to open up the country to a resurgence of tribal divisions, and he hesitated. After much hemming and hawing, Vieira finally relented, stating: "We are going to open up the system so that the people can chose the party that works best, but this must not be a tribal party." General elections were again slated for March 1994 and Vieira, as a good indication of his popularity, was reelected by 52 percent of votes cast, beating opposition leader João De Costa.

Guinea-Bissau continues to be one of the world's smallest and poorest nations. It enjoyed an unusual degree of political stability for a West African state, but the system started unhinging after June 1998. At that juncture, President Vieira blamed General Ansumane Mane for conducting gunrunning operations for separatists in southern Senegal. Mane denied the charges and marshaled his forces. A bloody civil war erupted. Vieira, whose corrupt regime had lost significant public support over the years, slowly lost control, and, in May 1999, he was finally overthrown and allowed to flee to Portugal. That October Guinea-Bissau attorney general Amine Saad formally applied for the extradition of Vieira to face charges of corruption and misuse of public funds—he still remains at large. General Mane, meanwhile, permitted new elections in January 2000 and they were won by KUMBA YALÁ of the Social Renewal Party.

Further Reading

Adebajo, Adekeye. *Building Peace in West Africa: Liberia, Sierra Leone, and Guinea-Bissau.* Boulder, Colo.: Lynne Rienner Publishers, 2002.

Forrest, Joshua. *Guinea-Bissau: Power, Conflict, and Renewal in a West African Nation.* Boulder, Colo.: Westview Press, 1992.

Galli, Rosemary, and Jocelyn Jones. *Guinea-Bissau: Politics, Economics, and Society.* Boulder, Colo.: Lynne Rienner Publishers, 1987.

Lobban, Richard, and Peter M. Mendy. *Historical Dictionary of the Peoples of Guinea-Bissau.* Lanham, Md.: Scarecrow Press, 1997.

Lopes, Carlos. *Guinea-Bissau: From Liberation Struggle to Independent Statehood.* Boulder, Colo.: Westview Press, 1987.

Vike-Freiberga, Vaira (1937–) *president of Latvia*

Vaira Vike-Freiberga was born on December 1, 1937, in Riga, Latvia. Her nation is nestled on the southern coast of the Baltic Sea between Estonia and Lithuania, and has existed as a distinct state since the Middle Ages. Once part of the czarist Russian Empire, Latvia gained its independence in November 1918 in establishing itself as a republic. However, in June 1940 Soviet troops brutally reoccupied the region and reconstituted it as a communist-style people's republic within the Soviet Union. After a devastating German invasion in 1941, Communist authority was finally reestablished in 1944, by which time almost 10 percent of the population had perished. Latvia was also subject to mass immigration and settlement by Russians in an attempt to dilute and possibly eliminate the native culture. However, by 1988 Premier Mikhail Gorbachev had relaxed traditional state control over the republics, and long-repressed anti-Russian feelings emerged. In 1989 the Popular Front of Latvia (PFL) was established and, following the Communist coup against Gorbachev in August 1991, Latvia again declared political independence from Russia. It is now governed as a republic, and administered by a president, a prime minister, and a parliament, the Saeima. Latvia has since struggled to establish good relations with its giant neighbor, but the presence of millions of Russians—nearly half the population—remains a source of continuing political tension and cultural turmoil.

Vike-Freiberga's family fled the Soviet onslaught in 1940 and lived many months in a German refugee camp. After the war they relocated first to Morocco and then to Canada, where she worked by day and attended school by night. An accomplished student, Vike-Freiberga gained admittance to the prestigious University of Toronto, where she obtained a master's degree in psychology, and then the University of Montreal, from which she holds her Ph.D. Presently, she is fluent in five languages: Latvian, French, English, Spanish, and German. Vike-Freiberga taught at the University of Montreal from 1965 to 1998, where she gained renown as an expert on Latvian culture and folksongs. In 1998 she renounced her Canadian citizenship and ended 50 years of exile by returning home. That same year she also assumed control of the Latvia Institute in Riga, which was dedicated to the preservation and dissemination of Latvian culture. It was while working at this post that Vike-Freiberga was drafted into the 1999 Latvian presidential race after being urged by fellow academics to run. After several secret ballots she emerged triumphant on June 17, 1999, becoming Latvia's first female president and the first female head of state in Eastern Europe. "We are the inheritors of our past, but we are not slaves who should live in the shadow of our past," she lectured. "We are the builders of our own future."

Vike-Freiberga came to power during a time of increasing friction with Russia. Conservative elements in the Saeima, alarmed by the continuing presence of thousands of Russian-speaking residents and the threat they posed to Latvian culture, passed restrictive language laws mandating the use of Latvian in public and business dealings. The government of Russia protested what it viewed as discrimination against its kinsmen and threatened a complete economic boycott. The European Union (EU), to which Latvia aspired to join, also criticized the move as inconsistent with their requirement

necessitating protections for minority rights. Vike-Freiberga, given her multicultural background, immediately sent the law back to parliament for reconsideration. She ultimately signed a less-repressive version, one that did much to diffuse European and Russian critics of Latvia's cultural rehabilitation. There was also a similar tussle over citizenship and naturalization, which she also handled deftly, in recognition of the sizable Russian minority. Conservatives have since labeled the president a "leftist" in her approach toward Latvia's former occupier, but Vike-Freiberga's own experience as a member of a linguistic minority renders her more sensitive to the issue than her countrymen. And, in addition to five languages already mastered, she is struggling to learn Russian!

However friendly to Russia on linguistic matters, Vike-Freiberga is determined to shore up Latvia's hard-won independence. She actively courts EU membership and the country might be allowed to join as early as 2003. Latvia is also determined to join NATO, a prospect that Russia strongly opposes but one that Riga views as essential to the continuing survival of the nation. "NATO's security umbrella is extremely important to Latvia," she declared. "We are in a geographical location that has been the cause of periods of occupation and aggression coming from large countries." However, most Western leaders balk at the notion of offending Russia by placing a powerful military alliance on its doorstep, so membership may not be forthcoming soon. Nonetheless, Vike-Freiberga is eager to demonstrate Latvia's reliability as a military ally and deployed troops in the Balkans as UN peacekeepers. Her government has also actively pursued good relations with neighboring Estonia and Lithuania, with whom Latvia shares historical, economic, and cultural ties. Vike-Freiberga continues as a popular and effective Latvian leader of her little state. She will be up for reelection in 2003.

Further Reading

Donson, John R. *Language, Ethnicity, and the States in Latvia.* Salford, England: University of Salford, 2000.

Eglitis, Daina S. *Imagining the Nation: History, Modernity, and Revolution in Latvia.* University Park: Pennsylvania State University Press, 2002.

Jubulis, Mark A. *Nationalism and Democratic Transition: The Politics of Citizenship and Language in Post-Soviet Latvia.* Lanham, Md.: University Press of America, 2001.

Murphy, Sean. "An Interview with Latvian President Vaira Vike-Freiberga." *Current History* 180 (November 2001): 392–394.

Neimanis, George J. *The Collapse of the Soviet Empire: A View from Riga.* Westport, Conn.: Praeger, 1997.

Pabriks, Artis, and Aldis Purs. *Latvia: The Challenges of Change.* London: Routledge, 2001.

Vranitzky, Franz (1937–   ) *chancellor of Austria*

Franz Vranitzky was born on October 4, 1937, in Vienna, Austria, into a working-class family. His father was a former Communist who transferred his allegiance to the more mainstream Socialist Party. Vranitzky attended the Vienna University of Economics in 1956 and four years later obtained his degree. He commenced a career in finance by working at the Austrian National Bank, rising to vice president. In 1970 he initiated his political career by serving as an economic adviser to Vice Chancellor Hannes Androsch, who also served as a mentor. By 1976 Vranitzky shifted back to the commercial sector by becoming deputy director of Creditanstalt Bankverein, Austria's largest bank, where he proved uniformly successful. For this reason he assumed control of the Länderbank, the second-largest bank, in 1981. As director general he was tasked with reviving the institution, now almost bankrupt through assumption of bad loans. Vranitzky prevailed upon the government to bail out the bank with tax money and cut all ties to unproductive firms. The actions essentially turned the bank around within three years. His success was widely hailed, and in September 1984 Chancellor Fred Sinowatz appointed Vranitzky minister of finance. Despite socialist leanings, he conducted governmental affairs in a business-like, nonideological manner, and he successfully reduced the national debt, scaled-back national borrowing, and eliminated an unpopular savings tax. Vranitzky's conservative policies caused friction with many within his party, but the measures also improved Austria's economic health. In June 1986 the victory of People's Party candidate Kurt Waldheim over Socialist Kurt Streyer for president induced Chancellor Sinowatz to resign. Vranitzky, a dapper, urbane figure on the political scene for nearly a decade, was appointed to succeed him on June 16, 1986.

No sooner had Vranitzky assumed power than a small coalition partner, the right-wing Freedom Party, elected the far-right nationalist JÖRG HAIDER as its leader. Vranitzky, cognizant of Austria's Nazi past, dis-

solved the coalition rather than work with Haider, and new elections were called. Surprisingly, Haider's party doubled in strength from 5 percent to 10 percent, which forced the Socialists to enter into a left-right "Grand Coalition" with the conservative People's Party. Vranitzky then worked amiably with President Waldheim until startling revelations about Waldheim's World War II career surfaced. Charges included Waldheim's presence with units accused of war crimes in the Balkans, which he previously denied. An international storm of protest ensued, and Austria faced a wall of diplomatic isolation. Waldheim remained unapologetic and defiant, intent upon completing his full term in office. Vranitzky, whatever his personal feelings on the matter, dared not criticize the head of his only coalition partner. It was only after intense international pressure that he conceded. He stated: "The president has not been very accurate with the truth in the course of all these events." It remained an awkward situation for many years to come.

The Waldheim affair proved seriously distracting for Vranitzky, but it did not prevent him from addressing Austria's greater problems. These included modernizing and liberalizing the economy, paring back the generous welfare state to reduced spending, and preparing Austria for entry into the European Union (EU) in 1995. He approached these various austerity measures pragmatically and efficiently, although the head of the Socialist Party, former chancellor Bruno Kreisky, accused him of abandoning party principles before resigning in protest. Vranitzky simply shrugged off such criticism as old-fashioned and, when he became chairman in May 1988, the party renamed itself the Social Democrats. Clearly times had changed, and Vranitzky was determined to lead his party into the new era. His political position—and Austria's—improved significantly in May 1992 when Waldheim stepped down and was replaced by a new president, THOMAS KLESTIL. The two men enjoyed a much closer rapport, and Vranitzky could finally turn his complete attention to national affairs. He enjoyed considerable success and great national popularity over the next five years, but in 1996 Haider's Freedom Party again gained additional seats at the expense of the Social Democrats. Vranitzky suddenly faced the prospect of entering into a coalition with Haider in order to stay in power. This he refused to do and, in January 1997, he resigned and was replaced by Finance Minister VIKTOR KLIMA. However, Vranitzky's 10 years as chancellor are regarded as highly successful for his party and country.

Though out of office, Vranitzky continued serving in several high-visibility positions. In 1998 he became a United Nations special envoy dealing with the Albanian-Serbian crisis in Kosovo. Ever quick to repudiate Austria's Nazi legacy, in March 2001 he further pledged to support the Jewish Welcome Service, which invites Jewish visitors from around the world to promote a positive view of Jewish culture in Austria. Vranitzky sees it as a valuable counterweight to the view of unsavory Austria projected by Haider's Freedom Party. "In the 21st century, the wounds of our country must be healed," he insists.

Further Reading

Bischot, Gunter, Anton Pelinka, and Ferdinand Karlhofer, eds. *The Vranitzky Era in Austria.* New Brunswick, N.J.: Transaction Publishers, 1999.

Lauber, Volkmer. *Contemporary Austrian Politics.* Boulder, Colo.: Westview Press, 1996.

Luther, Kurt R. *From Moderate to Polarized Pluralism? The Austrian Party System in Transition.* Keele, England: University of Keele, 1997.

Neisser, Heinrich. *Austria's Role in the New Europe.* Stanford, Calif.: Hoover Institution, 1994.

Sully, Melanie. "The 1995 Austrian Election: Winter of Discontent." *West European Politics* 19 (July 1996): 633–649.

Wade, Abdoulaye (1926–   ) *president of Senegal*
Abdoulaye Wade was born in Kebemer, Senegal, on May
29, 1926. His homeland is a former French colony located on the Western coast of Africa and one of that continent's few functioning democracies. It acquired
political independence in April 1960 and implemented a
constitution creating a strong presidency and a national
assembly. Senegal's first leader was the legendary Léopold
Sédar Senghor, a founder of the Socialist Party, who ruled
until being defeated by ABDOU DIOUF in 1980.
Throughout this period Senegal was ruled as a one-party
state, but the constitution was nonetheless revised six
times, reflecting a cautious, incremental approach toward
multiparty democracy. In 1982 the nation tried a political union with the English-speaking enclave of The
Gambia, which juts 300 miles into Senegal's interior, but
the arrangement collapsed after 1989. This awkward geographical placement has also facilitated a small but constant separatist movement in the Casamance region,
which occupies the southernmost reaches of the country. Senegal, while not rich, is better off than most of its
neighbors, enjoying the blessings of a relatively stable
polity, religious harmony (being 92 percent Muslim),
and a productive agricultural sector. The arrival of genuine democracy in March 2000 therefore seems the logical conclusion of many long-established trends—and
the work of one very persistent individual.

Wade was well educated by African standards, having completed his primary studies at home before leaving to study at the Lycée Condorcet in Paris. He
subsequently attended college at Besancon, acquiring a
Ph.D. in law and economics. Wade then returned home
to open a legal practice and to teach at the University of
Dakar. In 1978 he joined the Senegalese Democratic
Party (PDS) and won a seat in parliament. In parliament
he became a vocal critic of the Diouf regime for its alleged corruption and nepotism. Furthermore, Wade ran
for the presidency in 1978, 1983, 1988, and 1993, losing each time. Twice, in 1988 and 1993, Wade publicly
accused Diouf of stealing the election through voter
fraud, although, possibly to placate public murmuring,
he was twice appointed a governmental minister.
Nonetheless, in February–March 2000 he ran a fifth
time for president, especially as the Diouf regime was
reeling from a bad economy. The public was apparently
ready for a change. On March 19, 2000, Wade received
58.5 percent of votes cast in a runoff election, becoming
the nation's third president in its 40-year history. This
event also terminated four decades of Socialist rule in
Senegal, and it was greeted with wild celebrations. "You
can rely on me," Wade promised. "I am a candidate of
the poor, farmers, youth, women, and executives who
all long for change at the highest office." Significantly,
when Diouf chose to relinquish power peacefully, he

became only the third African head of state to do so in 40 years.

Wade entered power with Socialists still controlling the National Assembly and a new body, the Senate, which Diouf created a few years previously. However, he adhered to a campaign pledge to submit constitutional reforms to a public referendum. These changes called for elimination of the Senate and return to a unicameral legislature, the transfer of certain presidential powers to the prime minister, reduction of the term of office from seven to five years, and a limit of two terms in office. The measure was overwhelmingly passed by 94 percent of the popular vote. Moreover, rather than try to rule with his hands tied, Wade called for early elections in April 2001 to consolidate his support. Cashing in on his great popularity, the PDS won 89 of 120 available seats, giving the government a working majority. Since then Wade's greatest task revolves around diversifying the agrarian-based economy, which is heavily dependent on peanut production and, therefore, highly susceptible to drought. Cash crops like cotton, rice, and sugar are being encouraged, and the government is also pledged to support extensive reforestation to correct logging abuses.

To date Wade has had little success resolving the rebellion in the Casamance region, which has also led to complications with neighboring Guinea-Bissau and Mali. However, he has been active in promoting African unity and has traveled extensively throughout the region encouraging creation of a West African confederacy. Nor is he disposed to be a prisoner of the past. Whereas many African countries complain about European colonialism and demand monetary compensation for slavery, Wave openly ridicules the notion. "If one can claim reparations for slavery, the slaves of my ancestors, or their descendants, can also claim money from me," he insisted, "Because slavery has been practiced by all people in the world." Wade has also proven friendly toward the United States, has condemned the attack upon New York's World Trade Center, and defended the U.S. campaign against Afghanistan. However, as a Muslim, he strongly supports Arab perspectives on the Middle East and concludes that "the United States must impose on the Israeli people the existence of a Palestinian state with borders recognized by everyone." At 75 years of age, Wade paradoxically remains one of Africa's oldest leaders and among its most newly elected. His rise confirms Senegal's peaceful transfer to democracy and he is possibly Africa's most shining personification of tenacity and dedication to freedom.

Further Reading

Evans, Martin. "Briefing: Senegal: Wade and the Casamance Dossier." *African Affairs* 99 (October 2000): 649–659.

Gellar, Sheldon. *Senegal: An African Nation between Islam and the West.* Boulder, Colo.: Westview Press, 1995.

Novicki, Margret A. "Abdoulaye Wade: Democracy's Advocate." *Africa Report* 36 (March 1999): 41–44.

Schaffer, Frederic C. *Democracy in Transition: Understanding Politics in an Unfamiliar Culture.* Ithaca, N.Y.: Cornell University Pres, 2000.

Villalon, Leonardo A. *Islamic Society and State Power in Senegal.* New York: Cambridge University Press, 1995.

Wahid, Abdurrahman (1940–) *president of Indonesia*

Abdurrahman Wahid was born in Jombang, East Java, on August 4, 1940, the son of a Muslim religious teacher. His homeland was then officially known as the Dutch East Indies and had been colonized and controlled by Europeans since the 18th century. However, the islands were attacked and occupied by Japanese forces during World War II, which severely compromised Dutch control of the region. Following a brief war for independence, the Dutch East Indies gained their political independence as the Federated Republic of Indonesia in December 1949. Today it is the fourth-most populous nation in the world, with 216 million people settled upon an estimated 13,000 islands. Furthermore, it is an incredibly diverse assemblage, representing 300 different ethnic groups and 200 different languages. The majority religion is Islam, but small communities of Christians and other faiths are also present. The Indonesian constitution allows for a strong president and a People's Consultative Assembly that elects the chief executive from the largest party then in power. However, throughout most of its history, Indonesia has been administered by two notable strongmen, Sukarno and SUHARTO, who, aided by the strong military, ruled with an iron hand. Suharto was forced to resign from office in 1997 in the face of impending economic crisis. His successor, Vice President BACHARUD-

DIN JUSUF HABIBIE held on to power for just two years before being deposed in the nation's first democratically held national elections.

Wahid belongs to a long line of distinguished Muslim theologians, and his grandfathers helped establish the Nahdlatul Ulama (NU), a school for religious studies, in 1926. He attended a religious school in Cairo, Egypt, in 1964, and subsequently studied Arabic and European philosophy in Baghdad, Iraq. Wahid came home in 1971 and taught at a small university while also becoming associated with the NU, which had grown to encompass 30 million members. In this position he became a vocal critic of Suharto's dictatorship, and he was also outspoken in his advocacy of religious and racial tolerance. Consequently, he was temporarily forced out as head of the NU, but in 1998 Wahid helped to found the new National Awakening Party (PKB) to combat authoritarianism. By this time, he had also acquired the reputation of a brilliant scholar whose personal conduct was above reproach and was popularly known by the title of *Gus Dur* or "older brother." During the October 1999 national elections for a new president, the favored candidate was MEGAWATI SUKARNOPUTRI, head of the rival Indonesian Democratic Party and daughter of the late dictator. However, Wahid, as head of the PKB, managed to outmaneuver Sukarnoputri's supporters and defeated her in the assembly 373 votes to 313. This reverse angered Sukarnoputri's supporters and they poured into the streets by the thousands, but Wahid cleverly diffused the crisis by appointing her vice president. He thus become Indonesia's fourth president and the first one democratically elected in his nation's 50-year history.

The Indonesian people were weary of military rule and they held high expectations for Wahid's administration. He certainly started off strongly by appointing a civilian defense minister and pensioning off senior officers viewed as either too corrupt or overly ambitious. He proved especially keen to rid himself of General Wiranto, who had cruelly occupied East Timor and orchestrated violence against the inhabitants. The president also determined to promote ethnic tolerance, even at the expense of some of his more devout Muslim supporters. "Those who say I am not Islamic enough should reread their Koran," he declared. "Islam is about inclusion, tolerance, community." This stance was becoming increasingly essential, for fighting between Christian and Muslim communities was rampant and prompted seces-

sionist movements on Sumatra and East Timor. He then pushed bold, liberal measures to decentralize power from the capital to the regions and grant new freedom to minority religious. However, Wahid himself suffered intermittently from poor health, was nearly blind, and often made bizarre statements in public. He also proved himself stubborn and short-tempered in his dealings with other politicians. Consequently, within a few months of taking office, no less than 22 ministers resigned from his cabinet. Amid growing perceptions that the 61-year-old former teacher was actually senile, there was a movement to impeach him in the People's Consultative Assembly. Wahid grew increasingly unstable and tried to declare a state of national emergency, and he even solicited the military's help in suspending the assembly. They refused to comply and the vote to impeach him passed on July 18, 2001.

Wahid refused to exit gracefully. He holed himself up in the presidential palace for three days, without water or electricity, until soldiers arrived to remove him by force. It was then announced he would leave Indonesia "for medical treatment" in the United States over the next several months. This was accomplished peacefully and the once-honored religious scholar was unceremoniously replaced by Vice President Sukarnoputri. Wahid returned soon after, but in January 2002, the ailing ex-president was closely interrogated by police officials in connection with blackmail allegations made by Hutomo "Tommy" Mandala Ptura, son of ex-dictator Suharto, who is himself under arrest for corruption. Wahid's trial, if any, remains pending.

Further Reading

Barton, Grey. *Gus Dur: The Authorized Biography of Abdurrahman Wahid.* Jakarta: Equinox Pubs., 2002.

Bouchier, David, and Vedir Hadiz. *Indonesian Politics and Society: A Reader.* London: Routledge, 2001.

Budiman, Arief. *Indonesia: The Uncertain Transition.* London: C. Hurst, 2002.

Heryanto, Ariel, and Sumit K. Mandal, eds. *Challenging Authoritarianism in Southeast Asia: Comparing Indonesia and Malaysia.* New York: RoutledgeCuzon, 2003.

Honna, Jon. *Military Politics and Democratization in Indonesia.* New York: Routledge, 2003.

King, Dwight Y. *Half-hearted Reform: Electoral Institutions and the Struggle for Democracy in Indonesia.* Westport, Conn.: Praeger, 2003.

Kingsbury, Damien. *The Presidency of Abdurrahman Wahid: An Assessment after the First Year.* Clayton, Victoria: Monash University, 2001.

Malley, Michael S. "Indonesia in 2001: Restoring Stability in Jakarta." *Asian Survey* 42 (January–February 2002): 124–132.

Romano, Angela. *Politics and the Press in Indonesia: Understanding Evolving Culture.* Richmond, Va: Curzon, 2002.

Wajed, Hasina (1947–) *prime minister of Bangladesh*

Hasina Wajed was born in Tungipara village on September 28, 1947, in what was then British-ruled India. However, when Great Britain granted India political independence in August 1947, the British partitioned the subcontinent into largely Hindu and Muslim enclaves. This gave rise to the new state of Pakistan, divided between East and West Pakistan, and separated by over 1,000 miles of Indian territory. Though both were overwhelmingly Muslim, the two halves possessed markedly different languages and cultures. Moreover, the haughtiness displayed by West Pakistanis toward their poorer, less developed consorts fueled an eventual move toward separatism. This transpired in late 1971, when a third war between India and Pakistan resulted in independence for East Pakistan, which was renamed Bangladesh. It remains one of the world's poorest nations and, with a population of 120 million crowded into an area the size of Wisconsin, the most densely populated. Located on the Bay of Bengal, the area is also susceptible to violent, annual cyclones, which frequently kill hundreds, even thousands, of people. Since its inception, Bangladesh has also wrestled with the twin evils of poverty and political instability, which resulted in three military coups and three slain prime ministers in 30 years. Currently, the country is administered by a parliamentary system in which the majority party or coalition in the Jatiya Sangsbad (People's Assembly) chooses a prime minister. This official, in turn, appoints a Council of Ministers to assist running the country. Bangladesh is an overwhelmingly Muslim country by character, yet it differs from most in having established traditions of women in high office.

Wajed was the daughter of Sheik Mujibur Rahman, a military officer who was also the first leader of Bangladesh. She graduated from Dhaka University in 1973, and two years later fled the country after a coup that killed her father and three brothers. She remained in self-imposed exile until 1981, and returned home to claim the mantle of leadership within the Awami League (AL), a moderate Muslim organization. Since then, Wajed has proven steadfast in her determination to revitalize her father's political legacy and to punish his murderers. She gained election to parliament in 1986 as head of the AL and served as the nation's youngest-ever head of the political opposition. In December 1990 popular unrest resulted in the end of military rule and a return to democracy. In the February 1991 general elections, the winning party proved to be the Muslim-oriented Bangladesh National Party (BNP) under BEGUM KHALEDA ZIA, the nation's first female prime minister. However, she could did little to revive the nation's sagging economy and was also beset by allegations of corruptions and fraud. Therefore, when national elections took place in June 1996, the Awami League ended two decades of opposition by taking the majority of seats in parliament. Wajed was consequently sworn in as the nation's second female prime minister on June 23, 1996.

Wajed came to power at a difficult period for Bangladesh, as the country's long-standing problems of endemic poverty, overpopulation, illiteracy, and corruption were never more prevalent. Nevertheless, she invited BNP leaders to serve in her administration and called for a government of national unity to promote badly needed progress. "We will heal the wounds, not create new ones," she stated, "unite the nation, not divide it." But Wajed was also determined to pursue justice and she arrested several army officers believed responsible for the deaths of her father and brothers. Equally pressing was the state of the economy, which was poor and hit heavily by the Asian currency crisis of 1997. Wajed, fortunately, had eliminated the AL's previous emphasis upon socialist economics and embraced free markets, privatization, and foreign investment. The result was an impressive 7 percent growth rate for several months until a terrible cyclone in 1998 severely devastated the country. Bangladesh has since recovered much of the ground lost previously, but it remains overwhelmingly dependent upon foreign aid and assistance to survive.

Wajed continued to rule more or less competently, but she embarked upon a very shrill campaign of insults against BNP leader Begum Khaleda Zia, her predecessor. Both women hold each other's family responsible for the death of their fathers and other relatives. Their mutual antipathy glossed over the fact there were very few ideological differences between the two parties, save for the AL's slightly more pro-Indian stance. Nonetheless, Bangladesh experienced a rise in both Muslim fundamentalism and public violence. Many people were killed in a series of bombings and shootings that the government seemed unable to curtail. At this juncture, Wajed declared the existence of a BNP plot to assassinate her and she had the assembly pass a special provision granting her a personal bodyguard for life. Meanwhile, the economy began spiraling downward under the weight of deficit spending and unemployment approached 40 percent. During the next election cycle of October 3, 2001, Zia's BNP managed to capture a majority of seats in parliament, thereby ensuring her reinstatement as the new prime minister. Wajed stepped down accordingly, but her contentious tenure is full of historic significance. It marked the first time in Bangladesh's tortured political history that a sitting prime minister completed a full five years in office.

Further Reading

Ahmed, Nizam. *The Parliament of Bangladesh*. Aldershot, England: Ashgate, 2002.

Ahmed, Rafiudden. *Religion, Identity, and Politics: Essays on Bangladesh*. Denver, Colo.: Academic Books, 2001.

Jahan, Rounaq. *Bangladesh: Promise and Performance*. London: Zed Books, 2001.

Kabir, Muhammed G. *Changing Face of Nationalism: The Case of Bangladesh*. Denver, Colo.: Academic Books, 2001.

Seabrook, Jeremy. *Freedom Unfinished: Fundamentalism and Popular Resistance in Bangladesh Today*. London: Zed, 2001.

Walesa, Lech (1943–) *president of Poland*

Lech Walesa was born on September 29, 1943, in Popowo, Poland, the son of wealthy farmers. After World War II Soviet armies occupied Poland and they installed a Communist dictatorship. Walesa proved himself adept mechanically, so the state-run education system directed him to receive vocational training as an electrician. By 1967 he was working at the Lenin Shipyard and gradually became involved in trade union activity. The government was then under increasing distress owing to the inefficiency of a socialist command

economy, and it was forced to raise food prices in 1976. This act produced massive unrest among the workers, and Walesa quickly emerged as a leading advocate of confrontation with government officials. He was consequently fired and spent the next four years editing an illegal underground newspaper. Walesa also began circulating among various Catholic intellectuals to better coordinate a national, working-class reform agenda. When the government again raised food prices in 1980, Walesa jumped the fence at the Lenin Shipyard to launch a new national worker's organization, Solidarity. The movement spread quickly and a nationwide strike was called in July to underscore their demands. This was the first time a labor movement defied Communist authorities behind the Iron Curtain, and it garnered international attention. By August 1980 the government was forced to recognize Solidarity as a legitimate trade union, independent of government control. Its celebrity soon attracted millions of adherents across Poland as Walesa toured and championed worker's rights and economic reform. He had also become a world celebrity of note, and in 1981 Walesa flew to Rome and conferred with his fellow Pole, Pope JOHN PAUL II. Expectations for dramatic change were at a fever pitch.

Walesa's activities constituted a direct challenge to Communist authority in Poland and elsewhere. Communist leaders in the Soviet Union were especially worried that Solidarity might topple the entire Polish government, and they applied pressure upon military leaders there to take charge. Accordingly, in December 1981 General Wojciech Jaruzelski declared martial law, outlawed Solidarity, and had Walesa arrested. Nonetheless, Walesa received the Nobel Peace Prize in 1983 and he was hailed as the Communist bloc's leading reformer. From a Polish standpoint, he had also functioned as a symbol of national resistance to Soviet-imposed communism. Walesa was eventually released from detention but in 1988 another series of price increases unleashed a pent-up wave of strikes across Poland. The country literally ground to a halt as riot police engaged in daily confrontations with angry workers. Walesa, meanwhile, used this unrest as leverage during negotiations to legalize Solidarity again as an independent trade union. He prevailed and by 1989 the reform-minded Soviet premier, Mikhail Gorbachev, also began withdrawing troops from Eastern Europe. This act added greater impetus to the establishment of free elections and multiparty democracy in Poland and Eastern Europe. On

June 4, 1989, Walesa helped arrange the coalition that brought Tadeusz Mazowiecki to power as the first prime minister not a member of the Communist Party in 40 years. The following December Walesa was himself elected president of Poland with 73 percent of the popular vote. He was a national hero by any standards.

Once empowered, Walesa embarked on an ambitious program of human rights and economic liberalization. But, over the next five years, Poland struggled with a difficult transition from communism to capitalism. Unemployment rose, as did inflation and the national debt, and the country's leaders fought each other over what to do next. Walesa, a strict Catholic, also alienated millions of younger voters by his strident opposition to abortion (previously legal under communism). By 1995 his poll ratings were only 16 percent but he was determined to run for office again. His opponent, ALEKSANDR KWASNIEWSKI, a former Communist official, was handsome, telegenic, and articulate, the complete opposite of the gritty, low-brow Walesa. When the runoff vote was held on November 19, 1995, Kwasniewski won with 52 percent of the vote. However, Walesa won a personal victory of sorts when the new leader continued his reform policies toward democratization, increasing privatization, and membership in NATO. Walesa refused to accept defeat gracefully, however, and in 2000 he again campaigned against the incumbent, raising the specter of a return to communism were he to be defeated. The old Solidarity message no longer resonated with voters, unfortunately, and Walesa, the former national hero, received only 1 percent of the vote. At that point he announced his withdrawal from politics altogether. "The election result has indicated that I should step to the side of the political scene and withdraw from current activities," he reasoned. Walesa emerged from obscurity in May 2002 to announce that he will join the corporate board of an American computer company in Charlotte, North Carolina, which is owned and operated by a Polish emigré.

Further Reading

Boyes, Ruger. *The Naked President: A Political Life of Lech Walesa.* London: Secker and Warburg, 1994.

Kurski, Jaroslav. *Lech Walesa: Democrat or Dictator?* Boulder, Colo.: Westview Press, 1993.

Sanford, George. *Democratic Government in Poland: Constitutional Politics since 1989.* New York: Palgrave, 2002.

Simpson, P. "The Troubled Reign of Lech Walesa in Poland." *Presidential Studies Quarterly* 26 (Spring 1996): 317–336.

Walesa, Lech. *The Struggle and the Triumph: An Autobiography.* New York: Arcade Publishing, 1993.

Zubek, Voytek. "The Eclipse of Walesa's Political Career." *Europe-Asia Studies* 49 (January 1997): 107–124.

Wangchuk, Jigme Singye (1955–) *king of Bhutan*

Crown Prince Jigme Singye Wangchuk was born at the Dechchenchholing Palace, Thimphu, Bhutan, on November 11, 1955, the son of King Jigme Dorji Wangchuk. Bhutan is a small, landlocked enclave nestled in the Himalayan Mountains between India and China. This ancient Buddhist kingdom traditionally reveres isolationism, but in 1865 it accepted British protection in exchange for internal autonomy. When Britain abandoned Southeast Asia in 1947, its role was replaced by India. Bhutan remains one of the few remaining absolute monarchies. It totally lacks a constitution and until only recently was devoid of elected officials. Politically, economically, and socially, it is caught in a developing battle between cherished traditionalism and the encroachment of modernity. A National Assembly was finally created in 1953 by the elder King Wangchuk, and he endowed it with the ability to impeach and remove a monarch by a two-thirds vote. By 1965 the king added a Royal Advisory Council and a Council of Ministers to assist him in his rule. Three years later Bhutan was given an eight-man High Court to weigh decisions and appeals by local headmen and magistrates. Political organizations are also outlawed although an opposition party, the Nepalese-based Bhutan State Congress, maintains headquarters in India. Bhutan is one of the world's poorest nations, with an economy based entirely on farming and herding. Yet it prides itself on maintaining a distinct Buddhist culture that transcends material goods in favor of national harmony. "In five or 10 years we'll look back and see how happy we are," King Jigme has stated. "To us, happiness means religion, culture, and heritage, not only our standard of living."

Jigme was educated at home before attending a private school in Darjeeling, India. Thereafter he completed advanced studies in England before returning home in 1971. After passing through the Ugyen Wangchuk Academy for religious instruction, he became crown prince in line to succeed his father. This transpired unexpectedly in June 1972 as the king died suddenly while out of the country, and the 17-year-old prince was crowned *Druk Gyalp* (Dragon King) in an elaborate state ceremony. King Jigme is determined to continue his father's course of gradually opening up Bhutan to the modern world, though in such a manner as not to imperil its cultural uniqueness. He also declared his determination to establish, by degrees, a constitutional monarchy. Furthermore, the young king clearly restricts his responsibilities to the secular realm, while all religious matters remain the purview of the *je khempo,* or head of the monastery. In 1988 the king took reforms a step further by declaring that his council of ministers, previously appointed, were henceforth to be chosen by secret ballot in the assembly. King Jigme also surrendered some of his absolute powers to rule in conjunction with the assembly and council. "The future destiny of the country must be shouldered by the Bhutanese and should not be in the hands of one individual," he reasoned.

Historically, Bhutan places great emphasis on preserving its national character and culture, so most modern influences are either discouraged or outlawed. The nation did not acquire its first television station until June 1999, the same year that the global Internet was finally allowed. However, the king insists that men and women continue wearing their traditional, national attire for everyday living. Jigme, furthermore, declines to occupy his lavish palace and sets a more modest example by living in a smaller house with his four wives and children. Tourism is promoted as a source of income but is tightly regulated and controlled to minimize its impact on society. Bhutan also reinforces its reputation for isolationism by minimizing its contact with foreign countries. Aside from an embassy in New Delhi, which accepts responsibility for Bhutan's interests abroad, diplomatic exchanges are rare.

Despite a traditional Buddhist culture that stresses harmony, and a strikingly beautiful geographic setting in the Himalayan Mountains, all is not bliss in Bhutan. For many years migrant workers from Nepal were allowed into the country as guest workers, and many have since settled and taken up citizenship. Given the poverty of their homeland, many wish to avail themselves of the free health care and schooling provided to all Bhutan's people. However, the Nepalese, who are Hindu, loudly assert they are the victims of discrimination in political

Jigme Singye Wangchuck *(Consulate General of the Kingdom of Bhutan)*

and economic arenas. Tensions crested in 1988, when a government census felt that the influx of foreigners might overwhelm the traditionally small Bhutan population. A system of forced eviction and deportation then unfolded, which led to violence and the rise of armed resistance. An even greater danger has been the arrival of rebel groups fighting for independence from India, the United Liberation Front of Assam and the National Democratic Front of Bodoland, which have ensconced themselves in rugged Bhutanese terrain for refuge. In December 2001 the king warned the rebels to evacuate their training camps and leave peacefully, lest he order his own security forces into action. However, because the rebels are better armed and trained than Bhutan's 2,000 police and 4,000 soldiers, military assistance from India may have to be employed as well. The traditionally placid, solace-loving "Land of the Thunder Dragon" has proven reluctant to do this. The issue presently remains unresolved.

Further Reading

Ahsan, Syed Aziz-al, and Bhumitra Chakma. "Bhutan's Foreign Policy: Cautious Self-Assertion." *Asian Survey* 33 (November 1993): 1,043–55.

Basu, Gautam K. *Bhutan: The Political Economy of Development.* Denver, Colo.: Academic Books, 2000.

Hickman, Katie. *Dreams of the Peaceful Dragon: A Journey through Bhutan.* London: Phoenix, 2002.

Hutt, Michael. *Bhutan: Perspectives on Conflict and Dissent.* Gartmore, England: Kiscadale, 1994.

Rustomji, Nari. *Bhutan: The Dragon in Crisis.* New York: Oxford University Press, 1978.

Wasmosy, Juan (1938–) *president of Paraguay*
Juan Carlos Wasmosy Monti was born on December 15, 1938, in Asunción, Paraguay, the son of a politician. He was educated locally and in 1962 acquired his degree in civil engineering from the University of Asunción. Wasmosy then pursued careers in construction and cattle-raising, becoming one of the country's wealthiest businessmen. His building endeavors climaxed during the 1970s with the erection of the Itaipu and Yacyreta hydroelectric dams, two of the world's largest, on the Paraná River. He also developed an abiding relationship with General Alfredo Stroessner, who controlled Paraguay after toppling its elected government in 1954. However, when General ANDRÉS RODRÍGUEZ overthrew Stroessner in 1989, Wasmosy promptly switched sides. As a lifelong member of the Colorado Party, he entertained political aspirations but waited until democracy had been finally restored. This transpired in 1993, when Rodríguez, now president, stepped aside and called for new elections. Wasmosy then endured a bruising nomination campaign against Luis M. Argana, who may have actually won the contest. Wasmosy, however, enjoyed the patronage of Rodríguez and military commanders like General Lino César Oviedo. Backroom machinations ensured that Wasmosy became the party candidate in December 1992, although questions persisted about his legitimacy. He subsequently endured a public relations backlash by trailing competitors from the Authentic Liberal Party and the National Encounter Party, until a last-minute rally by Colorado loyalists carried him over the top. On May 9, 1993, Wasmosy won with 40 percent of votes cast, making him the first democratically elected president in Paraguayan history. He was also the first civilian executive after four decades of military rule. He assumed power on August 15, 1993. Paraguay was then in desperate need of social and political modernization, but the president cautioned fellow citizens against dramatic reforms. "The vast majority of public employees are Coloradans," he observed. "There would be a great deal of social trauma if there were a sudden change."

Wasmosy was fully committed to the principles of neoliberalism and embarked on programs promoting greater liberalization and privatization of state assets. Reforms were clearly necessary to boost the economy and lift half of Paraguay's 4.2 million citizens out of poverty. He also sought to enlarge the nation's participation in Mercosur, the Latin American common market, for expanded trade. But Wasmosy remained discreet enough to acknowledge his debt to the military and promoted General Oviedo head of the First Army Corps. This decision was denounced as proof of pandering to the generals, but Wasmosy realized that the military had yet to adjust to the reality of civilian rule. Reform-minded politicians remained upset by this cozy relationship between the president and the generals who, many suspected, engineered his candidacy in the first place.

By 1996 Wasmosy felt that democracy had been safely installed in Paraguay, and that year he ordered Oviedo to retire. When the general angrily refused and demanded Wasmosy's resignation, a political crisis ensued. Civilian leaders feared a return to military rule, but bloodshed was averted through a timely agreement. The president could have Oviedo's resignation in exchange for his new appointment as defense minister. Having dealt with the general from a position of weakness, this seemed the most reasonable alternative to a coup. Wasmosy's deal may have placated the military, but it sparked outrage from the public. They took noisily to the streets, accusing the president of submitting to military blackmail. Countries such as the United States also weighed in, threatening to withdraw their ambassadors if Oviedo were not dropped from the government. Under intense political pressure, the president prevailed upon the general to resign and submit to arrest. In the national interest, Oviedo complied, but he was subsequently released and banished to Brazil.

Wasmosy completed the remaining two years of his tenure without incident, and in May 1998 he was succeeded by Raúl Cubas Grau. He also received the traditional sinecure as senator for life, granting him immunity from prosecution. However, Wasmosy's business dealings while in office came under official scrutiny, and, in May 1999, the Senate stripped him of parliamentary immunity. A congressional investigation subsequently turned up evidence of fraud, and, on April 2, 2002, Wasmosy was found guilty of illegally acquiring $20 million from the state bank. He was sentenced to four years in prison but, in view of advancing years and declining health, this was reduced to house arrest and an $800,000 fine. The former executive is also required to report to police headquarters weekly and not leave the country.

Further Reading

Fournier, Dominique, and Sean W. Burges. "Form before Function: Democratization in Paraguay." *Canadian Journal of Latin American and Caribbean Studies* 25, no. 49, (2000): 5–32.

Lambert, Peter, and R. Andrew Nickson. *The Transition to Democracy in Paraguay.* New York: St. Martin's Press, 1997.

More, Frank. "The Political Economy of Peripheral States in a Post–Cold War World: The Case of Paraguay." Unpublished Ph.D. dissertation, University of Miami, 1993.

Valenzuela, A. "Paraguay: The Coup That Didn't Happen." *Journal of Democracy* 8 (January 1997); 43–55.

Vergara, Isaias M. *Paraguayan Policy toward the New Organization of American States.* Virginia Beach, Va.: Regent University, 1997.

Weizman, Ezer (1924–) *president of Israel*

Ezer Weizman was born on June 15, 1924, in Tel Aviv, then part of the British-controlled protectorate of Palestine. He was also nephew of Chaim Weizmann, a leading Zionist figure and the future first president of Israel. Weizman was raised in Haifa where he joined the Haganah, the underground Jewish army, but he became interested in flying. When World War II broke out Weizman gained his pilot's license and joined the Royal Air Force as a fighter pilot. After service in Egypt and India, he resigned in 1946 and the following year commanded a squadron of Piper Cub aircraft, the nucleus of the Israeli air force. Throughout the war for independence Weizman performed many harrowing supply missions behind enemy lines, usually without orders,

becoming renowned as a dashing—and occasionally insubordinate—officer. He remained in the military after independence was won, trained at the Royal Air Force Command College, and, by 1966, had advanced to chief of operations of the Israeli Defense Forces. The following year he advocated decisive, preemptive air strikes against superior Arab air forces while they were still on the ground, and these missions, brilliantly executed in the 1967 Six-Day War, virtually assured Israeli victory. However, Weizman, a flamboyant, outspoken individual, accumulated his share of enemies on the way to the top, and in January 1968 he was passed over as chief of staff. Feeling his military career had ended, Weizman summarily resigned his commission to enter politics.

Given his background, Weizman initially evinced a strident, hard-line stance against concessions to the Arabs, even in the interest of peace. He consequently joined the right-wing Gahal faction of the conservative Likud Party and served in the administration of Golda Meir as her minister of transportation. However, Weizman resigned when the prime minister offered the Arabs a cease-fire, and he subsequently warmed up to another hard-line figure, Menachem Begin. Weizman then directed Likud's startling successful campaign of 1977 that threw Labor out of power for the first time in 29 years, and Begin appointed him minister of defense. In this office he was responsible for peace negotiations with another dashing fighter pilot, Anwar Sadat of Egypt, that resulted in the 1979 Israel-Egypt Treaty. Thereafter, Weizman gradually moderated his stance toward his enemies, insisting: "We must be sensitive to any hint of peace and open our hearts to any Arab attempt to put an end to the wars." Outspoken as always, he found himself increasingly at odds with Begin and other hard-line cabinet members, so he resigned from office a second time in 1980.

After several years in private business, Weizman continued his political transformation by joining the centrist Yahad Party in 1984. When national elections produced a tie, which in turn resulted in a national unity government between Likud and Labor, he held down a number of ministerial positions. He also formally completed his metamorphosis by transferring to Labor, mostly because of its greater receptivity to peace efforts. By the 1990s Weizman had established himself as a proponent of "land for peace," advocated Israel's withdrawal from the Syrian Golan Heights, and even clandestinely met with Palestine Liberation Organization chairman YASSER ARAFAT. Such independence brought him nothing but condemnation, and in 1992 Weizman withdrew from politics, ostensibly for the last time. However, his stature as a war hero and his continued national popularity resulted in his nomination to serve as Labor's candidate for the presidency in 1993. Weizman won easily and went on to transform this largely ceremonial office into a bully pulpit for various issues. Foremost among these was his continuing insistence on reaching out to the Arabs in search of peace and normalized relations. Nor was he shy about taking on hard-line politicians such as BINYAMIN NETANYAHU or ARIEL SHARON. "I have never ducked a fight," he insisted, "and I am not going to start now." In 1998 Weizman was easily reelected president and he continued his one-man campaign for increased dialogue with Israel's enemies. He further gained the public's esteem for incessantly visiting wounded soldiers and terrorist victims in the hospital. However, in January 2000 it became known that he had accepted $450,000 in gifts from French businessman Edouard Saroussi between 1988 to 1993. The mere hint of corruption in the presidency was enough to generate calls for Weizman's resignation and he withdrew from office, under intense public pressure, in July 2000. In light of his advanced age and hero status, the government elected not to prosecute this controversial political maverick. True to his reputation as a dashing pilot, Weizman has never hesitated to forsake the "rules" when it suited his agenda. Curiously, his successor was the low-key, nearly inscrutable MOSHE KATSAV.

Further Reading

Avnery, Uri. *Ezer Weizman: The Peacemaker.* New York: Church Peace Union, 1979.

Gidron, Benjamin, and Stanley N. Katz. *Mobilizing for Peace: Conflict Resolution in Northern Ireland, Israel/Palestine, and South Africa.* New York: Oxford University Press, 2002.

Timerman, Jacobo. *The Longest War: Israel in Lebanon.* New York: Knopf, 1982.

Weizman, Ezer. *The Battle for Peace.* New York: Bantam, 1981.

———. *On Eagle's Wings; The Personal Story of the Leader of the Israeli Air Force.* New York: Berkeley Publishing Corporation, 1979.

Wijdenbosch, Jules (1941–) *president of Suriname*

Jules Albert Wijdenbosch was born in Paramaribo, Dutch Guiana, on May 2, 1941. His homeland, a small parcel of land sandwiched between Guyana, French Guiana, and Brazil, had been a prosperous Dutch colony since 1667 and over time acquired a very heterogenous population. Ultimately, the populace consisted of local Amerindians, imported African slaves, indentured Indian servants, and a smattering of Chinese and Europeans. Dutch Guiana obtained self-government in 1945, and it was declared an independent nation of Suriname in 1975. By the terms established by the 1987 constitution, the country is governed by a parliamentary system consisting of a unicameral legislature, the National Assembly, and a president who emerges from the largest party of coalition then in power. The chief executive is head of state, head of government, and head of the armed forces. He also appoints the Council of State, a senior advisory body. However, since 1975 Suriname has endured several military coups that overthrew popularly elected regimes. In 1980 Colonel Desi Bouterse toppled the government, installing a military regime that lasted until 1987. Three years later Bouterse again intervened until new elections were mandated in 1991. Politically, power in Suriname is shared between a number of ethnically based parties, with the African-oriented National Democratic Party (NDP) being the largest. As such, Suriname remains badly split along color lines, and this ethnic dilemma remains an obstacle to national consensus and the resolution of important issues.

As a young man, Wijdenbosch served in the harbor office of Paramaribo as the ranking customs house officer. Afterward he ventured to the Netherlands, where he worked as a public servant in Amsterdam, and he also studied political science. Returning home in the late 1970s, he joined the NDP and struck up cordial relations with Colonel Bouterse, the future dictator. Following the 1990 coup, Wijdenbosch became vice president in the administration of NDP candidate Johan Kragg, and by 1996 he served as NDP chairman. In 1991 a new president, RUNALDO VENETIAAN, held power, and he severely curtailed the military's influence on the government. Colonel Bouterse was forced to resign the following year, but he has since installed himself as head of the NDP opposition in parliament. During the next election cycle held on May 23, 1996, the NDP won only 16 of 51 seats, but Wijdenbosch conducted deft political negotiations. Consequently, he managed to craft a five-party coalition and became prime minister. However, this was accomplished only after Wijdenbosch agreed that his mentor, Colonel Bouterse, was not to hold office in the government. "I shall endeavor to forge the Suriname people into a truly democratic nation in which the quality of life of every citizen is equal and guaranteed," he pledged.

Wijdenbosch inherited an impoverished nation, for Suriname remains one of the hemisphere's poorest countries. Almost 63 percent of its population resides below the poverty line and the economy continues to be dominated by the mining of bauxite, the supply of which is approaching exhaustion. However, from the onset Wijdenbosch came under criticism for extravagant spending. In August 1997 he dismissed his minister of finance for complaining about his purchase of a new presidential yacht. Amid rising protests and a sinking economy Wijdenbosch called for early elections to bide for additional time, but opponents began agitating for his resignation. When this failed to materialize, a national strike brought the country to a virtual standstill in May 1999. The president's cabinet then resigned en masse in further protest. Furthermore, on June 1, 1999, the National Assembly passed a vote of no confidence against Wijdenbosch by a vote of 27 to 14. This is usually sufficient to induce a leader to resign from office, however, because the opposition failed to muster the two-thirds majority needed to impeach him, Wijdenbosch ignored the proceedings entirely. He simply reappointed a new cabinet and tried to address his sinking political fortunes by reforming the economy.

A major obstacle to Wijdenbosch's success was Colonel Bouterse. In July 1999 a Dutch court sentenced Bouterse in absentia to 16 years in prison for cocaine smuggling. However, Wijdenbosch refused to extradite him to the Netherlands, which imperiled continuation of Dutch foreign aid. Various human rights groups also want to try the colonel on murder charges arising from his earlier coups. Under intense pressure to resign, Wijdenbosch quit the NDP instead and formed his own organization, the National Democratic Platform 2000, to retain power. Elections were finally held on May 25, 2000, and Venetiaan's New Front coalition, consisting of three parties, captured 33 of 51 seats. He then replaced Wijdenbosch as the president of long-suffering Suriname on August 12, 2000, having pledged to fight corruption, enhance economic development, and reduce the national debt. Wijdenbosch's tenure in office must be considered one of the more embarrassing episodes in that nation's brief political history.

Further Reading

Dew, Edward M. *The Trouble in Suriname, 1975–1993.* Westport, Conn.: Praeger, 1994.

Ledgister, F. S. J. *Class Alliances and the Liberal Authoritarian State: The Roots of Post-Colonial Democracy in Jamaica, Trinidad and Tobago, and Suriname.* Trenton, N.J.: African World Press, 1998.

Penta, Karl. *A Mercenary's Tale.* London: Blake, 2001.

Premas, Ralph R. *Identity, Ethnicity, and Culture in the Caribbean.* St. Augustine, Trinidad and Tobago: University of the West Indies, 1998.

Sedoc-Dahlberg, Betty N. *The Dutch Caribbean: Prospects for Democracy.* New York: Gordon and Breach, 1990.

Y

Yalá, Kumba *president of Guinea-Bissau*

Kumba Yalá was born in Portuguese Guinea to the influential Balante tribe, although his exact birth date is unknown. His country was then a small strip of land on the west coast of Africa, hemmed in between Senegal and Guinea, and it formed part of the Portuguese Empire. In 1956 a liberation movement arose, the African Party for the Independence of Guinea and Cape Verde (PAIGC), which conducted low-level guerrilla warfare against Portuguese troops until their withdrawal in 1975. The new nation of Guinea-Bissau was then established as a one-party republic, although over the next 30 years it suffered from intermittent military coups and seizures of power. However, in 1984 a constitution was adopted that mandated a unicameral legislature, the National Assembly, which in turn elected a 15-member Council of State. From their ranks a president of the council was then chosen, who also serves as head of state, commander in chief, and head of the PAIGC. Furthermore, in May 1991 single-party rule was eliminated, and three years later the first democratic elections were held. But, in June 1998, the country suffered its latest coup at the behest of General Ansumane Mane, a hero of the war for liberation, who ousted sitting President, JOÃO VIEIRA. An 11-month civil war ensued that cost the lives of 2,000 people before stability was restored. Mane then allowed for a new round of national elections

in January 2000, but he was determined that the military should be allotted a major role in any post-coup administration.

As a young man, Yalá attended the University of Lisbon, where he majored in philosophy and law. After returning home he joined the PAIGC, but grew disenchanted with the policies of President Vieira and challenged him for the presidency as leader of the new Social Renewal Party (PRS) in 1994. Yalá was defeated but remained an outspoken critic of what he considered a corrupt regime. As the 2000 national elections approached, he crisscrossed Guinea-Bissau bedecked in his trademark red hat—a Balante symbol of responsible manhood—and gained a national following. A major reason for this surge in popularity was the excellent performance he gave during Africa's first televised political debate with Vice President Malam Bacai Sanha. In November 1999 the first round of elections placed Yalá first with 38.5 percent of votes cast while Sanha took second place with 23.4 percent. However, during the presidential runoff held in January 2000, Yalá swept the country with 72 percent of the vote. Moreover, during subsequent legislative elections, the PRS took 38 of 102 seats, the largest share. "I am appealing to all the people, the main stakeholders of change in the country," Yalá announced. "The national reconciliation process has to succeed because we are compelled to shoulder our responsibilities of developing our country." His success finally marked the return of democracy to Guinea-Bissau.

Yalá faces the unenviable task of governing one of the world's poorest nations. Its poverty is compounded by the fact that the many wars and coups of late devastated the national infrastructure, making recovery all the more difficult. Presently, Guinea-Bissau continues to be dominated by an agricultural export economy, centered principally around cashews, which makes it vulnerable to fluctuations in world market prices. Moreover, the civil service is in tatters, being perpetually on strike over money owed for several months. Yalá is therefore fortunate that his election was sufficiently free and fair to encourage economic assistance from the International Money Fund (IMF) and the European Union (EU). A bigger challenge was placating the military, which has a long and unsavory reputation for making or breaking administrations. Yalá therefore appointed several ranking officers to posts within his cabinet. The troublesome General Mane, however, turned down an invitation to serve as a presidential adviser and chose to hover in the background.

Yalá, a mercurial, sometimes unpredictable man, has since enjoyed stormy relationships with his cabinet. In November 2001 he dismissed his foreign affairs minister, and has also removed several top judges on suspicion of corruption. In December 2000 he weathered a military coup orchestrated by General Mane, which was put down by troops loyal to Yalá, and the general was killed. Though victorious, the president subsequently explained to high-ranking Islamic clerics that he was not inciting violence against Guinea-Bissau's Muslims, who, unlike his Balante tribe, constitute a majority of the population. "We are all one people," Yalá declared, "our lines of origin cross ethnicity and religion. And we must keep it like that." But in December 2001 he sacked Prime Minister Faustino Imbali for criticizing his regime. "The dominate political context in the country nowadays was one of crisis in government," he insisted, "which had to be overcome to prevent the negation of the social, economic, political, and cultural objectives outlined by the government after the last elections." Despite the apparent instability in his government, and his ham-fisted handling of affairs, Yalá still retains a degree of national popularity. If he can stamp out corruption and military intervention, he will have provided a lasting service to the political and social institutions of Guinea-Bissau.

Further Reading

Adebajo, Adekeye. *Building Peace in West Africa: Liberia, Sierra Leone, and Guinea-Bissau.* Boulder, Colo.: Lynne Rienner Publishers, 2002.

Bigman, Laura. *History and Hunger in West Africa: Food Production and Entitlement in Guinea-Bissau and Cape Verde.* Westport, Conn.: Greenwood Press, 1993.

Forrest, Joshua. *Guinea-Bissau: Power, Conflict, and Renewal in a West African Nation.* Boulder, Colo.: Westview Press, 1992.

Handem, Alfredo, "Civil Society and Gender Relations in Guinea-Bissau." Unpublished master's thesis, University of Arkansas, 1999.

Miller, John. *Report and Proceedings, Conference on Good Governance, Guinea-Bissau.* Cambridge, Mass.: Abt Associates, 1998.

Yeltsin, Boris (1931–) *president of Russia*

Boris Nikolaevich Yeltsin was born on February 1, 1931, in the village of Butko, Siberia, a frontier region of the now-defunct Soviet Union. He matured into a burly individual, hot-tempered and outspoken in a political culture where docility was the expected norm. Yeltsin studied engineering at the Ural Polytechnic Institute and eventually joined the construction industry in Sverdlovsk. Despite the stifling bureaucracy and incompetence characterizing Soviet management, he flourished as a manager and was allowed to join the prestigious Communist Party in 1961 at the age of 30. Success only stoked his political aspirations, and over the next two and a half decades Yeltsin established himself as a hard-drinking, no-nonsense administrator, autocratic by nature but absolutely intolerant of corruption. Such was his reputation that in 1985, Premier Mikhail Gorbachev, another reform-minded Communist leader, invited Yeltsin to Moscow as the nation's new secretary of construction. It was anticipated that his gruff, outspoken nature would help Gorbachev's attempts at national reformation.

To a man of Yeltsin's plebeian background, Moscow proved the antithesis of everything he had been taught to believe as a Communist. The local party structure was hopelessly corrupt and, worse, flaunted its extravagant lifestyle with limousines, cut-rate party stores, and other benefits far beyond the average Soviet citizen. Yeltsin, true to form, lambasted his counterparts for their indulgences, and deliberately rode the public transport system, mingling on a daily basis with common people. Such behavior made him a celebrity to reckon with, and by 1986 Yeltsin was elected head of Moscow's Communist Party, first secretary of the Moscow party, and a member of the influential Politburo. Gorbachev was then engaged in a careful process of *perestroika,* or restructuring, to both modernize and ameliorate the infamous excesses of Soviet rule. However, he had to walk a fine line to placate conservatives in the party, and change proved slow. Such tardiness angered the impatient Yeltsin, who, in October 1987, publicly railed against the Central Committee's sabotage of badly needed reforms. Such outlandish behavior was unprecedented, and Yeltsin was immediately stripped of both his rank within the Politburo and his secretaryship of the Moscow party. Gorbachev thereupon reassigned him as deputy minister of construction to keep this troublesome maverick from further mischief.

Yeltsin clearly had other ideas and began slowly reconstructing his political fortunes. He capitalized on his reputation as a populist and gained election to the newly created Congress of People's Deputies. Moreover, he defeated his handpicked party opponent by 90 percent of the popular vote. He used his position as a bully pulpit, and he castigated party regulars for their lavish lifestyle and resistance to change. Yeltsin's popularity ratings soared in consequence, and in 1990 he gained a seat in the Supreme Soviet, which was chaired by Gorbachev. The two men, so much alike, clearly possessed differing visions for their country and were headed down a collision course. The clash came in July 1990 during the 28th Congress of the Communist Party, when Yeltsin and his fellow reformists assisted Gorbachev in forcing the retirement of arch-conservative L. K. Ligachev. He then boldly—and typically—strolled over to the podium, denounced the communist system, and resigned from the party altogether.

Yeltsin's belligerence toward the political establishment rendered him the most popular figure in the Soviet Union, and he began attracting international attention. In June 1991 he beat out six other candidates to become the first elected president of the Russian Republic, created as a parallel government to the Soviet regime. In another display of independence, Yeltsin commenced discussions with the three Baltic states to accommodate their demands for greater autonomy from Moscow.

These actions forced Gorbachev to accelerate his own pace of reforms, and by August 1991 he also began negotiations with all 15 republics in the U.S.S.R. to enhance self-governance. Hard-line ideologues within the party found this intolerable. Feeling that further change threatened the existing political order, on August 19, 1991, they staged a coup by detaining Gorbachev in his vacation home and attempting to reassert Communist control. However, they totally neglected Yeltsin, which proved a fatal mistake. When informed of events, he hurried back to Moscow and joined milling crowds surrounding the White House, site of Russia's parliament. Armed only with a bullhorn, he climbed on back of a tank and denounced the plotters, urging the population to turn out in protest. "We are dealing with a right-wing, reactionary, anticonstitutional coup," he bellowed. They responded by the millions while army troops refused to move against them. Within three days the coup collapsed completely and Gorbachev was released. However, the political gravity had shifted decisively over to Yeltsin, and in the fall of 1991 the Russian parliament outlawed the Communist Party while the republics began declaring independence from the unraveling Soviet Union. By January 1, 1992, the U.S.S.R., one of history's bloodiest experiments, had voted itself out of existence. Yeltsin continued as president of Russia, which became a member of a new entity, the Commonwealth of Independent States.

Now in control, Yeltsin wasted no time throwing off the shackles of the Soviet past. He commenced a new program appropriately called "Shock Therapy" to liberalize the economy, sell off inefficient state-owned assets, and embrace free-market capitalism. Unfortunately, this triggered a round of high inflation and currency devaluation as the national economy stumbled. The Russian parliament also proved recalcitrant and, in October 1993, Yeltsin dissolved the assembly and called for new elections. However, many hard-line opponents of privatization refused to leave the White House and they staged an illegal sit-in. Yeltsin, true to his increasingly autocratic nature, ordered troops to storm the very White House that he once defended. Such strong-arm tactics tainted his reputation, and the public responded by electing a very hostile assembly dominated by neo-Communists. Now the economic crisis was compounded by political gridlock. Russia also became embroiled in a bloody and unsuccessful war in the breakaway region of Chechnya.

The ensuing strife took its toll on Yeltsin's health, for he drank heavily and suffered several heart attacks. In 1996 he appeared headed for electoral defeat, but he rallied himself momentarily, campaigned vigorously, and defeated his Communist challenger, GENNADI ZYUGANOV, by a narrow margin. The extent of his health problems was kept a closely guarded secret.

Despite economic turmoil at home, Yeltsin enjoyed greater success on the international scene. Numerous arms treaties with the United States were successfully concluded, which led to reductions in nuclear weapons. He also saw the eastward expansion of NATO as inevitable, and, through hard bargaining, Yeltsin arranged for Russia to have a seat on the alliance's decision-making council. Throughout the bloody Balkan difficulties he also made Russia's displeasure with the bombing of Serbia known. Thereafter, Yeltsin tendered the use of troops as peacekeepers, but he refused to place them under NATO or international control. This defiance placated nationalists at home who felt the nation had lost its standing as a great power. But the greatest obstacle facing Russia remained the economy, which remained sluggish and also led to rising disparities in wealth. But Yeltsin, a consummate politician, was determined to demonstrate that he was in command and twice fired his entire cabinet. The churlish, unpredictable leader suddenly announced his resignation on New Year's Eve, 1999, and he was replaced by VLADIMIR PUTIN, a former KGB operative. "Russia must enter the new millennium with new politicians, new faces, new intelligent, strong and energetic people," he announced. "I must not stand in its way, in the way of the natural progress of history." Yeltsin lives in private retirement, somewhat discredited by his boorish handling of parliament and the economy. He currently draws a generous pension from the state and was granted immunity from prosecution by Putin. But his heroic stance outside the White House in August 1991, armed only with a bullhorn, renders him one of the most influential figures in recent world history. Yeltsin remains a hulking personification of the legendary Russian bear.

Further Reading

Aron, Leon R. *Yeltsin: A Revolutionary Life.* London: HarperCollins, 2000.

Breslauer, George W. *Gorbachev and Yeltsin as Leaders.* New York: Cambridge University Press, 2002.

Felkay, Andrew. *Yeltsin's Russia and the West.* Westport, Conn.: Praeger, 2002.

Hesli, Vicki L., and William M. Reisinger, eds. *The 1999–2000 Elections in Russia: Their Impact and Legacy.* New York: Cambridge University Press, 2003.

Kagarlitsky, Boris. *Russia Under Yeltsin and Putin: Neo-Liberal Aristocracy.* Sterling, Va.: Pluto Press, 2002.

Medvedev, Roy. *Post-Soviet Russia: A Journey through the Yeltsin Era.* New York: Columbia University Press, 2000.

Polsky, Yury. *Russia During the Period of Radical Change, 1992–2002.* Lewiston, N.Y.: Edwin Mellen Press, 2003.

Smith, Kathleen E. *Mythmaking in the New Russia: Politics and Memory during the Yeltsin Era.* Ithaca, N.Y.: Cornell University Press, 2002.

Yeltsin, Boris. *Midnight Diaries.* New York: Public Affairs, 2000.

Z

Zahir Shah, Mohammed (1914–   ) *king of Afghanistan*

Mohammed Zahir Shah was born in Kabul, Afghanistan, on October 30, 1914, the son of a high-ranking government minister, Mohammed Nadir Shah. He belonged by birth to the majority Pashtun tribal grouping, which formed part of the 255-year old Durrani dynasty. Zahir Shah was educated locally and, when his father transferred from home as minister to France, he accompanied him. He finished his education by attending the Pasteur Institute and the University of Montpellier. Back in Afghanistan a simmering tribal dispute resulted in a brief civil war and Nadir, now victorious, was pronounced king. The 18-year-old Zahir Shah also became an assistant minister of defense and education. On November 8, 1933, Nadir was assassinated and Zahir Shah was enthroned in his place, although real power lay in the hands of a regent, Sardar Hashim Khan. Over the next four decades Zahir Shah ruled capably, if cautiously. He steered a studiously neutral course during World War II, and during the cold war Afghanistan became one of few nations to receive financial aid from both the Western and Soviet blocs. However, his reign was beset by long-standing tribal factions and palace intrigue. In 1956 his cousin, Prime Minister Sardar Mohammed Daud, precipitated a crisis with Pakistan over the sovereignty of tribes living along the border region. It took several

months of intense wrangling before the Khyber Pass was open again to Afghan commerce, and thereafter the king looked askance at Daud's machinations.

Despite Afghanistan's status as a deeply conservative Muslim state, Zahir Shah also tried serving as a modernizing force. In 1964 he promulgated a new constitution guaranteeing civil rights, the separation of powers, freedom of the press, and voting rights for women. However, Daud's persistent meddling led to another quarrel with Pakistan and the king demanded his resignation. Thereafter he broke precedent by appointing a new prime minister and a council of ministers, none of whom was related to the royal family. This brought a temporary halt to family infighting and ushered in a period of peace and prosperity for most Afghans. However, in July 1973 Zahir Shah ventured to Italy for eye surgery, and he was ousted in a coup arranged by Daud. This event triggered a spate of coups and countercoups that culminated in the Soviet invasion of Afghanistan in December 1979. The king, who was stripped of his citizenship, remained isolated in Rome for the next three decades. He was a helpless onlooker as his country degenerated into a vicious cycle of violence and destruction.

The Soviet occupation of Afghanistan finally ended in 1989, which triggered another round of internecine civil strife between competing groups of Mujahideen, or freedom fighters. However, by 1996 a new group, the

Taliban (militant Islamic purists) shot their way into power. The new leader, Mullah OMAR MOHAMMED, imposed a strict theocratic dictatorship that forbade women from being educated and repressed religious and political beliefs. Worse, he sheltered Saudi international terrorist Osama bin Laden and his al-Qaeda network. On September 11, 2001, bin Laden's operatives destroyed New York's World Trade Center, and President GEORGE W. BUSH demanded the extradition of the terrorists for trial. When Mullah Omar refused, the Americans commenced a military campaign that toppled the Taliban by December. The problem then arose of installing a legitimate Afghan government that would be acceptable to all the traditional feuding parties.

Zahir Shah watched these events closely because, as king, he realized he served as a symbol of national unity to all Afghans. After 20 years of virtually incessant warfare, the country was in desperate need for stability. He was invited home by HAMID KARZAI, the newly appointed interim leader and a fellow Pashtun. The old man was naturally elated. "I go back with eagerness," he told reporters, "I go back with happiness and joy." On April 19, 2002, King Zahir Shah was conveyed by the Italian air force to Kabul, where he touched down for the first time in 30 years. A throng of thousands greeted the aged monarch with cheers and flowers, which moved him to tears. Given his age, and the labyrinthine nature of Afghan politics, the king was authorized only to open and preside over a Ioya jirga, or grand assembly, to chose a single leader. On June 10, 2002, this body was opened by the king to thunderous applause, but he himself expressed no desire to return to the throne. "I never wanted to impose myself on the Afghan people," he insists. "I awaited them to give the signal that they are ready to accept me to go back." It is the king's stated hope that a new period of peace has been ushered in, despite the reappearance of tribal warlords and continuing assassination attempts. Reconstruction has since commenced in this war-ravaged nation. But Zahir Shah remains content to serve as a symbol of reconciliation and healing. "I am not here to seek the monarchy, but to help my people and to be close to them," Zahir Shah declared. "I am here to spend the rest of my life with my people."

Further Reading

Edwards, David B. *Before Taliban: Genealogies of the Afghan Jihad:* Berkeley: University of California Press, 2002.

Magnus, Ralph H. *Afghanistan: Mullah, Marx, and Mujahid.* Boulder, Colo.: Westview Press, 2002.

Rashid, Ahmed. *Taliban: Islam, Oil, and the New Great Game in Central Asia.* London: I. B. Tauris, 2002.

———. *Jihad: The Rise of Militant Islam in Central Asia.* New Haven, Conn.: Yale University Press, 2002.

Roberts, Jeffrey J. *The Origins of Conflict in Afghanistan.* Westport, Conn.: Praeger, 2003.

Rubin, Barnett R. *The Fragmentation of Afghanistan.* New Haven, Conn.: Yale University Press, 2002.

Zedillo, Ernesto (1951–) *president of Mexico*

Ernesto Zedillo Ponce de León was born on December 27, 1951, in Mexico City, the son of an electrician. He was raised in the town of Mexicali, near the U.S. border, before pursuing economics at the National Polytechnic Institute. Zedillo proved extremely adept as a student, and he subsequently won a government scholarship for advanced studies at Yale University. In 1981 he received his doctorate in economics, and he returned home to work at the Bank of Mexico. Zedillo rose through the ranks, and by 1988 he was appointed by President CARLOS SALINAS DE GORTARI to serve as his secretary for programming and budget. As secretary he designed a new national development plan that facilitated the growth of free-market economics and the privatization of government-owned industries. In January 1992 Salinas appointed Zedillo secretary of education, in which capacity he instituted moves to decentralize the system and revamp the nation's textbooks. In all these capacities he performed satisfactorily, acquiring a reputation as a highly intelligent technocrat who was quiet, unambitious, and incorruptible. In November 1993 he was tapped to serve as the presidential campaign manager for Luis Donaldo Colosio of the Institutional Revolutionary Party (PRI), which had dominated Mexican politics since 1929. The PRI was notoriously corrupt in power and routinely stole elections to perpetuate its tenure and patronage. However, when Colosio was suddenly assassinated on March 23, 1994, PRI national leaders were hard-pressed to find a suitable replacement. At the urging of Salinas, they selected mild-mannered Zedillo as their candidate.

Zedillo's appointment as the nominal head of the PRI was curious, since he never held elected office before. Moreover, he was bland, uncharismatic, and totally outside the typical mold of Mexican politicians. The country also faced a major embarrassment in the form of an Indian uprising in poverty-stricken Chiapas province, a direct challenge to national authority. However, Zedillo was fortunate in facing two equally stumbling opponents from the conservative National Action Party (PAN) and the radical Revolutionary Democratic Party (PRD). Furthermore, in a complete departure from the usual PRI politics, Zedillo had campaigned on a platform promising the freest and most honest election in Mexico's history. His message resonated with voters and on August 21, 1994, he was elected president by the slightest margins, gaining only 50.18 percent of votes cast. This strongly suggested that the PRI was losing its grip on the electoral process.

Zedillo was sworn in on December 1, 1994, and faced an imminent economic crisis. The free borrowing policies of Salinas triggered a near-collapse of the banking system and the peso suddenly lost half its value. The ensuing stock market crash threw Mexico into a steep recession, which was only ameliorated by an emergency $20 billion loan from the United States. Zedillo also had to enact strict austerity measures, which inflicted considerable pain upon the poor nations but finally stabilized the situation. True to his pledge, the president then embarked on an extensive plan for political reforms, to eliminate corruption and make elections fairer and more honest. He also made sweeping changes in the notoriously corrupt Mexican justice system, and he solicited military help for the ongoing war against drug smuggling. In 1996 he signed a peace treaty with the Zapatista rebels of Chiapas, although the military was so angered that they considered toppling him. By 1997 Zedillo's political reforms bore fruit, though not in the manner the PRI anticipated. That July the PAN took control of the legislature, the first time a Mexican executive had to deal with a hostile legislature since 1919. Nonetheless, despite grumbling from party loyalists, Zedillo hailed the outcome as proof that Mexican democracy was more responsive to the will of the voters.

For all the good work Zedillo accomplished during his six years in office, he still presided over a nation rife with corruption. In January 1999 he went on television to announce that Raul Salinas, brother of the late president, was arrested for the murder of a leading PRI politician. Carlos Salinas then went on a hunger strike protesting his arrest, before Zedillo exiled him to the United States. To many Mexicans it appeared that the PRI was back to running affairs as they always had— above the law and for personal gain. In 2000 Zedillo was constitutionally prevented from seeking a second term in office, so he handed the party's baton off to Francisco Labastida Ochoa. At that time he made the prophetic declaration: "The July 2000 elections will confirm that Mexico is a democratic nation." However, the PRI's opponent this time was the charismatic and outspoken VICENTE FOX of PAN, who went on to win the election handily. Thus the PRI's 71-year dominance in Mexican politics came to an ignominious end. Nevertheless, Zedillo was graceful—even grateful—in defeat. "I believe all of us, absolutely all of us, have to acknowledge one fact," he declared. "Mexico has completed its journey towards democracy." The changes he wrought, especially those criticized by his own party, finally bequeathed to his nation a new political age.

Since leaving office, Zedillo has concentrated on activities abroad in the field of international business, and his talents remain much in demand. He has served as a member of a UN panel to proffer advise on financial matters in developing countries, on the board of a major U.S. railroad company, and as head of Yale University's center on globalization.

Further Reading

Camp, Roderic A. *Politics in Mexico: The Democratic Transformation.* New York: Oxford University Press, 2003.

Chand, Kikram K. *Mexico's Political Awakening.* Notre Dame, Ind.: University of Notre Dame Press, 2000.

Hodges, Donald C. *Mexico, the End of the Revolution.* Westport, Conn.: Praeger, 2002.

Langston, Joy. "Why Rules Matter: Changes in Candidate Selection in Mexico's PRI, 1988–2000." *Journal of Latin American Studies* 33 (August 2001): 485–511.

Purcell, Susan K., and Luis Rubio-Freidberg. *Mexico under Zedillo.* Boulder, Colo.: Lynne Rienner Publishers, 1998.

Rodriguez, Victoria E. *Women in Contemporary Mexican Politics.* Austin: University of Texas Press, 2003.

Zeman, Miloš (1944–) *prime minister of the Czech Republic*

Miloš Zeman was born on September 28, 1944, in the German—formerly Czech—town of Kolin. His small, landlocked country had once been part of the Austrian Empire, but in 1918 the Czech Republic and Slovakia were merged into a new country, Czechoslovakia. In 1938 the Czech region, home to a large population of

Sudeten Germans, was absorbed by Nazi Germany while Slovakia became an independent state. By 1945 Soviet troops had occupied both sections, united them, and in 1948 installed a Communist-style dictatorship. In 1968 Czech Communists under Premier Alexander Dubcek tried mitigating party doctrine, and his "Prague Spring" was summarily crushed by Soviet troops. However, this oppression inspired creation of several dissident groups who refused to be silenced, and who subsequently orchestrated the so-called Velvet Revolution. Following the withdrawal of Soviet forces from Eastern Europe in 1989, Czechoslovakia held democratic elections, and Communist rule ended. Three years later, after a fallout between the two regions, the Czech Republic and Slovakia again parted company as independent nations. Presently, the government of the Czech Republic is based on a parliamentary system whereby a prime minister is drawn from whatever party or coalition holds the most seats. Several parties are present, but national politics are largely dominated by the leftist Social Democratic Party (CSSD) and the right-wing Civic Democratic Party (ODS). The Czech Republic also enjoys one of Eastern Europe's highest standards of living, a robust, free-market economy, and a well-deserved reputation for precision-made machinery and optics.

Zeman attended the Advanced School of Economics in Prague before joining the Communist Party in 1968. He became swept up in the liberalizing reforms sweeping the country, and, after the Soviet occupation, he was expelled from the party. For many years thereafter he worked as a researcher for different economic concerns, and in 1989 Zeman joined the Obcanske (Civic) Forum, an opposition group. He commenced his political career the following year by gaining appointment as head of the Federal Assembly budget committee. A talented political operative, he next joined the CSSD in 1992 and within a year had emerged as party leader. As a result of close elections in 1996, the ruling ODS allowed leading CSSD members to occupy important governmental posts, and Zeman served as chairman of parliament. As a result of close national elections in 1998, when neither the ODS nor CSSD could form a coalition government, both sides decided to join ranks as a single-party minority government. On July 17, 1998, Zeman was sworn in as the new prime minister, although little hope was held for the viability of his administration.

In power, Zeman continued the policies of his predecessors, especially full Czech membership into NATO (granted in 1999) and the European Union (expected in 2004). The overall economic picture is bright, and the country registers an annual growth rate of 5 percent. However, Zeman's tenure in office has also been marred by several controversies with neighboring countries. In September 2000 his government decided to proceed with construction of the Temelin nuclear power plant, located about 40 miles from the Austrian border. Given the age and problems associated with the plant's Soviet design, the decision sparked massed protests in Austria, especially from the followers of far-right leader JÖRG HAIDER. "The sooner Austria gets rid of Mr. Haider and his post-fascist Freedom Party the better," Zeman casually remarked, which further strained relations. When Haider threatened to veto Czech entry into the EU if Temelin becomes operative, Zeman agreed to allow inspection and monitoring of the facilities by outside authorities. The plant is still not online because of ongoing technical difficulties.

Miloš Zeman *(Embassy of the Czech Republic)*

A more emotional problem dates back to the dark days of World War II. After the conflict ended in 1945, the Czechoslovakian government expelled millions of ethnic Sudeten Germans from the country. Since then, many survivors and descendants are pressing for reparations for property lost as a condition for Czech entry into the EU. The Czech government under Zeman, who personally characterized the refugees as "Hitler's fifth column," soundly rejects such thinking. "According to Czech laws many Sudeten Germans committed treason, a crime which at that time was punishable by death," he insisted. "If they were expelled or transferred, it was more moderate than the death penalty." Equally controversial were the president's remarks during a recent visit to Israel in February 2002. At that time he declared that "Israel should not be forced to negotiate with [Palestinian leader YASSER ARAFAT, just as the allies were not forced to negotiate with the Nazis." The result was vociferous condemnation of the Czech Republic throughout the Arab world, and many EU leaders were equally aghast. It particularly raised hackles in Germany, where Chancellor GERHARD SCHROEDER angrily canceled a scheduled visit to Prague. The controversial Czech prime minister has since announced his decision to retire from politics when his term expires in late 2002.

Further Reading

Eyal, Gil. *The Origins of Post-Communist Elites: From Prague Spring to the Breakup of Czechoslovakia.* Minneapolis: University of Minnesota Press, 2003.

Innes, Abby. *Czechoslovakia: The Short Goodbye.* New Haven, Conn.: Yale University Press, 2001.

Kopecky, Petr. *Parliaments in the Czech and Slovak Republics: Party Competition and Parliamentary Institutionalization.* Burlington, Vt.: Ashgate, 2001.

Orenstein, Mitchell A. *Out of the Red: Building Capitalism and Democracy in Postcommunist Europe.* Ann Arbor: University of Michigan Press, 2001.

Shepherd, Robin H. E. *Czechoslovakia: The Velvet Revolution and Beyond.* New York: St. Martin's Press, 2000.

Stein, Eric. *Czechoslovakia: Ethnic Conflict, Constitutional Fissure, Negotiated Breakup.* Ann Arbor: University of Michigan Press, 2000.

Zenawi, Meles (1955–) *prime minister of Ethiopia*

Legesse Zenawi was born in the Tigrean town of Adwa, Ethiopia, on May 8, 1955. He subsequently adopted the name Meles in honor of a fallen war hero. Ethiopia, one of the world's oldest centers of civilization, is located on the Horn of Africa, astride the Red Sea. Unlike many other African countries, and save for a brief period under Italian domination, it was never colonized by Europeans. However, it is a parched, dry region and highly susceptible to drought. Ethiopia is also home to 12 distinct ethnic groups and 75 languages, which traditionally militates against national unity. When unity was maintained throughout most of the 20th century, it was at the behest of the powerful Amhara group—and at the expense of others. For many years Ethiopia was led by Emperor Haile Selassie until a military coup headed by Colonel Mengistu Haile Mariam toppled him in 1974. The new leader installed a brutal, Marxist-dominated dictatorship, and he ruled the country with an iron hand. His one-party state was replete with firing squads, mass collectivization of agriculture, and the deaths of thousands of citizens. Soon Ethiopia was regarded as a pariah nation, whose only reliable ally was the Soviet Union. However, Mengistu's oppression led to the rise of numerous resistance groups who, over the next 15 years, sought to wrest their respective regions away from the central government. The gradual collapse of Soviet support left the Mengistu regime increasingly vulnerable to attack, and in May 1991 he fled the country for Zimbabwe. By July of that year a new transitional government was in place, and Ethiopia began reasserting itself among the community of nations.

Zenawi completed his secondary education at the General Wingate High School before attending the University of Addis Ababa to study medicine. Though a committed Marxist, he was outraged by the abuses perpetuated by Mengistu and in 1971 he joined the Tigray People's Liberation Front (TPLF). A seesaw guerrilla war ensued for many years, but by 1989 Zenawi had emerged both as the head of the TPLF and a military commander of note. He was among the victorious leaders who stormed the capital in 1991, whereupon a transitional government was installed. In recognition of his contributions, the newly elected Council of Representatives appointed Zenawi president. Here he helped draw up a new constitution, which arranged a federal republic with nine ethnically based states. Ethiopia's first multiparty elections then took place in July 1995 and the following month the new Council of the People's Representatives appointed him the nation's first prime minister. At that time Zenawi assured his war-weary countrymen, "We are now able to make the transition to a fully democratic government which will satisfy the wishes of our peoples and their centuries-old longing for such a system."

Zenawi presides over one of Africa's poorest regions. Ethiopia is a predominately agricultural nation, highly dependent on coffee exports as a cash crop. However, this former Marxist has since renounced his views and fully embraced free-market economics. His priorities in office have been to diversify the economy, placing renewed emphasis on industrialization; and attracting foreign investment. To that extent he has been highly successful, and the Ethiopian economy has since been touted by the World Bank and International Monetary Fund (IMF) as a model for developing nations everywhere. His achievements have also been welcomed with relief by his countrymen, and, on May 14, 2000, they overwhelmingly elected him to another five years in office.

Ethiopia, unfortunately, continues to suffer from the effects of leftover conflicts. The northernmost region of Eritrea never accepted domination by its southern neighbor, and it waged a war of independence until Mengistu was ousted in 1991. Zenawi, as head of the transitional government, then allowed it to pursue independence. However, ongoing border disputes have since flared into all-out war, and, in May 1998, forces directed by President ISAIAS AFWERKI invaded Ethiopia. Fighting was intense and 2,000 lives were lost before a cease-fire was announced in March 2002. Thereafter, the disputed region has been patrolled by UN peacekeepers until official borders can be properly demarcated. That same spring the Norwegian government announced it was donating $1 million to assist in the demarcation process, provided Zenawi's government continues to support peace, stability, democracy, and human rights. Ethiopia's record on all these counts is far from perfect, but it is improving. Furthermore, since the September 11, 2001, attack on New York's World Trade Center, the prime minister subordinated his troops to the American Central Command, based in Tampa, Florida. In March 2002, General Tommy Franks arrived in Addis Ababa to confer with Zenawi about combating terrorism. Apparently, the prime minister requested assistance in fighting the renegade al-Itihaad group, a Somali-based Muslim fundamentalist group with ties to Osama bin Laden's al-Qaida terror network. Meanwhile, the country continues savoring its relative peace and prosperity, long absent after three decades of turmoil and repression. Zenawi is slated to run again in 2005 and, if he can maintain current trends in stability and economic growth, his reelection seems all but assured.

Further Reading

Donham, Donald L. *Marxist Modern: An Ethnographic History of the Ethiopian Revolution.* Berkeley: University of California Press, 1999.

Fessehatzion, Teke. *Eritrea and Ethiopia: From Conflict to Cooperation to Conflict.* Lawrenceville, N.J.: Red Sea Press, 1999.

Gilkes, Patrick, and Martin Plant. "War in the Horn: The Conflict between Eritrea and Ethiopia." London: Royal Institute of International Affairs, 1999.

James, Wendy, ed. *Remapping Ethiopia: Socialism and After.* Athens: Ohio University Press, 2002.

Pausewing, Siegfried, ed. *Ethiopia since the DERG: A Decade of Democratic Pretension and Performance.* New York: Zed Books, 2003.

Tesfaye, Aaron. *Political Power and Ethnic Federalism: The Struggle for Democracy in Ethiopia.* Lanham, Md.: University Press of America, 2002.

Vestal, Theodore. *Ethiopia: A Post-Cold War African State.* Westport, Conn.: Praeger, 1999.

Zeroual, Liamine (1941–) *president of Algeria*

Liamine Zeroual was born on July 3, 1941, in Batna, Algeria, then a French colony. In the 1950s he immersed himself in the anticolonial feelings sweeping North Africa and joined the National Liberation Army at the age of 16. After independence had been won in 1962, Zeroual pursued advanced military studies at the Moscow Military School in 1965 and the War College of Paris in 1974. Once home he served in a succession of increasingly important military posts, including command of all airborne forces and head of the Batna Military School. His reputation as a competent military professional led to his appointment as commander of all land forces in 1989, as well as deputy chief of staff. However, Zeroual had profound disagreements with President Chadli Bendjedid, and he resigned from the service that year. His final assignment was as ambassador to Romania, 1990–91. During Zeroual's absence Algeria was convulsed by civil war. Like all Muslim countries, it had experienced a surge in Islamic fundamentalism, brought on in large measure through poor handling of the economy and widespread poverty. After severe rioting in 1988 the political monopoly of the National Liberation Front officially ended, and a period of multiparty democracy ensued. However, the biggest beneficiary proved to be the Islamic Front of Salvation (FIS), which swept the June 1990 municipal elections. Legislative elections were scheduled for June 1991, and FIS's success emboldened them to campaign nationally. At this point the military intervened to reassert control and political activity was suspended until December 1991. When elections finally transpired, FIS won decisively, capturing 188 seats out of 430 in the National Assembly. Because the fundamentalists were now well positioned to seek a two-thirds majority, enough to amend the constitution, the army again intervened on January 11, 1992. This time they forced President Bendjedid to resign and substituted an eight-member High State Council to run the country. They then commenced a search for an acceptable executive officer.

Military usurpation of the election triggered a violent reaction from the FIS and other extreme Muslim groups. They commenced a savage guerrilla war by targeting soldiers, police, civilians, and especially foreigners, with terrorism. Not surprisingly, the military clamped down severely on all social unrest and the killing continued. A state of emergency ensued while the High State Committee proved unable to produce a candidate with sufficient political legitimacy to run the country. Therefore, on January 31, 1992, they called Zeroual out of retirement and installed him as president for a three-year transition period. "We will mobilize all our means to fight violence and stop bloodletting," he warned extremists. "The use of violence as a form of political expression or as a way to acceded to power could never be tolerated."

Once in power, Zeroual offered to establish a dialogue with the FIS and any other group willing to listen. None were. In light of the nation's economic distress he also moved quickly to conclude a debt renegotiation package with the International Monetary Fund (IMF) to ease conditions. However, Algeria also devalued its currency by 40 percent and eliminated subsidies on basic commodities. The result was an increase in consumer distress, which occasioned greater sympathy for the Muslim extremists. The vicious cycle of terrorism and re-

pression continued without interruption until November 1995, when Algeria's first direct presidential elections were scheduled. Unfortunately, the majority of parties decided to boycott the process, and Zeroual ran unopposed. Voter turnout was exceptionally high and he won 61 percent of ballots cast, which gave his regime the veneer of legitimacy. "I invite Algerian youth who are misled to look closely into the ruling passed by their people and to return to the correct path," he declared. "The state will continue its fight against the remnants of terrorist violence that target the homeland." The government then tried but failed again to establish a dialogue with the Islamic radicals, and the fighting continued. This prompted Zeroual to propose sweeping constitutional changes to be approved in September 1996. These modifications concentrated power into the hands of the executive at the expense of the legislature, in such a manner that no bill could pass without a three-fourths majority. Moreover, the president would appoint one-third of the upper chamber himself, ensuring that he could block any laws not to his liking. Muslim fundamentalists were now stymied in parliament, even in the unlikely event that they gained control.

Zeroual seemed increasingly in control of Algeria's civil war when, in September 1998, he suddenly and inexplicably resigned two years before his term expired. He then scheduled new elections for April 15, 1999, which were won by the present executive, ABDELAZIZ BOUTEFLIKA. Much speculation was given as to the reasons behind his retirement, but the consensus is that the former military man was ultimately sidelined by poor health. And, because by that time 75,000 people had been killed in sectarian violence, perhaps Zeroual wished to distance himself from a war that appeared unwinnable.

Further Reading

Derradji, Abder-Rahmane. *A Concise History of Political Violence in Algeria, 1954–2000: Brothers in Faith, Enemies in Arms.* Lewiston, N.Y.: Edwin Mellen Press, 2002.

Guess, Marc C. "The Emergence of Political Islam in the Arab World: Comparative Studies of Algeria and Jordan." Unpublished master's thesis, American University, 1996.

Roberts, Hugh. "Commanding Disorder: Military Power and Informal Politics in Algeria." London: I. B. Tauris, 2002.

Viorst, Milton. "Algeria's Long Night." *Foreign Affairs* 76, no. 6 (1997): 86–99.

Volpi, Frederic. *Islam and Democracy: The Failure of Dialogue in Algeria, 1988–2001.* Sterling, Va.: Pluto Press, 2002.

Zhirinovsky, Vladimir (1946–)

Russian politician

Vladimir Volfovich Zhirinovsky was born on April 26, 1946, in Alma-Ata, Kazakhstan, then part of the Soviet Union. His father, a Jewish lawyer, died while he was an infant, and he was raised by his mother, a cleaning lady. Zhirinovsky also endured a difficult childhood of growing up Russian while surrounded by Kazakhs, and the experience embittered him. Nevertheless, he passed through Moscow State University with a degree in Oriental languages. He worked several years for various publishing and international trade concerns, becoming fluent in German, English, and Turkish. Prior to the breakup of the Soviet Union in December 1991, Zhirinovsky evinced no interest in politics but, like many nationalistic Russians, he was greatly affected by his country's loss of international stature. That year he founded the ultraconservative Liberal Democratic Party (LDP) and ran for the newly created post of Russian president, finishing a surprising third behind BORIS YELTSIN and Nikolai Ryzhkov. This strong showing catapulted him into the national limelight, allowing for all-important media coverage. Zhirinovsky soon emerged as Russia's most volatile politician, telegenic, outlandish, and dauntingly unrestrained in his political invective. Brimming with resentment and becoming an expert finger-pointer, he was blatantly anti-Semitic and flaunted his prejudice like a badge of pride. Worse, Zhirinovsky's antics appealed to a large cross-section of the population, particularly in the countryside, who shared his anger over the fallen Soviet Union.

Many politicians dismissed Zhirinovsky's antics as little more than political theater, but his sometimes defiant nationalism, coupled with barrages of threats against perceived enemies—foreign and domestic—continued resonating with the public. Events crested in December 1993 when the LDP garnered 23 percent of the votes, nearly 12.3 million ballots. Zhirinovsky, now elected to the Duma (parliament), commanded no less than 65 seats, the second biggest voting bloc after Gennadi Zyuganov's Communists. From this position of strength, he posited himself and his party as a "third way" between the reformers and the Communists. His message was certainly abetted by the poor state of the Russian economy, floundering under the weight of free-market reforms and high unemployment. Under such circumstances, Zhirinovsky's foghorn belligerency found fertile soil in which to grow. Among his many threats were seizing Alaska back from the United States, declaring war against Japan, and dropping nuclear waste on Germany. The Jewish community in Russia, having borne the brunt of czarist and communist discrimination for decades, became understandably alarmed by his progress and immigration to Israel increased several fold. Russia's pent-up hatreds had apparently come home to roost.

The LDP's political fortunes apparently peaked in 1995 when they gathered only 11.1 percent, second to Zyuganov's resurgent Communists. But Zhirinovsky continued with his one-man diatribe against Jews, the West, and traitors, praising Adolph Hitler and declaring his support for Iraqi dictator SADDAM HUSSEIN. In 1996 he ran for the presidency of Russia, but tallied only 5.7 percent and was forced to drop out. He nevertheless maintained his high media visibility, railing against Yeltsin, and insisting Russia will not enjoy peace until its military forces "wash their boots in the Indian Ocean." His inflammatory shock tactics have since lost most of their effect, for the LDP's numbers remain abysmally low. Zhirinovsky, however, thrives in the niche he carved out for himself, a cheerleader for ethnic hatred and nationalist extremism. Over the years his taste for controversy remains little diminished. In July 2001 he admitted that his father was Jewish, and he immediately downplayed it. "Why should I reject Russian blood, Russian culture, Russian land, and fall in love with the Jewish people only because of that single drop of blood that my father left in my mother's body?" he asked. Several months later he criticized the Roman Catholic Church for creating four new dioceses in Russia, claiming that "this is the reason why Orthodox churches are being destroyed in the Balkans and seized in western Ukraine, and Catholic priests are getting more and more influence in Moscow, St. Petersburg, and across Russia." In 2002 he declared the American-led war against international terrorism in Afghanistan a failure and he anticipates an invasion against Iraq soon. "We can benefit from this situation and make money on arms supplies to another country, too," he asserts. Zhirinovsky is presently deputy speaker of the Duma, but he has failed repeatedly—perhaps understandably—to rise to full speaker. He remains firmly entrenched as Russia's apostle of hatred, and its solitary guardian of the lost and, to him and his supporters, the much-lamented Soviet imperial past.

Further Reading

Humphrey, Caroline. *The Unmaking of Soviet Life: Everyday Economies After Socialism.* Ithaca, N.Y.: Cornell University Press, 2002.

Karetisev, Vladimir P. *Zhirinovsky!* New York: Columbia University Press, 1995.

Koman, A. "The Last Surge to the South: The New Enemies of Russia in the Rhetoric of Zhirinovsky." *Studies in Conflict and Terrorism* 60 (Summer 1996): 279–327.

Nichols, T. "An Electoral Mutiny? Zhirinovsky and the Russian Armed Forces." *Armed Forces and Society* 21 (Spring 1995): 327–347.

Sawka, Richard. *Russian Politics and Society.* New York: Routledge, 2002.

Solovyev, Vladimir. *Zhirinovsky: Russian Fascism and the Making of a Dictator.* Reading, Mass.: Addison-Wesley, 1995.

Zhirinovsky, Vladimir. *My Struggle: The Explosive Views of Russia's Most Controversial Political Figure.* New York: Barricade Books, 1996.

Zhu Rongji (Chu Jung-chi) (1928–)

prime minister of China

Zhu Rongji was born in Changsha, the capital of Hunan province, China, on October 1, 1928. Hunan is also the birth place of Mao Zedong, the father of modern Communist China. Zhu was orphaned at an early age and raised by his uncle. He joined the Communist Party while studying electrical engineering at Quinghua University, from which he graduated in 1951. Over the next few years Zhu served in numerous positions with state power concerns until 1957 when, during Mao's "Hundred Flowers Campaign," he criticized the party for revolutionary excesses. This outspokenness resulted in a bout of "political rehabilitation" in the countryside, where Zhu was forced to feed pigs and clean toilets. Fortunately, he was considered "rehabilitated" by 1962 and appointed to the national economy bureau of the State Planning Commission. However, Zhu had lost none of his confrontational demeanor and in 1966, during opening phases of the catastrophic Cultural Revolution, he was again branded a "rightist" and sentenced to more rehabilitation. He remained thus disposed until 1975, when a minor post with the Power and Communication Engineering Company was proffered. The turning point in Zhu's career came in 1978 with the rise of DENG XIAOPING, a radical reformer, who was seeking brash, young technocrats to completely overhaul the creaking Communist state.

Zhu successfully served in a number of increasingly important economic positions under Deng, whereby he discarded traditional, centrally planned economics in favor of a capitalist, free-market model. In 1987 he gained appointment as mayor of Shanghai, long regarded as the most advanced economic sector of China, but then floundering under excessive bureaucratic control. In quick order, Zhu cut back regulations, invited in Western investors, and privatized various ailing and state-owned government interests. He pursued reform with such single-minded ferocity that Westerners nicknamed him "One Chop Zhu," for his uncanny ability to obtain quick results. The outcome was spectacular, and Shanghai became a showcase for Deng's new economic policies. More important, during the large student protests following the 1989 massacre at Tiananmen Square, Zhu refused to call on army troops to restore order; rather, he allowed the crowds to dissipate their anger and disband on their own. In recognition of his success, Zhu was elevated to one of six vice prime ministers within the State Council in 1996. More than any other individual, he now became specifically tasked with doing for China what he had already achieved in Shanghai.

Over the next eight years Zhu rigorously pursued capitalist reforms, again with excellent results. Taxes were trimmed, the bureaucracy streamlined, and free-market growth and profits encouraged. Consequently, the Chinese economy started expanding at unprecedented annual rates of 10 percent. Inflation, which had been rampant at 24 percent, was lowered to a mere 3 percent by tough austerity measures that also brought the national debt under control. By 1997 the Chinese economy performed so well that it was largely unaffected by the Asian currency crisis of that year, which had devastating effects on Japan, Korea, and other regional powerhouses. The government applauded Zhu's success by appointing him prime minister (premier) in March 1998, making him the third most powerful leader behind President JIANG ZEMIN and parliamentary leader LI PENG. In this capacity, Zhu flew to the United States in 1999 to appeal for China's entry into the World Trade Organization. This, however, would entail some serious economic concessions, including the elimination of import tariffs and subsidies for businesses. It also ensured a spell of social hardship, including greater unemployment, until the economy righted itself. But Zhu correctly gauged that membership in the WTO meant greater access to world markets, increasing emphasis on competitiveness, and long-term economic growth. In 1991 the United States finally granted China formal admission. The two national economies are now more closely entwined than ever.

Despite resounding success on the economic front, China faces several seemingly intractable problems. First and foremost is the issue of corruption, which is widespread and threatens to sap the nation's vitality. In March 2000 Zhu addressed the national legislature and promised to enact tougher laws against graft, which, in China, is a capital offense punishable by death. There is also the problem of Taiwan, which the Chinese Communists regard as a rebellious province and are determined to reunite with the mainland. Zhu has variously restated the hard-line party stance on the issue, but he has been circumspect about advocating military force, which would trigger an armed confrontation with the United States. More disturbing is the rise of Muslim fundamentalism in China's westernmost provinces. Religious unrest and agitation for a separate state will undoubtedly be dealt with harshly by Chinese officials, as will the issue of terrorism. Zhu officially lent his support for the American war against the Taliban regime in neighboring Afghanistan, but he stopped short of endorsing an invasion of Iraq. In January 2002 he also paid an official state visit to India, becoming the first high-ranking official to do so in a decade, where he conferred with Prime Minister ATAL BEHARI VAJPAYEE on ways of combating terrorists. Zhu has favorably impressed most Western heads of state with whom he has dealt, and is regarded by observers as charming, intelligent, and humorous. He is expected to resign from politics in 2003, along with Jiang and Li, to make way for more vigorous successors, better able to cope with a rapidly changing world.

Further Reading

Chen, Xiaowei. *Occidentalism: A Theory of Counter-Discourse in Post-Mao China.* Lanham, Md.: Rowman and Littlefield, 2002.

Dickson, Bruce J. *Red Capitalists in China: The Party, Private Entrepreneurs, and Prospects for Political Change.* New York: Cambridge University Press, 2003.

Leung, Pak-Wah. *Political Leaders of Modern China, 1840–2001: A Biographical Dictionary.* Westport, Conn.: Greenwood Press, 2002.

Pieke, Frank N. *People's Republic of China.* Aldershot, England: Ashgate, 2002.

Zhang, Xudong. *Whither China? Intellectual Politics in Contemporary China.* Durham, N.C.: Duke University Press, 2002.

Zweig, David. "China's Stalled 'Fifth Wave': Zhu Rongji's Reform Package of 1998–2000." *Asian Survey* 41 (March–April 2001): 231–247.

Zia, Begum Khaleda (1945–) *prime minister of Bangladesh*

Begum Khaleda Zia was born on August 15, 1945, in Dinajpur, East Pakistan. At the age of 15 she finished school and entered into a traditional arranged marriage. Her husband, Ziaur Rahman, was a captain in the Pakistani army. In 1971 a civil war was fought with Indian aid and East Pakistan declared its independence under the new name of Bangladesh. Ziaur, now a rebel, emerged as a war hero and rose rapidly to the rank of major general. In this capacity he supported a coup in 1975 that placed him in charge of the country. Zia, as a traditional Muslim woman, evinced no interest in politics and remained at home to raise her children. In 1977 Ziaur was elected prime minister through a national referendum while Zia became the nation's first lady. He also founded the Bangladesh National Party (BNP) to consolidate control. However, in 1981 Ziaur was assassinated in a military coup and was succeeded by General Hussein Muhammad Ershad, who seized the reins of government and declared martial law. Zia always suspected him of engineering her husband's death. This act induced her to become politically active, and in 1982 she secured appointment as vice chairman of the BNP. For the next eight years the otherwise shy housewife emerged as a major opposition figure to Ershad's regime, and she led repeated boycotts of sham elections.

Becoming chairman of BNP in 1984, Zia next called for international sanctions against the government, which finally succeeded in forcing Ershad from power in December 1990. He subsequently received a 20-year jail sentence for corruption and other charges. A caretaker government then emerged to orchestrate new national elections held in 1991. Not surprisingly Zia, Ershad's most unflinching adversary, easily won the election, becoming Bangladesh's first female prime minister. After BENAZIR BHUTTO of Pakistan she was only the second woman in a Muslim country to hold the post.

Coming from a nation rife with crime, corruption, and poverty, Zia had campaigned on a platform of change and equity. "I'm going to prove that a clean government in this country is possible," she announced,."All you have to do is to ensure accountability of the government to the people." Zia came to power in one of the world's poorest nations. Bangladesh is overcrowded, underdeveloped, and frequently lashed by violent cyclones that kill thousands annually. However, she tackled her responsibilities with relish. Mindful of widespread illiteracy and impoverishment among Bangladeshi women, she embarked on education and vocational training for both genders alike. She also sought foreign assistance for the establishment of small loans to assist female-owned businesses. Zia also championed moves toward greater liberalization of the economy and privatization of state-run enterprises. She tried constantly to attract foreign investment to facilitate this transformation, but when it proved not forthcoming the economy stalled. By 1994 Bangladesh remained in a serious recession and Zia's popularity sank. She was especially assailed by her political rival, HASINA WAJED of the Awami League (AL), who positioned herself to run for prime minister. Zia's attempts to rule were also complicated by the rise of Muslim fundamentalist parties in her coalition, which blanched at the notion of women in political office. Throughout 1995 Bangladesh erupted in an ongoing series of riots and political violence that took hundreds of lives. This disorder proved beyond Zia's ability to control, so in March 1996 she handed power over to a caretaker government. The BNP subsequently lost the election to Wajed's AL, who became the nation's second woman executive. Zia was angered by allegations of voter fraud and her party boycotted the parliament over the next 14 months.

For five years, Zia served in parliament as head of the opposition. Wajed, it turns out, enjoyed little success in redressing Bangladesh's chronic economic and societal problems. Zia carefully bided her time and, in elections held on October 5, 2001, she won a decisive victory over her AL opponents. The period up to the elections was marred by violent protests and confrontations, killing hundreds. But ultimately the BNP coalition won 185 out of 283 parliamentary seats, to an AL tally of 63. The scale of the defeat is viewed as a verdict against the violence, corruption, and crime that Wajed's administration could not resolve. Zia was then sworn into office a second time on October 11, 2001, while opposition leaders remonstrated about polling irregularities and boycotted the ceremony. Intent upon restoring some semblance of order to the nation, she next conferred with Shantu Larma, a former rebel leader, in April 2002. At that time they discussed continuance of a five-year-old peace accord reached with the previous administration. Zia had previously threatened to rescind the accord during the election, but now she seems content to maintain present accommodations. For the meantime her greatest priority is restoring the breakdown of law and order that has swept the countryside and threatens national stability.

Further Reading

Ahmed, Nizam. *The Parliament of Bangladesh*. Aldershot, England: Ashgate, 2002.

Kabir, Muhammed G. *Changing Face of Nationalism: The Case of Bangladesh*. Denver, Colo.: iAcademic Books, 2001.

Ryan, Paul R. *Bangladesh 2000: On the Brink of Civil War; Fragments from Inside a Coming Explosion*. Cummington, Mass.: Munewata Press, 2000.

Seabrook, Jeremy. *Freedom Unfinished: Fundamentalism and Popular Resistance in Bangladesh*. New York: Zed Books, 2001.

Zafarullah, Habib. *The Zia Episode in Bangladesh Politics*. Denver, Colo.: iAcademic Books, 2000.

Zyuganov, Gennadi (1946–) *Russian politician*

Gennadi Andreyevich Zyuganov was born on June 26, 1946, in Mymrino, Orel (Russia), then part of the Soviet Union. He studied to become a teacher, like his father, at the Orel Pedagogical Institute while also joining the Communist Party youth division, Komsomol. Zyuganov was staunchly Stalinist by persuasion, and he rejected any allegations of repression and genocide as propaganda. He stopped teaching to pursue politics by the late 1960s, and over the next two decades emerged as a mid-level party bureaucrat. In this capacity Zyuganov excoriated the glasnost (reform) policy of Premier Mikhail Gorbachev as detrimental to both communism and Russia. His close identification with other conservative elements led to an appointment on the Central Committee just as Gorbachev's efforts were unfolding. "What we can see today can be called a national calamity, comparable with the civil war or the invasion of Hitler's fascism," Zyuganov emoted, "Glasnost has grown into a hysteria and has become a weapon of ideological war against the people." Zyuganov's hard-line stance won over many admirers in conservative circles even though, as a political figure, he came across as wooden and dull. Following the failed coup against Gorbachev in August 1991, Russian president BORIS YELTSIN immediately outlawed the Communist Party. Within five months the tottering Soviet Union voted itself out of existence and the Communists, who had enjoyed absolute authority since 1917, suddenly found themselves out in the cold.

Zyuganov, a staunch party operative, may have been sympathetic toward coup leaders, but he was never implicated in the plot. He thus became the logical candidate to resurrect the party's fortunes when Yeltsin restored its legality in 1992. His new organization, the Communist Party of the Russian Federation (CPRF), exhibited a unique melding of past principles and current realities. Zyuganov retained his prior emphasis on state control of the economy, but he made generous allowances for private property and the role of religion. Moreover, his new ideology was strongly tinged by old-fashioned nationalism, placing Russia at the center of world events and firmly at odds with Western economic and cultural encroachment. He also rejected the free-market capitalism espoused by Yeltsin and Prime Minister VIKTOR CHERNOMYRDIN, calling for its disbandment. "Capitalism does not fit the flesh and blood, the customs and psychology of our country," he thundered. "It is not taking root now, and it will never take root." Zyuganov's message was abetted by the miserable performance of the economy, which remained in a deep recession. Yeltsin's health was also problematic and he appeared politically vulnerable. These circumstances spurred Zyuganov to run for the presidency in 1996 with great expectations.

During parliamentary elections in June 1996, the invigorated Communists won 35 percent of votes cast, making them the largest single bloc within the Duma (parliament). The following July he finished a surprising close second to Yeltsin and, because neither man won a clear majority, a runoff vote was scheduled. At this juncture, nationalist candidate ALEKSANDR LEBED, who ranked third and disliked the Communists, folded his tent and endorsed Yeltsin's candidacy. The president was then easily reelected although Zyuganov finished a strong second with 40 percent of the vote. This tally, as events subsequently proved, marked the high tide of Communist fortunes in the new age of freedom.

Zyuganov continued to oppose Yeltsin and proved a formidable obstacle to his reform efforts. In August 1998 he effectively blocked Chernomyrdin's reappointment as prime minister and forced Yeltsin to accept the more orthodox YEVGENY PRIMAKOV instead. The president's health, and the national economy, continued deteriorating and raised the specter of new Communist attempts to seize the presidency in 2000. But Yeltsin, himself a clever operative, deflated their chances by dramatically resigning on New Year's Eve, 1999, and appointing Prime Minister VLADIMIR PUTIN as acting executive. Putin, a former Communist, promptly coopted Zyuganov's calls for national greatness and renewal, stealing the left's thunder. Elections held on March 26, 2000, confirmed his success when Zyuganov won only 30 percent of the vote—still sizable, but declining. Apparently Communist appeal was restricted to an older generation of voters yearning for the Soviet past and attracted few newcomers. Zyuganov's inability to win also caused dissension among rank-and-file members, but discipline prevailed among the old guard and in December 2000 he was reelected first secretary. Despite the apparent eclipse of communism in the emerging Russia, Zyuganov bristles at the thought of political irrelevance. "The ideas of socialism and justice in this country are not simply alive, they are in the soul of every person," he declared on the 10th anniversary of Yeltsin's banishment of the Communist Party. "Its strength, influence, and authority show that decrees are unable to influence the feelings of people." Nevertheless, intraparty discontent abounds and led to formation of a splinter group, the New Communist Party. Their leader, Andrei Brezhnev, son of the late premier, feels himself better capable of promoting leftist ideas.

Further Reading

Karatnycky, A. "Gennady Zyuganov: Russia's Pragmatic Extremist." *Freedom Review* 27 (May–June 1996): 27–40.

Miller, A. H., V. L. Hesli, and W. M. Reisinger. "The Russian 1996 Presidential Election: Referendum on Democracy or a Personality Contest." *Electoral Studies* 17 (June 1998): 175–196.

Murray, John. "Still No Truth in the News? Coverage by Izvestiya of the 1996 Presidential Election." *Journal of Communist Studies and Transitional Politics* 15, no. 2, (1999): 1–40.

Phillips, Hugh D. *Leaving the Past Behind: The Russian Presidential Elections of 1996.* Washington, D.C.: Kenan Institution, 1999.

Smith, Kathleen E. *Mythmaking in the New Russia: Politics and Memory during the Yeltsin Era.* Ithaca, N.Y.: Cornell University Press, 2002.

Zyuganov, Gennadi. *My Russia: The Political Autobiography of Gennadi Zyuganov.* Armonk, N.Y.: M. E. Sharpe, 1997.

BIBLIOGRAPHY

Current Biography. New York: H. W. Wilson Co., 1940– .

Eccleshall, Robert, and Graham Walker, eds. *Biographical Dictionary of British Prime Ministers.* New York: Routledge, 1998.

Encyclopedia of World Biography. Detroit: Gale Group, 1998– .

Fredriksen, John C. *America's Military Adversaries: From Colonial Times to the Present.* Santa Barbara, Calif.: ABC-Clio, 2001.

Glickman, Harvey, ed. *Political Leaders of Contemporary Africa South of the Sahara.* New York: Greenwood Press, 1992.

Hamilton, Neil A. *Founders of Modern Nations: A Biographical Dictionary.* Santa Barbara, Calif.: ABC-Clio, 1995.

———. *Presidents: A Biographical Dictionary.* New York: Facts On File, 2001.

Hutchinson Encyclopedia of Modern Political Biography. Boulder, Colo.: Westview Press, 1999.

Jackson-Laufer, Guida M. *Women Rulers through the Ages.* Santa Barbara, Calif.: ABC-Clio, 1999.

Kavanagh, Dennis, ed. *A Dictionary of Political Biography.* New York: Oxford University Press, 1998.

Laybourn, Keith, *British Political Leaders: A Biographical Dictionary.* Santa Barbara, Calif.: ABC-Clio, 2001.

Lentz, Harris M. *Encyclopedia of Heads of State and Governments, 1900 through 1945.* Jefferson, N.C.: McFarland, 1999.

Leung, Pak-Wah. *Political Leaders of Modern China: A Biographical Dictionary.* Westport, Conn.: Greenwood Press, 2002.

Magill, Frank N., and John Powell. *U.S. Government Leaders.* Pasadena, Calif.: Salem Press, 1997.

Newsmakers. Detroit: Gale Group, 1985– .

Palmer, Alan W. *Who's Who in World Politics: From 1860 to the Present Day.* New York: Routledge, 1996.

———. *Who's Who in Modern History.* London: Routledge, 2001.

Powell, John, ed. *Biographical Encyclopedia of the 20th Century World Leaders.* 5 vols. New York: Marshall Cavendish, 2000.

Purcell, L. Edward, ed. *Vice Presidents: A Biographical Dictionary.* New York: Checkmark Books, 2001.

Uwechue, Raph. *Makers of Modern Africa: Profiles in History.* London: Africa Books, 1996.

Vazquez Gomez, Juana. *Dictionary of Mexican Rulers, 1325–1997.* Westport, Conn.: Greenwood Press, 1997.

Wilsford, David. *Political Leaders of Contemporary Western Europe: A Biographical Dictionary.* Westport, Conn.: Greenwood Press, 1995.

INDEX BY COUNTRY

JAPAN
Hashimoto, Ryutaro
Hosokawa, Morihiro
Koizumi, Junichiro
Miyazawa, Kiichi
Mori, Yoshiro
Murayama, Tomiichi
Obuchi, Keizo

JORDAN
Abdullah II
Hussein I
Rania al-Abdullah

KAZAKHSTAN
Nazarbayev, Nursultan

KENYA
Moi, Daniel arap

KIRIBATI
Tito, Teburoro

KOSOVO
Rugova, Ibrahim

KUWAIT
Jaber III

KYRGYSTAN
Akayev, Askar

LAOS
Khamtay Siphandone

LATVIA
Vike-Freiberga, Vaira

LEBANON
Hariri, Rafiq al-
Hrawi, Elias
Lahoud, Emile

LESOTHO
Mosisili, Pakalitha

LIBERIA
Taylor, Charles

LIBYA
Qaddafi, Muammar

LIECHTENSTEIN
Hans Adam II

LITHUANIA
Adamkus, Valdas
Landsbergis, Vytautas

LUXEMBOURG
Juncker, Jean-Claude

MACEDONIA
Gligorov, Kiro
Trajkovski, Boris

MADAGASCAR
Ratsiraka, Didier

MALAWI
Banda, Hastings
Muluzi, Bakili

MALAYSIA
Mohamad, Mahathir

MALDIVES
Gayoom, Maumoon Abdul

MARSHALL ISLANDS
Note, Kessai

MALI
Konaré, Alpha

MALTA
Fenech-Adami, Eddie

MAURITANIA
Taya, Maaouya

MAURITIUS
Jugnauth, Anerood
Ramgoolam, Navinchandra

MEXICO
Fox, Vicente
Salinas de Gortari, Carlos
Zedillo, Ernesto

MICRONESIA
Falcam, Leo A.

MOLDOVA
Lucinschi, Petru

MONACO
Rainier III

MONGOLIA
Amarjargal, Rinchinnyamiin

MONTENEGRO
Djukanovic, Milo

MOROCCO
Hassan II
Mohammed VI

MOZAMBIQUE
Chissanó, Joaquim

MYANMAR
Aung San Suu Kyi
Than Shwe

NAMIBIA
Nujoma, Sam

NAURU
Dowiyogo, Bernard

NEPAL
Koirala, Girija Prasad

NETHERLANDS
Balkenende, Jan
Kok, Wim
Lubbers, Ruud

INDEX

Boldface numbers indicate main entries.
Italic numbers indicate photographs.